POLIS

Polis

A NEW HISTORY OF THE ANCIENT
GREEK CITY-STATE FROM THE EARLY
IRON AGE TO THE END OF ANTIQUITY

JOHN MA

PRINCETON UNIVERSITY PRESS
PRINCETON & OXFORD

Copyright © 2024 by Princeton University Press

Princeton University Press is committed to the protection of copyright and the intellectual property our authors entrust to us. Copyright promotes the progress and integrity of knowledge created by humans. By engaging with an authorized copy of this work, you are supporting creators and the global exchange of ideas. As this work is protected by copyright, any reproduction or distribution of it in any form for any purpose requires permission; permission requests should be sent to permissions@press.princeton.edu. Ingestion of any IP for any AI purposes is strictly prohibited without a license to do so; licensing requests should be sent to DigitalLicensing@press.princeton.edu

Published by Princeton University Press
41 William Street, Princeton, New Jersey 08540
99 Banbury Road, Oxford OX2 6JX

press.princeton.edu

All Rights Reserved

First paperback printing, 2026
Paperback ISBN 9780691260037

The Library of Congress has cataloged the cloth edition of this book as follows:

Names: Ma, John, author.
Title: Polis : a new history of the ancient Greek city-state from the early Iron Age to the end of antiquity / John Ma.
Description: Princeton : Princeton University Press, [2024] | Includes bibliographical references and index.
Identifiers: LCCN 2023042361 (print) | LCCN 2023042362 (ebook) | ISBN 9780691155288 (hardback) | ISBN 9780691255484 (ebook)
Subjects: LCSH: City-states—Greece—History—To 1500. | Greece—Politics and government—To 146 B.C. | Greece—Social conditions—To 146 B.C. | BISAC: HISTORY / Ancient / Greece | POLITICAL SCIENCE / History & Theory
Classification: LCC JC73 .M3 2024 (print) | LCC JC73 (ebook) | DDC 938—dc23/eng/20231214
LC record available at https://lccn.loc.gov/2023042361
LC ebook record available at https://lccn.loc.gov/2023042362

British Library Cataloging-in-Publication Data is available

Editorial: Rob Tempio, Chloe Coy
Production: Erin Suydam
Publicity: William Pagdatoon (US), Charlotte Coyne (UK)
Copyeditor: Alison S. Britton

Jacket/Cover Credit: Bernard Gagnon / Wikimedia Commons

This book has been composed in Arno

GPSR Authorized Representative: Easy Access System Europe
Mustamäe tee 50, 10621 Tallinn, Estonia
gpsr.requests@easproject.com

To Fergus Millar
The last democrat

CONTENTS

A Note on Transcription ix
List of Illustrations and Maps xi
Preface xv

PART I. IN SEARCH OF *POLIS*   1

1   In Search of *Polis*   3

**PART II. BEFORE THE *POLIS*:
POSSIBILITIES—1100–700 BCE**   21

2   To New Beginnings   25

3   Diversity and Community   51

**PART III. MAKING THE *POLIS*: COALESCENCE,
COMMUNITY, AND JUSTICE—675–450 BCE**   69

4   Institutions, Community, Ideology: 1, 2, 3, *Polis*   75

5   600–450 BCE: Development, Complexification, and Citizenship   101

6   The Travails of Integration   128

**PART IV. FRAMING THE "CLASSICAL"
POLIS—480–180 BCE**   153

7   Political History (1): *Archē* and *Autonomia* in the Hundred Years' War   159

8   Political History (2): *Politeia* and *Stasis*   179

| 9 | The Great Convergence | 203 |
| 10 | The Qualities of the *Polis* | 229 |

PART V. POLIS AND IMPERIUM—180 BCE–400 CE — 259

11	The Indian Summer of the *Polis*	263
12	The Ends of Liberty	301
13	*Polis*, People, and Power in the Roman Empire	334
14	Cooptations, Prolongations, and Endings	368

PART VI. MAKING SENSE OF POLIS — 403

15	*Polis* as Society	409
16	*Polis* as Ideals	439
17	*Polis* as Interests	459
18	Bad *Polis*: The Realities of Power	480
19	Worst *Polis*: *Polis* as Injustice	501

PART VII. POLIS OF OUR WISHES — 539

| 20 | *Polis* of Our Wishes | 541 |

Abbreviations 555
Notes 557
Chronology 623
General Map 627
Bibliography 629
Illustrations Credits 709
Index 713

A NOTE ON TRANSCRIPTION

AS IS ALWAYS SAID, there is no logical way of transcribing nouns and names from Greek to English. I have tried to reproduce consistently some features of the ancient Greek, especially the long vowels ē and ō (but not in adjectives in English), for all except the most canonical of place-names and authors. The effect is, I hope, one of distanciation rather than distraction.

LIST OF ILLUSTRATIONS AND MAPS

0.1.	Orientation map	627
1.1.	View of Irakleia	4
1.2.	Map of Cyclades	5
1.3.	Inscription concerning goats, Hērakleia	7
1.4.	Reconstruction of Priēnē	9
1.5.	Territory of Priēnē	10
1.6.	Distribution of *poleis* by size of territory	15
2.1.	Some sites in the Mycenaean world	26
2.2.	Protogeometric tomb, Athens	31
2.3.	Settlement, Protogeometric Athens	33
2.4.	Lefkandi, Protogeometric monumental tomb and cemetery	34
2.5.	Habitat in Argos, from Mycenaean to Geometric	39
2.6.	Settlement and territory in the Korinthia	41
2.7.	Bronze panoply, Argos	45
3.1.	Plain of Thespiai	63
3.2.	Amphoras from mass burial, Paros	65
4.1.	Law from Drēros	76
4.2.	Chigi jug	91
4.3.	Vroulia	94
4.4.	Monument of Glaukos, Thasos	97
5.1.	Temple of Apollōn, Corinth	102
5.2.	West Pediment, Old Temple of Athēna, Akropolis, Athens	102
5.3.	Law from Chios	108
5.4.	Boundary stone, Thebes	116
5.5.	Spear buttspike, Arkadia	117
5.6.	Kastro (modern toponym), Siphnos	122

5.7. Treasury of the Siphnians, Delphi	123
5.8. Treasury of the Siphnians, Delphi	123
6.1. *Kouros*, Athens	129
6.2. Sculptural group, Samos	130
6.3. Statue of Nikandrē, Delos	131
6.4. Cremation trench, seventh-century BCE Athens	132
6.5. Votive plaque from Sounion	133
6.6. Funerary stele, Kerameikos	135
6.7. Lead figurines, Sparta	146
7.1. Map of Athenian empire	163
7.2. Map of places mentioned in Athenian casualty list, 459 BCE	165
7.3. Greater Thespiai	171
8.1. Plan of Olynthos	181
8.2. *Klērotērion*	184
8.3. Attic grave stele	188
9.1. Funerary relief, Western Asia Minor	207
9.2. Territory of Teōs	209
9.3. Territory of Chorsiai	211
9.4. Decree of Entella	214
9.5. Fourth-century coin of Knidos mentioning Democracy	219
10.1. Stele recording land conveyance to a civic subdivision at Kolophōn	234
10.2. Strongbox, Lokroi	238
10.3. Dikastic *pinax* (?), Myrina	243
10.4. Hellenistic gravestone of couple	246
10.5. Curse tablet, Attica	252
10.6. Fountain, Priēnē	256
11.1. Late second-century BCE hymn from Delphi	273
11.2. The shrine of Klaros in the late second century BCE	274
11.3. Priēnē, north stoa and decrees	280
11.4. Column for Menippos, Klaros	282
12.1. Sebasteion, Aphrodisias	308
12.2. Relief from Sebasteion	309
12.3. Coin of Hierapolis showing Marcus Aurelius	310

12.4. Aphrodisias "archive wall"	312
12.5. Coin of Kolophōn showing delegates of Ionian League	316
12.6. Southern Ionia and the *Trachōn*	322
13.1. Library of Celsus, Ephesos	335
13.2. Temple of Zeus, Aizanoi	336
13.3. Coin of Smyrna showing Antinoos	337
13.4. Portrait of priest of imperial cult, Athens	340
13.5. Honorific statue base, Thessalonikē	349
14.1. Apameia, colonnaded street	370
14.2. Askalon, pilaster from council house	371
14.3. Gerasa	372
14.4. Territories of Kanatha and Soada	373
14.5. Palmyra in geographical context	378
14.6. Palmyra, urban center	382
14.7. *Agora* of Palmyra	383
14.8. Funerary relief, Palmyra	385
14.9. Funerary portrait, Egypt	394
14.10. Portrait of Late Roman governor, Aphrodisias	398
15.1. Panopeus	412
15.2. Rhodes and its territory	421
15.3. Qartaba pillar	437
17.1. Territory of Prousa	461
17.2. Territory of Aigai	472
18.1. Bronze honorific statue	494
18.2. Land use on modern Irakleia	496
19.1. Priēnē built environment, reconstruction	503
20.1. Volney at Palmyra	553
20.2. Sunrise over Irakleia	554

PREFACE

THIS BOOK on the Greek city-state started off as the 2011 Eitner Lecture at Stanford University; I am grateful to that institution's Department of Classics for the invitation and the kindness of its hospitality. I also thank Al Bertrand, then Rob Tempio at Princeton University Press for giving it a home. The idea of a "synoptic, diachronic survey of civic culture from soup to nuts" emerged in discussion with Josiah Ober a few years before the Eitner Lecture, so it is fitting that the manuscript was finalized during another visit to Stanford in May 2023, during a conference in honor of his work and its creativity. The book's inspiration also goes back further and in stages. Fergus Millar's work on empire and local community, but also his personal convictions about the importance of autonomy and democracy, were one source. I wish I could have told him how much the book owes to him. Another inspiration is the teaching of Philippe Gauthier, convinced of the resilience of local communities in spite of historical shifts (e.g., Gauthier 1984). After a seminar by Gauthier, I was lucky to have a long discussion on the importance of the second-century BCE moment for our understanding of the *polis* with a student of his, Paraskevi Martzavou, whose insightfulness and passion have sustained this project throughout the years. A third source is, indeed, the work of Josiah Ober, starting with his astonishing *Mass and Elite in Democratic Athens* (1989), at whose heart burns a fire of democratic confidence and optimism. The present work is centered on issues of autonomy, democracy, and political equality as traits of the *polis*—especially outside Athens.

This non-Athenian focus reflects older sources of inspiration. These include reading (at the start of graduate work) a few pages by Robin Osborne in his *Classical Landscape with Figures* (1987) on a specific episode involving goats on a small island in the Cyclades sometime in the first half of the third century BCE (the relevant inscription is mentioned in chapter 1), or listening (as an undergraduate in 1990) to Simon Hornblower teach a class on the *polis*, including the example of Aigosthena on the Megarian-Attic border. Both showed the power of specificity at a small scale to illuminate big historical questions, though my first trip to Porto Germeno (ancient Aigosthena) had to await the summer of 2000, with Paraskevi (as did a visit to Panopeus, another site pointedly treated by Hornblower in his class and Osborne in his book). Earlier still, the experience of growing up as a metic of sorts in the old city-state of Geneva was a living lesson about the importance of local history as an expression of autonomy. Yet the experience of Geneva also illustrated difference, exclusion, and their distorting effects. The memory of both the empowerment of participation and the uncertainties on the margins in a certain type of local community helped me frame another central theme of the present work (though one which is explicitly treated only in the latter part of it): the ethical costs of community.

The influences listed above determine the focus of the book: local self-governance as autonomy or agency, and the consequences of struggles for the definition of political power within the community, across a wide timespan. Though I cover what are conventionally known as the "Archaic" (i.e., 700–480 BCE) and "Classical" (480–323 BCE) periods (well documented in literary sources and hence well studied in modern Classics departments in the United States where this book was finished), I also emphasize the "post-Classical" period (another conventional appellation), and somewhat reorganize the traditional periodization to produce a sort of "long classical" period, 350 BCE–300 CE. In this I follow Gauthier's insight that the *polis* cannot be understood without engaging with the rich documentation left by individual city-states in and as their public inscribed record. The great specialists of Greek epigraphy, Louis Robert and Adolf Wilhelm, showed earlier the potential of such material for a political and social history of the Greek cities in time, down to the Roman empire (though this lesson has to be gleaned as *Lesefrüchte*; Robert treated the "goat inscription" from Hērakleia in an arresting article: below, p. 4). The extraordinary work by Alain Bresson constantly demonstrates how epigraphy (in skillful combination with other sources) can provide powerful analyses of the polis' socio-economic history.

Any view that the *polis* ended with the "Classical" period is dispelled by the epigraphical material; any conception of ancient history or the Classics that does not give a large place to the post-Classical *polis*, beyond the old Athens-Sparta couple in the fifth and fourth centuries BCE, is necessarily incomplete. The history in this book is "Classical" in that it concerns people and places that have been valorized in a recent cultural tradition in the West, philological or contextualizing in that it situates this "Classical" history in precisely documented material and social worlds, and "philosophical" (for want of a better word) in that it is interested in questions of power, actions and causality, and value. But the result at least aspires to be a non-Classical account of the Greek city. I hope the book might interest specialists of the Hellenistic period (in connecting their period with the whole of ancient history), Classicists (in recalibrating and recontextualizing the contexts for the production of the Classical canon), historians (in providing a narrative of a type of city-state), philosophers (in historicizing the *polis*), social scientists (in showing how certain issues involving power, interests, and ideology worked out in ancient practice), and modern citizens.

The treatment in this book is still an exercise in linearity, a work of "lumping" rather than "splitting," an attempt to use long time (but not teleology) as a historiographical tool—ultimately producing on a large scale a unitary image of the *polis* similar to that which was proposed by M. Hansen, the director of the Copenhagen Polis Centre, which produced a great sum of knowledge on the *polis* of the "Archaic" and "Classical" periods. The interest of a unitary picture of the *polis* lies in its focus on the themes of political power and its consequences—or, more explicitly, on the history of the ideas and the practice of liberty and democracy as possibilities in contexts of change; in a big neo-Aristotelian history based on a roster of detailed examples, following the examples of Gauthier and Ober, or Millar, with particular focus on institutions as loci of power and justice, but also of negotiation and interests. The costs of the exercise (apart from the way in which scale exaggerates any faults in writing or conception) are inherent to its Aristotelian focus on citizenship. One is the focus on political and social forms, rather than a holistic urban history: if the history of the *polis* does not fetishize the city as such, its practitioners still have to remind themselves to work on settlement, economic patterns, and social relations, as well as the unitary phenomena of political institutions and discourse. A second cost of the Aristotelian mode is an insistence on inclusion and exclusion as a central polarity in the *polis*. The study of polarity, once an innovation in Greek history, is now a conservative position, as I realize while reaffirming the consequences of institutional and ideological power as determinant rather than the more fluid reimaginings of the *polis* as a field of interactions between associations and social actors, as has been excitingly proposed in recent scholarship. The centrality of civic institutions and ideology, moreover, comes with a cost in terms of social injustice: here my treatment of these topics, at the end of the book, opens some space for the return of the repressed alluded to earlier. I hope my explicit discussion of all these issues will at least have clarifying effect.

Another form of conservatism is that, even while trying to renegotiate the boundaries of traditional periodizations, I often follow the tenor of the existing scholarly treatments. For instance, the study of the Early Iron Age is dominated by a detailed and fascinating social archaeology of settlement and ritual practice, documented in materialities. In contrast, the "Hellenistic" period, conventionally defined as the period dominated by big monarchical states before the irruption of Roman power, offers a rich epigraphical documentation that allows for diverse readings of institutional works and ideological claims. I tried to combine different types of material (by emphasizing literary or epigraphical sources for the earlier periods, and gesturing at social archaeology for later periods), within the general landscape of subfields; often I felt the lack of fully joined-up, interdisciplinary resources to study most periods of Greek history. Writing on a large scale means striding alongside the various "great divides" that criss-cross the field, rather than bridging them. The reproduction of the scholarly focuses on the sub-fields in the history of the ancient world is a last, ironical form of Aristotelianism in the present book, a reflection of its inductive mode. What remains here is still a long love-letter to the discipline of ancient history within and without Classics. In other words, it represents a sum of things that "the field knows."

During the long period of working on this book (which moved with me from the UK to the United States, and grew during a world pandemic), many debts were incurred; I can discharge only some of them here. Institutionally, I thank Corpus Christi College, the Faculty of Classics at Oxford University, and Columbia University, for support. A Mid-Career Fellowship of the British Academy in 2012 helped the project on its way. The School of Arts and Sciences and the Stanwood Cockey Lodge Fund at Columbia University generously supported the later stages of research and writing. The Sackler Library at Oxford and, for the later years, Columbia University Libraries, especially Butler, Avery, Burke, and Lehmann libraries (with Karen Greene, then Jeffrey Wayno as specialized curators in relevant fields) were the practical instruments for research; especially during the onset of COVID-19, practical and imaginative librarianship played a vital role.

As for individuals, the list could be endless, but I would particularly like to thank, for inspiration or generous help, Mustafa Adak, Nino Ampolo, Nathan Arrington, Vincent Azoulay, Ryan Boehm, Alain Bresson (for generosity and inspiration), Richard Billows, Nick Cahill, Laurence Cavalier, Charles Crowther, Felice Costabile, Francesco de Angelis, Christine Delplace, Aneurin Ellis-Evans, Jaś Elsner (who suggested the dedication of the book; see Millar 2002b, 8–10), Sylvian Fachard, David Fearn, Marcus Folch, Blair Fowlkes-Childs, Pierre Fröhlich, Eleni Gizas, Stathis Gourgouris, Ben Gray, Klaus Hallof, Patrice Hamon, Alex Herda, Jeff Hurwit, Jesse James, Philippe Jockey, Georgy Kantor, Moritz Kiderlin, Alex Knodell, Mait Kõiv, Georgia Kokkorou-Alevras, Elif Koparal, Antonis Kotsonas, Shenda Kuang, Eri Lemos, Giovanni Lovisetto, Polly Low, Thierry Lucas, Menas Ma (for discussions), Vassiliki Ma (for discussions), William Mack, Angelos Matthaiou, Andrew Meadows, Jean-Charles Moretti, Sarah Morris, Marc Müllenhoff, Dimitris Nakassis, Josh Ober, John Papadopoulos, Robert Parker, Denis Rousset, Catherine Saliou, Mustafa Sayar, Klaus Schnädelbach, Matt Simonton, Bert Smith, Dan Sofaer, Colleen Swift, Peter Stewart, Peter Thonemann, Michalis Tiverios, Shante Tucker, Riet van Bremen, Hans van Wees, Umberto Verdura, Alex von Kienlin, Lela Walter-Karydi, Ute Wartenberg, Mark Whittow (much missed), Gareth Williams, Jean-Baptiste Yon, and Jim Zetzel.

The establishment of a formatted and checked bibliography is due to the extraordinary courage, skill, and eye of Umberto Verdura, as well as to the efforts of Dan Sofaer and Nicholas Koudounis. Jazmin Lara contributed to the index, and to final corrections, judiciously and carefully. All aspects of the illustrations were handled with consummate care, patience, and art by Giovanni Lovisetto. The work required versatility but also required forbearance because of the tricky tasks involved in getting unusual or out of the way pictures (necessary for the book's non-classicizing agenda). I am grateful to Chloe Coy at Princeton University Press for the expert guidance on editorial matters, and Angela Piliouras for the practical work of making a book out of the manuscript. Finally, I thank my family for their patience during the long writing of this long book and notably my mother, Hsinkai Li, for steady encouragement to finish the thing.

POLIS

PART I

In Search of *Polis*

1

In Search of *Polis*

> The human being is by nature an animal that lives in a community of citizens.
> —ARISTOTLE, *POLITICS*

The Goats of Hērakleia (ca. 270 BCE)

In 1895 or 1896, the French scholar Jules Delamarre, while exploring the island of Amorgos, studied a worn and fragmentary inscription found in modern Irakleia, a small islet in the Eastern Cyclades (or more dramatically, the *Erimonisia*, the "desert islands"), located to the south of Naxos and to the west of Amorgos (figs. 1.1, 1.2).[1] The text, though fragmentary, is nothing less than extraordinary in its implications. In short, it concerned the struggles of a community on ancient Hērakleia to reach a decision about goats; and it deserves full quotation.

```
            [καὶ τὸν Ἡρακλε]-
α καὶ τοὺς ἄλλους [θεοὺς τοὺς τὴν νῆ]-
σογ κατέχοντας, εὐορκοῦντ[ι μέν μοι εὖ]
εἴη, ἐφιορκοῦντι δὲ τἀναντία τῶν [ἀγαθῶν]·
ἐὰν δέ τις βιασόμενος αἶγας εἰσάγ[ειν ἢ]                4
τρέφειν ἐν τῆι νήσωι παρὰ τόδε τὸ ψήφι[σ]-
μα καὶ τὸν ὅρκον τῶγ κωλυόντων τινὰς
κτείνει, ἐπεξιόντων αὐτὸν οἵ τε προσ-
ήκοντες τοῦ παθόντος καὶ τὸ κοινὸν τῶν             8
νησιωτῶν ἅπαν· ὅ τι δ' ἂν εἰς τὴγ κρίσιν
ἀνήλωμα γίνηται, τὸ μέρος ἕκαστον εἰσ-
[φ]έρειν· ἀναγράψαι δὲ τόδε τὸ ψήφισμα τὸν
[ἱ]εροποιὸν Ἐπιστροφίδη<ν> εἰς στήλην λιθί-       12
νηγ καὶ στῆσαι εἰς τὸ Μητρῶιον· τὸ δὲ ἀνή-
λωμα τὸ εἰς τὴν στήλην καὶ τὴν ἀναγρα-
φὴν ἔστω ἀπὸ τοῦ κοινοῦ. ταῦτα δ' εἶναι εἴς
τε φυλακὴγ καὶ σωτηρίαν Ἡρακλειωτῶν             16
πάντωγ καὶ τῶν οἰκούντω[ν ἐν τῆι νήσωι].
```

FIGURE 1.1. Irakleia, in the Little Cyclades. The view is taken towards the east and includes some of the agricultural land of the island. To the left, one of the two harbor inlets; cf. fig. 18.2. Photo by Z. Tankosic.

> [... I swear by... and Heraklē]s and the other [gods] who hold sway over the island, and if I keep to my oath, may it turn out [well] for me, and if I break my oath may it turn to the opposite. If someone, in trying by force to introduce goats or to raise them, in contravention of this decree and the oath, should kill some men among those who try to prevent it, let the relatives of the victim and the whole commonwealth of the islanders prosecute him; as for whatever expense is incurred for the judgment, let everyone contribute his share; and let the *hieropoios* inscribe this decree on a stone stele and set it up in the shrine of the Mother of the Gods; let the expense of the stele and the inscription come out of the public treasury. These matters are to be considered as concerning the protection and safety of all the Herakleiotes and of the inhabitants [of the island].[2]

As analyzed in a luminous article by French historian Louis Robert, the inscribed document, datable to the first half of the third century BCE on paleographical grounds, preserves the end of a momentous decision by a political community, the Herakleiotes. In a formal meeting (the details of which are now lost), framed by the working of their institutions, the Herakleiotes decided not to keep goats on the island. They further took care of the implementation of this decision, through the imposition of an oath to respect the decision (this is where the preserved text starts). They also offered the guarantee of communal prosecution in case any attempt at stopping the introduction of goats onto the island resulted in death. The decision mobilized common institutional resources—deliberative, judicial,[3] financial, but also ideological. Its measures were formally declared necessary for the community's safety (*phulakē kai sōtēria*), a legal category protecting it against amendment or reversal, but also an invocation of the public good.[4] The document, transcribing the whole transaction of the

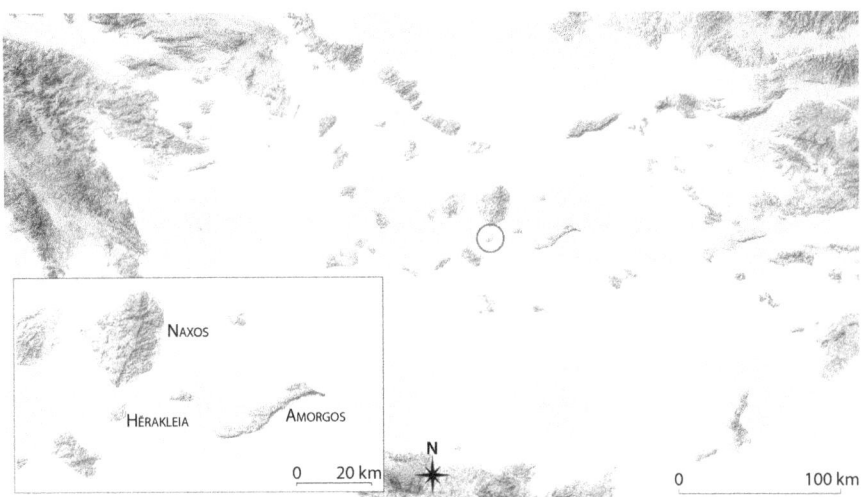

FIGURE 1.2. Hērakleia in its geographical context.

meeting in its institutional setting (including the motion as proposed, and almost certainly procedural details such as the proposers of the motion and the presiding bodies at the meeting), was inscribed in permanent form and displayed in a sacred space, the shrine of the Mother of the Gods, as a record and as a monument of the political community in action. Such inscribed decrees are a major source for the history of ancient Greek communities and their account echoes down this book.

Robert contrasted the ancient community with the later fate of the island, as seen by early modern travelers: a "goat island" used as pasture by absentee landlords, with no human inhabitants except for two or three shepherds. Hence, in Robert's view, the fragmentary decree showed an episode in "the eternal war between peasant and shepherd." The choice seems to be a political community, or something like the island of the Cyclops—a desert with goats and a few shepherds.[5] Yet the alternative is more complex. The local historian Ph. Gavalas gives a glimpse of the harrowing agrarian history of the island. The peasants seen by the German archaeologist L. Ross in 1840 were sharecroppers installed by an absentee landlord, the monastery of Panagia Hozoviotissa on Amorgos, on emphyteutic leases involving the surrender of half the harvest. (Interestingly, the leases stipulated the ownership of plough-oxen, a cow, and a donkey, but make no mention of goats: were they banned or supplementary to the lease requirements?) In the 1860s, the conditions were harsher still, with the monastic landlords granting harsh short-term leases and sometimes farming out the whole island to entrepreneurs, leading to multiple conflicts, defaults, and lawsuits.[6] In contrast, third-century BCE Hērakleia was neither a wilderness of many sheep and a couple of herdsmen, nor a depressed feudal world of sharecropping peasants dealing with absentee landlords and hostile laws, but the site of an egalitarian political community with the collective capacities to decide its own fate.

What should we call this political community? It regulates itself; it can take independent decisions in deliberative assembly, without referring to a higher authority (hence the *phulakē* clause safeguarding the measures). It has institutions—political, administrative, judicial, religious—and controls its own spaces, from a whole territory to the shrine where the decree was inscribed. It is immediately tempting to call it the *polis*, or city-state, of the Herakleiotes.[7] However, it is also true that the word *polis* never occurs in our fragmentary text. Instead, it mentions legal action taken by "the whole *koinon* (community) of the islanders," and at the end, "all the Herakleiotes and those who inhabit the island." Hence, another interpretation would be to see this decision as taken by an association of inhabitants on the island (dealing with encroachment by herd owners on Amorgos) rather than a city-state, since the term *koinon* can be used for groups and associations, as proposed by C. Constantakopoulou. Another possibility, tentatively mentioned by P. Fröhlich, would be that the decree was passed by a local subdivision or official body within a larger *polis* (for instance Amorgos).[8]

My own understanding of the nuanced poetics of community in the decree is the following. There exists a corporate group of entitled and enfranchised men, the *Herakleiōtai*, with a reified name (an *ethnikon*, to use the technical term) which shows that they claim to be the stakeholders of political community on the island—in other words, that they constitute a *polis*. That they can take their own independent decisions, wielding a *phulakē* clause (of a type that is only found used by *poleis* as states) shows that they are a *polis* endowed with state capacities, drawing notably on common funds (*koinon*, a term which can designate things owned by the *polis* but also the *polis* itself as community).[9] The introduction of goats is an internal affair (since those who do it would infringe their own oath), and hence the decree is about an effort at autoregulation by a community of citizens.

But there also are other people on the island, who do not have access to state institutional power—women, children, foreigners, enslaved people—and appear in the last clause as the inhabitants of the island: the *phulakē* clause concerns more than just the *polis* or the *dēmos* (the People constituted by citizens), but all inhabitants. Analogously, the *polis* of Magnēsia on Maeander, in western Asia Minor, celebrated rituals in honor of Zeus Polis-savior, "for the safety (*sōtēria*) of the *polis*, the territory, the citizens, the women, the children, and the others living in the city and in the territory."[10] The *polis* of Hērakleia is a set of political institutions but also a society, whose welfare is directly concerned by the decree formally passed by the Herakleiotes. The "whole *koinon* of the islanders" is a striking expression, insisting not just on the community (*koinon*) that is represented by the group of citizen Herakleiotes but putting forward a new, more capacious category of all those that occupy the island. The practical purpose is to explain that everyone in the social assemblage on Hērakleia will be liable for taxation—an exceptional levy, *eisphora*—to cover the judicial costs potentially involved in enforcing the ban; but this sense of the broader community

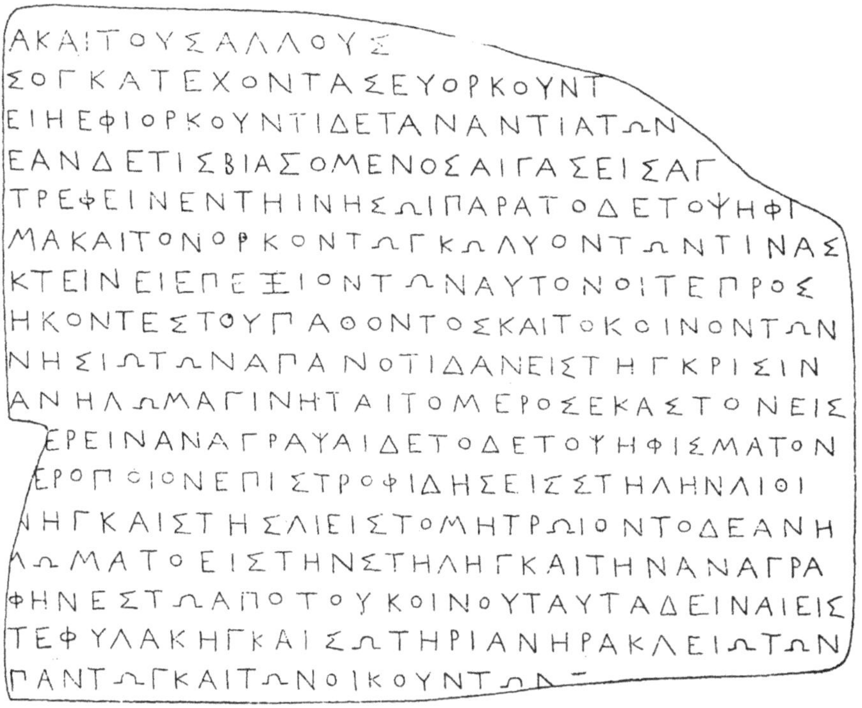

```
ΑΚΑΙΤΟΥΣΑΛΛΟΥΣ
ΣΟΓΚΑΤΕΧΟΝΤΑΣΕΥΟΡΚΟΥΝΤ
ΕΙΗΕΦΙΟΡΚΟΥΝΤΙΔΕΤΑΝΑΝΤΙΑΤΩΝ
ΕΑΝΔΕΤΙΣΒΙΑΣΟΜΕΝΟΣΑΙΓΑΣΕΙΣΑΓ
ΤΡΕΨΕΙΝΕΝΤΗΙΝΗΣΩΙΠΑΡΑΤΟΔΕΤΟΥΗΦΙ
ΜΑΚΑΙΤΟΝΟΡΚΟΝΤΩΓΚΩΛΥΟΝΤΩΝΤΙΝΑΣ
ΚΤΕΙΝΕΙΕΠΕΞΙΟΝΤΩΝΑΥΤΟΝΟΙΤΕΠΡΟΣ
ΗΚΟΝΤΕΣΤΟΥΓΛΑΘΟΝΤΟΣΚΑΙΤΟΚΟΙΝΟΝΤΩΝ
ΝΗΣΙΩΤΩΝΑΠΑΝΟΤΙΔΑΝΕΙΣΤΗΓΚΡΙΣΙΝ
ΑΝΗΛΩΜΑΓΙΝΗΤΑΙΤΟΜΕΡΟΣΕΚΑΣΤΟΝΕΙΣ
ΕΡΕΙΝΑΝΑΓΡΑΨΑΙΔΕΤΟΔΕΤΟΥΗΦΙΣΜΑΤΟΝ
ΕΡΟΠΟΙΟΝΕΠΙΣΤΡΟΦΙΔΗΣΕΙΣΣΤΗΛΗΝΛΙΘΙ
ΝΗΓΚΑΙΣΤΗΣΛΙΕΙΣΤΟΜΗΤΡΩΙΟΝΤΟΔΕΑΝΗ
ΛΩΜΑΤΟΕΙΣΤΗΝΣΤΗΛΗΓΚΑΙΤΗΝΑΝΑΓΡΑ
ΦΗΝΕΣΤΩΑΠΟΤΟΥΚΟΙΝΟΥΤΑΥΤΑΔΕΙΝΑΙΕΙΣ
ΤΕΦΥΛΑΚΗΓΚΑΙΣΩΤΗΡΙΑΝΗΡΑΚΛΕΙΩΤΩΝ
ΠΑΝΤΩΓΚΑΙΤΩΝΟΙΚΟΥΝΤΩΝ
```

FIGURE 1.3. Fragmentary decree of the Hērakleians on goats. From Delamarre 1902.

also emerges in the unusual extension of the *phulakē* clause to concern the safety of all the inhabitants. The very complexity of the relations between the political community of adult male citizens, and the rest of the human society within the same space, is an indication that we are looking at a *polis*.

The goal pursued by the political, shared effort of the *polis* of Hērakleia is not completely clear: why was the decree a matter of common safety, to the point of imposing an oath and expecting violence? Robert's picture of "the eternal war between herdsman and farmer" is too simple, since the traditional Mediterranean architecture combines gardens, intensive agriculture, and animal husbandry, including the raising of sheep and goats (that convert waste and scrub into important byproducts such as manure, fibers and protein).[11] Under the mask of civic consensus, what were the stakes? The question takes on greater urgency if we look at conditions on the island, with its 18 square kilometers, one good water source (on top of the highest eminence in its center) completed by cisterns and by a few wells sweet or brackish, limited arable land (one swathe from north to south, one small strip next to one of the harbors), and plentiful scrubland (fig. 18.2).[12]

The mystery thickens when we realize that the inscription with the decree barring goats is the only written artifact from the *polis* of Hērakleia (fig. 1.3); there are no other documents, and no record of material remains (such as the monumental shrine of the Mother of the Gods serving as an archive for inscribed public archives, let alone private housing, urban or rural). Did the *polis* manage to maintain itself after this particular crisis, recorded in an inscription, now broken, as isolated as a meteorite? At least, the document shows clearly the *polis* as a political form (decision-making, law, ideology), as a social form (small property owners free from direct control by landowners but subject to communally decided restraints on rights), and as a social relation (political community of adult male citizens, within "the whole *koinon*" of society). These three aspects form the theme of the present book.

Priēnē (120 BCE), Panopeus (160 CE), Palmyra (250 CE)

At Priēnē, in Asia Minor, there is no doubt that we are looking at a *polis* (fig. 1.4).[13] The term appears frequently in the rich epigraphical documentation from Priēnē, sometimes as an absolute to designate the political community in action: a priest might receive specific portions "from the animals which *polis* sacrifices" (*hōn polis thuei*; the Greek leaves out the definite article).[14] This documentation allows for rich, yet uneven history, with a notable emphasis on interactions with other *poleis* and on honors for deserving citizens (especially toward the later second century BCE). Much of this evidence was discovered during the great excavation of the urban site (1895–98). The German excavators uncovered and explored the urban fabric of Priēnē, its fortification system (including a redoubt on a cliff high above the city), its public spaces (*agora*, theatre, gymnasia, *stadion*...), its main shrine, dedicated to Athēna, its private housing, organized in equal-sized blocks, and some of the material culture produced in this setting. The publication (Wiegand and Schrader 1904) recreates a densely packed world of forty hectares laid out on an orthogonal plan against a stiff slope. From the excavation emerged the image of a rational, egalitarian, harmonious, indeed beautiful city in its dramatic natural setting, which some scholars implicitly or even explicitly designated as emblematic of *polis* culture; notably, W. Hoepfner and E.-L. Schwandner focused on the equal-sized "normal" and normed houses within modular habitation blocks alternating with large public spaces in a regular grid plan, as the symptom and the setting of an egalitarian, democratic polity.[15]

Continuous interpretive research and recent excavation on the site have sharpened this image without abolishing it. For instance, among the greater detail about the material lives of the Prienians, we learn not only that the denizens of this seaside city consumed vast quantities of seafood, including shellfish, but also that consumption of animal protein varied between private contexts (where mutton and pork was eaten) and official contexts such as the *agora* (where beef was consumed in common feasts, reflecting public resources). The distinction mirrors the public-private principle which structures the urban fabric. Most importantly, the urban

FIGURE 1.4. Imaginative reconstruction of Priēnē. Pen-and-ink drawing by A. Zippelius (1908).

fabric of Priēnē fits within a protracted history: the city, the urban center of an old *polis*, was rebuilt ca. 350 BCE on an extensive plan, which filled out slowly and with modifications to the original grid, starting with the public spaces. The city underwent a building boom in the late second century BCE, accelerated by the need to repair the damage caused by an earthquake ca. 130 BCE. Much of the large, monumentalized public spaces date to this time—for instance, the reshaped main public square (*agora*), separated from the utilitarian food market, or the refined spaces of the Lower Gymnasion.[16] The evolutions that appear in the building activity coincide with the debates and shifts in political language, as can be seen in the epigraphical material of the same decades (below, pp. 279–81).

But the *polis* of Priēnē was more than just the spectacular urban settlement. From the top of its akropolis, its citizen militiamen could survey other parts of the *polis*—a rural territory (fig. 1.5) in the Maeander valley (which was at least partly farmed by subordinate villages, the "Plainsmen"), at the mouth of the Maeander where the *polis* controlled saltpans, and also in forbidding Mt. Mykalē. The urban site was laid out on the steep south side, but the *polis* also controlled part of the

FIGURE 1.5. Territory of Priēnē, and neighboring *poleis*, based on Müllenhoff 2005, fig. 50.

milder northern slopes down to the sea.[17] This territory, of around 450 sq. km, is still poorly known as concerns ancient settlement and occupation. There is no clear image of what "the whole community of those who inhabit the territory" looked like, even though there are occasional mentions of "dwellers-by" (*paroikoi*) who might be resident foreigners in the urban center, or rural inhabitants.[18] At least it is clear that the territory of Priēnē was limited by that of other *poleis*—the island *polis* of Samos (that had continental holdings), Ephesos, Magnēsia on Maeander, Myous, and Milētos. Priēnē's relations with these neighbors would be close but occasionally conflictual, even involving open clashes; a dispute with Samos over frontiers and holdings on Mt Mykalē would last from (it seems) the eighth century to the second century BCE.[19]

These are the *poleis* Priēnē could even see from its urban center or at least its territory, but the Prienians had formal, highly normed relations with many other *poleis*—for instance, to provide arbitrators for internal disputes or to ask for arbitration in inter-state disputes. This form of *peer-polity interaction* involved mutual recognition by actors in a system of *poleis*, and indeed is one way in which we can see both the existence of a category of *poleis*, and one mechanism for recognition of the category as a status.[20] For instance, when a *polis* asked for one of its festivals to be acknowledged as having equal status to the ancient, prestigious panhellenic festivals, usually on the grounds of some religious event that could justify the recognition of the *polis* as "holy and inviolate," such a diplomatic transaction involved sending sacred ambassadors (*theōroi*) to peer polities, namely other *poleis*. The transaction, and the monumentalized record of responding entities (that had received the *theōroi* by appointing *theōrodokoi*, "sacred-envoy-receivers"), constitute prime evidence for *polis*-hood as being a formalized status, distinct from existence as an urban settlement.[21] Some contexts of local peer interactions could thicken to the point of taking the form of federal institutions, which still depended on the existence of building blocks endowed with stately powers of decision.

In practice, "peer-polity interaction" was made of multiple, overlapping *ad hoc* networks that each city constructed for itself. The *theōrodokoi* lists for different *poleis* exhibit divergence in their networks of contacts, rather than a single uniform list. As far as we can tell, Priēnē's network of formal *polis* contacts never stretched to Macedonia, in the North Aegean. But the experiences of communities there were shared with Priēnē, at least by the late second century BCE when Priēnē underwent its building boom. For instance, the city of Lētē, occupying a strategic ridge on a road leading from the Thermaic Gulf to the inland highlands and toward Thrace, but also controlling part of the fertile plain around Lake Bolbē on the other side of the pass, can be called a *polis* and shared in the common experiences of the network of *poleis*. It is true that it had a long, pre-*polis* history with its own specificities.[22] We can see it as a town of the Mygdonians (a Greek-speaking *ethnos* in a complex region) through its coinage in the sixth century BCE. In the fourth century, Lētē appears as a city colonized by the kingdom of Macedonia with elite settlers, whose customs and especially whose material culture is documented in epigraphical and archaeological material—a *polis* of sorts, but as part of a royal-national state. Two remarkable artifacts (of world-historical cultural significance), a large gilt bronze crater masterfully decorated with Dionysiac scenes in high relief, and a book of learned commentary on a mystical poem (the second earliest book attested in Europe), were found in the tombs of elite settlers, at Derveni (a modern toponym, whence the shorthand "Derveni crater" and the "Derveni papyrus," under which these artifacts are well known and exhibited in the Archaeological Museum of Thessaloniki).[23]

But by the late second century BCE, Lētē called itself a *polis*, with the normal institutions of People (*dēmos*), Council (*boulē*) and magistrates, public spaces (including an *agora*), and ceremonies to honor benefactors, a major preoccupation of Lētē as of Priēnē and indeed all other *poleis*. One of the benefactors Lētē honored was a Roman officer who in 119 BCE protected the *polis* (and other *poleis* in Macedonia) during a Celtic invasion:[24] a major development in the history of the *polis* was the rise of Roman power, which integrated the *poleis* into a monarchical world empire. In more peaceful times (22 BCE), market-commissioners dedicated an entrance, probably to the *agora*, "to the gods and the *polis*."[25]

In 121/2 CE, the *polis* honored with a statue another benefactor, a Roman citizen (a descendant of the settlers who came to the area in the second and first centuries

BCE), M' Salarius Sabinus, inter alia, for accepting to sell foodstuffs at an artificially depressed price "during the passage of the armies of the Lord Caesar"; part of the statue base was found in 1916 by British soldiers (Highlanders of the Black Watch regiment) digging trenches on the strategically important ridge where the city was located.[26] The presence of a Roman citizen and Roman armies on the march attest to the perennity of Roman power, but the document also shows the continuity in the need for the community to interact with its wealthiest members.

The second century CE was a time of stability, in which the *poleis* of Greece, the islands, and Asia Minor underwent spectacular urban development, with some exceptions. Priēnē is one (it never developed the colonnaded streets that adorned other cities, and indeed its neighbors such as Ephesos and Milētos). Likewise, the small city of Panopeus, in Phōkis, lacked spectacular spaces or monuments decorated with marble, in the second-century CE style, as noted by the traveler Pausanias, who affected to wonder "if one can give the name of *polis* to those who possess no government offices, no *gymnasion*, no theater, no market-place, no water descending to a fountain, but live in bare shelters just like mountain cabins, right on a ravine."[27] But this introduction is a play on the "checklist" of items that make for a *polis*: Pausanias then lists markers of *polis* status (borders, representation in the regional federation of Phōkis), and even more, the mythical past that manifests Panopeus's antiquity, naturalness, and worth (below, p. 410). He does not, however, mention the powerful fortification walls of the city, still partly extant today (fig. 15.1).

Panopeus in the 160s CE was doubtless a *polis*; but what would Pausanias have thought of the city of Palmyra in southern Syria, on the edge of the steppe, in the same decade or perhaps later (ca. 200 CE)?[28] It boasted monumental public spaces, ornaments, an *agora*, and magistrates' offices and the colonnaded streets which were set up in the Roman-imperial *poleis*. In its official epigraphy, the Palmyrenes call themselves a *polis*, are citizens (*poleitai*) and have institutions, such as the People (*dēmos*), Council (*boulē*), and office holders. The institutions also appear transcribed in Aramaic, as *dmws* and *bwl*, since the *polis* of Palmyra inscribed official documents in Greek and in Aramaic, uniquely for the cities of the Roman Near East. The term *polis* is not transcribed in Aramaic, but is once translated by *gbl*, a polysemous term that indicates a human grouping as well as a territorial one. The term appears in 51 CE, in the full expression, using the Aramaic ethnonym, *gbl Tdmory' klhn*, "the community of the Tadmorians, all of them," in a striking echo of the expression, three centuries earlier, of the "whole community" of islanders in a decree passed by a *polis*.[29]

From Hērakleia, a small island (indeed small-island) community in the early third century BCE to Palmyra in 250 CE, a great trading city in an Eastern province of the Roman empire, we have covered a vast range of historical, social, and ecological circumstances: is there any justification for applying, like a wet blanket, the term of *polis* to a whole range of different communities?[30]

In Search of *Polis*

In this book, I will argue that the *polis* can be defined with a unitary definition—but that this definition, to be capacious enough to cover historical, geographical, and ecological diversity, has to admit significant ambiguities.[31] Hence, *polis* means, initially, an urban settlement of contiguous habitations, a town, and this concrete definition was never forgotten.[32] But the city can give its name to human community, designated with a special name derived from the place (such as the Herakleiotes on their little Cycladic island). The full title of a Levantine city was "the people of the Laodikeians in Phoenicia, the holy and inviolate (*polis*)," *ho dēmos tōn Laodikeōn tōn en Phoinikēi tēs hieras kai asylou*: the *polis* appears in the same breath as a masculine plural noun designating a mass of citizens ("the Laodikeians"), and a feminine singular noun designating the placename ("the holy one"), both united grammatically.[33]

The members of this community control a territory, so that the name of the *polis* can also designate the whole territory as well as the city: in the constant wars of the fourth century BCE, when an army marches "into Phleious" or "into Aigosthena," it crosses the border of the land controlled by those *poleis*.[34] In practice, the territory is usually small, at least in modern terms. Perhaps a quarter of all poleis had territories of 25 square kilometers or less (like Hērakleia); perhaps 90 percent fitted within a territory of 500 square kilometers or less (table 1.1, fig. 1.6; see also figs 9.2, 9.3, 17.1–2, 18.2, for concrete instances).[35] Priēnē was located at the upper end of this range, a striking corrective for the temptation to call it a "small *polis*." The exact relations of power, access and membership between the city, the territory, and the members of the *polis* beyond any theoretical and ideal equation of all three, will constitute a *leitmotif* of this book.

Secondly, at least in the Greek context, a *polis* is self-governing, and exists as a state, with institutions and power. Stately competencies can be illustrated at Hērakleia by the single document that survives, but also at Priēnē by the rich epigraphical evidence, and at Palmyra by the extensive law on customs dues. This point has in fact been in dispute, either on the grounds that the *polis* was a "stateless" social organization, or that it lost its nature as a self-governing organism in the second half of the fourth century BCE. This theme will constitute a central area of concern in this book. It is true that the *polis* is qualitatively different from the contemporary state, with its extension, autonomy, and self-awareness. Furthermore, the *polis* is unlike the modern state of Hobbes's *Leviathian* as embodied sovereignty, or even the hierarchical, stratified "early states" of neo-evolutionist theory, as proposed for ancient Mesoamerica or Mesopotamia.[36] Rather, the *polis* defines itself as commonwealth (*koinon*), a community (*koinōnia*) of citizens, a constitution (*politeia*)—at least, these are the terms that Aristotle explicitly deploys to describe the rise and the essence of the *polis* in his *Politics*. It can hence be described as an auto-instituted organism, using concepts developed by social theorists such as C. Castoriadis or P. Clastres.[37]

Table 1: Territorial size and population estimates for a hypothetical total of 1,100 Greek city-states.

Polis size	Area km²	Estimated population range	Estimated average population	Polis count known size	Polis count total (est.)	Total pop. (1,100 poleis)	% total pop. (1,100 poleis)	% polis count (1,100 poleis)
1	25 or less	525–2,500	1,000	148	277	277,000	0.03	0.25
2	25–100	875–10,000	3,500	256	483	1,690,500	0.20	0.44
3	100–200	3,500–25,000	7,000	95	144	1,008,000	0.12	0.13
4	200–500	7,000–50,000	17,000	107	124	2,108,000	0.26	0.11
5	500–1,000	17,500–75,000	35,000	53	59	2,065,000	0.25	0.05
6	1,000–2,000	35,000–100,000	65,000	10	10	650,000	0.08	0.01
7	Over 2,000	75,000–250,000	150,000	3	3	450,000	0.05	0.003
Total				672	1,100	8,248,500		

From Ober 2015, Princeton University Press, whose notes (lightly edited) I reproduce here: *Polis* sizes 1–5 based on *IACP*. Size 6 = Argos, Byzantion, Ēlis, Eretria, Kyrēnē, Megalēpolis, Milētos, Pantikapaion, Rhēgion, Rhodes. Size 7 = Athens, Sparta, Syracuse. "Estimated average population" based on Hansen 2006, modified by results in Hansen 2008. "*Polis* count known size" includes 636 *poleis* in the *IACP* whose size in known or plausibly estimated, along with 32 additions in Hansen 2008 and 4 additions from E. Mackil (per litt.). 109 "size 1 or 2," 37 "size 2 or 3," 11 "size 3 or 4," 8 "size 4 or 5" (including Pergamon and Xanthos from Hansen 2008) are divided evenly between the two relevant categories. "*Polis* count total" assumes that the distribution of known-size *poleis* is modeled in the total count as follows: size 1 and 2: 53% of total are known; size 3: 65% of total are known; size 4: 86% of total are known; size 5: 89% of total are known; size 6 and 7: 100% of total are known. N.B. Hansen 2008 additions to the *IACP* list of sized *poleis* include 29 size 4 *poleis* and 3 size 5 *poleis*, but no size 1–3 *poleis*.

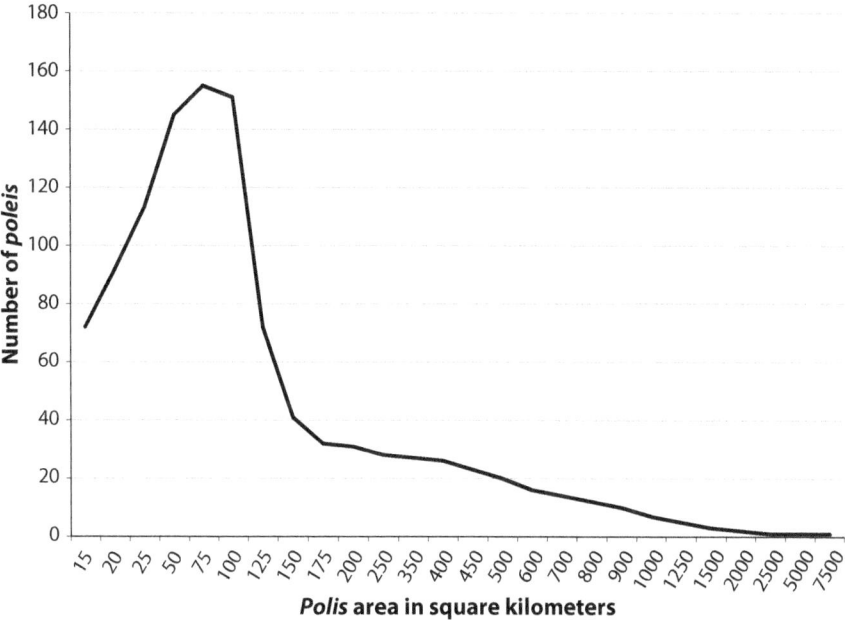

FIGURE 1.6. Distribution of *poleis* by size of territory. From Ober 2015.

However, the *polis* also clearly appears as endowed with a whole apparatus of means and monopolies: for instance, institutions in the form of clearly defined and formalized powerholders; collectively decided, uniquely legitimate and binding rules; collectively raised and pooled resources, extracted within a formally defined territory; public goods; exclusivity on the granting of rights, the awarding of distinction, the meting out of punishments; the means of coercion, or at least the claims to legitimate coercion; claims on its members, and the outward pursuit of external violence and power, two interrelated phenomena.[38] At a minimal level, the *polis* as apparatus can be described as some form of state, exercising governmental functions. The possession of these capacities amounted to a recognized status. The difference between a *polis* and a *kōmē* (village) was one of sovereignty, not of settlement size or degree of urbanization;[39] this is shown by the protocols of peer-polity interaction. Settlements that lost *polis* status ended up peripheralized, and hence could end up shedding urban traits of infrastructure and autarky-directed complexity.[40]

The problem of the stateness of the *polis* raises further issues. If the *polis* was a state, the emergence of governmentality is transformative and constitutes a major explanatory challenge (when and why does the state emerge in "archaic" Greece?). Conversely, if the *polis* was not a state, then its apparatus of governmentality needs minimizing or explaining away; for instance, by anthropologizing it as a religious and ritual phenomenon, or emphasizing social connectivity, a move fraught with theoretical difficulties and contradictions of its own. In this book, I will continuously argue for the centrality of stateness as a definitional characteristic of the *polis*, and for its persistence throughout its history;[41] this stance determines the shape of the narrative (as summarized below). But I will do so in awareness of the *polis*'s peculiarities as a state—namely, its closeness to social organization, its thinness, its ideological totalizing. The tension between the *polis* as a social organism (which can be described in terms that P. Clastres developed specifically to describe society as a something existing *against* the state) and the *polis* as governmentality, is a major concern of this book throughout its structure (as summarized below).

If we accept the state-like nature of the *polis*, two consequences follow. The first was clearly seen by Aristotle and recurs as an obsession in the *Politics*. In self-governing polities, membership gives access to institutions, and institutional power decides on matters such as dispute resolution, property rights and, especially, the distribution of common burdens: hence the composition of the citizen body is a social but also a political issue, bearing on the pursuit of interests by constituencies, especially the rich and the poor. The traditional alternative between oligarchy and democracy is rooted here; other ways of distributing power (for instance, by excluding the rural population) are also possible. In any case, the relationship between socioeconomic elites and the community, the *dēmos*, both in the sense of the whole body of citizens, and in the sense of the nonelite, will have to be negotiated toward some form of durable social bargain.

The second issue raised by stately self-governance is that of its extension and its limits. As state, the *polis* tends toward autonomy, yet the latter concept is fraught with problems. An autonomous *polis* must negotiate and maintain its existence within collaborative frames that should be compatible with local self-governance. Furthermore, a *polis* must find a way to coexist with other autonomous *poleis*, which can involve relations of force and hence the possibility of hegemony and even subordination—a problematic relationship. Finally, the autonomous *polis* must deal with large supralocal, imperial powers and find accommodations that preserve some margin of agency within which stateliness can be exercised: I will contend that the *poleis*, in dealing with large, supralocal, patrimonial formations, strove to keep acting and being considered as states down the centuries, until the end of Classical Antiquity. All these historical situations illustrate the nature of autonomy as a consequence of stateness but also as a source of tensions and ambiguities.

The free citizens that constitute the *polis* are free adult men—stakeholders in institutional power, slaveowners, heads of their households. The *polis* had a multilayered existence as a society, both as the organization of social relations around the constitution of a *dēmos* of citizens (what I will call *civic society* later in this book), and the impact of the mechanisms of inclusion and exclusion on the wider human ecology within the *polis*'s boundaries (what I will call *civil society*)—the poetics of *to koinon* in Hērakleia illustrate this tension, which is inherent in the *polis*-hood. In other words, it is easy, and tempting because of the profusion of evidence (especially documentary), to write an institutional history of the *polis*, and a history of the relationship between *polis* and power; it is more challenging to write a social relationship of the *polis* and of the impact of citizenship, and a history of the *polis* in its relationship with more diffuse forms of power.[42] Finally, the *polis* is the story of the city-state in Greek-speaking lands, starting in an Aegean-centered geography (mainland Greece, the islands, Western Asia Minor), but extending to other Balkan regions (notably Macedonia or Ēpeiros) and, spectacularly, to the western Mediterranean, the Black Sea, the Levant, and northern Africa, and hence involving both settlement by groups of Greek immigrants and the adoption of *polis* forms (along with the Greek language) by local communities.[43]

The definitions above are partly taken over from a comprehensive attempt to study the *polis*, as undertaken by the Copenhagen Polis Centre under the direction of M. Hansen, culminating in the sum represented by the *Inventory of Archaic and Greek* Poleis (2004), a majestic, team-authored survey of the 1,284 examples which the Centre found as examples of the form, beyond the well-known cases of giant *poleis* such as Athens or Sparta, which are very present in the literary sources and overrepresented in modern treatments of ancient history. Notably, the centrality of urbanness, the coterminality of territory, and especially the stately nature of the *polis* as organization, are investigated with great thoroughness and subtleness. The present book diverges from the Copenhagen version in placing autonomy at the heart of any definition of the *polis*, whereas M. Hansen argues, typologically, that it was not a necessary feature.[44] I propose to see its importance, but also its contradictions, as a crucial factor of the history of the *polis*. The centrality of stateness and autonomy, but also the nature of social negotiation and bargaining, appear clearly in a long history of the *polis* like the one I will construct here. These themes already receive much attention in Max Weber's treatment of the ancient city, as ruled by a closed political group defined by status (*Bürgerstand*) as a group of peers (*Verband*).[45]

The deep temporality of my account is a second divergence from the work of the Copenhagen Polis Centre. I aim to look for a continuous, yet evolving history of the *polis* beyond the periods where its apogee has traditionally been located, namely the archaic (700–480 BCE) and Classical (480–323 BCE) periods; indeed, many treatments of the *polis* are centered on these conventional periods.[46] Traditional periodization, I argue, prevents the clear perception of issues such as autonomy and stateness. A great deal of this book is devoted to producing a new narrative of the *polis*. In elaborating this "biography"—if it is possible to write the biography of a form of human organization, while avoiding the pitfalls of the humanizing metaphor (birth, youth, growth, decline)—I have centered my attention on the issues highlighted above—issues of politics, power, social bargaining—in the hope of producing narratives that are at least partly analytical.

I summarize the shape of the narrative below (pp. 403–7), so here will simply mention that my main argument is that after the collapse of quite different forms of political organization (part II), centuries of experimentation (part III) around central political ideas, and of conflict around the issues of autonomy and social power led to a "great convergence" of *polis* forms (part IV), starting ca. 350 BCE, to produce a relatively uniform, stable organism centered on communitarian, democratic forms and bargains between the community and its elites. The causes for the great convergence are contingent (the failure of local hegemony, the rise of empires, the success of *poleis* at preserving their autonomy), but also must be connected to deep structural features. The community of Hērakleia is but one example of the constitutionally minded, democratic *polis* that emerges from the great convergence, as was the diffusion and harmonization of *polis* forms, across the Aegean but also Asia Minor and the Levant.

This *polis*, whose emergence Aristotle witnessed, was a pervasive, normative form of political and social organization during an extended period, 350 BCE to 100 BCE, which might be considered a "long classical" period. It endured, with modifications and simplifications, into the Roman empire, down to 400 CE (part V). My periodization is influenced by the careful work of the epigraphist and historian Ph. Gauthier, as well as that of the historian F. Millar, whose great works on the Roman empire or the Roman Near East are also essays on the *polis*. Hence my periodizing scheme places the long ages of the developed *polis* (350 BCE–400 CE) at the heart of the history of the *polis*, unlike the traditional periodization of the Copenhagen Polis Centre's explorations. My belief is that this viewpoint allows for crucial insights into the definitional and conceptual issues involved in studying the *polis*.[47]

My extended narrative is above all inductive, drawing on evidence to seek patterns, but is also eclectically structured by the relevant theoretical tools: a constructivist study of ideology and language, informed by speech-act theory; an Aristotelian conviction that political institutions (in the sense of constitutional arrangements) and law matter, as shaping the parameters of social interaction; a "new institutionalist" awareness of interests, constituencies, path-dependency, and individual choices in the aggregate, especially in the pursuit of economic profit. I believe all these tools cohere in offering the possibility of a viable working model of the *polis*, where the Aristotelian emphasis on state power and institutions does not displace but helps to explain social history (chapter 15). At the end of this book (Part VI), I try to revisit the *polis* from a series of theoretical viewpoints, in a series of chapters that amount to a rolling conclusion. My aim is notably to gather, each time, the threads of events into coherent explanatory schemes. Thus, I spin out an idealist history of institutions and ideology (chapter 16), followed by a new institutionalist history of the *polis* as successful collective action or even "good institutions" in economic terms, notably engaging with recent accounts of *polis* history as that of a sustained economic boom (chapter 17). I also test my model of a democratic *polis* against grimmer possibilities, that of continuous violence as the price of collective action, and that of hidden oligarchical powers (chapter 18)—possibilities for which evidence is still scanty. Finally, I let the repressed social history, notably inhabited by those excluded by the construction of the political community and citizenship (such as women, foreigners, or enslaved workers) burst out to the forefront (chapter 19), drawing on recent work on gender or slavery, to attempt the hard exercise of remembering—and evaluating—the place of domination and violence in the *polis*.

The Aristotelian focus of the book is compatible with my interest in the *polis* as form, as an abstraction. But the theoretical interests are balanced with a constant engagement with detailed exemplification. The cases of Hērakleia, Priēnē, Lētē, Panopeus, and Palmyra, touched upon lightly above, illustrate the method, the sources, and the interest in institutions but also geography and ecology. The history of the *polis* must be written from such testcases, rather than the great and famous *poleis*: the "Third Greece," in Hans-Joachim Gehrke's striking, if problematic, formulation. We should look even further, to include places such as Kyaneai, in Lykia, which barely turns up in the canon of ancient Greek literature, but is an extraordinarily well-documented case of how the adoption of *polis* forms affected landscape and settlement.[48] Such examples serve to constitute a broad basis for the interpretive essays of part VI, even if they cannot match the systematic register of *poleis* established for a limited time span in the *Inventory of Archaic and Greek* Poleis. But they also serve the double, and contradictory, purpose of embedding the existence of the *polis* as a political and social form in a long, concrete history, and of illustrating the texture and singularity of each one of the *poleis* as part of this account.

PART II

Before the *Polis*: Possibilities

1100–700 BCE

Endings and Beginnings

The *polis* had a beginning; its particular characteristics emerged out of historical processes over centuries, from ca. 1100 to 700 BCE, and evolved during the sixth century BCE. "Beginnings" does not mean "origins." The beginnings of the *polis* do not necessarily hold the answers to our questions about its nature and its workings; the *polis* itself should be viewed as a historical process, and a fortiori as a historical development in which certain paths evolved or emerged. But this development offers a diverse, complex image of various interrelated phenomena: integration, structuration, consolidation, institutionalization, and ideological debates. In this chapter, I propose to explore these phenomena, starting from the Late Bronze Age—a millennium and more before the time of the islanders of Hērakleia, the *agora* of Hellenistic Priēnē, and the *gymnasion* of Roman-era Lētē that opened this book. In doing so, I will try to trace a number of developments—some due to continuity and development, some to surprising persistence, and some to extinction: rather than trace a clear path of development, I insist on this initial diversity as the crucial feature. Specifically, a number of related phenomena in the Greek world, during the half-millennium between 1200 and 700 BCE (the "Early Iron Age") led to the emergence of political communities: urbanization and consolidation; the negotiation of relations between communities and their elites; the integration and structuration of territory around proto-urban nuclei; and the structuration of communities in supralocal entities. These phenomena reinforced each other: the structuration of territory helped create the community within which negotiations took place, which in turn helped define spatial relations in political terms.

"Birth of the *polis*," "emergence of the city-state"—such themes are exciting and indeed central to the study of ancient history, but none of the phenomena is straightforward, especially because of the nature of the sources. The only surviving written, articulate sources of any length date to the end of the period within which these processes took place, namely some point within the second half of the eighth century BCE. They are, of course, poems, which fall into two pairs. The first pair is the *Iliad* and the *Odyssey*, two epic poems of exceptional length and beauty (almost certainly by two different authors, though later ascribed to a single "Homer"). These monumental texts celebrate the war-deeds (*Iliad*) or adventures (*Odyssey*) of heroes from an age explicitly said to be much older and better than the time of the poems' audience, and hence portrayed with archaizing traits: for instance, in the world of the heroes, bronze is used of weapons and tools and iron is a rarity, unlike the widespread use of iron in the real world of the eighth century BCE. There probably is only a tenuous relationship between this fictional world and the civilization that actually came before the Early Iron Age, the palatial civilization of the Late Bronze Age. The second set of texts is constituted by the shorter poems of Hesiod, written in the same meter as the two epic poems but treating different subjects (the *Theogony* presents cosmology, the *Works and Days* is a work of wisdom poetry on justice and order). The poems' style and repetitive texture, and even subject matter make it clear that they draw on a tradition of oral poetry (in which a performer deploys a repertoire of stock phrases, scenes, and themes to generate pieces), even if they must have been written down as fixed texts; by content, it is also clear that they are influenced by (or reuse, or draw on) much older Near Eastern texts and themes. These sources are difficult to use—the "historian's headache" indeed, as K. Raaflaub warned; much of the above (date, authorship, oral tradition leading to written texts, Near Eastern "influence") is open to controversy, and the basics of where and how to place these texts as historical documents are shaky.[1] This has a direct impact on the question of what sort of society these texts describe and imply. But the ideological force of these texts only makes them the more interesting—especially if they date to the later eighth century BCE, which saw considerable social diversity.

The other great text that tells us about the world before the *polis* is the material evidence, archaeological and art historical, of Early Iron Age Greece. Sustained systematic excavation, rescue excavation, and surface survey, especially of the intensive type, have provided a considerable body of evidence (which increased tremendously in the second half of the twentieth century, in an impressive success story in the practice of "classical" archaeology).[2] The patterns that emerge out of this evidence constitute an archaeology of social structure (especially through the funerary evidence), and an archaeology of social space, through the investigation of built-up spaces and houses within settlements, and of settlement distribution across territory. In addition, the period concerned (and its subperiods: see Chronology, p. 623) witnessed evolution in the visual arts (indeed, the various phases have traditionally served to define these subperiods). The period is characterized by richly figurative artifacts such as great painted fired clay vessels and bronze figurines. This world of images (funerals, armed men, horses, ships, dances) suggests the possibility of an archaeology of social meaning that might join up with the portrayed or inferred social worlds of the epic poems.[3]

All of the phenomena outlined above occur in a specific space-time largely defined by the archaeology. The core geography for these phenomena is constituted by the islands off western Greece, the Peloponnese, central Greece (Attica, Euboia, Boiōtia, Phōkis), the Aegean islands, Crete, and the western coast of Asia Minor; the northern Aegean; and Italy and Sicily.[4] This geography of social change and emergence exhibits a considerable degree of regional diversity, and the patterns and rhythms of development move with different intensities across time, a state of affairs compounded by the incomplete retrievability of the archaeological evidence (and its shaping by research practice—the surface surveys of different types, rescue excavations, and rare systematic excavations). But within these variations, the general story seems to show common traits across this geographical area; at least, the issues are the same, and the phenomena and the outcomes, even in their variation, are related and connected in deep and instructive ways. These connections appear the more striking when contrasted with Thessaly and Macedonia, where sociopolitical development seems to have followed a steady pattern of evolution, mainly in hierarchized and stratified directions, from the Bronze Age onwards (with a complex political pattern of urbanization of its own, and interactions with processes going on in Southern Greece).[5]

The chronological frame for the interlocking phenomena mentioned above is constituted by the five centuries between 1200 to 700 BCE, the period from the end of the Bronze Age to the Early Iron Age;[6] they can be sub-periodized into a two-stage collapse (1200-1100 BCE), a short period of abeyance (1100-1000 BCE), and finally a period of stabilization and integration (1000-700 BCE), with accelerating change and interaction in the decades after ca. 750 BCE.

Texts and images have been made to speak of a long, empty "Dark Ages," followed by an across-the-board "Renaissance" or structural revolution in the second half of the eighth century BCE. Within this scheme, the exact details of social structure might have been an egalitarian Dark Ages followed by an aristocratic eighth century BCE, or an elitist Dark Ages followed by an egalitarian eighth century BCE; but always privileging the suddenness and transformative nature of change.[7] Various elements of this (long satisfying) scheme have been challenged by new evidence: the supposed "Dark Ages" of empty landscapes, pastoralism, and mobility have yielded before a sense of continuity in settlement and agrarian economy, and generally the impression of poverty in the "Dark Ages" (indeed the very notion of "Dark" Ages) has come under attack.[8] The developmental sketch given below tries to integrate some of these exciting nuances in the story of the "birth of the *polis*."

But the joined-up interpretation of the whole of the material evidence is no more straightforward than the historical reading of the Homeric and Hesiodic poems. In the absence of written sources for the majority of the period, the interpretive models are those of prehistoric archaeology, depending on sophisticated methods to handle data or to read images, and drawing on models from social anthropology (sometimes applied with a degree of scholasticism or vagueness). These traits are, of course, those of archaeology as a discipline; the specificity in the case of the study of the centuries between 1200 BCE and 700 BCE has been a tendency to elaborate neat developmental narratives, leading toward the recognizable forms of the *polis*, with notably a proto–middle class appearing from the very start. The oddity of this combination (sophisticated archaeology with traditional narratives) stems from the central problem of studying the *polis*: political investment and desire. In the following pages, I abandon the preordained narrative of full-fledged emergence of a *polis* middle class, to explore a gradual, uncertain, obscure process, around two main themes: the processes of integration and structuration operating at many levels, and the mutually dependent constitution of elite and community.

2

To New Beginnings

> It is so difficult to find the beginning. Or, better: it is difficult to begin at the beginning. And not to try to go further back.
>
> —L. WITTGENSTEIN, *ON CERTAINTY*, 471

Palaces and Beyond (ca. 1400–1200 BCE)

A thousand years and more before Hērakleia and Priēnē: the jump back in time takes us to the Late Bronze Age, a world of palace-centered polities in the Aegean, participants in the brilliant concert of ancient Near Eastern powers of the second millennium BCE. At least, this is what the most obvious, spectacular, and coherent evidence suggests. By the fourteenth century BCE, such polities appear in the archaeological and documentary record as "early states" centralized around palaces that acted as the seat for power elites, headed by single rulers. The best-known examples are the well excavated sites of Pylos, Mykēnai, Tiryns, or Knōssos (fig. 2.1). Other, less well-known palaces occupied the sites of the Akropolis of Athens, the central hill of Thebes, and its neighbor Orchomenos. Recently, another palace has been discovered south of Sparta (at a modern village, Agios Vasileios).[1] These polities controlled extensive, well-populated and hierarchized territories. The palatial states also managed land tenure, making temporary grants of estates (or estate income) to individuals or shrines, in negotiation with rural settlements (designated with the term *damos*).[2]

Such structures allowed the efficient extraction, concentration, and disbursement of resources and surplus in the form of rations paid to officials and workers; the raw materials extracted could be further processed by specialized workers within the palace system. The bureaucratic records of these palatial economies, kept in a syllabary script (Linear B), form the only written evidence available—the first written material in Europe (the system is best attested at Pylos, in the Western Peloponnese but, excitingly, has also appeared at Thebes).[3] A measure of Late Bronze Age state power is given by the mobilization of labor for major works such as fortifications or hydraulic projects (as in the area of Lake Kōpais, near Orchomenos).

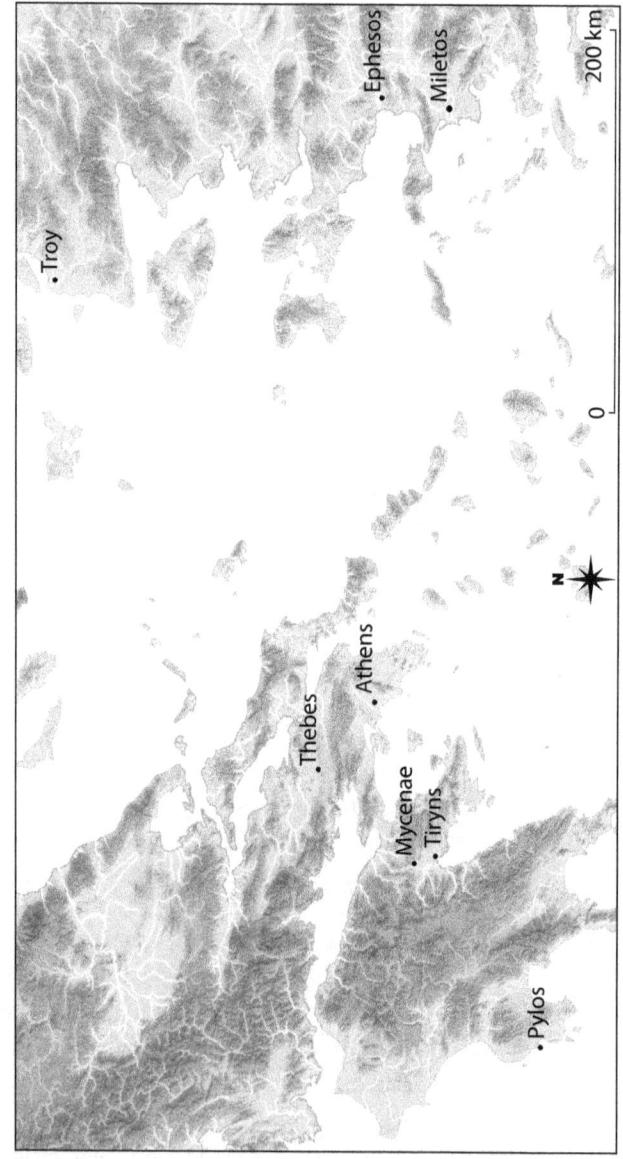

FIGURE 2.1. The Mycenaean world, and some of the well-known palatial centers.

The position of the ruler (*wanax*) and the ruling elite is made clear by their material culture: fortified palatial architecture, monumental tombs, high-status manufactured artifacts (bronze weapons, gold tableware and personal ornamentation, gems), graceful figurative art (for instance in the form of frescoed elite residences) and imported Eastern luxuries. All these traces of a high lifestyle, ideologically marked, are attested abundantly in many sites (they dazzle museumgoers and site visitors). This is most notable at Mykēnai, the site whose early excavation history led to the common designation of this civilization as "Mycenaean." The palace at Mykēnai is surrounded by a massive ashlar wall that incorporates earlier grave precincts (seventeenth and sixteenth centuries BCE); the main gate is decorated with a famous twin-lion relief (now headless), influenced by Near Eastern and Anatolian models. The palace storerooms contained luxury imports from the East and from Egypt; the structure was surrounded by massive, corbelled tombs.

The existence of a class of specialists in violence is suggested by Mycenaean art and artifacts, as well as the records of the distribution and maintenance of equipment by the palatial states.[4] Such equipment included the war chariot, which thus appears as a marker of warrior violence (as on the earlier funerary markers from Mykēnai), a Near Eastern–inspired artifact, and a product of palatial processes, economic and political. Elite culture certainly gave a central place to violence, which enabled control and acquisition, be it of local surplus or of captives. The status and position of the remainder of the population in these state formations are less clear (subordination, serfdom, a spectrum of varied statuses and groups?).

This system of polities, located in mainland Greece and Crete, looked outwards to a Late Bronze Age world of exchange and diplomacy among great hegemonic powers and local principalities.[5] Eastern goods were procured through overseas trade; the need for resources, especially metals, led to Mycenaean settlement throughout the Aegean, for instance in the Chalkidic peninsula in the northern Aegean.[6] Finally, a strong and organized Mycenaean presence in western Asia Minor, around Milētos, is attested both archaeologically and in the texts of the Hittite empire based in central Anatolia. The Hittite state interacted and competed at a high level with a Mycenaean entity, the Aḫḫiyawa (probably a transcription of "Achaians," a vocable used in the later Homeric poems to describe their heroes as an ethnic group). The Aḫḫiyawa ruler may have been based in a palace state in mainland Greece (perhaps Mykēnai).[7] The conflict (that perhaps inspired, distantly, legends about the Trojan War) illustrates the nature of the Mycenaean polities, and their success.

Even this sketch shows how difficult to understand the Mycenaean world is; indeed, the Hittite rulers may have misunderstood its political geography as dominated by a single ruler, rather than as a multi-palatial landscape.[8] Tempting as it is to see in the palatial polities of mainland Greece and Crete in the palatial period forms of "early states" based on extraction for the benefit of dominating elites, much remains obscure about them. The process of construction of these early states and their elites remains unknown: they succeeded an earlier phase of palatial polities centered in Crete (the "Minoan" culture), which had succeeded the looser social organization of the third-millennium Aegean and collapsed in the mid-fifteenth century BCE.[9] Most strikingly, for all their pomp, overseas connections, and bureaucratic organization, it is clear that the Mycenean entities constitute a system of microstates, especially compared with the Hittite or even North Syrian palatial polities—to the point that an expert on the period termed them "Potemkine" palaces ("disappointingly small").[10] Pylos may have ruled over several "provinces"—amounting, in the end, to an (admittedly very rich) corner of the western Peloponnese. Mykēnai might have dominated the Argolid (with another palatial settlement at Tiryns) and little more; this might be reflected, ultimately, in the small size of the palatial complex. Orchomenos probably controlled parts of the uplands of Phōkis but these areas lay close by, and Orchomenos had to contend with the close neighborhood of Thebes.

But even small size did not mean that these micro-polities were immediate expressions of sweeping palatial power, and the model sketched out above must be nuanced on the ground. Even in the Argolid, dominated by Mykēnai, the political economy and social structure might have not been structured simply by the palace and its needs.[11] A fresco at Pylos represents Mycenaean warriors overcoming figures dressed in shaggy animal skins: members of a marginal, untamed community, as marked by their rough clothing, contrasting with the sophisticated woven clothes produced in the ambit of the palaces (the fresco was paired with one showing ships, as if to emphasize the faraway horizons of the warrior elite).[12] The northwest Peloponnese (future Achaia) seems to have been devoid of palaces altogether.[13] Further afield, in the north Aegean, the Cyclades (notably at Naxos), or the western coast of Asia Minor, we find non-palatial forms of social organization, even if these were often culturally influenced and economically in contact with the Mycenaean lands.[14]

Historiographically, the palatial system appears as the antithesis of the later forms of the *polis* (the first time that we will define the *polis* in relation to political Others—a trope borrowed from *polis* discourse itself): monarchical, hierarchical, bureaucratic... The temptation has hence been to write up the death of this palatial "Other" as the necessary precondition for the rise of the *polis*.[15] On closer, more nuanced inspection, important themes appear in the world of the palaces that will play an important role in our story. The first is small size and regional structuration. There is no need to argue that the palaces reflect unchanging geographical determinants—or, conversely, that they precisely determined subsequent settlement patterns. Mykēnai would later be a small place and end up taken over by the rampant city-state of Argos. The fragmentation of the political landscape into micro-units is immediately recognizable as a feature in *polis* history. Within these micro-units, the relationship of settlements would require definition between integration, negotiation, and domination. Likewise, the relationship between micro-units, once their boundaries were defined, would need settling (domination, hierarchy, or parity being some of the possibilities for this relationship).

The second important theme is the presence of social complexity alongside the ownership and power structures of the palace. The palace, its ruler, its elites, its specialists in violence, dealt with other constituents: the *damos*, but also various types of property owners, sometimes endowed with corporate identities, as shown by the study of the terminology of land tenure and of production.[16] These widespread local landowners (perhaps linked with the *damos*) attested in the archives might be linked to a large element of sub-elite individuals whose tastes and consumption can be guessed at in the material record. This sub-elite class will play an important role in the future development of communities, in the rest of this chapter (and beyond).

Collapses and Aftermaths (1180–800 BCE)

The Mycenaean system disappeared in two steps. The first was the generalized and violent end of the system of palatial polities shortly after 1200 BCE; the causes are more likely to have been internal questions of sustainability than external invasion, though Mediterranean-wide factors may also have been at play, as suggested by the general context of upheaval and systemic collapse that saw the end of the Hittite superpower, as well as the destruction and abandonment of the extensive, wealthy city of Troy VIIa, one of the successive settlements on this famous site.[17] The Mycenaean centralized state structures fell into disuse for good. The collapse of control would have allowed, for a while, some local groups or even whole regions to enjoy a lifestyle characterized by leisure, warfare, and Eastern luxury goods, that had earlier been the preserve of the palatial elites.[18]

The material culture of this phase (designated, in the precise if dry patois of the archaeologists, as Late Helladic IIIC, or as "LH IIIC"),[19] shows many continuities with the Mycenaean age. These local groups might be descendants of the subordinate power holders and violence specialists of the *qa-si-reu* type appearing in the Mycenean documents (the word is the same as the later *basileus*, "king"). Such post-Mycenaean post-palatial groups (sometimes designated with the evocative name of "the last Mycenaeans") are notably attested archaeologically by rich funerary material that suggests available resources after the end of control; for instance, in Achaia in the northern Peloponnese, Eastern Lokris in Central Greece, or indeed in the Argolid after the end of the power of Mykēnai proper.[20] The ruined palatial site at Tiryns was partially reoccupied and reworked as an assembly place for a local community. Other sites were settled densely, and present a proto-urban appearance, for instance on the great island of Naxos, or on a seaside hill on the island of Euboia, a place called Lefkandi in modern times. The latter site (which we will revisit often) exemplifies one particular case of post-Mycenean dynamism— namely the communities of Euboia, whose inhabitants were active and adventurous, with a presence in the northern Aegean that prefigures their later ubiquity.

The second, minor collapse came in the form of the interruption of the postpalatial activities (by ca. 1100 BCE), as seen in the abandonment of sites such as Tiryns. The impact of this phase was diverse.[21] Crete enjoyed a soft landing and rapid recovery characterized by continuity or rapid rebirth of settlement, a pattern also seen on the island of Naxos.[22] At Athens, settlement continued on and around the Akropolis. Multiplication of simple tombs hints not so much at widespread impoverishment as the widespread access to status and recognition by nonelite groups, in the form of formal burial, as a consequence of the absence of the palatial polities or their powerholders.[23] In other regions, socially significant phenomena such as large scale settlement structures, elite consumption, and status-conscious burial vanish; for instance in Lakōnia, the Argolid, Boiōtia (past and indeed future powerhouses).[24] The result is a century-long period of obscurity and paucity in the archaeological record, which shows a drop in observable material remains and especially of imported commodities. Hence, this period is perhaps the only one that can still be called a "Dark Ages" (a name once popular for the whole timeframe after the end of the palatial polities). How should we interpret this abeyance? One possible story is that of abandonment and depopulation as a result of final collapse: a great dying-out of the productive population, coupled with a massive migration, the whole phenomenon ending in the extinction of overseas trade, social simplification, and widespread poverty.[25] Another possibility is a widespread pattern of population and settlement shifts across a destabilized landscape with concomitant fluidity in power structures—a time of fallow rather than impoverishment.

It is also possible that the material traces of human activities in this period are escaping our notice and hence getting underrepresented in our interpretations of the transitional period after the Late Bronze Age.[26] Hence another interpretation: this period might be one of creativity and rich social interactions free from the extractive state structures, violent elites, and luxury consumption of the Mycenaean period. In other words, the very obscurity of the record might reflect a successful escape from the palace.[27] This sense of a break with the past is grounded in the shift in material culture. The group inhumations of the Mycenaean period disappear, enabling the generalization of individual graves, usually cremations. Iron, rather than bronze, becomes widespread for weapons and tools. A distinctive ceramic style develops, hence the conventional name for the period, the "Protogeometric" based on this style (fig. 2.2), quite different from Mycenaean painted pottery in appearance and in technique (it is characterized by mechanically drawn circles and half-circles).[28] The Protogeometric pause may have been generalized across the Aegean. Whereas the islands led a subdued existence in the time of the Mycenaean palatial polities, the following period sees them exploding into inventive solutions for, and full participation in, the creation and negotiation of society and community that characterizes the following period.

The Protogeometric period, and its individuals and communities (of whatever form and nature), might represent "a bolt for freedom by many state subjects and

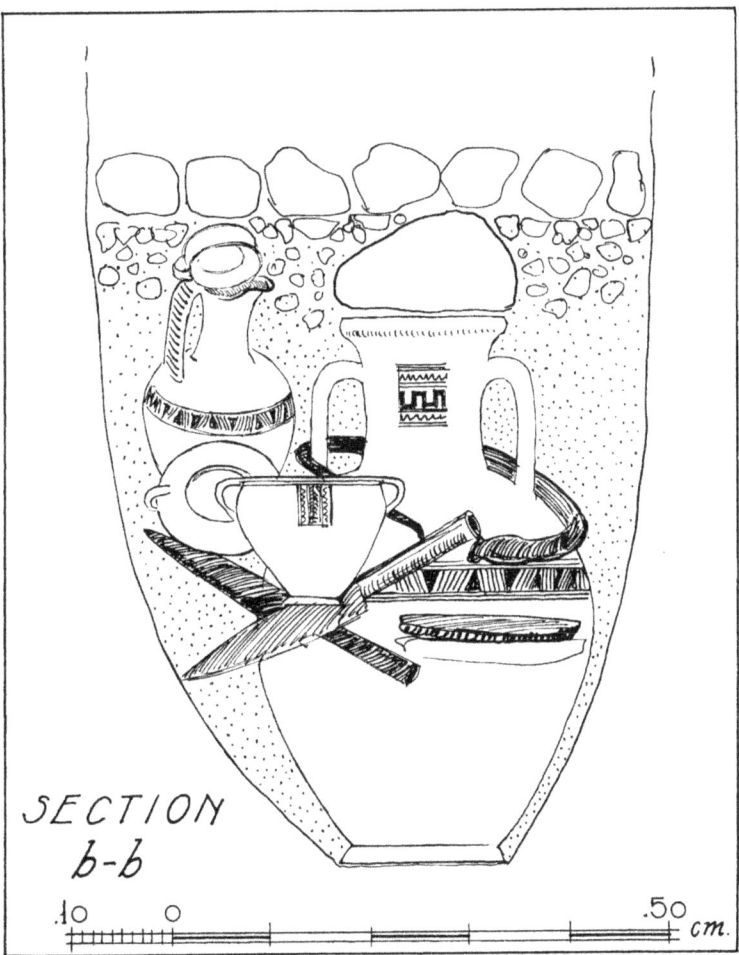

FIGURE 2.2. The "Protogeometric" style. Tomb of a "warrior-craftsman" from the site of the Athenian Agora, ca. 900 BCE.

an improvement in human welfare," of the sort that has been studied by anthropologists.[29] A sense of the period's communal creativity was notably adumbrated by C. Starr (1961). This period may have laid the grounds for a particular political anthropology, characterized by the absence of deeply embedded hierarchies, the weakness of elites, and the prevalence of multiple claims to power and recognition. These traits shaped the societies studied in the rest of this chapter, and indeed in the rest of this book; they also determined the particular nature of statehood in the *polis*, as different from the entities studied in theories of the early state, which focus on the consolidation of ruling classes, bureaucratization, and hierarchization.

This period of abeyance hence must be studied with the following period of increased activity, from ca. 900 BCE onwards, which is conventionally termed the "Geometric" period or, more simply, the Greek "Early Iron Age,"[30] because this period shows the outcome of the creative Dark Age pause. The increased activity may suggest an increase in population—or simply more visible, sophisticated social organization. In the first part of this period of development (900 BCE–800 BCE), three major themes deserve close attention: the emergence of loose settlements; the intensification of overseas contacts and trade in a general context of mobility and even migration; and more generally, the constitution of social relations between community and elite, as can be read in the whole material record.

The first theme, settlement, constitutes the physical context for the story of change in the Early Iron Age. Settlements are widely attested, often in places earlier occupied in the Bronze Age, sometimes in new locales—"big sites" rather than towns, which share central characteristics in their organization.[31] From the archaeological record (based on rescue excavation and surveying rather than systematic excavation), a major form of settlement seems to be groupings of scattered clusters or compounds of oval or apsidal one-room buildings.[32] Such settlement is extremely widespread. We can detect versions in Argos, Corinth, Thespiai, or Eretria;[33] at Ithakē off the coast of the western Peloponnese, in the Cyclades, on Crete, and in Asia Minor[34]—in other words, across the whole geography of future *polis* development. The widespread evidence for "clustervilles" suggests their currency as a feature in the Early Iron Age. A reminiscence of the type glimmers, distantly, in later overseas foundations. For instance, the organized plan of Megara Hyblaia, a settlement founded later in Sicily by migrants from mainland Greece ca. 725 BCE, is laid out as a regular grid with several axes, but grouped widely spread-out small houses, each within its plot, and at some distance from the others.[35] Likewise, Thasos, founded by settlers from Paros in the early seventh century BCE, was structured around two nuclei.[36] The clusters of houses were multifunctional; at Ōrōpos and at Eretria, iron working took place among and in the habitations and their annexes.[37] The houses of the living were surrounded by burials; indeed, it is often the sporadic dispersal of grouped burials that suggests the existence of the clusters of habitation, in the absence of remains of houses.

In other cases, the clusters are quite widely separated, as at Naxos (where two cemeteries, on either side of the akropolis, hint at two settlements—or perhaps three, if the akropolis itself was also occupied).[38] The clearest case is Athens.[39] There the spread is wide but can be read with some precision. Old settlements on the north and south slope of the Akropolis continued; clusters of settlement and artisanal activities operated on the future site of the Agora, while new clusters of settlement, as suggested by cemeteries, appeared further out to the south, northwest and northeast (fig. 2.3). The whole ensemble is too widely spread out to be considered a single "clusterville" (as shown by a glance at the map or an attempt to walk from site to site across modern Athens); rather, a galaxy of settlements, with con-

FIGURE 2.3. Protogeometric Athens as seen in its burial grounds, between the rivers Eridanos (north) and Ilissos (south): the circles represent "mortuary spaces" of greater or smaller extent. The Akropolis (with later temples), Classical fortifications, and Roman-era precinct of the Olympieion are left for orientation purposes (based on Dimitriadou 2019, fig. 3.47).

centrations large (to the northeast and northwest), small (south of the Akropolis), and straggling (along the river Ilissos, toward the harbor at Phaleron). A cluster located at the modern "Academy of Plato," 3 kilometers northwest of the Akropolis, offers a particularly striking example, which seems fairly typical of the shape and nature of these settlements: an apsidal house, a large cultic structure, and interspersed burials.[40]

The spatial organization and modes of social organization of the Early Iron Age clustervilles remain obscure. Notably, common open spaces and structuring principles are difficult to trace.[41] Some of the houses are larger than others and linked with ritual activities such as feasting or sacrifices: this eminence seems to suggest social differentiation, and perhaps the presence of chieftains or elite families. In some cases, their sites were later converted to communal cult places in the form of

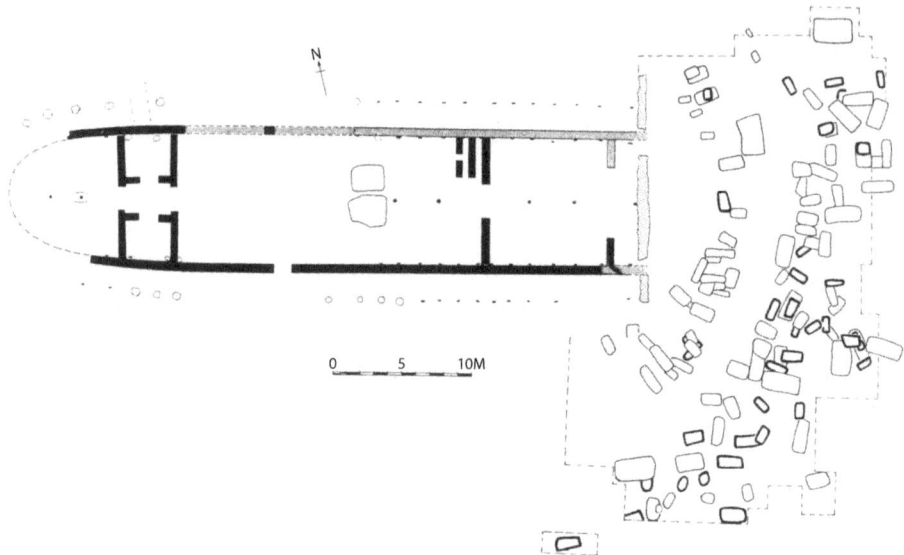

FIGURE 2.4. Funerary monument (ca. 975-950 BCE) and cemetery, Lefkandi.

monumental temples.[42] Such "manors" appear at Emborio and at Zagora. A more detailed example comes from Eretria, where an important cluster of large houses may have been the seat of a dominant family or elite group.[43] The elite nature of this cluster is suggested by the size of the houses, the possible functioning of one of the houses as a feasting hall, and finally by a rich tomb (dating to ca. 760 BCE) excavated nearby. This tomb contained golden offerings, imported goods from Attica and from the East, and a crater decorated with images of a stallion covering a mare. The iconography perhaps alluded to familial transmission of qualities, and certainly celebrated the raising of horses (a theme that already appears, faintly, at the end of the Protogeometric period).[44] On Euboia still, but much more spectacular, around 950 BCE a man and a woman were interred at Lefkandi (along with four horses) with lavish grave goods, under an apsidal longhouse, probably purpose-built for funeral rituals; the structure was then itself covered with a mound (fig. 2.4). In other places, large houses suggest eminence, but the lack of excavation evidence for the totality of the sites leaves it unclear whether we are looking at a "ruler's dwelling" or the dwellings of individual families among many such families of "Big Men."[45] We might wonder whether the Akropolis at Athens was occupied by a Big Man or succession of Big Families, in special houses, thus acting as the main, proto-urban nucleus for the constellation of scattered settlements mentioned above.[46]

The material base for these settlements is difficult to determine: the metalworking in the compounds at Ōrōpos implies surplus, acquisition, and the exchange of labor, but the economics of these activities is unknown. The problem is made more puzzling by the apparent absence of settlement in much of the countryside during the Protogeometric and Geometric periods.[47] Notably, the question of the fate of the Mycenaean *damos* or rural community, endowed with some form of legal personality and agency, remains unclear. The outer clusters of settlement at Athens suggest position on the axes of communication with the inner Attic plain (in the north) or the coast (in the south), and the wealth evidenced and celebrated by the cemeteries suggests access to resources and surplus of the countryside. One grave, that of the "Pregnant Rich Lady" (cremated and buried on the Areiopagos ca. 850 BCE), combines high-quality pottery, gold jewelry, a necklace of imported faience beads, a chest decorated with five miniature granaries (celebrating landed wealth), and seals (used by the lady as a steward of domestic wealth).[48]

The nature of the relationship between different places is equally obscure, yet answers on this matter would directly illuminate questions of economic activity and political relations. The metalworking activities in the compounds at Ōrōpos might be related to the bigger, well-connected settlements across the strait in Euboia.[49] In any case, the Early Iron Age "clustervilles" are clearly not the villages posited as the origin of the *polis* by Aristotle,[50] but a loose form of semi-nucleated settlement, readable in the evidence, widespread, and still poorly understood.

As in the earlier, post-Mycenaean period, the Euboian communities opposite Ōrōpos were extremely active in the Early Iron Age.[51] The north Aegean *koinē* of the post-palatial period continues and intensifies in this period, as attested by the wide distribution of Euboian pottery. The latter is well attested in the eastern Mediterranean—Kilikia, Cyprus, Northern Syria, Tyre, sites in modern Israel— in the tenth century (ca. 950–900 BCE), in the form of drinking vessels and amphoras. Conversely, Eastern luxury goods are found at Euboia, for instance at Lefkandi from ca. 1000 BCE onwards. Such contacts intensify in the following ninth and early eighth centuries. Finally, a new phenomenon at this time is the appearance of Euboian ceramics in the western Mediterranean, on Sardinia and in Central Italy (Veii).

These movements of goods also implied the movement of people, probably in collaborative contact with members of the Semitic-speaking communities that Greeks called "Phoenicians," from the central Levant coast. The development of the Greek alphabet, probably ca. 800 BCE, is one of the results of such contacts. An eighth-century BCE sherd bearing Phoenician writing has duly been found at Eretria, the Euboian community that succeeded Lefkandi when the latter was abandoned; this example is joined by a further twenty-five inscribed sherds, from the late eighth century BCE, in Euboian script, found at the Eretrian-founded settlement of Methōnē in the northern Aegean.[52] As part of cultural exchange, various myths and ideas may have been transmitted at this point; they were promised to a long and rich future within Greek culture.[53] The pattern of far-flung movement and exchange hence participates in a very long, very deep history of Mediterranean exchange, community formation, and landscape creation (in which the Phoenicians play an early, major, and constitutive role as traders, settlers, and cultural models, from the Levant to Spain).[54]

Euboians settled in the Chalkidikē from the tenth century BCE onwards (the settlement at Methōnē belongs to this Euboian presence)[55] and, remarkably, in the western Mediterranean at Pithēkoussai (modern Ischia off the entrance to the Bay of Naples) by the early eighth.[56] The broad mechanism at work might be the acquisition of metal and enslaved people from the North Aegean, to exchange for Eastern luxury goods manufactured especially in northern Syria but carried by Phoenicians;[57] the later phase of trade and settlement in the western Mediterranean may have been stimulated by similar activities by Phoenicians, but also driven by the quest for metal to feed into this system. The transport of Euboian decorated pottery and agricultural produce may have piggybacked on these exchanges. The high status of some of the individuals involved is demonstrated by the princely style of their burials at one of the settlements they founded in the West, namely Kymē (future Cumae), on the Campanian coast.[58]

The case of Euboia is quite exceptional by range and ambition of its contacts, and by the pattern of far-flung settlement. But trade and mobility were not restricted to Euboians. The island of Andros, where clustervilles are known at Yspili and Zagora, sent out settlers to the Chalkidikē peninsula, perhaps in search of metals, notably at the site of later Akanthos.[59] Most strikingly, migration seems to have taken place, probably in the eleventh and tenth centuries, from mainland Greece and the islands to Asia Minor. This is attested at Milētos (the origin of the migrants is not clear), and Aiolis and parts of the later Ionian coast from Boiōtia (Mēliē, opposite Samos, was probably peopled by such migrants; fig. 1.5). Milētos and Mēliē, Early Iron Age settlements, duly follow the clusterville model of spatial organization.[60] This phenomenon was later confusedly conceived as an "Ionian Migration" from Athens to western Asia Minor, but the processes driving these movements—a "Boiotian *koinē*," an "island *koinē*"?—are even more obscure than the Euboian activity. They may reflect economic expansion and demographic growth, and networks of contact and initiative between communities in the Early Iron Age Aegean.[61]

Seafaring acquisitiveness, the quest for metals, the consumption of imported prestige goods: all these phenomena raise again the question of social structure—how the wealthy get their means, how they relate to their society, and generally how the Early Iron Age settlements are constructed socially and politically beyond a very visible and energetic elite. The problem is already raised by the possible interpretation of some houses as "manors" or "ruler's dwellings," and especially by the opulence much in evidence in sites of the former post-palatial *koinē*, for instance at Atalantē in East Lokris,[62] or Lefkandi. As already mentioned above, a man and a woman received ca. 950 BCE a monumental funeral (the man cremated, the woman inhumed, accompanied by rich offerings and even the sacrifice of horses), within a Big House-like structure, which was later covered with a mound (fig. 2.4). In the following century or so (down to ca. 820 BCE), this monumental burial was itself the focus of a dense burial ground, constituted by burials of both genders and all age groups. In many tombs, offerings were extremely rich, including fine imported pottery, weapons, jewelry, and Near Eastern luxury goods (in one case, an assemblage of all these categories of artifacts). The Lefkandi burial ground suggests a whole social group, claiming proximity to the couple of the monumental funeral.

A similar phenomenon can be seen in the islands; for instance, in the old cemeteries at Naxos (at Grotta and the modern Cathedral Square). These had been in existence since the Protogeometric period, one located among ruined Mycenaean structures. Now in the Early Iron Age, they filled up with funerary enclosures, constantly maintained and used for cremation, burials, and, especially, ritual feasting on specially built platforms. This latter communal activity, presumably by family groups, gradually crowded out actual burials.[63] Likewise, the small tomb shrines at the site of Xobourgo on the island of Tēnos received forms of ritual cult that suggest they were used as focal points for families or groupings in the ninth-century BCE settlement.[64] At Minōa, on the island of Amorgos, a cemetery grouping of cremations (from the tenth to the eighth century BCE), including the "warrior" burial of a man with iron weapons but also the burial of a young child, might represent an elite group in the settlement.[65]

How do these special groups fit within their community? The Lefkandi cemeteries, alongside opulent burials, also contain less distinguished, simple tombs. In Athens and Attica, groups of tombs, notably on the north slope of the Areiopagos hill, with women and children distinguished by rich offerings (painted pottery, gold jewelry, Eastern imports), and men by warrior accoutrements such as swords or equestrian equipment (fig. 2.2),[66] become common in the ninth century BCE, suggesting wealthy and powerful families. One such tomb is that of the "Pregnant Rich Lady" mentioned above. Even these groups of tombs include more modest burials; "elite" tombs are absent from the central settlement around the Akropolis, a short distance away from the Areiopagos. Indeed, some groups of burials may have espoused an austere stye of burial (for instance, in the Kerameikos). Are the rich burials and the warrior burials in Athens and Attica the sign of a ruling class? In other places, such as Argos or the Corinthia,[67] the funerary material is uniformly poor, or austere: is this a sign of the absence of a ruling elite, or an affectation by the ruling elite itself?

We will encounter these problems repeatedly in the cultural politics of the *polis*. In the meantime, we still do not know how to make sense of the diversity of burials at Lefkandi next to the very luxurious and monumental burial of one couple, the funerary enclosures of Naxos, the diversity of Athens, the austerity at Argos. We would like to know if we are looking at the reinvigorated descendants of post-palatial local elites, or newly settled groups, or experimentation within communities emerging from the Protogeometric pause.[68] What we do see is micro-nucleated implantations in loose local connections. These were somehow supported by the surrounding countryside whose surplus was processed and stocked in compounds; some of their denizens are seen enjoying the products of overseas trade. The workings of these proto-urban settlements combined inherited egalitarianism with internal differentiation of wealth and status, perhaps within familial groups uniting non-elite, elite, and "superelite" households. These groupings, in turn, must have interrelated through collaboration and competition. These are not quite towns, and certainly do not look like *poleis*: the organization by clusters and without strong functional differentiation is very different from the later spatial regimen of the Classical *polis*.

A certain degree of fluidity in power relations within these loose settlements may have been the norm: hence the absence of any clearly legible social stratification, and also the slow evolutions that can be detected on the ground. The latter can be seen in cases such as the rise of rich graves in Athens, or the constant accumulation of funerary enclosures above Protogeometric-era tombs in Naxos, until the enclosures finally seemed to have entertained only a dim relation with the earlier "founder" tombs and enclosures on top of which they were erected. The lack of a clear legibility of hierarchy is itself highly suggestive about the nature of the Early Iron Age clusterville. What emerged out of the Protogeometric pause was a pattern of settlements involving acquisitive elites involved in (and perhaps summoned into existence by) the trading and raiding opportunities of the Mediterranean—but as part of complex social landscapes.

Consolidation, Structuration, Change (800–700 BCE)

From 750 BCE and onwards, a number of suggestive changes can again be read in the archaeological record; taken together, they sketch a picture of steady community consolidation. Immediately obvious is the more-ness of archaeological evidence: more tombs, more pots, more painters producing decorated pots, more built structures, more (and more varied) exports of high-quality ceramics to the East, more movement of goods and people toward, and settlement in, the Northern Aegean[69] or the western Mediterranean. The pottery of the Late Geometric period (750–700 BCE) shows a huge increase in numbers of found objects, but also of different workshops and of painters. But what does this intensification in the material record actually reflect? A. Snodgrass posited a startling demographic explosion, and some degree of demographic increase is likely; but the changes also must be the index of social change and negotiation.[70]

At the level of settlement structures, the centuries-old organization in clusters and compounds evolves toward more integrated forms.[71] Thus at Argos, the pattern of scattered burials, suggestive of clusters of houses and tombs across a loosely textured site, is replaced by the grouping of tombs in specialized cemeteries, as appropriate for more differentiated and nucleated settlement. The most important of these cemeteries is located in the southern part of the settled zone. This southern

FIGURE 2.5. Argos: from the Mycenaean (left) to the Geometric period (right), the settlement undergoes expansion. Habitat (squares) and burials (triangles) are scattered and mingled. From Piérart and Touchais 1996.

area also attracted a concentration of housing. This area would later transform into the *agora* or public square of the city; an open space, monumentalized and regularized by terracing, taking over from the older cemeteries and housing, and marking the outcome of the processes of nucleation as the emergence of public spaces and a differentiated proto-urban tissue (fig. 2.5).[72]

Similar outcomes appear at other sites, for instance at Ōrōpos, where an open space emerges within the housing,[73] or at Corinth, where burials start concentrating in differentiated cemeteries. Athens sees growth and reorganization: the southern flanks of the Akropolis served as an extensive cemetery, beyond which started a zone of terraced cultivation, after the abandonment of the once prosperous settlement on the coastwards road.[74] On the island of Paros, the site at Koukounaries, dominated by a Big House, was abandoned for a new settlement further downhill, with regular housing and open public spaces.[75] Such consolidated, reorganized proto-urban-like sites may have been marked off and protected by walls, in a further formalization of settlement: indeed, Ōrōpos was surrounded by a wall in the eighth century BCE, as were Asinē in the Argolid, and Old Smyrna in Asia Minor.[76]

The most visible marker of communal investment and common identity was the building of a monumental temple, attested in many Early Iron Age communities, often taking over from older Big Houses. Around 725 BCE, the elite housing quarter in the center of the inhabited zone at Eretria was cleared out, and the area taken over by a large building that must be the first of several successive temples of Laurel-bearing Apollōn.[77] A similar and similarly dated temple duly appears at the new settlement at Koukounaries on Paros.[78] The Akropolis in Athens emerged as a cult place at this time; it was distinguished by rich offerings, including monumental bronze tripods, and was the central cult place for the whole Attic plain in the eighth century BCE.[79] A comparable phenomenon is the end of the small "family" shrines at Xobourgo on Tēnos, during the Late Geometric period: a cluster of small shrines was replaced by a single cultic installation, with an *eschara* (sacred hearth) and a bench for gatherings.[80]

Examples could be multiplied, many as suggestive as those evoked above.[81] The construction of communal shrines went hand in hand with politically suggestive changes in settlement pattern, as can be seen at Zagora on the island of Andros. Here, the possible dominance of a "ruler's dwelling" is superseded by the foundation (around 750 BCE) of a whole series of Big Houses on the *megaron* plan (an elongated plan with porch and succession of rooms, privileging a central hall), perhaps reflecting the distribution of elite feasting as a ritual of power among a broader group; in a later phase (around 725 BCE), the plan of these houses is modified to a more complex, courtyard-centered, multiroom plan suited for a multiplicity of social roles between public and private—indeed, such will be the plan of the house (*oikos*) in the Classical *polis*. This is also the normative plan adopted when the settlement is extended further downslope.[82]

New Koukounaries on Paros and New Zagora on Andros were abandoned by the early seventh century BCE, as were other sites (often sites that were well organized and nucleated at an early phase, a paradox that needs elucidation).[83] This abandonment coincides with the consolidation of big sites. Such processes are well attested in Crete, where they begin slightly earlier than in the rest of the Aegean,[84] in a complex dance of settlement, evacuation, and consolidating. The result was a descent from the "refuge sites" of the post-palatial period to big sites. In mainland Greece, the Korinthia offers a complex and well-documented case of this phenomenon (fig. 2.6).[85] There, simultaneously with slow expansion and differentiation in the urban center of Corinth, activity intensifies at two shrines—the shrine of Poseidōn at the Isthmus (Isthmia), and the shrine of Hēra at Perachora across an inlet of the Gulf of Corinth. A third shrine, at Solygeia in the southeastern part of the territory, also appears ca. 700 BCE.

Such "extra-urban" shrines might be interpreted as staking claims of the community to a definite territory, and hence attest the emergence of the complementary integration of urban settlement and rural territory that will prove so fundamental to the *polis*.[86] Both the first temple on the urban site of Corinth and the first temple at Isthmia (with a 100-foot long altar) were monumentalized in the early seventh century (ca. 680 BCE). Apart from the complex case of Corinth, there are many other examples of extra-urban shrines which suggest a dynamics of consolidation of,

FIGURE 2.6. Settlement and territory at Corinth and the Isthmos from Late Mycenaean to Late Geometric. After C. Morgan 1999a, figs. 15, 16, 17.

and within, a territory (for instance, Mykēnai, Samos, Milētos, or Phaistos on Crete).[87] A smaller site on Naxos, Hyria (modern toponym), 2 kilometers south of the main settlement on Naxos, deserves particular attention for the clarity with which it illustrates the sequence and its outcome.[88] This is an old Mycenaean, then Early Iron Age site. During the Early Iron Age, the site seems a modest one, with a small built structure and limited traces of ritual activity, but ca. 730 it was distinguished by a larger temple and the archaeological remains point to increased ritual activities, inside and outside the temple. The temple was later one of the official shrines of the *polis* of Naxos, as explicitly attested by epigraphical documents. The sequence at Hyria seems clearly to show ritual activity at a shrine outside the main settlement as an expression of the community, as seen in intensified communal activities, greater ritual needs, perhaps simply more people in the settlements—a process that will lead to later *polis* forms.

It is important to bear in mind that these shrines are often older than the processes of settlement consolidation that usually took place or intensified in the decades after ca. 750 BCE. For instance, the shrine at the Isthmos is an Early Iron

Age site, which in fact appears before any traces of settlement at Corinth itself, and probably acted as a regional focus for settlements across the future Corinthia (whereas the shrine at Perachora does admittedly emerge ca. 775–750 BCE). "Extra-urban shrines" are not quite satellites thrown out as markers of control by emerging urban communities, but places with their own history and function. The shrine at the Isthmos served for ritual feasting but also for dedications of tripods, bronze bowls, weapons, and long bronze pins. The shrine at Perachora, which also served for communal dining, received rich dedications in the form of gold offerings and Eastern objects (especially in the seventh century BCE). The presence of ritual meals and gatherings in both shrines only emphasizes the difference in dedicatory assemblages in each site. The old shrine at Isthmia served for display of wealth by one or several groups in the area (perhaps the elites of the emerging urban site), in a prestigious regional site that also was located on a main axis of macroregional communication. In contrast, the shrine at Perachora may have served rural elites, or perhaps the elites at Corinth in their interface with the world of the sea. In other words, the looseness of interaction we see in the world of the Early Iron Age "clusterville" still seems to have obtained in the eighth century BCE.

The case of the Corinthia offers an illuminating model for other cases where "extra-urban" or "territorial" shrines preexist settlement. Thus in the territory of Milētos, in addition to the shrine at Didyma, two shrines at some distance from the main settlement site—one at Zeytintepe (modern toponym) south of Milētos, one at Assēssos to the northeast (fig. 1.5)—mark preexisting settlements of Protogeometric date, and hence of the same age as the main settlement itself.[89] The shrines must have played an important role in mediating negotiation and integration. The same must have held true in the case of Titanē,[90] in the northeast Peloponnese. There the local shrine, as a recipient of dedications and cultic activity, probably helped integrate the two very old settlements at Titanē and Sikyōn in a single entity (the future *polis* of Sikyōn, which we will revisit below), as the outcome of negotiation between preexisting entities (perhaps across the whole territory), rather than the projection of claims by the inhabitants of a central settlement on a smaller one.

The end result of these complex processes of negotiation was some form of integration and consolidation in ways that constructed spaces of community. Integration could intensify local claims to distinction, precisely in reaction to the creation of multi-settlement entities. At a rural site on the island of Naxos, Tsikalario (modern toponym), from the eighth century BCE onwards, local elites built a large cluster of monumental burials with enclosures and mounds, organized in what are perhaps family groups, to match the forms of funerary display practiced in the main settlement.[91] On a smaller geographical scale, rich peripheral tombs ("estate tombs") appear at Argos, precisely at the time when the main settlement is reorganizing itself.[92]

Processes of structuration between settlements also took place on a broader, regional scale. In the Argolid, the shrine of Hēra functioned as a shared focal point for other communities as well as Argos, namely the settlements on the ancient sites of Tiryns and Mykēnai.[93] (It would later be claimed by Argos as a part of its hegemonic ambitions over the region). Shrines thus played an important part in relating settlements in a nonhierarchical way within broader regional structures, which would evolve into identity groupings of varying tightness. The most important and widely ranging of such "inter-state" sanctuaries are the great shrines of Olympia and Delphi.[94] Olympia has a long history as a settlement and a shrine, from the eleventh century BCE at least—starting off as a site for ritual activity and dedicatory display for local elites from Ēlis, the area (later a *polis*) where Olympia is located; the shrine never lost this local, microregional attachment. But from ca. 725 BCE onwards, even while the activities of these local elites intensified, visitors from wider afield used the shrine for dedication and display, especially of bronze objects: Messenian and Argive dedicants are thus well attested. Likewise, eighth-century BCE Delphi served as a regional shrine for Phōkis, but also for communities around the Corinthian Gulf. Such regional contacts could result in the creation of local "horizontal" identities across localities—which led to the *ethnē* ("nations" or "tribes") attested in the later historical record, or to formalized institutions of interaction, such as the Delphic Amphiktiony.[95]

Simultaneously, wide-ranging contacts could end up reinforcing local integration and distinctiveness, a phenomenon we might term "Coldstream's paradox," named after N. Coldstream, the scholar who described it best. The late eighth century BCE is both a time of increasing interregional connection and of very distinctive local styles in pottery (Coldstream counts eleven local schools, all linked to sites that develop as *poleis*).[96] Territorial organization and structuration happen both at the level of the units that emerge as *poleis*, and at a broader regional level; in a sense, the structuration of *polis* territories is also a process of regional structuration at a local level.

It is not the case that the *polis* grows out of primitive "tribal" structures. The emergence of *polis* (city-state) and *ethnos* (regional state) go hand in hand.[97] Regional and supra-regional identity are compatible, as overlapping "tiers of identity" (C. Morgan) within networked activities. Where the boundaries were drawn depended on specific circumstances, including geography, whose determinative force should not be exaggerated. Thus, a strong Corinthian integration coexisted with connections across the Corinthian Gulf around Delphi, without these connections leading to integration. In contrast, settlements around Delphi, in close contact with each other, later enjoyed a shared existence as the *ethnos* of the Phokians. The late eighth century BCE thus witnessed interlocking processes of community generation. At the local level, we have seen the integration of local settlements into communities; at an intermediate level, we can guess at the relations of communities to form regions. Beyond such relations, there existed interregional connections that led to wider identifications (on the base of dialect and cult) within an overarching ethnogenesis; that is, the definition of a group of communities speaking the same language and recognizing each other through an architecture of appurtenances. The end result was, of course, a group that we call "the Greeks" (using a name derived from the Latin appellation for Euboian emigrants), but which reified itself under the name of *Hellēnes* only gradually and after much local debate (the term is not used this way in early Greek literature).[98]

Social Complexity in the Early Iron Age

Within settlements, the dynamics of integration and consolidation must have raised questions of social relations. Display by members of certain communities in interregional or local shrines made visible the status and wealth of these members in relation to peers in other communities and to nonpeer members in their own communities. The question of social structure in these communities is directly posed by the archaeological record, especially burials. The considerable rise in the number of tombs in the course of the eighth century BCE, noted above as at least a partial index of population increase, has been interpreted by I. Morris as an indication of the generalized widening of full membership in the community, reflected in formal, archaeologically retrievable funerary rites. In fact, the phenomenon could be indicative of the constitution of community itself. But it is also striking that the increase in the number of tombs goes hand in hand with a considerable diversification of funerary practice (unlike the relatively unified practice of the Protogeometric period, and to a considerably greater degree than during the Middle Geometric period). Part of diversification was the appearance of some groups practicing a strong degree of status affirmation.[99]

This triple phenomenon (increase in burials, diversity, increase in distinction markers) can be observed notably at Athens after ca. 750 BCE, when the growth in archaeologically recorded burials and the gradual melding of the various clusters of settlement into a continuum coincide with a high variety of funerary practice; and spectacularly, such markers of distinction as huge funerary vases, painted notably with scenes of funeral rituals (lamentations before the body lying in state) and processions by chariots and armed men, the latter with helmets sporting crests like ponytails, paired spears, swords jutting out horizontally from the belt, and hourglass-shaped shields.[100] These vases, produced by a small number of virtuoso workshops, seem to be the expression of specific groups making claims to status. However, even these signs of status undergo increasing diversity, with new shapes and themes appearing toward the end of the eighth century BCE (hunting, boxing, Eastern-inspired ornament). This diversification seems to reflect increasing social complexity and a diversity of claims.[101]

A particularly instructive example of social complexity and diversity comes from Argos.[102] There the recorded tombs increase nearly threefold during the Late Geometric period; funerary practice diversifies; grave goods reappear after the Early Iron Age "austerity." Some tombs are poor, involving the placing of remains in simple ceramic vessels, within fields of similar burials and without goods. Other tombs take a previously known form (the cist grave, where stone slabs outline and cover a stone box embedded in the ground) and develop it to much larger proportions. Yet other tombs are distinguished by the inclusion of metal offerings, especially weapons. One very large tomb, 3 meters long, contained a rich array of offerings: fine painted pottery, a bronze helmet, a bronze corslet, two iron axes, twelve iron spits, two iron firedogs shaped like ships, and gold objects (fig. 2.7).[103] The Argos warrior tomb makes claims to high status based on wealth in three metals, seafaring, violence, and aristocratic lifestyle alluded to by the firedogs and the spits, used for the consumption of meat at feasts. This tomb gives us a full elitist package and provides a context for the interpretation of Late Geometric pottery at Argos: the most frequent themes are horses and dancing women, but other themes such as seafaring or expressive collocations of Near Eastern–inspired animal motifs also make claims to distinction. A more basic reflection of high status is found in the impressive size and healthiness of the human remains in these "Big Graves."[104]

Athens and Argos thus provide two particularly rich and instructive examples of the twin phenomena of increase in tombs and increase in status display; they are also attested, with some variations, at Corinth (starting slightly earlier),[105] or Medeōn in Phōkis[106] (a very small site but connected to Corinth across the Corinthian Gulf). This local mirroring of phenomena attested elsewhere, in larger sites, might be used to argue that the growth in burials and in status distinction markers was a generalized phenomenon, which probably took place across the central geography of *polis* development, even though it is not yet

FIGURE 2.7. Bronze panoply from a Late Geometric tomb, Argos. 750-700 BCE. Archaeological Museum Argos (B. 26-28).

directly attested in many places (for instance, the islands or Asia Minor, or even relatively well-known places such as Eretria).

Medeōn also shows traces of another phenomenon that was probably elitist in its import, namely cultic offerings at a Mycenaean tomb. Tomb-cult offerings in Mycenaean structures are well attested across Greece—in the southwestern Peloponnese (Messēnia), in the Argolid, in Attica (indeed before the eighth century BCE), or in Crete.[107] This phenomenon seems to claim a connection to the past, and hence a statement about the distinction and quality of those making the gesture—perhaps as a way of rooting the power of certain groups through proclaimed continuity with putative ancestral figures in the spectacular Mycenaean tombs. Beyond this specific type of offerings, dedicatory behavior in general was a way of displaying wealth and status: in the Corinthia, the shrine at Isthmia is the only site where we see the dedications of weapons, tripods, and cauldrons at Isthmia (already mentioned above), hinting at the specialization of the shrine within the territorial structuration, but also at its function as the stage for the eminence of a group or class within the area.

All of these phenomena are claims to status and distinction: whatever the nature of the archaeological evidence (tombs, dedications, images); these phenomena are material traces that suppose gestures, actions, spectacle—processions of armed men following horse-drawn parade chariots to a cremation funeral followed by a feast and drinking party, dedications of precious objects, visits and offerings at old tombs, the eating of roast meat washed down with wine alongside peers, the acquisition and consumption of disposable wealth. But these gestures need to be considered carefully, replaced within the context of the social structure of the late eighth-century BCE communities. What work do such claims do, in relation to the rest of the community (or at least those buried in "nonelite" graves)? They might represent a response—a reassertion of primacy, a reaction of resistance, an attempt at control?—by certain groups, emergent during the Early Iron Age but now faced with rising pressure from below toward the inclusion of lower classes. This would be the story of struggle, indeed of revolution, as indexed by the evolution in funerary practice.[108]

Another interpretation, proposed by S. Houby-Nielsen, is that the increase in tombs reflects shifts within the ruling elite itself: we would have to imagine them as no longer choosing main representatives for formal burial at privileged sites (such as the Kerameikos), but favoring burial by whole family groups. This might fit the increase in archaeologically visible child burials among the new funerary landscape of the late eighth century BCE, which perhaps reflects the concern for the formal burial of elite families rather than access to such burial by the whole population at large.[109]

All these issues can be seen at Eleutherna, in Crete. There the record of an excavated nekropolis (Orthi Petra, a modern toponym) on the edge of the settlement hill suggests shifts within the local elite. The nekropolis was long dominated, from ca. 875 BCE onwards, by a single group (presumably a family) with graves clustered around what seems like a "founder's grave," and a special space reserved for the cremations of this group. In the late eighth century BCE, after a century and a half, this arrangement came to an end when the nekropolis was taken over by multiple cremations, covered by tumuli, and themselves the focus of further clusters of graves—including children's burials in ceramic vessels. These newcomer burials obliterated the older cremation area; in reaction, a new privileged cremation area was set up next to the older family plot, which continued in use with further burials clustered in the area. This plot was further marked out by a funerary monument, in an attempt by the original group to assert distinction in the face of change.[110]

The whole sequence at Eleutherna suggests that the eighth century BCE saw the accession of more people to burial in a privileged space—but that these were elite groups: the new cremation burials are very rich, as shown by the offerings, the tumuli, and the way in which they served as a focus for others. Under one tumulus covering a couple, the deceased male's burial included iron weapons (large sword, knives, bronze spear head) and, exceptionally, the presence of a headless, bound male corpse, probably of a captive executed before the pyre. This must reflect the position of the deceased as member of a warrior group: the execution recalls the heroic funeral of Patroklos in the Iliad, and generally the ceremony involved displayed the "mastery over life and death" (C. Morgan) of this man, and perhaps of the group or class he belonged to.[111]

Can the case, very spectacular but also very peculiar, of Eleutherna help to understand processes across the eighth-century BCE Aegean? At least Eleutherna, with its picture of an elite cemetery taken over (it seems) by other elite groups offers a possibility, and it is fruitful to see in the diversity of the evidence across the Greek world a multiplicity of interactions and pressures: there is no reason why tomb-cult, painted ceramics, and dedication at shrines should all reflect the claims of the same social class, rather than the positioning of multiple groups. Diversity of choices, statuses, and roles may be behind the considerable variety in the ceramic material from Naxos in this period.[112] Diversity may be the result of debates within the elite, or between elite groups, or between elites and slightly less elite groups—as a result of increasing integration that created the need to find ways to express relations to and within the community.

Such debates might lie behind phenomena in the material record: for instance, we can see an intensification of family principles of burial organization in Crete at the same time as community integration takes place.[113] In the so-called West Gate Cemetery at Eretria,[114] at the same time (ca. 725 BCE) that the central area of elite housing was converted to a communal shrine of Apollōn, a very rich burial took place on the western edge of the settlement, in a carefully built stone cist that contained the remains of a male within two large bronze cauldrons, and an important set of all-metal offerings: golden objects, four swords, six spears (five iron and one bronze). This warrior burial was joined by five adult and nine children's burials.

The cluster is likely to be a family plot, surrounding a "founder's" tomb on a significant site, namely the edge of the settlement that faces toward a rival community, Chalkis, the other great Euboian city, with whom Eretria fought a protracted war at this time (the Lelantine War). The later city gate would be erected at this site, which indicates that this Late Geometric burial ground was located on the road out of Eretria.

The richness and nature of the offerings in the warrior tomb suggest the deceased man's high social status, his access to imported goods and to metals, and his specialization in violence. The position of the tomb shows his status as the protector of the community against the competing community of Chalkis (and its own warrior elite); finally, the clustering of other tombs around the warrior tomb shows how his status and position within the community was exploited by a particular group to make claims about their place. The man buried in the warrior tomb belonged to a social group that the poet Archilochos, writing (and singing) over fifty years later remembered with awe as "the lords of Euboia," *despotai Euboiēs*, skilled in the grim work of the sword.[115]

Similar dialectics of status and community can be read in the funeral scenes depicted on the large funerary vases in Athens. At one level, the *prothesis* scene shows the deceased laid out on a couch and mourned for, and hence celebrates the elite individual. However, the vase does not celebrate his being or his deeds but shows such a moment of communal mobilization—the procession of armed men—whose parade is as important as the individual. Yet this image is not simply "the community"—it is a particular segment of the community displaying, and being displayed displaying, its capacity for armed violence, and hence its status in the community; or perhaps the image claims that this segment is a synekdoche for the community, an act that only raises the issue of the relations between groups within the Late Geometric communities.

The outcome of the processes visible for the late eighth century BCE was the gradual end of the variety and diversity, and the end of funerary display: this evolution is very visible in Attica, Corinth, and Argos. It may hint at community control of display and the end of sustained claims to elite status within the community; the general end of tomb cult—a short-lived phenomenon—points in the same direction. This development is not universal: at Samos, an aristocratic burial ground operates from the ninth century BCE down to the seventh century BCE without much discernable change.[116] Furthermore, much elite display may have migrated from funerals to dedications in shrines, as at Corinth where greater restraint in funerary practice in the late eighth century BCE is matched by increasing wealth in dedications. The end of diversity, therefore, does not simply introduce egalitarian practice, but ushers in situations where the same dialectical claims are made as before.

However, the affirmation of community was a broadly determinant outcome, and it often can be seen to impose itself on elite claims, sometimes literally, in the cemeteries that we have earlier seen as sites of affirmation by elite families or groups. At Naxos, the practice of cremations and enclosures stops at one of the sites (Grotta) in the main settlement. At the other site (Cathedral Square), most of the competing funerary enclosures were covered with a single large mound. The area is located close to the later *agora* of the *polis*—the main public space of the city-state of the Naxians.[117] The same evolution can be seen at Eleutherna, where the Orthi Petra cemetery received a 3.80-meter tall stone marker sunk in a great boulder (still visible today, hence the modern toponym) and a construction (a shrine or cenotaph) with relief decoration of warriors; these monuments determined the subsequent orientation of pyres and tumuli, and acted as markers of public presence in this space.[118] By the early seventh century BCE, the whole area was blanketed by a single tumulus. Around the same time in Eretria, the West Gate cemetery was covered by a triangular monument (perhaps the base or internal structure for a tumulus) next to a building used for ritual feasts and gatherings.[119] Likewise, at Minōa, the "elite" cemetery (with its warrior burial) ceased to receive further burials, was surrounded by an enclosure that was included in a new fortification wall around the city, and indeed was located immediately next to the city gate; at the same time, the city received a new shrine at the top of its hilly site. All these phenomena took place at the same time, at the end of the eighth or the start of the seventh century BCE.[120] Paradoxically, the outcome of processes of aristocratic display or competition was the imposition, indeed perhaps the development, of communitarian solutions that can be read on the ground with stark clarity.

Settlement and Community: An Archaeological Narrative

The archaeological evidence for the centuries 1100–700 BCE, in spite of impressive diversity, does suggest a unitary story; at times, the diversity is itself a crucial part of this story. The collapses of the Late Bronze Age world were followed by a brief period of post-palatial local elite brilliance, which itself vanished. After a long Protogeometric pause, the Early Iron Age is characterized by the loose settlements of clusters grouping housing, economic activities, religious and group activities, and burials. These clustervilles were probably occupied by elite families and organized in communities with diverse forms of social organization (chieftains, competing Big Men, stratification between wealthy elite and nonelite, family groups).

Around 750 BCE, a number of phenomena occur simultaneously: demographic growth, the intensification of overseas links, consolidation within and between settlements, and a diversity of forms of display and of competing claims to status, ending with the sudden communitarian takeover of some elitist spaces. The simultaneity of these phenomena and events is shown by their presence in certain well-documented sites, repeatedly referred to above to illustrate phenomena, but which are equally instructive when considered holistically as equations or testcases for the evolution of communities in the second half of the eighth century BCE. The story of Eretria offers one such equation. Another case is Argos, where we can read everything all at once: increase in number of tombs, settlement consolidation and organization, and elitist claims in the form of warrior tombs and aristocratic imagery. Likewise, the multiple phenomena at Naxos seem the fragments of a single story. The diversity of painted ceramics hints at varied styles and claims in the island. Aristocratic funerary precincts in town are balanced by great tombs in the countryside. An extra-urban shrine hints at the consolidation of territory, the final covering up of the family precincts in town hints at the consolidation of community.

How does this single story cohere? The most important feature in the diversity of phenomena and of possible interpretations for these phenomena in the late eighth and early seventh centuries BCE is the simultaneity of community definition and of claims to distinction. Community and would-be elite emerge at the same time (out of the common trunk of the Early Iron Age societies), and their emergence is mutually dependent.

3

Diversity and Community

> It appears to be a latent property of large villages to metamorphose into what anthropologists call corporate communities.
>
> —J. BINTLIFF, "CITY-COUNTRY RELATIONSHIPS IN THE 'NORMAL POLIS'"

Elites and Community in Early Greek Epic Poetry

The only continuous written sources for the later eighth century BCE are the epic poems of Homer and the didactic poems of Hesiod. For all their difficulties as historical documents, they provide sustained political statements about communities, values and action.[1] These statements are of crucial importance to try to interpret the life of the settlements whose very complicated archaeology I have summarized above.[2] Notably, the poems present us with a picture of elite individuals and families within their communities, the *aristoi* or *aristees* ("best men"), and the *basileis*, usually translated "kings," a title descended from the palatial and post-palatial local power holders (*qa-si-reu*). Their activities are the main focus of the *Iliad* and the *Odyssey*, and appear as an important, if peripheral, concern in the Hesiodic poems. The most striking feature about this portrayal is the tension between two elements, namely a lordly society, complete with economic and social structure, aristocratic ideology and values, and on the other hand, a very strong, explicit sense of community and public interests.

The lordly element is dazzlingly obvious in the Homeric poems. In fact, it is the point of the poems. The best men, the kings, live a lifestyle predicated on richly funded leisure, especially evident in two forms. The first component of lordly leisure is warfare, a symphony of intercommunal violence (ambushes, cattle raids, piratical razzias, duels, protracted massed battles, attacks on settlements), whose *leitmotiv* is the production of *kleos*, *kudos*, glory, for the lords, and the accumulation of *timē*, honour. Glory and honour can be obtained by killing and stripping opponents, or by obtaining plunder. The markers of this life are spoils displayed, exploits or lineage loudly celebrated (*euchos*, boast, is used as an equivalent to *kleos*),[3] or material tokens such as gifts, shares of animal protein publicly handed over and consumed in the feast, portions of booty—all these belong to the same economy of status. The obsession with status explains the portrayal of battle in the *Iliad*, which fluctuates between close *passes d'armes* and frequent long stretches where an individual hero slaughters numerous opponents, *seriatim* or in a mass (the *aristeia* or "excelling" of a hero).[4] Such a model of battle does not lead to decisive outcomes, but provides the necessary churning background for great deeds and their remembrance. A need to acquire but also to preserve glory explains the surprisingly bleak, cold-blooded calculations of the lords on the fighting field, balancing risk, opportunities, choices (fighting, running away, rallying, ganging up on opponents), in the shadow of the imperative of reputation and status.[5]

In the *Iliad*, when faced with a multitude of enemies, Odysseus literally speaks to his heart:

> Woe, what has befallen me? A great evil it is if I be alarmed and fear the mass. Yet a worse evil it is if I am taken alone: Zeus has frightened off the other Danaans. Why has my heart said this to me? I know that cowards keep away from war, but that whoever excels in war must stand his ground strongly, whether he be hit or he hit another.

In the long, excruciating fight before the Achaian camp, the hero Glaukos, struck by an arrow, immediately leaves the field (leaping off the Achaian wall which he was fighting to seize), lest he vouchsafe an enemy the occasion to boast by being wounded.[6] Glaukos's decision to abandon the fighting line to avoid status depletion makes sense in terms of managing status like a capital rather than contributing to collective outcomes. The *aristoi*, in addition to perfoming in combat, are also one of the things fought over, commodities in the economy of *kleos*: to kill and strip a rival, or conversely, to avoid this fate, are prime motivations. When Sarpēdōn falls, he tells his companion Glaukos to summon the Lykian leaders to fight over his body and avoid *oneidos*, reproaches.[7] Battle in the *Iliad* is a construct; it portrays a medley of Bronze-Age and fantasy equipment rather than the iron implements known to have existed in the real Early Iron Age. Yet the portrayal reflects the nature of a historical type of loose, warrior-centred warfare (between leaders and their gaggles of followers) that is paralleled anthropologically, and, most importantly, displays a coherent ideology.[8]

The second component of the lordly style is a developed image of the good life, based on consumption and cognate activities that mark out a class. One such activity is relaxed feasting in (relatively) luxurious buildings and surrounded by high-status objects such as crafted and fitted furniture. Another is gift-exchange during travels—embedded within high-status praxis, including such agreeable moments as sacrifice, hunting, music, sung poetry, and sport. These activities are present in the lifestyle of the warrior heroes of the *Iliad*, sometimes as routine activities that build the backbone of social life, sometimes as special, set-piece occasions like the varied funerary contests held by Achilleus after Patroklos's funeral.

Similarly, the *Odyssey* devotes huge attention to a portrayal of the leisurely lifestyle. Tēlemachos's travels in search of his missing father Odysseus fit this pattern of elite networking and gift-exchange. Menelaos wishes he could travel with Tēlemachos and harvest gifts from guest-friends: tripods, cauldrons, mules, gold . . . In fact, young Odysseus had himself visited his grandfather Autolykos, to receive gifts, partake in meat-heavy feasting, and hunt in Parnassos (where Odysseus was gored above the knee by the quarry, a huge boar).[9] Odysseus's ill-advised venture in the Cyclops's cave (against his companions' advice, he disastrously insists on waiting for the man-eating giant to return) is motivated by the hope for precisely this sort of gift.[10]

The feast is an integral part of the lifestyle: Odysseus and his companions spend a whole year feasting with the wind-god Aiolos and his children (who, indeed, do nothing else). The Phaiakians and, back in Ithakē, the numerous suitors who stay in Odysseus's house, eating and drinking their way through his fortune, offer idealized (or caricatural) images of a life of easy consumption. The link between consumption and status is made clear by the simple detail of Nestōr's steward-woman packing a meal for Peisistratos (Nestōr's son) and Tēlemachos—she makes sure to prepare the "food which the Zeus-fostered kings eat," which reflects almost unconsciously the idea that the *basileis* must eat different, better food than the rest of society (and much of the *Odyssey* can be read as a celebration of that fact).

The *Iliad* and the *Odyssey* are fantasies: the grim, hypertrophied image of suffering and war, or the dream-like images of constant play and feeding, are literary exaggerations that perform precise roles in the economy of the poems as literary texts. However, their very nature as fantasies makes them instructive as historical documents. To start, the warlikeness of the *basileis* or the *aristoi* is the foundation of their elite status. War, conceived as extreme physical and moral hardship (*ponos*) is the test of essential character in an unflinching theatre of distinction. Those who fight (and die) are "all the best men," *hossoi aristoi*.[11] Warfare is centred around the *aristoi*, who stand out and fight, while the *plēthus*, the mass, flees. The retreat of an *aristos* is a momentous event, much commented on by onlookers and by the Homeric narrator.[12] This naturalization of social difference through war is clear in the very frequent similes in the *Iliad*, where heroes are compared to ravenous predators. The heroes' bodies reflect their inherent capacity for violence (sheer size, muscular physique, meaty hands), as does the casual habit of bearing arms.[13] The naturalness of violence as social order is enshrined in the portrayal of the strength and violence of the gods, starting with Zeus, the ultimate *aristos,* as described wryly by his wife, the goddess Hēra.[14] Finally, warlikeness and prowess, in allowing the accrual of the rare commodity of *kleos*, give access to an even rarer commodity, memory and hence immortality—manifested in elite artifacts such as the funeral mound or indeed epic song itself.

The other feature of elite leisure, the easy lifestyle of feasting, is equally ideological. In the *Odyssey*, the Phaiakian lords, after having their fill of the feast and of song and dance (notably listening to song by a professional songster), go out for some sport, and one of the Phaiakian lords taunts Odysseus (still incognito, reluctant to take part in the sport):

> Stranger, I do not think you look like a man who knows about the many contests which men practice, but rather like the man who plies about with a many-benched ship, a leader of sailors who are in fact dealers, mindful of his wares, watchful of his cargo and of grasping profits—you do not look like one who takes parts in contests (*athlētēr*).[15]

The taunt tersely states a claims to social distinction by contrasting play with the need to make a living through the work of trucking and bartering, and by naturalizing the leisure and wealth of the lordly class. Odysseus duly responds by hurling a quoit over the bounds of the playing field, which is in fact the town's *agora*; he is assuaged with gifts, which acknowledge him as a fully entitled, leisured and propertied member of the privileged class.

Generally, and as in the case of violence, the easeful life of the lords recalls the life of the gods, and the love of feasting and spectacle shown by the latter—the gods, "who live at ease," an analogy which naturalizes the power and concomitant benefits enjoyed by the *basileis*. A lord is one "honoured like a god" by the *laos*, the people, and whose godlike intervention saves the people.[16] The algorithmic relation of warfare, easeful style, and *laos* is laid out in a speech by one of the *basileis*, Sarpēdōn, during a hard fight in the *Iliad*:

> Glaukos, why are both of us honoured most with a seat and meat and very many cups in Lykia, and why do all look upon us as gods? Why do we cultivate a great estate (*temenos*) along the banks of Xanthos, fine with vines and wheat-bearing land? It is time, then, for us to stand, first among the Lykians and face fiery battle, so that the stout-cuirassed Lykians may say, "Not without glory do our kings rule in Lykia, and eat fat sheep and drink excellent wine: with all that, their strength is noble, when they fight first among the Lykians."[17]

This statement of the social contract, with its fond vision of *noblesse oblige*, is ideological (it even shows us a lord imagining how his power is viewed by the people—with admiring consent and consensus). It raises the issues of "Homeric society," which the poems portray, directly or implicitly, in some detail.[18] The *basileis* clearly have followers or retainers (*hetairoi, therapontes*): this is the "people of the companions" (*ethnos hetairōn*) which receives and pampers the heroes, in battle and in peace. One such companion is Glaukos, Sarpēdōn's man, whom we have just seen listening to Sarpēdōn on noblesse. The workings of this world are shown by a scene at the end of the *Iliad*, showing the god Hermēs, pretending to be one of Achilleus's retainers. When Priam offers a gift, the "retainer" politely but emphatically declines—it will not do for him to accept a gift out of sight of Achilleus, for this would amount to despoiling his quite redoubtable boss—at the risk of immediate physical retribution if found out, namely a beating at the boss's hands. The social relation of retainerdom is also seen in the *Odyssey*, for instance in the flashy-dressing, arrogant young men whom the suitors have as personal servants (a feature reminiscent of later, stratified societies).[19] Agamemnōn is murdered by Aigistheus alongside his companions, thus sealing the destruction of his social persona as well as his physical person; Odysseus, stuck on Calypsō's island, is bereft of ships and companions, the two things necessary for his activity as *basileus*.[20]

Such retained men are bound to their lord by links of obligation, because they partake of the lord's food (both Sarpēdōn and Glaukos are fed from the former's estate), either in the feast or by direct gift of sustenance and shares of booty. Odysseus's faithful swineherd, Eumaios, in fact himself the son of a *basileus,* remembers a poignant detail from the moment of his kidnapping, the empty porch of his father's house, with the cups and the tables from the meal enjoyed by "the men who partook of the feast (*daitumones*), and served my father."[21] More succinctly, Tēlemachos tells a foreign beggar (in fact his own father Odysseus in disguise), "I will leave no man who touches my grain-measure remain idle."[22] The "beggar" and Eumaios are non-elite individuals: the networks of obligation or simply patronage stretch below the level of the warrior companions. When the suitors, on Ithakē, learn that Tēlemachos has left the island in search of news of his father Odysseus, one of them asks where Tēlemachos found companions (literally his *kouroi*, "young men")—was it among his *thētes* and *dmōes*? The two words designate non-elite, unfree statuses ("labourer," "villain"), under some form of obligation or retainership to Tēlemachos and his house; Eumaios illustrates the status, with his unfree status but his hope of being set up with house and wife to live next his master.[23] In the meantime, before this wish should come true, Eumaios, set up to work after being given clothes, shoes and food by the mistress (Odysseus's mother), has slaves (*dmōes*) working for him, and indeed companions (*hetairoi*) of his own. From his work as an unfree man for his masters, he derives food and drink, and the wherewithal to give something to "those who deserve his respect" (*aidoioisin*), perhaps an indication of a circle of dependents of his own, and hence a glimpse of a pyramid of obligation from lord to retained men to lesser retained men to lesser dependants.

Though the poems devote much attention to ties of dependency, this picture cannot be generalized. The whole of Homeric society is not a feudal pyramid structured regular ties of obligation.[24] Even the idealized world of epic is not a harmonious hierarchical order, but is diverse and open to conflict and contestation. The number of retained *hetairoi* and *therapontes* seems small (often made up of refugees, exiles, guest-friends); in many cases, the participants in the feast are autonomous agents, participating in feasts as acts of social reciprocity and competition, and not as retainers in a generalized feudal-style pyramid. Other retainers are specialists, such as the heralds who serve as the king's mouthpiece in communicating with other lords or with the community, and, the rest of the time, serve the king during the repetitive and interminable feasting.

Thus Odysseus, when he returns in disguise to his homeland of Ithakē, invents a fictive biography for himself, as a Cretan freebooter, whose story shows the fluidity of status, in a competitive world in which diverse sources of distinction operate. The bastard offspring of a lord "who was honoured like a god among the people for his fortune and his glorious sons," he compensates for a disadvantageous share of his father's inheritance by a good marriage, on account of his reputation for bravery and prowess at war (*rhēxēnoriē*, literally "the power to break men"). Neglecting work on his land, he specializes in warfare, leading nine expeditions of chosen men, for ship-borne forays and ambushes: "soon my house grew great, and then I became an awesome and respected man among the Cretans."[25]

In addition, it is very unclear whether we should imagine, even within the idealized world of the epics, a full extension of statuses of dependency down to a broad class of rent-paying peasants to support the lifestyle of the elite. The *basileis* clearly own land, exploited for their benefit by unfree labour. In the *Iliad*, Trojans and Greeks fight over the dead Patroklos "as when a man gives the fat-soaked hide of a bull to his people (*laoi*) to stretch," no doubt unfree labourers; Achilleus's richly wrought shield contains an image of reapers working a kingly estate (*temenos basileion*), under the eyes of the *basileus* himself who "stood among them in silence, holding his sceptre and rejoicing in his heart."[26] The images are those of estate owners deriving wealth and power from their ownership; however, the harvest in the second image is carried out by *erithoi*, a word of unclear derivation which clearly means "hired men," just like the word *thētes*.[27] The latter is used alongside *dmōes* (slaves, like Eumaios) to describe the dependents which might have provided Tēlemachos with travel companions. The implication is that the *basileus*'s household workforce combines unfree labour and hired labour, in varying proportions, but does not have vast numbers of serfs at its disposal.

The *basileus* is primarily a land-owner rather than a feudal lord sustained by serf populations;[28] his house, in the main settlement, serves to accumulate produce brought from his estate in the countryside (*agros*) into the settlement (*polinde*, "towards the town"). The house itself, surrounded by an enclosure, is an economic unit with its own workforce to process the produce; it might be ringed by orchards, olive groves, gardens and vines.[29] These sources of wealth are supplemented by acquisitive operations of piracy and plunder such as cattle-rustling—and also profit-generating exchange, especially through sea-borne trade.[30] The picture in Hesiod's *Works and Days* agrees with this situation: Hesiod himself is not a peasant, but the free owner of an estate made up of several plots, which he exploits with a mixture of enslaved and hired labour; the economy described by Hesiod does not show the stresses and specializations that would be expected if Hesiod had worked as a peasant owing rent in kind to a landlord.[31] The Hesiodic farmer, like the Homeric hero, also engages in exchange, notably overseas, with a view to making profit and increasing wealth.[32]

It is true that the *basileis* are shown making levies off the people, to replenish their own fortunes;[33] they live off the "fat of the people," or "drink the people's goods" (*dēmia pinein*), in a striking phrase which condenses the feasting lifestyle and the levying of surplus. Menelaos uses the phrase in a battle speech which links levy-fed consumption with the right to rule, and the obligation to be brave in battle.[34] This practice seems to be sporadic, rather than the established extraction of rent (for instance, Hektōr levies food off his people, but it is to feed the allies fighting for Troy).[35] The practice has symbolical force, but it also falls within the realms of the lordly politics by which the *basileis* rule their communities, and indeed relate to each other.

The picture here is also one of diversity, rather than of a universal system of pyramids of statuses and powers: the epic poems do have clear notions of monarchical rule, but constantly subject it to contestation and debate, and indeed the plots of the *Iliad* and the *Odyssey* can be said to revolve around such debates.[36] Both poems constantly present images of monarchy: Agamemnōn in the *Iliad* (indeed, most of the heroes are kings at home, though subordinate to Agamemnōn in the context of the expedition to Troy), Odysseus, Alkinoos in Phaiakians. Alkinoos's position as ruler is constantly emphasized: he descends from the founder of the settlement, his personhood founds the power of the Phaiakians, and his eminent position is symbolized by his dazzling palace, whose water-supply is used to irrigate his household productive gardens, with another stream flowing from the palace to a public fountain, in a clear image of the settlement's dependency on the ruler's gift.[37] On Ithakē, Odysseus's family is acknowledged as "more kingly" than the others, and hence difficult to get rid of (hence the problem posed by Odysseus's protracted absence); Penelope and others remember him as the good king, as caring as a father, and Odysseus himself describes the prosperity of the land where a good king rules, a picture which is also found in Hesiod (with its corollary, the ruin of the land ruled badly).[38]

Yet single rule is problematic in the Homeric world: more frequently, the plural *basileis*, the kings, is found, rather than the singular *basileus* (and Hesiod's harangue is addressed to *basileis*, though admittedly this could be to a whole class of rulers across the world rather than multiple lords within a single community). The authority of Agamemnōn, even in the special case of the expedition to Troy, is constantly under challenge (hence the story of the *Iliad*). On Ithakē, there are many *basileis* who can also be said to rule, are looked upon as gods by the people, and consider the possibility of being recognized as the dominant leader. In the absence of Odysseus, they court his wife in the hope of replacing him as ruler, and in the meantime consume Odysseus's wealth by daily feasting, in a move that both diminishes the material basis of Odysseus's eminence and caricatures the kingly feast that manifests the ruler's superiority and status. In Phaiakia, Alkinoos rules along with the glorious kings, *basileis*, *hēgētores* (leaders), *medontes* (carers for the people), and the twelve lords who sit in council with Alkinoos.[39]

Just as the story of the Cretan freebooter hints at a fluid society with competitive claims to status, epic poetry offers various images of political power—single rule, *primus inter pares*, competitive conflict between Big Men.[40] The dominant mood is a competitive, distrustful morality, maximizing gain and accrual of benefits in material and symbolical form, insisting on strict reciprocity, obsessed with status and getting on top. In the *Iliad*, during the funerary contest after Patroklos's funeral, Achilleus has to arbitrate between the claims to status emanating from touchy, competitive peers). Likewise, in the non-heroic world of Hesiod's *Works and Days*, competition and acquisitiveness are taken for normal, and relations with kinsmen and neighbours is strictly utility-driven rather than altruistic.

The consequence of this type of morality is a winner-take-all rawness to social and political relations, conceived as the pursuit of interests by individuals for themselves and their houses—the situation Hesiod laments as the reign of *cheirodikai*, "justice through force of hands," during the iron age in which he lives.[41] In the *Iliad*, both Achilleus and Hektōr's wife Andromachē worry that after the death of the lord in the family, there will be no one to protect his kin (an aged father, or an orphan child) from depredations and mistreatment at the hand of neighbours. The *Odyssey* is likewise a poem about force: on Ithakē, the situation boils down to a contest of brute strength. The suitors do as they please: they threaten to punish an Ithakan by "fining" him, because they do not like what he says. There is no one to protect Odysseus's minor son from depredation, exactly as Andromachē had feared for her child: Tēlemachos himself is too young to bodily, physically, violently drive away the suitors from his house. The suitors often state that their numbers and sheer physical strength allow them to get away with doing what they want. Odysseus will get his revenge by force, through the suitors' murder. Afterwards, he observes that murder usually results in exile from the community—unless one has many helpers. Odysseus duly defeats the suitors' kinsmen by force of arms, alongside his father and his son.[42]

One particular aspect of this rawness in social relations is the collective dominance of the powerful. The levying of gifts and goods, though punctual, reflects the lords' capacity to do so, as specialists in violence, and makes their dominance visible to all. Their wealth, confidence, and continuity as a group allow them to try to control political process. An assembly of warriors before Troy ends with actual violence meted out publicly by a king, Odysseus, to a man of the *dēmos*, Thersitēs, when the latter dares challenge Agamemnōn.[43] The lords monopolize the key social functions of religious ritual or arbitration of disputes—with the concomitant benefits, such as sacrificial meat or fees (construed as gifts or prizes) for arbitration. The latter practice is portrayed admiringly in the *Iliad*, and bitterly by Hesiod, who complains about the "gift-eating kings" who gave an unjust decision.[44] Little wonder that Hesiod, when speaking of the possibility of justice, lapses into the cynical tale of the Hawk and the Swallow, in which the predator tells the weaker bird to submit to the law of the strongest.

The Claims of Community in Early Greek Poetry

And yet, raw competition in Hesiod's Iron Age is not the whole story. The world of Homer and Hesiod is also about community. Tēlemachos did not chose his companions out of his small circle of dependents and slaves: he went *ana dēmon*, throughout the people. The *laoi* are occasionally a lord's companions or dependents, but mostly are the human element of the whole community.[45] The *basileus*'s position occasionally appears to be dependent on community decision: the royal *temenos* is sometimes revealed to be a grant from the people as a collective reward. Achilleus taunts Aineias: did the Trojans promise an estate as a reward for killing Achilleus?[46] One expression of community is the existence of the *polis* as a nucleated settlement: it is considered anomalous that Laertēs, Odysseus's father, never comes *polinde*, to town. Settlement is the setting for the community, to the point that *dēmos* can mean the people but also the place.[47] The community is visible in activities shared between the households: a marriage is a public event, and even more dispute resolution, decided by a panel of *basileis* but in the *agorē*, before a mass audience.

The word *agorē* designates any sort of meeting (Zeus holds an *agorē* of the gods in his own palace, Hektōr holds an *agorē* outside the walls of Troy).[48] A specific meaning is a public open space for common meetings. A major activity for the *basileis* is attending the assembly in the *agorē*, as seen in the movements and the time management of the suitors and of Tēlemachos on Ithakē, or in the background to the swineherd Eumaios's poignant memory of his father's house: the porch is deserted because the feast-partakers have arisen and left for the assembly place, "to their seats and to the opinion of the people." Some meetings are restricted to the *basileis* such as Agamemnōn's field councils, and the more normal council of *basileis* around Priam or Alkinoos. The councils are conceived as meetings of elders, as can be seen at Troy. A subtle reminder of the seniority of the council is the special beverage served by Agamemnōn at the feast of his inner circle of *aristoi*, the *gerousios oinos*, the "elders' wine." But the elders' council is related to concerns of the whole community: they are called *dēmogerontes*, elders of the *dēmos*, sitting with King Priam, and a *dēmogerousios horkos* (oath of the elders of the *dēmos*) can represent the whole community. Hektōr, just before his final fight with Achilleus, futilely ponders whether the Achaians would accept reparation guaranteed by such an oath.[49]

Aside from these restricted councils, the whole community can meet. The assembly of the people has a variety of functions—consultation, debate, witnessing adjudication or reparations. Most basically, it gives community sanction for actions, decisions, or proposals, by acclamation or by issuing its own decisions—*themistes*, a word that designates rules or laws as well as judgments. A simile in the *Iliad* compares the neighing of Hektōr's mares with the crash of a Zeus-sent storm, "when he is angry against men who in the assembly issue crooked judgments (*themistas*) and drive out justice with no regard for the wrath of the gods."[50] In contrast to the ideological statements linking prosperity or catastrophe with good kingship, this description of politics places the common fate in the hands of men and their decisions. Finally, in addition to such political institutions, the Homeric *polis* is organized by common religious activities, prayers and sacrifices followed by feasts:

Tēlemachos chances upon such a public sacrifice in Pylos, with the people arrayed in nine subdivisions on the seashore. (Admittedly, the feast itself gives a privileged place to the ruler, Nestōr, seated with his sons and his *hetairoi*.)[51]

At its strongest, the sense of the public good (the concept is not exaggerated) exercises a powerful influence over the whole community. For all their individual differences, the political force of *Iliad*, *Odyssey*, and the Hesiodic poems is communitarian. The main theme is the relationship between the rulers and the *laoi*, the whole community for whose welfare they bear responsibility—a relationship that can often turn tragic, as in the *Iliad*, when the faults of the great men, linked to their competitive claims, end up destroying the people.[52] The complement to the heroes' competitive claims is the sense of obligation toward the community, exemplified by Hektōr, who is moved by the need to protect his family and land but also a desire to fulfil commitments to the whole community. Failure to do so entails shame at the thought of having destroyed and not protected the *dēmos*, a shame as powerful a motive as the desire for *kleos*. This commitment is acknowledged by the whole community at Hektōr's funeral, when Kassandra calls out: "Trojan men and women, come and look at Hektōr, if ever during his lifetime you rejoiced when he returned from battle, since he was a great joy to the *polis* and the whole *dēmos*."[53]

But the sense of community goes beyond the portrayal of communal indebtedness to the services and prowess of the great men: it works together with an understanding of the difference between public and private. In the public assembly, Tēlemachos twice refers to his concerns about his father's whereabouts as a private matter (*idia*) rather than a public one, embarrassingly unlike an uncontrovertibly public matter such as military invasion by an external enemy, as mentioned by another public speaker at the same meeting.[54] The opinion (*phēmis*) of the people forces the Cretan freebooter to go on the expedition to Troy (in Odysseus's invented, but plausible tale). The community's anger (much feared)[55] exposed an eminent Ithakan to the danger of lynching and the redistribution of his property when he attacked the Thesprotians, a people friendly to Ithakē, on a freebooting expedition. Anxiety about the people (*dēmon hupodeisas*) and its massive reaction moved the miscreant to take refuge with Odysseus.[56] The community has clear interests and collective transactions (in this case, it has concluded ties of alliances with another community) that override the elite individual's desire to engage in the normal activities of his social class (freebooting to increase his wealth, and hence his standing, the possibility to engage in competitive display, and to transmit this possibility within his house); these interests are expressed by collective opinion (thus deciding what is legitimate and not) and result in direct action.

The concept of community is worked out in detailed, semi-formalized social arrangements. Intercommunal warfare, illustrated by Nestōr's account of a conflict between the Pylians and the Epeians, involves a clear concept of well-defined and integrated communities to the point of collective responsibility and agency. Damage inflicted by any Epeian on any Pylian can be requited by seizure carried out by the Pylians against all the Epeians (and the proceeds given back to individual Pylians who have suffered losses). In practice, this nexus of social relations is worked out in bovines. Individual Epeians steal oxen from individual Pylians, a Pylian expedition defeats the Epeians and plunders them, the booty is distributed to individual Pylians at the invitation of the victorious hero Nestōr, proclaimed by a herald in the public space of the *agorē*. In this context of well-defined communitarian concepts, spaces, and practices, the importance of the assembly and of dispute resolution in assemblies is less surprising: disputes are brought into the middle, *es meson*, as Menelaos demands during the contest after Patroklos's funeral.[57]

The analysis proposed above, in reading the epic poems, is composite—trawling at an angle across two very different epics, the *Iliad* and the *Odyssey*, and supplemented by the resulting picture with yet another, equally different poem, Hesiod's *Works and Days*. This may be justified by the broad agreement of the three texts in what they show and what they imply. My analysis is also artificial, in that it reads the action and the ideas in the poems according to two categories, presented separately: the lordly and the community-centered. In the two epic poems, the two themes are interrelated, in complex and dynamic ways that determine the economy of the poems and indeed their power as literary texts. But the importance of community is not an illusion. The world portrayed is a world of human communities: its opposite is the island of the Cyclops, described in the *Odyssey* as a place where giant, violent, lawless (*athemistes*) beings live in separate compounds with their families, in a pre-social universe without any need to work and without norms and justice, nor any means or need to interact with communities outside their immediate horizon—"they have no counsel-bearing assemblies (*boulēphoroi agorai*) nor laws (*themistes*), but inhabit the tops of high mountains in hollow caves; each lays down rules (*themisteuei*) in his family, and they do not care for each other."

To be specific, the world of the Homeric epics is about the city: the community finds its expression in a nucleated built environment, defined by walls, sharing public spaces—a human artifact that is the setting for norms, obligations, and community power that enforces these things, and which symbolizes them. This artifact—at the intersection of competitive elite claims, complicated lordly politics, clear communitarian norms, and practical physical realization of these norms, even in the absence of formalized political institutions—is the Homeric *polis*.[58]

Archaeological Readings of Early Greek Poetry

The big challenge here is to understand the relation of the story that emerges from the archaeological record (1100–700 BCE) and of the textual evidence from the eighth century BCE (the Homeric *polis*). This is hardly an immanent relation, and the exercise of mapping material record and epic poetry onto each other is fraught with difficulties. One way would be to look for layers of reference in the Homeric epics. A first layer would be Late Bronze Age reminiscences (certain traits of political geography, artifacts such as the boar's tusk helmet or the big shields); it is nonetheless clear that the political organization of the Mycenaean palace polities is not reflected in the epics.[59] A second layer would be the memory or even a commemoration of the warrior elites and principalities of the post-palatial period (the last Mycenaeans of LHIIIC), especially as concerns the sense of a world divided into multiple polities ruled each by a single king and his family.[60]

Yet another layer would be the world of the Early Iron Age compounds and settlements, in loose communities. These might be read against the raw competitive ethics and distrustful interactions between individuals and families that constitute one strand in Homer and Hesiod, and the competition between lordly individuals with small retainerdoms. As mentioned above, some of the clustervilles seem dominated by elites. The spatial organization of Achilleus's camp, as described in the *Iliad*, with its outer circle and its restricted access to the king's actual dwelling, is matched by the organization of Emborio on Chios. But the archaeology might also be read in terms of communitarian politics, like those of the epics. We might wonder if the "chieftain's houses" identifiable at some sites were in fact communal buildings, in light of the communitarian politics of the *Odyssey*. A chance remark by Tēlemachos attests the existence of the *dēmios oikos*, the "public house," whose nature is unknown: a shared feasting hall or meeting place, perhaps storing public goods?[61]

This layered reading can be considered archaeological in two senses, both as a relation of texts to material record and as a separation of the text into groups of traces of chronologically successive periods. Such a recapitulative reading does not ultimately account for the function performed by the poems (with their varied reminiscences) in their original context, the late eighth century BCE. The politics of epics should precisely be related to the tensions and changes of the moment of consolidation around nucleated settlements.[62] This period precisely shows the coexistence of the same two elements as in the poems. The first is the claim to power by an elite, in forms inherited from the Early Iron Age as well as new forms developed in the decades after 750 BCE, relating to leadership in war or supposed descent from a heroic past. The second is a set of communitarian practices and consolidation, readable in the changing face of the big nucleated settlements.

Early Greek poetry, and more specifically Hesiod (set in the present rather than a heroic past), also helps to understand the archaeological record in another fashion, namely by shedding light on the process of consolidation within territories. As mentioned earlier, A. Edwards has conclusively established that Hesiod does not describe relations between dependent peasants or tenants and landlords, but between a community of free landowners, Askra (which seems to be organized as a loose cluster), and the *basileis* residing in another settlement, which must be Thespiai.[63] However, it is also clear that Askra is not completely independent from Thespiai. Even if there is no mention of regular levies or taxes, there is some form of relation between small Askra, in its desirable valley with a local shrine,

FIGURE 3.1. View from the vale of the Muses, toward Askra (second hill from the left) and Thespiai, in the background.

and big Thespiai in its plain that acts as a central place for a number of smaller settlements and is inhabited by more prosperous landowners with aspirations to elitist stylings (fig. 3.1).

The dispute between Hesiod and his brother is adjudicated by *basileis* in Thespiai, to his disappointment and anger; hence his injunctions to the *basileis* to respect justice, and his images of prosperity or catastrophe being linked to the quality of the kings' justice. Hesiod hence documents the relations between nucleated settlements, and the process of integration that is going on all over the eighth-century BCE world—with the political joining up of smaller clusters of settlements with big sites as documented by "rural" or "extra-urban" shrines.

Most importantly, Hesiod shows us how the process is fraught with tension and negotiation, as can be seen in his appeal to values and justice, precisely to attenuate any free-for-all morality. The might-is-right of the cautionary tale of the Hawk and the Nightingale is in fact rejected, even though Hesiod subscribes to competition, utility, and mistrust within his own community. The aim is to mediate the process and prevent it from turning into the mere capture of an outlying community by the Thespian elites.[64] Such processes of negotiation, in turn, must have taken place between integrated communities: Thespiai's dealings with other such larger communities such as Thebes contributed to the structuration of the regional entity known as Boiōtia.

All these processes were not always peaceful, especially since the elites of the eighth-century BCE communities were, or aspired to be, warrior elites. Hesiod's wariness about the relations between his community, Askra, with the big site of Thespiai is about the exact form that integration will take; the tensions in the relation between elite and nonelite are also about settlement hierarchy (in fact, as a potentially recalcitrant settlement node, Askra would be destroyed by the Thespians in the fourth century BCE). In other cases, integration and structuration of territory did take the form of armed conquest and subordination. Eighth-century BCE Sparta reduced some populations in Lakōnia to serfdom, and other communities to some form of dependency. The movement of expansion must have driven the conquest and subordination of the Messenian plain, west of Lakōnia,[65] with the resulting abandonment of evolving settlements in Messēnia (such as Nichoria) and the end of tomb cult offered in Mycenaean graves. Both phenomena indicate the destruction of a local elite involved in the same processes of settlement consolidation and territory structuration as in the rest of the Greek world.[66]

As we will see in the next chapter, these sorts of processes of conquest were not rare in the "Archaic" world, and constituted one of the main paths of *polis* development. Even more brutally, some emerging settlements were destroyed as part of the processes of community definition. Around 700 BCE (if the dates given by the literary tradition are trustworthy), the settlements of Asinē in the Argolid and Mēliē in Iōnia were destroyed by neighbors.[67] Both were centuries old. Asinē had a history stretching back to the Bronze Age, and in 700 BCE was as large, complex, and important as its Argos. Mēliē was a Protogeometric foundation of the same age as the neighboring Greek settlements that ganged up to destroy it and reuse its territory as the site of a shared shrine, the future Paniōnion, which indicates its function as a focus for relations between the communities in Iōnia (fig. 1.5). These acts of constitutive proto-"foreign policy" ca. 700 BCE must have been conducted by armies, made up mainly of members of the community's elite, equipped with crested helmets, heavy metal armor, the (by now fairly standard) large round shield decorated with personal blazons, two spears and sword which appear on contemporary visual documents (fig. 3.2).[68]

Unity and Diversity in the Early Iron Age

How did these territorial structures of hierarchized settlements with a nucleated, ordered Big Site at its center come to arise? This question amounts to asking, at the end of our examination of the archaeological and the textual evidence and our attempt to read the two types of evidence together: what is actually going on in the Greek Early Iron Age? The whole process is surprising enough for Chester Starr to have described it as a virtual "miracle."[69] Earlier, I examined various archaeologically

FIGURE 3.2. The two special amphoras from the mass graves at Paros, showing fighting scenes. 725-700 BCE. Paros Museum 3523-4. H. 49 cm. Photograph Renaud Hirsch.

based narratives: an egalitarian "Dark Ages" followed by an aristocratic Late Geometric bloom or, alternatively, in I. Morris's influential model, a stratified "Dark Ages" of *aristoi* supported by serf-like *kakoi*, followed by social revolution and egalitarianism in the eighth century BCE.[70] The problem is that we are not quite sure about the nature of the "Dark Ages" societies (there is no evidence for serfs, for instance), nor of the social changes in the eighth century BCE, especially when the latter is so diverse.

My own sense of the landscape and of the shifts during the whole period between 1000 and 700 BCE would run, cautiously, as follows. After the final collapse of the post-Mycenaean world, various loosely organized agrarian settlements emerge or survive, colonizing what seems to be an empty countryside and occupying privileged sites. Some settlements are occupied by remnants of Mycenaean and post-Mycenaean elites with aspirations to distinction expressed through violence and luxury. Others are the abode of new men inventing their own identities and styles. Some are inhabited by descendants of producers in the Mycenaean and post-Mycenaean systems, which have now broken away and live in free, egalitarian "yeomen" settlements. There might already exist settlements made up of diverse groups, negotiating their relations. What matters is that the Late Bronze Age collapse does not seem to have allowed for the survival of extractive state structures. Lesser structures of exploitation, such as local principalities or big landowners, also seem to have vanished or declined.

The diversity of these settlements may be reflected in a range of political set-ups—and in instability at all levels—in relations between elite groups and between different elite and nonelite groups. Eliteness is manifested competitively and performatively through a display and through extra-community interaction with other elite groups; all these gestures signify and create social difference. Equally varied is the economic basis of these settlements. One source of surplus is the exploitation of the countryside through enslaved or enserfed labor according to historical accident or the capacity of local elites for violent capture. Other sources of surplus (across expanding horizons, and probably elite-driven) were agricultural produce, raw materials, manufactured goods, plunder, and enslaved men and women. Some elite leaders had enough surplus to create small groups of followers without ever entrenching their position.

The major question is that of the nature of the eighth-century BCE consolidation of communities out of the loose settlements and political styles of the earlier periods (Protogeometric and Early Geometric). It is clear that the "clustervilles" and loose settlements, representing the choice of Early Iron Age groups to live in rough proximity, gave rise to interactions, experiments, and debates about common interest, gradually tending toward consolidation and integration. However, the causes and processes remain obscure. Population growth and climate change may have driven the process; less dramatically, density of interaction within the loose settlements may have reached a tipping point requiring new solutions. Finally, local elites and their needs may have played a precipitating causal role. But we should be wary of overstating the position of the elite: their claims may only have reinforced the affirmation of community, and conversely, elite visibility may be a response to try to achieve distinction in the face of deep trends toward consolidation.

By 700 BCE, we see a "core geography" (southern Greece, islands, some parts of western Asia Minor) dotted with (but perhaps not completely structured by) a fair number of communities (say, over 150). These are internally organized around a central nucleated big site with differentiated spaces (public, sacred, private, cemeteries). Such communities include other secondary sites apart from the central proto-urban site. This territory may be defined by rural shrines (sometimes connected to a secondary site). Thus structured, the communities also relate to other communities, either by inter-elite contacts or by ritual and dedicatory activities at shared sacred sites (in fact, the activities of inter-elite networking and regional cultic gestures largely overlap). The interaction is sometimes violent, taking the forms of wars of conquest or protracted struggles for resources. The latter process is illustrated by the dimly attested Lelantine War, fought over a fertile vine-growing plain between the two great Euboian cities, Eretria and Chalkis, and involving not just the warrior elites of the two communities but also allied communities across the Greek world.[71]

Another way of considering the story up to 700 BCE is to reexamine individual testcases—for instance, the islands of Naxos and Paros at this latter date, neighboring islands. These have often supplied instances of Early Iron Age phenomena; when pulled together in single locales, the individual phenomena add up to suggestive pictures. On Naxos, as we have seen, the practice of enclosures above a jumble of older cremations and enclosures was coming to an end, and the whole area of one cemetery (at the modern Cathedral Square) covered with a mound. The process marked the end of closely competing funerary display and group rituals and replaced them with a single monumental structure on a vaster scale, which served the whole community.

The same process of community assertion can be seen in the development of a shrine outside the main settlement site and, by reaction, in the insistence by some rural elites to continue grand burials with enclosures in the old fashion. Social diversity is reflected in the great diversity of pottery styles. At the same time, the whole community managed to mediate between different groups, to the point that the Naxians embarked on assertive, aggressive behavior in the region, perhaps as a reflection of their success at forging a common identity, or perhaps precisely to transcend local tensions. Thus, the Naxians are present at Dēlos in the early seventh century BCE and are attested as enemies of the inhabitants of the neighboring island, Paros.

As for the Parians, we can tell that by 700 BCE, they had moved away from such settlements as Koukounaries in the north of the island, to a site that would remain that of the later *polis* (modern Paroikiés). Though little is known about this newly founded settlement in terms of spatial and social organization, a recent discovery provides an arresting glimpse into the life and values of the community.[72] A mass grave, dating to ca. 700 BCE, contains in two pits the cremated remains of 150 young men, in as many clay amphoras (fig. 3.2). Each amphora is decorated individually but is similar to the others, in a visual statement of solidarity and collective identity in which each man participates. Furthermore, each amphora is closed with a drinking cup whose decoration matches the amphora, in a reference to the drinking feast that was one of the means for bonding between elite individuals. Both burial pits were marked by massive stone pillars (one bearing a relief of a seated goddess). The war in which these men died fighting for their community (the battle scenes may show fighters protecting herdsmen) may well be the protracted conflict against prosperous, expansionary Naxos.[73]

It is likely that this mass burial contains the dead of a single event, namely the death in battle of fighters for the community, commemorated *en masse* rather than by their families within enclosures. This practice would be important for the Classical *polis*, and the Paros *polyandrion* (mass war grave) has been interpreted as showing the existence of a proto-democratic ethos in Late Geometric Paros. This interpretation is overstated and teleological (viewing the Parian mass grave from the perspective of democratic war funerals of Classical Athens). In its eighth-century

BCE context, the *polyandrion* celebrated a town-dwelling social elite that claimed to represent the community it defended. It also made place for elite leaders, buried in two special amphoras, much larger and with painted decoration showing war scenes (involving the armored fighters equipped with large round shields, known from other contemporary documents) and funeral processions. The Paros *polyandrion* reflects the existence of Paros as a consolidated community, but also as a place for elite claims and styling. The Naxians were also organized in the same way, judging by a Parian poet of the subsequent generation evoking "Megatimos and Aristophōn, tall pillars of the Naxians," now dead and under the earth. These were heroic leaders in war (who perhaps fell fighting against Paros), perhaps commemorated with literal pillars to which the poem might allude.[74]

The similarity of the two cases of Naxos and Paros reinforces the impression of widespread similarities in community consolidation (albeit with local variants and developments: the processes may have started much earlier in Crete, at the very end of the eighth century BCE in the Cyclades). I have argued above, within the "soft landing" model of the "new Dark Ages" that the Mycenean collapse was not followed by widespread regression, but by the empowerment, prosperity, and agency of countless small settlements of different nature, which join up in tentative patterns of structuration that developed during the eighth century BCE, without any clear direction of development but much complexity and experimentation. The story of the emergence of community is precisely not determined by the top-down phenomena of early-state theory, but of the long processes of negotiation within and between communities in a post-early-state world. But at the end of these processes, whose diversity and multidirectionality I have traced in the previous chapter, the outlines of convergent, mutually reinforcing solutions started to emerge.

The impression of uniformity should not be exaggerated at this stage; I have studiously avoided the word *polis*, or even proto-*polis* (just as I have felt uneasy writing about "the Greek world" at such an early stage). Even by the end of the eighth century BCE, we can guess that many solutions coexisted—ranked societies, princely societies, exclusive societies, egalitarian societies dealing with elitist reactions. The diversity reflects the political choices that communities would have to make in the following centuries. Likewise, even the most developed public forms in these communities do not amount to formalized political and civic institutions along principles of power-sharing and accountability. The emergence of such institutions and such principles, the construction of statehood, and generally the working out of the various problems posed by the diversity and possibilities of the Late Geometric period are the main themes of the next section, and indeed the rest of the book.

PART III

Making the *Polis*: Coalescence, Community, and Justice

675–450 BCE

SOMETIME AROUND 500 BCE, the people of Ēlis had a text incised on a bronze plaque and set up in the shrine of Zeus at Olympia, which they controlled. The text is now terribly fragmentary,[1] but it is clear that it regulated the behavior of the foreigner (*xenos*) in the shrine. If he performed the right sacrifice, he could participate in some event or festival; if not, he was to pay a fine to Olympian Zeus. The rule referred to, or was justified by, traditional practice (*ta patria*); but in itself, as a written text it embodied authority—the authority of a community characterized by a clear, bounded sense of membership and its consequences, and also of its right to decide on rules, enforcement, and punishment. This sense was made visible through the crucial technology of writing within public space: the community was not only able to exercise its authority, but also determine how to display it. Such bronze-inscribed texts are frequent in sixth-century BCE Ēlis, one of many communities that are known to have used written law. The technical term for legal texts in Ēlis is known: *wratra*, the "spoken thing," which still refers to the origins of law in an authoritative utterance, but here applied to an abstract concept that is no longer a speech-act by a single authority, but the result of a decision-making political process.

But the bronze plaque on which this law is inscribed has another historical lesson to give, in addition to the implications of written law for the constitution of community: one need only flip over the two surviving fragments. The Eleian regulation was inscribed on a recycled piece of bronze from one of the wide supports of a monumental tripod, an aristocratic dedication of the eighth century BCE, characteristic (as we have seen above) of the competitive display of the *basileis* that dominated the integrated communities of that period.[2] The exact processes, material and social, that evolved over two centuries from aristocratic dedication to inscribed communal object are irrecoverable, but their implication is clear. The evolution from the world of tripod-dedicating *basileis* to the world of written law issued by authoritative bodies is the story I propose to explore here.

This evolution is richly documented: in addition to the archaeological and visual record that tells us so much about social relations, the Greek communities used writing to produce an abundance of documents—from public documents inscribed on the permanent media of bronze or stone (figs. 4.1, 5.3, 5.4), to private inscriptions (religious or funerary) that tell us much about the values and aspirations of men and women in the seventh and sixth centuries BCE, and poetical texts of very high quality, known to us by indirect but continuous transmission down the ages. This very abundance is instructive about the greater social complexity of the communities in the Greek world in these centuries. A particular product of the processes of social evolution, and the documentation of these processes, is the monumental prose text of Herodotos, an immense *exposé* (*apodexis*) of his enquiries about his world (including the non-Greek peoples around the Greek world), its political structure, and its political history. This text, produced in the second half of the fifth century BCE, looks back on two and a half centuries of social, institutional, and political development, painting a vast panorama drawing on local oral traditions of the life of the *poleis* that emerged out of the nucleated communities of the late eighth century BCE.

When we look from the world of Homer and Hesiod to the world of Herodotos, the contrast poses the parameters of the story in terms as stark, though infinitely richer, as the inscription of law on a reused bit of Geometric-era tripod. The world of Herodotos is a world of great creative and artistic achievement—the colonnaded temple, or free-standing sculpture in stone and in bronze suppose considerable technological expertise and boldness. It is a world of *poleis*, a system of state powers that exists both at a local level of *polis* territories and at the macro level of regional networks (with a variety of possible organizational forms), and at the super level of a community of Greek communities sharing self-aware cultural traits that form a boundary around *to Hellēnikon*, the "Greek thing."[3] These powers exercise considerable agency in the form of a rich pattern of interaction that spans the spectrum from religious diplomacy to endemic low-level hostilities to outright big wars. The biggest of these wars was the successful effort of many of these communities, in a temporary macro network, to fight off the repeated attempts at territorial conquest or at least hegemony on the part of a supralocal empire, the Achaimenid state (indeed, this success played a major role in defining *to Hellēnikon*).

The narrative of that success is told by Herodotos (and in fact forms his main theme). If the figures given for the Persian armies are fanciful, the numbers involved on the Greek side tell their own story.[4] In 494 BCE, at the sea battle in front of the islet of Ladē, the *poleis* of western Asia Minor, in revolt against the Persian empire, lined up a fleet of triremes, large warships that required considerable financial means to build and operate and considerable manpower to take into battle (170 rowers and 30 more men: crew, officers, marines, missle troops).[5] The island *polis* of Chios put out 100 triremes, the Milesians 80, the Samians 60. That the Ionian fleet was defeated by the imperial forces of the Achaimenid state does not diminish the scale of the resources that some of the Ionian *poleis* could mobilize. In 480, the Greek fleet that overcame the Achaimenid invasion force at Salamis was made up of respectable contingents such as the 40 triremes of the Corinthians, or the 30 triremes armed and manned by the island *polis* of Aigina; even these contingents were dwarfed by the massive fleet of 180 ships sent by the exceptionally large *polis* of Athens. The numbers are the more impressive for the trireme having been adopted extremely recently by the Athenians.

Land forces deployed by the Greek *poleis* at the same time, however, give the same impression of numbers—of which we can be sure, this time, that they were all citizens, enjoying a certain social standing since they could afford infantry armor and weapons. At Plataiai in 479, the *polis* of Sparta could line up 5,000 heavily equipped men-at-arms (*hoplitai*)—having already lost an elite force of 300 Spartiates at the famous battle of Thermopylai the previous year; it also commanded 5,000 more men-at-arms from the various *poleis* that constituted, under Spartiate leadership, the regional entity that contemporaries called Lakedaimōn, inhabited by the *Lakedaimōnioi* (which I will call the Spartans, following modern usage). The Corinthians also put 5,000 hoplites in the field, the Sikyonians and the Megarians 3,000 each; the Athenians, again, put the largest contingent of 8,000 hoplites. These numbers should be completed by the citizen rowers and marines that the Athenians, Spartans, and other Greek cities sent out at the same time as the Plataiai campaign, to fight the Persians on sea. The city-state of Argos did not participate in the war against the Persians; about the same time, it is said to have lost 6,000 hoplites, massacred after defeat by a Spartan force, a number that is commensurate with those known for the Plataiai campaign (and from a massive cache of Corinthian armor dedicated at Olympia as victory booty, it is clear that the Argives inflicted a defeat on a large-scale Corinthian army slightly earlier). Even though there is no information (the picture in the epics is fanciful), it is impossible to imagine the warbands of the *basileis* in eighth-century BCE Argos or Sikyōn adding up to three or six thousand heavily armed men: to boil down to raw numbers the story of some Greek states' victorious resistance against the Persian great king allows us to see the path since the time of the first nucleated settlements of the Protogeometric period, from Early Iron Age clustervilles or even "Homeric" semi-states to developed city-states with considerable resources in manpower. Who these men-at-arms were, in terms of social position and political power within their communities, is a crucial aspect of the history of the early Greek *polis*.

It should immediately be added that not every city-state could come up with such resources. At Ladē, next to the eighty Milesian triremes, the Prienians fought in twelve triremes, and next to the Prienian flotilla, the citizens of Myous, a small *polis* on the gulf between Priēnē and Milētos, had provided three ships (fig. 1.5). At

Salamis, many of the fleets provided by Peloponnesian city-states were counted in the single figures (such as the eight ships from Epidauros or the five units of Troizēn); some of the island *poleis* provided pentekontors, antiquated small ships fitting fifty oarsmen (of the same type used by adventurous seafaring trader-warriors in the Geometric period)—the Melians sent two, the Siphnians and the Seriphians one each.[6] The great land battles also saw, alongside the large contingents, far less numerous bodies of heavy infantry, aligned by the smaller poleis. The disparity is instructive for two reasons. First, it shows the unevenness of size and power between various city-states, and various regional networks of city-states (such as the entity "Lakedaimōn"). This particular texture will not only explain a lot in terms of the course of narrative political history (which is about the power relations between the big and the small), but it also raises the simple question of causality, process, and environment: as Herodotos asked at the very start of his *Enquiry*, why are some *poleis* big, and some small? Second, the unevenness also must make us wonder about how, exactly, the concept of *polis* works, if it can describe Myous, which provided three ships at Ladē, and Chios, which was able to equip thirty-three ships for every Myesian unit. In what ways are Myous and Chios alike, and in what ways different?

But both Myous and Chios qualify, unreservedly, as *poleis*—city-states. In the previous chapter, I hesitated (to say the least) to grant either title to any of the settlements that emerged at the end of the Early Iron Age, after protracted processes of consolidation. To justify the facility with which I have now used the terms to describe Myous and Chios, Siphnos and Athens, Sikyōn and Sparta, is the aim of the present chapter. The big question here is that of the emergence of the *polis*, in its multiple forms—state, city-state, citizen-state, political community, political society. How, when, and why did the *polis* emerge in the Aegean world? One way to answer these questions is diachronic, as an analytical narrative situated in time, with a more or less clear shape—a starting point (the communities of 750–700 BCE) and a finishing point—the *poleis* that can be seen in Herodotos's panorama, especially in the late sixth and early fifth centuries BCE. The specific questions concern the modalities of institutionalization, social dynamics, and structuration—how the *poleis* came into being as states, what role was played by elites and elite competition, and how people and communities organized their relations in space and time. In what follows, these themes will first be studied separately, before examining the relation (causal or otherwise) between all three.

As always in this book, but especially in these chapters about the early phases of the *polis*'s life as a social form, the pitfalls are some major historiographical temptations. One of these is originalism; namely, seeking a definitive explanation for the essential nature of the *polis* in its supposed birth. The other is teleology, looking only at those features that make sense as explanations leading toward a final end that is strongly valued—in our case, democracy; indeed, all of Greek history becomes the story of the "origins of Greek democracy," or the birth of a "culture of freedom" characterizing the story of the West and its success.[7] And as always in this book, the way to avoid, or simply void, the origins-teleology trap is to explore specificities diachronically. In particular, we need to explore the specificities of the early *polis* as state form, by looking at processes and outcomes with an awareness of the diversity of possibilities and roads taken. This will mean trying to discern the workings of institutions or laws in contexts that often seem riven with competition and political conflict between elite groups whose interaction takes on historically specific, overtly political but informal shapes (dining or drinking groups, name-calling, pageantry . . .).[8] To speak of such elite groups raises the question of their definition, composition, and position. This question in turn generates questions about the position of the elite, and the nonelite (another category that needs defining), and the relations between the two within the early *poleis*. These synchronic questions about institutions and about political relations, feed back into the diachronic narrative of the emergence and consolidation of the *polis*: to think about the relations between state power, elite competition, elite and nonelite relations, requires the mapping out of these relations in space and in time, through the study of processes of structuration and of historical outcomes.

The twenty-five decades between 700 and 450 BCE are conventionally called the "Archaic period." The term itself is quaint, and fraught with problems. It not only places the *poleis* of this period on a linear teleological path of stages; it also qualifies these stages with a metaphor of growth, and specifically describes this period as archaic, and hence primitive, only in relation to what follows, which is valorized as "classical," and hence mature and fully developed, and indeed most worthy of consideration. All the same, the terminology and the periodization have the advantage of marking out a clear and coherent period in the story of the *polis*: this period's characteristics differ from the Early Iron Age that preceded it, and from the highly political, articulate, and focused period that followed. It is clear that writers and thinkers in this latter period—for instance, Thucydides or Aristotle, and in fact Herodotos—found the earlier political practices and discourses quite difficult to understand (even if one of the goals pursued by Herodotos, living in the early stages of a century of world war and Athenian hegemony, was to try to resurrect the "Archaic" period in all its violent complexity and singularity, indeed even to construct the "Archaic" in its strangeness when contrasted with the age of large-scale hegemonical competition in the fifth century BCE).[9] Furthermore, the "Archaic" label in fact forces comparison by contrast with other forms of "archaic" state, conceptualized (as we have seen) by historians and anthropologists as based on centralization and capture. These features are present, at least as possibilities, in the story of the "Archaic" *polis*, but they are not the whole story, and it is striking that students of "archaic" states have neglected the emergence of the Greek *polis* precisely because it does not fit their models (the way out is to argue, wrongly, that the *polis* was not a state).

Finally, the "Archaic" label, in its conventional currency, conjures up immediate and familiar images that summarize the historical specificity of the period, and its intriguing nature as an "archaic" state driven by a diversity of evolutionary pressures—the bronze-clad hoplite grasping two throwing-spears behind the bowl of his big round shield; the "aristocratic" feaster reclining on his couch among his equals, around a mixing bowl, listening to or producing song; the characteristic artistic productions of the period (figs. 4.2, 6.1 through 6.3, 6.6), such as decoratively surcharged vase painting, freestanding sculpture of youths and girls (*kouroi* and *korai*), or large ornate temple buildings. The world and the political styles within which these images fit are the subject of the following chapters.

4

Institutions, Community, Ideology

1, 2, 3, *POLIS*

> Government is everywhere antecedent to records ... for 'tis with commonwealths as with particular persons, they are commonly ignorant of their own births and infancies.
>
> —LOCKE, *SECOND TREATISE OF GOVERNMENT*,
> CHAPTER 7, SECTION 101

Community and the Possibility of Law: The Case of Drēros

Drēros was a small city in Eastern Crete, known to us through some sporadic but extremely instructive archaeological soundings on the hilltop site.[1] Private housing seems to have covered the site in a dispersed pattern. Though unwalled, the city was clearly defined, and an early cemetery has been excavated outside the built-up area, with tombs from the Protogeometric onwards (they show a small spike in social differentiation in the eighth century BCE, as expected).[2] At the center of the settlement lay an open public space, linked by a street to the temple of Apollōn and a public building of some sort. The walls of the temple were inscribed with public decisions or rules concerning the commonwealth. Five of these probably date to the seventh century BCE. Four of these, in various states of preservation, legibility, and intelligibility, must date to the last part of that century, but the earliest (ca. 650 BCE–630 BCE, judging by letter forms) is complete (fig. 4.1), relatively unambiguous in interpretation, and justly famous for its astonishing implications about *polis* history.[3]

Carved in big letters that snake back and forth, in the early Greek fashion, across the face of a 1 meter-long block of local stone, it reads as follows (rather than transcribe the dialectal forms, here I quote the original Cretan dialect in Greek, and translate):

ἅδ' ἔϝαδε πόλι· ἐπεί κα κοσμήσει δέκα ϝετίον τὸν ἀ-
                   θιοσόλοιον
ϝτὸν μὴ κόσμεν, αἰ δὲ κοσμησίε, ὀ(π)ε δικακσίε, ἀϝτὸν ὀπῆλεν διπλεῖ κἀϝτὸν
ἄκρηστον ἦμεν, ἅς δόοι, κὄτι κοσμησίε μηδὲν ἤμην.
ὀμόται δὲ κόσμος κοὶ δάμιοι κοὶ ἴκατι οἱ τᾶς πόλ[ιο]ς.

FIGURE 4.1. Law on the office of *kosmos*, Drēros, temple of Apollōn Delphinios. Ca. 650 BCE. All three fragments (a-b, top half; c, bottom half) belong to a single long block of hard limestone (L 175 cm), on which the text snakes around existing flaws in the stone.

Thus it seemed good to *polis*—when a man has been *kosmos* (high official), within ten years, let him not be *kosmos*. If he acts as *kosmos*, whatever judgment he renders (or "whenever he judges"), let him pay double, and let him be *akrēstos* (useless) for his lifetime (*added above the line*: god-accursed), and whatever he has done as *kosmos*, let it be nothing. (*punctuation mark*). And the swearers (are): the *kosmos* and the *damioi* ("men of the people," *probably officials*) and the Twenty of the *polis* (*probably the Council*).

This inscription embodies a formally proclaimed and permanently publicized common decision: it is what pleased the *polis*—the first time that the word appears in a document, and indeed the first time we can say unequivocally that it is used to describe more than just a physical settlement (as in Homer). It concerns the term of officeholding by the *kosmos*, a high official whose importance is attested for later periods in Crete (the term is related to the concept of order, also *kosmos* in Greek).

From the inscription itself, it is clear that a major part of the official's activity is judicial, arbitrating disputes within the community. The double payment inflicted as a fine might concern the amounts of reparation and fines that the *kosmos* himself has decided, but is more likely about the fees and gifts that litigants have brought for him in payment for the public function or office he fulfills.[4] The *polis* forbids any member to hold this office twice within ten years. Any man who should try to do so (or try to usurp the office's functions to exercise adjudicatory functions, as seen by G. Seelentag) has no right to sit in judgment legitimately (or even legally). He cannot issue publicly recognized decisions, since the community decides that they are to be quite literally "nothing." In addition, the culprit is disbarred from ever holding office again: he is to be "useless." The *polis* further enshrines this disposition by imposing an oath on the executive holders of specific offices: the *kosmos* himself (or itself: this may be a collective noun, designating a college of several *kosmoi*), the *damioi* who are perhaps those who administer the people's property (and hence will levy fines in the name of the *polis*), and the "Twenty of the *polis*" whose fixed number suggests a council.[5]

The law, in its very confidence, raises a series of questions that might give pause to any potential enthusiasm in seeing this document as the birth act of the *polis*. We do not know how such a decision was enforced; how the fines were levied; how successful the prohibitions were. We might note the implication of disorder and precariousness that shadows this text—the temptation to monopolize the position of *kosmos*, or to act like a *kosmos* without formal appointment, and the need for threats to keep this from happening. Indeed, the disbarment from office was reinforced by a later addition, threatening the culprit not only with being "useless" but also "cursed by the gods" (as F. Ruzé and H. van Effenterre have interpreted this difficult line of the inscription). Even if we can be sure that we have not recovered all of the public documents from Drēros (the seventh-century BCE documents were found where they had fallen, to the bottom of a disused open cistern of much later date), it is immediately clear that the text is not a "constitutional law" defining powers, but an *ad hoc* measure regulating some problematic situation.[6] All these remarks might suggest a picture of competitive, mutually suspicious elite individuals within an unsystematically integrated, weak community, striking individual bargains as part of continual transactions. This view is not far removed from the competitive, mistrustful world of the Early Iron Age. It is just as well to propose such a view of the "Archaic" *polis* at this point: the effect is to temper any teleological enthusiasm and to enjoin caution when trying to gauge the implications of the document from Drēros.

Yet these astonishing implications are equally worth exploring at some length. In this, the earliest documentary record of a *polis*, a document that explicitly talks about *polis* and *damos*, there are officials: the *kosmoi* (administrators), a council whose number is fixed and hence embodies some form of institutional representationality. The Drerian officials hold power on terms decided by the community, according to permanent, public, known, and stated rules. To occupy this function is to be "useful," to be disbarred "useless." Rules and roles entail acceptance, for the good of all, of annual rotation and power-sharing. The possibility that the same man can occupy this position annually but several years in a row, does not fit the spirit of the rule, and hence the loophole or logical problem is closed through a new rule established by common decision. The new rule makes allowance for the desire to serve again (or the need to have people serve again, if the ranks of potential candidates are small) by limiting the exclusion to ten years. The decision must have been taken in the assembly, by a vote upon a formal proposal and after deliberation (why as many as ten years?). It can be called both a law and a decree, to use the distinction developed in the Classical period—it has general force, but it is the result of a one-off decision by the people.

Since this rule might be contentious and constrains the potential individual pursuit of interests and power, the community deploys technological, institutional, and ideological means—writing, display, monumental space—to achieve publicity and authority. The rule is backed up by the gods in the form of the temple where the rule is written, and the curse that it invokes. Ideologically, just as the rule implies a sense of public interests, the fact of a common decision by all that constrains everyone individually implies shared power. The community decides the terms of office, the punishment, and the identity of things and people: "let this be nothing," "let him be useless." In the terminology of speech-act theory, the community has the monopoly on performative utterances, those words that actually change the world. Of course, the performative utterance does not do anything in itself and has to be carried out—hence the added-on curse, both as a threat and as the authorization of self-help and violence against the guilty man, thus legitimizing or delegitimizing behavior and individuals in the city.[7]

The implications are not lessened by the view that the Drerian law is an *ad hoc* decision. By filling a gap or solving a problem, it is equivalent to a thinking through of how to manage the workings of institutions in light of social practice and desired political goods: who shall hold the desirable (and lucrative) position of *kosmos*, in view of the multiple possible holders, the presence of competition between individuals and families, and the need of the community to have a workable process for the public adjudication of disputes? It is also certain that the powers of the *kosmos*, at this stage, were not defined by a written constitutional law. But this only makes more visible, and impressive, the assumptions about public authority. The Drerian law on the non-iteration of the *kosmos* assumes shared knowledge and agreed practice about what a *kosmos* is and what he can do: it operates in relation to a wide-ranging frame of reference, which regulated precise issues (what a *kosmos* does, how many people sit in the council, who the *damioi* are, and what they are allowed to do), but has broader implications in that it embodies the ideology of communal authority.

The contrast with the world of the Homeric *basileis* is enormous. Of course, in the nucleated, consolidated settlements of the late eighth-century BCE we have already seen the popular assembly, the council, the open resolution of disputes by prominent men in return for fees, and the ideology of community interests regulating elite actions. Yet in the world of Homer and Hesiod, the *basileis* sit in judgment based on their own status and fame. The assembly meets infrequently, and at the whim of individual *basileis* (Achilles in the *Iliad*, Tēlemachos in the *Odyssey*). Its decisions can be bypassed by groups, families, and individuals pursuing their own interests (such as vendettas or piracy). It does not have the openly recognized authority to constrain individual action, though it can exercise moral pressure or more direct forms of community violence. The council is informally constituted of great men whose status and number fluctuate. Charismatic individuals can propose, at their discretion, to impose fines to express displeasure and enforce control.[8] Such fines reflect certain privileged individuals' own power, embodied by their capacity for violence, and also perpetuate this power; they are not very different from the informal taxation levied by the *basileis* because they can.

In contrast, the Drerians' decision already supposes enough structure in the community to keep precise records; it is also likely that a *kosmos* in office will give his name to the year, and hence that time is administered and publicly shaped by the community. Public affairs are managed by public officials and bodies elected by the assembly: this rule necessarily means that the assembly meets at fixed points during the year to elect magistrates—and, we can be sure, to debate and decide public matters. Fines, as punishment or as a deterrent, are decided by the community, which also determines the amount. One consequence should be borne in mind: the fining of culprits must produce a body of common property, owned by the community (hence the *damioi*, in charge of the people's goods). How will common property be used? Collective action leads to more collective deliberation.

The most important fact about the Drerian law on the *kosmos* is precisely that is not a constitutional law, establishing the office. It shows the acceptedness of the power of the community to regulate itself at all levels—the place and mode of dispute resolution, elite behavior, sanctions. The Drerian law reflects the prevalence of a communal ideology, namely that the public good requires public decisions. Furthermore, the historical consequence of the Drerian law taking the presence and good workings of institutions for granted is that they must already have been in operation for some time. In this document, the opening three words are *hâd' ewade poli*—literally "Thus it pleased *polis*," omitting the expected definite article. The absolute usage hints that the Drerians were speaking of their *polis* as something more than just the physical city.[9] Another law from Drēros (ca. 600) starts with a similar formula (*poli ewade*); though the substance is almost completely lost, it concerns some action that is allowed in wartime: "let the *agretas* (literally "gatherer"—a military official?) not punish him."[10] This document, too, shows public authority over legitimacy and punishment, and shows another official as part of a seventh-century BCE "constitution of the Drerians."

The laws from Drēros contain a whole functioning world of institutions and laws, suggesting a shift to a form of stateness sometimes before the appearance of written law. How much earlier is anyone's guess: a few decades would take us to the first half of the seventh century, say around 670–660 BCE. Elsewhere on Crete, similar epigraphical evidence suggests a widespread and rapid shift to stately forms at some point in the seventh century BCE.[11] At Gortyn, even though the formula "thus it pleased *polis*" is absent, fragments of late seventh-century BCE law show the existence of interlocking institutions within a context of community regulation of behavior. Dispute resolution takes place in the *agora*; the *titas*, a financial official, levies fines in case of noncompliance with laws. One law seems to concern the regulation of building in public space—a perennial and essential concern of community, here enforced by the large fine of one hundred cauldrons.[12] This Cretan legal material grows richer in the sixth century BCE (see below); the seventh-century BCE start of law at least offers one possible anchoring point in the history of the *polis*, through the emergence of political institutions. Yet for the seventh century BCE, this material seems as isolated as a few asteroids; the question is if and how we can generalize from the temple of Apollōn at Drēros in the seventh century BCE.

An Archipelago of Institutionalization

Elsewhere, without being attested by documentary evidence comparable to the extraordinary traces of state formation at Drēros, the presence of regular institutions is suggested by fragments of literary texts. Alkaios, a citizen of the *polis* of Mytilēnē on the island of Lesbos (ca. 600 BCE) writes in his poetry of the things he misses, while in exile:

> I, the wretch, live the rustic's life, pining to hear the Assembly and the Council summoned by the herald; those things which my father and my father's father enjoyed until their old age, among those citizens harming each other—from those things I am disbarred.[13]

Alkaios knows that Mytilēnē has lived as a *polis* with political institutions for two generations before him, which hints at an early seventh-century BCE date for the formation of Mytilēnē as city-state, compatible with the indications in the law from Drēros. We know that Mytilēnē at the time of Alkaios received a set of laws (due to the action of his opponent, Pittakos): these included a law on the registration of land sales with officials (the *basileis*, literally "kings," and the *prytanis*, literally "ruler").[14] Such services may well have been offered for fees, like the arbitration provided by the *kosmos* at Drēros; in both cases, we see institutions playing a role in the economic life of the community.

Another instructive piece of late seventh-century BCE evidence comes from the temple of Artemis at Ephesos. There, a single financial document incised on a sheet of lead, shows the shrine and the *polis* interacting over complex financial transactions. The city transferred bullion as gifts to the shrine; the latter also enjoyed income from indirect taxes and rents (a naval tax, salt-pans and "the spear," perhaps a share of booty from raiding, or a tax on the sale of such booty).[15] The document does not give names of officials, since it is a piece of temporary accounting and recordkeeping on a cheap, reusable material (indeed, one side was erased and reinscribed); but it is clear that it is part of a whole series and must have involved institutionalized administrative processes and officeholders. The picture is consonant with the financial administrators that appear in the laws of Drēros and Gortyn at the same period.

Across the Aegean from Ephesos, Tiryns, in the Argolid, provides a tantalizing glimpse of institutionalization. Directly inscribed on Late Bronze Age masonry in a winding web of lines, a long inscription preserved a set of rules. They concern the responsibilities of officials called the *platiwoinarchoi* ("leaders of the wine-proximate men"?), who exercise power, can levy fines, and are answerable for their actions. They operate together with other officials (*hieromnamōn* or "sacred remembrancer," *epignōmōn* or "controller") against a backdrop of public goods, fines, written law (*grathmata*), and assembly meetings (*aliaia* and even *ochlos*, "crowd"). This inscription, whose appearance is so primitive but whose institutional content seems so sophisticated, might date to the seventh century BCE (judging by the letter forms), making it another document offering a single glimpse of well-established institutions and governance in an early *polis*.[16]

The seventh century BCE also saw the creation or formalization of a complex set of institutions at Athens, documented through a bundle of disparate evidence.[17] Three separate annual offices—the "king" (*basileus*) with religious functions, the "warleader" (*polemarch*), and the ruler (*archōn*)—were completed by a college of six "ordinance-setters" (*thesmothetai*) who fulfilled arbitration and judicial duties; the whole set of nine officials was later called *archōns* and conceived of as a single body with differing attributions. These officials were no doubt chosen by an assembly of citizens and operated in conjunction with a council, regrouping former officials and known by the name of the "Hill of Ares" (*Areios Pagos*). Later historiographical traditions proposed a narrative scheme to explain the emergence of these institutions, involving a passage from monarchical power held by the families of mythical kings, lifelong office, ten-year stints in office, and finally annual office.[18] These accounts (which reflect fourth-century BCE attempts at creating a rational narrative of Athenian origins along "aristocratic" lines) show, as does all the other seventh-century BCE evidence, the obscurity of the emergence of state institutions.

In addition to the nine *archōns*, officials called *naukraroi* (meaning unclear: ship-chiefs? temple-chiefs?) are known to have managed divisions called *naukrariai* and to have been led by their own presidents (literally "rulers," *prytaneis* in the plural) in structures that represented the various communities across Attica. They are said to have administered Athens at the time of a failed attempt at seizing power by an elite individual, the Olympic victor Kylōn, probably in 640 BCE: it was the *prytaneis* of the *naukraroi* who negotiated (the soon violated) safe conduct for Kylōn and his partisans.[19] What matters is the existence of a complex institutional system that was linked to public needs, perhaps financial in nature. This institution might have started with the financing, through levies or taxes, of communal or semi-communal fleets for expeditions; the institution perhaps evolved to cover the more general management of public goods or resources. Financial functions might also explain why the *naukraroi* were involved in negotiation with Kylōn: public treasure might already have been accumulated in the shrine of Athēna on the Akropolis, which Kylōn tried to seize.

Rather more fully than these snippets of information, another public institution attested for early Athens is a board of *ephetai* (also called "the Fifty-One") that could be called on to judge homicide cases. They are attested in a law, inscribed in 409/8 BCE, but officially described as the homicide law of Drakōn,[20] an Athenian appointed as legislator in 621/0 BCE (if we follow the date that later generations assigned to this event). The reinscription of this law even assigns it to a precise "axle"; that is, a wooden beam as part of a whole set, containing a full law code:

First axle.
And if someone kills someone not out of premeditation, let him go into exile; and let the kings (*i.e., the successive holders of the office of* basileus, *or another panel?*) judge guilty of homicide the perpetrator or the planner, and the *ephetai* are to decide. Let there be reconciliation, if there is a father, a brother, or a son, if unanimity is reached, else the objector is to prevail. If there are no such relatives, then up to first cousinhood and first cousin, if all wish there be a reconciliation (let this happen), else the objector is to prevail. If there is no one among such relatives, and the killer has killed unwillingly and the fifty-one *ephetai* decide that he has killed unwillingly, let ten *phratores* (members of local communal organizations called *phratries*, a word akin to "brotherhoods") let him in; and let the Fifty-One chose these on the basis of worth. And those who committed homicide earlier are to be held liable to this ordinance (*thesmos*). There is to be a proclamation against the killer in the *agora* (by relatives) up to first cousinhood and first cousin; cousins and their sons, sons-in-law and fathers-in-law and *phratores* will share in the prosecution... (*gap*)... If someone kills a murderer or is responsible for his death even though the murderer is keeping away from borderland marketplaces, contests and Amphiktionic rites (administered by the federal body with oversight at the shrine of Apollōn at Delphi), the perpetrator of such a deed is to be held liable as if he had killed an Athenian; the *ephetai* are to decide. It is to be allowed to kill or seize the murderer in the (Athenian) territory. (*fragmentary:*) If someone starts an unprovoked fight... kills him... the *ephetai* are to decide (*gap*)... if he is... or if he is a free man. And if someone kills another when the latter is forcibly and unjustly plundering or seizing property, let the death not be liable for compensation.

This law, passed at one precise moment (hence the clause about retroactivity) regulates behavior in case of homicide. This had always been an important issue for the Homeric communities. The judgment scene on Achilles's shield, portrayed in the *Iliad*, concerns a homicide[21] and issues of revenge, violence, and compensation overshadow the end of the *Odyssey*, when three generations of men in the same aristocratic house (Laertēs, Odysseus and Tēlemachos) have to consider how to confront the relatives of the suitors whom Odysseus has just slaughtered in his hall. The issue matters for all, because of the risk that violence will spiral out into a cycle of vendetta. (Indeed, the suitors and Odysseus's family face off in actual battle in the city before divine intervention puts a stop to the bloodshed). The Athenian law quoted above shows an extensive effort at regulating violence, considering and answering various questions that arise out of the basic situation—what can and should the community do about cases of homicide in its midst? It lays out clear channels for resolution after involuntary homicide, involving relatives and social groups that enjoy the right of asking for punishment of a killing or of consenting to the return of a killer.

The law decides on legitimate and illegitimate behavior, both in matters of procedure and of substance—for instance, the law defines legitimate self-defense or uses a legal analogy to define the act of killing a man guilty of homicide outside Athenian territory as illegal and subject to the same penalties and procedures as straight homicide of an Athenian. Conversely, and logically, action against killers who return to Athenian territory in spite of exile is legitimate and allowed. In all these matters, decision-making is framed by public officials, the *basileis* and, especially, the panel of fifty-one *ephetai*.

A seventh-century BCE date for this law cannot be considered absolutely secure. It rests on the attribution in the fifth-century BCE document, when the Athenians believed in two law codes, each by single lawgivers, Drakōn and the later *archōn* Solōn, surviving on the same medium of inscribed beams. The systematic, thought-through and coherent workings of the homicide law cannot have been produced in response to any single crisis (as forcefully underlined by M. Gagarin), and they do not resemble the mode of legislation attested in Crete (and elsewhere), namely single enactments, often by the *polis*, aimed at specific issues. But the differences should not be exaggerated. Both Drakōn's and Solōn's codes, attested through a variety of fragments, seem to have been a collection of measures responding to a variety of problems; in that respect, every single *thesmos* is not different from the laws attested in Crete. Conversely, the laws in Crete accumulate in inscribed form on the temple walls, thus forming quasi-codes. Most significant is the pervasive concept of public authority deriving from the community and exercised in the community's interest, through common institutions whose power is taken for granted.

Finally, a seventh-century BCE context for institutionalization is implied by a poem that belongs to a group traditionally ascribed to the Spartan poet Tyrtaios.[22] Tyrtaios locates the workings of institutions in the past as the result of a founding oracle from Apollōn: kings (here called "leaders"), elders initiating (or ruling) a Council, and an Assembly responding with straight decisions, by majority.

> They heard Phoibos and brought back from Delphi oracles of the god and words of sure fulfilment; for thus the lord of the silver bow, far-shooting golden-haired Apollōn, answered out of his rich shrine: the beginning of counsel shall belong to the god-honored kings whose care is the lovely city of Sparta, and to the first-born elders; after them the men of the people, answering them back with forthright ordinances, will say honorable things and do what is right, and not give this *polis* a crooked counsel. So shall the mass of the people (*dēmos*) have victory and power (*kartos*); Phoibos has declared this to the *polis* in these matters.

The same elements are found in a short, mysterious prose text, quoted by Plutarch in his biography of the mythical founder of the Spartan constitution, Lykourgos. The text is described as a *rhētra*, or pronouncement (of the people), and mentions, as measures started under Kings Polydōros and Theopompos, the division of the people into subdivisions, the establishment of certain public shrines, and the holding of regular meetings of the Assembly after gathering the tribes, as well as the same various powers of kings, Council of elders, and Assembly as in the poem by Tyrtaios. The text specifies that *kartos*, power, will be enjoyed by the people, but also assigns some authority of "setting aside" or "standing apart" to the kings if the decision is crooked. This text was probably found by Plutarch in his source, the Aristotelian description of the Spartan constitution. It seems to reflect an original Spartan document but almost certainly not a written law of the seventh century BCE. We may be looking at a written document of the sixth century BCE that purports to record an older decision, and perhaps even incorporates authentic fragments of earlier decisions—a "retro-charter."[23]

It seems clear that in the later seventh century BCE, at the time of the poems probably written by Tyrtaios, and even more so in the sixth century BCE, there was a clear consciousness of the *polis*'s institutions, a feeling that they must have started at some point in the past—and no clear sense of this starting point. There rather floated a mythological vagueness about origins, which is universally found in the "Archaic" *polis*. Hence the idea of institutions created as a balanced ensemble, upon the authority of an oracle of Apollōn implemented wholesale (the retro-charter adds further refinement in the distribution of power that the charter tries to pass off as original, and spurious association with the two eighth-century BCE kings who initiated Spartan expansion). The existence of the two kings is a Spartan peculiarity that defies explanation (the Spartiates themselves had mythological etiologies for the institution); nonetheless, the case of Sparta suggests formalization and institutionalization of power in the first half of the seventh century BCE, with an explicit if qualified acceptance of the *dēmos*'s ultimate authority.

The words used to describe this situation, *damos* and *kratos*, are of course the same as in the compound *dēmokratia*. This does not mean we should call the early Spartiate state democratic, but the association is striking because it articulates the idea that the People, the community, should decide on common matters, an idea that underlies the Drerian decree analyzed above. The same ideology can be seen in the names of some of the Spartan kings, which, from the seventh century BCE onwards, often have an element in *-damos*, reflecting a proclaimed awareness of the People in the Spartiate polity.[24]

Defining Communities: Tribes, Family Groups

The emergence of institutions, though widespread, is everywhere obscure. The interval between the acceleration of integration and consolidation of the late eighth century BCE, and the institutionalized communities of the late seventh century BCE, remains utterly opaque. It is easy to suppose that the processes of institutionalization must have prolonged community integration. Yet what we see in the seventh-century BCE *poleis* is a fictional society—namely, the union of groups that seem organic but are in fact integral parts of the institutionalized political community. The incomplete law of Drēros mentioned above was passed after consultation (?) of the *pulai* (a dialectal variant on the more usual *phulai*), civic subdivisions that are conventionally translated as "tribes."[25] Another late seventh-century BCE Drerian law might mention two other subdivisions: the *hetaireiai*, groups of companions, and the *agelai*, literally the "herds," groups of young men.[26] In Sparta, along with other divisions called the *obai* that were geographical districts or villages (their number and nature are unclear), tribes are mentioned as part of the founding institutions of Sparta, perhaps as part of local consultation comparable to the procedure involving the *pulai* of Drēros. Tyrtaios mentions the Spartiates's battle array in three separate contingents, "Pamphyloi, Hylleis and Dymanes," bearing the names of the three tribes known in a variety of *poleis* that shared a proclaimed identity as "Dorians" on the basis of dialect.[27] Similarly, the *polis* of Megara may have had a similar double system of five local units coexisting with the three Dorian tribes.[28] Other *poleis* shared, among the cultural traits that made them Ionian, four tribes. At Athens, this number might explain the twelve *naukrariai*.

The giveaway is the presence of identically named and numbered tribes across a number of cities. They are not age-old gentilician structures, remnants of warrior bands, or survival of clans or local villages; they are not primitive institutions that might reflect the prehistory before the *polis*. Their invention represents as much of a rupture as the emergence of political institutions. The tribes might have emerged in response to the situation during the Early Iron Age, namely as a world of clustervilles and loose settlements of the Geometric period. Literary sources allow us to guess the uneasy relations between families and social groups within these settlements, and the equally tense relations between big sites (for instance, Thespiai) and smaller sites (for instance, Askra). Once we are looking at "tribes," or "herds" of young men, we must suppose a *polis*-wide reorganization of the population. A notable part of the reorganization focused on *rites de passage* that integrated the young into the community—for instance, in the tribal regiments, based on the tribal system. The creation of community by formalizing and structuring group identity is strikingly embodied by an exhortation of Tyrtaios addressed to the Spartiates: "You are the descendants of unconquered Hēraklēs, so be bold."[29]

In the *Odyssey*, the *laos* of the Pylians, headed by Nestōr and his family, is portrayed as lined up in nine groups (literally "sittings," *hedrai*) of five hundred men each, awaiting the distribution of shares of public sacrificial victims that each group has provided, nine oxen per sitting.[30] Notable are the equal size, the constitutive role of these groups, and the way in which they make community visible as a framework for ritual activities of sharing. All that is needed is the fiction that these are age-old, ancestral groups, yet plugged into the workings of political institutions, for the *polis* to be invented before our eyes as an entity both greater than, and organically organized by, tribes, districts, "brotherhoods," "companionships," "herds." As a creation of the *polis*, tribes and their divisions had to be equal in size and distribute the population among constructed kinship groups; yet the process happened early enough, and naturally enough, for the members of the *poleis* to have considered them as ancestral ways of belonging to the *polis*, which displaced the earlier clustervilles and family groups.

The invention of groups and the distribution of the population into them may have taken place at the same time as the invention of government in the early seventh century BCE. Indeed, the working of state institutions probably required the distribution of the population into such groups to ensure an openly fair sharing of power. Hence the consultation of tribes at Drēros, perhaps as a mechanism for deliberation and assent. It is also likely that the "Twenty of the *polis*" were chosen on the basis of fairly distributed recruitment by tribe. In other words, the obscure leap to the horizon of state institutions also was a leap into a form of social organization that undergirded the state.

In addition to the tribes, subdivisions, and other groups, the early *polis* was structured by kinship groups, more or less fictional. They probably existed in the Early Iron Age communities as they came together, and the question of their relationship to the institutionalization of the *polis* must have been defined and negotiated. In Athens, "brotherhoods" (*phratriai*), "clans" (*genē*), and indeed other social groups played an important role in defining membership and cultic activities.[31] The multitude of such groups can be seen in later Athenian legislation attributed to the legislator Solōn in the early sixth century BCE. The law also makes clear the ultimate necessity of framing their existence within the institutions of the *polis* (a crucial theme of the future history of the *polis*: see below, chapter 15). The Solonian law hence gives a sense of the tensions and conflicts that had to be negotiated from the very start, at the time of the creation of the double frame of political institutions and fictional social groups:³²

> If a village (*dēmos*) or members of a phratry or performers of sacred ceremonies or messmates or members of a burial corporation or thiasotai or those who go away for plunder or for commerce arrive at an arrangement among themselves, it shall stand, unless public written documents (*dēmosia grammata*) forbid it.

Dining, Drinking, Singing Together

Dining groups constitute a particularly important category among the social forms in the early *polis*. In Sparta, the *pheiditia* (messes) were later an integral part of citizenship, and somehow bound with military organization. The poetry of Alkman refers to common meals (*sunaiklai*) and to the provision of food (bean porridge, white meal, and honey) whose very simplicity symbolizes communal sharing as members of "the people."³³ In Crete, the "men's hall" probably intermeshed with the "companionhoods" and the system of *rites de passage* attested for youths. Later evidence suggests that the Cretan dining halls were the scene of the redistribution of the products of levies (but the sources of these are unclear: rent from subordinate groups within the community? tribute from subordinate communities? taxation of citizens?).³⁴ At Azoria, a large hall was probably used for civic dining, and is associated with facilities for storage of large amounts of food and drink.³⁵

Even if such institutionalized common messes are not known elsewhere, the importance of the dining group is widely attested. An Athenian law, perhaps due to the lawgiver Solōn in 594 BCE, forbids the man guilty of homicide to have a share in libations, wine-mixing bowls (*kratēres*), sacrifices, and the *agora*,³⁶ encapsulating the way in which the early "Archaic" *polis* existed through social practices of sharing. Such dining groups may have met in an open space northwest of the Akropolis, once it was cleared of workshops and cemeteries, as suggested by finds of drinking cups, miniature votive shields (hinting at military membership of the *polis*), and ceramic counters that might be linked to voting or to distribution of goods.³⁷

Conversely, the *polis* could represent itself as a drinking group of the whole of the population of its members.³⁸ Some institutional manifestations looked like the dining group: office holders or councilors would hold feasts and drinking parties in the *prytaneion*, literally the "house of lords," patterned on private dining halls but serving public needs. The public area of Drēros, in addition to the temple of Apollōn with its publicly written law, also included a building with facilities for dining, which may be an example of a *prytaneion*. The poetess Sapphō describes (ca. 600 BCE or later?) the provision for a public *sumposion* in the *prytaneion* of her city of Mytilēnē (the same city where Alkaios mentions the Council and the Assembly as ancestral institutions). The officials and councilors were served wine by beautiful, well-born youths, citizens like Sapphō's much-loved brother Larichos.³⁹

A striking expression of the links between drinking group and *polis* can be found in the songs performed in banqueting contexts. The poetry of Sēmonidēs expresses group solidarity in grim poetry about death and forgetfulness, or (in the longest surviving poem) by lampooning the race of women as animal and different from that of men, an early example of the misogyny that was part of the self-definition of the in-group of citizens (below, pp. 504–6).[40] The female associations implied by the poetry of Sapphō at Mytilēnē, or the lyric of Alkman in Sparta, mirror the solidarity-fostering male groups within the *polis* (down to the socially approved and framed homoerotic emotions).[41]

The songs attributed to Archilochos deserve particular attention for giving a view of the *polis* from the banqueting hall. Publicly expressed grief for the death of immediate companions lost at sea is the occasion for solidarity of the close circle, a solidarity so close it takes on bodily form: their lungs, swollen with expressing grief, mirror the dead men's fate, establishing a bridge between the living and the dead, and most importantly, bonding the living companions. Yet beyond this immediate circle, the *polis* and its denizens will echo this grief felt by a restricted circle:

> Periklēs, nobody among the *astoi* will feast and reproach our laments and our grief, nor will the *polis*, for such were the good men who, the wave of the crashing sea washed away, and we have our lungs swollen with weeping . . .

The song insists on the powerful closeness of a particular group, perhaps a drinking group or "companionship," bound by solidarity and endurance, yet interlocks this group with the *polis* at large, made up of similar groups who meet for drink and song, and who are aware of each other.[42]

Song, performed before the group, ensures that action in the *polis* is subject to public judgment, and sometimes censure. Hence the variety of Archilochos's poetry, incorporating comments, critique, playacting, and explorations of issues that bind individuals and community.[43] One of the functions of song is indeed to mediate between communal pressure, group solidarity, and individuals such as the singer and the companions to whom he calls out. A tremendous poem evokes a gale, speaking to a companion whose monument was set up in early Thasos (below, p. 97): "Glaukos, see: the deep sea is already rough with waves, the cloud stands upright above the heights of Gyrai, a sign of a storm, and from the unforeseen comes fear."[44] Later readers, at least, did not hesitate to see this poem as a metaphor for a threat to the whole community: the earliest example of the metaphor of the ship of state.

The meal- and drink-sharing group acts as a political gathering in other ways. It involves order, equality between participants, and hence a reflection on membership and on the proper use of resources available. A fragment of Archilochos is addressed to an unwelcome guest whose behavior is also a sign of antisocial desire to consume without making a contribution, "drinking much unmixed wine, you did not contribute the worth (*timon*, cognate with *timē*, "honor, value") . . . , nor did you come . . . invited like a friend, but your stomach led your mind and your spirit astray into shamelessness."[45] The communal meals and drinking parties are conducted on the basis of contributions by participants, which are the counterpart of the distribution of shares in food or in mixed wine. There is no question of consumption at the expense of the others: such consumption is a mark of a shameful lack of restraint, and hence of disengagement from communal values of sharing.

Defining Communities: War

The issues faced by the emergent political communities, and the choices they imposed on themselves, are strikingly visible in the case of the communities' way of war. Poetry sung in the drinking party (*sumposion*), as in the case of some strikingly vivid pieces by Archilochos,[46] and figured pottery, give an idea of the seventh-century BCE fighting. Most men go forth in heavy equipment, with helmet, corslet, and round two-handled shield—a panoply that has largely been standardized since ca. 700 BCE; others fight with lighter variants. The heavy men-at-arms carry two spears, at least one of which will be thrown at the enemy (the poet Kallinos calls upon the young men to come up with "one last throw," even when dying) and the other used in close fighting under the concave shelter of the big shield. Generally, the fluid battlefield involves a considerable amount of missile warfare. In Tyrtaios, the *panoploi* (fully kitted-out fighters) are aided by *gymnētes* (literally "naked" fighters) who throw stones, under the cover of shields (their own or those of the *panoploi*?).[47] Seventh-century BCE vases frequently show archers taking part in fighting. One *aryballos* even shows a man-at-arms who has shed his helmet and propped up his shield with a stick, and presently is preparing to use a sling to take a potshot into a melee of close-in fighters. The impression of diversity is heightened by depictions of men riding horses into battle—not to serve as cavalry, but to dismount and fight on foot.[48]

The face of battle recalls that in the Homeric poems, the men-at-arms with their round shields and two spears resemble the armed men processing, sometimes fighting, on Attic funerary pottery of the Late Geometric period; indeed, such processions also appear in "Archaic" art (for instance, on Spartan *pithoi* of the seventh century BCE).[49] But the values have undergone a massive shift since the eighth century BCE. The communitarian elements are strongly favored. The Athenian Tellos, recorded by Herodotos perhaps as a seventh-century BCE fighter for his *polis*, died in battle and was honored with a public funeral.[50] This ethos (reminiscent of Hektōr in the *Iliad*, or the "pillars of the Naxians," Megatimos and Aristophōn) is now generalized to all members of the community. Kallinos's young men are told to fight for their families and their land, without fear of death, secure in the knowledge that the strong-minded man who falls in battle is "missed by the whole *laos*, for they look upon him as a tower."

Equally important is the diminution of the theme of fighting as the arena for the test of individual valor and the winning of *kleos* in a complicated equation.[51]

Nowhere is this clearer than in the lines of Tyrtaios's tremendous (if slightly repetitive) battle poetry:[52]

> For it is fine to fall among the front fighters, as a brave man, fighting for one's fatherland . . . Bravely let us fight for this land and for our children. and let us die without sparing our lives. Young men, come and fight, staying next to each other, and do not begin the shameful rout or the panic, but make your heart big and strong in your chests, and do not value your lives as you fight against men, and do not flee and abandon the older men, whose knees are no longer limber, the old men . . .
>
> Now be bold, for you are of the race of Hēraklēs, and Zeus has never deceived when he nods assent. Do not fear the mass of men, do not give in to fear, and let a man hold his shield straight against the front-fighters, considering his life hateful, and the black spirits of death as dear as the rays of the sun . . .

The deployment of bravery and aggressivity in the face of the horrors of edged-weapon warfare is not devoid of personal glory. Death in battle is extolled as something lovely and admirable, rewarded with *kleos*, heroic burial, and descendants to remember him. Yet this state of being admired and glorious is open to all those members of the *polis* who listen to the poem. The focus is the community: the brave but unnamed man who dares "to look at bloody murder and seek the enemy by standing close to them," shows *aretē*, valor, as "a common good for the *polis* and the whole *dēmos*."

The heroes have been resorbed in the mass of fighters, and the mass of fighters has access to the same rewards as the heroes, as members of the community, as long as they fulfill expectations that are now transformed into norms rather than options on the heroic menu. It is likely that the micro-feudalisms that sustained the *basileis* of Homeric society vanished alongside the heroic claims and calculations about lordly glory.

The link between fighting, membership, and community can be read on several Corinthian vases (dating to around 630 BCE).[53] These combine (from the top down) main registers showing heavily armored fighters, middle register images of heroic hunting and riding by youths (sometimes marked off by mythical scenes or beasts), and low friezes showing hare hunting by boys with hounds (fig. 4.2). Whatever the exact meaning of the collocation, the vases show images of order, the division of the community into definite age-classes, collective activities such as hunting and, as the culmination of the process, the status of the fighting man taking part in the communal activity of warfare.[54]

War was constitutive of the *polis*, internally and externally, in the spheres of institutions as well as civic ideology and representations. Internally, war had constitutive effects because it made members commit themselves to the defense or pursuit of communal interests, and in the name of an ideology of devotion to the whole community, to the point of death. It is this joint effort that makes Tyrtaios address

FIGURE 4.2. Corinthian jug representing heavy infantry combat, myth and hunting. Ca 640-25 BCE. H 26 cm. Villa Giulia, Rome. 22769. After drawing in E. Pfuhl, *Malerei und Zeichnung der Griechen* (Munich, 1923).

the whole Spartiates as descendants of Hēraklēs, one and all. As seen above, the representation is one of individuals defending their own families as part of collective effort for "the land" (*gē*), the fatherland (*patris*), and the *polis*, in return for collective recognition. In practical terms, this mobilization required institutional forms. The tribal divisions attested at Sparta (by Tyrtaios), the "war leader" perhaps in office at Athens (and perhaps a system of "families" used to levy fighting men across the territory) illustrate the solutions that the *polis* came up with to fulfill the needs and the possibilities posed by the communal effort of war.[55]

Externally, war was the expression of the *polis*, as the main form of "foreign policy." The latter term is justified, just as the term of state is justified for these entities that wielded legitimate violence internally and externally. Armed conflict represented competition between organized communities: the Naxians and Parians, the Chians and the Erythraians, the Argives and the Spartan entity. Examples could be multiplied (indeed such conflicts are often the only history we have for the early history of some *poleis*).[56] In other cases, the size of the combatants was disproportionate, as when the cities of Iōnia (having earlier resisted incursions and raids by the Kimmerians) faced military pressure from the Anatolian kingdom of Lydia. This is the first occurrence of the theme of the relation between the *poleis* and supralocal empires of domination—a theme that would characterize the history of the *polis* to its end.⁵⁷

Whether against neighboring *poleis* or big states, war determined the shape of *poleis* in two ways. First, violent conflict would decide which of two *poleis* owned borderland and border communities with their populations: the outcome fixed the territorial boundaries of *poleis*, as the limits for internal *polis* development. Secondly, the outcome of conflict might decide on the subordination, freedom, or dominant position of a community: the Epidaurians dominated the island of Aigina, before the latter broke free (inaugurating a period of hostility between the two *poleis*); Argos captured and sacked Nauplia, at the end of the Argive plain— part of a long story of Argive affirmation as a regional power.⁵⁸

The constitutive nature of warfare for the early *polis* is clearly seen in the case of early Sparta, which was a conquest state made up of the coming-together of five local communities, the subordination of local producers to serfdom (the "helots" known from later sources), and an expansionary drive to establish control over two neighboring landscapes. The first was the regional nexus of *poleis* in Lakōnia constituting a regional state, the *Lakedaimōnioi*, which the Spartiates headed. The second was the Pamisos valley where Sparta left some communities to develop into dependent *poleis* but which was mostly reduced to a mosaic of estates distributed to all members of the Spartiate community.⁵⁹ The processes, initiated already in the eighth century BCE as part of the phenomenon of consolidation in the region (above, chapter 3), was furthered and shored up throughout the seventh century BCE. It would allow the Spartiate state to expand north, in conflict with Arkadian *poleis* and the other large Peloponnesian *polis*, Argos.

All these events are partly documented in the poetry of Tyrtaios: for all of its communitarian insistence on the nobility of death to defend "this land" and each man's family, it also was about the rise of the Spartiate *polis* as conquest state. Tyrtaios celebrated the constitutive aspects of conquest and expansion; namely, in the past the seizure of rich lands, the expulsion of Messenian elites, the reduction of some Messenian producers to sharecroppers toiling like donkeys and forced, in an act of symbolic violence, to observe mourning for their masters when the latter died. In his own time, Tyrtaios speaks of great battles against a whole array of Peloponnesian *poleis* joining forces against Sparta. These aspects also united the Spartiate community, knitting state and society—or rather celebrating their equivalence.⁶⁰

The significance of these processes of subordination needs to be considered later. For now, what matters is the answer suggested by these political processes to the question, "Why did early "Archaic" *poleis* fight wars?" The reason was not a scramble for scarce resources. Survey archaeology suggests a landscape dotted with nucleated settlements and not yet fully occupied; that would take place from 550 BCE onwards (below, chapter 5).⁶¹ As the case of Sparta makes clear, *polis* warfare is part of a series of processes of affirmation and competition by emerging states, and generally of structuration.

Materializing the *Polis*

Seventh-century BCE consolidation can be further read in the archaeology of urbanization, in tandem with the evidence for institutionalization. Many of the central sites that are at the heart of territorial consolidation underwent significant monumentalization.[62] Eighth-century BCE temples, which clearly mark consolidated communities but whose appearance and construction were close to that of normal houses, were replaced by constructions of stone, timber, and terracotta. The wattle and daub, thatched-roof temple of Apollōn at Eretria underwent the change around 650 BCE. The shift toward monumentality was widespread. A stone temple for Apollōn was built at Corinth (early seventh century BCE), with limestone courses (probably completed by mudbrick) and a tiled terracotta roof; the shapes already announce those of the classical Greek temple, defined by size, roof and pediment, masonry, and façade.[63] On Naxos, the peri-urban temple of the late eighth century BCE was rebuilt, on a larger scale, with the same internal arrangements but the added feature of an outer porch t gave the temple a monumental façade.[64] Another early example is the temple of Artemis at Ephesos, built ca. 660–640 BCE in stone with an internal timber colonnade, and rebuilt a few decades later.[65] In Crete, at Gortyn, a temple of Apollōn Pythios (second half of the seventh century BCE) was built on a new site below the range of hills occupied in the Early Iron Age; more generally, the urbanization and organization of big central sites can be read all over the island.[66] The appearance of the monumental temple doubtless reflected and contributed to changes in religious practice,[67] as part of a more general movement toward monumental building in and by communities.

Monumental temples and public buildings are part of a physical record of intensified integration. Terracing work could regularize the *agora*'s open spaces at the heart of communities, as seen on the hilltop *polis* of Thēra, or at Latō in Crete.[68] The construction of the temple of Apollōn Pythios at Gortyn was accompanied by the abandonment of the widely separated clusters on the heights, and the shift of the inhabitants to consolidated nucleated settlement in the same area as the temple.[69] A similar movement toward urbanization occurs at Larisa, in Thessaly, where settlement shifts from a Geometric hilltop location to a plains site that will grow during the sixth century BCE into an organized, monumentalized city with clearly laid out units.[70] Eretria built its first fortification wall, surrounding and defining the vast area of the urban settlement, during the early seventh century BCE. The trace enclosed the site of an elite burial field around a "princely" tomb, now covered with a mound and a cultic structure: the development suggests that the private cemetery now became a public shrine of some sort.[71]

A particular case is the small local settlement established on a virgin site at Vroulia (modern toponym) on southern Rhodes, giving a clear image of social order (fig. 4.3).[72] The site has been fascinatingly clarified by recent work.

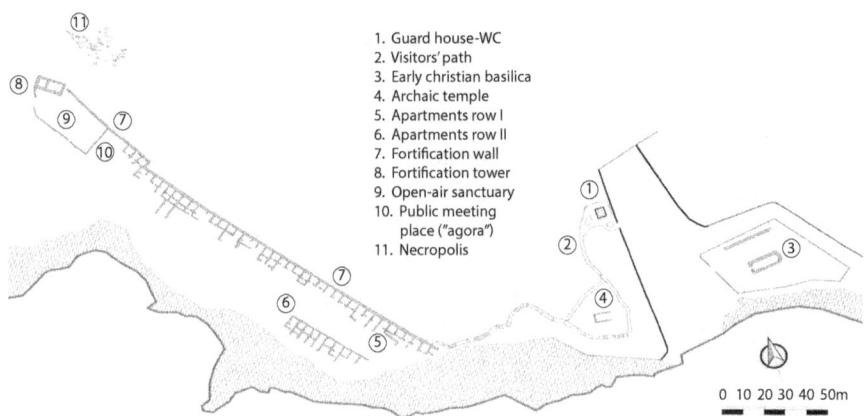

FIGURE 4.3. Map of the ancient settlement at Vroulia, southern Rhodes. From Kaninia and Schierup 2017.

The settlement is defined by a wall, which ensures defensibility and separates inside from outside, giving the community a physical boundary. Inside, the members inhabit private housing that is strikingly uniform and contiguous; they share public spaces for meetings or for cultic activities. Outside, the members bury their dead in cemeteries, grouped in clusters. The settlement at Vroulia was not a *polis*, and never became one. A nucleated place within the territories of one of the *poleis* on the island of Rhodes, it may have received a military garrison or a trading post rather than an agrarian community. Its interest is in laying out clearly and simply the relationship between spatial organization, durable built structure, and community integration. The settlement seems a physical manifestation of political community, in the form of public spaces, buildings, and the wide streets that unify them for the benefit of people: it illustrates the characteristic seventh-century BCE development of regular sites built around a certain idea of community. A fragment of Terpandros, a seventh-century BCE Spartan poet, associates the wide spaces of the city with war and justice. In the poetry of Archilochos, the city is more than just an assemblage of houses protected by their individual enclosures: it is also a site for common living—a place of wandering, of beauty, and even of implied love, a thing that can be threatened or damaged by war.[73]

What Was a *Polis*?

What was a *polis* in the seventh century BCE? A set of local relations between nucleated communities, articulated through the following means. Firstly, political institutions and law. Secondly, invented (yet organic) forms of kinship, alongside various networked social groups. Thirdly, ideological images and symbolic gestures promoting unity. All these means had to be deployed to try to work out the relationship between the big site, the *asty* or town, inhabited by an elite of *astoi* (not quite citizens, not just "townsmen"), the countryside, and the other nucleated settlements. The resulting bonds constituted the whole community.[74] Kallinos calls upon the youths to rise and fight out of shame before the "dwellers-around" (*amphiperiktiones*), perhaps inhabitants of the territory who look to the urban elite of *astoi* to represent their interests in war. This process of integration was basic to the *polis*: it can already be seen in the negotiation between Thespiai and Askra in the eighth century (above, pp. 62–63).

In the case of the comparatively huge territory of Attica, structured in the relation between the town of Athens and outlying communities (existing at least since the Geometric period, and perhaps founded by settlers from the town), the processes may have taken time (though later Athenians attributed the unity of Attica to the hero Theseus, in a typical mythological explanation for obscure historical processes). The archaeology of Attica suggests diversity and the absence of fixed hierarchies: the high-status cemetery at the Kerameikos is balanced by the large, marginal settlement at Phaleron by the sea, the "Geometric" style is replaced by the experimental, exuberant "Proto-Attic," cult places appear across the region.[75] By the time of Drakōn's homicide law, there was a clear sense of the territory. Perhaps around the same time, the Athenians fought a war with the Megarians over Eleusis, a community lying between Megara and Athens town (this is the conflict in which Tellos, the Athenian, is supposed to have died), and the conflict already supposes an Athenian state extending over the same territory as later.[76] It is out of this territory that Athenians will come to resist the attempt by Kylōn at proclaiming his sole power, occupying the central shrine of Attica on the Akropolis.

Furthermore, because the *polis* was a process of structuration between communities, the question that needed settling was where this structuration would stop: this explains the importance of settling border affiliation, and the temptation to conquer or destroy neighboring communities if they were small enough and not open to contestation or claims by other *poleis*. But such relations were not necessarily hostile: *poleis* also found a range of ways of structuring their relations, in forms of interaction that could lead to regional entities articulated in more or less formal ways. The state of Lakedaimōn, a constellation of "dweller-around" (perioikic) *poleis* around the *polis* of Sparta, is one example; it structures the relation between *poleis* on the model of the relation between big site and smaller sites within the *polis* territory.

Lakedaimōn is unusual by its considerable size and the complex relations between Sparta and the other *poleis*,[77] but it belongs to a generalized spectrum of possibilities in the articulation of territory and communities. We can see that even a small *polis* like Drēros was constituted by this process of articulations. A fragmentary, late seventh-century BCE law from the wall of the temple of Apollōn ends with the clause "since the Prespidai and the Milatioi have started" and perhaps begins with the formula "it was decided." These are certainly communities over which

Drēros claims authority—but which also have some recognized agency in the community, since a law or decree was passed upon their initiative. The first might be a community within Drerian territory, the second is almost certainly the inhabitants of Milatos, at this point a subordinate community that later achieved its independence and indeed fought wars with the Drerians over borderlands. A small *polis* such as Drēros, just as Sparta (and indeed probably every *polis*), faced the same necessity to structure and negotiate relations with communities around it; and just as Sparta, made the most of this necessity.

Finally, processes of structuration could lead to relations between *poleis* in the form of recognition and contrast. This is the function of the widespread tribal names and structures, such as the three "Dorian" tribes or the four "Ionian" tribes: along with dialect and cult, they offered recognition signs between various *poleis* scattered across the Greek world.[78] Between the widespread shared identity embodied by traits like tribal names or cults, and the closely integrated relations created by power relations between *poleis* and smaller *poleis*, there also existed a level of regional interaction and networking between *poleis* that jointly administered shrines or festivals in "federal" institutions of varying complexity. For instance, a number of *poleis*, and regions, combined to administer the great shrine of Apollōn at Delphi.[79] Later regional entities such as the Thessalians, Boiotians, or Phokians, grew out of inter-*polis* networking in the early "Archaic" period.[80]

Who Was the Seventh-Century BCE *Polis*?

The narrative above is unitary and focuses on political forms. Its central thesis is that the early "Archaic" *polis* of the seventh century BCE develops out of the communities of the late eighth century BCE, and that many of the trends are the same. What, then, is new about the seventh century BCE—new enough to warrant the name of *polis*? The survey of the early "Archaic" communities given above suggests three major shifts. The first is the emergence of political institutions of power sharing and government, and of written rules that depend on and underlie institutionalization. The second is the end of lordly politics, as visible in warfare. Finally, the third shift is the invention of multiple forms of fictitious kinship or association within *poleis* (patterned on preexisting associations) to ensure that the various groups that formed the *poleis* were bonded in imagined communities. Imagined descent bonds also provided means for *poleis* to relate to each other, sometimes by playing on kinship and similarities, sometimes by insisting on differences.

Various historical phenomena sound cautionary notes against assuming the universality and the robustness of the *polis* form. The archipelago of evidence is widely but thinly distributed, and the seventh century BCE is also characterized by diversity and messiness, as suggested by the archaeology of Attica. Alongside the documentary evidence for law (which, in hard epigraphical form, is almost entirely limited to Crete for the seventh century BCE), there are traces (in later

INSTITUTIONS, COMMUNITY, IDEOLOGY 97

FIGURE 4.4. Monument for Glaukos, set up by the sons of Brentēs, Thasos. 650–600 BCE. The inscribed marble block (H 51 cm, w 31 cm, d 18 cm) is built into a later monument under the shelter of a portico on the *agora* of the city.

literary evidence) of political competition and of dominant individuals or families: the Penthilidai at Mytilēnē, the Bacchiads and then the Kypselids at Corinth; see further below, chapter 6.

Another phenomenon suggesting that unevenness and diversity within seventh-century BCE communities can be found is in the ventures that were later remembered as organized expeditions sent out by *poleis*, and which have been studied in modern times under the not completely satisfactory name of "Greek colonization."[81] The poetry of Archilochos, a Parian who settled on Thasos, refers to a life of raiding and running warfare against non-Greek indigenous populations ("Thracian dogs"), seafaring, and the companionship of small groups. One such companion, Glaukos, was honored with a monument by "the sons of Brentēs" (fig. 4.4). The archaeology of Thasos, and especially of its urban fabric, is loosely organized around two "clusters" (themselves continuing older, Thracian settlements) in the old style. The northernmost quarter had its own cemetery (including the monument set up by a group for one Glaukos, known from the poet Archilochos, one of the settlers). It filled up with a loose network of houses and streets in different orientations.[82]

A similarly loose and "polycentric" plan appears at Naxos in Sicily in the seventh century, and it is tempting to see the same informality and messiness in other places. Incomers from the island of Andros settled at several sites: Argilos, Stageira, Akanthos, and Sane next to Mt Athōs.[83] Settlers from Sparta seem to have set out for southern Italy at the end of the eighth century BCE, on the site of Taras (modern Taranto), as suggested by much later, colorful accounts in the literary sources and the archaeological evidence. The relationship between this supposed expedition and the structuration of the Spartiate *polis* and its power across the southern Peloponnese is unclear.[84] The islanders of Thēra sent out a settler expedition to

Northern Africa (modern Libya), where they founded the city of Kyrēnē (ca. 630 BCE), the story being told in two versions, one Theran and one Kyrenaian, both carefully recorded by Herodotos.[85] The Propontis and the Black Sea were the setting for other settlement ventures that left from Milētos, or Megara, throughout the late seventh and early sixth centuries BCE. At the same time, the Ionian city of Phōkaia sent out settlers to found Lampsakos, on the Hellespont—and to Massalia, in what is now southern France (Marseilles).

These settlements are part of broader, older, stories—Mediterranean-wide connectivity, the search for commodities and raw materials in exchange for manufactured goods or Mediterranean produce, and urbanism in the first millennium BCE.[86] For instance, the settlement of Kyrēnē was established in what looks like an area of long-standing and diverse contacts between Greeks and Libyans, as shown by pottery finds.[87] This view would tend to downplay the specificity of the seventh-century BCE settlements, and inscribe in a long story of mobility and exchange (certainly, this is how archaeologists have written this story).

However, even these new communities can be viewed as part of the story of the *polis*. The poetry of Sēmonidēs and especially of Archilochos, adduced above as examples of the community consciousness in the dining groups, were written by participants in new settlement ventures—Sēmonidēs's Amorgos (settled by Samian incomers), and Archilochos's Thasos. The latter was taken over by settlers from Paros. We have seen how Paros, at the time of Archilochos's birth (ca. 700 BCE), was already structured by a long history of community-building, leading to the strong sense of solidarity and common purpose made visible in the two mass graves of Parian war-dead (fig. 3.2). This conclusion is supported by the physical layout of the new settlements. On Thasos, the space where the monument to Glaukos was set up later became the monumentalized *agora*, or public square, of the *polis*. If the public function of this space was already operative in earlier times, the site was chosen by the sons of Brentēs precisely because it was a communal space, within which they wanted to make their commemorative gesture. The messiness of private housing coexisted with a sense of common identity, and even common institutions such as festivals and contests.[88]

The evidence for consolidation supports I. Malkin's view that the new settlements operated as consolidated communities, comparable to the early *poleis* of continental Greece, the islands, and Asia Minor.[89] We see established settlements, founding other settlements in well-chosen sites, that can in turn continue the swarming process. Thasos, the initial foundation reinforced by waves of settlers from Paros, sent out groups on its own that founded cities on the mainland, probably in conditions of violent conflict against the Thracian inhabitants.[90] Corinth is said to have founded Kerkyra, which in turn founded Epidamnos.[91] This pattern of swarming can be seen in Sicily, where the settlements that appear during the late eighth century BCE generated further seventh-century BCE settlements by sending out population groups to seize and occupy sites.[92] If Early Iron Age Megara was made up of two discrete clusters sharing a common open space, its late eighth-century BCE foundation Megara Hyblaia in Sicily had a set of different grids meeting in an *agora* (which was monumentalized in the second half of the seventh century BCE) and multiple cemeteries outside the urban space. Megara Hyblaia's "sub-foundation" of Selinous in the mid-seventh century BCE was distinguished by a regular grid plan that the city would fill out.[93] The commonality involved in such ventures reflected and intensified integration, which is likely the result of continuous demographic growth.

It remains obvious that the history of the *polis* in the seventh century BCE will always be very obscure. Development toward *polis* forms must have been uneven and diverse,[94] as suggested by the material record and indeed the ecological diversity of the landscapes where *polis* consolidation occurs; what does it mean when the same suggestive phenomena of urban consolidation occur in the Thessalian plain or on an island? The consolidation of the urban Naxos ca. 700 BCE (with the end of competing elite burials) precedes similar phenomena at Eretria by decades. The evidence across all genres seems to gather in the latter half of that century, and perhaps in its last decades. This pattern can be widely observed in Crete,[95] the mainland, and the Cyclades.[96] The crucial moment of the emergence of the possibility of the *polis* as a horizon remains obscure in its details (just as C. Wickham describes the rise of the medieval commune in Italy as elites "sleepwalking" into institutional arrangements).[97] This uncertainty is one major problem with the elaboration of a unitary definition of the early *polis* as institutional form.

The other problem with a unitary account is that we do not know who was included within the *polis*'s forms of participating, belonging, and sharing. Who could vote or hold office at Drēros or Athens, who could attend the Assembly at Mytilēnē, who drank with Archilochos, who risked their lives in fighting for the community—the interrogation "what was a *polis*?" also poses a question about "who was the *polis*?" Some practices suggest inclusiveness. The diverse battlefields offered a place for both heavy men-at-arms and the light-armed fighters, both exhorted by Tyrtaios to fight bravely in Sparta's desperate battles.[98] We nonetheless might wonder if the men-at-arms were drawn from the elite, or at least the prosperous property owners in the early *poleis,* and what the political consequences of army service were.

Other processes raise the question of the degree of integration within the community: integrative structuration between big sites and smaller sites involved issues of membership and access. Cult activity continued at the old shrine at Koukounaries, on Paros, after the foundation of the new city (at modern Paroikies): did the shrine serve the inhabitants of the urban center, as a reminder of their control of the island, or rural populations?[99] Similarly, how did the inhabitants of Askra relate to the urban center at Thespiai, a hundred years after Hesiod, when *polis* institutions solidified?

The fragments of a seventh-century BCE law from Gortyn regulate judicial process and impose a fine (?) paid to "the whole *polis*" (*pansa polis*)—but who makes up this entity? The same law mentions someone receiving *wastia dika* in the *agora*, an expression that seems to designate "the trial reserved to the townsmen (*astoi*)." Is the implication that there existed at Gortyn legal rights enjoyed only by the urban elite within the *polis* as opposed to the rest of the inhabitants of the territory? It is likely that the same urban elite enjoyed the consumption of supplies in the Cretan dining halls. They may have controlled access to, and consumption of, oriental luxury objects on normed, egalitarian terms that display and reinforce community, for a group of equal but privileged citizens defined against the rest of the *polis* (see further below, chapter 6).[100] The early *polis* of the seventh century BCE affords arresting glimpses of institutional forms, which only raise the question of social relations. We do not know whether the members of the *polis* are a restricted urban elite, or a broader, more inclusive group. The possibility is that the same political forms and phenomena covered widely differing social realities, which raises the major problem of the function and representativeness of political institutions. These issues would be the subject of much debate and conflict in the following centuries.

5

600–450 BCE

DEVELOPMENT, COMPLEXIFICATION, AND CITIZENSHIP

> A projection of familial and tribal forms, the city subverts the authentic substance of the parochialism that favors kinship ties with a mysterious inwardness and rescues tribal institutions as ecumenical forms of civic administration. The Greek democrat, Kleisthenes, is almost a symbol of these shrewd maneuvers, maneuvers by no means unique to the Athenian *polis*.
>
> —M. BOOKCHIN, *FROM URBANIZATION TO CITIES*

More *Poleis*, More *Polis*

One way of telling the story of the *polis* in the sixth century BCE and beyond is to trace continuities and intensification. In contrast to the often sparse situation in the seventh century BCE, this is a moment when the *polis* becomes much more visible.[1] Notably, the *polis* develops in the same areas as in the previous century, namely urbanization and materiality, state institutions and law, and the construction of community.

The material remains are the most spectacular aspect. Early "Archaic" temples are replaced with larger, mostly stone buildings, according to the wealth and the ambition of the communities where these temples are located. The temple of Apollōn at Corinth replaced the earlier edifice (fig. 5.1) ca. 570 BCE. About the same time, a monumental temple was built on the Athenian Akropolis (fig. 5.2), the so-called "Bluebeard Temple," to use the modern name derived from a monstrous, triple-bodied figure that decorated its western pediment.[2]

On the island of Samos, at the "extra-urban" shrine of Hēra, the early temple was replaced by a much larger edifice, ca. 570–550.[3] Most famously, the temple of Artemis at Ephesos was reconstructed on an enormous scale, in marble with lavish adornment; the venture received support, financial and technical, from the Lydian ruler Kroisos.[4] Such structures now exhibit the developed forms of the classical

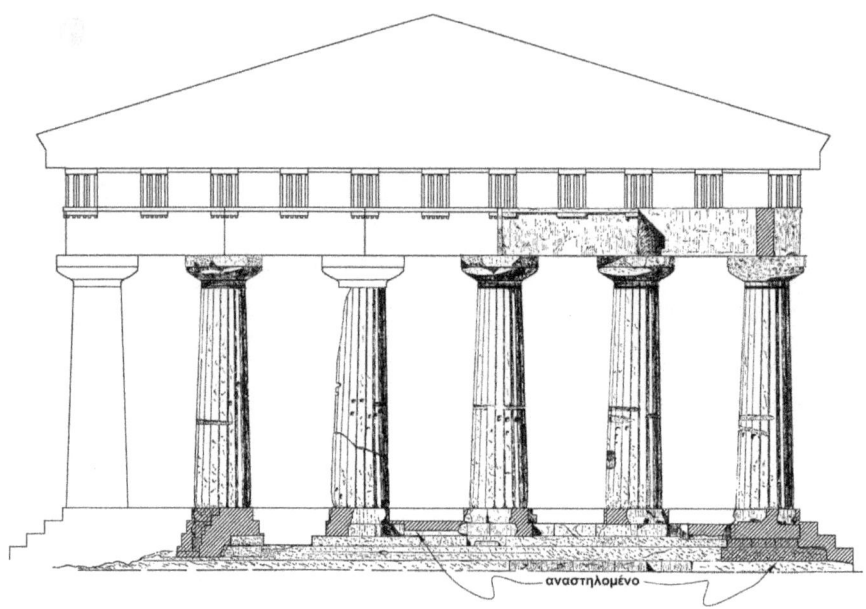

FIGURE 5.1. Temple of Apollōn, Corinth. Ca. 650 BCE.

FIGURE 5.2. West Pediment of the Old Temple of Athēna, Akropolis, Athens, with from left to right, fragments of limestone sculptural groups representing Hēraklēs and a Triton, two lions attacking a bull, and a three-bodied being. Traces of polychromy survive. Ca. 570 BCE. H 144 cm, length 1410 cm (surviving). Akropolis Museum Akr. 3.

Greek temple, with a colonnade surrounding the main building. The development of a widely accepted, "normal" plan for the temple is itself one of many signs of the way in which *poleis* existed in imitative and competitive awareness of each other.[5]

The enlargement and increased monumentalization of temples belongs to a general trend in continuous building activity in the sixth century BCE in public spaces.[6] For instance, the civic zone at Megara Hyblaia grew yet more buildings;[7] likewise, in Metapontion, the urban center was shaped by multiple temples aligned on the urban grid, and a large circular meeting place.[8] In Crete, a number of urban sites underwent remodeling and systematizing. The city of Azoria was reorganized around a unified plan that combined permanent private houses with a public zone of civic buildings. These included a shrine, an *andreion*, and a public hall for ritual and communal activities.[9] In mainland Greece, the *agora* in Peloponnesian cities such as Corinth, Argos, and even Sparta is formalized during the first half of the sixth century BCE, with the installation of specialized spaces for meetings, open-air venues for choral performances, and tracks for footraces.[10] In a less spectacular, but equally significant fashion, the early sixth century BCE saw the Ionian towns finally get rid of the remnants of the old style of clustered settlement in favor of an integrated, coherent urban fabric.[11]

Such settlements were protected by careful fortification works. In mid-sixth century BCE Asia Minor, such precautions were accelerated by the presence of predatory formations: the Lydian kingdom (who acted as patrons of the temple of Artemis at Ephesos), then the Achaimenid empire, but also local strongmen. The Phokaians are said to have fortified their city at this time with profits from trade with Spain (indeed, with help from an Iberian king), and part of the wall has been excavated. The already impressive curtain is reinforced, at its base, with an inclined masonry mass, as protection against battering engines.[12] The Phokaian wall covered a considerable circuit, probably enclosing far more than the built-up area of private housing and public buildings. The same is true of the circuit walls of other *poleis*,[13] for instance that constructed ca. 550 BCE around the town of Samos, showing the same monumentality and ambition as the architecture of the temple of Hēra.[14]

A particularly interesting example of public building is the provision of waterworks to urban centers through the major investment in the work of capturing a source, managing water adduction, delivering water in monumental surroundings, and evacuating the flow. On Samos, spring water was brought to the city by terracotta pipes laid in a kilometer-long tunnel hacked through a mountain by a remarkable feat of applied mathematics.[15] The work was counted by Herodotos as one of the three greatest works by all the Greeks, and he names the architect, one Eupalinos of Megara (3.60); it shows the same bravado as the monumental construction on the temple of Hēra, and the great wall circuit. Similar engineering works and provision of public water are known at Naxos, Aigina, Eretria, Corinth, Megara, Athens (where the waterpipes and fountain houses are familiar from the archaeological evidence);[16] all seem to date to the later sixth century BCE. Public water supply has sometimes been associated with the "tyrants" ruling various cities; this may have been the case at Athens, but not necessarily at Corinth or Megara (where the blocks are inscribed with the abbreviated name of the city or its members, not any single ruler). At Samos, as noted by H. J. Kienast, the tunnel and water adduction seem to have predated the tyranny of Polykratēs. The material outlay and technological knowledge are astounding; even more noteworthy is the deployment of means and *nous* by city-states to achieve the explicit provision of public goods to the whole community.

In addition, it seems accompanied by a generalized intensification of rural occupation and utilization, as suggested by survey archaeology.[17] This new blanket of settlement contrasts with the relatively empty landscape of the Early Iron Age. The *monde plein* of the sixth century BCE (which would continue for at least three centuries) must reflect continued demographic growth since the Early Iron Age, leading to the expansion into marginal, underutilized areas within bounded civic territories. In the case of Sikyōn, the process is attested by archaeology but also by a written document (below, p. 110). Urbanization is likely connected with rural development. Urban centers provided the market infrastructure for exchanges vital to rural utilization at all levels (from the production of elite wealth on cash cropping estates, to the needs of smaller, polyvalent farms), but also the institutions that regulated exchange, the status of those actors involved in exchanges, and their access to political power. These are all cardinal issues of the sixth century BCE.

Law and State in the Sixth Century BCE

The evidence for written law now turns into a dense field of nomothetic activity, an intensification that continues into the early fifth century BCE. This intensification takes two aspects. The first is the multiplication of attested laws from single *poleis*, visible for instance in Ēlis, as exemplified by the bronze fragment mentioned above (p. 69). At Gortyn, the process led to an early fifth-century BCE "Great Code." The second is the appearance of laws, often singly or in small numbers, in far more numerous places than before. The sixth-century BCE laws show the same major characteristics as earlier ones, but in more complex, developed, and self-aware forms. They strive for universalizing force and comprehensiveness, with far-reaching authority within society. The authority of the law rests on rationality and openness, but ultimately on the will of the community as the source of power, as made clear in more systematic inscribing of such measures. Enforcement is also made more explicit.

For instance, at Gortyn, a now fragmentary law formally regulates the behavior of officials—notably by specifying the delay before individuals can hold office again: three years for the *kosmos*, ten years for the *gnōmones*, and five years for the "officials for foreigners." The law extends the principle of rotation of power-holding and the imposition of delays. These are different according to the office, which must reflect a rational, deliberate decision by the community in response to the needs and possibilities of recruitment. This law is part of a whole set of rules and regulations.[18] One of these stipulates that a certain behavior must be published with a fine of fifty cauldrons "each time"; the *kosmos* in office is to levy the fine, and will be personally answerable for this action, to the extent of owing the fine himself if he does not proceed to recover the amount. In such cases, the *titas* will be responsible for levying the fine off the *kosmos*; but if the *titas* fails to do so, he in turn will have to pay it himself, now doubled. This Gortynian law shows a spirit of systematization, as seen in the various delays before iteration of office, and extension, as seen in the solutions for the enforcement of law. Whereas at Drēros in 650 BCE, the community said, through a law, "let him (the man who serves as *kosmos* twice) pay double," the later law from Gortyn is the product of people who have asked themselves how this would happen and thought about stages of possible enforcement with the consequence that the various enforcing magistrates are now themselves accountable.

The tendency of sixth-century BCE legislation toward complexity is noticeable (even if simple laws merely stating an interdiction continue to exist, and indeed will never completely disappear from the inscribed record).[19] When the *polis* of Eleutherna decided that people should not get drunk, it qualified the prohibition with the permission for grown men ("runners") to do so in company at the shrine of Zeus of the Headland. The law further added the proviso that this permission did not apply for priests, who had to follow an ancient ritual (*to archaion*).[20] As in the case of earlier measures, the fact that many laws were produced in response to specific issues does not diminish their rationality. They show the purposive effort of communities to think of solutions to problems that emerged as part of whole systems of institutions and laws at work—systems that the additions reinforce and define.[21]

Rationality appears in two laws from the Argolid (Argos and Mykēnai) that address the problem of how to judge cases during periods when there is no college of *damiorgoi*.[22] What matters is less the possibility of a vacancy than the will to provide for continuity of authority in such cases, by following the people's will ("the said things," as the law from Mykēnai puts it, referring to a body of tradition and accepted practice known and uttered by all). The same rationality and systematic spirit appear in a long series of "curses" inscribed at Teōs on a single document ca. 475 BCE (with a variant version known from another copy). By this means, the *polis* threatens with destruction the perpetrators of a whole series of state crimes (their descendants are also included in the curses). Though ritual in nature (the curses are performed by the magistrates yearly, by reading off the inscribed stone), the long document is also a systematic gathering of all the various types of treasonous crime the community can think of, or think through, and is akin to a law code in its attempt to summarize a whole field of issues and problems.[23]

Laws talk about laws, or law. They refer to other laws as laying down the pattern for procedure and punishment, in cross-references that are also legal fictions. In a Lokrian city, the penalty reserved for any man who proposes to redistribute plots allotted off public land will be carried out "according to the law on murder"; namely, a curse on him and his family, the confiscation of his property, and the demolition of his house. The Lokrian law, however, does allow for the case when such a redistribution might be judged necessary, in time of war: such a decision is delegated to a body of two hundred men chosen "on merit," on a majority vote, who might decide to actually proceed to further land grants.[24] The exact details of the procedure are (as so often) desperately obscure, but the spirit of completeness is obvious (the terrible penalties of the law might have to be lifted in case of emergency—but how should this be done? what is the source the legitimacy of law, and of changes to the law?).

Equally striking is the practical reflection on the validity of the law—how far the law should stay unchanged, how law itself can be changed, or control its own modifications.[25] In Ēlis, one legal text mentions some rights (*zikaia*), that are to conform with "the ancient writing" (*to archaion graphos*—perhaps a collective noun designating the whole body of preexisting written law), and forbids the modification of any previous law—unless the Council and the People decide to do so in a mass meeting. Another Eleian text (probably a gathering of various rulings with authoritative force) lays down that any judicial decision taken by an individual will be void if it is given "in violation of the writing" (*par to graphos*). The law, and the community through the law, takes pains to affirm the authority of written law over the various elite individuals holding office. Yet the law itself also adds that "the public decree (*wratra damosia*) will be effective, in matters of judicial decision." That is, the people's assembly can issue decisions that will override public law, since written law is merely an expression of the people's will.[26] The conundrum of the potential conflict between written law and the Assembly's decree is inseparable from the coexistence of community-issued authoritative law and the freedom of the decision-empowered Assembly. The Classical Athenian democracy puzzled over the same conundrum and ended up solving it in exactly the contrary direction: law prevailed over decrees. The issue continued into later centuries, a sign of its indissociability from the condition of the *polis*, and of the willingness of sixth-century BCE communities to grapple with such political and institutional problems.

What written law does is to give body to common authority—vested in more and more officials, who enjoy powers in virtue of their position. At Argos, in the early sixth century BCE, a carefully carved text recorded the making of sacred objects in the shrine of Athanaia—and the *damiorgoi* in whose year of office this happened. These sacred objects were public property, and hence their use was regulated by a law: that they belonged to everybody did not mean that anybody could use them. In the complex formulation of the law:[27]

> These objects of the goddess, let the private individual (*widhiastas*) not use them outside the shrine of Athanaia Polias (protector of the *polis*), but in public contexts (*damosion*) let people use them for rituals. If someone should violate this rule, let him pay the penalty (?), and let the *damiorgos* force him to do so (*epanankasatō*). Let the *amphipolos* take care of these objects.

The mandate of compulsion is very clear: it presents a confirmation of the stateness of the early *polis*, which seems hinted at in suggestive documents of the seventh century BCE but is pervasive in the sixth century BCE. Another document from Ēlis, this time a convention between Ēlis and a smaller community, envisions what should happen if "the writings" should be destroyed "by a private individual (*wetas*), an official, or a community (*damos*)." The man acting in his own capacity and the official wielding authorized power are clearly conceptualized—as is the collective personhood of the *damos*.

To an even greater degree than its forebear, the sixth-century BCE *polis* is not a "tribal" or "stateless society,"[28] but a state. Its manifestations can sometimes be surprisingly complex: an agreement between a Cretan *polis* and one Spensithios starts as follows: "Gods. It pleased the Dataleis; and we, the *polis*, namely five men from each tribe, have granted to Spensithios ..."[29] As seen in the previous chapters, it is not an "early state" in the sense of the product of elite capture and complexification of structures in response to the requirements of domination. On the contrary, the diversification and multiplication of offices reflect the needs of community. For instance, at Datala, Spensithios will now act as the *poinikastas* and *mnēmōn*—the scribe or archivist (literally the "man who does Phoenician things," as writing was still designated), and "remembrancer" of the community. There is a need for recordkeeping and public writing, fulfilled by a permanent official, to ensure continuity and consistency in the *polis*'s decisions. The particular status of Spensithios in representing the interests of the community is also manifested by his duty to step in in case there are no public priests for any particular cults, and perform the sacrifices at public expense.

Both the scribal function, and the rather *ad hoc* priestly function, are responses to public needs. At Drēros, the appearance of a body of "straighteners" who have the power to issue their own decrees (*ewade ithyntasi*, "it pleased the Straighteners"), perhaps responds to the need to hold other officials to account (the practice is well known from later *poleis*, and indeed is a crucial part of *polis* institutional and political culture).[30] At Sparta, during the sixth century BCE, a new body of annual officials, the ephors, "overseers," enjoyed wide powers within the polity. Herodotos shows the ephors forcing one of the kings to take a second childbearing wife to supplement his childless wife ("Do these things and do not act against them, lest the Spartiates think of something else for you," probably enforced abdication or exile, as attested later in Spartan history); indeed, the ephors personally witness the second wife's giving birth.[31] The creation of the ephors must respond to the need, experienced by the majority of the members, for a body of officials, chosen widely (across the population, five in total) so as to enjoy a community mandate, to counterbalance the power of the families that supplied the two kings. The visual equivalent of the stateness embodied by the *polis*'s officeholders is their representation as sitting men, a body posture that grants them "particular authority" (A. Duplouy).[32]

The processes of responses to community needs, in the same spirit of completeness and systematization as seen in the sixth-century BCE laws, can generate a whole web of institutions that act as an emanation of the *polis*. A single law from Chios, carved in big, legible letters on the four sides of a stone prism (fig. 5.3) ca. 550 BCE,

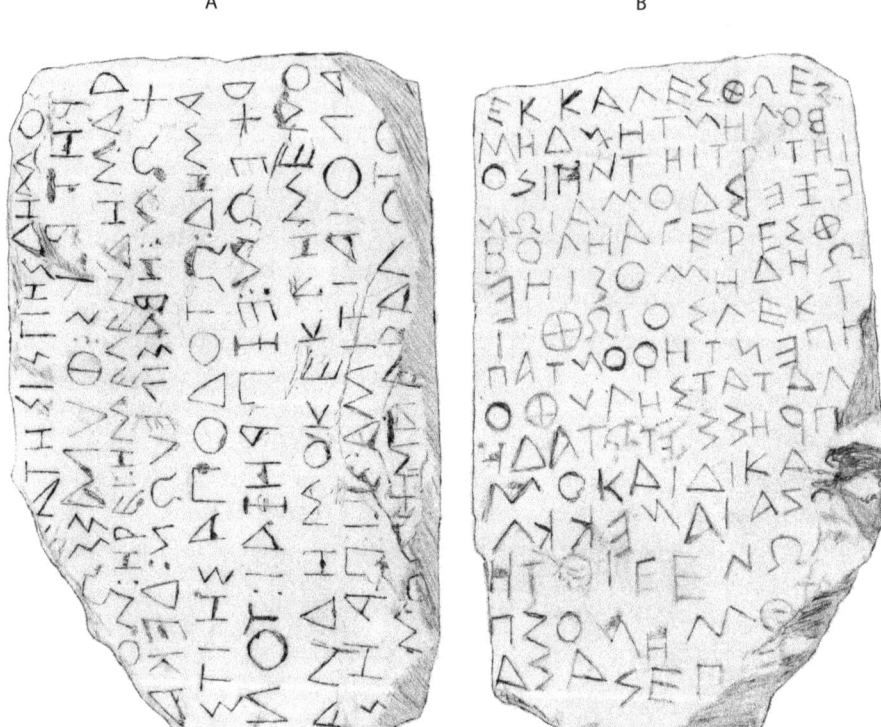

FIGURE 5.3. Two of the three inscribed faces of a law from Chios (on a block of red trachyte, H 74 cm, W 45.5 cm, D 17 cm). Mention is made of "the decisions of the People," office holders (*dēmarchos* and King), and of a Council of the People. Drawing by L. H. Jeffery.

traces the powers and duties of officials. One official guards "the people's utterances" (*dēmou rhētras*). Two types of main officials, the *dēmarchoi* ("rulers of the *dēmos*") and the *basileis*, are subject to fines in case of some failing (bribery?), to be paid to the goddess Hestia (the hearth goddess). The fines are to be exacted by another official before the assembled people (and it seems this official is himself liable to pay double the amount if he does not exact the fine). The judicial decisions by officials are not final but can be appealed against before a body called the *bōlē dēmosiē*, the "Council of the People," made up of fifty councilors per tribe, meeting regularly to "do all the People's business, and especially to judge cases on appeal."[33]

A similar process of judicial appeal, and a similar institution of a people's council, are attested in Athens, as innovations introduced by the legislator Solōn. The latter's own poetry describes tension between various segments of the Athenian population, and thus adds a sense of the conflictual situations that might have motivated the legislative extensions and systematizations in the sixth century BCE *poleis*, as attested in the epigraphical record. In turn, this record shows how the famous "Solonian reforms" are typical of sixth-century BCE legislation in their rationality, systematic nature, and stateness.

Polis as Public Goods and Political Economy

Though the *polis* as state is a close emanation of the needs of the community, this does not diminish its presence as state, with autonomous means (see generally chapter 15). This is particularly clear in the case of public goods—not simply through the provision of waterworks or monumentalized common spaces, but in the form of the creation and provision of public property and finances, *ta dēmosia*. A cache of inscribed bronze leaves from late sixth-century BCE Thebes, though very corroded, gives a sense of state administration and finance. We can guess at the handling of proceeds of taxes or dues in cash (after the deduction of a 10 percent levy for sacred purposes), the record of land tenure, the sale of confiscated property, and the financing of public feasting by officials.[34]

From such fragmentary sources, it is clear that the *polis* derived income from a variety of sources. The fines paid by delinquents could be paid in cattle; if paid in metal, they must have accumulated in sacred or public treasuries. Shrines themselves generated rent from sacred land, to be administered by priests, who themselves were public officials.[35] Most importantly, the *polis* collected taxes, which replaced the informal levies raised by the *basileis* (above, chapter 3). The existence of publicly collected taxes is implied by the grant of *ateleia*, exemption from *telos* (literally "service"): this is one of the privileges granted to Spensithios, the public writer and remembrancer of the Dataleis (along with his salary in kind).

Specific details emerge out of a more detailed grant of privileges given by the *polis* of Kyzikos to one Manēs, some of his relatives, and his descendants (the inscription recording the grant describes as what *polis*, in the absolute, gave him, just as it mentions that *dēmos* swore an oath over a sacrifice, and that *polis* gave him this inscription). Manēs is to enjoy *ateleia* and food at the Prytaneion; but he still must pay the *naussos* (harbor tax?), the fee for using the public scales, a tax of one-fourth, and sales taxes on horses and enslaved persons.[36] In this document, the *polis* occupies a public space, enjoying monopoly on legitimacy and on the provision of paid services, such as a harbor installation or set of public scales whose trustworthiness is recognized, and indeed which serves as a standard for the rest of the community.

The indirect tax on commercial transactions can also be considered as a fee enabling the presence of the state as a legitimate guarantor of the validity and trustworthiness of such transactions, notably by the provision of institutions for redress and enforcement. In Crete, contracts, deposits, and salaries are one of the explicit concerns of written law.[37] These functions are of course not unique to the Greek city-state; what matters here is the sixth-century BCE *polis* visibly occupying a level of stateness that enables it to fulfill such functions. In practice, taxation on the profits of Mediterranean-wide exchanges provided the income for the public building works that are such a visible feature of the early *polis*.

Apart from indirect taxation, the *polis* also collected direct taxes off wealth and income (something that is often unnoticed in modern literature on the *polis*).[38] The salary of the public writer Spensithios was paid by the community; the immediate form this took was that Spensithios could levy a certain number of "jugs" of must from any vineyard he chose, a direct form of extraction which might be patterned on how the community raised taxes. More systematic forms of direct taxation are implied by the description, in Herodotos, of the prosperity of the Thasians ca. 500: the income from their silver and gold mines (directly exploited or farmed out?) was so high that they could avoid levying taxes off agricultural income (*karpoi*).[39]

The unmistakable assumption is that many *poleis*, not blessed with Thasian-scale windfalls, had to resort to some form of direct taxation from the harvest and the vintage, in kind or in cash, to finance state operations. The principle at least can be seen in a document (a bronze tablet) from a large rural site in the territory of Sikyōn. This document gives a list of seventy-three members (ca. 500 BCE) who have a share of the *hestiatorion* (dining hall) with its paraphernalia (including a communal oil-press), "as long as they live there and pay their *telē*."[40] These are presumably to be contributions by all people who share in this installation and the feasting that goes on there, perhaps as part of their membership of the local community and the *polis* more generally.

The principle is that of direct common contributions, just as the common dining groups in Archilochos's time expected members to make direct contributions to the shared meals, a practice that continued in those sixth-century BCE *poleis* that retained and formalized dining groups as constitutive parts of the *poleis* at Sparta or in Crete. Spensithios, in addition to such privileges as the exemption from taxes and a salary directly paid in kind, was also expected to contribute ten "double-axes" of meat to his "men's club" (*andreion*) as his *dikaia*, "rightful share."[41] Citizenship was hence associated with contributions. An early fifth-century BCE law that regulates the sending of settlers from East Lokris to Naupaktos imposes penalties on any settler who leaves Naupaktos without paying his taxes (*lipoteleei*): back in Lokris, he will be excluded from membership until he pays his legal dues to Naupaktos (*ta nomia*, "the legal things").[42]

Some public "income" was directly consumed or used, as with Spensithios's salary in kind (he also received a suit of clothes at public expense). The commodities accumulated by the Cretan *polis* were redistributed in the *andreion*, in public fashion—as part of communal feasts, but also to support or compensate individuals working for the community with maintenance and salaries (*tropa*, *misthos*), in ways regulated by law (at Axos, such people were free of taxation but still had to contribute toward common sacrifices).⁴³ The Krotoniate doctor Dēmokēdēs is said by Herodotos to have been retained publicly at Aigina, against the huge fee of one talent a year, topped by the Athenians who lured the doctor over by offering 10,000 drachmas.⁴⁴

The possibility of public maintenance and pay would be a major part of the institutional repertoire of later *poleis*. Fines levied in cattle were sacrificed and consumed or distributed by the citizens: at least, this is suggested by the etymology of one of the words used for fining or confiscating, "herd-eating" (*pamatophagein*). The word appears in the early fifth-century BCE law from Lokris, mentioned above, in a clause threatening severe punishment to whoever tampers with the law or fails to give satisfaction to plaintiffs: "let him lose his citizen rights and let his property be confiscated (literally "subject to herd-eating").⁴⁵ Other items of direct consumption were the regular meals held by magistrates, and indeed privileged members of the *polis*, such as victorious athletes or special benefactors (as mentioned above, free food and drink at these meals was part of the gifts from the Kyzikenes to Manēs).⁴⁶

Another form of public expenditure was presumably the provision of public goods, such as monumental temples or city walls, even though in this period the modalities of contracting, labor, and payment are quite unclear. Elite families may have taken on duties of supervision of such tasks, presumably because they had the international contacts, social capital, and simply economic power to pay for contracts and work in advance. Yet an inscription recording the completion of the temple, cult image and precinct wall for the deity Aphaia, in the territory of the island *polis* of Aigina (ca. 550 BCE) recorded the priest and the deity, but also listed the buildings and the precious material used (ivory):⁴⁷ public expenditure required public oversight and accountability. The provision of public goods such as monumental buildings, in addition to increasing civic consciousness, necessitated the development of civic institutions such as the officials ensuring accountability, surveyed above.

Yet another item of collective expenditure was warships and naval warfare, if these were to be provided on any sort of scale beyond the level of freebooting and privateering, and especially once naval technology progressed from the fifty-oared ship to the large, complex three-banked trireme. Building this oared longship, optimized for speed and ramming, and even more, maintaining and manning it, required the deployment of economic means on a level that only the *poleis* as states could afford.⁴⁸ The Corinthians did so early on. Likewise, the various *poleis* of Asia Minor mounted substantial fleets to fight against the Achaimenid empire (above, pp. 70–71); and most famously, the Athenian *polis* built and manned a huge fleet of triremes in 480 BCE. This war effort was financed with the proceeds from silver mines in the Laureion, at the southeastern tip of Attica. We know, in this particular case, how the state collaborated with rich Athenians in a sophisticated financial scheme to carry out the actual building.⁴⁹

The *polis* was hence a form of political economy. As such, it also played a role in economic life—a striking example is the regulation of property, labor, productive activity, and exchange attributed to Solōn.[50] Most importantly, the *poleis* adopted coinage in the course of the second half of the sixth century BCE.[51] This crucial economic institution grew out of the intersection of several older practices. First, the Near Eastern practice of using cut and weighed bits of precious metal (usually silver) as tokens for transactions (a Late Geometric golden hoard in Eretria may attest to this practice in mainland Greece). Second, the use of iron, in the form of spits or axes, to store value, to display value in the form of dedications, or to conduct exchanges. Third, the (still poorly understood) practice of issuing standardized units of coinage in the form of blobs of electrum, an alloy of gold and silver, stamped with the marks of the issuer: this started between 650 and 630 BCE in Western Anatolia.[52]

Coinage appears across the landscape of *poleis* in a variety of forms, for instance in the metal used (electrum, or mostly silver), the weight standard, the volume of coinage issued or the size of the actual coins. The diversity reflects the diversity of the *poleis* and their opportunities: coinage may have performed differently in the Northern Aegean, Athens, Aigina (with a massive output of coins and a widespread standard), or the islands (where coinage was widespread). The form, if not the standards, rapidly stabilized into what is recognizably the coin, as an artifact—a round flan of precious metal, stamped on both sides with motifs that identify the issuer and mark the latter's guarantee of value.

In terms of economic impact, coinage may have played an important role in facilitating market exchanges and the economic growth that many see as a characteristic of the sixth century BCE.[53] In the context of the extension of stateness by the *polis*, coinage is a function of the *polis* as guarantor of transactions, or simply of justice, in the social space that it fills. Furthermore, coinage is a function of the *polis* as provider of public goods, since coinage allows fines and taxes to be levied or estimated more effectively, and public income to be stored handily and to be disbursed—for instance, for wall-building or fleet-building. The Phokaians' massive wall is explicitly said by Herodotos to have been financed by access to sources of silver in Spain, and the large issue of silver coinage on Naxos may be linked to its powerful fleet.[54] By guaranteeing transactions and facilitating state payments, coinage gave the *polis* a strong economic, but also ideological presence.

Polis as Constructed Community

In addition to intensified monumentality and increased stateness, the third development in the sixth century BCE is the continued consolidation and construction of community, a development that gave sense to stateness but was also a reflection of it. As in the seventh century BCE, the *poleis* managed groups within the community in order to multiply bonds of imagined kinship and shared locality, and to negotiate a place for preexisting groupings such as families or dining and drinking groups.

The formalized dining groups known from Sparta and Crete give a more detailed picture of the politicized practices in such contexts. Painted drinking vessels from Lakōnia give a powerfully normed image, a Spartiate look, of men in shared activities such as hunting or fighting in a heroic style that has been adopted by the whole community: the visual universe of the *syssitia* reinforced civic ideology.[55] On Crete, the transactions between Spensithios and the *polis* of Datala (discussed above) show the importance of the *andreion* for membership; the continued importance of communal feasting in the Cretan *polis* left impressive remains in the early sixth-century BCE feasting hall in Azoria. There, fourteen crater stands, fragments of armor, and storage jars for victuals attest to regular feasts of warrior citizens.[56]

In other *poleis*, even without the full integration and formalization of the earlier dining groups of citizens, feasting together remained an important activity to create bonds between citizens. The tribes and their subdivisions ("brotherhoods") offered a framework for shared activities such as warfare, festive activities, or even distribution of land, as seems to be the case at Himēra ca. 500 BCE.[57] The importance of tribes in structuring the human community in *polis* forms can be seen in the willingness of some *poleis* to reshape tribal organization. The *polis* of Kyrēnē entrusted this project to an external arbiter, Dēmōnax of Messēnē, in order to integrate immigrants. Every tribe was to have three parts—of Theraians, Dorians, and Islanders—achieving the integration of the population within units that only had meaning within the *polis*.[58] A similar arrangement may lie behind a tale of tribal names brought in at Sikyōn.[59] The Sikyonian reform, at least for the historian Herodotos, was echoed in the most famous, best-documented example, namely the introduction of ten new tribes in Athens by the reformer Kleisthenēs in 507 BCE, constituted by a complex distributive system of subdivisions ("thirds" and "demes," local villages) that covered the whole territory.[60] A similarly ambitious reform may have taken place, slightly later (and perhaps under Athenian inspiration) at Eretria.[61]

Citizens and Others

The result of continued and increasingly complex consolidation was to create a concept of citizenship—clearly defined membership of a *polis* linked to identity and translated into the form of political participation and a share of various public realms, such as religious activities.[62] Membership entails privileges—participatory and legal in nature; these privileges construct citizen status. One consequence is the protection of citizens against violence or oppression by other citizens through the presence of laws, processes for redress, and sanctions for violation. The reforms of Solōn, in the very early sixth century BCE, forbade the enslavement of an Athenian by another Athenian (notably by prohibiting the practice of taking out loans against the security of the person); they also defined the minimum privileges attached to the status of citizen—the possibility of appeal to the courts and of participation in the Assembly.

Another consequence of the construction of citizenship, and the delineation of a status of full members, was exclusion of others from this status. This difference was especially stark between the free and the unfree. Solōn's laws excluded slaves (as well as other categories deemed unworthy) from gymnastics and homoerotic pederastic relations with free boys: such activities were the preserve of the free-born citizenry.[63] The *polis* of Chios, which in a law passed ca. 550 BCE (above) shows such concern with protecting the "utterances of the people," controlling the power of officials, and offering citizens avenues for redress and appeal, was also supposed to have been the inventor of chattel slavery. Certainly, in the fifth century BCE and later, the *polis* depended on enslaved labor, of which it made massive use for wine-growing in its agricultural territory.[64] Other Ionian cities may have equally resorted massively to enslaved labor as implied in a chilling fragment of the poet Hipponax: "If they catch foreigners, they sell them on: Phrygians to Milētos to grind barley . . ." The structure of the Greek makes clear that this is only the beginning of a list of enslaved captives from the populations of Asia Minor, sold to the various cities.[65]

By the sixth century BCE, the shape and the consequences of citizenship are clear to see, in contrast with clearly designated people who do not enjoy this status: not just foreigners, but also immigrants, such as an elite Naxian *metaoikos* ("person who lives with"), who lived and was buried at Athens in the late sixth century BCE. His monument (speaking in its own voice, as is common in Greek funerary epigraphy), describes him as follows:[66]

> I stand as the tearful, sorrowful, and lamenting memorial in stone of the deceased Anaxilas. He was a Naxian, and the Athenians honored him as a *metaoikos*, outstandingly, on account of his moderation and virtue. Hence Timomachos erected me, a majestic funerary gift, because he was repaying gratitude to the son of Ariston, who had died.

Mobility and immigrants had always been (and would continue to be) a crucial part of the ancient Aegean; the consolidation of membership into citizenship would formalize the status of the mobile and the settled as nonparticipants in the community. Hence the pointed contrast between the Naxian identity of Anaxilas, and the Athenian community (named in the plural), a contrast mediated by the term *metaoikos*. Hence, also, the insistence on the valor of the immigrant, recognized by the Athenian community. The praise thus acts as a justification for the long-term presence of an outsider. The gesture is that of a private individual who is claiming communal acceptance for his friend, the Naxian foreigner, and trying to bridge the gap between citizen and immigrant with his majestic monument, set up in the very old and elite Athenian cemetery in the Kerameikos. The contrast between citizens and immigrant would harden into a legal distinction after 507 BCE, with the Kleisthenic reforms and the consolidation of citizenship at Athens after a period of autocratic rule by the Peisistratid family (indeed, the epitaph for Anaxilas the *metaoikos* might reflect this new status). This distinction echoes down the centuries of *polis* history.

The same concepts of citizenship and outsiders can be seen in the case of groups of Eleians residing in Sparta and Euboia, the *epiwoikia* ("group of additional dwellers in a place").[67] The term implies a well-defined group of citizens in Sparta or in the cities of Euboia, and a status of long-term foreign resident, the Eleians having gone to settle but not having gained access to membership. But the institution implies that the Eleians are likewise a well-defined group with privileges and rights. The term *epiwoikia* in fact appears in a citizenship grant by the Eleians: the new citizens became members of a civic "tribe" at Ēlis and also could "share in the *epiwoikia*," which is itself a privilege of Eleian citizenship. In Sparta, one Eleian divination specialist, Teisamenos, requested Spartiate citizenship as an exceptional gift in exchange for special powers (he is supposed to have been told by the prophetess at Delphi that he would win five great victories).[68] Teisamenos might have been a member of the long-term residents at Sparta granted formal recognition as foreigners, and hence precisely desirous "to be given a share of everything," in the striking formulation of Herodotos.

The identity of the citizens is fostered by institutional bonds and shared practice; it is also expressed in symbolic terms, especially through myth, whose civic use is particularly well attested in the sixth century BCE in visual art, in poetry, and in the accounts that are preserved in Herodotos. The large stone temples might act as supports for reliefs or sculptures, on metopes or in pediments. Some of these images might be described as high art or even sacred art, with representation of the divine and of shared myths. Other images told local myths that expressed the specificity and exclusivity of place, and its connection with the human community. For instance, when the temple of Aphaia at Aigina (above, p. 111) was replaced by a spectacular new building, the east pediment showed the rape of the nymph Aigina, the namesake of the island and mother of the Aiginetan hero Aiakos.[69] At Argos, in the *agora*, a sacred enclosure commemorated "the heroes (who died) in Thebes"; that is, the famous seven mythological figures who marched against that city (fig. 5.4). These figures may have been honored with choral song on a nearby dance floor.[70] Poetry from this period—surviving, fragmentary, or merely alluded to in later sources—gives a sense of this performed literary production, across a variety of genres, literary forms, and occasions, devoted to the collective celebration of local myth.[71]

Networking *Poleis*

Myth expressed local identity, as well as claims to a place within a network of communities and identities. The construction of community was also an external one of definition in relation to other *poleis*. Such phenomena of interaction could be strongly competitive, as part of the confrontation between *poleis* as states endowed

FIGURE 5.4. Reconstruction of inscribed limestone boundary marker of the sacred precinct of "the Heroes (fallen) in Thebes," agora of Argos. Ca. 500 BCE. H 63.5 cm, w 31.5 cm, d. 30.5 cm (The stone is represented standing in the fourth-century CE ground level as found during excavation.) Conceived by Anne Pariente, created by Aristophanes Konstantatos.

with a will to power. Argos, city of heroes, claimed be the greatest *polis* in the Peloponnese, as its historical right. These claims were met by resistance from other states, military and symbolical: at Sikyōn, the various changes in cultic practice and tribal structure may have been destined to contradict Argive claims.[72] The Argives defeated the Corinthians in a great battle sometime in the late sixth century BCE— unmentioned by extant narrative sources, the event is known by a large dedication of armor at Olympia.[73] Beyond Sikyōn, Corinth, or other cities of the northeast Peloponnese, the major rival of Argos was the Lakedaimonian regional entity, led by the *polis* of Sparta. This powerful entity achieved crushing successes over Argos from the mid-sixth century BCE onwards, culminating in the Spartiate king Kleomenēs's masterful offensive and bloody victory over the Argive men-at-arms at Sēpeia (494 BCE).[74] The Spartans expressed their own claims to supremacy in mythological terms, by recuperating and reburying the supposed remains of the hero Orestes.[75]

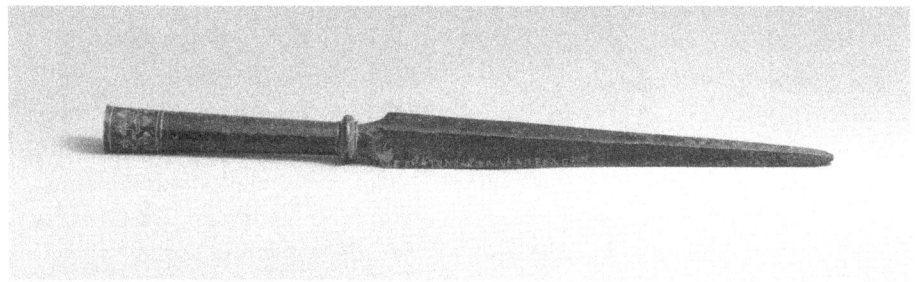

FIGURE 5.5. Bronze buttspike captured in a victory over the city of Hēraia (Arkadia) and dedicated to the Dioskouroi. No provenance. Ca. 500 BCE. L 42.3 cm.

The power competition between Argos and Sparta is the best known and most spectacular of the sixth-century BCE inter-*polis* conflicts, but this sort of competition, in the form of *polis* wars of varying intensity, took place everywhere. The shrine at Olympia in fact preserved an archive of wars between the *poleis* in the sixth century BCE. In addition to dedications from the giant battle waged between Argos and Corinth, dedicated armor recorded battles fought between cities in Boiōtia. Inscribed armor attests a victory of Orchomenos over Korōneia, a victory of Korōneia over an unnamed foe, a similar victory of the Tanagraians, a victory of very large Thebes over very small Hyēttos.[76] The *polis* of Kleōnai, in the northeast Peloponnese, lost a battle in the early sixth century BCE (when the victor dedicated the breastplate of a Kleonaian fighter) but won a battle around 520 BCE (when the Kleonaians dedicated a greave captured from their opponents). The Arkadian *polis* of Kleitōr (no giant) boasted in a dedication at Olympia of the violence it inflicted on its neighbors.[77] From the same context of Arkadian intra-*polis* warfare comes a decorated spear-butt, unfortunately without any ancient provenance because it was acquired on the antiquities market. It is inscribed as "dedicated to Kastōr and Polydeukēs, (as booty) from the people of the *polis* of Hēraia," *ieros Tundaridaius, ap' Eraeōn*, in local dialect (fig. 5.5).

Such local conflicts took a variety of forms. In the western Mediterranean, the *polis* of Zanklē (on the site of modern Messina in Sicily) defeated that of Rhēgion, on the other side of the Strait; Rhēgion later conquered Zanklē—and further defeated the powerful city of Gela. The Ionian *poleis* regularly conducted low-level hostilities against each other, even when under Persian control.[78] Athens and Aigina fought a long-lasting, on-again off-again war, involving local alliances, seaborne expeditions, and vicious engagements.[79] At this time, the Aiginetans, in the early fifth century BCE, rebuilt the temple of Aphaia on a massive scale, with new pedimental sculpture showing martial scenes drawn from the Trojan Wars,[80] reflecting the pervasiveness of war as a mode of interaction between communities, just as it had played a crucial role in the definition and structuration of these communities (above, pp. 89–92).

Sparta's success against Argos was due not just to the integration of Lakedaimōn and the reduction of Messēnia in the seventh century BCE, but in the successful maintenance of an open and extensible network of power in the Peloponnese, creating formal links and ties of political obligation that could be drawn on for military manpower.[81] In 479 BCE (at least in Herodotos's account), the Peloponnesian *poleis* were used to common expeditions abroad (*koinai exodoi*) under Spartan leadership.[82] In contrast, in spite of constant military efforts, Argos never managed to fully integrate the Argive plain, let alone create a sustainable network of political connections in the eastern Peloponnese or the Peloponnese in general, and its decisive defeat by Sparta in the early fifth century BCE accentuated centrifugal tendencies in the Argolid.[83] On a smaller scale than the Sparta-centered network, Ēlis successfully created an entity combining a state at its center with a periphery of lesser settlements of *polis* status, but politically subordinate to varying degrees: the "alliance" (*sunmachia*) of the Eleians, which had an eventful history in the subsequent centuries.[84]

Inegalitarian entities such as the Spartan or Eleian alliances were created by military pressure, but another way in which structured relations of inequality between bigger and smaller *poleis* could arise was the occupation of a neighboring space through the establishment of secondary settlements by a large *polis* (above, pp. 98–99). The island *poleis* of Thasos and Samothrakē, in the north Aegean, controlled mainland territories through fortified establishments that they considered "their" *poleis*— Sanē or Mesēmbria were "cities/forts of the Samothrakians," Strymē was one of the "mainland cities of the Thasians," and when the Persian king Xerxes marched past Thasos, the Thasians received him "in the name of the cities on the mainland."[85] In a similar fashion, Kyrēnē controlled a number of surrounding cities, usually offshoots founded by Kyrēnē (Barkē, Taucheira).[86] In addition to these mini-empires created by secondary settlement, it is also likely that some *poleis* imposed relations of dependency on smaller ones. Such relations are well attested in the fifth century BCE, for instance in Boiōtia, or in Arkadia:[87] the dependent *poleis* of Thespiai are probably referred to as "those with the Thespians" in an early fifth-century BCE arbitration.

Beyond the power relations between big and small, links between *poleis* could lead to the regional groups of local communities finding common identities and founding formal institutions.[88] On the island of Lesbos, the cities "established a great precinct, as a common thing, and put in it the altars of the blessed immortals," in the words of the poet Alkaios (who took refuge there during a period of exile).[89] The joint foundation probably took place in the late seventh century BCE already. At this shrine, located at Messon in the middle of the island (as we know from later inscriptions), the *poleis* of Lesbos held yearly festivals with competitions for women, as recorded by Alkaios in a poem of haunting beauty:

> ... there women of Lesbos with trailing robes go to and fro as they are judged for beauty; and around rings out the marvelous sound of the sacred yearly shout of women.

At a more developed level of institutionalization in the course of the sixth century BCE, Thessaly or Phōkis were regional units, made up of cities but endowed with a strong common identity, expressed through shared shrines and institutions that led to political action—especially expansion and war.[90] The Thessalian entity reduced neighboring communities to inequal ties, of the type Sparta imposed on its neighbors. The Phokians, however, resisted Thessalian power in a series of engagements (the wall at the famous pass of Thermopylai was built by the Phokians to prevent Thessalian incursions, so Herodotos assures us).[91] The successful resistance is contemporary to the production of a regional Phokian coinage, which may reflect federal institutions.[92] In addition to these large regional organizations, the account of Herodotos mentions a large number of smaller regional groupings around Thessaly and Phōkis.[93]

Another example is the region of Boiōtia, which deserves particular attention. As mentioned above, it is true that some *poleis* (Orchomenos, Thespiai, Thebes) directly controlled others as their dependencies. Boiōtia nonetheless was bound by a common identity, reflected in the ethnic name, central shrines, and even common finances and cooperative coinage (late sixth century BCE?) with shared types, issues being distinguished by city initials. E. Mackil observes that the cities that started the joint coinage were Thebes, Tanagra, and Hyēttos, "precisely the cities that along with Orchomenos were engaged in active conflict in the previous quarter century";[94] in fact, the collaboration may represent the outcome of victorious pressure by Thebes.

In 519 BCE, the *polis* of Plataiai, which was culturally part of Boiōtia, chose an alliance with Athens.[95] The aim was to escape being "pressured by the Thebans" (*piezeumenoi hupo Thēbaiōn*); they might also have wanted a free rein to control their own dependent settlements along the southern flank of the Asōpos valley. The alliance triggered a military intervention by the Thebans. But the Plataians also wanted to avoid "contributing to the Boiotians" (*es Boiōtous teleein*), which must mean more than just participate in networks of collaboration, as E. Mackil suggests. In a document dating to ca. 500–450 BCE, a Boiotarch is mentioned; that is, an elected official for the regional entity, thus strengthening the likelihood that this federal institution existed already in 479 BCE when Herodotos mentions it.[96] The institutional solutions developed for the *polis* were hence scalable to broader units, and there must have been formalized, regular institutions that were developing, or being imposed, in the late sixth century BCE: a nascent Boiotian League (even if the details of its institutional structure are totally obscure).

The document in question was found at Thebes, but is written in the variant of Boiotian dialect used at Tanagra, and indeed names a Theban as the beneficiary of a particular legal privilege (the right of priority in recovering debts).[97] Hence it is clear that the *polis* of Tanagra granted an enforceable right to a citizen in another Boiotian city, to which the document was sent and where it must have been registered in some fashion (it was found in the shrine of Hēraklēs at Thebes). The whole transaction seems dated by the Boiotarch and belongs to a formal framework of rules instituted in the Boiotian League. This is more than just economic collaboration: the latter is made possible by the existence of *polis* institutions and their scalability.

Military threats from outside the world of the Greeks mobilized such regional structures. Some *poleis* of the western coast of Asia Minor, bound by a joint identity as Ionians and a shared shrine, mounted a joint effort to rebel against Persian control, with structures of deliberation and decision-making. On a larger scale, many Greek cities of the mainland joined up in a temporary supra-regional structure of military alliance to resist the Persian invasion of 480. This structure combined the principles of unequal relations in the form of overall command by Sparta, with the common decision-making structures and shared purposes that characterized many of the regional "federal" entities. This exceptional, *ad hoc* arrangement shows how essential the principle of structuring local units into bigger related ensembles was to the workings of the world of the late "Archaic" *poleis*. As the sociologist E. Durkheim observed in a careful review of the legal historian H. Francotte's work on state formation in ancient Greece, the processes of local structuration of communities were scalable outwards into "bigger and bigger social formations."[98]

But connectivity between the late "Archaic" *poleis* extended to a richer register of interactions than state violence and organized power structures. The Peloponnese, in spite of the big-power competition between Sparta and Argos, and the successful establishment of a Sparta-centered system, was also structured by ties between *poleis*, especially in the large mass of *poleis* and subregional entities that made up Arkadia in the central Peloponnese, or in the northern coastal region of Achaia. A striking illustration of this connectedness is the network of roads, detectable archaeologically if difficult to date, that linked many Arkadian cities, and is not likely to have been an imposition of the Spartan state because it served local communication.[99]

This network of roads was likely matched by sacred connections, as attested by a difficult early fifth-century BCE festival calendar from Arkadia, which involved the participation of multiple cities.[100] The Delphic Amphktiony, though formally organized as a representative council of *poleis* involved in the administration of the shrine, can be viewed as a particular form of transregional connectivity, involving communities grouped by broad classifications that could be regional (for instance the Boiotians or Lokrians) but also descent-based (namely the Dorians and the Ionians).[101]

The most important and durable aspect of the consolidation of *poleis* and their interaction is the pattern of mutual, self-aware recognition as peers. Peer-polity interaction is intensely visible in the material culture of the *poleis*, as exemplified by the monumental temples and their rapidly codified features and large-scale stone sculpture (the so-called *kouros* type showing a muscular naked youth, and the *korē* type showing a richly dressed woman: see chapter 6, figs. 6.1, 6.2, and 6.3). The spread of *polis* institutions themselves, such as written law and governmentality, is part of the same phenomenon.[102] Interaction and mutual recognition took place in venues such as large "international" shrines and festivals; competition in formalized athletic and equestrian contests by members of the *polis* elites was understood to grant glory and fame not just to the individual victors, but also to their communities, which they represented.[103]

The publicness of the victories won by elite competitors was explicitly celebrated, and negotiated, in the poetry produced by specialized artists such as Pindar or Bakchylidēs, who combined local myth with an awareness of the network of *poleis*.[104] Such poetical celebrations hence imbricated the international network, local identity, and internal political relations in ways that raise the question of the power balance within the *polis* in the sixth and early fifth centuries BCE.

Sixth-Century BCE Communities: Toward Democracy?

The sixth-century BCE communities already exhibit the *polis*'s development—as city, as state, as commonwealth, as part of multiple external processes of relating, competing, and structuring. A sense of the specificity of the "Archaic" city-state can be gained from many examples: a particularly instructive one is the case of the island *polis* of Siphnos. The origins of the *polis* on this small island are unknown: though a settlement is known in the Late Bronze Age (at modern Agios Andreas) and a LHIIIC successor, the transition to the Early Iron Age town at the magnificent site of Kastro (modern toponym, fig. 5.6) is obscure, with no evidence for consolidation or the rise of political institutions.[105] What we do have is a vivid image of the island in the late "Archaic" period, ca. 530 BCE, from a number of sources. In Herodotos's account,[106]

> The affairs of the Siphnians at that time were at the greatest height of prosperity, and they were the richest of the islanders, since they had gold and silver mines on the island, to such a point that out of the tithe of the income from the island's resources, they dedicated a treasury in Delphi, equal to the richest, and, by themselves, distributed the revenue for each year. When they were having the treasury built, they asked the oracle if their present prosperity would be able to hold for a long time. The Pythia gave them the following oracle: "When the common hall (*prytaneion*) in Siphnos should become white, and the *agora* white-browed, then it will be time for the wise man to beware of the wooden host and the red herald." At the time, the Siphnians had an *agora* and a *prytaneion* built with Parian marble.

The moment is typically Herodotean, the sympathetic yet clear-eyed portrayal of great prosperity before a history-changing setback (the razzia by Samian exiles ca. 525 BCE). This moment exemplifies the monumentalization, in shining stone, of the common spaces in the *polis*, enabled by a particular windfall, and as an expression of community. The provision of public goods through *polis* finance is concomitant with the distribution of publicly owned resources to every citizen.

FIGURE 5.6. View of Kastro, the site of the ancient urban center of Siphnos.

The practice (analogous to the distribution of shares of meat from public sacrifices) can be read as a reflection of the nature of the *polis*, as the expression of a community of citizens who each directly have a share of common goods, in an immediate relation that characterizes the thinness yet pervasiveness of the state. The Athenians may have done the same with the income from their silver mines, and indeed considered doing so with the windfall of 483 BCE, before deciding to use it on a fleet of triremes.[107] Furthermore, the Siphnian *polis* also minted a small-volume coinage from the silver of the mines, perhaps used for distributions to the citizenry rather than trade purposes.[108] In addition, towers start to appear in the late sixth century BCE in the territory of the island, perhaps linked to the need to control enslaved labor, especially in marginal land[109]—a typical feature, as we have seen, of the agrarian systems that emerged at the same time as the definition of citizenship as membership in a privileged group.

The treasure house built by the Siphnians at Delphi expresses the *polis*'s self-image as a consolidated, unified community (fig. 5.7). The small, highly ornate building bore a frieze on all four sides with mythological scenes, in a combination of narrative scenes and static processional compositions,[110] dignified and fitting for the sacred context. One of the scenes (the north portion of the frieze) represents the battle between the Olympian gods and the Giants, characterized by their heavy arms and armor; the battle symbolizes the victory of order and justice over disorder and violence (fig. 5.8). Strikingly, the first god to be shown is Hephaistos, the artisan god, with his furnace and bellows, an unusual representation. Suitably

FIGURES 5.7–8. The Treasury of the Siphnians, Delphi. After Daux and Hansen 1987, fig. 133, 135.

for a thank-offering, this image alludes to the mining and smelting activity from which Siphnos's wealth flowed. The diversity of the gods, including the artisan Hephaistos, perhaps also alluded to the success of the *polis* in integrating diverse social groups in a victory over the threat of injustice as represented by the violent, warlike giants in armor. Beyond the iconographical message of the frieze, the texture of the building displayed Siphnos's position in the world: the architectural ornament was made out of fine Naxian marble, the sculpture out of superfine Parian marble, but the base of the treasury was made out of plain Siphnian marble, a display of Siphnian identity in the shrine of Delphi where Greek states showed off their specificity and their belonging to the network of peers.[111]

In comparison with the early "Archaic" *poleis* of the seventh century BCE, the sixth-century BCE *poleis* show two important areas of expansion. The simplest is expansion in numbers of settlements and hence of people: in the present state of the evidence, survey archaeology shows the widespread multiplication of nucleated sites, and generally of traces of occupation (including farmsteads) in the countryside surrounding the original nucleated sites, big and small, which made up the communities from which the *poleis* developed.[112] One *polis* where the pattern of implantation in the countryside is well investigated is Sikyōn.[113] The regulation from a Sikyonian rural site discussed above (p. 110) gives direct written evidence. Since traces of occupation at the site, modern Thekriza, only start in the early fifth century BCE, it is likely that the regulation lists the initial settlers (seventy-three in number), and mentions the institutions that shape their membership. At Sikyōn, the process of internal colonization of the rural territory came with political organization, mirroring the institutions of the *polis*. The causes and significance of this expansion are difficult to determine exactly. A possible interpretation might be that *polis* institutions and ideology shaped increasing wealth and population growth by directing the exploitation of resources, especially land, according to political norms of membership and status.

The second expansion in the sixth-century BCE *polis* is the strengthening of norms in the direction of egalitarianism, visible societally and expressed politically and constitutionally in forms that could be called proto-democratic.[114] The sixth century BCE is the moment when funerary practice finally stabilizes around generally accepted forms: restraint, no grave goods, and widespread access to formalized burial (as visible notably in the inclusion of children's tombs). Restraint and the rarification of aristocratic burial in mounds can be seen in Crete or in Thessaly.[115] When the small Boiotian *polis* of Akraiphia first becomes significantly visible in the sixth century BCE, it is through its cemeteries that show a broad base of homogeneous tombs (albeit with great variation in the actual content of the grave goods).[116] This outcome suggests the generalized acceptance of access to *polis* membership among a broad segment of the population.

Egalitarianism can also be read in the archaeology of the landscape. A striking package of egalitarian traits characterizes Metapontion in southern Italy. Universal formal burial and social homogeneity characterizes one of the cemeteries of the *polis*, a rural nekropolis (at modern Panatello) in use from the early sixth to the early third centuries BCE. The rural territory was intensively occupied in the sixth century BCE, especially in the last decades that saw new and sudden expansion into hitherto unexploited plains. The occupation took the form of small and medium-sized plots exploited by farmsteads, giving the impression of "a well-to-do, but remarkably egalitarian society."[117] The same pattern seems to be readable in the *chora* of Chersonēsos, in the Crimea: a socially egalitarian occupation of land resources, starting in the sixth century BCE.

The urban site of Metapontion, as mentioned above, counted among its public buildings a very large amphitheater-like structure (60 meters across). This structure may have served as a political meeting place, which would suggest a large and active body of citizens, and the importance of the popular assembly in the polity.[118] There is more explicit evidence for democratic institutions during the late "Archaic" period, in the sense of constitutional arrangements centered around sovereign decision-making by the *dēmos*, the people in the sense of the whole community, but also of the majority of nonelite citizens in the community; this principle could be expressed and worked out in different forms and with different levels of intensity.

Thus on Chios, we have seen the fragmentary "constitutional law" that mentions the people's utterances (*dēmou rhētrai*), accountability before the people in case of fining by officials, and the people's council. The institution of the ephors, in Sparta, is part of this trend; if the so-called Great Rhētra is a sixth-century BCE "retro-charter," as suggested above (p. 84), its final statement of *kratos*, power, residing in the *damos*, people, is an explicit statement about the awareness of the centrality of popular sovereignty. In sixth-century BCE Ēlis, laws could be changed only "with the council of the Five Hundred and the People in full number," *damos plēthuon*.[119] If the *platiwoinarchoi* laws of Tiryns (above, p. 81) should date to the sixth century BCE, as is possible on the basis of the script (say 570 BCE or perhaps later), we might see more traces of "democratic" practice in the clauses that seem to indicate popular sovereignty and accountability (an official handles public goods "according to the decision of the people"), and in the control exercised over the officials through penalties for failure to comply with law.[120]

There are indications in literary sources of "democratic" constitutional reforms in a sizable number of cities across the Greek world, to be placed mostly in the sixth century BCE.[121] The most important, and best attested, is the case of Athens in (and after) 507 BCE, where intra-elite competition led to the proposal and implementation in the face of factional opposition and even Spartan intervention, of reforms including the introduction of new tribes, the empowerment of local communities (the demes) as a constituent building block of the *polis* and the site for admission to citizenship status, the enshrining of assembly sovereignty in the constitution, as seen notably in the power of the Assembly to impose a ten-year exile (without property loss) on any citizen by a secret ballot (the votes were written on *ostraka*, sherds, hence the name of the practice, *ostrakismos*).[122]

The question is (again, unavoidably) who or what "the people" is. The Spartan "retro-charter" in assigning the *kratos* of the *damos* to its ancestral constitution, reflects an awareness that common decision-making is coherent with the political turn, when institutions and ideology moved away from the lordly assumption that the better sort should rule. Communal affairs are decided by the community: the tautology lies at the heart of what the *polis* is and is expressed by such documents as the constitutional law from Chios. But the *dēmos*, the commons, are never simply the whole community; they also mean that part of the community which has a simple majority, and hence by definition cannot be the elite. Thus, the development of communal politics also had an anti-elitist, populist tone.

This tone is illustrated by a vituperative poem by Hippōnax, calling for the death of one Eurymedontiadēs, whose sonorous name is elitist in tone ("Son-of-he-who-has-broad-cares": descent, the physically imposing dimension of "breadth," and care for the community, all make heroic claims). The poem starts with a parody of epic, then veers into political invective. "Muse, tell me of Eurymedontiadēs," who is to be put to death "in a vote, by the popular will," *dēmosiēi boulēi*: the words are the same as the terminology to designate the "popular council" in the contemporary Chian law, but here unmistakably describe the volition of the masses. The literal meaning of the word for vote, "pebble," and the scene of the execution, the seashore, refer to death by stoning, one of the traditional means to express popular anger. The reason for this savage wish is that Eurymedontiadēs, a monster of gluttony ("Charybdis of the sea") does not eat in an orderly way, *kata kosmon*: the crime of excessive consumption is a way of designating an elite lifestyle, perceived as greed and exploitation (as in the "gift-eating *basileis*" criticized by Hesiod).[123]

Similarly, various political rituals or ceremonies, obscurely attested in Megara (the "return of interest," open feasting in the houses of the rich), may be populist in intention in a carnivalesque vein.[124] Egalitarian or populist ideology could be expressed in less benign forms, for instance in real political violence between rich and poor, which is attested at the very end of the "Archaic" age, with violence against "the fat."[125] The term is recorded by Herodotos in his account of a popular uprising at Aigina; the elite is said to have overcome its opponents, and executed 700 of them.[126]

The populist vein is developed in post-Kleisthenic Athens, where the insistence on popular sovereignty developed into a strong populist politics (that contributed to the style of politics prevalent in democratic Athens). The new democratic politics are visible in the pursuit of elite rivalries through competition before popular arenas such as the Assembly and the courts, the inclusive tone of the chariot monument set up in 506 BCE to commemorate the victory of the "sons of the Athenians" over the arrogant violence of the Boiotians and the Chalkidians, or in the antielite rhetoric of graffiti on the *ostraka* used in votes to exile Athenian politicians:[127]

This sherd says that out of all the accursed leaders, Xanthippos son of Arrhiphrōn does the most harm.

Our story hence is no longer just that of the rise of stateness, but also that of the path taken by the state within the political economy of the community. Once the various elements of stateness that appear in the seventh century BCE are consolidated in the sixth century, the questions of justice and equality become much sharper. A seventh century for the *polis*-hood, a sixth century for democracy? Aristotle did speak of democracies for the constitutions that followed an initial stage of monarchy (while hedging his judgment by specifying that these ancient "democracies" were in fact moderate, censitary regimes).[128] Of course, the story is too pat, if only because historical realities do not fall neatly into centuries. Local variation is not necessarily the problem. The phenomena in places that are often described as anomalous, such as Sparta, Crete, or Thessaly, can be shown to be less exceptional than thought or to be part of broader phenomena (subjection, regionalism, law, decision-making) whose historical coherence can be unpacked.

The real issue is the way the story above has unfolded as the working out of the coherence of state institutions[129]—once the *polis* turn is taken, and communities have seen the resorption of the lords and the emergence of political institutions (alternance of power holding, authority, and decision located in community choice), political spaces (shared and meaningful spaces, soon monumentalized), and finally political ideologies of belonging together through bonds and activities of sharing. Even if this sketch of fast-moving structural transformation were true, the questions of process and causality would need to be inked in. More importantly, the role of political conflict and the place of elites are questions that are directly raised by the mere description of the *polis* as the expansion of the state into egalitarian and proto-democratic forms. To take for granted the resorption of the lordly is perhaps to speak about hamlets without their princes: again, the question is—what happened to the *basileis*? To examine the themes of conflict, competition, and elites may help with issues of causality, and sharpen our understanding of the early *polis*.

6

The Travails of Integration

> Grind, mill, grind; for Pittakos did grind while ruling as king over great Mytilēnē
> —FOLK-SONG, LESBOS

The Signs of Eliteness 650–500 BCE

The archaeology of "Archaic" Greece abounds in the monumental and the spectacular, embodying the display of private wealth and status. Monumental marble sculpture was set up in shrines by individual donors; it coexists with and eventually takes over from older forms of display such as the metal tripods favored during the Early Iron Age. At Samos and at Sounion in southern Attica, early marble statues of naked youths (*kouroi*) reach huge sizes, over 5 meters. Other, especially later examples (fig. 6.1), though smaller, retain impressive dimensions, and are heavily invested in status markers such as refined hairdos in ringlets (and razor-styled pubic hair). Statues could be combined in groups, like the family portrait showing a rich Samian, reclining, with his wife (sitting) and three daughters (represented as *korai*) and young son. The whole group bears the signature of the artist, Geneleōs (fig. 6.2)[1]. A female standing statue (*korē*), slightly over-lifesize (fig. 6.3) but shown with the refined hairstyle and ornate clothing befitting her wealth and status, was set up probably ca. 630 BCE at Dēlos by a Naxian family, proud of the exceptional qualities of Nikandrē. The lady is named in relation to male relatives in the verse inscription, where the statue itself speaks (without quite making clear what it represents—the dedicator or the goddess?):[2]

> Nikandrē set me up to the far-shooting archer goddess (Artemis). Daughter of Deinodikos the Naxian, she was outstanding among all other women, and the sister of Deinomenēs.

The Akropolis of Athens preserves an astonishing array of sixth-century BCE marble statuary (discarded and buried after the sack of the city by the Persians, in 480 and 479). The remains of what must have been a veritable forest of statues give a vivid impression of luxury and refinement embodied in body poise and materialized

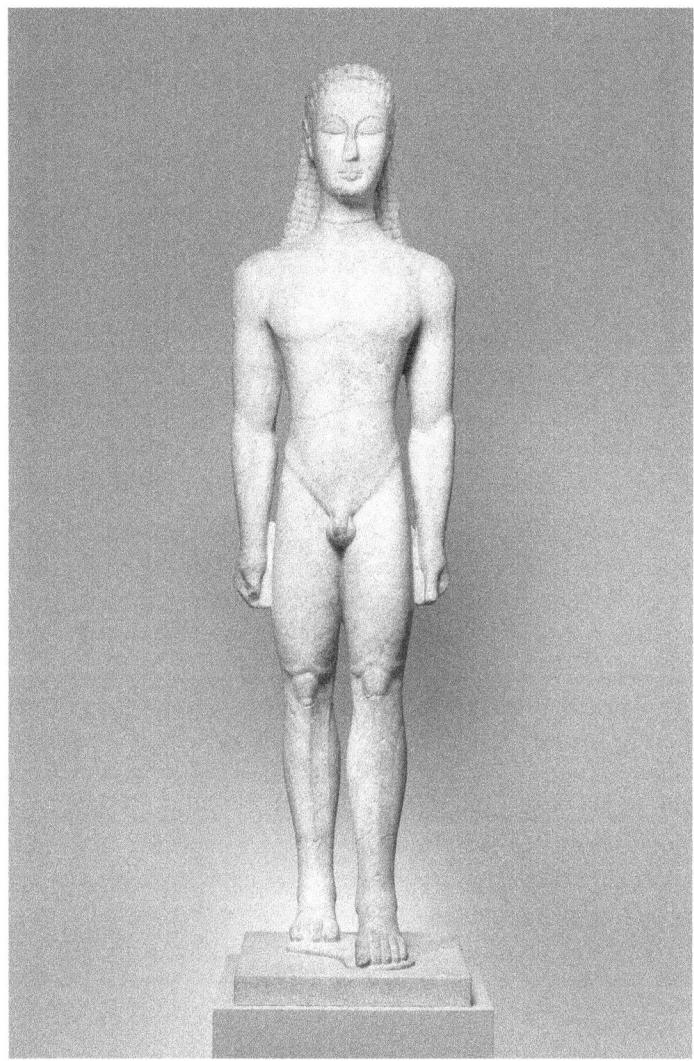

FIGURE 6.1. Large-scale marble *kouros*, Sounion, Attica. Ca. 600 BCE. H 305 cm. National Archaeological Museum, Athens, F 2720.

by the profusion of vestimentary decoration. The marble was brightly colored to imitate high-status clothing—as indeed it was on the *korē* of Nikandrē.[3]

The inscription on Nikandrē's statue shows the function of monumental dedications: to claim eminence. Competition explains the great diversity of cultural forms in the seventh and sixth centuries BCE. It has been singled out by O. Murray as the characteristic of the "Archaic" age, a view developed, with immensely refined readings of material culture by A. Duplouy, from the "Dark Ages" to the early fifth

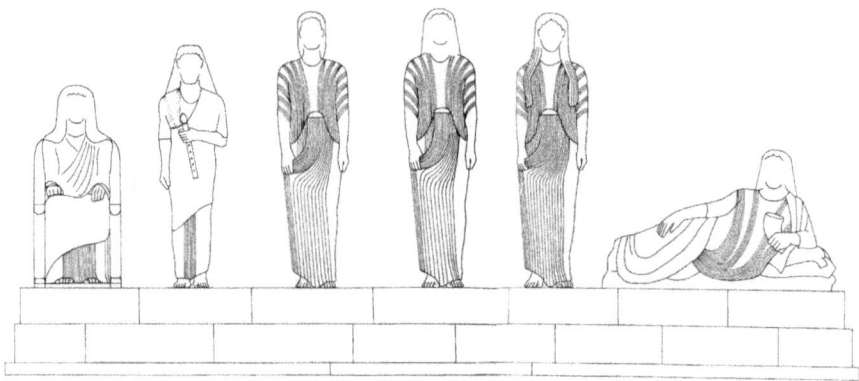

FIGURE 6.2. Reconstruction of family statuary group by E. Walter Karydi, Heraion, Samos. Ca. 550 BCE.

century BCE.[4] Competition and diversity are particularly visible in funerary practice. In Attica, some families practiced spectacular funerals involving feasting and vase offerings. The latter were displayed in front of massive trenches, then destroyed and buried in them, as part of cremation rituals (fig. 6.4).[5] Display in elite funerary practices is widely attested—at nearby Megara, for instance, but also across the Aegean, for instance at Klazomenai (in the form of spectacular painted sarcophagi and Lydian-inspired mounds, ca. 630 BCE). In the same timeframe, mounds and large funerary vases bearing reliefs illustrated elite Spartans' claims to eminence.[6] Generally, the very popular genre of inscribed funerary epigram rarely speaks of the *polis* but makes heroizing claims about individual eminence and worth.[7] Even at Metapontion, generally distinguished by its egalitarian culture, some tombs are distinguished by exceptional size, fabric, and quality of grave goods.[8]

Other ways, time-honored or innovative, of pursuing superiority obtained. Elites strove to claim good birth (even descent from a god or from foreign heroes, in contrast with nonelite locals);[9] to gain athletic victories in contests; to dedicate foreign objects (oriental or "orientalizing"); to engage in visible forms of religious practice (seventh-century BCE Attica undergoes an explosion in archaeologically visible ritual activity);[10] and finally to partake in an ostentatiously luxurious and exclusive dining style.[11] The exclusive, closed world of the banquet was the setting for the songs of Theognis, looking out critically onto the *polis*, claiming good birth as the true source of excellence, and lamenting the loss of trustworthiness among companions in a new world where wealth was the measure of a man's worth.[12]

The exclusiveness of the *sumposion* and its function as a manifestation of power are particularly well illustrated in the material record. For instance, two huge mid-sixth century BCE burial mounds from the Kerameikos cemetery in Athens contained the common burials of (mostly) men, in graves characterized by luxurious grave goods drawn from the world of the banquet (perfume vases, ivory couches)—perhaps the collective burial of a group of men (not necessarily kinsmen) bound by the *sumposion*.[13] An extraordinarily suggestive assemblage is provided by the impressive structures excavated at the end of the foot of Mersinlitepe, in the central highlands of the territory of Milētos, on a route connecting the city with the great shrine of Didyma. This ensemble, including a hall and a treasury or storeroom (?) within a large precinct (90 by 40 meters), was adorned with a semicircular base, 15 meters across, supporting a dozen sitting statues; the precinct wall was further decorated with half a dozen sphinxes. The excavated material abounds in storage and consumption equipment, establishing that the structure served for banqueting.[14] It may be better, both in the case of the Kerameikos mounds, the listeners of Theognis, and the Milesian hill-top precinct, to speak of groups making multiple claims to status, rather than simply "dining groups."

The various forms of competition were (by definition) about achieving recognition, acknowledging superiority, and hence social prestige (A. Duplouy). This was an activity reserved to individuals and groups constituting a social elite—if only because luxury feasting, dedicating exotic objects, training full-time for athletics competition, and so on, required time, resources, and wealth. Kleisthenēs of Sikyōn, whom we have already seen as sole ruler over his city (above, p. 113, n.59), is said to have held a competition to find the best husband for his daughter. The suitors were tested in the feast and in athletics, on specially built facilities, and belonged to the noblest, wealthiest, and most powerful families in their own cities, across a wide swathe of the Greek world.[15] The story (told in loving detail in an excursus by Herodotos) goes that the suitors were feasted and evaluated for a year; Kleisthenēs favored an Athenian, Hippokleidēs—before the latter, in a drunken revel, complete with upside-down table dancing, "danced away his marriage," as Kleisthenēs blurted out during the revel. The splendidly insouciant reply, "No matter for Hippokleidēs," passed into proverb.

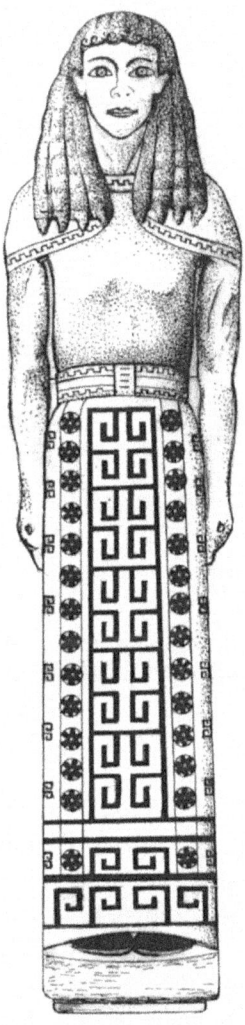

FIGURE 6.3. Marble *korē* of Nikandrē, 650-625 BCE. Dēlos. H 175 cm. Reconstruction of polychromy by G. Kokkorou-Alevras; drawing A. Drigopoulou.

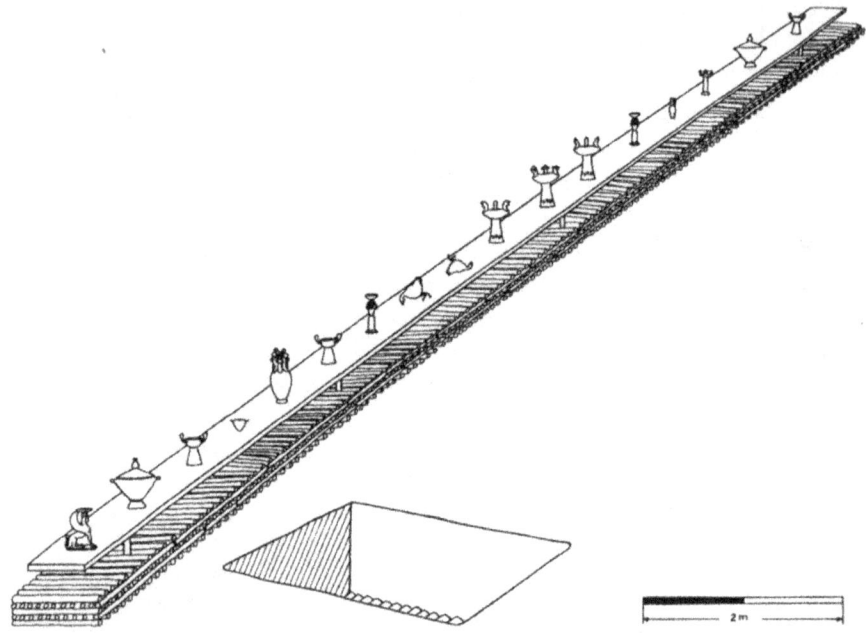

FIGURE 6.4. Reconstruction, offerings trench, and cremation pit, as component parts of an elite funeral in seventh-century BCE Athens. From Houby-Nielsen 1996, fig. 5.

Competition and Acquisitiveness

It is tempting to see Hippokleidēs's repartee, and indeed his joyful inebriate exuberance, as signs of the innate social confidence of the aristocrat. But this would be to fall into the trap of essentialism: the whole diverse context of competing claims to status is itself revealing of the absence of any ancient, entrenched aristocracy of birth. Just as the high competitiveness of the already idealized world of the Homeric hero is based on the absence of an immobile nobility, "Archaic" competition is predicated on the need for individuals and groups to achieve distinction performatively, by doing or saying things that create eliteness rather than reflect preexisting, universally recognized essences, even if essentializing is part of the strategies of eliteness. There was no aristocracy of birth that had held over from the Early Iron Age, because even that period did not know any entrenched class, and generally because historically, elite groups are constantly renewing themselves, demographically and socially; there was no ancient stranglehold of aristocratic power to be broken.[16] Instead, there were elite families and houses (well documented in early Athens) under constant pressure to compete, and positioning themselves in relation to each other and to the community. Hence the terms "aristocracy" or "nobility" are highly problematic if applied to the elites of the "Archaic" communities (and indeed much of ancient Mediterranean history).[17] Theognis's

FIGURE 6.5. Terracotta plaque from Sounion, showing fighters with round shield and two spears, on longship. Ca. 650 BCE ? National Archaeological Museum, Athens, 14935.

complaint that birth is forced to yield before wealth is not the lament of an old aristocracy faced with a breakdown of hierarchies, but an attempt at positioning one group in face of other claims, an act of competitive posturing as a strategy to draw boundaries of belonging and trust around a group.[18]

The competition of elite groups drove social and political processes. Competition required wealth (even if the latter functioned as a sign of innate quality): hence the continuation of the old practice of predation and freebooting. The prosperity of the Siphnians, in Herodotos's story (above, pp. 121–24), came to an end when the island was ravaged and the public treasury emptied for ransom by a band of Samians (who bought an island with the proceeds, before sailing off to Zakynthos and finally Crete). These freebooters came from a community that had long had a habit of piracy and plunder.[19] Privateering is envisaged by the Athenian law on associations (attributed to Solōn) as one of the possible purposes of formal association (above, p. 87). A plaque from the shrine of Athēna on Sounion showing heavy-armed fighters lining up on a ship, might represent such a group (fig. 6.5).[20] Whole communities could engage in low-level plundering, as in the case of the Ionian *poleis*, or Athenian-settled Sigeion and Mytilēnē.[21] Freebooting provided elites with wealth in the form of portable goods and especially enslaved humans, and perhaps also with direct access to mineral and timber resources in the North Aegean, in collaboration with non-Greek adventurers and craftsmen (drawn from western Asia Minor).²² This pattern prolongs the behavior of Early Iron Age elites: freebooting may have driven the earlier parts of the settlement expeditions.²³ Elite acquisitive behavior may also have driven local imperialism, in search of tribute and rent specifically to support the leisurely lifestyle and display habits of elites. The most spectacular case is that of the Spartiate conquest of nearby Messēnia; other cases might be the Thessalian drive to conquer and peripherize their neighbors or even the very obscure control of Aigina by Epidauros.²⁴

Elite acquisitiveness could drive violence inside the community, as in the case of the domination and exploitation of a segment of the population. Sparta again illustrates the phenomenon, since (as mentioned above, p. 112) it early on seems to have reduced producers among the population of Lakōnia into a subordinate status of serfdom, as rent-paying helots (though attached to privately owned estates), before extending the status to Messēnia. Helotage-akin social arrangements involving serfdom may have been widespread, and attestations are too frequent to be associated with any particular region, or simply brushed aside.²⁵ A different, more varied, but structurally analogous situation seems to have prevailed for a period in Attica, where subordinate sharecropping status (or corvée labour dues?), as well as debt bondage are attested for the late seventh century BCE. How these statuses emerged is still very unclear (presumably in connection to structural scarcity and patronage rather than continuity from the distant Early Iron Age), but their origin in elite acquisitiveness is unmistakably condemned by Solon's poetry.²⁶ The same concern with elite acquisitiveness as a source of violence and unrest in the community appears elsewhere, for instance in Theognis's sympotic poetry: without escalating to the level of wholesale subordination of producers, social violence and unjust seizures are directly attributed to the greed of "bad men" in the community.

Freebooting and communal violence were not simply about economic profit. During Athens's war against Aigina, the latter was aided by 1,000 Argive volunteers led by one Eurybatēs ("Wide-walker," a sonorous, heroizing name), an Olympic victor who also practiced single combat. Such freebooters sought adventure and military glory that could be translated back into status back home. Eurybatēs combined several claims to distinction—freebooting, athletics, heroic-style fighting (he was duly killed in the last of multiple duels fought against Athenian opponents).²⁷ Conquering and ruling over other communities, apart from yielding income (whose presence is moot in many cases outside of the Spartiates' direct control of Messēnia), may have expressed the political superiority of *polis* elites, in the form of military success and violence (rather than simply the state affirmation that I traced earlier). The importance of a capacity for violence in elite self-definition can be seen in the very impressive but rather grim funerary relief (made ca. 560 BCE) found near one of the massive collective burial mounds in the Kerameikos (fig. 6.6). The bearded, long-haired mature figure holds a staff in one hand, and the jutting scabbard and grip of a sword punctuates his strongly muscled silhouette, which distantly echoes such representations two centuries earlier (above, p. 44, on the "Geometric" Age).²⁸

FIGURE 6.6. Funerary stele, Kerameikos, Athens. Ca. 570 BCE. From Kübler 1973, after Kerameikos Museum P 1132. The height of the preserved section of the sculpted panel is 181 cm; the original stele probably measured 191 cm, and the full monument, including stepped base and crowning elements, must have reached 4 m. After Kübler 1973, 185 fig. 19.

Polis of Strife

Competition was not only about prestige, or the wealth that enabled display: it was political, and hence about power. In the most direct form, elite competition involved groups in raw power conflicts over control of the *polis*. The poetry of Alkaios, in early sixth-century BCE Mytilēnē, concerns the struggles between factions. Political enemies such as Pittakos, once a friend and a companion, now a trampler of his oaths and an opponent, are abused. Their banquet is full of merchants and braggarts, and in contrast to the supposedly well-born Alkaios and his friends (the ancient scholars' notion that Alkaios was noble must come from their literalist reading of his poetry), Pittakos is low-born, *kakopatridas* (his supposed father's name, Hyrrhas, is probably an insulting invention derived from "ugly"), a pot-bellied, foot-dragging dusky diner (the insults were duly collected by later philologists).[29] The "dusky dining" might be an allusion to Pittakos's refraining from the elitist practice of boisterous returns from banquets, illuminated with lamps and torches (the *kōmos*), just as he is said to have imposed a law punishing more severely drunk perpetrators, and restricted mourning at funerals.[30]

Elitist practices—song, banquets, drunken *cortèges* in the public urban spaces of street and piazza—create solidarity within a faction; conversely, name-calling bodily delegitimizes political opponents by denying them the signs of distinction. The cultural practices of competition work to political effect: hence the profusion of names for political factions. The *Dourikleioi* (Spear-Famed Ones) at Megara are one example, as are groups with highly positive names such as "The Ever-Sailors" (*Aeinautai*), "Wealth" (*Ploutis*), and "Might" (*Cheiromacha*) at Milētos. Three factions were known in early sixth-century BCE Athens—the Plainsmen, Coastmen, and Beyond-the-Hills-men—each led by a family (described with much later, and obfuscatory, detail).[31] Other names preserved for early Athens might also be factions and groups, rather than the official orders of a hypothetical Drakonian constitution, as later tradition had it.[32] Political invective probably satirized this practice. On Samos, the name "Fishermen" might ridicule a group with local ties to the sea (or freebooting?), and the " *muthiētai*" or "*mytharchoi*" might be the "speech-izens" or "speech-archs" (combining *mythos*, speech, with compounds that evoke the words for citizen or for ruler: members of the *polis* as pure wordmasters).[33] Such new formations evoked the names of groups, but to derisive and divisive purpose rather than as the foundation for group solidarity and the claim to rule. The drinking groups and associations that we saw earlier as a constituent part of the early *polis* could also prove factors of instability and conflict (see below).

Factions waged armed conflict over control of judicial and political office—the regulations, attested in Cretan cities, against repeated tenure of office suggest one way in which groups could monopolize power by the capture of accepted, legitimate positions of power in the community. Such groups, often familial, are widely attested, with varying degrees of certainty (the evidence is often no more than fleeting mention, as mere names, in later anecdotes)[34] from the seventh century BCE onwards. The two royal dynasties in Sparta may have been familial groups of this type, monopolizing a particular type of office, at the time of the probable coming together of the five communities that ultimately produced the *polis* of Sparta.[35] Groups of families in power are attested at Mytilēnē (the Penthilidai) and at Corinth, where the Bakchiads operated as "monarchic men," intermarrying, controlling office, and holding a limited Council of 200 members. Around 650 BCE, they were ousted by a single family, the Kypselids, from the name of the first leader, Kypselos. The family stayed in power for nearly a century.[36]

Single rule appears as a possible option in a variety of forms. In some cases, a family or individual manages violent but lasting capture of mechanisms of power, creating the basis for rule over several generations—the Kypselids in Corinth, the much later Peisistratids in Athens, and far less well-known dynasties such as the Orthagorids in Sikyōn (where the colorful Kleisthenēs ruled). Such rule is accompanied by the charismatic trappings of monarchy[37] around the person of the ruler: Kypselos at Corinth, the founder and ruler of Kyrēnē Battos, and the would-be Spartan tyrant Damaratos (an exiled king) are presented in stories echoed by Herodotos as miraculous children, among folktales and charismatic stories of ruler birth.[38] As a baby, Kypselos was miraculously saved from murder. Battos stuttered (and his descendants ruled over Kyrēnē with the native trappings of power, albeit in conflict with the citizens).[39] Damaratos, in virtue of an ambiguous birth story, might be the son of a deity. Damaratos had been exiled on the initiative of his rival and co-king, Kleomenēs, whose charisma and personal power may be seen as another case of a monarchical tendency which, in this particular case, was probably cut short by assassination by rivals or collective murder. The association of the Athenian ruler Peisistratos with Hēraklēs (he mounted a pageant to suggest he was brought back by Athēna to the city), or with Kronos, the deity who ruled over a Golden Age, similarly works by the manipulation of myth and ritual to achieve charisma.[40] Conversely, the invective in Alkaios against Pittakos, who achieved single rule, might be aimed at converting the monarchical figure into that of the physically hateful scapegoat (*pharmakon*), and thus denying legitimacy and charisma.[41]

However, Pittakos is supposed to have retired from power after giving out legislation in Mytilēnē. He can be considered to have belonged to another type of political actor. Such individuals held single rule temporarily, often as an emergency measure, within improvised terms—*aisymnētēs*, arbiter, and lawgiver. Solōn (whose poetry shows his self-styling, refusing sole rule, but occupying a particular place as a mindful, authoritative, and just arbiter between the various actors in the *polis* whose shape he manipulates by edict) can also be considered as one of these "Archaic" figures of individual rather than collective power.[42] Indeed, "installing an *aisymnētēs*," "rising in revolt with a view to the power of an *aisymnētēs*" and "exercising the powers of an *aisymnētēs*" were all activities cursed by the *polis* of Teōs, in yearly public ceremonies, during the early fifth century BCE.[43]

A third type of situation is that where no single family or group managed to capture power, control of the *polis* circulated between elite factions in situations of continuous, low-level violent conflict, involving various competitive strategies, concrete or symbolical. The best-known case is that of the three factions in Athens, between which power alternated (Peisistratos came to power twice, before finally rooting his control). The story of various factions in conflict over power at Mytilēnē, in the time of Alkaios, might also be about the alternation of rule between competing elite groups. The corollary of victory in this type of competition might be the temporary expulsion or exile of the defeated groups (as in the case of Alkaios, much of whose poetry at least purports to be written in exile).[44] Such a process took place in Athens in 508 BCE, when a returning group, under their leader Isagoras and with military aid from Sparta, expelled their rivals, the Alkmeonids led by Kleisthenēs, who had just proposed a package of reforms in the Assembly; this was probably understood by his enemies as an attempt at charismatic single rule.

Seizing and holding power was part of the history of the "Archaic" *polis*; under the name of *tyranny*, single rule was a major topic and source of concern for the citizens of the various communities in the Greek world—as shown by the claim oft repeated in poetry, "I do not wish/care for an opulent tyranny," starting in the seventh century BCE already.[45] In the eastern Aegean, families and individuals could hold on to power with the help of foreign rulers: the Lydian king gave a large sum of money to Alkaios's faction, and the Achaimenid ruler controlled the Ionian *poleis* by supporting local families in positions of rule, as bosses or vassals (the powerful tyrant of Samos, Polykratēs, or the tyrant of Milētos, Histiaios, suffered the fates of Near Eastern client kings—the first crucified, the second summoned to court for a long-term stay as a heavy favor, or a precaution).[46]

In the western *poleis*, especially in Sicily, single rule was a widespread and long-lasting phenomenon into the fifth century BCE; the rulers' power was noted by the much later historian Thucydides.[47] The Sicilian tyrants notably practiced imperialism on a large scale, which affected the *poleis* by conquests and deportation of populations from defeated *poleis*. For instance, the tyrant Gelōn moved to his capital of Syracuse the inhabitants of old *poleis* such as Kamarina and Megara Hyblaia (the latter, whose extensive site we have seen as an example of early urbanism, never quite recovered); Gelōn's successor Hierōn continued the policy on an even vaster scale.[48] Elsewhere, the emergence in Macedonia of the long-lived dynasty of the Temenids, in combination with local urban settlements, may be considered as a particular example of this monarchical style (albeit with its own developmental path).[49] Indeed, the sole power exercised by the Spartan war-leader Pausanias over the large alliance of Greek states gathered in a super-federation to fight against the Achaimenid invasion, in 479 BCE, shows that charismatic single rule was part of the political repertoire of the early Greek world.[50]

Additionally, the violent seizure of power was part of the history of the *polis* because of widespread, long-lasting conflict with alternance between rule, exile, and bargaining (as illustrated by the case of Athens):[51] such struggles might give a glimpse of what constituted politics as usual, namely turn-taking of powerful men and their supporters. Hence "tyranny" appears as a coalescing process of collaboration between powerful men, rather than simply the domination of one man and his family.[52] A particular case is the sixth-century BCE Peloponnese, where Sparta, using its particular resources of abundant manpower, seems to have intervened in factional fights to expel entrenched families, only to install and support friendly factions in a softer form of rule. This development parallels the constitution of more formal links of alliance and subordination between the big Spartan power and the Peloponnesian *poleis*.[53]

Polis History beyond Elites

The importance of elite groups in the textual and archaeological record is undeniable. Equally undeniable is the role of elites in determining "Archaic" politics, through their competitive behavior, their economic acquisitiveness, their need to rule (including through "tyranny"), and their factional conflict over communal goods and public institutions. The important question is whether this story is the real story, the only story, of the "Archaic" *polis*; alternatively, we should examine the question of the relation between the elites' story and the arc sketched out previously of the logic of the development of state institutions, public goods, and communal ideology. The two narratives overlap exactly. The seventh century BCE is both the time of the emergence of constitutional arrangements and of elite display in the shape of great antiquarian tombs. The sixth century BCE sees urban monumentalization and consolidation of the state toward arguably democratic forms, conjointly with elite politics of tyranny and faction-fighting. On Samos or at Athens, the monumentalization of great civic temples or the adduction of water for monumentalized public distribution, which speak of common purposes, civic finances, and communal pride, coincide exactly with the rise of spectacular private dedications in the form of marble sculpture. Periods of tyranny in both cities have no visible impact on such private gestures;[54] freebooting continues at all times.

The unsettling overlap sharpens the question of its nature, and generally of the place of the elites in relationship to the development and the history of the *polis*. One possible narrative is entirely elite-centered. The twin developments of state institutions and written, public regulation can thus be interpreted as responses to deep-seated elite conflict over power within the community, or to elite issues such as property disputes. The *polis* appears as unsystematic *ad hoc* arrangements to defuse conflict, reserved to a small social elite because of the use of the restricted technology of writing (itself an elite matter because of limited literacy), and deployed to counter any social change that might threaten the elite's position.[55] State institutionalization coincides with, and indeed facilitates, the ubiquitous iniquities of elite acquisitiveness and rule. This model has been applied to a number of *poleis*, including early Sparta (where, it must be said, the evidence for conflict is mostly late, and hence where this interpretation is unconvincing).

More generally, elite interaction might be considered as constitutive of the *polis*: the structures of the "Archaic" *polis* would hence have emerged as the product of elite practice, custom, interests, and social organization in families and networks.[56] Whatever the origins of *polis* institutions, we might choose, in a cynical or realist mood, to consider the latter weak and inoperative in the light of the evidence for endemic and long-lasting political conflict. In Athens, in spite of the existence of institutions and written law, political history is marked by the tyranny attempt of Kylōn (put down by a popular uprising and by the execution of the faction by the Alkmeonids acting privately, and not by magistrates of the city), by the constant struggle between the three factions, and by a successful tyranny which, it is said, exercised power without affecting the regular functioning of institutions, courts, and laws. In this view, "Archaic" Athens looks less like a state than a chieftain society, shaped and dominated by the power relations of elite groups and families:[57] this seems the real world of *polis* politics and actors, and the force of law and institutions a mere shadow, without reach or bite. Even the reforms of Kleisthenes might be seen as aiming at entrenching the control of a particular family, the Alkmeonids, by weakening the power bases of rivals and somehow giving an institutional advantage to Kleisthenes's family.[58]

In this model, elites appear disengaged from their communities, which are merely the arena for competition with rivals. What is more, these same elites derive much social capital and power from their interactions with other elites outside the *polis*, or in the form of acquisitive freebooting, or through display of luxury and claims of high birth with divine ascendants.[59] The tale of the suitors of Agaristē, at Sikyōn, exemplifies the international horizons of "Archaic" elites, horizontally integrated across regions, and disembedded from their communities. The early *polis* becomes the playground for wealthy, land-owning elite bullies, the scene of their standoffs, the battlefield for violent bosses.[60]

Yet an elite-centered narrative cannot satisfactorily account for the character and the outcomes of *polis* development. Notably, it cannot account for the exact shape taken by the changes, namely rotation, multiplication, and collegiality of public office, and written public regulation. We do not see phenomena that elite dominance would lead us to expect, such as the entrenchment of class interests, the rise of a society of orders, delicate bargaining between families or groups, or complex common-law arrangements. On the contrary, the epigraphical evidence and the traces in the literary evidence, both contemporary and later, show the suddenly detectable appearance of public institutions and rules for power-sharing, the clear location of legitimacy of power in communal interests, and universally applicable rules, communicated to the whole community which they concern.[61] In Drēros, the possibility of elite members repeatedly holding the office of *kosmos* was countered with an *ad hoc* law that grew out of agreed norms about power-holding, and ensured that the spirit of that rule was applied consequently.

Furthermore, arguments about the restricted, and hence restrictive, nature of literacy in the "Archaic" Greek world are untenable. Even in the case of Crete, where such claims of law-as-mystification have been pushed strongly, there is evidence for widespread familiarity with writing and reading. The presentation of early law also suggests the intention of communication to a wide audience (large lettering, punctuation, accessibility in public spaces, technological solutions such as prismatic inscription or spinnable beams for all-round legibility).[62] As argued above, the significance of the *ad hoc* character of laws of the "Archaic" *polis* should not be exaggerated: the laws respond to specific problems, but as part of coherent ensembles, whose tendency is to converge around principles of clarity and publicness.[63] The coherence of *polis* institutions, ideologies and regulations can be seen in the cogent development of stateness throughout the sixth century BCE. A striking example of this cogency is the set of reforms implemented by the Athenian *polis* at the end of the sixth and in the early fifth centuries, the "Kleisthenic reforms," which precisely did not introduce any long period of factional domination by the Alkmeonids.

Any interpretation of the *polis*, with its institutions, rules, and ideologies, as a weak state or simply as irrelevant beside the reality of elite assertion, is also difficult to hold in view of the centrality of public claims. If need be, the popular community could reimpose its will through lynch law. This is the significance of early Greek law and its curses upon evil doers, as at Teōs (above, p. 105): not a sign of state weakness as much as the threat of general community violence upon elites. Freebooting could fit within *polis* norms, when negotiated as a way out of conflict—a variant on exile to solve deadlocked internal situations.[64]

Even factional politics were cast in *polis* terms. The doings of factions can be condemned in terms of the public good. Archilochos already stigmatizes a group of exiles who, after being brought back to Thasos, "pursued their own interests and inflicted woes on the commons (*xun' epoiēsan kaka*)."[65] Such values exist in the Homeric polities; in the "Archaic" *poleis* they are the hegemonic discourse. Elite groups such as Alkaios and his companions articulate themselves in terms of the community. In exile, Alkaios pines for the *polis* and its institutions; his vituperative attacks on Pittakos or other tyrants are couched in the communitarian language of justice and injustice that is so important to the *polis*: Pittakos devours the people *ou kan nomon*, with disregard for the law. Even the poetry of Alkaios's aristocratic faction reaches for the legitimacy and publicness that the law confers. When Theognis complains about *kakoi*, the vile ones, taking over, his discontent is framed in terms of the corruption of justice for all, rather than simply the end of power for a social order.[66]

"Tyrants," too, can be couched in ideological terms that agree with *polis* norms. Oracles about Kypselos speak of fairness, one of the concerns of *polis* ideology, and the injustice of a small faction (the group calling themselves the Bakchiads), soon to be crushed, chastised by the rolling rock of justice, announced by the pregnant

Labda, Kypselos's mother). "She will give birth to a millstone; it will fall among the monarchic men, and it will bring justice to Corinth." The oracles about Kypselos speak of justice, one of the concerns of *polis* ideology; similarly, the Leōphilos, "People-friend" whom Archilochos imagines exercising sole power might be an imaginary tyrant-like figure.[67] Even Alkaios must admit that Pittakos was chosen by the whole community in a mass meeting (*aollees*).[68] Traces of Pittakos's self-presentation suggest that he posed as the protector of public interests against factional politics and elite claims, like Solōn later did. Sole rule was justified by public concerns.

In institutional terms, the Megarian tyrant Theagenēs's seizure and slaughter of the oxen of the rich might reflect the application of laws, in view of one of the uses of the verb "herd-eating" to describe fines imposed by the city (above, p. 111). The act might have represented, or been represented as, the implementation and reinforcement of *polis* norms against elite claims (for instance, involving pasturing rights on common land).[69] Some of the later tyrants of Samos made gestures that fitted within communal ideology: offering to place power "in the middle," or dedicating the fine tableware of the preceding tyrant Polykratēs.[70] The continuity of law and institutions in Athens in the time of Peisistratid dominance,[71] rather than showing the weakness of the *polis*, invites us to try to understand violent, theatrical politics within institutional workings. Indeed, the time when Alkaios remembers his father and grandfather enjoying the Council and the Assembly meeting (above, p. 80) would likely also have been the time of the ascendancy of a single family (the Penthilidai), in a context of factional struggle.[72]

Social Complexity and the Travails of Integration

It is clear that the early *polis* is not a direct function of elite claims and competition. Yet to insist on the stateness of the *polis* and the robustness of its rules-bound institutions and communal ideologies is not to deny the importance of elite behavior in shaping the *polis* and its practices. In the story of the *polis*, the rich will always be with us. The crucial question, however, is that of the place, and the nature, of these wealth and power elites, once the communities take the developmental path of strong integration that characterizes the *polis*. Phenomena such as the parallel development of public building and spaces and private dedication (within public spaces) are not just juxtaposed within the same historical time-space: their relation, because it is paradoxical, must be dialectical.

The origins of the *polis* lie in the long integration and structuration of communities during the post-palatial Early Iron Age, with an acceleration of visible processes in the eighth century BCE. The *polis* itself arises from exploration and choices consequent on strong integration—power-sharing among the whole community, in the name of the whole community, the *dēmos*. The consequences of the processes are visible materially and ideologically, as well as the crucial leap across the threshold of stateness; yet the processes themselves, and their causality, remain desperately obscure (one of the attractions of an elite-centered history is to elide the problem by consistently denying the existence of statehood for the *polis*, from its origins onwards).

The immediate consequence of integration and structuration is the constitutive question of membership: who was the *polis*? Who was the *dēmos*? What are the relations within the various elements that make up the *polis*? Social complexity and conflict over membership are a consequence of *polis* formation—the first and recurrent problems that the *polis* has to solve. Hereditary monarchy, sole rule by a closed group of "monarchical men," the signorial turn of tyranny—constant temptations or possibilities during the story of the "Archaic" *polis* and of the *polis* in general—are part of the mix of complexity, partly because they are always possible outcomes of competitive politics (someone or some group might prove stronger than rivals) but also because they propose a solution, namely the promise to simplify the problem of social complexity and justice by guaranteeing it through unchallenged authoritarian, Hobbesian force, justified through the charisma and the personal qualities of the ruler (even while potentially leaving institutions in place). Hence the constant appropriation of discourses of justice by the tyrants or single-rule men (lawgivers, arbiters) of the "Archaic" age.[73]

Yet social complexity itself would not go away because of Kypselid justice or Peisistratid consolidation. It was an inherent part of the *polis*, from the moment of structured integration of different but overlapping social elements during the Early Iron Age. Integration itself raised the question of social roles and eminence—who was best among the community?—and hence created the arena for multiple forms of competition between families, groups, classes, and places. Competition was supported and fueled by consumption and expenditure, creating the need for acquisitiveness, which could take place at the expense of nonelite members of the community: this type of behavior raised issues of justice and membership (what were the rights of the nonelite members of the community in relation to the elite?). Elite claims never simply played off against other members of the elite: they also raised the question of the consequences of distinction, in the form of the right to rule within integrated, structured communities: should the wealthier, braver, athletically stronger, have more rights within just communities based on strong notions of the public sphere? Was this a question of individual power or of the rights of whole groups or classes within the *polis*?

The means to achieve integration could in themselves create tensions and conflict. The invented groups such as tribes, "brotherhoods" or localities, the dining groups that offered synekdoches of the whole *polis*, raised the question of which groups represented the *polis*. Synekdoche generated its own centrifugal dangers: factions structured themselves into named bands or banqueting groups along the same principles of invented names and created bonds as the organic yet artificial groups that were supposed to be both constitutive of the *polis* and secondary to it. Such factional groups could claim representativeness, as can be seen in Alkaios's poetry, where his particular group imagines itself as holding legitimacy and justice, a claim that is not just a strategic positioning with the field of political conflict, but also a reflection of the very way the *polis* structures itself. Hence the consequence of factional politics, namely the exclusion through exile of those not belonging to the right groups that think of themselves as the *polis* through a process of synekdoche.[74]

In surveying competition and conflict as consequences of integration, the general interpretation I suggest for the unsettling overlap between elite-centered phenomena and community affirmation is exactly the contrary of the elite-driven narrative. Conflict, competition, elite claims were functions of community consolidation; paradoxically, they are as much indices of *polis* formation and stateness as written law or the formalization of public spaces during the seventh and sixth centuries BCE. The central paradox of eliteness being secondary to community formation would be worked out in later centuries; in the "Archaic" period, it posed problems that political communities had to solve.

Solutions: Closed or Open?

One solution to the travails of integration was to consolidate strongly a small group of stakeholders chosen on grounds of birth and especially wealth, and to exclude the rest of the population of the territory. Within the small group, power had to be shared equally, and social homogeneity imposed to ensure solidarity. In spite of the exclusive structure, a certain amount of porosity would obtain, and an open-ended menagerie of noncitizen statuses stretched far out, from second-class "inferior" citizen families, serf classes covering a variety of conditions (sharecropping, privileged groups), to subordinate (perioikic) *poleis* and allies bound in unequal agreements. The best-known examples of this type of *polis* based on exclusion and strong integration are Sparta and the Cretan cities, where all these traits appear.

In practice, these small groups are often urban elites, developing symbolical signs of recognition and belonging.[75] The full development of the model is particularly well illustrated by the Cretan cities of the early fifth century BCE, such as Gortyn, known by its extensive law code.[76] The model may have been operative elsewhere, for instance in Thessaly (where serfs, perioikism, and expansionism are very prominent traits in the late "Archaic" period). The settlements founded by small traveling groups in the Early Iron Age on the coasts of Asia Minor, or from the Late Geometric period onwards in Sicily and Italy, or in north Africa in the seventh and sixth centuries BCE, may have created social structures of integrated groups and dependent rural populations.[77] The Bakchiads, "monarchical men" in Corinth, may simply have been a restricted citizen group, surrounded by inferior families that in some sense belonged to the community, but were excluded from full power.

In this model, the restricted group has to present itself as the whole community. Hence the tamping down of elitism, or rather the diffusion of certain elitist traits (for instance, the ethos of endurance as a sign of innate superiority, access to chosen luxury markers as the prize and the sign of entitlement) alongside the promotion of egalitarian discourses of moderation and the fiction that the group of citizens is made up of commoners. The claim to divine or heroic descent is widespread among the closed citizen body, and civic subdivisions, real or invented, serve to tighten the bonds of group solidarity. This political style is most obvious in Sparta, the city of the *homoioi*, the "Alike Ones," even if there must have been disparities in wealth in the "Archaic" period already.[78] Spartiate political style underlies the egalitarian tone of Tyrtaios (above, p. 90), the "austerity" of Spartan visual arts,[79] or the playacting of Alkman and his tripodful of soup:[80]

> and some day I shall give you a great tripod bowl in which you may collect (...) It has still not been over a fire, but soon it will be full of bean soup, such as Alcman, who eats everything, loves warm after the solstice: he eats no delicacies but looks for common fare like the people.

The Spartiate concern for justice is based on the successful playacting that constituted their orderly world.[81] The sudden and very localized explosion in dedications of small, modest lead figurines at the shrine of Orthia (fig. 6.7) is probably related to the shifts in Spartan self-representation (over 68,000 of these figurines have been found for the sixth century BCE, a bafflingly high figure).[82]

This political style did not preclude a certain amount of variation in levels of luxury and display, as visible in dedications in Spartan shrines. Such dedications reflected the considerable disposable wealth available in "Archaic" Sparta, ultimately derived from the exploitation of a serf population. The parallel case to the world of social playacting of Sparta is to be found in Crete. There, the noticeable austerity in material culture, increasingly visible in the seventh and sixth centuries BCE, must likewise express the solidarity of the restricted citizen group that lives off rent from the countryside and its peasants; "orientalizing" art is deployed in specific contexts to bolster group solidarity (for instance, on large storage vessels used in the *andreion*, the communal dining hall).[83] Egalitarian, "middling" political culture played a crucial role in nonegalitarian, exclusive versions of the *polis* where access to membership was strictly controlled.

The other, diametrically opposite path was to structure the *polis* through wide inclusiveness, by the integration of a large segment of the adult male population as citizens, in strict distinction to noncitizens, namely foreigners and especially the enslaved. The "open" *poleis* were inclusive socially, by the acceptance of nonelite members without having to satisfy a fortune criterion, and geographically, by the full integration of members of smaller settlements around the big site (rather than reducing them to subordinate status). Certain privileges, linked to citizenship, will be widespread among the population; for instance, a share in sacrifices, communal feasting, or festival activities, and participation in decision-making and judicial institutions, indeed in the basic level of political power in the *polis*.

FIGURE 6.7. Lead figurines, shrine of Artemis Orthia, Sparta. Late seventh-sixth centuries BCE; the objects measure around 4-5 cm in height.

One consequence is a combination of widespread rights with a high level of social diversity within the *polis*. The various forms of invented bonds (tribes, "brotherhoods") are meant to bridge differences in determined ritual and institutional contexts, but coexist with many other forms of sociability. The dominant political culture will tend toward communitarian, egalitarian, and even proto-democratic forms, as seen above—in such areas as burial practice, private housing, and public spaces. It will also tend toward the diminution of elite extraction of rent off producers, because the latter, as citizens, are protected by institutions and have access to decision-making and rules-making.

In this open context, precisely because of easy access to public goods and political rights, elite competition, claims, and assertiveness will exist in very visible forms: these are *elitist*, in that they claim eminence, but as part of competition within terms defined by the community. The reforms attributed to the lawgiver Solōn, in Athens, gave citizen rights to the free population of Attica by suppressing some form of sharecropping or corvée arrangement, and hence ending a peasant status that gave a wealth elite power over other nonelite members of the community. The measures clarified the problems of membership in an inclusive direction. At the same time, an institutional reform introduced ranking by wealth, into four classes: *thētes* (the old word for agricultural workers), *zeugitai* ("yoke-men"), *hippeis* ("horsemen"), and the top level of *pentakosiomedimnoi* ("500-measure-men"). The formal stratification itself is an elitist feature, meant to give shape and measurability to status competition by directly and clearly translating land-owning value into social worth, especially since the categories were then translatable into political office.

This arrangement also represented part of the Solonian bargain between different constituencies, involving the grant of political rights to the poor and the monopoly of offices by constitutionally defined groups. Solōn's own impressive political poetry is worth quoting:[84]

> I have given the masses as much privilege as is sufficient, neither taking away from their honor nor adding to it. And as for those who had power and were envied for their wealth, I saw to it that they too should suffer no indignity. I stood with a mighty shield cast round both sides and did not allow either to have an unjust victory.

Whatever the details of the classification and its consequences in terms of officeholding, it is also clear that most of the classificatory attention goes to the very wealthy, whose social position is classified very finely, in contrast to the undifferentiated mass of thetes who must have made up most of the community.[85]

Elitist competition within inclusive *poleis* can also take the form of luxurious display, especially in the culture of the *sumposion*, the orientalizing drinking party, or the dedication of large-scale marble sculpture. Strikingly, both forms of display are very well attested in Athens precisely at the moments when the *polis* extends and formalizes its inclusiveness, after the "Solonian reforms" of the early sixth century BCE and the "Kleisthenic" reforms (tribal and institutional) at the end of the sixth century BCE.[86] Around this time, vase painting with military imagery may also reflect the social claims to eminence of particular classes within the competitive, unstable world of Athens after Solōn: this interpretation is boosted by subtle distinctions in the equipment of the armed men (for instance in helmet crests), or in the way in which the men-at-arms are paired with images drawn from myth, hence lending them prestige and alluding to lordly status.[87]

Elite competition, as a structural feature of such open systems, can move in three ways. It can create the parameters for political life, in the form of competition between elite groups; this may have constituted the normal model for politics, but with the constant threat of boiling over into full factional fighting, with stages of exile and expulsions, and even of escalation into more or less long-lived episodes of sole rule by arbiters or tyrants. Alternatively, elite competition could boil down into forms of self-fulfilling cultural display, such as closed *symposia* characterized by song and luxury, which existed as bonded "aristocratic" groups in parallel to the institutions and political culture of the *polis*. Elitist culture thus would appear as a reaction to inclusive developments in the *polis*, to stake out claims to essential distinction, exclusiveness, and quality. This model is well attested in the Classical period but may have been part of the diversity of some "Archaic" *poleis*, as might be detectable already in Theognis's poetry (ca. 550 BCE) or in late "Archaic" Athens.

Finally, elite competition might, in some ways, be a sign of the good integration of elites within inclusive *poleis*. Forms of competition, even though diverse, might also be about collaboration—for instance, in the production of normed images and in the search for negotiated spaces of eliteness that admit of community approval. This is strikingly illustrated by the politics of athletic victory. The latter offers an obvious image of eliteness at the most basic level because of the leisure needed for training and travel, but also because of such values as the glorious body of the athlete, his innate qualities of strength or courage, or the wealth exhibited in horse- and chariot-racing. Yet the celebration of victory took place through community rewards (participation in state-sponsored banqueting by magistrates) and, as we can see in the surviving early-fifth century BCE victory poems by Pindar, acts of celebration balanced individual eminence, family claims, and a sense of limitations and negotiation. The victor engaged the community in an exchange of services and toil against recognition, in a reciprocal relation of *charis*, "grace," "gratitude"; his claims were expressed with self-imposed limits, through awareness of mortality and the need for self-restraint.[88]

Another example of social diversity leading to integration might emerge from the landscapes of dedication that opened this chapter. Individual sculpture dedications, in shrines like the Samian Heraion or the Akropolis in Athens, end up by joining forces to produce gorgeous, varied landscapes that manifest the city's wealth and prosperity under the protection of a patron deity. The concern with family continuity, individual economic gains, and the transmission of property, which underlies many dedications, may be an elite concern but also promises the continuity of the *polis*, made up of individual families and their local rootedness. Furthermore, the record of dedication on the Athenian Akropolis shows not only the display of large-scale marble sculpture of standing naked men and elaborately dressed women, but an extraordinary diversity: *kouroi*, *korai*, horsemen, scribes, expensive dedications by craftsmen and traders celebrating their economic successes and patrimonial *avoir*, and a profusion of simple terracotta dedications reflecting non-elite participation in the most visible of *polis* spaces.[89]

Politics in the Early *Polis*

The two models sketched out above (restricted *polis* with an egalitarian middling culture, inclusive *polis* with diverse culture including an elitist strand)[90] are simplifications of complex situations on the ground. In many cases, it is not quite possible to say that, for example, "Corinth was a type 1, Samos was a type 2 *polis*." There are also many features that do not quite fit this scheme: for instance, the *Pansitimidai*, "descendants of those who have all honors" at Tegea, who seem to constitute a privileged status group; or the existence of elite individuals enjoying citizenship in multiple cities, hinting at status fluidity in and between *poleis*.[91] It is not possible to say whether Ēlis, which was an expansionist city as well as a proto-democratic one, started off as a closed-shop *polis* of the Spartiate type (my model does not have predictive power). Without precise evidence, it is difficult to see where to place such details as the "poor citizens" of Thasos contrasting with the fancy hairstyle of a friend of Archilochos, or how to analyze the social structure of "Archaic" Aigina.[92] In any case, law, institutions, and communitarian ideologies were shared traits across all types of *polis*.

Most importantly, inclusiveness took place along a spectrum; the question of where to start and where to stop including individuals in the body of fully enfranchised members remained live throughout the history of the *polis* (see below, chapters 15 and 19). The consequence is that "restricted" and "inclusive" *poleis* are points on a continuum, and that they are forms within the same *polis* logic that develops throughout the "Archaic" period. In Southern Italy, Rhēgion, Lokroi, and Krotōn exemplify polities that draw on both possibilities: they included thousands of individuals within a broad-based franchise—but kept the citizen body within fixed numbers, and hence closed.[93]

The two main stories around the development of the *polis* in the period are the rise of stateness in the form of institutions, law, and ideology, and the negotiations around inclusiveness and exclusiveness, with the concomitant adjustments in elite ideologies and discourses—the history of the state, and the social history of power. The intersection of these two *intrigues* ought to give a full history of the "Archaic" *polis*. In practice, this is rarely possible, because of the diversity of situations and the lack of evidence. The actual outcomes and choices depended on local factors—the capacity of elites for violent capture as a consequence of and requirement for acquisitiveness, the effects of elite competition on the wider population, contingent choices such as the role of individual elite leaders—and could vary considerably, from place to place and within places, throughout time.

For example, Attica underwent early consolidation (geographical and social), then a diverse seventh century BCE that has proven extraordinarily difficult to read (we have seen phenomena such as political institutions and law; an attempted tyranny foiled by popular reaction and elite reaction; diminution of detectable graves, which must reflect some social shift; antiquarian continuity of dedication on the Akropolis; and religious expansion). The outcome of the seventh century BCE seems to be increased elite pressure on nonelite classes; concomitantly, elite display comes back spectacularly with large-scale sculptural dedication. The reaction to that moment was not exclusion, but, in the "Solonian" reforms, fundamental political inclusion matched with compensatory elitist spaces. This situation in turn led to increased elite competition (ultimately dominated by one particular group, the Peisistratids), but also intensified community integration and citizen definition, down to the final "Kleisthenic" reforms. This story illustrates various possibilities within the parameters of the "Archaic" *polis*.

Analogous, yet variant, stories might be written for other *poleis*, according to the available evidence, again showing the possibilities of the *polis* forms in the "Archaic" Greek world. As we have seen, Sparta appears as conquest-state with a middling ideology for the core members, surrounded by unequals. Megara seems structured by intense negotiations between elite and nonelite, but shows continued monumentalization, which hints at stateness and publicness; it thus fits within my model of state formation driving social bargaining and conflict.

Other places offer complex pictures that my models help understand and clarify, if not necessarily classify too neatly. Argos appears as a well-integrated *polis* with institutions and laws; outside the circle of citizens, the *polis* probably had serfs (the "naked ones," *gymnētes*, or the "household men" *woikiatai*) and subordinate communities (the "slaves" who took over the city after the defeat at Sēpeia).[94] It nourished ambitions of conquest in the Peloponnese, and organized its public spaces in shapes that reflected these ambitions but also furthered, in concrete ways, the process of state formation. Sikyōn controlled a large and complex territorial state, perhaps structured by unequal relations between the urban elite and the inhabitants of the rural small sites (the "Club bearers" and "Sheepskin wearers," *katōnakophoroi*).[95] Early on, it was dominated by a single family with high political ambitions, but finally underwent expansive growth in the sixth century BCE in its territory, which suggests egalitarian developments as well as further state institutionalization. Even those places where we only catch only snapshots (sixth-century BCE Akraiphia known through its cemeteries and the shrine of Apollōn Ptōos with its varied offerings; Siphnos in its happy days) allow us to ask questions about development, choices, and outcomes.

Looking backwards from 500 BCE, the major point that requires explanation remains the emergence of stateness as a consequence of integration. Looking forward, the great question will be that of inclusion and exclusion, predicated on the paradox that the definition processes of elite and community were inextricably linked and mutually reinforcing, as well as antithetical.[96] The paradox would play itself out in the practical and theoretical debates about democracy and oligarchy of the following centuries. The question already appears in the populist politics of Kleisthenic Athens, and generally in the conflict between the poor and the "fat" that starts appearing in the early fifth century BCE.

In the meantime, the diversity and intensity of debates in the early *polis* gives the period its experimental feel, along with the *Belle Epoque* quaintness and histrionic quality of much of its politics. Even the rise and rise of stateness is an insistent note, expressed through law and institutions, in the ongoing debate on community. Solōn, who is said to have framed laws and institutions and elaborated a powerful, if nuanced, solution to the problems of elite competition and acquisitiveness, took a stance on community, in an explosive poem that speaks of community, conflict, social tensions, law, and justice:[97]

> Now our *polis* will never perish by the destiny of Zeus or the will of the happy immortal gods—for such is the great-hearted guardian, mighty-fathered daughter, that holds her hands over us. It is the citizens themselves, for the sake of profit, who will ruin the great city by their folly. Unrighteous is the mind of the leaders of the commons, and they are about to suffer many woes on account of their great violence, for they know not how to hold them from excess nor to order present joys in the peace of the feast . . . they grow rich obeying unrighteous deeds . . . they steal from each other with no respect for sacred or public goods, nor have heed of the august foundations of Justice, who is aware in her silence of present and past, and in time comes always to avenge. This wound comes to every city, inevitably, and the city falls quickly into evil servitude, which arouses discord and civil war that destroys the lovely youth of many. For in gatherings that wrong its friends, the lovely city is quickly brought low by its enemies. Such are the evils which then are rife among the *dēmos*, and many of the poor go to a foreign land, sold and bound with unseemly fetters, there to bear perforce the evil works of servitude. Thus the common woe comes to every house, and the courtyard doors will no longer keep it out; it leaps over the high wall, and always finds you, even if you go hide in the chamber. This it is that my heart bids me tell the Athenians, and how Bad-lawness gives a city much trouble. But Good-lawness (*eunomiē*) makes all things orderly and adjusted, and often lays fetters upon the unrighteous; she makes the rough smooth, stops excess, makes outrage wilt; she withers the growing blooms of ruin, she straightens crooked judgments, she mollifies overweening deeds; she stops the deeds of faction, she stops the anger of dire strife; and under her all is made perfect and senseful among men.

A similar point is made in a brief quotation from the poet Simonidēs, who worked for rich patrons as well as cities: "*polis* teaches man" (*polis andra didaskei*).[98]

PART IV

Framing the "Classical" *Polis*

480–180 BCE

A GROUP of *poleis* in central Greece called themselves with the collective name of Lokrians (*Lokroi*)—meaning that they shared a common identity, customs, cult, and institutions at the local and the regional levels.[1] To be more granular and grounded, the Lokrians fell in two groups, perhaps 50 kilometers distant as the crow flies: the Western (Ozolian) Lokrians in the rocky region west of Delphi, on the Corinthian Gulf; and the Eastern Lokrians in the highlands and valleys north and northwest of Boiōtia, parallel to the Euboian Gulf. West and East Lokris were separated by Phōkis and Boiōtia (and smaller regional units); and they were themselves divided into further subgroups. This state of affairs is rather difficult to explain but must reflect processes of movement and ethnogenesis during the Early Iron Age. (We have seen Eastern Lokris as the setting for LHIIIC warrior groups, in the brief post-Mycenaean moment: above, p. 29).

These regional groupings were never prominent players on the international stage of ancient history, but their story reflects the major developments in the history of the *polis*. We have seen Lokrian communities exemplifying the rise of law during the "Archaic" period; to this theme, we might add the sending out of settlers and the regulation of the institutional consequences, add the complex regional networking, and the use of myth and shrines to construct bonds within and between communities. That is, both Lokrian entities exemplify the complexity and inventiveness of the "Archaic" period and its emergent political communities. Both subsets of Lokrians shared institutions and a cultic identity, as can be shown notably by official documents of the sixth but (remarkably) also of the early second centuries BCE; defaulting on tax payments in any Lokrian community could be punished by exclusion from the Lokrians as a whole (a status described as being *apoloqros*, "de-lokrianized").[2]

Though two Lokrian subgroups were bound by identity and institutions, toward the end of the "Archaic" period (say, ca. 500 BCE), they were already organized along different lines, a situation that reflects the two great outcomes of institutional and ideological development (as explored in the previous chapter). Eastern Lokris was dominated by one large *polis*, Opous, located at modern Atalanti. Other, smaller poleis existed as dependent states, led by the local hegemonic power: the whole ensemble appears as "the Opountians and the Lokrians with the Opountians," and Opous translated its dominant position into a mythical claim to be the mother-city of all Lokrians, and more concretely in the levying of tax or tribute on other Lokrian communities.[3] This kind of power structure is known for other "Archaic" states, such as Ēlis or Sparta, or various Boiotian places, such as Thespiai; it was one of the major ways in which "Archaic" communities could relate to each other. The dominant *polis*, Opous, was elitist and restricted full membership to the "Thousand," perhaps connected to the "Hundred Houses" known for Lokris.[4] This sort of arrangement, too, is a familiar type of organization and indeed almost expected as a corollary of dominant *polis*-hood. Eastern Lokris probably supplied cavalry to the Spartan-led alliance in 431.[5] The elitist, domination-centered political setup of Eastern Lokris was compatible with a sense of being bounded by law, order, and justice, as shown by the funerary epigram of the Opountians killed at Thermopylai: "Opous, *mētropolis* of the Lokrians endowed with straight laws (*Lokrōn euthunomōn*) misses these men, fallen for Greece fighting against the Medes."[6] The personal self-fashioning of "Archaic" East Lokrian men seems to have been austere, as suggested by a sixth-century BCE stele showing the deceased in a simple *himation* and propped against a staff.[7] Ostentatious lawfulness and austerity are familiar from other closed polities, such as Sparta (above, chapter 6).

Western Lokris does show some signs of such a political culture, with a few examples of dependent communities or of elite groups in the Hellenistic period.[8] But generally, the landscape is structured differently from Eastern Lokris. There is no sign of a single dominant community: a number of small places share institutions and a regional structure (which in fact allows for local variation and even breakaway dynamics, around Amphissa), but exist as independent statehood-endowed communities. The "village named Polis," as Thucydides rather disdainfully names the settlement that served as the urban center for a community called the Hyaians, duly appears in the third century BCE in the documentary evidence as a city-state (the Polieis, alongside the Hyaians).[9] There is not much evidence for the institutional, social, and political organization of these small *poleis*, but it is likely, if only on grounds of their small size, that their political culture was not aristocratic and exclusive, but inclusive and participatory, structured around membership and integration. A recently published bronze tablet, inscribed and reinscribed, probably from Western Lokris is almost certainly an allotment token. Such artifacts were used to assign citizens by lot, for jury-courts and officeholding, a practice derived from democratic Athens: its provenance is highly suggestive for the inclusive nature of the West Lokrian *poleis*.[10] Western Lokris thus represents another form of structuration, external and internal, in the world of the early *polis*—built around peer polities that are themselves internally organized as integrative and egalitarian.

The elite-driven, center-and-periphery, domination-and-dependency model in Eastern Lokris, and the inclusive, dispersed, multiple equipollent-actor model in Western Lokris, represent two possible ways of relating and structuring *poleis*—two different paths, familiar to us from the "Archaic" period. Both regional entities underwent a continuous development, and lived a political history of their own, notably in the form of temporary absorption by other larger, more aggressive regional entities—the Boiotian Confederation or the Aitolian League—and in the form of interaction with a large autocratic state, the Antigonid kingdom based in the northern Aegean. But this history had a clear outcome: one of the models, the one represented by Western Lokris, won out. In the long run, the world of *poleis* would be one of many entities, interrelated and in equilibrium, and running their affairs along (roughly) inclusive and participatory lines, whereas the old model would become marginalized and rare, with pockets of survival and mutation. This pattern was pointed out a century ago, in a few sentences, by the great epigraphist A. Wilhelm—a specialist of the very detailed work on documentary evidence, which is so important to the sense of the *polis* phenomenon.[11]

This pattern can stand in for the main development that I will describe and explore from a variety of angles in this chapter: the generalization of the internally inclusive peer polity as the outcome of the interaction of a world of city-states, as a sort of collective experiment on a broad geographical scale, which is that of the geography of the *polis* (from Sicily to the Levant, from the Black Sea to Egypt) and over several centuries. The postulates of unity across diversities in time and space here work to reveal conflict but also the long harmonization of *polis* forms, internally and externally, in observable shapes, which this chapter aims to record and to describe, as a crucial moment in the history of the *polis*. This is the result of the phenomena of integration and community building that started at the end of the Late Bronze Age (chapter 2) and continued, with various travails and possible paths in the "Archaic" period. The solutions that emerged out of collective experimentation and interaction, once stabilized, would prove successful and long-lasting.

The timeframe is a long one, and it saw major transformations in the political history of the ancient Greek world over three and a half centuries.[12] This long period is the time when the city-states in the Aegean (and rather further afield) produced a large number of durable, high-quality artifacts, many of which have been preserved—a rich body of literary works for public performance, or alternatively deeply concerned with public matters such as the high politics at the center of narrative history; texts, state-related or private, inscribed on stone or on bronze to ensure publicity and eternity; public monumentalized spaces and buildings, sacred or non-sacred; artworks in a naturalistic idiom of great sophistication; and luxury or high-quality consumer goods. Much of this material, as it survives, and in spite of the haphazard nature of survival, constitutes the immediately familiar face of the ancient Greek world, as a valorized and canonized cultural object in the modern world.

The quality and quantity of this material reflect high material prosperity and economic development.[13] At a basic level, its presence shows continuous development from the earlier *poleis* and their cultural production—and also provides us with the evidence to write a history of the developed forms of the *polis*. The available evidence is distributed unequally—with a very heavy concentration of the literary, documentary, archaeological, and art-historical evidence in Athens, at least for the fifth and fourth centuries BCE, and the emergence of a much broader evidentiary footprint (usually documentary) in the third and second centuries BCE. Of course, the distribution of availability reflects a number of serendipitous factors—for instance, the modern choices of sites to excavate, the historical survival of monuments or inscriptions, the ancient variation in preference for an epigraphical habit of permanent publication of public documents, and the vagaries of repeated canon formation and preservation that determined the transmission of literary texts.[14] The problems of survival, retrievability, and excavation have already figured as an important problem in interpreting Dark Ages or Early Iron Age Greece (above, chapters 2 and 3). But the distribution and patterns of the available evidence, with caveats, do reflect historical processes, even if the evidence is shaped by later factors. The early importance of Athens is a major feature of the landscape of the *poleis* and reflects the successes and opportunities of its history; this Athenian predominance remains problematic for the interpretive strategies of a holistic history of the *polis*. The evolving shape of the traces left by the *poleis*, as obvious from collections or surveys of different types of evidence, also reflects the evolution and harmonization of the world of the *poleis*, and its connectedness.

These developments take place on a particular historical rhythm, which is influenced by, but not the same as, the normal periodization of ancient history. These are determined by high politics but whose application to *polis* history is only partly satisfactory. The evidence can thus be read at both levels—as a reflection of the traditional periodization and the pressures of political history, and as the outline of a long *polis* history that transcends this periodization. The traditional approach distinguishes between a Classical period, determined by the history of the Greek city-states, and a Hellenistic period, determined by supra-polis state formations, namely the large imperial states that succeeded the Persian empire after the latter's destruction.[15] This diptych can be described with greater definition by dividing the span between ca. 450 and 100 BCE into a high Classical period (ca. 480–400 BCE) and a late Classical period (ca. 370–300 BCE); and a high Hellenistic period (300–200 BCE) and a later Hellenistic period (150–31 BCE), which is characterized by Roman victories and domination over the eastern Mediterranean—with each of these subperiods melding into each other over transitional decades.

The broad outlines of political history within each of these periods are fairly well known, with different levels of detail according to the availability of sources and the history the type of sources allows us to write. I will often be using these conventional terms in this book: it is worth writing the history of events within these periods, even on the terms of traditional political history, for several reasons. The individual *poleis*, and even the *polis* as a political and social form, were deeply involved as actors in the event-history of the traditional periodization. Hence the familiar story shows us the *poleis* in action, with a vividness and a precision much greater than what we glimpse for the earlier period, greater even than Herodotos's detailed narrative of the *poleis*'s resistance to the Achaimenid empire, and his myriad details concerning the communities of the seventh and especially sixth centuries BCE. This story, if pitched at the right angle and level of detail, and if followed patiently over the centuries, helps us understand the problems faced by the *poleis* in their actions and in their world, and indeed to conceptualize their actions as historical problems.

However, as we can see in the case of West Lokris, but also in ubiquitous testcases, the agonizing history of hegemony and debates about membership and politics in the fifth and fourth centuries BCE led to harmonization in the following centuries, which is why the history of the *polis* that merely looks at the "Archaic" and Classical periods (like that offered by the Copenhagen Polis Centre) is incomplete without this continuation, even if the macro-conditions changed considerably with the presence of large supralocal states in the eastern Mediterranean. Indeed, the power of these states was itself shaped by the agency of their local interlocutors, drawing on resources and forms developed steadily throughout the periods of conflict and interaction. For this reason, in what follows, I propose to gently let go of the traditional periodization, arising from political history as well as the fetishization of texts and artifacts of the fifth and fourth centuries BCE. Instead, I propose to study the period 480-150 BCE as the story of two successive historical objects. The first is a "Hundred Years' War" (ca. 464–362 BCE): the concept is calqued from the devastating high-medieval conflict in Western Europe, to describe an equally devastating and tragic period of external conflict and internal unrest (chapters 7 and 8). Like its medieval parallel, the *poleis*'s long and extensive "big war" was a total event, with profound impact on political geographies, internal politics, the mechanics of state violence, economies, and demography; and yet it also opened the possibility of local agency and collaboration. The second is a great convergence of *polis* forms, producing a developed form of *polis* centered around autonomy and democracy—which it would be tempting to call "classical" but for the confusions such a name would cause with the traditional periodization (chapter 9).

This developed form of *polis*-hood is documented through the built environment, visual and sculptural imagery, and especially the political discourses it created during the third and second centuries BCE (the period traditionally known as "Hellenistic," and which I will occasionally refer to as such). During this period, we are confronted with a ubiquitous, uniform, and powerful image of the *polis* as, or at, the end of history—an image that deserves to be explored and nuanced (chapters 9 and 10), but which forms the heart of this book. As well as the network of dispersed, equal West Lokrian *poleis,* the decree of the island *polis* of the Herakleiotes, or the town plan of Priēnē, evoked at the start of this book, belong to these images. The importance of this period for *polis* history was emphasized by one of its greatest historians, the French epigraphist and institutional historian P. Gauthier (1935–2013).[16] In what follows, by offering an analysis that considers together the "Classical" and "Hellenistic" periods as part of the same dynamic, I attempt to apply the paradigms developed by Gauthier to recenter and rebalance Greek history.

7

Political History (1)

ARCHĒ AND *AUTONOMIA* IN THE HUNDRED YEARS' WAR

> The era that followed the Peloponnesian War, while catastrophically disordered from a Hobbesian "imperative of central authority" perspective, marked the apex of the classical Greek efflorescence.
>
> —J. OBER, *THE RISE AND FALL OF CLASSICAL GREECE*

The Hundred Years' War

In 459 BCE, the Athenians fought the Corinthians in battle twice in a row, a feat the more notable for being performed by the reserve forces of the youngest and oldest citizens, while the main body of mature Athenian fighting men was away. After the first, indecisive engagement, the Athenian scratch force set up a *tropaion*, a temporary monument made of despoiled arms and armor, claiming the victory. The Corinthian fighting men, under the scorn and taunts from their older peers, returned to the field after twelve days and set up their own counter-*tropaion*. But the Athenian force, stationed at Megara, rushed out, cut down the Corinthian working party, tore down the Corinthian monument, and routed the rest of the Corinthian force. During this second battle, a large group of defeated Corinthians blundered into a piece of farmland surrounded by a ditch. With a line of heavy men-at-arms, the Athenians hemmed them in at the open end of the estate, and, surrounding the plot with light infantry, exterminated the Corinthians under a blizzard of hand-thrown stones.[1]

This bloody incident exhibits features familiar from earlier modes of fighting between cities. The semi-ritualized nature of battle, which does not preclude real bloodletting, is a well-known theme in Greek history. The taking of spoils is paralleled in the local wars of the sixth century BCE (above, p. 117). Light infantry appears in Tyrtaios's poetry or in the tale about Kleisthenēs, tyrant of Sikyōn, called a mere stone-thrower in an oracle about his purported "tribal" reforms (above, p. 113). Yet there also is much that is new here. The battles occurred during the siege of Aigina, which the Corinthians tried to pressure the Athenians into lifting; the Athenian scratch force was stationed in Megara, now an Athenian ally. The horrible outcome hence belongs to a narrative of Athenian victory and even conquest, within a rapid evolution of high politics that would deeply impact the world of the *poleis*. Finally, the battles at Megara exhibit extraordinary, spectacular violence, of a type that would frequently blight the subsequent decades.

The atrocity at Megara took place at the start of a century or so of warfare, as part of a complicated high politics of power competition. This century is the stuff of traditional narrative history of the "Classical" period of Greek history, as documented in literary and epigraphical sources. These help produce a detailed narrative of so many wars—the First Peloponnesian War, the Athenian-Peloponnesian War (traditionally called the Peloponnesian War in modern scholarship, reflecting pro-Athenian focalization), the Corinthian War, and so on. But the complex conflicts might gain from being considered together as a single, long, terrible event—the Hundred Years' War of ancient Greece (ca. 464–362 BCE), which pitted against each other the great hegemonical or would-be hegemonical powers of Athens and Sparta (and later Thebes), with their respective allies and dominions.[2]

Of course, the analogy between the ancient cluster of wars and the medieval conflict might run the risk of seeming a mere *jeu d'esprit* prompted by the similarity in length of time. But it reflects something of the perception of at least some participants and witnesses. The historian Thucydides conceived of the clashes starting in the 460s (and even the tensions that began immediately after the defeat of the Achaimenid invasion of mainland Greece) as leading directly to the massive Athenian-Peloponnesian war, a world war that lasted from 431 to 404 BCE (with an "uneasy truce" between 421 and 413 and a bloody aftermath of civil war in Athens under Spartan protectorate). Thucydides's continuator Xenophon, in his *Greek Affairs* (*Hellēnika*), picked up Thucydides's unfinished narrative (with a self-effacing "and after these events"), and prolonged it with a survey of the multiple conflicts of the first half of the fourth century BCE, down to the indecisive battle of Mantineia (362 BCE). This date lies close to the ending point of another set of *Hellēnika* by the polymath Kallisthenēs of Olynthos, namely 357/6 BCE, the outbreak of the Third Sacred War, which would see the irruption of the Temenid monarchy of Macedonia into the world of the mainland *poleis*. The date also saw the start of the so-called Social War, an uprising marking the point when Athens finally lost control of most of its Aegean dominions (the war ended with Athenian discomfiture in 355 BCE).[3] Finally, this moment also saw the imposition of peace in Sicily, after decades of warfare and unrest, under the leadership of the Corinthian statesman-adventurer Timoleōn.[4]

Admittedly, the whole period 462–362 BCE (or 357, or 355) has not often been taken as a block by modern historians, who follow the lead of the ancient literary sources.[5] All the same, the expression "Hundred Years' War" conjures up images from its very formulation or by association with the high-medieval conflict,[6] which prove fruitful when looking at this particular portion of Greek history: diplomatic complexity and intractability; big wars and big battles, traditional warfare versus new tactics, including the use of specialized missile troops and mercenaries; the ground note of rural devastation (*chevauchées* in the fourteenth century CE, agricultural ravaging in antiquity); the importance of the nexus between money, the state, and long war; international bipolarity (here Plantagenet versus Valois, there Athens versus Sparta) but also local multipolarity in spite or because of the bipolar dynamics (hence the often vicious games played by Thebes, Arkadia, or Thessaly in the fifth and fourth centuries BCE, and by Burgundy, Britanny, or Spain in the fourteenth and fifteenth centuries CE).

The overarching classification as a single prolonged conflict precisely has the virtues of drawing attention away from individual vicissitudes (often bafflingly tangled, especially in the fourth century BCE), to larger factors and developments; namely, the temptation of empire and its costs in an age of world war. This age terminated with confusion and exhaustion, even if its echoes resonate down the 350s and even beyond. One such echo occurred in 324 BCE, when the Macedonian king (and conqueror of the Achaimenid empire) Alexandros III returned the island of Samos to its original inhabitants, the Samians whom the Athenians had expelled from the island in 364 BCE in order to colonize it (installing a *klērouchia*). When the Samians streamed back to the island, an Athenian force rounded them up and shipped them to Athens for execution, a fate thwarted only by the intervention of a Chalkidian friend of the Samians. The event is a last reminder of a terrible century of Athenian acquisitiveness and violence.

Yet the incident at Samos also hints at other developments. Conspicuous among them is the domination by supralocal kings, a phenomenon that would characterize the third century BCE; consequently, the *poleis* would have to find avenues of negotiation with such figures. Just as important is the existence of collaboration between *poleis*: once reinstated in their island, the Samians recorded the assistance they received from many other cities during their forty-year exile, in the form of acts of kindness to separate groups, which they choose to remember as sustaining the whole Samian community.[7]

Hence the fate of the Samians shows that there was more to this period than state violence (and civil war). The *polis* of Chalkis, on the island of Euboia, had escaped Athenian control at the end of the Peloponnesian War and, along with its neighbor and rival Eretria, lived an eventful political history of its own; likewise, the cities that helped the exiled Samians were moved by considerations of their own (including humanitarian concern) rather than the dynamics of high politics. The peer-polity interaction that characterized the earlier period, though it came under the terrible pressure of events, continued to function; indeed, political history and its vicissitudes had different repercussions, as their effects were distributed unequally across the vast, complex landscape of *poleis*. The survival and growth of a network of mutual help among *poleis* are also part of the story of the terrible hundred years and more of *polis* history this chapter (and indeed this section of the book) are concerned with.

The Short Fifth Century BCE in the Shadow of Athens

Our story starts after the defeat of the Achaimenid attempt at conquering mainland Greece. The fifth century BCE witnessed a tumultuous political history conducted on a large scale, and with greater means, than earlier—as noted by Thucydides, an eyewitness, minor participant, and major historian of the period. A salient feature of these decades is the competition for hegemony on a variety of scales: Athens was a major actor, at the level of high politics, but exercising durable impact on the whole spectrum of *polis* interactions. Athens had played an instrumental role in the defeat of the Persian expedition in 480–479 BCE on account of its massive fleet, which itself reflected Athenian advantages, structural and conjunctural, at this point in history. The most basic of those was the earlier discovery of a motherlode of silver ore. But it was the development of state institutions and collective consciousness that allowed these resources to be concentrated and deployed collectively rather than distributed to stakeholders; and the strong integrative ideology and constitutional practice of Kleisthenic Athens energized and mobilized the demographic resources of the very large Attic territory. In the first half of the fifth century BCE, the Athenian state occupied a leading position in the alliance of Greek states (in the Aegean) that kept on fighting the Achaimenid empire.[8] Perhaps unsurprisingly, Athens capitalized on this position, early on and with great energy and consistency, to further its own interests.

The outcome was the emergence, rapid consolidation, and extensive operation,[9] during the "short Athenian century" (478–404 BCE), of a large-scale, supralocal formation, in which hundreds of local communities in the Aegean islands, the northern seaboard, and the coastline of Asia Minor (fig. 7.1), paid cash tribute to the Athenian state. The latter largely monopolized the means of strategic violence in the form of a powerful war fleet, financed by tribute. Contemporaries simply referred to the Athenian *archē*, or rule (as in "the cities that the Athenians rule over").

Archē translated into various consequences, practical and ideological, over the local communities; the crudest of these was economic exploitation, in the form of the extraction of surplus, indirect taxation, and the seizure of landed assets by the state or private individuals, perhaps through economic pressure in response to tribute requirements, but most blatantly as punitive confiscation (for instance, after the revolt of Mytilēnē in 427 BCE).[10] Constant extraction produced astonishing levels of surplus—spent down on big projects or in wartime, often at a dizzying rate. The levying of tribute was also the reflection of an Athenocentric conceptualization of space.[11] The Athenians created an identity based on their political successes, but expressed in symbolic and religious terms of primacy over the rest of

FIGURE 7.1. The Athenian Empire and its tributary cities. From Low 2008, map 1.

the Ionian identity-group to which they belonged.[12] Combining empire and religion with shocking directness, Athenian gods and heroes (such as "Athēna who cares for Athens," "Iōn at Athens" and the Eponymous Heroes of the Athenian tribes) were big landowners in the territory of subject communities (notably receiving a tithe of confiscated property after revolt); boundary-stones from their estates have been found and studied by modern archaeologists.[13]

The prosperity and power of fifth-century BCE Athens during the "short Athenian century" are evident. Athenian prosperity is illustrated by the city's building activity, which transformed its aspect. An obvious example is the astonishing ensemble of marble building on the Akropolis, with three showpieces. The first was the monumental entranceway, or Propylaia (built 437–432 BCE). The second was the temple itself, the Parthenon (finished in 432), which served as a treasure house and a showcase for a lavish, colossal statue of Athēna in ivory and gold (the metal itself, attached in sheets to a timber shell, represented a considerable asset in itself). The third was another colossal statue, in bronze, of the same goddess, *Athēna Promachos* (front-fighting).[14] Further building activity shaped the public spaces, political and sacred, of the city, and also impacted the rest of the *polis*, in the form of temples and shrines at important sites: Sounion on the southern tip of Attica, Rhamnous, Eleusis, old sacred sites which received new sacred buildings.[15]

Athenian *archē* is also visible in the consumption of imported goods brought to the entrepot harbor of Athens, the Peiraieus, alongside imported grain, all this paid for by the cash extracted by the Athenian state and doled out to its citizens in return for military or political service. Fifth-century BCE Athenians were aware of this political economy and celebrated it, as we can see from the fragment of a comedy that jokily mingles actual goods with descriptions of political troubles:[16]

> Tell me, Muses dwelling in Olympia, which goods Dionysos has brought here on a black ship from the time he started trading on the wine-dark sea. From Kyrēnē silphium stalks and ox-hides; from the Hellespont mackerel and all kinds of dried fish; from Thessaly coarse salt and sides of beef; and from Sitalkēs an itch for the Spartans; and from Perdikkas many lies. Syracuse provides pork and cheese, (*lacuna*) . . . as for the Kerkyrans—may Poseidōn destroy them on their smooth ships, for they have a double heart. These goods from these places: and from Egypt, sails for rigging and cables, and from Syria, incense; fine Crete sends cypress for the gods, Libya plenty of ivory to buy, Rhodes sends raisins and dried figs which make good dreams, and from Euboia we get pears and fat apples—and slaves from Phrygia, and mercenaries from Arkadia, and Pagasai gives slaves and branded rascals; and the Paphlagonians provide acorns of Zeus and shiny almonds, for those are the ornament of the feast . . . (*text is corrupt*) the fruit of the palm and fine flour; Carthage, carpets and cushions.

The passage by the comic poet Hermippos reworks old images of plenty and happiness, which show the positive value ascribed to leisure and consumption as one of the consequences of political domination. Such aspirations contributed to shaping civic practice and discourses within Athens.[17] Some of the luxury items mentioned can be matched in documentary records, for instance the sale of the property of wealthy Athenians condemned for sacrilege in 414 BCE, including the famous Alkibiadēs (a great owner of cushions and fine furniture). The document corrects the impression of simplicity that later Athenians fondly liked to assign to their fifth-century BCE ancestors (and also shows the widespread landholdings that a rich Athenian could own in Euboia outside Athens).[18] The wealth of the richest Athenians, due to multiple interests inside and outside Attica, would persist long after the period of Athenian domination had disappeared (the politicians of fourth-century BCE Athens are noticeably wealthy, and invested in moneylending and long-distance trade).[19]

A more basic reflection of Athenian power and wealth is the increase in the number of citizens during the fifth century BCE. The Athenian heavy infantry had

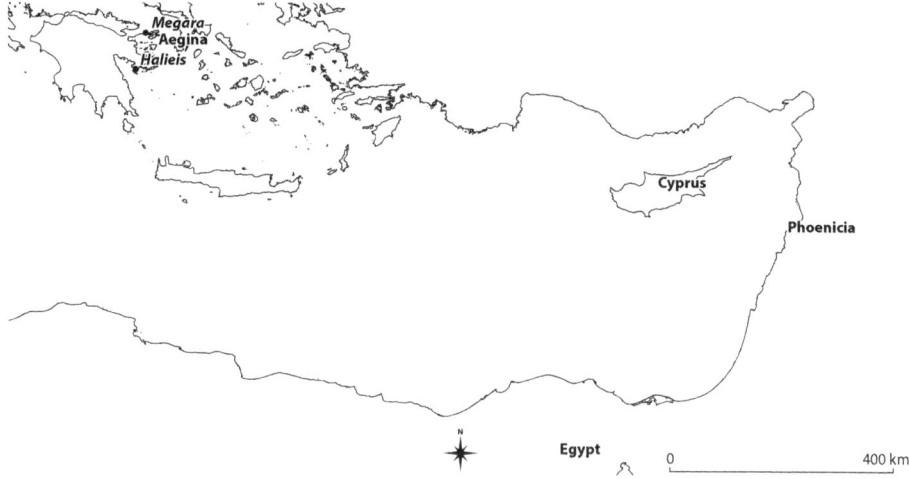

FIGURE 7.2. Places named in the heading of a tribal casualty list from Athens of 459 BCE (Osborne and Rhodes *GHI* 109).

numbered 9,000 in the all-out effort to defeat an Achaimenid landing force at Marathōn in 490 and 8,000 at Plataiai in 479; in 431 the figure reached 13,000 (counting only the men-at-arms between the ages of twenty and fifty, and hence leaving out perhaps 10,000 more "young and old," like those who perpetrated the atrocity at Corinth). The latter figures imply an enormous total adult male citizen population, of 60,000 or more.[20]

The troubles cheekily included by Hermippos among other imports echo, in their scale and geographical distribution—the Northern Aegean coast, the rival power of Sparta, Kerkyra near northwestern Greece—the hyperactive foreign policy and reach of the Athenian state in the fifth-century BCE. The same sense of reach and business is given by a public inscribed list of war casualties from 460 BCE, mentioning theatres of operation off mainland Greece, in Cyprus, Phoenicia, and Egypt (fig. 7.2).[21] The western areas of the world of the Greek *poleis* were also part of Athenian interests: involvement took the form of diplomatic contacts, colonizing ventures, and several military expeditions (the last one, sent to Sicily in 415, ended in disaster after a three-year-long battle before Syracuse).

The Athenian state was restless politically, economically self-interested and exploitative, dominant through overwhelming military means concentrated and deployed at a supralocal level, and coherently organized in administrative forms of control and extraction, to the benefit of a privileged ethnic group. In other words, it can usefully be described as a hyperpower with hegemonic ambitions, and as an empire or quasi-empire.[22] One of the inspirations was the example of the Achaimenid empire, a structure of domination and extraction to the profit of a class of Iranian masters.[23] It operated on an unprecedented scale, financial and geographical, outstripping any of the Late Bronze Age polities, and also the activities of the early *poleis*. The scale of Athenian strategic dominance in the eastern Mediterranean and the economic impact of imperial policies were also instruments of Athenian power. A highly visible case in point is to be found in the exclusion of Megarians, by then hostile to Athens, from all markets in the Athenian empire, at the outcome of conflict (the "Megarian decree" was one of the factors that precipitated coalition warfare against Athens). A slower event, but one with deep impact, was the disruption of economic connectivity between the Peloponnese, Crete, and Northern Africa, to the point that importations to Crete drop off throughout the "Athenian century": B. Erickson does not hesitate to see this as the effect of a deliberate, long-term Athenian policy of embargo.[24]

The Athenian empire had a heavy impact on many *poleis* that had earlier enjoyed prosperity and political agency—not just the rather small island-polis of Siphnos (above, pp. 121–24), but also major *polis* actors, with their own areas of control and initiative. Thasos lost its subordinate settlements on the continent, as well as its mines. Naxos revolted and was reduced by a siege; it is possible that the Athenian control of Dēlos, where it installed the treasury of the military alliance (478–445 BCE), disrupted the ancient interests of the Naxians in the sacred island. Aigina was besieged and reduced (as mentioned above, the atrocity at Megara happened after an attempt to relieve the siege).

Those cases are known only through scant notes in Thucydides; better known is the fate of Samos. The latter city revolted in 440, after the Athenian empire intervened in Samos's dispute with Milētos "over Priēnē"; that is, in a local conflict involving the perennial Samian claims on the mainland against those of Priēnē (the latter city being supported by its neighbor and sometimes ally Milētos). A faction seized power, freed the city from the Athenian garrison (which it handed over to the Achaimenid satrap)—and promptly resumed war with Milētos. A subsequent Athenian expedition was led by the Athenian college of generals (including the leading politician Periklēs as well as the tragedian Sophoklēs): it caught and defeated a Samian fleet as it returned from its attack on Milētos, and the Athenian empire relentlessly ratcheted up pressure, summoning successive Athenian and allied fleets to a total of 179 ships, if the figure in Thucydides's account is to be believed. In spite of some localized, temporary successes, the Samians succumbed to a siege and blockade of nine months, illustrated by savage repressive violence on the part of the Athenians.[25] The Samians were made to slight their sixth-century BCE fortification walls, surrender their war fleet, and pay back in installments the expenses incurred by Athens in war. In 439 BCE, Periklēs gave the oration over the Athenian war-dead, a patriotic ritual that belonged to the register of imperial auto-celebration perfected in fifth-century BCE Athens.[26]

The Samian war illustrates the disparity between the local horizons of conflict and agency, and the terrifying power and violence that the Athenian empire could bring to bear even on large actors within its space. The breaking of great *poleis*, with their own old histories of connectivity, expansion, and power, was in itself a demonstration of the qualitative superiority of the Athenian empire. Moreover, this sort of activity by the Athenian empire took place at a high level of interstate violence: at the end of the short Athenian century, after naval defeat, the population of Athens was caught in an agony of fear that it would be treated with the same devastating violence that it had meted out to other Greek states.[27]

For the short Athenian century is not just the story of the *archē* and resulting prosperity of the hyperpower. It is also the story of the reaction, namely resistance against imperial encroachment. Resistance took the form of competitive strategies of other *poleis* and especially of the *polis* network set in place by the peer-polity interactions of the sixth century BCE. The reaction took the form of three decade-long episodes of coalition warfare (460?–446, 431–421, 415–404 BCE), each of these increasingly well-organized and determined, against the Athenian empire (fig. 7.1). The effort was coordinated and even directed by the Spartan state, at the head of the formal confederacy of states that it led in war and that grew out of the unequal alliances set up in the sixth-century BCE Peloponnese (above, chapter 5)

After a protracted stalemate between the land-centered coalition and the seapower-based Athenian empire, and many strategic attempts at breaking the stalemate, the Athenian empire was finally defeated and dismantled. The determinant factor was a massive injection of Achaimenid money (after some hesitancy) on the side of the anti-Athenian, Spartan-led coalition. Persian gold enabled the Spartans to build up sufficient naval power to match and finally overcome the Athenians at sea, on the strategic element that had up to that point given them dominance and initiative.[28] The Spartan naval effort provoked, and was aided by, the mobilization of local communities from 412 BCE onwards (after the shocking defeat of the Athenian expedition to Sicily), especially those which had been under Athenian control. Furthermore, Spartan intervention created conditions in which these communities could reassert independence and stop regular payments of surplus, in the form of tribute or indirect taxation, to the Athenian imperial state (and indeed to the Persian state, a situation that was to prove troublesome subsequently).[29] The result was to unleash, or intensify, a diversity of messy local dynamics in the following years.

The Short Fourth Century BCE

The short Athenian century was itself followed by a short fourth century (404–362 BCE). This period is notable for the confusion of its multipolar competition over *archē* between the biggest actors—Sparta, Thebes at the head of the Boiotian League, Athens, and the regional entity of Thessaly. Furthermore, these decades were also a time of general confusion and conflict at many levels.[30] The apparent anarchy, however, was structured by deep features of *polis* history.

After the destruction of the Athenian empire, the Spartan state managed to maintain hegemony, in various forms and with varying degrees of success, for nearly three decades. Spartan hegemony took a number of forms: direct tributary control, garrisoning, integration within the Peloponnesian League, indirect influence and, especially, the intervention in local dynamics to dissolve preexisting and threatening regional structures, such as the Boiotian League. A crucial role was played by Achaimenid backing in the form of subsidies for a fleet but also authoritative pronouncement and arbitration (as dictated by the "King's Peace" of 386 BCE): the wars between the big Greek city-states were also a process by which their world was converted into a periphery of the Achaimenid system. The Spartans had to face repeated and prolonged episodes of coalition warfare directed against their power (just as the Athenians had), in 394 to 386 BCE, in 378 to 375 BCE, and almost immediately afterwards, from 375–371 BCE.[31] The conflicts opposed the overstretched Spartan state to various actors, especially the resurgent power of Athens, leading a broad naval league explicitly directed against Sparta. Equally active against Sparta, Thebes led a reconstituted (but far from unanimous) Boiotian League. The outcome was the loss of naval capacity for the Spartans after a series of defeats at sea and comprehensive defeat on land by the Theban-led coalition at Leuktra in southern Boiōtia (371 BCE) and Mantineia in the central Peloponnese (362 BCE).

The geographical distribution of the battlefields is itself revealing of the loss of Spartan power. The consequences were the dismantling of the old system of Spartan power, which had been set up in the seventh and sixth centuries BCE. The system had been based on several mutually reinforcing elements. First and most basic was the possession and exploitation of rich peripheral territory in the southern Peloponnese (especially Messēnia) through helotage. Second, and closely related, was the direct control of perioikic cities as part of a large, federal-like entity. The third ring in the circles of Spartan power was the indirect control of most Peloponnesian *poleis*, through divide-and-rule, prisoner's-dilemma techniques (specifically the collusion of local elite groups, the carefully gauged distribution of benefits in return for collaboration, and the application of violence on specific local actors by using other local actors). The latter techniques had been extended by the Spartan state to many other *poleis* in the Greek world—the cities of Iōnia after the Athenian defeat in 404 BCE, and indeed Athens itself; Boiotian cities (including Thebes); and Olynthos in the Chalkidikē, on the Northern Aegean seaboard.

The aftermath of Spartan collapse in 371 BCE saw an Athenian attempt at pursuing the old Athenian interests in the Aegean while continuing to direct a naval league of island *poleis*.[32] The seizure of Samos and expulsion of its inhabitants took place in 366 BCE, about the same time when Athens intervened to break up a confederacy of cities on the island of Keōs, and forcibly redirect export of local ruddle production to Athens exclusively.[33] A competing Theban effort at filling the void led to rather quixotic efforts at building a fleet and attracting Persian patronage (367 BCE) and at fostering Spartan-style zones of control, influence, and collusion in the Peloponnese and Northern Greece. By the end of the 350s BCE, it was clear that both the Athenian and the Theban attempts had failed. The islanders constantly strove for their freedom, and major members of Athens's naval league in the Aegean revolted, leaving the League much diminished.[34] Theban military supremacy by land soon reached its limits, both in the Peloponnese and in Central Greece, where it was contested with a surprising degree of success by the Phokians, who drew on the sacred treasures at Delphi to finance a high-performing army of mercenaries.

The faltering of Theban military capacity sheds light on determinant factors during the short fourth century BCE. One is the contradictory coexistence of undiminished financial needs for the conduct of hegemonical politics (through naval means or hired professional infantrymen), with the absence of financial means comparable to those enjoyed by the Athenian empire in the preceding century. The Spartan system did attempt a system of financial contributions from its subordinate allies,[35] and the Athenian naval league of the fourth century BCE also depended on contributions. But the limited realities of the period are shown by the often crude, smash-and-grab nature of naval expeditions at the very end of the fifth century BCE and throughout the short fourth century, and generally the much smaller size of military ventures (Athens in the fourth century BCE could mobilize 6,000 hoplites, and that with difficulty, a far cry from the demographically abundant imperial city of the fifth century BCE).[36] The lack of means for even the Athenian state in this period to meet the logistical and financial needs of the great game is noted by contemporaries such as Xenophon, the pamphleteer and historian, and Dēmosthenēs, a major politician of late Classical Athens.[37]

Another important factor is the sheer dynamism and complexity of local politics (in the sense of interactions between smaller *poleis*), especially once a number of paralyzing factors had dwindled away. One of these factors was the fifth-century bipolarity between the complementary enemies, Sparta and Athens. Even more important was the end of the deadening effect of Athenian direct control, and of the Spartan system of power in the Peloponnese. Once freed, Peloponnesian affairs notably involved incidents of protracted microregional warfare around the shrine at Olympia, control of which was disputed between Ēlis, a variety of communities inside Ēlis claiming their independence, and the Arkadians, Sikyonians, and Messenians. The presence of the latter two *poleis* illustrates how local conflicts embroiled actors outside their immediate context.[38] The conflict led to a running battle in the Olympic shrine itself, during the Olympic festival of 364 BCE and its athletic contests. At a higher level of politics, the battle of Mantineia in 362 BCE involved the Spartans against the Thebans, but also a whole host of other powers—Arkadian cities on either side, the new cities of Messēnē and Megalēpolis, founded to check Spartan power, and even Athens, once an ally of Thebes, but now fighting on the Spartan side. The battle ended with a Spartan defeat but also with the death of the able Theban commander Epameinōndas, one of the creators of the Theban expansion; the aftermath, as Xenophon tersely notes, was more *tarachē*, disturbance, for the whole Greek world.

Big and Small in the Hundred Years

The opposition between big and small is a leitmotif during the political history of the Hundred Years. The Athenians provoked hatred by their attitude to *mikropolitai*, the inhabitants of small cities; the Persian king's peace promised freedom to *poleis* big and small—and has to be seen as part of the long history of the *polis*.[39] The dynamics of big and small were present from the start of the story of the *polis*. Hesiod's wariness about the *basileis* is also a story of the relation between a big site (Thespiai) and a smaller one (Askra); early *polis* history is largely about structuration within *polis* territories and between *poleis* as unequal relations of domination and dependency (above, chapter 3).

The old story of the relations of power and dependency between big and small continues throughout the Hundred Years: the story of Thespiai illustrates this clearly (fig. 7.3). This *polis* was a dominant player, controlling smaller settlements either as dependent *poleis*, or as sub-*polis* establishments within its territory: in the 470s BCE, an arbitration involving various Greek states mentions "the Thespians and those with them." The expression shows that Thespiai headed a hierarchical federation of local *poleis*, which they led in terms of foreign policy. Perhaps a century later, a dedication showed Thespian control over the sacred vessels in a number of smaller settlements within the greater Thespian territory.[40] In the early fourth century BCE, Thespiai seems to have destroyed Askra, the old settlement where Hesiod had lived, as part of its drive toward territorial control.[41]

But Thespiai was also a smaller *polis* than Thebes, albeit large enough to be a problem: hence the Theban effort at breaking Thespian power, which culminated in the destruction of the urban site and the expulsion of its inhabitants. Nor was Thespiai unique in Boiōtia: the grand old *polis* of Orchomenos claimed mythic eminence in Boiōtia, controlled other smaller Boiotian *poleis* such as Chairōneia or Hyēttos—and suffered the same fate as Thespiai.[42] The Theban domination of Boiōtia, always latent in the "Archaic" and high Classical periods, was realized in the late Classical period (in the period of liberation and then expansion after 378 BCE) by such events; Xenophon's habit of speaking of policies of the "Thebans" rather than of the Boiotian League, though technically loose, reflects Theban predominance.

Hierarchical structuration can be seen, during the Hundred Years, in the case of a number of large *polis* actors already familiar from the "Archaic" period. Largest and most successful was the enormous state formation of Sparta, leading subordinate *poleis* and non-Spartan allies in a hegemonical alliance. But Sparta was not unique in this respect, and it is worth mentioning examples of this sort of arrangement because it gives a sense of the baseline of inter-*polis* relations in this period. Ēlis controlled a number of subordinate *poleis* in the northwestern Peloponnese, a situation that created continued unrest and tension with neighbors and with Sparta.[43] In the crisis that precipitated the "Peloponnesian War" in 433/2 BCE, the

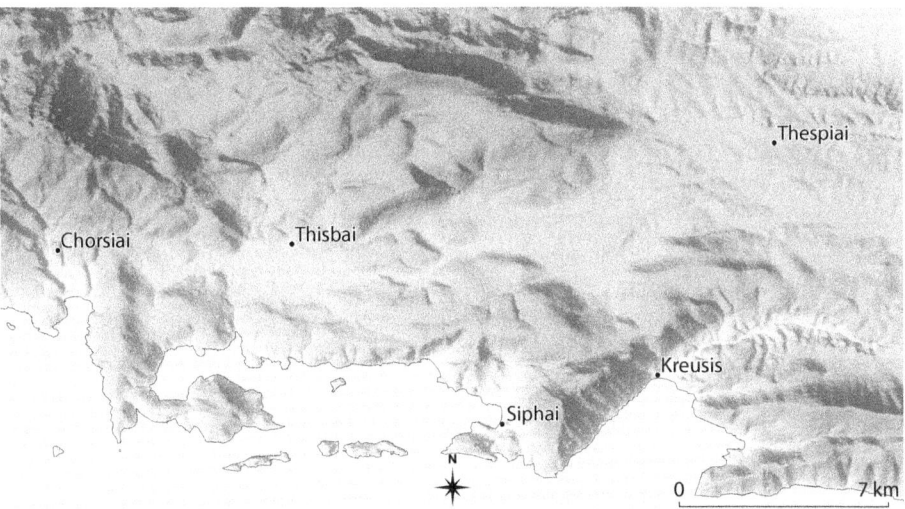

FIGURE 7.3. The Greater Thespiai: A Boiotian city and its neighbors in the Classical period.

Corinthians drew on the resources of a number of *poleis* over which it enjoyed some form of domination or preeminence, either because these were Corinthian foundations, or because of Corinthian influence.[44] The Thessalian city of Pherai claimed to rule over a territory that included other *poleis*;[45] the situation is the same as that of Opous's dominant role within eastern Lokris (see above, p. 154).

In the Chalkidikē peninsula, the *poleis* joined together in a federal formation around Olynthos, an earlier city that was enlarged to serve as the central Big Place for the federation, and indeed dominated it as the Thebans did the Boiotian League: Xenophon likewise speaks of the "Olynthians" when describing the expansion and power of the Chalkidian League (not to be confused with Chalkis in Euboia, of course). For the Olynthos-dominated league proved to be a powerful, ambitious state, expanding to include many local (non-Chalkidian) city-states, and indeed cities taken from the neighboring kingdom of Macedonia.[46] At a smaller level, Mantineia, in Arkadia, tried to dominate or absorb neighboring *poleis* (Helissōn was annexed and assimilated to a *komâ* or village, like the four or five original settlements synoikized to form the city).[47] Mytilēnē dominated a number of *polismata* on the mainland and even tried to synoikize the cities of the island of Lesbos in 428 BCE as a prelude to revolt from Athens; the same sense of superiority might appear in a fleeting mention of possible Mytilenaian leadership of the island in 389 BCE, this time with Athenian support.[48] Similar relations are also apparent in Sicily and southern Italy, where big *poleis* such as Syracuse dominated smaller ones, often in connection with the aggressive policies of monarchical rulers (a pattern already evidenced in the late sixth and early fifth centuries BCE); for instance, Syracuse controlled the (Hellenized) settlement of Morgantina, but passed it on to Kamarina in return for payment.[49]

Yet even against this baseline, the extraordinary nature of the imperial experiment in *archē* conducted by Athens during the short Athenian century is starkly apparent. Athenian power was qualitatively different from the old-style hierarchical formulas. The scale involved, the financial resources, the sustained state violence and pressure that these resources enabled—all of these were perceived as different and overwhelming by contemporaries, as portrayed by Thucydides. The Athenian historian weaves together descriptions of Athenian imperial hyperpower by Athenians (such as Periklēs) and a variety of non-Athenians (observers, victims, opponents), such as the Corinthians on the eve of war, the Boiotian general Pagōndas leading an army against a bold Athenian invasion, the citizens of the small island *polis* of Mēlos trying to resist violent conquest and dispossession, or the Syracusans resisting a conquering armada of Athenians and allies.[50]

The Athenian successes (in spite of the defeat that concluded the short Athenian century) constituted an example, or temptation, for many—hence the hegemony-driven high politics of the fourth century BCE. The Athenians' attempt at recovering their interests in the Aegean in the 360s BCE can be seen as a "ghost of empire" (E. Badian)—the lack of real means makes the repeated efforts (and the sporadic successes) all the more noticeable.[51] The Spartan attempts to expand their system outside of the Peloponnese took place on a staggeringly ambitious scale, beyond anything tried during the dynamic sixth-century BCE adventures; the Theban power drive started with a crushing of local peers unlike the normal competition between Boiotian *poleis*, and created lasting ill will in Boiōtia and the Greek world. Even if most *poleis* did not have access to the resources for imperial or quasi-imperial ventures, the ideals and aspirations embodied by the Athenian experiment influenced political language and ideas—and more directly, the violent power politics of the big *poleis* had an impact on the world of local inter-*polis* interaction.

The impact of Athenian inspiration and failure left a deep mark on the whole of the Hundred Years. The activities of the Spartiate power elite, and the state they led, can be seen as more than just the maintenance of the old system of power. In the 470s BCE, the rise of Athenian imperial power by itself destabilized the old structures of Spartan power in the Peloponnese. In the late fifth and early fourth centuries BCE, the Spartan state intervened to crush attempts at building local, unequally structured formations by Ēlis, Mantineia, Olynthos, and Thebes: the techniques that were deployed (massive force, siegeworks, local collusion), and the intolerance of local powers reflect an imperial vision, as does the assumption that Spartan *fiat* could decide on local status (the Athenian empire had been based on the same assumptions).[52] The systematic extension of the framework of the Peloponnesian League to broader geographical horizons, with the necessary shifts in structure, can also be seen as a response to the Athenian example and to the possibilities opened by Athenian activities. Below the level of the state, the taste of individual Spartans (elite and nonelite) for activities abroad reflects the possibilities offered by empire:[53] economic profit, status promotion, and adventure, all concrete forms of imperialism on the ground. The Thebans' brave attempt at *archē* beyond the control of Boiōtia (combining Athenian-style naval means and Spartan-style interventionism) was a deliberate attempt to occupy an Athenian-like position of dominance, and to "remove the Propylaia to the Kadmeia," the ancient mound that was the heart of the city of Thebes.[54]

In practice, the aspiration to empire took a great variety of forms, some surprising. Thucydides shows the Spartans offering the Athenians joint hegemony over the Greeks, and the Syracusans dreaming of hegemony with the Corinthians and the Spartans as being one of the outcomes of their defeat of the Athenian armada in 415-413 BCE.[55] The *polis* of Syracuse would go on to exercise hegemony over many *poleis* of Sicily and southern Italy, in an extraordinarily messy history involving the destruction of *poleis* and the deportation of populations. This story starts in the early fifth century BCE with its "tyrants," but its later developments were made possible by the high politics of the Hundred Years' War.[56]

One consequence of the heightened scale of politics because of hegemony is the presence of monarchical behavior as an option to which domination might lead. In an Athens which compared itself to a monarch, the decade-long high tide of Athenian imperialism coincided with the dominant position of one individual, Periklēs, repeatedly elected to the generalship.[57] The Spartan war-leader Lysandros, after the defeat of Athens, engaged in monarchical behavior (such as restoring by fiat local statuses or personal political patronage), and his status was recognized by unprecedented gestures in the form of honorific statues or even cultic honors.[58] Spartan institutions and pressures soon cut Lysandros down to size; but the figure who was instrumental in controlling Lysandros, the king Agēsilaos, proved to be an even more charismatic and powerful individual in fourth-century BCE Spartan history.[59] Agēsilaos's opponents, the Theban military leaders and politicians Epameinōndas and Pelopidas, also illustrate the age's tendency toward powerful individuals characterized by their love for war and hegemony, and their disregard for local constitutional niceties.

Among the many powerful individuals active in the fourth century BCE,[60] the most monarchical were the dynasts or strongmen of certain cities of Thessaly, of whom the most formidable was Iasōn of Pherai. Iasōn used a standing force of mercenaries and tactical innovations to gain supremacy over other cities of Thessaly, and hence the ancient position of *tagos*, leader, of the whole of the Thessalian regional entity, and of the traditionally dependent communities on the edge of Thessaly. Xenophon portrays his expansionist ambitions, based on his use of the resources of tribute, dependent manpower, aristocratic cavalry for shock troops, and strategic resources in foodstuffs and timber to create a large army and sizable fleet in order to seize *archē* in Greece; he also portrays Iasōn's skillful diplomacy in the aftermath of the Spartan defeat by the Thebans at Leuktra.[61] Iasōn was murdered during a cavalry muster in 370 BCE, but his combination of autocratic power, imperialist ambition, proactive diplomacy, and overwhelming military means would prove the winning solution at the end of the late Classical period, in the hands of the tyrants of Syracuse, Dionysios I and Dionysios II (as well as the adventurer Timoleōn, who was not far removed from a tyrant himself), and especially of the Argead kings Philippos II and Alexandros III (whom modern historians describe as Alexander the Great). Yet if instead of looking forward, we cast a glance back at earlier periods, we see that Iasōn worked within the traditional framework of power in Thessaly, namely the expansionist ambitions of a regional entity with serfs and dependent populations of "dwellers-around" (*perioikoi*). What Iasōn illustrates is the way in which the inspiration of Athenian *archē* exacerbated preexisting structures of power, such as the hierarchical regional relations and the monarchical-despotic tendencies in Thessaly.

It is equally important to realize that the presence of hegemony exacerbated other preexisting features, namely the possibility of small-scale politics as reactions and resistance to dominating drives: the dynamics of "big and small" could cut both ways. Attempts at regional dominance were countered by choices that can be observed even at very local levels, in cascades of breakaway dynamics. In response to pressures from Athens, regional units tried to create coherent entities that might have sufficient joint resources to resist or to act independently, such as the federal formations of the Chalkidians, of the Keian *poleis*, or the *poleis* on Lesbos under Mytilenian leadership. The Arkadian *poleis* joined in a league in the aftermath of Leuktra, perhaps with encouragement from the Theban leaders who started the Boiotian involvement in the Peloponnese. In turn, these regional units were met by recalcitrance from local *poleis* who preferred to avoid integration within these regional units, such as Mēthymna on Lesbos, Akanthos in the Chalkidikē peninsula, or Poiēssa on Keōs; Tegea and Heraiōn (a large and a small Peloponnesian city) resisted integration in the Arkadian League.[62] The behavior of Thespiai or Orchomenos, in Boiōtia, is another example of breakaway dynamics within a bigger entity, the Theban-led league, which was both a Theban power venture and a form of resistance to the pressure exercised by the Spartan state.

Poleis in Collaboration beyond the Ironies of Autonomy

In spite (or because) of these complicated eddies, the "federal" solution of regional structuration, with political institutions and ideological bonds, proved popular during the Hundred Years, developing trends that were already strong in the "Archaic" period. The Arkadian League or the Boiotian Leagues showed great inventiveness in constitutional matters, looking for forms within which to pool resources and to achieve working political representation of regional populations: the results were refined constitutional arrangements for deliberation, problem-solving, and implementation.[63] The Boiotian League in particular elaborated a complicated system of rotating representation, which were mirrored at the local level. These arrangements were simplified when the league was recreated under Theban leadership, but with the same need to ensure some form of representation for all member *poleis* through subdivisions and institutions. This particular aspect was to develop with great success during the following centuries in a number of regions.

Not all structuration had to be oppressive, even during the turbulent Hundred Years. An *ad hoc* arrangement such as the alliance of *poleis* in Asia Minor, led by the Spartiate king Agēsilaos in his war against the Persian empire, produced a number of solutions for the distribution of burdens, representation, and dispute resolution, that were essentially benign (even if the war itself was one of the forms taken by Spartan expansionism and adventurism in the fourth century BCE).[64] From this viewpoint, the Athenian "empire" itself might be understood in this context as a form of supralocal structuration and negotiation. At the very least, it started this way, as the continuation of the wartime alliance against the Persian empire, and also relied on federal institutions of consultation. Even in its developed, quasi-imperial, para-Achaimenid form, it could always be seen as an extreme version of structuration around a *polis*, in a sort of super-federal state.[65] In the fourth century BCE, at least for several decades or so (378–338 BCE), as we have seen, Athens reverted to this type of organization to create the naval league that resisted Spartan imperialism, with multilateral guarantees and constitutionalism.

Imperial aspirations mattered and affected many individuals and communities, yet the history of the Hundred Years cannot be reduced to the violent spasms of power competition, large scale or micro-imperialist, as portrayed in Thucydides's story of ships, walls, money and power—the story that he tries to naturalize in his brilliant reconstruction of early Greek history as driven by power dynamics, in the opening chapters of his history of the Athenian-Spartan War. To follow this construct unreservedly would be to fall into the real "Thucydides trap"—the belief in an unreservedly realist world structured by violence and self-interest. It is tempting to see Thucydides himself as trapped into naturalizing the particularly intense violence of the conflict between Athens and the Peloponnesian League (just as A. de Custine's vision of an essentially autocratic Russia might be naturalizing the particular situation under Nicholas I).

The same holds true for "Xenophon's trap," an equally tragic picture often in the ironical mode, showing a messy conflict of actors big and small (tellingly, the same ironical mode is adopted by Thucydides in Book 5 of his historical work, when exploring power politics in the Peloponnese at a time of Spartan weakness and general flux).[66] This picture of violent anarchy, on close reexamination, proves to be much more nuanced and complex, with plenty of scope for interaction along the lines of accepted norms and practices. In this world, there is a place for treaties (whose clauses were often enforced through collective violence by the wronged or their defenders, and always insisted on), arbitration (frequently resorted to, and not always ineffective), religious norms, kinship diplomacy, shared Greekness, and the reputation of *polis* actors before their peers.

Very often, political actors in difficult situations were faced with a diversity of solutions, varying from moral conduct to brute force to institutionalized compromises. The people of Mytilēnē fought enthusiastically against Spartan-led hegemony, under Athenian leadership, and influenced others to do so: the point is not so much to resist Spartan encroachment (from which geography protected the Mytilenians) as a real sense of commitment to international norms (indeed, after the Spartan defeat, the Mytilenians questioned the rationale for the continuing of the Athenian-led alliance).[67] The Athenian assembly and its politicians, or the Spartiate assembly and the various power-holders in the Spartiate elite, had to take such factors into account; even if Athens or Sparta, or smaller powers, ended up choosing to pursue self-interest, this choice always came at a cost, and the accounts of Thucydides and Xenophon, rather than the cold celebration or jaded retelling of *Realpolitik*, might be seen as its condemnation as violent, unsustainable transgression of norms.

The mounting costs of raw power politics doomed imperial aspirations, starting with the Athenian *archē*. Resistance was coordinated, as we saw above. Coordination took part under the leadership of big *poleis*, but around norms, especially the norm of *autonomia*, which we might translate as self-government and determination— perhaps even republican government. M. Hansen has strenuously argued for downgrading the importance of *autonomia* as unessential to the *polis*; yet the whole tragic narrative of the Hundred Years proclaims its importance.[68] Indeed, the narratives of Thucydides and Xenophon can be viewed as engagements with, or meditations on, the importance and conundrums of autonomy; hence Xenophon's interest in the possibility of agency for a small *polis* such as Phleious in the Peloponnese, between big powers and internal factions.[69]

The concept of autonomy appears during the fifth century BCE, probably as a reaction to the development of Athenian hyperpower.[70] The coalition wars against Athens, Sparta, or Thebes might be seen specifically as articulated efforts of the whole *polis* network at regulating and limiting power politics, especially since the latter had a vicious accelerating effect on local relations and structures. This local effect could also be limited by the application of norms. The *poleis* of northwestern Greece, after fighting an eye-wateringly horrible war as proxies of Athens and Sparta, reached their own agreement, explicitly refusing participation in the big powers' war; the treaty was still being renewed more than a century later. Similar processes took place in Sicily, after a period of exacerbated local warfare because of Athenian involvement in disputes between *poleis*.[71]

None of this should engage us to exaggerate the benign nature of the phenomenon. The norm of autonomy was itself riddled with paradoxes and ironies. Its existence forced compromises and ironies. Diplomatic negotiations invented situations where cities were both autonomous and tribute paying (as was the fate of Aigina after its conquest, or the cities of the North Aegean in the truce of 421 BCE);[72] ugly compromises such as the peace of 405/4 BCE between Dionysios I, the tyrant of Syracuse, and the Carthaginians, involved some *poleis* reduced to occupying defenseless sites and paying tribute to Carthage, some living autonomously (including the *polis* of Leontinoi, resurrected after a long period as a fort of Syracuse), and confirmation of Dionysios's personal power over Syracuse.[73] The principle of autonomy for cities big and small, as enshrined in the King's Peace of 386 BCE, allowed Spartan intervention in local politics in a variety of locales: Ēlis, Boiōtia, Mantineia, the Chalkidikē, and often with a remarkable degree of cynicism.[74] The protection of the autonomy of small *poleis* took place at the expense of larger *poleis*, or groups of *poleis*, through the action of a large, overwhelmingly powerful state: autonomy allowed for conquest and oppression.

In the case of Mantineia, the Spartans, pursuing their own goals of control in the Peloponnese after eight years of warfare, went so far as to break up the *polis* into constituent subparts and reverse urban concentration, in order to create elite-dominated clusters.[75] Mantineia also must have lost control over smaller *poleis* that it had absorbed, such as Helissōn. The latter's integration with Mantineia had been regulated by an agreement between the two communities, big and small, and the inscribed version partly survives (the inhabitants of Helissōn appear in a dialectal form that I reproduce below). It illustrates how the norms of *polis* life—in this case, not autonomy, but *polis*-hood itself—can be used to mediate power relations:

> Agreement between the Mantineians and Heliswasians [in good faith]. It was decided by the Mantineians and the Heliswasians: The Heliswasians are to be Mantineians, equal and the same, sharing in all things even as the Mantineians, bringing their territory and *polis* to Mantineia to the laws of the Mantineians and, while the *polis* of the Heliswasians is to remain as it is for all time, they are to be a *kōmē* of the Mantineans. There shall be a *theōroi* from Helissōn as from the other *poleis*; they are to make sacrifices in Helissōn and receive *theōriai* as before. Heliswasians and Mantineians are to pursue legal claims against each other according to the laws of the Mantineans from the point when the Heliswasians become Mantineians—after that point—but decisions in cases concluded previously are not to be subject to legal challenge. Whatever contracts the Heliswasians happen to have concluded amongst themselves before they became Mantineians are to remain valid for them according to the laws that they had when they joined Mantineia . . .

The agreement exploits the ambiguity of the term *polis*, both state and urban settlement, to negotiate the integration of the people of Helissōn into the community of the Mantineians to whom they contribute "their territory and their *polis*," while retaining some religious institutions.[76] Far from showing that a community could become a *kōmē* (village) of a *polis* and yet retain *polis*-hood (as M. Hansen writes), the document represents a compromise or a fudge, allowing the Mantineians to annex Helissōn, and the inhabitants of the latter to try to misrecognize annexation.[77] No doubt the Mantineians hoped that the compromise would last long enough for the annexation to solidify: their strategic use of *polis*-hood is a small-scale equivalent to the Spartan leveraging of *autonomia* to impose control on cities such as Mantineia itself.

Yet the care taken by the Mantineians to find compromise it still revealing of the importance of *polis* self-determination: the Heliswasians did not agree to outright annexation but wanted to keep at least the possibility of believing in their existence as a *polis*, and the Mantineians had to acknowledge this wish, and hence had to cast their power in acceptable terms, both locally and in terms recognizable in international terms. Away from the vicissitudes of domination, the workings of the peer network of *poleis* became features of routine. Relations were increasingly regulated by norms of reciprocity and obligation, commitments, and peer links, which created multilateral connections within the network of *poleis*.[78]

One symptom of the operation of international norms and autonomy is the economic boom that starts in the mid-fourth century BCE. In contrast with the boost that empire and tribute gave fifth-century BCE Athens, this phase of economic growth is more distributed, encompassing the islands.[79] It results from greater availability of income across the Aegean, rather than its concentration in an imperial capital; the Aegean was free not just from the burden of Athenian tribute, taxation, and acquisitiveness, but also from the distorting effects of Athenian strategic power. Economic growth also resulted from the operation of norms of cooperation, not the bursts of violence between cities. The economic efflorescence of the later fourth century BCE is as premonitory as the temptation to monarchy: it announces an age of *polis* prosperity, solidarity, and collaboration—in the long run.

8

Political History (2)

POLITEIA AND STASIS

It would not be wise to hate a stranger because his interests are opposed to ours, whereas it is natural and reasonable to hate a fellow citizen who stands against what one thinks is useful and good.

—A. FRANCE, *FARINATA DEGLI UBERTI, OR, CIVIL WAR*

Inside the *Poleis*

In 392 BCE, during a war between Sparta and a coalition of *poleis* including Athens, Thebes, Argos, and Corinth, a grim episode of civil war took place in the last-named city. In a single coordinated attack during the festival of Artemis Eukleia, the pro-war party in Corinth fell upon the proponents of peace. At a signal, as Xenophon describes the scene, "these men drew their swords and struck those they had been told to kill: one while standing among a circle of friends, another sitting down, another in the theater, some while sitting as judge in the contests." The scene presents a selective tableau of death caused by the neutron bomb of factional conflict going off during a civic festival. Some were killed among the statues and the altars in the *agora* (a frequent feature in stories of massacre among citizens). Some young men, who had stayed in the *gymnasion* and escaped the first wave of slaughter, took refuge on the Akrokorinthos (the huge rocky citadel above the city) and negotiated safe passage; they later appealed to Sparta for intervention on their side, especially when their opponents brought the city into *sumpoliteia* (political union) with Argos.[1]

Just like the atrocity at Megara in 460 BCE, the episode at Corinth had earlier antecedents; for instance, the slaughter of pro-Athenian democrats by the elite at Aigina (above, p. 126). In the context of the Hundred Years, it acts as a reminder that the *poleis* were not monolithic entities, and as an invitation to explore political and social life within them. The massacre and its aftermath offer a macabre reminder of what constituted normal life in Corinth: the unifying rhythms of the civic festival, the sociability of small circles and age groups, the built spaces of the urban center, the institutions of the state.[2] All of these elements continue trends and phenomena apparent in the late sixth century BCE. They are characteristic of the developed forms and discourses of the *polis* in the fifth and fourth centuries BCE, as documented in a rich archaeological, epigraphical, and literary record across the Greek world, from Sicily to Asia Minor and the Black Sea—a world richly saturated in *polis*-hood.

It is not my purpose here (in spite of my love of testcases) endlessly to illustrate the *polis*'s various material, institutional and discursive manifestations in and around the Hundred Years, but it is important to notice how, for all their variety, they point toward a unitary phenomenon of the *polis* as city and as state. For instance, Argos appears to us endowed with the trappings of *polis*-hood. It embellished and formalized its *agora* with a colonnaded meeting hall. To the east, the nearby steep slope was cut back to provide a large-scale public meeting place with seating (a "theatre" or assembly gathering place), and a smaller open space for judicial meetings was carved out further along the same slope.[3] Olynthos, center of the federation of cities in the Chalkidikē, offers the spectacle of a new city plan, laid out in a careful grid alternating equal plots of housing and big public spaces (fig. 8.1).[4] To the west, Kamarina, a city in Sicily with a complicated story of foundation and refoundations, affords a glimpse of a complex civic organization in fifteen "brotherhoods" (*ph(r)atrai*) and lower subdivisions ("twenties"). Kamarina's system of civic subdivisions is documented by a cache of small lead plates or strips, bearing the name, patronymic, and *phratra* of individual citizens: such objects were used in the *polis*'s institutional workings, namely allotment for office or jury service.[5]

Similar, though simpler, lead tablets found from Styra, in Euboia, may have fulfilled the same functions (they occasionally mention civic subdivisions).[6] On the same island of Euboia, but on a vaster scale, Eretria broke free during the travails of the Athenian state in 412, and expanded its territory (to the point of absorbing Styra). The territory had to be reorganized to articulate the human community and the rural territory, so as to make it into civic space: the Eretrias was organized into six tribes, which grouped local settlements (*dēmoi*) chosen from five subdivisions (*choroi*), thus unifying territory and people through the mediation of civic structures.[7] Likewise, the complex organization of the population and territory of Argos (in tribes and "brotherhoods" but also in villages) can be related to the vicissitudes of high politics and expansion.[8] Monumentalization, expansion, and civic subdivisions reflect normal structural features of the "Classical" Greek world: demographic plentifulness, and a booming economy based on cash crops, monetization, division of labor, and slavery. We will return below to the relationship between these features and the political and social form of the *polis* and its institutions.[9]

But in 392 BCE, the swordwork of murderous partisans as they swooped down on the sociability of a festival and the civic spaces of the city was anything but normal. The situation is explicitly described by Xenophon as conflict between "the

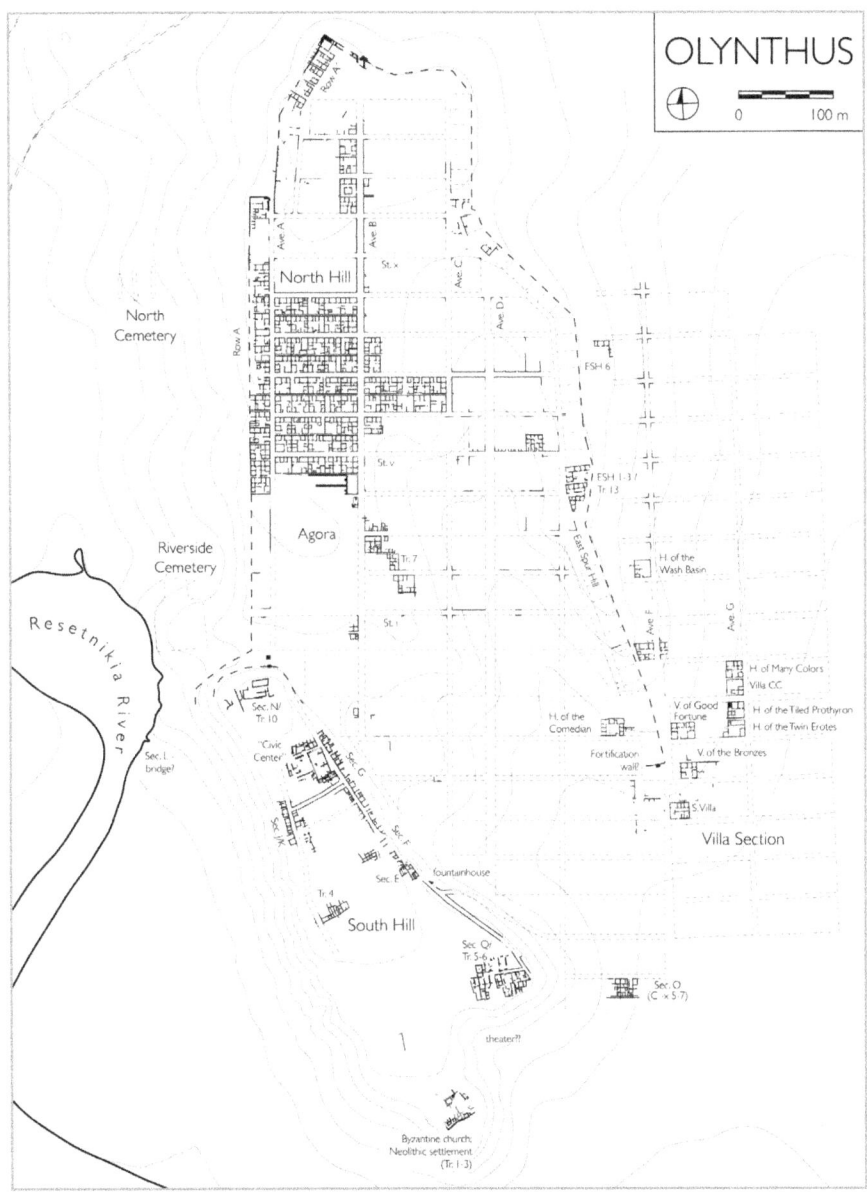

FIGURE 8.1. Plan of Olynthos (before 348 BCE). From Cahill 2002.

best" (*hoi beltistoi*), whom he tendentiously also would like to be "the most numerous," partisans of peace with Sparta, and another faction that he stigmatizes as partisans of war corrupted by Achaimenid subsidies, but which might well be a pro-Athenian democratic party. The Hundred Years were also the time of the sharpening of questions that we saw in abeyance at the end of the "Archaic" period—who is a member, who should rule, why, and how. The alternative between the different solutions, exemplified by the two best-documented and most emblematic cases, "Classical" Athens and Sparta, is the theme of this chapter—alongside the travails that the alternative inflicted on other *poleis* during the Hundred Years.

The Constitution of the Athenians

It is of course a cliché in ancient history that Athens is the best-documented Classical city-state.[10] What matters here is that the mass of evidence allows us to tell the detailed story of this one *polis*, the Athenians at a particular period (480–322).[11] A crucial moment came with the adoption during the fifth century BCE of a whole package of measures that widened political participation and access to power. Censitary barriers to state office were loosened and finally ignored.[12] The state resorted to the systematic use of the lot to choose officials, such as the Councilors; concomitantly, we see a multiplication of these officials,[13] both in the functions fulfilled and in the number of officials in each function, and the frequent rotation of officeholders. There were some exceptions (notably the board of ten generals, repeatedly electable), but it is remarkable that the crucially important 500-strong Council, or the old and prestigious offices of *archōn*, were filled by lot out of a preselected list. In the case of the Councilmen, this took place according to a system of quotas structured by the system of ten tribes and uniting the whole Attic territory in special subdivisions drawing from town, inland, and coastal regions.

Furthermore, citizens received compensation or pay (*misthos*) for office (yearlong) or for service, for instance for a day's service in the jury courts, but also for service as a priest or as a poet writing works for festival performance;[14] even attendance at the Assembly was eventually compensated. Finally, judicial matters were routinely referred to very large jury courts that represented the citizen body (Dēmosthenēs could address the Athenian people, as represented by Council and Assembly, while speaking before a court),[15] and general administrative oversight was transferred from the old standing Council of the Areiopagos to the Council of Five Hundred or the courts. Such oversight notably involved the continuous examining and controlling of power holders: officeholders were subject to testing before office (*dokimasia*), the public auditing of accounts and examining of behavior upon exit of office (*euthunai*), and the constant confirmation of suitability during office.

A history of Athenian constitutional development can be fitfully outlined. Some changes occurred during the first half of the fifth century BCE, but the main body of institutional innovations took place during the two crucial but quite mysterious decades between 460 and 440 BCE. The intellectual and cultural genealogy of Athenian constitutional practice remains obscure: the availability of money, in the form of imperial tribute, undoubtedly played an enabling role. It is also clear that far from being a smooth institutional development, the history of Athenian democracy was notably marked by two terrible if short-lived coups, after setbacks and final defeat in the Peloponnesian War, in 411 and 403 BCE, by narrow cliques.

The trauma of those oligarchical episodes had a deep impact on public discourse, civic spaces, and institutional practice, all of which were reshaped in their aftermath.[16] A codification of all Athenian laws took place after the first coup; after the second, the principle of the primacy of laws over decrees was confirmed and turned into a major principle of the workings of Athenian democracy. Laws themselves were not passed by the Assembly, but by a special body of Legislators; the enforcement of laws and decrees was entrusted to the law courts, which were smaller than the full Assembly and drawn from a different pool of citizens (since there was a minimum-age limit on service in the jury panels). These changes have suggested to some scholars a shift in the nature of the constitution, from popular sovereignty to the sovereignty of law.[17] In the latter half of the fourth century BCE, various innovations—the consolidation of financial administration, the resurgence of the Areiopagos—change the tone of Athenian administrative and political practice in an elitist direction.[18]

Yet the implications of these shifts should not be exaggerated.[19] The impression is one of unity across developments, as noted already by the Aristotelian treatise on the Athenian constitution. The law courts were understood to represent the People's power in the *polis*, under different institutional forms than the Assembly. The practice of pay, which was inaugurated so radically during the fifth century BCE, continued in the form of assembly pay introduced soon after the last oligarchical coup, and maintained long after.[20] Crucially, decisions were consistently taken by public vote in mass gatherings upon proposals by individual politicians who faced the uphill task of convincing the mass of their worth and of their proposal's benefits. This structural feature explains the populist parameters of Athenian political life, the intense competition between politicians using all institutional resources at their disposal, and the increasing power of the People or bodies representing the people. This style of politics can be called "demagogic," to use the phrase for "leaders of the people." The term is applicable not only to the boisterous politicians who succeeded Periklēs during the overheated early years of the Peloponnesian War, but to all Athenian leaders or would-be leaders, whose success depended on continuously persuading the Assembly to vote for proposals, establishing an acceptable persona, and disqualifying rivals through rhetoric accompanied by political maneuvering.

As well as a political arena, the Athenian *polis* was also an administrative entity, whose stateness was materialized in the steady establishment of permanent (and self-consciously impressive) buildings relating to the operations of administration, adjudication, and recordkeeping.[21] Stateness also appears in the managing of the citizen body: admission of new citizens was handled by the Council and controlled by official written registers. The state exercised coercive powers over this population,

FIGURE 8.2. Fragment of *klērotērion* (allotment machine), marble. This particular specimen dates to the second century BCE. Athenian Agora, I 3967. Athens.

levying taxes and enforcing obligations—for instance military service—according to formalized rules. State obligations generated forms of avoidance and evasion: the point is not that all Athenians were perfect citizens, but precisely that the pursuit of private interests implied the existence of a sphere of publicness that affected individuals.[22]

Stateness could be further seen in the activities of officials whose powers are catalogued by the Aristotelian treatise, and which appear at work in the documentary evidence. Usually in colleges or boards, they exercised authority (underwritten by punitive powers) over grain supply, the market, roads, market transactions, and myriad aspects of life in the town and countryside. An emblem of the complexity and autonomy of state apparatus is provided by the *klērotērion*, the machine for distributing service randomly, as used in the operations of allotment that were crucial to the state's workings (fig. 8.2). Its operation is described in the Aristotelian treatise, over a surprisingly long and detailed stretch in the last preserved section of the text.

In particular, the machine was used to allot jurors for the courts. The surviving body of speeches given before these courts (written by professionals for clients, or by Athenian politicians such as Dēmosthenēs or Aischinēs) give a sense of the power of the Athenian *polis* to affect behavior through rules and sanctions.[23] The courts (intervening if state-appointed arbitrators failed) decided on the basis of precedent, procedure, and articulate legal argumentation (*logos*); indeed, the jurors swore to observe criteria of relevance.[24] In 330 BCE, Aischinēs attacked a decree in honor of Dēmosthenēs by arguing that a general clause mentioning Dēmosthenēs's services was a lie, and hence that the decree was invalid, in accordance with a general rule that statements of fact in a decree should be true (naturally, this allowed Aischinēs to impugn Dēmosthenēs's whole political career, and Dēmosthenēs to turn the tables by defending his record with great eloquence). Alongside this line of attack, the main thrust of Aischinēs's prosecution was a legal point, namely that Dēmosthenēs could not have been voted a crown before rendering his accounts as a magistrate. The riposte was equally substantive: it pivoted on the argument that Dēmosthenēs had been honored for benefactions as a private individual, albeit during his term of service as a magistrate.[25]

Immediately noticeable are the storms of forced sophisms in legal argument and interpretation, the presence of contradictory statements, the dubiousness of testimony, and the protracted duration of proceedings across repeated lawsuits.[26] Yet these do not mean that law in Athens was completely open, but merely that litigants sued to win and used all the resources of legal interpretation to do so. The very presence of a complex law code generated possibilities to be exploited by professionals, the *logographoi*, speechwriters who combined a specialization in the rhetorical presentation or reshaping of facts with awareness of points of law. The multiplication of avenues for legal action is also a result of the procedures available within the Athenian system.[27] The procedural thicket is not a sign of chaos or statelessness but a normal feature of the interaction of multiple authoritative rules.

The nature of Athenian stateness should be carefully calibrated. The *klērotērion* was operated by members of the courts, themselves selected at random: there was no technician in charge of the workings of the machine. The state was strong, but also thin: the operation of the laws and the courts depended on voluntary prosecutors, and the operation of politics on volunteer politicians. The consequence of the state's thinness was to make it immediately responsive to popular decisions, whose primacy was enshrined within its structure, and to always favor political over merely administrative solutions. The official lists of citizens registered the results of decisions taken by a majority vote of the members of the demes, the local subdivisions of the Athenian state.[28] Judicial decisions were explicitly and immediately a manifestation of the People's power, in that they cast the realization of state power into the crucially important form of mass decision-making on the basis of laws that were themselves said to manifest and safeguard the People's will.[29]

Such statements belong to a rich vein of ideological statements about the People and their power.[30] Forensic oratory offered narratives of events, displays of character, and arguments about likelihood and consistency, all framed to as to reproduce democratic ideology. The tenets of this ideology are the moral right of the People, a mass of political equals, to decide on important matters and to judge individual character in relation to the safeguarding of the community as a whole. Forensic oratory amplified the "demagogic" style of decision-making by elite competition before the People. Democratic principles articulated in political speech, as well as explicit reflections on the Athenian system,[31] determined the character of Athenian state practice. *Dēmokratia* took the form of mass participation at all levels, as a distributive tool and a reflection of popular sovereignty, throughout the history of Classical Athens.[32] The importance of participation and distribution can further be seen in specific practices such as the frequent meetings (forty times a year by the 330s BCE) of the mass assembly, the rather freewheeling additions to proposals put before the Assembly, or the constant tinkering with institutions to direct them toward a greater circulation of power (for instance, the modification of the procedures for presiding over the Assembly).[33] The assumptions behind democratic practice and its institutional logic were well understood by critics of democracy: Plato attacks the very epistemological basis of mass decision as a political principle in his fictionalized portrayals of Sōkratēs—for instance, the latter's defense speech before a democratic court—or in the long debate about truth, knowledge, and rhetoric with followers of the sophist and rhetor Gorgias.[34]

Political Culture and Social History at Athens

In action, these principles and practices ensured the constraining of Athenian elites through multiple avenues. The exacerbation of competition in high-stakes, all-or-nothing politics[35] conducted in the Assembly and in the courts prevented elite collaboration, though there subsisted a world of elite groups and cliques that were feared and disliked (their potential was realized violently in the oligarchical coups of 411 and 403 BCE).[36] The resolution of disputes between rich Athenians over property and money in the courts involved appeals before popular audiences as a necessary complement to legal argument, thus embedding elite Athenians in their communities, in dialogue with the *dēmos* and on the *dēmos*'s terms. The volunteer prosecutions, in a system of thin stateness but constant distrust and surveillance and multiple procedural avenues for legal action, fulfilled this democratic function; hence the attempts by rich Athenians to disengage from the workings of the courts. The political setup continued to constrain elites, even after the abeyance of the direct mechanism of *ostrakismos*, the voting out for ten years of any individual the assembly decided to exile by secret ballot.[37]

One very practical result of popular power was the distribution of financial burdens (especially of war and of festival life) to fall on the wealthy. This could take the form of one-off wealth taxes levied on property (*eisphorai*), or of the provision, on an apparently volunteer basis (in fact upon compulsory and regulated assignment by state officials) of public services (*leitourgia*), such as the equipping of a warship or the training and equipping of a chorus for festival competition.[38] These burdens shaped elite behavior (and they were to play a crucial role in shaping the subsequent history of the *polis*). The evasion of such duties was denounced in the high-stakes game of elite competition within democratic politics; conversely, members of the Athenian elite could refer to financial services when asking for favor in the courts.³⁹ Furthermore, politicians could refer to a list of services, notably but not exclusively financial, to actively and formally request honors from the people in assembly.⁴⁰

The practice of honors is likely to have been present in the fifth century BCE already, and probably descends from the precedent of public tokens of distinction granted during the "Archaic" period to special individuals. Honorific practice grew denser in the fourth century BCE, and was the subject of much debate, self-interrogation, and recrimination between politicians. By the second half of the fourth century BCE, exceptional service could be rewarded by the "greatest honors," *megistai timai* (front seating in the theater, free meals in the *prytaneion*, and expensive portrait statues in bronze). Less grandly, panels of officials often received praise, crowns, and small gifts of money to perform sacrifices. Honors rewarded service, but also the general attitude of zeal (*philotimia*, literally "love of honors") toward the community, which was both the recipient of benefaction and the granter of status and recognition.⁴¹

In addition, the democracy developed particular discourses on citizen identity that were manifested throughout Athenian culture in text, space, image, and monument.⁴² These proclaimed the uniqueness and exclusiveness of the citizen body, conceived as autochthonous, thus appropriating elite tropes of worth. The restriction of the citizen body to individuals born of two citizen parents (451 BCE) made it a privileged body of power holders.⁴³ Athenian artistic production engaged with these images; for instance, in the great festivals that were the venue for the regular performance of dramatic and poetical literature, paid for by rich *leitourgoi*.⁴⁴ Publicly commissioned art for sacred buildings on the Akropolis⁴⁵ or for monuments on the mass graves of the war dead,⁴⁶ further publicized civic ideals.

Private cultural production also engaged creatively with Athenian civic identity. Painted pottery, an Athenian specialty (exported on a great scale to the eastern and, especially, the western Mediterranean), presented a nexus of images that showed and commented on the *polis*, lived and imagined, with such contained vividness that they have often served as a proxy for ancient Greece in modern imaginations.⁴⁷ Private graves, after a period of austerity at the start of the fifth century BCE, could be decorated with gravestones bearing reliefs that showed the deceased in civic or familial contexts (fig. 8.3).⁴⁸ Even the prose writings that constitute what we call philosophical texts (perpetuating the categories constructed by one of the writers, Plato) were deeply involved with, if critical of, democratic ideology and practice, as we have seen.⁴⁹

Whether public or private, Athenian texts and images combined to form a space of representation and debate about citizen status, defined by its exclusiveness and its difference from strategically represented and essentialized others such as enslaved persons, foreigners, and women. Abetted by the resources and dominant position (real or remembered) of the Athenian state, a powerful sense of Athenian specificity, derived from the local identity embedded in the territory and myths of every *polis*, developed into a sense of uniqueness and superiority.

FIGURE 8.3. Athenian grave stele, marble. 375-350 BCE. H 142 cm, W 81 cm. Now in the Metropolitan Museum of Art, New York.

In practice, the system generated paradox and tension. The essential political transaction was the intervention of the individual, as public-spirited politician, prosecutor, or provider, before a mass audience that judged him. At the same time, the Athenian political discourse constructed negative figures of manipulative orators and malicious, venal prosecutors (*sukophantai*). Politicians and litigants had to negotiate identities between these contradictory paradigms. Politicians claimed themselves fearless figures of integrity who did not bend to the will of the *dēmos* but spoke harshly and frankly to it (hence the apparently antidemocratic stances of a politician like Periklēs, but also in the populist, and popular, comedies of Aristophanes). Litigants ostentatiously claimed reluctance and clumsiness, rather than the eagerness and expertise that were structurally part of the system.

The overbearing power of the *dēmos* coexisted with a number of contradictory features. The celebration of elite individuals took place in the shadow of the constantly restated reality of popular sovereignty; the latter took diverse institutional forms that could prove uneasily compatible. Popular power obtained alongside a lack of responsibility on the part of the Assembly (in a system obsessed with individual accountability). Radicalness and exceptionalism coexisted with a militant conviction of traditionalism and unthinking veneration of the good old days. Finally, an ideology of transparency, fictional face-to-face solidarity and maximal citizen investment combined with a reality of self-interested individuals within a huge geographical space, where bonds were looser than civic ideology claimed. In 411 BCE, the oligarchical plotters expertly exploited these contradictions to hijack the democratic system.[50]

Such contradictions are a consequence of the systemic complexity of Athens as a *polis*. The multiplicity of Athens is partly reflected in its official articulation into 140 demes (often of considerable size) as well as a multitude of subdivisions ("thirds" within "tribes," brotherhoods, clans). But the diversity of the Athenian *polis* should not be reduced to these state structures (see below, chapter 15); it is also visible in the workings of a complex society, grouping individuals and households, with their own interests, spheres of action, and networks.[51] Private honorific statues mimicking but also departing from the public genre in celebrating individual achievement and family wealth,[52] the proliferation of lavish private grave monuments,[53] the flourishing of associations, and many other social phenomena suggest that the relationship between Athens as civil society and the Athenian state system was less isomorphic than it might seem (or we might wish; see further below, chapter 15).[54] One of these problems is whether Athens was raw with honor-driven competition, or if diversity was overcome and harmonized into collaboration.[55] This is only one question raised by the combination of radicalness and complexity that characterizes the history of the Athenian *polis*—a history that still largely remains to be written.

Dēmokratia and the *Polis*

It is all too tempting to view Classical Athenian democracy as closely related to empire. Yet it also grew out of the practices of late Archaic "Kleisthenic" Athens, which themselves belong to the diverse register of political forms developed during the seventh and sixth centuries BCE (above, chapter 6), and notably the register of open, inclusive, socially diverse regimes. Such archaic democracies also continued to develop, as pointed out by E. Robinson, who studied both the early democracies and the other "Classical" democracies beyond the case of the Athenian giant.[56]

Some early democracies continued to operate successfully, as in the case of Ēlis, whose sixth-century BCE culture of popular decision-making was prolonged by the later democratic regime explicitly attested in literary sources. In other cases, democratic institutions emerged out of the end of older arrangements. The process is usually obscure, as at Leukas, an island *polis* where an archaic system of restricted citizenship based on ownership of one of the "original plots" in the territory somehow changed to an open franchise without property qualification. (Nearby Zakynthos also is casually mentioned as a democracy in the fourth century BCE.) At Kyrēnē, monarchy disappeared, to be replaced by democratic institutions that coexisted dialectically with elitist activities such as aristocratic leadership in war, athletics, display in the form of benefactions or dedications, and banqueting in small groups. The complex dialectic is characteristic of the political and social life of Classical democracies.[57]

Without imposing a strict checklist, Robinson defines these Classical democracies institutionally, in terms of open access to citizenship and popular government (as exemplified by widely held but constrained political office and large popular courts). The sparse evidence allows him to locate 52 democratic *poleis* in the fifth and fourth centuries, a figure that Hansen strikingly expands to 109, often by pursuing the implications of indirect evidence. This figure constitutes a majority of the 198 cities for which any indications on constitutional arrangements are known (indeed, one should remove the princely city-states of Cyprus as outliers, bringing the total ratio to 109 out of 190).[58]

The relationship of these democracies with the high political history of the Hundred Years' War is less than clear. In some cases, Athens clearly imposed democratic institutions, as in various cities of western Asia Minor during the fifth century BCE, or on the cities of Keōs during the time of the second Athenian sea hegemony (above, p. 168).[59] Athenian-style institutions appearing in the islands are also suggestive of direct influence or imposition. Yet it is questionable whether all of the eastern Greek cities endowed with democratic institutions were democracies as an aftereffect of Athenian imperialism. Teōs and its foundation Abdēra had courts of 200 and 500 jurors, respectively; Thasos had courts of 300 citizens.[60] Such arrangements might continue institutional developments and concerns already visible in early fifth-century BCE Teōs and generally in the eastern Aegean.[61] Rhodes, Kōs, Kymē are attested as democracies in the fourth century BCE, when Athenian power over the far eastern Aegean had long waned.

Another group of democratic *poleis* is located in the Peloponnese; the best documented is Argos. Reemergent after defeat and disorder at the end of the Archaic period, Argos is clearly a *dēmokratia*, with decision-making institutions as well as large estates under popular control: the abundant rents on these estates financed public goods. This is the time of the monumental buildings mentioned earlier (theatre, meeting hall, public spaces).[62] A cache of financial documents, incised on bronze plaques and dating to the early fourth century BCE, illustrates democratic institutions at work: a multitude of officeholders, their frequent rotation, the enforcement of accountability on these officials, and transparency in the handling of public funds. As C. Kritzas observed, hundreds of Argive citizens took part in the administration of their *polis*, and they almost always are identified by their civic subdivision, in democratic style, rather than by their father's name. This documentary evidence confirms the impression that emerges from Thucydides's narrative: for instance, Thucydides mentions that the Argive *polis* has a special procedure for trying generals *extra muros* upon their return from campaign, a practice that hints at close control of officeholders and demagogic politics.[63]

Other Peloponnesian democracies are less well documented. The big, expansionary city of Mantineia is explicitly described as a democracy (before Spartan intervention, and after freedom from Spartan control).[64] Phleious and Sikyōn seem to have been democracies (or had periods of democratic government; see below on the ambiguous figure of Euphrōn of Sikyōn). Likewise, the thirteen cities of Achaia are said to have been democracies (perhaps illustrating a phenomenon of small, equal polities with nonelite culture, comparable to western Lokris). Another regional cluster of democratic *poleis* is to be found in Sicily and Southern Italy.[65] In the aftermath of a period of domination by powerful monarchical figures, Syracuse, the greatest *polis* of Sicily, had a democratic constitution for much of the fifth century BCE, complete with demagogic politics and officeholding by large boards; other Sicilian cities such as Selinous, Leontinoi, Himera, or Gela underwent periods of democracy. Rhēgion, Epizephyrian Lokroi, Krotōn, and Taras are all attested as democracies during the fifth century BCE, after periods of closed rule by small groups in the late Archaic period.

It is difficult to write a unified history of Classical democracy. The influence of Athens is undeniable in many cases. Argos, at the time of the development of its democratic constitution, was an ally of Athens when the latter was inventing the forms of "radical" democracy. Even the democracy of Thebes, after the city rose against Sparta in 378 BCE, is likely to have reflected Athenian support (this included a safe haven for the Theban exiles who freed their city). But the forms of Argive or Theban institutions do not look like direct copies of the Athenian constitution. Features such as demagogic politics, voluntary prosecutions, or *leitourgia* might be structurally part of democratic *polis* life rather than immediately Athenian in inspiration.[66] The presence in various *poleis* of *leitourgiai* such as the provision of choruses implies the habit of having rich men pay for services in contexts of competition for honor before the *dēmos*.[67] Nor is there any easy way to connect the Athenian practice of *ostrakismos* with the temporary exile of politicians at Syracuse (where the names of candidates were written on leaves in the procedure of *petalismos*), at Megara, or in Chersonîsos on the northern shore of the Black Sea, a Megarian colony. A potsherd found there bears a name, insults, and the exclamation *itō*, "let him go."[68]

Whether or not directly influenced by Athens, the practice fitted in with local democratic cultures that grew out of the inclusive, broad-based, egalitarian polities of the late "Archaic" period (as at Megara), or out of constitutional upheavals of the early Classical period (as at Syracuse). Democratic ideas may be reflected in the thinking of the famous itinerant "wise men" (*sophistai*, performers and teachers) active on the festival circuit. Two of the Sophists came up with thoughtful justifications for the distributive and participatory practices of *polis* life, for consultation, deliberation, and argument as good modes of living in common, and for the rational capacities of all participants in this project. Prōtagoras (ca. 485–420 BCE) and Dēmokritos (ca. 460–380) came from the democratic *polis* of Abdēra.[69] Among many fragments from Dēmokritos's lost writings that deal with political issues, his description of "poverty" in democracy as a better choice than prosperity alongside the powerful prolongs late Archaic thoughts about restraint, community, and citizenship, in explicit connection with the values of democracy and freedom.

Prōtagoras is portrayed by Plato as mounting a strong defense of the universal sharing in political capacity, and hence the legitimacy of wide political participation (even by bronzeworkers or shoemakers). This *prise de position* takes the form of detailed argument, as well as a myth that is likely a quotation or paraphrase of Prōtagoras's actual writing. Its power is undiminished by the particular context (the teachability of virtue) within which Plato frames it:

> . . . in the beginning men dwelt scattered, and there were no cities; so they were destroyed by the animals on account of being in all ways weaker, and the craft of making things was enough to provide food, it was lacking when it came to fighting war against the animals, for they were lacking in the political craft (*politike techne*), of which the art of war is a part. So they sought to gather together and save themselves by founding cities (*poleis*). Now whenever they gathered, they harmed each other because they did not have political craft, and hence scattered again and perished. So Zeus, fearing that our race would utterly be destroyed, sent Hermēs to bring respect and justice to men, so that there would be order and binding ties of friendship in the cities. And Hermēs asked Zeus how he was to give justice and respect to men: "Should I distribute these out like the crafts have been dealt out? Those arts were distributed in this manner: one man possesses the medical craft is sufficient for many individuals, and so with the other craftsmen. Should I place justice and respect in this way among men, or should I distribute them to all?" "To all," said Zeus, "and let all have a share. For cities cannot be, if only a few have a share, as with the other crafts. And lay down a law from myself, to kill him who cannot share of respect and justice, as a disease of the *polis*."

The crucial question, which cannot be easily answered in detail, is whether the institutional arrangements and ideology of democracy accompanied, or fostered, the social and economic phenomena known from Athens. These include the absence of formal overlordship by urban elites over dependent peasantry, the diminution of elite acquisitiveness as a result of nonelite access to political process, the slowing down of wealth accumulation and inequalities, and the promotion of equality through the provision of public goods (including subsidized access to political process) by redistributing surplus extracted from the wealthy.[70] Cautiously, we might infer from the presence of liturgies and demagogic politics that nonexploitative social relations and redistributive institutions were an important complement of the practice of popular power in cities characterized by *dēmokratia*.

From Oligarchy to *Oliganthrōpia*: Classical Sparta

The articulation of democratic practice and ideology was matched by another type of regime—the rule of the few, the better, the rich. To use the term current in the Classical period already, this was oligarchy, based on political inequality and the institutionalized restriction of access to power, based on wealth criteria. This type of régime—like *dēmokratia*—was rooted in the diversity of the "Archaic" polities, and specifically in the old practice of "closed" citizenship, internal hierarchies, exclusion from power, and domination over individuals and communities that are part of the *polis* without open access to full membership (above, chapter 6). "Archaic" Argos fell into this category, before the upheavals at the very start of the fifth century BCE that led to the elaboration of the Classical democratic régime. Notoriously, the Cretan cities also perpetuated a closed form of social organization during the fifth century BCE.[71]

Equally notorious, the Thessalian *poleis* continued along similar lines of restricted aristocratic régimes ruling over second-class citizens (including artisans) and, especially, over a rural population of serfs (*penestai*) with no access to citizenship.[72] A sense of the complexity as well as the restricted nature of the social organization in a Thessalian city can be gained from the *polis* of Mētropolis, where a family group, the Basaidai, controlled a number of privileges, including access to a *taga*. Once interpreted by L. Moretti as the city's chief magistracy, the term in fact seems to designate public land held by a civic subdivision. In the third century BCE, as we know from an inscribed agreement, the Basaidai negotiated with four families for access to the *taga*; the five families constituted a privileged *sungeneia* or fictive kingroup.[73]

The most obvious, if perhaps not the most typical, representative of the new oligarchical polities that evolved out of the closed system was Sparta, whose power and size allowed it to play a major part in the power politics of the fifth and part of the fourth centuries BCE (above, chapter 7), drawing especially on the manpower of the other *poleis* in Lakedaimōn, and generally of the majority of the Peloponnesian cities under Spartan control. Even though its story is much more obscure than that of Athens (because of lack of evidence, Spartan secrecy, the "Spartan mirage" of positive or awesome images about the Lakedaimonian polity, and the subsequent reception of those images),[74] it is clear that Spartan history was hardly immobile. Most importantly, the case of Sparta illustrates how the old, exclusive model evolved in parallel with and in reaction to the contemporary evolutions of the "open" model toward democracy.

It is true that Classical Sparta retained the social structure developed during the "Archaic" period. It restricted citizenship to a rentier class of landowners that was supported by the serf labor of helots (even if the treatment of this class increasingly took on aspects of chattel slavery, such as ownership and sale, as part of the intensification of the power of private property in Sparta).[75] The product of helot labor allowed citizens to enjoy leisure while paying dues in kind to state institutions. That is, Classical Sparta retained the relationship of overlordship and elite appropriation that had been a widespread phenomenon in earlier periods, but which tended to disappear with the spread of democratic constitutions descended from the "open" polities of the sixth century BCE. The resulting leisure allowed members of the citizen group to devote themselves to specialized elite activities, and generally to the leadership of the unequal pyramid of hegemony and power in the Peloponnese and beyond. Spartiate life took place within frameworks defined by the community, notably the famous state education, an elaboration of a number of community practices (warrior bands, *rites de passage*) that had played integrative functions in the archaic *poleis*.[76] The Archaic-style political histrionics remained visible, symbolizing the egalitarian solidarity of the citizens as "the People" through features such as costume,[77] the limited usage of each other's property, status markers through violence, and political manipulation of festival and ritual.[78]

Yet the old structure did not prevent the development and evolution of institutional practices. On the one hand, in spite of quaint-looking practices such as voting by acclamation, the assembly of citizens should not be considered powerless: it elected officeholders and voted on matters of state such as warfare and high politics. Even charismatic kings such as the swashbuckling adventurist Agēsilaos needed to work around the Assembly and state institutions. Assembly decisions often led to punitive measures against the kings, implemented according to the rule of law: several kings were fined or exiled. Internally, the Spartan state conducted its affairs (including public finances) through written records and accountability, like any other *polis*, and it should not be viewed as a nobly primitive or backward polity.[79]

But alongside the effective working of political institutions, what characterizes Sparta is a dynamic of competition and inequality.[80] The Spartiates had always known economic inequality, in spite of equal access to public goods and rationed luxury (paralleled in other "Archaic" *poleis* as part of a particular type of citizenship regime, as we have seen). Some Spartiates were very wealthy (above, p. 145); the fifth-century BCE Spartiate Lichas was famous for his lavish hospitality and his horseracing activities (he was literally whipped out of the Olympia of 420 when trying to crown his charioteer, whose chariot had been entered into the contest as a Boiotian team to bypass a ban on Spartan competitors).[81] Such activities are an index of the emergence of a wealth elite. The process and modalities are not completely clear, though the factors were undoubtedly elite acquisitiveness, inheritance strategies that allowed families to trap and transmit property, and the influx of wealth at the end of the Peloponnesian Wars (above, p. 167). The concomitant feature of impoverishment of nonelite Spartiates is equally difficult to explain, but it offers a clear hint of the acquisitive pressures on the part of the rich, perhaps involving lending and foreclosing, especially with the influx of money in the form of Achaimenid subsidies or of the profits of war and empire (above, chapter 7).[82]

The consequences of continuously increasing economic inequality were threefold. The first was the exclusion of poor Spartiates from full citizenship because of their failure to make the considerable contributions to the communal messes. The system of communal feasting as a participatory activity was a development out of the practices and ideologies of the Archaic *polis* (above, chapters 5 and 6) that resulted from and reinforced the solidarity of the integrated (and constantly performed) citizen group. Economic exclusion from full citizenship operated alongside other forms of exclusion, on grounds of unworthiness—especially cowardice in battle—which indicate how its roots are the principle of fair distribution of burdens. The outcome was a large group of second-class citizens, the "Inferiors," which shared the burdens of citizenship (especially military), but none of the advantages; namely, access to the elite lifestyle and political rule enjoyed by the "Alike Ones" (*homoioi*). The Inferior status may have been formalized only in the fifth century BCE with the increasing demotion of Spartiates on economic grounds.

The second consequence was the restriction of political power to the dwindling group of *homoioi*, since they monopolized office and decision-making within the Spartiate state. The drop in citizen numbers (*oliganthrōpia*, "lack of men") was a political rather than demographic phenomenon. The third consequence was the prevalence of corruption—not just in the form of illegitimate economic gain-seeking through gifts, bribes, and graft, but more generally in the form of fixing outcomes within the small power elite or bypassing institutional and political process. The Spartan state needed to raise special wealth taxes (*eisphorai*), just like Athens, to finance hegemonical war, but such taxes were particularly difficult to collect in Sparta—because of the solidarity of the rich elite of full citizens, and the absence of institutions to enforce state decisions on the rich and influential.[83] Patterns of personal patronage involving wealthy and powerful Spartiates (including the kings themselves) are also a result of the concentration of economic wealth and political power within the restricted group of full citizens.

These political processes explain certain characteristics of Spartan political life, discussed earlier. Most obvious is the tendency toward adventurism in "foreign policy," the aggressive *fuite en avant* in the fifth and especially the early fourth centuries BCE, down to the epochal defeat at Leuktra in 371 BCE. War allowed the Spartan system to mobilize its subordinate elements: helots, perioikic cities, subordinate allies and, within the Spartiate *polis*, the Inferiors. In addition, foreign wars allowed profits from plunder or systematic extraction to flow to all the elements of society. In addition to channels for social aggression and material profit, war offered avenues of social promotion for veterans of contingents of fighting helots, installed as military colonists on the edge of Lakedaimōn, or for Inferiors enjoying military command or governorships abroad.[84]

Another characteristic of Spartan political life is constant resistance to the pyramid of power. The revolt of the subordinate allies belongs to a continuum with unrest by Inferior citizens, the centrifugal tendencies of perioikic cities, and the uprising of helots, be it the integrated serf populations of Lakōnia proper or the subject communities in Messēnia. In the main, these forms of resistance were successfully controlled by the Spartan system through a variety of means: the divide-and-rule prisoner's dilemma-style techniques already mentioned (p. 168), but also assassination, arrest, torture, and extrajudicial execution (as happened during unrest in Sparta immediately after Leuktra).[85]

All the characteristics of the Spartan system are illustrated by one episode and its repression—namely, the conspiracy mounted by one of the excluded, a man named Kinadōn, in 395 BCE; this is recounted in an extraordinary piece of narrative by Xenophon.[86] Kinadōn, as an Inferior, had army experience, and his planned uprising of all the armed elements in Spartan society—Inferiors, *perioikoi* but also helots—shows the central place occupied by the military factor in uniting the divergent elements under Spartiate leadership. His resentment at being excluded from the full citizenship enjoyed by the *homoioi* was the result of the dynamics of inequality in plutocratic Sparta. When the conspiracy was denounced, the Spartiate state mobilized its full capacity for secrecy and restriction: the ephors did not even mobilize the "small Assembly," an institution so restrictive that we in fact have no idea of what it did within the Spartan constitution. The ephors acted fast and ruthlessly: Kinadōn was lured into a trap and arrested by a regiment of Spartan cavalry, on the pretense that he was about to carry out a police mission for the ephors, a role he had fulfilled before. The details of the sting are instructive: alongside the routine use of literacy in administration and repression at Sparta, they show the necessity for constant surveillance and repression in the Spartiate state, and the use of Inferiors as muscle for social control and as collaborators in the system of their own oppression. The punishment of Kinadōn and his associates illustrates the violence, symbolical and actual, underlying Spartan government (they were put in a wooden collar immobilizing the hands and driven around the city with whips and goads, presumably until their death).

Spartan realities did not quite amount to a crisis—we are rather peering into the workings of an apparatus whose internal dynamics compelled certain types of behavior, and whose continued operation was prone to extreme brittleness (as shown by the unraveling of the system after 371 BCE). The story of Sparta exhibits constant conflict and tension, plutocratic power, and the moralizing rewritings of economic inequalities characteristic of plutocratic societies. It is true that Sparta was a peculiar polity, with many special solutions and irregularities in its pyramid of power and circles of influence (for instance, privileges for groups of helots or certain perioikic communities). All the same, in spite of its peculiarities (which grew out of the fairly common solutions that it embarked upon during the Archaic period), Sparta serves as a particularly potent example of the workings of internally unequal polities, a perception already shared at the time.

Classical *Oligarchia*

As Sparta shows, the old model of restricted-access citizenship kept evolving in the fifth and fourth centuries BCE into articulate and sophisticated forms, just as the "open" polities (such as Athens) did during the same period. Classical oligarchies[87] are well attested in the narrative sources ("ruled by the best") and in the philosophical analyses of *polis* constitutions (especially by Aristotle). In constitutional terms, oligarchy meant a set of restrictive practices and arrangements[88] such as a censitary barrier to office or even citizenship,[89] an Assembly with restricted powers, a small Council with permanent membership and wide authority, and the strong executive and judicial power of a small number of elected and unpaid officials. These features all share the characteristic of making "some men deliberate about all things," as Aristotle puts it.[90] The Boiotian Confederacy, as it operated between 446 and 386 BCE, gives one example of such features uniformly imposed across all of its *poleis*. A high property qualification excluded more than half the male population from the franchise, and the full citizens belonged to four Councils working in a complicated system of rotation (one Council served as the administrative body for the three other Councils, decisions being taken by all four Councils).[91] Generally, the evidence, though patchy and unsystematic, suggests that oligarchical régimes were widespread, especially during the late fifth and early fourth centuries BCE.[92]

Oligarchical practices were underpinned by representations of closed polity as order, balance, self-control, and even justice. These descended from aristocratic self-representation, as developed during the Archaic and early Classical periods: signs of distinction (lifestyle, luxury, athletic competence) operated as proofs of the essential superiority of the "beautiful and good" (*kaloikagathoi*), as illustrated by Pindar's victory poems in the early fifth century BCE.[93] Another source was the concept of order as a collective good produced by the wise solidarity of a small ruling group and resulting in the community's happiness (*eudaimōnia*). Chios, an oligarchical city, is presented in these terms by Thucydides at the eve of its revolt from Athens in 412, a city combining prosperity, prudence, and stable *kosmos*.[94]

Such representations were not just ideological statements on the part of dominant groups, but also claimed that the few wielded power on grounds of merit.[95] The rich were more deserving of power on practical grounds: they were more capable to rule, since they were supposedly less corruptible and corrupted, and they were more competent, since they had the leisure to cultivate their abilities. In addition, they were more deserving of power on moral grounds, because they made greater contributions to the *polis*, in financial terms and through military service as the heavy men-at-arms that were the main tactical means of the Greek states. Oligarchy claimed a form of proportional or "geometric" equality that respected the differences or inequalities in ability and merit between individuals.[96]

The "few" self-servingly portray themselves as the "best" (*beltistoi*). The simplicity of the idea (and the blatancy with which it expresses the self-interest of the wealthy) should not obscure the sophistication and inventiveness with which oligarchical discourses and ideas were developed. Apart from the concepts about geometric equality and the entitlement of the wealthy, majority rule could be represented as the selfish pursuit of profits by the poor, and the democratic institution of mass decision as the unjust exercise of tyrannical power through coercion. Likewise, the lot or pay for service was illegitimate, unrepresentative, and morally corrupt and corrupting.[97] The moral and aesthetic language of oligarchy was complemented by a language of castigation for democratic practice and especially for its leaders—demagogues, *sukophantai*—criticized as the *ponēroi*, the wicked, in contrast with the *chrēstoi*, the useful ones. The critique was the more powerful for being sensitive to democratic anxieties about demagogues and *sukophantai*,[98] as illustrated by the clever deployment of such themes by violent oligarchical coups in Athens. More directly, democracy could be portrayed as irrationality and madness.[99]

Finally, oligarchical discourses proposed positive images. Oligarchy was equivalent to restraint (*sōphrosunē*) in contrast with the irrationality and ignorance of democracy (such as at Athens where the people embarked rashly on an expedition against Sicily, and refused responsibility for the subsequent disaster).[100] The "Few" constructed complex constitutional schemes around the rationality of numbers. Oligarchical thinkers painted images of order and ("geometric") justice holding sway in an idealized Sparta; they appealed to the reinvented past of the "ancestral constitution." These images, too, drew their power from their link with sources of cultural prestige in ancient Greek culture—the elitist Homeric poems, the "Archaic" groups with their names and numerical schemes, and the Spartan mirage. The oligarchical regime in Athens in 403 BCE organized a full muster of the population—structured in a body of full citizens, 3,000 strong, parading in the *agora*, while inferior citizens still under military obligations gathered in other places. The unequal statuses, visualized through hierarchical spatialization between citizen center and inferior periphery, may have been inspired by the Spartan model.[101]

The thought-world of oligarchy thus represented a political creation that appears as articulate and imaginative as democratic practice. Its discourses and ideas exercised a great hold, as perhaps shown by the widespread presence of oligarchical regimes. Yet a few features need emphasizing if we are to understand the historical nature of Classical oligarchies. For all its cultural nostalgia and its genealogical relation with the closed polities of the "Archaic" period, Classical oligarchy was a new phenomenon, an explicit reaction to the self-aware practice of *dēmokratia*, defined against it and often thought through as a deliberate, systematic rebuttal of democratic claims. The second feature is that for all its high-mindedness, oligarchy in practice was torn by contradiction and inconcinnity. Essentialist claims to excellence were belied by the realities of faction politics. The aestheticized images of harmony had to coexist with the violence essential to oligarchical discourse. Such violence was deployed to disqualify common practices of decision-making that were at the heart of *polis* processes and to vilify the democratic leaders (who were often from the same social background as oligarchs).

Most seriously, the dynamics of restrictiveness were plagued by uncertainty about how to manage the travails of inclusion and exclusion that were one of the great problems of the *polis*. The small, exclusive oligarchical citizen groups hesitated between imposing (democratic-style) equality among their members (and thus operating as small democracies), and giving free rein to the principles of personal excellence implied by class dominance. The latter solution risked leading to more exclusivity within the group and potentially to small cliques that were vulnerable to revolution and overthrow.[102] The contradictions had to be managed by a number of risky strategies of violence and social control, to preserve the concentration of power and prevent collective action by the disfranchised.[103]

Paradoxically, the very nature of Classical oligarchy as antidemocracy ensures its maximum legibility in democratic Athens itself.[104] The historical figure of Sōkratēs, for instance, was probably perceived as an antidemocratic thinker, and his trial and execution a consequence of this perception;[105] antidemocratic ideas are also surprisingly present in the comedies of Aristophanes, performed in front of mass audiences at *polis* festivals.[106] Athens itself underwent oligarchical episodes—the short-lived coups of 411 and 404 BCE, already mentioned. We have seen that the long shift in discourses and attitudes in the second half of the fourth century BCE (visible for instance in the greater power of the old permanent Council of the Areiopagos) that culminated in a Macedonian-backed, censitary oligarchy in 322 BCE, followed by a strong democratic reaction (when the old general Phōkiōn was tried and executed for treason), itself followed by a strongman regime under the philosopher Dēmētrios of Phaleron.[107] The latter evolution, toward greater power for officials combined with considerable unease about the position of elites in the polity, may have been one result of the increased leitourgic pressure on the wealthy, as required by the combination of grand ambitions and lack of funds after the collapse of the last serious overseas imperial venture by Athens in 357–355 BCE, when Athens's allies bolted for good. These episodes illustrate both the violence (in the form of executions or expulsions) and the instability (in the form of internal conflict) of actual oligarchical solutions.

The Divided *Polis* and the Temptations of *Stasis*

The presence of a streak of oligarchical choices even in Athens reveals the continuous dichotomy between democracy and oligarchy, yet also their close relation. The reaction to the oligarchical coup of 411 BCE was couched as a careful subversion of the oligarchs' own scheme of a limited franchise of 5,000 full citizens, thus exploiting the ambiguities in oligarchical discourse. Furthermore, the case of Athens shows that the dichotomy did not quite produce purely "democratic" *poleis* and "oligarchical" *poleis*. Like Athens, many cities experienced episodes of both.[108] Mantineia was governed according to a democratic constitution, with attendant features such as demagogic politics and judicial practices—except for an extended period (385–370 BCE) when the city was split into four smaller subparts, each of which was ruled by the landowners in "aristocratic" regimes.[109] Argos, a democratic *polis* with peculiar features of its own, also underwent violent oligarchical episodes. If Kymē, Erythrai, Kōs (to take only three examples of eastern Greek city-states) were democratic cities (as can be shown from epigraphical documents, or as is explicitly attested by Aristotle), they also knew periods of oligarchical rule, as a direct reaction to demagogic politics in the Assembly and in the popular courts.

To speak of "episodes" is a bloodless way to refer to the actual form that constitutional alternance usually took—namely political violence, often shockingly bloody. The grim episode of slaughter at the festival of the Eukleia at Corinth (above, p. 179) shows civil war to be a major part of the tragedy of Greece's Hundred Years' War. The conflict between oligarchical and democratic factions in Argos was exacerbated by the presence of a large contingent of full-time soldiers who were paid for and maintained by the *polis*, but harbored oligarchical sympathies (because of their social origin). The culmination of the protracted conflict was an attempted oligarchical coup (itself in reaction to demagogic policies), the repression of the coup by the execution of thirty of the "eminent ones" (a codeword for the wealth elite), followed by the mass condemnation and execution of 1,200 wealthy citizens. This atrocity was unique only in that its victims were bludgeoned to death (the savage episode is recorded in the term *skytalismos*, the "clubbing" used to refer to it).[110] Civil war (*stasis*) on Kerkyra, during the Peloponnesian War, also saw terrible violence between the oligarchical and democratic factions, escalating from judicial conflict to urban warfare to mass executions. Thucydides provides a careful, clinical narrative, as well as a powerful analysis of the corrupting effect of civil war and violence.[111]

Indeed, *stasis* occurs at multiple points in Thucydides's narrative: the conflagration of 431 had its origins in the involvement of big *poleis*, including Athens, in the politics of the small *polis* of Epidamnos, wracked by civic strife and expulsions. The Ionian *polis* of Kolophōn, during an episode of *stasis*, split into two towns, old Kolophōn and Notion; the latter underwent a secondary split between two factions, separated by a wall across the urban site, as a physical marker of the divided *polis*.[112]

Such internal violence was occasioned by conflicts between factions that promoted competing constitutional solutions and economic policies (democracies promoted demagogic control of the wealth, redistributive taxation, and the occasional confiscation of estates; oligarchies protected the property and contractual rights of rent-seeking elites). Violence was also fostered by structural features within the political culture of the *polis*.[113] Genealogically, the nature of membership in the *polis* was determined not just by essentialist tropes of identity and harmony (as fostered by discourse and ritual), but also by the sense of the justice of claims and entitlement as part of stakeholding in common public goods, especially since the latter were financed by individual but unevenly distributed contributions. The dual nature of citizenship explains why claims to entitlement could be so easily expressed in moral terms, with the consequent exclusion of opponents to such claims: hence the resort to casting-out through symbolical violence (in demagogic rhetoric or in oligarchical imagery) or actual exile, and hence the all-too-often realized possibility for escalation into real violence.

The unpacking of these contradictions underlies the dichotomy between democracy and oligarchy; but it also shows how democracy and oligarchy belong to a same continuum of *polis* culture. This continuum is clear in the way in which many "oligarchical" constitutions depend on the very practices and bodies (Assembly, Council, accountable officials) that are known from democracies but are more generally fundamental to the nature of the Greek city-states. Conversely, the language and interrogations of the oligarchical episodes in Athens, even if they were violently rejected by the democracy and assimilated to tyranny, left traces in the discourses, practices, and obsessions of the fourth-century BCE democracy, because they addressed central problems of the *polis*.[114]

To speak of this continuum does not diminish violence and conflict in the political history of the Hundred Years—a tragic, ironical history of constitutional practice as well as of discourse, ideology, and ideas about the right way to live in a *polis*. The temptation of authoritarian simplification was a response to the risk of debates about constitutional matters escalating into civil war and violence. A small military treatise of the Arkadian commander and politician Aineias of Stymphalos is obsessed with the danger of factional fighting, the need to repress it by direct police control, and the enforcement of civic harmony by imposed measures (for instance, the resort to debt relief to assuage tensions between rich and poor). The *polis* appears in this text as a world of political suspicion, requiring muscular intervention. Such security measures worked in the short term, as shown by the prevention of stasis in Phleious when it was under siege by the Spartans.[115]

The authoritarian temptation could evolve into monarchical solutions. Tyrannical episodes or actual regimes are sporadically known throughout the period between ca. 450 and 350 BCE, most spectacularly in Syracuse, where democratic politics led to a demagogue, Dionysios, seizing power and maintaining his family in control of the city from 405 to 344. Dionysios I also pursued hegemonic politics in Sicily and southern Italy (a powerful reminder of how power politics also favored monarchical solutions); his influence led to the resurgence of a series of tyrannical regimes in other Sicilian and Italian *poleis*. Indeed, we might choose to consider the Corinthian adventurer Timoleōn, who overthrew the tyranny in Syracuse and led the Sicilians to victory against the Carthaginians, as a strongman in the tyrannical mold—except for the more civic style in which he chose to present himself.[116]

Nor was tyranny limited to the western *poleis*, where there had been a long and spectacular tradition of such monarchical figures. In mainland Greece or in Asia Minor (for instance at Hērakleia Pontikē), their presence was abetted by the frequent use of professional soldiers, necessary to compete in the "big war" of the Hundred Years.[117] A Corinthian, Timophanēs, attempted a tyrannical coup at the head of 400 mercenaries in 366 BCE (the attempt was checked when his brother, none other than the future Syracusan strongman Timoleōn, killed him with his own hand). In Sikyōn, tension between oligarchs and democrats led to complicated regime change and the tyranny of a leading citizen, Euphrōn.[118] Euphrōn was expelled by an Arkadian force led by Aineias of Stymphalos (the military writer), returned, was murdered by elite, antidemocratic Sikyonians, and buried in the *agora* where some other Sikyonians honored him; his grandson was later a Sikyonian politician honored by the Athenian *polis*. The case of Euphrōn of Sikyōn shows the complexity of internal politics and the way in which the old princely solution could be embedded within the debates and conflicts of the age. If monarchical authoritarianism was a possible outcome both of hegemonical power politics and of local factional conflict, what other solutions did the political resources of the *poleis* offer?

9

The Great Convergence

> A blithe view of the history of modern democracy would see this change in expectations as following docilely in the wake of a prior shift in moral and political conviction. It would see democracy's triumph as the victory of a compelling formula for just and legitimate rule, aptly rewarded after a discreet interval by the happy discovery that such rule holds few terrors for the rich, and promises at least some benefits to practically everyone. But with the partial but weighty exception of the United States, that was scarcely the history which in fact occurred.
>
> —J. DUNN, SETTING THE PEOPLE FREE. THE STORY OF DEMOCRACY

Hegemony, Autonomy, Faction: The Infernal Equation

For a summary of the complexities and *aporiai* of the political history of the *polis*, we can turn again to Mantineia—would-be hegemonic city, democratic in the fifth century BCE, oligarchic in the early fourth century BCE. The processes that led to the shifts in Mantineia's history are interlocked and highly instructive. The breaking up of the *sunoikismos* that had created a large urban locus of democratic institutions and politics, the dissolution of democratic institutions, and subsequent oligarchical rule by local landowners—all these were imposed by Spartan intervention and the result, as intended, was compliance with Spartan foreign policy, as shown by Mantineia supplying troops to fight in Sparta's wars. Mantineian oligarchy was a direct result of Spartan strategies of control aimed at solving the recurrent problem of Mantineian recalcitrance and indeed expansionism. But its precarious nature as a solution imposed from outside (albeit with internal elite collusion) became clear a mere thirteen years after the creation of oligarchy. Immediately after the battle of Leuktra in 371 BCE, the *polis* of Mantineia reconstituted itself as a democratic state with a fortified urban center. When the Spartans demanded the demolition of the new wall and the dissolution of the reconstituted city, the Mantineian authorities replied that this was impossible because it was the will of the whole people.[1]

The case of Mantineia shows the imbrication of the prevailing paradoxes in the world of the Classical *polis*, which I have explored above (chapters 7 and 8).

The first set of paradoxes is the coexistence of norms of international life with the temptation of hegemony and the consequent instability. We have seen how autonomy was an ideal for the city-states, but also closely related to domination. The second set of paradoxes is linked to the working out of the practices and ideas involved in *dēmokratia* and *oligarchia*. Both types of regimes had their own contradictions and inconcinnities, and both, though explicitly defined one against another in an unstable, often very violent relation, shared deep characteristics within the same *polis* model (which did not preclude, and perhaps helps explain, the violence of internal conflict).

In an infernal equation, the desire for hegemony prompted intervention in local dynamics to foster the local autonomy (for instance, that of the Akrōreian communities on the edge of Ēlis against Ēlis itself) but also to support factions within communities. The Spartan state fostered oligarchies—simply put, small elite groups that would support its policies and force adhesion to them. This was the case in Phleious, or Thebes (the oligarchical faction was installed by a scandalous Spartan *coup de main* in 382 BCE) or, indeed, Mantineia.[2] The policy was almost certainly already in place in the sixth century BCE (as seen in the case of Corinth); in the Classical period, it took on a particular moralizing and ideologically colored aspect. In turn, the Athenians supported, with no great consistency, democratic factions and regimes during the time of its imperial power and in the aftermath;[3] the democratic regime at Argos may have favored the emergence of democracy at Mantineia in exchange for collaboration with the conquest of the Argolid in the early fifth century BCE (a good illustration of the imbrication of issues of hegemony with the different constitutional choices).[4] Alternatively, external powers could support a very small group, or indeed an individual (single rule remained a possible model for the *polis*) for pragmatic reasons, as happened in Euboian cities where opposing tyrants were supported by the competing powers of Athens and the Theban-led Boiotian Confederacy. In the Peloponnese, the kings of Macedonia, Philippos II and Alexandros III, favored local tyrants in the Peloponnese.[5]

Concomitantly, the very presence of large hegemonical powers exacerbated local intracommunal tensions into overt violence between factions, due to the possibility of overwhelming opponents with external support. Hence a grim story of uprising, murder, exile, and confiscation.[6] However, control founded on such violence could only be sustained by the continued support of the external power in return for collaboration and subordination. Factional domination was brittle: the association with foreign domination gave purchase for further intervention by other external powers to restore autonomy, and further delegitimized the faction that could be cast as collaborating with the enslavement of its own *polis*. Furthermore, stasiotic violence inevitably generated exiles, who developed a desire for revenge, the moralizing frame within which their own actions could be construed as liberation and justice, and an eagerness to appeal for help from other powers. The infernal algorithm of *stasis*, autonomy, and hegemony can be seen clearly at work in Thebes. There, the seizure of power by a Spartan-backed faction was checked, only a few years later, by the liberation of the city in a daring coup by an Athenian-backed faction, which led to the resurgence of the city and, not coincidentally, to the reaffirmation of Theban power that gave a pretext for Spartan intervention in Boiōtia to protect the autonomy of the smaller Boiotian cities.[7] (This is also the context for the start of a democratic regime in Thebes).

The violence and confusion of the imbrication of external politics and internal struggles was felt by contemporaries: the tragic or ironic narratives of the high politics found in Thucydides or Xenophon are matched by their attention to the violence of *stasis*. It might be tempting to interpret the Classical period as the story of a mounting crisis of an exhausted *polis* world,[8] culminating in the end of Greek freedom when the Macedonian kings Philippos II and Alexandros III simplified the mess of politics by defeating most *polis* actors. The Argead rulers imposed an institutional and political framework of control over the cities of mainland Greece and, astonishingly, embarked on a massive, all-out eastwards expedition whose effect was the overthrow of the highly successful Achaimenid state and the takeover of its extractive structures.[9] The spoils of conquest were divided among the powerholders of the Macedonian conquest apparatus, who competed amongst themselves for the largest share, and in so doing created a post-Achaimenid world of military states—the Hellenistic kingdoms.[10]

Yet this outcome, unexpectedly, would also offer dynamic new possibilities for the world of *poleis* because of the emergence of a multipolar, multiscalar world system and because the Greek culture of the *poleis*, by a historical accident, was promoted to a hegemonical status as the common idiom of the big power players in this system. In the long run, the *polis* form (in its discourses, institutions, and materialities) would spread across the eastern Mediterranean, overlaying and then displacing other cultures (for instance, the urban practices of the Levant and the Near East: chapter 14).

Factors of Convergence (1): The End of Hegemony

The Macedonian conquests, over the decades between ca. 350 and 280 BCE, undoubtedly constitute a major historical watershed—but within this context, the life of the *poleis* evolved according to its own logic.[11] This evolution is visible across the documentation for the *poleis*: from 350 BCE onwards, a process of institutional and ideological convergence affected the Greek city-states in their interactions and in their internal workings. The different rhythms of this convergence reflect the diversity and large number of the *poleis* involved, as well as the impact of the changes at the level of high politics; but generally, the phenomenon of convergence was structured by three interrelated evolutions.

The first of these is the end of hegemony as a possibility for the *poleis*, as a direct result of the rise of large supralocal monarchical states—an evolution that had surprising consequences for *polis* freedom. The extraordinarily dynamic and populous Argead kingdom, then the Hellenistic empires, mobilized money and manpower on a regular basis and on a scale that was simply impossible to match for any single *polis* or alliance. The competition for high political hegemony, where the means, stakes and costs had been rising steadily throughout the fifth and fourth centuries BCE, evolved to a scale beyond that of *polis* agency. Athens, during the latter part of the fourth century BCE, in spite of the absence of imperial revenue, built up a fleet of 400 warships, which it did not have the manpower or the money to fully man. The destruction of the last Athenian war fleet during an uprising against Macedonian control in 322 BCE, along with the decisive defeat of land forces raised by a coalition of *poleis*, confirms the overwhelming disparity of power between the big monarchical states and the *poleis*.

Such disparities were reaffirmed continuously. In 262 BCE, an alliance of Greek city-states led by Athens and Sparta fought a war explicitly described as a struggle for freedom, which ended in defeat by Macedonia (and the garrisoning and direct administration of Athens under Antigonid control).[12] Likewise, in 222 BCE a resurgent Sparta, its potential unlocked by social reform, was massively defeated by Macedonian intervention, as part of a general failure of resistance to the Macedonian superpower.[13] Finally, in 146 BCE a confederation of Peloponnesian cities, the Achaian League, was comprehensively crushed by the power that ultimately succeeded the Hellenistic kings—namely, the Roman Republic.

It is undeniable that the overwhelming military dominance of the Hellenistic supralocal states could be translated into conquest, control, and exploitation at the local level. The cities faced administrative control, tribute, and indirect taxation; the supralocal state wielded the right to define local existence within a register of statuses and within spaces of control. Some *poleis* were clearly subordinate or subject to and integrated within the direct administrative and fiscal reach of a big state: this is true for the way large Hellenistic empires such as the Seleukid or the Ptolemaic domain operated, but even more so for smaller states such as the Attalid, which were fiscally intensive and very present in the local sphere. Other *poleis* were called autonomous and free, but their freedom was defined by royal *fiat*: the horizon of royal meant that royally granted freedom was revocable.[14]

Nonetheless, a number of factors contributed to the limitation of royal power in dealing with the Greek city-states (even the "subject" or "subordinate" cities that were integrated within the kingdom). The *poleis* were all militarized (aligning militiamen, elite troops and even their own fleets), heavily fortified, and endowed with a strong sense of identity, interests, and continuity. Some funerary reliefs of the third and second centuries BCE (for instance in Iōnia) include in the portrayal of a luxurious feast (of heroizing overtones, the so-called *Totenmahlrelief*) the weapons of citizen militiamen. Such images remind us of the continued importance of the military factor in civic identity, individual and collective (fig. 9.1). The existence of local military means meant that the constant exercise of force against the cities was not sustainable

FIGURE 9.1. Funerary relief from Ionia, marble, ca. 200 BCE? Once in the collection of the Evangelical School, Smyrna; now lost. H 93 cm, L 99 cm. Pfuhl and Möbius 1979, no. 1861.

for the Hellenistic states. In addition, no single kingdom achieved overwhelming dominance over the others, and every kingdom was intent on causing difficulties to its rivals: the coalition of Greek states in 267–262 BCE and the resurgent Sparta of the 230s BCE were financed by the Ptolemaic kingdom, just as Athens after 229 BCE (when it got rid of its Macedonian garrison) was supported by Ptolemaic subsidies.[15] The imperialist king Antiochos III had to negotiate with the *poleis*, even during his campaigns of conquest, or reconquest, in Asia Minor (218 BCE, 204 BCE, 197 BCE); while fighting a war against the Roman Republic and its Attalid ally in Asia Minor, a single, midsized town, Notion (one of the two *poleis* in the bipolar state of Kolophōn), held off the great king (as he styled himself).[16]

The need on the part of the big supralocal empires to conciliate the *poleis* gave the latter considerable leverage to extract concessions and to create spaces for agency at their level. At the very least, interaction between ruler and *polis* had to follow the channels of civic language forged during the long interlocking debates held theoretically and concretely on the matters of community and international relations throughout the fifth and fourth centuries BCE.[17] Was this the best the *poleis* could do? It is important not to minimize the Hellenistic kingdoms' power to control but also not to scoff at this level of *polis* autonomy. The necessity to bargain with stronger extra-local powers had always existed for local states in the ancient Aegean world (and beyond), and the *poleis* were remarkably successful at playing the long game and achieving freedom. The fact of subordination at one point in a *polis*'s history did not preclude initiative and liberty as soon as the supralocal power faltered: large *poleis* such as Smyrna or Lampsakos achieved breakaway freedom from the Seleukid empire when dynastic strife weakened Seleukid control in Asia Minor.

The end of hegemony for certain *poleis* generalized the possibility of autonomy for all *poleis*: the big supralocal states tolerated, indeed fostered local freedom but not hegemony, to avoid the emergence of power bases or the disruption of imperial control and taxation. Furthermore, the end of hegemony spread to *poleis* that were not in the direct ambit of the Hellenistic empires, and specifically affected one particular type of relation that was common in earlier periods—namely, the unequal structuration into relations of domination by big *poleis* over subordinate or generally dependent *poleis*. As already noted, the "dependent *polis*" has been much insisted upon by the scholars of the Copenhagen Polis Centre as proof that *autonomia* was not an essential part of what it meant to be a *polis*; the decline and disappearance of this category, however, is an important process in the history of the Greek city-states and argues against the view from Copenhagen. The outcome suggests that Aristotle was correct to place autonomy at the heart of what it meant to be a *polis*: it is military capacities that allow the *polis* not to be a slave, but self-sufficient (*autarkēs*).[18]

The process was distributed unevenly. Dependent cities survived in both regions of Lokris, or on the borderlands of Ēlis, or in Ēpeiros—for a while.[19] The *polis* of Epidauros was taken over by Argos, with Macedonian support, after 338 BCE—for a few decades.[20] The Rhodian state, a very large and powerful island *polis* made up of the integration of three earlier, smaller *poleis*, ruled over many cities on the mainland; it also ruled over the *poleis* of Lykia and Karia—again, for a while, specifically between 188 and 167 BCE, before the Roman Republic made the Rhodians give up their control over these *poleis*, which then became autonomous.[21] The Lykian cities had earlier expressed interest in being allies of the Rhodian *polis*, but categorically not in being subject to Rhodian orders, a good illustration of the expectation of autonomy in dealings between *polis*-shaped entities.

In most cases, the old dependent cities either broke loose—this is what happened to Helissōn, integrated as a still existing *polis* by Mantineia in the fourth century BCE, but a fully autonomous *polis* in the Hellenistic period—or were integrated fully into the larger *poleis*, as civic subdivisions. The expansion of medium-sized and large *poleis* is a well-attested phenomenon in the Hellenistic period and prolongs the microimperialism of the "Archaic" and Classical periods. Milētos took over two *poleis* in its

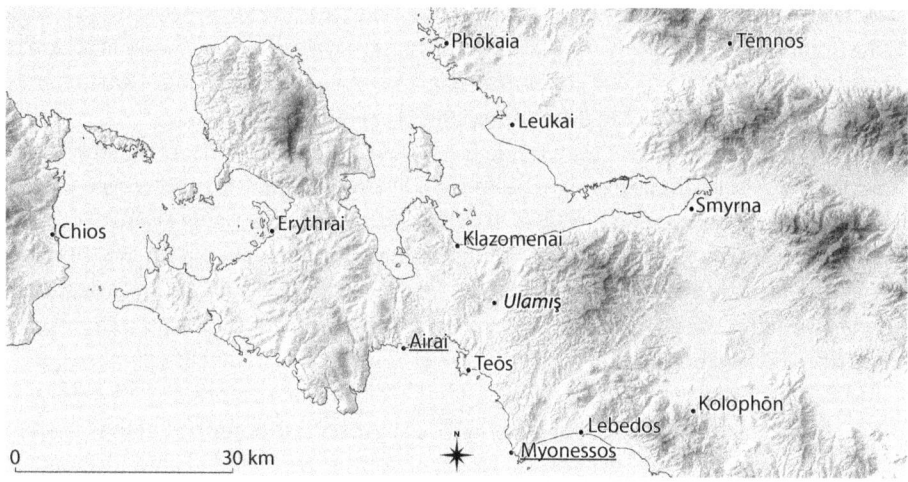

FIGURE 9.2. The territory of Teōs and its neighbors.

area (Myous, under ecological pressure because of the silting of the Meander Delta, gradually absorbed and keeping some form of corporate existence for decades after formal annexation: fig 1.5; and Pēdasa, taken over in one negotiated transaction).[22] The relatively modest *polis* of Teōs took over three or perhaps four smaller *poleis* in its hinterland, including Kyrbissos which it held with a permanent garrison of twenty citizen militiamen (fig. 9.2).[23] But crucially, that expansion now did not involve subordination, but took the form of the integration, not the subordination, of smaller *polis* units by the means of political union (*sumpoliteia*).

A particularly eloquent example of the new climate is to be found in central Greece, where Boiōtia had long been organized in groups of *poleis* structured unequally.[24] We have already seen Orchomenos controlling Chairōneia; likewise, the territory of the *polis* of Tanagra contained a subordinate *polis*, Mykalēssos, and perhaps another one, Pharai. The great rival of Thebes, Thespiai, ruled over four other *poleis* (Thisbē, Chorsiai, Siphai, and Eutrēsis), as well as the non-*polis* settlement of Askra; an early fifth-century BCE diplomatic document, found at Olympia, could speak of "the Thespians and those with them." Even Plataiai, the breakaway Boiotian *polis* that did not want to belong to the Boiotian Confederacy, controlled four smaller *poleis* in the Asōpos valley. In this landscape of *poleis* and unequally structured clusters of *poleis*, the "Hundred Years" unfolded along several interlocking storylines. One was the integration of the Boiotian city-states within a broader regional political structure with representative institutions. The other was the support of Sparta for individual Boiotian *poleis*, especially the larger *poleis* such as Thespiai (above, p. 170), in the name of local autonomy and to counter Theban ambitions—which must have been problematic in view of the "Greater Thespiai" or the "Greater

Plataiai" created by controlling smaller *poleis*. Finally, the Thebans attempted to lead the Boiotian cities to greater hegemony at large, as part of a politically unified region with federal institutions but under unambiguous Theban domination—which necessitated breaking rival big *poleis*, especially Thespiai and Plataiai.

The Theban effort failed. As a result, the League underwent a first reorganization under Macedonian control, which ended Theban domination and resurrected Thespiai and Orchomenos. Thebes itself was destroyed after rising against Macedonian control in 335 (the citizens of Thespiai and Orchomenos participated in the sack), and only refounded in 316 by Kassandros, one of the Macedonian dynasts who held sway after the death of Alexandros III. After some hesitancy (and a complex history of resistance and revolt against royal control, when Thebes was besieged and captured twice), the newly refounded Thebes was admitted to a Boiotian League in which the dependent cities had disappeared. As in the rest of the Greek world, they were either integrated into large *poleis* as civic subdivisions, or broke away to full autonomy and participated in the political and military institutions of the League. The *poleis* that were once dependent *poleis* within the Greater Thespiai were fully autonomous—tiny Chorsiai (fig. 9.3) was, at least formally, fully equal to its somewhat larger neighbor Thisbē, or indeed any other Boiotian *polis*; Thisbē was formally separated from Thespiai in a new system of districts.[25]

The League offered a framework for interactions between the cities— Orchomenos and Chairōneia struck an agreement about their military obligations to the League, and Orchomenos also seems to have concluded some form of treaty or convention (involving religious and financial clauses) with the small *polis* of Kyrtōnes (in another district of the League).[26] This development, a combined simplification and rationalization of the Boiotian *polis*-scape, represents a remarkable act of collaboration and restraint on the part of the big cities.

The path of the Boiotian *poleis* is part of a wide story—that of the Hellenistic period as the great age of city-state freedom.[27] Autonomy mattered greatly to the *poleis*, and this concern, which continued the struggles and debates of the "Hundred Years," can be seen in the celebration of the recovery of autonomy by *poleis*. The Eretrians, ca. 343 BCE, founded a great festival (the *Artemiria*, to spell the name of this festival of Artemis in its local variant), explicitly in connection with their prosperity and the "self-sovereignty" of republican government (they considered themselves *autokratores*). Furthermore, in 285 BCE, when they regained freedom, ancestral laws, and democracy upon the departure of a Macedonian garrison, they celebrated the day by adding elements to the tradition festival of Dionysos (the date of their liberation).[28] The citizens of Priēnē, in the early Hellenistic period, prefaced all their documents with the clause "When the Prienians were autonomous . . . ,"[29] and resumed relations with Athens (including the Athenian cleruchy on Samos, shortly before its dissolution).[30] Kolophōn invested in hugely ambitious fortifications as a mark of its regained autonomy. Admittedly, Kolophōn lost its freedom and indeed its existence as *polis* due to royal intervention shortly afterward; but it regained

FIGURE 9.3. View of part of the territory of Chorsiai, as seen from its akropolis, showing hillsides, agricultural plain, and harbor.

polis-hood again, and continued a complicated existence in the Hellenistic world, in *sumpoliteia* with Notion (or "Kolophōn-by-sea"), the city that resisted Antiochos III.[31] The rise of the long inscribed honorific decree for citizen politicians as a canonical form of civic expression is also linked with the generalization of autonomy, one of the major values celebrated in the praise of good citizens.[32]

One of the consequences of the generalization of autonomy and the end of dependent *polis*-hood was to facilitate participation in large federal states uniting autonomous cities within common decision-making processes and institutional frameworks to produce highly effective shared goods on the social, economic, and political fronts.[33] The end of hegemony solved many of the tensions that had held back earlier federal formations (above, chapter 8), in Arkadia or in Boiōtia. The distributive institutions (especially military) and delicacy of precautions in the new Boiotian League illustrate this phenomenon. Other leagues emerged during the third century BCE and enjoyed considerable success: the Achaian League in the Peloponnese, the Aitolian League in central Greece, the Akarnanian League along the western edge of the Corinthian Gulf.

Such federal structures were organized around an assembly of individuals from the various constituent communities, a board of elected officials reproducing at a higher scale the normal forms of *polis* organization. They also introduced various institutional and legal commonalities between member communities, such as property or citizen rights, and indeed a degree of uniformity in local practice. Finally, they also were animated by an extended form of *polis* ideology based on communitarian engagement: this extension was aided by the generalization of democratic forms, a development that the leagues themselves nurtured by their institutional practice. The Achaian politician Margos of Karyneia spent his whole life doing what was right (*ta dikaia*) for the Achaian state (*politeuma*): Polybios's language draws on the civic register of description of good citizenship and applies it at the federal level.[34]

These leagues often achieved enough critical mass to resist encroachment by the Macedonian kingdom and to act as political powers in their own right, in direct interaction with the larger supralocal states, partly shaping the political history of the Hellenistic world (especially in mainland Greece). The Achaian and Aitolian Leagues, rivals, also shared the characteristic of actively seeking more members to expand; the Aitolian League granted membership to communities in the Aegean, such as the island *polis* of Chios, and the Achaian League pressured communities into joining—including Sparta (which soon broke away). Likewise, the Boiotian League at times managed to incorporate *poleis* on the edge of the regional entity of Boiōtia—Megara, Aigosthena, Eastern Lokris, and the great Euboian cities of Chalkis and Eretria (for instance, the celebration of the latter city's freedom from Macedonian control in 285 took place when part of the Boiotian League).[35]

Yet the decision whether to join a league was the result of more than simply pressure from large state formations, and the leagues should not be seen as infringing local autonomy or reintroducing hegemony (much less as frames within which *poleis* were no longer autonomous, as M. Hansen erroneously writes).[36] Anaktōrion had long been a Corinthian possession, but its entry into the Akarnanian League was a result of the end of dependent *polis*-hood, and the availability of political choices.[37] It is true, however, that by the late third and the early second centuries BCE, the Aitolian and Achaian Leagues, partly by the very fact of their success at playing high politics in the same international space as the great royal states, shifted toward expansionism, often violent and aggressive—which did much to cause unrest in the Hellenistic world of those decades, even as it served the interests of the leagues' political elites in terms of power and raw acquisitiveness.[38] But this moment, too, came to an end.

The other consequence of autonomy was the spreading and the thickening of the network of peer-polity interaction, already pervasive during earlier centuries. The simplification of the status of *poleis* and the generalization of sovereignty multiplied the number of actors that had access to recognition and agency within the multi-actor network. Peer-polity recognition and interaction meant the availability of multiple channels for interaction, collaboration, and harmonization—myth and kinship, shared identity, or simply a perceived ethical norm for diplomatic exchange, already present in the fifth and fourth centuries BCE. As we have seen, the

Prienians, autonomous after the end of Achaimenid control in Iōnia, resumed contacts with Athens on the other side of the Aegean. In 205 BCE, the *polis* of Kytenion, which claimed to be "the *mētropolis* of the Dorians"; that is, the original heartland of those Greeks who identified themselves as Dorians and which was further integrated within a large, powerful federal state, the Aitolian League, went on a fundraising drive to rebuild its walls. This took the form of an embassy sent to all *poleis* that were related to the Kytenians in terms of mythical kinship.[39]

Such campaigns are known in the "Archaic" period or the Classical period, for instance around Delphi; the Hellenistic period sees particular communities mounting very ambitious diplomatic enterprises to achieve recognition of their territory and shrine as sacred (enjoying *asylia*), and their festival as equivalent to a particular old Hellenic festival; in practice, this meant sending teams of sacred ambassadors to ask every relevant member of the world of the *poleis*. The peer-polity nature of the network means that such campaigns imitated and influenced each other—and proliferated.[40] The whole texture of *polis* life was shaped by the interaction between free peers: the circulation of individuals, the appearance of the cities, and the bargaining between neighbors about economic matters.

It is true that armed conflict between the *poleis* was not a rare occurrence, reflecting the availability of military means and the margin for local initiative. But this does not mean that the *poleis* lived in a world of constant anarchy and predation: the end of *polis* subordination as an option had transformed inter-*polis* warfare to one of a range of negotiated options in interstate relations.[41] Warfare also gave the occasion for cities to collaborate and help each other, just like other crises. The *polis* of Entella, in western Sicily, had occasion to pass decrees to thank many of its neighbors for assistance during war as well as grain shortages, in the first half of the third century BCE (fig. 9.4).[42] The Entellans were notably helped by neighbors when they were "wandering" after expulsion; likewise, the city of Stymphalos, in the Peloponnese, helped the citizens of Elateia when the latter were driven out of their city, on the grounds of myth-mediated "kinship" between the two cities.[43] Peer-polity interaction thus allowed cities to try to resist the pressures of high politics; it also created strong horizontal links of solidarity that crossed the boundaries of supralocal states (even if the latter tried to control peer interaction by fostering networks within their own realms, through the promotion of the exchange of arbitration panels for local disputes, or regional federations).[44]

Factors of Convergence (2): A Democratic Turn

The operation of peer-polity interaction was favored by the second major historical development that formed part of the great convergence: the generalization of *dēmokratia*, with the result that most *poleis* could talk to each other because they knew that they were dealing with peers. This process was itself the result of a number

FIGURE 9.4. Decree incised on bronze, Entella (Ampolo 2001, A2). H 18.2 cm, w 11.5 cm.

of historical trends. An obvious trend is the gradual disappearance of full-blown *stasis*, and factional fighting complete with murder and expulsions, along ideological lines and with outside involvement. Such episodes did persist, notably in the Peloponnese;[45] they involved the intra-elite competition unavoidable in local politics, and class tensions over issues such as debt and contract enforcement. The

Spartan resurgence of the third century BCE under the reforming king Kleomenēs III, directed against the Achaian League, was accompanied by a strong class-warfare element that created considerable disturbance among the Peloponnesian cities; the implications for the social history of power in the Hellenistic *poleis*, and indeed for the political sociology of the *polis* in general, will need consideration later (chapters 10, 18, and 19). In Kynaitha, a *polis* of the Arkadian uplands and a member of the Achaian League, an Aitolian incursion exacerbated factional fighting involving exiles, and blew up into an episode of civil war and massacres. Hellenistic Sparta was regularly racked by factional fighting and exile.[46] Likewise, the destabilizing presence of the Aitolian League seems to have encouraged unrest in the cities of Macedonian-controlled Thessaly.[47]

Yet the landscape of exiles and struggles for power in the Peloponnese does not seem to have been created by ideological struggle between oligarchical and democratic factions. The competition between Hellenistic kings in mainland Greece, on the Thracian seaboard, in the islands, in Asia Minor and the Levant, certainly involved local supporters and factions[48]—but did not provoke full-blown civil war because there was no ideological divide within the *polis* paradigm. Naturally, unrest and disputes did not disappear from the *poleis*, but were often solved by appeal to outside arbitrators, a solution fostered by the Hellenistic kings (to preserve peace in the communities they ruled over), but also by the peer-polity network: *poleis* resorted to panels of "foreign judges," sent by other *poleis*, to arbitrate cases (usually involving economic matters such as contracts or debt) between citizens.[49] The success of foreign judges as a civic practice illustrates how the developments of royal presence and peer-polity interaction combined to create favorable conditions for the spread of democracy by tamping down the disputes that were one of the elements of the vengeful equation of the Classical period. The long arc of *polis* history bent toward a generally democratic future free from *stasis*.

It is quite true that the kings initially did support a variety of regimes in addition to local democracies. As hinted at earlier, Lysimachos not only deported the population of Kolophōn after defeating the Kolophonian effort to defend their refounded city, in order to increase his new city of Arsinoeia (a refoundation of Ephesos), but he also endowed this city with an oligarchical constitution with a restricted franchise and limited decision-making bodies.[50] The royal foundation of Ptolemais in Upper Egypt also saw an oligarchical coup, uniquely documented in an inscription.[51] In the Peloponnese, the Argead rulers and their Antigonid successors supported small factions and tyrants in a number of cities (in spite of engagements taken in the settlement of 338 BCE), into the third century BCE.[52]

All the same, such solutions would turn out to be unsustainable. The oligarchical régime at Ephesos-Arsinoeia proved a dead-end; the Peloponnesian tyrannies vanished in the second half of the third century BCE, when *poleis* were absorbed into the increasingly successful Achaian League. The end of tyranny could be peaceful, with tyrants abdicating and turning into politicians in their newly Achaian cities; or violent, with the murder or execution of tyrants. What matters is the great republican surge of these decades, which substantially loosened Macedonian control in southern Greece, and led to the end of oligarchy in the Peloponnese.[53]

Both outcomes illustrate the multiple failures of oligarchical and signorial solutions during the early Hellenistic period. (I borrow the term "signorial" from the historiography of the medieval Italian city-state: it describes personal despotism, specifically as a stage in the development of the city-state, the death-knell of the earlier *popolo* movement, and a response to endemic factionalism.)[54] Ideologically, single rule was decisively associated with tyranny, the latter having been defined in the late Classical period as oppressive and unjust (thus moving from the technical definition of the "Archaic" period to, basically, our understanding of "tyrannical"). In Sicily and southern Italy, the collapse of Syracusan tyranny was followed by a shift to democratic regimes, as can be seen in the case of the *polis* of Epizephyrian Lokroi (in modern Calabria).[55] There, the workings of the democratic city are illustrated by financial documents of the late fourth and early third centuries BCE. Hellenistic cities collaborated to put down tyrannies, in an effort to ensure the democratic and autonomous norm. The Ephesians aided democratic Prienian exiles in the early Hellenistic period; the militia of the small Karian city of Amyzōn marched out to turf out a tyrant from a neighboring *polis* sometime in the third century BCE; and the Lykian cities, in the early second century BCE, collaborated to fight against Rhodian-backed tyrants.[56]

Such a form of collaboration illustrates the imbrication of local autonomy (with military means) and the normalization of democracy. Furthermore, oligarchical rule was identified with tyranny because of factional violence and injustice. In Athens, the faction of 403 BCE was named the "Thirty Tyrants," and post-403 legislation drew on images of tyrant-slaying that had been developed earlier in Athenian political culture.[57] Just as oligarchical violence was cast as unjust and oppressive, democratic ideology also valorized and legitimized its own violence as nonfactional, communitarian, and liberating: such acts of tyrant-slaying, faction repression, and communal uprising directed against tyrants or tyrant-like oligarchs, were conceived as founding acts of *polis* liberty, embedded within constitutional measures by decree and by honorific practice, and valorized by civic rewards.[58]

Democratic action drew its force from links with the rough self-help that had been one of the manifestations of community, from the beginnings of the *polis* (for instance, in Odysseus's Ithakē: above, p. 60, or in early fifth-century Teōs: above, p. 141). The representation of this violence oscillated between the heroic gesture of one man to the implication and uprising of all citizens (again, a legitimizing and valorizing of one of the modes of democratic violence, the upsurge of collective violence against a small minority). At Eretria, a law against tyrants specified that in case of overthrow of democracy, every citizen should take arms, "thinking himself [able to fight]"—the verb used, *hegeimenon*, also designates the act of leadership, as if every citizen were his own general, and the *polis*'s freedom was founded in the sum of individual acts of autonomy.[59]

The shifts and appropriations involved in democratic valorization, and its foundational value, can be seen in a remarkable document from Erythrai, where a democratic city restored the statue of a tyrannicide, a citizen named Philitēs:[60]

> It was resolved by the Council and the People: Zōilos son of Chiadēs proposed. Since those in the oligarchy took away from the image of the statue of Philitēs, the killer of the tyrant, his sword, thinking that his pose was directed against them in general; in order that the *dēmos* be seen to take great care and to remember forever its benefactors, living and dead; with good fortune; be it resolved by the Council and the People; the *exetastai* in office will contract out the work, having made an inquest with the architect, about how it should be realized as it was before; let the monthly treasurer be at their disposal; let the *agoranomoi* take care that the statue be clean of patina and crowned always on the first of the month and the other festivals. (*There follows a decree about the details of how to pay for all this*).

At Erythrai, the tyrannicide's liberating violence was felt as a threat by an oligarchic faction—showing how oligarchs themselves acknowledged the force of the assimilation of tyranny and oligarchy (at least this is how the democratic *polis* imagined its foes). The oligarchs' reaction was to remove the tyrannicide's sword, in an act of mutilation bordering on sacrilege, and perhaps accomplished in secrecy: the gesture united the factional group by the bonds of a shared gesture of defiance toward the community, which it hoped to cow by this gesture of secrecy and unaccountability. The restored democracy reestablished its links with the heroic gesture of the tyrannicide by the restoration of the monument itself, by the way in which the crowned statue looks like the mass of crown-wearing citizens at each festival, embedding the tyrant-slayer's gesture within the whole community of potential defenders of the democracy, and by the way in which the democracy punctiliously insists on transparency and accountability, in contrast with the exclusionary, cliquish secrecy of "those in the oligarchy."

Oligarchy died a double death with irreversible results. The new militant oligarchy, as a confident set of propositions about the just *polis*, which had developed in response to *dēmokratia*, retreated into texts or stances, then simply disappeared;[61] the old style of closed polity, with various forms of playacting to ensure the solidarity of the small citizen group and the exclusion of others, gradually vanished. Far from being a text written during the twilight of the city-state (as, for instance, P. Pellegrin has repeatedly written),[62] Aristotle's *Politics* constitutes an invaluable witness situated at the start of the great convergence in the second half of the fourth century BCE. It is true that some of the terms of the debates and conversations in Aristotle's ragbag, seminar-like text are still influenced by the elite-centered and oligarchical questions raised during the fifth and fourth centuries BCE: Aristotle was still a man of his class (wealthy, elitist). Such hoary questions (taken a bit too seriously by modern historians of philosophy or political theory) include the constitutional issue of law versus decrees, the philosophical conundrum of "rule by the best," the self-serving interrogations about the place of the virtuous in a hypothetical "best constitution," and the point-scoring, gotcha-critique of democracy as equivalent to tyranny because of the threatened spoliation of the rich and of the supposed lack of restraint and materialism of the populace of the poor.[63] Equally, Aristotle is aware of the monarchical and signorial possibilities and temptations of the same period.

But under these debates, the historical assumptions and general framework are those of the generalization of democratic practice. Aristotle's famous critique of Sparta, in *Politics*, Book 2, reflects assumptions about the importance of equality, the necessity of redistributive taxation and levies to produce public goods, and the crucial role of the *polis* as state—all areas that were blocked by Spartan plutocracy (above, p. 195).[64] In addition to his awareness of autonomy as a principle of *polis*-hood (above), Aristotle's discussions of citizenship and the access to rule grudgingly or unconsciously acknowledge the gravitational pull of democratic ideas and consensus; for instance, the principle that all men can judge all things and hence the *dēmos* should control the great affairs of state, the nature of the *polis* as the *koinōnia* of all free men irrespective of wealth, the practice of wide access to office and accountability, the possibility of pay for political service, the constraining of inequality and wealth elites—even if the seminar-like nature of the text includes much pushback against these ideas, or attempts to nuance them out of sight.[65]

Likewise, the *Politics* are full of references to the spread of democracy: an awareness that craftsmen are no longer being excluded from citizenship, examples of old-style constitutions or censitary barriers falling into abeyance or dwindling[66]— even if Aristotle also invokes examples from the "Archaic" *polis* and finds much nuance and diversity in actual practice. In the end, and for all his hesitations, Aristotle seems to favor a form of constitution that he cannot quite bring himself to call *dēmokratia*, describing it as *politeia*, an inherence to the possibilities of the citizen-state and a corrective to the aberration that his elite-centered and philosophical frameworks force him to see in democracy (we could translate it by "republic," which has the same mealy-mouthed effect). *Politeia* is close to rule by the masses, as Aristotle admits;[67] and is the result of compromise and negotiation—a concept that may prove useful for the interpretation of the great convergence.

The vanishing of the old closed style participates in the generalization of democratic regimes in Asia Minor, sponsored by Alexandros III in his takeover of the Ionian and Aiolian coast in 334: "let the constitution (*politeoma*) be a democracy (*dēmos*)," as he wrote to Chios (in an admittedly complex document that also dictated military contributions, imposed a garrison, and involved the League of Corinth, founded by Philippos II in 338, as well as his own jurisdiction, in Chian internal affairs).[68] This support of *dēmokratia* and autonomy had its roots in the specific need to obtain local support and consent in the aftermath of the removal of Achaimenid control and of the local oligarchical factions mostly favored by the Achaimenid state

FIGURE 9.5. Bronze coin (*dichalkon*), Knidos, 350-300 BCE. Obv. head of Aphroditē with caption DAMOKRATIAS; rev. ship prow above club. Ca. 17 mm. BnF Fonds général 491.

at that point in time. It also tied in with the old theme of the liberation of the Greeks of Asia,[69] fittingly for the pan-Hellenic motive of Alexander's expedition.

Autonomy and democracy were next adopted as slogans and policies by some of Alexander's successors, such as Antigonos the One-Eyed and his son Dēmētrios the Besieger, or their rival Ptolemy I (the dynast based in Egypt but nurturing ambitions in the Levant and the Aegean). Whatever the realities of the implementation of the royal slogans (in practice, these early successors often infringed local freedom and intervened in local politics),[70] the effect of royal support for democracy was the extension of democratic regimes beyond the original area of Alexander's policy (Iōnia and Aiolis) and the acceleration of the phenomenon of institutional convergence throughout the Hellenistic world.

Around 300 BCE, the small island *polis* of Tēlos, with the help of arbitrators from neighboring Kōs, brokered a settlement with its oligarchical faction (imposing various tasks as part of the reconciliation); the outcome was explicitly described as strengthening democracy.[71] A bronze coin, probably struck at the time, celebrates the local regime: its main side bears the head of Athēna and, split between the projecting flanges of an aegis, the legend *DA-MO-KR-AT-IA-S*, "of democracy," perhaps meaning "in a time of/under democracy." Suggestively, the monetary legend is exactly paralleled in bronze coins of Knidos, dating perhaps to the mid-fourth century BCE (fig. 9.5).[72] The generalization of democracy was hence the result of three contemporary, interlocking phenomena: the demise of oligarchy (more or less violent), the construction of new civic possibility through reconciliation, and the frequent underwriting of these two phenomena by outside powers.[73]

Processes of Democratic Diffusion

In addition to democratic ideology and discourse (seen especially in the case of the ideological disqualification of hegemony), the great convergence took the form of the widespread adoption, adaptation, and normalization of democratic institutions.[74] Whereas in the fifth century BCE, the *polis* of Ioulis simply published regulations on funerals, later additions to the original document were formulated as decrees, laying out the procedures of popular decision-making in a public manner that seems to matter as much as the actual content of the decrees or laws.[75] More generally, the epigraphical sources hint at large mass assemblies, the lack of censitary barriers, demagogic politics, popular courts, pay for service, accountability of magistrates and public control over them, transparency and publicity, and a culture of reciprocity balancing individual services and collective honors: such features become well attested throughout the world of the *poleis* (see further below).[76]

The process can be illustrated in general terms at Thasos, where, after three decades of civil strife and rapid regime change, a democratic polity emerged out of reconciliation: the moment in the early fourth century BCE is documented in an inscription in which the qualifiers of the various factions were erased, testament to the reconciliation's success. The aftermath saw an intense period of institutionalization and rule-making along democratic lines.[77] A small *polis* in western Sicily, Nakōnē, tried to overcome civil strife with the help of arbitrators from its neighbor Egesta: it passed a decree creating new civic subdivisions, the "elected brotherhoods" of five men each (one from each faction, and three neutrals): an original, extreme solution that combines a civic ideology of kinship-like commitment and a confidence in complex institutional solutions.[78] The decree from Nakōnē is unique for now; in addition, the artifact bearing it appeared without provenance on the antiquities market and the site is not localized. We can still tell that it was passed by the normal sequence of proposal by the Council and popular vote in the Assembly. The same holds true for the decrees from neighboring Entella (above, p. 213).[79]

We can turn to three further examples for detailed illustration of the diffusion of democratic culture, and its continuity. The first is a decree from Hellenistic Athens. Dating to 228 BCE, it mentions the reasons why the people should honor a good citizen:

> since the laws too order that those whom the *dēmos* of the Athenians has honored with food in the *prytaneion*, for setting up trophies on land or on sea, or bringing back liberty, or putting their own fortune at the disposal of the common safety, or becoming benefactors and good advisors, should be taken care of, with their descendants, by the *boulē* and the *dēmos*, and that the people should give a dowry for their daughters' marriage according to its wishes and for the restoration of the benefactors' private fortune, according to the value of the benefactions of each . . .

The tone and issues are very similar to the tone of discussion in late Classical Athens, and the nature of service is political, as leader, or as politician, or as benefactor: the relationship between benefactor and community is not about elite dominance, but community reward for devotion to the *dēmos*, a general principle of the political culture of the age.[80]

The second example is the continuity in the story of Kymē. This Aiolian *polis* is described by Aristotle as particularly democratic, to excess, provoking a subsequent oligarchical reaction (during the late fourth century BCE?).[81] The reaction was obviously reversed, since in the early Hellenistic period the *polis* had a democratic constitution, as seen in a document mentioning the Kymaian law against *hubris* (haughty violence—such laws are typically democratic). Another document is a decree regulating the powers of the important office of *stratēgos* (general), which nearly amounts to an "anti-tyrannical," anti-oligarchical law of the type widely known in this period, since the general is to be punished (amongst other crimes) if he fails to help the democracy or hands the city keys over to those who wish to overthrow the democracy. Both of these documents explicitly describe the *polis* of the Kymaians as free, autonomous, and democratic.[82]

My third example is late Classical Kōs. This is another *polis* described by Aristotle as excessively democratic; in the Hellenistic period, Kōs appears endowed with clear democratic institutions and practices.[83] When a special commission submitted to the Assembly the draft proposal for a regulation concerning the perks to be enjoyed by the priestess of Dionysos Thyllophoros, a citizen speaker proposed a considerable amendment on substance, namely that the priestess should contribute toward the upkeep of a small shrine—and managed to get this proposal passed by the people, thus imposing a real financial burden on the family that would buy the priesthood.[84]

The democratic qualities expected from the Koan citizen are made explicit in the oath sworn by the members of Kalymnos, a neighboring island taken over by Kōs in a local process of expansion and synoikism (cf. pp. 209–10):[85]

> I will remain in the established democracy and in the restoration of the *homopoliteia* and the ancestral laws which there are on Kōs and the decrees of the *ekklēsia* and the *diagraphai* concerning the *homopoliteia*; I will remain in the friendship and alliance with King Ptolemy and the agreements which the *damos* has agreed with the allies; I will not install an oligarchy or a tyranny or any other constitution apart from democracy on any account, nor will I allow anyone who does so, but will prevent as much as possible, and I will not betray any of the forts or the akropolis nor myself nor abetting another on any account, nor will I allow Koan land to become smaller, but I will augment it according to my powers; I will be a just judge and a fair citizen, voting and putting to the vote decrees without favor in the matter of that which seems to me advantageous to the *damos* . . .

Koan citizenship meant an explicit commitment to preserving the constitution as a democracy, defined in opposition to the equivalent and disqualified practices of tyranny and oligarchy. Democracy was linked with the freedom of the *polis* and indeed its desire to affirm itself as a state, through expansion and foreign policy. Citizenship at Kōs also meant the exercise of civic activities that belonged to the democratic political culture of the Hellenistic *poleis*: acting as a judge in the popular courts, voting as a citizen in the Assembly, putting matters to the vote as a magistrate before the Assembly. All of these activities took in the awareness of the duties to act for the good of the *dēmos*, equated to the common good, thus realizing the old equation between the majority, the common mass, and the community—an equation at the heart of the democratic *polis* and the *polis* in general (above, p. 124). The realization of this equation, just as the generalization of autonomy, is significant for the nature of the Classical *polis*.

When the cities of Milētos and Hērakleia under Latmos struck a peace treaty after fighting a local war, they entrusted arbitration about a disputed piece of territory to a *polis eleuthera kai dēmokratoumenē*, a free and democratic city (or "republican" state, to use this classic terminology), whose judgment would be acceptable as that of one of their peer cities.[86] The expression does not mean that there are *poleis* that are not free and not democratic, but that these are essential qualities of *polis*hood in the Hellenistic period. In the Hellenistic period, *dēmokratia* can in fact mean both freedom from external control, and a democratic régime: in both cases, it is the *dēmos* that decides. The convergence between the two concepts already appears in the reply given in 370 BCE by a reconstructed, freshly democratic city of Mantineia to the Spartan demand that the rebuilt walls be dismantled and the city dioikized (above): this is impossible, because it goes against the *dēmos*'s will. This particular case shows how the defeat of Sparta in 371 BCE, and the dismantling of its system of control through oligarchical factions and collusion, played an important part in the great convergence. By 319 BCE, the Macedonian dynast Polyperchōn promised the cities who should rally to him "autonomy and democracy," together, an early but explicit connection of the two concepts.[87] Such examples raise the question of the shape of the great convergence as a historical phenomenon, and the imbrication of freedom, democracy, political events, and cultural history.

The Great Convergence and the History of the *Polis*

It is clear that the first stage of the convergence took place between ca. 350 and 280 BCE, as noted by P. Carlier.[88] The end of hegemony in the aftermath of Leuktra (and the end of Syracusan hegemony in Sicily and southern Italy), the creation of the Hellenistic empires, and the emergence of the norms of autonomy and democracy, all took place during this time span, and are most visible in parts of mainland Greece (with a lag in the Peloponnese), the islands, and Asia Minor. It is equally clear that the late fourth century BCE played a crucial role both in defining the terms of the debate, and in starting the processes of convergence: the celebration of autonomy and the democratic practice so visible in cities of early third-century BCE Asia Minor (Kymē, Priēnē, discussed above) prolong developments visible in the second half of the fourth century BCE, for instance at Eretria, which proudly proclaims its *autokratoria* or political self-sufficiency and which protects democracy through its anti-tyranny law (above, pp. 216–17). The case of Eretria suggests that the roots of the great convergence lay in the generalization of autonomy and democracy as the most desirable forms for the *poleis*. An oligarchical pushback seems to be detectable in late fourth-century BCE Athens (above, pp. 183, 199), in various forms, and in the cities of Asia Minor. This pushback was decisively undone by a combination of royal support for autonomy (after some hesitation) and internal evolutions in the *poleis*.

The gradual disappearance of "tyrannies" and oligarchies throughout the Greek world, and the constant interaction between kings and cities within a shared moralizing language, further drove the extension of the *polis* model during the third century BCE. The *polis* of Larisa, in Thessaly, provides an illustration. Larisa had once been the seat of a powerful monarchical family, the Aleuads; after a typically eventful history it was absorbed, with the rest of Thessaly, into Macedonian control in 352 BCE. Yet under Macedonian control, it developed *polis* institutions of its own, which show local specificities (power of the *tagoi* combined with authority of the Assembly and frequent rotation of officials such as the treasurers) and a strong sense of local autonomy. True, the *polis* was part of the Antigonid state: it produced a high-ranking officer of Philip V and had to admit new citizens upon instructions by that king. The Larisaians nonetheless did so with reluctance and even resistance and made a point of issuing their own decree to validate, on local terms, the royal instructions.

This type of distancing, space-opening, agency-creating behavior is exactly the same as can be observed for other *poleis* in their dealings with Hellenistic kings, and its presence at Larisa is another instance of the convergence of *polis* behavior,[89] of the way in which dealing with kings along pre-scripted lines produced spaces of autonomy. The pattern is observable throughout the Hellenistic world in the third century BCE, and on the part of all kinds of cities—old Greek city-states, new royal foundations, non-Greek communities adopting *polis* forms (below)—for instance, the communities of inland Karia, behaving like *poleis* and insisting on being treated as such by the royal authorities.[90] In the Seleukid empire, "imperial" cities such as Sardeis or Antiocheia in Persis (a new city founded by a Seleukid ruler) also became accepted as a *polis* by other Greek *poleis*. Sardeis was to entertain relations with Delphi, a prestigious old Greek city; it was treated as a *polis* by the Seleukid ruler Antiochos III, when it was reconquered after the defeat of a usurper. By the early second century BCE, Sardeis sent out foreign judges and passed honorific decrees for citizen benefactors, like other Greek *poleis*.[91] Antiocheia in Persis was treated as a "kindred" city by Magnēsia on Maeander (which had contributed colonists to the royal foundation), when the Magnesians asked for acknowledgment of their shrine of Artemis as holy and inviolate, a typical transaction of the peer-polity network; the Antiocheians responded with a long, formal decree that shows the workings of civic institutions and ideology.[92]

The diffusion of the *polis* mode allows us to trace the convergence of *polis* institutions, and its intensity. Non-Greek communities adopted *polis* forms, and were acknowledged as *poleis*: by 100 BCE, the result was the increase of the world of the Greek *poleis* by several hundred new *poleis*, either old communities that bought into the *polis* world, or royal foundations that converged into the network. The phenomenon starts at the same time as the great convergence, ca. 350 BCE, when cities in Karia and Lykia start inscribing decrees in Greek that reflect *polis*-style decision-making institutions. The language of these documents is the Ionian dialect, and the calendar uses Ionian months, showing the influence of the Greek city-states of western Asia Minor; the general context, however, makes it clear that the adoption of *polis* institutions was strongly encouraged by the Achaimenid governors of Karia and Lykia (belonging to a single family of local strongmen, the Hekatomnid dynasty), and that the new *poleis* worked within Achaimenid administration.[93]

An inscription in Greek informs us that "when Pixōtaros son of Hekatomnos became satrap of Lykia, he appointed Hierōn and Apollodotos governors (*archontes*) of Lykia, and Artemēlis as governor of Xanthos, and it seemed good to the Xanthians and their dwellers-around—to set up an altar to the King of Kaunos and Arkesimas," and so on (the cult of these two deities was endowed with land, and the enforcement of the endowment underwritten by the satrap). The satrap in fact issued a *datah*, to use the technical, Iranian term for "law," in Aramaic (one of the administrative languages of the Achaimenid empire), restating and confirming the arrangements decided by the "lords of Orna" (*b'ly 'wrn*), using the Lykian name of the city. The satrap's edict was inscribed on the same stone slab as the decree in Greek. The same slab bears the decree in Lykian, as decided by the citizenry (?), designated by the local term *arus*, and the dwellers-around (the term is translated into Lykian). The trilingual document is a striking piece of evidence for the adopting and adapting of *polis* forms within a world empire, showing pressure from above as well as the integration of a rural or dependent population.[94]

These early cases show different mechanisms for the diffusion of the *polis* model. One mechanism was patronage by supralocal states: the Achaimenid state or its provincial representatives (surprisingly), and later the Hellenistic kingdoms. During the third century BCE, a large number of Karian, Lykian, and Levant-based communities produce Greek-language decrees that suppose *polis* institutions and indeed explicitly show their workings. The dynastic culture of local bosses in Lykia, based on fortified sites and celebrating their capacity for violence, vanishes, replaced by *polis* institutions.[95] The phenomenon is further attested in inland Anatolia or Kappadokia in the second century BCE, often in contexts associated with royal power (for instance, Attalid Asia Minor or smaller realms such as Bithynia or

Kappadokia).⁹⁶ In other words, the close relation between Hellenistic kingdoms and Greek city-states was reflected in the transformation of local communities, encouraged to adopt Greek political forms or even refounded as royal cities with Greek names and institutions.

Another mechanism for the diffusion of the *polis* model was peer-polity interaction. This could take the form of the influence of *poleis* upon their neighboring communities. Asia Minor was the most important scene for this sort of interaction (Iōnia, Karia, and Lykia, but also Pamphylia and Kilikia).⁹⁷ In the fourth century BCE, Sardeis had relations with the nearby *poleis* of Milētos and Ephesos, even if the Milesians were not quite sure how to refer to the institutions and governance of the Lydian city.⁹⁸ Similar interactions may have taken place in the Greek West, in Sicily and southern Italy (for instance, Morgantina seems to have become a *polis* in the late Classical period).⁹⁹ Connections could also happen between widely separated communities, for instance Sardeis and Delphi, in the sixth century BCE already. By the third century BCE, certain non-Greek communities, once they had adopted *polis* forms, received recognition and acceptance within the network of *poleis*, with surprising fluency and facility, as can be seen across the Hellenistic world.

For instance, at some date between 240 and 200 BCE, a man named Diotimos from Sidon in Phoenicia competed in the contest at the Nemeia, in the Peloponnese, one of the prestigious old festivals of Greece; his victory in the four-horse chariot race was commemorated by an honorific statue set up by the Sidonians, with an epigram that describes Sidon as the mother-city of Thebes.¹⁰⁰ The document—the earliest Greek inscription from the region—shows *polis* institutions and language, and acceptance within the festival circuit that was one of the structuring features of inter-*polis* life. In 201 BCE, the Karian city of Alabanda, refounded by the Seleukid empire as an Antiocheia, asked for recognition of its shrine and territory as *asylos* (inviolable), a typical transaction in the peer-polity network of *poleis*: the transaction is known from the responses from two prestigious places, Athens and the Amphiktiony of states that governed the oracular shrine at Delphi.¹⁰¹ The fundraising drive of Kytenion (above, p. 213), a perfect example of peer-polity interaction, is in fact known from a single response to it (a polite refusal)—that of the Lykian city of Xanthos. The Kytenians had no hesitation in approaching a Lykian city as part of the network of *poleis*; the Xanthians, at this point, were perfectly conversant in the conventions of inter-*polis* dealings.

What these cases show is that peer-polity interaction, using all the resources within Greek culture for identity formation and intercommunity structuration, accelerated the adoption of *polis* forms with enormous facility, and offered considerable advantages to both the communities acknowledged as *poleis* and the *poleis* that did the acknowledging and hence found new interlocutors and partners.

In spite of the richness of the documentary evidence, much remains puzzling about the wide adoption of *polis* forms and the ready acceptance of new members into the family of *poleis*, especially in view of negative (if nuanced) earlier views of non-Greek cultures and individuals.[102] What does it mean when the first inscribed document in Greek from a small Anatolian site or an old Phoenician city is a perfectly drafted honorific decree? The impact on the non-Greek communities, and the inner dynamics, remain obscure, notably in terms of local power relations. What was imported of the culture and political economy that went together with *polis* institutions? Did elite power in dynastic Lykia (for instance) disappear to be replaced by democratic practices, in a widespread social revolution? In the case of Phoenicia, we see participation in Greek culture and the emergence of *polis* institutions appear at the same time. Diotimos of Sidon, victor at the Nemeia, was in fact the descendant of the old ruling family of Sidon and he held a local magistracy called *dikastēs*, judge, in the Greek inscription—probably the translation of a Semitic institution (*shofet*).[103] Processes of becoming a *polis* were nested within the broader historical processes that constituted the great convergence. Any causal questions about the widespread adoption of *polis* forms are similarly part of the broader question of the causes of the great convergence of *polis* forms.

Explaining Convergence

My answer to the question "why the great convergence" has been narrative and high political. The defining moments are the unraveling of Spartan dominance at Leuktra in 371 BCE and the subsequent generalized failure of hegemony; the evolution of Athenian democracy in the second half of the fourth century BCE; and finally the strategic needs of the Macedonian ruler Alexandros III, then of the competing successor kingdoms to secure local support, create legitimacy when dealing with the Greek states, and foster administrative simplification within their territories. These events partly help to explain the runaway phenomenon of *polis* autonomy. But a purely event-driven perspective is less good at accounting for the persistence and ultimate generalization of democratic practices. Why did the Hellenistic kings' attempts at backing tyrannies or oligarchies not cause a generalized signorial turn comparable to what happened in medieval Italy (when democratic and autonomous *commune* were replaced by tyrannical and expansionary *signorie*)?[104] That this development was a possibility in this history of the *polis* is shown by the landscape of Sicily and southern Italy in the first half of the fourth century BCE, with its combination of strongmen, mercenaries, factional fighting, and Syracusan hegemony (above, p. 174); or by the case of Iasos in Karia, around the same period when we see the city split between partisans of a pro-Athenian, democratic city and those of the local Persian-backed strongmen, the Hekatomnids.[105]

Likewise, the role of the network of cities in ensuring homeostatic uniformity as an important factor in fostering both convergence and diffusion raises questions about why these two phenomena took place. Various items of political culture were clearly influenced by Athens or derived from the developments in the Athenian laboratory and diffused through peer-polity interaction (after a period of direct imposition by Athens in the fifth and early fourth centuries BCE). Examples of Athenian influence can be seen in the constitutional realm: they include the name of certain magistracies like the *euthunoi*, the use of Attic words for certain constitutional procedures,[106] and the formulation of amendments from the floor. Furthermore, many features of law and judicial practice show Athenian influence.[107] On an abstract plane, we can see Athenian influence in the moralizing political vocabulary for the character of good citizens, the liturgical system, the shape of the honorific decree (with its hortative clause aiming at publicity and exemplarity), the system of greatest honors for the greatest benefactors (free maintenance, honorific seating, bronze portrait statues), and perhaps even the habit of extensive epigraphical publication.[108] However, to point to such features does not answer the question of causality. Furthermore, this phenomenon should not be exaggerated—Athenian and Athenian-inspired practices are part of a much broader *polis* culture, which grows out of the general democratic *koinē* of the Classical period. The varied legal systems in many *poleis* can show complexity and sophistication without any sign of Athenian inspiration.[109] Even in the case of institutions or laws that parallel things known at Athens (for instance, communal care for war orphans on Thasos, or the anti-tyrannical law of Eretria), idiom and ideology reflect engagement with issues of statehood, community, and popular power, but not a specific Athenian model. The question is why the general debate on these issues led to democratic convergence.

Some of the answers to this question lie in the interlocking of the vicissitudes of political history, the working out of the *polis* as a set of consistent and sustainable discourses and ideas centered around autonomy and democracy, the advantages afforded by the *polis* and the ecology of *poleis*.[110] The generalization of democracy among the *poleis*, by restraining elite acquisitiveness, ensured the availability of surplus among the mass of citizens, for consumption or investment. The abatement of hegemony and power politics, by abolishing extraction and tribute and fostering avenues for arbitration and negotiation, created a network of peer polities whose economic exchanges were fueled by the available income among their citizens. The result was the noticeable economic uplift of the world of the *poleis*, from 350 BCE onwards.

Another factor that explains the great convergence is simply that of compromise and negotiation throughout the late Classical and Hellenistic periods; this aspect prevents us from viewing the story of the *polis* merely as a success story. The autonomy of the Hellenistic *polis* came in many shapes and forms—often that of a legal fiction within the space of the kingdoms, fostered for reasons of administrative convenience and imperial legitimacy; the question was the elaboration of a compromise that sufficed for many of the snowballing positive effects of autonomy in a network of *poleis* without threatening royal control, to which the overall collaboration of *poleis* may have contributed by fostering stability. For the citizens of Samos, recovering their *polis* from the Athenians was the beginning of their freedom—thanks to royal intervention, which they gratefully acknowledged in civic ritual.[111]

Many of the democratic features of the Hellenistic *polis*, such as the Kymaian law against *hubris* or the oath of the Kalymnians upon joining the *polis* of Kōs, reflect the presence of royal power (above)—in the case of Kymē, the assistance of the dynast Philetairos, honored with cultic gestures; in the case of Kōs, an unequal alliance with Ptolemy II, which appears in the oath itself (just as it does in documents of democratic and self-governing Milētos under Ptolemaic control).[112] Other democratic features, such as liturgies and honorific culture, or indeed many institutional practices, continue without change in Athens in periods of oligarchy (as well as foreign control).[113] The continuity might mean that democratic forms had achieved such currency that even narrow regimes had to use them (see below, chapter 16).

Another interpretation might be that the common *polis* forms that emerged ca. 300 BCE were sufficiently open and flexible, because of their diverse genealogy, to accommodate all kinds of social and political realities on the ground. Aristotle's *Politics*, in reflecting on means of stability, proposes that democracies should allow officeholding by the wealth elite or that oligarchies should allow wide access to power, implement protection against elite violence, and support redistributive practices. These proposals might reflect the actual negotiations and compromises that were part of the great convergence.[114] The resulting institutional *koinē* realized the potential of the *polis* as a state, through the expression of the authority of the political community of citizens, beyond any difference between oligarchy and democracy. The common *polis* forms born of the great convergence hence are a sign of the success of the great convergence—but also of its cost (to which we return below in chapters 17 and 18, as part of a wider examination of interests and incentives in the history of the *polis*).

10

The Qualities of the *Polis*

> How strange does this freedom seem to us [i.e., the freedom of the Ionian cities in the Hellenistic period]. Our acquaintance with this period is so poor and empty, that one is tempted to see in a renewal of civic liberty nothing more than another deformation as part of the terrible chaos of the political relations of the time. Yet let us be wary of preconceptions: for sure, the ancient self-obsessedness with original freedom no longer exists, but the vigorous efflorescence of material interests, a general prosperity based on multifarious activities, and the claims of a more rational evolution, rich in needs and pleasures, will always produce a state of society that can only be prevented by external circumstances and temporarily from asking for political self-government.
>
> —H. G. DROYSEN, *GESCHICHTE DES HELLENISMUS*

Reading with the Grain of the *Polis*

The outcome of the great convergence was a network of city-states sharing a political culture that developed out of the earlier debates and contradictions. This political culture shows great unity, stability, and coherence. At least, such is the picture that can literally be read out of the record of the *poleis*, especially the great archive of official literature constituted by public monumental epigraphy but also the public built environment and its normed elements.[1] Often this record is fragmentary—as in the case of the shard of a decree from the island *polis* of Hērakleia, which opened this book and where we see courts, an official called the *hieropoios* ("maker of sacred things") hinting at organized finances among other civic institutions, a main shrine, an Assembly, ceremonies such as oaths, laws, and monumental inscription of binding legal texts. Yet this culture in fragments seems to cohere enough to allow us to reconstruct one continuous political discourse, shared between a plurality of *poleis* and hence to speak of the politics of the *polis* in general. The grid plan of housing, implying egalitarianism, can be detected widely from Priēnē (above, p. 8) in Asia Minor to the south Italian *polis* of Hērakleia, where it replaced a more diverse townscape.[2]

This evidence comes from what is traditionally called the "Hellenistic" period (323–31 BCE).[3] Once regarded as the age of the *polis* decline, it should rather be interpreted as the time of strong civic governance and agency, in the aftermath of the great convergence and thanks to a bundle of historically favorable contingencies that the *poleis* made the most of (above, chapter 9). The type of *polis* that emerged in this period, and the issues it dealt with, would endure until the end of the ancient world: such issues included negotiating relations with supralocal powers, talking to peers, managing the place of economic elites in a context of popular sovereignty, and mobilizing and federating constituent elements of civil society.

At the same time, the stability of these solutions raises problems of its own. The sustainability and wide transmissibility of *polis* forms might have depended on their capacity to simplify issues into normed discourses, institutions, and practices, the more powerful for being universal. Such a simplifying trend should not obscure the continued social questions about wealth inequality and the economic life of the *poleis* as urban settlements, nor the potential costs of Aristotelian solutions.[4] The transmissibility of *polis* institutions (discussed previously) can most obviously be explained by peer-polity interaction and royal patronage. Yet, as we have seen, these factors do not address the question of the internal impact on local societies (for instance in Lykia or in Karia) of the adoption of democratic institutions or mass-elite bargains such as liturgies or *eisphora*, notably because they imply the surrender of power by any entrenched local elites.[5] We will have to bear these issues in mind even as we survey the qualities of the *polis* and will revisit the themes surveyed here (namely ideology, practices, and inequalities) at the end of this chapter and, at greater length, at the end of this book (chapters 17–19). For now, this chapter will start with a survey of *polis* forms; these reprise earlier institutional and ideological developments (and hence will seem familiar), but also respond to historical changes in and around the *polis*.

Identity and the Construction of Community

By 300 BCE, *poleis* were the result of long processes of incorporation and integration, naturalizing and articulating territory, urban centers, secondary settlements, inhabitants, and the local past. The ubiquitous discourse of mythical kinship worked on the fiction that the whole group of citizens of a *polis* could be conceptualized as descended from a mythical founder. This extremely widespread conceit extended and generalized aristocratic tropes of descent to the whole community. Whereas the "Nēleidai" had designated a particular group of families in "Archaic" Milētos (supposed descendants of the hero Nēleus and immigrants from Pylos), by the Hellenistic period the name had been appropriated to mean all the Milesians as a group, judging by a poetical but very public monumental text.[6] In institutional terms, the descent trope was expressed in the widespread practice of legally restricting citizenship to individuals born of citizen father and mother, as it had been in democratic Athens. One consequence of the generalization of democracy is that the citizen body in the *poleis* was (at least in theory and as an image of itself) united, bonded—and exclusive.[7]

Polis identity was the boundedness of a human and physical entity in its specialness. On Nisyros, the city walls were surrounded by a zone of public land—at first five feet, later extended to fifty, making clear the symbolical boundedness of the *polis* (as well as fulfilling a practical function against encroachment on the fortifications, a vital part of the city's military capacity).[8] Symbolically, boundedness was made visible in *polis* rituals and religion, centered around cults particular to each place. The citizens of the island *polis* of Hērakleia solemnly swore not to keep goats by the island's tutelary deity, Hēraklēs. Religious specificity determined a rich calendar of festivals that reinforced community through shared experiences in time and space and rituals such as meaningful processions.[9]

Festivals also were the scene for competitions and display, especially of literary works written for performance. Such works included pieces of antiquarian research, compilations of local history (read out in formal contexts), locally embedded poetry, and drama.[10] The majority of this cultural production is lost, since it never was canonized and transmitted as high culture.[11] The same function was performed by art and monuments that expressed various themes of local identity, such as military prowess, the glories of past history, the specificities of epichoric versions of mythology, or famous cults and religious manifestations. In Asia Minor, the third and second centuries BCE saw competitive religious monumentalization, comparable to competitive temple-building in the sixth century BCE.[12] What is clear is that the expression of the strong integration of the *polis* communities served both as markers and means of internal cohesiveness, and as tokens for participation in the processes of structuration and peer-polity interaction that were a vital part of being a *polis*. Myth and historical memory could be manipulated: this was not a sign of decadence or cynical frivolity, but of the vitality and usefulness of myth and memory in fostering shared understandings as the basis for community, just as in the sixth or fifth centuries BCE.[13]

In the aftermath of the great convergence, myth no longer needed to be deployed to express dominance and hegemony. In the second century BCE, the citizens of Argos set up a monument on the supposed tomb of the mythical king Phorōneus, founder of the city, first inventor of policed life, husband of the goddess Peithō (Persuasion), and sire of other important mythical figures—amongst others Apis, the first ruler of the Peloponnese and Niobē, first mortal woman to lie with Zeus and hence to create the race of heroes.[14] This mythical identity displaced earlier assertions of the right to rule over the Peloponnese in favor of subtler claims—one of Phoroneus's children gave his name to the region later known as Achaia, and founded Sikyōn. These stories located Argos in a contemporary world: rather than the old Dorian identity that had been the cornerstone of claims to hegemony and conflict with Sparta, the Argives alluded to an Achaian identity that aligned them with the rise of the Achaian League in the third-century BCE Peloponnese. It is true that this new identity was also competitive, as seen in the various claims to primacy and specialness. But the stakes were not hegemonic: they fitted within a world in which many other *poleis* claimed specialness.

In other words, *polis* identity concerned agency within a world of autonomous peers, another reflection of the great convergence and the joint, reciprocating processes of harmonization and differentiation, visible across the cultural landscape of the third and second centuries BCE. A sense of this world of cities can be gained from a fragment of a third-century BCE travelogue, moving from *polis* to *polis* (including a striking panorama of Athens). The phenomenon of "kinship diplomacy" is another illustration, but generally older institutions such as *proxenoi* flourished in the aftermath of the great convergence.[15]

Internally, the *poleis* as integrated communities were structured by multiple ways of belonging that evolved out of the earlier symphony of groupings, subdivisions and synekdochic associations (above, pp. 85–89, 112–13, 143, 180). Such subdivisions articulated the unity of people, space, and time.[16] The bounded group of citizens was made up of tribes that were divided into smaller units, bearing names relating to the mythical past of the *polis*, as a shared element of identity. The Xanthians were divided into tribes of which two bore names derived from heroes linked to Lykia (Sarpēdōn, Iobatēs), thus linking the civic practice of the Hellenized city with an old mythical Greek past.[17] The territorial organization of Athens into demes and tribes continued to operate during the Hellenistic period, albeit with mutations.[18] It is likely that in at least some *poleis*, the Athenian-style system of having citizens present their offspring for acceptance by civic subdivisions as a gateway to citizenship was in operation. This is suggested by citizen grants by the *polis* of the Thasians: the newly admitted Thasians would join a *patra* after convincing it to accept them,[19] a specific instance of the usual formality of scrutiny and decision applied in the case of citizen children presented by their family for formal acceptance by the *polis*.

Similar systems are attested everywhere, and their rationale, genealogy, and local meanings can often be guessed. A comparable complexity can be seen at Milētos, where the citizen population was divided into ten tribes, along the Athenian model with which it shared names, probably a trace of Athenian control in the fifth century BCE. The citizen body further divided into pseudo-gentilician groups, and the territory of Milētos was divided into five large divisions called *dēmoi* that grouped multiple settlements. These divisions bore local names: for instance, the *dēmos* called *Lerioi* grouped not only the citizens on the island of Leros, but all three islands that constituted Milētos's maritime territory. Likewise, the *Argaseis* or *Teichiesseis* bore the names of old settlements abandoned by the Hellenistic period (in the "Archaic" period, Teichioussa had been the seat of the aristocrat Charēs, who claimed status as "ruler").[20]

The layeredness of the system was the result of a complex local history, and this complexity was lived as multiple ways of belonging that reflected continuity and fostered multiple ties. The archaeology of the secondary settlements in *polis* territories is unevenly known: it is documented in some detail for Attica, but still rather obscure for most other *poleis*.[21] Strikingly, on Paros, the old site at Koukounaries that had been the main settlement during the Early Iron Age (above, pp. 39–40), continued as an extra-urban shrine and an administrative center for a rural settlement, as shown by the discovery of sealings that must have come from official documents in a local archive.[22] The importance of formally recognized, institutionally integrated territorial subdivisions cannot be exaggerated: they show the existence of citizens living in the countryside but participating in the *polis*, rather than working to provide rent to masters in a consumer city.[23]

Civic subdivisions had a corporate existence of their own, with their own cults, finances, property (estates, buildings, objects), assemblies, and ritual life. The life of individual subdivisions can easily be illustrated. At Teōs, a *symmoria* honors its four presidents; nearby, at Kolophōn, a *genos*, the Geleontes, handles complex financial affairs pertaining to real estate, as inscribed on a stele (fig. 10.1). The island deme of the Lerioi (mentioned above), existing within the Milesian *polis*, celebrated a rich cultic calendar.[24] A particularly instructive example comes from the *polis* of Mēthymna, on Lesbos, where in the third century BCE the *chellyastyes* (literally "thousandths") held periodic assemblies and sacrifices to "ancestral gods" (complete with distributions of meat).[25] The documents of the *chellastyes* show unity of practice as well as local variation: the Prōteis' great festival involved a sacrifice to Zeus Sotēr, the Phōkeis celebrated Dionysia at which the main event was the carrying around of the god's cult image on worshippers' shoulders. Modularity and variation emphasize the function of civic subdivisions, which was to articulate a sense of belonging within the *polis* at large within institutionalized forms and make it experienceable and imaginable.

At the same time, civic subdivisions played an important part in the functioning of the *polis* as state (on which more below). At Epizephyrian Lokroi (a foundation of the Lokrians in mainland Greece), the phratries and their common treasury were directly administered and supplied by the central financial administration of the *polis*.[26] Civic subdivisions almost certainly served as the basis for the units *of polis* militias; neighborhoods (*amphoda*) are also attested as the units for urban defense.[27] The networked architecture of civic subdivisions smoothed out tendencies toward centrifugality or clustering, a structural risk in the relations between urban center, rural territory, and secondary settlements. This risk existed especially in larger *poleis* and once *poleis* started to expand by negotiating the absorption of smaller *polis* units (above, pp. 208–9).[28] The integrating and uniformizing effect of the network of subdivisions is hence a function of the great convergence, namely of the assumption of citizen equality and the end of relations of subordination within *polis* boundaries.

The integrating effect of the network of subdivisions may have been of further consequence in accommodating another aspect of the great convergence, namely

FIGURE 10.1. Marble stele bearing documents of the tribe of the Geleontes, Kolophōn. Ca. 200 BCE. H 1.91 m. Shrine of Apollōn, Klaros.

the disappearance of subordinate statuses in the Hellenistic *poleis*. Groups of serfs such as the helots at Sparta, or the *laoi* ("peoples") in Asia Minor, seem to have rejoined the citizen body or at least vanished as separate, formal categories (with the concomitant generalization of chattel slavery as the basis for the economy).[29] Indeed, it is tempting to see the active part played by civic subdivisions, partly local, as a sign of the enfranchisement of rural communities and their integration within the polity (along the model best known in Athens from the very late sixth to the late third centuries BCE), and hence a confirmation of the absence of formal overlordship by elites over rural populations.[30]

Civic subdivisions were not the only associations in the *poleis*.[31] The proliferation of private associations in late Classical Athens has already been noted (above, p. 189); it continued into Hellenistic Athens, and is matched by a rich associative life in other cities, such as Rhodes or Milētos.[32] The epigraphy of the associative phenomenon, like that of the civic subdivisions, points toward integration within the *polis*; this development may in fact have been heavily influenced by the final and harmonized forms taken by the civic subdivisions.[33]

The effect of the great convergence was the wide acceptance of civic parameters, and the easing of the travails of integration and concomitant uncertainties about the relations between groups and community. Absent the great debates about the right form of constitution, in the aftermath of the significant extension of citizenship status and its privileges, and as a consequence of the decoupling of claims to excellence from political domination, associations and groups vied for distinctiveness without centrifugality. Various bodies of armed men, or organized groups of young men, which had proven points of instability in earlier periods, appear during the Hellenistic period as corporations within the *polis*, and in harmony with its workings. The cavalrymen of Athens passed a decree in 281 BCE praising their officers' democratic and law-abiding spirit, in marked contrast to the oligarchical dirty-war violence of the elite horsemen of 411 and 403 BCE. Young male citizens were socialized and integrated into civic workings, in various stages that descended from the old structures of youth and transition in the "Archaic" communities: boyhood, a short transitional adolescence or *ephēbeia* between sixteen and eighteen, and a long period of being part of the "young men," *neoi*, between twenty and thirty years old.[34] The latter formed the nucleus of the *poleis*'s militias.

Of course, there was nothing necessarily inclusive and collaborative about civic subdivisions and associations: tribes and local groups had existed in exclusive *poleis* exploiting rural populations, and associations had acted as the vehicle for faction in civil war. But the effect of the great convergence was to harness the integrative potential of such institutions. The Hellenistic city evolved ritual, institutionalized means of unity, as visible in the seams of interaction and exchange between civil society and organs of state government in the *polis*. The *neoi* of Kolophōn, 153 strong, went as a body to petition the city council to honor their gymnasiarch, an official in charge of the public spaces and buildings reserved for collective physical and educational activities, the *gymnasion*.³⁵ More dramatic is the behavior of associations in Troizēn, in 146 BCE, during the crisis of a conflict between the Achaian League and the Roman Republic: forty-one associations, in their variety (cultic groups whose names reflect local traditions and history, alongside villages and civic subdivisions, *patriai*), responded to a decree of the *polis* concerning common defense, by giving up their corporate property (*koineia*) and land that the city needed for new fortification works; the unity of purpose is shown by all the decrees of the associations being inscribed on a single stone slab.³⁶

The Workings of Stateness

State institutions³⁷ were self-consciously the shape that membership in the *polis* took, as noted by theorists such as Aristotle, or actual documents of the *poleis* such as the oath sworn by the Kalymnians upon entering the Koan polity (above, p. 221) to respect the constitution and the *polis*'s safety and to act well as a juror, a voter, and a magistrate. The state existed as a separate sphere and a personality endowed with its own agency and tropes, and whose interests, hovering above the interests of each of its members, needed defending and promoting. *Qua* state, the *polis* expressed the autonomy of the community in relation to external actors, and hence interposed itself between large supralocal states and the local level of communities and individuals. Internally, the state stood as the expression of common interests and identities.³⁸ The results of the great convergence were the uniformatization of institutions, their diffusion, and their legibility as part of a coherent system of *polis* workings, most richly documented in the third and second centuries BCE.³⁹

The epigraphical material characteristic of this period allows for an exploration of the texture and the diversity of state practice across the world of *poleis*. The complexities of procedures involving civic institutions and bodies appear in many documents. When Ephesos settled problems of debt in the aftermath of war, when Samos regulated the public purchase of grain and controlled the activities of small retailers in a great shrine, or when Paros laid out the modalities of public archiving, these *poleis* intervened as states, and documented the processes self-consciously.⁴⁰ Such legal and institutional texts show how *polis* officials, usually serving in boards,⁴¹ managed complex local affairs beyond the civic rituals, dedications, sacrifices, and easeful feasting that continued to enjoy a lively presence in the *polis*.⁴²

The *polis*'s magistrates were the *polis* in action, in the form of a network of differentiated positions with clearly defined powers and privileges, mapped out in the civic time of the *polis*'s calendar.⁴³ When *ad hoc* jobs had to be done in the *polis* (building works, dedications within a shrine), the task was entrusted to specially chosen commissions whose powers were defined and regulated since they were, like other magistrates, an *archē*, wielders of rule in the community.⁴⁴ Such powers were defined by rules and laws, which we can suppose, from incidental but frequent references in the evidence, to have been gradually extended throughout the Classical and Hellenistic periods and covered explicitly much of the spheres of action of magistrates and lawcourts.[45] The magistrates themselves passed on to their successors a body of rules, precedents, and state papers (along with tokens of power, such as the city's keys) that acted as a cartulary with guidelines for authoritative, empowered action within the community.[46]

The result was the automaticity of stateness. Magistrates vetted matters of state,[47] enforced the law (as had always been their function),[48] imposed punitive fines, and protected public interests or spaces through action or prosecution.[49] As in fifth- and fourth-century BCE Athens, the *boulē* or Council, a large standing body, took an active role in affairs of the state.[50] A sign of automaticity is the minute at the bottom of a decree passed in Halikarnassos, noting how magistrates duly took the decision to the courts for a second vote, no doubt in accordance with law.[51] The law courts had their own autonomous existence, reflecting another sphere of state operation and legitimacy, regulated by its own complex rules and based on the use of documentation. A good example is the long roster of possible legal procedures mentioned in a law of Thasos, fixing holidays when judicial proceedings are not allowed: magistrates with strong judicial powers coexisted and interacted with a complex set of different procedures for pursuing cases before law courts.[52]

Magistrates, as part of the state, handled public monies on the basis of official decisions. This activity constituted a great part of state operations, and enabled public goods of all kinds, from public works (see fig. 10.6) to government and foreign policy; along with state papers, magistrates passed on remaining funds to their successors. When the Oropians decided to refortify the city ca. 300 BCE (a practical decision typical of the great convergence and its affirmation of *polis* autonomy), the officials elected for this purpose were given access to "all of the *polis*'s incomes," except for sacred expenditure, payments for attendants (either temple servants or public employees), and any other expenditure stipulated by law or in a decree (*kata nomon ē kata psēphisma*). The vital provision of security at Ōrōpos still had to leave space for essential operations—the running of the great shrine, the Amphiaraion; basic functions carried out by paid employees; and, in a typical piece of *polis* ideology, anything else decided on by the sovereign People, expressed in different legal forms. Even religious and priestly matters were handled and financed by the state and its officials, the increasingly important and widely attested *naopoioi* ("temple builders").

The handling of public monies required and generated much official documentation and archival material—this phenomenon is very visible at the intersection of money and religion, for instance on Dēlos, or in the records of the loans taken out by the *polis* of Epizephyrian Lokroi (mentioned earlier).[53] There the bronze tablets recording the loans and the institutional transactions were kept in the shrine of Zeus Olympios, together with bullion and coins, in a massive stone box whose huge lid weighing over a ton was winched up when loan records were deposited (fig. 10.2).

As exemplified by the case of the fortifications of Ōrōpos, the sources for these public goods were "the incomes of the *polis*," an expression that designates organized public

FIGURE 10.2. Strongbox for public finances (and archival documents), Lokroi Epizephyrioi, *in situ* and complete with lid. From Costabile 1992, fig. 1.

fiscality within the territory. In the third century BCE, even the tiny island *polis* of Hērakleia had a state treasury, *to koinon*, "the common thing." The state derived income from its own resources (real estate or farmland, leased out against cash rents), but it also imposed levies on revenue streams within its ambit, including indirect taxation on commercial activity and direct tithing of agricultural production. It further could levy poll taxes and wealth taxes on property in case of emergencies (*eisphorai*, "contributions"). The *polis* of Teōs taxed productive activities in its territory: plow and draught animals, working slaves, pigs, sheep, wool, weaving, dyeing, market gardening, beehives, were all taxed. In addition, all inhabitants paid a poll tax that financed a public doctor.[54] The *polis* also collected fees for public services, especially dispute resolution: litigants paid fees (*prytaneia*) to the *polis*, which could use this income for its own purposes.[55] It is not clear whether on the island of Hērakleia, the payment of "costs" involved in court cases are the deposit of *prytaneia* paid by litigants, or the levying of a special tax (*eisphora*) to allow for the court to meet; the uncertainty at least summarizes the options that the *polis* had.[56] Religious services, provided officially by the *polis*, also incurred fees and taxes to finance such public goods.[57]

All these income sources formed a civic budget, sometimes called the *dioikēsis* or *oikonomia* (the "administration"), managed by financial officials who wielded great power in the *polis* (the first such officials are the very prominent politicians of late fourth-century BCE Athens, such as Euboulos and Lykourgos) but were also closely controlled. The budget itself could be planned and regulated by law and decree. At Xanthos, in 205 BCE, a nine-year plan for the *oikonomia* prevented the Xanthians from making any grant to the embassy from the Kytenians asking for a donation (or so, at least, the Xanthians claimed; they ended up taking out a loan to be able to offer funds).[58] When the citizens of Pēreia agreed to the integration of their *polis* into a neighboring *polis*, Melitaia, they took care to map their civic territory but also to list the "disbursements made by the *polis*"; that is, public expenditure for the *gymnasion*, sacrifices, heralds, and the magistrates.[59] The union of the two communities would take place with the proviso that the Pereians kept track of their territory to be able to reclaim it in case the agreement ceased, and on the condition that the specific public expenditure of Pēreia was maintained in the shape of its earlier commitments. The agreement shows us how a *polis* existed as a spatial territory but also specifically as public property (leased to obtain public income) and a schedule of payments out of public financial means.

Sources of civic income were supplemented by *leitourgia*, the direct provision of services by the rich in semi-voluntary forms. The system is best known for fourth-century BCE Athens (above, p. 186) but also operated intensively to finance the cities after the great convergence. Teōs, in addition to a comprehensive network of taxes (above) also imposed such duties on its elite: the latter paid for the costumes and training of choruses at festivals, financed teams for torch races, and provided free oxen for public sacrifice, among other services.[60] At Priēnē, *leitourgia* included the provision of warhorses and warships and, most onerously, the advance provision of large sums of cash in the name of the payers of property tax (the liturgists being expected to recover their own outlay from these payers). This practice (*proeisphora*) combined public taxation with the personal contribution of wealthy individuals, in a fashion typical of the thinness of the *polis*'s actual bureaucratic resources, to meet immediate needs in cash.[61]

Further financial resources could be raised through such voluntary action, for instance by gifts or promises (and the *eisphora*, as a one-off transaction, could be represented in this guise). Unsurprisingly, the collection of voluntary contributions took place in highly visible collective forms, as shown by the long inscribed lists of donors.[62] The Kolophonians financed a massive urbanization and fortification program at the end of the fourth century BCE by such means. Frequently, individuals made loans to the *polis* (rather than simply making financial gifts, on top of the burden of public taxation): the walls of Ōrōpos were financed by loans, and part of the exceptional leeway granted to the special commission in that *polis* in matters of civic finance was to enable the repayment of these loans, another illustration of the imbrication of individual initiative and state process. Such financial arrangements allowed the *poleis* to carry out a rich building activity that finalized the processes of urban monumentalization initiated centuries earlier.[63]

The Practice of Democracy

We should minimize neither the stateness of the *polis* nor the democratic nature of its workings. Popular sovereignty was distributed across the *polis*, through the stately forms that were collaborative, mutually dependent, and dynamically related—namely, the Assembly, the Council, the officeholders, and the law courts.[64] A comic literary composition by the third-century BCE poet Herōdas portrays a law court scene, with rhetoric striking themes familiar from earlier Athenian rhetoric, namely the democratic composition of the court and its vital role in defending the city's interests.[65] Much thought went into the relation between all the institutional elements. The issue was the same as during the conflicts of the "Hundred Years"; namely, how exactly popular sovereignty would be expressed in the balance and the tension between the three potentially contradictory and constantly reciprocating elements. If the popular assembly was sovereign, what was its relationship to the laws and to the courts? What was the relationship between *psēphisma* (decree of the people) and *nomos* (law) as an expression of popular sovereignty? What place for the automaticity of state functions?[66]

Constitutional experimentation and self-correction are most visible in the case of fifth- and fourth century BCE Athens, through the rich epigraphical documentation. Similar processes can be guessed at for other *poleis*, for instance Iasos or Milētos, through changes and adaptations of processes to manage institutions and timeframes (for instance, in order to allow time for the possibilities of scrutiny, challenge, or prosecution that were such a crucial part of the political culture). The processes of experimentation would culminate in the late Hellenistic institutional intensification (below, chapter 11). Constitutional processes were also continual learning processes, as can be observed in small, incremental changes in procedure (Iasos provides a well-documented case).[67]

The main venues for decision-making remained the Assembly and the cluster of institutional processes around it. As the embodiment of the community's access to power, the Assembly was itself at the heart of arrangements to ensure openness, access, and authoritative presence. It met frequently, so that its authority was a practical reality, not just a symbol of community power—forty times a year in Classical Athens, twice a month in Samos or Kōs, once a month in smaller places such as Iasos or second-century BCE Delphi. As the gathering of (potentially) the whole citizen body, it always concentrated large numbers of citizens. Mass had a symbolical force, but also the practical effect of the involvement of numbers so large as to constitute a very representative sample in big *poleis*: the three or four thousands known for Halikarnassos or Magnēsia on Maeander, the thousand or so guessable for Priēnē, Kolophōn, or Delphi, or even the hundreds of citizens meeting in the Assembly places of small *poleis* on the mainland or the islands.[68] The island *polis* of Anaphē had a healthy democratic culture—for instance, submitting decisions of the Council to ratification by the Assembly; one decree was passed by "all the votes, 95."[69] Similar numbers might have voted the decree of the Herakleiotes forbidding the raising of goats. The model of mass decision-making by voting was the only acceptable one. Propositions to the Assembly were themselves the result of deliberation and votes by the Council or the boards of magistrates. Decision-making involved a cascade of meetings and votes.

The actual processes involved varied in the handling of the meetings, but also the type of voting—by show of hands, or by secret ballots, for instance when confirming earlier decisions (it is the record of the counting of ballots that allows us to occasionally see the remarkable size of the meetings).[70] At Mantineia, care may have been taken to seat the voters in randomly distributed areas in the theater to avoid clustering by deme and by tribe and hence grouped voting.[71] In practice, the processes of deliberation, meeting, and voting to generate decisions may have been inflected to produce unanimous, or nearly unanimous decisions.[72] Citizens had access to decision-making processes: in the most direct way, by speaking in the Assembly, and by elaborating motions or proposing amendments to motions elaborated by the panels of magistrates and the Council. A wide range of speakers and proposers emerges, even if star politicians and speakers, or even generations of such figures, can be discerned (the same pattern operated in fifth- and fourth-century BCE Athens).[73] Athenian-style riders are occasionally known; more generally, motions and riders by private individuals speaking from the floor may be invisible in surviving decrees, because they were incorporated into the main motions; the resulting decrees appear as unitary documents.[74] Occasional decrees recording motions as emanating from "the People" may reflect a process of amendments from (indeed "by") the floor during debates (though they perhaps simply reflect multistage decision procedures).[75]

The agenda and the processes in the mass decision-making process were handled by the Council (which usually put motions to the Assembly, or sometimes simply referred matters to it) or by the magistrates. Hence the importance of individuals' access (*prosodos, ephodos,* or written *prographē*) to the boards of magistrates, and especially to the Council, to raise concerns or to propose specific items for debate and decision.[76] Two inscribed decrees from Kōs (honorifics) record the individual who approached the board of magistrates with a proposal that made its way to the agenda of the Assembly—the avenue by which "private" associations could interact with state institutions, as in the case of soldiers or the 153 *neoi* of Kolophōn (above, p. 235).[77] Access to the *boulē* might also be open to individuals. At Iasos, a decree on sacred matters asked the relevant officials (*neōpoiai*) to submit a proposal (*ephodos*) for the financing of repair work in shrines, but also allowed any private, non-magistrate individual (*tōn idiōtōn ho boulomenos*) to make additional proposals on this matter.[78]

Such approaches, made by groups or individuals, are often explicitly said to have impacted on public decision-making and reflect access to the *polis*'s institutions. The evidence seems to indicate a widespread responsiveness, consonant with the general ethos of openness. Magistrates constantly refer matters to the Assembly, often for administrative decisions; they do not seem to capture or control processes and issues, an outcome which was perhaps also precluded by the wide range of speakers and avenues for initiative and the interplay of institutions.[79]

Popular sovereignty determined the shape of the institutional state in accordance with practices and principles that emerged from earlier debates about power and rule. These principles include mass participation, scrutiny and control of power holders, and the prevalence of the public good over individual interests. In the *polis*, the forms of power-holding that gave it existence as a state were widely distributed among the community of citizens, notably through extensive collegiality. Most *archai* were multiple affairs, and the single emergency magistracies of the Classical period, let alone the various monarchical solutions, were abandoned. This holds true for minor officials, but also for officials in charge of major business of state, namely finance or military affairs such as defense works or active operations (in practice often joined with day-to-day administration).[80]

Within these boards, power was further distributed by short tenure. Financial administrators and military officials might serve for a semester or even for one third of the year (which also reflects the individual burdens involved).[81] This practice was the development of the rotation of formalized and institutionalized office that constituted the crossing of the stateness boundary by the "Archaic" *polis* (above, pp. 80–85). In practical terms, it multiplied the distributive effect of extensive collegiality, so that in the smaller *poleis*, every citizen must have had some experience of the state as administrative practice and as authority over the community.[82] Further circulation of power was ensured by the widespread use of the lot for magistracies and important bodies such as the Council (as attested at Milētos, according to a "law of the Council," *bouleutikos nomos*).[83]

Allotment was particularly used for the courts. The practice is attested throughout the Hellenistic period (with a noticeable increase in evidence for the second century BCE).[84] A striking illustration comes from the city of Myrina, where some citizens had themselves buried with the bronze allotment tickets necessary for the system to work (fig. 10.3): political participation in the *polis* and its democratic institutions was an essential part of individual identity, as sealed and deposited in the grave.[85] Another example comes from Amphissa in West Lokris (the regions discussed at the start of this section: above, pp. 153–55). In 283/2 BCE, the Athenian tribe Hippothōntis honored one Phyleus for being a good priest of Asklēpios and also for good service in supervising the allotment of jurors (hence indicating a specific office in the early Hellenistic period, after the less specialized practice of the fourth century BCE); in this capacity, Phyleus had received official praise from the Council and the Assembly. Evidence for allotted courts in Athens continues down to the late Hellenistic period, a century and a half after Phyleus's service.[86]

The courts also illustrate another institution for the distribution of power, namely pay. Payment or compensation for attendance and service is well attested

FIGURE 10.3. Bronze tablet bearing name and patronym (probably a juror's allotment ticket), from tomb at Myrina. From Pottier, Reinach and Veyries 1887, fig. 21.

for the courts and onerous service such as embassies; it is likely that the court fees on the small island *polis* of Hērakleia were used to compensate the service of officers or jurors. Service on the Council probably also entailed pay (as on Rhodes), and other offices. Even Assembly attendance may have been paid, as certainly happened at Iasos in the early third century BCE.[87]

Distribution of power belonged to a wider political culture of openness and access. One immediately obvious instance of this political culture was the ubiquitous expectation of initiative by citizens in pursuing and prosecuting delinquent magistrates. This was a particularly significant, publicly oriented form of voluntary prosecution as part of the judicial system (with local variations and nuances).[88] The Iasian decree on sacred matters mentioned above (*I. Iasos* 219) also allowed *tōn idiōtōn ho boulomenos* to denounce before officials the priests or any other officials in case any of the written, legal regulations were not being followed.[89] This right belongs to the normal register of state activities, alongside the activities and the powers of magistrates and the involvement of wealthy elite citizens. When the city of Dēmētrias organized a procession to consult the oracular shrine of Apollōn Korōpaios in its territory, order was kept by officials with rods and the right to exercise physical violence but sworn in before the Assembly and liable to prosecution for misconduct by their successors or, indeed, any citizen (ca. 100 BCE).[90]

Voluntary prosecution of magistrates is particularly well attested when public monies or investments are involved and is also noticeable as part of the democratic intensification in the second century BCE. When the island *polis* of Ioulis received a large private donation to finance temple building (250–200 BCE), the *boulē* elected by secret ballot a commission to handle the cash and lend it out at interest, and all processes were closely controlled by magistrates endowed with punitive powers; indeed, the magistrates themselves were liable to voluntary denunciation and prosecution by any citizen.[91] Officials and their acts were scrutinized by a number of actors before, during, and especially after their tenure of office, not only in relation to the handling of public monies, but also with an eye to general suitability and behavior.[92] In Teōs, magistrates rendered public accounts for public monies every month. In the Macedonian *polis* of Beroia, the gymnasiarch, at the end of his term of office, submitted the financial accounts for his administration and every citizen was empowered to take part in the public auditing of these accounts (*suneklogizesthai*).[93]

The practice of publicity and transparency, reflecting the general distribution of power among the community of citizens, explains the centrality of public writing. This fulfilled a practical function. In Hellenistic Milētos, a number of decrees were normally exposed on wooden tablets for perusal as part of a multistage decision process that invited public scrutiny, involvement, and confirmation.[94] The handling of public goods left public texts (as they had in Classical Athens).[95] An example comes from second-century BCE Lampsakos, where money was distributed as part of a festival of Asklēpios, according to lists of citizens. The lists were to be established by magistrates "in full view" (*eisobdēn*), and the magistrates had to swear before the Assembly to having observed this stipulation—after which the lists were duly published for inspection.[96]

But public writing also performed monumental and ideological functions: they were seen as well as read,[97] symbolizing and embodying the open, transparent nature of the state, as well as the cohesion of the community. Public writing was there to be inspected (*skopein*), and hence part of a world of communication and debate, also embodied in practices that bridged the gap between oral and written, such as official reading out of decrees in public, and listening to citations of the law or readings of documents in the courts. Finally, inscribed texts of the *polis* gave in themselves proof of the community's authority, its power to make things happen (*gignesthai*), since they always include a full description of institutions at work, including the decision to publish the text.

Commitment and Rewards

The above survey of the institutional workings of the *polis* that emerged out of the great convergence of the late fourth and early third centuries BCE is necessarily selective and impressionistic. All the same, it is clear that these institutional workings share a common set of presuppositions that can be further read in the public documents, the literature, the shared rituals, spaces,[98] and monuments[99] of the *polis*. The first is a very strong sense of public goods, constantly stated, implied, and enacted through access, distribution, and publicity. Its generalization is a reflection of the harmonization of *polis* institutions after the violent debates on the "right" constitution and the struggles for control of the public sphere. The second presupposition is that publicness, realized through institutions, is a good in itself or rather reflects the reality of basic goods that emerged during the great convergence—the equality and freedom of the individual citizens, the autonomy of the *polis* as a state, worked out in the accepted forms whose justice embodied the good life in common. These two presuppositions might be called communitarian, in that they locate the measure of moral goods in the political community (see further below, chapter 16).[100]

A cardinal site for the expression of *polis* ideology was the honorific decree, by which the community rewarded deserving citizens with honors (crowns, proclamations, statues), and indeed with the decree itself, which provided a monumental narrative of recognition.[101] In spite of their overwhelming presence in the surviving epigraphical record, such transactions were rare occurrences in civic routine but their visibility gave them emblematic force in making explicit values and expectations, and their location within the community. In Asia Minor, in Smyrna and neighboring *poleis*, gravestones of the third and second centuries BCE include engraved crowns in prominent places (fig. 10.4): this feature, imitating the representation of honorific crowns on public documents, places public recognition at the heart of individual identity at the moment of death.[102]

Yet it is equally clear that publicness drew meaning from an articulated sense of the private.[103] The complementarity of both spheres appears in Attic oratory of the fourth century BCE, or in the ubiquitous habit in public epigraphy of including an initial clause of appraisal of individual behavior *koinēi kai idiai*, in public and individual dealings. It also appears clearly in the urban fabric of the cities, which contrasts the tight grid of private houses with the open and clearly signaled public spaces. The inclusion of the weapons of the citizen soldier on funerary reliefs of the third and second centuries BCE showing private banqueting scenes displayed the interdependency of private and public, individual, and collective (see fig. 9.1 for an example from an Ionian *polis*). Private worlds of relaxation and luxury coexist with reminders of service as citizen militiamen who protect the *polis* as autonomous space. The pivotal place of private property reflects the balance of public and private: even if the whole of the *polis*'s property could be conceived as the sum of each individual's possessions (as witnessed by the collective conception of public debt),[104] the *polis* did not collectivize property. Public goods were financed by contributions levied off private fortunes, but confiscation was unknown, and emergency needs were met by enforced purchase of private property or compensation for the latter's use.[105] So civic commitment had to be balanced with articulacy about reasons and rationality about the benefits that the individual citizen derived from membership and stakeholding. The relationship was conceived as reciprocity, as appears clearly from a common feature in civic honorific texts, the so-called hortative clause declaring that a *polis* passed such decrees "in order that we too be seen clearly to honor fine men (*tous kalous kagathous*), and to incite many citizens to a similar reasoned choice (*prohairesis*)."[106]

The latter term designates a rational, considered choice (it figures prominently in philosophical language, as well as the moralizing political discourse of the mid-fourth century BCE, as attested in Athens). The offering of symbolical honors for services was extended to foreign benefactors from other *poleis*, a good illustration of the facilities offered by peer-polity interaction. Furthermore, honors were offered to powerful actors from outside the network of the *poleis*, namely the officers of the royal states or even kings themselves.[107] This allowed *poleis* to deploy particular discursive strategies to embed or socialize potentially threatening actors in

FIGURE 10.4. Marble funerary stele from western Asia Minor (Smyrna), showing man, woman, enslaved attendants. Ca. 150 BCE. H 151 cm.

terms of *prohairesis*, the rational choice to perform services. It is true that these strategies developed into their own forms (for instance, ruler cult belongs to the roster of honors developed by the cities to interact with foreign presences);[108] but the application of civic honors to non-civic actors also reflects the *poleis*'s confidence in the validity of its whole system of recognition.

The proclaimed rationality of the relations between individual and community shows the potential tension or contradiction between reciprocity and communitarian commitment (see further below, chapter 17). Were good citizens good because of the habitus of moral investment, or because of reciprocal self-interest and the exchange of dues? The two are inconsistent, and B. Gray has shown how in case of conflict, as was so common during the late fifth and fourth centuries BCE, the inconsistency could exacerbate internal tensions into full-blown conflict.[109] Yet after the great convergence, in the new democratic *koinē* these tensions could ease. Honors for good citizens had a protreptic effect that was both rational and communitarian: in ensuring social reproduction of good citizens by imitation, they also had precisely the educative and socializing effect that communitarianism was based upon.[110]

The insistence on *prohairesis* naturalized civic behavior: the avoidance of profit-maximizing by rich citizens (who are said to prefer the public good, or public praise, to private profit),[111] when presented as the result of deliberate policy and choice, assumed the public good as an undeniable given, in virtue of which individual choices took place and led to commitment and voluntarism. By describing as reciprocal transactions by which material benefactions by individuals were balanced by symbolical returns (crowns and honors) from the community, the *polis* reaffirmed the communitarian principle of its right to decide on virtue and rewards, and generally the primacy of community. In embedding pure economic goods into a moral economy of reciprocity, the exchange of benefactions for honors showed the unsurpassable generosity—of the *polis*.[112]

Polis, Elites, and Political Economy

The passing of the honorific decrees was a social drama in its own right.[113] In second-century BCE Aigialē, a *polis* on the island of Amorgos, the *prytaneis* presented the *chorēgoi* (rich citizens who had paid for the expense of a chorus performance at a festival) before the Assembly, for a debate about their merits and about the possibility of rewarding them with a crown.[114] Honors for such apparently humdrum occasions such as exiting office, leasing public property, or lending money to the city show the importance of civic honor for individual citizens.[115] The fact that the highly conspicuous honorific material focuses on the good actions and attitudes of active and wealthy citizens [116] raises the problem of the place of elites in the *poleis* for the "great convergence" as for earlier periods. How did elite distinction fit within *polis* institutions characterized by wide distribution of power and democratic norms?

The answer to this question has oscillated in the recent study of the Hellenistic *polis*. All divergent interpretations have, nonetheless, placed heavy emphasis on the honorific transactions under the (modern) name of "euergetism"—the exchange of benefactions (especially economic) by elite actors for symbolical requital by the community, as indications of potential dominance by elites, albeit within civic norms and playacting.[117] This emphasis may be misleading: so-called euergetism should be viewed within the context of the power structures of the *polis* and its long history (and in my view the term should be reserved to describe social interactions in the *polis* of the Roman empire: see below, chapter 13).

For sure, there were rich and very rich citizens in the *poleis*, even if the exact social and spatial distribution remains obscure. As always, the rich constituted a minority and wealth bought leisure and access to privileged goods such as education and expertise, social confidence, charisma-laden lifestyle, international links, mobility, and opportunities.[118] Such wealth was based on cash-crops grown with enslaved labor for trade (especially long-distance), rent from property, industrial production in workshops staffed by large teams of enslaved workers, and moneylending at interest. All these activities separated the leisured and wealthy from the rest of society, namely the "little big men" of the sub-elite, a middling group of working farmers, artisans, and small *rentiers*, and various groups of poor citizens, urban and rural. Of course, the citizen elites were also elevated above the non-free and the noncitizens. Some, but not all, rich families visible in the private and the public spheres succeeded in maintaining their socioeconomic level over generations.[119]

In the particular context of the great convergence, the inclusiveness of the democratic *poleis* caused the same pattern of elite affirmation as seen in earlier periods (above, chapter 6), namely a multiplication of elitist claims to distinction, couched in communitarian terms as defined above (even though conspicuous consumption and display in the domestic, funerary, or votive spheres continued in the Hellenistic period).[120] Equally important was the institutional context, within which elite behavior can most fruitfully be interpreted. Members of the civic elites assumed leadership roles, often traditional: military leadership, civil office, priesthoods, financial contributions. These are the roles mentioned in the Athenian decree of 228 BCE as "setting up trophies on land or on sea, or bringing back liberty, or putting their own fortune at the disposal of the common safety, or becoming benefactors and good advisors." The economic role, as donors, is not the principal one.[121]

Elite roles were constrained by the *polis* context in three major ways. First, the *poleis* as public spaces were saturated with communitarian ideology of integral commitment and rational choice directed toward the public good, to the point of individual sacrifices of personal welfare and economic resources. This applied for generalship, political speaking, and officeholding. A telling example comes from the practice of civic finance. As wealthy individuals, officials might be called upon to make loans to the *polis* during their year of service; indeed, they probably were under substantial practical and ideological pressure to do so and meet any shortage in public liquidity out of their own pocket. In this case, there might be a strong expectancy that they would forfeit any interest off their loans, so as to avoid any hint of profiting from their own administrative acts and as part of their general devotion to the public good.[122] At least, such public-minded behavior would be noticed, putting pressure on other officeholders.

Second, elite roles were embedded in the particular institutional set-up of the democratic *poleis*. Conformity to *polis* norms was not only ideological but politically determined, in that civic virtue (*aretē pros ton dēmon*) was a practical necessity for elite citizens. These might have to adduce proof of good democratic, public-minded character in case of litigation before a mass court of citizens. Such popular courts ruled on issues of taxation and leitourgic duties that were a great part of elite life; furthermore, they decided on issues of property that directly affected the life of elite individuals and families. The combination of intra-elite enmity, voluntary prosecution, and the multiplication of occasions for prosecution of officeholders kept the elite continually exposed to potential legal jeopardy.

Beyond the courts, elite political careers depended on forging a plausible persona and reputation, based on concrete indications of good character. This sort of persona can be seen in the case of the political competition between leading citizens in late Hellenistic Mylasa.[123] The great convergence led to the end of *stasis*, but the generalized democratic model must have involved constant competition between politicians speaking before the People, and often impugning their rivals' character on ideological grounds, in aggressive moves reminiscent of the "demagogic" politics of Athens.[124]

Third, the activity of wealthy citizens took place in the general institutional framework of scrutiny and accountability. All honorific decrees were passed after a report and a request—sometimes by semi-organized constituencies (above, p. 235) but often by the honorand himself. Such reports, presented to institutionalized bodies (starting with the Council), resemble the written reports and requests that were part of the state apparatus of the *polis*. Dēmosthenēs, in a speech arguing for the importance of honors for benefactors, quotes from the application for an honorific statue written by the Athenian general Chabrias in 375 BCE.[125] Such applications belong to the wider context of explanatory and justificatory speech-acts produced in public by individuals, in the courtroom, in front of civic bodies such as the Council, or before the People itself, before, during, and after the exercise of power in the *polis*. Such speech-acts could lead to blame or punishment, as well as rewards (such as the crowns or praise that might follow on the satisfactory rendering of accounts by officials).[126] The "hortative clause" that explains the intention of honorific decrees—to make visible the capacity of the *polis* to return marks of gratitude for services and to provoke emulation—is itself part of the wider practice of public scrutiny.

Elite benefaction can be clearly interpreted as part of the wider political economy of the *polis* rather than as an alarming sign of elite domination. It also has a history that, like all other constituents of the great convergence, evolved during the earlier periods of "Archaic" experiment and "Classical" conflict. As already mentioned, the notion of elite service and community reward, and indeed of eliteness as constituted by community recognition, is present from the Early Iron Age communities (above, chapter 3). The first "hortative clause" turns up on a victory monument from Athens dating to the early 470s BCE, during the early Athenian campaigns against the Persians.[127] There, honor is explicitly said to be a *misthos* (salary), given *ant' euergesiēs*, in exchange for doing good to the *polis*. The specific nexus of honors and punishments as incentives for the elite and as a frame for their institutional embedding, must have emerged during the development of radical democracy in Athens.[128]

After its apparition in the fifth century BCE, the nexus of scrutiny and requital is richly documented at Athens in the documentary (and especially the forensic) material for the fourth century BCE, much of which was explicitly formulated as a debate about the right ways to punish and to honor citizens. The rise of the honorific decree for individual benefactors, the formalization of high honors for the great military leaders and politicians (maintenance, front seating, and bronze honorific statues), and the spread of routine honors for magistrates[129] may have been part of the implicit bargains offered to fourth-century BCE elites. They were balanced by scrutiny, accountability, and pressure on elite individuals within the democratic polity.

The great convergence, which saw the diffusion of the democratic model, also entailed the spread of this particular political economy. An index of this phenomenon is the wide distribution of the honorific decree or the honorific statue in the late fourth century BCE. Honorific culture represented accommodation to the more or less mild oligarchical pushback of the late fourth century BCE.[130] The latter phenomenon petered out, partly because the democratic norms proved most successful and efficient, partly because of lack of royal support or tolerance. What remained was a set of relics such as the aristocratic-flavored language of *kalokagathia*, the mention of fathers (or ancestors), and the focus on individual agency and impact, characteristic of the honorific decree. All those traits were leftovers from the fourth-century BCE fascination with great men (and would prove long-lived).[131]

The various strands of this civic culture harmonized and balanced out. A complex transaction in Ioulis, already analyzed above (p. 243), involved the *polis*'s collective desire to carry out public works on shrines, wealthy citizens making a gift, the involvement of civic institutions of decision-making, administration within rules and norms, the election of officials out of the wealthy citizens, and the right of *ho boulomenos* to supervise and prosecute. We have seen how the equilibria of the great convergence were predicated on a moral sense of the public goods embedded in and defended by the *polis*, its norms, laws, institutions, identity, and ideology. As in the Hērakleian decree about goats (above, pp. 3–8), the interest of *to koinon* superseded all; restraint and collaboration were expected and opposition to common decisions was *bia*, illegitimate violence. Hence patronage, the translation of economic power into political power, was voided in the *polis* (since, as we have seen, the Spartan model of oligarchical inequality ended in erratic failure in the first half of the fourth century BCE). The ideological and institutional setup prevented elite capture and hence precluded any possibility for elite distinction to serve as the basis for the dismantling of the democratic control and redistribution.[132]

The *polis* was also about the managing of tensions. As mentioned earlier, at the end of the third century BCE, the Xanthians laid out a binding multiyear budget in which special wealth taxes (*eisphorai*) were clearly announced but also limited. The Milesians, when in need of funds because of a prolonged shortfall in tax revenues, avoided decreeing an *eisphora* (which would hit the rich citizens) but also retrenching the public expenditure of salaries (which would affect the poorer citizens but also generally threaten democratic participation). The *polis* of Milētos hence resorted to a sophisticated (if somewhat alarming) financing scheme—raising loans which were reimbursed as lifelong pensions.[133] Optimistically, the citizens of Iasos exhibited striking confidence that in the *polis*, equilibrium and justice as balancing acts could lead to the good life: an inscribed list of citizens testified that they "gave money willingly out of their own fortunes, wishing to increase the democracy as much as possible, for the grain-buying fund, in order that the *dēmos* always live happily (*eudaimonōs*), in abundance of grain, when there will take place a distribution of grain to all the citizens out of common means (*ek tōn koinōn*)."[134]

Image, Reality and the Return of History

Institutional workings, ideological equilibrium, and *eudaimōnia*: the account above is a maximal account, written as a reflection of the fascinating discourses of the *polis* and of their utopian qualities. Did this *polis* actually ever exist? It has been claimed (and I am in general sympathy with this claim: below, chapter 17) that the good institutions and social solidarity of the *polis* lead to a remarkable degree of economic prosperity, supercharged by the consumption of citizens in the third and second century BCE.[135] The result seems to be the "end of history," as if the *polis* were the sum of its successes, leading to stability. But we might want to pause and examine the self-image of the *polis* more closely, and perhaps stop reading with the grain so assiduously.

A starting point might be found in Athens just before the great convergence, and more precisely in the deme of Halai Aixōnides, where in 363/2 BCE, the good demarch Euthēmōn, by his voluntary example and by proposing a new decree, reformed the finances of the deme, notably by imposing procedures for handling public monies and documenting public expenditure. More documents suggest a small political crisis. A contemporary decree (badly preserved, but naming Euthēmōn), passed after a report by one Nikomenēs, enjoined the deme authorities to pronounce

FIGURE 10.5. Lead curse tablet, found in Attica. Mid fourth-century BCE. L 14.1 cm. From *IG* 3 appendix 24 (Wünsch).

curses in order "that such things never happen again." The deme elected a commission to dedicate a statue of Aphroditē on the Akropolis, which might be linked with rituals of reconciliation (all twenty-four members of the commission received honorific crowns, including Nikomenēs and Euthēmōn). Most strikingly, a contemporary curse tablet includes Euthēmōn and Nikomenēs among the intended victims of its magic binding spells, reflecting the frustration and ill will of adversaries, perhaps sidelined by Euthēmōn's exemplary and do-gooder reforms (fig. 10.5).[136] Its private binding spell stands in contrast, with targeted individual malice, to the public curses performed by the deme to protect collective interests.

The good citizen and the good institutions were normative images, which yet do not completely occlude the realities of conflict and of politics, even in the post-convergence *polis*. The allusiveness of the documentary material often prevents us from perceiving what political conflict was about. Economic tensions between rich and poor, or disputes about property rights, or institutional dysfunction, can be guessed at. Some form of unrest (*tarachē*) was stifled in the *polis* of Minōa by a combination of ritual, political negotiation and royal intervention, without the actual terms of the conflict ever being made clear in the decree recording its end.

Nor is this case unique.[137] More frequently, decrees mention the bad actions of "some men" (*tines*), unnamed antisocial actors whose deeds need the remedy of proposals and interventions by good citizens.[138]

Even though the earlier "infernal equation" of hegemony and stasis had vanished, the *polis*'s balancing acts did not remove the possibility of conflict. The institutionalization of transparency, scrutiny, and exemplarity, the very high premium placed on voluntary prosecution, the central role played by popular courts and mass decision, the structural necessity for aggressive demagogic politics—all these features were part of the genealogy of the *poleis* in the great convergence and essential to their workings, their character, and their success. But by nature, these features encouraged conflict. Structural conflict was taken for granted between members of the elite, whose competition was an essential part of the functioning of the system of voluntary leadership and policing; indeed, "demagogic" conflict might have been, paradoxically, one of the tools to produce the smoothed-out consensual decrees that we possess (the other tool being constant deliberation and bargaining in preliminary meetings to produce propositions, and then in the Assembly meeting itself: above, pp. 240–41). The system also generated tension between the community and individuals, since an ideology of commitment and the primacy of community claims placed ethical pressure on economic transactions and pursuits.

Although this particular political culture was functional in a large *polis* such as fourth-century BCE Athens, in smaller *poleis* the adversarial style and the ethical claims may have placed constant stress on communal life. Hence the widespread evidence for troubles centering around the courts in the Hellenistic period, and the resort to panels of foreign judges to resolve gridlock (a specific application of the collaborative network of peer-polity interaction as well as an illustration of the high value placed on consensus). In Erythrai or in Dēmētrias, such courts resolved political problems (a denunciation that generated near-*stasis*, a conflict between a decree and a law); more generally, foreign courts took on backlogs of cases, either arbitrating or adjudicating long-standing conflict.[139] We will need to look back on the island of Hērakleia and wonder about the goat-raisers whose choices were now cast beyond the pale, and whose actions would be characterized as violence and designated as the authorized target of self-help and community prosecution (see below, chapters 18 and 19).

In addition to its operation as a network of institutions, the *polis* existed as a society. As Aristotle observed, by its very nature it was *plēthos*, plurality; the *polis* existed as a set of "free spaces" for individuals and groups to interact, rather than necessarily be governed by the constitutive protocols of *to koinon*: this fact was as crucial to the operation of the collective as the public/private dichotomy.[140] In reality, as well as being a bounded, autonomous institutional field of political equality, the *polis* was "lumpy." Associations were undoubtedly part of civic institutions, and associative practice and discourse imitated civic *praxis*.[141] Yet at the same time, they are not reducible to that role. Associations ensured religious, funerary, economic, and collaborative functions that did not necessarily fit within the civic framework of membership and public goods; as social organizations, they offered spaces for relations of hierarchy and patronage of the type that was precluded by the institutional and ideological setup of the *polis*.[142] Households represented further *loci* for emotional ties and social dramas, such as the transmission of property. These were issues that the *polis* took an interest in but did not lie completely under its control; for instance, private consumption, family commemoration through statues in shrines or the *agora*, or the increasing popularity of adoption belong to a social history that was not immediately dependent on the political world of the *polis* (see further, chapter 15).[143]

For all the power and pervasiveness of civic ideology, individuals preserved their agency as rational actors. Good citizens, when serving as magistrates, refrained from taking interest on monies they lent to the *polis* (above, pp. 248–49); this implies that from the moment they stepped down from office, they usually charged interest on their loans to the city. When the important decree of democratic Kymē limiting the powers of the *stratēgos* (above, p. 221) was inscribed, the *polis* needed to take a small loan to cover this item of expenditure: it is hard not to notice that the man who provided the funds was in fact the treasurer (and also the proposer of the decree; we might wonder if he did not charge interest on this loan, since the decree is silent on this matter). The Milesian financial measures to meet a shortfall in tax revenue avoided disturbing the social compact between rich and poor (above, pp. 248–49)—by putting in place extremely favorable terms for lenders, who were repaid through a life pension that after ten years would start to yield a profit: no wonder that many citizens subscribed to the scheme in their children's name, making an utterly rational investment.[144]

The *polis* existed both as a heightened, utopian, political image and as a complex realist interaction of actual social actors. The problem of the relationship between these is one of the great themes of my survey of *polis* history, but it is particularly visible in the case of the post-convergence *polis*, where public institutions and ideology have achieved a finished, stereotypical, and widespread form. It is noticeable that the thickening of the fabric of associations in the *polis*, and the increasing visibility of private family display, emerge clearly from the mid-fourth century BCE onwards; that is, at the precise moment when the great convergence of *polis* institutions gets started. Furthermore, notably in a genealogical perspective, it might be worth asking if the *polis* as state was not a particularly powerful form of symbolical overlay or playacting, in the direct line of the playacting that helped bind the disparate elements that came together in collaborative state and community forms in the early "Archaic" period.

The particular conditions of the third and early second centuries BCE (the "Hellenistic" period) added to the structural pressures that the *polis* had to face. The period is characterized by additional complexity and opportunities, in the form of increased mobility and elite contacts. The *poleis* thus had to find a place for resident foreigners and immigrants, which boosted the associative phenomenon but also influenced affected civic structures such as citizen education or euergetical transactions (see further, chapter 15). Foreign youths joined the ranks of the *ephēbeia* in large cities such as Athens or Pergamon, and foreign benefactors financed festival activities at Iasos.[145] New political and economic opportunities reinforced the position of the elites. The latter gained positions of influence through contacts with the big kingdoms (witness the Athenian Kallias of Sphēttos, officer in the Ptolemaic court but also benefactor at home);[146] by drawing on capital for loans and investments, and agricultural wealth for the production and export of cash crops, elites may have increased their wealth in the world economy of the Hellenistic period.[147]

The result may have been elite reaffirmation, visible in multiple suggestive phenomena. One case is that of the "private" honorific statue. The genre had emerged in the particularly contested social landscape of mid-fourth century Athens; its intensification at the end of the third century BCE, and its take-off during the following period, indicates the desire of individuals and especially families to display their disposable wealth. In addition, such monuments usually commemorated the transmission of property within elite families (sometimes with explicit indication that statues were set up after inheritance), and hence the social reproduction of wealthy households. The increasing visibility of such monuments, in shrines and in the *agora* of Hellenistic *poleis*, marked the acceptability of statements about family wealth. In addition, family monuments imitated public honorific monuments and sometimes associated private and public monuments in portfolios of statues, which reversed the normal statements about the primacy of the public by integrating public honors within the facets of elite individual identity, in a striking act of appropriation.[148] It is tempting to read this phenomenon with others such as the collaboration of elites in furnishing "foreign judges" to their cities, bypassing democratic courts and accountability with well-to-do specialists,[149] or changes to the language of praise, to wonder if the relics of elitist culture in the *polis* were quite successfully constrained by the *polis*.

These questions gained sharp relief from ca. 150 BCE onwards (during what is conventionally termed the "late Hellenistic" period): elite affirmation coexists with the continued operation of *polis* institutions and ideology, and indeed their intensification, visible in Athens but also across a large number of *poleis*. The debates and negotiations of the late second-century BCE, fueled by economic overheating and massive political change, illustrate the tensions inherent in the *polis* that emerged out of the great convergence (see below, chapter 11). Just as Aristotle's *Politics* reflects the start of the great convergence, Aristotelian themes of citizenship and ethical fulfilment in the *polis* appear in the late second century BCE. The echoes are strikingly illustrated by Priēnē. The city was rebuilt on its new grid plan ca. 350 BCE, an early instance of the strongly ideological materiality of the *polis*, and its late fourth-century BCE decrees speak of democracy, equality, and autonomy,

FIGURE 10.6. Fountain in Priēnē (actual state, as photographed by John Ma in 2007, and reimagination by E. Neumann, in Krischen 1938).

as inherent parts of *polis*-hood (fig. 1.3). A fountain, still visible in the ruins of the city (fig. 10.6), exemplifies public goods, but also the rule of law, since it was accompanied by an inscription specifying its use (no private laundering or ritual cleansing at this public, shared facility), and enforcing penalties by means of law, namely denunciation according to "the law on denunciations (*nomos phasikos*)."[150] Two centuries later, the very long decrees passed for great benefactors illustrate the tensions and the heightening of civic ideology, embedding active and wealthy individuals in a discourse of good citizenship. We will return to these decrees below, as evidence for the shifts and tensions within the late Hellenistic *polis*; here they remind us of continuities in discourse and values.

These decrees are inscribed on walls of the north stoa of the *agora* of Priēnē (see fig. 11.3, see also fig. 19.1). This space illustrates the history of the *polis* in many instructive ways. The crucial private/public dichotomy is brought out by the contrast between open public space and tightly knit private housing. In the late second century BCE, the Prienians separated the practical activities of food selling into a special market next to the political and presentational *agora*—a very Aristotelian statement of the division between politics and mere practical or profit-oriented activities.[151] The *agora* was taken over by honorific statues, public and (strikingly) private, thus reflecting the elite reaffirmation of the late third and early second centuries BCE. Yet all the statues were moved and reorganized by the *polis*, which placed them in a single row of statues. This ensemble staged an image of community that was civic and communitarian, yet also tending toward elitist messages about the preeminence and agency of the wealthy. The potentially elitist yet carefully negotiated statement was in turn challenged by other monuments, set up by prominent Prienian families, occupying highly visible sites in the northern side of the *agora*: these might represent a "super-elite" within the *polis*.[152] The *agora* remains frozen in the state of flux and development of the early first century BCE: the subsequent hardships, and the backwater status of Priēnē during the Roman empire, mean that the means and the will for elite display and competition in civic spaces were lacking. Its fossilized record of social competition and change during the second century BCE, and the implied impact of subsequent events, raises the question of the historical processes that altered the "Aristotelian" *polis* of the great convergence.

PART V

Polis and Imperium

180 BCE–400 CE

SOMETIME IN THE 30S BCE, the citizens of Patara, in Lykia, honored one of their number. Idagras had competed as a boy in athletic contests and won victories in all-out close combat (*pankration*) at events near and far (Lykia and Rhodes, but also the Nemea and the Argive Heraia in the Peloponnese). He thus had participated in an old, aristocratic-tinged activity that manifested his leisure and wealth, in a way that claimed to represent his community; such claims were a direct descendant of the competitive, performative claims to distinction that created civic elites in the "Archaic" and Classical *poleis*. The adult Idagras held office in the federal league of the Lykians, and represented it on embassy, thus fulfilling the roles expected of wealthy and educated members of the community.

In exchange for which services, as part of the processes of auditing and examining that lay at the heart of the political culture of the *poleis*, and probably upon application by Idagras himself, his city honored him with a bronze portrait statue and a gilt crown (his honors are known from the inscribed base of his statue). The measures were contained in a decree of the Patarans, passed "upon the proposal of the people"—which means that the decree was voted twice, a practice typical of the constitutionalism of the developed *polis* (above, chapter 10). The statue of course is forever lost, but we can be fairly certain that it represented the honorand using the familiar visual tropes of good citizenship: grave face, restrained body (even if exhibiting traces of a glorious and muscular past), civic dress-code (see fig. 18.1). All these features are characteristic of the public life of the *poleis*, and their presence in a Lykian city is the result of a long-lasting and deep embedding of civic culture in this Anatolian region.

Yet the honors for Idagras also reflect a changed world. He was a "Pataran and Roman," a Roman citizen, having received this status by a grant from one of the dynasts of the last decades of the Roman Republic, the triumvir Mark Antony, whose *nomen* he bore—M. Antonius Idagras, the Roman, the Greek and the Lykian aspects of his identity and his status all combining in his composite name. The embassies on which he served did not go to other cities, but to the powerful figures of Roman commanders in the field, the Greek expression (*autokratoras*) translating the Latin *imperatores*. M. Antonius Idagras's successful embassies secured privileges, described as "gifts" (*dōreai*); for instance, being excused from having to provide 600 citizen soldiers to fight for Rome (perhaps in one of the conflicts between Roman dynasts that made up the civil wars of the first century BCE).[1]

The situation in which a Greek city expects grants, conceived as gifts, from the ruling power reflects the unilateral power of Rome in the eastern Mediterranean (in fact in the whole Mediterranean); where once ambassadors from Greek cities went to other cities, or to Hellenistic kings and their officials, they now went to Roman officers, or to the center of power, to the city of Rome itself. This historical sea-change overlaps with the latter part of the great convergence in *polis* institutions. The intensification in accountability and institutional functions, the careful articulation of communitarian values, the debates about these values as exemplified by good citizens being publicly rewarded—all these late Hellenistic phenomena occurred in the world changed by the intervention of Rome (chapter 11).

To notice this overlap raises a series of historical questions. The first is the nature and the rate of change that Roman presence brought about—and indeed the nature of the "coming of Rome" itself. By the time of Idagras's honors, Rome had been a dominant presence in the eastern Mediterranean for a century and a half. This question has been probed by scholars seeking to elaborate a sophisticated, pericentric model of interaction between the Roman power and the states of the Hellenistic world. It is particularly fruitful in allowing us to write a history that is not simply the story of Roman imperialism seen from the point of view of the victors and exclusively concerned with their agency and motivation.

The second question is the significance of the elements of continuity so evident on Idagras's statue base: what did Roman control change in the *polis*? The question concerns the fate of the *poleis* of the great convergence: what happened to the equilibria of autonomy and democracy that the *poleis* achieved and maintained with great efforts? Conversely, we might ask a third question: to what extent did *polis* culture shape the forms taken by the Roman "conquest," and subsequently, by the Roman empire?

The questions sketched out above took on particular urgency with the emergence of a world empire ruled by a military monarchy (the process was underway at the time of M. Antonius Idagras, whose patron was the unsuccessful rival to the victorious dynast Imperator Julius Caesar, later Augustus). The Roman empire saw an extension of power as well as an intensification of the state's ability to integrate and instrumentalize local communities. If we should no longer fix the endpoint of the *polis* at the battle of Chairōneia in 338 BCE (when the kingdom of Macedonia defeated a coalition of *poleis* including Athens and Thebes, putting an end to the tragic century of hegemonical competition), what should we say of the battle of Aktion (31 BCE), which marked Augustus's victory? Hence I propose to look at various aspects of the *polis* within a world empire: the fate of local autonomy (chapter 12); the evolution of civic life between the glare of elitism and democratic institutions (chapter 13); the diffusion of a form of *polis* life in the Roman Near East and its cooptation by the Roman state, and the slow end of the *polis* form, coinciding with the end of Classical antiquity (chapter 15). It is an extraordinarily rich period, notably in the density of documentary and material evidence, in the presence of informative literary sources, and in the extension of *polis* life from the Adriatic to the Syrian steppe and Egypt.

11

The Indian Summer of the *Polis*

> In the second century and in the first, the Greek cities were increasingly embroiled in various conflicts, wars of Rome in the Aegean and Asia Minor, wars of Mithridates, wars between Romans; a dangerous life, for many ending in agony. The life of the city continues in the same framework and with the same ideas. What brings about more and more impactful changes within civic life is the appearance and the development of the practice and the system of the *euergetai*.
> —LOUIS ROBERT, "THÉOPHANE DE MYTILÈNE À CONSTANTINOPLE"

Polis and Spear-Crowned Power

In 128/7 BCE, a chorus of Athenian boys, sent by their city to Delphi, prayed for divine favor over Athens, Delphi, the professional guild of Dionysiac Artists (one of whom had composed the hymn and directed its performance), and for the "spear-crowned power of the Romans," flourishing with ageless might.[1] By then Roman intervention in the eastern Mediterranean was nearly a hundred years old and had led to a changed world. The establishment of military dominance by the Roman Republic took place in a relatively short time span (220–168 BCE), which the Achaian politician and historian Polybios, a contemporary, witness, and victim of the process, described poignantly: "Who would be so dull or indolent as not to wish to know how and by what type of constitution nearly the whole inhabited world succumbed and fell under the sole rule of the Romans in less than fifty-three years?"[2] Polybios later extended his purview to the years 168 to 146 BCE, to describe the further development and extension of Roman power.

In spite (or because) of the heat of argument over a century and more of grand debate on "Roman imperialism in the East,"[3] it is clear that the general contours of the phenomenon fall in place within a unified if unarticulated story of Roman imperialism. The disagreements amount to emphasizing different aspects of this phenomenon (rather like the tale of blindfolded men describing an elephant). The first aspect is the violent, domineering characteristics of Roman intervention and its aftermath. The second is the concern for preexisting norms, especially for the discourse of liberty that developed as part of the great convergence of the late fourth and third centuries BCE. The third is the unsystematic, often disengaged attitude of the Roman Republic and its elites toward the Hellenistic world. The dynamic combination of these three characteristics explains the particular outcomes of the late Hellenistic period and the way they affected the *poleis*.

The first aspect, ubiquitous violence, is prominent in Polybios's narrative. Even a sideshow like the First Macedonian War was a brutal affair of sieges and sacks and left bitter memories. At the end of the Third Macedonian War, the Roman victory at Pydna saw the wholesale slaughter of the Macedonian citizen soldiers. A year later, in 167 BCE, the victor of Pydna, Paullus Aemilius, led his troops in a punitive expedition to harry the lively post-monarchical federal state of Ēpeiros for leaning toward the Antigonids. Seventy cities were devastated.[4] Even if the late third century BCE had seen a recrudescence of interstate violence (the Epeirote federal shrine had been sacked in 219 BCE by the Aitolians) and even if Hellenistic international politics were harsh,[5] the violence of Roman intervention on and around the battlefield was noticeably extreme. Though Rome initially did not follow up conquest with annexation, "smash and leave" (A. Eckstein) still involved a considerable amount of smashing. This was carried out with gusto by the members of a militaristic society that entertained constant and maximal suspicion toward potential threats, along with a legalistic conviction of the justness of Roman causes, to the point of solipsism.[6] Roman intervention was also a case of "smash and grab" because military victory was an acquisitive bonanza.[7]

Violence was also present in between battles, sieges, and razzias. The Roman Senate sometimes pursued aggressive policies with ruthless cynicism and bad faith, deliberately and openly leveraging local politics and unrest to obtain advantage over political targets.[8] The aftermath of victory was the assumption of the victor's performative right to decide and dispose, and hence the precarity of local statuses. The concept is a version of the "surrender-and-grant" model that was central to Hellenistic kingship.[9] With variants (notably in the extensive powers wielded by commanders in the field), the major outcome of Roman imperialism was to extend, systematize, and universalize the performative assumption grounded in military conquest.

Thus in 196 BCE, Flamininus and a Roman commission decided on the liberty of the Greeks who had been ruled by Philip V and another Roman commission settled the affairs of Asia Minor in 188 BCE after defeating the Seleukid ruler Antiochos III. The rights of victory were permanent, and Roman grants reversible. Just as the Roman Senate had granted the cities of Karia and Lykia to Rhodes in 188 BCE, it intervened a decade later, in 177 BCE, to modify the terms of the grant (by specifying that the Lykians were to be treated as subordinate allies but not as subjects). Yet another decade later, the Senate reversed the grant altogether, by declaring the freedom of the cities of Lykia and Karia. No direct military victory or conquest explains by what right the senate decided not only to free Karia and

Lykia (part of the spoils of the victory over Antiochos III), but also Stratonikeia, an earlier Rhodian conquest. Nor is there any direct legal reason allowing the senate to grant Dēlos (a free city!) to the Athenians—but also to stipulate that it would be a free port. Equally moot is the justification for the orders issued to the Achaians, who had not been a defeated party in the Third Macedonian War, to surrender a list of men perceived as dangerous to Rome (the hostages included Polybios). The possibility of the Senate interfering with the local arrangements of their "allies" is assumed by a Roman law of 100 BCE, precisely because this law, for the time being, exempts concerning from its provisions "whatever peoples and nations bring tribute, incomes or soldiers to a king or to kings or to peoples with whom there is friendship and alliance with the Roman people."[10] Such was the *maiestas* of the Roman people, which defeated foes and allies alike agreed to respect.[11]

The outcome of Roman violence was, most obviously, the destruction of the Hellenistic concert of great powers.[12] In 169 BCE, during a successful invasion of Egypt, the Seleukid ruler Antiochos IV received envoys from the Greek cities, some attempting to broker a settlement, others entrusted with separate affairs. The Achaians came to discuss participation in their festival in honor of the former Antigonid ruler, Antigonos Dōsōn—a very Hellenistic moment, combining the importance of festival culture, ruler cult, and the complicated politics of the Peloponnese. Antiochos IV duly set aside 100 talents levied from Egypt as gifts for the Greek cities.[13] Yet this was one of the last moments of the old Hellenistic world, with its multipolar diplomacy and interactions. The following year, during his second Egyptian campaign, Antiochos IV was humiliated by the Roman envoy, C. Popilius Laenas, who brought the Senate's orders for Antiochos to evacuate Egypt and demanded an answer on the spot. When the king asked to consult his friends, the Roman responded by tracing a circle in the sand around the king, and demanding that the latter give his answer before crossing the line.[14] In continental Greece, the defeat of Macedonia in 196 BCE, even before the destruction of the Antigonid kingdom, put an end to the world created by the ascendancy of Philip II starting in the 350s BCE (with the quasi-integration of Thessaly in the Macedonian space, and domination of southern Greece by a combination of direct control and interference with local politics).

The other great losers in the process were the regional leagues. The Aitolian League had developed into an acquisitive, predatory state run to the benefit of its central elites; its enemy, the Achaian League, had pursued a no-omelet-without-broken-eggs policy of unification of the Peloponnese to be able to project power in the Hellenistic world (comparable to the Theban project of unifying Boiōtia in the fourth century BCE).[15] Their disappearance would have significant consequences for the world of the *poleis*. From now on the "Hellenistic" world bathed in a sea of Roman power, where realist behavior would be removed from the grasp of all players, and banished to a peripheral badlands of small, competing kingdoms and *poleis* (Kappadokia, Bithynia, Pontus—as well as the post-Seleukid Levant).[16]

The *poleis* recognized that the axis of the world had tilted. Honors—statues, cult, festivals—were offered to powerful individual Romans in the field or to Rome in general, just as they had been offered to the Hellenistic kings.[17] Concretely, from the 180s BCE the recognition of Roman power took the form of the constant dispatch by the Greek cities of embassies traveling all the way to Rome, their audition by the Senate, and responses, sometimes in the form of envoys or delegations sent to specific cities or regions, or on whole circuits of inspection. This pattern rhythms the account of Polybios. A particular instance is the sad recurrence of embassies sent by the Achaian League to try to obtain the liberation of the hostages they provided after 167 BCE.[18] By the end, the embassies were instructed carefully to avoid disagreement or argument with the Senate.[19]

The Achaian League did attempt resistance when confronted with Roman demands, by ignoring them or trying to fit them within the legalistic frame of the Achaian constitution. But not only did this attitude antagonize the Senate and ultimately contribute to the harsh treatment of the League; it also gave rise to internal conflict between legalists and partisans of compliance. The unipolar field of Roman power distorted politics in the Greek cities, partly by reintroducing *stasis* but especially by giving those with Roman support (such as the Achaian politician Kallikratēs) a massive advantage, to the point that cities started to anticipate Roman wishes.[20] Likewise, the presence of Rome distorted the interaction between cities, since the unfolding of disputes was subject to Roman approval and Roman support could decide the outcome: Achaian reprisals against Athens (when the Athenians refused to compensate exiled Delians) were only conducted once Roman agreement was secured.[21] The Athenians initially interceded for the city of Haliartos, sacked by a Roman army during the Third Macedonian War, but soon modified their suit to ask (successfully) for Rome to give them the territory of Haliartos.[22]

Rome and the Liberty of the *Poleis*

It is a paradox that the second great characteristic of "Roman imperialism" is the fostering of local liberty.[23] In 133 BCE, when the last Attalid king, Attalos III, bequeathed his kingdom to the Roman Republic, the Senate proclaimed the freedom of all the Greek cities that had belonged to the king. This is attested in Asia Minor but also for overseas possessions of the Attalids such as the island of Andros.[24] Even Pergamon, the former royal capital, rejoiced in its "ancestral democracy."[25] The Roman Senate had earlier made some effort to adhere to norms in its international dealings, which it conceived in terms of obligations and reciprocity, generally conceptualized as forms of trust and friendship.[26] In addition, Hellenistic rulers and supralocal powers had long expressed their power through the discourse of freedom and its defense, which offered a suitable space for local legitimacy and negotiation as well as a tool for high political competition.

After the grim experiment of the First Macedonian War, the Roman Senate as well as Roman officers operating in the Hellenistic world found that the pre-scripted discourse of freedom constituted unavoidable precedents (alongside the discourse of benefaction, within which the *poleis* coopted Rome and Romans—hence honors for them as "common benefactors"—but which Rome itself did not really adopt).[27] The adoption of this discourse by Romans in dealing with the Hellenistic world was the result of multiple local initiatives, such as the extraordinary embassy from Lampsakos that pressed Roman officials and the Roman Senate to protect its democracy and autonomy.[28] The parameters of the great convergence not only survived the arrival of Roman power, but shaped it: yet again, the *poleis* of the great convergence were able to make their own luck.

Hence, one effect of the Polybian moment was to intensify the generalization of autonomy that characterizes the great convergence of the late fourth and third centuries BCE. Perioikic cities finally disappear in Lakōnia (helotism would linger on until the end of the first century BCE). Likewise, subordinate statuses vanished in Crete.[29] The cities of Messēnia, though grouped around the big central city of Messēnē, were not bound by relations of domination.[30] The end of perioikism favored developments such as those visible in second century BCE Thessaly. There, the cities freed from Macedonian control as well as the old relations of subordination between communities and within communities created their very active league, structured around the cult of Liberator Zeus in memory of the proclamation of Greek liberty in 196 BCE.[31] Other smaller leagues emerged; for instance, the Magnesian League around Dēmētrias, or the Oitaians and the Perrhaibians, on the periphery of Thessaly (the Thessalian League later absorbed the latter two). The Thessalian *polis* of Larisa participated fully in inter-*polis* networks, as shown by the epigraphical record; so did the Thessalian League or the Magnesian League.[32] Inscriptions show how the leagues and their constituent cities were involved in each other's business and disputes, and awarded each other recognition and honors.

Such activities perpetuated the peer-polity interaction of past centuries; indeed, the pressure of Roman intervention and of dangerous events fostered collaboration between cities, along the familiar lines of inter-*polis* kinship. In the 190s BCE, the *polis* of Stymphalos helped refugees from Elateia, to whom they considered themselves related through their respective mythical founders. Heroic envoys from Teōs repeatedly intervened to help the embattled city of Abdēra, founded by Teians nearly four centuries earlier.[33] Peer-polity interaction functioned intensely during the 180s BCE—a dense life of conflict, negotiation, and exchange sprang up in Asia Minor, for instance in the Maeander valley, spanning the spectrum from treaties of collaboration to border disputes pursued by arbitration to full warfare between coalitions, and involving such *poleis* as Milētos, Hērakleia under Latmos, Priēnē, or Magnēsia.[34] The resort to "foreign judges," called in to judge civil cases, flourished.[35] After the withdrawal of Rhodian control over southwest Asia Minor, the

Karian and Lykian cities enjoyed their liberty. The Karian *polis* of Apollōnia under Salbakē—once a military colony founded by the Seleukid empire—expected its ally, Kibyra, to come to its aid if anyone marched against its territory or its *dēmokratia*. Similar sentiments were expressed in nearby Pisidia, where Adada and Termēssos swore to aid each other if anyone tried to suppress the cities' "laws, incomes or *dēmokratia*."[36]

As for the Lykian cities, they formalized their relations in a federal league, whose institutions were described ca. 100 BCE by the geographer Artemidōros of Ephesos. They included a federal council, college of magistrates, and even a federal law court; at all of which cities were represented by delegates chosen in numbers proportional to their size (a federal solution already attested for the fifth-century BCE Boiotian League). The Lykian League's origins lay in some cities' resistance against Rhodian control; after independence, it duly conducted its own foreign policy, including wars and expansion. A glimpse of the league's activities can be caught in the decree passed by the small *polis* of Araxa for one of its citizens, Orthagoras, an officer and politician in the league, who fought against Rhodian-backed tyrants but also against the northern neighbors of Lykia.[37] The Lykians offered cultic honors to Rome in recognition of the grant of freedom in 167 BCE but also made the most of their freedom to conduct an eventful political life.

One factor that gave a head start to local liberty was Roman neglect. As M. Holleaux established (at the start of modern debates on Roman imperialism), the Roman state formation was not animated with a driving desire or consistent plan to conquer the Hellenistic world or the Mediterranean space. Structural features encouraged disengagement, notably the short term of service by Roman magistrates in the field and the multiple theatres of involvement that resulted in a collectively short attention span in "Eastern" matters. Q. Metellus Macedonicus gained his nickname for his role in crushing the uprising in Macedonia in 148; yet he never returned to Greece after that time. In many cases, Roman pressure and instructions were not followed through on the ground—or rather, follow through involved local actors and their live interests, and hence negotiation, litigation, boundary-pushing, and consultation. As mentioned above, in the 150s BCE, when Athens behaved injuriously toward the expulsed Delians or the Oropians, the injured parties, with considerable support from the Achaian League (another instance of the pressure of events provoking the solidarity of peer-polity interaction), referred the matters to Rome and obtained favorable decisions. These opened the way to further negotiation on the ground.[38] Around the same time, a dispute between Priēnē and Ariarathēs of Kappadokia escalated to the point of low-grade warfare, even though the matter had been referred to Rome for arbitration and a decision—which remained *lettre morte* in the actual local contexts.

Hence the Polybian sea of power allowed for archipelagoes of local initiative and freedom—the more so for liberty being an official policy of the Roman Republic. The very security of Roman control allowed for a certain looseness in implementation and attention. This period of abatement in itself marks an important stage in the history of the *polis*, both externally and as concerns the evolutions of the great convergence in *polis* life.

Indian Summer (150–86 BCE)

Though partially masked by the power politics and large-scale warfare of the Polybian moment, civic phenomena reemerge strongly during the second half of the second century BCE and onwards. The intense workings of the *polis*, internally and in peer networks, form the "Indian Summer" of the *polis* during the late Hellenistic period (ca. 150 BCE onwards), to use the conventional periodization.[39] We should not focus simply on Roman power (as in collections of documents on "Rome and the Greek *poleis*"): this neglects all the other evidence for the life of the Greek *poleis*.[40] The Indian Summer prolongs the local freedom that is one of the features of the early second century BCE. Yet the Indian Summer of the Greek cities was also a period of tension and unease surrounding the twin issues of local agency and democracy. Roman presence, however discreet, was ineluctable, and its cumulative impact led to encroachment, exploitation—and a terrible first century BCE.

In 144/3 BCE the Roman proconsul of Macedonia, Q. Fabius Maximus, in a letter to the citizens of Dymē, could speak of the settlement of Greece as the restoration of freedom in the continuation of the earlier policies. Proclaimed attention to the freedom of the Greeks coexisted with the proconsul's intervention within the city of Dymē to stop some form of unrest, probably linked to debt.[41] Mainland Greece was not annexed to the province of Macedonia but started a new provincial era of its own in 145 BCE; at least initially, there is no clear evidence for any form of Roman administration, control or extraction in the form of tribute or taxation. Though the *polis* of Epidauros had participated in the Achaian War and fought against Roman armies, it would conclude an alliance with Rome as a free city, as we know happened in the case of other Greek *poleis*.[42] It seems that the *poleis* of mainland Greece were granted their freedom and left in an ambiguous situation.

The situation was similarly ambiguous in Asia Minor after 133 BCE. The bequest of Attalos III explicitly granted freedom to all the Greek *poleis*, a prolongation of the Attalid policy of favorable relations with the *poleis* (including the devolution of royal land to *poleis* and the encouragement of *polis* development in Mysia).[43] The commission of Roman senators who arrived in Asia Minor to settle the details, set up a structure to consult the *poleis* (the "council according to the Roman lawgiving," as a contemporary document from Pergamon names it). The *poleis* actively resisted the Attalid pretender Aristonikos-Eumenēs III. Civic troops fought for the Romans. The small city of Mētropolis in Iōnia (a royal foundation!) sent out its militia, led by a local notable, one Apollōnios, to join the Roman legates. Aristonikos's fleet was held in check by the Ephesians' ships of the line.[44] After the final Roman victory and the creation of the province of Asia, the general freedom of the *poleis* seems to have been respected.⁴⁵ The bequest of 133 BCE set Mētropolis free, along with all the other *poleis* in the Attalid kingdom; the city honored its fallen with an inscription on the base of the statue of their commander, who also was killed leading his fellow citizens.⁴⁶ Apollōnis, a royal foundation and once a subordinate city in the Attalid-controlled Lydian plain, must have gained in 133 BCE the freedom that it enjoyed in the first century BCE.⁴⁷ Another *polis*, Kolophōn, insisted, in the decree for a leading politician, Menippos, that the city's autonomy was separate from the province—and hence that its boundaries were secure, and its jurisdiction separate from the sphere of activity of the Roman proconsul and from the practices of Roman law.⁴⁸

Roman provincialization did not amount to territorial annexation by Rome, and could be conducted with explicit attention to civic autonomy,⁴⁹ as under the governor Q. Mucius Scaevola (the Younger) sometime in the early 90s BCE.⁵⁰ The model of generalized autonomy was later applied to Kyrēnē and its region when it became a Roman province (96 BCE).⁵¹ Civic freedom was paradoxically an integral part of Roman provincialization. The application of the autonomy principle is reflected in the mainly military forms taken by the Roman *provincia* in the north, a space of military activity against the Balkan communities, and hence one that left the *poleis* to their own devices. Furthermore, it is clear that Roman provincialization in Greece, Macedonia, and Asia Minor coexisted with the general freedom of the island *poleis* of the Aegean.⁵²

Whatever the legal arrangements, there was much leeway in the world of the *poleis* in the later second and early first centuries BCE. This is particularly noticeable in Asia Minor. By the later second century BCE, the cities of Karia and Lykia had decades of experience of freedom. The temple of Hekatē at Lagina, in the territory of Stratonikeia, was probably built during those decades; its frieze probably shows local myth, in celebration of Stratonikeia's pride and place in the region and in the world.⁵³ A sign of agency is the resurgence of military activity, realizing the potential of the inter-*polis* alliances that appear earlier. The Thebans proved highly aggressive toward their neighbors, especially Phōkis and Euboia, in echoes of their behavior during the fourth century BCE.⁵⁴ Asia Minor was a veritable hotbed of small local wars. The *poleis* in the small federal state in the Kibyratis were ferociously independent, and entered conflict, sometimes armed, with their Lykian neighbors.⁵⁵ Low-intensity wars flared up regularly between neighbors—Magnēsia and Priēnē raided each other around 140 BCE; Kolophōn and Mētropolis, neighboring *poleis* that we have seen proclaiming their freedom, clashed when Kolophōn seized men off its neighbor's territory. Eurōmos and Mylasa clashed over obligations and disputes once an attempted union between the two *poleis* failed; Stratonikeia fought with neighboring Keramos, Mylasa, and Rhodes.⁵⁶ Eurōmos garrisoned its frontier, and Sardeis and Ephesos kept troops (as they detailed in an alliance concluded in 90 BCE).⁵⁷

Some *poleis* even had fleets, like the Ephesian fleet that defeated Aristonikos; warships appear at Kōs or Halikarnassos.⁵⁸ Aristotle had earlier commented on the desirability of a fleet for cities (with strictures on how to crew the ships). Whether civic fleets were generally feasible in Asia Minor and the islands in the time of the Hellenistic empires is moot. The second- and first-century BCE fleets, though doubtless small, illustrate the leeway enjoyed by the *poleis*, and the way in which the new conditions allowed them to fulfill notions developed theoretically by Aristotle.[59]

Militarization is often reflected in the civic culture of the period. The imagery on funerary reliefs from second-century BCE Samos frequently includes, as part of luxurious feasting scenes, presentations of weaponry—offensive arms, modern helmets, body armor, and shields both in the old Greek style and in the new center-grip Celtic style. These are not marks of heroic status, but the actual equipment worn by citizen militiamen; indeed, the *polis* of Samos consolidated its control over the neighboring island and the city of Minōa on not-so-neighboring Amorgos, prolonging an expansionary process started in the late third century BCE.[60] The case of Samos is striking for the frequency of the military motif; it is well paralleled, as we have seen, in Iōnia for the same period (above, p. 206; for a particularly large and elaborate example, see fig. 9.1). The young men graduating into adult citizenship (ephebes) of Milētos received weapons as prizes. Civic troops also appear in Greece, at Thebes or Athens: the ephebes of late second-century BCE Athens, albeit a small, select group, continued military training, including with heavy mounted weaponry (even if they had to pay for the engines to be refurbished to standard).[61]

More often, conflict could be solved by negotiation. The phenomenon is widely attested in the later second century BCE, in Asia Minor as well as on mainland Greece. The armed violence between Magnēsia and Priēnē moved to arbitration by a third party, Mylasa (appointed by the Roman Senate), just as later the Prienians and Milesians went to arbitration under Roman auspices, before a panel convened at Sardeis; the conflict between Stratonikeia and Rhodes went to arbitration by Bargylia. Around 140 BCE, the city of Milētos arbitrated a dispute between Messēnē and Sparta by sending a 600-strong panel of judges.[62] By the early first century BCE, the Arkadian *polis* of Phigaleia appointed a local citizen, Archippos son of Agallos, as "advocate for the ... judgments" (he notably represented his city in a long-standing dispute with another Arkadian *polis*, the border city of Lepreon).[63]

The reemergence of the Thessalian *poleis* or Sparta as autonomous actors allowed these communities to participate in institutionalized structures of exchange and mutual help; for instance, in the practice of asking for or supplying panels of "foreign judges" to arbitrate in cases of internal dissension or backlog in judicial cases (this, too, is a development of a phenomenon already apparent in the 180s BCE). As one example, in 109 BCE, Larisa provided five judges to Athens—to adjudicate cases between citizens of Athens and citizens of Sikyōn, according to a judicial agreement, probably passed after the end of the Achaian League in 146 BCE. The second century BCE was the great age of "foreign judges" and the links they forged between *poleis*.[64]

More generally, the "Indian Summer" was saturated in the phenomena of peer-polity interaction, which the pressure of events in the late third century BCE and the Roman conquest had intensified. At Priēnē, the active citizen Herōdēs was honored for traveling to "Athens, the *mētropolis*" on sacred business and staying on to negotiate other matters. Another Prienian (his name now lost) was particularly active:

> he went on embassy often to the Milesians over the troubles that arose for the city, and likewise to the Magnesians (on Maeander), and also to the Samians over the dispute over the territory and over the demand for the murderers, and also for going on embassy to the Trallians over the troubles that arose for the city often and without shunning any difficulty; likewise towards the Alexandrians in the Troad, the Ephesians and the Mylasans, and also to the Erythraians in connection with the dispute with the Milesians and likewise to the Sardians, and to the Kolophonians in relation to the business with the Magnesians . . .

The Cretan embassy that showed up at Kolophōn with an ultimately successful claim for some sort of payment belonged to the same register of activity.[65] The vitality of civic life invites us to nuance any alarmist view of the "end of autonomy" in the second century.[66] From the 140s onwards, free cities across Asia Minor struck coins on the Attic standard, all using the same device of a wreath surrounding the motif on the obverse, combined with reverses showing the patron deities of each city.[67]

Beyond conflict, negotiation, and bargaining, peer-polity interaction in the second century BCE takes the vivid forms of cultural interactions, curating imagined links between *poleis* and strengthening local identities. The old, familiar forms of traveling historians and wandering poets are clearly attested in the later second century BCE, through the honors voted for them.[68] Such gestures involved individuals but also official contacts between *poleis*, since the decrees for the performers were sent to their home *poleis*. One prominent part of the connective tissue of peer-polity interaction had always been religious and, as shown by the local deities figuring on the reverses of the various wreath-bearing coinages, the religious element is particularly visible in the later second century BCE, to the point that the period has been characterized as a religious renaissance.[69] Priēnē invited all related *poleis* to join in the celebration of its festival of the Panathēnaia, which the city announced it was celebrating with sacrifices and contests "in a manner worthy of Priēnē" and its kindred.[70] More ambitiously, the city of Kolophōn relaunched its festival of the Klaria, with proclamations addressed "to all men."[71]

There is particularly rich evidence for religious activity and innovation in late second-century BCE Athens. The reform of civic festivals such as the Theseia and the Thargelia was explicitly framed in terms of ancestral piety toward Apollōn, and of a glorious Athenian past going back to the Persian Wars.[72] A large team of citizen virgins wove the tunic (*peplos*) given yearly to the old wooden statue of Athēna Polias, and their fathers reported to the Council and asked for honors. The practice, an innovative addition to a very old *polis* cult in Athens, created a new body of young citizen women that balanced the rejuvenated *ephēbeia* of young men.[73] The old cer-

FIGURE 11.1. Fragmentary inscription with hymn to Apollōn, 128 BCE, carved on blocks of the Treasury of the Athenians, Delphi. The last three lines contain a prayer for the power of the Romans.

emonial embassy to Delphi, the Pythais, was revived in great splendor, the three- to five-hundred strong delegations getting larger and more lavish at each iteration (138/7, 128/7, 106/5, and 98/7 BCE). They involved members of the old priestly families, less well-off Athenians, and professional performers, the artists of Dionysos.[74] The hymn to Apollōn mentioned above, celebrating Roman power, is a performance piece from one of the Pythais-delegations. Like another one from a similar occasion, it survives with its musical notation (fig. 11.1), so that we can actually hear the sound of the late Hellenistic boom in religious and ritual activity.

There are many more examples of the religious aspect of the "Indian Summer." The reorganization of the entrance festival for Artemis of the White Brow at Magnēsia on Maeander was documented in a full dossier.[75] The citizens of Bargylia, in Karia, spent much energy on devising ways of increasing the honors of their goddess, Artemis Kindyas and her divine power, with a silver fawn carried at processions and a complex system of public subsidies for civic subdivisions to raise oxen for a parade and sacrifice.[76] In Thessaly, the *polis* of Dēmētrias regularized and solemnized the rituals for the consultation of the oracular shrine of Apollōn Korōpaios in

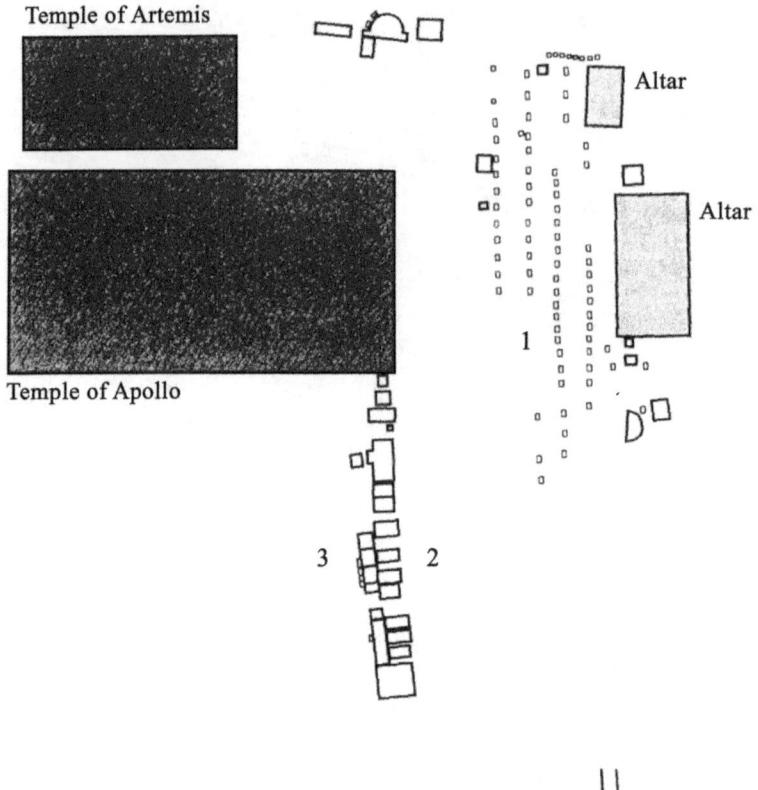

FIGURE 11.2. Shrine of Klaros by the first century BCE. 1. Installations for sacrificial victims (rings for retaining ropes); 2. Row of honorific statues, facing east (including monument of Menippos: fig. 11.3); 3. Row of older monuments, including *kouros* and Geleontes inscription, facing west. After Ferrary and Verger 1999, fig. 3.

the civic territory (ca. 100 BCE).[77] A striking example is the case of the "Mysteries of Andania": the *polis* of Messēnē took over a cult in its territory, hitherto administered by an individual: the mysteries were closely related to the invented traditions important to the identity of the city, newly founded after the destruction of Spartan control in 371 BCE.[78]

Religious activity brought about a boom in building activity. At Xanthos, the temples of Apollōn, Artemis, and Lētō were rebuilt in the second-century BCE, but in ways that preserved the much older buildings as antiquarian monuments.[79] Another example comes from Kolophōn. As part of the monumentalization of the shrine of Klaros, an area with older monuments and "Archaic" *kouroi* was set apart, creating a memorial landscape in parallel to the honorific array of monuments such as those for Menippos and Polemaios (fig. 11.2).[80]

The stele of the tribe of the Geleontes (above, p. 233). was one of the older monuments relocated to this area. In addition, the religious revival boosted antiquarianism. The handover of the mysteries of Andania to the *polis* was accompanied by a dossier drawn from historical and antiquarian sources by the last familial priest. The "Temple Chronicle" of Lindos, a list of dedications in the shrine starting in mythical times, completed by a list of the apparitions of the goddess, celebrated history of Lindos through famous monuments but also focused on lost (often invented) dedications. It acted as a meta-dedication that completed the existing monumental landscape of Lindos.[81] Similarly, the *polis* of Halikarnassos reinscribed, ca. 100 BCE, an older list of priests of Poseidōn that stretched backed to the foundation of the city (the surviving fragments cover at least 827 years).[82]

The second-century BCE moment[83] thus echoes the energy of the *polis* world ca. 300 BCE, when the removal of Achaimenid taxation and the end of hegemony-centered big *polis* struggles led to renewed confidence and prosperity. To continue one of the themes of this book—the relationship between the physical aspect of urbanism and the political history of the *polis*—the late second and early first centuries BCE see the intensification of civic edilitary investment on a massive scale, and often imitating the airs of royal prestige building. At Priēnē, the *agora* was reorganized and rebuilt, with a new monumental stoa lining the north side of the civic space. As mentioned above (p. 256), a new food market was built next to the reorganized *agora*. A massive new *gymnasion*-cum-*stadion* was laid out on the southern edge of the whole city. The shrine of Athēnaiē saw continuous work, on the temple itself but also the hall lining the southern side of the terrace; even the precinct itself was enlarged in the early first century BCE.[84]

The vitality of the network of *poleis* and the clear definition of *polis* life also help us understand, as a peripheral effect, the continued interest of the remaining Hellenistic kingdoms in fostering *polis* life for instrumental purposes, as in Ariarathid Kappadokia in late Seleukid and post-Seleukid Babylonia, or in the Seleukid Levant under Antiochos IV (which led to local unrest, recorded in history as the "Maccabean revolt").[85] Indeed, the disappearance of Hellenistic kingship did not put an end to the process. Settlements of military colonists, drawn by the Attalid kingdom from the highlands of Mysia and implanted in eastern Lydia, soon turned into *demoi* after the end of the Attalid dynasty and, in the first century BCE, into the league of the *Mysoi Abbaeitai*, with a federal assembly, constituent member cities, and evident familiarity with the formal language and ideology of the Greek *poleis*.[86] The story of these *polis*-aspirational communities would continue in the following centuries.

The scheme outlined above can be confirmed from other viewpoints. One is the special case constituted by Hellenistic Crete. A striking feature here is constant violence, as noted by contemporary observer Polybios: intra-*polis* strife and faction; inter-*polis* warfare, often surprisingly brutal and leading to conquest or even the destruction of *poleis*; inter-*polis* power, in the form of dependency for the smaller *poleis*. The island of Kaudos, though endowed with *polis*-hood, was dependent on Gortyn, to whom it paid a cut of all its revenues, including its juniper-berry crop.[87] In other words, Crete stayed in line with its "Archaic" potentialities (a path aggravated by its isolation during the Classical period). Yet later on, Cretan cities were not isolated from the rest of the Hellenistic world. Disputes were solved by arbitration, by other cities or within federal structures. The various campaigns for recognition of *asylia* mounted by *poleis* in Asia Minor took care to involve the Cretan *poleis*, especially since *asylia* amounted to protection from piracy and depredation.[88] Cretan *poleis* were thus part of Hellenistic peer-polity interaction and imitated it locally. By the late Hellenistic period, Cretan *poleis* look increasingly normal to the point of adopting various democratic forms.[89]

The Great Intensification: Democratic Institutions and Ideology in the Late Second-Century BCE

The Bargylietans' desire to increase the honors of their goddess Artemis Kindyas involved civic institutions mobilized massively in ways that both used their resources and displayed their effectiveness. Likewise, the reorganization and ordering of the oracle of Apollōn Korōpaios, proclaimed as a reflection of the city's grateful piety and antiquarian attachment, involved civic institutions:[90] pay for office, record-keeping, legal compulsion and penalties, accountability of officials before the assembly. The document recording the reorganization spends much time on such measures as the pay for the security detail chosen from the citizens, or the procedures for possible prosecution. The consultation was closely supervised by the priest, but also the three generals and the four "law-guardians" (*nomophylakes*): all eight officials put their seals on the vessel where the oracular responses of the god were kept before being handed out to consultants. A very similar institutional process can be seen at work in the case of the mysteries of Andania, which laid out the responsibilities of civic officials, including a body of initiates that acted as the decision-making institution in control of the cult.[91]

Such civic workings were the direct prolongation of the diffusion and constant reinforcement of democracy in the third century and early decades of the second century BCE. In Magnēsia on Maeander, if officials failed to read out the new decree on the *Eisitēria*, they were liable to prosecution "by anyone who so wishes among the citizens, who have the right to do so, upon reward of half the penalty."[92] The clause spells out the universal right of citizens to conduct volunteer prosecutions—and in this case, to participate in the policing of the conduct of officials. The same institution appears in the enforcement clauses of the law concerning the cult of Apollōn Korōpaios, or in second-century BCE Athens.[93] The *dēmokratia* that Pergamon entered after the end of the Attalid monarchy was both its independence and its existence as an internally democratic state, both being an expression of the people's power.[94]

In democratic cities, old and new, the Assembly and the courts were understood as expressions of the power of the people (as nonplussed Roman observers noted in the case of Rhodes in the late second and the first centuries BCE).[95] The courts could be drawn by lot (as at Rhodes) and quite large (the largest Milesian court was 600-strong, as called upon for the arbitration between Sparta and Messēnē in 140 BCE), which implies a substantial pool of jurors among the citizenry.[96] In Athens, we catch glimpses of the courts at work, still following the laws and institutions of the fourth-century BCE, with a strong public commitment to democracy: a decree was inscribed "so there nothing illegal or inexpedient might occur, but that the democratic and equal [body of the courts?] might remain safe."[97] Surviving examples of allotment machines, a strongly democratic technology, date to this time.[98]

The end of the big regional leagues further drove democratic intensification. These large formations harmonized institutions. Local eccentricities in institutional culture vanished in places such as Argos or Troizēn, replaced by the uniform protocols of *polis* decision-making. The *polis* of Delphi, once freed from Aitolian control, appears as a democratic city with a universal franchise and strong popular institutions.[99] The cities of Thessaly, after the end of the Antigonid state, start to look like normal *poleis*, with both specificities and conventional traits (the combination is typical of *poleis* everywhere). At Larisa, honorific decrees had to be confirmed by the Assembly after a period of reflection, as in late Classical Athens; various matters were confirmed by secret ballot.[100] The codification of laws at Larisa must belong to the same movement of democratic and institutional intensification (we know that the laws of Larisa took up at least fourteen inscribed stelai).[101] The processes of normalization are well illustrated by Pythoion, a small *polis* to the north of Thessaly, on the western slopes of Mount Olympos. The city had once belonged to the kingdom of Macedonia, as shown by the estates of Macedonian officers and the presence of royal land. After 197 BCE, Pythoion joined the Thessalian League, and the first known decrees from the *polis* of the Pythoiastai are proxeny decrees (ca. 180–170 BCE), with their own local formulas (the decree is said to be passed by the *koinon* rather than the *dēmos*), and also with recognizable *polis* institutions and gestures: honors, inscription of decrees "so that it may be possible for whoever wishes to look at it (*epiblepein*)," and payment out of public funds by civic officials.[102] Macedonia, once the seat of the Antigonid kingdom, also saw the emergence of a *polis* culture, growing out of preexisting *polis* institutions but also converging with the general shape of institutional practice.[103]

We should not call second-century BCE democracy a watered-down version. The workings of democratic institutions were accompanied by a strong and finely differentiated understanding of the formal consequences of having popular sovereignty following through the different forms of assembly, courts, council, and offices. Yet another decision of the citizens of Dēmētrias concerning the cult of Apollōn Korōpaios (the maintenance of the sacred grove) was passed on to the relevant officials to be registered formally as a law, literally "as having the position of legislation" (*nomothesias taxin*).[104] More generally, in a development of the political culture of the great intensification of the early second century BCE, institutional pathways were often carefully inscribed and displayed as a mark of good polity, displaying formal correction in following rules. This was an age of legalism in procedure (for instance, in respecting *ennomoi chronoi*, the respect of legal delays or constitutional safeguards before implementing honorific grants—as can be seen in second-century BCE Larisa). Indeed, we see procedure getting more complex and punctilious in decrees from the *poleis* of Lampsakos or Assos in the Troad (ca. 130 BCE).[105] Equally noticeable are the consequences of popular sovereignty: state power, the wide distribution of offices (as seen in late Hellenistic Priēnē), citizen politicians, the absence of dominant families or of formal social stratification,[106] the routine accomplishment of official duties by citizen magistrates (as noted in terse honorific decrees of a sort familiar since the late fourth century BCE).[107]

As earlier, the wealthy and leisurely paid for a major part of the workings of democracy through a mixture of taxation, targeted financial obligations (*leitourgiai*), or semi-formalized but expected voluntary gifts in a private or official capacity (in the form of loans, cash advances, or outright donations). The rich festival life of Athens was financed by citizens grouped in colleges of payers, comparable to the fourth-century BCE Athenian *symmories*.[108] In Priēnē, rich citizens were subject to a number of financial burdens, either as straight-up obligations or as part of office (ranging from cash advances to public coffers to the fitting out of a warship). The holder of the priesthood of Dionysos Phleos, in addition to the normal perks of office, could be exempt for life against a hefty payment (12,000 drachmas or more, with a 10 percent immediate down payment). A rich Prienian, Athēnopolis, paid 12,002 drachmas, a rational cost-benefits calculation that shows how real the financial burden of taxation and liturgies was.[109] Strikingly, the procedure of *eisphorai* (special wealth-taxes), burdensome on the rich, appears in Macedonia ca. 100 BCE, part of the democratic culture in that region after the end of the Antigonid monarchy.[110]

Admittedly, there is some later literary evidence for Roman support for institutional change, namely in the introduction of a censitary barrier to office in Thessaly after 196 BCE and in the Peloponnese after the dissolution of the Achaian League in 146 BCE.[111] The general shift in the name of the city councils from *boulē* to *sunedrion*, observable in Boiōtia after 171 BCE and in the Peloponnese after 146 BCE, has been interpreted as a sign of oligarchy imposed by Rome (the secretary of the *sunedrion* seems to have exercised wide responsibilities in the Peloponnesian *poleis*). But the evidence is thin and inconclusive. There is no evidence for restricted franchise. The Council does not seem to wield particularly wide powers in the Peloponnese, to the detriment of the People. The colleges of magistrates (*sunarchiai*) that appear in the Peloponnesian cities do not seem like oligarchical bodies, but simply a local variation on the generally democratic practice of the *poleis*, as is visible elsewhere in this period.[112] Boiotian and Peloponnesian *poleis* had to reinvent institutional practice after the dissolution of federal structures, just as the

Thessalians did; but they did so in ways that tied into the trends of the great convergence. These were also reflections of the lack of direct Roman interest or involvement during the Indian Summer of the poleis.[113]

Elitism and Elites in 100 BCE

At the same time, there emerged new forms of discourse celebrating the attitudes and actions of wealthy, leisured citizens, suggesting to some scholars (such as Ph. Gauthier, whose work has illuminated the history of the *polis*) a watershed ca. 150 BCE.[114] The most characteristic of these forms is the long biographical decree, often stretching over hundreds of lines of extended narrative devoted to the character and actions of a good citizen, honored for political activity and services. At Priēnē, a whole series of these decrees was inscribed on the sidewalls of a new portico in the *agora* (fig. 11.3).[115] It is the wordy biographies of worthies such as Polemaios or Menippos of Kolophōn that tell us about the *poleis*'s sense of their freedom or the workings of their institutions.[116]

In the long decrees, good, pious, well-disposed, well-educated men, worthy of their ancestors, demonstrate ethical dispositions toward fulfillment through virtue in preference to any practical profit (*to lusiteles*).[117] The good citizen will accomplish many things during his political life—but also dip deep into his purse. After his victory in athletic games, Polemaios of Kolophōn provided victims for the celebratory sacrifices in his hometown and paid for distributions of cakes and sweet wine (*glukismous*), in order to make all partake in his ethical disposition in life (*tēs tou biou prohaireseōs*), manifested through a "sharing out of the abundance from his fortune" (*metadosin tēs apo tou biou chorēgias*). The word *bios*, designating both the ethical life course of the benefactor and his fortune, shows how moral behavior in the grand decrees takes on monetary form (just as *chorēgia* is borrowed from the language of financial obligation and gifts). Similarly, a citizen of Epidauros, Aristoboulos, behaved in public-minded ways to the point that he actually "damaged his *bios*."[118]

The transactions came in various forms. Benefactors could offer one-off financial gifts. Thus in ca. 100 BCE, the city of Eretria received a considerable gift of 40,000 drachmas from the gymnasiarch Theopompos, to invest in a foundation. Around the same period, Augis lent his city of Argos 10,000 drachmas free of interest, to allow the city to celebrate their festival in honor of the Roman general Flamininus. At other times, great benefactors waived compensation[119] for office (Moschiōn of Priēnē only drew part of his ambassadorial compensation when he traveled as far as Alexandria and Petra). They sold grain at low prices, or made gifts of both cash and grain; spent liberally when in office. A female benefactress, Archippa, offered a considerable gift to her city, Kymē (documented in eight honorific decrees). She funded the building of a new council house, inaugurated with sacrifices, banquets, and distributions of sweet wine. Furthermore, she repaired

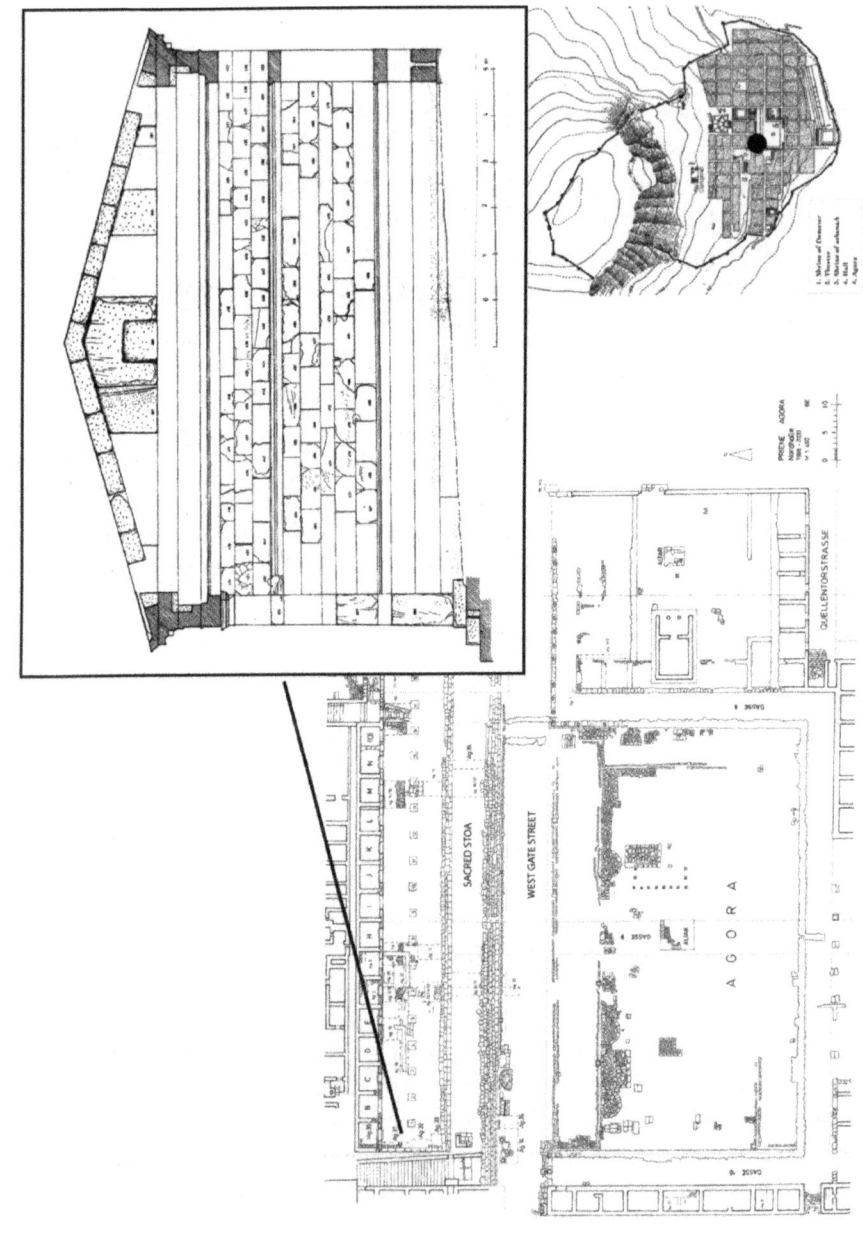

FIGURE 11.3. The late second-century BCE "great decrees" of Priēnē in their context, the north portico of the *agora*. After von Kienlin 2004, plate 50.

the council house's roof herself, actually having the timber and materials handled by her own people. At the end of her life and in spite of illness, Archippa financed major building works in the *agora* out of the sale of two estates; she further left monies to establish permanent revenue to be used for twice yearly sacrifices in the council house, and to maintain the building.[120]

Of course, the expectation of material contributions by good citizens is nothing new; for instance, it was an important part of the style of the good citizen in mid- to late fourth-century BCE Athens, alongside other signs of political commitment. Likewise, the expectation that certain types of public office would incur costs is already present earlier. But the sheer density of financial and material gifts by late second-century BCE benefactors is striking, as a far-reaching consequence of the conflation of office and *leitourgia*.[121] The *agōnothetai* of the Theseia at Athens met out of their own pockets the costs incurred by the festival (including compensation paid out to the councilors);[122] the office of president of the contest worked as a *leitourgia*, in shifting the burden of the festival's costs directly onto a citizen. Strikingly, a scheme to raise money from serving magistrates for a cash gift to Delphian Apollōn during the Pythais ran into difficulties, with defaulting magistrates or low payments; the burden had to be taken on by two individuals, Sarapion of Melite and Medeios of Peiraieus, not coincidentally the most prominent citizens in Athens ca. 100 BCE.[123]

This development was exacerbated by the absence of royal benefactors once Roman intervention had removed the great Hellenistic states from the scene, and not occupied the resulting void. The end of monarchical patronage, which had benefited free and subject *polis* alike, and the promotion of subject *poleis* to freedom, created sudden financial needs that were filled by citizen benefactors.[124] At Priēnē, the large, modern lower *gymnasion*, voted by the people, could not be finished "because of the woes that had befallen the kings who had made promises towards the costs"; Moschiōn stepped in to pay for at least some of the work.[125] In Kolophōn, the people voted to continue the monthly "royal feasts" for the young men, thus continuing and appropriating a ritual that had almost certainly expressed gratitude to a royal benefactor; these feasts were funded by a combination of public funds and large contributions by the monthly officials. Menippos met the whole expense for some of these feasts.[126]

The increased emphasis on elite giving shifted agency and control toward the rich, active citizen.[127] Polemaios of Kolophōn, by going on embassies to Rome, "allowed the other citizens to remain in their homes without being bothered, while he tackled the danger on behalf of all, by land and by sea, exposing his life, his soul and his whole life on behalf of the people." His fellow citizen Menippos was praised as "having presided over his fatherland in the most perilous circumstances." This very phrase was inscribed on the six-meter-tall column that bore his gilt bronze statue (fig. 11.4).[128] When the Kymaian benefactress Archippa had her workmen move and stock building materials in public space, the measure temporarily surrendered

FIGURE 11.4. Honorary monument for Menippos of Kolophōn (modern restoration), shrine of Klaros. The base, inscribed with a long decree, bears a column, which once bore Menippos's gilt bronze statue. Photograph J.-C. Moretti.

control of public space to a rich citizen, with no thought of accountability. Gifts came with strings attached: Archippa asked for her accountant to be given citizenship, and shaped arrangements for the investment of her cash gifts.

Giving to the city, on a considerable scale and repeatedly, allowed late second-century BCE benefactors to experiment with civic discourse and imagery and to push them in elitist directions. The banquets and distributions of cakes and sweet wine, as private gifts, were not bound by civic protocols that privileged institutionality and egalitarianism. Rich benefactors' jollities took place in accordance with their own reimaginations of community, along hierarchizing schemes, by setting the councilors and officeholders apart from the rest of the citizenry. The Prienian Herōdēs invited the city's magistrates and their sons to partake of refreshments in a distinct group.[129] Conversely, elitist experiments eroded the distinction between citizen, foreigner, and slave.[130] At Priēnē, a benefactor offered a public breakfast party with a tot of unmixed wine: he threw open his own house "as a common good for all on the same conditions." In the heterotopia of the benefactor's home, "it was possible to put little weight on the fate of the slave or the condition of the foreigner."[131]

Concomitantly, prominent citizens made a great deal of their family relations in public spaces. The benefactions of Archippa involved her male relatives, who were also honored alongside her. The weddings of great men were the occasion for feasts offered to the community. These were recognized by the *polis*, certainly after being mentioned by the benefactors themselves, in speeches or written requests for honors. The religious revival in Athens involved family relations. The *ergastinai* weaving Athēna's peplos were honored on the request of their fathers. A priest of Asklēpios felt free to name his sons as key-holders for the shrine. On the Akropolis, the statue of a fourth-century BCE priestess was refurbished and reinscribed by her descendants in the second century BCE, displaying continuity in family piety.[132] The increased visibility of the *genē*, kinship groups claiming ancient link with priesthoods and religious rituals, was another aspect of the boost given to elite families by the intense religious life in late second-century BCE Athens.

A growing emphasis on family relations and their display is suggested by the intensification of private dedications and family monuments, visible for instance in second-century Delphi or Rhodes.[133] A huge monumental mausoleum in the territory of Milētos (near modern Akbük), sitting atop a forty-meter-high hillock and adorned with columns and represented shields, belonged to a wealthy family of this period.[134] The prominence of elite families in semi-formalized contexts of feasting and giving, but also in a variety of other social contexts such as the religious life or the votive and monumental landscape, is reminiscent of the "Archaic" period, notably the sixth century BCE, with its strategies of family prestige, and the second half of the fourth century BCE, when the form of the private family statue crystallized.

Grand benefactors were rewarded with grand honors. Archippa, the benefactress of Kymē, was allowed to put her name on the *bouleutērion* she had built; she was honored with a statue group representing her (crowned by the *Dēmos*) and her male relatives and paid for by her brother. The setting up of this monument was commemorated by sacrifices and sweet wine provided by Archippa, a further step in the spiral of giving and recognition. The three hundred-odd lines of the eight decrees in her honor were carved in crisp, carefully laid-out lettering on two pillars, perhaps the door jambs of the council house.[135] Such practices were widespread. At Aigai, the council house was dedicated by a benefactor honored with a statue for him and five members of his family in an enormous niche in the building.[136] The gymnasiarch Theopompos at Eretria was honored alongside his family: statues he set up of his relatives were dedicated by the People, in addition to two bronze statues of him.[137] In Priēnē, benefactors were honored with multiple statues—bronze, gilt bronze, marble—and public funerals where they were crowned by the community and individual citizens if the latter so wished.[138] The effect was to create a specific group of good citizens, defined by wealth, leisure, and public-spiritedness: Archippa was granted a public burial "as for the other *euergetai*."[139]

The question is that of the cumulative effect of the largesse and visibility of wealthy citizens, the experiments with elitist discourse, the honorific forms of the grand decree, and the multiple honorific statues. Was the general tendency an aristocratizing dynamic in the Greek city-state, tending toward the creation of a distinct ruling class in the late Hellenistic *polis*?[140] In Athens around 100 BCE, officeholding, religious roles, economic benefaction and social distinction went together, and were concentrated in a restricted number of families. The evolution is visible in the case of the Pythais delegations to Delphi, or, especially, in the "little world" of the Athenian *ephēbeia*: the prosopography of the ephebes and their magistrates, the *kosmētai*, overlaps significantly with that of the officeholders and benefactors.[141] In classic Aristotelian fashion, the issue is one of wealth and its role in the *polis*. We should pause at the facility with which the benefactors lend or give money to their communities. Menippos of Kolophōn promised to spend one talent (6,000 drachmas) on building work in the shrine—and exceeded his promise.

The availability of cash hints at considerable fortunes in the late Hellenistic period. This may be the result of a number of connected developments. The prosperity of the market economies of the late Classical period (sustained by *polis* institutions and networks) must have continued during the third century BCE in conjunction with the operation of the royal economies of the big post-Achaimenid states. In the late second century BCE, the civic elites perhaps boosted their fortunes by occasionally taking over royal land or estates; the cities may have assimilated local estate holders into their citizen bodies.[142] The skill of the civic elites at investing, handling, and lending cash likely led to the wealth accumulation implied by the grand benefactions of the late second century BCE. It is conceivable that increasing wealth inequalities led to concentration of landed wealth. This is suggested by some survey evidence, especially in mainland Greece, though the evidence is very far from decisive.[143]

In the case of Athens, it is clear that the gift of Dēlos in 167 BCE led to an economic boom on the island, because of its status as a tax-free harbor (declared by the Roman Senate); the profits were channeled back to Athens, and notably served to underwrite the religious and festive revival.[144] They also jumpstarted the exploitation of the silver mines in Laurion, in the southern tip of the Attic peninsula (just as other moments of bonanza had done). The 130s BCE saw a long-lasting slave revolt in the mining district, perhaps reflecting pressure to increase production.[145]

The new style of gift-giving and honors seems a response to the wide availability and increasing concentration of money: hence the general insistence on the monetary forms, big and small, taken by civic virtue, or on the surprisingly specific celebration of financial measures as a benefaction. Polemaios of Kolophōn offered debt relief to fellow citizens (duly noted on officially registered contracts), provided friendly loans to refugees, and maintained his guarantee for contracts between citizens, thus helping *hoi ergazomenoi*, "the workers," an expression designating investors and businessmen. The decree for Menippos mentioned, among his benefactions, his care when holding office to keep civic harmony and protect private property.[146] Should the new civic style in the late Hellenistic *poleis* simply be considered as the voice of the new money talking?

Democracy and Elitism in the Late Second Century BCE

As our earlier history of the *polis* shows, from the "Archaic" period (say the seventh century BCE) onwards, democratic and communitarian gestures are not enough, in themselves, to prove the complete presence of democratic institutions and ideology. Conversely, the elitist style or discourse surrounding the practice of civic benefactions are not enough to prove that *poleis* had turned into wealth-dominated oligarchies during the second century BCE. The risk is accepting the grand decrees as a clear indication, in themselves, of an oligarchical turn, in the light of which other phenomena can be interpreted: the life of the *gymnasion*, familial dedications, or the shape of second-century BCE *polis* architecture.[147] Both institutional-democratic acceleration and increased elite visibility can be seen in the very late third and especially the second centuries BCE: the conjunction is a familiar one from earlier periods in the history of the *polis*. A further crucial connection exists between the external agency of the *polis* and the internal hegemony of the People—a connection expressed by the Hellenistic usage of *dēmokratia* for both. Popular sovereignty took the form of self-rule by the *polis* and, internally, the right to regulate individual behavior and to make claims on its members.

As a reminder of the complexities of *polis* culture in the late second-century BCE, we might reread the grand decrees as evidence for the functioning of civic institutions as well as for elitist discourse. What did the late Hellenistic benefactors actually do? The Kolophonian politician Polemaios, elected to office, collected and handled public monies honestly and competently in the course of his duties; perhaps in commemoration of this, he dedicated an incense burner out of his own funds.[148] At Epidauros, Aristoboulos, who did not hesitate to deplete his own fortune for the city, sold grain at a low price, held office in a just manner, paid his liturgies completely and generously, and accepted missions and embassies. He also paid for public building works or repairs, on top of the whole package of civic obligations.

At Priēnē, we can see a bit more in the details of the way in which private giving occurs on top of a dense pattern of liturgical obligations, public expenditure, and office-related expenditure.[149] The long decree for Moschiōn of Priēnē presents a blizzard of giving and largesse, but closely examined it reveals, across a long political career, a combination of service and officeholding (burdened with an expectation of personal expenditure), tax-related liturgies, loans, and some outright gifts and emergency relief.[150] The total amount of direct monetary and frumentary gifts is smaller than the loans and liturgies, though Moschiōn also waived pay and assumed costs. The decree for Moschiōn focuses on his individual actions, but it is likely that the contributions and loans he made were in response to appeals from the People. Likewise, we occasionally guess that his actions on embassies were achieved alongside fellow citizens, or that the hospitality he offered Roman troops was part of a city-wide effort. The act of giving was embedded in a broader context of officeholding, obligations, and public-minded conduct and service.

The grand decrees constituted an elitist genre that described the performance of civic obligations, the conformity with democratic norms, and the acts of supererogatory, ostentatious giving on the same level, as a sign of inherited dispositions, breeding, wealth, and virtuous character. Elitist discourse converts wealthy, leisured, active citizens into distinguished leading members of the community—into an elite. This sort of operation, aiming at generating distinction, is part of an old story—one which was an important part of the prehistory and the origins of the *polis*, and coterminous with the processes of popular sovereignty and communal capacity to constrain the wealth elite. Notably, the claim to recognition on the basis of service, economic signs of public-spiritedness, and the lavish performance of liturgies, are central features of Athenian democratic practice in the fourth and probably already the fifth centuries BCE.

As always, the elitist goal of achieving distinction meant accepting norms decided by the People: the relation led to dialectical problems. Moschiōn achieved distinction through his actions, but in practical ways that were defined and constrained by compliance with democratic institutions and communitarian norms of popular sovereignty, enforced through accountability and political equality and resulting in redistribution. The constitution of, and access to, elite status was controlled by institutional and ideological mechanisms that lay in the hands of the *polis* and specifically of the People. Yet the institutional frame and the *polis*'s norms could potentially serve as the vehicle for the consolidation of elite power through the restriction of office to the wealthy, the dependency of the People on savior-like gestures by the elite (aided by elitist discourse), and the implicit acceptance of such ideas because they were couched in a democratic language. Such a scenario in turn might trigger democratic efforts at containing oligarchical drift and enforce certain political equality.

This whole dynamic is part of the condition of *polis*-hood—and will continue in muted and mutated forms under the Roman empire. What was specific about the late second century BCE? The emergence of the grand decrees along with accumulations of honorific statues public and private, suggesting a socially exclusive class of benefactors, point to a historical moment of particular complexity in the dialectics of mass-elite negotiation.

A simplified model of the politics during the "Indian Summer" suggests itself along the following lines. The defining characteristic is the assertion of *polis* identity and agency in the aftermath of the brutal Polybian moment. But the process also entailed costs at a time of economic pressures. The latter resulted from the end of royal subsidies (not replenished by the Roman state), the lack of subordinate *poleis* (*perioikoi*) and subordinate peasant communities as sources of revenue, and finally, the costs of constant rounds of inter-*polis* disputes and competition. As we have seen, Priēnē engaged in massive building work—for instance, in the *agora* and on the lower *gymnasion*—as well as festival activity and diplomacy, at a time when it endured territorial losses in disputes with neighboring *poleis*, and when its native plainsmen may have lost their subordinate status—perhaps to turn into the private tenants of rich Prienian land-owners.

Because of the nature of the peer-polity system, no *polis* withdrew from its activities on the international scene; and because of the legacy of strong democratic, redistributive institutions, the *poleis* met these needs by appealing to the wealthy, leisured citizens, who achieved recognition as a civic elite on the condition of agreeing to contributing service and money. At Argos, Augis's loan of 10,000 drachmas helped the city celebrate the festival of the *Titeia* after a crisis in funding: the combination of pressure on public resources and increased available private wealth may be typical of the moment. Increased reliance on elite sources of funding for the manifestations of civic identity explains the sense of entitlement of the benefactors, and community acceptance of their elitist experiments.

But the latter were matched by the intensification of state discourse, institutional workings, and democratic practice in the late second and early first centuries BCE. Athenian elitism and Athenian democratic forms, notably in the courts, are richly attested at the same time (above, p. 277). The grand decrees at Priēnē were balanced by terse, old-style honorific decrees for good magistrates. The long decree for the gymnasiarch Theopompos at Eretria informs us both about his gift to the *gymnasion* and the detailed provisions taken by the city to ensure the transparent handling of the monies: the whole poetics of the document and its publication are also a debate about the place of elitism and the power of institutions.

A particularly instructive case can be found in Pergamon, around 130 BCE, as brilliantly studied by P. Hamon. An inventive gymnasiarch, Mētrodōros son of Herakleōn, took the young men to accompany all funerals, "which resulted in the most humble being honored in this way as much as those who were in positions of preeminence." This honor was probably extended to all (male?) citizen funerals, thus offering to all a mark of distinction usually given to great benefactors in the late Hellenistic period: for instance, it is one of the honors offered routinely to the group of top benefactors at Priēnē.[151] In addition to the egalitarian extension of distinction to all citizens, the measure might also have had the effect of making clear the boundaries of the citizen body after the upheavals of the war of Aristonikos when the citizen body was extended, and at a time the ephebate itself, paradoxically, was flexible in admitting foreigners.

The measure thus reaffirmed democratic exclusiveness (by making clear boundaries), inclusiveness (by assimilating new citizens to old), and egalitarianism (by making rich young citizens and non-citizens parade at the funerals of poor and rich citizens alike). Mētrodōros's innovation allowed him to achieve distinction by blunting other elite citizens' claims to preeminence. Very classically, the competitiveness of elite citizens has the effect of extending democratic and egalitarian practices; just as classically, Mētrodōros is honored more generally for his sense of equality (*isotēs*) among the ephebes but also toward the *polis* at large.

The liveliness, dialectical imbrication, and tensions of the political debate between elitist discourse and democratic practice, argue that the spirit of the age was not an oligarchizing tendency. In spite of neo-archaizing strategies of prestige, competitive or collaborative, civic elites did not manage to convert distinction into power, and there is no oligarchical breakthrough to the level of institutional capture—no timocratic stranglehold on the workings of power in the *polis*, not even in the Peloponnese after 146 BCE (above, pp. 278–79). A fragmentary decree from late second-century BCE Athens mentions democracy, access to offices chosen by lot, an attempt by evil-minded men (*kakotropoi*) to change things, the decisive intervention of advocates to defend the *polis*, the reaffirmation of measures established by the Areiopagos, and the entrenchment and protection of certain laws.[152] The situation implied is tense and contested, as befits a large, complex, evolving city-state where elitist discourse and measures and democratic practices are both strongly active, but there is no clear indication of an oligarchical coup, slow or otherwise, or of gradual drift into oligarchy.

The "Indian Summer" was also an age of reflection about the *polis*, just as the tense fourth century BCE led to the birth of articulate political philosophy in the age of Plato and Aristotle—often oligarchical in bent, in response to democratic practice. The prominence of the Areiopagos in both late fourth- and late second-century BCE Athens confirms the parallel. The "Indian Summer" saw a revival of Aristotelian discourse about individual and community, as shown by the attempts, in the grand decrees, to frame elite behavior in terms of character, civic virtue, and self-accomplishment through devotion to the public good. This was both an attempt to justify elite position and eminence, and an effort to come to terms with the constraints imposed by democracy on elite behavior.

As earlier, democratic ideology was mainly expressed in institutional practice and discourse, and elitist ideas were explored in philosophical texts and discussion. The philosophers Panaitios (a Rhodian active in Athens) and his pupil Poseidōnios (a citizen of Apameia in northern Syria, installed and naturalized in Rhodes) engaged with political issues in different ways—Panaitios in his discussion of the duties of the good citizen and the ethics of action, Poseidōnios with a savage critique of democratic ideology and its contradictions.[153]

At the turn of the second century BCE, the Roman Senator M. Antonius visited the Athenian politician Menedēmos, in whose house he heard the latter argue about the old question of the relation between philosophy, rhetoric, and virtue. Menedēmos explicitly appealed to the example of Dēmosthenēs to prove the ethical worth of rhetoric. He referred to the world of active civic politics rather than philosophical argument. Menedēmos duly went on embassy to Rome and stayed with his eminent Roman friend. His activity as ambassador and the cultivation of Roman contact is typical of the life of the civic elites of the second and first centuries BCE. This world offered a model for Cicero, who engaged with Panaitios, M. Antonius, and his Athenian friend Menedēmos. It is worth remembering that the debates of the second-century BCE *polis*, rather than simply "Hellenistic philosophy," influenced Roman political thought.[154]

Hegemony to Empire

The apparent disengagement of Roman domination might be an illusion—or a more encompassing form of power. "Free" *poleis* constantly lived with Roman encroachment. After the end of Hellenistic multipolarity, the spaces for *polis* agency were overshadowed by the universality of the Roman monopoly on performative definitions. In Asia Minor, the Roman Senate decided on the distribution of whole regions: Phyrgia and Lykaonia were given to one of the peripheral small kings, then taken back and placed under Roman administration (the exact status is unclear); Pamphylia (with its Attalid *poleis*, whose status is also unclear) was put under the purview of a separate governor, who had Kilikia as his *provincia*.[155] Just as the Boiotian and Achaian Leagues were dissolved in 171 and 146 BCE respectively, the small Kibyratan league may have been abolished by Rome around 102 BCE.[156]

Local freedom meant litigating out a situational space of freedom, a bundle of negotiated privileges within the flow of Roman power.[157] This meant constant hard work, as shown by the exertions of the Kolophonian statesmen, Polemaios and Menippos.[158] The latter defended the autonomy, the rights and the privileges (*philanthropa*) of their city against a plethora of threats: depredation by Roman agents, intervention by the governor, and threats to the judicial independence of Kolophōn. All these threats were fended off by embassies undertaken by the Kolophonian politicians, to representatives of Roman power in Asia Minor (the *hēgoumenoi*, "leaders"), or to Rome itself, where Polemaios and Menippos traveled—the latter no less than five times. When Menippos saved a Kolophonian citizen summoned to Rome for capital punishment, and the integrity of Kolophonian legal autonomy, the embassies from friendly *poleis* congratulated the Kolophonian *dēmos* and sacrificed with them in rejoicing; when Menippos obtained a *senatus consultum* stipulating that "it does not belong to the governor to issue judgments nor to meddle outside the province," the Kolophonians celebrated the ruling as "appropriate for our democracy and most fine." Yet the struggle against the encroachments of Roman power was not necessarily successful. At Ephesos, another free city of Asia Minor, an officeholder, one Periklēs, intervened to prevent a Roman quaestor from recovering a runaway slave from the asylum of the shrine of Artemis—and was summoned to Rome for trial.

Roman military campaigns and their consequences did not abate. When Ti. Didius, the governor of Macedonia, conquered in 101 BCE the Chersonēsos and the Kainikē, regions of Thrace ruled by a local ruler since the destruction of the Antigonid kingdom, the senate constituted a new sub-province, attached to but not incorporated within the province of Macedonia.[159] This administrative measure is recorded in a Roman law of 100 BCE concerning the provinces. The consequence of the Roman monopoly on the performative was the unilaterality of Roman decisions. Roman power directly concerned everyone: copies of the law were found in the free *poleis* of Delphi and Knidos. A decree of the Amphikitionic League concerning the Dionysiac artists carved out an exception for any possible objection from Rome, and the senate intervened to settle the dispute between two associations of Dionysiac artists in Greece.[160] Rome reserved the right to decide and to define, and also to take, from everyone. The *senatus consultum* confirming the liberty of the city of Termēssos pronounced it clear from levies and contributions, except if duly stipulated in the Roman *Lex Porcia*.

That the governors were military commanders and that many of their actions were *ad hoc*, wartime consequences of the nature of their command (*provincia*) do not reduce the unilateral assumptions behind their behavior, nor their disruptive impact. In 133 BCE, the civic militia of Mētropolis, celebrated by the newly freed city, had fought as part of a local army levied by Roman consuls. The free *poleis* of Asia Minor were subject to the same pressures as the *poleis* of Macedonia, provincialized in 148 BCE, in the rear of an active theater of Roman operations and hence subject to providing supplies and troops. In this province, the *polis* of Lētē treated the Roman quaestor Q. Annius's decision not to levy troops and supplies to fight against a Galatian incursion as an act of remarkable humanity.[161] The power of governors stretched to the islands, never formally provincialized but included within a space of Roman hegemony. There, the governors assumed roles earlier taken by Hellenistic kings. A proconsul of Asia, L. Quinctius, was honored as a savior and a benefactor by the island *polis* of Tēnos; another island *polis*, Andros, sent a judge to Adramyttion as part of a panel of foreign judges organized by Cn. Aufidius, the legate of the proconsul of Asia.[162]

In the Athenian Agora in front of the large portico erected by an Attalid ruler, the city set up a speaker's platform for Roman officials (its foundation still visible now), namely the proconsuls of Asia or Kilikia, on the way to their province. One of them, L. Gellius, offered to arbitrate the disputes between the different philosophical schools of Athens.[163] This offer (received and remembered with ridicule) did not flow from any formal authority on the part of the proconsul in the free city of Athens. It nonetheless reflected the Roman governors' power for intervention and the universal performative assumption at the heart of Roman power.

Significantly, the principle adopted by the *poleis* appointed to arbitrate in disputes between poleis was *uti possidetis* at the moment of Roman power. This was the criterion applied in the dispute between Magnēsia on Maeander and Priēnē (as noted above, the Prienians lost). The set formula probably reflects instructions or influence from the Roman Senate; the criterion of the arrival of Rome for legitimate territorial demands marked a simplificatory end of history for the *poleis* and their complex multiple stories. Under the Roman empire, it was still remembered that the *polis* of Chios, in reward for steadfastness as an ally during the war against Mithradatēs VI (below, p. 293–95), received confirmation from the Senate that "they would use the laws, customs and rights that they enjoyed when they entered the friendship of the Romans."[164] The impact of Roman presence can further be seen in the transformation of the procedures of arbitration into a two-stage affair (involving first an examination of the receivability of the request, then the delegation to arbiters bound by the initial decision): this reflects the practices and schemes of Roman private law.[165]

Peer-polity interaction, occurring within the ambit of a universalizing and unilateral imperial power, served to affirm and propagate this power. Because of the Roman monopoly on decisions and the granting of privileges, access to Roman patronage was crucial.[166] The consequence is that all *poleis* had to lobby Roman powers and their representatives and all had to aim for the favored status of friends, which was determinant of privileges and rights. Hence, peer-polity interaction made all free *poleis* strive to affirm their status as friends of Rome and equated freedom with friendship of Rome. The communities of Asia Minor under incipient Roman rule joined as a federal association (*koinon*), attested from 98 BCE onwards: this included *poleis*, *dēmoi*, and *ethnē* (the *polis*-aspirational settlements of inland Asia Minor), and "the men admitted on an individual basis into the friendship of the Romans" (*hoi kat'andra kekrimenoi en tēi pros Rhomaious philiai*) as well as "the other Greeks."[167] The cause for the conflict between Sardeis and Ephesos may well have been the question of precedence at the festival celebrated by the *poleis* of the confederation in honor of Q. Mucius Scaevola.[168] In this world, free *poleis* and their citizens could directly serve as vehicles of Roman decisions and instructions, as Rhodes and perhaps Menippos, the tireless defender of Kolophonian interests, may have done, again using the network of inter-*polis* contacts to transmit Roman power.[169]

More formally, Roman power imposed structures of control. The aftermath of conquest and the transition to *provincia*-status entailed an administrative process from the outset. Macedonia was structured by an east-west road that joined it with the Adriatic, the Via Egnatia, already started by the proconsul Cn. Egnatius in 146/5 BCE.[170] Asia Minor similarly received a road, built by M' Aquillius starting in 129 BCE, after the end of the War of Aristonikos. The declaration of liberty for the *poleis* was followed up by administrative measures implying permanence and practicality.[171] The province of Asia served as a laboratory for control and exploitation, enhancing forms and solutions that had served the provincialization of Sicily in the third century BCE. It now seems likely that the division of Asia into districts (*dioikēseis* in Greek, *conventus* in Latin) centered on individual *poleis* chosen as administrative nodes, dates to the early years of the formation of the province and that the system took over Attalid structures.[172] Later on, these districts are attested as judicial districts and fulfilled other administrative functions. In the assize centers, the Roman proconsul heard disputes and rendered judgment, applying the principles of Roman law that the Kolophonians kept at bay but which played an important part in making rule systematic and visible,[173] alongside road-building and the organization of space.[174]

In addition, *poleis* served economic functions for Roman officeholders and their troops. The presence of the latter seems to have a visible impact on the coinage production of some poleis.[175] Ephesos, like other *poleis*, continued to issue a cistophoric coinage (inherited from the Attalid kingdom); for a brief period in 121 BCE, the proconsul actually issued Ephesian *cistophoroi* in his name, presumably to pay for troops. A spike in the production of this cistophoric coinage at the end of the second century BCE, culminating in 100 BCE, might be linked with the campaign of M. Antonius against pirates. The same pattern can be glimpsed later on Thasos (where Q. Braetius Sura, the legate for the proconsul of Macedonia, struck coins in his name) or even in Athens, where large volumes of the "New Style" Athenian coinage seem to have been produced over four years (126/5 to 123/2 BCE) to be dispatched to the *provincia* of Macedonia for operations on the northern frontier.

Administrative control and judicial *quadrillage* were accompanied by financial extraction. At the same time as the road building and the setting up of the *conventus*, the Roman Republic took over the Attalid system of taxation, namely an indirect system of tolls and a direct tithe on agricultural production. The tolls concerned all movement in and out of the former royal land. Even if the *poleis* were "outside the province," as the Kolophonian decree for Menippos bravely states, they could not avoid contact with this network of taxation; indeed, many *poleis* (such as Ephesos) precisely served as the points where tolls were extracted for the Roman state. The levy on agricultural production almost certainly concerned the former royal land that became property of the Roman Republic; this probably included urban settlements whose *polis*-forms had been sponsored by the Attalid kingdom. But the measure also concerned the *poleis* set free in 133 BCE, because they had administered, claimed, or taken over royal land, throughout the Hellenistic period and especially during the late Attalid devolution. Much of the status of these holdings would have to be litigated by the *poleis*.[176] Roman tax farmers pursued profits aggressively, often challenging the status or ownership of resources in the *poleis*'s territories. Wetlands that had once belonged to the Attalid kings but been "returned" to Ephesian Artemis, were claimed by the tax farmers, before an embassy to Rome fended them off. The embassy was led by a leading Ephesian citizen, Artemidōros, fulfilling the familiar role of defender of civic interests in addition to his interests as a geographer and writer (as mentioned above, he wrote a description of the Lykian League). Likewise, a Prienian "great benefactor," Kratēs, opposed some publicans' claims over Priēnē's saltpans.[177]

Q. Mucius Scaevola the Younger was honored by the *poleis* for restraining the tax farmers as well as his respect for local autonomy.[178] But restrained governors and greedy publicans were aspects of the same Roman power.[179] The proconsul of Macedonia was required by the law on provinces of 100 BCE to spend sixty days in the newly conquered Kainikē and Chersonēsos and organize matters including the farming out of taxes and their ultimate collection. Tax farmers extracted; the Roman state provided the political and institutional framework. Especially important was the jurisdiction of the governor, who adjudicated disputes between the *poleis* and the tax farmers. In the complex affair of the Prienian salt-pans, Kratēs traveled to the assize centers of Pergamon and Laodikeia on Lykos. Ideologically, the proconsul's jurisdiction made Roman authority visible; concretely, it served the needs of the tax farmers and facilitated the installation of Roman and Italian entrepreneurs in the Hellenistic world.[180]

"Roman" businessmen spread across the communities and territories of the Hellenistic world, notably on Athenian-ruled Dēlos where they may have conducted the slave trade.[181] This development reshaped the economy of the Mediterranean in complex ways.[182] Publicans, businessmen, and even officeholders of the Roman state were part of a system of profit-seeking in constructing the "eastern provinces" of Roman dominion. In 167 BCE the Roman Senate, briefly refraining from exploiting the Macedonian mines, reflected that the arrival of tax farmers was incompatible with civic freedom—a rare moment of awareness of the impact of imperial profit-seeking. In 88 BCE, during war between Rome and the last king capable of independent action, Mithradates VI, the furious massacre of eighty thousand Italians in the *poleis* of Asia Minor in 88 BCE gives a sense of the oppression wrought by the empire of control and exploitation.

The Trap of Roman Power

Roman power from the late second century BCE onwards accomplished what was only potential in the time of the Hellenistic kings: the transformation of freedom into a status within a horizon of control in a universal empire. This was the trap of

Roman power, the long-term realization of Polybios's fears: a generalization of subordination, albeit masked by the vitality of the *poleis*'s Indian Summer. The contradictions are plain to see. Kolophōn was the fatherland of citizen politicians defending the freedom of their city against the encroachments of Roman governors; but the shrine of Klaros where Polemaios and Menippos were honored also became the setting for honorific statues for Roman governors. M. Antonius was honored, in 102 BCE, with a column exactly like those bearing statues of the citizen politicians who had tried so hard to keep governors at bay.[183] Ephesos appears in many guises: as a free *polis* defending its interests and its dignity, a seat where Roman governors and officials spend time, an important stage in the Via Aquillia, and the residence of numerous Italian businessmen.[184]

In particular, Athens was the setting for an intense religious, patriotic, and antiquarian revival, an economic powerhouse as a result of the free market on Dēlos, a society marked by elitist display, a polity characterized by democratic reaffirmation, and a stopover for Roman officials on their way to their provinces of Asia or Kilikia. The city struck a new coinage that celebrated its success and identity and served its economy; but also delivered volumes of this coinage for Roman campaigns in Macedonia. The Athenian Agora received a new archive building reflecting the judicial and law-centered culture of late Hellenistic democracy, but also a platform to give the speech of passing Roman officials a privileged place, even if they did not have formal legal authority over the *polis*.

The contradictions burst into an obscure, extraordinary conflict at the start of the first century BCE. Mēdeios of Peiraieus, one of the generous citizens of Athens who relieved magistrates from the burden of contributing toward the Pythais, and perhaps the most eminent Athenian of his time, ended up occupying the archonship for the three years 91 to 88 BCE. Was his behavior motivated or justified by claims to power in proportion to his financial contribution as a great benefactor and his sense of elite status? If so, the bald claim to entitlement and power underestimated the strength of the democratic element in late Hellenistic Athens. Some Athenian citizens led a reaction, couched in democratic and constitutional terms, and combined with an appeal to the victorious Mithradatēs VI and the rejection of Roman hegemony.[185] Athēniōn, the leader of the democratic reaction, apparently gave the decisive speech in the Agora from the speaker's platform. The events are known through a hostile and satirical account by the philosopher Poseidōnios: it is possible that Athēniōn was not an impoverished, illegitimate teacher of philosophy, but a philosophically trained leading citizen of the type familiar from the "grand decrees." The democratic and redistributive language, the patriotic-antiquarian portrayal of the Athenians as the Kekrōpidai (lampooned by Poseidōnios), might reflect the democrats' program, and Poseidōnios's portrayal of Athēniōn's "tyrannical" regime, complete with massacres and confiscations, might be the polemical distortion of a series of democratic measures such as the reinvigoration of the popular courts, war taxes on fortunes, punitive enforcement, and the distribution of grain to citizens.[186]

The result was renewed Roman violence during the First Mithradatic War (88–85 BCE), fought by Sulla with a savagery that had not been seen since the initial arrival of Roman troops in 211 BCE. Athens itself was besieged and sacked in 86 BCE, as was the Lokrian *polis* of Halai. Surviving Halaians, the anecdote goes, offered the convalescent Sulla a gift of fish, and after a terrifying quip ("So are there still Halaians left?") were granted their city back.[187] The anecdote reflects the Roman assumption of now universal rights founded in violence and victory. The blanket assumption of freedom was replaced with decisions according to service or harm to Roman interests. The *poleis* of Greece and Asia were subjected to direct payment of tribute and war contributions on top of indirect taxation. The Thebans lost half their territory for turning their coat rather too often during the campaign.[188] The independent *polis* of Hērakleia Pontikē had never belonged to the province of Asia; though an ally of Rome, it had provided assistance to Mithradatēs under compulsion, and as a punishment, it was subjected to taxation and publicans.[189] The Herakleians resented these as contrary to "the character of the constitution" (*ta ēthē tēs politeias*) and as the beginning of slavery. They responded by murdering the publicans and made them vanish; the gesture proved futile, merely provoking tighter control by Rome. In contrast, those *poleis* that had remained loyal to Rome (for instance, Kyzikos, Rhodes, the Karian *poleis*, and the Lykian League) were rewarded with freedom and privileges—always subject to Roman approval. In Karia, the *polis* of Tabai, though explicitly declared to be free as a reward for their resistance to Mithradatēs, had to ask for permission to fortify a site in its territory.[190] The Lykian League fought hard alongside Rhodes (its earlier overlord) to defend Roman interests, and hence enjoyed its freedom as a reward for service as a faithful ally. The League honored the city of Xanthos with a colossal bronze statue for services in the war, "in defence of the hegemony of the Romans and the liberty of all the Lykians." The League later swore to respect and defend the majesty of Rome, in a treaty concluded in 46 BCE, in the time of the dictator C. Julius Caesar.[191]

The aftermath of the First Mithradatic War simplified the ambiguities surrounding freedom that had characterized the late second century BCE, by assimilating almost all *poleis* to a subordinate status, apart from a small category of privileged free communities.[192] The old, formerly "free" *poleis* and the communities of inland Anatolia that aspired to *polis* status were alike subordinate and tributary; the Anatolian communities gradually gained acceptance as *poleis* during the first century BCE. Aizanoi, in Phrygia, would emerge as a highly successful *polis* during this period, thanks to favorable measures taken by the Senate.[193] The status of *asylia* (inviolability of territory), once obtained by the canvassing of multiple peer-polities, was now granted directly by the Roman state and its representatives. The Roman commander Sulla and his lieutenant Lucullus wrote to the Kilikian *polis* of Mopsouhestia to declare the inviolability of the local shrine of the Egyptian gods. Sulla further recognized the *asylia* of the shrine of Hekatē and the territory of Stratonikeia in Karia and did the same for the shrine of Amphiaraos at Ōrōpos in Boiōtia; both acts were confirmed by the senate. (The status of the Amphiaraion was unsuccessfully challenged by tax farmers on the grounds that Amphiaraos was not a god but a hero.)[194]

The Roman state further favored the foundation or establishment of *poleis*, as administrative interlocutors and fiscal entities, in areas that came under its control, such as Bithynia or the Levant (we will encounter these cities again under the Roman empire). In the Levant, the Roman state intervened in a complex landscape of post-Seleukid entities, in the 50s BCE, to (re)establish and foster cities using the language, institutions, and discourses of the Greek *polis*. These activities were felt on the coast from northern Syria to Raphia and Gaza, and on both sides of the Jordan in the interior, and reshaped the whole region into what would gradually turn into a "Roman Near East" (see below, chapter 14).[195]

Though these simplifications came from the application of the logic of Roman power to the historically complex landscape of *poleis*, the context of the first century BCE was also a time of considerable disorder in Roman practice itself. As a Roman annalist described the First Mithradatic War, Sulla "reduced the poleis into his own dominion," reflecting the personal nature of the decision-making.[196] One effect was the diffusion and confusion of Roman authority, especially because of the disappearance of the central decision-making role of the Senate in favor of extraordinary commands and because of the conflict between individual powerholders during the Roman civil wars.[197] Another impact was the periodic recrudescence of violence and coercion: local material and human resources were tapped by the various parties in the Roman civil wars. When the Lykian *poleis* and Rhodes refused to aid Brutus and Cassius, Caesar's assassins, they were sacked and despoiled. Sometime after this, the citizens of Patara were asked to supply 600 soldiers (they escaped this request thanks to the efforts of their fellow-citizen, M. Antonius Idagras: above, p. 259). The press-ganging of Greeks by Antony's troops for service or corvée labor was recorded vividly by Plutarch, whose grandfather was among those impressed to carry supplies overland to Antony's camp when the news of the latter's final defeat at Aktion arrived.[198] In Plutarch's own *polis*, Chairōneia, even more dramatic events had taken place fifty years earlier. The commander of a Roman detachment, stationed in the city during the initial operations against Mithradates VI, tried to rape a young Chaironeian, and the latter had murdered the Roman officer and his entourage, which brought a series of troubles on the city.

As the Roman power to grant and define by *fiat* was distorted or hijacked by the personal power of the dynasts of the late Republic, access to such figures gained enormous importance. Theophanēs of Mytilēnē obtained the resurrection of his city (punished for siding with Mithradatēs VI) through his friendship with Pompey; Caesar was moved by his friends Mithradatēs of Pergamon and Theopompos of Knidos to grant freedom and tax immunity to their *poleis*.[199] These very great benefactors often received important honors, including cultic honors, in their home *poleis*.[200] Theophanēs can be seen at two moments in the epigraphical record: when he was honored, early in life, for holding office as a *prutanis* with piety toward the gods, as a fairly normal civic official—and, later when as a friend of Pompey he "got back from the Romans, common benefactors, and the city and the territory and the ancestral freedom, and restored the shrines and the honors of the gods."[201] When Sulla pardoned the Halaians, he affected to treat the fish given to him as intercessors on the Halaians' behalf: the joke works because of the reality of Roman dynasts pronouncing on matters of life and death based on the intercession of their Greek friends.

Important and well-connected men could exercise tyrannical power within their home cities, as happened in the case of Kyrēnē and other cities in Libya (if we read between the lines of the literary and epigraphical sources).[202] For a few decades, Sparta would be ruled by a single man, Euryklēs, and his descendants. Tyrants are known elsewhere in this period (for instance at Magnēsia on Maeander or on Kōs), a sign of the distorting effect of the immense power of individual Roman powerholders, and the concomitant possibilities for their Greek partisans and friends.[203]

The Roman dominion continued to foster economic exploitation: the first century BCE is an age of the Italian businessmen as well as the military dynasts. Moneylending to the *poleis* took on particular importance because of the increased and generalized demands of Roman taxation, as well as the exactions in kind and in blood. Whereas the *poleis* had avoided massive indebtedness, now the Italians lent to them at very high interest rates (48 percent is attested).[204] The moneylenders were closely linked to the Roman power elite. The creditor of Salamis in Cyprus, M. Scaptius, enjoyed the support of M. Brutus (and specifically tailored *senatus consulta*) in his efforts at recovering debts. The simple reason for Brutus's support was that Scaptius was handling the senator's own money.[205] Cicero intervened to put pressure on two free *poleis*, Alabanda and Mylasa, which owed money to a friend of his. He tried to ensure, through a local agent, one Euthydēmos, that the *poleis* would send advocates (*ecdici*) for legal proceedings rather than ambassadors to argue before the senate.[206] Whereas the free *poleis* resorted to the normal diplomatic, political avenue, Cicero intervened to shut down this avenue and move the affair to the courts, institutionally set up to favor the Italian capitalist.

Such incidents are instructive as to the close and personal connections between the structures of government and the "informal" dimension of economic exploitation by Italian businessmen. Scaptius had obtained a formal appointment as a *praefectus* and used a cavalry squadron to try to chase the money owed to him. At Lampsakos, an Italian businessman used official help to recover a debt from the city (in the affray, a lictor was killed by Lampsakene citizens, who were duly prosecuted).[207] Romans and Italians appear as landowners in the *poleis* in contravention of the rule that limited ownership to citizenship; they either reinvested proceeds in landed estates, or seized land offered as security for loans.[208] The Roman citizens who appear making offerings in the shrines of Greek *poleis*, or being buried in their cemeteries—for instance in Macedonia, at Thessalonikē or at Létē—belonged to communities of such Italian settlers in the eastern Mediterranean.[209]

The *Polis* in the First Century BCE

The life of the *poleis* in the first century BCE was not simply a series of violent episodes of anomie; it also prolonged the open-ended possibilities of the "Indian Summer." The cities continued to deal with Roman provincial administration with its routine combination of judicial and military activities. After the sack of 86 BCE, Athens dealt with Roman officials, often honoring them with statues set up in prestigious sites in the Agora.[210] The governor's work is documented by Cicero, proconsul of Kilikia in 51 BCE. Cicero traveled to his province through Asia Minor;[211] his inaugural edict proclaimed the continuation of the younger Mucius Scaevola's policy of allowing the *poleis* to judge their own cases as a sign of their autonomy. Cicero also prided himself on turning down a very large cash gift from Salamis in Cyprus, and on not having suitors to him vetted by a chamberlain (*cubicularius*) but being as approachable as he was when standing for office.

More telling is Cicero's open declaration of oversight into civic finances, in spite of the proclamation of autonomy (Cicero duly forced civic magistrates guilty of embezzlement to return monies). He had earlier treated the issue with telling irony toward the *poleis* ("Never mind—at least they think they have *autonomia*," using the actual Greek term). The details about the relations between Cicero and the *poleis* of Kilikia can be paralleled with the care taken by P. Servilius Isauricus to restore or proclaim the freedom of various *poleis* in Asia (46–44 BCE). The governor also restored buildings and offerings: like judicial freedom, these material forms of civic pride act as symbols and manifestations of autonomy and its importance.[212]

Some years after a Chaironeian youth had murdered his Roman would-be rapist, the neighboring *polis* of Orchomenos went to the governor of Macedonia to accuse Chairōneia of anti-Roman sentiments. The incident shows the continuation of disputes between *poleis*, since Orchomenos and Chairōneia had a long-standing disagreement (perhaps territorial).[213] Even in the grim first century BCE, some degree of agency remained for the *poleis*. Agency extended to include military capabilities. The Smyrnians contributed their fleet to help Rome in its struggle against its Italian allies in revolt and liked to remember this as a genuine and free act of assistance.[214] Some *poleis* chose to resist outside foes. The citizens of Thasos held out against the troops of Mithradatēs VI and drove back a Thracian expedition, and Karian *poleis* such as Aphrodisias, Alabanda, and Mylasa tried to oppose the Parthians who swept in to Asia Minor in 43 BCE, led by the Roman desperado Labienus.[215] Mylasa was led by Hybreas, the local democratic politician: he enacted the city's autonomy by showing fine resolution before the Roman renegade, in the old civic tradition of frank speech and, admittedly, with the traditional result of catastrophic violence.

Elite politicians continued performing services for their cities. Around 50 BCE, the island *polis* of Paros honored one of its citizens, for thrice undertaking a difficult mission to Crete about the reimbursement of a loan.[216] Similarly, Mylasa honored Iatroklēs for public service (an embassy to a Roman governor, without taking compensation or office), benefactions, and economic services (loans and debt relief) toward fellow citizens and foreigners alike—exactly the same package, in the 70s BCE, as in late second-century BCE Priēnē, and described in the same Aristotelian-flavored discourse.[217] In the first half of the first century BCE, the Pergamene Diodōros Pasparos, apart from securing important advantages on an embassy to Rome, performed the duties of a gymnasiarch, including lavish building work in the *gymnasion*—for which benefactions he received important honors that are amplified versions of the honors for the grand benefactors of the late Hellenistic period.[218] The small *polis* of Pagai, on the northern shore of the Megarid, honored a citizen, Sōtelēs, for a rich series of gifts, including banquets.[219]

The imbrication of benefactions, institutions, and participatory activities can be seen in the Prienian decrees for the last of their grand benefactors, one Aulos Zōsimos, duly honored with decrees couched in Aristotelian language and with multiple honorific portraits. He was in fact an Italian businessman and a Roman freedman.[220] The difficulties of Roman rule may occasionally have tipped the balance toward giving outsize influence to providential individuals. At Sparta, the pressure of Roman demands led to the magistrates asking the rich for contributions—and the latter to nominate one individual, Diotimos, as having shown unique generosity in the past: one expects that Diotimos's financial actions granted him at least some form of extra influence in his city.[221] Such shifts may have combined with the distorting effect of access to the Roman dynasts, and help understand the sporadic appearance of signorial families (above). Even without the latter dramatic developments, increased dependency on elite figures in the first century BCE, beyond even the evolutions of the second century BCE (above, pp. 279–85), may have helped certain families entrench their power. At Aphrodisias, a decree passed ca. 50 BCE speaks of "the first and most glorious citizens," descendants of "the greatest ancestors, founders of the city."[222]

Even then, civic institutions proved resilient enough to continue to balance elitist claims. The honors for Diodōros Pasparos at Pergamon were passed in due accordance with institutional process. Assembly politics and rhetoric are attested in the hostile testimony of Cicero (in fact, the best evidence for assembly politics in the Indian Summer comes from his caricature).[223] Hybreas of Mylasa was a democratic politician, of nonelite birth, and Mylasan political life was marked by his rivalry with Euthydēmos, a wealthy citizen also active at the level of the federation of the province of Asia (and had acted in cahoots with Cicero: above, p. 297). Their rivalry was conducted in competition in the assembly, through rhetoric and contrasting political styles: Hybreas called his haughtier, high-handed rival "an evil necessary to the city."[224] In civic administration, financial office could involve the large numbers and frequent rotation in the Classical style, as seen in Tēmnos; popular juries continued to operate as the basis of judicial autonomy.[225]

An image of the Greek *poleis* brought to their knees by Roman violence and "pasha" rule was painted by M. Rostovtzeff, as ending the economic prosperity and civic freedom of the *poleis*, to which Rostovtzeff was so attentive. The picture is in fact at least as old as Plutarch or Strabo, who records the end of history in the first century BCE and its aftermath. In Strabo's account of Pisidia, the Selgians, after their past of independence, are now "fully subject"; the variegated ethnic history of Asia Minor comes to an end with provincialization.[226] Yet Strabo's account of Greece and Asia Minor is still structured by the endurance of the *poleis*, in whose history Roman decisions are simply a point in continuity of time. The continued agency and self-awareness of the *poleis* in the face of subjugation by Rome explain the cultural efforts at finding ways to define local identity as proxies for autonomy.[227] By the end of the short first century BCE, the Roman civil wars had led to the destruction of the old Roman ruling class and the advent of a military monarchy at the center of power. That the universal empire of Rome affected the life of the Greek city-states had been clear for 150 years. The question would now be that of the evolution of this relationship; and of the possibilities for the cities, as ever, to be a party in the making of their own history, both without and within their boundaries.

12

The Ends of Liberty

> The early Roman Empire rested on a network of cities, which were capable both of conspicuous expenditure locally, in the form of public buildings, shows and festivals, and of carrying many of the functions of government, but by the fourth century their capacity to perform these roles had dramatically declined. Both the capacity and the decline depended in part on the availability or unavailability of the richer classes to undertake expenditure associated with public offices or with liturgies. These remarks are of course mere common-places.
>
> —F. MILLAR "EMPIRE AND CITY, AUGUSTUS TO JULIAN: OBLIGATIONS, EXCUSES AND STATUS"

Greek *Poleis* in a Roman Empire

For an initial sense of the place of the *poleis* within the high Roman empire (31 BCE–284 CE) with its cortège of emperors and dynasties (in the traditional narrative),[1] we might turn to the travels of a tireless Ephesian in the third century CE. As we know from his now fragmentary statue base, the man traveled "often" on official business to the emperors in "the queen-city Rome," but also to Britain, Germania Superior (where he met Caracalla at a shrine of the healing god Apollōn Granios), Sirmium, Nikomēdeia, Antioch, and "even Mesopotamia." The same man acted as a local officeholder and as an advocate for the *Koinon* of Asia (the league of the *poleis* in the province).[2]

A contemporary, the eminent jurist Licinius Rufinus, operated at a much higher level in the social and political hierarchy of empire. He started his career in high imperial office and saw the interactions between emperor and local community from the center, as a "friend of Augustus"; adlection to the Roman Senate led to the governorship of Noricum, a military province, and involvement in high politics of imperial succession in 238 CE (when he was part of a senatorial delegation opposing the military emperor Maximinus). But he also was a benefactor in his hometown of Thyateira, where he was honored with statues by professional associations as well as by local notables. In addition, he served as an advocate for the

Macedonian *koinon* in a dispute with the Thessalian *poleis* over their contributions, for which service the high priest of the *koinon* honored him with a statue.[3]

Continuities are obvious. Menippos and Polemaios of Kolophōn had also traveled to Rome on embassies. But the scale is now much vaster, that of a world empire—from the Atlantic to the Euphrates, from the Rhine and the Danubian lands to the mid-African deserts. The *poleis* were part of an entity of 60-odd million inhabitants, organized in provinces, cities, villages, imperial estates. They dealt with the empire's administrative architecture, which included a heavily militarized frontier defended by a standing army of Roman citizens and noncitizens organized in standardized units, such as those that Caracalla would have led in Germany or that Licinius Rufus commanded in his province. It was centered on the metropolis and Italy, highly urbanized and hungrily consuming goods from across the empire. The whole structure was bound by a thin administrative apparatus inherited from the hegemonical Roman Republic, such as the cities of the eastern Mediterranean had dealt with in various forms, some evanescent, some heavy-handed (above, chapter 11). The question is what it meant to be part of empire. In this chapter we will explore the organicity and subsidiarity of the links between central state and local communities, as well as the coexistence of a "global" Graeco-Roman high culture with myriad local variations.[4]

Specifically, the question of the Greek cities within a world empire raises the issue of the long impact of integration—without prejudging of the issues with general statements about the thinness of empire or the collusion of local elites. I want to avoid, from the start, summaries such as "the Roman empire was a mosaic of cities, because the emperors had no other choice" or "Greek aristocrats were partners of empire." Urbanization, and urban culture, took different faces in the Western provinces (where it was actively fostered by the Roman state, in particular forms of "municipal" organization) and in the Greek East, where it existed as the outcome of the processes of evolution, convergence, and adaptation traced in this book.[5] But the experiences of the nameless Ephesian notable point to the unifying structures of Roman power and monarchy—Roman law and citizenship—that ultimately were extended to the whole free population of the empire in 212 CE.[6] Notably, empire imposed its forms across the space of its power. It is crucial to keep in mind this fact of imperial rule while studying the long history of the *polis* in its diachronic continuity.

It is still worth insisting on the many ways in which the *poleis* under the Roman empire existed as city-states along familiar lines. The story of the Greek city as urban built environment reaches a triumphant crescendo in the great building boom of the second century CE.[7] Civic institutions continue their expansion in northern Syria, the Dekapolis, and the Phoenician coast and, in the third century CE, Egypt—a theme to which we will return separately (chapter 14). New cities were founded or recognized, in Asia Minor or in Greece, down to the third and fourth centuries CE, in a continuation of the late Hellenistic processes. Hērakleia under Salbakē and Sebastēpolis in Eastern Karia, Atyochōrion in Phrygia, followed by Tymandos and Orkistos in the same region, Aidēpsos in Euboia: these are merely some examples (see further below, pp. 323–24).[8]

Like all *poleis,* these new cities structured territory with a central urban site and satellite villages. This basic form can be seen in the layered landscape around Hadrianoupolis, in Paphlagonia. There, a particular area with its villages had been assigned, perhaps in the first century BCE already, to one of the provinces (Pontus or Paphlagonia), in a typical piece of Roman administrative intervention. The area later was integrated around a *polis,* Kaisareia (whose full name, the *Proseilēmmenoi Kaisareis,* "Assigned Kaisareians," takes over a piece of administrative terminology and makes it into a sign of local particularism). The *polis,* in normal fashion, comprised an urban center and peripheral villages. Under Hadrian, the city was refounded and became the *"polis* of the *Kaisareis Hadrianoupolitai."* As part of the refoundation, the territory may have been extended to include more places, such as an older settlement at Kimista (if that is the right ancient name), which became a village in the territory of Hadrianoupolis.[9]

Old or new, cities continued to govern themselves, passing decisions and legislation, curating access to their citizen body and managing their own resources. After an earthquake, the city of Laodikeia on Lykos restored itself "by its own means," as Tacitus noted.[10] These resources included the city's rural hinterland. The system of civic subdivisions that organized the citizen body, for administrative and ritual purposes, extended into the countryside, as can be seen in Nikomēdeia in Bithynia.[11] Hence cities continued to contend with other cities over borderlands; there was no loss of interest in the *polis*'s rural territory as part of a supposed decline of the *polis*.[12] The traveler and geographer Pausanias recognized the small city of Panopeus, in Phōkis, as a *polis,* because it had recognized borders (and sent envoys to the Phokian League).[13] Cities sent men out to fight—in the civil wars of the empire (in which the 600-strong contingent from Patara almost served), against invaders in Greece (the Elateians were led out by a local notable, an Olympic victor, as if it were the sixth century BCE), as allies in the Roman empire's Eastern Wars. The Thespians sent a body of young men, complete with secretary and doctor, to fight in Lucius Verus's Parthian campaign.[14]

Civic images, so important as expressions of *polis* identity, are attested in this period through coinage, built spaces and buildings, and sculpture. Some honorific portraits of the second century CE exhibit continuity, in the all-important manner of portraying bodies and faces, with earlier norms and values.[15] The *polis* continued to produce and display itself through texts such as inscribed honorific decrees, laws, and (superseding the decrees) statue bases. Some of these texts concern specific continuities from the "Indian Summer" of the second century BCE, and the resilient reactions to the troubles of the terrible first century BCE. The "great acceleration" of civic culture in the late Hellenistic period left deep traces. Laws at Gytheion or on Chios concerning the new phenomenon of ruler cult under the

Julio-Claudian emperors could exhibit the old sense of civic history and punctilious attention to institutional procedure, accountability, and open distribution of power, inherited from earlier periods. In Athens at the time of the emperor Augustus, mass meetings of the Assembly were still held, and a law shows the city reasserting its control over the shrines in its territory, thus reconnecting with late Hellenistic traditions of civic affirmation through religious activism.[16] Even if inscribed honorific decrees grow rare in the record, there are clear hints that decrees continued to be passed and civic ideology to operate. A speech by the philosopher-rhetor Cocceianus Diōn (or "Dio Chrysostom" as he is traditionally called in the literary canon), given around 98 CE in his home city of Prousa in response to honors, is based on all the tropes of the honorific transaction as developed during the great convergence. These include family precedents, individual excellence in the service of the community, essentialized communitarian goodwill, *eucharistia* or "exchange of graces," and the bigness and generosity of the *polis*.[17]

This speech belongs to the most remarkable body of evidence, the extraordinarily rich literature of the Greek world under Rome (sometimes unhelpfully called "Second Sophistic" after a particular literary practice, improvised declamation by specialized performers or "sophists"). Indeed, the time of the Roman empire might be the period in which the Greek cities are best known, or at least most visible. In the corpus of speeches by Cocceianus Diōn, we find not only philosophical essays but also display pieces on political themes, and speeches in his own hometown of Prousa before the Assembly and the Council, of a type not preserved outside fourth-century BCE Athens. We can hear, in these Roman-era speeches, themes developed throughout the history of the *polis* (for instance, images of political unity: the beehive, the ship, sickness and health).[18] We will repeatedly encounter Cocceianus Diōn and his corpus of political speeches in the course of our exploration of the Greek cities during the Roman imperial era.

But all these densely attested poliadic phenomena, even though they look familiar and prolong earlier historical moments, are intimately linked with the presence of the Roman empire. The building boom was financed through institutions that were closely controlled by the Roman state (below, pp. 320–21), and generally can be viewed as part of an empire-wide urbanistic surge. The extension of the network of cities and the creation of *poleis* in Egypt were more or less directly fostered by the Roman state. The forms of local conflict were channeled and indeed generated by the conditions of empire (below, pp. 327–28).[19] The power of the Roman state in determining winners and losers in the eastern Mediterranean is noticeable during the first century BCE. This holds true for whole communities, such as Sparta, Aphrodisias, or Aizanoi (in contrast, Athens chose the wrong side in the final episode of Rome's civil war).[20] When in the first century CE, some free cities such as Kyzikos or Rhodes, or the free Confederation of Lykian cities, tried to assert their freedom—for instance, through their right to try and execute Roman citizens[21]—the consequence was loss of freedom through provincialization.

Such doomed assertions of autonomy allow us to see the continued presence of a widespread diaspora of Roman citizens living in the cities of Greece and Asia Minor (see above, p. 293). These Romans took part in the lives of the cities, notably by exercising a formal role in political decision-making.[22] The accession of the emperor Gaius was saluted at Assos by a decision, passed by the Council, the resident Romans, and the people, to send an embassy chosen among the Romans and the Greeks, and to swear an oath of loyalty.[23] At Marōneia under the emperor Claudius, a remarkable "perpetual decree" allowing the emergency appointment of ambassadors was passed upon the proposal of a number of bodies, including the resident Romans (who thus must have gathered separately and voted on a draft).[24] Unusually, a benefactress was honored by "the Greek and Roman women" at Akmoneia in 6/7 CE, an example of the presence and participation of Romans in the social life of the cities.[25] Resident Romans also frequently appear alongside the Council and the People as bodies responsible for honorific statues. Even more striking is the participation of Roman citizens in the *gymnasion* at Thespiai or Mytilēnē.[26] The impact of the social presence of Roman citizens in the civil spaces of the *polis* remains to be investigated in detail; it reflects the stresses placed on the *polis* as a political organism by its integration within a world empire with its own system of statuses and stakeholders.

These two elements—the high-handed (at times heavy-handed) *fiat* of the Roman state and the settlement of Roman citizens—combined massively in the form of Roman colonization and city foundations across the old Greek world, a phenomenon that should be distinguished from the continued spread of urban forms evoked earlier.[27] Under Caesar and preponderantly under Augustus, colonies of Roman veterans were installed in the Peloponnese (three colonies: Dymē, Patrai, Corinth), the northern Aegean (Diōn, Kassandreia, Philippoi), and in Asia Minor, both in the northwest corner of the province of Asia (three colonies), in Bithynia-Pontos (three more colonies), and in Pisidia and Galatia (nine colonies in total). In addition, Roman veterans were settled without the formal installation ("deduction") of a colony at Termēssos, where Augustus granted them tax exemption (as confirmed under Claudius).[28]

The best-documented and studied example of the impact of Roman colonies is the case of Patrai, which received vast lands on both sides of the Corinthian Gulf, taking over the territories of old *poleis* that lost their existence as autonomous city-states. The Roman veterans installed at Patrai must have received large estates created by the extinction of the *poleis* and the expropriation of their citizens. The consequence was a significant reshaping of the social and human landscape of the northern Peloponnese, with concomitant effects on the rest of Greece. The colonies were inhabited by Romans and enjoyed a special legal status (Cocceianus Diōn mentions how Apameia had an *exairetos politeia*, an exceptional constitution, in contrast to its close neighbor and rival Prousa).[29] They were characterized by special institutions of a type better known in the western parts of the Roman empire (such as two chief magistrates, the *duoviri*); their inhabitants used Latin in their inscribed documents, public and private.[30]

The Italian "diaspora" and Roman colonization thus appear as symbols of the impact of Roman high-handedness, intensified by the imperial monarchy. Yet these phenomena, too, underwent changes of their own: the Italians gradually were absorbed into the *poleis*, even though they could impose their own images and policies through euergetism (for instance, at Ephesos, the Roman Vibius Salutaris invented a whole set of rituals that colonized local civic texture with his own conception of world and *polis* into civic texture).[31] The Roman colonies adopted the Greek language (even officially) and Greek civic ideologies and images, and were accepted in the peer-network of *poleis*.[32]

The continuity of basic urban phenomena and, even more, of civic ideologies, speaks of the resilience and the vitality of *polis* forms within a world empire. But we are constantly confronted with another history, in which *polis* forms lead back to empire. The sense of the Roman empire as an end of history, on a global scale, surfaces in the monumental geographical work of Strabo, writing under the emperors Augustus and Tiberius. Strabo's evocations of local *polis* history and agency all too often end with the statement that the present is now that of Roman power and administration.[33] Of course, the great convergence of *polis* forms had precisely developed in an age of supralocal empires that the *poleis* learned how to deal with. Those mechanisms were still deployed by the local communities, but with what efficacy? The sketch given above oscillates between looking at forms of continuity and detecting the deep pressures of imperial integration. In the present chapter, the theme I will investigate is that of self-governance ("republican" forms, if you wish), especially in the light of my insistence that autonomy is an essential part of the *polis*, as realized during the great convergence.

Theoi Sebastoi and the Impact of Monarchy

At the top of the ecology of interlocutors that the *poleis* had to deal with or think about, there were gods—namely, the Roman emperors. The *Sebastoi* ("Venerable ones," translating into innovative Greek the equally envelope-pushing *Augusti* in Latin) were gods in their lifetime—at least at the local level of the cities, with no need for official posthumous divinization by the Senate in Rome.[34] The statues of Roman emperors joined the statues of the gods in temples, as happened at Priēnē in the Temple of Athēna. The latter was rededicated to Athēna and Augustus, and received a series of statues of Roman emperors next to the colossal image of Athēna (the head of the emperor Claudius survives).[35] The portraits of Roman emperors systematically appeared on the cities' coins, alongside or instead of the gods (see fig. 12.3); more explicitly, the Greek cities spoke of the emperors as gods, repeatedly and extensively, in ways deeply embedded in the fabric of their social life.[36]

The shape and history of the phenomenon are clear. Ruler cult in the Greek provinces of the Roman empire did not occur in isolation but came after three centuries of cult for Hellenistic kings, Roman officials, and Rome itself. It also coincided with organized cultic honors for the emperor in the western provinces. As S. Price observed, it is absent from the countryside, unless promoted by denizens of a city. When the shrine of a rural shrine in the mountain south of Prousa was adorned by two donors with a colonnade in honor of Trajan's Dacian victory (a gesture that is adjacent to ruler cult), the two men took care to specify that they were citizens of the city, and to distinguish their gesture from the world of rural cults and religion.[37]

The phenomenon started with a bang under Augustus. The Greek cities offered an exuberant range of cultic honors to him, to members of his family, and to his immediate successors and their families, often by adding elements of the ruler cult to existing festivals. Such additions are signaled in the festivals' names; for instance, the *Kaisareia Erōtideia Rhōmaia* of Thespiai, celebrating Augustus with Eros and Rome. Another method was to assimilate members of the Julio-Claudian dynasty to patron deities. Still at Thespiai, Augustus's wife, Livia, was the goddess Memory, or more precisely *Sebastē Ioulia Mnēmosynē* (Augusta Julia Memory), for the city's territory included the vale of the Muses, that deity's artful daughters (in the Early Iron Age, they had deigned to visit the poet Hesiod, from nearby Askra). Another assimilation to an age-old deity can be seen at Mytilēnē: Claudius's wife, Agrippina, was associated by the Mytilenians with the "Aiolian Goddess *Karpophoros*" (Harvest-bringer), honored in the old, shared shrine in the middle of the island of Lesbos.[38]

Ruler cult was ubiquitously integrated into *polis* life. Civic gestures such as dedicating objects or buildings to the city and its specific local gods became imperialized by the association of the emperor to the recipients of dedication.[39] An illustration of the local contexts for ruler cult is provided by the world of fish-mongering at Ephesos. A building for the payment of fish taxes (*to telōneion tēs ichthuikēs*) was dedicated by the fish traders "to Nero Claudius Caesar Augustus the emperor, his mother Julia Agrippina Augusta, Octavia his wife, the People of the Romans and the People of the Ephesians." Later, at the same spot, a lady dedicated a statue of Isis to "Artemis of Ephesos, Imperator Titus Aelius Hadrian Antoninus Caesar Augustus Pius, the first and greatest *mētropolis* of Asia, the twice temple-warden of the emperors, the city of the Ephesians, and the people in charge of the *telōneion*."[40]

Ruler cult also was a set of images, traces, and expressions about the emperor, his family, and his power in the world and in time. Much more grandly than the Ephesian fishmongering facilities, the temple of the emperors at Aphrodisias was approached through an extraordinary monumental avenue, dedicated to the *polis*'s patron deity Aphroditē, the *Theoi Sebastoi* and the People. The approach was framed by two highly ornate façades, each paid for by a different family, on the northern and southern side of the open space (fig. 12.1). The aligned reliefs, on two levels, represented the emperor among cosmic deities and a series of nations

FIGURE 12.1. Sebasteion, Aphrodisias.

subjugated by Rome (northern façade), the emperor's rule over the world (as exemplified by Claudius ruling over sea and land, or vanquishing Britannia), and scenes from myth (southern façade: fig. 12.2).[41] Imperial dominion is shown sublimated in divine form among the gods, or as mythologized idioms and next to mythological scenes.

The imperial cult, even though initiated by the cities themselves, was deeply linked with the political and social structure of the Roman empire. It involved elite patronage, civic institutions, large-scale federations of cities, and Roman governors in close interaction with the cities. In its ubiquity and embeddedness, ruler cult was not simply a set of honorific responses to specific benefactions or an instrument in diplomatic transactions (though it also played this role, as Hellenistic ruler cult had done). It also worked as a structural feature of the Roman world, acknowledging and transmitting the transformative impact of monarchy and manifesting loyalism as part of a monarchical culture. The cities showed great interest in dynastic politics, awareness of the influence of individual members of the court (for instance, empresses) and responsiveness to the inclinations of individual emperors.

The massive and exclusive nature of Roman power, combined with the monarchical revolution at the end of the first century BCE, intensified the functions played by ruler cult in the Hellenistic period—namely, it helped to make sense of dominion as part of shared gestures across an empire.[42] Ruler cult expressed a communal understanding of dependency before Roman power; it did so by focusing on the status of the imperial monarchy, which is analogized though ritual, image, text, and monument, to godlike scale, power, and permanency. Such operations reflected in local terms with expressive organicity an ideology of unifying

FIGURE 12.2. Sebasteion, Aphrodisias. Marble relief from South building, showing the emperor Claudius godlike and ruling over land and sea. H 360 cm.

world rule and peace. The ideology of world peace can be seen when in 9 BCE, the cities of Asia Minor briefly tried to coordinate all their calendars to start with Augustus's birthday.[43] It is no wonder that in the province of Asia, the local, civic forms of ruler cult tended to harmonize, notably along the model of the big institutions of ruler cult at the level of the *Koinon* of Asia, as discussed by G. Frija.

Universalizing won out, as befitted a world empire. After the diversities and raptures of the Julio-Claudian period, ruler cult underwent simplification. Most cities had priests of generalized *Theoi Sebastoi*, the august or imperial gods. The priests managed cultic forms at the local or federal level; their prestige was made visible through characteristic dress and insignia such as image-bearing crowns (fig. 12.2).[44] In practice, the ruler cult ended up being structured around festivals for the emperor, with processions, portable statues, prayers, and sacrifices.[45] At Oinoanda, a new festival founded by the local benefactor C. Julius Dēmosthenēs and named after him, included, as a matter of routine, a golden crown for the president of the contest

FIGURE 12.3. Bronze coin of Hierapolis-Kastabala, bearing on the obverse the emperor Marcus Aurelius (ruled 161-180 CE) sitting on a magistrate's chair, holding a globe and crowned by Victory, and on the reverse a bust of Dionysos. Diam 30 mm. *RPC* 4.3.6180. Münzkabinett, Staatliche Museen zu Berlin 18304385. Photograph by B. Weisser.

(*agōnothetēs*) with a portrait of Hadrian and an image of ancestral Apollōn. The *agōnothetēs* alongside all the other officeholders performed rituals to the emperor and the ancestral gods at the start of the year on the "Augustus day"; special officials (*sebastophoroi,* or "Augustus-bearers") carried in procession the statues of the emperors (*sebastikai eikones*). Those images were so familiar that their exact role did not even need to be specified. Events could include a contest for speeches in praise of the emperor and his family.[46] More solidly, ruler cult took the material forms of built shrines, with temples dedicated to the emperors, or associating the emperors with preexisting cults (as happened earlier with festivals). Some of these temples were the result of common decisions and financing by regional, "federal" associations of cities, which contributed jointly to building costs and to cult (below, pp. 316–18).

The divinization of the emperor expressed a simple fact. The reach of Roman power was universal, making itself felt into provinces that, constitutionally, were governed as "public" provinces by the Senate rather than directly by the emperor, for instance Asia Minor.[47] A coin of Hierapolis, in Kilikia, shows the emperor Marcus Aurelius on a judge's chair (*sella curulis*), holding the globe in his right hand, and crowned by victory (fig. 12.3).[48] Cocceianus Diōn, in a speech in his hometown of Prousa, modestly deprecates his efforts in securing advantages for the city: they happened as if he had prayed and the gods carried out the practical work.[49] The god-like performative efficacy of imperial grants and pronouncements is reflected, more simply, in the widespread usage of calling the emperor—and especially the letters and documents that carried his decisions—"divine" (*theios, theiotatos*).[50]

Cocceianus Diōn explicitly stated that benefits came "from the rulers," *para tōn kratountōn*, by then a venerable expression to designate the universal hegemony of the Roman state. Tangibly, the emperor gave gifts of cash or materials for building. "Aiolian Harvest-bringer" Agrippina offered very concrete funds to endow the gymnasiarchy of Mytilēnē in perpetuity. Cities could consider themselves as re-created by their imperial benefactor and founder (*ktistēs*), for instance when aided after earthquake damage. "Refounding" occasioned the addition of an imperial name (e.g., *Kaisareis*) to a preexisting *ethnikon*.[51] Hadrian (prolifically attested as a *ktistēs*) seems to have been particularly generous with gifts to the cities—such as Smyrna, Ephesos (the recipient of "unmatched gifts"), or Athens, where Hadrian finished the temple of Zeus Olympios started by the Peisistratids over six and a half centuries earlier, built other temples and a monumental precinct (the so-called Library of Hadrian).[52]

But the Roman emperor's power, as heir to the power of the kings, was also the power to decide on local statuses. A list of benefactions at Smyrna ends with the list of "all the things which we obtained from the lord Caesar Hadrian through Antonius Polemōn": among other gifts a million and a half *denarii* and ninety-six marble columns for a bath building, but also a second grant of the status of "Temple Warden" (of the provincial imperial cult), a sacred contest, and tax exemption.[53] Performativeness was now concentrated in the monarchical figure of the emperor (the place of the Roman Senate rapidly dwindled during the first century CE, though it did rule on the *asylia* of the cities of Asia in 22 CE).[54] The emperor decided directly on the very existence of a *polis* as a corporate, recognized entity with institutions. Hadrian confirmed the *polis* status of Narykos in Lokris in response to an embassy that adduced the existence of institutional markers (rather like the borders and delegates of Phokian Panopeus) as well as cultural claims.[55]

Hence the importance of personal connection with the emperor. Cocceianus Diōn's grandfather had planned to secure freedom for his home city thanks to his imperial connections (he had written a speech but died before he could attempt the crucial embassy). Later, Cocceianus Diōn attempted to use his personal relations with the emperor Nerva in the same way, but failed.[56] Still in Bithynia, Nikomēdeia obtained benefits from the emperor Commodus thanks to the intercession of the emperor's favorite, the Nikomedeian Saōteros, as commemorated on an issue of bronze coinage captioned "All is well in the world"—and, conversely, lost its privileges when Saōteros fell from favor (as alluded to sardonically in the coinage of Nikomēdeia's neighbor and rival, Nikaia).[57]

Apart from the prestige, liberty was desirable because it entailed freedom from tribute and extensive jurisdictional competences.[58] A dossier of imperial letters, from the first century BCE to the third century CE, was inscribed at Aphrodisias as a celebration of the city's liberty (fig.12.4).[59] Trajan informed the Smyrnians that they could not force citizens of the free cities to contribute to a temple financed by the cities of Asia, especially since Aphrodisias did not belong to the official list of

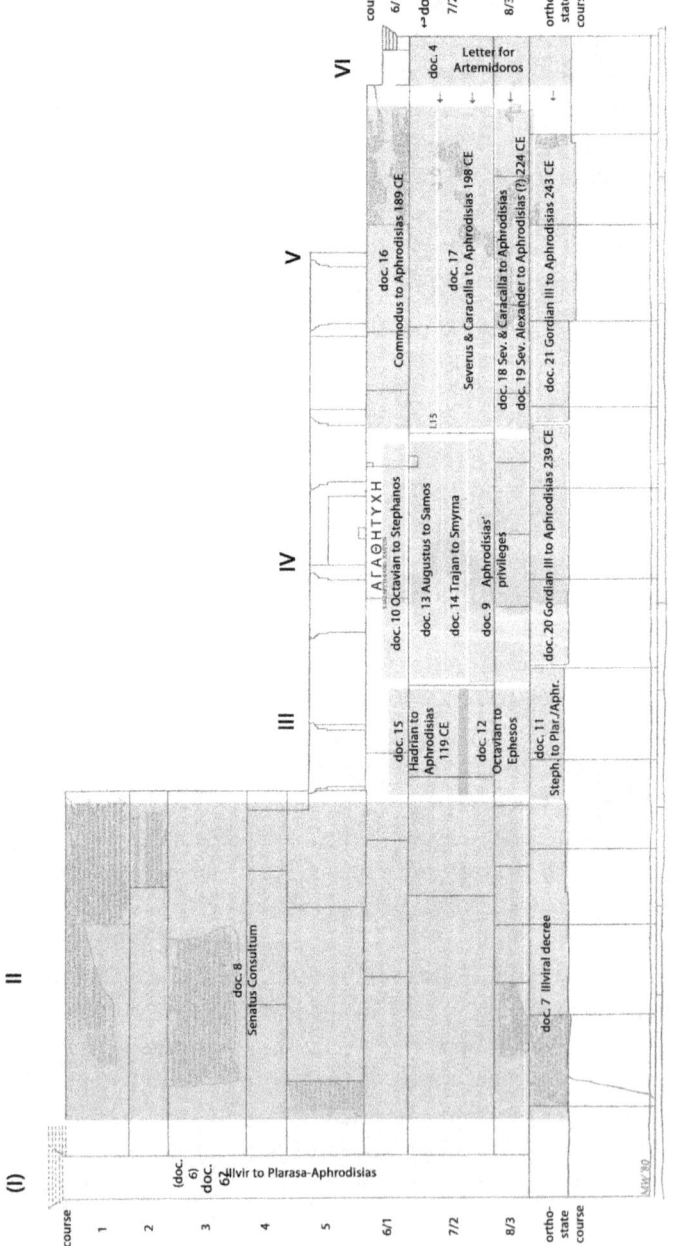

FIGURE 12.4. Aphrodisias, "Archive Wall" of imperial documents in favor of the city, after Kokkina 2015–2016.

provincial cities (*formula provinciae*). This particular pronouncement concerning an Aphrodisian resident at Smyrna, was paraded by the city of Aphrodisias as a confirmation of their liberty. A hundred and twenty-odd years later, Gordian III acknowledged that Aphrodisias, a free city, was not bound by a decision of the cities of Asia concerning relief for earthquake victims (but nonetheless asked the Aphrodisians to willingly contribute out of humanity). The visit of Roman governors to Aphrodisias was considered problematic, even upon invitation by the city, not only in the eyes of a governor (who wished to be sure that there was no "civic law, senatorial decree or divine [i.e. imperial] letter" preventing this), but also by the emperor Commodus.[60]

But though the privilege of liberty could give pause to the emperor himself, its origin as an imperial benefaction was never in doubt. On the same Aphrodisian archive wall, a letter of Octavian already described the freedom enjoyed by Aphrodisias—"the highest privilege (*philanthrōpon*) of all"—as a mark of his special favor, which he refused to the Samians, in spite of their petition and their enlisting of the patronage of Octavian's wife, Livia (the letter is in fact addressed to them, a copy being sent to the Aphrodisians).[61] Nero confirmed the liberty of Rhodes early in his reign, and in his penultimate year, during his tour in Greece, granted freedom and tax exemption to all cities in continental Greece (the province of Achaia)—privileges that Nero's successor, Vespasian, reversed for fiscal reasons. Hadrian, upon his accession, received an embassy from the small island of Astypalaia and responded by confirming the city's liberty (he later noted that the Astypalaians could not pay a congratulatory gift of "crown money").[62] The Astypalaians had enjoyed a treaty with Rome, but this does not seem to have played the role of legal precedent; likewise, the hesitant governor writing to Aphrodisias did not refer to the treaty concluded in the first century BCE, but proclaimed his warm feelings toward "the cities honored with liberty by the ancestors of our lord, the Emperor Alexander, who himself confirms it and increases the rights in which you rejoice."[63] The free cities of Aphrodisias and Stratonikeia had earlier set up statues at Ephesos in which they described themselves, paradoxically but tellingly, as "free from their origins, thanks to the grace of the emperors."[64] Conversely, the emperor's decision could deprive cities of freedom, as happened to Kyzikos (above), or assign some cities as subordinate to others. Cocceianus Diōn hoped to get the emperor to assign to Prousa neighboring cities and their territory, such as Apollōnia under Rhyndakos and the small *polis* of Germanikē. These cities' harbors would have allowed Prousa to bypass having to deal through unfriendly Apameia. The city of Diokleia, in Phrygia, honored the emperor Septimius Severus, "New Hēlios," for giving them some form of precedence over a group of communities in their region, the Moxeanoi.[65]

Freedom stood at the apex of the system of grants affecting status; for instance, promotion to center for the governor's assizes in Asia Minor (*dioikēsis*)—Cocceianus Diōn at least obtained this privilege for Prousa and also congratulated the city of Apameia for being a *dioikēsis* center, in an ironical speech.[66] The *polis* of

Hierapolis honored Antoninus Pius with a statue group showing the emperor standing in a chariot after an ambassador obtained confirmation of the status of the Hierapolitan public bank being used to handle tribute payments to the Roman state (the ambassador also paid for the chariot, though not the whole group).[67] The same privilege (as well as the status as assize center) probably appears in a long list of acclamations inscribed in Pergē around 276 CE:

> Grow from strength to strength, Pergē, the only inviolate one!
> Grow from strength to strength, Pergē, to whom (the emperor) Tacitus [...]!
> Grow from strength to strength, Pergē, Temple-Warden since Vespasian!
> Grow from strength to strength, Pergē, honored with a sacred flag!
> Grow from strength to strength, Pergē, honored with silver coinage!
> Diana of Ephesos, Diana of Pergē!
> Grow from strength to strength, Pergē, treasury of the lord!
> Grow from strength to strength, Pergē, first of the assize centers!
> Grow from strength to strength, Pergē, where consulars compete for honor!
> Grow from strength to strength, Pergē, where consulars preside over contests!
> Grow from strength to strength, Pergē, best of Pamphylia!
> Grow from strength to strength, Pergē, which has never lied!
> All the rights guaranteed by a decree of the Senate.[68]

The reference to the Senate is not an antiquarian throwback, but a reference to a specific institution, the granting of the status of "Temple-Warden" of the imperial cult to a city, a decision in which the Senate played some role (as it did in the grant of *asylia*). The acclamations show how the various statuses, gifts, privileges, and honors all result from a grant by Roman power as part of a single field, which was more than the sum of the myriad interactions between the *poleis* and the emperor. Still, Antoninus Pius, when responding to a letter from the Ephesians (complaining that their titles had not been acknowledged by the Smyrnians), was clear that these were "the names which I myself decided you should use."[69]

The hundreds of festivals and contests in the Greek world were now dependent on pronouncements from the emperor for their exact status (for instance, as "sacred" games, indeed even equivalent to the old prestigious contests of the Olympia-Delphi-Nemea-Isthmia circuit) and the legal consequences. Some contests were "eiselastic"; that is, victors had the right to a festive entrance back in their home city (as they "introduced" their crown)—and to a pension. Trajan, weighing whether the pension should be paid from the moment the victory was announced in the city or from the festival entrance, pronounced for the latter.[70] Hadrian reversed this decision as part of a series of pronouncements issued in 134 CE in which he laid down rules concerning the rights of the performers (organized as a guild) and attempted to organize and regulate (not quite successfully) the succession of a number of contests in a unified cycle to facilitate the movements of the participating artists.[71] For all the complexity and messiness of the festival calendar (even or especially after reorganization), Hadrian's letters illustrate the complete evolution of the old, all-important network of peer-polity interaction (where the status of festivals was decided by direct, diplomatic appeals to each individual member of the system) into a unified system with the emperor at the center. Hadrian personally received the representatives of the guilds and of the *poleis* at Naples, before issuing his decisions. The absorption and transformation of peer-polity interaction was one of the impacts of monarchy.

The unilateral power of the emperor to decide statuses generated hierarchy. As we saw, Pergē claimed to be first of *conventus* centers, the *mētropolis* of Pamphylia, and indeed the first city of that province—all statuses granted by emperors. "First city" or "*mētropolis*" were formal titles, held in virtue of an imperial grant (thus Ephesos was "the first and greatest *mētropolis* of Asia" from the 140s CE onwards). Smaller *poleis* were content with humbler claims, which confirm the operation of a unified field of statuses: in the mid-third century CE, on local coinage, Nysa called itself "sixth (city)," and its neighbor Magnēsia the "seventh (city)" of Asia, or perhaps more likely within a minor category of cities, apart from the great and prestigious cities that collected the grander titles of *mētropolis*, "first" cities, and Temple Wardens of the imperial cult.[72]

Titles as "*mētropolis*" or "Temple Warden" were integrated within formal structures of interaction between *poleis*. These had evolved out of peer-polity interaction to create confederations endowed with state-like forms, the *koina* of the Classical and Hellenistic ages (above, pp. 175–75, 210–12)—or indeed, the "Archaic" period. The Lykian League continued to exist after the provincialization of Lykia, with its own institutions and even some authority in matters of indirect taxation.[73] The Ionian League, grouping thirteen *poleis*, is attested from the "Archaic" period to the third century CE, over a millennium; the league itself, and cities within the league, struck coins celebrating the existence and identity of the Ionians (fig. 12.5).[74] Other surprisingly small and obscure *koina* kept on operating in the Roman empire, such as a confederacy of Phrygian cities, the *koinon* of the cities on Lesbos, or the Arkadian *koinon*.[75]

Like other features of the *polis* world, "federal" formations, even if they kept political institutions,[76] were profoundly transformed by the impact of monarchy, and further served as mediators between subject communities and Roman monarchical power.[77] Augustus, Nero, and Hadrian directly intervened in the membership of the Delphic Amphiktiony. Augustus gave no fewer than ten delegates out of the traditional twenty-four to his newly founded city of Nikopolis (the "Victory City" commemorating his defeat of this rival Marcus Antonius at Aktion), by taking away the delegates once sent by Thessalian-controlled communities. The decision is a telling sign of the monarchization of institutions, as well as a reflection of Roman power to change local structures. Nero increased the number of delegates sent by the Thessalians, inflating the traditional number of delegates to as many as thirty-four. Hadrian reversed Nero's measure, bringing the total number down to

FIGURE 12.5. Bronze coin, Kolophōn, bearing the portrait of Trebonianus Gallus (ruled 251–253 CE) on obverse, and on reverse a scene of the delegates of the Thirteen Ionian Cities offering sacrifice before the temple of Apollōn at Klaros (cf. fig. 11.2). Diam. 34 mm. BnF Fonds général 338. RPC 9.600.

thirty.[78] Another example is provided by the *Koinon* of Syria, organized in the northern Levant around a number of subdivisions (*eparchiai*). This seems an early creation of the Roman empire reflecting the provincialization of the area but persisting in spite of subsequent administrative reorganization.[79]

A major function of the leagues was imperial cult, at a regional or provincial level, celebrated by a high priest.[80] The function could also be designated by an honorific title as chief official of the league (Helladarch, Makedoniarch, Asiarch, Lykiarch, Bithyniarch, Kilikiarch . . .). Its holders (and their wives) were considerable personages, sometimes in office "for life" (i.e., at their discretion), and liable to very heavy personal expenditure, for instance by providing gladiator shows and wild beast hunts, *kunēgēsia*.[81] The orator Aelius Aristeidēs, nominated by his adopted homeland of Smyrna, strove to evade the burden of the high priesthood of the province of Asia Minor.[82] But the high priesthood had its advantages, often serving as a stepping stone, after a few generations, into the elite of the empire and imperial service.

The title of "Temple-Warden" of the imperial cult was awarded to a *polis* where a league would build a temple to a specific emperor in the name of the whole region and financed by contributions from all the member *poleis*.[83] The honor could be awarded cumulatively: Ephesos, Smyrna, Pergamon were all "thrice Temple-Warden," and Sidē lay claim to a sixfold title. League members also made regular financial contributions (designated with the same verb as in earlier periods, *suntelein*) for federal festivals. In 255 CE, the Lydian *polis* of Philadelpheia refused to pay its contributions to the *mētropoleis* of Asia toward imperial high priests and festivals, on the grounds that it, too, had once enjoyed that status. Characteristically for the Roman empire, the Philadelpheians obtained an exemption from such contributions by dispatching an ambassador (a friend of the emperors) who went to find Valerian and Gallienus in Antioch. Courteously, the imperial decision was phrased as a legal fiction: the exemption was to be considered "as if the *mētropoleis* had voted to grant you this."[84]

"Federal" imperial cult reflected the structuration of relations, involving *poleis*, leagues, and the emperor. These relations evolved in time. Starting under Augustus, the Thessalian League (renamed "Augustan Thessalians," *Sebasteoi Thessaloi*) offered imperial cult centered on the great city of Larissa but also reproduced at the level of individual cities. In addition, the league celebrated imperial cult festivals in Hypata, the latter reflecting the integration of the surrounding perioikic communities, with their traditions, into Thessaly. By the second century CE, as everywhere else, the imperial cult grew more unified and simplified, with high priests and federal festivals. At the same time the Thessalian *koinon* seems to have drawn inspiration from the practices at the Delphic Amphictiony, of which it was a member and, conversely, tried to introduce its own innovations into imperial cult practices at Delphi. By the third century CE, the Thessalian cities were contributing to the imperial cult as celebrated by the Macedonian *koinon* (reflecting their own integration into the province of Macedonia).[85]

An elaborate illustration of the structuration of relations, and the role played by the imperial cult, is provided by the "super-League" of pan-Hellenes constituted during the first and second centuries CE by a number of smaller leagues: the Achaian (which enjoyed some form of precedence), Boiotian, Lokrian, Euboian and Phokian.[86] In 37 CE, the small Boiotian *polis* of Akraiphia sent a delegate, Epameinōndas son of Epameinōndas, in the name of the Boiotian League, to the meeting (*sunodos*) of the super-League, at Argos, to swear loyalty to the new emperor Gaius, sacrifice for his safety, and celebrate a festival in his honor in the presence of the Roman governor.

When the super-League further voted to send an embassy to Rome, the envoys from the larger Boiotian cities declined to serve, a situation the super-League interpreted as the Boiotian League defecting from its common obligations. The Akraiphian Epameinōndas shouldered the burden, traveling as part of the delegation that went to Rome and returned with an imperial letter of thanks (Gaius declined all statues, except for those set up in Olympia, Nemea, Delphi, and the Isthmos, the four great old pan-Hellenic shrines, and crucially, confirmed the right of the super-League to continue to meet). In recognition of his services, Epameinōndas received honors from the super-League, which were notified to the Boiotian League; the Boiotian League met during the federal festival of the Pamboiōtia to vote honors of its own, and the individual Boiotian cities and even villages followed suit, starting with Thebes.

The whole dossier (decree from the super-League, imperial letter, decree of the Boiotian League, decree of the *polis* of Thebes, and relevant covering letters) was inscribed at Akraiphia. The documents clearly map out the hierarchical integration of the small *polis* in the empire through two layers of federal institutions, and its activities, diplomatic and cultic (the super-League soon instituted a direct imperial cult of its own). The subdivisions of the province of Syria (above), obscurely attested and still dimly understood, may have worked in the same way. More directly, the emperor Antonius Pius rebuked the citizens of Ptolemais-Barkē for sacrificing at the Capitol in Rome on their own: the *ethnos* of the Greeks of Kyrēnaikē was already represented by an official delegation, which duly sacrificed during the festival of the Capitolia.[87]

The regional and supra-regional leagues were of varying antiquity (some going back to the "Archaic" period, some to the late Hellenistic) and authenticity, but all were open to intervention by Roman *fiat* and all were coopted by the Roman empire. The functions of deliberation and representation within cultic and festive activities directed at the Roman center and the figure of the emperor, though they emerge from below, were supervised by the Roman state (as shown by the presence of the governor at the meeting of the super-League of Greece, in 37 CE). They could even be deployed by the Roman state, as shown by the case of the Panhellēnion founded by Hadrian (not to be confused with the southern Greek super-League discussed above). This was a peer-polity organization but on a vast scale, made up of dozens of cities in Greece, Asia Minor, and Kyrēnaikē. The Panhellēnion was founded by Hadrian and admitted members on the basis of Greekness. Its activities centered around Athens, an important site for cultural Hellenism since the late second-century BCE. Delegates met in Athens, at the temple of Zeus Olympios finished by Hadrian, to supervise a festival, celebrate the imperial cult, and pass decrees, including honorific decrees for the emperor, which were communicated back to member cities but involved the emperor himself.[88]

The imperialization of regional leagues is one illustration of the impact of monarchy on the world of the *poleis* and the reorientation of the world around the godlike power of the emperor. But the performative assumption also entailed a claim to practical ownership of the world. The leagues themselves, apart from proffering symbolical recognition of imperial power in cult and diplomacy, also acted as its instruments,[89] across the whole empire, east and west. In other words, the forms that reflected the godlike power of the emperor to define statuses also participated in the implementation of control and exploitation that gave very real form to this power and provided the economic basis for it.

Provincializing the *Polis*

The emperor's godlike power took the concrete forms of administrative apparatus—which are both very human and exceed human experience in abstraction and scale.[90] The Greeks in their *poleis* lived under "the rulers." The expression *hoi hēgoumenoi* (or equivalents) is attested from the mid-second century BCE to the second century CE, when it is used by Plutarch or Cocceianus Diōn to refer to Roman power and specifically to the Roman governor. "Remember the boots above your head," is Plutarch's injunction to the local officeholder. Even though the latter wears the crown of local civic dignity (literally a *timē*, an honor), his gaze is to remain fixed on the footwear of the mighty figure sitting on a raised platform. The striking vignette makes the same point about Roman power as the imperial cult—but in relation to the specific institutions of close-up Roman governance.[91] These are the boots of the senator (*calcei*), and not the sandals of the Roman soldier. Even though we should not exaggerate the degree of demilitarization of the "Greek" provinces of Greece and Asia Minor,[92] the main forms of contact between the Greek cities and the Roman empire took place within its administrative structure. Administrative structure was the concrete expression of the Roman imperial state's rights and, for all the thinness of means, the Roman state acted with coherence and continuity to establish its control over the local communities and to intervene within them.

This governmental intensity[93] started with the emperor himself, who regularly issued *mandata* to all of his governors, instructions about actions that the governors were expected to execute or matters to attend to. In addition, the emperor probably received a stream of queries from the governors and responded with decisions and further instructions. The correspondence between the emperor Trajan and the younger Pliny during his governorship of Pontos and Bithynia gives a clear idea of this phenomenon (even if he served on a special mission).[94] In turn, the governors published part of these *mandata* and issued edicts setting out a framework of legal principles and measures applying to their province. The conception is that of a space subject to the general flow of power—implemented through the regular circuit of the province from assize center to assize center, as in the time of the Roman Republic (above, p. 292).

The judicial competences of the cities fitted within this space. Even if the *poleis* still had their courts, their competences were shaped by their status (subject cities did not control capital cases nor try Roman citizens), and hence a constant reminder of the performative power of the Roman empire. This power meant that, in spite of the Roman empire's attempt to distribute judicial competences between the governor and the local communities, litigation tended to gravitate back toward the governor, as the strongest source of decision, to the point that the Roman state had to manage such expectations.[95]

Finally, the governors occasionally authorized local decisions, in law or decree form, especially if they involved financial matters (below): for instance, gifts for festivals and celebrations at Ephesos or Oinoanda were the subject of authorizations by the governor. In one case, the governor's opposition to honors for the benefactor Opramoas of Rhodiapolis was itself overturned or overcome (by appeal to the emperor?).[96] We are not quite seeing bureaucracy at work, but a routine, regular attention from the center, generating the concrete manifestations of state.

The great power of the governor—present, occasionally honored as a savior for services, often hated and contested—is not a reflection of the importance of the powerholders but of the reach of the Roman state.[97]

The issuing of regulations by emperor and governor (followed up by the governor's rounds) was not purely ritual or passive. One area of particular attention was the finances of the cities.[98] The Roman state could audit these through different mechanisms; for instance, by entrusting this duty as an express mandate to the governor. Pliny's special governorship in Bithynia and Pontos entailed particular attention to such matters. The governor's efforts were assisted or replaced by specially appointed commissioners, such as locally appointed *curatores/logistai* or senatorial *correctores* for the free cities (one example is Pactumeius Clemens, a senator from North Africa, who in the second century CE repeatedly exercised this function for a group of free cities in Greece, then in Syria, and in Kilikia).[99]

Such activity generated actionable knowledge, as seen in Pliny's effort at recovering public monies, and the Roman state could intervene without the (rare and fiddly) processes of inspection. At Beroia, the proconsul of Macedonia intervened to rearrange financial matters (including preexisting foundations but also taxes and fees, for instance from municipal watermills): the aim was to ensure the oil supply of the *gymnasion*, in decline for lack of funds.[100] The *dioikēsis* (financial settlement) of Prousa's financial affairs, planned by a governor, might have been a general rearrangement of taxes and rents, causing much local unease.[101]

Most importantly, Roman officials exercised oversight over local decisions involving income and expenditure. A hectoring, nervous oration by Cocceianus Diōn enjoins the Prousan citizenry to behave decorously at the occasion of a visit by the governor to hear a proposal concerning the market officials in Prousa, doubtless with financial implications; indeed, the governor had authorized this special meeting of the Assembly. Earlier, at Aizanoi, under Tiberius, a decision concerning a priesthood and tax exemption drew the attention not just of the proconsul of Asia Minor but also of the imperial financial manager (*procurator*), again because of financial implications.[102] At Sardeis, at least one of the public funds was subject to "the care and the permission of the emperors."[103] This level of interest in local finances and the civic budget seems unparalleled for earlier periods of supralocal control over the *poleis*. Even if there had been precedents, and even if intervention was rare or the result of local appeals (below, pp. 325–26), the systematic nature and ambition of Roman practice are remarkable. The existence of imperial oversight is a mark of the administrative integration of *poleis* in a world empire, to a much greater extent than under the third-century BCE kings or under the "empire of domination" model that obtained in the first century BCE.

Control reflected the rights of ownership. World mastery was symbolized by the imperial claim to treasures, curiosities, or samples of the best produce. The perfumes that the people of Tithōrea, in Central Greece, distilled from their excellent olive oil were sent to the monarch (*hōs basilea*) as a regular homage.[104] More concretely, the emperor owned natural resources (including such resources on the territory of *poleis*—and indeed across the whole imperial space: silver mines in Spain, gold mines in Dacia, marble quarries . . .).[105] Ownership, as the underlying reality under political control, created the right to extract surplus, in the form of cash, goods, and services. Extraction is symbolized by the regular gift of actual, high-value gold crowns offered by local communities, then cash payments *in lieu*. Tellingly, the latter were formalized as regular imperial taxes. Budgetary oversight and occasional interventions were clearly about curating local resources as a sustainable source of imperial income. The extraction of surplus is in fact muted in the evidence from the Greek cities of the Roman empire: we more often hear of tribute remission after natural disasters.[106] Yet extraction was a massive part of state operations, involving indirect taxation on goods and transactions, collected through private tax-farming in collaboration with the emperor's patrimonial officials (*procuratores*), and direct taxation collected by the cities on the basis of assessments carried out by the cities themselves.[107]

The latter practice illustrates the crucial role played by the local communities in the imperial system. Individual landowners owed tribute to the Roman state coffers but paid it to (or through) their *polis* (as is explicitly attested in the testamentary foundation of one C. Julius Epikratēs at Nakrason in Lydia). Likewise, cities collected the imperial poll tax off citizens and their families (in some cases, meeting the cost out of special funds gifted by benefactors).[108] Hence a *polis* had to pass on the proceeds of taxation to the Roman state, such as the 500 drachmas that the citizens of the island *polis* of Gyaros found burdensome (the geographer Strabo met their ambassador, hitching boat rides to go petition the emperor Augustus at Corinth for a lower tribute rate). The actual cash was concentrated in special centers, sometimes coinciding with the assize centers (Pergē boasted of this function—above, p. 314). The network of cities was used operatively for the funneling and handling of imperial taxation.[109]

The cities thus acted as instruments in their own exploitation. The instrumentalization of the *poleis*, both at the individual level and as part of networks, can further be seen in their provision of services for the Roman state's operations and infrastructure. For instance, the cities provided labor for road building (fig. 12.6). The remote upland city of Amyzōn built a stretch of the mountain road (the *Trachōn*, "Rough One") between Ephesos and the Maeander Valley, under the supervision of an imperial procurator, a good instance of the imperialization and patrimonialization of the process of exploitation under the monarchy.

The road lies quite far to the northwest of Amyzōn, and shows the imperial gaze on the landscape, distributing tasks among communities drawn from a catchment area between the Ionian coast and the Maeander floor: the *polis* of Amyzōn built "the portion incumbent on it." Likewise, in 93 CE, the *polis* of Kolophōn participated in the restoration of a road in the long plain south of Smyrna. "Imperator Caesar, son of the divinized Vespasian, Domitian Augustus, invested with tribunician

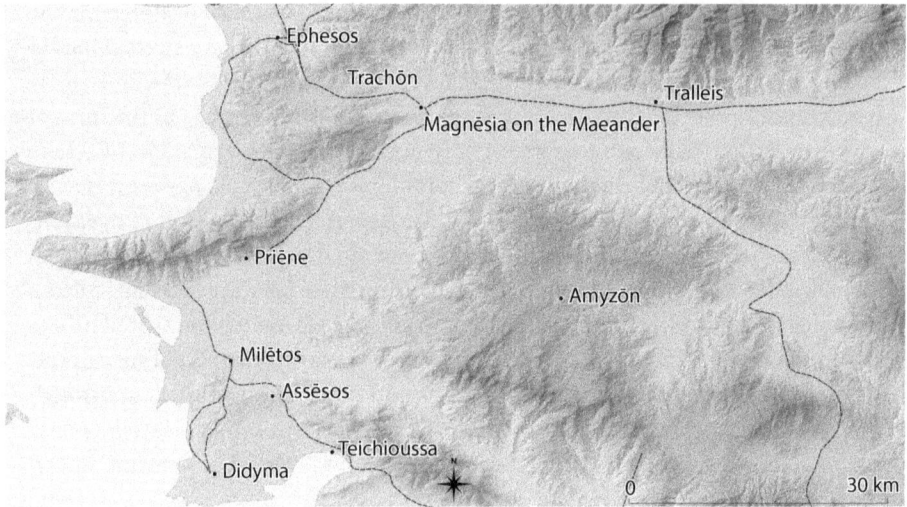

FIGURE 12.6. Amyzōn and the *Trachōn*.

power for the 13th time, consul for the 16th time, perpetual censor, father of the fatherland, restored the roads," as the milestone tells us in Latin and in Greek; in the latter language, a terse two-word indication completes the story, *Kolophōniōn ergasamenōn*, "the Kolophonians having done the work." Under the same emperor, the citizens of Indeipedion were called upon to build a five-mile stretch on another road (some 15 kilometers away across the Lydian plain).[110]

Built by the mobilization of corvée labor, such roads were explicitly termed imperial (*tas basilikas kai leōphorous hodous*, "the royal highways," in the words of a proconsul of Asia under Caracalla). They constituted and structured empire by carrying men, money, and information on behalf of the Roman empire. The city of Euhippē complained about official travelers straying from the royal highway and descending upon it with their demands.[111] Even without the excesses which Euhippē suffered, the burden of administration was shouldered by the cities. The latter provided resources and facilities for the official transportation system (*vehiculatio*) of the imperial state: beasts of burden, chariots, fodder, accommodation. This took according to specific and graduated rules (concerning compensation or gratuity), issued from the emperor and the governors (the system, unsurprisingly, was frequently abused by the state's men).[112]

The *poleis* served as nodes of empire: the routes and communications went from city territory to city territory, as units of space and bundles of resources along the way. The Roman empire hence harnessed to its own uses the nature of the *poleis*, as urban centers structuring human and physical geography. A.-V. Pont writes memorably of "cités-outils," cities as the tools of empire. But the register of services (*formula, kanōn*) was applied to "all the cities and the villages." In another consequence of world ownership, the Roman empire pushed intervention further, down to the lower levels of structuration, dictating arrangements in the rural countryside that the *poleis* claimed as their own. The Roman state, even as it acknowledged the existence of the *poleis*, pierced the shell of *polis* integrity, bypassing civic political mechanisms to tinker on the ground.[113]

Furthermore, functions linked with the empire's exercise of violence, control, and punishment were ensured by local communities. In Bithynia, cities guarded prisoners for the Roman empire or in collaboration with it, using specialized public slaves and thus allowing the Roman state to spare its specialized, full-time legionary and auxiliary troops (as noted by Trajan in a letter to Pliny). The stately nature of *polis* institutions, including means of violence and coercion, simply made available local means of enforcement for imperial use, and "prisons ... represent a prime instance of the interdependence of city institutions and of provincial government" (F. Millar).[114]

In Asia Minor, security was ensured by *eirenarchs*, officials provided by cities "in charge of the peace" but chosen by the governor, as a service to the imperial government; the office seems to have been created and imposed by the Roman state across the cities of Asia Minor.[115] The sophist Aelius Aristeidēs successfully evaded attempts (including lawsuits) to appoint him eirenarch for the city of Hadrianouthērai, a fairly recent foundation where the office must have been included as a necessary part of the machinery of local administration from the start.[116] At the head of local police forces, the eirenarchs hunted bandits but handed over their catch to the governor for trial, as seen in the edict of the proconsul of Asia, T. Aurelius Fulvius Boeonius in 135/6 CE.[117] Though the Roman state relied on local means of enforcement, it wielded the ultimate authority to interrogate and decide on punishment.

Finally, the cities assisted the Roman state in executing punishment, by flogging and assigning prisoners to public works, *opus publicum* (Pliny was nonplussed to find that Nikaia and Nikomēdeia actually used prisoners as remunerated public slaves, rather than for forced labor). The cities also provided the facilities for execution in the arena, as gladiators or by wild beasts, at events put on by civic magistrates or the officials of the regional *koina*. Cities thus provided infrastructure for the operative violence of the Roman state, from coercive punishment to spectacular executions.[118] A good example of the instrumentalization of the *poleis* is their role in the persecution of Christians, in response to directives from the Roman state. As seen in the grim narratives of the Acts of the Martyrs, the eirenarchs and his men arrested Christians, to be executed by gladiators, beasts, or torture during festivities celebrated by civic or federal officials. The enthusiasm with which the *poleis* carried out these horrible tasks was a result of their identification with the Roman order.[119]

The role of cities as instruments of governance explains why the Roman empire actively fostered their foundation. At the same time the Paphlagonian city of Kaisareia was being refounded as Hadrianoupolis (see p. 303), Hadrian founded three cities in Mysia, an under-urbanized area of northwestern Asia Minor grouping plains and wooded highlands. The first was Hadrianouthērai ("Hadrian's Hunts") in the plain (the city whose eirenarchy Aelius Aristeidēs so persistently evaded); the other foundations were Hadrianeia further east, and Hadrianoi in the upper Rhyndakos Valley on the southern flank of Mount Olympos.[120] Still in Mysia, over a century earlier, a city foundation on a vast scale had grouped a number of settlements into a single unit (these settlements later broke loose from the Augustan-era foundation). The Roman state saw the cities as a way to control and organize the landscape.[121] Hence the Roman state's acceptance of, indeed support for, the *polis*-formation phenomenon in inland western Asia Minor, already started in the late Hellenistic and the first century BCE (above, chapter 11); and indeed, the support for *polis*-formation in the Levant (below, chapter 14). A recently attested city foundation on the island of Kephallēnia (under Hadrian, perhaps inevitably) suggests that the fostering of new cities as part of administration was not limited to Asia Minor and the Levant.[122]

Since cities were instruments of empire, the Roman state practiced routine and deep-reaching intervention in their workings, in addition to financial oversight. The provincialization of Lykia and its *koinon* of cities in 43 CE was described as the intervention of Claudius's divine foresight to free the Lykians from strife, lawlessness, and banditry and create "concord and the right administration of justice and the ancestral laws of the constitution, entrusted to councilors chosen out of the best men, away from the undiscerning mob" (see further below, chapter 13). In practice, this meant direct reshaping and uniformizing of local electoral law through Roman edicts, *nomothesiai*.[123] The Roman empire often tried to reshape the *poleis*'s constitutional arrangements, notably by changing the Council from a rotating office to a lifelong body (the failed Augustan foundation in Mysia, mentioned earlier, might have had a list of councilors "selected" for life).[124] Furthermore, Roman pronouncements reworked local law, as at Athens, where Hadrian, under the cover of proclaimed traditionalism, imported Roman practice into the regulation of oil production and sale.[125]

This, then, seems the end of liberty in the Roman empire: transformation of the *poleis* into subjects, elements, and instruments of empire, under the heavy hand of the Roman emperor. All the phenomena described above—regulation, extraction, instrumentalization, and intervention—are the practical effects of the performative right to decide things by *fiat*: the power to decide on local statuses and conditions, and the implied ownership of the world. Thence flows the power to claim property and services (or to choose not to claim them, as a privilege that reaffirms imperial performativity); thence the right to use local communities unaccountably, for the ends of the imperial monarchy, and to sculpt the shape of local communities to fit the ideas of the imperial user and their practical needs. Conversely, the massive capture of *polis* workings and resources, alongside the embedding, ideological and practical, of the Roman state in the texture of the *polis*, ensured the conditions for the felicity of the empire's performatives—issued by the emperor, echoed and restated by the governors, implemented by the governors and the procurators. The impact of monarchy is unevenly present in the sources, which are largely the articulation of the relation between city and ruler in the old style, with less light shed on the structures of control and exploitation, often unsayable for the subjects and taken for granted by the imperial state. Even so, the outlines are clear: the installation of monarchy marks a watershed in the history of the *polis*, as seen in the subsequent three centuries of empire—which appear as a story of sustained coercion.

Statelikeness and Autonomy

In this landscape of Roman power, what place for the old ambitions of the city, namely republican self-government and agency toward peer competition? We have seen the *poleis*, managed and exploited, as constituent parts of empire. Their autonomy was essential for the system of power to work. But the paradoxical result was to allow for constant initiative from the local communities. One of the signs of the *polis* in operation had always been its diplomatic activity, and in this period also, we see the constant sending of embassies and requests. The local communities constantly generated the business of empire, by addressing embassies and requests to the emperor himself (a development of the "Polybian moment" and its embassies to the Senate: above, chapter 11). The nameless Ephesian I mentioned at the start of this chapter, who traveled to Rome but also to Britain and to Mesopotamia, was busy with just such activities.

The concrete forms of imperial government were directly shaped by local initiatives, and hence affected by *polis* ideology and values, and especially the *polis*'s sense of itself. This is the "petition-and-response" model of empire, proposed by F. Millar whose great work on *The Emperor in the Roman World* is also an essay on the Greek city.[126] Most of the "constitutions" of the Roman emperors, gathered by J. Oliver (1989), are responses to petitions. Hadrian received an embassy from the "new" city of Hadrianopolis Stratonikeia, in northern Lydia (new only in the sense of being refounded with the imperial name). Upon petition, he granted the city ownership of "the taxes from the territory" but also intervened in a small-scale, individual affair, ordering a noncitizen property owner to repair a dilapidated house or sell it. Hadrian also answered two further embassies from the city, in which they informed him of their good relations with governors—typical examples of the dealings between city and emperor.[127] The "eternal decree" passed by the *polis* of Marōneia in Thrace to authorize the emergency dispatch of ambassadors without consulting the Assembly (above, p. 305) reflects the importance of embassies as means of communication.[128]

It cannot be overemphasized that the forms taken by the cities' activism are diplomatic, descended from, or converging with, the old forms of correspondence between Hellenistic kings and *poleis*, where, whatever their status—subject, subordinate, "free" or genuinely independent—*poleis* were addressed as self-governing entities in their own right. Even in the Roman empire, the *polis* never quite forgot its origins as a *state*. It was the *patris*, or fatherland, of its citizens; it kept its *Staatsfähigkeit*, its stately capacities, to use the striking expression of D. Nörr's brilliant and controversial essay (1966) on the *polis*'s enduring sense of itself as a political rather than an administrative unity. Legally, ideologically, subjectively, *poleis* behaved as if endowed with autonomous stateness. Against Plutarch's injunction that civic politicians should defer to Roman powerholders, an honorific decree of Xanthos, praised a local politician for behaving morally in his activity as a citizen (*politeia*) and for "exercising full power in the interests of the *polis*" (*authentounta huper tēs poleōs*), which I interpret as forcefulness in representing the *polis* in external relations with the Roman empire.[129]

In addition to the diplomatic address to the Roman emperor, *Staatsfähigkeit* appeared in the taking of common decisions, the management of public goods (from territory to endowments to shared spaces), the pursuit of a rich life of social relations, interests, and conflicts mediated by institutions. These activities took place in a monumental urban setting that was the concrete venue and the metaphorical image of political status and worth. Petition and response thus participated in the active claim to statehood. It represented an attempt to negotiate the *polis*'s position when faced with the integrative and provincializing tendencies of the Roman empire, by affirming its legitimate interests and its right to defend them visibly and constantly in a struggle against the loss of political status (*Entpolitisierung*, as Nörr writes). In practice, it meant that the cities constantly negotiated and bargained with the Roman state, aiming at achieving not just a space of autonomy but also at alleviating the burden of empire. Petition and response embodied a broad effort of the cities to create their own luck, once again, as they had done during the third and second centuries BCE, and indeed repurposing many of the instruments developed during that time.[130]

The image of stateness underlies the *poleis*'s discourses. Petition and response is known through the honorific celebration of civic leaders who went on embassies, and through the responses of the emperors. One instance of stateness might be the ruler cult itself. Above, I traced the spread and the shape of this practice, which metaphorizes the overwhelming nature of Roman imperial *fiat* and embeds dynastic loyalism in civic texture. But historically, one of the ruler cult's functions had been ideological, in S. Price's interpretation (already adumbrated by D. Nörr); namely, to sublimate imperial power away from local political work, and isolate it as something different and remote that allows space for *polis* agency. Imperial cult was a political, strategic declaration of incommensurability.[131] It framed propositions about the nature of monarchical rule—beneficent, universal—which aimed at assigning a role to the rulers, comparable to the philosophical discourses on kingship by Cocceianus Diōn of Prousa or the rhetorical *morceau* of praise of Roman hegemony delivered at Rome by Aelius Aristeidēs in 144 CE.[132] Such discourses aimed at a double effect: internally, in the mental landscape of the citizens of the *poleis* and help them come to terms with the coexistence of local statelikeness and supralocal power; and externally, to create discursive parameters within which Roman power might take place.

The desire for stately recognition poured into the sustained "status races" between cities, such as that between the three great cities of the province of Asia—Pergamon, Smyrna, and Ephesos (above, pp. 313–15). The well-traveled third-century CE Ephesian ambassador who journeyed "often" to Rome and to other locations, went on his last known embassy to the emperor Macrinus, "concerning (Ephesos's) status as first city (*prōteia*), and the other privileges (*dikaia*)." The man was praised for literally winning the case (*neikēsanta*). Such statuses had not only to be obtained through petition and response, but also defended (as in the "Indian Summer" of the late second century BCE)—and competed for against rivals. This is the meaning of the aggressively celebratory note in the acclamations for Pergē (above, p. 314) in the context of Pamphylian competition for status. Pergē's claim to be the only inviolate city, first of assize centers and best of its province, unlike other cities and their untruthful claims, was directed against its rivals such as that other old and great Pamphylian *polis*, Sidē.

Cocceianus Diōn might claim the Romans mocked such competition as "Greek follies";[133] this did not mitigate the intensity with which the feuds between *poleis* were pursued down the centuries. But competition should be understood as part of a broad spectrum of peer interaction. Other speeches by Cocceianus Diōn show how at one end of the spectrum, inter-*polis* interaction took the form of hegemony—actual in the case of Rhodes over the remnants of its continental dominion; attempted in the case of Tarsos over the smaller cities of Kilikia; symbolical in the case of cities claiming advantages, real or not, from functions in Roman governance, such as assize centre or "bank" for tributes.[134] At the other end of the spectrum, cities collaborated: competition was balanced with efforts at concord, celebrated on occasional issues of local bronze coinage. The participation of Sparta in a network of peer interaction in the Roman period saw the reemergence of collaborative institutions such as the sending of foreign judges.[135]

A particularly important medium for stateness of the Greek cities in the Roman empire was found in the resources of local communal identity, developed since the "Archaic" period.[136] The *poleis*'s self-imagination as descent groups with mythical founders (gods or heroes)[137] gave rise to public art (at Aphrodisias or Pergē: fig. 12.2),[138] civic coinage (showing local myth, often obscure to modern scholars),[139] and festivals.[140] The celebration of local identity, in visual media and in discourse, acted as a proxy for autonomy, but also as its ideological justification: a *polis* was special, old, greater than its constituent citizens, worthy of special attention on the grounds of its mythological and religious identity.

All these factors justified the right to self-actualization through self-government. The *polis* of Panopeus, though small and undistinguished in terms of its cityscape, could claim political institutions—and considerable antiquity as the site of the claybed whence mankind was remade after the Flood (see further below, chapter 15).[141] Cocceianus Diōn spoke, at times seriously, to his fellow citizens at Prousa, as to a unique city; to others, he only engaged with local myth by preterition, but his very irony shows the importance of myth for the corporate identities of *poleis*. Cultural identity formed the basis for *polis* pride or even arrogance, grounded in the size and antiquity of the cities: a *polis* could imagine itself as the best, first, most ancient *polis* (as Sardeis did).[142] The Rhodians, in Dio's vision, embodied a special dignity in their very dress and bearing, indissolubly linked with their historical greatness as a free *polis*.

Cultural identity was the medium for inter-*polis* competition. Tarsos and Aigeai both claimed foundation by Perseus, and curated sacred images that the Argive hero had left behind on his expedition against the Gorgons. But it was also the medium for contact and collaboration. A famous orator from Aigeai, P. Anteius Antiochos, traveled to Argos to present his researches on the foundation of his city by Perseus, an example of the persistence of the discourse of kinship identity into the Roman period. A particular example is the continued celebration of the kinship between Sparta and cities in Asia Minor.[143] The modularity and mutual relatability of *poleis*, thanks to the widespread model of mythical foundation, belonged to a more general participation in a widely shared Greek identity, which remained strongly recalcitrant to absorption within an imperial identity. The sense of ethnic apartness from Rome and of historical distinctiveness undergirded the multiple variations of local civic identity.[144]

The Ambiguous Fate of Liberty

The above represents an ideal sketch of civic autonomy, written out of *polis* discourse. Yet local bronze coinage in Asia Minor, while insisting on the identity and specialness of the *poleis*, also evokes the ineluctable figure of the emperor who often granted the right to celebrate local festivals (figs. 12.3, 12.5). Local manifestations of autonomy did not make empire disappear. Proxies for autonomy remained proxies, and the energies of civic affirmation accepted and strengthened the framework of empire. All the elements in the traditional arsenal of *polis* identity have to be viewed realistically in the shadow of empire—a strong, interventionist presence, capable of considerable intrusions at the local level and of cooping local agency as part of governance. The workings of *polis* autonomy were preemptively priced into the practice of empire: this applies for petition and response as well as peer-polity interaction.

For by its nature, petition and response was predicated on the performativity of the imperial pronouncement. *Prōteia* and privileges, all the way to liberty, were granted by the emperor (and often emperor-centered, as in the case of the imperial cult). Competition for privileges reaffirmed the fundamental fact of imperial performativity. Cities in priding themselves on being assize centers, tried to reconceive their instrumentalization as marks of worth, but reaffirmed the presence and legitimacy of empire. The resort to the emperor or the governor over local disputes of precedence was couched in the forms of statelike diplomacy, but, actualizing the fears of the civic leadership, simply invited the Roman state in.[145] So did petition and response more generally, by its very nature.

The Severan codification and formalization of the relations between empire and subject were less a sudden *Entpolitisierung* of the *poleis* (as Nörr wrote), than the finalization and formalization of structural tendencies in the Roman empire. Petition and response also allowed the empire to show itself repeatedly, consistently, as a field of rationality, legal-mindedness and responsiveness—and hence legitimize and formalize its presence. Symbolically, petition and response, though meant as an expression of stateness, in fact put the cities in the same situation as individual subjects who also had access to the emperor through direct appeal (a conflation of monarchical practice and of Roman legal privileges)—a powerful sign of subordination and integration.[146]

Viewed coldly, the Roman empire appears as the end of the line for civic autonomy. The situation superficially resembles that of the late fourth to the early second centuries BCE, just like Roman-era ruler cult resembles Hellenistic ruler cult. In that period, cities had faced supralocal empires and found ways of collaborating and preserving autonomy through negotiation and patience. Such was the story of the cities of Iōnia or Karia, of the islands, of mainland Greece, and even Macedonia and Thessaly, and it continued into the "Indian Summer" of the cities. But under the Roman empire, the whole context changed in profound ways. In this world, it seems that the *poleis*'s old tricks worked to strengthen and extend the force of empire, actual and ideological. As C. Brélaz has observed, the devolution of police functions to the local communities instrumentalized the latter, integrated them within the Roman state and allowed for the appearance of autonomy.[147]

For François Jacques, the French historian of cities in the Roman empire (especially the western provinces), the fate of local autonomy was to simply become a form of imperial governance, harmonized within its workings, as seen for instance in the subsidiarity and complementarity of the administration of justice or in the interlocking of fiscal administration.[148] Jacques was all too ready to criticize Nörr's vision of empire and city as opposed entities, a vision that Jacques assigned to a nineteenth- and twentieth-century German interest in the relationships between local entities and a strong federal state. And yet Jacques himself might have been writing with his own sympathy toward a powerful, unitary state, in the French tradition. He willingly admitted the validity of Nörr's vision for areas with a strong *polis* tradition as opposed to western regions such as Roman Africa; and most importantly, he never questioned the importance of local autonomy as part of the empire. We might go further than Jacques, or even flip his position. We should stop taking for granted or natural the way in which the Roman empire was based on the autonomy of local communities. The latter state of affairs was a result of the tenacity of the *poleis* in negotiating with the empire, and making sure that, given its overwhelming potential, its power would stop at the level of the *poleis*, and that the *poleis* would be the only interlocutors of empire, even at the price of the latter's embrace.

In this way, as Paul Veyne wrote, the *polis* spread to the whole Roman world. His magnificently phrased conclusions are worth quoting:

> what inspires these cities [the *municipia* of the Roman West] is the old Greek ideal of the independent *polis*.... We should not wonder at this unusual spectacle presented by "Roman" cities which call themselves independent of Rome or, even better, allies of Rome. As we saw, this concept is Greek in origin; and in fact, it is worth repeating that the whole municipal life of the Roman empire, in short that which we call the urbanization and Romanization of the West, is, truth be said, merely a chapter in the history of Hellenism. Cast aside all questions appertaining to the State (itself a distant, lightweight confection), namely the condition of the different categories of cities after conquest; forget about the matter of institutions (quattuorviral, duoviral constitution, etc). Consider that which was nearest, more concrete, and most quotidian about life for the immense majority of the population: the narrow framework of the city-state, the pressure of public opinion, the civic ideal, the relations of notables and populace, festivals and collective ceremonies, the care for urban environment, the rivalries with neighbouring cities and disputes over prestige or titles, the pride in the local past, euergetism, the system of benefactions offered by notables to their cities (with their subtle, complex workings), which appears under the same guise in the Roman cities and in the *poleis*: in all this, the Hellenistic world perpetuates itself and conquers the West through Rome.[149]

The strange persistence of autonomy holds as true for the *poleis* as the *civitates* of Gaul, North Africa, or Spain. The western *civitates* behaved with a sense of their corporate identity and their right to speak to the Roman state as self-possessed actors, which is utterly familiar to the student of the Greek *polis*. The main issue was not about individuals "becoming Roman" (the focus of recent scholarship on "Romanization") but about the capacity of local communities to find their voice in dealing with empire.[150]

For instance, the *civitas* of the Aedui in Gaul centered around their city of Flavia Aeduorum (modern Autun), defended their interests through ambassadors; at least, this is attested in the late third century CE by two surviving speeches of exactly the type known by rhetorical treatises and implied by honorific inscriptions for civic ambassadors (like the Ephesian at the start of this chapter).[151] The convergence between western cities and eastern *poleis* is strikingly illustrated by Q. Trebellius Rufus of Tolosa (modern Toulouse) in the province of Narbonensian Gaul. This man, who held Roman citizenship and held equestrian office in the

Roman administration during the late first century CE, was high priest of the ruler cult in his western province—but was also honored in Athens, where he held the eponymous archonship, a priesthood of the ruler cult and a traditional priesthood, and where he was honored with multiple honorific statues. The city of Athens had no problem in mentioning how Trebellius Rufus had been honored in his fatherland, a city at the other end of the Roman empire. The provincial League of the Narbonensians, and the authorities of Tolosa, wrote letters in Greek to the magistrates of Athens: Tolosa was integrated within the old structures of peer-polity interaction, extended to the world empire, just as the *civitas* of Vienna (the former Gallic nation of the Allobroges) claimed mythical kinship with the *polis* of Biennos in Crete.[152] One of the speakers for third-century CE Flavia Aeduorum was the descendant of an Athenian settled in the Gallic city, but the extension of the *polis* model did not await that moment, nor did it depend on direct immigration of articulate notables from the East. The extension of *polis*-hood constitutes a major historical phenomenon within the history of the Roman empire, and a partial reflection of the way in which the *poleis* made the empire in their image, albeit at great cost and with profound changes.

The lesson of a *polis*-centered vision of the whole Roman empire is to establish, in actual terms, a practicability of civic autonomy, even in the shadow of empire and in full awareness of the Roman state's ambition to govern and power to coopt. The Roman state might have depended on other instruments than the cities—for instance, villages or local magnates as direct individual interlocutors. Indeed, it partly attempted to do so, working at levels below the network of bounded, self-governing cities, as in the case of the imperial transport system (above, pp. 322–23). That it generally did not was the result of civic activism: the latter established cities as the partners of empire, rather than the subjects of its exploitation and the victims of its indifference. That petition and response became the standard way of interaction between empire and subject did not have to happen inevitably: the cities made it happen, embassy by embassy.

It was the *poleis*'s collaborative activism that established petition and response and peer-polity interaction as the inevitable forms that empire would try to coopt. Once the cities' indispensability was established, the dependency of the empire on their workings meant that in practice, the ubiquity and power of the imperial state could be as much of a fiction as civic autonomy. The whole jungle of privileges and *prōteia* never constituted a fixed system of statuses; rather, these were fluid and open to multiple interactions. Civic competition for status and recognition multiplied titles and claims, and generated subfields of interaction and competition. The "secondary scale" of titles in Asia known for the "sixth" and "seventh" cities of Asia (above, p. 315), depended on imperial *fiat* but complicated, in its proliferation, any sense of imperial unity, constituting instead a multitude of *ad hoc* subfields.[153] As F. Millar notes, "it is not without significance that [the third-century CE senatorial historian of Bithynian origin Cassius] Dio regarded the struggles of cities for primacy and honorific titles with profound scorn—city titles, he notes in a passing comment, used to be awarded by the Senate, while now cities appropriate whole lists of titles as they please."[154]

The autonomy of the cities could achieve real effects because of stately identity and purpose[155] and the patchiness of imperial interventions. Local or regional collaboration could oppose the actions of the governor; petitions by the cities, as recognized actors in the empire, could play the system to slow down the operations of empire. Petition and response, horizontal peer-polity interaction, and manifestations of local identity entangled empire in the *poleis*'s workings, even playing the emperor against the empire, as the Aphrodisians repeatedly managed to do. In practice the *poleis*'s success at creating a complex, interlinked world and at negotiating with the empire allowed them to bargain for rebates on their tax burden or to protect their privileges. The measure of their success, ironically, would come at a time when the costs of empire spiraled, the Roman military proved insufficient in the face of attacks in both West and East, and the network of civic privileges proved an obstacle to emergency fiscality.[156]

Less dramatically, the imperial tools of subsidiarity and instrumentalization meant that the *poleis* enjoyed some leeway; within the Roman empire, this was perhaps the best that the *poleis* could effect for themselves. Left to their own devices, they ran their own affairs, for instance in judicial matters. We have seen the cities of Larisa and Hypata as the centers for ruler cult; they also appear in Apuleius's second-century CE novel as holding trials and running their own affairs (below, p. 352–54). Endowed with the capacity for violence (a distant reminder of the role of war in state definition), the *poleis* even might take arms when the imperial state faltered. Just as they had done during the Roman civil wars, they engaged in local conflict in times of dynastic strife. In 68–69 CE, or in 193 CE, cities pursued local rivalries as they had done in the first century BCE (and earlier). Nikaia, Nikomēdeia, Byzantion, all took an active part during the war that led to the establishment of the Severan dynasty, and local enmities determined partisanship. In the Levant, Laodikeia on Sea and Tyre espoused the opposite party to, respectively, Antioch and Berytos.[157] The cities did so even though they paid a heavy price after the reestablishment of order: for backing the losing side, Byzantion briefly lost its existence as a *polis*, becoming a subordinate settlement in the territory of Chalkēdōn.

This capacity for state-like military force proved useful when outsiders threatened the Roman empire or even broke past its frontiers, the cities fought by sending contingents, or organizing their defense. The military activity of some *poleis* went beyond administrative subsidiarity. A warband made up of Kostobōkoi (a Balkan nation), after marching from the Danube into central Greece, was destroyed by the mobilized citizens of Elateia in Phokis.[158] Just after the last great burst of civic activism and identity affirmation in the first half of the third century CE, the *poleis* would defend themselves against invasion during the military crisis of the late third century CE, under the leadership of local notables such as the Milesian

Markianos or the Athenian P. Herennius Dexippos, who wrote a Classicizing history of the invasions (see below).[159] But strikingly, they did so ensuring their own safety within a framework of proclaimed loyalism to the empire (hence confirming the pertinence of Jacques's insights about the cities' integration within empire).

The story of Greek *polis* and Roman empire remains ambiguous and incomplete, a story of imperial power and local agency. It is a qualitative story, of the balance between the pressures from above and below, and the resulting social and cultural history; I have offered multiple readings from within the knowledge represented by Roman statecraft, the idealistic assumption of *polis* stateness, and a realistic but ambiguous perspective on the actual capacities of the state and the constancy of civic activism.

The story of *polis* and empire also extends in space, with the model of the *polis* supported by empire in the "Roman Near East," whose social and cultural history was a central concern of F. Millar (below, chapter 14). Finally, it is a diachronic story, whose shapes change with the evolutions from the Antonine dynasty of the second century CE to the Severans of the third century CE, and the crisis of empire in the late third and early fourth centuries CE, which civic autonomy may have aggravated but which it also contributed to overcome, only for a resurgent, transformed late Roman state to tighten control on local autonomy (below, chapter 14).

All these contradictory phenomena are signs of the ambiguity of the relationship between state and *polis*—an ambiguity fostered by the long continuity of local autonomy, which the *poleis* defended using resources developed during the Hellenistic period. Importantly, the cities' efforts at preserving their agency and carving out livable local spaces were also about internal affairs, namely the conditions for sovereign popular government, in the prolongation of the great convergence of the third and second centuries BCE. When "the armies of Caesar" (Hadrian) marched through Macedonia demanding supplies in kind, the city of Lētē had to respond by mobilizing its own resources and negotiating solutions with its elites. It notably honored a benefactor, M' Salarius Sabinus (a descendant of Italian settlers) for not increasing the prices of the goods that he supplied to the city.[160] Under pressure from the empire, the city remained a political organism with the power to decide on its arrangements. In other words, the continuation of local political life was also one of the forms that the continuation of autonomy took, and the fate of democracy in the *poleis* under the Roman empire was bound with the defense of autonomy.

13

Polis, People, and Power in the Roman Empire

> Are you not the ones who praise us all day long, calling some champions (*aristeis*), some Olympians, some saviours, some nourishers? Then by Zeus and the gods, you will be convicted of false witness in your own court, and are you saying such things as now out of anger, or were you speaking that way earlier out of flattery? Are you now being deceived, or were you deceiving us then? Will you not put an end to the unrest and acknowledge that you have fellow citizens who are most graceful (*charientas*) and a city which could be blessed (*makarian*)?
>
> —DIO CHRYSOSTOM, ORATION 48

The Glare of Elitism

The *polis* of the Roman empire appears to us flooded in the glare of elitism, and it is all too easy to suppose that *polis* and elites were coterminous. For G. de Ste. Croix, it was axiomatic that this period saw the "destruction of democracy" (starting in the Hellenistic age).[1] In contrast, when seen from Late Antiquity with W. Liebeschuetz, the Roman-imperial *polis* appears as a haven of classical civism, full of elaborate care for lawfulness and constitutionalism.[2] In this chapter, I will argue for taking constitutionalism seriously, as springing from and impinging on social life. For it is all too tempting to discount constitutionalism when confronted with the more spectacular and concrete frontage of the Roman *polis* as built environment. To a certain extent, the Roman-imperial *polis* still exists. It is possible to deambulate in its great buildings or colonnaded streets, among the forest of honorific statues for its elites.[3] These monuments are often those of exceptional individuals, great benefactors enjoying Roman senatorial status, and living as members of the imperial aristocracy of a global empire, their very long names reflecting marriage and inheritance patterns among super-elite families (we will see many examples below).[4] In F. Millar's formulation, we are seeing "the classic pattern of the integration of the Greek upper classes into the highest orders of the Roman system."[5] The "Library of

FIGURE 13.1. The "Library of Celsus," Ephesos.

Celsus" at Ephesos was built in honor of the Sardian (not Ephesian) Senator Ti. Julius Celsus Polemaeanus, proconsul of Asia, by his son, Ti. Julius Aquila Polemaeanus, also a senator.[6] The building, exuberant and ostentatious in its architecture (fig. 13.1), was adorned with personifications of Celsus's virtues, captioned in Greek and in Latin. It also served as a monumental tomb for Celsus and occupied a focal point at the intersection of Ephesos's two major avenues.

On an even grander scale, the immensely wealthy magnate, orator, Roman consul (and son of a consul) L. Vibullius Hipparchus Ti. Claudius Atticus Hērōdēs rebuilt the Panathenaic *stadion* in Athens, complete with Pentelic marble seats, and gave the city a new *ōdeion* dedicated to the memory of his wife. In addition, Hērōdēs Atticus (to give him a shorter version of his name) offered buildings to several other cities and shrines in Greece;[7] from his "building program," it is clear that his particular interests were idiosyncratic, shaped by imitation of imperial patronage. Another example of the impact of the super-elite families on Roman-era cityscapes is the southern gate of Pergē, in Pamphylia, gathering images of the Olympian gods on the lower level and of founders on the upper level—twelve local heroes, but also two Roman senators: "Founder, M. Plancius Varus, of Pergē" and "Founder, C. Plancius Varus, of Pergē," respectively father and brother of the donor, a rich lady named Plancia Magna.[8]

The super-buildings of Ephesos or Pergē act as a shorthand for the wealthy citizens decisively shaping the cityscape. Examples could be multiplied: Asia Minor

FIGURE 13.2. Temple of Zeus, Aizanoi.

offers a particularly rich roster of such phenomena. The very orientation and shape of the urban center of Aphrodisias, in the first century CE, was determined when the imperial freedman C. Iulius Zōilos offered a temple of Aphroditē, one of the porticoes of the northern *agora*, and the decorated stage-front of the theatre. This towering figure of the early Augustan period was followed and imitated by other Aphrodisian families; for instance, the two families that set up the monumental, porticoed space ("Sebasteion") leading to the temple of the imperial cult (above, pp. 307–8, and figs. 12.1 and 12.2).[9] The same pattern of intense urbanization under the impulse of elite families can be seen at Aizanoi, which benefited from the early Roman empire in ways similar to Aphrodisias (fig. 13.2).[10] Among the marble splendors of Roman Ephesos, M. Claudius P. Vedius Antoninus Phaedrus Sabinianus, together with his wife Flavia Papiana financed a towering, extensive bath complex, on the northern edge of the urban site. The couple also rebuilt the council house on the Upper Agora, on an enlarged plan and with a lavish internal façade, whose aediculated ornamentation harbored statues of the imperial family personally set up by Vedius Antoninus. Imperial letters (from Antoninus Pius) in support of Vedius Antoninus's building activity were inscribed on the council house; his own public honorific statue was set up in front of the building.[11]

These massive architecture donations are the most spectacular examples of the practice of elite giving. The case of a husband-and-wife couple of benefactors at Patara, in Lykia, illustrates the mechanisms involved. Ti. Claudius Eudēmos left a

FIGURE 13.3. Bronze coin, Smyrna, bearing the legend "Antinoos, hero" on the obverse and "Polemōn dedicated to the Smyrnians" on the reverse. 39 mm. BnF Fonds général 2553. *RPC* 3.1975.

large sum of money to the city: the endowment, when invested, provided funds for extensive renovations and buildings in the city (in addition, they also paid for his honorific statue).[12] His wife, Claudia Anassa, funded an "eternal" gymnasiarchy; that is, left an endowment to meet the costs linked with the holding of that office. More modestly and hence more typically, the citizen of Lētē, M' Salarius Sabinus (above, pp. 11–12), offered 370 *denarii* for repairs to the *gymnasion*, as well as gifts to the citizens during feasts. The Pataran Ti. Claudius Eudēmos also gave six and a half drachmas to every citizen. The great benefactor of Smyrna (and celebrity rhetor) Polemōn probably offered distributions of cash to his city, in coins bearing the inscription "Polemōn dedicated (this) to the Smyrnians" (fig. 13.3).[13] We will revisit the case of M' Salarius Sabinus below, as an illustration of the practice of elite benefaction in return for civic honors, a development of the earlier practices.[14]

By this period, the term "honors" (*timai*) is often used to designate concrete statues, part of the honorific monuments that reshaped urban spaces. The *agora*, colonnaded streets, and piazzas of the small mountain city of Termēssos were dominated by multiple images of "celebrities" such as Atalantē, "daughter of Piaterabis, granddaughter of Pillakoas, great-granddaughter of Kinnounis, a widow, adorned with nobility and temperance (*sōphrosunē*), who has demonstrated every womanly quality, emulating by her exertions the accomplishments of her ancestors who frequently devoted themselves toward the *polis* with most conspicuous expenditures and in loans and in distributions and gifts and priesthoods."[15] The Anatolian names combine effortlessly with the civic language. Around the same time, at Patara, Ti. Claudius Eudēmos and his wife, Claudia Anassa, were honored with at least twenty-three statues throughout the city, in return for the benefactions mentioned above. The case of Opramoas of Rhodiapolis shows a benefactor as the direct beneficiary of significant urbanistic change. In the reign of Antoninus Pius, Opramoas, the great benefactor of the Lykian *poleis* and of the Lykian League (especially after an earthquake), was buried in a temple-like mausoleum in his hometown of Rhodiapolis, choking a plaza in front of the city's theater (and next to a stoa financed by him), on a terrace high above the *agora*. The tomb was covered on all four sides with sixty-four decrees, thirteen imperial letters, and nineteen letters from provincial governors, all in Opramoas's honor.[16]

When looking at monuments and statues, we are looking not just at inscriptions and monuments, but at people—wealthy men and women, their families extending vertically in time as well as horizontally through connections. Opramoas appears in the various documents in his honor as "son of Apollōnios son of Apollōnios son of Kalliadēs." At Oinoanda, the mausoleum built by one Licinnia Flavilla for her parents and ancestors, and taken over in the very early third century CE by her kinsman and heir Diogenēs, was covered (like Opramoas's mausoleum) with inscriptions on all four sides, tracing genealogies back over twelve generations.[17] The high visibility of elite women in the Greek provinces of the Roman empire is a reflection of the importance of women as a means to build genealogical connections between elite families.[18] The experience of encountering such families has led P. Thonemann to describe the history of small *poleis* of inland Karia as equivalent to that of single prominent families: the Carminii of Attouda, the Ulpii of Hērakleia under Salbakē.[19] In mainland Greece, we might likewise feel tempted to see the history of Messēnē as that of the Saithadai, or Sparta as that of the Euryklids.

Beyond families, we seem to be looking at a whole class. We know their faces, dress, and bodies, thanks to the well-preserved portrait statuary of the eastern provinces of the Roman empire.[20] Rather than trying to identify the individuals,[21] we can step back and take a good look at the genre and its implications. The high-quality marble *timai* (honorific statues) were sometimes financed out of the disposable surplus available to elite families. The fortunes of the civic elites in the Roman-era *poleis* continue and deepen the trend of wealth accumulation apparent in the second century BCE. Phenomena such as land ownership in multiple *poleis*, big estates administered by Roman-style managers (*oikonomoi, pragmateutai*), urban real estate, moneylending, and speculation on the price of grain attest the presence of a wealth elite in the Roman-era *polis*. Some scholars suspect changes in land tenure patterns, or even the wholesale destruction of the socioeconomic basis of the Classical-style *polis*, namely the existence of a middling class of smallholders.[22]

In addition to wealth, the statues show how poise and refinement were highly prized aspects of personal deportment. These traits appear in the biographies of star performers in the genre of rhetorical improvisation, which the biographer, the rhetor Philostratos, termed the "Second Sophistic."[23] The term described a specialized type of improvised performance, derived from Roman models of declamation (both in the genres and in the classicizing subject matter), and was practiced by very wealthy and eminent rhetors, often belonging to the Roman aristocracy: Hērōdēs Atticus was one such performer. This performative genre required lengthy rhetorical training, ease, competence within the Classical literary canon, and finally mastery of a carefully curated high literary dialect, namely Greek as written in fifth and fourth century BCE Athens.[24] But even without engaging in this highly specialized and competitive form, the elites of the cities across the whole of the Greek-speaking provinces of the Roman empire, prided themselves on literate education, rhetorical and philosophical. High culture, *paideia*, acted as a sign of distinction and prestige (as it had for the leading citizens of the *poleis* ca. 100 BCE).[25]

The wealthy claimed other aspects of the culture of the Greek cities. The legendary founders set up by Plancia Magna in the rebuilt city gate of Pergē (above) represented local history, culture, and identity, as did the heroes on the "Sebasteion" at Aphrodisias (on the south wing: figs. 12.1 and 12.2).[26] For Roman Greece, C. Dickenson has outlined, in the account of the antiquarian traveler Pausanias as well as in the documentary and archaeological record, a number of traits that reflect investment in the "heroic past": a sustained interest paid to heroic tombs (often invented or repurposed monuments) of figures from myth or from the prestigious, antiquarian-religious attention to bones and relics, and the practice of burying contemporary notables in heroic-style tombs within cities.[27] The city of Argos, with antiquarian monuments in its *agora* and a special category of honors "of Perseus and Hēraklēs" for benefactors, belongs to this trend.[28] Members of wealthy families claimed descent from historical or mythical figures. A notable in Roman Sparta claimed descent from Brasidas, the famous Spartan general of the fifth century BCE, just as Athenian grandees prided themselves on descent from luminaries of Classical Athens. Plutarch named one of his sons after Chairōn, the eponymous founder of his home city of Chairōneia.[29]

Foundation myths and invented traditions had long acted as an assertion of collective identity, as well as a means for interaction between cities; indeed, they continued to perform this dual role under the Roman empire, as one of the proxies for civic autonomy (above, pp. 327–28).[30] But the Roman Imperial *polis* saw elite families staking out claims upon this past, just as elite benefactors impacted public spaces.[31] Such claims are clearly related to elite interest in lineage and genealogy.[32] The politics of heroic ancestry in the city could be articulated explicitly. Some of Plutarch's friends claimed descent from the Boiotian hero Opheltas and, in virtue of this descent, "wanted to have more than others." Tellingly, Opheltas was a controversial figure, whose behavior was said to have led the Boiotians to condemn and renounce monarchy.[33] The bronze coinage struck by the cities (above, pp. 327–28) could be a vehicle for the celebration of members of the civic elites.[34] The religious activity of the Milesian Ti. Claudius Damas, twice prophet of the oracular shrine of Apollōn at Didyma, defender of the antique privileges of the priestly personnel, is reflected in the religious and antiquarian imagery of coinage struck under his supervision.[35]

FIGURE 13.4. Head from statue of priest of the imperial cult, Athenian Agora. S 3500. The preserved section of the head measures 35 cm; the small imperial busts in the crown, 5.3 cm.

Other claims were new. Many of the men and women shown in marble portraiture were Roman citizens, even if they usually eschewed representation with the Roman-style toga.[36] More generally, the styling of faces and hair is deeply influenced by fashions and models from the Roman metropolis and reflects conscious appartenance to a world empire. Some portraits show men wearing special crowns, decorated with multiple miniature imperial busts (fig. 13.4) linked with ruler cult and its festivities.[37]

Ideologically and institutionally, ruler cult was a way for communities to make sense of empire, negotiate their place within the Roman world, and proclaim their loyalty (above, pp. 326–27); but seen close up, sociologically, the ruler cult was associated with elite self-promotion, and hence elite claims about a hierarchical world-order binding together the godlike master of the world, the local notable and his community.[38] In the province of Asia and in Lykia, the extremely wealthy high priests of the provincial ruler cult often moved on to the ranks of the Roman upper class. At the level of the cities, cults for the emperors were celebrated by priests drawn from the elite, often serving for life. At Athens, an ancestor of Hērōdēs Atticus, Ti. Claudius Novius of Marathōn, was high priest of the imperial cult alongside other high offices of the *polis*. Similarly, the eminent citizen of Akraiphia, Epameinōndas, who represented the Boiotians in the pan-Achaian *Koinon* and was a benefactor of his city (above, p. 317), served as high priest of Nero and the *Sebastoi*.

The details of ruler cult had to be invented by individuals (often in collaboration with Roman officeholders) and provided the occasions for self-promotion by individuals and families. This is particularly clear at Aizanoi, where a family recorded on a private archive wall its initiatives in founding and expanding on imperial cult, and its direct contact with the Julio-Claudian dynasty.[39] At the same time, under Claudius, another family at Aizanoi financed cult for the *Theoi Homobōmoi Sebastoi*, the "Emperor gods who share the altars." This competition between elite families in coming up with initiatives for local imperial cult illustrates the way in which it allowed elites to display their connection with the world masters, and eminence in their own communities.

The marble faces of the elite ask to be seen as faces of power: in their thousands across the Greek-speaking provinces of the Roman empire, statues were accompanied by inscriptions listing offices and benefactions. Cocceianus Diōn of Prousa spoke of the elites' love of status (purple, public sacrifices) in the cities.[40] It is tempting to construct a model of elite entrenchment: in return for support from the Roman empire, local elites (it is to be supposed) fulfilled administrative functions for the empire and, as K. Hopkins claimed, shared the proceeds of rents and taxation.[41] One major issue here is how Roman Imperial–era elitism evolves out of earlier *polis* practices and institutions, namely the positioning of prestige and redistribution as part of the negotiation between mass and elite, within inclusive polities. Did these practices now function as instruments of the elite capture of *polis* institutions, discourses, and spaces, and as the celebration of elite rule in the cities? The answers to this question involve trying to discern the operation of civic politics beyond the glare of Roman-era elitism.

Stratified Polities?

For the dream-interpreter Artemidōros of Daldis, writing at the start of the third century CE, dreaming of statues usually designated one thing: the actions of the first men (*prōteuontes*) and the leaders (*hēgoumenoi*) of the city, the group that was usually honored with bronze honorific portraits. The presence of the powerful was obvious to the imperial-era dreamer. When a decree at Thespiai in Boiōtia was proposed by the "first men," there was no need to specify who these were.[42]

In some cities, restrictions were imposed on civic membership. Thus at Athens, an early first-century CE reform seems to have imposed membership of the fictitious kinship groups (genē) as a condition for citizenship.[43] The great Pamphylian city of Sidē may have had a privileged group of citizens with full voting rights, judging by the care with which, in the much smaller city of Karallia (in Kilikia), a Roman veteran is described as an "assembly-going citizen" (ekklēsiastikos poleitēs) in Sidē. Similar titles appear in other cities of southern Asia Minor.[44] A similar implication emerges from the mention of distributions to "those duly inscribed and those inhabiting the countryside" in Prousias on Hypios. It is possible that the increasing use of the ethnikon or mentions of citizenship inside cities and their territories indicates privileged statuses within the population.[45]

A particularly telling phenomenon is the civic ritual of distributions (dianomai).[46] In late second-century CE Sillyon, distributions of money and grain funded by a family of benefactors were given, in decreasing order, to councilors, elders, assembly-going citizens and their wives, simple citizens, an obscure group called the vindictarii, freedmen, and resident foreigners. In one distribution, the councilor received tenfold the amount reserved for the simple citizen.[47] The practice of distributions created privileged groups such as the five hundred "grain-dole recipients" (sitometroumenoi) of Oinoanda.[48] One hundred and fifty years later, in a festival similarly founded by an eminent Oinoandan lady, members of a privileged group of "five hundred" received ten denarii each, and members of the People (dēmotai) two denarii each.[49] The same concept appears at Delphi, where the city distributed lots of territory to its citizens: one share of forty plethra to each mere "man of the people" (dēmotēs), but one and a half shares to councilors and members of a privileged group of damiorgoi.[50]

The most privileged group was that of the councilors (bouleutai).[51] In the past, the democratic Councils of the Greek cities had operated with a scrupulous attention to the distribution of power (above, p. 342): renewed annually, chosen (often by lot) among the whole citizenry to ensure representation of the constituent civic subdivisions, compensated during their year's service to enable wide recruitment, the councilors operated within complex procedures to rotate responsibilities and power. In contrast, the evidence from the period of the Roman empire strongly suggests the widespread transformation of the Council into a closed body of permanent, lifetime members.[52] These made up a visible, definable group (the tagma bouleutikon): the Ephesian benefactor Vibius Salutaris was described as "our fellow citizen and a member of the Order of Councilors."[53] Such men enjoyed "bouleutic honors" such as those granted as a special dispensation upon the proposal of the "first men" to volunteers from Thespiai, fighting in one of M. Aurelius's wars.[54] The special honors for councilors (and magistrates), mentioned above, belong to this context. The development parallels the prominence of individual civic benefactors.[55]

A sign of the evolution is the occasional appearance, starting at the end of the second century CE, of "sons of councilors" (*patrobouloi*) as a defined group, young men assisting their councilor fathers and attending Council meetings as preparation for their future entry into the Council.[56] Without the status of councilor being formally hereditary, the institution of the *patrobouloi* indicates the widespread monopolization of access to the Council by wealthy families. Hence the description of a Xanthian notable as "a councilor from his ancestors onwards," *ek progonōn bouleutēs*.[57] Nor is this mere bluster: when family links can be traced (as in the abundant evidence from Patara), councilors in fact do descend from such ancestors.

Cocceianus Diōn's orations give a vivid sense of the masterful self-consciousness of the Council as leading element in the city, and the political competition surrounding the selection of councilors. The Roman governor of Bithynia, the younger Pliny, noted the desire of Bithynian elites to choose "the sons of honorable men rather than members of the common people" for the Council.[58] The same predilection can be seen in the spread of associations of elders (*gerousiai*), which evolved from a civic association to an official institution in the *polis* (though always keeping a strong ceremonial profile).[59] Similar dynamics can be seen at work in the reserving of certain offices to councilors (*archai bouleutikai* as opposed to *archai dēmotikai*) and the privileging of former magistrates as part of the order of councilors (*tagma bouleutikon kai archontikon*) during the third century CE.

The tendency was to create clear, formally enforced social barriers within the civic body. Hadrian, as a favor to two Ephesian sea captains, wrote to the magistrates and the Council of their home city to ask for their cooptation as councilors. The emperor undertook to pay their entrance fee if they should pass their review (*dokimasia*) and upon their "election" (*archairesia*).[60] The latter word had designated popular elections, but here probably was used for the selection by the Council and magistrates. The appropriation of the term in itself summarizes extension of elite power within the Greek cities under the Roman empire.

The shift in electoral practices and the introduction of entry fees to be paid by prospective councilors reflect the history of elite capture of institutions.[61] For instance, by the 60s CE, the city of Akmonia in Phrygia had a Council of Elders that admitted members upon payment of a fee.[62] The practice of entry fees is paralleled in the cities of the Roman West, notably in Italy, where curial elites exercised a stranglehold on institutional power. Some changes were clearly introduced in imitation of Roman practice, or even as the result of direct Roman intervention.[63] Roman attention to local constitutional arrangements went hand in hand with the first century BCE tightening of control (above, chapter 11). Already in 86 BCE, the settlement of Asia Minor by Sulla after the First Mithradatic War regulated matters relating to the holding of office.[64]

The clearest case is the set of rules (*Lex Pompeia*) imposed on the cities of Bithynia and Pontos when the region was reduced to provincial status by Pompey in 63 CE, and still operative nearly 180 years later when the younger Pliny governed the province. Here, access to the Council was defined as a lifetime appointment. Former magistrates were granted membership upon exit from office; membership of the Council was policed by special lifetime magistrates, patterned on Roman censors.[65] When Lykia was transformed into a Roman province in 43 CE, the Roman state reformed local institutions in favor of a wealthy elite, importing models and practices from the Roman West.[66] The ethos and praxis of Roman government favored local elites, as individual Roman governors openly stated.[67] The impact of these reforms can be seen both at the level of the federal organization of the new Roman province, and at the level of individual cities.

Thus institutional practice in second-century CE Oinoanda is patterned on Roman municipal law, at a level of detail that can only result from Roman intervention, the one-off "legislations" (*nomothesiai*) of Roman governors mentioned as binding models for new offices.[68] It is possible that similar provisions were imposed on the cities of the immense province of Galatia, formed under Augustus.[69] In addition, the Roman state probably fostered oligarchical institutions in new cities. A short-lived Augustan-era foundation in Mysia (above, p. 324) had appointed lifetime councilors.[70] It is all too tempting to suppose that these lifetime bodies now ruled their cities. A set of epigrams from Pergamon celebrates a local notable named Diōn (not the orator from Prousa): he "directed the city like a ship with his good advice," received an oracle from Delphic Apollōn promising him future commemoration and was "the Nestōr-like utterance of the Council."[71]

As for instigators or implementors of change, we might look to the members of the local elites, often enjoying close ties to Roman power, to which they paid ostentatious and self-promoting homage by holding priesthoods of the imperial cult (above, p. 341).[72] The Milesian "lawgiver" (*nomothetēs*) and high priest of the imperial cult, Ti. Iulius Dēmētrios, might have been responsible for oligarchizing reforms in his city in early first century CE.[73] Such men may have contributed to the diffusion of the new restrictive institutional *koinē*, especially since many enjoyed citizenship in multiple cities.[74] A son of C. Julius Dēmosthenēs, the benefactor of Oinoanda, was also a citizen of Patara in Lykia, where he set up a Council of Elders, an explicit example of the spread of the new institutions through the network of multiple elite involvements.[75]

This active participation of elites in institutional changes means that these were not simply impositions by the Roman state. They connected with shifts in the political culture of the *poleis* during the second and first centuries BCE (above, chapter 11). "I am aware, men of Tarsos, that it is the custom amongst you and amongst others for citizens to come up and give advice—not any citizens, but the prominent and the rich, and particularly those who have performed the *leitourgiai* well," said Cocceianus Diōn.[76] It is all too easy to interpret the "custom" as reflecting the dominance of the leitourgical principle, namely that members of the elite, as main contributors to public life, are entitled to rule.[77] Some members of the elite "performed all magistracies and liturgies," "spent generously on their magistracies," took on office, priesthoods "and all the other expenditures" (women and children could hence hold office by shouldering the financial burdens involved, often considerable, as in the case of the gymnasiarchy).[78] They promised gifts of money, or even buildings, in exchange for the honor of officeholding, worked their way through multiple civic offices, and held office repeatedly (*pleonakis*).[79] Such practices, already apparent in the Hellenistic period, grew widespread under the Roman empire: they constitute the broader world within which the elite entrenchment took place through institutional means.

The story is compelling, but perhaps not as clearcut as it might seem. Even in Bithynia, where civic life was shaped and recreated by the *Lex Pompeia*, the payment of entry fees by councilors was an exceptional measure, for admission of members outside the normal path of officeholding. In addition, there is no clear evidence for a formal censitary requirement for membership of the Council in the Bithynian cities, and the selection of "the sons of honorable folk" was an ideal that may have contrasted with the actual admission of nonelite members (as Pliny deplores).[80] Evidence for censitary requirements is overall surprisingly thin. When Cocceianus Diōn berates the Tarsians for allowing anyone to love them and be found worthy of the city for 500 drachmas, he is speaking of the old Hellenistic practice of selling citizenship, not of a censitary barrier (as has sometimes been claimed).[81] True, such barriers might have existed at Sillyon and Pōgla, with "assemblymen" distinct from the rest of the citizens, but this is likely a direct imposition by the Roman state during the provincialization of Galatia.[82] The hierarchical civic practices of third-century CE Pisidia or Lykia hence might be strongly localized and not a generalized norm. In addition, A. Heller has pointed out that inequal distributions seem to constitute shifting groups rather than reflect entrenched ones; that is, they perform distinction on a rotating and perhaps competitive basis (a phenomenon akin to the competitive *habitus* of the early *polis*?), alongside other forms of more egalitarian rituals in the old style.[83]

The rise of a western-style "curial" class in Asia Minor or Greece is difficult to substantiate. The title of "first men" of Thespiai and the bouleutic honors proposed for the young volunteers seem informal marks of status rather than legal privileges. Rotation rather than lifetime service on the Council continued at least in some *poleis* (it certainly did so in Roman Athens). That "councilor" is listed as a descriptor after a man's name does not necessarily imply a lifelong seat as opposed to occasional service on the Council.[84] Evidence is lacking for admission fees for the Council (and office-linked euergetism) in Macedonia, which suggests broader access to office than in a restricted model.[85] Most importantly, the Councils of the *poleis* of the Greek world retained their large numbers—600 is a frequently attested figure, and perhaps 1,500 at Ephesos—to the point of creating the need for further levels of distinction within the group of councilors.[86] This phenomenon reflects at least some degree of openness and broad recruitment.

It is vital, as we survey the tide of elite-centered phenomena, to notice their irregularity and diversity. Structurally, there were no entrenched aristocracies because of demographic patterns. Rich families died out or got diluted out of existence because of demographic overinsurance (in the form of multiple progeny breaking up property concentration). It is true that there are highly visible families over generations (such as the Vedii of Ephesos), or massively wealthy and active individuals at specific moments (such as Hērōdēs Atticus or Opramoas of Rhodiapolis), but such examples of temporary success are expected within a general context of constant demographic fragility and renewal among elites. At Sillyon, a woman held high office in the late second century CE as the last surviving member of a family that had prided itself on accumulating civic magistracies.[87]

Socially and economically, the civic elites but also the citizen bodies of the Roman-era *poleis* show widespread signs of diversity.[88] The grain riot at Prousa, in whose aftermath a young and brash Cocceianus Diōn gave an embattled, pugnacious speech, deserves attention because it complicates any simple picture of wealth and power in the city. Rather than the desperate uprising of a dispossessed urban poor faced with great landholders, the event seems to have unfolded across a complex social landscape of grain-growing estate owners, cash-cropping middling citizen farmers, and other types of wealthy elites, with competing interests negotiated politically in the Assembly.[89] Diōn's description of his own economic activity (vineyards, moneylending, suburban real estate) allows glimpses of the diversity and specialization that might underlie the conflict in Prousa. Diversity and the presence of smallholders are suggested by the spread and the type of epigraphical evidence from Bithynian cities such as Nikaia and Nikomēdeia, as well as Prousa. Elsewhere in Asia Minor, the professional associations attested in Thyateira (in Lydia) or in Hierapolis (in Phrygia) suggest well-established and prosperous artisans (even though the existence of such guilds might also indicate a lack of institutional power).[90] A similar picture of social diversity appears in several different regions: the Kibyratis, Central Lykia, or Karia. At Iasos, the spectrum of notables tapered off from great benefactors to middling landowners, all drawn from a variety of origins (including well-established Italian families).[91]

This diversity is reflected in the institutions of officeholding in the *poleis*. Rather than a single, monopolizable *locus* of political power, officeholding was widely distributed and collegiate—following the principles of the *poleis*'s institutional culture. The institutions of Oinoanda, as laid out in the dispositions for the festival founded by the benefactor C. Iulius Dēmosthenēs, are revealed to include a whole gamut of minor offices, none of which is known from the honorific inscriptions for great benefactors, but all of which must have been held by citizens of the *polis*.[92] The "first offices" mentioned in some cities imply the existence of exactly this sort of minor offices.[93] To dream of serving as secretary, town commissioner (*astynomos*), supervisor of education (*paidonomos*), supervisor of women (*gynaikonomos*), or market commissioner (*agoranomos*) announces nuisances, in the view of the dream interpreter Artemidoros ("it is impossible to serve as market commissioner without troubles, expenditures and blame"). Local officeholding was no sinecure.[94]

Because of the principle of collegiality, these offices required constant and widespread participation in the running of the *polis* as a communal project. Plutarch's treatise on local politics invited his reader not to spurn these activities, which perhaps did not necessarily demand full-time service from their participants and hence could be undertaken by individuals who did not enjoy elite leisure. Plutarch further admits that older citizens might refrain from routine officeholding and assembly interventions—which, again, implies younger, more active citizens involved in the normal operations of living as an active citizen in a *polis*.[95]

Offices in the urban center required participation across the citizen body, notably from the inhabitants of the countryside, as well as any "urban elites." This crucial factor has been emphasized in A. Heller's quantitative work on officeholders in the Roman-era *poleis*.[96] Heller's main finding, arising out of a massive and extensive survey of the epigraphical evidence in Roman Asia Minor, is that even if there existed families that repeatedly held office, most officeholders did not come from such families, but can rather be seen holding office once. The consequence is that officeholding was not monopolized by a small group of elites, and that the tempting equation of *polis* and leading family cannot quite be true. Heller's quantitative findings are confirmed by M. Bennett's observation that the eponyms on the bronze coinage of Roman Asia Minor are only rarely attested in the honorific epigraphy of the cities.[97] (In addition, it is likely that most coinage iconography was not influenced by the monetary officials' own preferences, or at most chosen by them out of a standard civic repertoire, a point that undercuts any supposed elite control of civic memory and imagery.)

These important quantitative findings can be illustrated by some examples. Among the rural notables of Central Lykia, some could serve repeatedly. One such man was Ermandyberis of Limyra, honored by his wife in his village, for repeatedly holding office in town: treasurer, *prytanis* during the celebration of a federal festival, official in charge of grain distributions, priest of the Emperors, *dekaprōtos* for twenty-five years, and "all the other offices and liturgies." In contrast, many others held occasional office. In Lykia, a man named Hierōn who served twice as village headman (*dēmarchos*, a rotating office) also held priesthoods in the city of Arykanda (incidentally a sign that the countryside was not necessarily occupied by disfranchised peasants). The same sort of activity appears in the case of a young villager from the edge of the territory of Pergē, who became a member of the *gerousia* in town and, for the privilege of serving as lifelong priest, paid that association 600 drachmas.[98] Apart from officeholding farmers, we find other "little big men" of the Roman-era *poleis*, craftsmen or merchants in magistracies or the Council: a painter, a slave-dealer, a purple-seller.[99] At an even less prosperous level, a poor citizen squatting on public land on the edges of civic territory (as imagined by Cocceianus Diōn for a Euboian city) might travel to town to participate in civic activities such as receiving a share in a distribution or taking part in a meeting of the Assembly (below).

Other avenues for access to office came from unexpected developments within elitist culture. "Eternal" offices held by very wealthy benefactors (such as Claudia Anassa, above, p. 337), grew out of iteration blurring into long officeholding, but ended up in the very practical form of endowed foundations whose income, disbursed in the name of the eternal officeholder, enabled wider participation in officeholding by meeting the costs of office. Such subsidies could widen access to offices such as the gymnasiarchy or the position of market commissioner, where personal expenditure for oil or grain was expected.[100] C. Iulius Dēmosthenēs's foundation at Oinoanda ensured that the official presiding over contests (*agōnothetēs*) would meet costs out of available income rather than as private benefactions. The measure closed off the possibilities of individual officeholders showing off their generosity but also freed officeholders from the pressure of personal expenditure as part of their duties.[101]

The evidence for social diversity among those running the *polis* invites us to look past the elitist glare of the honorific evidence. Some citizens were praised for promising benefactions to the city in return for election to office, holding multiple offices and eschewing their claims to compensation; others did not. When replying to city embassies, Roman emperors systematically reminded cities to pay travel expenses to ambassadors, unless they had waived reimbursement—the latter is often singled out for praise in the context of civic honors, which is a sure sign that we should not take such disinterested generosity for normal practice. The very fact of fulsome praise for constant, multiple, repeated officeholding and euergetical promises for office suggests that there were citizens who held office occasionally, in return for compensation, and without benefactions to their cities in the absence of any formal requirement to do so.[102] Cocceianus Diōn speaks, before the people of Nikomēdeia, of multiple avenues to acquire eminence and trust before the people: generosity, "flattery" (an old antidemocratic trope that here must mean the distribution of public goods as well as popular consultation), and wise philosophical advice. The tripartition is highly suggestive for the continuities in civic ideology, institutions, and practices.

You, the People: The Possibility and Practice of Democracy in the Roman Empire

In Roman Thessalonikē, at some point in the second or third century CE, an elaborate, multi-statue monument was set up for a benefactor and his family. "According to the decision of the Council, the fatherland (honored them)," runs the monumental inscription on the crowning element of the base (now kept in the garden of the Old Archaeological Museum of Thessaloniki, with no provenance). Council,

FIGURE 13.5. Marble base for multi-statue monument. Thessaloniki. Old Archaeological Museum / Yeni-Djami (*IG* 10.2.1.5 *1069, no inv. no.). "According to the decision of the Council and the People, the Fatherland (set up these statues)." Third century CE. L 210 m, H 30 cm, D 68 cm.

elite families: these are the familiar elements of the Roman-era *polis*. But the inscription was completed: carved on a molding, in much smaller letters, an addendum notes that the statues were set up by decision of the Council "... and of the People" (fig. 13.5), like the majority of honorific monuments from Roman Thessalonikē—as the outcome of a decision taken by both institutions.[103] We should not minimize the implications of this addendum: someone considered it important and considered that viewers might share this view. The *polis* in the Roman empire inherited not just the late second-century BCE elitist practices of status gradations and benefactor narratives, but also punctiliousness about constitutional procedure (above, chapter 11). We may assume that the complicated dialectic between elitism and constitutionalism was also one of the legacies of the late Hellenistic "Indian Summer." As we have seen, control over magistrates is even attested in decrees concerning the cult of the emperor,[104] in the familiar form of voluntary prosecutors enforcing laws and ensuring accountability.

The crucial detail about the earliest speech preserved among Cocceianus Diōn's speeches in his hometown (*patris*) Prousa (and indeed among his whole *oeuvre*) is not that it concerns a common grain riot, but that the aftermath of the riot was a special meeting of the Assembly. The solution mooted to face the crisis was institutional, namely the appointment of special commissioners over the market. Since these commissioners would unavoidably be called upon to contribute from their personal fortune to alleviate the frumentary crisis, the process had to be negotiated politically. The issue was the choice between exemption for those citizens who had already performed liturgies, and simply the most suitable candidates— namely, the richest.[105] The very existence of choice shows that there have been diverse proposals before the Assembly, and hence a lively debate during which Cocceianus Diōn himself has been impugned and called upon.

Specifically, the most likely sequence of events is the following. After the grain riot, the Council (recruited from the wealth elite) presented to the Assembly a preliminary motion (*probouleuma*) proposing the appointment of special commissioners but also exemption for those who had already served in *leitourgiai*. This motion from the Council was countered in the meeting by a citizen orator arguing for an unrestricted choice by the People (which would almost certainly tap the richest citizens, notwithstanding earlier financial burdens, on account of the present crisis and general need). The latter proposal might even be called demagogic: it reflected open debate in the Assembly and is predicated on the People's power to decide. The demagogic speaker proposed generalized burdens on the wealth elite, in order to promote the popular good without regard to the specific interests of the wealthy (they would have felt an understandable desire to avoid the double whammy of normal *leitourgiai* and service as special magistrates with many out-of-pocket costs). Cocceianus Diōn himself mentions demagogic politicians as "flatterers" in his survey of citizen speakers at Nikomēdeia (above, p. 348).

It is all the more remarkable to see such democratic practice in Bithynia, where Pompey imposed an oligarchizing constitution in 63 BCE. In spite of Roman intervention, Bithynian cities participated in a generalized *polis* culture where speakers in the Assembly could and did initiate proposals for deliberation and a participatory vote;[106] it is likely that the same held true for cities in Asia Minor and Greece, in spite of varying degrees of Roman interventionism. The importance of the Assembly is shown by the existence of a regular calendar of meetings, attested at Sardeis (where an honorific decree could not be passed for a magistrate in office, a rule that shows the survival of the punctilious constitutionalism of the Classical *polis*) or at Ephesos.[107]

Even if the Council or boards of magistrates usually put proposals to the Assembly, the People could directly order the Council or individual magistrates to consider matters or draft motions. The benefactress Lalla (ca. 150 CE) was honored by her home city of Tlōs, upon a motion drafted by the priest of the imperial cult— who had been commissioned to do so by the People's "shouting" during a meeting.[108] Cocceianus Diōn himself, while speaking before the Assembly, proposed "inviting" the Council to consider the individual promises of financial contributions toward his building projects: this can only mean *ad hoc* acclamations upon an informal motion by a speaker. Indeed, Cocceianus Diōn specifically mentions how "demagogues" do not hesitate to put proposals to the Assembly without passing through the Council (*aprobouleuta psēphismata*)—in contrast with a paradigm of good leadership embodied by Agamemnōn consulting the elders, as Homer portrayed in the *Iliad*.[109] The initial hearing of the martyr Pionios in the *agora* was cut short, lest it turn into an actual if unscheduled meeting of the People, complete with stormy "enquiry about bread."[110]

Indeed, in his narrative of an eventful meeting in a Euboian city, Cocceianus Diōn portrays several proposals by orators before the People. In real-world Prousa, the orator may himself have used a letter from the governor as the occasion to propose a motion in the Assembly about a building project in the city.[111] "Raving about the speaker's platform, while speaking or drafting proposals," was how Plutarch summarized the civic politician, alongside officeholding and embassies. The same Plutarch, in an elitist pamphlet on leadership in civic politics, recommends pressuring citizens to withdraw their proposals before they reach the Assembly, or rigging debates about proposals to try and control the agenda (on such maneuvers, see below, chapter 18). This projected informal power (whatever its reality or feasibility) in fact underlines the actual operation of democratic politics in the Assembly, and the absence of any formal elite control over proceedings.

Traces of anxiety about popular power appear in documents drafted by members of the elite when trying to control the fate of endowments they gifted to their cities. Thus the possibility of a proposal in the Assembly by a simple citizen (*idiōtēs*) was considered normal enough for second-century CE benefactors such as Vibius Salutaris of Ephesos or C. Iulius Dēmosthenēs of Oinoanda, in setting up festival endowments, to guard against the reallocation of funds by such avenues. The situation is itself typical of the inherent tension between state power, or even popular power, and the wishes of benefactors.[112] Indeed, an Aphrodisian notable took precautions, when leaving money to his city, to guard against public decision-making:[113]

> let it not be possible for anyone, neither magistrate, nor secretary, nor private individual, to divert, or transfer to another use, all or part of the capital or the interest, by directing matters individually through a vote or a decree (*psēphophoriai idiai suntassonti ē psēphismati*), or a letter, a decision, a registration or a riotous disturbance (*ochlikēs katabareōs*) . . .

The assimilation of demagogic policy and riot at least has the advantage of emphasizing a sense of the People's power in the political landscape of the *poleis* of the Roman empire.[114] As the statue base from second-century CE Thessalonikē reminds us, decisions by a *polis* were joint decisions by the Council and the People. Matters were ultimately decided by the People in deliberative meetings, as Cocceianus Diōn reminded the Assembly (when justifying the increasingly controversial building project he had proposed to the Prousans).[115] This seems to hold true down to the third century CE at least.[116] Decrees, when procedure can be traced, continue the tradition of constitutional punctiliousness that embodied the People's sovereignty and the rule of law—even in a simplified form, as can be seen in third-century CE Chalkis. There, a motion concerning a donation (and subsequent honors for the benefactor and his sons) obtained the Council's and the People's approval at the same meeting.[117] At Oinoanda, the whole dossier of decrees setting out the festival founded by the benefactor C. Julius Dēmosthenēs was given a final ratification by the Assembly.

Where the evidence is plentiful enough, we see that the Assembly met regularly, deliberated upon motions filtered by the Council but with some initiative and measure of control over the agenda, considered an ample spectrum of public business (albeit within the limits of Roman control and administration), managed its finances (including the minting of local bronze coinage, at times thanks to gifts by benefactors who petitioned for this honor),[118] enacted legislation, granted citizenship, voted honors, conducted diplomacy with the Roman state and with other *poleis*, and elected officials (even though the process was probably increasingly under the control of the Council).[119] The love of rhetoric typical of the age is less a sign of elite distinction expanding like an inert gas to smother public life, than a reflection of the necessity for persuasive and impressive speech before an alert, appreciative, empowered People. In the third-century CE, the rhetorical author Menander treats political rhetoric as a necessary skill to be deployed in real contexts of deliberation.[120]

These contexts were highly competitive.[121] The Assembly continued to grant honors and to judge claims to public recognition; it hence adjudicated in conflict between politicians. In spite of Plutarch's fantasy of elite collusion, competition before the Assembly led to the familiar all-or-nothing civic politics that were the corollary of "demagogy."[122] In the absence of a middle ground of compromise, political opponents were castigated for their bad character and intentions toward the commonwealth, and their lives scrutinized in public as an index of character. Cocceianus Diōn gives a lively portrait of the Assembly and its speakers in action, in his tale set in a Euboian city—and even more, in his own preserved speeches or fragments of political speeches,[123] where he attacks unnamed rivals as inherently inimical to the prosperity of Prousa, rejoicing in its woes, and bitterly opposed to himself because of his ambitious patriotism. Conversely, his own private life was exposed to criticism by political rivals. His long hair, fine purple clothes and beautiful house were castigated as signs of a tyrannical nature, and his rather messy financial affairs denounced as showing unfitness for public life and a comically flawed character.

Elite competition might also have taken place in another venue apart from the assembly, namely popular courts, in another continuity from the world of the Classical *polis*.[124] Such courts persisted (complete with jury pay) in Roman-era Rhodes, as noticed by Cocceianus Diōn.[125] The orator himself seems to have spoken in court in his home town of Prousa: he contrasts the shamelessness of those who attack the People from the very speaker's platform in the Assembly, with his own fate, impugned by his own rivals in a venue that is likely to be some form of civic court.[126] More directly, the Assembly sometimes also appears as a partner in judicial processes (formally led by the Council), for instance at Athens.[127] Lucius, the main character in Apuleius's novel *The Golden Ass*, finds nothing particularly surprising *per se* at being tried for murder by the Assembly in Hypata in second-century CE Greece, and he pleads vigorously, indeed melodramatically, for his life (the trial turns out to be a carnivalesque hoax, but Lucius did not find the proceedings suspect on institutional grounds). The same fate sometimes threatened Christians, since the *poleis* were a major tool for their persecution (above, p. 323).[128]

The composition of the Assembly and of the People it represented in the *poleis* of the Roman empire remains unknown. The sovereignty of the Assembly is not necessarily coterminous with the rule of the poor; the social question in the Greek provinces of the Roman empire adds another veil to the problem of the Greek *polis* as founded on the rule of a citizen body, however defined. Above, I drew attention to examples of a divide between urban citizenry and rural populations that seem not to have access to citizenship. Yet in other *poleis*, such as the Lykian cities mentioned above, rural communities were well integrated in the citizen body. Villages appear endowed with institutions and operating as civic subdivisions (for instance at Saittai, in Lydia, where village names were inscribed on theater seats).[129]

Overall, it is safe to say that the Assembly was neither subject to a crushingly small wealth elite, nor equivalent to it. Cocceianus Diōn spoke of "*polis* and People" in a single breath, to designate the regimes of Bithynia; the expression designates democracy.[130] When speaking before the Assembly, he gingerly deployed learned "Greek examples" (evoking "a man called Epameinōndas," "the famous Periklēs," "that famous Sōkratēs"): the audience members did not belong to a highly educated leisured elite.[131] The wide social composition of the People meant that it was always something bigger than the elite and its business; its interests were symbolized and embodied as the whole *polis*'s advantage, identity, and goods.

Shared Goods, the Common Interest and the *Polis* as Public Actor

Elite conflict, rivalry, and mutual recrimination played out in the Assembly around the notion of the public good, as seen in Cocceianus Diōn's extraordinarily vivid corpus of political speeches delivered in his home city of Prousa. The same principle moved the *polis* of Patara to honor one of its citizens in terms that emphasized service much more than personal qualities:[132]

> The Council and the People and the Elders of the Patarians honoured with the first and the second honours Iasōn, son of Dionysios, son of Dionysios, son of Xenoboulos, of Patara, excellent man by virtue of his ancestors, who provided many good things to the city, who served as priest of the emperors with piety and love of glory and great expenditure, who served twice as *prutanis* with love of honor and generosity, who served as treasurer with trustworthiness, who served as official in charge of security (*paraphylax*), who served as public purchaser of oil (*eleōnēs*), who also was commissioner in charge of public works and a humane member of the Commission of Ten guaranteeing the collection of taxes (*dekaprōtos*), who gave the city money for freedom from charges before the province, distinguished in all virtue and restraint (*pasēi aretēi kai sōphrosunēi*).

Honors constructed a civic elite, and defined eliteness in terms of the public good and the inherent greatness of the political community. These terms were accepted by wealthy and active citizens as the terms of their elite identity. Iasōn was almost certainly honored by Patara after he asked for recognition and listed his services in a speech before the city. The personification of the People as equivalent to the whole community (in visual form or in cult),[133] and the learned, mythologizing stories about foundation by heroes and gods, were other ways of expressing the collective bigness of the community, its primary nature and overriding claims to the devotion of its members. Hence the investment of the citizen body in disputes about titles or precedence.[134] For all of his oligarchical leanings, Plutarch agrees that the *polis* has more claims than any parent, on account of its antiquity and greatness.[135] The seamless combination of elitist and communitarian appears clearly in the celebration of a benefactor of Tralleis for holding office "gloriously and democratically," *endoxōs kai dēmokratikōs*.[136]

The existence of collective interests took the state-like form of an institutionalized public actor, as well as purely symbolical shapes. We have seen how the *polis* of Oinoanda scrutinized the festival, projected by and named after the benefactor C. Julius Dēmosthenēs. The *polis* tacked onto the original proposal a whole new set of rituals, involving the raising, parading, and sacrificing of oxen by civic subdivisions and villages in the civic territory. This addition shifted the tenor of the festival. The benefactor had planned a town-centered commemoration of his generosity and, characteristically, the hierarchical, elitist celebration of status; the *polis* managed to convert the project into an event mobilizing the whole territory, making visible the structuration of city and countryside which was such a vital part of the architecture of the *polis*, and insisting on the stake of villagers in the *polis*. That is, the *polis* intervened to make the festival a *polis* festival, of a type known in the late second century BCE (for instance at Bargylia, where the city funded the raising of oxen by civic subdivisions for a festival in honor of Artemis), and much earlier.[137]

In practice, the "public actor" took the form of the civic official, whose activism and stately character reaffirmed the primacy of collective interests. The (fictional) market commissioner at Hypata who punished an overcharging fishmonger by having his wares trampled publicly after their purchase by Lucius, the hero of a tale set in that city, did so with a proclamation of the city's majesty.[138] The comic side of the incident comes from the magistrate's gusto, the pettiness of the wares, and the contrast between the grand cliché of the *polis* as a site of justice and the situation of poor Lucius, who ends up without his fish (nor compensation for his loss). Justice and public-mindedness of good citizens are constantly praised in the Roman-era *polis*. The "democratic and magnificent" citizen of Tralleis mentioned above was also praised for defending the laws.

The description can be restricted to a mention of their fairness when in office, or explained at some length, as in the case of Q. Veranius Philagros, a good citizen of Kibyra:[139]

> The people honored Quintus Veranius Philagros, son of Trōilos, of the (Roman) tribe Clustumina, priest of Virtue (*Aretē*) for life, who went four times on embassy to the emperors to Rome, without compensation and with success con-

cerning the greatest matters, who served as public advocate for many great public affairs, out of which he provided enough money for the building (literally the founding, *ktismos*) of the city, and who won a hundred and seven public slaves and the estate K . . . a, and who was priest of Caesar Augustus and gave to the city over many years for distributions at feasts during the festival of the Kaisareia 54,000 Rhodian drachmas, and graciously forgave 100,000 Rhodian drachmas worth of debt for those which the People wanted, and who undid a great conspiracy which was greatly harming the *polis*; and, who, as the greatest of the matters obtained in his embassies, asked Tiberius Claudius Caesar to get rid of Tiberius Neikophoros, since the latter was extracting and taking 3,000 drachmas a year from the city, and to ensure that the sale of grain took place in the market place, at the rate of 75 *modii* for every *jugum* on the whole territory—for which services the city gave him the honours of the best man (*aristeus*).

This is not to say that all magistrates were just and conscientious defenders of public interests, and all members of the civic elite good citizens devoted to the public good. The "Granikeian Baths," a settlement in the immense territory of Kyzikos, endowed with hot springs and a market place, never received the periodical inspection of the city's market commissioner (leaving the local enslaved administrator to take over).[140] But what emerges from such stories of "running" rather than "ruling" the *polis*,[141] as seen in the long statue-base inscription for Quintus Veranius, is a set of norms about community, and the expectation that individual behavior, shaped by these norms, enables and gives shape to the "public actor" of the *polis*—both externally, in various proxies of autonomy, and internally, in affirming the presence of the *polis* and its collective interests.

As developed during the great convergence, ethical expectations imposed on citizens were especially reflected in economic gestures: benefactions, refraining from maximizing profit and self-interest in selling grain, and the individual assumption of public financial burdens. Indeed, the enslaved administrator of the Granikeian Baths organized the local landowners to provide donations, in a form of quasi-taxation, in order to provide public services. The landowners noted that the collective benefit was such that "they felt as if they were receiving rather than contributing"—a sentiment close to the interpretation proposed by D. Engels as the underlying secret to the economic success of the Roman-era *polis*: namely, collaborative restraint by public-minded, literally Stoic elites, to the benefit of the whole community including the elite individuals themselves.[142] The *polis* duly recognized the services of the administrator, providing a little narrative of the events at the Granikeian Baths, a narrative of the origins of political community itself.

The economic aspect of the power of the People appears much more directly in the works of Cocceianus Diōn. As already mentioned, the orator witnessed the Assembly of Prousa decree the setting up of a grain fund that benefited the whole civic population but undoubtedly was financed by contributions from rich citizens.

He personally organized, at personal cost in money and effort, a complex and protracted building project for his city, supposed to be funded by voluntary donations from fellow citizens. It is only by a slight exaggeration that he portrayed a speaker in his imaginary city's Assembly asking, point-blank, whether a citizen is willing to pay a talent to the city, on the mistaken assumption that he is not only rich, but has been withholding his wealth from the city and living off public land without paying rent, and that it is high time that he fulfilled his obligations toward his political community.[143] The incident is comical because the supposed "bad rich man" is in fact a poor, mountain-dwelling hunter, but the demagogic sentiments expressed would have been familiar to Cocceianus Diōn and his audience.

Public goods, in the city, were a concrete manifestation of the "public actor"— material goods that benefited collectively, but also reflected collective claims. Of course, the sources for these public goods included elite contributions. Grain funds (*sitōnika*) for the cities were an innovation of the *polis* under the Roman empire[144] but they must have been established by the same means as in the Hellenistic period—namely, semi-voluntary donations by wealthy citizens. Their frequency is a sign of the Roman-era *poleis*'s power to gather funds for common purposes. For the rich to dream of such schemes funded by a call for donations (*epidoseis*) announced ruin (a real prospect: Cocceianus Diōn's grandfather worked his way through two patrimonies to fulfil his duties, *eis philotimian*, literally "for the love of honor"). Similarly, to dream of office portended trouble and scrutiny—whereas to the poor, a dream of *epidoseis* announced abundance and wherewithal.[145] These donations are the descendants of the salary (*misthos*) once distributed by democratic cities, starting with Athens of the fifth century BCE, when the abundance of officeholding and the frequent, pay-generating naval cruises were a form of administrative and military Keynesianism.

However, in spite of the glare of elitism, it is clear that the Roman-era *polis*, just like the *polis* of the Hellenistic period, did not exclusively depend on the voluntary benefactions of the rich.[146] The *poleis* continued to raise their own taxes, especially indirect taxation on sales or transactions. The city of Oinoanda usually taxed the sale of cattle in town (it duly exempted the twenty-four oxen raised upon public mandate for the festival of the Dēmostheneia). Profit from transactions could range from the few hundreds of *denarii* raised at Hypata by fees for manumissions (shared between the city *gymnasion* and the public chest),[147] to very large sums in rich cities. At Ephesos, careful management by the "sophist" and local notable Ti. Flavius Damianos while holding high office (as "secretary of the People" at the apex of the Ephesian civic government) produced a surplus 127,816 *denarii*. These presumably came from the collection of indirect taxes and the levying of fees for stately functions offered by the *polis* of Ephesos, but might also represent public monies that were not spent when Damianos contributed his own funds.

Such income was produced by publicly owned assets. The *poleis* levied rent from publicly owned land, real estate, and facilities such as (remarkably) the municipal watermills owned and operated by the city of Beroia.[148] The glare of elitism should not blind us to the considerable importance and durability of such resources, pooled from many directions. The splendid "Library of Celsus," promised by one Roman magnate at Ephesos, was built by his son, but not quite finished. The important thing for our present argument is that the work had to be pursued by a local commission, managing the original foundation (and dipping into it), with financial assistance from Ephesian associations.[149] Institutions and civil society palliated the failings of elite giving.

Civic budgets allowed for the financing of public goods—monuments, festivals, cash distributions to citizens during these festivals, and compensation for public service.[150] These were the final materialization of the People's power in the *poleis*— created by a combination of public ownership and of collective claims on the fortunes of the wealthy, handled by the "public actor" of institutions and officeholders for the benefit of the People. "Shall we lose our own property?," shout the assemblymen of Prousa, interrupting Cocceianus Diōn's speech on some delicate financial matter involving officeholders, institutional regulation of the marketplace, elites, and the Roman governor.[151] When we see the Roman-era *polis* with its colonnaded streets and public buildings, what are we looking at? The People's answer was: its own goods, produced in the main by its own resources deployed for its advantage and in its image.[152] The picture is familiar, and echoes the practices of the *polis* as they emerged during the great convergence (above, chapter 10); under the Roman empire, they simply happened to be widely documented.

Polis and Politics in the Roman Empire

We have encountered two images of the Roman-era *polis*.[153] First, the city of wealthy elite families and their monuments, funded by their generosity and reflecting their eminence, values, and comfort. Then, we see "*polis* and People" exercising their power in the Assembly over the wealthy and extracting a share of elite surplus to lavishly finance public goods. The twin realities of elite power and people power paint a more complex picture than that of *de facto* elite domination and hierarchy under a façade of public-minded ideology.[154] Admittedly there is nothing inherently democratic about the notion of public good, public goods, public-mindedness, or the "bigness" of the public actor; the content and practical applications of this nexus of *polis* concepts had to be worked out in practice. These tensions were part of the condition of the *polis*, resulting from the embedding of elites in their communities and the link between elite status and community sanction; their presence is a sign of the way in which the story of the self-governing cities in the Greek provinces of the Roman empire is the continuation (and ultimately, the end-stage) of the story of the Greek *polis*.

Here the Roman state intervened: its reading of the forces in presence was simplificatory and decisive. One obvious explanation is fiscal and practical. The

Roman empire's primary aim was to preserve the viability of the cities as fiscal units feeding the empire's needs (above, p. 321). Taxation was collected by the cities: specifically, by local elites whose members, in colleges of ten or twenty men (*dekaprōtoi, eikosaprōtoi*),[155] were personally responsible for collection and transmittal of taxation revenue, and on occasion advanced in cash their community's tribute. The nameless Ephesian notable who went on such long journeys to defend his city's interests (above, p. 301) also served as a *dekaprōtos*; in smaller *poleis* such as the cities of Lykia, some went on serving in this capacity over decades.

However, the *dekaprōtoi* also illustrate the direction of Roman intervention at the local level. They took care of some elements of civic finances—managing the invested funds that were a crucial instrument in providing public goods, collecting taxes, and even advancing cash to cover certain civic taxes. A function created by the Roman state for its own fiscal needs also harnessed elite responsibility in local contexts, thus consolidating the principle of local *leitourgiai* imposed on the wealthy: the *dekaprōtoi* acted like the wealthy citizens who proffered cash advances (*proeisphora*) to cover special taxes in the Hellenistic cities. The *dekaprōteia* was a service that members of civic elites could promise to undertake (as the priests of Stratonikeia in Karia did); conversely, in 73 CE, a *dekaprōtos* in a city of Roman Macedonia obtained the office by promising a temple to Asklēpios, as if this was a civic magistracy or liturgy like any other. It appears often (for instance in Lykia) alongside other civic offices: "magistracies, prytanies, secretaryships, priesthoods of the Emperors, gymnasiarchies, treasurerships, police commanderships (*paraphulakiai*), curatorships, *dekaprōteiai*."[156]

The *dekaprōtoi* enjoyed status in their communities as a result of their responsibility in the literal sense of being able to provide security but also in the ideological sense of being trustworthy men of substance and property. In the Aegean island *poleis*, they appear as a group making proposals in the Assembly. But this responsibility did not directly translate into an institutional power base or solidify into the creation of an order; it resulted from the combination of the Roman state's enlisting of local elites with the *poleis*'s claims on these same elites. One Ephesian notable was honored for being *dekaprōtos* of Artemis's funds, at the local level, and *dekaprōtos* for the imperial tribute.[157] The pattern was a general one: the Roman embrace of the principle of services resting upon the rich included, indeterminately, services to the Roman empire and to the local communities, as formalized in Roman law during the third century CE.[158] The Roman empire further made sure not only that members of the elite shouldered financial and personal burdens, but also that they followed through with the promises (*epangeliai*), of benefactions in exchange for office or as standalone gifts, to the point that interest was due on unfulfilled promises.[159]

The *leitourgia*-system, as a meeting place of the Roman state's demands and the *poleis*'s traditional network of burdens placed upon the local elites, pinpoints the nature of Roman intervention in the constitutive debates of the *polis*. Rather than a conspiracy of powers (imperial state and local notables) to share the proceeds of rent,[160] the Roman empire appears as the interlocking collaboration of institutions—supralocal and local—to force local elites to make their surplus available with a view to feeding the empire but also to producing public goods at the level of the *poleis*. The effect was to limit the hijackability of *polis* institutions and goods. The Roman state took the ethos of the *polis* as seriously as the civic elites claimed to do. In enforcing *leitourgiai*, it compelled elite involvement in local communities. This spirit can be seen in the younger Pliny's scheme of forcibly loaning public monies out to citizens of the cities in his province of Bithynia with a view to generating public income. In this particular case, the emperor Trajan objected, but such a scheme might have been imposed for a while on the civic elite of the island *polis* of Andros.[161]

More generally, the Roman state further protected local finances and public property from encroachment and capture: "it is not right for public property to be held privately" was one of the principles enjoined upon the financial inspectors.[162] The Roman empire enforced accountability on those who handled public money (the emperor Antoninus Pius ordered the auditing of the former magistrates of Ephesos, including those deceased within ten years of his edict); it paid attention to the local collecting of public debts to the cities. The two operations were connected: the younger Pliny's efforts to recover public monies held by individuals in the cities of his province of Bithynia-Pontos arose from his mission to inspect local finances.[163] An inspection of the finances of Ephesian Artemis lead the governor Paullus Fabius Persicus to discover, and try to remedy, abuses by officeholders and the local elites.[164] Roman officials repressed repeated attempts on the part of the elites at creating tangible payoffs from the takeover of officeholding through *leitourgiai* and benefactions.[165]

A sense of elite burdens can be gained from Cocceianus Diōn's behavior. After initiating a building project in Prousa (to which he expected to contribute personally), he planned to retire from public affairs in order to concentrate on moneymaking to meet his costs. Likewise, the regulations for the festival set up by C. Iulius Dēmosthenēs at Oinoanda gave ample space for individuals involved in presidency to prepare for the burden, and shielded them from other offices.[166]

Faced with such costs, wealthy citizens might try to misappropriate public funds (as never-to-be-repaid loans or unaccounted-for project money);[167] they further might exploit office to produce favors for friends (for instance, in assigning lucrative contracts or duties such as remunerated embassies).[168] Public funds could be spent on amenities such as the *gymnasion* specifically to benefit the wealthy rather than the whole city.[169] Benefactors (such as Lalla of Tlōs) could keep the capital on their promised foundations, claiming to manage the sums as public money and paying fixed interest to the city—an operation that might have allowed wealthy citizens to use legal means to enforce the collection of their own loans (a perennial problem of moneylending elites).[170]

Another avenue for the recovery of the costs of elite power was increased rent-seeking (from landed property, speculation on staples, or money lending) in order to claw back the outlay on *leitourgiai* and benefactions. Here, too, civic elites met with limits imposed by the Roman state. In a measure directed against grain-hoarding and speculation, the emperor Claudius compelled the landowners of Kibyra to sell locally, in the city market, a fixed quantity of all grain grown in the *polis* territory. The measures applied (enforced sale) were drawn from Roman practice (comparable to the coercive purchase of oil at Athens, as laid down in a law imposed by Hadrian), but they came about as the result of local petition from the city (as conveyed in an embassy by the very active civic politician Q. Veranius Philagros: above, pp. 354–55), as part of a general effort to contain elite rent-seeking.[171] The values underwritten by the Roman state were thus those of the "public actor" with which it collaborated. When Hadrian banned the councilors of Athens from taking on tax-farming, the intention was to prevent self-dealing and the abuse of power, just as in the cities during the great convergence, magistrates were expected not to extend interest-bearing loans to the public treasury (above, pp. 249, 254) for obvious reasons of conflicts of interest.[172]

Such actions form the background to the claim, elaborated in the rhetorician Aelius Aristeidēs's tour-de-force encomium of Rome, that the Roman empire maintained social peace, notably by curbing the excesses of the rich.[173] The virtuous circle of the "good city" of publicly minded elites, deeply invested in the welfare of communities that exercised sovereign power over their members and their goods, was also the result of Roman intervention on one side of the balance of forces in presence in the *polis*. The result was the "beautiful city" of the Roman period, whose spectacular buildings we evoked at the start of this chapter (above, pp. 334–36). The monumentality of Roman Ephesos was the result of spectacular constructions by super-benefactors but also by a constant stream of *leitourgiai* and gifts by elite citizens—combined with the presence of the Roman governor of Asia, able to enforce *leitourgiai* and encourage elite disbursement toward public goods.[174]

Roman imperial control hence worked to slow down any oligarchizing developments of the leitourgical turn and the monopoly of office through wealth. Any purely fiscal interpretation of Roman administration is too limited, and the political culture and inheritance of the Roman state must have played a role in shaping its intervention. In the case of the regularizing and integrative pressures of empire from the first century CE onwards, two interlocking concepts are specifically relevant to the Roman state's attitude towards local communities. The first is its sense of public goods (*res publica*), as a reflection of popular sovereignty, embodied in ideology, official acts and even, at a formal level, the nature of the emperor's power: As F. Millar asseverates, "there is good evidence that the Roman emperors, as the inheritors of the powers of a *res publica* whose institutions still existed, did receive their powers through formal conferment by these institutions." The second concept is the continuity of local communities as self-governing city-states in the quasi-nation state constituted by the Roman Republic after the extension of franchise to the whole of Cispadane Italy; as such, their internal political and social order had to be preserved, in ways centered on the continuity of public goods.[175] In other words, the Roman state's intervention to preserve the local constitutional and political arrangements of the *polis* reflects multiple historical factors. The first was an imperial tendency to leave local cultures and polities as they were, as a condition for consent to empire and peaceful control. The second was the fiscal need to keep elites in a particular place where they were visible and subject to extraction, on terms that preserved local institutions. Finally, as just argued above, and most relevantly to the theme of the present chapter, a determinant role was played by the democratic tendencies of the Roman Republic. These were prolonged by the Roman empire's attitude of defending local political communities.[176] The result was the effective, if incomplete, protection of central elements of the democratic *polis* of the great convergence.

The Roman state powerfully affirmed the *polis* as a space of stateness and justice, both being manifestations of popular sovereignty. The latter already rested on a vigorous presence of the Assembly as the place of collective decision-making, delegation of authority, accountability for power held and public goods handled, and the honoring or punishing of individuals in highly competitive contexts—a package of traits inherited from the long history of the *polis* and sustained by elite buy-in (see above, chapter 10). The Roman state's willingness to intervene to curb elite power acted as a sufficient signal of its support for *polis* institutions and ideology. The resulting situation was a "tragedy of the elites": the very mechanisms for the capture of power by civic elites and their justification and legitimization tended to lock them into a situation of constant contributions to public goods and limited elite predation, within a context of democratic power underwritten by the supralocal state.

Political Life in the Roman-Era *Polis*: A Model

These parameters allow us to trace a model of political life in the Greek cities in the Roman empire, and the stakes around which its struggles were structured. Here again, the multivalence of the *leitourgia* came into play. As a sign of elite entitlement, it encouraged the wealthy in a sense of ownership over the public realm; as a marker of public claims on each individual citizen's wealth, it belonged to a political culture of intrusive accountability and scrutiny of elite behavior and character. In the Roman-era *poleis*, we can still clearly see mutual accountability enforced among the elites by the citizen politicians and officials; for instance, elite citizens policed each other while serving as *ekdikoi* (public advocates) acting to recover collective property through legal action,[177] or as magistrates intent on containing rent-seeking activities in the market. Civic politicians were put in the position of having to defect from collective elite interests (to defend these interests would have involved peaceful collusion in power, as Plutarch in his collection of *Political Precepts* wished wealthy, cultured citizens would engage in). Instead of collusion, notables engaged in harsh competition between them, a structural feature of *polis* life: they were reduced to attacking their social peers before the People in order to gain social capital and advantages.

Additionally, in our model, such behavior might in fact be considered as the prevention of other forms of defection, and hence as the convergence of elite interests and community functioning. Defaulting on *leitourgiai*, the diversion of public monies, the occupation of public property—these actions simply would have passed on to other members of the civic elites the defaulters' share of the burden of providing collective goods to the community, a duty to which the elites were committed on ideological, cultural, and structural grounds (namely in order to achieve advantages in political competition before the People). The pursuit and public denunciation of defaulters thus reinforced solidarity among the *leitourgia*-liable citizens, but also compliance with the social contract between rich and poor citizens around redistributed wealth producing public goods. Intra-elite competition further might ensure elite solidarity by preventing any single demagogic or euergetical figure from accumulating power; but, here too, elite competition further reinforced the power of the People, since its judgment would both provide the social capital for individuals to rise above their peers and the mechanisms to cut these individuals back to size in assembly politics.

In 18 CE, Tiberius's adopted son Germanicus traveled in the Greek-speaking provinces of the empire on a special mission: he is said to have "restored the provinces, exhausted by internal strife and the wrongs inflicted by magistrates."[178] The Roman state's intervention, for all its simplificatory pressures, was also complexifying; the resulting nuances of public life contributed to keeping the *polis* from falling into a death spiral of elite power working to strip away public goods. This political equation, partly familiar to us from the life of the *polis* in the aftermath of the great convergence (chapter 10), is portrayed imaginatively by Cocceianus Diōn in a Euboian city (*Oration* 7), where two speakers compete before the Assembly. One attacks, mistakenly if violently, the rustic, bewildered narrator of the tale of a visit to the city, as an antisocial rich man evading *leitourgia* and usurping public lands; the other defends the countryman, by directly challenging the first speaker, his political opponent. More darkly, a world of hatreds, dirty tricks, violence, and mistrust can be glimpsed in the dream life of the clients of Artemidōros of Daldis, and in the physiognomic advice proffered by the sophist Polemōn of Smyrna, no stranger to local civic life.[179]

Such sources illustrate the concrete existence, but also the price of the model of politics sketched out above. The most vivid confirmation is provided by the corpus of speeches delivered by Cocceianus Diōn at Prousa, completed by two letters of the contemporary governor of Bithynia, the younger Pliny. This body of material shows the philosopher-as-civic-politician caught in exactly the "tragedy of the elites" outlined above, and compelled, by the logic of the Roman-era *polis*, into a series of uneasily coexisting positions. When Cocceianus Diōn holds office, he defends public goods, attacks unnamed rivals, enforces accountability on the rich, chases public money in private hands, agitates to get elite financial commitments discharged, and generally protects individual members of the People as well as the People in general against elite acquisitiveness. But this behavior also exposes him to accusations of tyranny and highly personal attacks and character assassination (for instance, by dragging in his personal finances or his haughty lifestyle). In response, he is generally expected to maximize his legal advantage in political conflict (Diōn or another Prousan politician seem to have tried to have their opponent Flavius Archippos condemned to hard labor by the Roman state). As a rhetor in the Assembly, his philosophical stance becomes the demagogue's shtick—a past record and *doxa* of devotion to the *dēmos* and proof of his good character, as he prepares to set out arguments. In the specific guise of an embattled elite benefactor before the People, he promotes the interests and reputation of his class, defends his own interests by threatening to call in the governor to make sure other members of his donor class do not defect, and threatens to defect from the projected public project.

Finally, and most surprisingly, when Cocceianus Diōn ends up handling public money to build a monument (as a result of the building project that he championed before the Assembly, financed by his own startup donations pooled with other citizens'), he behaves as a rich man would, in maximizing his interests and his position—like many other wealthy Bithynians, he proves averse to accountability because he has put in his own funds, justifying his sense of ownership. Cocceianus Diōn went as far as to symbolically mark ownership by including within the public monument a private family tomb to his deceased wife and son. Ultimately, he had to be forced into rendering accounts by the intervention of the governor, the younger Pliny, after consultation with the emperor himself (in addition, the family tomb was close enough to the statue of the emperor to allow his enemies to accuse him of sacrilege, a vicious twist in the political conflict that also reflects the participation of local elites in an empire-wide monarchical culture).[180]

This model of civic politics is at odds with that one brilliantly and durably proposed for the post-Classical *polis* by P. Veyne (and followed, with variations, by subsequent scholars). For Veyne, *euergetism* was constituted by disinterested donations on the part of all-powerful elites who dominated their cities economically, politically, socially, and provided all public goods voluntarily. To our eyes, the various pillars of the untrammeled dominance of the *notables* are now far less obvious than it seemed to Veyne, and the elements of the model can no longer stand. Instead of entrenched civic landholding aristocracies dominating weak *poleis*, we notice the breadth and demographic fragility of the elites, the economic diversity of the cities, the persistence of institutional and ideological power wielded by the People's assembly, the realities of a considerable burden of redistributive policies enforced by elite competition and underwritten by the Roman state, and the abundance of public goods and resources. All these features made up the horizons of local civic politics in the Greek cities of the Roman empire. What, then, of euergetism, the activity of massive gift-giving (in the form of cash, endowments, gifts in kind, or building activity) that the great families engaged in?

It is clear that the opportunities of the Roman empire super-charged local benefactions, as practices by a highly resourced, imperially connected elite—for instance, the Roman senator from Athens, Hērōdēs Atticus (above, p. 335). But his case deserves close attention because (at least as told through multiple sources) it reveals the political economy of euergetism as a flight mechanism from the specific pressures of civic culture.[181] Philostratos recounts that Hērōdēs's father, the great benefactor (Ti. Claudius) Atticus, left a considerable foundation to be invested under the city's supervision in order to distribute the sum of "one *mna*" to every Athenian citizen in perpetuity. Hērōdēs himself convinced the Athenians to take a lump sum instead—but when individual citizens came to collect, far from disbursing the promised lump sum, he endeavored to show, by consulting his financial records, that they were each heavily in debt to him.

Having safeguarded his patrimony by this inspired piece of lawyering and accounting, Hērōdēs Atticus proceeded with his spectacular architectural benefactions to the city of Athens (above)—the marble Panathenaic *stadion*, the cedar-roofed *Ōdeion*—but on his own terms, unaccountably and personally, and therefore quite unlike the projected benefaction by his father, which would have placed funds into public ownership and administration for public distribution through institutional means. The *Ōdeion* was dedicated to the memory of his deceased wife Regilla; Hērōdēs himself was buried in a monumental tomb above the Panathenaic *stadion*, described in his epigram as his work: "Here lies Hērōdēs son of Attikos, of Marathōn—to him belong all these things—famous across the world." These buildings were part of a whole series of benefactions across Greece, in Boiōtia and Euboia as well as culturally prestigious locales—Delphi, Olympia, the Isthmos, Thermopylai.[182]

Euergetism offered spaces of flight from the local engagements and redistributive practices of civic culture. It performed as a model at the opposite of the leitourgical trap, based on the private practice of wealth; it claimed ownership of benefaction and its effects, and aimed at evading the constraints and accountability of *leitourgiai* and *epidoseis*. Hence the attractiveness of the imperial cult as the occasion for massive benefactions above routine elite contributions, linked with the prestige of the world monarch, and indeed often leading to high status in the form of membership of the imperial aristocracy and personal proximity to the emperor (above, p. 341). Hērōdēs Atticus laid claim to gratitude without accountability, redolent of an "Archaic" world of prestige and *charis*. A long epigram fondly imagines him communing directly with a grateful community coming out to welcome him in a formal ceremonial reminiscent of that deployed for the emperor or, earlier, for the Hellenistic kings.[183] The great families of Aphrodisias, so active in financing large-scale building in their city, or the most visible citizens of Iasos who offered repeated benefactions and went on long embassies without compensation, similarly kept aloof from officeholding and *leitourgiai* (the routine of which kept ticking along).[184]

But could euergetical expansion achieve escape velocity from the gravity of the *polis* model and its politics? As large-scale, noncompulsory generosity, euergetism was admittedly distinct from institutionalized and (semi-)compulsory elite contributions (*leitourgiai*, promises, *epidoseis*). Yet euergetism ultimately reflected the same ideology of engagement and devotion. The presence of virtuoso, large-scale voluntary benefactions, by the same actors or the same families over generations, maintained pressure on the rest of the elites to conform to the model of personal expenditure and of non-maximizing, supplementary generosity when dealing with the community. The activity in Ephesos of very big donors belonging to the Roman senatorial aristocracy influenced the local civic notables' behavior and kept them in line.

A more modest example than Hērōdēs Atticus might further illuminate the dynamics of euergetism. As we have seen at the start of this book, in the Macedonian *polis* of Lētē, one M' Salarius Sabinus (a rough contemporary of Hērōdēs) served as gymnasiarch and duly contributed funds for the repair of the *gymnasion* (the rather modest sum of 370 *denarii*) and cash for distribution at banquets; he also sold grain and foodstuffs below market price (*paraprasis*), especially when the city bought supplies for the Roman army. All these gestures (in addition to his activity as an official) were recorded when the city set up a statue of their "gymnasiarch and benefactor."[185] The city did not transfer the demands of the Roman state directly to its members, but drew on its own finances to purchase the supplies (thus respecting private property, as well as using the proceeds of common taxation to shield the poorer members); yet it depended on the collaboration of agricultural producers, especially the landowners in the rich plain of Lētē, to avoid inflation. M' Salarius Sabinus took the lead, keeping the prices low, hence helping the community constrain his peers—and gaining communal recognition above his peers. But why did the benefactor engage in euergetism? The answer embeds euergetism back into the frame of civic politics. Extra-institutional, supplementary generosity could give benefactors an advantage over political adversaries, hence reinforcing the inescapability of the whole leitourgical system, creating an inflation of benefactions mirroring the oft-noticed "inflation of honors," and embedding euergetism back into civic culture: this, too was part of the "tragedy of the elites."

The result of the embedding of *euergetai* was simply to expose them to public claims and processes. Cocceianus Diōn complains that the same Assembly that acclaimed benefactors as "nourishers" or "Olympians" of generosity could also howl in indignation when demanding public property or enforcing claims on defaulting donors.[186] Hērōdēs Atticus's claims to unaccountable generosity provoked constant and severe challenges during his whole life: the Panathenaic *stadion* was so named (it was claimed with bitter irony) because it was erected with funds truly belonging to all the Athenians, namely the despoiled legacy of Ti. Claudius Atticus that should have produced institutionalized public goods. Far from the harmonious concert of acclaim happily imagined in his welcoming poem, Hērōdēs 's life in Athens was marked by accusations of tyranny, multiple attacks and lawsuits by enemies, and the recruitment of personal enemies of his, the Quintilii brothers, to escalate proceedings to the level of the emperor himself (Hērōdēs unsuccessfully counterattacked with an accusation of conspiracy, and had to undergo a terrible, dramatic hearing before Marcus Aurelius at his winter headquarters of Sirmium).[187]

Even Hērōdēs's burial, seemingly a celebration of his exceptional status, was the result of a public claim: the *polis* granted him a public funeral, his bier was carried off by the ephebes and met publicly by crowds—against his personal wishes to be buried on his large, private, idiosyncratic estate at Marathōn, in a region where members of his household were already buried. As shown by other similar incidents, such enforced public honors belonged to the repertoire of collective claims on the person of elite citizens, imposing and framing recognition in communitarian terms.[188] So Hērōdēs was buried in a monumental tomb in the Panathenaic *stadion*, and seems to have received some form of heroic cult, as shown by an altar inscribed in a combination of archaizing spelling and grammatical punctiliousness, addressed to "Hērōdēs, Marathonian hero." Yet his name was subsequently erased, and the area of his tomb used for a low-status cemetery, hinting at rapidly shifting meanings of the monumental area. Even in the Panathenaic *stadion* , there was no clear and entrenched celebration of the power of an individual member of the civic elite, be it for as exceptional a figure as Hērōdēs Atticus.

The accusations against Hērōdēs Atticus, and the involvement of the Roman power, were not unique: his grandfather Hipparchos had ended in exile, his property forfeit to the emperor, on an accusation of tyranny.[189] At Ephesos, the notable Ti. Claudius Aristiōn, priest of the imperial cult (both at the city and the provincial level) and benefactor, was prosecuted by his enemies before the emperor Trajan (the younger Pliny happened to attend the hearing, where Aristiōn was judged to be "harmlessly popular"). After the ordeal and his exoneration, Aristiōn's euergetical activities continued unabated: he notably paid for fountain houses and an aqueduct, was a major contributor toward one of the city's bath complexes, and presided over the public commission that finished the "Library of Celsus" when (as we have seen) the super-benefactor's funds fell short.[190]

It is impossible to know how many other great benefactors were subject to the interconnected pressures of public accountability and elite competition—we mostly see such figures in their works, as in the case of the great families of Aphrodisias, and in honorific discourse. But the general context of civic politics suggests the communal entanglements that went with euergetism. The sophist Ti. Flavius Damianos appears in his biography by Philostratos as the builder of massive works at Ephesos (including a portico connecting the city with the shrine of Artemis); the bases of multiple honorific statues set up by civic groups for "this man, in all things incomparable," show him as a benefactor (promising a building in the Varian baths complex) but also as a leitourgist and generous magistrate.[191] The very large sums he recovered or transmitted to the public treasury during his tenure as secretary of the People might come from chasing down public monies in private hands. Damianos hence typifies the activities of publicly minded notables exercising their administrative and forensic talents against other notables to gain honor and recognition.

In other words, even the politics of euergetism merely reenacted the tensions of the elite *leitourgiai* above which it sought to rise, as an ironical *mise en abyme* of its dynamics. The "sophist" P. Anteius Antiochos of Aigeai, as we have seen, avoided assembly politics and officeholding, preferring to commune with Asklēpios in his shrine and offering unaccountable benefactions to the People;[192] all the same, he probably traveled to Argos on official business for his *polis*, with a mandate from his *polis*, and wrote a pamphlet, *Agora*, which might have been political in theme, on the civic life that he ostentatiously eschewed but could not escape.[193]

What do we see if we look past the initial glare of elitism that surrounds the *poleis* in the Roman empire? For all the modifications, simplifications, and developments brought about by Roman power, the political life of the Greek city-state remains recognizable from earlier times. Oligarchizing shifts and institutions (born of internal developments within *polis* culture as well as Roman intervention) coexisted with the strong, unyielding constraints of the democratic institutions, instruments and ideology inherited from the great convergence. The leitourgical trap, the tragedy of the elites, and the constant struggle of politics, acted as the meeting point of these tendencies. The upshot is that elitist claims can be seen as belonging to a repertoire of playacting determined by political institutions, dramatizing the stakes of redistribution, access, entitlement, and accountability. Both the elitist claims and the communitarian politics are familiar from earlier periods, but revealed through the diverse, fragmentary evidence of the Roman imperial period, in simplified forms and with stark clarity.

This model remains just that—a model: whether it seems reassuring, optimistic, or dark perhaps depends on one's starting point and political preferences (see further, chapter 20). At least it reintroduces conflict and instability (rather than simple elite entrenchment) in this chapter of the history of the Greek *polis*, as a sequence of long debates and conversations about politics. My simple contention here has been that the Roman-era city, with its colonnaded streets, great building works, and distributions of money, was not the result of a weak public sphere, but a reflection of the continued vitality of the *polis* as democratic form.

14

Cooptations, Prolongations, and Endings

> One did not need to be a Greek city to behave like one.
> —LUCINDA DIRVEN, "THE IMPERIAL CULT IN THE CITIES OF THE DECAPOLIS, CAESAREA MARITIMA AND PALMYRA. A NOTE ON THE DEVELOPMENT OF IMPERIAL CULTS IN THE ROMAN NEAR EAST"

The Roman Near East

The preceding two chapters have focused on a core geography of *polis*-hood, located in mainland Greece, the Aegean islands, the western and northern shores of the Black Sea, and Asia Minor. (Southern Italy and Sicily have dropped out of my story after the second or even the third centuries BCE.) Additionally, I occasionally adduced examples from the Levant and Near East. For instance, under the Roman empire, the organization of cities of Syria in a local league exemplifies (none too clearly) the modification of peer-polity institutions under the monarchy. My examination of the *polis* in the empire, but also of the empire as a world of *poleis* must now turn more squarely to these areas:[1] one of the questions is whether the cities of the Levant merely provide more exemplification, whether they show modifications to the basic model, or whether they reveal something about the close collusion between *polis* and Roman state. I will argue that the case of these cities gives an exceptionally clear sense of the impact of Roman state power on the *polis*, through its cooptation as an instrument of governance—a development that determined the fate of the *polis* as a political form, but also the shape taken by empire on the ground, in ways more legible than the imbrication of autonomy and empire seen in Asia Minor or Greece (chapter 12).

We find *poleis* in the Roman Near East, starting in northern Syria, as well as along the Levantine coast down to Gaza and also inland, in southern Syria and Palestine, including but not limited to the cities loosely called the "Ten Cities" (*Dekapolis*)—for instance, Skythopolis, Gerasa, or Kanatha.[2] This landscape was the result of a complex history of its own. Notably, it coincides with the extent of the Seleukid kingdom's control in the second century BCE. The area had been shaped by the late fourth- and third-century BCE foundation of Macedonian-style cities in northern Syria, their convergence with general *polis* norms, and the Hellenization of the Phoenician cities of the coast. In the late second century BCE, the area became a late Hellenistic badlands (above, p. 265), created by the decline of the Seleukid state and its conflict with rising local actors (the Hasmonean kingdom proved particularly successful among these post-Seleukid entities). In the mid-first century BCE, in a transformational event, the Roman state intervened to foster the reestablishment of Greek cities, notably those of the "Dekapolis."[3]

It is true that these *poleis* are not the only form of urbanism in this region. The late Hellenistic badlands had their own cities and monuments (below), often spectacular and distinctive. Later, the Roman empire imposed *coloniae*, settlements of Roman citizen veterans with a special status and their own institutions and indeed political culture. This took place on a vaster scale than in Greece and Asia Minor where we have already seen the phenomenon.[4] Berytos was founded on the site of an older Phoenician town, under Augustus, with military veterans, and remained strongly Roman throughout its history (as shown by its Latin inscriptions and coinage, and its famed schools of Roman law). Roman *coloniae* were founded at Ptolemais and Caesarea (the latter a rather Roman-looking or Romanizing city created by a client king, Herod the Great, recreated as *Colonia Prima Flavia Augusta Caesarea* by the emperor Vespasian): these foundations were linked to the military needs and administrative operations of the empire in the area of Judaea. Coins of Ptolemais bear legends in Latin and Roman motifs (the plowing that marked out the *colonia*; *vexilla*, flags of units detached from the legions).[5] The epigraphy of Caesarea is characteristically Latin and contains mentions of Roman institutions such as the decurions (rather than the Greek *boulē*), a *quaestor*, or a *haruspex*, a specifically Roman priest.[6]

The most striking example of such direct imposition of Roman urbanism in the region was the refoundation of Jerusalem (admittedly not a *polis*, but an oligarchically ruled temple-state) as the colony of Aelia Capitolina, after an unsuccessful Jewish revolt against the emperor Hadrian. Unlike Asia Minor or Greece, where colonies assimilated to the institutional practice of the *poleis*, the Roman colonies of the Near East kept their identity, and indeed offered a model for the Roman empire's dealings with the *poleis* of the Levant, in the late second and third centuries CE.

But these Roman cities and colonies existed as minorities within a broader world of *poleis*. Here I offer a survey of material forms, discourses, and, most importantly, the political practices implied by the latter, to illustrate how the cities in the Roman Near East prolong the normative forms of *polis*-hood, but within the nuances of local context.

FIGURE 14.1. Main colonnaded street, Apameia.

The Roman Near East as a World of *Poleis*

The cities of the Roman Near East generally adopted the style of monumental architecture and public ornament favored by the *poleis*, especially from the second century CE onwards.[7] The characteristic colonnaded avenue or *plateia*, "wide street," an essential element of this monumental style, may indeed have originated in the Levant.[8] The form is magnificently illustrated at Apameia in Syria (fig. 14.1): the main colonnaded road, 21 meters wide and fronted on both sides by 7-meter deep porticoes, crossed the city from north to south over 2 kilometers, the style of column varying (smooth, straight-fluted, spiral-fluted) from stretch to stretch.[9]

The archaeological remains of other "beautiful cities" abound in the region (excavated and reconstructed to varying degrees in modern times). If the Roman-era appearance of Antioch on the Orontes is poorly known because it lies under modern Antakya,[10] we can turn to Askalon and its sculpted pilasters from the rich sculptured ornament of a Severan period *bouleutērion*. Excavated from the sandy hillocks that cover the site, these offer a vision of Roman imperial ideology paralleled in other cities in the eastern provinces (fig. 14.2).[11] Such a "theater-shaped *bouleutērion*" is attested epigraphically at Kanatha in the Dekapolis (where a "sacred *plateia*" also appears).[12] The monumental shape of Kanatha is in fact visible in the modern settlement, mostly in the form of basalt buildings from the Severan

period: the *bouleutērion* complex but especially a terraced sacred ensemble with no less than four temples. Even more spectacular are the remains of other cities in the Dekapolis such as Skythopolis or Gerasa (fig. 14.3).

As elsewhere, monumentalization in the cities of the Roman Near East (often enjoying a long urban history before the Roman empire) can be interpreted as a proxy for *polis*-hood.[13] The monumental, often walled urban center acted as the focus for the processes of structuration that lay at the heart of the *polis*. The census of 6 CE, conducted by the Roman state, apparently found a population of 117,000 inhabitants for Apameia—which can only designate the whole population of a vast productive territory, in the middle Orontes valley, the modern Ghâb plain.[14] Antioch, as far as can be determined by literary and archaeological sources, controlled an expansive hinterland, stretching into the limestone hills to its north.[15]

Kanatha, in the foothills of the Hauranitis (modern Jabal al-'Arab / Djebel Druze) offers a particularly interesting and well-documented example.[16] It was the main urban settlement in a territory that included a mountain settlement such as Seeia (2.5 kilometers to the southeast), but also the lower country stretching westwards (fig. 14.4) where settlements such as Soada or Atheila benefited from building activity, especially to channel and distribute the waters from the mountain. Secondary settlements were

FIGURE 14.2. Sculpted marble pilaster; Victory alighting on a globe supported by a crouching Atlas. H 306 cm. Council-house, Askalon, ca. 200 CE.

FIGURE 14.3. The "Oval Piazza" at Gerasa. Drawing by W. D. Merrill, in Kraeling 1938, plan XV.

well equipped with monumental buildings, such as the temples at Seeia and Atheila, or the *nymphaeum* of Soada, dedicated by "the city," namely Kanatha.[17] A fragmentary dedication by this very "*polis* of the Kanathians" found at a nameless village (*kōmē*), the modern Kerak, 26 kilometers away, records public works under commissioners (*epimelētai*). They were certainly of the same type as those undertaken in other settlements, namely hydraulic distribution or religious building activity.

In the same village, an individual made a dedication to "Zeus Greatest, of Kanat(h)a."[18] The appartenance of the settlements to a civic entity structured around Kanatha was made clear by the remarkably active pattern of unifying gestures that criss-crossed the territory. The Soadans regularly trooped to celebrate a

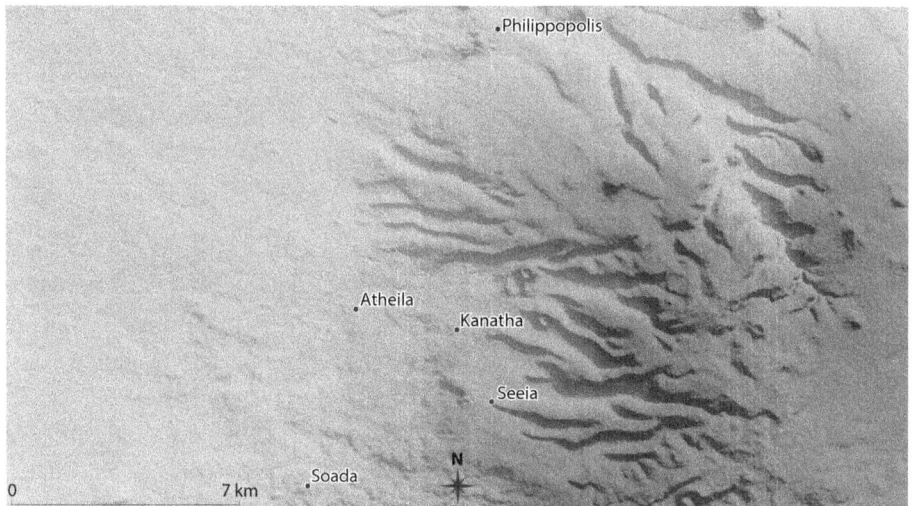

FIGURE 14.4. The territories of Kanatha and Soada. After Sartre 1981.

festival at an extra-urban shrine (complete with sacred grove) near Kanatha (at modern Dmeir es-Semeij), as recorded at the shrine, perhaps one of a calendar of collective pilgrimages and celebrations of villages around a central place.[19] Such transactions and relations reflect the constant problems and dynamics of urban center and rural territory.

The sense of belonging was expressed individually as well. A dedication was set up in a neighboring city of the Hauran by a "Sēnos Kanōthēnos," a Seeian from Kanatha. Much, much further afield, a merchant, Thaimos (nicknamed Ioulianos), buried by the river Saône near Lugdunum in Gaul, was described in his verse epitaph in Greek as "by birth a virtuous and kind man of Atheila," but also specifically as "a citizen and councillor of Kanotha near (?) Syria." The gravestone further bore a Latin epitaph, whose precise description of Atheila confirms its status as a village (*vicus*).[20]

Such phenomena of integration clearly parallel the situation in Asia Minor, as in the case of the festival of the Dēmostheneia at Oinoanda, where the villages contributed to and participated in the great sacrificial rituals (above, p. 354). As in Asia Minor or in Greece, territorial structuration raises questions about the distribution of power within the borders of the *poleis*. Some evidence (mostly from later periods, the fourth century CE and beyond) suggests large landholding and exploitation of tenants, notably around Antioch; but in the same area, evidence for prosperous villages (with monumental shrines in Greek style) implies smallholders with their own resources, organically integrated within the economic system of the city-state.[21] As in Asia Minor, village institutions, as seen in public epigraphy, mirrored the civic culture of the *polis* and suggest integration within the structures of citizenship.

The "mother-village" (*mētrokōmē*) of the Thelsēnoi, in the territory of Damaskos, had political institutions of its own (and presumably occupied a place in a local hierarchy of villages); the villages of the Hauran produced inscriptions in Greek, attesting "communal structures closely modelled on those of Greek cities."[22] These phenomena show the ubiquity of the *polis* model of common decision-taking, and the capacity of the inhabitants of the countryside to act collectively within the framework of *polis* territorial integration.

Territorial structuration into units made up of monumentalized urban center and rural hinterland created the familar network of cellular peer polities.[23] As in Asia Minor or Greece, civic autonomy was manifested by frontiers, monumentality, and local coinage (mostly bronze), which referred to local cults and legends (and hence fictitious descent as a shared collective identity).[24] The city of Sidon produced coins that notably bore the figure of Europe on the bull (as noted by the satirist Lucian);[25] the third-century CE coinage of Tyre refers to mythical episodes and connections (Kadmos teaching letters to the Greeks; Dido founding Carthage).[26] Even small cities like Balaneia, on the north Syrian coast,[27] or Kanatha[28] could produce local bronze coinage. Balaneian coinage figured a female figure wearing a turreted crown, the personification of the Fortune (*Tychē*) of a city (the statue was offered by a citizen in explicit recognition of the city's autonomy). A similar figure appears on the coinage of Kanatha under Claudius. The rare coinage of Apameia bears the name of its citizens in the plural (as normal), but coupled with an adjective in the feminine singular, as befits the corporate identity of the city: "Of the Apameians, the (city that is) holy and inviolate" (*Apameōn tēs hieras kai asylou*).[29] The adjectives constitute a religious-honorific title: as in Asia Minor, one way for peer polities to exercise agency was competition for honorific titles. Tyre and Berytos competed for the title of mother-city (*mētropolis*) of their region, Phoenicia (a subprovince of Syria, then a province in its own right), down to the fourth century CE at least, just as Antioch and Laodikeia did in their own subregion, northern Syria.[30]

As for other *poleis*, such forms of competition are themselves about mutual recognition. Skythopolis styled itself as "the city of the Nysaians, also called Skythopolitai (a city that is) holy and inviolate, among the Greek cities of *Koilē Syria*."[31] The built forms of the Roman-era "beautiful city" help construct a network of peers across the region or indeed the world of *poleis*: Apameia, Gerasa, Skythopolis, let alone Askalon or Kanatha, were noticeable because of their built ornament but also simply mid-range *poleis* among their peers.

In the context of competitive peer-polities, lettered men fulfilled the cultural needs of the cities by deploying literary panache and antiquarian learning, amidst festivals and other civic occasions for performance. Some local talents went on to world fame, such as Lucian, from the east Syrian city of Samosata.[32] Others would benefit their communities by serving on embassies, filling the archetypal role of the local notable which we have seen for the cities of other eastern regions of the Roman empire (above, chapters 10 to 13).

As already mentioned, the local leagues, as well as the pan-Syrian *koinon*, celebrated the imperial cult within a structure that mirrored the administrative structures of the Roman empire (above, pp. 316–18): agency and peer-polity interaction were subsumed within the manifestations of empire. Here, too, local bronze coinage bore the portrait of the reigning emperor. From the reign of the emperor Claudius, the citizens of Apameia became "Klaudieis Apameis," to which the place-name of "Antōninoupolis" was added under Caracalla, a century and a half later.[33] Likewise, Balaneia changed its name and its coins were minted not as those of the "Balaneōtai" but of "the Klaudieis, also known as Leukadioi," a sign of refoundation in honor of the ruler (and of complicated local rearrangements).[34]

In the Levant as elswhere, the Roman state intervened easily to reshape *polis* life. It reduced the extensive territory of Kanatha by elevating Soada to *polis* status.[35] A special envoy of Hadrian, P. Pactumeius Clemens, "settled" the accounts of the cities of the whole province of Syria, just as he did for cities in Greece and in Kilikia. At a more local level, a *logistēs*, one Claudius Agrippa, appointed by the emperor over the finances of a single city, Kanatha, approved the use of its financial resources for reconstruction work.[36] The city of Skythopolis, when honoring the reigning emperor Caracalla, simply called him "the lord" (*ton kurion*), in recognition of the power of the Roman emperor.

As for the internal processes in the *polis* of the Roman Near East, we can revisit the great colonnade at Apameia (fig. 14.1). Behind the colonnade lay the bath building (*thermai*) erected and dedicated on behalf of the emperor Trajan's well-being by the local super-benefactor L. Julius Agrippa.[37] The dedicatory inscription mentions that he bought the land, and not only the baths, but also "the basilica within them, the portico in front of them as well as the decoration and bronzework within them." The bathhouse was further the setting for honorific statues by individuals and groups celebrating the individual benefactor, as a private space of eminence; we have seen such spaces elsewhere, for instance at Oinoanda (above, p. 338).

L. Julius Agrippa was clearly an exceptional figure, intervening in exceptional times, namely the need for rebuilding after an earthquake. He styles himself, and is described by his city, as enjoying "royal honors," and descent from local dynasts: his style is a throwback to the great benefactors of the first century BCE, in its insistence on his capacity to fill royal-like roles and on his personal status as friend of the Roman people. This was a status inherited from his great-grandfather, one Dexandros, a friend of Augustus, first priest of the imperial cult in the province and benefactor of Apameia. The "royal honors" might indicate how L. Julius Agrippa's ancestors stepped in to fill the void left by royal subsidies and benefactions, as Menippos had done in his city of Kolophōn ca. 100 BCE (above, p. 281).

Yet in the Roman Near East, just as in other parts of the world of *poleis,* we see simpler offerings by officeholders and benefactors, such as the men paying for single columns at a shrine at Kanatha, donors giving the same shrine a gift of 500 *denarii*,[38] or the magistrates disbursing fixed sums of 1,500 *denarii* at Gerasa for building work dedicated to the imperial house and the concord of the people.[39] Such offerings reflect institutionalized pressures on citizens of means. Instead of claiming his exemptions, L. Julius Agrippa fulfilled *leitourgiai*, paying for various services and budget items; he further performed embassies to Rome, held office as market commissioner (when he paid a cash gift toward grain, and contributed several miles' worth of the building of an aqueduct) and served as secretary of the city for the exceptional term of a year (alongside a commission whose members he selected).

The pattern of generosities and officeholding (and during officeholding) is entirely characteristic of *polis* life in the Roman empire. The *leitourgiai*, enforced by the Roman state, continued into the fourth century CE when they are an important theme in Libanios's orations. The normal institutions of magistracies and Council are widely attested[40]—for instance in the tiny documentary dossier of honorific inscriptions from Balaneiai, or at Kanatha (the donor who paid toward the cost of the *ōdeion* did so while presiding over the city council), or again at Gerasa.[41] The exact details of constitutional arrangements are even more obscure than in Asia Minor, but attested figures of 600-strong Councils indicate broad recruitment, comparable to practice in the Aegean zone.[42]

From Gerasa, dedications to the imperial house and to the harmony of the People (*hē tou dēmou Homonoia*) hint at a civic politics of conflict and reconciliation.[43] An episode of conflict left traces in the apparently routine dedication of a public registry-house at Kanatha, set up for the safety of the emperor Hadrian during the year-long service of the market commissioner (*agoranomos*) and under the supervision of a multimember commission.[44] All the elements belong to the register of institutional workings, but one name was carefully chiseled out—the mark of conflict and condemnation (we could imagine a case of mishandling of public funds or failure to deliver on a promise, comparable to the cases alluded to in the speeches of Cocceianus Diōn).

It remains difficult to see the People, in the sense of the mass of nonelite citizens, in the cities of the Roman Levant—even more so than in the cities of Greece or Asia Minor.[45] A fragmentary mention of a *[dēmo]tikon sunedrion* (popular council) at Apameia remains unexplained and isolated. But what is clear is the presence of a public actor, the *polis*, as an expression of collective will that cannot be reduced to elite individuals and families, that has considerable economic resources of its own, and that wields the ideological and institutional power to impose certain types of public duties on its elites. Here too, the "beautiful cities" are the result of that political and social dynamic. The noticeable prosperity of Roman Syria might be linked to a successful balancing act—between city and countryside, and different social groups (elite and nonelite)—comparable to that of the *polis* in other regions in the Eastern part of the Roman empire (above, p. 355, drawing on the suggestive work of D. Engels).[46]

The picture given above is composite—just like the picture for the *polis* in the Aegean spaces and the eastern Mediterranean generally. It inscribes the history of the cities in the broader story of the Greek city-state in the Roman empire, as part of a picture of political communities that were, for reasons of path dependency and historical contingency, pluralist rather than merely elitist. A single document such as the honorific inscription set up at Athens by the city of "Tripolis in Phoenicia" in enough to show a whole package of open civic institutions, corporate identity, and involvement with a network of cities within a world empire.[47] I have examined several urban sites as taxonomic test cases for that story: Apameia, its colonnade and its benefactors; Balaneiai, its coins and its magistrates; Gerasa, its urban décor and the political turbulence that appears in the epigraphical evidence. Kanatha especially offers a multi-faceted image of a *polis* in its structured territorial geography of villages, monumental urban site, institutional environment, civic and religious identity, and its combination of elitist behavior with social diversity among the benefactors. These are all traits of *polis* life; it is hence at least possible that public life in Kanatha was completed by other traits such as *leitourgiai*, accountability, wide power sharing, and participation in decision-making.[48]

Yet Kanatha deserves more discussion. For sure, it can be adduced as an example of *polis* history, belonging to a world of *poleis* stretching from the Adriatic to Gaza. But it also is located rather far inland in its basalt mountain, in an Aramaic-speaking world with its own history—including a record of sustained encounters with the transformative presence of the Roman state. Such encounters are the theme of F. Millar's epochal *Roman Near East* (1993), a social and cultural history of the impact of empire.

The Aramaic-language inscriptions in the great shrine at Seeia, in the territory of Kanatha, and its complex basalt architecture drawing on Near Eastern models, act as a reminder of this history.[49] The earliest inscription, a bilingual Greek-Aramaic stele from 109 BCE, commemorated a priest "introducing" (probably in a procession) Baalshamim, Isis, Malakelaha and another deity whose name is now lost. The Roman-era pantheon of Kanatha included an Arabian god, Theandrios (also named "the god of Rabbos"), honored in an extra-urban shrine, and Athēna Gozmaiē, distinguished by her non-Greek epithet.[50] In the Roman Near East, the history of the *polis* is a specific phenomenon taking place not only in the coastal zone, but also in eastern Syria, Palestine, and Roman "Arabia." Writing *polis* history here means pondering the relationship of institutional forms with underlying cultural and social realities. Did the latter inflect the forms taken by the *polis*? What did the *polis* look like in Aramaic? Did *polis* institutions affect local societies in the Roman Near East? Such questions can be approached through the case of Palmyra, in the eastern Syrian steppe.[51]

Palmyra, *Polis*

In 137 CE, the Council of the Palmyrenes voted a decision (*dogma*) that had force of law, concerning the collection of indirect taxes in the city including customs dues on imported wares.[52] The document illustrates the character of Palmyra as a *polis*. Within its boundaries (*horia*), the *polis* exercises sovereignty: it taxes all

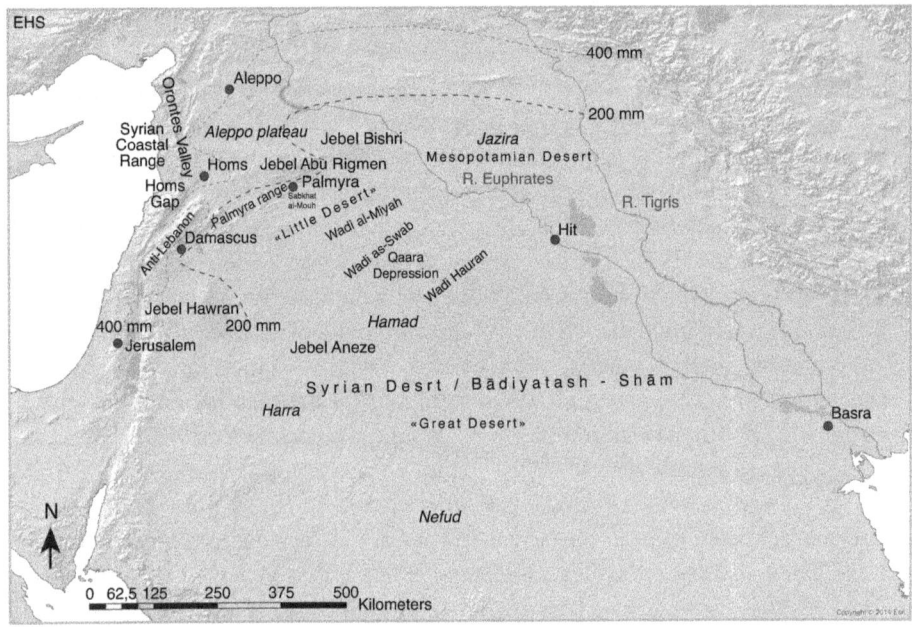

FIGURE 14.5. Palmyra in its geographical context. Map by E. Seland.

imports and exports into the city, if aimed at commerce, but exempts transactions involving the villages in its territory, as stakeholders in the community dependent on the circulation of goods but not deriving profit from it. On the same principle, inhabitants of the territory did not pay pasturing fees for using the commons.

The territory of Palmyra, including the well-watered highlands in its northern part (fig. 14.5),[53] received significant public investment in infrastructure, just as Kanatha's territory was structured by waterworks, roads, and shrines. In 198 CE, the city honored the "general" (*stratēgos*) Aelius Boras for keeping the peace "within the boundaries of the *polis*," which might mean the whole territory rather than just the urban center.[54] The territory was the setting for an agricultural festival in a fertile low-lying plain, 22 kilometers northeast of the city. The festival day (March 21, on the spring solstice day) is recorded on three (or four) monumental altars, set up at public expense and under the supervision of financial officials, by the *polis* to a deity called "Zeus Highest and Favourable" in Greek and "His-name-is-blessed" in Aramaic. The altars are carved with reliefs showing respectively a hand holding out a sheaf of wheat, a hand holding a tree, and an offering table.[55]

In the Customs Law, the *polis*'s statelike power is shown by the very terms in which the law is expressed as an embodiment of the *polis*'s force to intervene within its own space:

whereas in earlier times, most of the dues were not entered in the law on customs, but exacted by custom, since it was stipulated in the tax-farming document that the tax farmer should levy the dues in accordance to the law and to custom, and it frequently happened that disputes arose in this matter between the merchants and the tax farmers, be it resolved: that the magistrates in office and the *dekaprōtoi* shall determine the dues not entered in the law, and write them into the next tax-farming document.

The reaction of civic authorities implementing decisions by officeholders and involving various forms of public writing, illustrates the central concerns of the *polis* (above, chapter 5 for examples at the start of the history of the *polis*). Palmyra taxed profitable activities: the import or export of goods for sale, hay, and windfalls ("since there is trade in them"), the selling of clothes by street vendors, prostitutes, and workshops in the city's "bazaar" or retail center (*pantopōleion*). It further levied fees for the use of public goods, namely the commercial use of the two springs within the city. Disputes concerning the implementation of the law were to be adjudicated by officeholders, namely the *dekaprōtoi*, the board of financial officials, and the *syndikoi*, the city's advocates defending public interests—familiar to us from the cities of Roman Greece and Asia Minor.

Another example of the statelike presence of the *polis* in the economic realm is the existence of an *archeion*, literally the magistrates' office where official acts were kept, but by extension designating an office where private acts were officialized and registered for a fee, by the authority of the *polis* (as at Kanatha, or indeed other *poleis*). The *archeion* itself is named as an institution having the power to decide on the enforcement of the clauses in a private act.[56] The city's authority was backed up by its own military forces, just as cities of Asia Minor kept armed guards, or cities of Greece occasionally responded to threats by mobilizing their citizenry (above, pp. 323, 332).

Palmyra was a city of the Roman empire since the very early first century CE. Manifestations of local agency were deeply interwoven with imperial *fiat*. As can be seen in the text of the Customs Law, the full name of the *polis* is *Hadrianē Palmyra* (*Hadriana Tadmor* in the Aramaic), in memory of a visit and patronage by Hadrian, so that the citizens were *Hadrianoi Palmyrēnoi*. The city's precious two springs were officially the "Springs of the Waters of Aelius Caesar," named after Hadrian's adoptive son. The Customs Law combines the decree of 137 CE with an older, multilayered dispensation that cited Roman authoritative pronouncements as a substantive source of law. Hence the law preserves undigested pronouncements in the first-person singular ("I have edicted," "I have shown") going back to a Roman governor; it refers to decisions, taken in the first century CE by a member of the imperial house, Germanicus Caesar, and a governor, Cn. Domitius Corbulo. A particular tax in the new law is a calque of imperial practice, namely a tax collected by "Kilix, Caesar's freedman"; that is, a freedman *procurator* (manager) intervening within the city to collect taxes, just as a freedman *procurator* had interfered with the finances of Aizanoi in Asia Minor (above, p. 320).[57]

Palmyra belonged to the Roman province of Syria: it is hence unsurprising to see two other manifestations of Roman power, namely a *logistēs* or auditor of the city's finances,[58] and imperial cult offered in recognition to the emperor's all-powerful reach.[59] A local notable, Rabbelos son of Waballath, combined his office as symposiarch of the priests of Bel with a priesthood of the emperors and set up statues of the emperors Marcus Aurelius and Lucius Verus, given their official titles but also the simple appellation "the lords." The monument included a letter from the emperors, confirming (as a "gift") the city's right to offer twice-daily sacrifices to the emperors. The transaction illustrates the Roman state's control of local finances as well as the diplomatic functions of ruler cult.[60] The inscription for a statue of the emperor Hadrian, set up by a Palmyrene in the shrine of Bel, perhaps echoes public cult in speaking of "Imperator Caesar Nerva Traianus Hadrianus Augustus, master of the world and benefactor of the city."[61]

Without giving a full purview of institutions, the Customs Law of Palmyra calls upon many of the offices held in the city:[62] the *prohedria* or rotating presidency of the Council (probably of a smaller committee of *sunedroi*), the secretariat of the Council and the People, the eponymous magistrates, the public advocates, and the *dekaprōtoi* (strictly speaking a *leitourgia* rather than office, fulfilled by men underwriting various items of public finance: above, pp. 353–58). We thus have a sense of an institutional structure, but also of the revenues from indirect taxation and from semi-voluntary levies on elite surplus. A member of the Palmyrene elite of the early third century CE, Julius Aurelius Malichos, received testimonies "from the god, the Council and the most illustrious governor" for fulfilling the office of market commissioner (*agoranomos*) brilliantly, along with his father, who had "accomplished all the *leitourgiai*." Another *agoranomos* was honored for "saving great expenditure" for the city—in other words, for paying official outlays out of pocket rather than drawing on public funds (we have seen the "sophist" and benefactor Ti. Flavius Damianos probably doing the same at Ephesos—one example among many: pp. 356, 366–67).[63]

Malichos was honored with multiple statues in the *Tetradeios*, the four-sided *agora* that acted as an honorific and representational space (next to a commercial open space where the Customs Law was set up). Honorific statues from the *agora* commemorate officeholding, such as the gymnasiarchy and the *agoranomia*, as well as service as *proedroi* and *sunedroi*, the same offices that appear in the Customs Law. In contrast, honorific monuments set on consoles on the shaft of columns in the city's shrines and in its colonnaded streets celebrate the free-form benefactions of great donors independently from most forms of officeholding or *leitourgiai*. Malēs, nicknamed Agrippa, was honored by the Council and the People for serving as secretary when the emperor Hadrian visited, providing anointment oil for citizens and foreigners alike, and building "the temple of Zeus with its entrance and its other porticoes."[64] In 175 CE, another shrine, the great temple of Bel at the eastern end of the city, received six gilt bronze doors from two benefactors, the cousins Yarhibol and Awida, "generous in many affairs."[65]

At Palmyra, as elsewhere, we should peer beyond the glare of elitism generated by great benefactors, their virtuoso displays of gift-giving, and their families, in order to perceive diversity—between great givers and dutiful magistrates, but also within the social elite, as carefully studied by J.-B. Yon. The diverse social landscape included, besides a few super-benefactors, a distributed plethora of small office-holders, *leitourgoi*, occasional benefactors (including donors of cash gifts to the Council) and more modest donors (offering a few or even a single column for a street, comparable to the small donors at Kanatha). At the more modest level, benefactors engaged in much jockeying to achieve distinction, notably through the dedication of private honorific statues in shrines. The social landscape stands free of the imprint of any lastingly dominant families. In the funerary realm, the same picture emerges of a complex landscape combining very rich families (entombed in towering monuments) with middling families, in competing patterns of display, evolving taste, and pragmatic constraints.

It is true that at Palmyra as elsewhere, the People is harder to see than the elites. But political activities presumably took place before the People, when the latter passed decrees by voting on motions. Honorific statues were duly set up by the Council and the People, as the inscriptions record: that is, after a motion from the Council to the People.[66] The Customs Law was passed by the Council as an administrative measure of the sort that other *poleis* (even Classical democratic ones) could leave to the competences of the Council. Likewise, the frequent presence of honorific monuments set up by the Council alone are merely the manifestation of its corporate existence within the *polis* rather than the sign of the Council's political dominance. The Council's corporate identity appears in the clay tokens (perhaps tickets for gatherings or even feasts of councilors) showing the Council (*bwl'* in Aramaic transcription) personified as a female figure casting her vote in an urn.[67]

The Customs Law gives a sense of an active urban economy involving craftsmen and traders, and more generally of a division of labor (including enslaved labor). It also hints at a populous countryside of producers around the city. Rural producers and a diverse urban population may have made up the People when it met in assembly to vote decrees. Estimates of population for the urban settlement and the territory range into the five figures, and hence would support a citizen population, urban and rural, in the thousands, comparable to other *poleis* in the eastern provinces of the Roman empire.[68]

A trace of local politics may be read in the plan of the city itself (fig. 14.6), where the path of the long colonnaded main street had to take into account preexisting buildings, such as the shrine modern scholars assign to the deity Nabu. Though the new street itself was rerouted to avoid bisecting the shrine, it still passed over the entrance zone to the shrine's precinct, which had recently been remodeled to

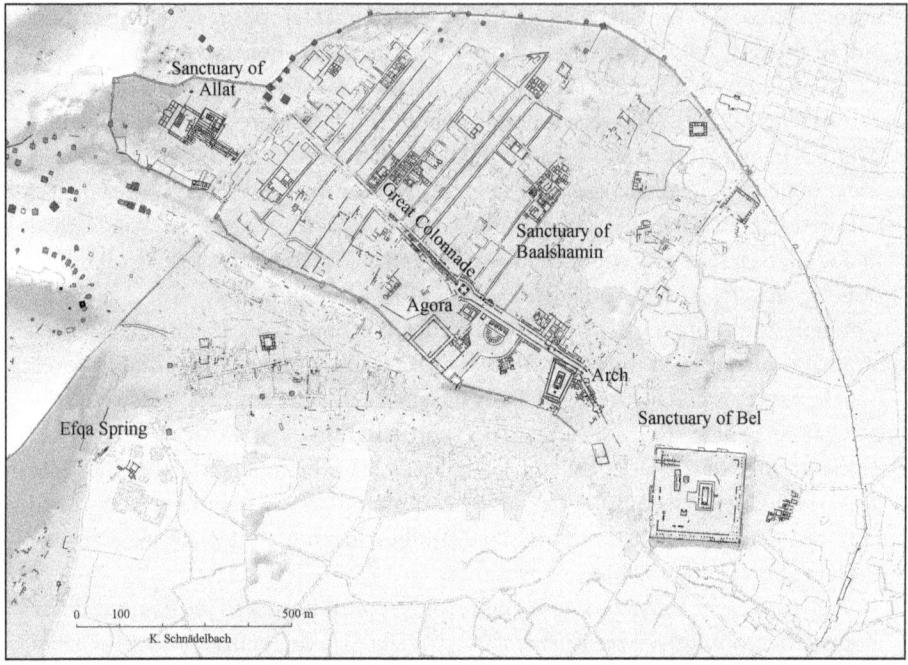

FIGURE 14.6. Plan of urban center, Palmyra. Plan by K. Schnädelbach.

face northwards: the shrine's new monumental gateway was demolished and replaced with a side entrance.[69] This outcome must have occurred after political conflict and negotiations between various constituencies, including elite families that had patronized the shrines. The whole piecemeal urbanization of the Roman-era city must have involved negotiations and conflicts of exactly the type documented in Cocceianus Diōn's speeches in his hometown of Prousa.

As in other Roman-era *poleis*, the Palmyrene "Great Colonnade" offers a concrete image of the *polis* community as an overarching power or public actor: disparate interests and ambiguous outcomes were subsumed and unified within the ethos of the *polis* as communal project.[70] The same ethos appears in the city's honorific culture, manifested in its statuescape.[71] The *agora* alone had over 200 honorific statues (fig. 14.7). Many of those were the bronze statues mentioned in the Customs Law as an import into the city, and only survive in tiny fragments because of the reuse of the metal. Others were in marble, and sufficiently large fragments survive to allow us to look at the faces of elite citizens from Palmyra. The fragments, but also a funerary painting representing such statues, show that the portraits were executed in the style and idiom developed for the Roman-era *poleis*, drawing on older models for the citizens' dress, the *himation* and restrained body stance. The inscriptions accompanying the statues celebrated the honorands' communitarian virtues of piety, generosity and love of *polis*.[72]

COOPTATIONS, PROLONGATIONS AND ENDINGS 383

FIGURE 14.7. The *agora* of Palmyra and its statues. Reconstruction by Thibaut Fournet (in Delplace and Denzter-Feydy 2005, 116).

Palmyra was a self-aware political community. In the precinct of the city's greatest temple, that of the god Bel, during the second century CE the city re-erected on column consoles statues that dated to a much earlier time, when the political community was coming together. One was the statue of Ḥašaš son of Neša, set by two groups "since he made peace between them," in November 21 CE; the other, the statue of Mokeimos son of Ogeilos, honored in March 51 CE by "the city of the Palmyrenians" or the "community of all the Tadmorians" in Aramaic (*gbl Tdmory' klhn,* a rare and soon superseded expression), since he had "pleased the city and the gods" and given various implements to the shrine.[73] Both texts show the city's sense of its own history and its desire to preserve and monumentalize this history within the context of the changing urbanism of the "beautiful city" so characteristic of the second-century CE Roman empire.

The "sons of Komare" and the "sons of Matthabol," reconciled by Ḥašaš, appear in the city as part of the four civic subdivisions or "tribes" (*phulai* in Greek): in second-century CE Palmyra (as in all other *poleis*) these tribes seem to be creations of the *polis*, with a territorial basis taking over or subsuming older civic groupings, and endowed their own cults and shrines. The civic community was hence structured by subdivisions, as in other *poleis*;[74] especially important benefactors were honored both by the city, and by the four tribes, thus offering a vision of the city in its constituent parts, upon an order (*prostagmati*) from the overarching institutions of the city, the Council, and People.[75] Such a performance of community is paralleled elsewhere in the Roman empire, for instance at Ephesos by the honors for P. Vedius Antoninus III.[76]

In the religious sphere, public cult and rituals celebrated at the level of the subdivisions as well as the whole community, made visible *polis* solidarity and integration.[77] Associations of priests were part of the network of civic sociability in Palmyra, just as for other *poleis* (below, chapter 15). Among these ritual activities, the Palmyrenes held public feasts, as documented in clay tickets for admission: some for limited associations or groups (such as the Council itself), others likely for larger admission, and involving free distribution of foodstuffs such as wine, financed out of public funds or donations.[78]

Palmyra, for all its geographical distance from the *poleis* of the Levant, appears as a particularly well-documented *polis*. In fact, Palmyra is simply the best-documented *polis* of the Roman Near East. Exploring Palmyrene epigraphy reinforces and extends the impression of normalcy that emerges from northern Syria and Phoenicia. This observation might seem paradoxical, when seen in the broader context of the cultural history of Palmyra, where the temptation has been to insist on the "eastern" nature of the city. Such an interpretation is echoed in popular representations of the city as "the Venice of the Sands," this pearl of the desert, the irreplaceable treasure, a place of exotic "wonders."[79] The recent devastation of the site and its modern museum has contributed to enshrining the sense of Palmyra as an exotic wonderland (in 2015 the terrorists of ISIS/Daesh executed the head of antiquities at Palmyra, Khaled al-Asaad, and proceeded to blow up the temple of Bel, the temple of Belshamim, and several great funerary monuments of the ancient Palmyrene elite).

Palmyra, of course, had its specificities. It was a *polis* whose temples combined, in very distinctive style, classical architectural ornament with traits such as an entrance on the long side (rather than the short), a flat roof, towers and stairs on the corners of the main body—for instance on the temple of Bel. Such temples were the privileged recipients of donations from individuals.[80] It was further a *polis* in an oasis, surrounded by steppe land, graced with camels (attested along with donkeys in the Customs Law). Finally, most noticeably and uniquely in the Roman Near East, Palmyra was a *polis* written in Greek and in Aramaic (as mentioned sporadically above): the Customs Law is known both through a Greek and an Aramaic copy, and the honorific inscriptions are, similarly, bilingual artifacts of a bilingual *polis*.[81]

The strangeness that transpires from the funerary portraits from Palmyra, with their fixed, frontal pose, staring eyes, and often embroidered clothing (fig. 14.8),[82] or from the Aramaic honorific inscriptions under the Greek, might foster the claim that Palmyra was not a "*polis*," but (say) a tribal society structured by clan hierarchies and clientage, and with *polis* elements operating as a veneer, or instrumentalized for the original non-Greek society's needs; or as a hybrid entity, combining the Roman, the Greek and the local, in a highly specific ecological niche between

FIGURE 14.8. Funerary relief, Palmyra. 181 CE. Limestone. H 51.8 cm, W 44.8 cm.

highlands, oasis, steppe, and long-distance connectivity.[83] Such claims, however, should be laid aside.

It is certainly true that even the epigraphical evidence from the *agora* offers an image of diversity beyond the interactions of *polis* life.[84] If roughly one third of the statue inscriptions from the *agora* reflect civic culture, another third refer to the ineluctable presence of the Roman state (in the form of soldiers from units stationed in the city or its territory, provincial officers, and emperors),[85] and the remaining inscriptions are set up to honor rich Palmyrenes who led or financed caravan expeditions across the steppe to trade in lower Mesopotamia or even beyond, to India (reached by boat over the "Skythian sea"). This long-distance trade played a vital part in the economic prosperity of Palmyra (and indeed in the economic life of the whole Roman empire).[86]

Yet the caravan inscriptions, for all of the exoticism of their subject matter, are a clear case of civic discourse in action: they reintegrate within a civic frame actors of a particular non-*polis* space of hierarchy and money—the caravanners, the caravan-leaders, the military escorts. The merchants issued honors in the normal, ethicized forms of personal devotion and willingness to subordinate economic self-interest to common interests. Indeed, the *polis* itself honored caravan leaders for their actions as good citizens on the same terms, recognizing the importance of the social transactions of the caravanners but prolonging and validating their recasing in civic terms. N. Andrade observed that the honorific discourse reframed faraway actions and events "as the exemplary deeds of citizens done on behalf of a *polis* and it situated competition for prestige, elite rivalries, and inter-familial contests before an audience of citizens that exercised judgment."[87] The *polis* form was adopted locally, within the framework of Palmyrene practice (such as the importance of the caravan trade for economic and social life), but the discourse of *politeia* (civility) shaped and transformed and indeed constituted the Palmyrene community: the *polis*, in its institutions, recognized and honored a good citizen (*agathon poleitēn*) such as Abgaros, son of Patroklos, in 84 CE.[88]

The Aramaic expressions for the political organs of the city-state are calques from the Greek: *bwl,' dms* (replacing the earlier Aramaic term *gbl*), for the Council (*Boulē*) and the People (*Dēmos*). The description of the good citizen as *philopolis* in Greek is literally translated as "who loves his city" (*rḥym mdynth*); the institution of epigraphical honors, though couched in Aramaic (statues are set up *lyqrh*, "for his honor," translating *teimēs heneken*, "for the sake of honor" in Greek, and replacing the earlier formula *lḥyyh*, "for his/her life"), was a new genre, created by the citizens of Palmyra to allow them to fulfil a central function in the political economy of the city-state between community and individuals, mass and elite.[89]

The public bilingualism of the *polis*, as much as an expression of local identity through institutional forms, might also have had the function of making those forms more widely legible, and hence encouraging the vital breadth of participation in them, especially in the absence of the deep Hellenization of the population, including the rural inhabitants of the villages, that is suggested by the epigraphical record for the "*polis*-land" of northern Syria or the Hauran. The presence of Aramaic inscriptions in the rural highlands north of Palmyra, as well as the use of the language by Palmyrene soldiers abroad, attest to a literate population that could read the *polis* in Aramaic.

Furthermore, the richly diverse artistic and material culture of Palmyra can be viewed as that of a *polis*, in which the public monumental architecture, the sacred buildings and reliefs, and the honorific statues in Greek dress are balanced against the traces of highly ornate private housing and the abundant funerary art: such tensions are part of *polis* life.[90] The funerary art, exhibiting local specificities separate from the Hellenized and Romanized surfaces of public life, exactly fits in the dialectic workings of *polis* culture in negotiating the dialectic between public and private, between family, individual, and community, and between the multiple horizons of the city.[91] The reclining, feasting figures wearing embroidered tight-fitting riding clothes coexist with himation-wearing male figures that allude to public life and good citizenship, and the world of the trans-steppic caravan trade was itself taken into account in the civic sphere. The priestly pillbox felt hat on some male funerary portraits manifests the deceased man's piety, his status—and also the communal engagement of his family, since priestly office involved public service and indeed the payment of a fee to the city, comparable to the *summa honoraria* familiar from other *poleis*.[92] The emergence of crowns and wreaths, on their own or as part of the priestly hat, possibly refers to public honors in return for institutionalized service. Palmyrene funerary imagery should be viewed as *polis* art, just as in the case of other well-documented bodies of funerary imagery from city-states with strong public spheres.[93] In contrast, the city of Hatra, at the other end of the Syrian steppe, in its public architecture, its funerary reliefs of armed men, and its displays of domination by a ruling class, looks markedly different from the *polis*-inflected institutions and material culture of Palmyra.[94]

Palmyrene specificities can be viewed as part of the continuum of *polis* history, rather than the sign of hybridity. The fluidities and specificities of its religious life do not need to represent a body of practices or notions foreign to the *polis* and its public life. Its bilingualism is reminiscent of (admittedly much shorter-lived) phases when Anatolian cities expressed themselves publicly in Greek but also in Karian or in Lykian. Its reluctance to engage in normal forms of peer-polity interaction such as the assertion of local cults and identity in bronze coinage or the celebration of athletic contests, are possibilities within the spectrum of *polis* behavior (just as the *poleis* of the islands did not celebrate such contests during the Roman period). Such variations are to be expected within the system of *poleis* and part of the process of diffusion of *polis* forms alongside the unity of civic institutions, whose transformational effect can be seen in the epigraphical documentation, in the monumental face of Palmyra as "beautiful city" and collective, long-term work of art, but also in its urban economy and in the development of its territory.

The "irreplaceable treasure" destroyed by Daesh in 2015 was a Roman *polis* of the second and third centuries CE, the outcome of a long development starting early in the first century CE. (The ancient city was excavated and curated in the twentieth century, and hence its scholarship is entangled with the story of late colonialism and of the nation-state in the modern Middle East.) *Polis* structures, without quite making the desert bloom, did foster the development of barley-growing, market-gardening villages in the Palmyrenian uplands, at the limits of the 200 millimeter annual rainfall, as part of an integrated civic territory during the two and a half centuries of Palmyra's existence as *polis* within a world-empire.[95] Palmyra as *polis* can stand for the coherence and normalcy of the *polis* model in the Roman Near East, as part of a story of the remarkable extension of *polis* forms, institutional and ideological—in Asia Minor and in the Levant, from the mid-fourth century BCE onwards.

Polis and Empire: Imperial Cooptation and Its Costs

Our exploration of the *polis* of Palmyra, its normalcies and its nuances, offers a suggestive model to understand another distinctive case, that of Hierapolis-Bambykē, a city with an ancient shrine of Atargatis. The cult, described by Lucian in his deeply unreliable, extraordinarily playful Herodotean pastiche, *On the Syrian Goddess*, is also known from representations on coins and reliefs. These show that the cultic standard (*sēmeion*) worshipped alongside Atargatis and her consort Hadad seems to have imitated the shape of a Roman legionary standard,[96] a reflection of the empire's presence in the Levant. The cult, with its Roman inflexion, existed within a city known through two epigraphical documents to have had civic institutions (Council and People acting collectively), an honorific culture, and civic subdivisions (specifically a phratry or "brotherhood" with its own magistrate and priest), in combination with a probable Roman military presence—exactly as in Palmyra.[97]

We will revisit the implications of the coexistence of local cult and high-normed political institutions (chapter 15). For now, it is the very normalcy of Palmyra as *polis* that deserves emphasis. Normalcy points to the impact of empire, rather than just the diffusion and development of *polis* institutions. One of the earliest documents of Palmyra as *polis* is a trilingual inscription, recording how the honorific statue of a benefactor of the city's shrines in Latin, Greek, and Aramaic was set up in 74 CE by the Council and the People—*Bule et civitas* in Latin.[98] Indeed the very name Palmyra (written in Greek) probably reflects a Latin translation of a popular etymology of the local toponym Tadmor. Whatever the mechanism (influence from above or response from below to perceived official direction), the inscription hints at *polis* forms being a product of Roman power. In another equally indirect indication of Roman influence, as discreet as a watermark, the ubiquitous Greek expression *teimēs heneken*, for the sake of honor, is in fact not usual in the Greek world, and is likely a calque of a Latin expression (*honoris causa*). The mechanisms remain hidden by which the Roman empire fostered *polis* life at Palmyra without direct intervention; but we are seeing the effect the cooptation of *polis* forms by empire: this is a major feature of the history of Roman imperialism in the Near East.[99]

The *polis* played a major part in the provincialization of Judaea, after the destruction of the aristocratic temple-city of Jerusalem with its national-religious community. One example is the refoundation of a local settlement, Mamortha in Samaria, as Flavia Neapolis, which struck its own coinage and whose citizens honored their patron, a former governor of Judaea, with a statue at Ephesos during his tenure as proconsul of Asia. The honorific inscription reveals the presence of Council, People, public decisions and civic resources (the Flavian Neapolitans sent were elected both as ambassadors and as commissioners handling the public monies allocated for the statue).[100] Another example is the Flavian-era foundation in southern Syria, Kapitōlias, endowed with an extensive territory administered by the new city.¹⁰¹ After the repression of a major Jewish revolt in the region by Hadrian, the area (as the Roman province of Syria Palaestina) was filled with Greek cities, in which Jews were a minority, and whose culture was "pagan": recognizably a *polis* culture with civic spaces, notable benefactors, officials, and local taxation. Exceptionally, we can glimpse this culture in sayings and pronouncements by rabbis in Tiberias or Sepphoris (as recorded in much later Talmudic compilations), alongside the epigraphical record.¹⁰²

The process of *polis* creation by the Roman empire continued in third-century CE Syria Palaestina. The intensification of imperialism in the Roman Near East was matched by increasing presence and number of *poleis*. Lydda became *Loukia Septimia Seouēria Diospolis*, Baitogabra became *Loukia Septimia Seouēria Eleutheropolis*. The dynastic title honoring the emperor Septimius Severus shows the direct intervention of the Roman state. Eleutheropolis was endowed with a considerable territory, including notably the village of Ziph, nearly 30 kilometers to the southeast. An ossuary from Ziph mentions a *prōtopoleitēs* (*rš mryn* in Aramaic, "leader of the lords"), first citizen—an example of a rural notable enjoying status in the urban center.¹⁰³ As attested at Beth Shearim, such villages could have *polis*-like institutions of their own—just like villages in Syria or Asia Minor.

Another old settlement, Emmaus, became a *polis* under the name Nikopolis, by decision of the emperor Elagabal. Yet the decision of the emperor was duly motivated by the petition of the inhabitants, whose case was pressed by the Christian Julius Africanus (a citizen of Aelia Capitolina).¹⁰⁴ This local initiative shows the desirability, even the normalcy, of *polis* status. Their petition presumably aimed at autonomy from control by Diospolis and Eleutheropolis, just as Soada freed itself from Kanatha. This sort of centrifugal movement is familiar from the history of the *polis* (see above, chapter 7, in the much bloodier circumstances of Greece's Hundred Years' War). This is the administrative structure that transpires from Eusebius's fourth-century CE *Onomastikon*, whose geography of a biblical Holy Land is mapped out on a contemporary network of cities.

The annexation of the territories of the Nabataean kingdom and the creation of the province of Arabia in 106 CE were similarly accompanied by the emergence of *poleis*. The Nabataean kingdom had its own urban forms and monumental environments, which can be considered local variants on Hellenistic culture. The kingdom's capital, the desert site Petra, with its distinctive religious and funerary architecture, illustrates the urbanism of the dynasty. But its complex post-Hellenistic visual registers¹⁰⁵ did not perpetuate themselves in the Roman Near East. Petra appears in the second century CE as a *polis*, with a Council that could validate private acts (it hence must have had an *archeion* or registry).¹⁰⁶ The life of the *polis* must have taken place within the empty stage left by the great buildings of the post-Hellenistic dynasty. The case of Petra parallels that of Kanatha, so clearly attested in the second and third centuries CE as a *polis* in its official language, institutions, and concerns. Kanatha was a civic community living within an older monumental shell or backdrop of sacred architecture, left by local elites close to the Herodian dynasty, rather than a hybrid community dominated by old priestly clans (or whatever).[107]

When the Roman empire expanded into the Middle Euphrates region, starting in 197 CE and throughout the following century, it again recast local urban settlements as *poleis*—Appadana (renamed Neapolis, "New City"), Karrhai, Doura-Europos, Hatra, Markoupolis.[108] These *poleis* used the Greek language for official business, as well as *polis* institutions, variously attested: the Council of Neapolis, civic subdivisions such as the "tribe Antōnia" at Karrhai, or at Markoupolis the *archōns* and the public registry that they managed through a financial agent (*pragmateutēs*, not attested for any other *polis*). Such processes of *polis* creation in the aftermath of war or in frontier zones, though obscure, must have taken place as top-down decisions rather than the horizontal diffusion of institutions familiar from earlier periods.

From the Severan period onwards, *poleis* of the Roman Near East were frequently given the status of *coloniae* (without actually receiving Roman citizen settlers), radically modifying their internal constitutional arrangements and legal status in the administrative structure of the empire. This promotion was notably granted to Palmyra, but also to the new *poleis* in the Mesopotamia: Nisibis, Karrhai, and many others.[109] Doura-Europos, in 254 CE, called itself the "*Kolōneia* of the Eurōpaioi of Seleukos Nikatōr, sacred, inviolate and autonomous," combining the old Macedonian-Hellenistic past of the city, the titles denoting status recognized by peers and by the empire, and the new, adapted title of Roman *colonia*.[110] The *poleis-coloniae* on the Euphrates represent a centrally imposed, regional modification of the *polis* forms, on top of the general simplifications that the pressure of the Roman state had effected (above, chapter 12). It is useful to call this local variant, in a region saturated with Roman military and state presence, a "Greco-Roman" *polis*, especially since it occurred after the near-universal grant of Roman citizenship in 212 CE. It illustrates the impact of imperial instrumentalization (above, chapter 12) on the forms of the *polis*.

A striking example of these processes, contemporary to the fostering of Greco-Roman cities with the title of *poleis* and *coloniae* on the Mesopotamian frontier, is to be found in Egypt.[111] In addition to the enormous city of Alexandria and a small number of communities with recognized status and institutions as *poleis*,[112] Roman rule in Egypt oversaw a transformative process of municipalization of the already existing urban centers (somewhat confusingly called *mētropoleis*) of the administrative subdivisions (*nomoi*). The formalization of a class of local land-owning elites was followed by the imposition of leitourgical duties and local officeholding encumbered with financial burdens.[113]

The outcome was a particular version of Roman-era *polis* life in the *nomos*-centers, which indeed often called themselves *poleis*, even though they did not enjoy a legally recognized personality, were directly administered by the Roman state, and had no territory. Membership of these towns was held by a privileged class of "metropolites" (formally registered and distinguished in fiscal policy from the native Egyptians of the countryside). A smaller social elite, defined by graduation from the *gymnasion*, provided local officeholders and leitourgists by cooptation. In any one town, the metropolites might number in the thousands, amounting to a substantial body of members. The social elite's contributions largely contributed to pay for public goods in the urban centers, including new monumental buildings in a Roman style (illustrated by the second-century CE remodeling of Hermoupolis).[114]

These communities dealt with the demands of direct imperial administration but also negotiated the local relations between collective obligations, popular pressure, and elite calculations. In the minutes of a rowdy meeting at Hermoupolis in 192 CE, one Achilleus was proposed for a *leitourgia* ("Let him be crowned with the office of *kosmētēs*: imitate your father, the lover of honor (*philotimos*), the fine old man") and tried to evade it by taking on a lesser one, but with a firm commitment to financial contributions. The proceedings concluded by another man undertaking, under personal guarantee, to ensure Achilleus would shoulder the burden of *leitourgia*—but not before being interrupted by an accusation of personal violence and haughtiness.[115] The scene offers arresting echoes of *polis* culture (paradoxically, it is only in Egypt, where the climate preserved perishable papyrus archives, that we have direct, verbatim records of public meetings). This phenomenon might be explained as the echoes of practice in the Greek *poleis*; or it could be the result of structural and institutional features, namely the pressures of *leitourgia* and accountability.

In the early third century CE, these urban communities were granted Councils and the status of self-governing *poleis* with their own financial resources and property—the "civic account" (*politikos logos*) or "household of the city' (*oikos poleōs*). This formalization recognized the privileged position of the metropolitan and gymnasial classes (and indeed drew in the richer members of the village populations into the urban groups).[116] Among their resources and incomes, the *poleis* could draw on fees and contributions paid by the elite, occasional euergetic contributions, rents from public property, interests off public loans, and local taxation, a striking illustration of their increased autonomy.[117] Public resources allowed these communities to give out cash or grain to large groups within the citizen body, in ways reminiscent of practices in the cities of Roman Asia Minor and Greece.[118] The *poleis* of Roman Egypt were run by their Councils, which managed local financial resources, regulated the local marketplace and economy, coopted its own members and magistrates, and (closely related) distributed duties and burdens among the population.[119] The power of the Council is visible in its multiple activities or in details such as the address of letters from Roman officials to "the magistrates and the Council."[120]

But the Councils also dealt with the People, whose presence may have been formalized alongside the creation of Councils. In any case, scenes of communitarian interaction took place in the third century CE *poleis* as they had in the *nomos*-centers earlier. At Oxyrhynchos, a local benefactor, Theōn, was the subject of a praise poem, celebrating his repeated gifts of anointing oil and of grain; the latter type of gift (either by direct distribution, or by acting as market commissioner, *agoranomos*) is mentioned as the normal contribution of rich, boastful men, in contrast with the gift of oil to the *gymnasion*, fitting for the educated Theōn.[121] The type of document is unique, the result of the preservation of perishable papyrus, but the transaction is quite reminiscent of benefactions to the cities of Asia Minor or Greece (and even the poetical form recalls the piece celebrating the return of Herōdēs Atticus: above, p. 364).

Raucously, the *dēmos* of Oxyrhynchos met during a festival (ca. 290 CE), coinciding with a visit of the governor of Egypt. As in the meeting at Greater Hermoupolis a century earlier, the minutes show an event replete with *polis* culture. The *dēmos* asked for permission to pass a decree for Dioskoros, the president of the Council (*prutanis*). The latter acknowledged the intention but asked for the honor to be deferred to another occasion, where such a decree could be voted in accordance with the city's laws. Dioskoros's punctiliousness recalls legal delays for honors in the Hellenistic period (above, p. 278). The whole event is drenched in loyalist and dutiful sentiments, proclaimed toward the Roman empire and the emperors ("The Roman power for ever! The lord Emperors!"), the governor ("prosperous prefect! Hail to the governor!," etc.), and especially and at great length toward the *prutanis*:

> "Ocean *prutanis*, Ocean, glory of the city, Ocean, Dioskoros, first citizen," "Hail the friend of his fellow-citizens, hail the lover of moderation," "who holds office for the people of moderate means (*metrioi*), who holds office with equity for . . . , who holds office for the city, who cares for the city, who loves moderation for the sake of the city, who is the founder of the city!"[122]

The acclamations give an image of hierarchy and deference to authorities from the civic magistrate to the Roman emperor. Yet the occasion (using acclamations to try to force through a vote and a decree in the presence of the Roman governor) is reminiscent of meetings in Roman Asia Minor. In the same way, honors for the benefactress Lalla, "mother of the city" at Tlōs, were the result of pressure exercised in the assembly through the medium of acclamation (above, p. 350). The title "Ocean," repeatedly bestowed on the Oxyrhynchan *prytanis*, like the acclamations that Cocceianus Diōn remembered warily, could quickly be replaced by popular anger at elite misbehavior or failure to keep promises (above, p. 365). The terms of the acclamations continue a version of *polis* ideology in celebrating equality alongside "moderation"; additional acclamations for the public advocates celebrate their crucial role in protecting public goods (as in Roman Asia Minor: above, p. 354).[123]

In addition to elements of *polis* institutions and ideology, the new cities of Egypt continued to exhibit corporate pride and affirmation (through competitive titulature, building activity, literature, festivals, athletics). The "ancient, venerable and splendid city" of Greater Hermoupolis was particularly famed for its athletes (who drew pensions off the city); it also repaired and refurbished the colonnades of the monumental center at great expense, thus pursuing its earlier taste for public building.[124] This particular Egyptian *polis*-hood, developed in the first three centuries CE, is the combination of the local management of elite burdens and communal pressures, and the imperial understanding of the uses of local autonomy.

Within its institutional forms, the life of Egyptian *polis*-hood can be illustrated by its cultural history. For instance, the funerary reliefs of Oxyrhynchos show its inhabitants in Greek dress, in a style reminiscent of the Palmyrene funerary reliefs:[125] the similarity is suggestive for the structural features of *polis* life in the Roman Near East and in Roman Egypt (cf. fig. 15.3). The famous literary papyri from Oxyrhynchos's rubbish dumps give a sense of the eclectic tastes and reading culture of its citizens. Nor was that city unique. As a papyrus find shows, a notable at Greater Hermoupolis around 100 CE read the Aristotelian treatise on the constitution of the Athenians as well as Dēmosthenēs's speech *Against Meidias* (21), in which the orator prosecuted a wealthy man for *hubris* against him during a festival, an outrage that affected the whole community.[126]

The practice of Greek culture situated the Egyptian cities within the network of *poleis* in the Roman empire; the literary culture of the *metropoleis* was promised to a rich future in the form of the Greek poetry written in late Antique Egypt, which is the avatar of the literary culture of the cities.[127] Even more famous are the painted funerary portraits from cities in the Fayyûm, which present us with the faces of the *metropoleis* in hauntingly naturalistic style—albeit fitted within the trappings of traditional mummification, a striking image of the complex position of the urban elites within the land of Egypt (fig. 14.9).[128]

In the Roman Near East, the diffusion of *polis* forms from the first century CE onward was a corollary of provincialization. The Roman empire used self-governance, territorial structuration, and a particular social compact to achieve local self-administration, which allowed for efficiencies in operations of conquest and control. *Polis* served as an interface with empire, as well as the medium for peer-polity interaction. Hence the version of *polis* culture diffused as a corollary of empire reflects the simplifications imposed by the Roman state. The divine surprise of the survival and the strengthening of *polis* culture came at a great price, as illustrated earlier—namely, cooptation as an instrument of a world empire (above, chapter 12). This development fostered forms of *polis* life in inland Asia Minor, in Thrace, in the provinces of Syria, Arabia, and Mesopotamia, in Egypt as part of a whole landscape of urbanized empire, from the Atlantic to the Euphrates; the phenomenon confirms the way in which the *polis* model imposed itself as the basic unit for imperial administration.[129] The consequences of the embrace of the Roman empire can most clearly be seen during the crisis of empire during the third century CE, and its aftermath.

FIGURE 14.9. Egyptian funerary portrait, encaustic on limewood panel (38 cm visible), inset in a linen-wrapped mummy (H 169 cm). Roman imperial period. Excavated at Hawara.

Endings and Beginnings: Beyond the *Polis*

In 324 CE, the inhabitants of Orkistos, in Phrygia, petitioned the emperor Constantine to be allowed to be a *polis* again, rather than a village (*vicus*) subordinate to the *polis* of Nakoleia. The Orkistans' existence as a *polis* is indeed attested earlier by a small body of epigraphical material. The emperor duly granted them the right to "enjoy the splendor of the laws and of the title"; that is, the concomitant privilege of local self-governance and *polis* status. The drama is familiar in *polis* history—the undoing of synoikism or attribution, as happened in the case of Nagidos and Arsinoeia seven centuries earlier (see below, p. 608, n. 59). Equally familiar was the care that the petitioners took to draw attention to the advantageous site of the settlement, as well as their past as a *polis* with its own magistrates, Councilors, and People. The justification of *polis* as a product of nature but also of institutional practice, recalls the way the people of Narykos had formulated their appeal to the emperor Hadrian when they had to prove their right to be a *polis* (above, p. 311). The whole back-and-forth of petition and response and of imperial instructions, passed down to an officeholder, are also familiar from earlier *polis* history.[130]

By the time of the petition by the Orkistans, the *poleis* had weathered a major crisis. Decades of attacks from outside the boundaries of the Roman empire reached into Greece and Asia Minor.[131] The cities faced these attacks directly, often conducting resistance on their own. The generalized military emergency faced by the empire required such measures, but the troops fielded by the cities were also a measure of their capacity for autonomy, even at such a late date. Episodes of resistance were directed by members of the local elite, just as in the 180s CE at Elateia (above, p. 332). At Milētos, one Makarios led the citizenry in mobilizing against a Gothic attack. The Herulians besieged Thessalonikē, and marching down the Greek peninsula, sacked Athens. The Athenian population, which had evacuated the city, fought back under the leadership of Herennius Dexippos, a local notable who had held priestly office—and who wrote a history of the Herulian invasion.[132]

The cities' resistance to foreign attack also took the form of intense manifestations of loyalism to the Roman empire, a striking illustration of how closely invested they were in its workings: the mid- to late third century CE flourishing of local bronze coinage and festival culture (above, pp. 327–28) manifested the cities' sense of autonomy and identity, but also of belonging to a world empire.[133] Yet the end of the third century CE witnesses the dwindling away of phenomena that had played a central role in the public life of the Roman-era *poleis*, such as local bronze coinage, massive civic building, and local festivals. The solid honorific culture that had celebrated the public-minded actions and attitudes of the civic elites also grows fainter in the surviving evidence.[134]

The end of the third-century CE crisis led to a wholesale, empire-wide reform, ushering in the "New Empire" of the next three centuries.[135] In the case of the cities, the administrative reforms tightened the Roman state's control over the local communities. The effect was to prolong, formalize, and intensify the instrumentalization of the cities, a process that had been ongoing since the emperor Augustus (above, pp. 318–28) and intensified during the Severan dynasty in the late second and early third centuries CE, as noted by D. Nörr (1966). The structures of the New Empire would increase the Roman state's control immeasurably.

The Orkistans regained *polis* status under Constantine in a changed world. As N. Lenski has observed, the emperor's decision, though espousing familiar forms of petition and response, was shaped by his religious policy, itself a response to the change brought about by the growth of Christianity.[136] In addition to traditional arguments, the Orkistans drew attention to their fidelity to Christ; indeed, their earlier loss of *polis* status and attribution to Nakoleia might be connected to the anti-Christian policy of the emperor Maximinus.

Constantine's activism is of a piece with the extension of state power under the New Empire, as seen in the multiplication of governors and the heightening of their competences, and the uniformization of local communities as instruments of empire. Imperial legislation uniformly concerned cities in the Eastern and Western provinces alike. The Late Roman state sequestered at least part of the civic incomes and properties (especially temple estates and foundations), sometimes under the heading of religious policy, as a corollary to the direct management of civic expenditure by the governor and other imperial officials.[137] It tightened the assignment of financial burdens, both locally and as part of imperial administration and tax collection, and multiplied legislation around the composition of the Council, or more precisely the now hereditary bouleutic class that was entitled to serve in the Council but also liable to leitourgic service. The Late Roman state also treated the councilors as a resource within instrumentalized cities—for instance, shifting them around to cover local needs.[138]

None of these phenomena was entirely new, but their consequences threatened to lead to the obsolescence of the old institutional forms of the *polis*.[139] The richest members of the local elites found an outlet in the aristocracy of imperial service, which exempted them from local service (thus breaking the compact enforced upon them by the earlier Roman empire). The takeover of much of local administration by the Late Roman state did away with civic officeholding (which vanishes during the fifth century CE) and the decision-making role of the Assembly. The outcome was the disappearance of local euergetism as the preserve of the local super-elite and of civic politics. The last honorific decrees, and indeed the last formal meetings of the assemblies, must have happened at the end of the third century CE. The disappearance of the sovereign, decision-making Assembly of the People is as obscure as the emergence of state institutions in the early seventh century BCE (above, chapter 4).

Yet some elements of the Late Roman city were still determined by *polis* life and ideology.[140] The embedding of the bouleutic element within its leitourgic obligations continued the practice of the earlier Roman empire. Indeed, the repeated imperial legislation enforcing these obligations were responses to appeals and petitions from the local elites, eager to avoid free-riding and defection among their class, as they continued running their communities.[141] The Late Roman state continued to listen to initiatives and petitions from the cities, and to sustain their public life. In 443 CE, Theodosios II, traveling to Aphrodisias to fulfil a vow, received petitions from the citizenry of Hērakleia under Salbakē, asking for imperial subsidy to help rebuild their walls, aqueduct, and other buildings fallen into disrepair. The emperor responded with a general ruling on the restoration of public property to the cities:

> since we strive with the greatest passion and all our strength to ensure that the cities subjected to our power enjoy a perpetual felicity ... we find no more salutary reason for recalling our former felicity than that there should be assigned to all the cities (*civitates*) the urban landed estates as well as the rustic ones and the shops which pertain to civic ownership rights, which have been occupied by certain persons in any manner whatever within thirty years to be counted back from the present time.[142]

Explicitly framed as a reaction to private acquisitiveness damaging the cities, the measure illustrates the continued relationship between the intentionality of the Late Roman state and the maintenance of public goods and life at the level of the cities.

By the early fifth century CE, repeated imperial legislation may have had an effect in stemming the defection of the councilor class and in keeping them embedded within local communities. The councilors themselves were now called the *politeuomenoi*, those exercising civic duties and caring for the public good through deliberation and willed consensus—the last descendants of the good citizens of the Classical city. Indeed, this is how Libanios paints them within his city, fourth-century CE Antioch.[143] The burdens of civic administration weighed heavily on this class of "middling" elite citizens—a prolongation of the leitourgic and euergetical pressure that bore down on elites in the *poleis* of earlier periods. The *ekdikos*, appointed by the Late Roman state, was supposed to defend the interests of the poor against the rich—a continuation of the mechanisms constraining local elites within the Roman-era *polis* (above, pp. 354, 361), and an echo from even further back, from the time of demagogic politics in the adversarial space of the courtroom and the Assembly.[144]

Furthermore, euergetical ideology and discourse, though no longer deployed for the very rich citizens by their communities,[145] applied to the governors honored with new statuary forms, as analyzed by R. R. R. Smith in the case of Aphrodisias (fig. 14.10).[146] The Late Roman honorific epigram, a highly recondite form written in antiquated language, recycled and reinvigorated the old tropes of elite service and community recognition.[147] Like many earlier benefactors, the governors usually paid for their own monuments, a clear sign of the genealogy and the function of the genre.

FIGURE 14.10. Marble statue portrait of Late Antique governor, Aphrodisias, North Agora. A "tall austere slender figure" (Smith 2002, 142) of 191 cm representing the late fourth-century or early fifth century CE imperial official Oecumenius.

In F. Millar's words, "the now Christianized Greek city, as the context for an urban community, as a physical structure, as a self-governing organization and as a channel for contacts with and communications to and from the Imperial power, played as essential a role as it had since the earliest stages of Roman rule."[148] Thus the church and its structure of governance and reproduction rested on the existence of a network of cities, shaped by the Roman state: as observed by F. Millar, lists of bishops participating in the great ecumenical councils give an overview of the continued existence of a landscape of *poleis*, with the recurrence of names familiar to the historian of the Classical *polis* and of its prolongations in the Roman Near East: Athens or Argos, but also Priēnē, Teōs, or Amyzōn; and also Diospolis (Lydda), Kanatha, and its neighbor Dionysias. Bishoprics were subordinated to a *mētropolis*, "mother-city," using the same language of hierarchies and status promoted by the Roman empire and growing out of the old peer-polity interaction. The bishopric/ *mētropolis* structure even oddly reproduced the phenomena of competition for status that characterized the *poleis* of the Roman empire (above, pp. 327–28).[149]

The Late Roman city performed something not unlike the same function as the *polis* once had, binding the elites to redistributive obligations to their local communities (as a corollary to their obligations to the Roman state). In the eastern part of the Roman empire, the old constricting limits of civic life acted as a temporary bastion against the rise of inequality, in contrast with the Late Roman West.[150] This Late Roman version of civic life, enforcing communal burdens, confirms the centrality of the obligation of the *leitourgia* to *polis* life: not a tool for untrammeled oligarchical dominance, but a form of embedding elites within their communities.

Although the role of the super-benefactors had been taken over by the governors, the councilors continued in the role of the civic *leitourgoi* familiar from the Roman-era *polis*. Indeed, it could favor flare-ups of civic life, as visible in fifth-century CE Stratonikeia in Karia, where a benefactor, Maximus, was honored with statues and inscriptions that drew on the old resources of euergetistic language:[151]

> You gaze upon me, Maximus, who have bestowed on the city and its inhabitants much of our toils [i.e. my wealth gained through toil]. Therefore the council and those citizens without wealth set me up with glorious stone portraits before the holy house of the God Christ. How good it is not to care for possessions.

This Late Roman form of urban and civic organization proved long-lasting and stable. Its solutions fitted comfortably the local elites (as noted by M. Whittow, who indeed thought this was the natural state of the *polis*).[152] The tension between the different functions of the Late Roman city, of civic constraint but also of elite affirmation, is inherent to the *polis* and confirms the last period of vitality of the old bargains. But the Late Roman city gradually and unevenly mutated into a "Late Antique" city, perhaps by the early sixth century CE.[153] The richest members of the elite, evading the burdens of the bouleutic class yet connected with the institutions of imperial power, seized control of power locally in oligarchical revolutions that erased the constitutional legacy of the *polis*, replacing the Council with less well-defined power groups: the bishop, the governor, and the "first men." These were the direct recipients of imperial orders, such as the letter sent to the city of Hadrianoupolis in Paphlagonia (for its earlier life, see above, pp. 323–24; indeed, the document is inscribed on the reused base for the statue of the emperor Commodus). Significantly, it was in the bishop's court, before "the landowners great and small," that the order was formally read out for them to disband their private armies of "lance-cavaliers" (*xylokaballarioi*).[154]

The grandees, powerful and prosperous thanks to connections within imperial service, and now recapturing local government from the bouleutic class, can also be seen in Antioch.[155] The Late Antique city that succeeded the Late Roman city was shaped by fluid, opaque forms of power.[156] Old constitutional forms were replaced by an ecology of competition and acquisition,[157] and by a dynamic, loose politics of big men (whether imperial officials or not) ruling their cities. The disappearance of the regimented public spaces of the *polis* followed: they had been one of the main public goods produced by the *polis*, from its appearance onwards. In the Late Antique politics, the popular will forced its way to the surface in the forms of acclamation and negotiation by riot and violence, even if associative life survived (for instance in the institution of the *neaniai*, the urban youth, often turbulent).[158] The class of councilors, devoid of power and purely attached to obligations, sank into obscurity and gradually disappeared, though councilors and *politeuomenoi* occasionally appear in hagiographical sources that show old cities in the background of the movements and actions of saints such as Nikolaos at Myra, in Central Lykia, or Thekla at Seleukeia on Kalykadnos.[159] This is the last glimpse of the old civic elites whose relationship to the community, public-mindedness voluntary or enforced, and proclivities to rule have played a central part in this book.

By the sixth century CE, the notables' function in the city had shrunk to the point that their contribution to local expenditure was minimal, compared to their continual role in imperial administration and tax collection (and their predatory presence as landlords). The bishops took over some of the roles of the civic elites: for instance, they represented local communities in embassies to the emperor, so long a central part of the public activity of local politicians and leaders.[160] Bishops also appear as builders and providers of public goods but with significant differences: they drew on church funds or contributions from the faithful, and their benefactions were addressed to a new constituency, namely the poor rather than the citizen body. An eloquent case is that of Theodoret, whom F. Millar describes as "defending his achievements in twenty-five years as bishop of Kyrrhos: among other things, two public stoas constructed out of church funds, two bridges, and the repair of the public baths and the aqueduct."[161] At this point, the status of citizen (*politēs*) disappears, replaced by a concept of mere inhabitant: this is the end of the empowered stakeholder, whose distinction from the rest of society formed the cornerstone of the political community since the seventh and sixth centuries BCE.

The end of the Late Roman city did not entail the end of urban settlement of towns or cities, documented vividly through their preserved remains. The Late Antique cities were marked by multiple keepsakes and legacies from the earlier form; Skythopolis provides a striking example.[162] The monumental cover of the cities, a legacy of the good life in common that characterized the *polis* as project, represented a material and aesthetic legacy that had to be negotiated.[163] Ephesos remained a great city, maintaining old monuments and building new ones— churches such as the Church of St. John, and the monumental *Arkadianē* street between the harbor and the theater. Priēnē, in contrast, shrank to a small settlement around its church.[164] Cities continued to live in close relationship with the countryside, as shown by the life of St. Nicholas of Holy Zion (living in the same area as the earlier St. Nicholas of Myra).[165]

The Roman state did not stop needing cities for imperial governance, and hence the local communities had some leeway in dealing with the supralocal empire. The site of Didyma, since antiquity an extra-urban shrine in the great territory of Milētos, gained its status as a city (*polis*) under Justinian in 553 CE, with the name Ioustinianoupolis. The promotion occurred because of local petition, and the city defended its interest by further appealing to the state, in order to negotiate a favorable status in regard to its taxation burden. The whole dossier, analyzed by D. Feissel, shows the formidable competences of the Justinianic state, but also the continued existence of cities with some form of agency, and a sense of the relative statuses of cities.[166] If we knew more about the internal life of these cities, perhaps we would perceive more echoes and images of what mattered about communal life and external relations. Yet the diversity of possible faces of urbanism in this period (some prosperous, traditional, and classicizing; others evolving rapidly away from old models) is itself indicative of the end of the unitary story of the *polis*.

The history sketched above is the story of the gradual end of the *polis* in two steps over 250 years (300–550 CE). The *événementiel* history of Late Antiquity finally caught up with the ancient city. The crisis of the second half of the sixth century CE, which confronted the emperor Justinian with plague and military disaster, led to another wave of reforms, stripping the cities of resources and autonomy. Whether the local communities might have survived these measures to reinvent themselves again by the reaffirmation of *polis*-like ideologies is a moot point, since the Late Antique world itself came to an end with a series of major shifts, namely the Slavic migrations into the Balkans and the arrival of Islam on the eastern Mediterranean scene. Even then, the impact of such events varied. The small settlement at Priēnē was abandoned during the seventh century CE; the fortification on top of the akropolis would be occupied during the Middle Ages. In contrast, cities in Syria continued to enjoy a vibrant life (Skythopolis would be laid low by an earthquake in 749 CE).[167]

The ancient city faded out of recognition. In the late tenth century CE, Sparta appears in the life of St. Nikon "Metanoeite" as dominated by magnates (*archontes*), who used the former *agora* as a polo field (and donated it to the saint to found a monastery).[168] Going forth, the *polis* and its discourses would continue in two forms. The first was the survival of some manifestations of civic autonomy within the Byzantine empire. The last *cité d'empire* might be Philadelpheia in Lydia (at modern Alaşehir in Turkey)—a city with a long history. It was founded by the Attalid kingdom; its life as a *polis* in the Roman empire is documented by the usual array of epigraphical, numismatic, and archaeological sources.[169] We have seen the city in 255 CE touchily refusing to contribute to the *Koinon* of Asia on the grounds that it had once enjoyed the prestigious status of *mētropolis* (above, p. 316). In the Middle Ages, it appears as a fortified Byzantine town with its territory, rural strongholds, ecclesiastical institutions, schools, and mercantile activity, surviving the vicissitudes of war and conquest, and presumably ruled informally by a combination of episcopal power and local magnates. Under its local oligarchy, the city fought against Turkish emirs in 1335 and 1348, commemorating in religious rituals the magnates killed in battle. Philadelpheia would prove the last free city in Western Asia Minor, falling in 1390 to the Ottoman sultan Bayezit I, who led a Byzantine contingent among his troops.[170]

The second way in which the *polis* survived was less concrete. Ideas of public good and civic community appear in Byzantium, though it is true that the explicit sources for them are usually the Roman republic, reflecting the Roman identity of the Byzantine empire. It is all the same legitimate to wonder what influence might have been exercised on the political imagination of Byzantium by the Greek literary canon, where the lion's share was taken by works written for performance in different venues, public or private, of democratic Athens.[171] The patriarch Photios, in the ninth century CE, read and excerpted a work of local history about the eventful life of a particular *polis*, Hērakleia Pontikē; the narrative, written by a citizen in the first century CE, covered in great detail moments of the city's attempts to preserve autonomy (see above, p. 295).[172] But the Byzantine space is characterized by the absence of any communal movement descended from *polis* praxis: there is no continuity or resurgence of the old city-state ideals, apart from odd survivals such as Philadelpheia. Over the final ruins of its history, the survival of the *polis* would occur in its reception, and its historiography (chapter 20).

PART VI

Making Sense of the *Polis*

MY STORY for the *polis* looks like this. It starts with the Late Bronze Age polities in mainland Greece. These polities are centered on extraction, stocking, and inegalitarian redistribution; they are led by figureheads living in palaces, consuming the product of international exchange, and engaging in international high politics across the Mediterranean. As polities, they were based on negotiation between the palatial elites and various productive constituencies. Viewed in perspective, they were small on the scale of the empires of the ancient Near East. Their collapse at the start of the twelfth century BCE had the effect of freeing local power actors— among these, the *basileis* of LHIIIC (the "last Mycenaeans"), not hereditary lords but rather freebooters or specialists in violence. Others might be agricultural villages: the relations between freebooters and producers must have been negotiated and fluid.

These societies in turn disappeared, yielding to a century-long pause (the "Protogeometric" period), which may have been a time of creative experimentation and prosperity rather than darkness (here I follow the visionary C. Starr rather than the influential A. Snodgrass). Out of this period come the **clustervilles**, constellations of houses and hamlets with no clear center, serving local elites with needs for resources (enslaved labor, metal) and international contacts, yet attracted to the proximity of their peers. The clustervilles somehow negotiated their relationship to a territory and its nonelite inhabitants. Athens provides a clear example (with widely spaced settlements, arranged around the Akropolis). This phase lasted from the tenth century BCE onwards, holding sway from Macedonia to Crete and from western Greece to Asia Minor. The clustervilles are networked to such a degree that changes occur across the board and swiftly.

By the mid-eighth century BCE (the "Late Geometric" period), many of these conurbations develop into proto-urban settlements where elites and nonelites meet, along a competitive rather than stratified model. This distinction is one of the original "folds" that will determine the history of the *polis*. Urban consolidation involved defining a central place, with spaces set aside as public: temples, shrines, public meeting places. The other constitutive process was **territorial structuration**; that is, the definition of relationship between the central settlement and the countryside with its inhabitants; the clarification of boundaries; and the negotiation of relations with other communities beyond the bounded territory. Such phenomena are visible in the same geographical space as above, with the addition of areas of elite acquisitiveness and settlement such as Southern Italy and the northern Aegean.

These proto-urban settlements must solve problems of **community and justice**: the problems are at the heart of monumental literary sources of the late eighth century BCE (the Homeric epic and the didactic poetry of Hesiod). The solution will be long, multipart, and consequential (the second "fold" of *polis* history). The first stage is the **obscure leap to statehood**, which is transformational and occurs around 675 BCE: it centers on institutions and law (written rules, accumulating around institutionalized practice). Especially important are the yearly magistracies as means of power-sharing. This revolutionary moment might have taken place in a few decades of the early seventh century BCE and is traceable all over the Aegean. Alternatively, it may have constituted a horizon to which communities acceded at different times during the seventh century BCE. The paradox is that the *polis* appears as political forms, but that the social relations in the *polis* remain obscure and may have varied considerably. Most visible are the traces of consolidation. Public spaces get monumentalized; public goods are raised and administered. Social ritual, organized around fictional kinship, dramatizes membership and hence stake-holding in the community. These processes will make visible, in metaphorical terms, the issues of **political power and entitlement** within the polity.

Working out the consequences of the leap to statehood and the establishment of public goods involved constant experimentation, and hence widespread instability as part of *polis* history. Monarchical rule is a widespread and long-lived possibility; but the model of equality between peers proved equally widespread and coterminously linked with the existence of institutions, law, and public goods. In practice, two types of *poleis* emerge. The first is based on **small, closed groups** that exercise domination over noncitizens, second-class citizens and subaltern communities ("subject *poleis*")—the effect of the successful capture of community by a small in-group that practices egalitarianism among itself. The second type often emerges after social upheaval, and is made up of **wide-franchise, open communities**, within which the old dynamics of display and competition continue, but subject to community validation as a result of political equality.

In the end, the egalitarian open model proved most successful, and a further stage in *polis* development is marked by the **generalization of egalitarianism** in the sixth century BCE, together with increasing sharpness in definition of state institutions and state powers, and increasing monumentalization of urban centers. At the same time, the sixth century BCE witnesses the politically constitutive exclusion of women from the public sphere and the widespread resort to slavery as part of complex economies. Economic development is visible in the filling up of the agrarian landscape with the farms and diversified holdings of smallholders (rather than large estates). The presence of elitist signs (big tombs, small banqueting groups) is not enough to prove the existence of elite-ruled polities; they rather reflect social complexity within broadly inclusive polities. This egalitarian model even influences the "closed" polities during the sixth century BCE.

The following **Hundred Years' War** (464–355 BCE) sees continuous violent conflict. Within the generally agreed-on framework of *polis* practices, **control of political institutions and entitlement to public goods** was the subject of disputes, formalized as a matter of the definition of the access group (small or large), often intersecting with questions of class. The small groups of the wealthy protected property interests through the repressive capture of institutions (ensuring the enforceability of contracts and shielding wealth from redistributive pressure). Alternatively, big citizen groups used political institutions to curtail elite power and enforce redistribution. (The alternative is starkly expressed, and explored at great length, in Aristotle's *Politics*). The internal debate (often conducted with knives, clubs, and confiscation) combined with external conflict between *poleis*, especially in the form of **superpower conflict**. The latter was initiated but not controlled by the Athenian hyperpower. The result was a **tragic equation** or **tragedy of powers** dominating most of the period.

Yet this tragedy of powers is not the only story. This period also sees demographic and economic development fueled by the potential of good political institutions (that is, the protection of private property, rule of law, peer-to-peer economies) as well as the systematic resort to chattel slavery within market-oriented economies linked with broader Mediterranean and extra-Mediterranean economic fluxes. This prosperity may partly have fueled the **great convergence** in political culture that takes place during the late Classical period (350 BCE onwards)—this is the third "fold" in *polis* history. Broadly democratic norms arise, at the same time that hegemony as well as the domination of "subject *poleis*" falter. The evolutions in high politics—the end of the great power politics for *poleis*, the choice of the competing Macedonian autocrats to support some degree of *polis* autonomy (as part of superpower rivalry), even though they also tried to control and tax the *poleis*—also had the paradoxical effect of reinforcing the omni-democratic (C. Müller), omni-autonomous convergence.

The *poleis* produced by the great convergence shared **democratic characteristics** that grew out of the debates of the previous period. In this context, the activities of local notables and elites are not, in essence, different from the models developed in the fourth century BCE (elite recognition and eminence defined by democratic institutions and ideology). The sense of "bigness" displayed by the *polis* was boosted by a sense of political autonomy and agency and manifested in symbolical forms of interaction and recognition ("peer-polity interaction").

These characteristics are visible throughout the third and early second centuries BCE, and proved stable, in a sort of "end of history." Certainly these characteristics persisted during the upheaval of the impact of the Roman hyperpower during the second century BCE—the "Polybian moment," followed by a well-documented and richly fascinating **Indian Summer** of the Greek city-states. During this period, the low visibility of Roman power in Greece and Asia Minor left space for a solid intensification of intra- and inter-polis life, fed by the accession of whole regions to the norms of the great convergence (Thessaly, Crete) and the resulting catch-up phenomena. One corollary of this intensification is the continued **diffusion of the *polis* model** throughout the eastern Mediterranean. The intensification of Roman power led to **a terrible first century** BCE. The impact on the cities was undoubtedly the increase of elite control in internal politics, but also the destruction of swathes of elite wealth.

Under the **Roman empire** of the first three centuries CE, the *polis* faced an integrative monarchical state that instrumentalized local processes for its own aims. The old mechanisms for the *poleis* to make their own luck, such as petition and response, ended up inviting the imperial state back in. Yet the *poleis* still managed to make themselves the privileged interlocutors of imperial power, finding spaces of **autonomy and stateness** (D. Nörr), through a variety of proxies and defense mechanisms. The outcome was a dialectical relationship between empire and city, in which the latter, while being coopted and instrumentalized, established itself as the privileged interlocutor of the imperial state. Internally, the **glare of elitism** should not blind us to nuance and democratic continuities. The local politician Cocceianus Diōn's awareness of the power of **"You, the People"** is a function of the continued capability of the *Dēmos* in assembly politics (H. Fernoux). The *polis* continued to lock the elites in by the very means the latter chose to express power; the Roman state sustained the *polis* by systematically enforcing elite *leitourgia*. At stake in civic politics was the question of elite defection from their commitments and potential exploitation of structural advantage, as debated in assembly politics. The famous and hyper-visible phenomenon of "euergetism" (benefaction by the very rich) has to be read within this context of elite acceptance of redistributive burdens (the **"tragedy of the elites"**), involving the concomitant effect of *polis* institutions and imperial intervention. This survival and continuation of the *polis* and *polis* issues within empire constitutes the divine surprise of this stage of its history.

Part of "*polis*-world," a major feature of the differentiated Roman empire, stretched into the Levant from Syria down to Gaza; the same processes, problems, and negotiated solutions obtained there as in Greece, Asia Minor, the islands, or eastern North Africa. Further inland, the civic forms of the *polis* are also well attested. The generalization of the *polis* model is hence highly visible under the Roman empire, and indeed a major part of the history of the Roman empire: Aramaic-speaking communities (Hierapolis, Kanatha, Palmyra) emerge from post-Hellenistic dynastic or priestly cultures to take on the standardized forms of the Roman imperial *polis*, with civic institutions. The case of Palmyra established the normalcy, rather than hybridity, of the *polis* in the Roman Near East. The phenomenon confirms the **cooptation** of *polis* forms by the Roman empire, which fostered *poleis* as part of imperialism and provincialization, as pointed out by F. Millar in his history of the Roman Near East (for instance, in Judaea in the aftermath of repeated revolts, on the Mesopotamian borderland, and in Egypt from the time of Augustus onwards).

The close relation between Greek *polis* and Roman empire played out in Late Antiquity, with the disappearance of the "Classical" forms of the *polis* in the new empire that emerged after the military and administrative crisis of the late third century CE. Notably, its close association with the pagan powers and the persecution of Christians disqualified the old *polis* in a Christian empire; its local resources were at least partly confiscated following the administrative reforms of the early fourth century CE. By 300 CE, civic institutions changed radically, with the end of the popular assembly, the diminution of local councils (which continued to shoulder the burdens of local administration as well as services to the imperial state), and the flight of the elites into the Church and high imperial administration. The **Late Roman city** was at first ruled by its local Councils with some survivals from the old institutions (for instance, the public advocates who defended public interests and the poor against elite acquisitiveness). As P. Brown noticed, this last avatar of the *polis* proved effective at preventing nascent feudalism in the eastern Mediterranean (as opposed to the western empire). Even this "curial" regime was replaced, around 500 CE, in **Late Antique cities**, by opaque, informal oligarchies of big men, outside institutional forms, and in collaboration with the imperial state and the representatives of the Church (W. Liebeschuetz).

Yet echoes of the *polis* persisted into Late Antiquity. One such **persistence** can be found in the built environment, sometimes carefully curated. Another is the use of euergetical language for governors and bishops, to cast them in the role of the old benefactors. A final persistence is the continued operation of bouleutic classes into the sixth century CE, occasionally glimpsed in literary sources, as local leading men and presumably still taking on the *leitourgia* burdens that originated nine centuries earlier in the cities of the fifth and fourth centuries BCE. This world came to an end with the radical changes of the late seventh century CE (Slavic invasions, Islamic conquests), which marks the end of a long history.

This is the shorter version of the long chapters above. An even shorter version would focus on three points: the obscure leap to the state in the seventh century BCE, the great convergence of the late fourth century BCE (and its consequences), the long transformation of the *polis* from the fourth century CE onwards. Hence a time span from 650 BCE to 500 CE, within which the six centuries between 300 BCE and 300 CE are crucial.

What is this narrative the history of? Above all it is the history of a *political form*, the *polis* of the great convergence, its development, diffusion, successes, and ultimate fate. The assumptions in this book have been Aristotelian, privileging questions of access to political power. These Aristotelian choices have clear consequences. As I stated in the introduction to this book, *polis* history is not quite urban history, but the history of a particular type of state organization, with institutional and ideological expressions as well as a bundle of social relations. The question is how to map one onto the other—state upon society. In what follows, I would like to explore as well as nuance, the Aristotelian viewpoint—namely, the centrality of institutional power for any attempt to understand the *polis* as society (chapter 15). Such an exploration is also a defense of an Aristotelian approach against recent conceptualizations of the *polis*—as network of associations, as a gender-inclusive whole, as a religious commonwealth . . . I argue that all those aspects are constituted by the political dimension of the *polis*, and that any notion of *polis* as civil society has to be analyzed using finer categories, which are secondary to the political and the institutional.

Nor are institutions simple. They embody claims about community and membership as moral entities; "virtue politics" produces the good life, which is after all one of the aims of living in a *polis* (chapter 16). But this definition of the outcome of ethical behavior as happiness shows the utilitarian calculus at the heart of virtue politics (chapter 17). Utilitarianism opens the door to self-interested, cynical interpretations of the "bad *polis*" as a community of selfish actors; and hence, in the balance of forces, of actual oligarchy (chapter 18). Even grimmer is the picture of the "worst *polis*" as potentially merely the safeguard of the dominating classes—patriarchal and slave-owning (chapter 19). All these critical approaches represent the costs of the Aristotelian *polis*.

The chapters in this section constitute a set of rolling conclusions to the book; though they were written as successive takes on the question of the nature of the *polis* (and the consequences to any answer to this question), they all sketch out simultaneous, coexisting, and interdependent answers. To a certain extent, this simultaneity implies a static, simplified object of enquiry—the political form that emerged out of the great convergence of the later fourth and early third centuries BCE and achieved remarkable stability in the following centuries (or so I claim). One element that counteracts the potentially general and static nature of the analysis is how each theoretical take implies different causality paths for the emergence of the *polis* as institutional and ideological form, its evolution, the ultimate convergence of local variations, and its subsequent history under the Roman and Late Roman state. Together, through these rolling conclusions, I try to offer a picture of the *polis* far from any "Greek miracle," aware of the question of injustices (inherent or contingent) in social realities but also aware of the potential of the *polis* as a political ideal.[1]

15

Polis as Society

> In the civic community, the producer's membership—especially in the Athenian democracy—meant an unprecedented degree of freedom from the traditional forms of exploitation, both in the form of debt bondage and in the form of taxation.... The old dichotomous relationship between appropriating state and subject peasant producers was compromised to a certain extent throughout the Graeco-Roman world whenever there existed a civic community uniting landlords and peasants, that is, whenever peasants possessed the status of citizenship.
>
> —E. M. WOOD, *DEMOCRACY AGAINST CAPITALISM*

A Political Form: Power, Stateness, Institutions

My history of the *polis* has three characteristics. First, it is narrative and descriptive (rather than driven by explanation, for instance within a rational-choice model).[1] Second, I assume the unity of the phenomena described in the narrative. Third, the narrative is structured by its attention to power, stateness, and institutions, on which other social phenomena are dependent, or of which they are functions. All three interlocking choices deserve some comment and critique.

To start with the immediate (though perhaps ultimately trivial) issues of form:[2] the long, continuous narrative aims at providing context within which individual cases might meaningfully fit, as connected parts in time and space—the island *polis* of Hērakleia ca. 250 BCE, Priēnē in 120 BCE, Panopeus in 160 CE, or indeed many places or incidents within ancient history, from the eastern Mediterranean, Sicily and Italy, the Black Sea area, or the Near East. But conversely, all of these accumulate as examples of the broad phenomena of community consolidation and structuration. The aim is to produce a revisionist narrative, or at least a recalibration. The study of the *polis* must integrate this long history: to focus on the "Archaic" and Classical periods (as the work of the Copenhagen Polis Centre almost exclusively did) produces a narrow view, skewed by the paradoxes and contradictions working themselves out over a tragic century or so (460–360 BCE). The recalibration proposed in this book takes us away from widespread images of the "death of democracy" after the Classical period, as proposed by G. E. M. de Ste. Croix and followed by P. Cartledge in his recent essay.[3]

The phenomena, and all those folds and watersheds that constitute my new narrative, need explaining. Why did the clusters and hamlets of the Early Iron Age consolidate into communities? Why the generalization of egalitarianism, why the tragic century of external and internal war of all against all, and, most importantly, why the great convergence? Why did the *polis* persist under empire—until it stopped doing so and changed out of all recognition? Some of the answers were grounded in the consequences of contingencies, such as the abrupt rise of the Macedonian-ruled empires (and the concomitant, paradoxical reinforcement of *polis* life), the irruption of the Roman state into the concert of eastern Mediterranean powers, or the changes in the Late Roman state. I will try to develop further answers from a variety of theoretical angles (idealist, constructivist; neo-institutionalist, economy-centered; radical and pessimistic, even very pessimistic). For now, what matters is to justify the fact that these answers are unitary, shaped by the other characteristics of my narrative: the postulate of unity, and the focus on political agency.

The postulate of the unitary existence of *the* Greek city-state, in the singular and the absolute, rests on the widespread currency of certain phenomena: institutional processes, political discourses, social relations, and the built environment of civic life. All these features exhibit broad similarities and remarkable stability, even if they change—usually across the board, as can be seen during the Hellenistic period and under the Roman empire. The stability of *polis* life as a world culture constitutes in itself a salient fact of ancient history. We are not dealing with an ideal type (let alone Max Weber's ideal type of the ancient city as nonproductive, status-obsessed, rentier-run).[4] Rather, it is a detailed inductive picture, combining an emic element of how citizens of *poleis* defined and spoke of their communities, and an etic collective of observable traits that the *poleis* share. There was a clearly defined category of *polis* as a self-governing city-state made of politically equal citizens and, especially in the Hellenistic period and the Roman empire, a city-state using the institutionalized practices and language that had emerged in the Greek-speaking lands of the Mediterranean.[5] In this context, *polis*-hood was also an official status that could be formally recognized by other *poleis*, as distinct from a mere settlement; or, once a world empire had emerged in the Mediterranean, that could be granted and guaranteed by the ruling power.

However, the end-result of formalization risks offering a mere checklist for *polis*-hood. Such a mental list underlies an oft-quoted passage of Pausanias about the Phokian *polis* of Panopeus (discussed a number of times earlier).[6] Yet this is a much richer passage than often allowed for, which deserves full quotation in all its strangeness and multistage complexity (rather than the truncated extracts that usually appear in earlier scholarship on the *polis*):

From Chairōneia it is twenty stades to Panopeus, a *polis* of the Phokians, if one can give the name of *polis* to those who possess no government offices, no *gym*-

nasion, no theater, no market-place, no water descending to a fountain, but live in bare shelters just like mountain cabins, right on a ravine. Nevertheless, they have boundaries with their neighbors, and even send delegates to the Phokian assembly. The name of the city is derived, they say, from the father of Epeios, and they maintain that they are not Phokians, but were originally Phlegyans who fled to Phōkis from the land of Orchomenos. A survey of the ancient circuit of Panopeus led us to estimate it at about seven stades. I was reminded of Homer's verses about Tityos, where he mentions the city of Panopeus with its beautiful dancing-floors, and how in the fight over the body of Patroklos he says that Schedios, son of Iphitos and king of the Phokians, who was killed by Hektōr, lived in Panopeus. It seemed to me that the reason why the king lived here was fear of the Boiotians; at this point is the easiest pass from Boiōtia into Phōkis, so the king used Panopeus as a fortified post. The former passage, in which Homer speaks of the beautiful dancing-floors of Panopeus, I could not understand until I was taught by the women whom the Athenians call Thyiads. The Thyiads are Attic women, who with the Delphian women go to Parnassus every other year and celebrate orgies in honor of Dionysos. It is the custom for these Thyiads to hold dances at places, including Panopeus, along the road from Athens. The epithet Homer applies to Panopeus is thought to refer to the dance of the Thyiads. At Panopeus there is by the roadside a small building of unburnt brick, in which is an image of Pentelic marble, said by some to be Asklēpios, by others Promētheus. The latter produce evidence of their contention. At the ravine there lie two stones, each of which is big enough to fill a cart. They have the color of clay, not earthy clay, but such as would be found in a ravine or sandy torrent, and they smell very like the skin of a man. They say that these are remains of the clay out of which the whole race of mankind was fashioned by Promētheus. Here at the ravine is the tomb of Tityos. The circumference of the mound is just about one-third of a stade, and they say that the verse in the Odyssey, "Lying on the ground, and he lay over nine roods," refers, not to the size of Tityos, but to the place where he lay, the name of which was Nine Roods.

For sure, as many scholars have observed about this passage, Pausanias confronts the *polis* of Panopeus with the Roman-era "checklist" of monumental buildings (itself drawing from a storied tradition going back to the seventh century BCE). But he does so in a richly self-reflexive move, playing with and transcending this trope by referring to other, deeper elements of *polis*-hood, namely institutionalized recognition within frames of interaction with other *poleis*. He mentions, with deliberate offhandedness, the great circuit of walls that embodied the city's integrity and political agency (fig. 15.1). He further investigates local connections to myth; the justifications for the *polis* status of Narykos, as recognized by Hadrian, are of the same nature: institutional but also mythical (above, p. 311).[7] That is, Pausanias is aware of the function of the checklist (to identify a *polis* by obvious signs),

FIGURE 15.1. Fortifications of Panopeus. Photograph Sylvian Fachard.

but also of its rationale and justification (i.e., the existence of a unitary object called *polis*), and the way in which these can be fulfilled by looking for other signs of *polis*-hood.

Pausanias also addresses the central problem of diversity in the landscape of *poleis*, as shown by his interest in the specific mythological connections of Panopeus: a mention in Homer, a location in a chain of song and dance connecting famous places, and local monuments and traditions. The latter connect Panopeus with the oldest times of mankind—the petrified remains of the clay whence the species was fashioned, and still smelling like human flesh. This diversity is part of the condition of the *polis* and forces us to confront the problems inherent in a major characteristic of my *polis* history, the postulate of uniformity. Even if the *polis* can be traced in highly legible forms of evidence (literary sources, the archive of monumental writing, increasingly standardized built environments), uniformity covers a considerable degree of difference (as noted by Aristotle already in the *Politics*).[8] The economic life of a *polis* depended on resources that varied wildly within the microecologies and connectivities of Mediterranean geography (so that territory size does not determine wealth).[9] The geography and ecology of the *polis* include the Aegean but also Southern Italy, the Black Sea, Northern Africa, Anatolia, the Levant, Mesopotamia, and Egypt. We have seen cities in dry geographies such as Attica or the Aegean islands, in wet geographies such as western Greece or the Balkan settings of the modern Albanian coast, in the alluvial plains of Macedonia or of Western Asia

Minor. We have seen cities of fishermen[10] and cities of farmers, even of caravan traders and camel-drivers. Does it matter that Palmyra was a *polis*?

Diversity was reflected internally in social relations, in crucial areas such as access to resources and economic power, and externally in the degree of agency a city could achieve. In addition, diversity played out in time, over centuries that saw important historical change—political, economic, and even climatic. What unites the island *polis* of Hērakleia ca. 250 BCE, which had a population in the hundreds in a territory of 18 square kilometers, and Ephesos under the Roman empire, with a spectacular monumental center, an urban population of at least 20,000, and a vast territory stretching into the Kaystros valley and along the Ionian coast?[11] It is not difficult to illustrate the disparity between the various elements in the same drawer labeled "*polis*." In the course of our narrative, places wink in and out of focus. We need only to look at the evidence and context for any one "Greek city," or region including several cities, to see diversity and change (as old Herodotos knew already).

The tableau of diversity has led W. Gawantka and E. Lévy to challenge the postulate of unity as the construct of modern political desire (see above, chapter 1).[12] In reaction, this book is premised on the existence of a common thread that connects the diverse communities in space and time. The story of the *polis* is precisely that of a construct, but of a normative one. The unitary phenomenon of *polis* forms integrates local diversity in two ways. First, it simplifies it into the "normal" institutions and parts, corresponding to generalized expectations as concerns both internal and external life. Second, it allows—indeed encourages—epichoric specificities to act as markers of distinctiveness and hence communal identity, within a network of peer-polities. The Panopeians' claim to be immigrants from Orchomenos, descendants of the infamous Phlegyans, establishes this border city's difference from the Phokians (to whose federal organization the Panopeians nonetheless belonged); the rival toponym "Phanoteus" claims the city for Phokis, as a foundation of the Phokian hero Phanotos (perhaps as part of a takeover of the city in the "Archaic" period).[13]

Beyond their precise political force, these traditions manifest Panopeus's great antiquity, its right to exist as a *polis*, and also the modalities of its existence as a *polis*. The attempt to connect the place, through visible and sensual signs, with the earliest times of humanity, might represent an effort to express the uniqueness of Panopeus in ways that briefly allowed its citizens to escape the issues of local politics (where belonging to the Phokian entity was both necessary and irksome). The various markers of the small city of Narykos, not so far from Panopeus, reflect the same sense of antiquity and uniqueness—and also the way in which specialness is involved in political life, since it allows the city to fend off the claim of hostile neighbors.

My final postulate is that the unity of *polis* forms rests on issues of political power. Panopeus's uniqueness, just as the proofs of Narykos's right to *polis*-hood, are part of this constructed, unitary history. One reason why this matters is that stateness creates the space for local self-government. The concrete forms taken by the latter were, externally, a striving toward some form of autonomy; and internally, a tendency toward the sovereignty of a community of equal citizens, as evidenced in ideology and in practice—and hence toward some form of democracy. This is the point of Pausanias's checklist of built environment, state institutions, and collective storytelling. Together, such features symbolize but also enact the essential traits of the *polis* as political community; namely, its existence as an autonomous entity, endowed with agency, intent on self-governance, and naturalizing the solidarity of its members through fictions and monuments. The checklist further allowed communities to recognize each other as peers—thus ensuring the broad unity of the phenomenon of the *polis*.

Autonomy and Politics

Autonomy has been one of the main focuses in this book. It is part of the characteristics of the early phases of *polis* formation, namely of the definition of communities and their territorial structuration: hence the importance of warfare, as one of the tools of self-definition. I have also argued that autonomy (as resistance to hegemony and subordination) is one of the leitmotifs of the tragic century (460–360 BCE) and that, after many vicissitudes and changes, it constituted a major outcome of the subsequent great convergence. Military means, human and physical (such as the walls of Panopeus but also the arms of citizen militiamen), remained essential to the *polis* for defense and affirmation throughout its history (above, pp. 266–71, for cases during the second century BCE).[14] Under the integrative pressure of the big Hellenistic states, and then the Roman imperial state, autonomy suffered serious, undeniable erosion; but this process also drove the emergence of various forms of proxies for autonomy, such as the claim to status and dignity through buildings, festivals, and competitions, and generally cultural identity (as at Panopeus or Narykos). These proxies themselves were, by then, very old expressions of the status of *poleis* as participants in a network of peers and also of claims to power and agency (as, for instance, in the Peloponnese down the ages).[15]

The importance of autonomy as an essential part of *polis*-hood has been denied by M. Hansen, on the grounds that some *poleis* were subordinate to others, not just in hegemonical structures or even in alliances or federal states (which strains the definition of "subordinate"), but also within direct, close bonds of subjection. For instance, Chairōneia, a *polis*, somehow "contributed to" its bigger neighbor Orchomenos, the regional entity of Boiōtia.[16] Throughout the present work, I argue against this view. I try to establish that autonomy is inseparable from the stateness that Hansen rightly places at the heart of *polis*-hood. The norm of autonomy made relations of subordination highly problematic, indeed unsustainable, and the tension between norm and hegemony structured the whole tragedy of the Hundred Years' War of the "Classical" period.

This is as true of the great hegemonical drives of the fifth and fourth centuries BCE as of the local relations of dependency. The latter was often a blip, a temporary bargain or a noticeable anomaly (the relationship between Mantineia and Helissōn illustrates all of these: above, pp. 177–78), and the collapse of hegemony, ultimately and by association, did away with the "dependent *poleis*" so central to Hansen's case.[17] To insist on the central importance of autonomy is not to argue (as German legal historian A. Heuss did) that the *polis* was so essentially free that there were no legal concepts to describe its subjection. On the contrary, such concepts did exist, as pointed out forcefully by E. Bickerman at his most legalist: *poleis* were integrated within empires along a scale of statuses and privileges granted by the ruling power and which, from the start, included the grant of the horizon of liberty itself.[18] But the existence of these concepts is itself predicated on the workings of a self-governing *polis*.[19] Subordination presupposes some bounded, self-governing entity to be subordinated in the first place (since a "subordinate *polis*" is not integrated like a village or civic subdivision). By its very definition, the subordination of the *polis* opens the way to contradictions and tensions that required a spectrum of solutions from dissolution and annexation to breakaway freedom, to proxies for autonomy and the constant, uneasy negotiation that characterizes the condition of the *polis* from the third century BCE onwards.

What was the point of autonomy? Of course, the most obvious advantage is freedom from external exploitation; if this ideal was not attained, proxies for autonomy established the right of the local community to bargain for better conditions, and the self-awareness to pursue collective goals in the face of external interlocutors big and small. Another important function of autonomy was internal to the political community. Autonomy crucially enabled communal decision-making on issues of governance,[20] membership, procedure, rules, adjudication, and the administration of public goods. These issues of state power (which constitute another central theme of this book) further intersected with the matrix of power between the rich and the poor. Such an analysis is a simplification of the diversities of local situations, but a simplification created by the ancient institutions themselves, and a crucial instance of the way in which the unity of *polis* forms tended to abstract debates and issues. In spite of local variation in naming and in institutional detail, the outcome of these debates was the constitutional "great convergence" starting in the late fourth century BCE, predicated on democratic institutions with the strong potential to limit elite domination, within an articulate communal ideology that tries to balance public claims and private property, economic inequality and political equality.[21]

The subsequent tensions, persisting into the Roman empire, are predicated on the nature of the great convergence as a social as well as an institutional phenomenon, through the practice of *leitourgia* and honours. The double nature, external and internal, of communal self-government explains why the expression "democracy" or "cities ruled by the people," *dēmokratoumenai poleis*, can designate both external autonomy and internal democracy (in our modern terminology).[22] When the first-century BCE geographer and historian Strabo narrated (or imagined) the early history of Mytilēnē, he summarized the actions of the politician Pittakos as "dissolving the family monopolies on rule (*dunasteiai*) and restoring autonomy."[23]

Both aspects, external and internal, are predicated on the operation of state power. To place stateness and power at the heart of *polis*-hood is to reaffirm a broader Aristotelian view, whose various tenets are of particular interest here in helping enrich but also confirm our interpretation of the *polis*. First, the Aristotelian focus on political power should be completed by the concept that life in a community raises moral issues—the "living well" (*eu zēn*) which is an important theme of the *Politics*. This aspect constitutes the theme of the following chapter of this book (and also overshadows the next chapters, on interests and domination). Second, an Aristotelian view posits that social relations in the *polis* can be meaningfully simplified to the inherent opposition between a leisured elite (defined by wealth, though often keen to claim innate superiority) and a majoritarian mass of free but not wealthy citizens. Third, the questions of access to and control of political power will directly affect the ways institutions are deployed around interests, especially as conceived by the group that "rules" constitutionally.[24] The *dēmos* will favor redistribution, and even more, will try to entrench protection from the rich:

> the poor, even if they do not share in honours, are willing to keep quiet, as long as no one exercises arrogant violence (*hubris*) or takes away anything of their property.[25]

The rich, conversely, aim to maximize economic power. They strive to protect property interests, limit redistribution, and ensure enforceability of contracts (especially in matters of debt and rent).

Finally, one of the main components of an Aristotelian approach is the democratic potential of *polis* forms and concepts that Aristotle grappled with when he wrote on the eve of the great convergence, preferring to speak of *autarkeia* and *politeia* rather than autonomy and democracy. We should perhaps not be so afraid of the latter terms since we mercifully do not live in the fraught world of the later fourth century BCE. Notably, the issues of elite honors and recognition, office-holding, and the distribution of the financial burdens of *polis* life are crucial, and are regularly mentioned in Aristotle's *Politics*, just as they constitute a resonant theme in *polis* history.

The Trouble with Aristotle: *Polis* as Society

An Aristotelian approach to the *polis* is deeply concerned with which group will rule over it or at least in it (the rich, the poor, the "best," an individual), and in whose interest. Hence, such an approach entails a constant awareness that institutions matter deeply for their practical consequences. However, it is immediately obvious that politics and more generally life in the *polis* were more than just a question of Aristotle-style institutions, be they deliberative, executive, or legal.[26] The Athenian Agora is clearly a site of government[27] and civic ideology,[28] monumental, inscribed, and enacted, the space of officeholding, inscribed law and honorific monument. Yet the Agora was also a space filled with the stalls, screens, and stands of retailers and craftsmen: a market for myriad commodities, a place to get services such as haircuts or commodities such as pottery or enslaved workers, and the venue for informal encounters. The members of the deme of Dekeleia in the mountain of northern Attica used to meet at a particular barbershop, next to the Herms (that is, pillar-statues of the god Hermēs set up by former magistrates next to the Stoa of the Archōn-King).[29]

The "Aristotelian" institutional workings of deliberation, administration, or adjudication not only took place cheek-by-jowl with daily social activities but were directly impacted by a sphere of extra-institutional power (D. Gottesmann) in the form of "stunts" or gestures such as supplication or social performances outside the institutional venues, or even before institutionalized entities such as the Assembly or the jury-courts. The performance of grief and mourning by the relatives of Athenian servicemen lost at sea after the battle of Arginoussai in 406 BCE influenced the outcome of the trial of the Athenian generals, accused *en bloc* of failing to save them. Reputation, public opinion, and gossip served to police the Athenian community in the absence of any strong administrative and coercive structure.[30] The city of Athens was a space of multiple extra-institutional, informal experiences and of interactions between individuals and groups involving citizens, immigrants, enslaved workers. These interactions cannot be defined by or limited to the terms of political institutions and formal citizenship, yet were constitutive of social life in what K. Vlassopoulos (taking a leaf from a book by the radical social theorists Sara M. Evans and Harry C. Boyte) termed "free spaces" of creativity and agency.[31] As B. Akrigg notes, Plato famously portrays in the opening of his *Republic* a scene where "elite citizens and wealthy metics mingle and are at ease in each other's company"—in the house of one Kephalos, a metic and the father of Lysias, also a metic and a specialist *logographos* who produced speeches for Athenian citizens to use in court.[32]

An extra-institutional viewpoint acts as an invitation to consider the *polis* not just as citizenship and access to political institutions, but to embrace its whole breadth as a society of associations, a field where individuals are members of multiple overlapping groups, reflecting multifaceted identities. After all, even Aristotle in the *Politics* admitted that not only were there multitudes of *poleis*, but that each *polis* itself was a multitude.[33] To reuse a term favored by Aristotle, the city is made up of *koinōniai*, or communities. These include the civic subdivisions that have been a familiar feature of our narrative of *polis*-hood. For instance, in the early *polis* we have seen kinship-based or kinship-adjacent groups—clans (*genē*), "brotherhoods," tribes—but also locality-based associations. The demes of Attica, formalized in the "Kleisthenic" reforms of 508 BCE and an integral part of Athenian society for the subsequent three centuries or so, are the best-known example. Local groups were organized in larger structures, such as the cultic association in northeast Attica, the Marathonian Tetrapolis.[34] Other associations grouped individuals around shared activities or interests (financial or professional): associative life is already taken for granted in a law attributed to the early sixth-century BCE reformer Solōn.[35]

Associations were everywhere in the *polis*. They could be as simple as a group of commensals or drinking partners; as focused as a funerary club (such as the *temenitai*, gathering citizens, foreigners, women, for religious activities including the maintenance of members' tombs);[36] as specific as an organization of metalworkers in Tlōs in 150 BCE, or of market gardeners in a city of Roman-imperial Asia Minor, Thyateira;[37] as elaborate as the associations in Hellenistic Rhodes whose multi-barreled names declared complex histories of formation and cultic practice.[38] One example is the *Eranistai Samothrakiastai Hermaistai Aristobouliastai Panathēnaistai hoi sun Ktesiphōnti* ("The Members of the Mutual Fund of Worshippers of the Samothrakian Gods, of Hermēs, founded by Aristoboulos, celebrators of the Panathenaia, under the direction of Ktesiphon"). Associations even had their own chapters. Thus the *Panathēnaistai systrateusamenoi syskanoi*, the "celebrators of the Panathenaia, on campaign together, who are tent-mates" formed their own *koinon*.

An essential part of the associative life was the feasting whose traces are ubiquitous in *polis* history.[39] Examples include the dining groups or "herds" of youth of Crete in the seventh and sixth centuries BCE; the festive gatherings of citizen, foreigner, and enslaved, paid for by benefactors in the late second century BCE; and the feasts celebrated in third-century CE Palmyra in honor of certain gods, and to which admission was gained by presenting clay tokens.[40] The associative phenomenon is thus a major part of *polis* history, in spite of all the changes in *polis* forms. It has rightly received sustained scholarly investigation (notably because it intersects with interest in the history of religions in the Roman empire, especially that of Judaism and Christianity). This phenomenon has usually received piecemeal, period- and context- specific explanations. But when we see that the associative phenomenon can be interpreted both as a reaction to democracy (in the Classical *polis*), and a reaction to oligarchy (in the Roman-era *polis*), we might realize that prevalence of the associative phenomenon might have some more general, structural connection with the *polis* form.

But what is left of the *polis* itself, if we disassemble it down to a field within which individuals associated at a number of levels and scales, and across multiple associations? A natural follow-up would be to say that, to all intents and purposes, these associations *were* the *polis*. After all, Polybios (albeit in a satirical portrayal) described late third-century BCE Boiōtia as overtaken by drinking and feasting associations ("there were many Boiotians for whom there were more dinners per month than days assigned in the calendar").[41] But what would such a statement as "the associations were the *polis*" mean? It claims that the associative level was where meaningful interactions occurred, notably in the realms of economic collaboration, religious performance, and the microdynamics of social power. It also posits that the associative phenomenon was constitutive of the *polis* in a more fundamental or real way than political and governmental institutions were. The choices and agency of social actors to interact with other actors, according to a number of factors (including discourses, ideas, or nonhuman conditions), seem to result in a criss-crossing, shifting network of constantly performed relations. But according to what principles? The answer can only be local and context-bound (thus challenging my postulate of the *polis* as a unitary phenomenon).

In this view (inspired by Bruno Latour's actor-network theory), the aggregate of relations is what really matters in the history of the urban settlements of the eastern Mediterranean.[42] The Roman-era *polis* might gain by being viewed as the aggregate of elite families, their power of patronage, and the social interactions of the professional associations. Indeed, the shrines and even the *agora* of many cities, from the fourth century BCE onwards, exhibit side-by-side honorific statues dedicated by the *polis* (represented institutionally as the People, or the People and the Council) and statue portraits set up by civic subdivisions, associations, or especially families: the *polis* appears as a field of multiple actors and transactions.[43] These manifestations are not devoid of a political dimension but they take place at a remove from the veil of formal political institutions of the *polis*. Indeed, we might choose to view these manifestations as the real locus of power and politics—as has been explicitly proposed for the "Archaic" *polis* (above, pp. 139–40) or the "Indian Summer" of the *polis* (above, pp. 284–85).

In such a deconstruction of the institutional view, there is no justification for the centering of the citizen as stakeholder with access to political institutions. Membership in the *polis* dissolves into a fluid play of multiple, indeterminate statuses.[44] The significant characteristic of Classical Athens becomes not the citizen/noncitizen dichotomy but the many gradations of privileges and spaces of agency for inhabitants, including resident foreigners and even slaves. As part of this picture of generalized fluidity, we might underline the fact that Athenian citizens could be punished by the forfeiture of political rights and access to the *agora*, or even subject to corporal violence in certain circumstances, thus blurring the distinction between enslaved and free.[45] In Classical Sparta, citizens who had proved cowardly in battle and went by the infamous name of "tremblers" could be partially disfranchised by losing the right to buy and sell, as well as being cut off from the contacts of normal sociability; such second-class citizens joined the ranks of "Inferiors" which included impoverished Spartiates but also bastard children of half-Spartiate birth (above, pp. 195–97). Another example of unevenness in the field of social status is the privilege given to Spartiates from the *oba* of Amyklai (a locally based civic subdivision) of attending the festival of the Hyakinthia, even when serving in the army (in 390 BCE, the practice resulted in a disastrous military defeat on the line of march).[46]

As with the case of the Spartiates from Amyklai, differences ran even within the group of fully enfranchised adult male citizens. Some of these differences were formalized: even in democratic Athens, census requirements for office never were officially abolished. Other differences were created by multiple differences and inequalities in wealth, leisure, access to resources and social capital. For instance, access to institutional workings must necessarily have been different for citizens according to proximity to the urban center that the *polis* never ceased being, and this difference was exacerbated by wealth and class. Rural wealthy citizens might have multiple residences or networks of guest friends to tighten bonds with the urban center; the rural poor, on the other hand, might show up in town a few times in their lives. This at least is how Cocceianus Diōn imagined a rustic citizen relating to the urban center of his *polis* (above, pp. 347–48). Under the Roman empire, the *polis* often appears under the guise of a bundle of multiple groups: the young men, the people who frequent the *gymnasion*, the old, the "other citizens," the dwellers-by, the foreigners, the Romans, the landowning noncitizens (often wealthy members of other cities). . . . [47] We will revisit these barriers and inequalities in the *polis* (chapter 19).

A particularly rich example of *polis* as social complexity is offered by Rhodes. This was a "new" *polis* created in 408 BCE out of the synoikism of three original *poleis* (Ialysos, Kameiros, and the spectacularly well-documented Lindos), but it also was a territorial entity comprising a center (the island) and outlying territories on the Karian mainlands and on the islands (fig. 15.2).[48] The tiny island of Symē or the long rocky island of Karpathos were both integrated into the Rhodian entity, but seem to have had "inhabitants" who were not full citizens.

Inscriptions document complex local organization and diversity: for instance, "those living in Symē" gathered in a corporation (*koinon*) to honor a full citizen of Rhodes, thus showing the coexistence of citizen and noncitizen in the same social space.[49] The members of Lindos (one of the three original *poleis* on Rhodes) defended their exclusive access to priesthoods and rites, against the claims of citizens from outlying regions on the island and on the Karian mainland. The mainland areas were annexed shortly after 305 BCE by the Rhodian state and assigned to demes belonging to one of the original three cities. Yet, the original Lindians successfully defended their nativist privilege, in a hearing before the Rhodian state (they celebrated their victory in a monumental inscription). As C. Thomsen notes, "not a single Lindian citizen from a deme in the Peraia or on Karpathos ever held an office or a priesthood in Lindos," but the original Lindians felt free to legislate concerning sacred matters in the overseas "Lindian" demes.[50] The consequence was that overseas Rhodians could hold office in the central Rhodian state, but were excluded from the original three cities; Rhodian citizenship was separated by history and geography into patterns of privilege and exclusion.

Furthermore, the diffusion of the *polis* model generated complexities and diversities in the citizen body.[51] An example is the presence, in second-century BCE Philadelpheia (in Lydia), of an "association of the citizens and of the ephebes under

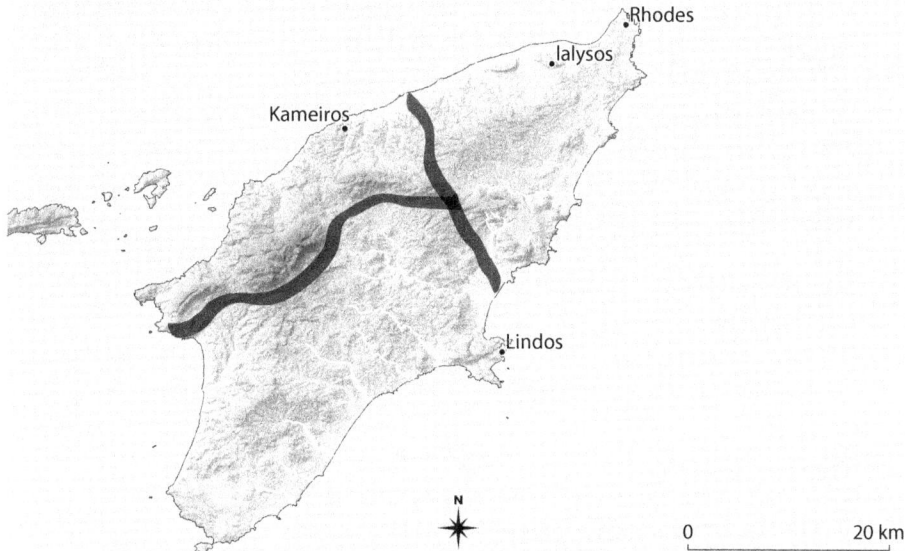

FIGURE 15.2. Rhodes and its subdivisions. After Thomsen 2020.

Nikanōr," honoring the latter official: these might be citizens of a Hellenistic military foundation installed in the midst of a rural settlement (the inscribed stele recording the honor was found 5 kilometers away from the city). The end result of the process was the situation, in at least some Roman-era *poleis*, whereby urban dwellers and members of the socioeconomic elite had become a formally recognized citizen body, with rights not enjoyed by the rural inhabitants (above, p. 342). Even without such formal statuses, civic ceremony distinguished between the Council, officeholders, members of special groups of grain-dole recipients, and other citizens. The *polis* begins to look more like an early-modern city, with a spectrum of statuses and privileges.[52]

Participation and Performance

If citizenship itself was not a matter of institutional definition, then what was it? To define membership away from merely institutional definitions shifts our focus to a wide array of participatory activities, which were political in the sense of community-forming, without being strictly about politics in the narrow sense. In 403 BCE, in a context of civil war, the historian Xenophon writes, Kleokritos, the herald of the initiates of Eleusis, a most august personage in Athens, invited the oligarchical party to lay down arms:[53]

> Fellow citizens (*andres politai*), why do you drive us out? Why do you want to kill us? We never did you any harm, but we have shared with you in the most

solemn rites and sacrifices and the most magnificent festivals, we have been companions in the dance and fellow festival-goers and fellow soldiers, and we have braved many dangers with you both by land and by sea in defense of the common safety and freedom of both of our parties. By the gods of our fathers and mothers, by our ties of kinship and marriage and comradeship—for all these many of us share with one another—cease, out of shame before gods and men, to do wrong against your fatherland . . .

This portrayal of citizenship in action is deeply political but not institutional in the strictest sense: it is about the public performance of gestures and activities. In addition to any institutional functions, and its workings as an open venue of fluid social interactions, the *agora* was often a space for the performance of rituals; for instance, the choruses, processions, and dances we can guess at in "Archaic" Athens or Argos, but also in later periods.[54] At Priēnē around 100 BCE, the *agora* could transform into a processional avenue with spectators on either side, some sitting under familial statue groups, others on a low flight of steps. The huge, portico-lined public square of third-century CE Smyrna was not only the setting for the informal interactions hinted at by graffiti, but also the venue for the execution of Christians, a type of event which constituted violent mass happenings in an urban context.[55] As we have seen, the performed nature of citizenship is a very striking feature of the early *polis*. This could take the form of social performance in the small groups of the feast and the drinking group, or of self-styling in body and vestments (for instance, regulated flaunting of markers of luxury such as horse-rearing or long hair) with a view to manifest and conform to group identity. In A. Duplouy's striking formulation, citizenship was a *habitus* rather than a matter of institutions.[56]

Such manifestations were performative (in the technical sense of Austinian speech-act theory, by which statements act on the world). Just as felicitous performance created eminence and distinction for competitive elites, it constructed the group and established membership in it, based on "uptake" (to use the Austinian term): that is, acceptance in the fluid world of interactions, associations and statuses.[57] *Polis* as the practice of a mode of life invites an anthropological analysis centered on identity, symbol, and memory—themes close to the so-called Paris School and its structuralist analysis of the *polis*. Nor are such phenomena limited to an "Archaic" period. The practice of citizenship is equally centered on participation in festival culture in later centuries, in fifth- and fourth-century BCE Athens, or during the "Indian Summer" of the second century BCE. At Kolophōn ca. 100 BCE, as we have seen, long honorific decrees for good citizens describe a whole register of actions: acting as an advocate for the city and holding office, but also sporting competition, sacred travel, sacrifices and dedications, money lending and pledges, festivals, public entertainment (*akroamata*), distributions of meat or cakes to citizens and foreigners alike, and lavish feasts for special age groups (the young and the elders). Similar pictures emerge from other cities in the Hellenistic period, in different contexts (for instance, Teōs in 203 BCE, when it reengineered its social life around ruler cult for the Seleukid ruler Antiochos III, or Priēnē in its honors for great benefactors).[58]

To appropriate an Aristotelian term once again (or simply to return the term to its original noninstitutional context), we might describe the *polis* as concerned with *koinōnia* in the sense of partaking or communion. Religious ritual and experiences formed a central part of *polis* as communion; indeed, religious ritual, especially animal sacrifice and the consumption of sacrificial meat, was a major part of the shared activities of the human community and of the institutional officeholders. Partaking in sacred matters is occasionally described as a constituent part of being a citizen, when citizenship is shared between communities or granted to individuals: new citizens are allowed to have "a share in the sacred matters, which all the other citizens share in."[59] Officeholders are honored for the successful accomplishment of the sacred duties of sacrifice and ritual.[60] The *polis* was what the *polis* did, and what the *polis* did was to worship and to honor the gods, through ritual events and material manifestations. "The core of the *polis* was its bond with the gods," as J. Blok writes.[61] Such concerns were the first item of business transacted in meetings in many *poleis* (a special mark of honor was to have priority access to the Assembly "after the sacred matters").[62]

One of the signs of the emergence and consolidation of the *polis* is the building of monumental temples to patron deities, which unifies the community and relates it to a network of its peers (through competition and by analogy),[63] and the religious nature of civic monuments and spaces never abates. The *agora* itself was a sacred space, filled with shrines. The city's main deity, honored in its most important shrine and festivals, could represent the community in visual shorthand (for instance, at Aizanoi; fig. 13.2); the synekdoche is already present on "Archaic" coinage (for instance early Athenian coinage with the head of Athēna) and lasts down to the cult of patron saints in Late Roman cities.[64] The nature of the *polis* as a compact between a human community and the world of the gods is visible not just in the participatory nature of *polis* religion, but also in the claims it makes on its inhabitants. Festival activities reached out to individuals within the whole diverse social space of the community; they imposed the physical, bodily, and spatial performance of participation in the form of leisure, special clothing or accessories such as crowns, and installations such as domestic altars.[65]

To see the *polis* as essentially a religious organization takes us far from Aristotle's institutional focus on political power. In this capacious performance- and participation-based model, the adult male citizen and his involvement in political institutions are no longer the measure for all things, or at least the touchstone for the nature of the *polis*. Women, for instance, are taken to be as full members of the community. Notably, citizen women fulfil an important part in the cultic affairs that are a central part of civic activities, as participants in festivals, or as holders of religious office.[66] The latter could be highly visible (as with the priestesses of Athens), or more discreet (as on Hellenistic Rhodes, where female deities were served by female priestesses, but without the latter being prominent in the honorific record).[67] The complementarity of male magistrates and female priestesses appears explicitly in the negotiations between the two *poleis* of Medeōn and Steiris in Phokis when the two cities joined in civic union (*sumpoliteia*): "let it not be possible to force the Medeonians to serve (*leitourgein*) in office at Steiris, if they have been *archōns, xenodikai*, exactors, *damiourgoi*, priests, hierarchs, and, among the women, if they have served as priestesses."[68]

Furthermore, citizen women transmitted citizen status through legitimate birth, in democratic Athens from 451 BCE onwards, as well as many other (perhaps most) cities in the subsequent centuries (for instance, Kōs or Rhodes)—this seems a clear indication of the full integration of women within the *polis* as community. By guaranteeing citizen status, they also transmitted the right to participate in the ritual life of the *polis* as sacred community of religious interaction with the gods. Crucially, women perpetuated the *polis* by biological and social reproduction, by bringing forth legitimate citizen children. They ensured the inheritance of citizen property and hence the continuity of households in the *polis*.[69] In this view of the *polis*, women are fully *citizens*, and even children are citizens, inasmuch as both groups participated in the *polis*'s religious life. Their presence as citizens and full members of the *polis* can serve as an emblem for a history of the *polis* as a society that is not dominated by adult male elite presences.[70] Hence, logically, women could be the recipient of citizenship grants in other cities; indeed, this is duly documented in epigraphical documents from the third century BCE onwards. In such a history, what need of Aristotle's focus on institutions, what need of the state at all?

Bringing the State Back In

There is much force to a critique of banal Aristotelianism in any history of the *polis*. The costs of my basic choice of looking at the *polis* not as a history of settlement and society but as a history of political institutions, have haunted this book, as continuously setting the limits of what can be said. An example of the dilemma is the way in which specialists in Hellenistic epigraphy are perhaps all too comfortable defining and identifying a *polis* with a stroke of the pen, in reference to a list (admittedly an inductively constructed and well-documented list) of institutions and status markers: a *polis* is not a village or a town, has political institutions, is recognized by peers and imperial masters. The catalogues of *theōrodokoi* (hosts for official sacred envoys) enumerate *poleis* as clearly defined political communities recognized by other *poleis*. This sort of history leaves out a lot, even if I have tried to pay some attention throughout the narrative to social relations, cultural identity, ecology, and economics. Yet this sort of critique within a "new social history" of the *polis* is also problematic in major ways. In what follows, I would like to make a plea for the centrality of the state, a plaidoyer for bringing the state back in, even or perhaps especially in a social-cultural history of the *polis*—but in full awareness of the consequences of this intellectual move.[71]

It is true that in the case of the *polis*, we are dealing with a distinctive type of state, reflecting its very nature and constitutive processes. The nature of the *polis* complicates any attempt to understand the importance of institutionalized state power, because of the immediacy of relations between state and members—a dimension that is itself deeply ideological (as all constructions of the state must be). The nature of the *polis* as citizen-state is manifested by its constant designation as a noun (the *ethnikon*) in the masculine plural: the Prienians, the Athenians, the Hērakleiotes. The trope is ubiquitous in narrative, but also in such media as civic coinage, where the *polis* (a singular noun) can be completed by the *ethnikon* in the plural, in hybrid grammatical constructions that show the equation between the abstract concept of *polis* and its sense of a community of citizens (see above, p. 374, on the case of Apameia in Syria). A striking image of this nature of the *polis* as society is given by the urban plan of Priēnē. As suggested by F. Rumscheid, Priēnē was not structured by public spaces of power but deliberately created as the sum of modules for private houses, themselves determined by the standardized size of the dining couches for small gatherings. The whole grid plan of Priēnē is generated by the needs of the citizen household and the face-to-face meetings of citizens in modular groups.[72]

The *polis* can be expressed as the sum of its members; alternatively, it can be described as "the common thing" of its members, the *koinon*, for instance *to koinon tōn Delphōn/Ilieōn* ..., "the commonality of the Delphians" or "... of the Ilians."[73] The word can be understood as describing community, but it also has the sense of the "common property" of that human community. The *polis*, a community, was materialized as the sum of the members' property, interests, and claims. The territory was the aggregate of its members' real estate, so that land ownership was long restricted to citizens. When the Ephesian priest of Artemis was allowed to own land at Priēnē, he was forbidden from holding property contiguous to the border, lest his ownership allow the Ephesians to claim his property as part of their territory. Conversely, a friend of the Seleukid king Antiochos I, given an estate from the royal land, was allowed to attach it to the civic territory of any city he chose.[74] This aggregative and immediate conception of the *polis* explains why public goods such as proceeds from mines or the windfall of elite gifts, were distributed to individual citizens, throughout the *polis*'s history (for instance above, pp. 122–23, 337, 342, 364).

The immediacy of the *polis* influenced its stately manifestations. An obvious characteristic of the *polis* is the thinness of its apparatus. In the *polis* there is no real bureaucracy. The "remembrancer" of Datala in "Archaic" Crete was not a scribe but a member of the political community, even if his functions were to be kept in his family (above, p. 107). The allotment machines in the courts of democratic Athens were not run by technicians, but by average members of the jury, who were drawn by lot (above, p. 184). Specialist bureaucrats with power are generally absent in the *polis* (though cities do have salaried doctors or architects); many state functions are devolved onto public slaves, which reify state functions as a function of ownership by the citizens rather than as an autonomous entity with the agency and the will to pursue its own separate interests and logic.[75] The Hobbesian Leviathan is not a figure that the ancient Greek *polis* would have recognized itself in, even if it could represent itself with personifications.[76] The normal regime of alternance in power-holding, the love of large colleges, the constant resort to accountability, are also functions of the immediacy of the *polis*.

The thinness of state operations in the *polis* is not a result of technological or conceptual limitations. The *polis* had emerged out of the ruins of palatial polities that had two markers of an entrenched, active state, namely monarchy and scribal bureaucracy at the service of extraction and accumulation (above, pp. 25–29). The important processes took place during the Early Iron Ages, where communities grew in the leaderless, nonhierarchical world of the "clustervilles" (above, chapter 2). This world may have been comparable to the Tupi-Guarani anarchic formations studied by the anthropologist Pierre Clastres,[77] in its characteristics of weak executive power, community claims on the service and property of the prosperous few, and internal solidarity (as seen notably in mass participation in external conflict). All these Clastresian traits would characterize the *polis* in its history; they survived institutionalization, or perhaps drove the particular path to institutionalization in the *polis*'s history.

In view of the immediacy of the links between *polis* and society, it has proven tempting to call the *polis* a stateless society.[78] In what precedes, following the analysis of M. Hansen, I have consistently argued against this interpretation on the basis of what I see as clear signs of stateness—starting with autonomy, but especially focusing on the existence of written laws, institutionalized forms of legitimate power, and automatic processes of governance. No doubt the immediacy of the relationship between *polis* and citizens shows that the *polis*, as a citizen-state, was also a "society-state" (to coin a phrase) in which Clastresian characteristics determined the face of the state and the level of its operations. Yet this immediacy did not diminish the existence of institutions, nor their precise goal, which was the administration, protection, and even production of *to koinon*, the shared goods of the citizen community. Immediacy cut both ways: because of the nature of the *polis* as community and as the aggregation of the citizens' goods, the *polis* could also issue claims on all of its members' activity and their goods, to protect itself as common project.[79] The sense of collective project was manifested in various forms of "bigness," such as vital common spaces and structures (walls, meeting places, shrines) and public goods (such as drinking water; fig. 10.6): these have been obvious features throughout my narrative of *polis* history.

"Society-state" is ideological. As a representation of the relationship between *polis* as state personality with means of enforcement and control over public goods, and *polis* as human society, it is based on identification and elision. The latter operations allowed the society of citizens to imagine itself as the synekdoche for the whole human ecology that lived in the territory of the *polis*. This identification was particularly intense in democratic *poleis* such as Athens, where the extensive franchise fostered the sense that the citizens were the whole society, to the point that M. Canevaro argues that there was no popular culture separate from official or elite culture, only a *polis* culture that was also the culture of the People, including that expressed by the political institutions of the city.[80] This culture, as we have seen, was generalized as *polis* culture, starting early on. The poetics of *polis* as society can be seen at work in the fragmentary document that opens this book, showing the *koinon* of the islanders taking a decision for the safety of "the Herakleiotes and all those who inhabit the island."

But this example only makes all the clearer that the *polis* as society-state is closely bound with institutional power—in fact, with power over the remaining, noncitizen members of society. Thus, the citizens of Hērakleia imagine themselves as the community of islanders, but are aware that they are taking decisions that affect others who do not have a say in the Assembly, the society of "all those who inhabit the island." The *polis* of Megara passed a decree validating an honorific decision taken by one of its *kōmai* (villages), Aigosthena: the decision was inscribed "so that the people knows how to honor those who do good for the *polis* or for the *kōmai*."[81] More starkly, the citizens of the new city of Aphrodisias-Plarasa duly passed a decree (88 BCE), decided by the Council and the People, to support a Roman governor during the First Mithradatic War by sending an armed sortie that included resident foreigners (*paroikoi*) and slaves. They declared that "our whole people, with wives, children and our whole livelihood" were ready to risk all for the Roman cause.[82] Neither the wives nor children, let alone the slaves and *paroikoi,* had any say in the decisions that directly impacted their lives. The point is that institutions mattered: elections, sortition, votes, officeholding, law-making, sitting in judgment, fining, taxing, expelling—all the operations of deliberation, decision-making, judicial decision, and implementation constituted legitimate governmentality and hence a very direct, binding form of power in the *polis* with far-reaching effect on its denizens.[83]

The existence of extra-institutional, informal interactions, structured by diversity and negotiation, does not cancel out the force of autonomous institutional power as wielded by the entitled group of citizens, and the concomitant asymmetries.[84] To ignore institutional power, or to minimize its reach, comes at the risk of several confusions. One is believing that the tautologous survey of extra-institutional interactions (which are, indeed, extra-institutional) amounts to demonstrating that they somehow displaced institutional power, or prevented elections from having consequences (to borrow an expression from modern political cant). The second is mistaking a number of social metaphors and performances for social reality, an error which amounts to merely fulfilling the ideological function of such metaphors.

Now the Aristotelian *Constitution of the Athenians* notes holy matters as an important concern of the Assembly—but the latter also handled matters such as defense, food supply, or edilitary administration. The grant of citizenship in the *poleis* often specified "participation in divine matters and office-holding" as the salient facts of civic activity.[85] Likewise, the public examination of citizen candidates for office made sure that they were good family men, that they participated in religion, but also that they served the *polis* in war and paid their dues and taxes.[86]

In what follows, I propose to show that the immediacy of the relations between state and society only reinforces the validity of an Aristotelian approach to the *polis*: rather than being shaped by social relations, institutional power, embodied in the state, constituted social relations and identities. For instance, *polis* institutions distributed, as the outcome of formal workings, crucial recognition in the form of honor in the community (*timē*), in preliminary evaluations (*dokimasiai*), in the examination of performance and expenditure (*euthynai*), and in honorific decrees (above, chapter 10).[87] To posit the primacy of the institutional entails clarifying the relationships of society and politics; the consequences of the exercise will also occupy us for the rest of this book.

The *Polis* as Civic Society

The *polis* generated its own metaphorical images as a *civic society* (to coin a phrase calqued on "civil society"). This was a function of stateness but also dissimulated it in multiple ways. One form of civic society was the ubiquitous interlocking and nested system of constituent subdivisions, which I have insisted on in my earlier account. These subdivisions include dining groups (whose formalization was an important part of the early *polis*), gentilic pseudo-kindreds ("brotherhoods," etc.) constituting larger "tribes" named after divine figures or legendary heroes, and local settlements or wards (often grouped in larger units such as "tribes"). Subdivisions only exist as parts of the civic whole, and fulfil vital functions for the *polis* as state. The most basic function fulfilled by "tribes" (and the like) is to mediate membership of the *polis* (as is clear from forensic evidence from Athens, but also the generalized practice of assigning new citizens to subdivisions and tribes).[88] Civic subdivisions also served to organize the citizen body for military duties, distribute fiscal burdens or material benefits, structure political institutions such as officeholding, service on the Council, or even pay for assembly attendance (as attested at Iasos).

Civic subdivisions also follow civic protocols—for instance, in keeping a regular schedule of meetings and ritual celebrations, respecting rules and laws, and implementing institutionalized scripts such as holding officeholders to account and honoring them. Above, we saw examples at Hellenistic Milētos, Mēthymna or Samos (p. 333). They especially worked to entrench civic institutions (mass decision, accountability, and redistribution), and civic ideology. When Aristotle proposed restraining elite officeholders' acquisitiveness by holding them accountable in the Assembly, he also imagined giving the "brotherhoods" an official role by entrusting them with public bookkeeping.[89]

Such subdivisions, though they look like descent groups or associations, are civic institutions in themselves from the time of the early *polis* down to the Roman empire.⁹⁰ In Roman-era Prousias on Hypios, city neighborhoods set up and no doubt worshipped at altars of Saviour Zeus "on behalf of the *polis*."⁹¹ As the Prousian neighborhood cults show, the function of apparent multiplicity was to ensure unity and solidarity out of the social diversity of the *polis*. In their constant coming together, the multiple subunits of civic society reenacted the obscure origins of the *polis* (as an institution, but also in the case of every individual city-state): rites were about rights, specifically the right to the city. A particularly elaborate and instructive example comes from second-century BCE Bargylia (above, p. 273). This Karian *polis* increased the honors of their deity, Artemis Kindyas, by distributing public funds to civic subdivisions and to the various bodies of civic magistrates in order to subsidize the raising of oxen for a bovine beauty contest and for ultimate sacrifice and consumption. The distribution took place according to a law of the city (duly passed through institutional mechanisms and involving an amendment). It benefited the tribes, the magistrates, the resident foreigners as a group.⁹² The parallelism between the tribes and the magistrates as constituent parts of the institutional workings of the *polis* is striking; metics are constituted as a quasi-civic group within the *polis*.

What the boutrophic subsidies at Bargylia show is the close link between ritual performance and civic institutions. Rituals mobilize institutional means but also act as a proxy for membership and access to institutions. The case of Bargylia also illustrates the propensity of institutions to metaphorize and to naturalize themselves. This analysis can fruitfully be applied to the ritualized performance of citizenship, as described above (notably for the "Archaic" *polis*): such performance is closely related to the institutional aspects of the *polis*. Rituals and performance enact the entitlement that is institutionalized citizenship, namely access to the protection of person and property, to decision-making, and to honor and recognition. This was already the central insight of the anthropologizing approach practiced by the "School of Paris" spearheaded by J.-P. Vernant and P. Vidal-Naquet, namely that rituals and discourse dramatized inclusion and reinforced solidarity among the citizen group.⁹³

Additionally, participation and rituals embody real goods in themselves. The *polis* provided consumables such as partaking of animal protein or diluted but vitamin-rich, psychotropic, and addictive ethanol-based drink,⁹⁴ paid for by political processes of redistribution or semi-voluntary elite generosity. Further public goods that flowed as a result of entitlement were economic, such as cash or grain (distributed for free or sold cheap thanks to collective means). Finally, the *polis* also provided, as an entitlement of membership, emotional satisfactions: the feeling of belonging to a community, the sense of ownership over space, territory, built environment, and history, or the collective and orderly communion with the supernatural in order to honor the gods, ask them for favors, and offer thanks.⁹⁵ The nature of the *polis* as purveyor of emotional or affective goods also appears in occasions of ceremonial mourning in public funerals (at Pergamon, provided for all citizens) or consolation decrees for the death of promising elite citizens.⁹⁶ Indeed, all those were part of the "good life" that the *polis* procured for its members (rather than the contemplative life that Plato and indeed Aristotle wished for), and gave participation and performance real substance and desirability.

The metaphors of participation were all the more important because the *polis* did not clearly define citizenship as a bill of rights (though a concept of *dikaia*, "just and right things," did emerge).[97] Participation in rituals offered a visible symbol of membership as well as a means of accrediting the members of the political community. The close connection between the *polis* as institution and the ritual performance of identity is visible everywhere, notably in the cardinal genre of the honorific decree. In this type of document, the city displayed itself as the play of institutions and politics, morphing into civic ritual and monument through stereotypical gestures such as the repeated proclamation of honorific crowns, or through normed repertoires such as honorific inscriptions or even portraits in painted or sculpted forms. The hot city of politics turned to the cold city of ritual and imagery.[98]

My account of the *polis* gives much attention to reading the literature of state found in the honorific register. A simple example, recently published, from the *polis* of Karthaia on the island of Keōs (early third century BCE) illustrates the proximity of ritual and political institutions. A citizen "receives praise for continuous service as a good citizen," on the following grounds:

> Since Theoklēs the *archōn* in earlier times shows continuous zeal for the people and now having entered the office of *stephanēphoros* he completely offers the sacrifices to the gods well and with zeal, and takes care of the citizens, spending on many items out of his own resources, and he administers all the other things related to his office well and with zeal . . .

Theoklēs's reward was to be a crown, a proclamation in civic festivals, and a yearly gift of fifteen drachmas for him to offer sacrifice—all three items of expenditure being met out of public funds and paid out by the city treasurer.[99] The importance of religion is obvious: sacrifices are mentioned first, as an important part of the duties. But they are not the only part and this decree does not show that the direct point of the *polis* was religious communion. Religious ritual is a sublimated, generalized, acceptable showcase for the administrative activities of the *stephanēphoros*; the decree shows the role of religion as a token and a proxy within institutional workings—and as an image or a mythology that *polis* gives of itself, to itself, and to others. The genre of the honorific decree is entirely about producing these stylized images of a "cold city" of ritual. As we have seen above, other sources allow us to reconstruct practical activities by officeholders (notably in the Roman-era city of Plutarch or Cocceianus Diōn); we will later try to revisit some images in search of what conflicts or tensions they might hide.

The workings of statuses and gender similarly should be viewed as functions of the *polis* as state and the centrality of the entitled adult male citizen. Diverse statuses in the *polis*, favored or indeed disfavored, were defined in relationship to citizenship as participation in institutions, especially judicial, but also political (since the noncitizens were defined by access to the former but not the latter). In other words, such statuses work by being like the "full" or "complete" citizen of Aristotle—or by subtracting certain properties of citizenship, such as socioeconomic rights but also participatory rights. The position of citizen women (*politides*) in the *polis* was likewise defined in relationship to male citizenship as held by participants in political institutions.[100] It reflects a civic order produced by negotiations between the citizen stakeholders in the institutions of decision- and law-making; women's roles and functions, notably in transmitting property and perpetuating citizen households, are ultimately regulated by those institutions. If we accept my suggestion that participation in ritual and performance are civic fictions, acting as very real metaphors for participation, female participation in these rituals at festivals or through the representative function of priestesses, can be viewed as another constituent metaphor of civic order. In the city of Medeōn (quoted above), the detailed and varied roster of functions fulfilled by men contrasts with the solitary mention of priesthoods for women.

The function of gender within debates about citizenship can clearly be seen in the generalized practice of defining citizenship through birth from two citizen parents (already mentioned above), a practice that was inaugurated in mid-fifth century BCE Athens but spread to other *poleis* during the great convergence.[101] This norm can be interpreted as democratic in that it extended to the whole population the elitist concern with birth, and hence constructed an aristocratic metaphor for citizenship consistent with the *polis*'s conception of itself as a descent group. This latter conception was itself an appropriation of aristocratizing claims of descent from a great founder (hence elite groups named in *-idai*, "descendents of . . ." a hero). The same process can be seen in the extension of the name "descendants of Aiakos" (*Aiakidai*) or "descendents of Nēleus" (*Nēleidai*) to the whole citizen body of Aigina or Milētos.[102]

The effect of this shift in definition was to reduce and diffuse elite power in multiple ways. Double citizen descent annulled the value of the foreign marriages that had been one avenue for elite distinction and international networking;[103] it made citizen women valuable independently of wealth. Secondly, double citizen birth had to be validated by civic institutions: it forced members of the social elite to canvass for legal recognition by the small-scale subdivisions that were the entry points to the citizen body, thus submitting the transmittal of property (both essential to elites) to the decision of citizen peers, who would be exercising political equality, and were necessarily nonelite in terms of wealth. In other words, the issues negotiated by the double citizen descent are closely bound to issues of political power in the Aristotelian terms of mass and elite.

The democratic nature of the institution of double-citizen birth is clearly shown by the decision of the elite, by late Hellenistic and Roman times, to pursue multiple citizenships.[104] Another elite strategy was to offer women and children for officeholding, *leitourgiai*, and benefactions, in order to recreate social distinction.[105] Elite women and children played roles in the power strategies of male citizens, reflecting the authority of the male heads of households (again, a very Aristotelian situation, but also a strategy of distinction that is already found in the variation in burial practice in the Early Iron Age and early Archaic period).[106] Gender is a token in issues of institutional and social power.

In short, I am here suggesting that a whole swathe of the phenomena grouped above under the portmanteau heading of "*polis*-as-society"—subdivisions, rituals, performed identities, statuses, gender—should be viewed as functions of the Aristotelian *polis* of political institutions and debates about power between mass and elite. Moreover, I am arguing that these functions were metaphorical, and hence ideological—and that much of the noninstitutional interpretations of the *polis* have merely taken the ideological force of these metaphors too literally (for instance in arguing that citizenship *was* performance, or that different but equal roles of citizenship were distributed by gender). Indeed, their precise function was to naturalize political relationships of obligation and participation into pseudo-organic, "social" relationships. Political metaphor transcended institutionality by reifying participation *per se* rather than political power, and hence mystifying the issues of power and access at the heart of citizenship. However, the realities of institutional power were clearly defined and starkly operative. The Milesians allowed their Olbiopolitan kinsmen free access to cultic participation but asked them to register if they wanted to actually participate in officeholding. They further expressly specified, when granting citizenship, that the latter gave access to cultic activities, officeholding "and all the other things."[107] The same expressions appear in grants of citizenship by Eurōmos or Eretria.[108]

Without wanting to diminish the central importance of religion, ritual, and belief as part of the real experience and emotional life of preindustrial communities (at the mercy of endless contingencies, starting with the vagaries of weather for agricultural production), and without wishing to adopt a purely functionalist interpretation of the sacred, I also propose seeing *polis* religion as performing the same mystifying role as other political metaphors. To see the *polis* as a group bonded by its relation to the gods was a heightened discourse about community, with political implications (without necessarily being the result of a deliberate, instrumentalizing choice). When the young citizen men of Athens graduated from their two-year military service in the *ephēbeia*, and swore an oath not to abandon their "sacred weapons" (*hiera hopla*), there was nothing sacred about the weapons in themselves (they were given to the ephebes from 335 BCE onwards, but the phrasing of the oath might be older). Sacrality is a metaphor for the interests of the community, defended by the citizens' bravery in warfare.

The ephebic oath hence allows us to appreciate the force of the expression *hiera kai hosia*, which the ephebes swear to defend and which is common in Athenian discourse to describe public life: "sacred things (*hiera*) and righteous things (*hosia*)." The latter expression does not imply that the *polis* is a religious association but uses religious discourse to give an exalted description of its civic workings. It is analogous to the bigness of the public actor in administrative dealings, or to the logical primacy of the *polis* in Aristotle's sociology of *polis* origins.[109]

The various elements sketched out above constitute a particular model of power. To use concepts developed within Foucaldian theory, what we see is singular to the *polis*. In contrast with the world of the "indifferent shepherd" of pre-Christian autocratic rule, the realm of the "good shepherd" of Christian kingship, or the *raison d'État*-focused model of modern governmentality,[110] the *polis* is structured by specific conditions (autonomy, political equality) but expresses them through the naturalizing and familial metaphors of civic society, which produce *civic capital*. I propose this term—a calque from "social capital" (M. Putnam), on which more below—to describe the conjunction of several phenomena.

First, civic capital describes the power of the "Aristotelian" *polis* to naturalize and embed itself by achieving credibility among its citizen population as well as the population at large that the *polis* represents. Next, the term designates the actual benefits that the *polis* distributes to its citizen stakeholders as symbols of participation as well as real public goods. Finally, civic capital includes the degree of access to institutional power afforded to citizens through participation in institutional processes as well as the workings of civic society. All these are illustrated in the case of the publicly funded ox-raising by the "tribes" of Bargylia or, just across the modern Gulf of Güllük, in the Karian *polis* of Iasos, by the recently published decree of a tribe, the Agelaeidai, in honor of their main official. This document illustrates the well-known imbrication and articulation of religious ritual, civic ideology and norms, and institutions. Most strikingly, the meetings of the "tribe" were supervised by officials named as the *prytaneis*, which might be the same officials the "tribe" chose to serve to preside over the Council and the Assembly, thus imbricating the civic subdivision closely into *polis* institutions, and creating avenues for access and interaction between the level of the subdivision and the structures of *polis* governance.[111]

Civil Society in the *Polis*

Though civic society presented itself as a whole world of social relations, its fictions left much out in the urban center and the rural territory of a *polis*. Groups and constituencies organized themselves in the forms of associative life that we mentioned earlier (clubs, cultic groups, and so on), and that have attracted a great deal of attention in recent scholarship. Even Aristotle, in a difficult passage about what constitutes a *polis* and distinguishes it from a mere society of humans, notes that "there arise in the cities connections, brotherhoods, sacrifices and pastimes for the sake of living together"; these are the products of friendship and sociability as well as practical collaborations for profit or protection.[112]

What is most remarkable is that these private associations, which we can consider part of *civil society* rather than the civic structures of state, nonetheless make a point of closely imitating the institutional forms and discourses of the *polis*. Just as civic subdivisions do, they gather in assembly, follow procedures and rules, pass resolutions after deliberations, manage common goods (funds or land), hold officials to account, and honor good members for generosity toward the commonality. Such institutional behavior is well attested at Athens, where religious associations, family associations, and groups of soldiers hold officials to account for their management of common finances, and honor them with decrees.[113] The practice is widespread: we have seen examples from Hellenistic Milētos or Rhodes, and from Roman-imperial Palmyra, where associations of caravan-merchants honored civic politicians as their benefactors but also as good citizens (above, p. 386).

Such forms of *koina* (associations) behave like the *koinon* or association par excellence, namely the *polis* itself. The values they celebrate in public, through honors, proclamations, monuments, and permanent inscriptions are civic, as observed by C. Thomsen when studying the "civic aspirations" of the associations of Hellenistic Rhodes.[114] A *thiasos* (religious association) at Kallatis, on the eastern coast of the Black Sea, honored a member who fought well for the *polis*, and similar associations at Argos celebrated the city's victory over the dynast Kassandros. Associations did not just promote their own interests but displayed their awareness of belonging to the *polis*.[115] They honor public figures such as benefactors or officeholders, contribute *leitourgiai* to the *polis*, or try to work as a quasi-civic subdivision in the absence of official subdivisions, as in the case of associations of soldiers, local citizens, and Athenian residents in the fortified settlement of Rhamnous in Attica. Another case is the group of "those living on Symē," not quite recognized as a corporate body by the *polis* of Rhodes after annexation, but capable of honoring Rhodian office holders (above, p. 420).[116]

The hegemony of civic models and *polis* ideology is evident. We precisely do not see informal, extra-institutional power, but quasi- or would-be institutional aspirations. One explanation lies in the effect of the great convergence. The latter universalized the discourse of common decision-making and accountability as the main means for political and social interaction. This discourse, conversely, had deep and ancient roots in majoritarian, consultative decision-making by small associations such as kinship groups (actual or fictive).[117] The *polis* model also spread by capillary diffusion, since it was reproduced in the workings of civic society in the assemblies and meetings of the civic subdivisions. The mimicry of the *polis* by the groupings of civil society can be considered as an imitation of the civic subdivisions, whose social impact they hence extended and magnified (this may be another aspect of "civic capital"). A final explanation is that the adoption of *polis* institutions and discourse, in the prolongation of the system of civic subdivisions, was the only way for nonpublic associations to achieve visibility and efficacy in the social space of the *polis*, for instance by distributing civic-like skills and competences, or giving groups the shape necessary for recognition within the *polis*.

The "inhabitants" of Symē, without any formal status in the huge *polis* of Rhodes, used institutional forms and civic ideology to interact with Rhodian citizens (and convert them from landowners into quasi-civic benefactors) and the Rhodian state. This example confirms that the medium and the price for access to social capital in the *polis* was mimicry of its institutions and the adoption of its structures, discourses, and its values. The result of this alignment of civil society on civic society is that at least in the most visible manifestations, civil society constructed itself as secondary to and articulated on the civic society of *polis* institutions. It is hence unclear how the level of "civic" interactions helped Rhodian elites to gain political ascendancy in the assembly at Rhodes (as C. Thomsen proposes); that is, how civil society allowed for conversion of informal power into "civic capital" or simply power. Civil society in the *polis* certainly worked to produce social capital (trust, bonds, access to formal and informal avenues of power), and we will return below to these aspects of *polis* life; but even this intermediate level, at the intersection of institutions and social practice,[118] appears saturated with the institutional and discursive presence of the *polis*, rather than pluralist.

In what precedes, I have proposed distinguishing between a civic society that naturalized institutional power and a civil society that aligned itself on civic society, in an acknowledgment of power in the *polis*. This simplification of social life has the advantage of helping us see more clearly what it is that we are trying to capture within the social histories we write for the *poleis*. The distinctions are important because it is all too easy to write about the fictions and metaphors the *polis* generates about itself as if these were its total social history, and because the *polis* itself was so closely bound with these representations of itself as society. I am hence arguing for a much more unitary vision of the *polis* than the recent emphasis on associativeness might allow for, or than the image proposed in 1965 by P. Jones for the medieval Italian city-state. Jones writes that the latter "was never unified, but always throughout an association of communities and powers." (It is only fair to say that this vision of the medieval city has in turn been challenged in recent scholarship.)[119] The multiplication of associations of workmen or professional artisans in the Roman imperial *polis*, in contrast with the generally guild-free social life of the *polis* in earlier periods (say the fifth century BCE, or the *polis* that emerges out of the great convergence) might be a response to exclusionary and oligarchizing tendencies during the Roman empire, creating the need for corporate entities for solidarity or bargaining, even if the drift toward oligarchy should not be exaggerated and democratic institutions remained present (above, chapter 13).[120]

The question remains of what social life existed beyond the field saturated by *polis* institutions and ideology; that is, in the "free spaces" (the workshop and the field, the barber's seat, the tavern, the street, the house) that K. Vlassopoulos sees as existing interstitially in the *polis*. This is a crucial question for the possibility of a social history of the *polis* that is not just the rehearsal of its fictions about itself as society; below, I try to explore some spaces where we can see life beyond the *polis*'s fictions. As we shall see, such spaces appear, surprisingly, in Priēnē, which we have often studied as a prime example of *polis* institutions and civic society. In addition,

B. Gray has argued that a considerable amount of thought and attention was paid to the costs of exclusion, and that the second-century BCE experiments in social practice were not (just) oligarchizing experiments run by elite citizens, but also attempts at inclusion and extension.[121] All the same, the impact on noncitizens of the structures of exclusion, their agency, and their negotiated realities, were perhaps ineluctable. The experiences of the noncitizen and citizen-adjacent will be the poignant themes of this social history of the *polis* outside of the *polis* (chapter 19). For the purpose of this chapter, what matters is that this tripartite division—civic society, civil society, social remainder in free spaces—allows for an exploded view of the *polis* rather than the confusions between social and institutional that I attempt to dispel in this chapter.

The Consequence of Institutionalism

Beyond the methodological and theoretical problems of a social history of the *polis*, my focus is the shape of the Aristotelian *polis*: constituted as a citizen-state, structured by political institutions around autonomy and democracy, but endowed with a mirror image in the form of rituals, performance, and associations. These constituted a civic society on which civil society aligned itself. This form, that stabilizes during the Hellenistic period, proved durable and suitable for diffusion in the Roman empire, especially in Anatolia, the Levant, and Egypt. There, the transition of local communities to *polis* status or the imposition of *poleis* on local contexts entailed a broad and general reshaping of landscape, settlement, and population, into the modular forms of the *polis* (above, chapter 14)—this holds true even for Palmyra, which uniquely promoted the local dialect of Aramaic to a public language while making it fit within the parameters of civic discourse. The significant impact of *polis* forms on the "Roman Near East" is a cornerstone of F. Millar's extraordinary survey of the region; the transformation of urban centers, the spread of *polis*-style institutions, including to the countryside.[122] But this reshaping was also shallow, leaving unaffected vast areas of social life. If men wore the *himation* and *chiton* in the poses of the restrained Greek citizen, and displayed themselves as officeholders and *leitourgoi*, women retained traditional costume and, presumably, cultural roles in the household, religious life, and local societies. The dichotomy is visible, famously, in the funerary reliefs from Palmyra (always labeled in Aramaic, the local language, rather than the Greek used in the public sphere alongside Aramaic), but also elsewhere in the Roman Near East. For instance, on a funerary column from Qarataba in modern Lebanon, the representation of voluminous local costume, complete with headdress, forces the two female portraits to be shown with much smaller faces than on the two male busts (fig. 15.3).[123] It constitutes one example of the social residue, sometimes considerable, beyond civic society and civil society.

This is the consequence of my focus on political institutions. Of course, engagement with noninstitutionalist social and cultural history enriches and nuances any

FIGURE 15.3. Limestone gravestone found near Qartaba, Lebanon, on the territory of ancient Berytos. H 197 cm. National Museum, Beirut, 3977.

institutionalist interpretation of the *polis*—and, ironically, brings us back to the broader concerns of the Aristotelian view. In arguing for the power of institutions to impose binding decisions, and hence the central importance of access to state institutions for the definition of membership, I have drawn attention to the *polis*'s desire to naturalize itself, by presenting itself through metaphors of participation and societal articulation and, consequently, the idealizing nature of *polis* institutions. Institutions make moral claims about community (which helps explain the religious bent of much of *polis* discourse and political rituals). Here we have returned to the question of the Aristotelian good life in the city, as a moral good. The ideal *polis* is a dominant feature of discourses about and by the *polis*, starting in the early poetry that was present at the emergence of the *polis*, but continuing into the archive of documents produced by the city-states of the great convergence. This cluster of ideas deserves careful unpacking (chapter 16). But the ensemble of political ideas is also an ideology, not just in the sense of a set of concepts and arguments but also as a discourse, often contradictory, that allows for power struggles and bargains: the study of the *polis* of institutions leads to an *institutionalist* inquiry, where we study the pursuit of interests within the bounds of rules and path-dependency (chapter 17): it will turn out that we have never left the Aristotelian city of rich and poor.

16

Polis as Ideals

> The State is indissociably a solution and a problem. A solution, because it is embodied in institutions, practices and rules, and a problem, because it only exists in relation to the permanently instable, and tirelessly reworked and debated, issue of the institution of the social sphere. Hence the history of the State is a *history-as-crossroads* (which is why it cannot be reduced to administrative history, which only catches the State in its "objective" moment). Moreover, it is the privileged meeting site for political philosophy and history.
>
> —P. ROSANVALLON, *L'ÉTAT EN FRANCE*

> Most Western intellectuals know little about philosophy, and care still less. In their eyes, thinking that political proposals reflect philosophical convictions is thinking that the tail wags the dog.
>
> —R. RORTY, *WHAT CAN WE HOPE FOR?*

Moral Claims in the *Polis*: Institutions, Ideology, and Virtue Politics

In the shrine of Klaros, two similar monuments commemorated the good citizens and politicians of Kolophōn, Polemaios, and Menippos at the end of the second century BCE (above, chapter 11). The monuments were composed of multiple parts. First came a solid cubic base, covered in a long civic text describing the actions of a good citizen and narrating, in procedurally detailed terms, the city's response—namely honors, including a portrait statue. On top of this base stood a column bearing a simpler inscription: "The People (has honored/set up a statue of) Menippos, son of Apollonidēs, natural son of Eumēdēs, who acts as a benefactor and who, in his relations with the political community (*politeia*) was zealous and a lover of the good (*philagathon*) and who was a leader of his fatherland in difficult circumstances."[1] This phrasing is a variant on the more common formula, "The People (has set up a statue of) So-and-so, on account of his goodwill and his excellence (*aretē*) toward the people." Finally, the monument was topped by the portrait statue itself, in gilt bronze (fig. 11.4). Under the Roman empire, the honorific decree and the inscribed statue base were collapsed into a single genre, in which the good citizen is qualified with adjectives and participial phrases summarizing the actions that lead to the honors. The statues of M. Antonius Idagras, of Patara (above, p. 259), or M' Salarius Sabinus, benefactor of Lētē (above, pp. 11–12), stood on such bases. Though plentiful in absolute terms, such statues were fairly rare relative to the daily workings of civic life, just like honorific decrees.[2]

Even though they were infrequently produced, such honorific monuments, in their exemplarity and articulacy, throw light on crucial features about the *polis*. To start with, both the decree and the statue inscription obviously stake out moral claims. The decree is explicitly and self-consciously cast as the worthy requital for good behavior and character, in a transaction that will have exemplary effect, inspiring others to good behavior. The sentiment is expressed in a stereotypical phrase that is part of the architecture of the honorific decree, the so-called hortative clause: honors are granted "so that the Council and the People be clearly seen to honor good men worthily of their good deeds," in the words of the decree for Menippos, or "in order therefore that the people be seen clearly to honor those who strive toward goodness and repute, and that many others strive to obtain such rewards, since good men are honored," to quote an even more elaborate version in a contemporary decree from Eretria.[3] The example of virtuous behavior rewarded is assumed to be a moral inspiration in itself, notably through the promise of recognition.

The honorific transaction is a political script that enacts a *virtue politics*, in the sense of a politics centered (at least ostensibly) on morally approved actions and attitudes as the heart of good citizenship and ethical personhood.[4] Virtue politics involves community, individuals, and actions in a relationship mediated by institutions and ideas. The latter two are, of course, closely bound together. Through rules and procedures, institutions embody values and morals; conversely, the latter are not simply discourse or ideas, but also made efficacious by their practical implementation through rules and institutions.[5]

One upshot is that we can revisit one of the scholarly debates about Classical Athenian democracy (in the fourth-century BCE) concerning the proper way to study that régime. Should Athenian democracy be studied as institutions and procedures (as argued for by M. Hansen or P. Gauthier)? Or is the most fruitful but also the methodologically best way to look at discourse and ideology (a view championed especially by J. Ober)?[6] The latter concept can be understood in the simplest sense of a set of ideas but also in the more complex, political sense of a reality created through norms. Specifically, with J. Ober, we can hold that Athenian institutions, political and judicial, were founded on the central idea of popular sovereignty, and were concerned with implementing the latter practically, pragmatically, and experimentally. To weigh in on a specific debate, we could even argue that the concept of popular sovereignty underlies the various fourth-century BCE shifts toward giving law and the law courts a place within constitutional workings, rather than reflect the "power of the courts" or the "sovereignty of the law" as M. Ostwald or M. Hansen hold.[7]

But we can equally posit that popular sovereignty was not materialized by mere performative hegemony in discourse and law (through some sort of magic inherent in democratic speech-acts).[8] It was realized and perpetuated by the working of the democratic institutions of Athens—namely the Assembly, broad access to office, accountability and transparency, the popular law courts, and the local assemblies at the level of the demes where issues of citizenship were negotiated in the first instance. Equally crucial was the willingness of citizens to participate in institutional work, as assemblymen, jurors, or as prosecutors or speakers in the Assembly (though the latter two in practice demanded skill, leisure, wealth, and social capital). Hence, we can follow J. Ober on the crucial force of ideology, and M. Hansen on the central role of institutions: what the old debate underlines is the importance of the dialectical interrelation between institutions and ideology. Where should we start? With ideology, because to study ideology helps understand the rationale of institutions. Any unified theory of the *polis* should start with the intellectual and moral content of institutions; that is, with the ideas behind virtue politics.

Articulating *Polis* as Ideas

It is perfectly true that there is no surviving treatise articulating a political philosophy of the democratic *polis*, whereas there are plenty of antidemocratic texts; for instance, the critical depiction of decision-making in the narrative account of Thucydides, or the comprehensive attacks on democratic decision-making as epistemologically flawed in philosophical dialogues by Plato (above, chapter 8).[9] There are strikingly few explicit statements of first principles, such as "all citizens are equal in dignity for the following, logically consistent reasons," to be found anywhere in *polis* culture. Yet there are clear indications about the values and ideas that accompany the development of the *polis* and the democratic politics of the great convergence. These ideas structure the latter's virtue politics, and may be read as parts of a long text about the *polis*, a text that it is possible and necessary to unpack.

Cardinal statements about community are already to be found in the political poetry of the "Archaic" age, such as that by the Athenian leader Solōn. His sense of commonwealth and the work of politics would be repeatedly quoted in subsequent texts because of their pithy summation of the ideas undergirding civic community. More explicitly democratic ideals are expressed in forensic and political oratory, such as produced in fourth-century BCE Athens by public speakers before the courts and the Assembly. We can be sure that they were also to be found in the *poleis* of the Hellenistic and Roman-imperial period, even though the oratory has largely not survived. The exception is the work of the Roman imperial-era rhetor, Cocceianus Diōn, who shows awareness of democratic *polis* rhetoric and indeed wrote speeches in this register during his none-too-successful career as a local politician (above, chapter 13). Indeed, the small body of political (and even forensic?) speeches surviving among his more literary offerings hints at the important role of political oratory in the post-Classical *polis* as sites of negotiation and enforcement of civic norms.

Another source documenting the *polis* as ideas is the discourse of public honors, performed in civic venues such as the Assembly or the theater, and inscribed on stone. B. Gray has shown how this material can be read as serious engagement with philosophical ideas about community and ethical behavior.[10] I have drawn on the body of political language in the civic decrees as the basis of the sketch of the qualities of the *polis* in the great convergence, which (I argue) produced a remarkably stable, influential, and even desirable political form (above, chapter 10). It is this moral quality of the *polis* I wish to articulate and revisit here.

As part of the same pattern of democratic reticence about explicitly stating any political philosophy, the statements in oratory and decrees mostly avoid engaging with substantive definition and analysis; such a pattern of avoidance is itself part of a communitarian politics (see further below). Their implications have to be unpacked and teased out of texts that are often flooded with democratic ideas without them ever being spelled out in detail. For instance, the guards of the towering akropolis at Priēnē honored their commander, Helikōn, for ensuring that they should "enjoy equality" and for "enjoining them to remember that there is nothing greater for Greek men than freedom," as they kept watch from the fort above the cliff and looked down on the *polis* and its territory (fig. 1.3).[11] These statements were unifying precisely because they are not unpacked or examined, but assumed to be consensually held. But to be accepted, they must have conveyed ideas (even unarticulated ones), and worked to make these ideas coalesce, or at least coexist.

In simplified terms, the *polis* places the public good as the criterion of virtue and valorizes, implicitly or explicitly, all individual efforts to promote it. The public good is that which benefits the whole community (tautologously); and, in the democratic polities that were the norm after the great convergence, the community's members are implicitly conceived as equal and free persons, endowed with dignity and worth.[12] The citizen's dignity was recognized in multiple ways. In the first place, dignity was enshrined in rulings against bodily violence as acts of belittlement (*hubris*) directed against an equal; such rulings are attested in Classical Athens but also in other *poleis*. This stand against acts of hierarchical humiliating contrasts with the social violence that is central to the world of the Homeric poems or the unequal model of polity in the Archaic and Classical periods (most notably Sparta).[13] Symbolically, as I argued above (chapter 15), equality and dignity were expressed in the form of the citizen's participation in civic activities (such as festivals, feasting, or sacrifices, from "Archaic" Greece in the seventh and sixth centuries BCE to third-century CE Palmyra).

Closely linked to citizen dignity and equality is the *polis*'s autonomy or independence. Of course, the most obvious aspect of independence is external agency at the level of the *polis* when dealing with peers or supralocal powers; above, I have insisted upon the essential importance of autonomy, either actual or in the form of enabling proxies. However, independence, as the self-governance of the People, also designates the people's rule inside the *polis*; both dimensions are described by the expression *dēmokratia* or *polis dēmokratoumenē* (above, p. 222). Independence thus doubly guarantees the individual freedom of each citizen—he is ideally free from orders from external masters, and free from hierarchy or domination by an economic and social elite. This idea is made explicit in the occasional claim that democracy allows everyone to live as they please (a sentiment that acts as a proxy for absence from domination).[14] This internal dimension of freedom is symbolized by democratic lifestyle (noted disapprovingly by antidemocratic thinkers who speak of unbridled license, but valorized in forensic oratory, which insists on egalitarian moderation and self-control).[15] Conversely, the restriction of external freedom in the Roman-era *polis* favored the rise of stratified social orders and, to a certain degree, of a culture of deference (above, chapter 13).

Protected and embodied by autonomy, the outcome of equality between members is the just community that the *polis* imagines itself to be in its discourse of civic order. In F. Ruzé's striking phrase, *eunomia*, orderly government, is a striving toward justice.[16] Civic justice as fairness is ultimately about access to institutionalized processes and public goods, as a sign of entitlement.[17] The implication is that individual welfare is a product of a just community and immediately bound up with the welfare of this community; hence communal solidarity is a logical necessity that affects individual well-being, not just a moral imperative. In Aristotle's words, "one should not consider living in reference to the political community as slavery, but as safety."[18] The sentiment is already present in Solōn's political poetry:[19] all citizens benefit from good civic order, for no person can escape public disorder. "Thus the common woe comes to every house, and the courtyard doors will no longer keep it out; it leaps over the high wall, and always finds you, even if you go hide in the chamber . . ." Likewise, the solidarity of individual interests within the community is a crucial theme in political and forensic oratory; for instance, in the Athenian politician Lykourgos's prosecution of an Athenian who deserted the city in time of emergency, or the Roman-era orator and author Cocceianus Diōn's speech to his fellow-citizens at Prousa, extolling the city's greatness upon being honored by it.[20] Here again, ideas are the basis for ideals—ideal behavior in citizens, ideal worlds as created by civic behavior.

The general consequence of these ideas is the primacy of community, a concept that structures Aristotle's *Politics* (Book 1), even as he develops a narrative scheme of the historical emergence of *polis* out of constituent parts (households, then villages). Acting in the interests of the whole community is logically the right thing to do, because each individual's existence is itself guaranteed by the community.

The idea appears paradigmatically in famous cases such as Sōkratēs's decision to obey the laws out of a sense of obligation even if they condemned him to death.[21] It also underlies more routine manifestations of civic life. Benefactors such as Polemaios or Menippos did the right thing in putting their lives and fortunes at the service of their fellow citizens in second-century BCE Kolophōn. Three centuries later, in second-century Lētē, M' Salarius Sabinus freely accepted to sell his grain, beans, and wine below market price according to the widespread practice of *paraprasis* (above, p. 365) in times of shortage; there was no need to explain why the benefactor felt he had to "prove useful to the city." Good citizens and lovers of the city, the recipients of honors and praise in Roman-era Palmyra filled civic office, undertook *leitourgiai*, and actively helped constituencies such as the caravan traders on their expeditions across the eastern steppe. On the basis of the epigraphical record of such actions, N. Andrade has described Palmyra as a living civic culture.[22]

Contribution (in money and in time) to the public good is justified by interlinked principles. The community's welfare represents the greatest good, and the burden of ensuring the material basis for this welfare should be distributed justly, as decided by the community itself, which considers that it has a moral claim on its members being and property.[23] In concrete terms, the burden is passed on to the wealth elite as having the most resources, a decision that is both practical and implicitly ethical: hence its mention in oratory and its celebration in honorific decrees for benefactors of the city, who also happen to be drawn from its wealthier classes. This is the essence of the *leitourgia* system, which combines with extraordinary service (euergetism) to create the political economy of the developed *polis* (above, chapters 10 and 13). But devotion is also expected of less spectacularly elite citizens, in the form of obedience to decrees and laws, service in war, and a reasoned choice to defend the community. The anti-tyrannical law of Eretria in the 350s makes clear: each citizen chooses, under his own leadership, to defend the constitution (above, pp. 216–17).[24]

The *Polis* from Democratic Politics to Communitarian Ideals

These ideas lay the ground for a *communitarian politics*, to use a concept developed in modern political philosophy.[25] In this world view, community is the appropriate entity to judge moral actions and the character of moral actors and does so on the criterion of service to the commonwealth: that is, of services and attitudes of which the community is the recipient. This idea is somewhat articulated, though not completely in good faith and in a polemic context, by Aristotle in a discussion of democracy: the definition of the just is that which seems good to the greatest number or to the people.[26]

Communitarian judgment appears in the forensic oratory of fourth-century BCE Athens (above, chapter 8) as well as in the long honorific decrees of the late second century BCE, which are imbued with moral judgment (above, pp. 279–84). The practice of public funerals for outstandingly good citizens[27] can be considered as a set of particularly communitarian rituals, in which community shows itself judging the whole quality of an individual's life, implicitly pointing to itself as the source of recognition and meaning for the individual and doing so in front of the individual's body, which was the concrete instrument and locus of his situated moral commitment to his community. In Mesambria, a city on the Black Sea coast, one Euphamos son of Pausanias was honored after his death with a public crown during his funeral, the announcement of his honors, and with "an acclamation among the whole people that he was blessed" (*makarixai de auton pandēmei*).[28] The same idea lies behind the reference to public honors on gravestones from second-century BCE Iōnia (in Smyrna and neighboring cities): honorific crowns frequently figured on such monuments, and the names of the deceased sometimes appeared in the accusative case, a trope imitated from the inscriptions captioning honorific statues (above, fig. 10.4).[29]

Such inscriptions beneath honorific statues provide in their stereotypical formulas another statement of communitarian morality; its content deserves to be unpacked. When the People honors an individual for goodwill and virtue toward itself, in a highly normed and widespread formula ("on account of goodwill and virtue towards itself," i.e., the People: *eunoias heneken kai aretēs eis heauton*), it does not necessarily deny the existence of virtue in the absolute (indeed decrees mention individuals striving for the greatest moral goods, *ta kallista / arista*), but it states that its concern is to recognize the deployment of a moral quality in a relationship to itself, which it can judge directly and inductively, without engaging in substantive or foundational debate about the definition of this quality.[30] As Aristotle notes, "it is necessary that the *aretē* of the citizen exist in relation to the *politeia*."[31]

This is basically the situation that Plato found infuriating (indeed, Platonic philosophy and its peculiarly insistent pursuit of foundationality and transcendence can be considered to have developed out of a critique of this position as instantiated in Classical Athens).[32] This situation is characteristic of, and consistent with, the pragmatic nature of communitarian morality. We see here another way in which the *polis* of the great convergence is close to Aristotelian philosophy and its nonfoundational, consensualist basis. Indeed, Aristotle resorts to an anthropology of the citizen as the starting point for enquiry into virtue, the virtues and the passions, in the *Nikomachean Ethics*.[33] *Polis* legal culture exemplifies the same communitarian principles. Ancient Greek law is heavy on procedure and hence the modalities of participation, but light on substance, which is left to the community to decide through praxis in the courts, and whose ethical basis is, again, not articulated beyond a sense of the public good.[34] The *polis*'s insistence on procedure ends up reinforcing popular sovereignty: hence, I interpreted the intensified attention to institutional decision-making during the "Indian Summer" of the *polis* as a sign of democratic resilience in the face of increased elite claims (above, chapter 11).

It is true that generally, communitarianism can come in all shapes and forms. For instance, there can perfectly well exist a communitarianism of strictly hierarchical societies, based on loyalty and acceptance of inequalities as just. It is likely that a monarchical system such as the Macedonian national kingdom led by Philippos II and Alexandros III worked along such lines, as manifested in the enthusiastic commitment of its stakeholders that proved one of the mainsprings of the kingdom's irresistible success. Echoes of this national communitarian commitment can be found in the later Antigonid kingdom (for instance, in Polybios's narrative of its military successes). In the case of the *polis*, communitarianism, from the great convergence onwards, is tightly bound with democracy, spreading just as democracy did during the great convergence. As J. Ober noted, the lack of foundationality that Plato was criticizing clearly constituted the specific epistemological basis of radical Athenian democracy.[35] *Polis* communitarianism reflects the power of the People to decide on the basis of its collective judgment and opinion: the language of decision is officially that which "pleased" or "seemed good" (*edoxe*) to the People. But the roots of *polis* communitarianism are deeper than the democratic turn during the great convergence: as F. Ruzé's study of *eunomia*, justice as politics, emphasizes, the emergence of political institutions during the Archaic period results from the need to express the will of the majority, the *plēthos* (mass).[36]

Here again, Aristotle's philosophical method follows *polis* tendencies, in his privileging of collective opinion (*ta endoxa*, cognate to the formula of *polis* decision-making, such as *edoxe tēi boulēi kai tōi dēmoi*, "it seemed good to the Council and the People").[37] This epistemological move amounts to a privileging of popular sovereignty, which itself is inherent to the *polis* and celebrated throughout its civic spaces. The collocation of honorific decree and honorific statue does not just demonstrate the concatenation of institutions and ideology but also celebrates popular sovereignty: the monument offers up a form of accountability. The People's will has indeed been materialized in the statue; the statue is explained by the institutional processes documented in the inscription.[38] In the words of Aristotle (as part of a passage of moral critique of popular rule): "democracy seems to be defined by two things, the fact that the majority is sovereign (*kurion*) and by freedom. Now equality seems to be just, and equality resides in the fact that what is pleasing to the masses (*plēthos*) should be sovereign."[39]

As we saw in the case of Classical Athens, popular sovereignty is also embodied in institutions of decision-making, administration, judicial decision, and accountability and transparency in handling public goods. Generally, moral judgment can sometimes be explicitly democratic, referring to service to the mass, or the extension of elite privilege to individuals (as in late Hellenistic Pergamon: above, pp. 287–88). However, *polis* communitarianism sublimates popular sovereignty to generally designate the whole community, by playing on the poetics of the People in an inclusive rather than oppositional sense. The honorific transaction, which has an emblematic force for *polis* values, focuses on rewarding eminent individuals who are often in dialogue not so much with the popular masses (who recede into facelessness) as with the *polis* as institutions and ideals. Instead of Ober's "mass and elite" so visible in democratic Athens during the fifth and fourth centuries BCE, the *polis* of the great convergence focuses on "elite and community."[40] By the Roman imperial period, honorific statues are often described as the result of gestures by "the Council and the People," thus privileging the institutional face of the *polis* rather than the People as both community and nonelite majority.[41] In other cases, the statues are said to be the result of a decision taken by the *polis*, not the *dēmos*. The choice of *polis*-centered rather than explicitly democratic discourse might reflect the compromises and negotiations that enabled the great convergence, and underpinned its stability and its capacities to continue drawing on the individual fortunes of the wealthy citizens, through liturgies and benefactions, to produce public goods (below, chapter 17).

The consequences of communitarianism are the following. The *polis* is a moral good, not simply because all communities are good and the judges of morality (along communitarian lines), but because of the fairness of its organization leading to socially and morally just outcomes; the *polis*'s morality and capacity for ethical valuations were inherently part of its workings, which explains the importance laid on rituals of recognition for good citizens. Concomitantly, *polis* politics are morally good (both in their processes and outcomes), and by their nature tend toward greater things than individuals can. Finally, life in the *polis*, on account of its moral nature, is the crucial setting for individual self-fulfillment. These ideas are articulated in Aristotle's *Politics*: though the treatment of the *polis* devotes much attention to issues of ruling and being ruled within discussions of institutional power in the *polis*, Aristotle also admits of the *polis* as centered on a higher good (*agathon ti kuriōteron*)—the famous statement that it creates conditions for livelihood (the social existence of welfare and security), but with the good life as its purpose.

Consequently, in the discourse of virtue politics, much stress is laid on individual commitment, even enthusiasm (*prothumia*) for the community and the common good, and an explicit recognition of its primacy. This sort of constant devotion to the public is a central civic ideal, expected of the city's members.[42] The logical idea of the primacy of community shades into this ideal of commitment inherent to the good citizen, to the point of personal cost. Benefactors are meant to have unhesitatingly chosen public interests over their own profit (*to idion lusiteles*), as many late second-century BCE decrees mention.[43] Moschiōn, one of the "great benefactors" of late Hellenistic Priēnē (above, chapter 11), was praised in those terms, notably for responding to an appeal for a grain fund:[44]

> when the people invited everyone individually to volunteer to contribute to the common store at the price which he wanted, he (Moschiōn), taking his brother as his partner, contributed . . . *medimnoi* to the *polis* at the price which the *polis* (?) chose, thus making himself a man unmindful of his own interest, but a follower of ambition towards the common interest (*ta koina*) . . .

The concept of the possibility of moral choice was also extended, with some success, to serve as the medium for interaction with external rulers in order to cast their actions within this moralizing framework, whose lack of substantive definitions left enough leeway for negotiation (above, pp. 245–47).[45] This attempt is an index of how effective the *poleis* found moral ideals in constraining power actors.

All the concepts unpacked above are constitutive of not just the political culture of the *polis*, but also its culture more generally. Where other hierarchical polities reserved crafts and aesthetics to the consumption of elites (the "Fabergé effect," in C. Broodbank's formulation, as duly observable in the material culture of the palatial period in mainland Greece or in the luxury goods consumed by the military aristocracy of later fourth-century BCE Macedonia),[46] the history of the *polis* features constant and increasingly elaborate public art (sometimes of great aesthetic value, sometimes not so much). Civic temples, urban grid planning, city walls, public spaces, and even private dedications within these spaces constitute a whole artistic artifact shared by the citizens.[47] The *polis* as art constitutes an actual public good in its own right, symbolizes the public goods that stakeholders have access to, and also represents the abstract "bigness" or priority of the *polis* over its constituent members. It is operative as part of the definition of the *polis* in its early phases (for instance, in sixth-century BCE Samos: above, p. 101), but especially for the Hellenistic *polis*.[48] We have seen it in our recurrent visits to Priēnē, where recent research has nuanced but not overturned our interpretations of the built environment as representing and embodying civic ideology (fig. 1.3; see further below, p. 537).

The idealized representation of the human form and specifically the highly normed protocols of citizen representation (against which elite play-acting strives to make itself seen), participate in and complete the same ideology (fig. 10.4). They constitute a "classical" style, born in civic contexts, and drawing on various registers to express *polis* values: equality between citizens, restraint as a way of being and relating to others, and the dignity of members of the political community. But we should already note that the classical style would prove pliable to use in autocratic regimes, from Augustan Rome to modern totalitarianisms, a disturbing appropriation of an expression of the *polis*'s strong ideological control over its individual, predicated on a morality of the public good (see further below, chapter 19).[49]

The *Polis* of Political Philosophy

In what precedes, I have looked at the *polis* under a number of interlocking guises—as the moral inspiration of virtue politics and recognition, as a logically coherent and compelling set of political ideas, as a democratic practice, and as a world of constitutive ideals and assumptions. J. Ober's *Demopolis* leverages the historical example of the *polis*, based on the concepts of freedom and equality but not on individual rights, to imagine the possibility of democratic practice without the necessity of liberalism.[50] Thus, defined by its central historical concepts and without importing the anachronistic, liberal notions of rights, the *polis* as a form of government appears as a chapter in the history of ideas, and a matter of political philosophy[51] that can be pursued as a sequence of cogent arguments that bind together the different aspects of the *polis* as ideas and as ideals.

If we start with *freedom*, the *polis* can be analyzed in the same terms developed by Philip Pettit to study "republican" governance as inherently moral. It is true that his conception reflects awareness of Roman and early modern history models, not the Greek *polis*. Pettit hence favors "nondomination" as enjoyed by citizens, rather than participation, with some interest in issues such as mixed constitutions and the like. But the whole Pettitian package is still most useful for our purpose here.[52] The consequence of the citizens' freedom is that collective choice, after deliberation, represents a moral decision taken by reasonable actors—but also, in the communitarian framework, that the *polis* acts as the reference for the morality of choices. Alongside disinterested goodwill (*eunoia*), the city also expects actions as the result of *prohairesis*, morally reasoned choice. This holds true for the city's great benefactors but also for all citizens choosing to stand and defend the community. Likewise, the effect of good civics (for instance, as embodied in the actions of good citizens) is to encourage (*protrepesthai*) them toward imitation of good citizens and the resulting diffusion of civic virtue.[53]

Another source of legitimacy for the *polis* lies in the central place it grants to individual dignity and worth of citizens, as we have seen above; it can be considered as a consequence of the citizens' *equality*. J. Ober goes so far as to find in the *polis* a practical and stable instantiation of the idealistic proto-Kantian position that individuals (or rather citizens) should be treated as endowed with inherent dignity and worth. All citizens in themselves are considered as deserving of disinterestedness in interactions rather than exploitation or domination, and of conditions that allow for their individual flourishing during their lifetime.[54] The value of dignity is not only central to individual fulfillment through recognition within a free community of peers, as instantiated in the honorific decree;[55] it also offers the reasoned basis for the institutionalized practice of political equality.

Political equality ensures such goods as access to decision-making and office-holding, and accountability; it also tackles the moral problem of economic inequality by putting superior wealth and resources to uses that result in advantages for the whole community. Another effect is the prevention of wealth concentration, which posed a moral threat to political equality. The choices embodied in the *polis* can be analyzed in the terms defined by J. Rawls:[56] what matters is the equality between citizens, and hence the need for the acceptability of the outcomes of complex socioeconomic realities in the *polis*. In Rawls's famous thought-experiment, any given society's arrangements should be acceptable for every member no matter where he might end up in a random reshuffle: though this experiment was never expressed in this way by a third-century BCE Rawls or in an honorific decree of the late second century BCE, it is at least a useful way to think about the way the citizens considered each other as members of the same political community.

To use a concept defined by H. Arendt, the *polis* is based on *power*, but in a very specific form. Arendt defines power as the collective capacity for action born of general participation and direct consent in polity, rather than violence and domination.[57] As part of this collective form of power, the *polis* expects from its members (and publicly rewards) the proffering of constant *eunoia*, disinterested goodwill. The latter characteristic is part of the canonical terms of praise for the civic benefactors, whom we have seen honored "on account of their goodwill and excellence towards the People": the words were used on statue bases but also proclaimed in gatherings.

Furthermore, to continue in an Arendtian vein, the aim of such politics is precisely not the social and quotidian dimension of managing to survive—that is the realm of mere *labor*. Instead, Arendtian power and politics require the communal work and striving to produce higher, immortal goods—an ideal befitting the "bigness" of the *polis*, which is immortal and greater than its members. (Revealingly, it is paralleled by the early modern Italian city's obsession with *grandezza*.)[58] Politics hence requires thinking beyond the limits of household interests and property, the realm of what political scientist R. Putnam has called the antipolitical or pre-political force of "amoral familism."[59] Since the *polis*, in Arendt's view, does not aim for basic survival but strives for disinterested common goals, it demands from citizens the civic courage necessary to free themselves from individual interests and think politically of what benefits the whole commonwealth, whatever the personal cost (we have already seen this concept as a logical consequence of the idea of the primacy of community: above, p. 447). In Arendt's terminology, this is politics as *work*.[60]

This whole model offered above is an idealizing composite of modern concepts that are often distantly inspired by the ideals of the *polis*, culminating in H. Arendt's concept of power and politics. For now, I will leave aside any relationship between this idealizing composite and its applicability or inspirational potential for modern or contemporary politics (see further below, chapter 20). In this chapter, the main value of the idealizing model is to help pinpoint and unpack clearly many aspects of *polis* life. For instance, the artistic production of the *polis*, as surveyed above: the bigness and aesthetic value of the *polis* as material forms are statements of its immortality, and hence of its priority to its individual members and of its claim on their contributions to a common political project that is morally superior to any individual interest. Likewise, ancient civic discourse and practice can be fruitfully analyzed in terms of Arendt's concepts of courage and political work (which themselves are schematizations of Aristotle's terms, produced at the start of the great convergence). A decree of the Lykian *polis* of Tlōs, passed after 167 BCE, honored a citizen in terms that are strikingly close to Arendt's concepts:[61]

> (the people decided to honour a benefactor) who proved a good man (*andra agathon*) and a benefactor of the people from his ancestors, who accomplished for the people and the *ethnos* (of the Lykians) many of its interests and the greatest deeds pertaining to glory, and fought bravely in the wars and accomplished

deeds of valour and preserved the laws and the ancestral democracy, and served as lifetime priest of Sabazios before the city, gloriously and generously, and in all his activity as citizen (*politeia*) behaved with endurance, success and justice.

Furthermore, Arendt's dichotomy between political work and quotidian labor offers a pat terminology to reconsider the *polis*'s monumental public spaces. In second-century BCE Priēnē, not only was the *agora* reorganized to group honorific statues, public and private, in a single series and inscribed with long honorific decrees couched in explicitly ethical language (see above, chapter 11), but the business of retailing food was shunted off to a specialized, practically oriented market next to the monumental civic *agora* (fig. 1.3).[62] Of course, historically, concretely, the *polis* existed in practical life, and the aims of the actually existing *polis* were quotidian, relating to security and welfare (for instance, ensuring sustainable access to food, in ecological conditions of uncertainty). Yet by casting such concerns in the moral terms of the public good and public spaces, *polis* ideology valorized them as politics.

This Arendtian sublimation of the quotidian dimension of politics as exemplification of the dignity of collective action and political courage can be illustrated out of the history of the *polis*. We can speak of Arendtian politics on the island of Hērakleia, where the citizens banned the raising of goats (above, pp. 2–8)—perhaps the protection of legume gardening and intensive agriculture with ox-drawn ploughs, against a minority of rich citizens trying to raise goats to produce animal protein and byproducts. Such a choice would be more lucrative for those who had the economic wherewithal to engage in export trade, but more demanding of finite common resources on the small island, as shown by the subsequent history of the island as a "goat island" run for the profits of a large landowner, the monastery of the Panagia Hozoviotissa on Amorgos, before it was resettled in the nineteenth century as, again, a small agrarian community.[63] The civic transaction by which the citizens of the *polis* decided to take the prosaic yet vital step of banning goats to ensure the *sōtēria* (safety, salvation) of the whole *koinon*, so that the community of islanders could survive, might be read as reflecting the courage of a citizen community to exercise power in the Arendtian sense, and the heightening, valorizing effect of politics in common to solve a practical problem posed by individual behavior.

An Idealist History of the *Polis*

The upshot of looking at the history of the *polis* through modern political philosophy is to reveal how the *polis*'s own discourse, if read with the grain, produces an idealist, utopian history: Hannah Arendt on Hērakleia. This image should not be dismissed out of hand as unrealistic and unconnected with real events. The utopian tendencies are already present in products of *polis* culture such as decrees or public speeches. Cocceianus Diōn's Prousa, as he claimed before the Assembly, was naturally a perfect city of noble-born descendants of Greeks, of heroes and wise men.[64] If all the elements surveyed above added up to a long-lasting political culture, the latter should be considered as having constitutive force; that is, real power in defining political subjects and their actions.

Furthermore, as I argue above, the ideas in *polis* culture are intellectually coherent, notably on the grounds for communitarian morality (beyond just stating that morals are a communal affair), and deeply appealing on moral grounds but also for reasons of emotional fulfillment through the recognition of individual dignity and worth according to service to the common good. A parallel for the compelling force of political ideas of justice can be found in the nineteenth-century spread of republicanism in the south of France, as studied by Maurice Agulhon in the case of the *département* of the Var. The region had traditionally been fiercely royalist, ultra-Catholic and reactionary (to the point of antirevolutionary and pro-Restoration violence); adhesion to the Third Republic heralded its transformation into an equally passionate world of grassroots republicanism at the village level, which lasted into the twentieth century. One explanation for the shift (on top of social factors and specific contingent factors) seems to be the sheer appeal of republican values and ideas, and their capacity to create a livable political culture and shared common spaces.[65]

How did the *polis*'s ideals and values arise? One answer has been to posit a transformational invention of politics. J.-P. Vernant and C. Castoriadis have written the story of the *polis* as that of the emergence of publicness (the placing of affairs "into the middle," *es to meson*, to use an expression found in Herodotos), and of a politics of the public good, created by the self-institutionalization of autonomous communities.[66] It is true there are differences between these two theorists of the *polis*. Castoriadis sees the emergence of the *polis* as logically and factually subsequent to the conceptualization of individual autonomy (which he tries to discern in early Greek poetry). Political institutions follow on from the definition of society through concepts and debates (for instance, about power relations and the law). In this philosophical, ideas-driven history, the *polis* is the daughter of reason. In contrast, for Vernant, "reason is the daughter of the *polis*," a result of the invention of politics sometime in the eighth century BCE. But both view the *polis* as a matter of the power of ideas to construct identity and community, and understand the history of the *polis* as the working out of the ideas of political community and public good: the political turn leads to democratic forms structured by the communal work of participatory power rather than violence—and to Greek culture in general. (Another trait shared by both scholars is a belief, more or less articulated and coherent, in the historical uniqueness of the "ancient Greeks" as a whole, and its importance for "Western Civilization"; the attractiveness of such nostrums has paled in recent years.)[67] The same approach is adopted by C. Meier or P. Vidal-Naquet, and the same celebratory notes resound from their pages.[68]

The history of the *polis*, as sketched out in this book (and summarized above, pp. 403–7, with its folds and its watersheds), could be viewed in a Castoriadian-Vernantian light, as the story of the political turn and its consequences. I have argued that we can read, in the archaeological record, a fairly long period of gradual coalescence of proto-urban settlements during the Early Iron Age, out of the disparate elements left over from the end of the Late Bronze Age palatial polities. The eighth century BCE, as seen in the archaeological but also the sparse literary and documentary record, is not quite the scene of a social and economic revolution, but sees the intensification of this movement, with concomitant social diversity. A crucial factor is the coexistence of community values (attested in the Homeric poems) with elite competition for the distinction but also the power of big men within communities (also attested in the Homeric poems as well as in the archaeology of the Late Geometric settlements). The emergence, during the cardinal period of the seventh century BCE, of institutions and laws (what I termed the "obscure leap to the state"), gave concrete form and power to community values. In Castoriadian terms, the latter produced the concrete institutional forms that instantiated intellectual or spiritual changes, and the rise of governmentality cannot have been independent from the values and ideas being debated in the communities of the early age: there must have been something for the Drēros law (above, pp. 75–80) to emerge out of, fully formed, as it appears in our evidence.

Yet the Drēros law rests on a network of already existing institutions: these represent commitments and bargains between the constituent parts of the community, especially the wealth elite and the nonelite, which institutionalization helped define—just as they gave visibility and substance to community values. The powers of the Assembly, the role and nature of officeholders, the social matter upon which their authority was exercised, the definition and relationality of good behavior on the part of individual members and hence the morality of the political community: these issues had to be clarified in relation to values, but also created a political realm of its own, whose ethical content would also have to be clarified. The issues were debated throughout the late "Archaic" travails of integration and the tragic "Classical" century, in a constant project of working out the consequences and issues of the political turn in terms of extension and implementation. As we have seen, this is a story full of stops and starts, violent episodes, and overshadowed by the distracting temptation of empire—but always remained the story of the potential of the *polis*.

An idealist history also might be written for the great convergence (even if Castoriadis and Vernant were classically uninterested in the centuries defined by the traditional periodization as Hellenistic, i.e., the period from 350 BCE to 100 BCE, because of the long characterization of this period as one of decline). The great convergence was favored by specific political contingencies (the failure of *polis*-driven hegemonies, the rise of extensive supralocal kingdoms after the destruction of the Achaimenid order) but it also represented the diffusion of a particular set of moral values and ideas about community. For instance, the central question of my history of the *polis*—why elites accept the burdens of office and taxation, while following a moral model of economic restraint and of communal generosity—is explicable in idealist terms, however one conceives of these theoretically: the force of moral ideas, the power of communitarian ideals, the constitutive nature of community and recognition. The international concert of *poleis*, united in a system of peer-polity interaction, reinforced the values of the *polis* by making it an arena for recognizing virtuous citizens on a world stage, and in generalizing the ethical model of the *polis dēmokratoumenē* as a human norm.

The compelling moral force of the *polis* and its ideas would explain its stability, based on intrinsic qualities of freedom and equality and also its attractiveness to local communities that adapted the *polis* model, from the mid-fourth century BCE onwards, in a long-lasting, enduringly consequential process that rolled across the eastern Mediterranean. It is true that the process was promoted by supralocal empires, starting with the Hekatomnid satraps, in Karia and Lykia during the late Achaimenid empire, and continued down the centuries until the instrumentalization of the *polis* by the Roman state in the Levant, Mesopotamia, and Egypt. But what matters here is that the *polis* as idea took root in these contexts, and that local communities such as the Aramaic-speaking city of Tadmor/Palmyra, adopted *polis* discourses and forms enthusiastically and durably; elites and communities entered a moralizing dialogue, centered on recognition and virtue politics, which imply the whole package of political ideals about individual and community, including solidarity, participation, and justice.

The outcome is what I earlier tentatively termed the "end of history" (above, pp. 247–51 and chapter 10 generally). The expression is modeled, self-consciously and uneasily, on the controversial concept put forward by F. Fukuyama in 1989, namely that liberal democracy represents an endpoint of political development.[69] Here I mean that the stable persistence of the ideals of autonomy and democracy ensured that local elites long continued to abide by virtue politics after the great convergence. This held true under the Roman empire, under imperial compulsion but also because of the continuing force of *polis* ideals. Civic values persisted into late antiquity, and indeed partly outlasted the institutional forms of the *polis* itself. The *polis* might be said to have disappeared when civic ideologies of devotion to the public good and of the primacy of community lost their hegemonic grip on small-scale social realities.

Idealism and Contradiction

It is noticeable that *polis* ideology is fraught with contradictions, in spite of the robustness with which it is professed and performed. Decision-making institutions are set up for deliberation, indeed conflictual debate, but the goal is the presentation of decisions as consensual and universally accepted. Decrees, at least in their published, permanent form, present motivations that are unitary and claim simple, universally accepted truths ("since . . ."), and move on to decisions and procedures; disagreement or adversaries are unnamed, appearing as *tines*, "some people."[70] The paradox, as noted by N. Loraux, is that the *polis* seems founded on politics as an idea yet shies away from them as threatening to the spirit of unity that is equally central to the *polis*.[71] Doubtless deliberation in the Assembly took place at Hērakleia, but the choices in the alternative (to allow or disallow the raising of goats) were starkly opposed in their consequences, as we have seen. Once the city of Hērakleia reached a decision, it tried to impose unanimity through the civic ritual of a collective oath, the monumental form of inscription in a shrine, and the proclamation that it concerned the safety of all. The image is that of unanimity obtained through political work. *Homonoia*, concord, was one of the *polis*'s ideals, celebrated explicitly through cult and discourse.[72]

Thus the *polis* of Melanippion, in southern Asia Minor, fondly imagined that recovering its freedom, external peace, and right to control its own property (admittedly in the extremely uncertain world of the early second century BCE), would suffice to ensure a "political life with concord" (*meth' homonoias politeuesthai*).[73] *Homonoia* also lies implicit behind the interlocking structures of fellowship that made up civic society (above, chapter 15). Images of concord and consensus cast a curiously depoliticized light on political decisions; the imagined *polis*, as in political rhetoric, manages to overcome inner conflict through the civic virtues—especially the courage—of its members.[74] The ideal was embodied in the concrete, institutional paths of decision-making that, as M. Canevaro has proposed, aimed at imposing consensus.[75] As in the "peaceable communities" of early-modern New England, the risk of conflict and paralysis seems to have led the citizens in the *poleis* to strive to reach and impose consensual decisions.

In addition to this central contradiction (which we might term "Loraux's paradox"), a similar contradiction exists between the claim that individual liberty is central to the *polis* and the equally crucial primacy of the community. This contradiction is explored in the dramatic poetic works performed at public festivals in fifth-century BCE Athens.[76] The surviving plays by the poet Aristophanes unerringly focus on the fragile seam between individual self-interest and the common good. In the *Acharnians* of 425 BCE, the antihero, dubbed with the provocative name *Dikaiopolis*, "Just-city," comes to the conclusion that the *polis* can do nothing for him (it is too corrupt in its workings, including the democratic institutions that are meant to represent the People and its interests), during the first phase of the Peloponnesian War. His reaction is to strike a separate peace with the Spartans, a decision whose individual economic benefits he selfishly keeps to himself and celebrates riotously at the end of the play (convincing even the chorus of Acharnians, members of a populous and warlike deme that is suffering from the conflict). The Aristophanic genre constantly engages with the contradiction of public good and private interest, whose unresolvable oppositions lead to riotous violence and outrage (*hubris*).

This is exactly the outcome that the *polis* tries to obviate, but whose ubiquitous presence in the comic universe—alongside obscene language, marginal paths, carnivalesque reversals, extreme fantasy, and utopian imaginings—reveals its nature as serious provocation.[77] We will return below to the question of interests in the *polis*, as revealed by Aristophanic comedy. The same interrogations appear in other fifth-century BCE texts, such as the speech given by the brilliant Athenian renegade Alkibiadēs at Sparta, where he declares that his own interests as an elite individual were no longer protected in democratic Athens, and hence that the rational compact of interests between individual and community no longer held true in his case.[78] Alkibiadēs reappears, poignantly, in Aristophanes's comedy *The Frogs* (405 BCE), where the tie-breaker question put to the two great, deceased poets Aischylos and Euripides in the underworld (in a contest of their worthiness to be brought back by Dionysos) is simply their opinion of Alkibiadēs (who had returned to Athens and led it with some success), "for the *polis* suffers birth-pains on this" (lines 1422–23).

The case of the elitist Alkibiadēs and his stormy relation with democratic Athens illustrates the class-bound rather than simply individual nature of the conflict between interests and common good, an insight that is central to Aristotle's analysis of power politics in the *polis*: since the rich and the poor pursue different interests, their respective control of the constitution will have, crucially, different outcomes. The insistence that individual welfare is bound with the *polis* order and its insistence on collective good tries to deny class conflict. *Polis* ideology in fact accepts the possibility of individual loss but tries to transcend it by justifying it intellectually or emotionally on the register of heroism, without quite erasing the contradictions. Underlying all these tensions is the unresolved contradiction between interests (*ta sumpheronta*, constantly discussed in *polis* discourse, for instance oratory or honorific decrees) and the claims of virtue, supposedly equated with the pursuit of collective *sumpheronta* in communitarian fashion, but without being able to erase the presence of individual interests, which are unescapably present because of the *polis*'s place for individual welfare and dignity as one of the goods it produces.

This range of possibilities raises yet another contradiction. Good citizens show enthusiastic commitment (*prothumia, ekteneia*) to the *polis*, to which they offer themselves (*heauton paraskeuazein*)—as the result of rational choice, reasoned moral decision-making (*prohairesis*), and imitation of exemplary behavior by other citizens, but also because of character (in the best of cases), ancestry, or else because of habituation (obtained through civic ritual) and education. Honorific decrees end up celebrating all of these motors as the sources of good civic behavior, without quite stopping to parse the dialectics and tensions between them.

In spite of the irenic tone of honorific decrees, the contradictions had earlier proven explosive, as shown by B. Gray in his study of *stasis* and exile. In the terrible civil wars of the *poleis*, especially during the Hundred Years' War (but also in some cases during the third century BCE), conflicts of interests coexisted with, and indeed were exacerbated by, multiple aspects of civic ideology: the reasoned equation of citizenship with entitlement to rule and public goods; the requirement for unanimity; the ideal of constant commitment as part of civic personhood. A constant danger was that there might prove to be no easy space for the mediation of conflicts, and that the most immediate avenue would be to cast political adversaries as essentially lacking in civic character and morals, and hence deserving of expulsion from the citizen body or actual extermination, since they could only be traitors and anti-citizens existing beyond the pale of the political community (see above, chapter 8) .[79] The abatement of explosive conflict, despite the unresolved nature of the tensions, constitutes another major puzzle of the great convergence.

Loraux's paradox, Aristophanes's carnival of *hubris* and utopia, Aristotle's class tensions, the honorific decrees' overdetermination of civic behavior, Gray's vision of *stasis* as an inherent insolvability of civic equations—all these are expressions of contradictions stemming from the *polis*'s capacious lack of foundationality, which we have discussed earlier: many of the constituent parts of *polis* ideology are tautologous. This image of contradictions seems to lie far from our first image of *polis* ideology as intellectually and morally compelling. We might therefore see the contradictions as bound with the dichotomies and tensions in the *polis* itself—elite and mass, individual and collective, city and countryside, the many diversities within each *polis* and between *poleis*. We could choose to focus on the incoherence implied by these contradictions, as signs of fragility. But alarm at the contradictions in *polis* ideology should not be exaggerated; they are, after all, not more contradictory than the quotidian "brain balkanization" entailed by any ideology (as P. Veyne expresses it).[80] Another way of describing the situation might be that the contradictions are there precisely because the *polis* is multiple, and because the elements of multiplicity have to be mediated and connected within the *polis*: openness of texture, tautology, lack of substance, and intellectual contradictions allowed for negotiation and integration.

We have seen diversity present from the start in the story of the *polis*—in the Early Iron Age communities or cities such as Akraiphia in the sixth-century BCE (judging by the city's cemeteries). Civic ideology allowed such communities to cohere by offering intellectual and moral grounds for doing so—but also required community cohesion in order to work at all. This explains the importance of constructing *polis* identity as something bigger than individuals, primary to them, rooted and natural, through social metaphors of shared descent from a founding figure (god or hero), deep and situated connection to place and time as expressed by myth, art and public spaces, and local historiography.[81] Such claims not only acted as proxies for the essential dimension of autonomy (as I have argued previously), but also constructed imagined communities as contexts for the communitarian-moral tropes of civic ideology. For instance, the claim of the *polis* to be a descent group was also connected with civic ideals: the authentic Athenian was supposed to have an innate sense of democratic values and public-mindedness (as argued recently by S. Lape; see further below, pp. 511–12).[82]

Furthermore, the elements of *polis* as society, outlined earlier (chapter 15), are coterminously linked with *polis* ideals and ideology. Civic subdivisions maintained the fiction of kinship and promoted equality and solidarity between citizens. Their mythical or localized names gave an image of antiquity, and hence a representation of the *polis*'s own antiquity and dignity (shared by all its members), and of its naturalness: these qualities reinforce the *polis*'s moral claims to priority over its members. The ubiquitous institutional practices among civic subdivisions (around public goods, decision-making, accountability, and honors) had the effect of further naturalizing the institutional practices of the *polis* (as well as entrenching them: above, chapter 15). The shared activities of *civic society* and its network of constitutive, officially recognized associations, offered institutionalized contexts for the affirmation of civic ideology beyond individuals and their families (Aristotle designates meetings, dining-clubs and other manifestations of sociability as inherently dangerous to tyranny).[83] This ideology had to be hegemonical within the community to function adequately, which explains its dutiful imitation by the associations and groups of *civil society* (chapter 15). This, too, was a crucial dimension of political work in the *polis*: not just deciding common affairs together, "in the middle," with a sense of the public good (and so on), but creating the sense of shared identity for the political community to exist at all.

Political work must mediate between three disparate things, in a triangular relation: firstly, civic ideology and its communitarian claims about the morality of the public good and public goods; secondly, civic capital and its construction of unity; and thirdly, the realities of diversity and plurality. Civic ideology exists as a horizon and goal for civic capital; the latter makes civic ideology viable; both civic ideology and civic capital manage diversity by masking it, transcending it, or embedding it within the *polis*. However, this intense need to transcend diversity does not make the contradictions or incoherences go away; it only raises the inescapable question of negotiations of interests, or of power in a much rawer sense than the Arendtian ideals. It is to this *polis* of self-interested actors we now turn, as we look harder at what lies beneath the tensions and contradictions of civic ideology.

17

Polis as Interests

> Even if it is very difficult to obtain truth concerning equality and justice, it is easier to do so than to exercise persuasion on those who are capable of excessive acquisition, for the weaker always seek equality and justice, and the strong do not care for these things.
>
> —ARISTOTLE, *POLITICS*, 6.3 1318B1

> Private property is (or should be) instituted only inasmuch as it serves the general interest, within a balanced set of institutions and rights which allow for the limitation of individual acquisitiveness, the circulation of power and the best distribution of wealth. The issue is how far such a political process should extend. That unease should surround it is understandable.
>
> —T. PIKETTY, *UNE BRÈVE HISTOIRE DE L'ÉGALITÉ*

Interests, Costs, and the Risks of Statehood

In the early second century CE, Cocceianus Diōn could extol his home city of Prousa as the site of civic virtue and greatness, while responding to an honorific decree—but also offer a sarcastic deconstruction of this image in less happy circumstances, while offering jaundiced comment on honors for a rival. Indeed, in his youth he had been forced to speak, none too graciously, in an emergency meeting of the Assembly after a grain riot (above, chapter 13, esp. p. 346).[1] After a city of good intentions, we find ourselves in a city of interests: the *polis*'s real citizens were all too human. In the terms defined by the sociologist J. Baechler, they were free and sovereign, self-interested and selfish, invested in their own individual welfare and safety. They rationally calculated risks, costs, and benefits; these are traits notably and durably characteristic of Mediterranean societies and their mutually suspicious actors. They had to earn a living, raise a family, maintain households, and make or lose fortunes (since civic virtue and engagement, though morally compelling and world-building, did not feed people or administer estates on their own).[2]

So naturally they trucked and bargained, chased returns, competed over resources and opportunities; they pursued economic interests (in contrast with the benefactors who behaved in exemplary fashion and took losses for the sake of the public good in accordance with civic ideals, or so we are asked to believe). They did so in an ancient Mediterranean world whose characteristics were alternances of scarcity and glut, specializable micro-ecologies alongside generalized consumption of the same staples, and the all-encompassing, connective elements of sea and wind. All these characteristics imposed the structural necessity of exchange for survival, but also offered the possibility of profit-chasing for enterprising individual actors.[3] This description of the *polis* fits within a new model for the ancient economy, based on exchange and profit rather than landownership and status—a model, however, that also integrates the workings of social institutions that imposed costs and choices on participants in a market economy. Hence the proximity of this model with histories written within the "new institutional economics."[4] The latter field of enquiry and theorization is not concerned with institutions as constitutional arrangements within the *polis* (studied for instance with such tenacity and investment by P. Rhodes or M. Hansen), but as long-standing features and practices within which the pursuit of utility (material or symbolical) takes place, be it individually or collectively.

The plurality of individual self-interested actors in the *polis* was compounded by a plurality of constituencies, pursuing overlapping but divergent interests within the same community.[5] In the *Politics*, Aristotle both recognized plurality as a condition of the *polis* (in response to theoretical constructions of *polis* unity such as that found in Plato's *Republic*), and was tempted to simplify the situation down to the opposition between the rich and the poor, and their struggle over institutional power. Without denying this opposition, we might note that even episodes of conflicts mobilized complex interactions between multiple constituencies. As suggested above (p. 346), the grain riot at Prousa involved several groups and their interests: grain-growing and exporting estate owners (who must have collaborated with the ship owners of neighboring Apameia in Bithynia), but also Cocceianus Diōn (who drew his income from vine-growing, cattle-raising, money-lending, and real estate investments near the hot baths in the suburb of Prousa), and finally a discontented "People." The latter group had its own complexities, since it may have included the urban population (including part-time farmers commuting out to fields around the city?) as well as cash-cropping middling agriculturalists in the villages of rural territory around Prousa (fig. 17.1).

Much earlier, perhaps ca. 600 BCE, Solōn had portrayed the diversity of economic life in the nascent *polis*:[6]

> Everyone has a different pursuit. One roams over the fishy sea in ships, longing to bring home profit; tossed by cruel winds, he has no regard for life. Another, whose concern is the curved plough, cleaves the thickly wooded land and slaves

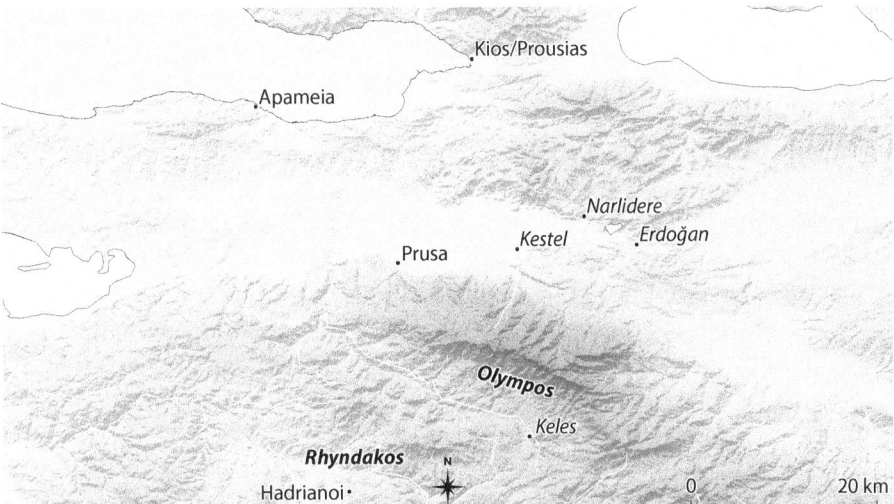

FIGURE 17.1. Prousa, its territory, its neighbors, in the Roman empire (including village sites known by modern toponym).

away for a year. Another who has learned the works of Athēna and Hēphaistos, the god of many crafts, gathers in his livelihood with his hands; another, taught the gifts that come from the Olympian Muses and knowing the rules of the lovely art of poetry, makes his living. . . .

Solōn's poem is a meditation on uncertainty: the general up-and-down vagaries of life, but also the pursuit of wealth and the social impact of acquisitiveness. Organized, settled urban society offered multiple opportunities for violent or at least forceful acquisition. The wealthy, through greater economic means and social capacities, could practice predation on the weak, defection from agreements, and freeriding (that is, overconsumption of shared goods). All these forms of social behavior involve force on the part of those trying to get away with acquisition— forcible seizure or overextraction, the role or threat of violence to create space for defection or overconsumption. The *polis* developed mechanisms against the manifold types of social violence—indeed, to a certain extent it *was* the mechanism against them, in that it constructed the means for regulation.[7] The Cretan city of Drēros, in the seventh century BCE (above, pp. 75–80) provided instruments for legitimate arbitration in economic disputes, in the form of rulings by the main officeholder, the *kosmos*, in exchange for fees. Such officeholders were not just informal arbitrators but must have issued judgments that were recognized by the whole community as uniquely binding. The *polis* hence helped ensure and regulate contracts between economic actors.[8]

An emblematic case is to be found on the island of Hērakleia, which we have encountered repeatedly in this book. The *polis*'s decision to ban the raising of goats (above, pp. 2–8, 451) was probably motivated by literal issues of overexploitation by certain individuals of shared pasture and perhaps of water sources on the island—the one spring, the several wells (sweet or brackish), and the rain-fed reservoirs. (Additionally, goats may have inflicted damage to individual property). When a community is caught in the throes of overexploitation, the result is that there is no advantage for any individual to follow the rules, but that everyone might reasonably choose to pursue his short-term interest, thus avoiding being a "sucker" and being caught as the last one to respect the rules. This pattern of behavior occurs even if the ultimate outcome is the destruction of the vital shared resource. This is literally a textbook case of the "tragedy of the commons," as defined (as a model or thought experiment) by the ecologist Garett Hardin in 1968; namely, the violent overexploitation of common goods by selfish individuals for their short-term gain with no regard for shared interests among the living and with future generations.[9]

The issue could not be solved by individual negotiations: it was probably situated in a space of conflict and unclarity of rules, and the conflicts were too urgent, too bitter for arbitration. The *polis* responded radically. It took the decision to shut down the behavior that enabled individual overexploitation, by declaring it illegitimate and subject to self-help measures in case of infraction. Furthermore, the *polis* threw the weight of community resources—ideological, symbolical-religious, and institutional—behind the enforcement of the decision. Even though these resources were thin (there is no police force or bureaucracy), they were performative and had practical consequences in making certain types of violence illegitimate, and in mobilizing institutions to protect citizens enforcing the communal decision. The stated aim was *sōtēria* (safety) for all, as one of the goods produced by the *polis* when faced with uncertainty and the clash of interests. Awareness of the latter allows us to guess at the precise conflictual context within which the work of Arendtian politics had to take place. The same concern for safety as one of the results of governance appears in some written consultations of the oracular shrine at Dōdōnē by *poleis*, asking by which sacrifices they might ensure this state of affairs (another concern is good weather and crops).[10] As shown by Hērakleia and its goat ban, the *polis* (in addition to external agency or ritual activities) worked through rules and institutions to counteract individual uncertainty by limiting predation, defection, and freeriding: this function is essential to its nature as state. In his essay on the Roman-era *polis*, D. Nörr noted the *polis* was not only an ethical discursive space, but also a practical regulatory one;[11] the insight echoes up and down the history of the *polis*.

One consequence of statehood, in the form of autonomous institutions, was the *polis*'s control over its own property and incomes. The *polis* as state was present in its own economic sphere, chasing returns (for instance, on money lent out at interest) or levying rent. The latter could take the literal form of income derived from *polis*-owned property, but also that of fees extracted for the use of facilities uniquely held by the *polis*. The *polis* also levied fees against the right to exercise profit-making activity within the *polis*'s spaces, urban and territorial and within reach of the *polis*'s power.[12]

Furthermore, movement of goods through the *polis*'s territory and disposal of it in retail spaces managed by the *polis* are all fair game for the *polis*'s expectancy of getting its own cut of individuals' profits. This is the implication of grants of the privilege of *ateleia* (tax freedom) on all imports as long as they are for personal household usage: any commercial or productive activity generated a profit on which the *polis* levied a tax (above, pp. 237–38).[13] Finally, and most directly, the *polis* could tax wealth in movable and immovable forms. In this respect, the *polis* looks at first sight like any state, namely a stationary entity that uses its unique position of force to extract profits, in negotiation with constituencies in the social space that it controls, sometimes justifying such levies as the fees for the provision of services or protection (and hence the reduction of uncertainty), but often just practicing extraction as the naked consequence of situational advantage.[14]

Yet we should not just see the *polis* as the biggest gorilla among other self-interested actors within a given social space. I have argued in the pages above that the *polis*, as a *koinon* or participatory community of citizens, is different in nature from predatory extractive states (be it "early states" or developed empires).[15] In the *polis*, revenue-raising activities are directly purposed toward the solidaristic provision of public goods (another *leitmotif* of the constitution and development of the *polis* throughout its history), through investment or redistribution. In turn, much of the *polis*'s activity is aimed at solving second-order problems of collective action and tragedy of the commons, created fractally by the very provision of regulatory solutions and public goods—a conundrum that lies at the heart of L. E. Ostrom's Nobel-winning work on collective action.[16]

In the case of the *polis*, the processes of "auto-institution," fundamental to Castoriadis's vision of the *polis* and its history, are themselves burdened with costs; for instance, the widespread participation of citizens in decision-making meetings, in the courts and in officeholding, and the increased contribution of certain elite individuals to communal purposes. These costs create problems of collective action: why should any individual actor be the first to take on costs, if the consequence is that he alone will have to suffer such disadvantages and the others enjoy the fruits of the new dispensation? Indeed, what incentives do any individuals have to bear costs, if they can freeride their way to benefits created by the cost-bearing actions and contributions of others? Why should individuals contribute to the costs of a common project if they can protect their own interests? How does a community make its members coordinate its actions in a way that enables it to exist at all, instead of a collection of individuals pursuing their interests in competitive ways that try to shift costs onto others?

In practice, the *polis* continually addressed all the problems outlined above, namely freeriding off public goods produced by collective effort, refusal to share in the costs of collective action, defection from engagements taken toward the community and its material needs, and acquisitive takeover attempts on public goods. Indeed, the institutions of seventh-century BCE Drēros can be considered as illustrating one solution to the problem of uncertainty and conflict in economic transactions. However, we clearly intuit that these institutions generated their own problem, namely the possibility of publicly sanctioned positions of power that could be monopolized (the possibility of "archaic tyranny"). This second-order problem had to be solved by the *polis* as state through its own means, namely the creation of legal rules to prevent monopoly and, under the umbrella of law, the coordination of different actors toward that goal (above, chapter 4).

The works of fifth- and fourth-century BCE literature offer a meditation on issues of freeriding and the second-order problems of collective action. Herodotos gives, under the guise of a narrative of the rise of the Near Eastern empire of the Medes, a political parable of the risks inherent to the rise of a regulatory authority, namely the permanence of hierarchy and dominance.[17] The Athenian civic poet Aristophanes also dramatizes problems of collective action (in spite of an ideology of the common good, which the comic genre revels in deconstructing: see above, p. 455).[18] For instance, as we have seen, the *Acharnians* seem to celebrate the private peace struck by its (anti-) hero Dikaiopolis, a defector from the common war effort against Sparta, in a riotous, carnivalesque riff on the tension between shared costs and individual benefits.

A particularly elaborate example is provided by Aristophanes's *Assemblywomen* (performed in 391 BCE). The poet imagines a utopian *polis* ruled by the good sense of women who have peacefully obtained power. There, all must contribute to a common store, from which they all draw in feasts. But whereas a good citizen (a "sucker"?) contributes dutifully, a rational calculator (or "bastard"?) prefers to hold back at the contribution phase yet joins in enthusiastically at the redistribution and consumption phase, claiming good citizenship at that moment. True, any serious meditation on the problem of freeriding is lost in the subsequent course of the play (when the action goes on to portray the free provision of male sexual partners to women, and concomitant problems of fairness in distribution), yet this riotous ending does not detract from Aristophanes's sense of the crucial problems of *polis* life. His work shows remarkable engagement, in a concentrated imaginary form, with the social and institutional practices in the *polis*. In the case of *Assemblywomen*, he notably draws on the importance of contributions and of feasting, which are a central part of *polis* existence since the "Archaic" period.

In concrete terms, as we have seen at multiple points in the history of the *polis*, good citizen politicians spend much of their time tracking down freeriders and defectors, and denouncing them before the Assembly and the courts. Acting as the watchdog of public interests constitutes a central part of "demagogic" politics and is linked with the all-or-nothing conception of civic virtue. Such was the activity of a Prienian, Apellis, who served for twenty years as the city's secretary, during which time he showed great zeal "concerning the common struggles (*agōnes*) of the People," meaning the lawsuits undertaken by the city to protect public goods.[19] Perhaps surprisingly, we have also seen this activity as an important part of leading civic politicians in the Roman-imperial *polis* (above, pp. 354–55), where acting as an advocate of the city (*ekdikos*) meant defending public goods from elite acquisitiveness or defection (in practice, occupying public land without paying rent, seizing public monies, or shirking leitourgical obligations or euergetic commitments). Cocceianus Diōn portrayed this behavior in his semi-imaginary Euboian city. A rustic type, living on his former master's estate, now confiscated, has the unpleasant experience, during a visit to the urban center, of being accused of exploiting public goods for his own benefit. Rather remarkably, the rhetor-politician himself engaged in dubious behavior as a civic leader handling public funds in Prousa, and his rivals must have pursued him in the courts and before the Roman governor.[20] These are the stakes of statehood, which explain the vital role of autonomy for the *polis*: the possibility not just of minimizing uncertainty, but of intervening in problems of collective action and freeriding.

The *Polis*'s Solution

So the *polis* as state was not a predator (in M. Levi's definition) and was more than just a guarantor of the security of economic transactions through law and public authority. What, then, was the *polis*? Its specific nature is reflected in the Clastresian characteristics of immediate correspondence to the *political community* as society (above, pp. 425–27)—notably the absence of entrenched governing elites, the circulation of power, the primacy of popular sovereignty, and finally the prizing of egalitarianism in the political realm and in the social sphere. The Herakleiotes did not appeal to an external sovereign to solve the tragedy of the commons; they *were* that sovereign, embodied as a community, a People. Even if popular sovereignty was fraught with contradictions and even if statehood entailed costs and subsequent problems of collective action, the nature of the *polis* lay in the act of self-institution, as defined by C. Castoriadis; namely, the formalization of common decisions to face down common problems and ensure public goods, starting with the safety of the community itself—the *sōtēria* that the Herakleiotes invoked as the goal of their decree, and that constituted a special category of decree in the institutional repertoire of many *poleis*.

At least, since the actual origins of the *polis* in general and each *polis* in particular were obscure, this was the constitutive self-imagination of the *polis*, enacted with each meeting of the People in Assembly. In addition, the immediacy of the bond between *polis* and society was institutionalized through the structures of civic society, the fictional kin-groups and associations that were a constitutive, official part of the *polis* and an essential vehicle for state operations, and whose ubiquity was mirrored in their imitation by the groups within civil society (above, chapters 15 and 16).

The result of the compromises, bargains, and social fictions that constituted the *polis* of the great convergence was a clear, stable solution to the collective action problems and the problems of the plurality of interests.[21] The obvious feature is the generalization of democratic institutions, predicated on popular sovereignty and political equality. Just as Aristotle predicted, if the outcome in social terms was to protect the poor from elite violence, in economic terms the outcome was a particular equation of redistributive pressures, namely, the inflexion of the ideological, coercive, and extractive powers of the state to shift the burdens and costs of common life onto the elite, especially in the form of *leitourgia*. In R. Osborne's modeling of the political economy of the *polis* (specifically for fourth-century BCE Athens, but the model can be applied in other contexts),[22] the set-up of political equality puts leitourgic burdens on the wealth elite, with a cascade of effects throughout the *polis* as political economy. The institution of *leitourgia* lies at the heart of the democratic community, in the name of an ideology that combines the sense of the public good with a class-bound awareness of elite resources and a sense of redistributive justice. Honorific decrees, though celebrating elite benefactors, are predicated on the same sense of rightful communitarian claims on elite property to generate public goods, through mechanisms such as accountability or the apportioning of distinction and *déchéance*.[23]

In our model, the elite finds itself under redistributive pressure from the democratic *polis* but is prevented from making up its losses by directly racking rents, because of the *polis*'s role in protecting the masses from any structures of dependency (this is very clear in the Roman imperial–era *polis*: above, chapter 13). The elite hence have to turn to the market economy, which their involvement boosts. Here, too, many consumers were citizens, and hence protected themselves from elite rent-seeking though the *polis* as state, which exercised regulatory power on the market through decrees and laws (for instance, through intervention to control prices, directly or indirectly). The regulatory effect was confirmed by the courts, which political equality placed in the hands of the mass of citizens. Notably, the power of elite-recruited magistrates to decide civil cases was much curtailed by their referral to courts above a low threshold (in accordance with the "Solonian" principle of systematically referring cases to the people rather than leaving them in the hands of wealthy, socially eminent officials).

An index of the absence of elite ability to aggressively chase profits or rents can be found in the realm of moneylending: "sticker price" interest rates were rarely adhered to, and haircuts and renegotiation were common.[24] The resort to foreign judges might reflect the attempt by the elites to bypass the effectiveness of *polis* institutions at limiting rent-seeking by the wealthy.[25] Political equality in the *polis* results in a situation that is not quite a safety net, but at least constrains the "natural" acquisitiveness and violence of the elites, exacerbated by the very pressures generated through political equality.

In addition, any attempts by the elites at capturing political institutions, colluding with a view to rent seeking, taking over public goods, or redefining public goods to their advantage, were made difficult by the *polis* through institutional and ideological instruments (namely the communitarian norms we have sketched in the previous chapter). Elite distinction was predicated on community recognition, proclaimed in honorific transactions and granted on terms of civic disinterestedness and devotion. The latter invariably took the dual form of competitive, superfetatious generosity that cemented the leitourgic burden, and of the denunciation of elite malpractice before the community. Institutionally, elites were thus incentivized to defect from their class interest to achieve individual distinction, which could be converted into emotional and ideological payoffs, but also practical advantages. These included social capital in intra-elite disputes that played out before the courts, and tangibly, minor benefits or perks to be derived from officeholding.[26] The mutual holding in check by wealthy citizens constitutes what I called the "tragedy of the elites" (studied at several points in this book, notably chapters 10 and 13). The *polis* model formalized and harnessed the structural tendency toward competition and strife among urban elites;[27] it also instrumentalized virtue politics into a means of socializing and integrating wealth elites within a political community.

Yet the full *polis* model also protected private property, even while making constant claims on elite wealth. This solution is a coherent extension of the principle of protection of citizens against tyrannical or elite power—for instance, against outrageous violence and acquisitiveness; the citizen's property was to be protected just as his body. The same claim to protection, extended by institutions and laws against seizure and expropriation, was also made by the wealth elite. Indeed, such claims had constituted an oligarchical critique of democracy as a form of tyranny, on the grounds that it used coercion to confiscate private property.[28] Likewise, democracy could be represented as a form of freeriding, allowing the poor to enjoy public goods provided by the wealthy, through economic contributions and services in office or in war, since the brunt of military effort was borne by self-equipped men-at-arms and cavalry.[29] This is the meaning of the Athenian oligarchs' clarion call (a sort of classist dog-whistle), at the end of the war with Sparta, to restrict citizenship to those who could "serve the *polis* with body and fortune." The developed forms of the *polis* did not practice expropriation and confiscations; such practices were associated with the civil strife of the Hundred Years (460-360 BCE) and died out with them (one exception is the radical social reforms in Hellenistic Sparta, which ended in isolation and catastrophe).[30]

The political economy of the *polis* after the great convergence hence reflects a number of compromises toward property rights, especially as enjoyed by the elite. Though there were forms of direct taxation on profits and property, often cast as emergency measures, especially during liquidity shortages for the *polis* state (*eisphora, proeisphora*), the most important form of levy on the wealth elite was *leitourgia*; that is, direct burdens taken on by members of the elite. *Leitourgia* represented a social pact, giving members of the wealth elite a measure of personal recognition and direct control over their redistributive burden. The institution allowed for the crucial perception of agency and participation in a common project in which the wealthy had to bear many of the costs, and where their role was ideologically and morally defined within the constraining limits of communitarian praxis.[31]

In addition, *euergesia*, namely the voluntary provision of benefactions, big or small, above the leitourgic burdens in exchange for honors, furthered this social bargain between mass and elite. By granting elitist honors and social capital, on ground constantly negotiated between the democratic community and the members of the social elite,[32] the euergetical exchange imposed the terms of strong communitarian restraint on the elite but also represented a communal signal or commitment to consistently respect elite property rights.

Indeed, the euergetical exchange legitimized the elite profitmaking that generated the surplus for public goods. Thus, in the second century CE, we have seen how the people of Tlōs acclaimed the benefactress Lalla, forcing a local official to draft a proposal that she be called "Mother of the City"—because she very kindly offered to manage the city's investment of her cash gift, as part of her moneylending business, possibly pocketing some of the profit as her fee, and possibly leveraging her situation in order to overcome protections for debtors (if we read between the lines; above, p. 359).[33] Of course, the balance between communal claims and elite profit-seeking was rife with tensions and risks, and the loudness of the honorific transactions and of virtue politics served to cover the tensions, as part of the continuous political work of the *polis* in action (see above, chapter 16).

The understanding of the democratic *polis* as a set of bargains necessary for the survival of the constitution is the mainspring of Aristotle's *Politics*. On the one hand, elite surplus will be subject to extraction (through direct taxation, confiscation, or the courts) to produce public goods, including pay for office or service. On the other hand, since excessive redistributive pressure will lead to elite defection, often violent, institutionalized guarantees have to be offered to the rich, who have to sure that the *polis* will not claim all of their property.[34] Mass-elite bargains were all the more necessary because the evolution of *polis* institutions (mostly) put an end to imperialism (or micro-imperialism), perioikism, and helotism as sources of income for the *polis* and its citizen stakeholders, and also because the city's own sources of revenue (taxation, rents), though significant, were insufficient to cover all of its fiscal needs.

The workings of the *polis* solution can be seen in many transactions and manifestations. For instance, the scrupulousness of *polis* finances in recording borrowing from sacred funds, interests owed to the gods, and eventual repayment of such loans (as in third-century BCE Epizephyrian Lokroi) acted as a further signal of the communitarian *polis*'s respect for private property (as well as a sign of the *polis*'s piety, as has often been said). Indeed, the money was probably handled by members of the civic elite, acting as officials and hence applying their own ideological principles of respect for the sanctity of contracts and loans (even if in practice, Zeus Olympios never quite got most of his money back).

At a more human level, we may return to the Roman-imperial city of Lētē, in Macedonia, with which we opened this book. As we have seen, the local notable M' Salarius Sabinus, in addition to offering services, cash, and benefactions as a gymnasiarch, was honored for his economic behavior (that is, he probably reminded the *polis* of this at the end of his officeholding, when rendering accounts before the assembly)—as a sign of his civic virtue. We can hence see him undertaking the burdens of office (and almost certainly *leitourgia*), but also responding to pressures from the community not to maximize his returns from his economic activity as estate owner and grain-grower, and hence selling at lower than market price.[35]

But in return for all these manifestations of disinterested commitment to his *polis*, his property, livelihood, and lifestyle were secure: this is illustrated by the city's response to the exigencies of the Roman state and its military machine. When the emperor Hadrian passed by, Lētē was asked for contributions in kind to the *annona* (military supply for the Roman army). The *polis* could only meet these by drawing on its own agricultural resources, which in practice meant the property of its individual citizens. But the *polis* did not meet the imperial demands by directly transferring the requisition down to its members, and hence levying or confiscating the necessary goods. Instead, the *polis* chose the path of *purchasing* the goods on the market. As a gesture of reciprocity, when Salarius Sabinus "provided" (against payment) wheat, barley, beans, and wine to the city, he ran true to form and accepted a lower price than the current one, thus contributing to controlling any spike in price that the sudden requisition threatened. The bargain between the *polis* and its elite held and was cemented by honors (Salarius Sabinus duly received an honorific statue); but all these repeated gifts in cash or in kind were predicated on Salarius Sabinus's right, as a large estate owner, to chase profits by following, and potentially manipulating the variation of prices on the markets. In the previous chapter, we looked at the *polis* as a proto-Rawlsian world of acceptable outcomes and of economic inequality accepted because it resulted in goods for the whole community; here we see that the Rawlsian decencies were outcomes of bargains between different constituencies and their interests.

From Civic Virtue to Virtuous Circle

The *polis* model sketched out above is the durable outcome of the democratic and autonomy-centered "great convergence." Emerging at the end of the tragic century of conflict, the *polis* solution developed during the third century BCE, and weathered robustly the shocks and pressures, exogeneous and endogenous, of the second and first centuries BCE (the "Indian Summer" of the *polis* and the short, terrible first century BCE, as I fondly called them: above, chapter 11). The proof of the institutional pudding lies in the economic lift-off, then efflorescence, of the world of *poleis* from the mid-fourth BCE century onwards, as reconstructed by such scholars of Greek history and especially the ancient economy as A. Bresson, G. Kron, and J. Ober.[36] "Wealthy Hellas," to use Ober's striking expression, is the concrete consequence of the actions of individual, profit-seeking, self-interested actors within an exchange-centered market economy shaped by the particular institutional set-up of the *polis*.

To start with, one consequence of the *polis*'s history was the absence of extractive "vampires" in the immediate social space; that is, no predatory state run for the benefit of a power elite, and no rentier class crushing a tenant peasantry. On the contrary, popular control of institutions ensured a degree of redistribution, direct, indirect, and in the form of financing of institutions and services. Structurally, as we have seen, the effect of political equality must have been to slow down the accumulation of wealth by an elite through capture of resources or rent extraction, and hence put a brake on any "natural" social inequality of the type that could have threatened political capture of institutions. The latter outcome is illustrated by the plutocratic fate and ultimate decline and fall of Classical Sparta, a fate that was avoided by the *poleis* of the great convergence.[37] Strikingly, the world of *poleis* knew shortages but not, it seems, famines, perhaps because of the political control on rent-seeking, accumulation, and speculation. A parallel might be found in the resilience and robustness of municipal economies in the Roman West.

More generally, the resulting distribution of wealth, although it is anachronistic to speak of a unitary middle class, would have favored a broad nonelite element in the *polis*. This included the "little big men" visible in the record of the Roman-era *polis* as occasional officeholders and rural notables (above, chapters 13, 14), but also a diverse group of families living above subsistence levels.[38] Their disposable income fueled a consumer boom as reflected in the "bourgeois" lifestyle that M. Rostovtzeff thought he could detect in the funerary art of *polis* citizens (fig. 10.4, cf. fig. 14.5), or in the growth in material culture tabulated and analyzed by I. Morris for early and Classical Greek history.[39] It is possible that nonelite disposable income was invested into productive sectors (cash-cropping, slave-operated manufacturing), thus generating yet more growth. At the same time, elites turned to market activities, trade in staples and commodities, real estate, or moneylending, in ways that may have dovetailed with nonelite consumption, production, and exchange in urban and rural contexts. All of these activities (elite and nonelite consumption, investment in the market, moneylending) generated profits that the *polis* taxed to finance public goods. This is a model of a virtuous loop created in the economy of the developed *polis*, through institutions that were developmental rather than extractive.

Another consequence of the constrained place of civic elites was the absence of patronage and deference in the *polis*, because of the lack of a wide gap between rich and poor.[40] Egalitarianism was reinforced by *polis* ideology, namely the concept of individual dignity and worth, and the unity promoted by the discourses and practices of *polis* as society. The latter rested on the fiction of the *polis* as a common descent group with shared moral character and a particular bond to place. Crucially, invented community acted as a way of overcoming contradictions in *polis* ideology (above, chapter 16). The all-too-necessary unity of the *polis* was enacted through multiple activities at the level of civic and civil society that served as symbolic proxies for full membership and stakeholdership: "brotherhoods," "tribes" and the like. The same function was performed by the sublimated image of the *polis* as a religious and religiously pure community. All these proxies offered constructed bonds beyond the family, in the form of commitments to multiple groups which only made sense as part of the overarching structure of the *polis*. Such "rational rituals" (to use the expression developed by M. Chwe) embedded individual actors in the civic community.[41]

Within this imagined community of bonds and rituals, unity was articulated as the characteristic of a community of free equals, through the ethical but nonuniversal and nonfoundational discourse of civic virtue, which was visibly rewarded through civic honors, valorized and reified in education, and diffused throughout civil society at the associative level. To use the model developed by Chwe, the *polis*'s rational rituals diffused common knowledge as well as common fictions: they made sure that all members knew the *polis*'s values of collaboration and solidarity, and that they all knew that other members knew, through visible, public participation in mass forms but also capillary contexts throughout *polis* as society. The impact is visible in the shape kinship took in the *polis*: S. C. Humphreys's analysis of the best known case, democratic Athens in the fourth century BCE, shows an absence of phenomena such as banking dynasties or lineage-based politics, a situation that suggests the disappearance of familism in this particular instance.[42] I would hypothesize that the same held true for most *poleis* after the great convergence and into the Roman empire.

As a result of rational rituals, civic identity encouraged solidarity between citizens, both as individuals and as members of constituencies (especially the Aristotelian categories of rich and poor). The ideas and ideals of civic virtue, proclaimed in the *polis*'s central institutions and performed at the associative level, had the practical effect of fostering social capital and especially trust between citizens. In G. Herman's somewhat idyllic interpretation of democratic Athens, public-mindedness, valued as undergirding the democratic polity as a whole, led to positive, respectful interactions between individuals who could commit to their Athenian counterparts as trustworthy partners rather than distrust them or rebuff them as potential adversaries. Game theory helps to understand this outcome as a conscious choice within the repeated interactions, to avoid defection from the common good.[43]

Civic trust lowered transaction costs in the *polis* in social and especially in economic dealings, in the *polis* as market.[44] We might draw a parallel with the famous analysis offered by R. Putnam for modern Italy, namely that the absence of clientelism and "amoral familism" allowed for the effective workings of good government, and hence economic and social development unblighted by corruption.[45] It is likely that the workings of the *polis* as a high-trust, low-defection environment

FIGURE 17.2. Aigai and the hinterland which it absorbed.

multiplied its institutional capacities as a legal entity guaranteeing the safety of persons, contracts, and property, with transparent, accountable, and non-capturable procedures and goods. The *polis*'s economy and prosperity would hence be explicable as the results of good institutions in the broadest sense, including the democratic bargains of the great convergence as well as the legal and administrative provisions that it offered, like any stately organization.

As an economic environment, the *polis* fostered investment and expenditure by secure, trustful citizens animated with a sense of stakeholding, belonging, and self-worth. The resulting profits and hopefully, growth, could further be taxed to finance public goods, which promoted the sense of belonging and proved the latter's practical benefits. In addition, the robustness of *polis* institutions encouraged growth of a different kind, namely territorial expansion through the takeover of smaller cities through *sunoikismos* (above, pp. 208–9). Synoikisms brought complexities and difficulties: the processes of economic integration also had political repercussions in terms of representativity and responsiveness of the *polis* to its constituent members and their interests. For instance, when Teōs or Aigai took over smaller neighboring *poleis*, converting them to settlements in their hinterland (fig. 9.2, fig. 17.2), they needed to rearrange economic fluxes involving such commodities as raw wool, timber, or firewood toward the urban center where the commodities were used or transformed into exportable goods. Part of the transaction also involved rebates and guarantees to the communities that joined the larger *poleis* and contributed their population, property, territory, and resources.[46] Such tensions had always been part of the *polis*, between town and countryside, the different forms of settlement in the countryside, and generally different constituencies within the *polis*. They were addressed by political processes and solutions in *polis* constitutional workings as well as civic solidarities. In that respect, the huge region-*polis* of Athens, with its two major urban centers, its myriad *dēmoi,* and the hamlets and farmsteads in the countryside, was not exceptional, and many cities had to confront the same problems of bigness.

The resulting complexities of scale might have contributed to the diversity and resources of the expanded *poleis* as well as to their economic life, mobilizing and reinforcing political processes of bargaining and decision-making: bigness fed back into the institutional workings of the *polis*. Some of these processes can be seen in the rather messy case of the baths at Thermai Granikeiai, on the territory of Roman-era Kyzikos but 40 kilometers far from the urban center, and neglected by the *polis* officials until a combination of local initiative and *polis* recognition regularized the local market and resulting economic growth (above, p. 355).[47] The challenges of bigness might have further stimulated institutional problem-solving and hence intensified the effectiveness of the *polis*. The end result of all these institutional processes was a prosperous social organism with high equality, high trust, good governance, and substantial levels of pay, perhaps comparable to other historical moments of prosperity. It is possible Classical Athens enjoyed a standard of living comparable to such as early modern Holland.[48]

The workings of *polis* institutions could be projected externally. They were modular and scalable, through processes of peer-polity interaction. Within leagues, *poleis* could collaborate through consultation and representative decision-making to harmonize institutions and lower transaction costs, as well as pool resources for goals such as diplomacy, bargaining, or violence for policy ends.[49] In addition, the existence of a network of *poleis* allowed for interaction between mutually recognizable entities practicing the same institutional culture, and hence enabling the extension of legal protection or facilities after negotiation and along pre-agreed forms (for instance, by granting tax exemptions or access to special expedited courts). It was the *poleis* that constituted the most versatile element in the economic networks. For instance, Kyrēnē, a grain-rich *polis* favored by exceptional ecological conditions in Northern Africa, exported grain during an Aegean-wide shortage in the early 320s BCE, the many recipients were mainly *poleis* (with a few dynasts benefiting as well). The event dramatically highlights the operation of an international framework for interaction between *poleis*.[50] Finally, individual members of a *polis* were recognizable to other *poleis* and could work institutionalized forms to facilitate movement. A doctor from the *polis* of Hyrkanioi Makedōnes in western Asia Minor could travel and ply his art among the cities of Lokris after receiving an honorific decree from one of them in the late second century BCE.[51]

Connectivity between *poleis* allowed for the operation of two divergent, but mutually reinforcing phenomena.[52] The first was specialization in cash crops, either because of exceptional ecological conditions favoring the production of a commodity, or because of a location enabling the export of a commodity at favorable costs. Favorable conjuncture allowed a *polis* to concentrate its economy around the production of the valuable commodity and to export it for cash, with which it could import staples. The commodity would be circulated among other *poleis*, as well as exported to regions outside the network of *poleis* (for instance, Thrace or the Black Sea) in exchange for valuable staples such as grain or enslaved labor, the first to feed the *polis*, the second to work intensively on the cash crop. The second way of riding connectivity was for cities to both export and import commodities (notably wine but also manufactured goods), which took on added value both through the costs of transport, and through nonlocal provenance that lent distinction, and hence culturally driven appreciation, to foreign goods. *Poleis* within the connected network of peers collaborated to consume each other's commodities and to export their own commodities, in ways that generated profit for all participants. Both modes of *polis* economics illustrate how being a *polis* allowed for fruitful participation in peer-polity interaction, leading to expansion and growth.

The collaborative network of *poleis* may have played a major part in sustaining their economic efflorescence between the third and first centuries BCE, a time of conflict and predatory imperial states. Indeed, the *poleis*, because of their corporate organization and their claim to autonomy, could bargain with empires, to try to negotiate rebates and lessen the impact of extraction. They existed as a network of small spaces of liberty (in contrast notably with the "royal land" of villages and even towns directly administered by empires), gradually extending to contiguity across the eastern Mediterranean world.

This, as we have seen, is how fourth- and third-century BCE Priēnē imagined itself in the flush of its newly gained autonomy. But the model of the *polis* presented here also invites us to imagine Priēnē as an economic space, even if it shunted its victuals market to one side and was much taken with representing civic honorific discourse in inscribed and visual form (fig. 1.2, fig. 11.3). We can view the urban texture of the city (an example of the "*polis* as life form" explored by A. Matthaei and M. Zimmermann) in two ways. First, it represents not just the communitarian primacy of the *polis* (above, chapter 16) but also its particular socioeconomic choices. The grid plan gives a sense of the city's egalitarianism, which results from political equality; the orderliness of the urban infrastructure of walls, streets, and open spaces is a reminder of the city's provision of collective goods through public finance—freedom (collective and individual), security, and the regulation of interactions in a transparent, shared mode. The city is also characterized by the beauty and durability of public spaces and monuments—the *agora* and its surrounding colonnaded porticoes and rooms, the two gymnasia, the shrines, especially the great shrine of Athēna Polias. These all act as reminders of the provision of public goods, but also of the overarching presence of community and its commitment as a space for social capital and trust.

Second, the provision of impressive public spaces and monuments was itself the "proof of the pudding," the direct result of the *polis* solution that favored the development of local economies through the restriction of rent-seeking and the creation of broad bases of wealth that could provide the resources—economic and social, public and private—to build Priēnē on its hillside. Indeed, the whole approach in this chapter has been focused on the "proof of the pudding," rather than follow the efforts of some historians to draw quantitative blood from the built and inscribed stones of ancient evidence. In the absence, for almost all *poleis*, of even the scanty figures known for Athens, we might start by looking for phenomena and posit a causal relationship or correlation between such phenomena as the hard surfaces of *polis* prosperity, constant demographic abundance without Malthusian consequences, and *polis* institutions.[53] Specifically, the economic liftoff and durable prosperity of "wealthy Hellas" (Ober) or "la Grèce des cités" (Bresson) should be related to political equality and its consequences.

I have further argued that this model holds broadly true for the *polis* after the great convergence, namely under the Roman empire. Even within an extractive world empire, at a time when a global wealth elite accumulated the spoils of extraction (starting with the Roman emperor himself), the political economy and the institutions of the *polis*, as developed in the great convergence, continued to operate effectively. This state of affairs and the historical logic that led to it are attested by multiple sources. True, the *polis* endured partly because it was underwritten by the Roman empire, which needed both its prosperity as a tax base and its autonomy as administrative relay. But *polis* institutions, in simplified form, were also robust enough to be diffused throughout the eastern Mediterranean, either through imitation or through imperial grant. Their coherence and operativeness can be seen in the success of urban life in the Roman Near East, which is an effect of the polis' success at harnessing local elite wealth to create local welfare and public goods.

Hence, I have proposed to see the beautiful city of marble, so visible an artifact in the landscape of the Roman empire, not as a reflection of elite domination but as an index of the persistence of *polis* solutions. D. Engels proposed a similar interpretation (elite restraint, wide distribution of wealth, economic growth) for Roman Corinth (which is admittedly not a perfect example because of its odd situation as a Roman colony in the province of Achaia; that is, as a city that might have enjoyed particular legal advantages). This democratic interpretation of the marble city might also apply to spectacular sites such as Roman-imperial Ephesos, Aphrodisias, or even Palmyra (figs. 12.1, 12.2, 13.1, 14.6, 14.7), as I argued above when surveying the changes that poliadization brought to that "caravan city." In other words, the continued prosperity of the cities into the Roman imperial period, in spite of the impact of an extractive global empire and its elites, might be a clue that the democratic economy of the *polis* was robust enough to continue its work.

The Road to Priēnē: A New Institutionalist History of the *Polis*

The economists D. Acemoglu and J. A. Robinson explain the success or failure of nations in terms of good institutions.[54] If we accept the picture given above of the *polis* as a sweet spot of institutions, a "Goldilocks" point when the right mixture of pressures and bargains led to buoyant growth, the urgent question is that of historical development—even more than in an idealist history of the *polis*, where the main transformative moment is the realization of the idea of the common good and the eventful working out of its ramifications. How can we write the history of the *polis* in new institutionalist terms of rational choice, costs, and collective action?

The first stop is that of the densification of settlement from "clustervilles" to nucleated settlements, at the end of the Early Iron Age. This process of coalescence, rather than merely an episode in the history of ideas in the form of a Castoriadis- or Vernant-style political turn, might be the result of competition and schismogenesis— that is, conflict over resources and borders between increasingly consolidated territorial units, in which the loose communities of the Early Iron Age, with their clusters of mutually suspicious big men and multiple claims to authority (as visible in the Homeric poems or in Hesiod), had to find means of coherence, collaboration and self-governance that would not expose them to predation or even violent takeover by their neighbors.

This, in practical terms, is the process of self-institution that Castoriadis posited at the start of the history of the *polis*. Communities that could not manage this process, for reasons of small size or internal conflict, were absorbed, destroyed, or subordinated by their neighbors. The discourse and "rational rituals" of fictive kinship groups emerged at this juncture, perhaps as a means to create civic capital without relying on preexisting competitive groups (local or kin-based) that would pursue their own interests as constituencies. The reasoned yet emotional appeal to the common good as constitutive of community also emerged at the same time, as a response to the same needs and a means to create the middle ground for effective common action.

The next stage is the emergence, during the "Archaic" period, of state institutions capable of adjudicating disputes, enforcing rules, and providing public goods. Such institutions also had to prove capable of meeting the costs out of community surplus, through some form of taxation or levy. It is important to bear in mind the diversity and fluidity of solutions in the "Archaic" *poleis*. Rather than a single form of extractive early state, the early *polis* could be organized as rule by a small set of families, rule by an individual, or a polity—and the last could itself be defined as the rule of a narrow group or a broad one broadly; all these forms could succeed each other, or even coexist messily, within the same *polis*.

As we have seen (chapter 6), two main types emerge during this period. Narrow, closed polities restricted membership to a small wealth elite dominating serfs and *perioikoi*; the broad polities included a more diverse population of wealthy, middling, and poor. These two types seem to have developed for contingent reasons, rather than because of ecological or geographical determination. Closed polities had very high solidarity and trust, high social capital, and low transaction costs among the citizen body; but the maintenance of the system entailed high political costs generally and, in the long run, led to low economic performance and political capacity, as illustrated by the woes of Sparta in the late fifth and fourth centuries BCE. In contrast, open polities had low political costs because of widespread inclusion, participation, access to institutions and legal protection of property, contracts, and person, effective protection of public goods, and generalized entitlement (among the citizens) to public goods. These phenomena occurred in spite of uncertainty and confusion about issues such as status or access to office, which were impossible to regulate satisfactorily. In such polities, social capital had to be constructed through ongoing political work or bricolage, which constituted undoubted costs of their own.

We also know the end of the story—namely, that the open polity model proved more resilient and successful, leading to the great convergence starting ca. 350 BCE (chapters 9 and 10). Rather than explaining this phenomenon by the sheer force of the *polis* idea and its moral consequences, it is worth trying to understand it within the terms defined at the beginning of this chapter, namely by positing that the *polis* was made up of rational, self-interested actors belonging to multiple constituencies. The events of the tragic Hundred Years that preceded the great convergence could be considered as repeated turns in a particular competitive game between and within *poleis*, in which various political and institutional arrangements were tested at multiple scales—leading to three noticeable developments. The first is the phenomenon of increased collaboration between *poleis*, according to rules, as a groundswell that takes place beyond the violent tragedy of hegemonical powers, big and small, which we have followed above (chapters 8 and 9).

The second is the convergence of political constitutions toward some form of democracy, especially noticeable as an outcome after violent conflict and upheaval. Epizephyrian Lokroi, after direct rule by the Syracusan tyrant Dionysios II and a period of civil conflict, emerged in the form of a democracy, with a sovereign popular assembly and civic institutions (as shown by the scrupulous accountability of its borrowing from the treasury of Zeus Olympios: above, p. 237).[55] The same pattern probably underlies the settlement struck on the small island *polis* of Tēlos ca. 300 BCE, after civil unrest between oligarchs and democrats, as brokered by external arbitrators (the surviving oligarchs publicly accepted leitourgical burdens as reparation).[56] The third is the widespread adoption of the *polis* form, with its institutional culture and social bargains, by non-Greek communities across the eastern Mediterranean, which seem to have adopted the *polis*'s solution in regulating the relations between mass and elite as well as its possibilities for interfacing between communities.

The multiple turns of the *polis* game had centered on conflict within communities, between the rich and the poor (albeit often represented and led by elite politicians) over the power of the state, because the *polis* as state had the coercive power to assign burdens, distribute the protection of laws and institutions, and open access to public goods. The *polis* carried out these operations while claiming a Clastresian social immediacy that made it immensely effective and legitimate, and hence exacerbated competition for control of its institutions (this is the institutionalist aspect of Gray's paradox, namely that civic ideology must divide as well as unite). Aristotle's *Politics* is precisely predicated on this conundrum of state power as represented by the constitution (*politeia*, which ranges from the basic definition of citizenship to issues of high office and legislation), as the prize of conflict between the two constituencies of rich and poor, those with great economic surplus and those who, by virtue of being free men, potentially only have a claim to membership in the political community. This is another example of a second-order problem created by the very solution to collective problems: the emergence of an agreed-on form of authoritative power generated and escalated conflict precisely because of the coercive and acquisitive potential inherent to problem-solving capacities.[57]

We have noted, with some astonishment, that the outcome of the multiple turns of the tragic game of powers in the fifth and fourth centuries BCE turned out to be a great democratic convergence (above, chapter 9). The path to convergence was in great part decided by contingencies, namely the failure of hegemony and the end of the deadly entanglement of external hegemony and internal conflict. Contingencies allowed the competitive forces within *poleis* to settle on the stalemate of "moderate democracy," which becomes general in the great convergence. As stalemates go, this was a productive one, grounded in bargains and compromises between political equality and economic inequalities. Such bargains include the leitourgical system or euergetism. The process of convergence was mediated by a shared institutional culture (inflected but not determined by the Athenian experiment in radical democracy) and in a set of ideas and discourses about the common good, with very deep roots (indeed, going back to the Early Iron Age) and refined constantly in the debates of the Classical period—that is, the values and ideals I have parsed earlier (chapter 16).

These ideas were not completely consistent (as we have seen), especially in light of the refined analytical political philosophy to which they were related (but which developed against it). But their nonfoundational nature and their capaciousness precisely could serve as the space for collective action within the *polis*, especially since their appeal was morally and intellectually compelling and highly effective at the small-scale level of the *poleis* that were structured in multiple ways as closeknit imagined communities. The workings of the *polis* at a small scale help us to understand why a political philosopher (albeit of an antidemocratic, Platonic persuasion) such as Plutarch retained strong links with his hometown, the *polis* of Chairōneia, where he remained and took on civic office, in spite of his global privileges as a Roman citizen, and his vast horizons.[58] The *polis* showed civic ideas in action, and working.

Peer-polity interaction, with its capacity to spread innovation quickly across a wide network, did the rest. It ensured the normativeness of the *polis eleuthera kai dēmokratoumenē* during the late fourth, third and second centuries BCE; Priēnē is but one example among very many. Hence the *polis* was indeed a matter of ideas, values, and intentions—within a specific historical, institutional context.[59] When this context changed in the fourth century CE, notably because of pressure from the Late Roman state, the various variables in the *polis* equation drifted apart, namely the familiar, millennium-old actors on the stage: the richest level of local elites, the "little big men" who had done so much to meet the burdens of the life in common, the collective body of the people in assembly, and finally the civic subdivisions and the local associations.

Interests and Ideals, and Beyond

It turns out that the *polis* of ideals and the *polis* of interests are the same: the former is not an airy sham, the "cover" for the hard-bitten realism of the latter. *Polis* ideals existed within a specific historical context of diversity and experimentation, driven by competition over interests by calculating actors and constituencies. It is true that the content of these ideals (notably the ideal of public good and virtuous citizenship) could exacerbate conflict, in a striking illustration of the interdependency of interests and ideals; but the ideals also could provide the solution to conflict, in the right combination of contingent conditions (the failure of hegemony) and structural factors (small-scale communities, peer-polity interaction). In this manner, civic ideals were also institutions, in the new institutionalist sense, shaping costs and benefits. Their compelling nature as ideas allowed for a space of collaboration and restraint, penalizing defection. Their normative nature as communitarian performance undergirded the actual institutions of popular sovereignty and the political economy of the *polis* within which interest-seeking had to work.

The picture given above might seem too good to be true: the history of the *polis* leads, through a series of divine surprises, to developed political and social forms located in an ideological and institutional sweet spot, as the "Goldilocks" great society where everything is just right and rewarded with economic lift-off and prosperity, the crowning achievement of the *polis* as proto-modernity. That civic virtue, democracy, good governance, egalitarianism, high trust, and market regulation should lead to happiness and prosperity perhaps sounds like a morality play, and looks a like a pat reflection of our own political investments and debates about the possibility of democracy, the feasibility of social democracy, the sources and costs of the holy grail of economic growth. This should give us pause, notably because this story is adjacent to stories about a "Greek miracle" and hence politically charged narratives about the genealogy of the success of Western Civilization (see below, chapter 20). In the rest of this book, I propose to reexamine this final picture, and the whole narrative that sustains it, to look at the *polis*'s involvement in multiple forms of power—not in its idealistic, optimistic Arendtian guise, but as a pessimistic story of conflict and domination.

18

Bad *Polis*

THE REALITIES OF POWER

> Citizenship is that particular point of view of the dominant, which constitutes itself as a universal point of view—the point of view of those who dominate the city and who have constituted their point of view as natural by representing the city as a unity.
>
> —F. ISIN, *BEING POLITICAL. GENEALOGIES OF CITIZENSHIP*

Forgetting "Goldilocks"

What should happen if we decide to read the *polis* against the grain, rather than as the sweet spot where political and social justice, civic virtue, institutionalist balance, and economic performance all meet and are revealed as the same thing? I have alluded to possible realist readings earlier, notably in the shadow of the qualities of the *polis* after the great convergence (above, chapter 10), or when touching on the subject of the diversities rather than the unity within the *polis* and between individual *poleis* (above, chapter 15). In this chapter and the next, I will insist squarely on the tensions, fracture points, and elisions in *polis* history: my aim is to uncover and explore social bads and their dialectical connection to the goods produced by the *polis*. The three main components of the *polis* of social bads are the following: first, structural conflict and violence; second, power imbalances as a consequence of economic inequality; third, the pervasive impacts of exclusion as one of the constitutive elements of membership. At this point, we must bid farewell to Aristotle's *Politics* (which I have repeatedly taken as a guide in tracing historical phenomena or interpretation). Whereas the *Politics*, on the point of confronting the *polis*'s essential link with control by social groups, finally moves to the sublimated level of ideal constitution-building in Books 7–8 (revisiting Platonic leitmotifs such as education, the soul, performance, philosophy), I propose here to take a walk within the *polis*'s penumbra of violence and injustice. But in fact, the gravity of history only takes us back to the very beginning of Aristotle's *Politics* and the constitutive elements of the *polis*, this time not as a sign of the *polis*'s bigness and primacy, but as sites of potential domination.

The social bads of the *polis* are plain to see, even or especially in a small community such as the island of Hērakleia, which appears at the start of this book and has recurred as an example of the *polis* at work. Above, I took care in pointing to Hērakleia as a striking example of politics in action. First, I tried to show on the small island, Arendtian power (rather than domination) achieving the safety of all through political work (chapter 16). Then, I read the social transaction of goat-banning as a clear case of a textbook collective action problem (the tragedy of the commons through overgrazing) being solved by coordination (chapter 17). The utopian form of the civic decree (a major source for the story told in this book) makes it easy to focus on *polis* solidarity. Yet the Herakleian decree is also astonishingly clear about the problems of violence and conflict surrounding communal action. Its poignant isolation also raises questions about the durability and sustainability, ecological and especially political, of the *polis* solution. Finally, through the very act of playing with the poetics of *koinon* and citizenship, the Herakleiotes also made clear that the political process may have concerned all the inhabitants of their small island world but were firmly in the hands of a particular group of stakeholders.

An awareness of the negative aspects of the *polis* has long been part of its historiography, connecting the *polis* with exclusion and exploitation, notably in the case of slavery (this trend starts with modern critiques of democracy as the rule of the "idle mob").[1] Here I follow the lead (though not the detailed treatment) of two provocative essays that exemplify the urgency of the task and its possibilities. The first is ancient historian J.-L. Roubineau's searing social history of the *polis* (2015), which challenges the paradigm of a unified, egalitarian, just community structured by democracy, and argues instead for an inegalitarian polity, starkly divided between rich and poor, riven with violence, tensions, and contradictions. The second is critical theorist E. Isin's genealogical enquiry into citizenship (2002), which traces the constitutive strategies of citizenship as "solidaristic, agonistic or alienating," with particular attention on the last category of othering as an essential part of the construction of political community. The city is a "difference machine" that creates forms of otherness that intersect with exclusion: some groups are constructed as "strangers" in the city's midst, but not outsiders.

This nonbinary approach invites us to reconsider the problem of *polis* as society (at which I have had a first pass above, from an Aristotelian and institutionalist angle: chapter 15). Indeed, Isin's sympathetic yet lucid riposte to the urban historian Lewis Mumford's celebration of the city serves as a fertile model if we are to reconsider critically the diachronic and synchronic history of the *polis* form:[2]

> Mumford was perhaps the best archaeologist of the city that the twentieth century witnessed. Yet Mumford was unable to free himself from a perspective that relentlessly cornered him into recovering the good or evil of the city, rather

than seeing that one was not possible without the other. That the city was a crucial condition of citizenship in that being a citizen was inextricably associated with being *in* the city was obvious to Mumford. That over the centuries struggles over citizenship have always taken place "over" the city too was also obvious. But that the city was neither a backdrop to these struggles *against which* groups have wagered, nor a foreground *for which* groups have struggled for hegemony was less so. That the city was the battleground *through which* groups defined their identities, staked their claims, waged their battles and articulated citizenship rights, obligations and principles was not at all obvious to Mumford.

The present essay does not quite fulfill the liberating potential of this programmatic, if somewhat sibylline, paragraph by Isin; nor do I feel able to offer a critical biography or a radical history of the *polis*.[3] But to look back on my whole long narrative with Isin-inspired lucidity about the relations between the various elements in the *polis* solution with a dialectical gaze, trying to avoid static miserabilism or incoherence, is simply a historical duty as well as a moral necessity.

Conflict, Consensus, Violence

The vision of *polis* institutions as working to create welfare is utopian, and the *polis* admits of conflict in multiple forms, exacerbated by political practice. Loraux's paradox (above, p. 455: the *polis* is conceived as centered on politics but *polis* politics themselves are presented as post-political and consensual) does not make conflict go away and may even exacerbate it. If we return to the island of Hērakleia, we must admit that for all the consensus implied by civic ceremony, it is also the case that Arendtian "civic courage," political work, and collective striving, in the end still meant that some citizens had to bear the brunt of a decision that irrevocably affected their livelihoods and habits. Civic decision-making had the potential to create winners and losers.

The celebratory, hortatory, exemplary, utopian genre of the honorific decree occasionally trails wisps of strife and resentment. The failure by the Macedonian *polis* of Morrylos to honor a good citizen (who offered a cow to the city) by actually having the crown proclaimed in front of the Assembly might be an oversight, or reflect hostility toward the honorand; the proclamation only took place when his son held office (by which time the cow had already calved).[4] A decree from Keramos, without entering into details, gives some intimation of political strife in coded language. It honors a citizen who behaved well when the city joined another, probably Stratonikeia: "when after this the citizen body fell in difficult circumstances, showing no fear of the inflexibility (*anatasis*) of some, he tried to increase greatly his goodwill toward the masses (*plēthos*) with an authentic and true spirit."[5] On occasions, the very urban landscape suggests conflict: we can speculate about discontent when considering the second-century BCE reorganization of the *agora* at

Priēnē (grouping all honorific statues in a single row), or the razing of the monumental gate of the shrine of Nabu at Palmyra, to make way for a new colonnaded street (above, pp. 381–82). Even when good citizens were honored for protecting public goods or limiting elite acquisitiveness (as often in the Roman-imperial *polis*), we might wonder if the situations admitted of complicated conflicts of interest, whose resolution involved costs and losses while hiding them under the civic harmony which was the official face of the city.

The arguments and appeals that were aired in the few hours of the citizens' meeting at Hērakleia are lost forever. What is clear is that all complexities got simplified and stylized into an exemplary image by the blunt instrument of civic ideology. On the surviving written document, we can only read the "cold," monumental text that the community left as a sign of unanimity. Civic ideology, the poetics of *to koinon*, and the moral claims of the *polis* as political community reduced differences and debate to silence. Awareness of imposed consensus as the aim of political decision-making may have exacerbated conflict and resistance to the processes. This situation might be precisely what the decree from Keramos, mentioned above, called *anatasis*—a "rigidity" or lack of willingness to accept consensus or compromise for the collective good, to the point of threatened violence.

Here, inter-*polis* collaboration, through panels of "foreign judges" from other cities, may have offered (or imposed) solutions for difficult political cases such as legal proceedings to annul a decree as illegal at Dēmētrias (*dikē huper psēphismatos hōs paranomou*, what Athenians called a *graphē paranomōn*), or "the case involving denunciations" that the Erythraians found fraught enough to call in judges from Priēnē.[6] Foreign judges could break an institutional impasse while avoiding blame resting on any individuals or groups in the city, or open resentment breaking out against any one side "winning" the debate—a reminder of the constant proximity of conflict in the *polis*.

More often, violence and discontent must have been precursors to and side products of decision-making: a decree from the *polis* of Minōa (on the island of Amorgos) speaks of *tarachē* (trouble) that civic ritual but also royal intervention helped contain.[7] Violence is present implicitly and explicitly, upstream and downstream from the Herakleiotes's decree. The ecological conundrum about goats was conflictual, leading not just to disagreement but to violence. Even after the decision not to allow the raising of goats was passed, the general effect was not instant. More hard work was involved in the aftermath of the political decision to keep the tragedy of the commons at bay, in order to give substance to the intention of preserving the island as a human community. The social magic of the decree (making some acts legitimate force and declaring others illegitimate and antisocial violence, *bia*) had to be implemented in practice by the action of some citizens preventing others from forcibly keeping goats, literally "with an aim to violence" (*biasomenos*). This individual action entailed the risk of injury or even death in physical fracas with those infringing the city's decision. The only power of enforcement here is prosecution, publicly undertaken by the community. The matter-of-factness with which such confrontations are considered implies that physical violence must have broken out before the Herakleiotes's decree against goat-keeping.

The case of Hērakleia highlights how the *polis*, for all its ideological strength as a state, could be startlingly thin on the ground when it came to enforcement. This is perhaps understandable in a tiny *polis* like Hērakleia, but self-help was also the rule for the enforcement of the law and especially the execution of judicial decisions in a large and well-institutionalized *polis* such as Classical Athens, and Aristotle recognizes the general difficulty of enforcing the law.[8] The *polis* offered regulatory solutions to uncertainty and conflict, but solutions raised further problems; the situation at Hērakleia, with conflict upstream and downstream from the intervention of the *polis*, was characteristic. A clue to the ubiquity of violence in the fabric of the *polis* can be gained from the widespread practice of officially suspending the right to seizure and self-help during religious festivals, which were meant to be spaces of rejoicing and communion.[9]

Violence and enmity were inevitable as consequences of regulation; they were part of the feedback loop of institutional workings. Conflict was channeled back to *polis* institutions of adjudication, either directly or after further rounds of physical violence. Intervention would instantiate the *polis*'s definitions of what was legitimate and what was beyond the pale (*hubris*), and what the practical consequences would be.[10] In the case of Hērakleia, the *polis*'s intervention about goats contained the potential for further conflict that could escalate to violence; but violence, in the aftermath of the *polis*'s ruling, would lead to further intervention and regulation in the form of judicial proceedings to which the *polis* itself would be a party. The *polis* was dialectically bound with a reality of conflict—preceding, underlying and flowing from the praxis of civic politics.

The effect of conflict as reinforcing rather than undermining the *polis* is a corollary to its success at establishing itself as the only possible social and political form, coterminously expressing society (as a Clastresian fiction: above, chapter 15), conceived as primary to the individual and claiming validity as a realm of justice and virtue (above, chapter 16). The weakening of familism as part of the moral economy of the *polis* also played into this phenomenon, by projecting family disputes into the public sphere where they were openly debated and received uncertain resolution: hence the prevalence of conflict and enmities within the family, so visible in Athens but also ubiquitous in the dreams interpreted by the second-century CE specialist Artemidōros.[11] Endemic conflict was hence the corollary of state functions with weak enforcement, but worked to reinforce the claims and presence of the state (thus perpetuating more conflict). Violence operated as a reflection of the *polis*'s ability to preserve itself as a state, as well as the price to pay for its regulatory functions.

Conflict was especially exacerbated by the democratic turn of the great convergence. As we have seen, constant elite competition, escalating to actual conflict, was one of the mechanisms by which elite collusion was kept low (what I have termed the "tragedy of the elites"). The process is clearly documented in Athens and might have been operative wherever there were large jury courts (in *poleis* down to the first century BCE at least). The upshot of the democratic dynamics of mass and elite (to echo J. Ober's influential formulation) is hence constant conflictuality among the members of the civic elite. Generally, the universal resort to volunteer prosecutions to ensure enforcement required and perpetuated the existence of personal enmities. The extraordinary virulence of attacks in litigation characterizes the legal style of the *polis*, as illustrated by Athenian forensic oratory in the fourth century BCE but also by the speeches of Cocceianus Diōn in Roman-era Prousa *ca.* 100 CE. The propensity for political enmity and judicial feuds is merely the most visible aspect of elite conflictuality; at times, enmity burst into physical violence that implicated public institutions of adjudication and only reinforced *polis* authority and ideology.

A well-documented case of the imbrication between private elite feuds and *polis* institutions and ideology is the lawsuit launched by the Athenian politician Dēmosthenēs against Meidias, for punching him in the face during the festival in 351/0 BCE.[12] Intra-elite violence, often cast in the form of *charivari*, is attested in the Roman-imperial *polis*; for instance, at Tarsos, Sardeis, or Knidos (where a nightly affray before a citizen's house led to a man being killed by a chamber pot, dropped along with the contents, from an upper floor window).[13] But even without reaching open violence (which attracted the attention of the Roman state: the affair of the chamber pot was referred to the emperor Augustus), enmity between individual members of the civic elites could take the more endemic form of dirty tricks, hidden hostilities, plots, slander. Such hidden enmities, and the desire to defeat enemies in the open contest of the courts and to seize their property, haunt the dreams of Artemidōros's clientele in late second-century CE Asia Minor (as a nightly menagerie of boars, wild asses, and other beasts).[14]

Elite conflictuality is a political choice resulting from institutional barriers to elite collusion, rather than merely a product of Greek "agonistic spirit." To be more specific, elite agonistic conflict was taken over and instrumentalized in the democratic *polis*. The presence of elite conflictuality enshrined conflict as the generalized norm for social relations, because this was the price to pay for preventing elite dominance.[15] In world-historical terms, I propose seeing in such intra-elite competition a structural feature of "municipal" politics, as an index of communitarian, public-facing polities with strong means of controlling elites. It shows up in other historical contexts; for instance, in the towns of eighteenth-century Provence, as analyzed by the great historian of French republicanism, M. Agulhon. Strikingly, other *polis*-like institutions are attested in this context, for instance *paraprasis* (wealthy citizens selling grain at low price upon request by civic authorities) or euergetism, and mechanisms of civic solidarity to weather crises such as food shortage or fiscal pressure from outside.[16] In this sort of polity, collaboration between civic leaders is rare because structurally difficult and lauded as a gesture of exceptional public-mindedness. In Magnēsia on Maeander, during the First Mithradatic War, in the face of danger the two main politicians agreed that one should withdraw to allow the other free rein in leading the *polis*.[17]

What took place in the island *polis* of Hērakleia was precisely not *stasis*, nor "normal" interpersonal violence in a face-to-face, preindustrial, Mediterranean society. The *polis* of Athens was notably free from concerns of personal "honor," as pointed out by G. Herman, as a consequence of the moral universe and the practical choices of the citizens;[18] the case of Athens illustrates the parameters of *polis* interactions. This characteristic only makes the presence of conflict in the *polis* the more salient. The solution the *polis* evolved to effectively produce public goods entailed heavy social costs. By this I mean not the "transaction costs" of institutional economics (above, chapter 17), but social burdens and bads generated by the *polis* and its workings: decision-making, enforcement, regulation, democratic politics, and redistribution, which all generated conflict and violence. The acceptance of these features shows that *polis* communitarianism, which placed the common good at the heart of its ethical system, was a form of utilitarianism with much leeway for actual violence in social relations.

The same spirit can be seen in the practical workings of the popular court system, so highly developed in democratic Athens and so central to the control of its elites (above, pp. 184–86). Founded on mass decision-making after hearing competing speeches, rather than as a technical process handled by trained legal officials applying substantive rules, the system visibly privileged the political aspect of adjudication and the application of rules. For all its ostentatious statements about following procedures, technicality, and substance as part of stateness (above, pp. 236–37), it remained strikingly open to manipulation, for instance through mendacious testimony (*pseudomarturia*), rumors, or the threat of vexatious prosecution. The "open texture" of democratic judicial institutions had the strong potential to produce unjust outcomes, which would still be sanctioned by the *polis* as inherently just in their very definition, because they were the product of communal decision. This is simply the logical result of communitarian politics.[19] The utilitarian calculus, and the obligation it imposed on the *polis* members who benefited from it, were recognized by Sōkratēs as he awaited execution (a scene we have earlier visited as a pure instance of disinterested individual commitment).[20]

The capacity of the *polis* to impose collective demands on the individual has often been commented on as characteristic of its nonliberal nature. This holds true even though, in its developed, democratic form, it purported to protect the dignity and the property of individual members, including and especially the poorest, against violence and dispossession by other members, and to allow people to "live as they please"—that is, free from dominance. The very instruments of collective action that protected dignity and freedom were hegemonical and holistic, namely the development of institutions as the proclaimed expression of the People's will and the utilitarian enforcement of the *polis*'s decisions to achieve collective welfare, at the cost of social bads that individuals would have to suffer.

The nonliberal character of the *polis* was famously commented on by two modern thinkers, both from the city-state culture of nineteenth-century Switzerland—namely, the writer and politician Benjamin Constant (1767–1830), and the historian Jacob Burckhardt (1818–1897). Constant, in a lecture delivered in 1819 (but based on thoughts elaborated in 1806), famously contrasted "ancient" liberty (predicated on the active participation of citizens in the autonomy of small states) and "modern" liberty (centered on the protection of individual rights in large nation-states).[21] Though he does not mention Constant, Burckhardt, in his great cultural history of ancient Greece (based on lectures delivered in the 1870s and 1880s) insists on the same contrast between modern freedoms and rights and the ancient conception of the *polis* as something greater than, and prior to, individuals and their households, for the individual "owes everything to the Whole" (*denn es verdankt dem Ganzen alles*) and can only achieve his full potential as a citizen in the political community of free citizens. Burckhardt passes judgment on the *polis* as a *città dolente* (repurposing a tag from Dante's *Inferno* as the epigraph to the relevant section), a "sorrowful city," born in the violent act of *sunoikismos* that transforms farmers into political beings, and where individuals are constrained and shaped by the collective.[22]

My purpose here can hardly be to critique the classical learning deployed by Constant or review the image of Greek history in Burckhardt's immense opus;[23] this is, after all, a book on the *polis*, not its reception or historiography (though see chapter 20). I simply note that this vision of the *polis* (alongside a sense of the importance of autonomy and the direct nature of participation in state institutions) was formulated by thinkers who had lived, intimate experiences of city-state culture, since both Constant and Burckhardt were members of the elites of Swiss cities. Constant was born in the Francophile and internationally connected elite of Lausanne, and Burckhardt came from the Basler aristocracy, witnessing both the loss of power by the latter and the end of the old Swiss confederation of city-states. In the case of Constant, critique was indissociable from deep sympathy, as shown by his engagement with two Genevese thinkers, Jean-Jacques Rousseau and J. C. L. de Sismondi (1773–1842), who were also deeply interested in the workings and the history of city-states. The title page of *Du Contract Social; ou Principes du droit politique* (Amsterdam, 1762) proudly bears the name of "J. J. Rousseau, citoyen de Genève." The work itself presents favorably, indeed as a logical form of sovereignty, a state structured around assembly politics, popular sovereignty, and performative utterances born of face-to-face politics—an image that goes much further in the direction of democracy than existed in the real city-state of Geneva.[24] As for the second author, Sismondi (as the Genevese writer, born Simonde, styled himself to claim descent from a medieval Pisan family), he penned a large-scale history of the medieval Italian city-states, which appeared in the decade preceding Constant's lecture on liberties. Both clearly were strong (though complicated) admirers of the civic ideology and democratic practice in small-scale city-states.[25]

This intimate, sympathetic familiarity with the history of city-states lends the critique elaborated by both Swiss writers particular interest. Constant and Burckhardt were convinced that the *polis*'s claims to primacy over the individual had serious consequences—Constant in speaking of the ancient city as *lacking* certain forms of individual liberties, Burckhardt in viewing the *polis* as a product of quite literally foundational and transformational violence. Their analysis helps pinpoint the presence of conflict and violence in the *polis* as an integral part of a nonliberal social pact. The ideological positions, practical choices, and social bargains that constituted the *polis*'s solution, especially with a view to ensuring and implementing political equality, had social costs, including a utilitarian calculus that endemic conflict, violence as part of processes, and potential harm against individuals were acceptable corollaries to popular sovereignty and its goods. Because of its communitarian postulate (equating the good with the collective will), the *polis* itself would be ill-equipped to repair that which its own actions and discourses had generated.

The Risk of Oligarchy

In the analysis offered above, I posit endemic conflict as the consequence as well as the cost of communitarian control of the elite. But did the mechanisms of elite embedding and control work as well as I have supposed throughout this book, in proposing a model predicated on the democratic turn of the great convergence? The central tension of the model is the coexistence of economic inequality and political equality; the tension is made stronger by the aspiration of the latter to limit "natural," "Mediterranean" social domination by the rich and indeed to limit economic inequality more generally through institutions, ideology, and regulation. To re-summarize the view espoused in the present book, the world of the *polis* is not that of a dizzyingly vertical "natural oligarchy," as proposed in earlier interpretations (for instance, P. Veyne's model of euergetism, penned in 1976), but exists without urban aristocracies or nobility.

This insight is central to J. Ober's *Mass and Elite* (1989), in which Ober articulated a model of popular sovereignty actualized in political institutions and ideology, thus combining institutional analysis with a Gramscian interpretation of civic communitarian discourse, but in the context of the implementation of popular sovereignty rather than of oligarchical dominance. Within this framework, elites constitute themselves through elitist behavior that either embeds them within the community or offers an outlet for symbolical competition and display. Similar interpretations were proposed in M. Giangiulio's essay on Greek democracy, or A. Bresson's synthetic treatment of the ancient Greek economy. This is the model I have tried to apply across the deep history of the *polis*. Here I am not proposing to reopen this debate, to revisit my thesis on the "death of oligarchy" in the great convergence; for instance, by arguing that the *polis*'s social elites, because they held office, paid liturgies and supplied politicians, in fact controlled all institutions of decision-making and adjudication, and that the *polis* "really" was an oligarchy under the cover of its institutional and discursive workings. This would constitute a sort of "zombie oligarchism" (that is often proposed as all too obvious a picture of power in the ancient city).

While I hope to have traced in sufficient detail the vagaries of civic institutions during the second and first centuries BCE, and under the Roman empire (notably with the hardening of privileges enjoyed by the Council), I also have argued for the durability and resilience of the democratic model predicated on the "tragedy of the elites" even in these periods. Furthermore, I have suggested the inability of elites to close the oligarchical loop by directly converting officeholding and leadership into a position of political power from which they could capture institutions to their advantage. Finally, I have argued (above, chapter 17) that the *polis* solution represented a social pact in which the nonelite felt that it was obtaining redistribution through democratic pressure, and the elite felt that it was practicing largesse and hence exercising influence.[26] Such an analysis is consistent with the "democratic elite theory" proposed by E. Etzioni-Halevy. This model holds that within democracies, elites endowed with superior economic means exist and can offer material inducements, but as autonomous and pluralist elites, are not embedded within the state and can be constrained within political and ideological norms.[27]

Yet we might want to reexamine the question of power in the *polis*. I propose to use the concepts developed by the political philosopher and sociologist Steven Lukes in a "radical view" of power as a 3-D entity (direct institutional power, control of the agenda, and control of the discourse). Let us grant that we can clearly see, in the *polis*, popular sovereignty in the institutional realm of one-dimensional power: the elites do not impose their will on the popular assembly but a plurality of elite individuals has to compete against each other before the assembly.[28] Likewise, let us accept that the elites do not achieve two-dimensional power, in the sense of imposing their will by controlling the agenda or the institutions that implement decisions, because of embedded elite competition and accountability. But what if elites were able to wield three-dimensional power in the *polis*—that is, the ideological power to control the discourse about issues and the perception of debates, so that upstream from any process of deliberation and decision, they could prevent their interests from being challenged, and the people's interests from being pursued or even articulated?

As I mentioned above, Ober's model of Athenian democracy holds that three-dimensional power lies with the People and its hegemonical control of discourse and ideology, thus trapping the elites in acceptance of democracy; indeed, the very discourse of elitism is one vehicle for this acceptance. In this book, I have further proposed that virtue politics, by valorizing the public good and communitarian morals, constrained and constructed the parameters of civic behavior, and indeed the outlook of citizens within their community (albeit at the cost of endemic conflict and violence, as I argue above). But at the end of his exploration of democratic sovereignty enacted in the popular courts, Ober considers, with noticeable unease, the possibility that democratic discourse was perhaps a front for much deeper, invisible operations of influence and manipulation by a wealth elite, a worry that should give us pause.[29] A fragment from an unknown poet, Theodōros, apparently recommended pursuing acquisitiveness while praising equality (a dictum considered as scandalous as Archilochos's description of masturbation or Euripides's justification for perjury).[30] What follows is a history of the *polis* in the subjunctive mode, notably for source reasons; it ponders a way of joining up dots of evidence into a pessimistic picture.

At the risk of tautology or banality, political equality did not make economic inequality vanish; that was precisely the central reality of the *polis*. Redistribution, regulation of elite acquisitiveness, the absence of direct dependency, all had an impact on economic inequality and fostered property-owning and resource access among the nonelite, but the scale of redistribution is impossible to measure. Even in the "radical" democracy of Athens during the fifth and fourth centuries BCE, a minority of families and individuals owned a plurality of the land—to give an idea of proportions, perhaps rather less than a tenth of the total population of Attica owned around a third.[31]

The inequality was probably more severe in the *poleis* of the Roman empire, where rich individuals could own land across the territories of several cities, and indeed some men acceded to the levels of the imperial aristocracy. Without reaching such heights of wealth, an individual citizen of Daulis still appears in possession of a single estate of 95 hectares, perhaps 1.5 percent of the city's total territory.[32] I have tried to qualify any excessive miserabilism by pointing to widespread evidence for "little big men" and smallholders (as documented in Roman-era Bithynia or Lykia). But wealth still gave leisure and resources. As we have seen when exploring civic politics in the Roman-imperial *poleis*, a notable at Tralleis in the early first century BCE was praised as having held office "splendidly and democratically," a phrase that encapsulates the tension between elitism and popular sovereignty. The notable's generosity and political activity as serial officeholder and ambassador were made possible by wealth and leisure, as in the case of almost all civic politicians. Moreover, he was honored at his funeral by at least six cities of western Asia Minor, perhaps for going there on embassies, or for helping citizens from those cities when they visited Tralleis. Elite status meant multiple connections outside the *polis*, even if outside ties were viewed with suspicion in the democratic *polis* as redolent of aristocratic affirmation and divided loyalties (indeed, the abatement of such connections was an important part of *polis* solidarity).[33] Such connections were diplomatic and honorific, but also came with economic advantages; they belonged to the greater social capital that the elite enjoyed alongside, and as a consequence of, its superior economic means.

I still maintain that there was no immediate route in the developed, institutionalized, forms of the *polis* for eliteness and distinction to be translated into formal, institutional mechanisms of political power; indeed, popular power was partly exercised by controlling the definition of eliteness, leveraging this position to extract surplus (as tax, liturgy, or euergetism) for redistribution. But the question remains of the indirect means by which capital—civic, social, and actual—could convert into informal power. A possible example is given by Xenophon, writing in the fourth century BCE but reimagining the Athens of the fifth century BCE, during empire and the beginnings of radical democracy: Xenophon shows us a coterie of rich men, turning a demagogue, a skilled speaker in the courts and the Assembly, by financial inducements and ideological conversion to their elitist *habitus* of small-circle sociability. Once turned, the former demagogue functions as his rich friends' watchdog, to ward off volunteer prosecutors by blackmail, namely through the threat of counter prosecutions (thus subverting the function of demagogues, as skilled speakers enforcing democratic norms on the elite).[34] The "watchdog" insulated wealthy individuals from the institutional effects of democracy. The operation was supposedly masterminded by Kritōn, the same man who recommended that Sōkratēs abandon his obligations to the *polis* by escaping his jail in disguise. Though the factuality of Kritōn's strategy is open to question, the anecdote shows one possible way in which the tragedy of the elites could be averted through the application of brute financial force and social capital.

Around the same time the anecdote is supposed to have taken place, sworn secret societies (*xunomōsiai, hetaireiai*) of young rich men worked to subvert the selection of officials and the operation of law courts in democratic Athens, probably through pay-offs and blackmail, the same tools supposedly employed by Kritōn's tame demagogue.[35] The power of money further appears in what at first sight constitutes a prime case of democratic control, institutional and ideological, of the elites; namely, the lawsuit pressed by Dēmosthenēs on the rich Athenian Meidias for personal violence. Dēmosthenēs presented the case as motivated by the desire to repress elite violence and arrogance—but agreed to drop the case against a significant financial settlement.[36] Such acts of economic power aimed at blunting one of the essential elements of the popular sovereignty in the *polis*, namely the policing of the elite by constant intra-elite conflict, fought out before the People in the Assembly or the courts. The transaction also makes litigation look suspiciously like a source of intra-elite extortion (verging on *sukophantia* or malicious prosecution motivated by gain), rather than the high-minded defense of the community, and specifically the *dēmos*, against elite violence.

The power of *polis* elites to influence outcomes by material inducements might have been multiplied by exploiting access to public resources through the monopoly of office, for instance in the form of public contracts or favorable leases on public land. Such favors, proposed by Plutarch in his treatise on political life,[37] do not amount to a direct capture of *polis* institutions, but a leveraging of the elites' economic advantages to allow them to gain social advantages, notably through officeholding. The latter was largely the elites' preserve, even though there were forms of compensation for service, and especially once officeholding converged with *leitourgia* because officeholding required leisure and out-of-pocket, nonreimbursed expenses. The question is whether this happened systematically enough to erode the separation of state and elites that is a main feature of democratic polities as outlined by Etzioni-Halevy, or whether the institutional mechanisms of control and accountability held fast.

Beyond their exercise of economic power, local elites also mounted ideological offensives, increasingly visible during the "Indian Summer" of the late second century BCE (above, chapter 11). The period exhibits phenomena such as large-scale benefactions, ritualized events making social hierarchies more visible at the cost of civic identity, narratives of individual benefactors helping their communities and individuals as signs of their personal virtue (through *leitourgia* but also gestures such as personal loans or financial backing). The decrees from Kolophōn for the politicians Polemaios and Menippos, or the "great decrees" of Priēnē, are spectacular examples of this last trope, as well as of the whole elite biographical genre. The great benefactors of the late second-century BCE "Indian Summer" and of the Roman-era *polis* constantly broadcast messages about their own eminence and virtue, and (implicitly) the virtues of their class. Even if their behavior was at least partly the result of constraints exercised by the *polis* and underwritten by the Roman state (above, chapter 13), did it not create possibilities for influence and "3-D" power for the benefactors and their ilk?

Radical power theory, as developed in Lukes's "3-D" model, forces us to rethink whether elite *bricolage*, economic power, and ideological offensives allowed the wealthy and well-resourced to control issues and outcomes—to capture the agenda. The question notably has to be asked over time, in relation to the possibility of elitism reaching tipping points in cultural change, or escape velocity from the ideological and institutional trap of *polis* forms. We do not have, for the *polis*, detailed cases for the exercise of power within political communities, such as modern sociologists can use as tests and seedbeds for social theory. As an example of such analyses, we need only point to the sociologist R. Dahl's vision of complex, multidirectional pluralism, which is based on a detailed study of decision-making in 1960s New Haven, Connecticut. Conversely, with a radically different conclusion, the sociologist B. Flyvbjerg offers a thick, ironical, Foucault-inspired description of urban planning and decision-making in the Danish city of Aalborg, specifically of the dismal failure throughout the 1970s of a well-meaning, ambitious plan of urban renewal in response to mounting automobile-caused problems of pollution and congestion. The agonizing fate of the "Aalborg Project" was determined by a coterie of powerful, well-organized interests: the local Chamber of Commerce, working hand in glove with the private bus company, a friendly mayor, the police department (which refused to enforce laws and helped stymie the planning process) and the local conservative newspaper.[38] On a grander scale, the ultra-rich exercise a disproportionate, yet stealthy influence in the policy debates and implementation in the contemporary United States, in a billionaire's "stealth politics" that is utterly deleterious to democracy.[39] The value of such examples is heuristic: was the *polis* like New Haven or like Aalborg?

The problems go beyond the bias of the monumental-honorific epigraphical sources that tell us about public life in the majority of smaller *poleis*. A genre predicated on recording and implementing decision-making cannot, by definition, describe which issues are prevented from being discussed, the central issue in Lukesian radical power theory. We lack the evidence to see Lukesian processes at work, or to sense, negatively, the gravitational pull of elite interests at work within the *polis*. We can see the *polis* of Lētē honoring estate-owning benefactor M' Salarius Sabinus for restraint in the market (*paraprasis*), and generosity in office; we can witness the *polis* of Tlōs acclaiming the moneylending lady Lalla for a gift of cash (in return for office), which the generous donor offers to invest for the city. But we do not know if, or how, the benefactors leveraged their wealth, social capital, or civic capital to achieve informal power in the furtherance of their interests, for instance by controlling debates and decision-making in ways that shielded their economic activities from scrutiny or obscured their impact on the small-scale society where they lived. In this context, the honorific statue (fig. 18.1) stands as the image and the instrument of the social influence of the elite rather than (or as well as) the ideological power of the community.[40] Or perhaps more accurately, the statue stands between us and any clear perception of Lukesian questions, blocking our view.

It is at least possible that the constant, normative deployment of elitist tropes (powerful individuals with agency, passive people as recipient) and of benefactions allowed well-resourced individuals to exercise influence even in the public sphere. On Paros, in the late second century BCE, Killos, son of Dēmētrios, held office multiple times, including the position as market supervisor (*agoranomos*) twice, applying the laws, ensuring the quality of bread and barley meal, and mediating in a case of labor dispute: he "took care that neither party should be wronged, forcing in accordance with the law one party not to keep aloof but to resume work, and the other party to pay their salary to the workers without lawsuit (*aneu dikēs*)."[41] The decree describes Killos acting justly and in accordance with the law, but might echo Killos's own notions of his authority, or the People's attempt to rationalize the behavior of a powerful actor (the latter occurrence is repeatedly and sadly documented by Flyvberg for 1970s Aalborg). The good *agoranomos* Killos acted selectively: he applied the law to force workers to resume their activities; he also prevented the workers from taking their dispute to the law courts, which were meant as a democratic venue for adjudication and regulation, and might have led to an outcome more clearly favorable to the workers.

An especially provocative case is that of the wealthy Athenians who in the mid-fourth century BCE invested massively in the grain trade but portrayed their capitalist, profit-seeking activities in the language of civic devotion to the public good, as grand actions befitting good citizens, while denouncing retailers (their partners and rivals for gain) as antisocial profiteers. Furthermore, civic discourse and claims allowed grain traders to downplay their international connections (that included relations with the rather unsavory Greco-Skythian kings in the Black Sea area). The

FIGURE 18.1. Bronze statue, likely honorific. Date unclear: first century BCE? H 181.4 cm. No provenance.

whole operation smacks of ideological misdirection by a skilled, articulate elite. In A. Moreno's striking formulation, the elite's involvement in the grain trade left not the fingerprints of capital, but the "glove-marks of ideology."[42]

We might turn, once again, to the island *polis* of Hērakleia and its lonely, fragmentary decree prohibiting goats. The decree suggests that the community, in the name of an ideology of the public good, constrained rich, antisocial, violent goat-raisers from devastating the commons, but above we wondered if beneath the Arendtian surface, the situation did not admit of complicated interests, as suggested by the glimpses of violent conflict (chapter 17). A glance at a map of land use on the island in 1990 (fig. 18.2) has no documentary value, especially when the population of the island was 100 inhabitants, but is highly suggestive of the possibilities and the possible tensions generated by the ecology of the island. This shows a tripartite division between a central swathe of cultivated land from north to south (wide at the top of the island where the good source of fresh water lies), a large zone of rough vegetation on the mountainous western part of the island, which is probably suited for ovicaprines, and a zone of "grassland" in the eastern part of the island, which might have admitted of a variety of uses.[43] Instead of supposing rich goat-raisers held in check by the political community, it is possible that the situation involved smallholders with a mixed economy (including ovicaprine husbandry), of a sort widely attested in the Mediterranean (and even specifically on modern Hērakleia)[44] being defeated by cash-croppers (especially winegrowers) with resources and connections beyond Hērakleia, and the competence to manipulate civic discourse. In this scenario, rich winegrowers control the ideological debate and are able to redefine the public good in ways that suit their specific interests, branding any opposition as antisocial, to the point of authorized violence against their opponents under the cover of *polis* legitimacy. Hērakleia appears as a microscopic, Cycladic Aalborg rather than as a realm of Arendtian politics and work.

The question is whether institutional path dependency (i.e., the way democratic institutions incentivized intra-elite conflict) and the ideological hegemony of communitarian discourse were enough to prevent such operations, or whether the former could be disarmed and the latter instrumentalized by determined elites pursuing direct goals. The concentrated action of elites stands in potential contrast to the reified but diffuse and impersonal structures of the *polis* as state or "public actor" that had to be animated by part-time officeholders (often members of the elite) or in periodic public gatherings.

Social Power in the *Polis*

We are confronted with a double uncertainty: first, about the existence of elitist attempts at Lukesian "3-D power," for lack of secure and diverse evidence; second, about their efficacy in creating space for patronage and influence within the *polis*. Such uncertainty might itself be part of the way informal power works, as opposed

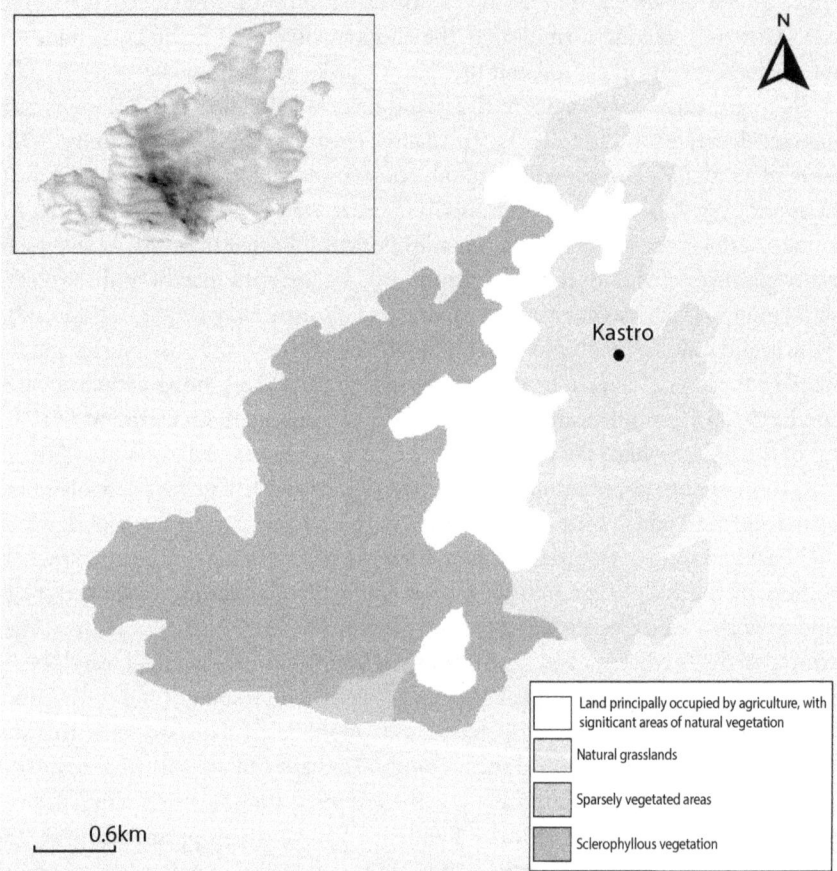

FIGURE 18.2. Land use on Irakleia in 1990. Data from Copernicus Land Monitoring Service.

to the transparency and accountability of rules-bound, collective institutions of the *polis*. The deme of Halai Aixōnides, shaken by crisis and scandal in the 360s BCE (above, pp. 251–52), may have seen attempts by individual members to capture public finances, through informal power and influence, and as a way to increase informal power by increasing means of patronage; hence the intervention of one deme member to bring in transparency and dispel opacity through measures that may have created further conflict (as shown by a curse tablet against the do-gooder).

However, we may be looking at the wrong place in continuing to survey the evidence for ways in which social capital impacted political and institutional power. Economic inequality also impacted informally and noninstitutionally on relations between actors with unequal resources. A document from Tralleis gives a sense of this dimension of power—precisely by claiming that it was kept at bay. In the late second century BCE, the Trallians honored foreign judges from Tēnos for justice, impartiality, and (judging from the fragmentary text) the determination to yield to the influence "neither of an office-holder nor of a rich man."[45] The implication is that members of the elite, either through their privileged access to official positions or through their economic power, tried to impinge on judicial processes: the impartiality of the external arbiter was not just a strategy to void local conflict, but a bulwark against the *social* power of the rich.

The traces of the informal power of the rich are faint, but suggestive. The liking of rich citizens for interpersonal violence and haughtiness is noted even in fourth-century BCE Athens, and is portrayed in Apuleius's novel set in Roman Greece, where elite young men might run amok in the streets of Hypata at night (a type of elite affirmation present already in the early *polis*, and repressed by archaic, "tyrannical" legislation: above, p. 136). A poor man might be driven off his land by his estate-owning neighbor, "powerful, rich and young, but misusing the prestige of his ancestry, predominant through factional intrigue and able to achieve easily anything in the city."[46] The great man portrayed by Apuleius can rely on economic resources, prestige, and networks of support, to achieve power—admittedly of a much rawer kind than Lukesian informal power, because exercised directly in social space rather than through political institutions; that is the point of such informal, face-to-face power, the more effective for being immediate. A young Cocceianus Diōn apparently told an angry assembly, during a grain shortage, "I own estates, all in your territory, and up to now no neighbor, rich or poor (and many such men live next to me) has accused me of seizing his property or evicting him justly or unjustly." That Dio can boast of such restraint as a positive trait implies that a rich man might well apply acquisitive violence to his neighbors.[47] Was such power facilitated by social and civic capital accumulated through officeholding, liturgies, and benefactions?

As we have seen, this is the sort of behavior that the *polis* solutions were meant to contain, from early times onwards, as illustrated by Archilochos's fulminations against anti-social behavior, or the literal curses against elite evil-doers at Drēros in the seventh century BCE or at Teōs in the fifth century BCE. One of the implicit ideas within civic thought is that the liberty of the citizen, sublimated into civic autonomy, implied freedom from domination inside the *polis*. The protection of public goods but also nonelite citizens against violence and acquisitiveness was one of the services that members of the elite performed as part of the definition of their eliteness in the *polis*, as can be seen even in the Roman empire (above, pp. 354–55). But even if fourth-century BCE forensic oratory is strategically phrased, and Apuleius's narrative is fiction, it is not too much of a stretch of the imagination to suppose that multiple factors might have limited, in this case as in other spaces of the *polis*, the capacity or willingness of the elite to police its own power. For instance, any individual member of the local elite might be too strong—too wealthy, too influential, too well-connected, endowed with too much social capital in his *polis* and others—for any other individual or group of individuals to willingly tackle in the arenas of the court and the Assembly. In other words, the slow accumulation of wealth might allow one individual or family to break through institutional barriers and endemic intra-elite conflict to consolidate positions of social power. Though the courts played an essential role in keeping members of the elite in check by subjecting them to community sanction, poor individual citizens might lack the wherewithal or social capital to protect themselves by initiating the bruising, time-consuming, resource- and expertise-intensive process of litigation.

Distance from the urban center must have complicated access to *polis* institutions of protection, accountability, and redress, especially if the local settlements within the *polis* territory had their own institutional life within which the sub-elite "little big men" might wield outsized face-to-face influence; differential access to institutions created diversity within the citizen body (above, pp. 420–21). As suggested by N. Jones, even in democratic Athens, the rural settlements and subdivisions (*dēmoi*) might have been the scenes of patronage and inequality—though this tendency must be counterbalanced by the workings of local political institutions and accountability, as in the case of Halai Aixōnides.[48]

However intriguing the possibility of rural elite power, the evidence for patronage and acquisitiveness in the Attic countryside is faint (as opposed to evidence for elitist display or *leitourgia*), though I have argued earlier that the nature of civic discourse would make such phenomena invisible. Because of the necessity for competition as part of the self-policing *polis* system, elite conflict and generalized violence was structurally part of the *polis* landscape, as I have emphasized: is it possible that episodes of injustice got lost within the broader context of conflict as an ineluctable part of civic politics and processes? Administratively, the *polis* deployed its stately resources to repress criminality (especially against property), and unrest—but such police powers, unsurprisingly, did little to directly impede elite violence such as that of young elite carousers or landowners. In turn, the presence of violence and uncertainty might have encouraged nonelite individuals to seek patronage and protection from members of the elite, especially if the latter managed to insulate themselves from the bite of *polis* institutions.

The *Polis* between Utopia and Domination: A Realist History?

The reconstruction above is speculative and subjunctive, animated by the suspicion that *polis* discourse might rationalize or cover up domination (rather than power, to continue using Arendtian terminology: above, p. 450), and sympathetic to pessimistic conclusions. On this view, the elitism that was a part of the *polis*'s story, from the open polities of the "Archaic" period to the great convergence, might have distended its boundaries to become an informal elite power living within the *polis*, even after the democratic convergence and beyond its institutional and ideological reach. Indeed, in this reconstruction, elite power would be a consequence of *polis* democracy: by putting the burdens of *leitourgia* and officeholding on the elite, by giving elites a communally sanctioned role in leading and policing civic process, *polis* institutions might have allowed members of the elite, and especially the elite as a class, to accrue civic capital that could be converted—not into direct institutional capture, but into social capital, thus evading *polis* institutional control, with a view to increasing elite capacities to influence politics and exercise social power in noninstitutional spheres. The protocols of popular sovereignty and especially the "tragedy of the elites," so visible in our sources, would hence represent the costs to pay for elite power, but also a shelter for the latter.

Is this picture accurate, historically possible, or helpful? It is at least useful as a skeptical pause, an invitation not to always take *polis* discourses at their own word. But as a test for this picture, it is worth asking a simple question: what would a skeptical or realist history of the *polis* look like? How does such a stance account for the various waypoints in the narrative given earlier in this book? How does a skeptical narrative account for the emergence of law and state forms in the "Archaic" period, the "putting in the middle" of decision-making and the definition of virtue politics, constitutional experiments (signorial turns, open and closed polities), the elaboration of a *polis* solution balancing elite and community claims of equality, and the diffusion of this model in a "great convergence" and its persistence in the face of empire?

It is certain that violence and the raw pursuit of power by individuals and groups play an important part in the event history of all the centuries in which the *polis* developed and spread; notably, violence and power manipulation were crucial elements of the "Hundred Years." But it remains difficult to construct the narrative of *polis* history solely as the preserve of violent, endemic competition between great men and the masses, and among great men, or of elites hoodwinking their communities behind the cover of claimed virtue and equality: such a history has poor explanatory power, and risks merely offering sniping sidelines or descending into cynical takes on decisions, processes, and outcomes in the *polis*. I earlier argued against such a cynical, elite-driven history in the case of the "Archaic" *polis* (above, chapter 6), rather making the case that institutions precisely arose out of and against pure elite power. I also tried to keep the possibility of Lukesian politics in the picture, when reconstructing the workings of the *polis* in and after the great convergence (notably in the Roman empire), as a field of uneasy questions (as gathered and summarized in the present chapter).

Violence and "3-D power" might be considered either as residues of phenomena that the *polis* tried to solve, and which admittedly could have powerful effects on individual members of the *polis*; or as secondary phenomena generated by the history of the *polis* proposed in the two previous chapters, and born of the insufficient reach of *polis* ideals in the sphere of the quotidian; or yet again as zones of risk and lapses that occurred when *polis* institutions and civic ideology flagged or weakened in the face of sustained elite pressures or simply of elite opportunism. All these possibilities open up vistas of other *polis* histories during and in spite of the great convergence. The secondary nature of these phenomena does not mean that they were unimportant as part of the lived social reality in the *poleis*. They may have existed alongside the structure of civic society and civil society (above, chapter 15)—in its interstices or in its dead zones, or in the "free spaces" outside the embrace of institutions and inclusion.

19

Worst *Polis*

POLIS AS INJUSTICE

La cité, ce mal nécessaire.
—E. WILL, IN LETTER TO PH. GAUTHIER (JANUARY 9, 1987)

Since the State emerged out of the need to keep down class conflict, and since it emerged out of the conflict of these classes, it generally takes the form of the State of the most powerful, economically dominant class, which by means of the state becomes the politically dominant Class, and hence acquires new means to dominate and exploit the subordinate class. Thus, the ancient state was above all the state of the slave-owners with a view to the domination of the slaves, just as the feudal state was the organ of the nobility with a view to the domination of free and subordinate peasants, and the modern representative state tool of the exploitation of salaried labour by capital.
—F. ENGELS, *THE ORIGIN OF THE FAMILY, PROPERTY AND THE STATE* (1881)

Polis as Exclusion

The citizens of the *polis* of Hērakleia, when they met in assembly, took a decision that affected "the *koinon* of the islanders," a description of the *polis* as commonwealth that idealized the citizenry as the inhabitants of the territory, just as the gods they invoked were "those who hold the island." Yet the decree itself declared its concern for the safety of "all Herakleiotes and those inhabiting [the island]," the latter group being distinguished from the group of citizens. Even though it is the latter who exclusively meet and vote, the noncitizens are affected by the decision. Apart from not raising goats, they will almost certainly have to contribute (as part of the commonwealth) to the levies to finance the court proceedings in which the *polis* will be a party in case of fatal conflict over illicit and indeed illegitimate goat-raising.

Though the group of citizens, *Hērakleiōtai*, is made up of the only ones entitled to take the decisions, it *represents*, in all senses of the term, the whole human community on the island, whose interests it defends. Our earlier confrontation with the violence, conflict, and possibility for manipulation involved in the transaction forces us to admit that the image of Herakleiote citizens defending the safety of all the inhabitants is a fiction. This sort of fiction, positing solidarity between citizens and the rest of the social population within a *polis*, can be seen in civic festivals—for instance, those documented in the second century BCE at Magnēsia on Maeander. There, the citizens decide on a festival for Zeus Sōsipolis (*Polis*-saving) that is meant to benefit the whole population; the citizens also stipulate the participation of everyone in the city. That the same mechanisms (citizen decision-making, population participation in solidarity) were used to force the integration of the population of a Seleukid colony in Jerusalem (including the Jewish population) is a reminder of the power differential involved in such events, under the ideology of solidarity.[1]

The inequality in power between different groups in the *polis* resulted from the basic, constitutive relationship of exclusion. This can be read in many other manifestations of civic culture. The beauty of the built environment at Priēnē (fig. 1.3), melding public and private, was a reminder that certain people were stakeholders in the *polis* and in its autonomous existence as materialized by its splendid, orderly, and perennial monuments (fig. 19.1)—but that others were not: the enslaved, the foreigners, the serf-like tributary "Plainsmen" in their villages (fig. 1.5).[2] Earlier (chapter 15), I affirmed the validity and the centrality of the Aristotelian conception of the *polis* as a political community of members having access to institutions of deliberative decision-making, government, and adjudication. I hence called for an Aristotelian understanding of *polis* as society (which I schematized as its civic, civil, and marginal forms). But this definition comes with an inescapable consequence: namely the exclusion, according to different modes, of women, children, enslaved people, strangers—and even, at least potentially or as a temptation, of certain groups of free-born native men, on grounds of poverty, occupation, or distance from the urban center.

Hence the *polis* was a patriarchy, an enslavement society, a nativist organization, and a polity haunted by the model of an urban aristocracy. In this chapter, I will explore these aspects as a further, interlocking set of social bads that potentially constitute the *polis* as tragedy. The consequences of this scheme combine with earlier structures of analysis to offer the possibility of a multidimensional vision of the *polis*.

Patriarchy, Age and Gender

As a patriarchy, the *polis* was a society of fathers, excluding children from the public sphere as immature, unfinished, and hence institutionally incompetent individuals.[3] These incomplete persons were managed within the household: as vehicles

FIGURE 19.1. The *agora* of Priēnē, as reimagined in Krischen 1938 (drawing by H. Horn). The late second-century BCE decrees were inscribed on the inside wall of the portico.

for property transmission (especially for the elite) and as sources of labor (especially for the poor). The management of the supply of children belonged to household issues of property and livelihood. In this context, some children (their plentiful ranks already ravaged by very high rates of disease and infantile mortality) were probably victims of physical violence, starting with exposure of unwanted infants (especially female), which usually led to death or enslavement.[4] A grim reminder of this violence is the well in which the remains of hundreds of infants and small children (including a battered toddler) were thrown along with sacrificed puppies as ritual offerings, in the Athens of the late second-century BCE Indian Summer, in a blind alley just off the Agora, filled with its institutional and extra-institutional interactions.[5] It is true that we do not know the social status of the children whose remains were thrown in the "Agora Bone Well," but it is likely that many were born to noncitizens (resident foreigners or enslaved residents), compounding their precarity and vulnerability. In addition, children of all social statuses were subject to routine physical punishment at the hands of adult male citizens, or at least with their approval and at their urging, as part of their education and upbringing. Finally, boys and adolescents were caught in nexuses of erotic and sexual relations, imposed by adult male citizens as part of their habitus, albeit fraught with anxieties and complexities.[6]

Patriarchy excluded women from political institutions as a matter of course. On the island of Hērakleia, the decision to ban the raising of goats, the binding oath, the prosecution in case of fatal outcomes of self-help, were all conducted by the adult male citizens, even if the decision affected all the inhabitants of the island; for instance, labor arrangements in the household must have shifted in consequence of the decision. Adult women of citizen households labored under life-long institutional incompetence in the decision-making realm but also in the legal sphere where, theoretically, they needed the approval of a male representative (*kurios*, literally "lord") for economic transactions. In Athens, women could only undertake transactions worth one *medimnos*—about 50 liters—of barley or less.[7] Yet, though legally property-less dependents, women were crucial for the transmission of property and the reproduction of citizen households, both economically and in terms of legal status after the generalization of the rule of descent from citizen parents as part of the definition of the citizen body (as we have seen: above, chapter 15). The structural importance of women for citizen households is reflected in the emergence, during the Hellenistic and Roman periods, of a terminology for female citizenship (such as the word *politis*, "she-citizen," or the use of female "ethnic" markers such as *Xanthia*, "female member of the *polis* of Xanthos").[8] I have argued above that these new markers do not remove institutionalized and constitutive subordination.

More directly, the importance of legitimate birth for the transmission of citizen status, the passing on of property, and the reproduction of households, entailed control of citizen women's sexuality, the valorization of their virginity when unmarried, and the protection of their fidelity after marriage.[9] An Athenian man of the early fourth century BCE, on trial for having killed his wife's lover (probably after entrapping him), claimed to have acted for the sake of the whole citizen body.[10] Later in the fourth century BCE, the comedies of the Athenian poet Menandros portrayed stories involving lovers, mistresses, rapes, and the concerns of citizen fathers and sons. The plays reflect anxieties about the reproduction of citizen households, especially at a time when frequent changes in political regime affected the composition of the citizen body.[11] Ideally (and ideologically), adult male citizens managed and controlled their women (daughters, sisters, others) as they moved between generations and households. Older men (in their thirties) married younger wives, often in their mid to late teens, when the latter could be controlled physically and psychologically. Xenophon provides a memorable (if fictional and idealized) description of such a teen bride received in her husband's house, in a dialogue between Ischomachos, an elite Athenian, and the hanger-on Sōkratēs:[12]

> "Ischomachos, I would gladly hear this from you, namely: did you yourself educate your wife to be of the right sort, or did she know how to take care of her duties when you received her from her father and mother?"
>
> "And just what knowledge could she have had, Sōkratēs, when I took her over? She was not yet fifteen when she came to me, and earlier she had lived under close care, with a view that she should see as little as possible, hear as little, and say as little as possible. Does it not seem to you a fine thing, if when she came the most she knew was how to produce a cloak when given wool, had seen only how wool-working tasks were not allocated to the female slave? Since she came perfectly well trained as concerns her stomach, Sōkratēs; which I regard as the greatest form of training for man and woman alike."
>
> "But in other respects, Ischomachos, said I, did you educate your wife yourself, so that she should be competent to perform her duties?"
>
> "No, by Zeus, Sōkratēs, at least not until I had first offered sacrifice and prayed that I might teach, and she might learn, that which was best for the both of us."
>
> "And then, said I, did your wife not join with you in these same sacrifices and prayers?"
>
> "Indeed, she earnestly vowed to the gods to behave as she should, and it was clear to see that she would not neglect the lessons she was being taught."

Noticeable is the teenage bride's socialization in matters concerning "her stomach"; that is, her appetite for food. "Archaic" poets such as Hesiod (in the eighth century BCE) or Sēmonidēs (in the seventh century BCE) attest the household head's control of access to nutrition. "Women stole food because they were kept half-starved by their husbands who resented their habit of eating," in M. West's sarcastic formulation: the reproach of overeating comes from a conception of women as consumers of household resources, supposed to be generated by the patriarch's labor.[13] Such casual misogyny participated in a broader ideological construction of gender, pervasive in *polis* culture. Sēmonidēs's portrayal of women as divided in animal-like species in his poetry, which was sung in men's gatherings, coincides precisely with the moment of *polis* consolidation. Later, "Classical' Greek art from the fifth century BCE onwards, represents female bodies in ways predicated on a male gaze, male desire or contempt.[14]

Conceptions of gender also presided over the distribution of male and female bodies in space. Ideally, women's work was confined to the house's interior, and even the special spaces within the house. In practice, even when they had to move outside the household, women's lives were segregated from the public world of men, and the *polis* institutionalized control over women's lives and movements by appointing special officials (*gynaikonomoi*, literally "administrators of women").[15] The minimizing of female agency and consent was one corollary of a gender regime that placed citizen women and their reproductive capacities in a nexus of status and property. Another was the production of romantic or sentimental myths that tried to camouflage the contradictions within this regime (while maintaining complicity with coercion, violence, and rape).[16] A third corollary was the wide availability of cheap prostitution, usually by enslaved workers.[17] The *sumposion* or drinking party, a crucial institution in the *polis* from its early days onwards, was a locus for adult men to perform solidarity through shared rituals, texts, and activities. These included the actual exclusion of citizen-status women, the exploration of self and other through song and through playacting on the boundaries of identity (including racial ones), and social and sexual commerce with female performers and sex-workers, of noncitizen and often non-free status.[18]

The latter women were often subject to physical violence; but violence was generalized in matters of gender. The boundaries defining female condition were policed through violence—actual (in a play by Aristophanes, an Athenian wife is threatened with a punch for asking about politics: below, p. 529)[19] and organized (Xenophon represents Ischomachos putting in great efforts to construct his teenage wife's agency and to constitute her whole world).

Polis as Enslavement Society

The adult male citizens, in addition to controlling women, were slaveholders, holding slaves as part of the household but also outside it.[20] Enslavement involved both legal ownership of enslaved human beings and their "social death" (O. Patterson) in the form of denial of all honor and personhood. Both manifestations were dialectically connected. Ownership led to the social death of the enslaved, who were often renamed by their enslavers as an initial act of erasure of social ties and subjected to ill-treatments expressing and enabling for their objectification. Conversely, the ultimate consequence of social death for the enslaved was being treated as an object or an animal, the "man-footed thing" (*andrapodon*, calqued off *tetrapodon*, the "four-footed thing"—an equivalent might be "manstock," as in "livestock").

Manstock had no recognized human honor but only value as a commodity, and hence was treated as such in economic transactions: it was sold, leased, or offered as collateral in financial transactions.[21] The *polis* was a complex slaveholder society, whose economic basis, workings, and self-imagination all rested on the enslavement of humans.[22] Slaveholding was widespread throughout the economy of the *poleis*, starting with the agricultural territory: the towers that appear in the islands (one is attested on Hērakleia), may have been connected with the control of enslaved workers. It is true that we cannot be sure exactly who owned the agricultural slaves that are abundantly attested in the literary evidence. But even if slave-owning was unevenly distributed within the agrarian population (poorer families may have relied on oxen, their own work power, family contributions, and mutual aid), enslaved workforces undoubtedly sustained the elite cash-cropping that was a vital part of *poleis* such as Chios, Kerkyra, or Rhodes.[23]

Enslaved workers were also a vital part of the nonagricultural economy, present in the large-scale enterprises of elite investors; for instance, workshops or gangs of specialized workers hired out for extractive activities such as mining but also moneymaking affairs such as prostitution (thus fulfilling the potential, for the enslavers, of the enslaved person as a chattel that could be exploited and made to yield income). Enslaved labor was also crucial in smaller affairs: individual craftsmen worked side by side with enslaved assistants but pocketed the latter's salary, "small investors" owned a slave and hired him out for fixed rent, enslaved craftsmen were set up to work independently but surrendered most of the proceeds. All these phenomena are well attested for the diversified economy of fifth- and fourth-century BCE Athens (flush with cash and slaves from empire and its aftermath),[24] but also appear in the diversified economy of a small, nameless *polis* that was unified with or annexed by Teōs (above, p. 209). From the temporary tax incentives offered by Teōs, it is clear that slaves could be hired out for labor, gather firewood, make charcoal, or generally work in an economy of "wood-selling" (*xylopōliē*), a cash-making, profit-driven sector crucial for a small mountain *polis* (even if we do not know the size or distribution of the enslaved workforce).[25]

Away from the world of profit chasing at different scales, enslaved workers performed labor in the household, as well as serving as status symbols for elite women and men. Gravestone reliefs (fig. 9.1, fig. 10.4) complement the civic imagery for their subjects (whose economic substance, social capital, and civic-mindedness are celebrated) with figures of slaves. These are shown at a smaller scale and with subaltern postures, showing their lack of social status and, more simply, tiredness and stress.[26]

Since slavery was interwoven in the economics of the *polis*, it also was integral to its political economy. In this book, we have emphasized the role played in the formation of the *polis* by two interconnected phenomena, public goods and redistribution of elite wealth; it is time to realize their dependency on enslaved labor. Public goods could be directly produced by enslaved labour. This is the case of the marble and metal ore mines that ensured the early prosperity of Thasos and Siphnos, and later the imperial might of Athens: the exploitation of such resources must have employed enslaved technicians and laborers on a large scale (the actual arrangements probably involved private contractors rather than direct use of enslaved labour by the *polis*). Public goods were also produced by the redistribution of elite wealth, tapped directly and indirectly by taxation, liturgies, services, and semi-voluntary benefactions, in order to provide public goods. This social resource was largely created by enslaved labor, agricultural or artisanal, on the estates or in the workshops owned by the elite. Slavery also sustained the "Mediterranean" regime that characterized the *polis*: enslaved labor, however distributed, made possible the cash crops (especially wine) that were exported to buy staple products such as grain, and more slaves, or that were exchanged between locales to generate profit and growth (above, pp. 473–74).

Because of their dependency on slavery, the *poleis* were avid markets for enslaved humans, procured from a variety of sources including under-urbanized regions such as Thrace, the eastern Adriatic coast, and inland Anatolia. These regions existed as zones of violence and enslavement that fed the need of the *poleis* in exchange for products of the *polis* economies such as wine or coined silver. This is only one way in which the phenomena of slavery are corollaries or effects of developments in civic practice. The consolidation of community solidarity and the absolute protection of the bodily integrity of citizens, whose status precluded the intracommunal enslavement of poorer members by the elite, entailed the need for enslaved labor from outside the *polis*, as a concrete consequence of civic ideals and institutions.

I earlier wrote about the importance of the citizen's dignity, as protected by *polis* law and institutions (above, chapter 16): a proto-Rawlsian good distributed equally among the citizens with political consequences, and a factor for the trust and commitment in the civic community, with a virtuous cycle of good economic and social outcomes. But a corollary of this landscape of dignity was the construction of a class of people denied dignity and honor within the community. The phenomenon is best attested in the case of early sixth-century BCE Attica, in the case of the "Solonian" reforms and the still poorly understood political turmoil that resulted (above, chapter 5). As E. Wood writes, "the relative unavailability of Athenian free producers for exploitation was itself a critical factor leading to the growth of slavery. In a sense, the free time of the poor was won at the expense of slave labor for the rich."[27] Similar situations (though the details are even more obscure than sixth-century BCE Athens) may be at work in the early *poleis* of Asia Minor with their serf populations, or at Chios, a center for winegrowing, an early example of institutional development and one of the earliest places to adopt chattel slavery (or so later Greeks affected to believe). M. Finley famously and influentially wrote that "one aspect of Greek history, in short, is the advance, hand in hand, of freedom and slavery,"[28] a view of "Archaic" Greek history and the rise of citizenship that has been nuanced but still deserves consideration.[29] M. Finley further quotes a figure of the German Enlightenment, the legal theorist Johann Friedrich Reitemeier, who in a history of ancient slavery published in 1789 pointedly associated subordination with "civil society" (*bürgerliche Gesellschaft*), since the latter is incompatible with universalism.[30]

Indeed, citizenship was defined in institutional and ideological terms as the apanage of freeborn members of the political community: for these men, freedom was the basic characteristic (as can be seen in Aristotle's *Politics*, where *hoi eleutheroi*, the free or rather the poor freeborn citizens, are the foundation of the democratic *polis*). We earlier defined this quality in terms of freedom from subordination to the wealth elite in the community, but the citizen's freedom also was conceived in terms of not being enslaved, and hence of potentially being slaveholders. The internal solidarity of the *polis* was about relations between mass and elite, but also about the control and exploitation of slaves. *Polis* as society was made up of members who aided each other in controlling slaves, Plato notes.[31] *Polis* as state deployed its institutions to control slaves, for instance by making escape difficult: Plato's ideal state expects active participation of citizens and magistrates in this task.

A concrete example comes from the cities of Milētos and Hērakleia under Latmos, which, in concluding peace after one of the local conflicts characteristic of the Indian Summer of the second-century BCE, made detailed provisions concerning the return of runaway slaves, including finder's fees, reimbursement for food, and the right to sell off unclaimed slaves (the task was entrusted to border guards, an office held by a tax farmer who expected to profit from his activities).[32] In addition, the *polis* managed and derived income from the exit out of slavery. The fees paid by the enslaved to purchase their (conditional and limited) freedom profited to individual enslavers (the money allowed them to purchase a replacement and perpetuate the system, as well as profit from it), but part of the fee was paid to the *polis*'s treasury. The second-century BCE institutionalization of Thessalian cities (which I draw attention to as the acceleration of *polis* normalcy in Thessaly after the end of Antigonid control in 196 BCE, above, p. 277) may have been financed by fees paid by manumitted slaves; this source of public income continued to be important subsequently.[33] Such processes were the first time that enslaved individuals dealt directly and as their own persons with the laws of the *polis* under whose protection citizen members flourished.

The practicalities of enslavement involved violence and degradation, which we can see in many forms, starting with the beatings and angry whippings that literary sources, from Plato to Galen, mention as a regrettable aspect of slave-owning (because it demeaned the *masters*). It is also Plato who explicitly tells us (through an oligarchical, might-is-right character in the *Gorgias*) that the enslaved were denied the ability to help their loved ones against harm—an unspeakably cruel, abusive yet routine consequence of slavery.[34] Physical harm abounded. In Athens and elsewhere, the testimony of slaves was admissible in court only under torture, "proven" as by a touchstone (the world *basanos* designates both) through the overwhelming ordeal of whipping or joint dislocation on the rack.

The resistance of the enslaved was often broken by specialized techniques of domination and management, or punished by death. At Amyzōn, a slave killed his master as the latter was sleeping and set fire to the house—the dead man's epitaph tells us that "for my sake, my fellow citizens crucified the perpetrator and left him for the beasts and the birds." The citizens undertook the punishment as a matter of public interest. The incident took place not far, in time and space, from the cities of Milētos and Hērakleia that struck an agreement about the return of runaway slaves, in the time of the free cities of Karia during the Indian Summer of the late second century BCE.[35] Another horrendous example comes from the fifth-century BCE, in the time of the Athenian empire: a man accused of murder and tried in Athens mentioned, as part of his argumentation, an 11-year old enslaved boy who stabbed his enslaver but lacked the nerve to finish him off: if the enslaver had died without his killer being known, every slave in the household would have been executed. "In the event, he was caught and subsequently confessed his guilt."[36] In a chilling omission, the speaker does not need to mention that the boy was certainly put to death.

Polis as Exclusion: Foreigners

By definition as an in-group of members enjoying the civic solidarity and the protection, direct and indirect, that resulted from access to institutional power, the *polis* was not open to foreigners, including long-term residents. This state of affairs resulted logically from the definition of the citizen body in terms of birth from citizen parents (above, pp. 230, 431).[37] In the *polis* foreigners could not own land (a restriction relaxed during the Roman empire or circumvented by multiple citizenship-holding by the elite). Additionally, they had no direct access to judicial institutions, needing representation by citizen patrons, known as "protectors," *prostatai*, in fifth- and fourth-century BCE Athens (just as citizen women needed representation by their *kurios* in matters of property and law). A piece of comic literature, set in Kōs, suggests that this practice was widespread (below). In Athens at least, resident foreigners paid a tax for the privilege of residence, even while being liable for financial service and even military duties.[38] The liability of resident foreigners for *leitourgia* reflects the wealth enjoyed by some of them, such as the rich individuals who appear in fourth-century BCE Athens, or the well-connected and wealthy foreigners in third- and second-century BCE Milētos and Knidos.[39] But this wealth was burdened with institutional incompetence and duties without rights.

The institution of resident foreigners was widespread (under different names— *metoikoi*, *paroikoi*—or periphrases). A dialogue of Herōdas in the third century BCE portrays resident foreigners in the democratic *polis* of Kōs for comic effect: the brothel-keeper Battaros, arguing a case in court against another foreigner (both have duly taken citizen "protectors").[40] Perhaps resident foreigners were also present in smaller *poleis*, such as Hērakleia. Certainly the institutional landscape makes frequent provisions for foreigners, resident or transient. For instance, in the *polis* of Bargylia, *metoikoi* were plentiful enough to constitute a quasi-civic body, which received subsidies for ox-rearing alongside civic subdivisions, for the festival of Artemis.⁴¹ In a peace treaty between Tēmnos and Klazomenai, provision was made for a special joint tribunal to judge any future disputes between those cities: the judges were to swear an oath to render fair judgment "for the Temnians and Klazomenians, and the *metoikoi* and the others of those living in both cities."⁴²

The arrangement is all the more striking because it existed in a Mediterranean world that was structurally based on high mobility and connectedness, where goods but also people circulated by choice and by necessity (above, chapter 17);⁴³ exchanges intensified during the Hellenistic period, from the late fourth to the late second centuries BCE, precisely at the time of the great convergence of *polis* forms and generalization of a democratic model that emphasized solidarity but also exclusion.⁴⁴ In a series of classic articles, Ph. Gauthier proposed an interpretation of the restrictive nature of *polis* citizenship as a reflection of the centrality of participation in communal activities and access to institutions (in contrast with Roman citizenship, which, Gauthier claims, operated as a status). Gauthier's view has been nuanced, notably as concerns the lived realities of citizenship and foreignness, but still usefully accounts for the closed nature of membership in the *polis* as political community.⁴⁵ It is significant that Gauthier elaborated this view on the basis of documentary evidence from the Hellenistic period (his area of particular specialization).

Citizenship, the result of birth from citizen parents, was emmeshed within civic institutions: the household, the subdivisions of civic society that had to accept the new citizen (a process best documented in Athens but probably widespread across the *poleis*), and central institutions that registered citizens for administrative and political purposes (especially services to the *polis*). Citizenship grants were bestowed by the whole community, by a vote: even if the practice grew more common as time went on (including women among the recipients), especially against payment of a fee, there never arose a formal avenue of automatic access to citizenship for strangers or for resident foreigners (among whom manumitted slaves were included).⁴⁶ This, too, is a consequence of an Aristotelian, institutionally focused *polis*.

The closed nature of the *polis* citizens as a group of entitled members explains its representation as an essentialized descent group. The mid-fifth-century BCE Athenian restriction of citizenship to those born of two citizen parents⁴⁷ was undoubtedly a response to the specific conditions and opportunities of the fifth-century BCE imperial democracy, but its influence among the *poleis* of the great convergence shows its adequation with civic ideology. Collective descent was reified and fetishized in the claims that *poleis*, as human communities, were somehow entirely and directly descendants from a founding figure. Such claims enabled peer-polity interaction (since *poleis* could construct relations amongst themselves as connected by relations of kinship between their mythical founders), and also strengthened internal solidarity, since mythical pasts expressed local identity and acted as a proxy for autonomy (notably during the Roman empire).

The resulting conception of the *polis* was a nativist ideology, or even a "racialist" conception of membership and community, in the striking formulation proposed by S. Lape for democratic Athens in the fifth and fourth centuries BCE. This nativism was part of the great convergence in *polis* practices and discourses, in that the conception of the *polis* as descent group expressed the democratic collectivization of aristocratic claims to noble ancestry (above, p. 431). It is no coincidence that local history, with its insistence on local identity, narratives, and the bond between descent groups' past and place, gains widespread popularity during the great convergence starting in the fourth century BCE.[48]

The fiction of collective descent was directly connected to the crucial role of civic virtue in the workings of the *polis*, conceived as a just polity because it represented the communitarian will of the many, but also because its individual members lived good and moral lives geared toward the common good (above, chapter 16). Nativism emphasized the innate qualifications of citizens to live just lives as stakeholders in a moral community; the trope underlies the general clauses of many honorific decrees. The concept implies that natural-born citizens are uniquely invested in the common good of their community through their connection with other members of the civic community, the community's memory, religious experience, and sense of place (as celebrated in rituals and monuments). The conflation of self-interest and morality is of course quite typical of virtue politics in the *polis*. Equally typical is another implication of nativism, namely the idealization of the *polis*. Individual citizens are just because the *polis* by nature, and hence every *polis*, is a venue for the performance of human excellence, in which citizens participate by their civic activity.

Nativist tropes are found in institutional practice: for instance, the insistence that candidates for office in Athens could trace descent from citizen ascendants for two generations on both sides, were registered in a local subdivision (deme), participated in cults of "ancestral Apollōn" and "household Zeus," paid their taxes, served in the military, and treated their parents well. Speakers before the *polis*, in assembly or in courts, spoke of the innate qualities of good citizens—the trope occurs in the Attic orators of the fourth century BCE as well as that none-too-successful local politician in Roman-era Prousa, Cocceianus Diōn—and excoriated asocial types as foreigners, outsiders hostile by nature to the political community. Democratic solidarity, as expressed and metaphorized in nativism, came at the cost of constructing strangers to the community and constantly excluding them.[49]

Town and Country

Even the native population in the *polis* was riven with potential divisions. Admittedly, it is tempting to posit a "normal" model of the *polis* (to use an expression coined by E. Ruschenbusch) that favors the integration of rural settlements and minimizes the opposition between city and country. This can be imagined in two possible ways.[50] In the first iteration of this model, applying especially to the case of small *poleis*, the territory is largely cultivated by citizen farmers, commuting (if necessary for hours) from a densely inhabited urban center to dispersed agricultural holdings, which allows for diversification and risk mitigation. This is how we might imagine the island of Hērakleia being cultivated (though the modern island was divided between four villages) or indeed any other small *polis*, a category abundantly illustrated in this book. The island of Hērakleia covers about 18 square kilometers, and, as mentioned earlier (chapter 1), the vast majority of *poleis* had a territory under 500 square kilometers, which would fit in a circle with a radius of 12.62 kilometers, so that most citizens could commute out to their fields.[51] If poor, the citizen farmer has no slaves or a few slaves who live with him; if rich, the citizen-farmer might have gangs of enslaved workers residing in the rural territory and taking care of his estates.

Second, since the territory of larger *poleis* cannot be conceived as being exclusively worked by town-dwelling farmers, their territories are ideally structured by a network of nucleated settlements, fractally reproducing at a smaller scale the central settlement and occupied by citizens. The denizens of these settlements were integrated within the *polis* by the formal recognition of their settlements as civic subdivisions of the whole, by financial compensation for political service and attendance in the urban center, and by institutional representation at the political center. The best-documented example is Athens in the fifth and fourth centuries BCE, after the "Kleisthenic" reform that formalized and capped a long process of integration. As we have seen, similar systems seem to have generally existed in large *poleis*, for instance at Argos, Eretria, Milētos, or Samos (above, chapters 10, 15). This type of organization represents a particular application of the civic society of subdivisions by which every *polis* was structured.

Thus E. Ruschenbusch and M. Hansen can consider that the *polis* was normally not a "consumer city" occupied by a small landed elite living on rents drawn from a mass of peasants, the latter being defined by their lack of political ability to take collective action and remedy their situation. Rather, the *polis* was typically inhabited by smallholding citizen farmers (*Ackerbürger*, to use M. Weber's term, perhaps to be translated as "farmer-burghers"), who commuted to their holdings (within three hours' walking distance from the center: compare figs. 9.2, 9.3, 17.1, 18.2).[52] This arrangement would allow the effective management of dispersed holdings, which were a response to risk but also the consequence of egalitarian inheritance practices. The ancient Greek city-state, on this view, looks radically different from the medieval Italian commune constituted by the domination of the rural *contado* by the urban center.[53] The urban concentration of the majority of the population of most *poleis* would explain the importance of institutional politics conducted in the urban center by and for the citizen population, which could directly participate in state processes. The democratic tendency of the *polis* could be explained by nucleated settlement: the mass of citizens making its presence felt, acceding to political power, using it to shape institutions and ideology in the *polis*, and retaining it in spite of oligarchizing reactions. Additionally, the concentration of many non-elite farmers in the urban center would have perpetuated democratic regimes, by continuously hindering, through regulation and redistribution, the creation of large fortunes.

However, this view of a "good *polis*" nucleated on an urban center where political power was exercised by the citizen community calls for a series of qualifications or nuances.[54] Hansen's elaborate model, complete with quantitative speculation, of a *polis* population largely concentrated in the urban settlement rests on shaky empirical grounds, namely, the supposed absence of dispersed rural settlement in survey archaeology (which has recently been challenged on methodological grounds),[55] as well an array of literary sources (which are inconclusive and impressionistic). Hansen's image seems unsuitable for Priēnē, for a number of reasons. First, the townhouses have no trace of working, storage, and manuring facilities (unlike the fourth-century BCE houses at Halieis in the southern Argolid). Second, the *polis* controlled a complex territory over a plain and a mountain (both sides) with secondary settlements,[56] subordinate villages of Plainsmen and perhaps even isolated farms that might have provided the rag-tag militia led by a Prienian in parallel with the formally mobilized citizen soldiers to fight against Celtic invaders.[57] This territory does not seem to be easily understood as a concentrated settlement of farmer-burghers.

Was even every small island *polis* organized along Hansen's model? This might have been the case of Hērakleia, on its island. On the other hand, I find it difficult to imagine a rich island such as Siphnos (with its 74 square kilometers) exclusively exploited out of the small urban settlement at Kastro (fig. 5.6).[58] Likewise, the territory of Siphnos's poorer, smaller (29 square kilometers) but rugged neighbor Seriphos is unlikely to have been exploited out of a single urban settlement perched high above the island's main harbor. Rather than reduce such territories to simple questions of size (as if the urban settlement were a point in the center of a circle with a radius of 5 kilometers, or 12, or whatever), we might conceive of complexity and irregularity even at a small scale. Many examples bear out a model of territorial complexity. A well-documented case is the *polis* of Kyaneai in Central Lykia, covering a territory of 136 square kilometers (at this point it is better to banish any thought of a circle with a radius of 6.58 kilometers). It is clear that the Yavu plateau, occupied by Kyaneai, was saturated with secondary settlements, villages, and especially farms, where the majority of the citizen population probably resided. Indeed, the multiplication of rural establishments is concomitant with the formation of the *polis* in the Yavu plateau and in Lykia generally.[59] Another example from Asia Minor is the foundation of Aphrodisias in Karia that was accompanied by a dense occupation of the valley within which the city was located.[60] Further up in the highlands of Karia, it is likely that the *polis* of Amyzōn had no urban center at all, but rather an important monumentalized shrine where the citizens periodically met. This dispersed population presumably occupied farmsteads and villages in Mount Latmos (one of them seceded during the second century BCE, which suggests distance and centrifugal tendencies).[61]

In mainland Grece, the territory of the small *polis* of Halieis was densely occupied, during the fifth and especially the fourth century BCE, with farmsteads of very diverse types; a secondary settlement and two clusters of farms were permanent settlements situated outside the immediate hinterland of the city.[62] Even the landscape of fourth-century BCE Attica was not simply divided into small nucleated settlements replicating the big central settlement, but occupied with a diversity of solutions, including loose villages, polycentric microregions, hamlets, and farmsteads.[63] Without trying to quantify and generalize, as Hansen does, I consider it likely that some degree of rural residency was a widespread phenomenon. This is not to argue in favor of the "consumer city" as the dominant model. Rather, structuration of the territory, notably through the extension of civic society to rural space, was the crucial element of *polis* life, with the effect that this required political work, tensions, and the risk of power imbalance; in other words, the relationship of town and country remained a *problem*.

The risk was particularly present because of the emergence of large *polis* territories through synoikism, with secondary settlements included within them (above, chapter 10). The phenomenon was a development of the older phenomenon of complex civic territories with secondary settlements, as can be seen at Priēnē (above) or Teōs, which in the fifth century BCE controlled three secondary settlements—Aroiē, "the fort," and "the island" (perhaps Myonessos, modern Üçgen Adası, 18 kilometers from the urban center).[64] By the late second century BCE, the territory of Teōs (fig. 9.2; perhaps 135 square kilometers) included up to five earlier *poleis* (Airai, Oroanna, Kyrbissos, and one or two more cities, as well as villages or farmsteads in the mountainous hinterlands).[65] Likewise, the *polis* of Aigai absorbed all the settlements in the Aiolian mountain (the modern Yünt-Dağ: fig. 17.2).[66]

On a larger scale, the territory of some city-states covered vast geographies across land and sea. The *polis* of Rhodes included not just the island itself, but a continental territory and a cluster of small islands, whose inhabitants were admitted to the citizen body.[67] One of these islands was Tēlos, which we have seen earlier as a striking example of negotiation between elite and *dēmos* during the "great convergence" of the fourth century BCE (above, p. 219), before its absorption by its big neighbor. At Milētos, the large number of citizens receiving a gift of grain in 160 BCE (perhaps 9,000 men) hints at the enfranchisement of the population of settlements absorbed by the *polis*, namely the mountain community of Pēdasa, once a *polis* but taken over by Milētos in the early second century BCE, and the "Milesian islands." The communities annexed by the *polis* of Milētos made up a great continental and maritime "territory."[68]

Under a "good *polis*" model, we would not hesitate to consider rural populations as well integrated in *polis* structures, through "Kleisthenic" institutions, and simply through direct participation of individuals in *polis* life. The elites of the Rhodian continental and maritime territories participated enthusiastically as semi-voluntary contributors (*leitourgoi*) and priests in the festival life of the urban center of the *polis*.[69] In Roman Asia Minor, we have seen rural settlements producing citizens who held office in the urban center. Such settlements were often officially integrated within the structures of civic society (above, chapters 13 and 15), as subdivisions of the citizen body and *polis* territory. In any case, many villages appear endowed with *polis*-like institutions to enable decision-making and produce public goods.

Yet, as we have seen when discussing power imbalances (above, chapter 18), the issues of the relationship between urban center and secondary settlements or dispersed farmsteads remained problematic, especially as concerns access to the political institutions located in the urban center, the connective ties of civic society, and the public goods managed by the *polis*.[70] Even on Ruschenbusch's or Hansen's optimistic "normal" models, in the best of cases, up to a third of the citizens resided in farms or villages in the territory. How often did they attend the Assembly, hold office, go to court, receive distributions or compensation? The poor hunter represented in Cocceianus Diōn's fantasy set around a Euboian *polis* (*Oration* 7) encounters the *polis* rarely—receiving a distribution of cash once during a visit to town, and another time getting involved in a full-blown Assembly meeting. What about the inhabitants of settlements absorbed by other *poleis*, for instance within the territory of Aigai or Teōs?

Subordination of those with diminished access to the center remained a possibility. The subjection of the countryside and its populations was present at the emergence of the *polis* (above, chapter 6) in many regions; for instance, the "Dustyfeet" of early Epidauros are likely a subordinate rural group, as Plutarch writes, rather than farmer-citizens commuting back to the urban center (as Hansen fondly supposes).[71] The relationship did not need to be named with a formal title: when Hērakleia under Latmos, in Karia, was shaken by a series of calamities (an earthquake and war ca. 200 BCE), its "villages and settlers" (*dēmoi kai oikētai*) ran away, perhaps serfs comparable to the Plainsmen of nearby Priēnē, or perhaps simply peasants in a relationship of economic inferiority to the city. In some *poleis* of Lykia, a class of *paroikoi*, "dwellers-by," seems to designate free, locally born residents who did not have access to full citizenship, as possibly implied by a recently published inscription from first-century BCE Xanthos mentioning citizens, *metoikoi*, and *paroikoi* as the free population of the *polis*.[72] Earlier, in Limyra, "*paroikoi* who have settled in the city" are mentioned, which seems to confirm the existence of second-class citizens in the countryside (and also their occasional migration to the urban center, where they existed as an undigested group, perhaps constantly renewed like rural immigrants to the cities of early modern Europe).

The appearance of differentiated classes of citizenship in some Roman-era *poleis*, or the use of the ethnikon or the marker "of the citizens" in official documents within *polis* territories (above, p. 342) might point to an evolution by which the urban citizens, precisely because they monopolized access to institutions and public goods, evolved into first-class citizens distinct from the rural, free, originally citizen, population. This rural population would have ended up occupying a position structurally similar to the *paroikoi* in Lykian cities. The situation might be comparable to early-modern Geneva, with its territory of 89 square kilometers for a population of 31,000 inhabitants, divided between an urban population of 20,000 and a rural population of 10,000. In the autonomous Genevese city-state, an elite of some four hundred *citoyens* enjoyed access to office and participation, whereas *bourgeois* only had the right to vote, a right denied the locally born *natifs* and immigrant *habitants*, let alone the peasantry of the countryside. This modern parallel allows us to wonder if, in the long history of the *polis*, the urban population's relationship with the rural populations was often an unhappy one, between the complex work of integration and the temptation of exclusion and subordination.[73] Even without formal subordination, the stark facility with which the inhabitants of the city ended up in possession of the harvest of the denizens of the countryside, as witnessed by Galen (with no comment on the mechanisms involved), acts as a reminder of the imbalance between town and country in the *polis*:

> Those who live in the cities, in accordance with their universal practice of collecting as soon as summer was over a sufficient supply of corn for the whole following year, took from the fields all the wheat, with the barley, beans and lentils, and left to the rustics only those leguminous products which are called starches (*ospria*) and pulses (*chedropa*), after they had taken away a good part of these to the city. So the people in the countryside, after consuming during the winter what had been left, were compelled to resort to unwholesome foodstuffs, through the spring, eating twigs and shoots of trees and bushes, bulbs and roots of unwholesome plants, and they fell upon the so-called wild vegetables, whatever one could get hold of, to the point of satiety; they ate them after boiling them whole like green grasses, of which they had not tasted before even as an experiment.[74]

Galen continues with a clinical description of the physiological damage inflicted by this diet, which he presumably witnessed during his rambles in the hinterland of his city, the *polis* of the Pergamenians, *mētropolis* of Asia, thrice-Temple Warden.

The Shapes and Proportions of Exclusion

It is impossible to quantify accurately and truthfully the distribution between the various categories in the population of any *polis*, even if ancient cities may have kept records for military or fiscal reasons.[75] In the case of Athens, it is plausible (if ultimately something of an educated guess) to propose figures as high as 60,000 adult male citizens after decades of imperial prosperity in the fifth century BCE, out of a total population of around 320,000 (if we were to count a total population of 240,000 inhabitants of citizen status, 30,000 resident strangers and 50,000 slaves), so that the *polis* was institutionally in the hands of an in-group of around 19 percent of the population. In the fourth century BCE, the adult male citizens perhaps dropped to 30,000, out of a citizen group of over 120,000, and a total population of (say) 200,000 (including 30,000 resident strangers and 40,000 slaves); the in-group of adult male citizens would have made up 15 percent of the total population.[76] It is unnecessary to specify that these figures are completely approximative, with no real parameters for slaves and foreigners; their point is to think about possible proportions.

In contrast, Sparta, a closed polity based on serf labor and leading a federal structure, would have been ruled by a fully enfranchised citizen group of 8,000 in the early fifth century BCE (judging by the numbers of Spartiate men-at-arms in battle, to which a number of old or disabled citizens should be added): if the total population of the Spartan entity (including populous Messēnia) added up to (say) 300,000, the ruling group of adult male Spartiates would have amounted to less than 3 percent.[77] But such calculations are complicated by the fact that many communities in the Spartan entity were subordinate "perioikic" *poleis*, and by the increasing presence of disfranchised Spartiates, marginal groups, and enfranchised helots: how do we quantify the Spartan system with its concentric circles of power? After the loss of Messēnia in 369 BCE, and the gradual amputation of Spartan territory, the process of concentration of wealth and exclusion of the poor continued in the city of Sparta, complicating any attempt to calculate the size of the elite in-group.

What might the proportions have looked like for a less extensive *polis*? There are no solid indications, so what follows is mere speculation. At a much smaller scale, the island *polis* of Hērakleia must have had a few hundred inhabitants—but how many exactly? It is true that in the nineteenth century the figure was around forty tenants and their families (207 inhabitants in 1879) but (as suggested above, chapter 1) this may reflect the peculiar conditions of abandonment because of pirate raids, followed by underdevelopment because of an oppressive regime of sharecropping (at 50 percent!) to the benefit of an absentee landlord, the monastery of Panagia Chozoviotissa on Amorgos, or lessors.[78] The situation may have had a long-lasting impact (the island had a mere 286 inhabitants in 1928). But if we are willing to suppose that the collective action efforts of the citizenry were successful and made a life in common not just sustainable but prosperous, without a feudal-style landlord taking the surplus, could we imagine (say) 500 inhabitants, of which over 100 were adult male citizens? For what it is worth, the German archaeologist L. Ross thought the spring at the high point of the island could easily sustain around a hundred families.[79]

Priēnē, ca. 270 BCE, might have had 1,000 adult male citizens, busy with politics and the numerous offices required by the *polis*'s institutions.[80] Many of these probably resided in the urban site and its 500 or so townhouses, though, as I argued above, a (substantial?) proportion of citizens must have lived in smaller settlements at Priēnē's harbor town, fortified places in the territory or perhaps even farmsteads on the northern side of Mount Mykalē (fig 1.5; though survey archaeology has revealed nothing).[81] But what number of slaves lived in the *polis*? What number of resident foreigners and freedmen? How many slaves worked in the citizens' fields?[82] Most importantly, what was the number of Plainsmen subordinate to the *polis*, and of the later *paroikoi*? As a thought experiment, we might people the beautiful city and its territory with 1,000 free adult women, 1,000 free children and elderly people of both sexes, 1,200 slaves, 300 resident foreigners, and 2,500 subordinate peasants of all ages, whose status contrasted with the adult male citizens. On this model, the citizen population of 1,000 men amounted to around 14 percent of the total population of 7,000 individuals living within the whole territory of the *polis*.

In the case of another small city, it is interesting to note that the small *polis* of Akraiphia had a population of resident foreigners (*pedawoikoi*). Dozens of these were granted the same fiscal situation as that of citizens, *isotelia*, in reward for their service in war (seventeen names survive, but the inscribed stone bearing the list is fragmentary). If we were to assume that a total of fifty-odd *pedawoikoi* were inscribed on the document (perfectly possible), that these were merely the most enthusiastic participants in the defense of Akraiphia (and hence that, for example, another twenty foreigners sat out the conflict or were not rewarded), we would have a population of seventy resident foreigners (and their families)—but out of what total population? The city was able to provide around twenty conscripts a year for the Boiotian federal army during the third and early second centuries BCE, which suggests a population of 700 adult male citizens—around 20 to 23 percent of a total population, which we could put at 3,000 to 3,500 across the whole territory.[83]

We could continue these experiments, looking for testcases and examples. For instance, for a large island *polis* such as Naxos or Thasos—this whole book abounds in *poleis* that we could try to see on the ground, rather than as examples of broad historical evolutions. None of these exercises is securely based, because of the absence of quantitative records, especially as concerns the question of numbers of slaves and foreigners. Nor is it quite clear what the significance is of often large figures for voters known to have attended assembly meetings in *poleis* of western Asia Minor (above, p. 240). It is true that they number in the thousands of citizens, and I used such figures to speak of democratic *poleis* in the great convergence; yet we do not know what the figures mean without a sense of the size and the structure of the rest of the population across the whole *polis*. For all the treasures of ingenuity and effort deployed to overcome the limitations in our evidence, the risk is that we have long moved from a subjunctive history to a subjective one.

In spite of the disparity between the very big *poleis* and the smallest ones, the proportions might have been roughly similar across the spectrum, namely an institutionally empowered group of adult male citizens making up about 15 to 20 percent of the total population (and a larger citizen group including children and women—perhaps amounting to rather less than half of the total population within *polis* boundaries). Rather than a tiny elite, the body of citizens in most *poleis* may have represented a sizable, highly conscious and privileged minority group constituted by inclusion and exclusion. An interesting comparison comes from the north Italian communes of the twelfth and thirteenth centuries. In these city-states, the class of well-to-do mounted citizen cavalry (*milites*) may have constituted 10 to 15 percent of the whole urban population, which implies a large adult male citizen population (amounting to a majority of the male population in the city). The subordinate countryside has to be taken into account and dilutes the proportion of citizens against the total population of the city-state without, however, amounting to domination by a narrow oligarchy.[84]

Exclusion and Domination in the History of the *Polis*

The picture above is a composite (like so much in the last part of this book), structured by the duality of citizenship and exclusion. More specifically, adult male citizen selfhood occupies its center, and is surrounded by the excluded—childish incomplete citizens, women entailed to perpetual juniority, enslaved manstock, resident foreigners with duties but no rights, rural *paroikoi* enjoying free-born citizen status but laboring under informal or institutionalized inferiorities. The principle of polar opposites that structuralist historians (the "Paris School") have seen as a cardinal phenomenon in ancient Greek culture, rehearsed the centrality of adult male citizen status, which is constitutive of the *polis*.[85] In C. Hedrick's striking reading of the Aristotelian model, the citizen lies at the zero-degree point of the *polis* as society.[86] The funerary reliefs showing a feasting scene (*Totenmahlreliefs*), as illustrated by a large and lavish example from an Ionian *polis* (fig. 9.1), can be reread in the light of the centrality of the adult male citizen. This figure occupies the literal center of the composition, reclining on a couch, the food laid out before him, holding silverware in both hands—an image of privilege; indeed, the visual trope is borrowed from representations of gods and heroes shown on votive reliefs as feasting in a reclined position, as they receive worshippers. The religious overtones are fitting for the funerary context and allude to the heroization of the dead (as do the horse head, the snake arching over the male figure's head to drink out of the bowl in his left hand, and the shrine-like architectural frame), but it is telling that they are deployed specifically and exclusively for the male figure. He is the only one to recline at the feast; he is surrounded by, and towers over, the stratified world of the household—a free woman sitting by the diner's couch, a free young man sitting at his feet, and the enslaved serving boy standing by the mixing bowl. We have seen that the couch is the usual furniture for the men's gathering in the *sumposion* that was an important part of the *polis*, to the point that the whole of Priēnē's democratic institutions at work: a multitude of officeholders, their frequent rotation, the enforcement of accountability on these officials, and transparency in the handling of public funds. As C. Kritzas observed, hundreds of Argive citizens took part in the administration of their *polis*, and they almost always are identified by their civic subdivision, in democratic style, rather than by their father's name. This documentary evidence confirms the impression that emerges from Thucydides's narrative: for instance, Thucydides mentions that the Argive *polis* has a special procedure for trying generals *extra muros* upon their return from campaign, a practice that hints at close control of officeholders and demagogic politics.[63]

Other Peloponnesian democracies are less well documented. The big, expansionary city of Mantineia is explicitly described as a democracy (before Spartan intervention, and after freedom from Spartan control).[64] Phleious and Sikyōn seem to have been democracies (or had periods of democratic government; see below on the ambiguous figure of Euphrōn of Sikyōn). Likewise, the thirteen cities of Achaia are said to have been democracies (perhaps illustrating a phenomenon of small, equal polities with nonelite culture, comparable to western Lokris). Another regional cluster of democratic *poleis* is to be found in Sicily and Southern Italy.[65] In the aftermath of a period of domination by powerful monarchical figures, Syracuse, the greatest *polis* of Sicily, had a democratic constitution for much of the fifth century BCE, complete with demagogic politics and officeholding by large boards; other Sicilian cities such as Selinous, Leontinoi, Himera, or Gela underwent periods of democracy. Rhēgion, Epizephyrian Lokroi, Krotōn, and Taras are all attested as democracies during the fifth century BCE, after periods of closed rule by small groups in the late Archaic period.

It is difficult to write a unified history of Classical democracy. The influence of Athens is undeniable in many cases. Argos, at the time of the development of its democratic constitution, was an ally of Athens when the latter was inventing the forms of "radical" democracy. Even the democracy of Thebes, after the city rose against Sparta in 378 BCE, is likely to have reflected Athenian support (this included a safe haven for the Theban exiles who freed their city). But the forms of Argive or Theban institutions do not look like direct copies of the Athenian constitution. Features such as demagogic politics, voluntary prosecutions, or *leitourgia* might be structurally part of democratic *polis* life rather than immediately Athenian in inspiration.[66] The presence in various *poleis* of *leitourgiai* such as the provision of choruses implies the habit of having rich men pay for services in contexts of competition for honor before the *dēmos*.[67] Nor is there any easy way to connect the Athenian practice of *ostrakismos* with the temporary exile of politicians at Syracuse (where the names of candidates were written on leaves in the procedure of *petalismos*), at Megara, or in Chersonîsos on the northern shore of the Black Sea, a Megarian colony. A potsherd found there bears a name, insults, and the exclamation *itō*, "let him go."[68]

Whether or not directly influenced by Athens, the practice fitted in with local democratic cultures that grew out of the inclusive, broad-based, egalitarian polities of the late "Archaic" period (as at Megara), or out of constitutional upheavals of the early Classical period (as at Syracuse). Democratic ideas may be reflected in the thinking of the famous itinerant "wise men" (*sophistai*, performers and teachers) active on the festival circuit. Two of the Sophists came up with thoughtful justifications for the distributive and participatory practices of *polis* life, for consultation, deliberation, and argument as good modes of living in common, and for the rational capacities of all participants in this project. Prōtagoras (ca. 485–420 BCE) and Dēmokritos (ca. 460–380) came from the democratic *polis* of Abdēra.[69] Among many fragments from Dēmokritos's lost writings that deal with political issues, his description of "poverty" in democracy as a better choice than prosperity alongside the powerful prolongs late Archaic thoughts about restraint, community, and citizenship, in explicit connection with the values of democracy and freedom.

Prōtagoras is portrayed by Plato as mounting a strong defense of the universal sharing in political capacity, and hence the legitimacy of wide political participation (even by bronzeworkers or shoemakers). This *prise de position* takes the form of detailed argument, as well as a myth that is likely a quotation or paraphrase of Prōtagoras's actual writing. Its power is undiminished by the particular context (the teachability of virtue) within which Plato frames it:

> ... in the beginning men dwelt scattered, and there were no cities; so they were destroyed by the animals on account of being in all ways weaker, and the craft of making things was enough to provide food, it was lacking when it came to fighting war against the animals, for they were lacking in the political craft (*politike techne*), of which the art of war is a part. So they sought to gather together and save themselves by founding cities (*poleis*). Now whenever they gathered, they harmed each other because they did not have political craft, and hence scattered again and perished. So Zeus, fearing that our race would utterly be destroyed, sent Hermēs to bring respect and justice to men, so that there would be order and binding ties of friendship in the cities. And Hermēs asked Zeus how he was to give justice and respect to men: "Should I distribute these out like the crafts have been dealt out? Those arts were distributed in this manner: one man possesses the medical craft is sufficient for many individuals, and so with the other craftsmen. Should I place justice and respect in this way among men, or should I distribute them to all?" "To all," said Zeus, "and let all have a share. For cities cannot be, if only a few have a share, as with the other crafts. And lay down a law from myself, to kill him who cannot share of respect and justice, as a disease of the *polis*."

The crucial question, which cannot be easily answered in detail, is whether the institutional arrangements and ideology of democracy accompanied, or fostered, the social and economic phenomena known from Athens. These include the absence of formal overlordship by urban elites over dependent peasantry, the diminution of elite acquisitiveness as a result of nonelite access to political process, the slowing down of wealth accumulation and inequalities, and the promotion of equality through the provision of public goods (including subsidized access to political process) by redistributing surplus extracted from the wealthy.[70] Cautiously, we might infer from the presence of liturgies and demagogic politics that nonexploitative social relations and redistributive institutions were an important complement of the practice of popular power in cities characterized by *dēmokratia*.

From Oligarchy to *Oliganthrōpia*: Classical Sparta

The articulation of democratic practice and ideology was matched by another type of regime—the rule of the few, the better, the rich. To use the term current in the Classical period already, this was oligarchy, based on political inequality and the institutionalized restriction of access to power, based on wealth criteria. This type of régime—like *dēmokratia*—was rooted in the diversity of the "Archaic" polities, and specifically in the old practice of "closed" citizenship, internal hierarchies, exclusion from power, and domination over individuals and communities that are part of the *polis* without open access to full membership (above, chapter 6). "Archaic" Argos fell into this category, before the upheavals at the very start of the fifth century BCE that led to the elaboration of the Classical democratic régime. Notoriously, the Cretan cities also perpetuated a closed form of social organization during the fifth century BCE.[71]

Equally notorious, the Thessalian *poleis* continued along similar lines of restricted aristocratic régimes ruling over second-class citizens (including artisans) and, especially, over a rural population of serfs (*penestai*) with no access to citizenship.[72] A sense of the complexity as well as the restricted nature of the social organization in a Thessalian city can be gained from the *polis* of Mētropolis, where a family group, the Basaidai, controlled a number of privileges, including access to a *taga*. Once interpreted by L. Moretti as the city's chief magistracy, the term in fact seems to designate public land held by a civic subdivision. In the third century BCE, as we know from an inscribed agreement, the Basaidai negotiated with four families for access to the *taga*; the five families constituted a privileged *sungeneia* or fictive kingroup.[73]

The most obvious, if perhaps not the most typical, representative of the new oligarchical polities that evolved out of the closed system was Sparta, whose power and size allowed it to play a major part in the power politics of the fifth and part of the fourth centuries BCE (above, chapter 7), drawing especially on the manpower of the other *poleis* in Lakedaimōn, and generally of the majority of the Peloponnesian cities under Spartan control. Even though its story is much more obscure than that of Athens (because of lack of evidence, Spartan secrecy, the "Spartan mirage" of positive or awesome images about the Lakedaimonian polity, and the subsequent reception of those images),[74] it is clear that Spartan history was hardly immobile. Most importantly, the case of Sparta illustrates how the old, exclusive model evolved in parallel with and in reaction to the contemporary evolutions of the "open" model toward democracy.

It is true that Classical Sparta retained the social structure developed during the "Archaic" period. It restricted citizenship to a rentier class of landowners that was supported by the serf labor of helots (even if the treatment of this class increasingly took on aspects of chattel slavery, such as ownership and sale, as part of the intensification of the power of private property in Sparta).[75] The product of helot labor allowed citizens to enjoy leisure while paying dues in kind to state institutions. That is, Classical Sparta retained the relationship of overlordship and elite appropriation that had been a widespread phenomenon in earlier periods, but which tended to disappear with the spread of democratic constitutions descended from the "open" polities of the sixth century BCE. The resulting leisure allowed members of the citizen group to devote themselves to specialized elite activities, and generally to the leadership of the unequal pyramid of hegemony and power in the Peloponnese and beyond. Spartiate life took place within frameworks defined by the community, notably the famous state education, an elaboration of a number of community practices (warrior bands, *rites de passage*) that had played integrative functions in the archaic *poleis*.[76] The Archaic-style political histrionics remained visible, symbolizing the egalitarian solidarity of the citizens as "the People" through features such as costume,[77] the limited usage of each other's property, status markers through violence, and political manipulation of festival and ritual.[78]

Yet the old structure did not prevent the development and evolution of institutional practices. On the one hand, in spite of quaint-looking practices such as voting by acclamation, the assembly of citizens should not be considered powerless: it elected officeholders and voted on matters of state such as warfare and high politics. Even charismatic kings such as the swashbuckling adventurist Agēsilaos needed to work around the Assembly and state institutions. Assembly decisions often led to punitive measures against the kings, implemented according to the rule of law: several kings were fined or exiled. Internally, the Spartan state conducted its affairs (including public finances) through written records and accountability, like any other *polis*, and it should not be viewed as a nobly primitive or backward polity.[79]

But alongside the effective working of political institutions, what characterizes Sparta is a dynamic of competition and inequality.[80] The Spartiates had always known economic inequality, in spite of equal access to public goods and rationed luxury (paralleled in other "Archaic" *poleis* as part of a particular type of citizenship regime, as we have seen). Some Spartiates were very wealthy (above, p. 145); the fifth-century BCE Spartiate Lichas was famous for his lavish hospitality and his horseracing activities (he was literally whipped out of the Olympia of 420 when trying to crown his charioteer, whose chariot had been entered into the contest as a Boiotian team to bypass a ban on Spartan competitors).[81] Such activities are an index of the emergence of a wealth elite. The process and modalities are not completely clear, though the factors were undoubtedly elite acquisitiveness, inheritance strategies that allowed families to trap and transmit property, and the influx of wealth at the end of the Peloponnesian Wars (above, p. 167). The concomitant feature of impoverishment of nonelite Spartiates is equally difficult to explain, but it offers a clear hint of the acquisitive pressures on the part of the rich, perhaps involving lending and foreclosing, especially with the influx of money in the form of Achaimenid subsidies or of the profits of war and empire (above, chapter 7).[82]

The consequences of continuously increasing economic inequality were threefold. The first was the exclusion of poor Spartiates from full citizenship because of their failure to make the considerable contributions to the communal messes. The system of communal feasting as a participatory activity was a development out of the practices and ideologies of the Archaic *polis* (above, chapters 5 and 6) that resulted from and reinforced the solidarity of the integrated (and constantly performed) citizen group. Economic exclusion from full citizenship operated alongside other forms of exclusion, on grounds of unworthiness—especially cowardice in battle—which indicate how its roots are the principle of fair distribution of burdens. The outcome was a large group of second-class citizens, the "Inferiors," which shared the burdens of citizenship (especially military), but none of the advantages; namely, access to the elite lifestyle and political rule enjoyed by the "Alike Ones" (*homoioi*). The Inferior status may have been formalized only in the fifth century BCE with the increasing demotion of Spartiates on economic grounds.

The second consequence was the restriction of political power to the dwindling group of *homoioi*, since they monopolized office and decision-making within the Spartiate state. The drop in citizen numbers (*oliganthrōpia*, "lack of men") was a political rather than demographic phenomenon. The third consequence was the prevalence of corruption—not just in the form of illegitimate economic gain-seeking through gifts, bribes, and graft, but more generally in the form of fixing outcomes within the small power elite or bypassing institutional and political process. The Spartan state needed to raise special wealth taxes (*eisphorai*), just like Athens, to finance hegemonical war, but such taxes were particularly difficult to collect in Sparta—because of the solidarity of the rich elite of full citizens, and the absence of institutions to enforce state decisions on the rich and influential.[83] Patterns of personal patronage involving wealthy and powerful Spartiates (including the kings themselves) are also a result of the concentration of economic wealth and political power within the restricted group of full citizens.

These political processes explain certain characteristics of Spartan political life, discussed earlier. Most obvious is the tendency toward adventurism in "foreign policy," the aggressive *fuite en avant* in the fifth and especially the early fourth centuries BCE, down to the epochal defeat at Leuktra in 371 BCE. War allowed the Spartan system to mobilize its subordinate elements: helots, perioikic cities, subordinate allies and, within the Spartiate *polis*, the Inferiors. In addition, foreign wars allowed profits from plunder or systematic extraction to flow to all the elements of society. In addition to channels for social aggression and material profit, war offered avenues of social promotion for veterans of contingents of fighting helots, installed as military colonists on the edge of Lakedaimōn, or for Inferiors enjoying military command or governorships abroad.[84]

Another characteristic of Spartan political life is constant resistance to the pyramid of power. The revolt of the subordinate allies belongs to a continuum with unrest by Inferior citizens, the centrifugal tendencies of perioikic cities, and the uprising of helots, be it the integrated serf populations of Lakōnia proper or the subject communities in Messēnia. In the main, these forms of resistance were successfully controlled by the Spartan system through a variety of means: the divide-and-rule prisoner's dilemma-style techniques already mentioned (p. 168), but also assassination, arrest, torture, and extrajudicial execution (as happened during unrest in Sparta immediately after Leuktra).[85]

All the characteristics of the Spartan system are illustrated by one episode and its repression—namely, the conspiracy mounted by one of the excluded, a man named Kinadōn, in 395 BCE; this is recounted in an extraordinary piece of narrative by Xenophon.[86] Kinadōn, as an Inferior, had army experience, and his planned uprising of all the armed elements in Spartan society—Inferiors, *perioikoi* but also helots—shows the central place occupied by the military factor in uniting the divergent elements under Spartiate leadership. His resentment at being excluded from the full citizenship enjoyed by the *homoioi* was the result of the dynamics of inequality in plutocratic Sparta. When the conspiracy was denounced, the Spartiate state mobilized its full capacity for secrecy and restriction: the ephors did not even mobilize the "small Assembly," an institution so restrictive that we in fact have no idea of what it did within the Spartan constitution. The ephors acted fast and ruthlessly: Kinadōn was lured into a trap and arrested by a regiment of Spartan cavalry, on the pretense that he was about to carry out a police mission for the ephors, a role he had fulfilled before. The details of the sting are instructive: alongside the routine use of literacy in administration and repression at Sparta, they show the necessity for constant surveillance and repression in the Spartiate state, and the use of Inferiors as muscle for social control and as collaborators in the system of their own oppression. The punishment of Kinadōn and his associates illustrates the violence, symbolical and actual, underlying Spartan government (they were put in a wooden collar immobilizing the hands and driven around the city with whips and goads, presumably until their death).

Spartan realities did not quite amount to a crisis—we are rather peering into the workings of an apparatus whose internal dynamics compelled certain types of behavior, and whose continued operation was prone to extreme brittleness (as shown by the unraveling of the system after 371 BCE). The story of Sparta exhibits constant conflict and tension, plutocratic power, and the moralizing rewritings of economic inequalities characteristic of plutocratic societies. It is true that Sparta was a peculiar polity, with many special solutions and irregularities in its pyramid of power and circles of influence (for instance, privileges for groups of helots or certain perioikic communities). All the same, in spite of its peculiarities (which grew out of the fairly common solutions that it embarked upon during the Archaic period), Sparta serves as a particularly potent example of the workings of internally unequal polities, a perception already shared at the time.

Classical *Oligarchia*

As Sparta shows, the old model of restricted-access citizenship kept evolving in the fifth and fourth centuries BCE into articulate and sophisticated forms, just as the "open" polities (such as Athens) did during the same period. Classical oligarchies[87] are well attested in the narrative sources ("ruled by the best") and in the philosophical analyses of *polis* constitutions (especially by Aristotle). In constitutional terms, oligarchy meant a set of restrictive practices and arrangements[88] such as a censitary barrier to office or even citizenship,[89] an Assembly with restricted powers, a small Council with permanent membership and wide authority, and the strong executive and judicial power of a small number of elected and unpaid officials. These features all share the characteristic of making "some men deliberate about all things," as Aristotle puts it.[90] The Boiotian Confederacy, as it operated between 446 and 386 BCE, gives one example of such features uniformly imposed across all of its *poleis*. A high property qualification excluded more than half the male population from the franchise, and the full citizens belonged to four Councils working in a complicated system of rotation (one Council served as the administrative body for the three other Councils, decisions being taken by all four Councils).[91] Generally, the evidence, though patchy and unsystematic, suggests that oligarchical régimes were widespread, especially during the late fifth and early fourth centuries BCE.[92]

Oligarchical practices were underpinned by representations of closed polity as order, balance, self-control, and even justice. These descended from aristocratic self-representation, as developed during the Archaic and early Classical periods: signs of distinction (lifestyle, luxury, athletic competence) operated as proofs of the essential superiority of the "beautiful and good" (*kaloikagathoi*), as illustrated by Pindar's victory poems in the early fifth century BCE.[93] Another source was the concept of order as a collective good produced by the wise solidarity of a small ruling group and resulting in the community's happiness (*eudaimōnia*). Chios, an oligarchical city, is presented in these terms by Thucydides at the eve of its revolt from Athens in 412, a city combining prosperity, prudence, and stable *kosmos*.[94]

Such representations were not just ideological statements on the part of dominant groups, but also claimed that the few wielded power on grounds of merit.[95] The rich were more deserving of power on practical grounds: they were more capable to rule, since they were supposedly less corruptible and corrupted, and they were more competent, since they had the leisure to cultivate their abilities. In addition, they were more deserving of power on moral grounds, because they made greater contributions to the *polis*, in financial terms and through military service as the heavy men-at-arms that were the main tactical means of the Greek states. Oligarchy claimed a form of proportional or "geometric" equality that respected the differences or inequalities in ability and merit between individuals.[96]

The "few" self-servingly portray themselves as the "best" (*beltistoi*). The simplicity of the idea (and the blatancy with which it expresses the self-interest of the wealthy) should not obscure the sophistication and inventiveness with which oligarchical discourses and ideas were developed. Apart from the concepts about geometric equality and the entitlement of the wealthy, majority rule could be represented as the selfish pursuit of profits by the poor, and the democratic institution of mass decision as the unjust exercise of tyrannical power through coercion. Likewise, the lot or pay for service was illegitimate, unrepresentative, and morally corrupt and corrupting.[97] The moral and aesthetic language of oligarchy was complemented by a language of castigation for democratic practice and especially for its leaders—demagogues, *sukophantai*—criticized as the *ponēroi*, the wicked, in contrast with the *chrēstoi*, the useful ones. The critique was the more powerful for being sensitive to democratic anxieties about demagogues and *sukophantai*,[98] as illustrated by the clever deployment of such themes by violent oligarchical coups in Athens. More directly, democracy could be portrayed as irrationality and madness.[99]

Finally, oligarchical discourses proposed positive images. Oligarchy was equivalent to restraint (*sōphrosunē*) in contrast with the irrationality and ignorance of democracy (such as at Athens where the people embarked rashly on an expedition against Sicily, and refused responsibility for the subsequent disaster).[100] The "Few" constructed complex constitutional schemes around the rationality of numbers. Oligarchical thinkers painted images of order and ("geometric") justice holding sway in an idealized Sparta; they appealed to the reinvented past of the "ancestral constitution." These images, too, drew their power from their link with sources of cultural prestige in ancient Greek culture—the elitist Homeric poems, the "Archaic" groups with their names and numerical schemes, and the Spartan mirage. The oligarchical regime in Athens in 403 BCE organized a full muster of the population—structured in a body of full citizens, 3,000 strong, parading in the *agora*, while inferior citizens still under military obligations gathered in other places. The unequal statuses, visualized through hierarchical spatialization between citizen center and inferior periphery, may have been inspired by the Spartan model.[101]

The thought-world of oligarchy thus represented a political creation that appears as articulate and imaginative as democratic practice. Its discourses and ideas exercised a great hold, as perhaps shown by the widespread presence of oligarchical regimes. Yet a few features need emphasizing if we are to understand the historical nature of Classical oligarchies. For all its cultural nostalgia and its genealogical relation with the closed polities of the "Archaic" period, Classical oligarchy was a new phenomenon, an explicit reaction to the self-aware practice of *dēmokratia*, defined against it and often thought through as a deliberate, systematic rebuttal of democratic claims. The second feature is that for all its high-mindedness, oligarchy in practice was torn by contradiction and inconcinnity. Essentialist claims to excellence were belied by the realities of faction politics. The aestheticized images of harmony had to coexist with the violence essential to oligarchical discourse. Such violence was deployed to disqualify common practices of decision-making that were at the heart of *polis* processes and to vilify the democratic leaders (who were often from the same social background as oligarchs).

Most seriously, the dynamics of restrictiveness were plagued by uncertainty about how to manage the travails of inclusion and exclusion that were one of the great problems of the *polis*. The small, exclusive oligarchical citizen groups hesitated between imposing (democratic-style) equality among their members (and thus operating as small democracies), and giving free rein to the principles of personal excellence implied by class dominance. The latter solution risked leading to more exclusivity within the group and potentially to small cliques that were vulnerable to revolution and overthrow.[102] The contradictions had to be managed by a number of risky strategies of violence and social control, to preserve the concentration of power and prevent collective action by the disfranchised.[103]

Paradoxically, the very nature of Classical oligarchy as antidemocracy ensures its maximum legibility in democratic Athens itself.[104] The historical figure of Sōkratēs, for instance, was probably perceived as an antidemocratic thinker, and his trial and execution a consequence of this perception;[105] antidemocratic ideas are also surprisingly present in the comedies of Aristophanes, performed in front of mass audiences at *polis* festivals.[106] Athens itself underwent oligarchical episodes—the short-lived coups of 411 and 404 BCE, already mentioned. We have seen that the long shift in discourses and attitudes in the second half of the fourth century BCE (visible for instance in the greater power of the old permanent Council of the Areiopagos) that culminated in a Macedonian-backed, censitary oligarchy in 322 BCE, followed by a strong democratic reaction (when the old general Phōkiōn was tried and executed for treason), itself followed by a strongman regime under the philosopher Dēmētrios of Phaleron.[107] The latter evolution, toward greater power for officials combined with considerable unease about the position of elites in the polity, may have been one result of the increased leitourgic pressure on the wealthy, as required by the combination of grand ambitions and lack of funds after the collapse of the last serious overseas imperial venture by Athens in 357–355 BCE, when Athens's allies bolted for good. These episodes illustrate both the violence (in the form of executions or expulsions) and the instability (in the form of internal conflict) of actual oligarchical solutions.

The Divided *Polis* and the Temptations of *Stasis*

The presence of a streak of oligarchical choices even in Athens reveals the continuous dichotomy between democracy and oligarchy, yet also their close relation. The reaction to the oligarchical coup of 411 BCE was couched as a careful subversion of the oligarchs' own scheme of a limited franchise of 5,000 full citizens, thus exploiting the ambiguities in oligarchical discourse. Furthermore, the case of Athens shows that the dichotomy did not quite produce purely "democratic" *poleis* and "oligarchical" *poleis*. Like Athens, many cities experienced episodes of both.[108] Mantineia was governed according to a democratic constitution, with attendant features such as demagogic politics and judicial practices—except for an extended period (385–370 BCE) when the city was split into four smaller subparts, each of which was ruled by the landowners in "aristocratic" regimes.[109] Argos, a democratic *polis* with peculiar features of its own, also underwent violent oligarchical episodes. If Kymē, Erythrai, Kōs (to take only three examples of eastern Greek city-states) were democratic cities (as can be shown from epigraphical documents, or as is explicitly attested by Aristotle), they also knew periods of oligarchical rule, as a direct reaction to demagogic politics in the Assembly and in the popular courts.

To speak of "episodes" is a bloodless way to refer to the actual form that constitutional alternance usually took—namely political violence, often shockingly bloody. The grim episode of slaughter at the festival of the Eukleia at Corinth (above, p. 179) shows civil war to be a major part of the tragedy of Greece's Hundred Years' War. The conflict between oligarchical and democratic factions in Argos was exacerbated by the presence of a large contingent of full-time soldiers who were paid for and maintained by the *polis*, but harbored oligarchical sympathies (because of their social origin). The culmination of the protracted conflict was an attempted oligarchical coup (itself in reaction to demagogic policies), the repression of the coup by the execution of thirty of the "eminent ones" (a codeword for the wealth elite), followed by the mass condemnation and execution of 1,200 wealthy citizens. This atrocity was unique only in that its victims were bludgeoned to death (the savage episode is recorded in the term *skytalismos*, the "clubbing" used to refer to it).[110] Civil war (*stasis*) on Kerkyra, during the Peloponnesian War, also saw terrible violence between the oligarchical and democratic factions, escalating from judicial conflict to urban warfare to mass executions. Thucydides provides a careful, clinical narrative, as well as a powerful analysis of the corrupting effect of civil war and violence.[111]

Indeed, *stasis* occurs at multiple points in Thucydides's narrative: the conflagration of 431 had its origins in the involvement of big *poleis*, including Athens, in the politics of the small *polis* of Epidamnos, wracked by civic strife and expulsions. The Ionian *polis* of Kolophōn, during an episode of *stasis*, split into two towns, old Kolophōn and Notion; the latter underwent a secondary split between two factions, separated by a wall across the urban site, as a physical marker of the divided *polis*.[112]

Such internal violence was occasioned by conflicts between factions that promoted competing constitutional solutions and economic policies (democracies promoted demagogic control of the wealth, redistributive taxation, and the occasional confiscation of estates; oligarchies protected the property and contractual rights of rent-seeking elites). Violence was also fostered by structural features within the political culture of the *polis*.[113] Genealogically, the nature of membership in the *polis* was determined not just by essentialist tropes of identity and harmony (as fostered by discourse and ritual), but also by the sense of the justice of claims and entitlement as part of stakeholding in common public goods, especially since the latter were financed by individual but unevenly distributed contributions. The dual nature of citizenship explains why claims to entitlement could be so easily expressed in moral terms, with the consequent exclusion of opponents to such claims: hence the resort to casting-out through symbolical violence (in demagogic rhetoric or in oligarchical imagery) or actual exile, and hence the all-too-often realized possibility for escalation into real violence.

The unpacking of these contradictions underlies the dichotomy between democracy and oligarchy; but it also shows how democracy and oligarchy belong to a same continuum of *polis* culture. This continuum is clear in the way in which many "oligarchical" constitutions depend on the very practices and bodies (Assembly, Council, accountable officials) that are known from democracies but are more generally fundamental to the nature of the Greek city-states. Conversely, the language and interrogations of the oligarchical episodes in Athens, even if they were violently rejected by the democracy and assimilated to tyranny, left traces in the discourses, practices, and obsessions of the fourth-century BCE democracy, because they addressed central problems of the *polis*.[114]

To speak of this continuum does not diminish violence and conflict in the political history of the Hundred Years—a tragic, ironical history of constitutional practice as well as of discourse, ideology, and ideas about the right way to live in a *polis*. The temptation of authoritarian simplification was a response to the risk of debates about constitutional matters escalating into civil war and violence. A small military treatise of the Arkadian commander and politician Aineias of Stymphalos is obsessed with the danger of factional fighting, the need to repress it by direct police control, and the enforcement of civic harmony by imposed measures (for instance, the resort to debt relief to assuage tensions between rich and poor). The *polis* appears in this text as a world of political suspicion, requiring muscular intervention. Such security measures worked in the short term, as shown by the prevention of stasis in Phleious when it was under siege by the Spartans.[115]

The authoritarian temptation could evolve into monarchical solutions. Tyrannical episodes or actual regimes are sporadically known throughout the period between ca. 450 and 350 BCE, most spectacularly in Syracuse, where democratic politics led to a demagogue, Dionysios, seizing power and maintaining his family in control of the city from 405 to 344. Dionysios I also pursued hegemonic politics in Sicily and southern Italy (a powerful reminder of how power politics also favored monarchical solutions); his influence led to the resurgence of a series of tyrannical regimes in other Sicilian and Italian *poleis*. Indeed, we might choose to consider the Corinthian adventurer Timoleōn, who overthrew the tyranny in Syracuse and led the Sicilians to victory against the Carthaginians, as a strongman in the tyrannical mold—except for the more civic style in which he chose to present himself.[116]

Nor was tyranny limited to the western *poleis*, where there had been a long and spectacular tradition of such monarchical figures. In mainland Greece or in Asia Minor (for instance at Hērakleia Pontikē), their presence was abetted by the frequent use of professional soldiers, necessary to compete in the "big war" of the Hundred Years.[117] A Corinthian, Timophanēs, attempted a tyrannical coup at the head of 400 mercenaries in 366 BCE (the attempt was checked when his brother, none other than the future Syracusan strongman Timoleōn, killed him with his own hand). In Sikyōn, tension between oligarchs and democrats led to complicated regime change and the tyranny of a leading citizen, Euphrōn.[118] Euphrōn was expelled by an Arkadian force led by Aineias of Stymphalos (the military writer), returned, was murdered by elite, antidemocratic Sikyonians, and buried in the *agora* where some other Sikyonians honored him; his grandson was later a Sikyonian politician honored by the Athenian *polis*. The case of Euphrōn of Sikyōn shows the complexity of internal politics and the way in which the old princely solution could be embedded within the debates and conflicts of the age. If monarchical authoritarianism was a possible outcome both of hegemonical power politics and of local factional conflict, what other solutions did the political resources of the *poleis* offer?

urban fabric could be said to be generated by the size and positioning of the couch (above, p. 425); here it is repurposed hierarchically for a family scene, to speak of patriarchal domination. Perhaps the *andrōn*, the men's dining room, did fulfill this telling dual role in real life—as the setting for the men's gathering that was a constituent part of the *polis*, and as the scene of family dinners in which the head of the household presided over women, children, and slaves, performing their different relations to him. Behind the reclining adult male appear his weapons emphasized by a frame and reminding us of his role as participant in the political community, and his entitlements as a citizen. The normative representation of household hierarchy, private luxury, and service as a man-at-arms is a final reminder of the exclusionary processes of class and leisure as a condition for participation in the *polis*.

All the *polis*'s bads, in the manifestations described above (violence, patriarchy, enslavement, exclusion) were interconnected in a cat's cradle of analogies, correspondences, relations, paradoxes, and nuances woven around the citizen. These form an anti-civic society generated by the *polis* and complementing the civic society of groups and associations by which the *polis* made itself visible (above, pp. 428–33). Male slaves can be called *pais* ("boy"), which expresses the lack of status of the enslaved and the children alike—and both are exposed to the punitive violence and sexual aggression of the adult male citizen; however, the citizen future of the boy modulates the forms sexual activity can take in his case. Women are excluded and subject to deprivation, and hence steal food and alcohol, for which exercise they need cunning, like slaves. Women are victims of boundary-policing violence at the hands of the adult male citizens, like slaves. Yet they are also part of the citizen household, and hence play their role in reproducing slavery and the exclusion of foreigners; in contrast, prostitutes and slaves were assimilated as deprived of sexual honor and subject to the same outrages.[87] Free noncitizens in the city are outsiders: ex-slaves and unenfranchised country-folk could be called *paroikoi*, perhaps in the same cities; in other cities, ex-slaves were assimilated to resident foreigners.

If the citizen body can be naturalized as a descent group, and even conceived as having innate qualities and capabilities, the excluded can also be conceived as inherently disqualified from citizenship. Hence the conception of women as lacking in self-control and deliberative reason, or the notion that slaves (often imported from outside the Greek world) came from ethnic groups that were suitable for being ruled, and hence slaves by nature. Both of these ideas are set out in Aristotle's *Politics*, and it is not coincidental that this work, devoted to the ramifications of citizenship, starts by repeating and formalizing the principles of exclusion found in the *poleis*.[88] As we have seen, the situation with country-dwellers was complex, between outright exclusion, exploitation, and othering in the early *polis* and integration within the citizen body as full participants in the political community by the time of the great convergence; in any case, town-dwellers, elite and nonelite, were deeply implicated in the countryside and its economic activities, be it as estate owners or as smallholders. At the same time, images of rural dwellers as either idealized, nonpolitical beings (exemplified by Dio's hunter), or comic, boorish figures lacking in urbanity, or as antisocial, profit-driven, selfish actors (exemplified by characters in Aristophanes's comedy, for instance in his *Acharnians*: above, p. 455), try to cast them as noncitizens, ostensibly not because of their residence but because of their nature and character.[89] The politics of negative images of rural populations is made clear by similar sentiments in the medieval city, where they were undoubtedly hardened by the urban domination over the countryside and hostility toward the poor: concepts of the public good and civic participation were defined against the figure of the peasant, imagined as incapable of disinterested and virtuous civic behavior.[90] Concepts of the public good, as we have seen, can exclude as well as unite, dominate as well as inspire.

This baroque intertwining of negative aspects of exclusion represents a final set of consequences of the Aristotelian definition of *polis* and *politeia*. Such costs are adumbrated in the dilemma of extension and access. If the *polis* is considered as a political community of participation by full members engaged in an ennobling common project (as H. Arendt imagined the *polis*), mobilized by solidaristic ideologies, and committed to moralizing ideals, there are two possibilities for the construction of the citizen body. The first is to try to widely empower inhabitants, in spite of multiple inequalities, to participate in the *polis*, a choice that requires much political work (notably in terms of institutional design) and pooled resources. The second is to exclude those who are unable to participate for various reasons: physical distance or, more insidiously, proclaimed defects such as lack of moral virtue or unsuitedness on account of economic disadvantages, the first often being used as an ideological cover for the second and enabled by moralizing virtue politics. This second solution is a temptation echoed in the latter parts of Aristotle's *Politics*. In Aristotle's wake, H. Arendt sensed this potential path when she viewed slavery as a solution to the dichotomy between mere labor and political work, namely the shunting-off of labor onto a specialized group.[91] The dilemma is inherent to *polis*-hood.[92]

The inherence of the ideology of exclusion explains its constant presence in the history of the *polis*. Enslaved labor probably played an important role in enabling the wealth and the lifestyle of the Early Iron Age elites, hence encouraging expansion and settlement in areas where metals and enslaved individuals could be acquired, in the western Mediterranean, the northern Aegean, the coasts of western and southern Asia Minor. Slavery is present at this formative phase, for instance in fostering group solidarity among acquisitive settlers, or in creating social difference between elite groups (enjoying access to metals, imported goods, and slaves) and local non-elite producers. The subsequent political problems would have to be solved through collective negotiation, leading to the community clusters that preceded the *polis*. In the early history of the *polis*, the construction of citizenship and a citizen group defined by political equality was accompanied by the definition of the household, the othering of women, the rise of chattel slavery, the simultaneous appearance of prostitution and elite pederasty,[93] and debates about the position of strangers and rural populations within the *polis*. Citizenship, the market, and the presence of strangers both in the *polis* and on the margins, all interacted in creating and defining the conditions of *polis* life.

The rest of the narrative of *polis* history can also be written as the history of exclusion. The pervasiveness of chattel slavery, especially among the "open," democratic polities, offered a powerful metaphor through which hegemony could be conceptualized—and rejected as beyond the pale for communities of free and equal men. This ideological move means that the existence of slavery contributed not just to the definition of the citizen, but also to the vigorous ideal of *polis* autonomy. I have argued that the latter played a central role in the great convergence of *polis* forms, in disqualifying imperialism amongst *poleis*, and in encouraging resistance and agency in the face of supra-*polis* powers, such as the Hellenistic kingdoms and the Roman empire. The invention, extension, and instrumentalization of *polis* nativism (and its corollary of exclusion) is part of the great convergence in *polis* forms. Nativism acted as a medium for democratization, inclusion, and peer-polity interaction, and is prolonged into the Roman-era *polis* as a proxy for autonomy and a justification for democracy.

The diffusion of chattel slavery (rather than serfdom) is equally part of the great convergence, and the spread at various times of *polis* forms into landscapes of slavery such as Thessaly, Mysia, Bithynia, Phrygia, the Levant, or Thrace must have complicated the trade in enslaved humans. Did the adoption of *polis* forms by local communities act as a defense against enslavement of local populations, or on the contrary facilitate it by giving enslaving local elites a cultural form (Hellenization) and an institutional form that allowed them to interact with their peer *poleis*? At any rate, the exportation of injustice and exploitation outside the boundaries of the citizen body was a corollary of *polis* solidarity, visible in the resort to chattel slavery but also the creation of subordinate hinterlands, as in the case of Rhodes but also Mytilēnē or Byzantion.[94] These maritime cities controlled continental hinterlands, but the same temptation to subordinate the countryside is present in landlocked cities with big territories, and we have seen the dilemmas posed by the unfinished integration of secondary settlements after the wave of *synoikismoi* during the great convergence, and the occasional appearance of *paroikoi* and second-class citizenry in the Roman-era *poleis* (above, p. 516).

Finally, if exclusion was inherent to the *polis* as form, the practices and ideology of exclusion and othering must have been part of the diffusion of the *polis*, alongside the political culture of institutions and social relations between mass and elite. This is suggested by details such as the citizens of Julia Gordos (on the eastern edges of Lydia) honoring a citizen in 75/6 CE for good civic behavior but also for having lived "the life of a household master," *oikodespotēn bion*, or the repression of prostitution and *kinaideia* (men as passive partners during penetrative sexual intercourse) in second-century CE Tralleis.[95] The contrast drawn between the "shamelessness" of "those who cannot hide that they suffered unspoken violence" and the ancestral restraint of the *dēmos* as it protects its shrines and its gymnasia, coheres with the classical regimen of citizenship, sexuality, and the body, seen in the case of Classical Athens. The same sexual protocols also occur at Beroia, in second-century BCE Macedonia, where the *gymnasion* was forbidden to artisans, madmen, and male prostitutes, and where the segregation of young boys from older adolescents may have to do with the control of sexual aggression and the management of the citizen body.[96]

For cases such as second-century BCE Beroia, first-century CE Julia Gordos, or second-century CE Tralleis, there is no unbroken chain of evidence of transmission of values from fourth-century BCE Athens, but rather the suggestion of a strong cultural constraint that can only come from the ideology of the *polis*. Values and ideology came alongside the institutional set-up of citizenship and exclusion. It is tempting to view the visual culture of the new *poleis* of the Roman Near East and Egypt, especially funerary imagery, as reflecting a version of the *polis* ideology centered on the citizen. At Palmyra, the representation of women bedecked with jewelry, rather than expressing some timeless luxury or enduring native identity (I have come close to suggesting this: p. 436, fig. 14.8, cf. fig. 15.3), might convey the wealth of the household and the role of entitled women in transmitting this wealth, and hence reproducing households. This applies especially to the elite households whose fortune was tapped by taxation, *leitourgia*, and benefactions to produce public goods, a political economy that is well attested at Palmyra.[97]

Distorting Effects

If we see the social history of the *polis* as shaped by the gravitational field of citizenship, arraying other relations around it in an "anti-civic" space, the activities of noncitizen actors, for all their diversity (see above, chapter 15), were subject to constant distorting effects rather than amounting to autonomous spaces of diversity, fluidity, and agency that might have constituted the "real" *polis*. This holds true in spite of the operation of multiple statuses, diversities, forms of immigration and settlement, zones of negotiation between the privileged and the marginalized, possibilities for self-affirmation by noncitizen groups, and the occasional public visibility and activity of women (as can be seen, for instance, in fourth-century BCE Athens, or Hellenistic Rhodes, or the cities of Roman-era Asia Minor).[98] The main intent and effect of the *polis* as institutions remained the concentration of benefits on the entitled in-group, and the shifting of costs onto the excluded, the enslaved, and the outsiders through violence, exploitation, or rent-seeking.

Concomitantly, the basic lack of access to the full package of rights and privileges that came with citizenship necessarily generated vulnerability and precarity, in different forms for transient foreigners, resident foreigners (dependent on citizen patrons and liable to special fees as well as duties to the citizen commonwealth), and the enslaved and ex-enslaved. The vulnerability must have been exacerbated when the categories of exclusion and subordination intersected, for instance for enslaved foreign women or children.[99] The provisions for ex-slaves guarantee their freedom against seizure, but conditionally. Freedmen and freedwomen must continue to contribute labor to their former enslavers on terms, owe them deference, and their freedom from seizure is guaranteed by the intervention of citizen volunteer prosecutors—that is, dependent on the willingness of the community of the free to intervene for them. The threat of re-enslavement must have been a real possibility, as shown by Athenian law, where this terrible fate is the penalty inflicted on freedmen who neglect their duties to their former enslavers, along with foreigners who impersonate citizens.[100]

Even if women of all statuses did work for a living, they did so under heavy burdens—the enslaved and the freed having to surrender at least a proportion of their earnings and their work as rent; the free laboring under the costs of social disapproval, limited opportunities, the weight of gender norms and expectations, and lack of access to credit and institutions. They were potentially condemned to what S. Ogilvie (in the context of female work in early modern Germany) calls a "bitter living"[101] through lack of access to the institutions that protected adult male citizens from exploitation and lowered their transaction costs (above, chapter 17).

Conversely, the in-group of citizens could treat the excluded (the enslaved, the women, the strangers, the disenfranchised rural populations when present), like so much else in their world, as occasions to make profits and levy rent—as a form of stock. This (definitely non-Kantian and horribly non-Rawlsian) outcome is one of the consequences of the new economic history of the Greek city (above, chapter 17), and of the export of inequality and exploitation to the margins of the *polis*. The view of the *polis* as a world where civic virtue and the rule of law ensured low transaction costs and prosperity for all—as visible during the third and second centuries BCE but also, I have argued in the wake of D. Engels, in the Roman-era *polis*—thus has to be reframed. The *polis* worked as a mixed regimen guaranteeing, for an in-group of citizens, rights and benefits (notably from public goods and redistribution) and allowing differential access to those rights for outsiders, who provided surplus to the in-group. Instead of a system where liturgies and euergetism allowed a wealth elite to exploit the poorer members of the political community (a possibility I explored above), the *polis* might have been a social pact between rich and poor members of the political community to share the spoils of membership, partly levied off the excluded and made to fructify within protected spaces.

The outsiders were not condemned to passivity, but their attempts at collective action, I have argued above, ended up reinforcing the order of the *polis*. Women acting as benefactresses and even officeholders, visible in the Roman-era city, exemplify not so much economic and political agency on the part of women, as their role in promoting the visibility of elite households. They represent an attempt on the part of the elites to increase their influence in the competitive "tragedy of the elites" that constituted the political economy of the cities;[102] or indeed to try to escape this framework. Forms of associative life created a rich civil society (above, chapter 15), but when the subaltern spoke, we must wonder what practical influence their gatherings and decrees had in compensating for the inherent disadvantages of exclusion from the citizen group. Rather than represent a visible counterpower to citizen centrality, or an appropriation of *polis* discourse by excluded groups, the ubiquitous imitation of *polis* institutions throughout *polis* society reinforced the entitlement of the citizens, notably by rehearsing the hegemony of *polis* ideology and reaffirming the *polis*'s claim to morality as embodied in civic participation, public-mindedness and recognition (above, chapter 16).

For instance, a Rhodian association of foreigners and slaves honored one of its members with praise and a crown for fortitude when contracted to remove the corpse of a doctor and burying it (perhaps during an epidemic) and making sure by his persistence and his courage in the face of personal enmities (*apechtheia*) that members of the association paid their dues and debts. The monumental inscription, the fine civic language, and the homage it pays to brave Chrysippos, house-born slave of Merops, truly reaffirm the positive contents of civic discourse. Yet this statement cannot undo the absence of citizen status for all the actors involved. They can only try to claim a citizen-like dignity that *polis* institutions deny them but whose valence the Rhodian association of slaves accepts and desires.[103]

Spaces for agency (as in civil associative life) or negotiation (as in festivals or venues for the enslaved to bargain for better conditions) reinforced the world that the adult male citizens made.[104] Often the subaltern are left to celebrate their hard work and skill, or faithfulness to masters—that is, values reinforcing the *status quo*. The fifth-century BCE epitaph of Mannēs, a Phrygian, perhaps a denizen of an informal settlement of Anatolian workers in Attica, shows his pride in his work— "By Zeus, I never saw a better lumberjack than myself"—but also records his death as a victim of the Peloponnesian War, in whose outbreak he had no say.[105] In reaction, marginal cultural forms tried to give space for other voices than those assigned to the subaltern by the order of the *polis*. The tales concerning the biography of a fictional slave, Aisōpos, show an ugly, disfavored individual, whose sharp wits afford him agency in his relations with his dull master. The stories are preserved in mostly Roman-era versions, but go back to the early fifth century BCE. When runaway slaves created their own maroon society on third-century BCE Chios, under the leadership of one Drimakos, they organized it as a monarchy rather than along the lines of the participatory democracies from which they had only known exclusion and bitter exploitation.[106]

The articulation of ethical stances distinct from the moral and political economy of the *polis* points to the limits of the reach of *polis* institutions and civic society. In addition to the subaltern discourses mentioned above, one particular example is the elaboration of bodies of moral thought that we see happening within rabbinical Judaism or early Christianity, on the margins of the *polis* world and its harshness.[107] Likewise, the emergence of highly sophisticated literate cultures in non-Greek languages such as Syriac or Coptic, in conjunction with the spread of Christianity and generally of new debates about the supernatural and the self-fashioning of humans in their relations with both the supernatural and human communities, are developments that happen away from the communitarian, moralizing discourses and contexts of the *polis*.[108] Though the *polis* played a major role in reshaping the Roman Near East, the social and cultural histories of the Near East in Late Antiquity show the limits of civic culture, as was already noticed by A. H. M. Jones when he somberly concluded his survey of "the achievement of the cities" (below).

One function that associations could have fulfilled was to try to elicit patronage, and hence find access to institutional processes through personal connections with members of the group of citizens—that is, precisely the sort of hierarchical, unequal, and noninstitutional processes that the *polis* discouraged among its own members. These may have existed in spite of civic ideologies (above, chapter 18), but would particularly have operated in the margins of the *polis*. Such processes might have been favored by members of the wealth elite, in spaces where democratic institutions had a weak reach (as I speculated above), to try to achieve social power. Disadvantaged individuals could try to hustle their way to profit from patronage and ultimately to gain access to the protections of civic status, as illustrated by the case of the prostitute Neaira (enslaved since childhood but managing to buy her manumission) and her progress within fourth-century BCE Athenian society. Neaira's story receives a lurid retelling in a piece of surviving forensic oratory from a court case against her, but can be reconstructed as the biography of one individual trying to work her way past the exclusionary structures of *polis* society.[109]

It has perhaps not been emphasized enough that the quest for patronage and protection, and hence privileged access to institutional advantage, necessarily generated competition among the excluded, thus perpetuating inequalities between individuals or groups, hindering any form of solidarity, and hence again reinforcing the *polis* order. This outcome is explicitly attested in third-century BCE Athens, at a time of renewed democracy and autonomy for the city: a travelogue (see above) comments on the difference between the *Athēnaioi*, citizens of Athens, generous and hospitable, and the *Attikoi*, noncitizen inhabitants of the area, who are suspicious, untrustworthy, and ill-intentioned. The difference is not natural or inherent, but due to the distorting effect of citizen status.[110]

Polis and Justice/Injustice

The political theorist E. Isin describes the city as a machine producing difference. In the case of the *polis*, difference was the basis for exclusion. Were exclusion, and the concomitant possibilities of domination, the *raison d'être* of the *polis*? If in their own way oligarchies are communities of political deliberation and participation among their members (albeit often unstable, dwindling, and self-devouring), it is conversely true that even the most inclusive democratic *polis* is an oligarchy, in that it limits its inclusion and excludes the majority of its territory's inhabitants from membership and stakeholding, on fictitious grounds of descent rather than on economic criteria. This was applicable even to a small *polis* such as that of the island of Hērakleia, where the citizens felt entitled to take a public decision concerning "all the inhabitants."

The constitution of the in-group of stakeholders is predicated on their freedom; that is, their freedom from rule—but also their own freedom to rule, as noted in Aristotle's formal description of the *polis* throughout the *Politics*. As argued above (chapter 16), this foundational characteristic of citizenship manifests itself in participation in decision-making and dispute resolution—and in the wide distribution of actual "ruling" over equals in the form of officeholding, through the principles of collegiality, accountability, and rotation. But the freedom of citizens (their not-being-ruled) was reflected in their own ability to rule over others in their household: wives, children, the enslaved, the strangers (be they immigrants or "strangers within"). These were ruled in different ways but always permanently by the entitled members of the *polis*.

Hence propensity to rule was inherent to the *polis*. It is present in the early history of the *polis*, for instance in the closed polities that restricted citizenship to a small urban elite, undergirded economically by the labor of subordinate peasantry in the countryside, and politically by perioikic settlements or subject *poleis*. The new *poleis* founded by settlers (notably in the northern Aegean, the Black Sea region, the western Mediterranean, or northern Africa), which are an important part of the early development of the *polis* form, may have lived off the subordination of non-Greek, native populations by the Greek settlers, as proposed by G. Zuchtriegel (who studies closely the case of colonization during the fifth century BCE and specifically the case of Hērakleia in southern Italy).[111] An explicit link between the freedom of the enfranchised and the fact of ruling over others is given by the multiple senses of freedom in "Archaic" and Classical Sparta—control over a serf-like population, participation in politics, leisure to conduct political and military affairs, and (as a direct consequence) hegemony over others. The local imperialism of other *poleis* with subordinate populations in the northeast Peloponnese: Argos, Sikyōn, Epidauros, in Crete, or in Thessaly, probably rested on the same principles.[112]

The temptation to rule underlay the drive to hegemony that plagued the long history of the *polis*, culminating in a "Hundred Years' War," before developments in high political history ruled out this possibility. Down the centuries, the inherent association between *polis*-hood and rule over others explains why the *polis* form proved a reliable tool of large-scale statecraft and especially empire, as a linchpin of the reorganization of Macedonia under Philip II, as part of colonial rule by Hellenistic kingdoms (with whom it shared at least a linguistic and ethnic background), or as an extension of provincialization in the Roman Near East, where new *poleis* governed vast territories with the support and ultimately for the benefit of the Roman state (above, chapter 14).[113] J.-M. Bertrand boldly suggested that the *polis* of Priēnē ruled over the Plainsmen as proxies or representatives of supralocal imperial power, since the Achaimenids and Alexandros III levied tribute off the Plainsmen even as the latter were under Prienian control.[114] The *polis* was the serviceable tool for the subordination of populations that lost the support of supralocal empires, as in the case of the Jews, or of groups perceived as enemies of the established imperial order, such as Christians.[115] We have seen how the Roman-era *poleis* served enthusiastically as the enforcers of persecution against Christians, to gruesome effect.

In the Aristotelian ideal of the *polis*, the adult male citizen's capacity to rule over his household is linked with his capacity to participate, as a deliberating person, in politics—in decision-making, adjudication, temporary rule over other citizens, and control of the public goods produced for the commonwealth by extraction of revenue from the elite, economic transactions in the *polis* and common property. It is worth considering the relationship in the other direction. Participatory politics, namely shareholding in the enterprise of preserving freedom (from slave-like subjugation) and of creating a life in common (through public-mindedness and virtue politics), might have acted as alibis for domination, patriarchy, nativism, and enslavement, by proving the innate moral entitlement of the adult male born citizen to rule over others (women, foreigners, and the enslaved), to take their labor, and to treat them like stock. Of course, no culture is responsible for its subsequent reception, but it is at least suggestive that in early modern and modern North America, the slave-owning gentry of Virginia and the aristocracies of the Deep South claimed classical republicanism as a model, in which a small enfranchised elite enjoyed political rights while exploiting an enslaved and racialized workforce.[116]

Citizenship made domination possible, not just by rejecting domination and exploitation outside the circle of members, but by giving members an ideological justification for their power to exclude and to exploit: the "virtue politics" of the *polis* (above, chapter 16), apart from enforcing solidarity between rich and poor, also ensured their solidarity against outsiders. Participation in politics was conceived as natural to adult male citizens, the fulfillment of their human potential, the reflection of their public-minded character (as illustrated by civic discourse about good citizens). But it was participatory citizenship that entitled the husband of Lysistrata, in Aristophanes's play of the same name, to threaten her with violence at the moment when she tries to breach the separation: he broodingly returns from the Assembly, and ostentatiously—indeed violently—denies Lysistrata's right to find out what happened by raising a fist over her.

Putting a wife back in her place allows the adult male citizen to continue exploiting her labor in the household (notably for care and housework). Conversely, men's failure at politics threatens their entitlement and, in Aristophanes's topsy-turvy fantasies (*Lysistrata, Assemblywomen*), opens the path to women's power. One way to consider the ritualized activity of politics, so visible throughout Athens as in other *poleis*, is as a theatrical demonstration of the entitlement to rule over others. More broadly, a great deal of civic culture seems to need the Other, often enslaved, as justification and as purpose. The "normal type" of the gravestone showing man and wife using civic tropes of restraint and order (fig. 10.4) might also have celebrated the right to rule and exploit the enslaved whose bodies show their lack of suitedness for the life of the free. Aristotle writes that dealing with slaves lacked anything heightened or inspiring (*semnon*), unlike the noble purposes (*kala*) of politics and civic activities.[117] The citizen slaveowner's dictum rings as a disconcerting echo to H. Arendt's definition of politics as ennobling work among citizens who participate in a collective, grand enterprise.

Citizenship had more practical applications. In Marx's and Engels's description, the *polis* as state was primarily directed against holding down the slaves.[118] This function also inflected the relationships between *poleis*: the peace between Hērakleia under Latmos and Milētos (above) drew on the resources of peer-polity interaction to allow the resumption of normal exploitation of the enslaved by curtailing their possibilities to escape and by returning escapees back to their enslavers. The skyline of island *poleis* with their solid, ashlar-built towers (Hērakleia, but especially Seriphos and Siphnos, give examples) might have reflected the security of slave-owning citizens, feeling justified in their rights by their membership of political communities.[119] In this interpretation, the decree of the Herakleiotes, in its commitment to find a political solution to conflict (and here we should be willing to take the document at face value, without looking for hidden dimensions of power), might have comforted the citizen stakeholders in their awareness that they exercised power in a reasoned, participatory way, that justified their power over the excluded—female, enslaved, foreign. As I suggested at the start of this chapter, the grounded yet sublime beauty of the city of Priēnē (figs. 1.5, 10.4, 19.1) might have communicated the entitlement of the citizens (as members of a community whose transcendent bigness was made visible through the built environment)—and hence their advantages over the excluded (including the rural inhabitants).[120]

One further function performed by political community as foundational exclusion might have been to solidify the social pact between elite and mass. In earlier chapters, we have seen this pact cemented by virtue politics and locked in by a delicate bargain involving economic inequality, political equality, rent-seeking and rent-limiting, property rights, and communal claims on individual property. The constantly enacted and proclaimed exclusion of others from membership in the city, and hence from the social pact of the *polis*, created practical advantages for the entitled, but also the shared ideological good of entitlement itself. One question we must ask is if citizenship, exclusion, and othering fulfilled the role of strengthening the power of the local elites within their *poleis*, through a sense of privileges shared between the rich and the poor, defined as a community against excluded others: this sense of membership and solidarity might have been used by the elites to distract attention from rising economic inequalities and rent-seeking within the *polis*.

This function might have been all the more important with the end of armed conflict between the *poleis* (and hence the absence of external enemies to foster solidarity), and the increasing share of wealth seized by wealthy elites with the resources to participate in the economic growth that the good institutions of the *polis* fostered, especially once global connectivity supercharged exchanges in the Hellenistic period, then under the Roman empire. Such an analysis is clearly inspired by pessimistic views on modern politics in the ailing democracies of the developed world (especially the United States, where racial politics and culture wars have been instrumentalized by wealth elites and their political henchmen to obscure and distract from class conflict).[121] Does it help to understand the ancient Greek *polis*? In any case, it invites us to look for connections between the various social bads produced by the *polis*, in their complex connection with the latter's social goods.

Writing Histories of the *Polis*

What would the good *polis* look like? I have been tempted to point to the island world of Hērakleia, perhaps, as a community of citizens making conditions and solutions for the common life, or the spaces of the autonomous and democratic *polis* of Priēnē, if our gaze peoples them with citizens. We can imagine the citizens living in an urban center and solving common problems as part of a project of political freedom and equality. They appear to us working as free, property-holding members rather than as rent-producers for an elite; living an egalitarian political culture of citizen dignity, restraint, and solidarity around ideals of the public good; and exercising collective agency in interacting with other city-states and in resisting or bargaining with bigger imperial entities, thanks to force-multiplying peer-polity bonds and federal structures. Citizens do so by participating in effective democratic institutions and rules born of centuries of experimentation and diffusion, successfully constraining and embedding the wealthy within law and redistributive practice. These good institutions produce literal public goods that alleviate poverty in the *polis*. The *polis* works to channel the rational pursuit of interests within institutions that reinforced general welfare. Its prosperity comes from ideals and institutions; it is mostly based on free labor rather than slaves.

And what of the bad *polis*? In these last two chapters, I modeled the *polis* as inextricably bound with endemic bads: riven with violence upstream and downstream from political processes, a violent rather than restrained society; insidiously affected by elite power in controlling issues and outcomes; and foundationally based on mechanisms of exclusion (formal or informal), to the benefit of a privileged in-group of adult male citizens, an urban elite enjoying access to participation in state institutions, and benefitting from the protection that institutions generate. Bad *polis* is especially dependent on widespread enslaved labor at all levels of society.

We now can understand why the *polis* is so ready for complicity with imperial control and exploitation. This, too, could be a description of the island polity of Hērakleia (perhaps riven by conflict, controlled at a deep level by a small wealth elite, and dependent on enslaved labor for cash crops), or the *polis* of Priēnē, with its small citizen body, enslaved workers, and dependent countryside.

It is clear that the good *polis* is the result of a coherent set of relations between its various features: political ideals of equality and solidarity both facilitated and were reinforced by democratic institutions and the good economic institutions (for instance, by fostering trust and coordination). It is equally clear that the three great bads of the bad *polis* (violence, elite power, exclusion) were interconnected, dynamically but jaggedly. Violence was endemic as part of *polis* workings, generated by political processes; but it also existed because of the necessity to create and police the boundaries of exclusion, and was visited on the marginalized (women, enslaved people, and the freed, at least as threats). The prevalence of conflict among citizens may have made violence against the excluded more acceptable, a fortiori, but the endemic exercise of physical violence against the excluded might also have made citizens all the more ready for violence against each other. Such violence might have played an important part in the acquisitive power of great men. Furthermore, exclusion was foundational for solidarity among citizens, but also created the need for patronage among the excluded, and hence the conditions for informal elite power. The connections between violence, power, and exclusion were (perhaps unsurprisingly) marked by anomie and contradictions.

Good *polis* and bad *polis* coexisted, but what were their relations? A critical view of the *polis* is to view the good as directly founded on the bad, in relations of causal dependency. A. H. M Jones, at the end of his great survey of the post-Classical *polis*, ends with a despairing indictment (often forgotten nowadays) of the *polis*, an image of failure and tragedy, for not sharing the advantages of urban life and of civic institutions with those on its margins—the enslaved, the rural peasantry, the populations who did not have access to the codes of Greekness within which the *polis* expressed itself with such articulacy and force. The critique rests on a conviction of the importance and dignity of civic participation, and sorrow at their not being shared more widely (befittingly for the social-democrat Jones).[122]

More vigorously, N. Purcell, at the end of his groundbreaking essay on "mobility and the *polis*," delivered a sobering assessment:

> [t]he *polis* in general, we might say, was a cul-de-sac, an unhelpful response to the challenges of the Mediterranean reality, if building large and relatively harmonious and inclusive societies is considered a worthwhile goal.[123]

The essay appears in a volume edited by O. Murray and S. Price on the "archaic" and "classical" *polis* conceived as a prequel—a homage but also a methodological and theoretical challenge to A. H. M. Jones's treatment, which had appeared fifty years earlier. Murray and Price's volume is bookended by Purcell's essay and a paper by W. Runciman, which echoes Purcell in calling the *polis* "an evolutionary dead-end," because its democratic institutions made it unfit to respond to the high-political challenges of the late fourth century BCE. This whole book has argued against this view and proposed an alternative scheme of the *polis*'s durability as a political and social form; but it still has to sail into the headwind of Purcell's daunting critique.

Critiques of the *polis* as injustice and violence are reminiscent of certain strictures formulated within liberal political philosophy. Especially relevant are political philosopher J. Shklar's protests at the blind spots of liberalism, because of abstraction (as in the case of J. Rawls's theory of justice), because of excessive faith in the power of "natural" social manifestations of community (as in the case of M. Walzer's shared understandings), or because of a willingness to accept the exclusionary costs of Aristotelian-style *polis* citizenship (as in the case of H. Arendt). All of these neglect the dimensions of suffering and injustice involved in actual instantiations of their political models. In the two latter cases, Shklar specifically excoriates romantic investment in the *polis* (in the form of a "quaint obsession with Athens"; the present book runs the risk of merely replacing Athens with the *polis* from the third century BCE to the third century CE as an object of obsession).[124]

A metaphor of a conception of "good *polis*" being based on or the same as "bad *polis*" might be found in a short story by science-fiction author Ursula Le Guin. In her "psychomyth" *The Ones Who Walk Away from Omelas*, Le Guin presents a utopian city, whose perfect happiness is based on the mistreatment of one child, living an awful, squalid existence "in a basement under one of the beautiful public buildings of Omelas." All the adult citizens know of the child's existence, and that "their happiness, the health of their children, the wisdom of their scholars, the skill of their makers, even the abundance of their harvest and the kindly weathers of their skies, depend wholly on this child's abominable misery"; indeed, confronting this fact and viewing the degraded child are part of the privileged inhabitants' coming of age. But a minority chooses to leave the city rather than accept the foundation of their happiness and live with it.[125]

This metaphor for the *polis* remains, however, an image or emblem, however useful it is to help us start viewing the *polis* critically. Such a miserabilist metaphor is problematic in several ways. First, it might assign excessive causal force to contingencies and secondary complicities. The *polis* did not invent patriarchy, abuse, violence, sexual exploitation, enslavement, othering, disenfranchisement, which are world-historical phenomena (and are for instance visible in the pre-institutional, pre-*polis* world portrayed in the *Odyssey*, or in large empires such as the Achaimenid, or in extensive social organizations such as the Celtic warrior nations of Western Europe during the Iron Age). It is true that the *polis* was embroiled and complicit in these practices, in ways that reflected and affected the political structures of citizenship. My earlier survey argues that *polis* ideals and institutions were potentially transformational, explaining the history and the stability of the *polis* as a political and social form. Here I have suggested that the conservative, consensual, communitarian nature of its ideology, and the pragmatic force of its institutionalist bargain (between *dēmos* dominance and elite persistence) all meant that the *polis* could not achieve any radical transcendence of its general world-historical context of gender inequality or enslavement. *Polis* ideology, institutions, and social rituals merely underlined the limited reach of social justice when distributed among a group of stakeholders, who would shape slavery and exclusion in the image of their world.

Second, as a metaphor, "bad *polis*" merely mirrors, in critical fashion, the self-satisfied and strategic imagination of the adult male citizens as the sole beneficiaries of a political community based on exclusion. It is a useful reminder of the violence and anomie that the utopian, stylized language of institutions leaves out; but its claims of dialectical connections between bad *polis* and good *polis* are complicated by the fictional nature of both. The realities of the *polis* might be less tragically simple, and the connection between goods and bads multiple and differential. This does not mean that we should reintroduce an image of the *polis* as ordered by multiple statuses or associative groups, an interpretation that I have argued against on institutional and Aristotelian grounds. But it does mean that the *polis* of institutions existed in close connection with another world, which took various forms. It appeared as the *polis*'s residue, its margin, its shadow, its double. It existed in the interstices and on the margins of public institutional workings. This is how I understand D. Kasimis's insight that the excluded, the stranger, is in fact intimately part of the *polis*, despite the nativist fictions that modern political theorists (such as M. Walzer) have agonized over.[126] But the presence of the stranger is often as a repressed or occluded presence, whose traces or even whose return we have to learn to see in the *polis*'s fictional shadow.

In practice, we can start by looking again at the parameters of the *polis* as form. Above, I sketched out three elements of the "good" *polis*: institutionalism (in the sense of good constitutional design), idealism (in the sense of a virtue politics of the public good), and interests (in the sense of an enduring solution to collective action problems). I have also explored three bads—endemic violence, elite "three-dimensional power," and exclusion and its consequences. The specific intensity of these six historical vectors, and their interaction, determine the history of the *polis* in general, but also the particular shape that any one *polis* took in the course of time, in relationship with larger causal factors that they influenced in turn. They also will have to be taken into account as part of social and cultural histories in which the *polis* form figures, because of the constitutive impact of its concerns (stateness, agency, the travails of integration, structuration between city and country, the relations between mass and elite).

Day to day, the structures of exclusion admitted of compromises and negotiations in the operations of the developed forms of the *polis*. The democratic ideal of dignity and its incompatibility with lordly violence, in spite of the divide between entitled citizen and non-enfranchised slave, percolated to concern all human denizens of the *polis*, as shown by tentative protections given to the enslaved from wanton violence because of the attempt to limit outrageous violence and the sense of superiority it implied.[127] The effect is conveyed by vignettes from the fifth century BCE: the angry observation, in an antidemocratic pamphlet, that in Athens one cannot punch people in the street because he cannot tell free from slave; the rallying of enslaved laborers to the side of the people in the civil war on the island of Kerkyra, in the knowledge that rule by a small group of the wealthy was simply worse for everyone.[128] Democratic inclusiveness had general positive impacts on the *polis* (just as oligarchical exclusiveness ended up affecting negatively even the members of the small enfranchised circle). G. Kron senses that "the democratic social and political rights enjoyed by Greco-Roman citizens must surely have had innumerable subtle effects," in extending some degree of legal protection to the whole of *polis* society.[129]

Small decencies and gestures of humanity appear in *polis* culture. In late second-century BCE Priēnē, benefactors extended civic ritual (often in a private context) to foreigners, *paroikoi*, and slaves, reflecting a knowledge that these conditions were contingent rather than a reflection of inherent inferiority, thus rejecting Aristotelian "slavery by nature" as a constituent part of *polis* practice, if not necessarily of *polis* ideology. B. Gray has seen in these occasions and others (as documented especially in the civil decrees of the late second and first centuries BCE), a discovery of the possibility of *philanthrōpia*, love of humanity, in the *polis*, as the result of serious thought about the problems of exclusion and the possibility of remedying them without watering down civic participation and equality.[130] In the case of many decisions taken by the assembly of citizens affecting all the inhabitants (as already mentioned, as a reflection of exclusion and privilege), the professed motivation was concern for the welfare of the whole population, as in the case of Hērakleia where the citizens at least claimed to act for "the *koinon* of all those inhabiting the island." Just as citizen dignity, if conceived capaciously, extended beyond the limits of the citizen body, the ideal of the public good included *polis* as society. The citizen body in assembly could be animated with a sense of its representativeness and its responsibility—to the benefit of those citizens who could not attend, and generally of the non-enfranchised.

Finally, and most significantly, the citizen body might have been more porous than nativist ideology admitted. Even democratic, fifth-century BCE Athens, where the rule of bilateral citizen parentage was introduced as a condition for citizen birth, underwent such explosive demographic growth between 480 and 431 BCE that it is very likely that many strangers were admitted into citizen ranks, presumably from immigrants and freedmen.[131] The constant accusations of foreign descent among the Athenian elite might betray this open secret (to the point that E. Cohen has supposed that birth from two *resident* parents—*astoi* in the text of the citizenship law of 451 BCE—was sufficient for admission to the city body).[132] The story of Neaira, for all of its obscurities (due to the source, a vituperative court speech) might reflect the porosity of the citizen body, policed by court cases and family feuds rather than systematic bureaucratic efforts, since these lay beyond the stately resources of the *polis*. The ideology of nativism, precisely because it was a fiction—usually expressed in mythological terms of distant descent from founding heroes or deities, rather than the historical concept of a documented group of settlers—could cover a much messier reality of informal acceptance and infra-institutional admission.

The performative nature of the mechanisms of admission to the citizen body may have favored this outcome. Acceptance into the small subdivisions that constituted "civic society" but also regulated citizen intake at birth depended on persuasive performance and uptake; so did participation in the *polis* rituals and institutions that made citizenship visible and were one of the perks of citizenship. The remote countryman portrayed by Cocceianus Diōn in his essay on *polis* life, the *Euboicus*, seems to have no problem in just showing up and receiving his share in a distribution in town (typical of the Roman-era *polis*), nor in taking part in an assembly meeting. His knowledge of himself as citizen is never questioned.[133] Had he in fact been the son of a freedman or immigrant, his track record of participation would have constituted overriding signs of his citizen status. The citizen body was hence constituted by democratic institutions and their performative power to create realities, and by the successful performance of citizen identity. The performative model of citizenship, proposed by A. Duplouy, offered a path of acceptance through fictions and consensus.[134]

The process might have taken place in large *poleis* (because of the sizable population and difficulty of keeping track, especially if there was movement within the *polis* and its territory);[135] but also in small *poleis*, thanks to the willingness of face-to-face communities to admit members whom they agreed upon. The sale of citizenship, attested occasionally, might have acted as a guaranteed admission to the civic body, in contrast with messier, more protracted processes, a fast-track or VIP solution. In these conditions, it is possible that immigrants or their descendants, or descendants of freedmen, or rural inhabitants moving to the urban center, succeeded in getting themselves absorbed into the citizen body.

All of these possibilities do not quite dispel the cloud of pessimism that overhangs this chapter. A fringe of small decencies did not change the way in which exclusion was woven into the fabric of the *polis*. In fact, decency might have veiled exclusion and hence made it more palatable for the victims. Professed concern on the part of the citizens for the welfare of the whole population of the *polis* was potentially self-serving and might have covered the distorting realities of power and violence wielded by the in-group of citizens—in other words, it might merely have been another of the alibis of "bad *polis*." The real possibility of a porous *polis* did not change the existence of institutions and laws, their distorting effect on the marginalized, and the necessity for hustling and patronage among the margins. Yet these pessimistic interpretations, in turn, are not the only possible ones: the socializing and humanizing effect of ideals might have created eddies and countereffects to the strict workings of institutions, the self-serving ideologies of the citizens, and the violent, exploitative pursuit of self-interest by the enfranchised. This set of interferences represents the practical interactions between the different parameters of "good" and "bad" *polis* I outlined above, and another complication to the project of writing the history of the *polis*.

A striking illustration of the return of the social within an Aristotelian history of the *polis* is provided by the site of Priēnē, with which we opened this book, and indeed which we have revisited repeatedly. Recent soundings on the northern edge of the site, at the foot of the cliff face of Tēlōneia, have revealed an astonishing fringe of workshops, rock-cut installations, and strikingly atypical ritual gestures. This occupation left evanescent traces that contrast with the solidly civic, aesthetically refined and unitary city laid out against the slope in an orthogonal rhythm of public spaces and private housing, and made of cut stone, images, and inscriptions, all of which present a familiar, even archetypal face of the *polis* (fig. 1.3).[136] Who the occupiers of the fringe zone were is unknown, as are the precise dating and duration of the occupation of the zone: was it a temporary occupation, an area of workshops and labor for the citizens, or a shadow of the *polis* inhabited by a marginal population? The unusual ritual offerings admit of different interpretations: is their anomaly connected to immigration or to spheres of activity not represented in the main urban center? After the present *voyage au bout de la nuit,* the anti-Aristotelian, messy fringe to the beautiful city adds yet another layer of complexity to the *polis* of Priēnē and to the history of the *polis* more generally.

Fringes might even exist at the center of the *polis*. As we have seen, an extraordinary decree from second-century CE Tralleis extols ancestral decorum (*kosmos*) and represses sexual disorder in the form of prostitution and some activity described as "shamelessness" and "unspeakable violence (*hubris*)." The decree expresses great indignation at license taking place in public spaces such as streets, gymnasia, or even shrines, "as if vessels for lustral water did not exist, nor laws." The decree can be read as a reaffirmation, through the civic institutions of the assembly meeting and the decree, of the old norms concerning the body and personhood of the adult male citizen (the undescribed "shamelessness" must designate passive homosexuality or male prostitution). But it also shows the existence of transgression and otherness within "free spaces" created even at the heart of the *polis*.[137]

In the present book I have argued for the durability of the *polis* form and its concerns (stateness, agency, the travails of integration, the relations between mass and elite, structuration, and territory) because of their constitutive impact. Here I simply end by gesturing at how to extend this history to include social history or urban history in all its richness and contradictions,[138] while maintaining the premise of the present book (and specifically of its concluding chapters), namely that social history and urban history can only be understood if the political and institutional forms that constitute social spaces, directly and indirectly, are taken into account as crucial and even primary factors—the Aristotelian starting point of the *polis* and its history. The consequence is to take urbanization as a political phenomenon rather than just a bundle of lively social and economic interactions or, worst, just a material epiphenomenon of built environments in their impressiveness and durability.[139] The further consequence is that the study of the city is also about the promise of political forms and their impacts and costs.

PART VII
Polis of Our Wishes

20

Polis of Our Wishes

> The Middle Ages invented communal society without any precise information on the Greek *polis*.
>
> —U. ECO, *TRAVELS IN HYPERREALITY*

> There were literally hundreds of small Greek "republics" of city-states, nearly all with a council (*boulē*) and assembly (*ekklēsia*), stretching from the Black Sea to Spain, and lasting into the Roman Imperial period. And for that matter, apart from the Greek cities of Italy themselves, many of the other numerous non-Greek communities of Italy were also "republics" with constitutions. But in the canonical history of democracy, these worlds of small, self-governing republics have no place.
>
> —F. MILLAR, *THE ROMAN REPUBLIC IN POLITICAL THOUGHT*

HOW SHOULD WE TALK about the *polis*? My first impulse has been to launch into a straightforward narrative. The exercise in linearity seemed to me worthwhile, in that it allowed for the elaboration at some length of a revisionist and recentered story of the *polis*. Because it was necessary to select, among all the events in a long stretch of time, features that seemed salient and to account for their durability, their articulation, and their evolutions, my narrative at least had some analytical pretensions. The centre of attention has been power relations—between mass and elite, between big and small communities, between local community and empire—as mediated by institutions, discourse, and ideology. All these features might seem to belong to a political form, but also have social consequences that can be described in detail. The final picture was of a type of local community, organized as a republic with state-like powers, striving to preserve self-government down the ages, working out the consequences of popular government, and managing forms of justice within the political community, often at high costs for those outside that community's boundaries.[1]

The narrative section might be called the biography of a political and social form, because of my interest in formal institutions (in the sense of constitutional arrangements) as shaping power relations. By institutions, I mean decision-making venues and administrative bodies, but also such constitutive elements as civic space or territorial structuration. The biographical metaphor should not be pressed too hard: even though *poleis* were often represented as personifications or allegories (the *Dēmos*, the city's Fortune, or a patron deity), there was no conception of the *polis* as a collective body in the Hobbesian manner, though it is true that in lawsuits, a *polis* could speak and be addressed in the singular.[2] For instance, the *polis* of Thronion, in a written statement filed with the Delphic Amphiktiony in a dispute over the apportioning of delegates to that body, seems to address its opponent, the *polis* of Skarpheia:

> it is right that I should hold and control the share that is rightly mine, and that I should appoint the *hieromnēmōn* and send him, whenever it is my turn to hold the hieromnemonship. But you, city of the Skarpheians, you contest this with evil meddlesomeness and sophisms, and you wish to take over unjustly my share of the hieromnemonship . . .

In any case, the biographical metaphor really stands for the whole concept of *polis*, rather than the ability of individual cities to personalize themselves. In this context, the biological metaphor of birth, growth, and death is not quite welcome, since it implies a natural, preordained *telos* of perfection and decay, which I tried to avoid in my narrative, even when speaking of the great convergence or the disappearance of *polis* institutions. But the biographical metaphor has the advantages of representing the story of the *polis* as a unitary one, which has been the main postulate of this book, and its main problem.

The unitary nature of the *polis* form enabled a series of takes on the final picture (of republican agency, democratic government, differential social justice) that seemed to me to flow from the theses propounded in the narrative. I hence offered a restatement of the advantages (and disadvantages) of an Aristotelian focus on access to power (chapter 15); an idealist history of "virtue politics" (chapter 16); a new-institutionalist analysis of bargains and interests (chapter 17); a cynical history of violence and oligarchical manipulation (chapter 18); and a critical (and even hypercritical) history of citizenship as complacency, exclusion, and domination (chapter 19). These takes coexist uneasily. An idealist history of the *polis* and a new-institutionalist one are optimistic. They posit that the *polis* had the transformative power to convert individual interested actors into public-minded collaborative citizens—an optimistic explanation for the *polis's* rise and especially its diffusion across different social and economic setups, which it reshaped in egalitarian and democratic directions. Optimistic histories of the *polis* see the latter as an historically instantiated case of democratic polity generating just outcomes, without the destruction of the rich, and producing well-being.

In contrast, a pessimist history, in placing domination and exclusion at the heart of the *polis*, not only can explain the widespread adoption of *polis* forms by elites as just a cover for their power, but also threatens to alter our perceptions of *polis* democracy. The latter might just have been the practice of a small elite of shareholders, and the excluded might have been left vulnerable and exposed to the distorting effects of the polarity between inclusion and exclusion. The crucial question is whether the social bads in the *polis* were a product of its setup, or part of the givens of the premodern world in which it emerged. A realist coda to the history of the *polis*, on the question of whether injustices in the *polis* were inherent or contingent, leads to the realization that the *polis* could transcend neither its circumstances nor the paradoxes of inclusion and exclusion. But the realities of interaction may have been more humane and more complex than the pessimist storyline allows; political equality might have found ways to touch those outside its immediate circle, especially during the Hellenistic period (as posited by B. Gray). After the narrative sketch of the first part of the book, the last part thus tries to offer criss-crossing paths in the history of the *polis*, and parameters to evaluate different moments in this history.

All that remains to do now is the following. First, to examine the *polis* in its world-historical contexts, both ancient and post-ancient: a fragment of global history. Second, to trace the reception of the idea of the *polis* in modern times: a piece of intellectual history, often crossing paths with a political history of modern Europe. Third, to interpret the historiography of the *polis* in its intellectual and social frameworks: a further fragment of intellectual history, or of the history of ideas in various contexts, scholarly as well as social. These three projects each constitute well-established research topics in their own right, with their own literature and agenda. Here, at the end of this book, since there is no time and space left and I have no training in the daunting fields and specialisms involved, I would merely like to sketch out some possibilities in each direction, in the light of the findings I hope to have reached and unpacked on the way.

The first project, then, is a global history of the Greek *polis*, or rather a global comparative history of city-states, within which the Greek *polis* might fit. A major attempt at such a history has been attempted by the leader of the Copenhagen Polis Project and historian of the Greek *polis*, M. Hansen, to whose exhaustive *Inventory* the present book owes such a great debt.[3] It is clear that the ancient Greek *poleis* were city-states, and all together made up a city-state culture or civilization, as defined by Hansen. It surely stands to reason that it is equally interesting and important to look at other parts of the world and other historical periods, and to see if city-states and city-state cultures can be found (or not), according to an ideal type resting on rigorous definitions elaborated by Hansen, with twelve criteria for city-states, and fifteen criteria for city-state cultures. The criteria include small size, political authority flowing from self-governance or independence, territorial consolidation (with frontiers), and structuration around a central urban place, a politically stratified population, strong local identity, and connectivity with other similar entities. Hansen farmed out the analysis to forty-two specialists who were strictly kept within the limits of his checklist. The approach is the same as that of the Copenhagen Polis Project, which it complements.[4]

The findings of the Hansen-directed survey are suitably diverse: across world history there are many cases of city-states linked in a city-state culture, and other cases that do not fit the ideal type. In particular, the case of the Greek *polis* perfectly fits the ideal type, and "[a]ll other city-state cultures are dwarfed by the ancient Greek city-state," as Hansen observes at the start of his own contribution; the main contribution of city-state cultures to world history are republicanism and federalism—familiar concepts to the student of the *polis*, but leaping, in the modern period, from the micro-state to the level of the territorial macro-state. However, the satisfying nature of the findings might be a giveaway that they are preordained by the parameters of the enterprise, and that the definition of the city-state model is itself initially inducted from, or defined around, the forms of the *polis* itself; a reflection of the project's intellectual dependence on the Copenhagen Polis Project.[5] Hansen's comparative history simply poses again the problem of the specificities of the *polis* form within world history.

It is true that the early *polis* exhibited a diversity that fits well within the wide spectrum of city-state solutions surveyed in Hansen's comparative history. Internally, the early *polis* was organized along various internal sociopolitical arrangements (that could be as different as internal subordination, signorial rule, or broad democratic decision-making). Externally, relations between *poleis* could take different forms, such as competition between hostile independent peers, collaboration, integration in federal schemas, subordination, or integration within power structures. However, as Hansen observes, the *polis* developed into a highly unitary form, centered on the features mentioned above: territorial integration, an exclusive definition of citizenship with the concomitant features of external independence and internal equality (the evolution described above as the great convergence). In addition, the *polis* was constantly characterized by distinctive political institutions: the Assembly, the Council, and magistrates who rotated in and out of their limited powers.

The consequences are traced throughout this book: various social goods shared between stakeholders in the political community, and concomitant social bads. These practices, which emerged out of contingent historical conditions, proved remarkably suited for local flourishing and resilience. As such, the political economy and institutions of the *polis* may be considered as sustainable forms for small-scale, local polities. Their prevalence in the *polis* world, and their long-lasting adoption around the eastern Mediterranean, bears out their power. Indeed, as P. Veyne (1961) memorably writes (above, p. 330), the *polis* form exercised deep influence on the texture of the Roman empire itself.

The point of a global comparative history is not to determine or celebrate "the *uniqueness, priority* or *superiority*" of the *polis*, to borrow a declaration of principle from J. Ober's *The Greeks and the Rational* (2022). The history of the *polis* represents a discovery (and consolidation) of democracy, not *the* discovery of democracy. That forms of democracy have been found experimentally, again and again across the history of humanity,⁶ should warn us off seeing in the history of the *polis* an instantiation (or a causal factor) for the supposed "Greek miracle" (of rationalism, philosophy, and so on), or a proof of Greek genius, as part of the history of the West and its world-historical successes.⁷ In addition, the elements of a critical history of the *polis* raise the question of the imbrication of empowerment and injustice, the possibility of real decencies, and the potential of political ideas beyond specific social contexts. Finally, the *polis* was not immortal, in spite of its resilience, as shown by its disappearance in the Byzantine empire, which did not undergo a communal movement and had to draw republican inspiration from Rome rather than the *poleis* (above, p. 402). In other words, the point of comparison is at least partly the investigation of internal politics, the history of sociopolitical institutions, the evaluatin of their social impact and costs, and the study of the sustainability and ultimate fate of internal arrangements.

Among the diversities of global city-state history, forms centered on autonomy and popular government do appear frequently in ancient Eurasia. The ancient Near East saw small self-governing polities in fourth- and third-millennium BCE Sumer, and city-states in Mesopotamia during the Neo-Babylonian period in the first millennium BCE. The Levant knew self-governing cities in Phoenicia. In the city-states of Early Historic India, between the sixth and the third centuries BCE, communal decision-making and social negotiation are attested.⁸ The point of this observation is not to trace whether the *polis* was influenced by or directly imported from the ancient Near East, but to trace the circumstances favoring the emergence of self-governing small polities, and the factors shaping internal political developments.

Furthermore, familiar issues of local self-governance and social negotiation between mass and elite make an appearance in later contexts—for instance, in European history. The city-states of medieval and Renaissance Italy show concern with internal power distribution, fairness, communal glory, and the ethical dilemmas of political individual: all this is very reminiscent of the world of the *poleis*. (Indeed, I have occasionally drawn on material from this world to shed light on the concerns of the *polis*.)⁹ The communes of medieval Flanders or southern Germany offer further examples of self-governing, quasi-democratic city-states.¹⁰ In the history of some early modern European cities, local governance and social debate are central problems: particularly important is the case of Geneva, with its absence of patriciate and contested electoral system.¹¹ Modern municipal life, such as can be seen in prerevolutionary Provençal towns,¹² exhibits institutions that resemble *leitourgia* (for instance, selling grain below market price), and intra-elite strife reminiscent of the world of Cocceianus Diōn. The self-governing towns of early modern New England, those "peaceable kingdoms," illustrate the strict processes involved in local consensual decision-making (above, p. 455).¹³ I have often drawn on these cases for parallels, but all of them, from twelfth-century Italy to seventeenth-century Massachusetts or eighteenth-century Provence, cannot be shown to be directly descended from the world of the ancient city, let alone the *polis*. There is no direct link between the ancient city, let alone the *polis*, and other forms of city-state life in European history or world history.[14] Discontinuity only sharpens the questions of emergence and development for the city-state form.

The question for global-historical perspectives on the *polis* is whether its emergence and development are contingent events, or represent structurally determined outcomes, or at the very least recurring possibilities for small-scale polities, as alternatives to any "natural" state of predation—the "early state" or more generally social organizations predicated on the dominance of violent elites.[15] The European examples show that *polis*-like structures can emerge and evolve out of local interactions between elite families and between town and country; yet the potential fragility of such structures is illustrated by the relatively rapid failure of the communal movement in Italy, where a signorial turn displaced the popular regimes, or by the incapacity of Italian civic oligarchies, consumed by class warfare and self-interest, to resist imperialism.[16] The failure of early quasi-democracies (to use S. Muhlberger's expression) in India further illustrates this point. The comparatively long and stable history of the *polis* after the great convergence hence raises the same questions about contingency and structure as its emergence.

Such questions are not unrelated to our hopes and fears about the possibility of democracy in the contemporary world, and our anxieties about whether democratic decencies are intrinsically linked to exclusion (below, p. 550). To write about the *polis* in a world-historical context requires combining the interest in power shown by historians of democracy (often relying on secondhand accounts) with the empirical mass of testcases gathered by Hansen's survey, beyond the latter's narrow parameters, while keeping at arm's length the celebratory temptations of the "Greek miracle," the ministrations of students of political thought invested in the story of freedom and equality (often as corollaries of celebrations of the West), and the desire to directly address the anxieties of the modern world. The challenges are of course the same as those involved in writing the history of the *polis* more generally.

The issue of discontinuity further raises the question of the reception of the *polis* as idea, which is the second project outlined above. As is clear in the case of the Italian communes, no direct continuity of institutional practice leads from the *polis* to European political history, the rise of the West, or modernity; and no clear path leads from Marathōn to modern democratic nation-states. Nonetheless, after the end of the ancient world, a particular set of cultural artifacts from the history of the *polis* was present during the history of western Europe. These included theoretical but moralized disquisitions on politics such as those from Plato, Aristotle, or Polybios, historical accounts written by Thucydides, or the moralizing biographies by Plutarch. The canonical nature of these texts (already selected, studied, and curated in antiquity), their explicit or implicit theoretical bent, their assumed factuality, and their often exemplary nature made them particularly suitable for study and interpretation. In addition, ancient art added usable tropes for moralizing reflexion. In other words, the stories, versions, and images that the *polis* gave of itself, notably because of the centrality of virtue politics, were read and scrutinized—by whom and to what effect?

It is important to bear in mind that these artifacts were consumed differentially, and in a variety of contexts, which covered the spectrum from progressive and revolutionary to absolutist and reactionary, and always on the scale of the whole European continent. Classical culture was never just about the Greek *polis*, since it included artifacts from ancient Rome (a quasi-democratic republic that underwent an autocratic revolution and transitioned to a world empire);[17] in addition, the entities of reception were themselves diverse in scale from city-states to kingdoms to large territorial states. Any history of reception that reduces the classical heritage to the story of republican government is too restricted and misleading. Classical culture was selectively reworked and put to perfectly effective use as the celebration of monarchy and hierarchy, in myriad forms from the Renaissance and early modern festivals studied by Roy Strong (1984) to the intellectual essays of the nineteenth-century reactionary thinker Joseph de Maistre.

But inevitably, some encounters with the Classics did lead to the *polis*. The story of these encounters, from the Middle Ages to modernity, exceeds the scope of the present book by far.[18] To be precise, it might be said (judging by contemporary work on the topic) that these encounters were constituted by a number of filters and addressed a specific form of the *polis*. First, the latter is largely simplified to focus on Athens and Sparta during the "Classical" period because of the survivals of the literary canon (including narrative history and philosophy as well as cultural masterpieces). Second, its study is largely mediated by the discipline of philosophy, and approached through the authorial category of "great Greek thinkers" (usually Plato or especially, Aristotle, available in a Latin translation since the mid-thirteenth century), whose thought can be combined or contrasted with the Roman history of Livy (especially the earlier books, devoted to a fictionalized narrative of the rise of the Roman Republic). Third, the study of Greek political philosophy thus constructed is further situated in particular historical contexts and debates. The *polis* as an object of study was constantly rethought in new contexts yet also passed on for further elaboration within a chain of interpretations by modern thinkers, such as Machiavelli or Montesquieu, Hobbes or Harrington, who reelaborated ancient ideas on issues of governance. Modern thinkers, as an interpretive community, collectively wrote an intellectual or philosophical history where the *polis* figured in various, often contradictory guises.

In these conditions, the encounter with the *polis*, focalized on Athens, mediated through antidemocratic "great thinkers," often took the form of suspicion against democracy as practiced in the *polis*, namely direct democracy with a strong element of class antagonism, so that historically grounded forms of representative government could be thought of as explicitly antidemocratic, moderate, and safe from the perceived excesses and tumults of popular government. And yet early-modern antidemocratic or even authoritarian authors were well aware of the durable power of "popular" conceptions of power, as Hobbes noted with characteristic sarcasm:

> In these westerne parts of the world, we are made to receive our opinions concerning the Institution, and Rights of Common-wealths, from Aristotle, Cicero, and other men, Greeks and Romanes, that living under Popular States, derived those Rights, not from the Principles of Nature, but transcribed them into their books, out of the Practice of their own Common-wealths, which were Popular; as the Grammarians describe the Rules of Language, out of the Practise of the time; or the Rules of Poetry, out of the Poems of Homer and Virgil. And because the Athenians were taught, (to keep them from desire of changing their Government,) that they were Freemen, and all that lived under Monarchy were slaves; therefore Aristotle puts it down in his Politiques, (lib.6.cap.2) *In democracy, LIBERTY is to be supposed: for 'tis commonly held, that no man is Free in any other Government.* And as Aristotle; so Cicero, and other Writers have grounded their Civill doctrine, on the opinions of the Romans, who were taught to hate Monarchy, at first, by them that having deposed their Soveraign, shared amongst them the Soveraignty of Rome; and afterwards by their Successors. And by reading of these Greek, and Latine Authors, men from their childhood have gotten a habit (under a false shew of Liberty,) of favouring tumults, and of licentious controlling the actions of their Soveraigns; and again of controlling those controllers, with the effusion of so much blood; as I think I may truly say, there was never any thing so deerly bought, as these Western parts have bought the learning of the Greek and Latine tongues.
>
> (HOBBES, LEVIATHAN, 2.21.9).

What relationship between the *polis* of the early modern philosophers and the historical *polis* as has been studied in the present work? At least, the modern "philosophical history" of the *polis* offers a point of comparison, to sharpen historical understanding of the ancient models, and facilitate better grasp of the operations of modern receptions.[19] On occasion, the world of the historical *poleis* could make a surprising appearance in modern debates, as in the case of the Lykian League, described by Strabo using Artemidōros's account of the league ca. 100 BCE, in its heyday during the Indian Summer of the *poleis* (above, p. 268 and generally chapter 11): Montesquieu's praise for Lykian federal institutions (in *L'esprit des loix* (1748)) drew the attention of James Madison, and they are discussed seriously in the *Federalist Papers*, specifically no. 9 (1787) and 45 (1788). It is pleasing, at the end of this book, that proportionality in the US House of Representatives was inspired by the ancient Greek *koina*, and specifically the practice of one regional league during the second-century BCE "Indian Summer" of the *poleis*, in an arrestingly precise echo from the real history of the *polis*.[20] A reminder of the more usual idealizations found in the "philosophical" history of the *polis* can be found in the note sent (on a Friday) by the French revolutionary Hérault de Séchelles, asking the curator of printed works at the *Bibliothèque Nationale* for help in drafting the Constitution of 1793:[21]

> 7 June 1793, year II of the Republic
>
> Dear fellow-citizen,
>
> Since I am tasked, alongside four colleagues, to present a plan for the constitution on Monday, I would like to ask you, in their name and mine, to furnish us immediately with the laws of Minos, which must be in a collection of Greek laws. Our need is urgent.
> Hérault.
> Greetings, friendship, fraternity to the worthy citizen Desaulnays.

However, the actual historiography of the *polis*, as an object of antiquarian and historical enquiry,[22] is deeply involved with the contexts of its production and hence itself a form of reception. Paradoxically, research on the *polis* appears after the disappearance of the actual city-state in Europe and the end of the oppositional dynamic between large supralocal state and local community, a dynamic which strongly recalled the confrontation between *polis* and empire throughout the former's history.[23] The Swiss thinkers Constant, Sismondi, and Burckhardt write at a time when their native city-states were being subsumed into the federal nation-state of Switzerland (above, pp. 487–88). What is clear is that the *polis*, characterized by its concern with citizenship and the internal balance of power within community, served as a proxy for debates on the nature of the nation-state and its government, especially representative democracy (even though representative government had explicitly been defined against *polis*-style direct democracy). This may hold as true for the radical British historian G. Grote, author of a vast history of ancient Greece in which democracy and Athens occupy the forefront, as for the French Republican Fustel de Coulanges, the author of an anthropological history of *The Ancient City* but also of an essay on Polybios and the end of Greek freedom.[24] Hence, no doubt, a particular interest in the biggest players among the *poleis*, especially Athens and Sparta during the Classical period, which could serve as vehicles (more or less explicit) to think about the fates of the great powers,[25] with especial interest in the case of complex nation-states formed out of regions and, indeed, the ruins of city-state cultures, such as Germany or Italy.[26]

Furthermore, the *polis* could also serve the nineteenth-century West as a medium to think about empire, colonialism, and race. The easy assumption of affinity between the Western nation-states and the *polis* facilitated this function; the Greek *polis* figured as a proxy for the rational and civilized, in contrast with the barbarian and the sub-political, as evidenced by the inferior form of sociopolitical organizations based on empire and village. The dichotomy is made explicit in Jouguet's study of municipal life in Egypt (1911), contrasting Greek town and Egyptian village, but also underlies the Orientalist contrast between city and despotic state in Max Weber.[27] Such strictures may be echoed in the image of the "Oriental," "Islamic" or "Arab" city as depoliticized and fragmented, as opposed to the rational, democratic *polis* taken as the implicit ancestor of the Western nation-state and its capitalist order.[28]

What about the present work? The account in this book was written in an inductive mode, so that I hope that the whole of my account is not simply a reflection of contemporary politics, especially in its deliberate focus on the post-Classical period and the documentary and material archive of *polis* life. In other words, I hope that exemplification does not serve the purpose of creating the effect of the real when an early modern-style focus on Plato and Aristotle no longer suffices. Yet it may not have been able to wholly avoid adopting a wishful mode, even within the space left by the avoidance of the celebratory tropes of the "Greek miracle" or the "Western tradition." At the very least, the main focuses in this work can be viewed in the light of contemporary concerns and debates—namely, a history of the *polis* as that of the relations between mass and elite on the one hand (and hence, a story of political equality and democracy); a history focused on the relations between city and empire (and hence on the conditions of local freedom); and finally, a critical history about the costs of exclusion and the need to confront them honestly.

On the first theme, namely the right form of political economy between mass and elite, the context stretches over the decades of the late twentieth and early twenty-first centuries, and includes the following watersheds. First, the failure of communism in 1989 and the glimpsed possibilities of a Fukuyamesque future characterized by liberal democracy. Second, the concomitant neoliberal movement and its suspicion of the State in the absence of the threat of communism (and subsequently, the opportunities for acquisitiveness and rent-seeking in the absence of the state). Third, the crisis of neoliberalism, heralded by the long-standing financial crisis of 2008 and the following decade; and fourth (and most urgently), the attempts to think of an alternative to neoliberalism ever since that moment. Within this contemporary context nests an anxiety about the possibility of a working economic order based on equality and about the possibility of democracy at all in the face of factionalism and plutocratic capture.

It is entirely fitting that J. Ober's transformational *Mass and Elite*, on the political economy of Classical Athens but also (I have argued in this book) relevant to the history of the Greek *polis* in general, appeared in 1989, the year of the fall of the Berlin Wall. In the more recent nexus of events and ideas, some of the impulse toward this book came from the new-institutionalist effort to show that Athenian and generally *polis* democracy were economically viable or even optimal solutions (Ober 2010), but also from the question of whether T. Piketty's ideas on the connections between politics and economic equality and inequality (2013) might help understand the ancient world.[29] The role of the state, the provision of public goods, the possibility of democracy in the form of control over elite power and of effective redistribution of elite wealth, the risk of elite capture of institutions, the problem of how to make the wealthy contribute a fair share to common social and political projects, are familiar topics of contemporary contention but also structure my analytical narrative.

Furthermore, the relationship between *polis* and empire, the second major theme of this book, may have taken on a greater poignancy in new post-modern conditions in which the nation-state itself is dwarfed by a few superpowers (China, the United States) or even transnational forces (the global corporation, globalization), even while other structures possibly sustain the nation-state (the European Union, perhaps?) or encourage the renaissance of smaller polities at the regional or even urban level. Local forms of citizen power take on new interest in this context, as well as the question of the suitability of the nation-state as the *locus* for a just social bargain (of the type swept away by the neoliberal revolution) or its problematic nature as the instrument for class interests.[30] It may be significant that the engagement with local geography and the archive of particularism that emerges from the many *poleis* that inscribed their affairs has been a specialization in modern European scholarly traditions—in Germany and Italy, as well as France and Great Britain, in countries that have grappled with problems of federalism national and supranational, as well as their own places within the post-modern world order. These countries have also a tradition of social democracy and municipal government, which could further account for their interest in successful democratic practice on a small scale. Of course, particularism, social democracy and municipal government also characterize a small north European country—Denmark, to the point that Fukuyama associated successful social democracy with "getting to Denmark" (though the failure of municipal urbanism in modern Aalborg offers a cautionary tale: above, p. 492). It is also the country where M. Hansen worked—the specialist in Athenian democracy in its institutional workings, and animator of the great Copenhagen Polis Centre that focuses on diversities and unities of the *polis* form, and which this book largely responds to.[31]

Finally, the interrogations, in the latter part of the book, about violence and especially exclusion, mirror contemporary interrogations not just about the feasibility of democracy and economic redistribution but of its hidden costs, and of the possibility of pluralist democracy centered on social and racial justice rather than the ethnodemocracy model that may have undergirded twentieth-century social democratic ventures, and which offers such an uncomfortable parallel to the exclusivist, nativist practices of the Classical *polis*.[32] It may not be a coincidence that the relevant chapters in this book grew while I worked and lived in the United States after 2015, at a time when the fragility of institutions and even democracy itself seemed tragically apparent, and in a general context of slow *stasis* in the United States and, by echo and imitation, in the United Kingdom. Yet the idea emerged earlier, in the late 1990s, while working on the Hellenistic *polis* (notably in France) at the start of the rise of far-right populism as a political force. These half-hearted attempts at the biography of this book, combined with timid introspection verging on *égo-histoire*, are as sketchy as the other elements of intellectual history offered here, and their uncomfortably allusive nature may make them rapidly incomprehensible for future readers. They only represent a first sense of the situatedness of the venture.

At least, the final exercises in doubt, born out of admiration for more radical social histories of the *polis* than that proposed in this book (I singled out the essay by J.-M. Roubineau), have the advantage of countering the risk of utopianism in a history of the *polis* (as visible in idealist accounts of the *polis* by figures such as Castoriadis or Vernant, which were all too willing to celebrate, reflexively, the *polis*'s uniqueness and its status as ancestor to the West: above, chapter 16). My general model of the *polis* as political and social form might prove useful, if only as an exemplification of political ideas and discourses which can be, and have been, studied and used independently of their precise historical context (even though those who applied these ideas were not always aware of the abstract nature of the exercise).[33] But its claim to historicity requires constant confrontation with its correctives. These can take the form of a subjunctive history or a critical one—or perhaps, more simply, the willingness to revisit the many examples and moments that this book is inductively built upon.

An effort to recalibrate the master narrative of the *polis* and perhaps of ancient history more generally, might see documents and incidents not just as exemplifications of broad schemes and phenomena, but also as one-off dramas that represented active choices within the possibilities of the *polis* form. This might hold true even for strongly normed interactions such as the honoring of the gymnasiarch M' Salarius Sabinus at Lētē in the time of Hadrian, or the reorganization of the urban plan of Priēnē in the late second century BCE, or the meeting of the citizens of the island *polis* of Hērakleia to decide on the contentious matter of refraining from raising goats. This history, too, is never quite free from desire: the paean to "the sovereign city-state" in history by G. Parker, while never flinching from the conflict and exploitation inherent to city-state cultures, celebrates the city-state as vibrant, organic, natural, sustainable, and especially nonideological—a contrast, a refuge, from the modern nation-state and its harshness.[34] Perhaps at the end of this book I might allow myself a measure of cautious sympathy for the forms of the *polis*, since their story is one of the possibilities of stable democracy born of political equality and social bargains; but I can only do so in full awareness of the social bads that accompanied these goods.[35]

As an example of the temptations and difficulties involved in studying the *polis*, we might turn to the French traveler and philosopher Volney. Constantin-François Chasseboeuf (to give him his birth name) visited the ruins of Palmyra in 1784. *Les Ruines*, his very long (and now rather forgotten) treatise on history, religions, and civilization (among other topics), published in Geneva in 1791, starts in that setting.[36] Sitting on a column drum at sunset, surveying the ruins from the heights above the western cemeteries, the author contrasts the populousness, prosperity, and material splendor of this ancient city with the present

FIGURE 20.1. Sunset over Palmyra (frontispiece of Volney, *Les ruines*, 1826 edition).

FIGURE 20.2. Sunrise over Irakleia. Photo by Z. Tankosic.

desolation. I remembered Volney when describing the creation of the *polis* of Palmyra within the Roman empire as a social organism but also as a prosperous, integrated territorial unit (above, pp. 377–87). Volney's comparison of the desolation of the Orient with the prosperity of the West (starting with his own country, the military, mercantile, and colonial power of France), leads not to colonialist celebration but to a fearful meditation on a possible future when the West will undergo a similar decline and fall. His melancholy thoughts are interrupted when an actual ghost or specter appears to lecture him on the causes of prosperity and decline: they lie not in destiny, nor in divine favor or ire, but in all too human and social causes (which the specter then lectures on at inordinate and, to be frank, not always illuminating length: fig. 20.1).

These, too, are thoughts I bore in mind as I related the prosperity of Palmyra and its territory to its adoption of *polis* forms, institutions, and discourses (above, pp. 387–97; not based, alas, on any visit to the site of modern Tadmur). But for my part, I fear no evening specter came to lecture me on the nature, meanings, and pitfalls of the *polis*—in the colonnaded streets of Palmyra, on the wooded ridges or the rich plain of Lētē in Macedonia, across the stern slopes that dominate the orthogonal urban site of Priēnē, or on the island of Irakleia at the hill of Kastro (modern toponym), which probably was the urban center of this microscopic city-state above its harbor. In the end, the determination of the meaning of the *polis* in world history, and of the best way to study the *polis* in time between the idealism of institutions, the violence of social forces, and the desire of the modern observer, is not through revelation, illumination, or haunting, but through political work.

ABBREVIATIONS

REFERENCES TO GREEK INSCRIPTIONS in published *corpora* follow the list of abbreviations (itself abbreviated as *GrEpiAbbr*) proposed by the *Association Internationale d'Épigraphie greque et latine* (*AIEGL*), in its January 2022 iteration, as can be found online at time of writing: https://aiegl.org/grepiabbr.html

BE
Bulletin Épigraphique, published yearly as part of the *Revue des Études Grecques*; cited by year and rubric number.

CT
Hornblower, S. 1991–2008. *A Commentary on Thucydides.* Oxford.

FGrH / *BNJ*
Jacoby, F. 1940. *Fragmente der griechischen Historiker.* Berlin.
Succeeded by:
Worthington, I., ed. 2007. *Brill's New Jacoby.* Online corpus.

IACP
Hansen, M. H., Nielsen, T. 2004. *An Inventory of Archaic and Classical Poleis.* Oxford.

Pack²
Pack, R. *The Greek and Latin Literary Texts from Greco-Roman Egypt.* 2nd Edition. Ann Arbor.

PAT
Hillers, D., Cussini, E. 1996. *Palmyrene Aramaic Texts.* Baltimore.

PCG
Kassel, R., and Austin, C., eds. 1983–1995. *Poetae Comici Graeci.* Berlin.

RPC
Burnett, A. M., Amandry, M., and Ripollès, P. P. 1992–. *Roman Provincial Coinage*. London and Paris. Also available as part of *Roman Provincial Online* project at Oxford University: https://rpc.ashmus.ox.ac.uk

RS
Crawford, M., ed. 1996. *Roman Statutes*. London.

SH
Lloyd-Jones, H., and Parsons, P. 1983. *Supplementum Hellenisticum*. Berlin.

Robert, *OMS*
Robert, L. (1969–1990). *Opera Minora Selecta. Épigraphie et antiquités grecques*. 7 vols. Amsterdam.

Wilhelm, *KS*
Wilhelm, A. *Kleine Schriften*. 1974–2008. Leipzig, then Vienna.

The title above is one recently given to a series of volumes gathering Wilhelm's writings, under different titles according to original publication. The relevant volumes in this book are:

1.1 *Akademieschriften zur griechischen Inschriftenkunde*, vol. 1, edited by W. Peek, Leipzig, 1974.
1.3 *Akademieschriften zur griechischen Inschriftenkunde*, vol. 3, edited by W. Peek, Leipzig, 1974.
2.1 *Abhandlungen und Beiträge zur griechischen Inschriftenkunde*. vol. 1, edited by W. Peek, 1984.
2.4 *Abhandlungen und Beiträge zur griechischen Inschriftenkunde*, vol. 4, edited by G. Dobesch, Vienna, 2002.

NOTES

Chapter 1. In Search of *Polis*

1. Delamarre 1902. The report of the findspot, by Delamarre ("the garden of a monastery" in the northeastern part of Irakleia, 1860) is misleading, since there is no monastery on the island (Ross 1843, vol. 2, 34–35; Gavalas 2010, especially 67–87). The stone likely came from one of two plots owned and directly exploited on Irakleia by the monastery of the Panagia Chozoviotissa on Amorgos (hence the garden *belonged* to the monastery). These plots (Docharies, Karpazas) are located at Livadi near the ancient site (Kastro), in the northeast of Irakleia: Gavalas 2010, 85–86, 204. On Delamarre's work on Amorgos, Haussoullier 1910 (more precise than *IG* 12.7, p. ix). The stone is now kept in the Archaeological Museum of Chora (Amorgos) with the rest of the Ioannidis collection, rediscovered by L. Marangou (as A. Matthaiou kindly tells me).

2. *IG* 12.7.509 (with *IG* 12 suppl. p. 146); Robert 1940–65, vol. 7, 161–70 (discussing the evidence of the travelers, esp. L. Ross); Chandezon 2003, no. 35, excellent, whose text I follow. Note the following: line 4: read βιαζόμενος as in *IG* 1.³ 256, line 9 (Ma 2012, 151–52)? Line 12 Ἐπιστροφίδης on stone.

3. The expenses incurred in trial might be court fees (perhaps even compensation for jurors in a popular court), or the deposit required from the parties to litigation (Chandezon 2003 *ad loc.*); on such fees, Migeotte 2014, 315–16.

4. Noted by P. Roussel 1911, 452–53, with older bibliography. On the formula, Swoboda 1890, 6–8; Wilhelm 1909, 180 (budgetary allocation) and *KS* 2.1, 247–48; Gschnitzer 2001–2003, vol. 2. 153–64 (the formula gives the decree priority over other decisions); Boffo 2011 (privileged category of decrees, classified as such; updates Gschnitzer's list). To Gschnitzer's and Boffo's lists, add *SEG* 60.760 (at Dionysopolis, in the Black Sea, decrees concerning the safety of the city are valid with immediate effect).

5. Robert 1940–1965, vol. 7, 161–70, drawing on the seventeenth-century French traveler Pitton de Tournefort; the same picture appears in the fifteenth-century traveler Cristoforo Buondelmonti, who saw multitudes of goats (Buondelmonti 2018, 21r). The island, though much threatened by piracy, still had inhabitants until 1701, by which time the various holdings had been gifted to the monastery of the Panagia Chozoviotissa on Amorgos: Slot 1982, 31; Borromeo 2004, 130 (based on reports from Jesuit missionaries in the seventeenth-century Cyclades; also Borromeo 2007, 912, 935, 946–47, 1042); Gavalas 2010. 63–65.

6. Gavalas 2010, 67–101; earlier, Kolodny 1974, vol. 1, 262–67, on the harsh agrarian history of the Small Cyclades, and vol. 2, 655–57, on the slow liberation of the sharecroppers on modern Donoussa, a neighbor of Irakleia.

7. So Roussel 1911, 450–55, followed by Robert 1940–1965, vol. 7, 161–70.

8. Constantakopoulou 2007, 205–14; 2012, 308–20; 2015; Fröhlich in *BE* 2013, 327. On associations, Fröhlich and Müller 2005; Taylor and Vlassopoulos 2015.

9. Robert 1966a, 89–90; *ISE* 2.99, lines 14–15 (also Migeotte 1984, no. 30): a decree of Krannōn (early second century BCE) is expressed with the formula "it seemed good to the *koinon* of the city" (*edoxe tou koinou tas polios*, in Thessalian dialect).

10. *I. Magnesia* 98.

11. Halstead and Jones 1989; Halstead 1996; Halstead 2014.

12. On traditional agriculture on the island, Kolodny 1974, vol. 2, 655–57 (parallel case of Donoussa); Connell 1980; Gavalas 2010 generally. The hypnotic documentary *Express Skopelitis* (2020), by Aimilia Milou, gives a sense of actual conditions in the Small Cyclades. For archaeological and historical research on the island, as well as its geography, in addition to Ross, Robert, Chandezon, quoted above, see Philippson 1959, 144–45; Philaniotou 2006; recently: Mavridis, Tankosić and Kotsonas 2018 (early occupation in cave to the west of the island). I regret not being able to take into account in this book the work of the *Small Cyclades Project*, as explained at https://smallcycladicislandsproject.org, notably on Irakleia.

13. Wiegand and Schrader 1904; *I. Priene*; Schede 1964; Raeder 1984; Rumscheid 1998; Rumscheid 2006; *I. Priene B-M*; Raeck, Filges and Mert 2020 (with a survey of recent research); *IACP* no. 861. On the reconstruction by the architect J. A. Zippelius, see the explanatory note by Wiegand 1910 and the interpretive, contextualizing essay by Kockel 2012.

14. *I. Priene B-M*, index, "πόλις: passim." Priest: *I. Priene B-M* 144, 146–49.

15. Fehr 1980; Hoepfner and Schwandner 1994, 188–225. Generally, Schede 1964; Rumscheid 1998.

16. Debates and new evidence in Raeck, Filges and Mert 2020.

17. Wiegand and Schrader 1904, 7–37 (esp. 28–31) and Plate I; Philippson 1912, 93–97; Thonemann 2011; Lohmann et al. 2014; Lohmann et al. 2017.

18. Gauthier 1988; Bertrand 2005a; Kah 2012 (on Priēnē, agnostic on the exact definition of *paroikoi* as opposed to *katoikoi*); and see pp. 510–17.

19. Magnetto 2008; on the importance of a continental territory for Samos, Carusi 2003, 212–16.

20. Ma 2003a.

21. Robert, *OMS* 1, 327–31; Perlman 1995; Rigsby 1996; Perlman 2000a (in the Peloponnese); *IACP*, 103–6; nuanced treatment in Raynor 2016 on the use of the *theōrodokoi* lists for Macedonia.

22. Papazoglou 1988, 213–15; Psoma 2006 denies the coinage to Lētē. On the site (above the actual village of Laina, north of Thessaloniki rather than at the village of Aivatli, renamed Liti in modern times) and the cultural history of the Macedonian settlers, Hatzopoulos 1996, vol. 2, no. 79; Hatzopoulos 1994; Tzanavari 2019. Duchesne 1875 is still worth reading; the site will be treated extensively in the forthcoming corpus of inscriptions from Central Macedonia by P. Paschidis.

23. Tombs: Themelis and Touratsoglou 1997. Crater: Barr-Sharrar 2008. Papyrus: Santamaría 2019.

24. *Syll.*³ 700 (no. 100 in forthcoming corpus of Central Macedonia).

25. Dimitsas, *Makedonia*, no. 678 (no. 106 in forthcoming corpus of Central Macedonia). A large funerary monument with a "frieze-like relief," whose surviving portion shows ten members of the same family (along with seven enslaved attendants and three horses), illustrates the social elite of late first-century BCE Lētē: Kalaitzi 2016, 234–37, nos. 141–43.

26. *SEG* 1.276 (no. 109 in the forthcoming corpus of Central Macedonia).

27. Pausanias 10.4.1–4; below, pp. 410–12.

28. Kaizer 2002; Sommer 2018; Smedile 2019. Palmyra as *polis*: Sartre 1996; see further, pp. 377–87.

29. *IGLS* 17, particularly no. 18.

30. For critiques of the notion of *polis* as excessively reified, Gawantka 1985; Purcell 2005; Vlassopoulos 2007a.

31. See already Lonis 1994, e.g., 11 (strong communitarian structures, territory organization, external sovereignty); the importance of autonomy and political status are central to Max Weber's conception of the ancient city (and the "western" city): Bruhns 2014, 1–16.

32. Brulé 2005; R. Frederiksen 2011.

33. *I. Delos* 1551.

34. E.g., Xenophon, *Hellenica*, 4.4.15.

35. Ober 2015, 21–44.

36. On the problematic, and potentially anachronistic, implications of modern notions of the state when applied to premodern societies, Schaub 2005. On early state theory: Yoffee 2005 (this body of theory intersects with the comparative history of the premodern city, on which see Yoffee 2015); more generally, Knodell 2021, 248–58 on points of comparative contact between the study of Early Iron Age Greece and other early complex societies.

37. Castoriadis 2008, with Pébarthe 2012; Clastres 1974, with Gourgouris 2019. See chapter 15.

38. Ando 2018a offers a sobering vision of the authoritarian and imperialist tendencies of the *polis* form.

39. Thus Herodotus 7.198–200, on the topography of the pass of Thermopylai, carefully distinguishes between *poleis* and villages in the landscape.

40. Reger 2004 on *sunoikismos*; *poleis* upon absorption can end up garrisoned, governed, or abandoned.

41. Hansen 2002a; Greg Anderson 2009.

42. For a critical, groundbreaking attempt, Roubineau 2015.

43. On geographies of Greekness, Malkin 1998, Morris 1998a, for the archaeology of both a core geography centered on the Aegean (see also p. 23), and other peripheral or different regional ensembles. Macedonia: Ma 2016b, summarizing work by M. Hatzopoulos; Ēpeiros: Papadopoulos 2016.

44. E.g., Hansen 1995.

45. See, e.g., Humphreys 1978, 159–74; Finley 1983, 1–3; Finley 1985, 88–103; Whittaker 1995; Capogrossi Colognese 1995; Capogrossi Colognese 2000 (232–59, summarizing Weber's views on ancient Greece); Hansen 2004; Bruhns 2014, 1–85; Bresson 2016, 8–11, 206–7, rereading and critiquing Weber. On Weber's changing ideas about the ancient city, Bruhns 1987–89. Weber's essay on the city is to be found in M. Weber 1999 (edited by W. Nippel as volume 22.5 of the *Gesamtaufgabe*).

46. Welwei 1998.

47. For a similar, though not identical, reperiodization of the ancient world (around a "long Hellenistic" period into the second century CE), Chaniotis 2018.

48. Region-*polis*: E. Cohen 2000; "Third Greece": Gehrke 1986, and in a different order of ideas, R. Osborne 1987; Kyaneai: already Robert, *OMS* 6, 169–75, but now especially, e.g., F. Kolb 2008.

Part II. Before the *Polis*

1. See, for instance, M. West 1978, 1997, 2011; Fowler 2004; Morris 1986; Edwards 2004; Raaflaub 1998 ("headache"); Wecowski 2011.

2. Interpretive essays in Snodgrass 2006; also Snodgrass 2000, 1981; Morris 1998a; Coldstream 2003; Lemos 2002. On surveying, Bintliff and Snodgrass 1988; Bintliff and Howard 2007. On housing, Mazarakis-Ainian 1997. For a general survey, Bintliff 2012.

3. Langdon 1998; Papalexandrou 2005; d'Agostino 2008.

4. Knodell 2021 insists on the importance of Central Greece, at the intersection of maritime and continental lines of communication.

5. On the geographies of the emergence of the *polis*, Snodgrass 1977; Morris 1998a; I here have lumped together Western Greece, Snodgrass's and Morris's "core," and Crete. Diversity: Whitley 1991. Northern Greece: Morris 1998a; Bintliff 2012, 221; and p. 23 on the evolution of the Macedonian state.

6. Whitley 2001, 77–102; Whitley 2004; Dickinson 2006.

7. Hägg 1983a; Morris 1987, 1998a, 2000; Snodgrass 2000; Morris 2006, 2009a.

8. Lemos 2002; C. Morgan 1999a, 2003; Papadopoulos 2003; C. Morgan 2009; contra, on quantitative grounds, Morris 2006.

Chapter 2. To New Beginnings

1. Dickinson 1994; Shelmerdine 2006. General treatments: Shelmerdine 2008, Lemos and Kotsonas 2019 for thematic and especially regional surveys; Dickinson 2019 for a nuanced, exciting essay; D'Ercole and Zurbach 2019, 71–243; Middleton 2020; Knodell 2021. Late Bronze Age Athens is anomalous in the absence of strong palatial structure: Papadimitriou and Cosmopoulos 2020. On the early Mycenaean period seen through a particular site (Pylos), Davis 2022 (also a reflexive essay on the field of Late Bronze Age archaeology).

2. Shelmerdine and Bennet 2008; Werlings 2010, 21–45.

3. Palaima 2003, a survey of the peculiarities and the workings of administrative writing in this period (with emphasis on the Pylian material); Sjöberg 2004 is more doubtful for Mykēnai and Tiryns. Thebes and Orchomenos: Aravantinos 2019, 764–68. "Redistribution in Aegean Palatial Societies" is discussed in an online forum under the aegis of the *American Journal of Archaeology* (115), 2011: https://www.ajaonline.org/forum/905.

4. The warrior ethos of Mycenaean society seems illustrated by the recently published sealstone showing a combat scene in dazzling detail, and found from a tomb near Pylos, dating to ca. 1450 BCE at the start of the Mycenean age (Stocker and Davis 2017; Davis 2022). However, conceptions of the Mycenaeans as "Vikings" or "warrior-bands" are overwrought: Dickinson 2014.

5. Vividly depicted in Broodbank 2013, 345–444, and in Cline 2021.

6. Snodgrass 2006, 144–57.

7. Mycenaean presence in Western Anatolia: Zurbach 2006. Aḫḫiyawa: Beckman et al. 2011; Blackwell 2021; Cline 2021.

8. Blackwell 2021.

9. Broodbank 2013.

10. Sherratt 2001.

11. The possibility of an open political economy in the Argolid is explored in Sjöberg 2004; on the complexity of Mycenaean economies, away from any simple, palace-dominated model, Nakassis 2013 (emphasizing elite diversity and local agency in Mycenaean Pylos), Nakassis 2020 (summarizing his earlier work).

12. Broodbank 2013, 412; Davis 2022, 52–53.

13. Arena 2015. On the diversity of the Mycenaean world more generally and the existence of nonpalatial regions or even polities, Knodell 2021, 63–115.

14. van Effenterre 1986; Gounaris 1999 (notably 102, on Melos); Berg 2019, 278–305.

15. E.g., Finley 1954; Vernant 1962.

16. Zurbach 2017; S. Wallace 2020.

17. Middleton 2020; Cline 2021. Destruction of centers, including the Akropolis, in Mycenaean Athens, is argued for by Ruppenstein 2020.

18. Lemos 2014.

19. Knodell 2021, 7.

20. "Last Mycenaeans": Desborough 1964. On the post-Mycenaean groups, e.g., Deger-Jalkotzy 1991, 1996; Kilian-Dirlmeier 1998; Morris 2000, ch. 4; Sjöberg 2004; Dickinson 2006; Crielaard 2006; Eder 2006; Lemos, Liveratou, Thomatos 2009; Middleton 2020; Knodell 2021, 116–50. On Eastern Lokris, Kramer-Hojos 2008, 129–32.

21. Generally, Deger-Jalkotzy 1991; Bintliff 2012, 207–33 (cautious about retrievability of evidence). The population of Mycenaean Askra, in Boiōtia, perhaps migrated to a more defensible site (the modern Pyrgaki), before returning to Askra in the Protogeometric period (ca. 1000–900): Bintliff and Snodgrass 1988, 61.

22. Crete: Kotsonas 2002; S. Wallace 2010; Gaignerot-Driessen 2016, 2018.

23. Dimitriadou 2019, 52, which I interpret in terms of widespread social recognition rather than mere impoverishment; Dimitriadou 2020. The equation of formal burial and social recognition forms the cornerstone of I. Morris 1987; Welwei 1992.

24. Lakōnia: Cavanagh et al. 2002. Argolid: Mee and Forbes 1997, 57–61. Boiōtia: Bintliff and Howard 2007. Other regions—e.g., islands: Gounaris 1999 (Mēlos, Keōs), 2005; Aigion: Papakosta 1991. Fluidity of power structures: Whitley 1991.

25. S. Murray 2017, notably 210–46; on migration, Yasur-Landau 2010; Kotsonas 2016 (against the concept of "Dark Ages"); S. Murray 2018 (in favor).

26. Lemos 2014.

27. On the potential unsustainability of palatial economies in the Mycenean content, Deger-Jalkotzy 1996; Weiberg and Finné 2018, 593–95, discussed by Cline 2021, 184–85. The image of communities "escaping" from extractive rule derives from Scheidel 2019.

28. Papadopoulos in Papadopoulos and Lord Smithson 2017, 23–28.

29. J. Scott, 2017, 206.

30. Starr 1961; Morris 2000; Lemos 2002; Dickinson 2006; C. Morgan 2009; Knodell 2021.

31. Big site: C. Morgan 2003, 45–106.

32. Generally, Mazarakis-Ainian 2012, 140–43. Athens: Dimitriadou 2019, 71–164.

33. Argos: Aupert 1982; Hägg 1982; Foley 1988; still accepted by J. Hall 1997b; Touchais and Divari-Valakou 1998. Corinth: Williams 1984; C. Morgan 1999a, appx. 4. Thespiai: Bintliff and Snodgrass 1988; Bintliff et al. 2007 (surface survey of site). Eretria: Mazarakis-Ainian 2012, 135–37 and Verdan 2013, 155 (however, willing to see Eretria as a structured proto-urban site, and the "clusters" as impressions gained from the modalities of archaeological excavation).

34. The evidence is gathered by Mazarakis-Ainian 1997. Note also the following—Ithakē: C. Morgan 2011 (elite longhouses near sacred area); Athens: D'Onofrio 2011; Eretria: Crielaard 2007; Ōrōpos: Mazarakis-Ainian 2002; Islands: Kourou 2011, discussing Zagora on Andros, Koukounaries on Paros, Xobourgo on Tēnos (all toponyms modern), and the town of Samos (see also survey of building forms in N. Burckhardt 2012); Crete: Gaignerot-Driessen 2016 on the primeval soup (my term, not hers) of loose clusters across the landscape of E. Crete (Mirabello Gulf) in the LHIIIB and LHIIIC periods. Asia Minor: Herda 2006; essays in part I of Cobet et al. 2006.

35. di Vita 1990; Greco 2020, 71–72. Naxos, in Sicily, was probably organized in clusters of houses, unevenly spread across the site: Pellagatti 1981.

36. Blondé, Müller, Mulliez 2002; de Polignac 2005.

37. Mazarakis-Ainian 2002; 2007; 2007–2008; 2012, 126–32. Eretria: Verdan 2013.

38. Charalambidou 2018.

39. Dimitriadou 2019, engaging with Papadopoulos and Lord Smithson 2017. Our understanding of early Iron Age Athens, and its relationship with an immensely complex Attic landscape, will be revolutionized by the publication of the massive conference hosted at the American School of Classical Studies in Athens in December 2022.

40. Mazarakis-Ainian and Livieratou 2010.

41. Generally, Longo 2009 (but most of the examples date to the Late Geometric, after 750 BCE); for the Athenian example (the area of the Classical-era Agora), Papadopoulos and Lord Smithson 2017.

42. Mazarakis-Ainian 1997.

43. Zagora: Coucouzeli 2007. Eretria: Mazarakis-Ainian 1987; Verdan 2013, 190–98 (elite group next to communal sacred space).

44. Psalti 2006; A. Psalti in Kaltas et al., 2010, 314–17; Simon and Verdan 2014.

45. E.g., Phaistos (Lefèvre-Novaro 2007); Aetos on Ithakē (discussed in C. Morgan 2009, 53–54); Koukanaries on the island of Paros (Schilardi 2002); Klazomenai in Asia Minor (Aytaçlar 2004), Ypsili (modern toponym) on the island of Andros (Televantou 1999, Televantou 2000): big houses near future site of temples.

46. Papadopoulos 2003, 297–316.

47. Mersch 1997; Bintliff et al. 2007; Bintliff 2012.

48. Papadopoulos and Lord Smithson 2017, Tomb 15, 124–76.

49. Mazarakis-Ainian 2002; de Polignac 2005, 65–66.

50. Though the settlements Aristotle imagines as existing in close proximity and interacting along set rules (without reaching the ethical and institutional level of the *polis*) might come close: *Politics* 3.9 1280b.

51. Popham and Lemos 1995; Luke 2003; Dickinson 2006, 197–218; Lane Fox 2008.

52. Bessios, Tzifopoulos, and Kotsonas 2012; Strauss Clay, Malkin, and Tzifopoulos 2017.

53. Lane Fox 2008.

54. López-Ruiz 2021.

55. Methōnē, Torōnē: Snodgrass 2006, ch. 8.

56. M. Frederiksen 1984, 62–64; Buchner and Ridgway 1993; recently, D'Agostino 2006; Lane Fox 2008, chaps. 8–9.

57. Dickinson 2006; *contra*, Papadopoulos 1996, 1997, 2005.

58. C. Morgan 2009.

59. Recent syntheses in Stephani, Tsangaraki, and Arvanitaki 2019, 55–103 (by Chr. Televantou, S. Paspalas, L. Palaiokrassa-Sakalidou, E. Tsigarida, K. Sismanidis, Z. Bonias and J. Perreault).

60. Herda 2006, 2009; Mac Sweeney 2013, 157–97 (with attention to local reworking of foundation stories).

61. Mac Sweeney 2013, 2017.

62. Already noted in Deger-Jalkotzy 1991, 62; A. Livieratou in Kotsonas and Lemos 2019, 822–23, on Atalantē and other Early Iron Age cemeteries in East Lokris.

63. Lambrinoudakis 1988, 2004; Charalambidou 2018.

64. Kourou 2011.

65. Marangou 2002–2005, 207–24.

66. For instance, "Tomb 13" (Papadopoulos and Lord Smithson 2017, 104–18: sword, spearheads, probable battle-axe, whetstone snaffle bits), with D'Onofrio 2011, 652–53 (on the long slashing sword in an Areiopagos tomb, which implies not just warrior status, but long-reach fighting from above, i.e. from horseback or a chariot); generally, Lemos 2007.

67. Argos: Diogo de Souza 2015. Corinthia: C. Morgan 1999a, 395–97, based on Dickey 1992 (unpublished Bryn Mawr PhD, *non vidi*).

68. On Early Iron Ages elites, Ulf 2007.

69. On Euboian settlement at Methōnē, Strauss Clay, Malkin, and Tzifopoulos 2017.

70. Snodgrass 1993: demography and social change. Eighth-century "revolution," Snodgrass 1977, 1981; Hägg 1983a; Morris 2009a (restating and enriching views proposed in Morris 1987). On demography, Snodgrass 1977; Morris 1987; Green 1990; C. Morgan 2003, 224; Scheidel 2003, esp. 126–31; Bresson 2007, 125; Morris 2009a.

71. Survey of the evolution of "big sites" in C. Morgan 2003, 45–71; also Vink 1997, de Polignac 2005, and Lemos, Livieratou, and Thomatos 2009.

72. Hägg 1982; Papadimitriou in Lemos and Jager-Delkotzy 2006.

73. Longo 2009.

74. Dimitriadou 2019, 242.

75. Schilardi 2002.

76. R. Frederiksen 2011, 131–32 (Asine), 188–90 (Old Smyrna).

77. Verdan 2013, 228–30.

78. Schilardi 1983, 2002, 2017.

79. Scholl 2006.

80. Kourou 2011; Kourou 2013, esp. 86–94.

81. The evidence is gathered in Mazarakis-Ainian 1997—for instance, Tegea in Arkadia (the temple of Athēna Alea), Thermon (where a temple replaced a "megaron," in an urban site that later was an important center for the *ethnos* of the Aitolians); see also Phaistos in Crete: Lefèvre-Novaro 2007. A large temple might have been erected in the late eighth century BCE at Teōs (Crielaard 2009a, 66 n. 212; an ashlar, seventh-century BCE successor to a wooden or wattle-and-daub building?), but the accompanying Late Geometric settlement is not known.

82. Coucouzeli 2007; Westgate 2015.

83. Lemos, Livieratou, and Thomatos 2009.

84. S. Wallace 2010; Gaignerot-Driessen 2016 (challenging the notion of "refuge site" in favor of systematic spread across inland landscapes).

85. C. Morgan 1999a.

86. de Polignac 1984 (Eng. tr. 1995).

87. See, for instance—Mycenai: Antonaccio 1995, 52–53 (a shrine of Agamemnōn, near a Mycenaean bridge over a ravine, and a shrine to Enyalios [the god of war] at Asprochomata [modern toponym] adorned with dedications of weapons and located on a road toward Corinth, suggest the affirmation of the community at Mykēnai, even though there is no real trace of a nucleated settlement); Phaistos: Novaro-Lefèvre 2007, 485–86; the most exciting example is the now-discovered shrine of Artemis at Amarynthos, whose relation to Eretria requires study and meditation.

88. Hyria: Lambrinoudakis 2001.

89. Senff 2006 (Zeytintepe); Herda 2009 (Assessos).

90. Lolos 2005, 2011.

91. Lambrinoudakis 2001, 2004; Charalambidou 2018.

92. Hägg 1983b.

93. J. Hall 1995.

94. C. Morgan 1990; Kyrieleis 2006.

95. Lefèvre 1998, Sánchez 2001.

96. Coldstream 1983; qualified by C. Morgan 1999b.

97. C. Morgan 1990, 2003, 2006.

98. J. Hall 1997a, 2002, esp. 125–71 on debates about who belonged to the *Hellenes*.

99. Morris 1987, 1998a, 2000.

100. Rombos 1988, Snodgrass 2008. On the hourglass-shaped shield, Greenhalgh 1973.

101. Rombos 1988.

102. Hägg 1983b; Pappi and Triantaphyllou 2011.

103. Courbin 1957. There probably were more gold offerings than recovered since the tomb was rifled in ancient times.

104. Pappi 2006; Pappi and Triantaphyllou 2011.

105. C. Morgan 1999a, summarizing Dickey 1992.

106. C. Morgan 1990, 121–22.

107. Coldstream 1976; Whitley 1994; Antonaccio 1995; Whitley 1995; van Wees 2006a.

108. Morris 1987, 1998a.

109. Houby-Nielsen 1995. The material from the Geometric necropolis on Samos might offer parallels. It combines expensive cremations, high-grade pottery, and child burials (summarized in Viglaki-Sofianou 2013).

110. Stampolidis 2004; 2008, 104–62; 2019, 139–48.
111. C. Morgan 2009.
112. Papadopoulos 2001.
113. S. Wallace 2010; Gaignerot-Driessen 2016.
114. C. Bérard 1970; Crielaard 1998 (elitist interpretation of the record at Eretria); Blandin 2007, 167–68 (cautious).
115. F3 West.
116. Tsakos 2007, on the nekropolis at Tria Dontia (modern toponym).
117. Lambrinoudakis 1988; Charalambidou 2018.
118. Stampolidis 2008, 135–38.
119. C. Bérard 1970; Blandin 2007, 168 n. 1880 (pointing out that the early seventh-century material is still very badly known).
120. Marangou 2002–2005, vol. 1, 207–24.

Chapter 3. Diversity and Community

Large villages to corporate communities: J. Bintliff, "City-Country Relationships in the 'Normal Polis.'" In *City, Countryside, and the Spatial Organization of Value in Classical Antiquity*, edited by R. Rosen and I. Sluiter, 27 (Leiden: 2006).

1. Hammer 2002, on the political nature of the Homeric poems. On the making of the poems, I follow M. West 2011.
2. E.g., Crielaard 1995 (perfect fit between archaeology of the eighth century and Homer); Dickinson 2006, 239–40 (pessimistic).
3. *Iliad*, 11.444–45.
4. Passes: e.g., *Iliad*, 14.401–507 for a prolonged sequence; 22.207: Achilleus will not let anyone throw at Hektōr, lest Achilleus lose priority of *kudos*. Generally, Di Donato 2003.
5. Van Wees 1994a, 1994b, 1996; Lendon 2005.
6. *Iliad*, 11.404–10 (another example is 17.90–105); 12.390–91.
7. *Iliad*, 16.491–501.
8. Latacz 1977; Van Wees 1996, 1997; Raaflaub 1998.
9. Tēlemachos: *Odyssey*, Books 3–4. Young Odysseus's travels: 19.394–466.
10. *Odyssey*, 9.229–30.
11. *Iliad*, 11.691, in Nestōr's description of protracted fighting by the Eleians against the Pylians, whose best men died at war. The *good* are those who fight.
12. *Iliad*, 15.295–305.
13. van Wees 1998.
14. *Iliad*, 15.108.
15. *Odyssey*, 8.159–64.
16. *Iliad*, 9.574–605 (speech of Phoinix to Achilleus, story of Meleagros).
17. *Iliad*, 12.310–21.
18. Finley 1954 is still essential.
19. *Iliad*, 24.432–36; *Odyssey*, 15.330.
20. *Odyssey*, 4.535–59, 11.412.
21. *Odyssey*, 15.468. In Phaiakia, the *basileis* are those who drink fine old wine and listen to song in Alkinoos's house: 13.7–9.
22. *Odyssey*, 19.28.
23. *Odyssey*, 14.62.
24. This is the main thrust of van Wees 1995.
25. *Odyssey*, 14.192–234.
26. *Iliad*, 17.389.
27. The classic passage on the status of the *thēs* is Achilleus's bitter statement that he would rather be a landless *thes* among the living than a *basileus* among the dead: *Odyssey*, 11.489–91.
28. Likewise, *Iliad*, 14.121–5, Diomēdēs's boast about his lineage celebrates his father's house, grain fields, vineyards, and herds, as well as his prowess; it does not mention serfs or subordinate inhabitants on the estate but seems rather to insist on direct ownership and management.
29. Enclosure: e.g., *Odyssey*, 17.264–68. Orchards: at least this is the case of Alkinoos's palace, as seen in *Odyssey*, 7.114–16.
30. *Iliad*, 7.467–75; *Odyssey*, 1.184.
31. Edwards 2004.
32. van Wees 2009b.
33. *Odyssey*, 13.14–15; 19.192; 22.55; 23.355.
34. E.g., *Iliad*, 16.437. Drinking the people's goods: 17.248–52.
35. *Iliad*, 17.225–26.
36. Osborne 2004; on the theme of Homeric kingship, Drews 1983, Carlier 1984; Ruzé 2003, 107–23 (originally published in 1989). L. Mitchell 2013 argues for the structural importance and durability of personal rule as a factor in Greek history (rather than "Big Men" or "chiefs" contrasted with "proper" kings).
37. *Odyssey*, 7.129–32.
38. *Odyssey*, 15.553–54, 16.401–2; good king: 4.690–95, 19.105–14, *Works and Days* 225–47.
39. Ithakē: *Odyssey*, 1.389–98; 15.510, 519–20; 16.76, etc. Phaiakia: 6.53, 7.146, 8.390, 13.12, etc.
40. A sign of this fluidity and ambiguity is given by a disagreement in an edited volume on Homer (Wace and Stubbings 1963, 438): whereas G. Calhoun, the contributor on "polity and society (the Homeric picture)," speaks of a simple organization with no en-

trenched nobility of birth, the editors of the *Companion to Homer* in a footnote to the same page draw attention to the importance epithets exalting divine birth and patronymics in Homeric society.

41. *Works and Days* 174–95.

42. *Iliad*, 22.489, 24.489; *Odyssey*, 2.187–94, 2.242–50, 16.71–72, 23.118–20.

43. *Iliad*, 9.50 (assembly of lords); 13.740 (council of the *aristoi*); all of *Iliad* 2 illustrates the working of lordly politics.

44. *Iliad* 18; *Works and Days*. In the *Odyssey*, the mention of arbitration is given as an indication of time (the sea-monster Charybdis spits out the spars of Odysseus's shattered ships at the time when a judge will take his lunch break, after judging "strong men in dispute").

45. Haubold 2000; Werlings 2010, 47–107.

46. *Iliad*, 6.194, 9.578, 20.184. The details and the implications of how this practice works (where does the community find the land for such grants? commons or uncultivated land?) are unclear: Donlan 1989. Odysseus wishes the Phaiakian lord happiness and the smooth generational transmission "of the property in your halls, and the share (*geras*) which the people has given."

47. E.g., *Odyssey*, 16.28.

48. *Iliad*, 20.4; 18.243–45.

49. Wine: *Iliad*, 4.259. Elders: 3.149–55; 11.372, where the hero Ilos himself, founder of Troy and its royal line, is called *dēmogerōn*; *Odyssey*, 2.14. Oath: *Iliad*, 22.119.

50. *Iliad*, 16.384–92; Ruzé 1997, 13–106 on Homeric decision-making; Hammer 2002 on the "plebiscitary politics" of the *Iliad*.

51. *Odyssey*, 3.1–35; 21.258.

52. Haubold 2000.

53. *Iliad*, 22.99–105; 24.703–6.

54. *Odyssey*, 2.10–80.

55. *Odyssey*, 14.239; 16.95, 275.

56. *Odyssey*, 16.420–30.

57. Papakonstantinou 2008, 19–46, and Hawke 2011, 52–100, on the importance of popular pressure and community participation in dispute resolution in the worlds of Homer and Hesiod.

58. Scully 1990, Hölkeskamp 1997.

59. But see I. Shear 2000, 2004; also Deger-Jalkotzy 1991.

60. Deger-Jalkotzy 1991.

61. *Odyssey*, 20.264–65.

62. Crielaard 1995.

63. Edwards 2004; I slightly differ from Edwards in my interpretation of the dispute, which I think has been decided by kings.

64. On mediation and the rise of the *polis*, de Polignac 2006.

65. E.g., van Wees 2003; Luraghi 2008.

66. de Polignac 1995, 143; Luraghi 2002.

67. Morgan and Whitelaw 1991; Herda 2006; Mac Sweeney 2013, 178–87.

68. Benaki Museum, ΓΕ 7675; Paros amphora: see below (Croissant 2008). Big round shields clearly appear on relief-decorated *pithoi* (large storage jars) from Tēnos from the late eighth century BCE: Simantoni-Bournia 2004, 136–38 and Simantoni-Bournia 2013, 102–3 (interpreting the shields as center-bossed contraptions).

69. Starr 1957.

70. Morris 1987, refined and amplified in Morris 2000; Tandy 1997.

71. Some thoughts in R. Frederiksen 2011, with ranges of possibilities and generally *Alba* 2008.

72. Croissant 2008, based on Zaphiropoulou 1994, 1999; Agelarakis 2017, studying the cremated bones (but with description of the find by Ph. Zaphiropoulou, 5–10).

73. The conflict is attested in Archilochos (F 89 West); Marcaccini 2001.

74. Archilochos F 325 West with Swift 2019 *ad loc.* on possible authenticity.

Part III. Making the *Polis*

1. *Nomima* 1.4 (*I. Olympia* 5, main fragment, and 6).

2. Likewise, another, rather earlier (say ca. 550 BCE), law was inscribed at Olympia on a piece of bronze cauldron (of the type supported by monumental tripods): *I. Olympia Suppl.* 1. On tripods, Papalexandrou 2005, 2008; for the typology of the genre, Maass 1978. I was unable to obtain photographs of *both sides* of the relevant fragments.

3. Herodotos 7.37.3, "the *poleis* of the Greeks" is a typical way of describing this world; 8.144.2; generally, e.g., J. Hall 2002; Vlassopoulos 2013.

4. Herodotos 6.8.

5. Zaccarini 2013, 16 on the ship numbers.

6. Herodotos 8.43–48.

7. E.g., Ober, Wallace, and Raaflaub 2007; C. Meier 2011. Against teleology, Seelentag 2015.

8. Connor 1987; Walter 1993; Forsdyke 2005b.

9. Herodotos's awareness, mostly unspoken, of fifth-century BCE big war, informs the treatment in Fornara 1971; see also Harrison and Irwin 2018.

Chapter 4. Institutions, Community, Ideology

1. Tiré and van Effenterre 1966, 85–88. Excavation and research on the site has resumed from 2009 onwards, by the French School at Athens and the 24th Ephorate of Prehistoric and Classical Antiquities. One important finding is that the best documented state of the *agora* is Hellenistic, much later than the period under consideration here: see for instance the report for 2013 (C. Bouras), available at https://chronique.efa.gr/ (accessed December 2023).

2. van Effenterre 2009.

3. *Nomima* 1.82 (same document, Koerner 1993, no. 90, and Gagarin and Perlman 2016, Dr 1); Ehrenberg 1937; Seelentag 2009; Werlings 2010, 170–72; Seelentag 2015, 139–63; Genevrois 2017, 147–49, 199–203; Meister 2020, 231–33; generally, Gagarin 2020a.

4. Sciachitano 2018 (favors fines; see A. Alonso Deniz, in *BE* 19, 401, adducing L. Dubois as noted in Genevrois 2017, 110).

5. Alternatively, the term *damioi* could designate representatives of the rural population: Genevrois 2017, 87–88.

6. Hölkeskamp 1992; qualified, gently but far-reachingly, by R. Osborne 1997 ("joining the dots" of law).

7. On curses authorizing self-help, R. Parker 1983, 193–96.

8. *Odyssey*, 2.178–193, where an aristocratic suitor threatens to fine someone for displeasing him in assembly speech.

9. Such absolutes occur elsewhere in the documentation for the early *polis*, as in the donation of Kyzikos to Manēs (see p. 109), and in the Eleian material: Minon 2007, 417.

10. *Nomima* 1.64 (Gagarin and Perlman 2016, Dr 2).

11. Runciman 1982 notes the suddenness of the shift to governmental structure; Gehrke 1997; J. Hall 2009.

12. *Nomima* 1.1; 2.23, 92 (also in Gagarin and Perlman 2016, G13, G15, G5).

13. Alkaios F 130B with Kantzios 2018; I understand "those things" as referring to the political activity (Caciagli 2011, 189) rather than a concrete good such as lost property or confiscated estates (e.g., D. Campbell, Loeb edition).

14. Dimopoulou-Piliouni 2015, 122–25.

15. Manganaro 1974; Kroll 2020.

16. *Nomima* 1.78 (favoring 600-575 BCE); also published in *SEG* 30.380; Koerner 1993, no. 31.

17. Hignett 1952 (skeptical); Stahl 1987 (general); Develin 1989 (not skeptical); Walter 1993, 176–209; Greg Anderson 2003 (much more minimalist than the picture offered here); Kienast 2005; Dmitriev 2018 (from kinship to institutions); Humphreys 2018, 627–36.

18. *Ath. Pol.* 2–8.

19. Herodotos 5.71; Thucydides 1.126. Kylōn's attempted coup has been downdated (E. Lévy 1978); discussion in Hornblower, *CT* 1.203–5. On the naukraries, Figueira 1993, 151–72 ("quasi-public" institution); Gabrielsen 1994, 19–24; Wallinga 2000; Ismard 2010, 299–305 (relating them to the distributed workings of the demes); my interpretation here is rather more "statist," following van Wees 2013.

20. *IG* I.^{3}104 (also Leão and Rhodes 2016, fr. 5a). On authenticity, and general workings and context, Stroud 1968; Gagarin 2008.

21. *Iliad*, 18.497–508.

22. Tyrtaeus 4; Werlings 2010, 196–204.

23. Plutarch, *Life of Lykourgos* 6; Nafissi 2009, 2010. The *rhētra*, on which many opinions have been expressed, is published in *Nomima* 1.61; see for instance Ogden 1994; van Wees 1999b. A parallel might lie in the mythologizing of Cretan laws and order, which may also reflect the effort at creating *post-eventum* foundation narratives for *polis* institutionalization (Gehrke 1997). The purported list of gifts by the hero Phanotos to his daughter, inscribed in the late sixth century BCE as etiological justification for contemporary ritual practice, might also offer a parallel (Rousset, Camp, and Minon 2015 whence, *SEG* 65.361).

24. Cartledge 1987, 23.

25. *Nomima* 1.64 (ca. 600 BCE); Seelentag 2015, 348–53.

26. *Nomima* 1.68 (also in Koerner 1993, no. 91; Gagarin and Perlman 2016 Dr3; Seelentag 2015, 496–99.

27. Will 1956, 44–53; J. Hall 1997a, esp. 9–16.

28. Plutarch, *Greek Questions* 17 (*Mor.* 295 B); analyzed by Walter 1993, 98–112 (N. Jones 1987, 95–96, is skeptical).

29. F 11.

30. 3.1–11.

31. Blok 2017, 107–16.

32. Leão and Rhodes 2016, fr. 76a.

33. F 95, 96; 19 describes a private *sumposion*.

34. Seelentag 2015, 374–443.

35. Small 2010; Haggis et al. 2011. The toponym is modern.

36. Leão and Rhodes 2016, fr 14.

37. Doronzio 2018, 201–11, though the ceramic chips (fashioned from broken pottery) have also been identified by J. Papadopoulos (2002) as discarded post-defecation wipes.

38. Wecowksi 2014.

39. F 203.

40. T. Morgan 2005.
41. Calame 1977 (trans. 2001), 1996; Lardinois 1996.
42. F 13 West (but contrast F11).
43. E.g., F 14, 109, 114, 177, 182. On Archilochos's *polis*, Kontoleon 1964; Pouilloux 1964; and the new essays collected in Katsonopoulou, Petropoulos, and Katsarou 2008 (*Paros II*).
44. F 105.
45. F 124.
46. E.g., F. 94, 95, 98, 111 (addressed to the *neoi*, the young men), 139, 146.
47. Tyrtaios F11, lines 35–38.
48. On archaic warfare, Greenhalgh 1973 on riders; van Wees 2000; van Wees 2004, 166–83; Cawkwell 2011, 416–37. A. Schwartz 2009 believes in a much more unitary picture of warfare, unchanging between 750 and 338 BCE, but the upper limit is too early (and the lower limit meaningless). Potshot: Rawlings 2000, 240.
49. Förtsch 2001, 99–102.
50. Herodotos 1.30, though the context is hardly secure: a chronologically impossible anecdote uniting the early sixth-century BCE figure of Solōn and Kroisos, the Lydian king who ruled in the second half of the sixth century.
51. See chapter 3, where this equation is assigned to the Early Iron Age; I follow Lane Fox 2008, 381–84.
52. F10-11 West; Werlings 2010, 184–86. On the institutionalization of heroic ethos in the Spartan army, van Wees 2006b.
53. Hurwit 2002 discusses these in their social context. On the most famous of these vases, the "Chigi *olpē*" or jug, found in a tomb in Etruria with material that can be mostly dated to the last quarter of the seventh century BCE, d'Acunto 2013 (interpretive essay); Michetti and van Kampen 2014 (on context). It might be tempting to place the Chigi jug around this low date (so d'Acunto), rather than ca. 650 BCE as often done. Notable among the other vases are a very small *aryballos* apparently found at Thebes, and now in the British Museum ("Macmillan *aryballos*," 1889.0418.1), and a fragmentary *oinochoē* excavated in a seventh-century BCE context at Erythrai in Asia Minor. Shanks 1999 offers readings of Corinthian iconography in terms of violence and aspirations in the early *polis*.
54. Schnapp 1997 on hunting and warfare as part of the social imagination of the *polis*.
55. On the obscure 360 *genē* of Attica, as a possible system for military mobilization, D. Roussel 1976; Humphreys 2018, 627–720.
56. Herodotos 1.16, 1.82. Jeffery 1976 provides much political narrative for the interaction of the early *poleis*.

57. Herodotos 1.6.3, 1.14–26.
58. Herodotos 5.83.1, with Figueira 1993, 9–33; Nauplia: Kelly 1976, 88.
59. On early Sparta, and the helots, see, e.g., Cartledge 2002a; Ducat 1990; M. Meier 1998; Förtsch 2001; Luraghi 2002; Kõiv 2003; van Wees 2003; Luther, Meier, and Thommen 2006; Ducat 2015 surveys the evidence anew.
60. F 5–7 West.
61. Foxhall 2013.
62. Lang 1996, Hansen 1997a ("Polis as Urban Centre"); Hölscher 1998 (overreliant on Pausanias, but vitally aware of the need to see the whole picture of the archaic *polis* as town: temples, meeting places, houses, tombs—rather than focus exclusively on the funerary material); Crielaard 2009b.
63. R. Rhodes (2003).
64. Lambrinoudakis 1991.
65. Kerschner 2020, 199–207. Perhaps the same thing happened at Teōs: Crielaard 2009a, 66.
66. Perlman 2000a; Marginesu 2005; Gaignerot-Driessen 2016.
67. Prost 2010a.
68. Hölscher 1998, 76 (Thēra).
69. Perlman 2000a; for parallels, Gaignerot-Driessen 2016 on the seventh-century emergence of *polis* structures in Eastern Crete.
70. Kotsonas 2002; also C. Morgan 2003, 89–91.
71. C. Bérard 1970; Blandin 2007.
72. Kinch 1914; Morris 1992 (exaggerating the difference between Vroulia and a "normal" *polis*); Lang 1996, 193–94; Wriedt Sørensen 2002 (dispelling Morris's interpretations of the funerary material as unsound); Lang 2007; Kaninia and Schierup 2017.
73. F 35, 37 (house and fence) 49, 82, 89 (shared spaces) West.
74. Bintliff 1994; Meister 2020, 115–57.
75. R. Osborne 1989; Arrington 2022.
76. Legon 1981; *IACP* no. 225. The war with Megara over Salamis, whatever its date, likewise supposes an extensive and integrated Attic territory.
77. Ducat 2008, 2010, 2018.
78. D. Roussel 1976 on tribal names as "recognition signs" between local elites across regions.
79. Forrest 2000 on amphiktionies as an important state form in the early archaic period (and even earlier); Sánchez 2001, 32–57 (placing the process too early, in my view).
80. C. Morgan 2003.
81. Boardman 1999; Graham 1983; Tsetskhladze 2006–2008, Adam-Veleni and Tsangari 2015.
82. Grandjean 1988, 469 (also Grandjean and Salviat 2000, 197); Owen 2009. On Thasos generally, Brunet et al. 2019.

83. Romiopoulou 1999 (Andrian foundations); Tiverios 2008, for an immense survey of the evidence; Zannis 2014, 233; Stephani, Tsangaraki, and Arvanitaki 2019 (recent synthesis, connected with an exhibition at the Archaeological Museum in Thessaloniki).

84. Coudin 2009, 75–99.

85. 4.145–67, and Meiggs-Lewis *GHI* 5 (same document *Nomima* 1.41), with Giangiulio 2001; R. Osborne 2009a, 8–16; Cawkwell 2011, 11–32.

86. Horden and Purcell 2000; Osborne and Cunliffe 2005; Etienne 2010; Broodbank 2013; van Dommelen 2017.

87. R. Osborne 1998aa.

88. Archilochos F 182 West.

89. Malkin 2002, 2003, focusing especially on institutional indices of formal foundation.

90. Archilochos F 291 (on Strymē, claimed by Thasos and Marōneia); Neapolis and Oisymē: evidence gathered in *IAGC* on these sites.

91. Thucydides 1.24.

92. Thucydides 6.3–5; de Angelis 1994 (on the particular case of Selinous, founded by Megara Hyblaia); 2016, 65–75.

93. Danner 1997; de Angelis 2003, 17–39 and 128–45, on Megara Hyblaia and Selinous (Megara Hyblaia, in the second half of the seventh century saw the construction of nine monuments, of which three were temples, but two more were public meeting places of some sort); R.-M. Bérard 2019 on cemeteries of Megara Hyblaia.

94. J. Hall 1997b argues for seventh-century Tiryns and Mykēnai representing a different type of urbanization, namely scattered with a central ceremonial nucleus (formerly the Late Bronze Age complex), but it is equally possible that the seventh-century situation reflects the weakness of these places in relation to Argos.

95. Kotsonas 2002.

96. Gounaris 1999; Mazarakis-Ainian 2017.

97. Wickham 2015.

98. E. Irwin 2005, on the diverse nature of fighters in the Tyrtaian battle line, and the implications of inclusiveness—but also of social differentiation—in early archaic Sparta.

99. Schilardi 2017, 100–1.

100. Brisart 2011; Seelentag 2015. On the "orientalizing kit," López-Ruiz 2021, 63–89.

Chapter 5. 600–450 BCE

City subverting parochialism: M. Bookchin, *From Urbanization to Cities. Toward a New Politics of Citizenship* (London, 1995), 39.

1. J. Davies 1997.

2. Hurwit 1999, 99–121; Etienne 2004, 41–48 or Paga 2020, 33–43, for (slightly different versions of) the architectural history of the Akropolis and its temples.

3. Franssen 2011.

4. Kerschner and Prochaska 2011; Kerschner 2020, 235–36.

5. Snodgrass 1986; Gruben 2001, 24–55; Spawforth 2006; Osborne 2009a, 248–52; Neer 2018, 126–40. On the technology involved in the canonical forms of the Greek temple, Coulton 1977.

6. Lang 1996; 2007; d'Ercole and Zurbach 2019, 488–521.

7. De Angelis 2003, 26–28.

8. J. Carter 2006, 195–210.

9. Haggis et al. 2011 (hesitant on using the word *andreion* for the dining hall; and generally, on Azoria as an example of the remodeling of Cretan *polis* centers around 600 BCE).

10. Argos: Pariente 1992. Sparta: the evidence is mostly from Pausanias, writing seven centuries later, but see the evocative use made by Hölscher 1998 (also on Megara); Förtsch 2001, 46–49, on sixth- and early fifth-century BCE building in the *agora*.

11. Tréziny 2006; Eren 2013.

12. Herodotos 1. 163–9 and Özyiğit 1994 on Phokaia.

13. Generally, R. Frederiksen 2011, completing notes in *IACP*; e.g., Pharaklas 1998, 4–7 on walls of Thebes at least by 479 BCE (upper and lower town).

14. Kienast 1978.

15. Kienast 1995.

16. Lang 1996, 118–27; 2007, 186–7; Avgerinou 2019, 46–48. Corinth: B. Robinson 2011, 131–41. Megara: Avgerinou 2016, 2019 (on the rediscovery of the underground water channel, which served until 1936). Wilhelm, *KS* 2.1, 35 n. 51, notes archaic blocks inscribed with the name of the city, and probably from hydraulic works: these would be direct evidence for the archaic water supply works, whereas the "fountain of Theagenēs" known archaeologically is a fifth-century building (Glaser 1983, 51).

17. Foxhall 2013; d'Ercole and Zurbach 2019, 523–41.

18. *Nomima* 1.82 (also in Koerner 1993, no. 121 and Gagarin and Perlman 2016, G14).

19. *Nomima* 2.82, for an example (Korōpē, ca. 550 BCE: prohibition on the removal of crops or objects from a sacred estate, upon pain of a fine paid in nature).

20. *Nomima* 2.98 (also Gagarin and Perlman 2016, Eleutherna 1).

21. Adak and Thonemann 2022, 104, note additional clauses added to a sixth-century law at Eretria (*SEG* 41.725, also in *Nomima* 1.91).

22. Argos: *Nomima* 1.100; Mykēnai: 1.101.

23. Adak and Thonemann 2022, docs 2–3, superseding earlier editions (*Nomima* 1.104–5; also in Meiggs-Lewis *GHI* 30; Koerner 1993, nos. 78–79; Osborne-Rhodes *GHI* 102); Herrmann 1981; Youni 2007.

24. *Nomima* 1.44 (also in Koerner 1993, nos. 47–48, the famous "Pappadakis bronze" published by N. G. Pappadakis in 1924; probably from Lokris and dating ca. 525-500 BCE). On cross-referencing or legal fictions, here and elsewhere, Bertrand 2000; Gagarin 2008, 142–43.

25. Veneciano 2014 on the congruence of *rhatra* (enactment or decree) and law in *Nomima* 1.109.

26. *Nomima* 1.108–9 (also in Koerner 1993, nos. 38 and 41).

27. *Nomima* 1.88 (also in Koerner 1993, no. 25; Nieto Izquierdo 2019, no. 6).

28. Morris 1987; Camassa 1993; Berent 2000, 2004; contra, Greg Anderson 2008. For further discussion, see pp. 424–29 and generally chapter 15.

29. *Nomima* 1.22 (also in Gagarin and Perlman 2016, Da1). On the tribes, Seelentag 2015, 366–68.

30. *Nomima* 1.27. On accountability, Fröhlich 2004.

31. Herodotos 5.39–40 (another example of oversight at 6.63); Richer 1998.

32. Duplouy 2006, 337 n. 125.

33. *Nomima* 1.62.

34. Matthaiou 2014.

35. van Wees 2013; Migeotte 2014, 126, 130, 237 (archaic examples, taken from a study of civic finances in later periods).

36. *Nomima* 1.32; dated to the sixth century BCE by the script (the inscription was recarved in the first century BCE—out of antiquarian interest?).

37. Perlman 2004.

38. Migeotte 1995. Against this misconception, see already Wilhelm, *KS* 1.3, 266–67, notably on late archaic ōon.

39. Herodotos 6.43.3. On the silver and gold mines of Thasos, some on the mainland and some honeycombing the akropolis of Thasos town, Grandjean and Salviat 2000, 177–80; generally, Brunet et al. 2019.

40. *Nomima* 1.75 (also in Koerner 1993, no. 23); Lolos 2012, 310–12, 405–8 (proposing to identify the group as a phratry and exploring possible localizations).

41. Seelentag 2015, 422–26.

42. *Nomima* 1.43 (also in Koerner 1993, no. 49), lines 14–16.

43. Aristotle, *Politics*, 2.9 1271a; Genevrois 2017, 99–102, on *dialusis* (distribution) of goods in the *and-reion* (seen in *Nomima* 1.28, also Gagarin and Perlman 2016 A1, Axos, where workers contribute for sacrifices but nothing else; Seelentag 2015, 309–12); generally, Seelentag 2015, 374–443.

44. Herodotos 3.131.1–2.

45. *Nomima* 1.43 (also in Koerner 1993, no. 49); Latte 1968, 280 and 295.

46. Athletes: Xenophanes 2 West and see chapter 6 on competing claims to distinction.

47. *IG* $4.^2$ 2.1038.

48. Van Wees 2013, notably on the provision of pay for rowers in sixth-century Eretria (*Nomima* 1.91).

49. *Constitution of the Athenians* 22.7; van Wees 2013, 64–68.

50. Leão and Rhodes 2016, fragments 60–68; Murray 1993, 199–201; Humphreys 2018, 18–61.

51. For recent synthesis, essays by J. Kroll, K. Konuk, P. van Alfen, and K. Sheedy, in Metcalf 2012; on the birth of coinage, Le Rider 2001; Schaps 2004.

52. van Alfen and Wartenberg 2020, strongly revising an earlier orthodoxy (Le Rider 2001) that saw the Lydian kingdom as guaranteeing the trustworthiness of a naturally variable alloy.

53. Bresson 2016, 260–78.

54. Herodotos 5.28–30; Pollux 9.83; Descat 2000; Sheedy 2012.

55. Osborne 1996–1997; Förtsch 2001.

56. Haggis et al. 2011.

57. *SEG* 47.1427. On civic organization in Sicily and southern Italy, see the papers published in *Mediterraneo Antico* 21 (2018), 1–132.

58. Herodotos 4.161–62; Hölkeskamp 1993.

59. Herodotos 5.67–68, with Forsdyke 2012, 90–112 for a possible reconstruction ("Dorianization" of the tribes at Sikyōn in the late sixth century, and satirical invented tradition to disqualify earlier civic subdivision as imposed by the tyrant Kleisthenes).

60. Herodotos 5.66–73; [Aristotle], *Constitution of the Athenians* 20–6; Lévêque and Vidal-Naquet 1964.

61. As explored in forthcoming work by S. Fachard and S. Verdan; see already D. Knoepfler, *BE* 14, 219.

62. Manville 1990; Walter 1993; Duplouy and Brock 2018.

63. Leão and Rhodes 2015, fr. 74.

64. Theopompos *BNJ* 115 F 122a; Thucydides 8.40.1–2

65. F 27 West. The connection between citizenship and enslavement of others is central to Finley 1980; Vidal-Naquet 1981; it is nuanced in Rihl 1996, and contested in D. Lewis (b) 2018 (use of enslaved labour, as property of the enslavers, is widespread in the ancient world, including "Homeric" society).

66. *IG* I.³1357, with Baba 1984 (perhaps too quick to see official "honors" granted by the Athenians), Papadopoulos and Lord Smithson 2002; cf. *SEG* 13.36 (Karian in sixth-century Athens, with a bilingual Karian-Greek tombstone).
67. *I. Olympia Suppl.* 5a with Siewert 2006 (the *epoikiē* is attested in the early fifth century).
68. Herodotos 9.33–36.
69. A. Stewart 1990, 137–38.
70. Pariente 1992, Marchetti 1994; *SEG* 37.283 (same document also in *Nomima* 2.44); found reused in the context of a fourth-century CE ritual zone, probably close to the original archaic shrine.
71. For surveys of the genres and contexts, Budelmann 2009; Athanassaki and Bowie 2011. For examples: Fearn 2011 (Pindar in his Aiginetan context); Lulli 2011 (narrative elegy in *polis* contexts). Much of the evidence concerns the early fifth century BCE, when the poetry of the great lyric poets Pindar and Bacchylides survives (e.g., D'Alessio 2004 on the hymns composed by Pindar for Argos, perhaps from the 460s onwards); Bowie 2014, on the Argive poet Sakadas and his song, performed to pipe music, on his city's role in the Trojan war, gives an earlier example.
72. Adshead 1986; Pariente 1992; J. Hall 1997a, 93–98. But as already mentioned (above, n. 59), Forsdyke 2012, 90–115, proposes a different reconstruction.
73. Jackson 2000; *I. Olympia Suppl.* nos. 131–42.
74. Spartan "foreign policy"—a somewhat anachronistic formulation, which I heard the Latinist R. G Nisbet (1923–2013) mock as an absurd, hackneyed topic taught in Greek history during his undergraduate days in the late 1930s—is a major theme in Herodotos: 1.65–67; 3.39–56; 3.148; 5.39–54, 64–65, 69–76, 90–93, 97; 6.48–85, 92, 105–8; 7.133–34, 204–6, 239; 9.19, 28, 37, 77.
75. Herodotos 1.66–68; Boedeker 1993; Welwei 2004; J. Hall 2007, esp. 333–37.
76. *I. Olympia Suppl.* nos. 120–24, 127, 129–30, 145–46. On such material, Schröder 2020, 37–53. Local wars in Boiōtia: Buck 1979, 96–101; Mackil 2013, 23–26.
77. Nielsen 2002, 193–95, 348, on Pausanias 5.23.7 (dedication); generally, 131–33, 186–87, on the "evidence of considerable inter-Arkadian warfare" (228).
78. Herodotos 6.43.
79. Herodotos 5.89–90, 97; 6.49–50, 87–94; 7.145; Figueira 1993, 33–60, 113–49.
80. Watson 2011.
81. The cases of Tegea (Herodotos 1.66–68, with Braun 1994) and of a *polis* on the border with Ēlis, the Erxadieis, give a sense of the forms taken by relations between Sparta and Peloponnesian communities (*Nomima* 1.55); Cawkwell 2011, 53–73 for a (probably correct) minimalist view.

82. Herodotos 9.26.2.
83. J. Hall 1995; Piérart 1997; Frullini 2021.
84. *Nomima* 1.52; *SEG* 50.458 (same document *I. Olympia Suppl.* 2); *I. Olympia Suppl.* 5a (where the revenues of Kykysion, a small *polis* taken over by Ēlis, seem to be assigned to a single individual!); Taita 2007.
85. Herodotos 7.59.2, 108.2, 109.2, 118.2.
86. *IACP* nos. 1025, 1029; Strabo 17.3.21 (*polichnia* belonging to Kyrēnē).
87. Hansen in *IACP*, 87–95; *I. Olympia Suppl.* 5 (Thespiai).
88. Mackil 2013; Beck and Funke 2015.
89. Alkaios fr. 129, 130b; L. Robert, *OMS* 2.801–31; Ellis-Evans 2019, esp. 227–28 (whence I borrow translations).
90. Franchi 2016, 65–97. Phōkis: McInerney 1999, 2013 (on the crucial role of the shrines on the Eastern fringes of Phōkis, especially at the site now called Kalapodi). Generally, on "federal shrines" (across periods) Funke and Haake 2013.
91. Herodotos 8.27–28 (war), 7.176 (wall); Ellinger 1993; McInerney 1999, 173–78; Franchi 2016, 235–327 (on memorial aspects of the accounts of the war).
92. McInerney 1999, 178–81.
93. Herodotos 7.132.
94. Mackil 2013, 22–33 (the late sixth-century coinage is discussed p. 26), 185–92, 247–49; Mackil 2014.
95. Herodotos 6.108; Ducat 1973 attempts to reconstruct sixth-century Boiotian history, and Theban pressure.
96. *SEG* 60.509; Herodotos 9.15.1.
97. Aravantinos 2014, 201–2.
98. Durkheim 1901.
99. Pikoulas 2000 (who does, however, believe in a centralized process driven by Sparta).
100. Carbon and Clackson 2016. The text, illegally excavated, is devoid of any context.
101. Sánchez 2001.
102. Snodgrass 1986, reprinted in Snodgrass 2006, 234–57.
103. C. Morgan 1990; C. Morgan 2003; Hornblower and Morgan 2007; Nielsen 2007; Nielsen 2014.
104. Kurke 1991; Fearn 2011.
105. Vlachopoulos and Charalambidou 2019, 1010–12; earlier, Brock and Young 1949; Sheedy 2006–2007; Christophilopoulou 2007, on housing at Siphnos (some eighth-century and mostly seventh-century BCE houses). Generally, *IACP* no. 519 (G. Reger).
106. Herodotos 3.57.2–4.
107. van Effenterre 1979 proposes that these cases, which look like handing out individual shares of surplus, in fact designate the constitution of public funds, owned by all, and the provision of public goods for

everyone (such as the monumental civic buildings at Siphnos).

108. Sheedy 2012.

109. N. Ashton 1991 with Lohmann 1996; Morris and Papadopoulos 2005 (on Ashton's Towers 18, 36 and especially 48).

110. Brinkmann 1994; Neer 2001, who interprets the program as aristocratic (using an interpretive grid developed by L. Kurke).

111. Daux and Hansen 1987, 25–32 (the peculiarities of Siphnian marble "make the blocks of the walls of the Treasure-house of the Siphnians stand out among all other stones at Delphi").

112. Bintliff 1994; Bintliff 2012, 234–51. Foxhall 2013.

113. Lolos 2011.

114. E. Robinson 1997, arguing powerfully for widespread democracy in the late archaic period; Ober, Wallace and Raaflaub 2007, for a general survey.

115. Kotsonas 2002.

116. Andreiomenou 1994.

117. J. Carter 1990 (quoted 430); somewhat modified in J. Carter 2006 (where the case of Chersonēsos is also considered). Zuchtriegel 2018, 129–36, offers a different interpretation (with oligarchy, stratification, and subordinate countryfolk in the sixth century, followed by revolution, land redistribution and urban-dwelling small holders in the very early fifth century BCE).

118. J. Carter 2006, 199–208, though registering doubts about the political function of the structure (by D. Mertens).

119. *Nomima* 1.108–9 (also in Koerner 1993, nos. 38 and 41); Minon 2007, 417; Veneciano 2014, esp. 214–15.

120. *Nomima* 1.78 (also in *SEG* 30.380, Koerner 1993, no. 31); script: Jeffery 1990, 443.

121. Gathered in E. Robinson 1997.

122. Herodotos 5.66–73; [Aristotle], *Constitution of the Athenians* 20–26; Lévêque et Vidal-Naquet 1964; Manville 1990; Greg Anderson 2003. Ostracism: Siewert 2002; Forsdyke 2005a, esp. 144–67; Kosmin 2015; Sickinger 2017; Węcowski 2022 (showing how the procedure forced elites to collaborate and compromise rather than face the daunting prospect of the actual vote to exile).

123. Hipponax F 128.

124. Plutarch *Greek Questions* 17 (*Mor.* 295B-C); Figueira 1985, Forsdyke 2005b.

125. Herodotos 5.30.1 (Naxos); 5.77.2–3 (elites of Chalkis); 6.91.1 (Aigina), 7.156.2 (Syracuse).

126. On Aiginetan social relations, Figueira 1981, esp. 321–43; Watson 2011 (though perhaps too optimistic that the failure of the popular uprising shows the solidity and acceptance of oligarchical rule).

127. Herodotos 5.77, *IG* 1.^{3} 501 (also in Meiggs-Lewis, *GHI* 15); Paga 2020; Ostrakon: Siewert 2002, T1/153 (S. Brenne), though here I translate as in in Meiggs-Lewis, *GHI* 32.

128. *Politics*, 4.13 1297b.

129. Runciman 1982 seems to consider the rise and development of the *polis* as a foregone conclusion, once consolidation and external pressures led to the formation of state functions.

Chapter 6. The Travails of Integration

1. Duplouy 2006, 195–97.

2. Athens, National Archaeological Museum 1; Richter 1968, 26 no. 1; Hansen, *CEG* 403 (earlier *IDélos* 2); Donohue 2005 (220–21 on the way costume and styling may have also situated Nikandrē as much as her name and her inscription).

3. Brinkmann 2003 (catalogue nos 21–117); Franssen 2011; Pandermalis 2012; Kokkorou-Alevras 2018 (on Nikandrē). The current display in the Akropolis Museum gives an impressive sense of the collective effect of the sculptural dedications.

4. Murray 1993, 201–19; Duplouy 2006; Giangiulio 2017; Meister 2020, especially 223–71.

5. Houby-Nielsen 1992; Doronzio 2018, esp. 154–57.

6. Discussed and contextualized by Duplouy, Mariaud and de Polignac 2010 in Etienne 2010, 276–309. On Klazomenai, Ersoy 2007, 175.

7. E. Irwin 2005, 63–81; Duplouy 2006, 119–50; R. Thomas 2007, notably 161–64 (and esp. fig. 42 for the "immense grave marker" of Damotimos of Troizēn).

8. Carter et al. 1998; but contrast Zuchtriegel 2018, 132 (interpreting such tombs as a sign of social stratification and tyranny).

9. Duplouy 2006, 37–71; Meister 2020, especially 223–71 on the institutionalization of elite competition as part of *polis* formation. For instance, the Athenian "tyrant" Peisistratos's name was a reference to a son of the Homeric Nestōr, and a claim of descent from that hero (Herodotos 5.65); an eminent citizen of the island *polis* of Tenedos, when holding office, commissioned a piece from the poet Pindar, which mentioned his athletic victories and his descent from a Spartan and a Theban hero on either side of his genealogy (*Nemean* 11). See also R. Smith 2007; R. Thomas 2007.

10. Osborne 1989, with thoughts on the seventh century in general, to be read with Etienne 2010.

11. Murray 1990 and 1993, 207–12, on the *sumposion*; Kurke 1991, 1999.

12. Figueira and Nagy 1985.

13. Houby-Nielsen 1995; Duplouy 2006, 143–47.

14. Duplouy 2006, 204–6, 213–14, brilliantly reinterpreting and contextualizing Tuchelt, Schneider, and Schattner 1996 (who publish the ensemble as an "Archaic Cult Complex"); I derive the contemporary toponym (Mersinlitepe) from the latter publication, in preference to the pre-1922 "Kokkinólakka" for the narrow plateau at the end of which the complex is located. On the topography and history of the "Sacred Road" between Milētos and Didyma, see Schneider 1987 (precise on the site of the complex) and the critical article by Slawisch and Wilkinson 2018 (with material gathered on the website of the Panormos Project, www.panormos.de, accessed October 2023); generally Slawisch 2009 on the region from the sixth to fourth centuries BCE.

15. Herodotos 6.126–30; Papakonstantinou 2010.

16. D. Roussel 1976, sharply analytical; Bourriot 1976, exhaustive and careful on the evidence. *Genos* is either a broad term meaning descendance or, in the Classical period (especially in Athens), a technical term designating a cult group; Humphreys 2018, esp. 632–62.

17. Stahl 1987; Stein-Hölkeskamp 1989; Fernoux and Stein 2007; Fisher and van Wees 2015.

18. Nagy and Figueira 1985; Lane Fox 2000; van Wees 2000.

19. Herodotos 3.58–59; piracy in general, 3.39.3–4. The inscribed sitting statue *IG* 12.6.561 (earlier publications *Syll.*[3] 10, Meiggs-Lewis *GHI* 16) certainly concerns property seized forcibly by the Samians or a Samian, but the interpretation is problematic: Αἐάκης ἀνέθηκεν | ὁ Βρύχωνος ⋮ ὅς τῆι | Ἥρηι ⋮ τὴν σύλην ⋮ ἔ|πρησεν ⋮ κατὰ τὴν | ἐπίστασιν, "Aiakēs son of Brychōn dedicated (this), he who burnt the booty for Hēra according to the vision" or "who exacted for Hēra (a tithe of?) the seized property during his tenure as supervisor" (by far preferable); Carty 2015, 53–63.

20. Plaque: Doronzio 2018, 21–22 (Athens, National Archaeological Museum 14935, discussed in Arrington 2022, 235–36).

21. Herodotos 5.94.2; Ellis-Evans 2017, 35–37.

22. Herodotos 1.64.1, [Aristotle] *Constitution of the Athenians*, 15.2; Zannis 2014.

23. Rihll 1993.

24. Herodotos 5.83.1; Figueira 1981, 183–92 on Aigina as originally marginal community to Epidauros; Figueira 1993, 9–33 (the evidence for Argive direct control of Aigina seems to me weaker than Figueira allows for).

25. The evidence is varied, but cumulatively suggestive: Van Wees 2003 on evidence for subordinate classes at Argos, Epidauros, Sikyōn, Lokris, Thessaly, Crete, Sicily (at Syracuse), Asia Minor (Priēnē, Hērakleia Pontikē), and perhaps Kyrēnē; Luraghi 2009 (on functionality of unfree labour); Hodkinson 2009, 430–31; Ducat 2015 describing helotism as slavery (with individual masters), but governed by collective and political practice (also D. Lewis (b) 2018); on the nature of helotage as serfdom, Hunt 2017.

26. Solon F4, 36 West; [Aristotle], *Constitution of the Athenians* 2, 6. 12. On the situation before Solon's reforms, the freeing of the "sixth-parters" (*hektēmoroi*) by the "shaking-off-of-burdens" (*seisachtheia*), to use the colorful language of the early sixth century, and the consequences of this reform, scholarship abounds; see, e.g., Gallant 1982; Wood 1988; Manville 1990; Rihll 1991; Rhodes 2006; Roubineau 2007; Faraguna 2012; Zurbach 2017, 331–97; Guia Valdéz 2019; Humphreys 2018, 18–61.

27. Herodotos 6.92.

28. Houby-Nielsen 1995, on Kübler 1973 (where the archaïzing, unusual features of the stele receive comment); van Wees 1998 on the trappings of violence and body language.

29. Alkaios F 140, 70 (where I understand *philōnōn* as "lovers of the sale"), 130, 429.

30. Plutarch, *Dinner of the Seven Wise Men* 12 (*Mor.* 155F), Cicero, *On the Laws*, 2.26.65–66, with Dimopoulou-Piliouni 2015, 117–27.

31. Megara: Plutarch, *Greek Questions* 18 and 59 (*Mor.* 295D, 304E) with Legon 1981, 104–35; Figueira 1985; and especially Forsdyke 2005b. Milētos: Plutarch, *Greek Questions* 32 (*Mor.* 298C) with Ruzé 1985; *Aeinautai* also appear at Eretria: *SEG* 34.398. Athens: Herodotos 1.59.2, [Aristotle], *Constitution of the Athenians* 13.

32. Humphreys 2018, 546–47.

33. Anakreon F 16 Bergk, 31 Gentili; Ma 2016d, 636 n.6 (but see Marzari 2006 for a different interpretation, with *muthos* equated to "secret" and hence conspiracy).

34. The evidence is gathered in Berve 1967; de Libero 1996.

35. D. Roussel 1976, 53–55.

36. Herodotos 5.92; D. Roussel 1976, 51–61; Ruzé 1997, 289–95; Kõiv 2019 (arguing that the Bakchiads and Kypselids were basically similar, and presented or conceptualized using the same traditional narrative schemes).

37. Brilliantly explored in Ogden 1997.

38. Herodotos 6.67–70; Burkert 1965; Murray 1993, 147–50.

39. L. Mitchell 2013, 124–25; Kurke and Neer 2019.

40. Herodotos 1.60.1–5; Connor 1987; Blok 2000.

41. Ogden 1997, 97–99, 148–49.
42. On Solōn as a tyrant-like figure in his use of political language, E. Irwin 2005.
43. Adak and Thonemann 2022, docs 2–3 (superseding *Nomima* 1.104, as well as Meiggs-Lewis *GHI* 30; Koerner 1993, no. 78; Osborne-Rhodes *GHI* 102).
44. On the importance of exile in "Archaic" politics, Forsdyke 2005a.
45. Archilochos F 19 West, Phokylides F 4, Solon F 23.
46. Alkaios F 69; Graf 1985; Luraghi 1998.
47. Luraghi 1994 (arguing for an influence of the Eastern Mediterranean "tyrants" on their Sicilian counterparts); Braccesi 1998, esp. 5–65; Thucydides 1.17.
48. Demand 1990, 45–54; Lomas 2006. On Megara Hyblaia after its emptying and extinction as a *polis* in 483 BCE, Tréziny 2018 (the later settlement had no corporate existence until the late fourth century BCE).
49. Ma 2018.
50. L. Mitchell 2013; Kõiv 2016; Dreher 2017.
51. É. Will 1998, 125–29, on a particular case (Miltiades in Peisistratid Athens).
52. Greg Anderson 2005; for a parallel, T. Scott 2012, 53, for the way in which factional fighting in fourteenth-century Italy could produce terrible chaos—but also, eventually, durable alliances between families, which then formed the basis for despotic rule.
53. Herodotos 5.92a; Cawkwell 2011, 33–53.
54. Franssen 2011 on the paradox of "Archaic" votives.
55. Hawke 2011, heavily dependent on Tandy 1997 for his vision of a crisis in the early "Archaic" period. This crisis may be a phantom, derived from a brilliantly schematic narrative of economic change in the eighth century. See also M. Meier 1987 for early Sparta.
56. D. Roussel 1976, e.g., 31 (general statement: *polis* constituted "d'abord par et pour l'aristocratie"), 200 (leadership roles), 229 (on tribal names explained by elite contact between communities), and really *passim*.
57. Greg Anderson 2003, on the weakness of the early Athenian state.
58. Stanton 1984.
59. Stein-Hölkeskamp 1989; pushed most strongly by Kurke 1991; Morris 1996; Morris 1998a; Kurke 1999; against whom see Hammer 2004.
60. van Wees 1999c.
61. For a critique of an elitist view of the emergence and function of archaic law, Harris and Lewis 2022.
62. Restricted literacy: strongly argued for by Whitley 1997 (notably on the basis of the scribal contract between the *polis* of Datala and the "Phoenician-letters specialist" and remembrancer Spensithios: see p. 107); broader literacy in Crete: Perlman 2002, 2014; W. C. West 2015 for informal writing at Azoria (sixth century BCE). Legibility of laws: Gagarin 2008; Gagarin and Perlman 2016, 53–55.
63. Gagarin 2008.
64. E. Will 1955–1957.
65. F 93a West. Alkaios F 444 seems to describe a private war fought by Archeanaktides and his companions, perhaps exiles.
66. F 177 West; but I am not completely sure that the mechanism for the *kakoi* taking over is the courts (so Papakonstantinou 2008). Archilochos divides the deeds of men into wicked and lawful (*leōrga kai themista*), which at least illustrates the concepts, without necessarily concerning civil strife (F 177 West).
67. Archilochos F 115 West.
68. F 70, 348.
69. Aristotle, *Politics* 5.5 1305a; Forsdyke 2005b is wary.
70. Herodotos 3.142–43. Detienne 1988, 74–81.
71. [Aristotle], *Constitution of the Athenians* 16.8.
72. Kõiv 2016, 33, discussing Mitchell 2013, 83 n. 44.
73. McGlew 1993, Greg Anderson 2005.
74. This interpretation is inspired by B. Gray's understanding of exile, exclusion, and conflict as products of the very ideologies of commitment at the heart of the *polis*: Gray 2015. On the poetics of *damos* in Alkaios, Werlings 2010, 144–58 (the invective in Archilochos against a man who turned away from the oath and the table might describe a similar situation: F 173 West).
75. I here adapt a thesis put forward by Meister 2020 (especially 135–50, itself adapted from Duplouy's interpretive models), that distinction develops as an urban phenomenon, marking the dominance of the urban elites over the countryside.
76. Gagarin and Perlman 2016 G72.
77. Herodotos 7.155.2; Zuchtriegel 2018; Marini 2018.
78. A tale of trickery in Herodotos (6.62) involves a Spartiate and a king of Sparta exchanging gifts drawn from their "treasures" (*keimēlia*). Hodkinson 2000, especially 400–5, 413–15, argues for partible inheritance involving female heirs tending to maintain some parity in landed property before the fifth century BCE, but also for the presence of established and powerful elite lineages.
79. Förtsch 2001.
80. F 17, with Ehrenberg 1933; Förtsch 2001, 4–8; Werlings 2010, 189–96.
81. Nafissi 1991.
82. Dawkins 1929, 249–84; Osborne 1996–1997.
83. Brisart 2009, 2011.
84. [Aristotle], *Constitution of the Athenians* 7.3; Solon F5 West (translation D. Campbell).

85. [Aristotle], *Constitution of the Athenians* 7; Foxhall 1997; Prost 2010b; nuances in Ismard 2010, 71 n. 125.
86. Franssen 2011 (dedications); Lynch 2011 (*sumposion*).
87. On military imagery on black-figure vases, Lissarrague 1990; Osborne 2018, 87–97.
88. Kurke 1991.
89. Keesling 2003; Scholl 2006 (esp. on nonelite offerings); Raubitschek 1949. Again, the Akropolis Museum gives an idea of nonelite presence through dedications.
90. Ruzé 1997 (on "Dorian" and "Ionian" models).
91. *Pansitimidai*: *Nomima* 1.77; cf 21 (privileges for officeholders in northeastern Peloponnesian *poleis*). Citizenship: *IvO* 260; *Nomima* 1.80.
92. Thasos: F 109, 117 West. Aigina: Figueira 1981; Fearn 2010, 2011.

93. Giangiulio 2015 gives much space to the South Italian *poleis*, and their proto-democratic culture; Giangiulio 2018 on the *poleis* with closed-number citizen bodies; also Robinson 1997, 71–78 (skeptical views, based on source criticism of the literary evidence, in Lombardo 2005).
94. Piérart 2020, 67–75; *SEG* 26.449 (Argive *archos*).
95. Ducat 1974, 1456; Garlan 1995, 104–11; Ducat 1990, 111–12 and 1994a, 19–20; van Wees 2003; compare the "Dusty-feet" of archaic Epidauros: Plutarch, *Greek Questions* 1 (*Mor.* 201E). Theopompos *BNJ* 21 F 176 and 311 describes the sheep-skin dress as imposed by tyrants on rural inhabitants, to keep them from entering the city.
96. Meisters 2020, especially 224–41.
97. Solon F 4 West.
98. Simonides F 15 West.

Part IV. Framing the "Classical" *Polis*

1. On the Lokrians see Daverio Rocchi 2013 (general); Lerat 1952 (Western); Nielsen 2000, Pascual and Papakonstantinou 2013, Zachos 2016 (gazetteer), Rousset 2020 (Eastern).
2. *IG* 9.1² fasc. 3, 706: this inscription concerning the dispatch of maidens to Ilion to atone for the rape of Kassandra by the hero Ajax (the lesser), records privileges for the East Lokrian city of Narykos (within which a group took on the duty of supplying the maidens), but was found in West Lokris (Oiantheia, perhaps originally set up in the shrine of Athēna at Physkos, as suggested by G. Klaffenbach). Exclusion for nonpayment of taxes: *Nomima* 1.43 (or perhaps simply punishment by being "removed from the Lokrians," *apo Loqrōn*).
3. *IACP* no. 386 on Opous (Th. Nielsen); *IG* 9.1², fasc. 5, for testimonia and epigraphical documents relating to Eastern Lokris. Opountian federation: see for instance the honors granted by the Opountians and the Lokrians with them: 1909–10, 1912, 1917 (second-century proxenies), also *IG* 9.1², fasc. 1, 72 (honorific statue, set up at Thermos in Aitōlia, late second century BCE). The lack of inscribed civic documents from the Eastern Lokrian cities on their own is very noticeable. Tribute: this is how I interpret the levying of disputed funds in Xenophon, *Hellenica*, 3.5.3. Beck 1999 offers a nuanced picture of the position of "Archaic" Opous in East Lokris.
4. *Nomima* 1.43 (also in Körner 1993, no. 49); Wilhelm, *KS* 2.1, 401; but see Giangiulio 2018, 285–87 (preferring to see the Thousand not as an oligarchy but the whole citizen body). Hundred Families: Polybios, 12.5.6.

5. Thucydides, 2.9.3 (simply speaking of Lokrians); but cavalry from East Lokris is most likely on the basis of the geography, and because West Lokrians appear as light-armed fighters in 3.97.2.
6. Page 1981, XXIII (perhaps a Hellenistic composition).
7. *IG* 9.1 ed. 2, fasc. 5, no. 1906 (with plate 7); but see discussion by D. Knoepfler, *BE* 15, 322, who would assign the relief to Hyēttos in northern Boiōtia.
8. Lerat 1952, vol. 1; The dependent position of these *poleis* is shown by their dating official documents (inscribed at Delphi) by the eponymous magistrates of larger *poleis*. A second-century BCE decree of Oiantheia apparently mentions a group called the *megaloi*, "big men" (literally), alongside the *polloi*, but it might be a misreading for a title of officials (*SEG* 54.452, with D. Rousset in *BE* 05, 225).
9. Thucydides 3.102.1; later evidence in *IAGC* no. 160 (D. Rousset). The Hyaians presumably found themselves another urban center unless they existed as a dispersed polity (still a *polis!*).
10. Kroll 2015 (*SEG* 65.2037)
11. *KS* 2.1, 401–2, on Lokris and "the revolutions of the fifth and fourth centuries."
12. Hornblower 2011, for a study of the Greek world within a broad context.
13. Ober 2010, de Callatay 2012.
14. On canon formation, Kaldellis 2012, Netz 2020.
15. Ma 2012.
16. Gauthier 1984, 1987–1989, 1993, all gathered in Gauthier 2011.

Chapter 7. Political History (1)

Apex of efflorescence: J. Ober, *The Rise and Fall of Classical Greece* (Princeton, 2015), 222.

1. Thucydides 1.105–6, with Rood 1998, 240–42. On the "First Peloponnesian War," D. Lewis (a) 1997, 9–21.

2. See already Roberts 2017 for a long Peloponnesian War "with no winners, only losers."

3. Rood 2004; Rood 2007; Tuplin 2007 (albeit making the point that Xenophon's ending point may be ambiguously open-ended; the ambiguity does not accompany the ending point of Kallisthenes's history).

4. Plutarch, *Life of Timoleon*; Westlake 1952; Talbert 1974; Smarczyk 2003; Congiu, Micchiché, and Modeo 2011; Santagati 2018.

5. As far as I can tell, the conceit does not figure in the foundational narratives of G. Grote (1846–1856), E. Meyer (1884–1902), or J. Beloch (1893–1904) for the relevant period.

6. I cannot pretend to any expertise but have consulted Contamine 1992; D. Green 2014; Prestwich 2018; as well as dipped into J. Sumption's multivolume narrative account (1990–2023).

7. *IG* 12.6.42 (Antileōn of Chalkis, friend of the Samians), 17–41 (exile-related decrees); Shipley 1987, 155–68; Habicht 2006, 51–52.

8. Plutarch, *Life of Kimōn*; Zaccarini 2017.

9. Thucydides 1.99. The problems are those of the exact chronological shapes of the process: a long-accepted scheme based on the epigraphical evidence posited a watershed in the very early 440s, but the downdating of many epigraphical documents forces a rethinking of this scheme (Meiggs 1972; Rhodes 2008; Papazarkadas 2009; confirming intuitions of H. Mattingly; Tracy 2014, 2016). Yet the structural features favoring Athens, the presence of massive military means in the service of the long-term pursuit of Athenian interests emerged before the wartime conditions of the 420s BCE: Kallet 2013.

10. Thucydides 3.50.2 for the *klērouchia* on Lesbos installed after a revolt; Gauthier 1966; Brunt 1993, 112–36 (originally 1966); Figueira 1991; Salomon 1997; Pébarthe 2005; Moreno 2009; Pébarthe 2009; Igelbrink 2015.

11. For the inscribed lists of the one-sixtieth of tribute contributions offered to Athēna, community by community and region by region, Meritt, Wade-Gery, and McGregor 1939–1953; on the massive block on which a first series of lists was inscribed, Miles 2011.

12. Rosivach 1987; Smarczyk 1990; Connor 1993; Constantakopoulou 2007. The image of Ionian haplessness in Herodotos may reflect fifth-century perceptions (1.143, 6.11–14).

13. Smarczyk 1990; *IG* 12.6.238–51 (Samos); *IG* 4.^{2} 2 792–804; Thucydides 3.50. I would also see the boundary stones on Naxos as related to an Athenian settlement (Papadopoulou 2016, whence *SEG* 66.978), which would explain the situation portrayed at the start of Plato, *Euthyphro* (Athenian landowner on Naxos).

14. Hurwit 1999; Holtzmann 2003; Hurwit 2004. L. Kallet-Marx 1989 shows that the Parthenon was probably not directly and solely financed by tribute; Migeotte 2014, 571–75 on the diverse sources of income for the Akropolis building program (including the one-sixtieth from the tribute and surplus from various budgets).

15. Lapatin 2007; T. Shear 2016.

16. Hermippos, *PCG* 5, F 63; Gilula 2000; Pellegrino 2000, 195–225 (text and commentary).

17. Commodities flooding into Athens are noted by a fifth-century BCE antidemocratic pamphlet ([Xenophon], *Constitution of the Athenians*, 2.7) and in Thucydides's portrayal of Periklēs's praise of Athenian power during his speech over the war dead of the first year of the Athenian-Peloponnesian War (2.38). See further Braund 1994; Ceccarelli 1996; Pellegrino 2000.

18. Osborne-Rhodes, *GHI* 172; Moreno 2007, 77–143. On furniture, cushions and suchlike, including Alkibiades's soft furnishings, Andrianou 2006; Wilhelm, *KS* 2.1, 178–85.

19. Rhodes-Osborne *GHI* 51 (the *polis* of Arkesinē, on the island of Amorgos, honors the Athenian politician Androtiōn, resident on the island in some official capacity, for a loan). The affair between Ōreos and Dēmosthenēs, reported in a highly unfavorable light by Aischinēs (3.103) presumably concerns a similar loan.

20. Thucydides 2.13; Gomme 1933; Hansen 1985; Akrigg 2019.

21. Osborne-Rhodes, *GHI* 109.

22. Meiggs 1972; Finley 1978; Figueira 1991, 1998; Low 2008 (variety of essays, bibliography); Ma, Papazarkadas, and Parker 2009; Powell and Meidani 2016 for the story seen from outside Athens.

23. Briant 1996, Raaflaub 2009.

24. Megarian decree: Aristophanes, *Acharnians*, 515–66; Thucydides, 1.67.4; Plutarch, *Life of Perikles*, 29–31; McDonald 1983. Crete: Erickson 2005.

25. Osborne-Rhodes, *GHI* 138; Thucydides 1.115–17; Plutarch, *Life of Perikles* 28; Σ Aristophanes, *Wasps* 283; Shipley 1987, 116–19.

26. Plutarch, *Life of Periklēs* 8.9; Aristotle, *Rhetoric* 1.7 1365 a31-33, 3.10 1411 a2-4. On Athenian funerals for the war dead, Loraux 1981 and 1993; Clairmont 1983; Arrington 2015.

27. Xenophon, *Hellenica* 2.1.31, 2.2.3, 2.2.10.
28. Aegean as Athenian lake: Thucydides, 3.22.2.
29. Thucydides, 7.28.4 (indirect taxation instead of tribute).
30. On Xenophon's sense of events, Tuplin 1993; Dillery 1995. Carlier 1996 presents a series of explorations of fourth-century BCE history. For a unique view of Athenian decision-making, see the collection of decrees magisterially presented by Liddel 2020.
31. On fourth-century BCE political history, e.g., Ryder 1965; Hamilton 1979; Cartledge 1987; Hornblower 1994; Buckler 2003; Buckler and Beck 2008 (collected essays); Cawkwell 2011 (older essays); Hornblower 2011; Gartland 2016a.
32. On the Second Athenian Confederacy, see the paper republished in Cawkwell 2011.
33. Rhodes-Osborne, *GHI* 39–40; Brun 1989; Osborne 2000; Lytle 2013.
34. Debord 1999, 378–83, 393–4, 398–9 on the small and midsized *poleis*'s "permanent quest for freedom, which might seem pathetic to modern observers."
35. Xenophon, *Hellenica* 5.2.21.
36. Cawkwell 1996.
37. Xenophon, *Ways and Means*; Dēmosthenēs, *Philippics* and 19.291; *IG* 2.^{3} 1.2 (S. Lambert), Lambert 2018.
38. Xenophon, *Hellenica* 6.5–7, e.g., 7.1.26, 7.4.12–35; Diodoros 15.78.1–3; *I. Olympia Suppl.* 11.
39. Xenophon, *Hellenica* 5.1.31; Amit 1970, for a treatment of a few salient cases, and the introduction of the concept of big and small; Daverio-Rocchi 2008; also the collection gathered by I. Savalli-Lestrade in the journal *Topoi*, vol. 18 (2013).
40. Ma 2013b (though other interpretations of this material are possible), 2016a.
41. *IACP* p. 433.
42. Diodoros 15.79; Dēmosthenēs 19.112, 141, 235. Tuplin 1986; *IACP* nos. 213, 222 (M. Hansen); Gartland 2016b.
43. Ruggeri 2004; Roy 2009a. For earlier periods, Taita 2007.
44. Thucydides 1.26–30, 2.30 (Sollion). The numismatic record briefly records Corinthian influence: Kallet and Kroll 2020, 82–87.
45. Graninger 2011a; *IACP* no. 414.
46. Xenophon, *Hellenica*, 5.2.12–13; Zahrnt 1971; Hatzopoulos 1996, vol. 1, 176-9, on the power and potential of the Chalkidian League; Ma 2016b (homage to M. Hatzopoulos's model).
47. Thucydides 4.134 (Mantineia's allies), 5.33 (Parrhasians subjects of Mantineia); Rhodes-Osborne, *GHI* 14; Moggi 1976, 146–47; Hodkinson and Hodkinson 1981.
48. Thucydides 3.50, 4.52; Xenophon, *Hellenica* 4.8.28; Ellis-Evans 2019, 155–97.

49. Thucydides 4.65.1.
50. Thucydides 1.68–71, 4.92, 5.86–111 (with James 2024, compelling); 6.33–34 with 4.59–64 and Cuscunà 2004.
51. Badian 1995.
52. Mantineia: Gillone 2004; Xenophon, *Hellenica* 2.2.9, 2.37 for grants of *polis* existence; *IG* 1.29, 1454 for Athenian practice.
53. Xenophon, *Constitution of the Spartans* 16; Plutarch, *Life of Agis* 5.1; David 1979–80; Hodkinson 2000, 423–32.
54. Aischinēs 2.105; Cawkwell 2011, 299–333 (originally 1972).
55. Thucydides 4.17; 7.56.
56. The vicissitudes are summarized in *IACP*, 182–248 (T. Fischer-Hansen, T. Heine Nielsen, C. Ampolo).
57. Thucydides 1.122.3, 124.3; 2.63.2; 3.37.2; Periklēs "was becoming" sole ruler: 2.65.9.
58. Statues: Biard 2017, 55–61; honors: Habicht 2017, 1–4; *IG* 12.6.334.
59. Cartledge 1987 offers a biography of this extraordinary figure as a way into the whole history of the fourth century.
60. Ferrario 2014.
61. Xenophon, *Hellenica* 2.3.4; 6.1.2–16, 6.4.21; Westlake 1935; Sprawski 1999, 2004, 2012.
62. Xenophon, *Hellenica* 6.5.6, 22. On Keōs, Rhodes-Osborne, *GHI* 39–40; Brun 1989; Lagogianni-Georgakarakou 2007.
63. Corsten 1999; Mackil 2013; Gartland 2016a.
64. Xenophon, *Hellenica* 3.4.16.
65. Morris 2009b.
66. Tuplin 1993.
67. Rhodes-Osborne, *GHI* 31 (367 BCE); Brun 1988.
68. Hansen's views are summarized in *IACP*, 87–94; rejoinders and refutation in Fröhlich 2010.
69. Musti 2000; Bearzot 2004; Daverio Rocchi 2008; Phleious: Xenophon, *Hellenica* 5.2.8–10, 5.2.10–17 and 21–25, 7.2.1–3.1; Pontier 2007; Fontana 2010, 2014; Alcock 1991 on the urban site.
70. Ostwald 1982; E. Lévy 1983; Dmitriev 2011, 16–66.
71. Thucydides 3.114.3. Treaty renewed: *SEG* 63.391 (P. Funke, K. Hallof).
72. Ostwald 1982, 28; Thucydides 5.18.5
73. Diodoros 13.114.1 (*Staatsverträge* no. 210).
74. Narrative accounts in, e.g., Ryder 1965; Cartledge 1987. Ēlis: Roy 2009a, 2009b (especially on source problems). Boiōtia: Ma 2016a.
75. Xenophon, *Hellenica*, 5.2.1–12; Ephoros, *BNJ* 70 F 79 (V. Parker); Diodoros 15.5.4; Strabo 8.3.2; Moggi 1976, 140–47; Bearzot 2004, 37–43; Funke 2004.

76. Mack 2013, 91–95; 2015a, 218–21.
77. Fröhlich 2010, 663–64; likewise, the case of Pagai in the Megarid: an urban settlement (*polis*), it was formally and politically a subordinate village of Megara, until it gained independent *polis*-hood in the Hellenistic period (*IACP* no. 226, R. Legon).
78. Low 2007; Hunt 2010; Mack 2015a.
79. Rutishauser 2012; Ober 2015.

Chapter 8. Political History (2)

1. Xenophon, *Hellenica* 4.2–4; Salmon 1984, 354–62; Boehm 2021; on context, Cartledge 1987, 363–65; Bettalli 2012.
2. *IACP* no. 227 (R. Legon), though the evidence for Classical Corinth is thin on account of the destruction of the city in 146 BCE and the disappearance of documentary material.
3. Piérart and Touchais 1996, 46–52. On Argos generally, Bearzot and Landucci 2006; Piérart 2020.
4. Cahill 2002; Nevett et al. 2020.
5. *IACP* no. 28 (T. Fischer-Hansen, T. Nielsen, and C. Ampolo); Cordano 1992; O. Murray 1997; Cordano 2011; Cecchet 2017, 69–73; Osborne and Rhodes *GHI* 124. On civic organization in Sicily and southern Italy, see the papers published in *Mediterraneo Antico* 21 (2018), 1–132.
6. *IG* 12.9.56; Cordano 1992, 85–86; Masson 1992.
7. Knoepfler 1997; Fachard 2012, 47–51.
8. Piérart 2020, 283–85.
9. Bresson 2016 on both structure and institutions in the economy of the Greek cities.
10. D. Lewis (a) 1997, 60–324; Strauss 2013; Hansen 1991.
11. E.g., Ober 1989; Boegehold and Scafuro 1993; Boedeker and Raaflaub 1998; Munn 2000; Osborne 2010; Azoulay and Ismard 2011; Cataldi 2018; Akrigg 2019.
12. These were the last remnant of the façade of a ranked society set up by the Solonian reforms: above, p. 147, with Prost 2010b.
13. [Aristotle], *Constitution of the Athenians* 24; Thucydides 8.53.3; Hansen 1980.
14. Wilson 2000, 64–65.
15. On representation, Ober 1989, 2006, 212–47; nuanced in Blanshard 2004. Dēmosthenēs 19.10.
16. Osborne 2007; Wilson 2009; J. Shear 2011.
17. Ostwald 1986; Hansen 1989a, 2010.
18. Eder 1995; Rhodes 2009, 28–43; Tiersch 2016; Lambert 2018. The fourth century BCE also sees concentration of wealth by its end: Cl. Taylor 2017, 149–94.
19. Ober 1989; Millett 2000.
20. Hansen 1991, 150; 240–42 (pay for courts, Assembly and Council, but not attested for officeholding).
21. Sickinger 1999, Pébarthe 2006.
22. Christ 2006.
23. S. Johnstone 1999.

24. Rhodes 2004a; differently, Lanni 2006 (tension between discretionary power of democratic courts, the sense that mass decision-making was the best avenue for fair outcomes, and the need for reliable legal process).
25. Aischinēs 3; Dēmosthenēs 18; MacDowell 2009, 382–97.
26. Osborne 1985a; D. Cohen 1995. As well-studied examples of feud-like, protracted, tit-for-tat litigation, Andokidēs 1, Lysias 10, Dēmosthenēs 21, [Dēmosthenēs] 59.
27. For instance, Dēmosthenēs's prosecution of Meidias, using a particular procedure relating to the disruption of a festival rather than a straight public case for *hubris*, shows awareness of the multiplicity of avenues—and the problematic nature of the consequences (Dēmosthenēs 21).
28. Ismard 2010; Kierstead 2017.
29. Dēmosthenēs, 19.40; D. Cohen 1995; Lanni 2006.
30. Ober 1989, which amounts to a reading of Athenian political culture; D. Cohen 1995; S. Johnstone 1999; Pieperbrink 2014; Filonik, Griffith-Williams, and Kucharski 2019; Edwards and Spatharas 2020.
31. Brock 1991.
32. Sinclair 1988.
33. Wildcat amendments: Osborne 1990b; Rhodes with Lewis 1997, 22, 27; for an example, *I. Eleusis* 28a-b (same document in Osborne-Rhodes, *GHI* 141), a decree on the first-fruit offerings to Eleusis, passed on a draft proposal by a special board and augmented by a proposal from an individual, the seer Lampōn (440-435 BCE?). On institutional self-correction, Gomme 1951; on Assembly procedures, Hansen 1991, 140–41.
34. Ober 1998, 2001; Allen 2010.
35. Dēmosthenēs 20.108 (*hamilla tōn agathōn*); in 330 BCE, Hypereidēs described how a rival politician, Diōndas, initiated fifty *graphai* (public lawsuits), including fifteen against Dēmosthenēs alone (*Against Diondas* 3).
36. Thucydides 8.65–66 gives a striking portrayal of elite groups collaborating to paralyze, then subvert and overthrow the democratic regime; Bearzot 2013, 25–81 on "how to overthrow a democracy" in 411 BCE. On the coup, then the reconciliation after 403, Azoulay 2019; Azoulay and Ismard 2020.
37. Above, pp. 125–26; Węcowski 2022.

38. Wilson 2000; Christ 2006, 2007; Fawcett 2016.

39. Credit accumulated for use in the courts: the trope is frequent in the fourth century BCE forensic rhetoric but indubitably present in the fifth century already (Thucydides, 7.15.2).

40. Gauthier 1985 closely studies the Athenian phenomenon of *aitēsis*, the public request for rewards on account of public gratitude (*charis*), in the Classical period and down to the late third century; Deene 2013 (noting Athenian reluctance to grant honors for citizens acting in their private capacity).

41. Whitehead 1993.

42. Loraux 1993; Boegehold and Scafuro 1993; Loraux 1996; Boedeker and Raaflaub 1998; Arrington 2015.

43. C. Patterson 1981; Boegehold 1993; Lape 2010.

44. Vernant and Vidal-Naquet 1973 (translated by J. Lloyd, 1988); Winkler and Zeitlin 1990; Goldhill and Osborne 1999; D. Carter 2011.

45. Holtzmann 2003; Hurwit 2004.

46. Clairmont 1983; Arrington 2010; Low 2010; Arrington 2015.

47. Bérard and Vernant 1984; Lissarrague 1990; Oakley 2004; Lynch 2011 (for a well contextualized group); Osborne 2018.

48. Morris 1987, 154; Shapiro 1991; Morris 1993; Bergemann 1997.

49. Ober 1998; Allen 2010.

50. Thucydides, 8.65–66; also 6.27–28, 53, 60–61 for an earlier example of democratic paranoia, the quest for those responsible for mutilating images of the god Hermēs in Athens in 415 BCE. On face-to-face relations, Finley 1983 (as long as we bear in mind that face-to-faceness was a fiction); on the cascade of incertitude that oligarchical terror created within the Athenian citizen population, and the paralyzing effect this had on coordination between democratic citizens, Teegarden 2014, 18–26.

51. E. Cohen 2000; Couvenhes and Milanezi 2007; Ismard 2010, notably on the religious sociability grouping communities and people in non-state-sponsored formations (223: "Tous les chemins ne mènent pas à la cité!"); Azoulay and Ismard 2011.

52. Ma 2015a, 198–99.

53. Bergemann 1997; Marchiandi 2011.

54. Ismard 2010, arguing that associations (and the *phénomène associatif*) problematize the distinction between public and private, and indeed the centrality of the role of the *polis* as state actor.

55. D. Cohen 1995; Herman 2006.

56. E. Robinson 1997, 2011; also Giangiulio 2015.

57. E. Robinson 2011, 134, discussing the views of A. Laronde.

58. Hansen 2013, indispensable review of E. Robinson 2011, using *IACP* index 11 (1138–40).

59. Brock 2009.

60. *SEG* 31.985; D. Lewis (a) 1984; Rhodes with Lewis 1997, 296, 393–94.

61. Teōs: Adak and Thonemann 2022, docs 2–3, which supersede earlier editions (*Nomima* 1.104–5; also in Meiggs-Lewis, *GHI* 30; Koerner 1993, nos. 78–9; Osborne-Rhodes, *GHI* 102; above, pp. 107–8, on Chios (admittedly an oligarchy in the fifth century); Osborne-Rhodes, *GHI* 132, from Halikarnassos, contains an entrenchment clause showing awareness of the problems of popular sovereignty coexisting with legally authoritative texts (comparable to archaic Ēlis: above, p. 106).

62. *SEG* 54.427; Kritzas 2006; Piérart 2020, 71–73, 113–27, 153–65.

63. Thucydides 5.60.6.

64. *IACP* no. 287, p. 519; E. Robinson 2011, 34–40.

65. Giangiulio 2015.

66. Aristotle, *Politics* 5.4–5 1304b-1305a with E. Robinson 2011, 152–56.

67. Wilson 2000.

68. *SEG* 49.1031, summarizing Vinogradov and Zolotarev 1999 (*non vidi*).

69. E. Robinson 2011, 143, 211.

70. On these phenomena at Athens, Wood 1988, Manville 1990, Ober 2015.

71. Gargarin and Perlman 2016, 77–86.

72. *IACP* nos. 403; Larisa (p. 696), 413, Pharsalos (p. 703), with sources; Westlake 1935; Ducat 1994b; Helly 1995, 345–47; Ducat 1997; Mili 2014, 53–97.

73. Agreement: *ISE* 2.97; R. Parker 2010; B. Helly in *BE* 15, 394, on Helly and Tziafalias 2013 and its relevance to the Basaidai of Mētropolis. Documents from third-century BCE Atrax suggest similar complexities involving tribes, civic subdivision, and *genos* (*Inscr. Atrax* 1, 2).

74. Ollier 1933–1943; Rawson 1991; Hodkinson and Powell 2002; Hodkinson, Morris, and Christesen 2012.

75. The mechanisms—based on violence and the fostering of collusion—for social control of the helot class are clearly attested during the Classical period: Ducat 1974, 1990; Luraghi and Alcock 2003. I suggest seeing the increasingly free exercise of private ownership rights over helots (whose origin as a class lies in a serfdom arrangement) as an exacerbation of their state of dependency and the "social death" (O. Patterson 1982) they suffered, but also as a reflection of the increasing development and dysfunction of the Spartan economy, and the privileging of property rights as a function of the power of the wealthy (Hodkinson 2000). For the argument that helots were simply slaves, D. Lewis (b) 2018.

76. Xenophon's *Constitution of the Spartans* gives an idealized but instructive picture of Spartiate life within its state frameworks.

77. Hodkinson 2000, 209–26.

78. Thucydides 5.16.2–3 (return of exiled king Pleistoanax "with choruses and sacrifices similar to those when they set up the kingship upon the foundation of Sparta").

79. Spartan literacy: e.g., Xenophon, *Hellenica* 3.3.8–11; Cartledge 1978 ("public functionaries were called upon to perform routine acts of literacy on a day-to-day basis"); Boring 1979; A. Powell 2001, 238–41 (routine use of writing contrasted with image of repugnance for books and terse oral style). Accountability: Aristotle, *Politics* 2.9 1271a, *Rhetoric* 1419 a.

80. Hodkinson 2000; Ducat 2013.

81. On the "Pindaric" style of Lichas's hospitality, and the repute it brought Sparta, Xenophon, *Memorabilia* 1.2.61; on the whipping incident, Thucydides 5.50.4, Hornblower 2004, 273–86.

82. Oliva 1971; Hodkinson 2000; Bresson 2021.

83. Aristotle, *Politics* 2.9 1271b; Hodkinson 2000, 189–90; on public finances in Sparta, survey in Rohde 2017.

84. The Theban complaint in Xenophon, *Hellenica* 3.5.12, that Sparta sends out helots as harmosts (governors) must be an exaggeration; Cartledge 1987, 92–93.

85. Cartledge 1987, 164, on Plutarch, *Life of Agesilaos*, 32.

86. Xenophon, *Hellenica* 3.3.4–11; Ducat 2013, 2016; P. Davies 2017a.

87. Brock and Hodkinson 2000; Bultrighini 2005; Simonton 2017.

88. Gehrke 1985, 315–20; Ostwald 2000, especially on the "crucial role of property," and pessimistic about the possibility of reconstructing oligarchical constitutional practice in detail.

89. Aristotle, *Politics*, 5.2–4 1301a-1304a.

90. For instance, Xenophon *Hellenica* 5.2.30; generally, Whibley 1896, 139–77 (strongly qualified by R. Wallace 2013); Aristotle, *Politics* 6.14 1298a.

91. *Hellenica Oxyrrhynchia* 11.2–4; Cartledge 2000; Corsten 1999, 27–33; Mackil 2013, esp. 22–46.

92. Teegarden 2014 (the earlier figures for the "Archaic" period are somewhat meaningless), drawing on the *IACP*.

93. Fearn 2009; on the term, Bourriot 1995; Roscalla 2004. But see also Kurke 1991.

94. 8.24.4 with Hornblower *CT ad loc.* (adducing 8.9.2, as proof of oligarchical régime).

95. Brock 1991; Cartledge 2000; Brock and Hodkinson 2000; Leppin 2013.

96. Harvey 1965, 1966.

97. See the anti-Athenian, antidemocratic pamphlet ([Xenophon], *Constitution of the Athenians*) conventionally called the *Old Oligarch*, with Bertrand 1989 and Ober 1998, 14–26; Aristophanes, *Acharnians* (with Sommerstein 2005); Xenophon, *Memorabilia* 1.2.40–46 with de Ste. Croix 1981, 414–16; Plato, *Gorgias*.

98. Rosenbloom 2004a–b.

99. Thucydides, 6.89; Plato, *Gorgias* 455a-461b (and *passim*), *Republic*, Book 8; Ober 1998.

100. Implied by Thucydides at 6.6.1, made explicit at 8.1.1 ("they were angry against those of the *rhētores* [orators] who had shared their enthusiasm for the expedition, as if they had not voted it themselves").

101. Xenophon, *Hellenica* 2.3.20.

102. Cliques: Gehrke 1985, 318.

103. Teegarden 2014; Simonton 2017.

104. Rhodes 2005.

105. Stone 1988; Scholz 2000; Nails 2009; Ismard 2013.

106. Sommerstein 2005.

107. Habicht 1997a, 53–66 (2006, 71–84); O'Sullivan 2009 (inserting Demetrios in debates and evolutions within Athenian democracy); Allen 2010; Faraguna 2011; Faraguna 2016; Leão 2018; Faraguna 2018. Areiopagos: Hansen 1991, 290–94. The execution of Phokiōn in 318 BCE (Diodoros 18.66–67; Plutarch, *Life of Phokion*, 33–38) is presented in our sources as a moment of radical democracy comparable to the trial of the Athenian generals in 406 BCE (Bearzot 1985, 214–41; Tritle 2014, esp. 123–40).

108. Lintott 1982; Gehrke 1985; Gray 2015. Hansen in *IACP*, 124–29; Loraux 1997 (2002), on the close link between politics and *stasis*; Arcenas 2018 (quantitative analysis showing that stasis was neither endemic nor infrequent).

109. See above, pp. 189–93.

110. Diodoros, 15.57.

111. Thucydides, 3.69–85.

112. Thucydides, 1.23; also 3.34 (Kolophōn), 4.66; Xenophon, *Hellenica* 2.2.6 (part of the violent alternance on Samos).

113. Berent 1998 (within the "stateless society" paradigm that I have argued against in this chapter); Loraux 1997 (2002); Gray 2015; Börm 2019 (explanation through innate competitiveness of Greek elites).

114. Finley 1971; Mossé 1978.

115. Whitehead 2002; Barley and Pretzler 2017; Xenophon, *Hellenica* 5.3.23, 4.3.22; generally, Piccirilli 1974.

116. Berve 1967, 221–82; Caven 1990. Timoleōn: Santagati 2018.

117. Berve 1967, 283–85.

118. Xenophon *Hellenica* 7.1.43ff

Chapter 9. The Great Convergence

Blithe view: J. Dunn, *Setting the People Free. The Story of Democracy*. 2nd ed. (Princeton, 2019), 125–26.

1. Xenophon, *Hellenica* 6.5.3–5; *IACP* no. 287 (Th. Nielsen).
2. Xenophon, *Hellenica* 5.2.36, 5.3.25. Phleious: Pontier 2007; *IACP* no. 355 (M. Piérart).
3. Brock 2009.
4. Strabo 8.3.2 C337; Bearzot 2006, 114–16.
5. Berve 1967, 300–310; Knoepfler 2002, 196–98; Knoepfler 2004; S. Wallace 2016. On single rule, S. Lewis 2004, relating to the case of Euphrōn of Sikyōn.
6. Lintott 1982; Gehrke 1985, especially 268–308.
7. The sources for the coup are multiple and contradictory: Ryder 1965, 53–54; R. Kallet-Marx 1985; Tuplin 1993, 147–49; Stylianou 1998, 231–43. Boiōtia: Ma 2016a.
8. E.g., Momigliano 1934.
9. On the Achaimenid empire and its extractive structures, Briant 1996 (Eng. tr. 2002). Macedonian takeover: Briant 1982; Billows 1995.
10. Bikerman 1939a; Ma 2013a; Brun, Capdetrey, and Fröhlich 2021; Fischer-Bovet and von Reden 2021. For specific examples, Bagnall 1976, Hölbl 2004 (Ptolemies); Bikerman 1938; Capdetrey 2007; Kosmin 2014; Feyel and Graslin-Thomé 2017 (Seleukids); Thonemann 2013 (Attalids).
11. Gauthier 1984, which inspires my essay on the "great convergence" (Ma 2018).
12. Habicht 1997a, 142–72; Habicht 2006, 161–92; Oetjen 2014.
13. Cartledge and Spawforth 2002, 35–53. Generally, É. Will 1979–1982, vol. 1, 359–96; Kralli 2017; Shipley 2018, 62–71.
14. Bikerman 1938, 1939a; Ma 2002; Capdetrey 2007; Feyel et al. 2012. On the Attalids, Kaye 2022.
15. É. Will 1979–1982, vol. 1, 153–207.
16. Livy 37.26.4–8, 37.31.3; C. Jones 2019b. Admittedly, the Kolophonians are portrayed by Livy (no doubt repeating his source Polybios) as terrified by the siege (appealing to the Roman commander for help), and Antiochos III lifted the siege only after his fleet (commanded by Hannibal) was defeated; local autonomy existed in the interstices of superpower warfare. Notion has recently been the object of surveying by a team under the direction of C. Ratté and F. Rojas (https://sites.lsa.umich.edu/notionsurvey/, accessed May 7, 2023).
17. Ma 2002.
18. Aristotle, *Politics* 4.4 1291a; Ma 2000.
19. Lokris: above, pp. 153–55. Psōphis was an Arkadian *polis* "politically united" with Ēlis in 219 BCE: Polybios, 4.70.2, in fact probably a perioikic city, as shown by Roy 2000 and 2006 (an Eleian court sat at Psōphis)—until Philip V gave them their independence (Polybios, 4.73.8). Ēpeiros: Milan 2018 proposes seeing Kassōpē as a large territory with a main eponymous *polis* and secondary *poleis*, in the mid-fourth century BCE and perhaps down to the late second century BCE (*SEG* 36.555).

20. Kritzas and Prignitz 2020, 12–23.
21. Polybios, 22.5; Zimmermann 1993; Adak 2007 on the unsustainability of Rhodian rule.
22. Myous: Herrmann 1965, 90–103 (Herrmann 2016, 274–86), confirming W. Ruge's reconstruction of the history of Myous and its relations with Milētos; Mackil 2004, 494–97; Thonemann 2011, 334–38; Boulay 2014, 66–67 (perhaps excessive in calling Myous a mere *chōrion*, but summarizing the uses to which Milētos, then Philip V put the *Myēsia*); *SEG* 59.1357 (W. Günther: Myesians being admitted to full citizenship in Milētos; somehow related to the *sumpoliteia*). Pēdasa: *I. Delphinion* 149 (with P. Herrmann, *I. Milet* 6.1, p. 184); Gauthier 2001a; Wörrle 2003, esp. 1368–70. Milētos also controlled islands off its shore, e.g., Leros: Thonemann 2011, 283–86; *IG* 12.4.4, pp. 1255–86. Generally, Herrmann 2001 on Milētos.
23. Robert and Robert 1976; Reger 2004.
24. Evidence gathered in *IACP*, pp. 437–61 (M. Hansen).
25. Corsten 1999, 27–61; Knoepfler 2001b; Ma 2013b; Mackil 2013, esp. 346–98; Kalliontzis 2020, 98–144.
26. Kalliontzis 2020, no. 39 (fragmentary, but I do not think it shows a relationship of dependency, as Kalliontzis suggests).
27. Bravo 1968, 357–68, insists on the importance of civic freedom in J. G. Droysen's history of the Hellenistic world (first ed. 1836–1843), the pioneering historian of the Hellenistic period (whence the epigraph to this chapter); Rostovtzeff 1941, e.g., 665–95.
28. *LSCG* 92, with Knoepfler 2001a, 203; *IG* 12.9.192, with Knoepfler 2014b on the improved festival for *dēmokratia* regained (*SEG* 64.778).
29. *I. Priene B-M*' 15–19; Crowther 1996.
30. *I. Priene B-M* 5. On the Athenian settlement on Samos, see p. 113.
31. Robert and Robert 1989, 77–85; Maier 1959–1961, no. 69 with Vecchio 2019; Gauthier 2003; Rousset 2014. On recent research on the topography, Gassner, Muss, and Grammer 2017. On fortifications in this period, generally McNicoll 1997.
32. Forster 2018 (as can be seen in early Hellenistic Athens but also many other regions, such as the Iōnia, the islands and the Black Sea area), e.g., 478–81.
33. Mackil 2013.

34. Polybios 2.10.5.
35. Kalliontzis 2020, 128–39.
36. E.g., in *IACP*, p. 87 (type 7).
37. *IG* 9.² 1 583, same document also *I. Olympia Suppl.* 13.
38. E.g., Ferrary 1988, 69–73; the behavior of the big leagues comes close to the model of international anarchy proposed in Eckstein 2006, 2008. Competition by the leagues, esp. in the Hellenistic Peloponnese: for the political history, Kralli 2017; Shipley 2018.
39. *SEG* 38.1476; Ma 2003a, 7–11; Rousset 2004–2005 (I thank Alain Bresson for discussion of this text).
40. Rigsby 1996; Knäpper 2018. The exact practical ramifications (as opposed to symbolic dimensions) of *asylia* remain unclear.
41. Ma 2000; Chaniotis 2005a; Boulay 2014; Eckstein 2008 picks up on the presence of *polis* warfare but exaggerates the violence and scope of it.
42. Ampolo 2001 with *SEG* 41.1185 for concordance to 30.1117–18, 1120–23, 35.999.
43. *SEG* 25.445; Ma 2003a, 30–31; C. Jones 1999a, 33.
44. A recent example of royally fostered resort to "foreign judges" can be found in Debord and Fröhlich 2018 (judges from Kolophōn sent to Aigai, all within the Seleukid realm).
45. The examples are usefully collected in Börm 2019, but interpreted rather differently here; Shipley 2018, 134–58, postulates the persistence of *stasis*, admits an "attenuated record" but interprets it as a phenomenon of the evidence rather than as a sign of abatement.
46. Polybios, 4.17–19. Sparta: Polybios, 4.22–24; Cartledge and Spawforth 2002, 35–72.
47. Helly 2009.
48. *RC* 17 (same document *I, Ephesos* 1485): a King Antiochos mentions a personal guest-friend (*idioxenos*) in the city of Ephesos; at Iasos in 190 BCE, the pro-Seleukid faction expelled the supporters of Rome: Livy 37.17.5–6, Gray 2015, 254–58. More usually, members of local civic elites often hold posts in royal administration or gain prominence as intermediaries with royal courts: Savalli 1998, Paschidis 2008.
49. Royally sent arbitrators: *IG* 11.4.1052, 12.4.135a, 12.5.1065, 12.7.221. Foreign judges: Robert *OMS* 5, 137–54; Gauthier 1994; Crowther 1995; Crowther 2007a; Cassayre 2010, 127–75; Magnetto 2016; Börm 2019, 171–200 (crisis of institutions faced with structural intra-elite strife).
50. G. Cohen 1995, 177–80.
51. *OGIS* 48 (also in *I. Egypte prose*, no. 4); Kayser 2017 (40–41 on the oligarchical coup and protests by the *neōteroi*).
52. Dēmosthenēs 17; Polybios, 2.41.11–14; Shipley 2018, 97–126 (interpreting the "tyrannies" as part of normal civic politics). Berve 1967, 393–405.

53. Polybios 2.41–43, 2.59; Holleaux 1921, 121–22, on the "republican movement" of resistance against Macedonia (the felicitous expression is borrowed from J. Beloch).
54. P. Jones 1997; Paton and Law 2016.
55. del Monaco 2013 (*IG Locri*); del Monaco 2018; *IACP* no. 59 (Fischer-Hansen, Nielsen, Ampolo).
56. Priēnē: *I. Priene B-M* (same document *I. Ephesos* 2001). Amyzōn: Robert and Robert 1983, no. 23. Araxa: *SEG* 18.570, with Zimmermann 1993 on date.
57. J. Shear 2011; Azoulay 2014a; Teegarden 2014, 15–53.
58. Knoepfler 2002, notably 163–64; Teegarden 2014, to whose examples one might add *CITh* 3 1, lines 31–35 (Thasos, early fourth century: decree with rewards for whoever kills a tyrant or oligarch); *I. Adramyttion* 34, lines B 55–8 (same document *OGIS* 4, lines 106–10; law "concerning whoever tries to overthrow the democracy (*damos*)" on the *polis* of Nasos, in 318 BCE); *SEG* 64.1229 (law limiting the powers of the generals at Kymē: see below) with Hamon 2008, 102–3; and Hamon 2012, 354 n. 14.
59. *SEG* 51.1105, line B23.
60. *I. Erythrai* 573; Gauthier 1982, 215–21; Teegarden 2014, 142–72.
61. Veyne 1976, 201–2; Ober 1998.
62. Latterly, Pellegrin 2017, 59–66.
63. Carlier 2005 on all these theoretical constructions.
64. *Politics*, 2.9 1270a-1271b.
65. All men can do all things: *Politics* 3.11 1281a-b. Control of great matters: 311 1282 a-b. All free men: 3.6 1279a.
66. 3.4 1277b (artisans); 4.4 1290b (Thēra), 5.3 1303a (Ōreos, Amprakia).
67. 5.7 1307a.
68. Heisserer 1980, 79–95 (also in Rhodes-Osborne *GHI* 84 A); generally, Shane Wallace 2018.
69. Seager and Tuplin 1980; Jehne 1991; Debord 1999, 236.
70. *RC* 1 (earlier publication *OGIS* 5); *I. Iasos* 2–3; Diodoros 20.37.2 (unsuccessful appeal by Ptolemy in mainland Greece, at Sikyōn; É. Will 1979–1982, vol. 1, 69–72); Gruen 1984, 132–57; Dmitriev 2011.
71. *IG* 12.4 132; Habicht 2007, 129–30; Simonton 2019.
72. Tēlos: Stefanaki 2008, and Brett 1950, 70, on Athēna as *Polias*, the protector of the city. The coin is known in two examples, which between them allow the reconstruction of the astonishing legend: Berlin Münzkabinett 18205268, once in the collection of F. Imhoof-Blumer, who read the legend: Imhoof-Blumer 1890, 154, no. 460, [ΔA]|MO|K[P|AT]|IA|Σ; *Numismatische Abteilung der Schweizerischen Kreditanstalt Bern* 40

(May 1983), 16 no. 98: [ΔΑ|ΜΟ]|Κ[Ρ]|ΑΤ|ΙΑ|Σ. I thank Ute Wartenberg for help with these coins. On Knidos and its bronze coinage, R. Ashton 1999.

73. On reconciliation and creativity, see the dense network of essays collected in Cataldi, Bianco, and Cuniberti 2012.

74. Rhodes with Lewis 1997 surveys the mostly epigraphical evidence and offers a synthesis in which institutional convergence appears clearly.

75. Osborne and Rhodes, *GHI* 194.

76. Mass assemblies: Robert, *OMS* 3, 1499–1502; Rhodes with Lewis 1997, 510–12; Canevaro 2018b. Pay: Iasos *ekklesiastikon* (Rhodes-Osborne, *GHI* 99, which we now know dates to the early third century rather than the time of Alexander: Fabiani 2015b, 259, 289–91); Rhodes: Grieb 2008, 263–353. Accountability: Fröhlich 2004, Feyel 2009.

77. *CITh* 3, starting with the reconciliation act at no. 1.

78. *SEG* 30.1119; Gray 2015, 35–78.

79. The very fragmentary honorific decrees from Krotōn, *SEG* 64.857–58 (third century BCE, inscribed on bronze) confirm that the great convergence in *polis* institutions touched the cities of Italy and Sicily.

80. Gauthier 1985; Ma 2015a.

81. Robinson 2011.

82. *SEG* 59.1407, Hamon 2008.

83. Robinson 2011; S. Sherwin-White 1978, 175–223; Rhodes with Lewis 1997, 237–38; Carlsson 2004; Grieb 2008, 139–98.

84. *IG* 12.4.304 (ca. 220 BCE), see also L. Meier 2012, no. 31; the financial burden is still in vigor in the first century BCE (*IG* 12.4.326).

85. *IG* 12.4.1 152 (earlier publication *Tit. Calymnii* XII).

86. *I. Delphinion* 150, lines 84–85.

87. Diodoros 18.54–56, 64.3.

88. Carlier 2005, 273.

89. *IG* 9.2.517 (*Syll.*³ 543); Bertrand 1990.

90. Robert and Robert 1954; Robert and Robert 1983; van Bremen and Carbon 2010.

91. Gauthier 1989 (who would date the emergence of Sardeis as a *polis* to the disappearance of Seleukid power in Asia Minor between 246 and 226); Rigsby 1991, 50–52, pointing out that there certainly existed local institutions in pre-Seleukid Sardeis; also Briant 1995. On Hellenistic Sardeis generally, Berlin and Kosmin 2019.

92. *IG Iran Asie centr.* 52–53 (earlier publications: *RC* 31–32; Rigsby 1996, 69–70; *I. Estremo Oriente* 250–51).

93. *SEG* 40.991–92, also Debord and Varinlioğlu 2001, no. 90–1, with van Bremen 2013a; O. Henry 2013; Fabiani 2015a; Rix 2016.

94. Metzger et al. 1979; the texts can be found at http://www.achemenet.com/fr/tree/?/sources-textuelles/textes-par-regions/anatolie/lycie (accessed June 2023); Rhodes-Osborne, *GHI* 78 for the Greek text. See also Briant 1998 (republished and translated by A. Kuhrt in Briant 2017); F. Kolb 2018, 209–22.

95. Dynastic culture: e.g., Childs and Demargne 1989; Carstens 2009, 52–61. For the evolution of settlement in Lykia, illustrated by a particular case, the city of Kyaneai and its territory in central Lykia, F. Kolb 2008; for the replacement of Lykian dynastic culture by *polis* culture, F. Kolb 2018, 709–25.

96. Robert 1963, 471–540; Michels 2009, especially 334–39.

97. On the institutional *koinē* of southern Anatolia (as seen in the widespread eponymy of the *dēmiourgos* in Pamphylia, Pisidia, and Kilikia), Robert 1963, 478–79; it is unclear when these institutions spread.

98. Early links: Herodotos 1.54; Gauthier 1989, 160–65; *I. Ephesos* 2; Milētos, where the Milesians mention "the envoys chosen by the Sardians" as the equivalent of the ambassadors formally elected by the Milesian assembly.

99. Purcell 1994; *IACP* no. 3, Morgantina (T. Fischer-Hansen, T. Heine Nielsen, C. Ampolo).

100. *SGO* 4, 20/14/01; Bikerman 1939b.

101. *CID* 4.99 (earlier *OGIS* 234).

102. Vlassopoulos 2013.

103. Habicht 2007, 125–27; Bonnet 2015, 260–65.

104. Generally, T. Scott 2012; Paton and Law 2016.

105. Fabiani 2014, 2015a.

106. Meritt, Wade-Gery, and McGregor 1939–1953, vol. 3, 149–54; D. Lewis (a) 1997, 51–59; Robert 1940–1965, vol. 11–12 (on Athenian-influenced formulas on Paros); Fröhlich 2004, 116, 304, 314.

107. The mid-fourth century Abderitan law on the right of return of enslaved people or beasts of burden after purchase, in case of undisclosed illness seems closely influenced by Attic law: *I.AegThrace* E 3, with *BE* 68, 115 (summarizing the analysis of the legal historian I. Triantaphyllopoulos), Hypereides 3.14–15 (Philips 2013, no. 309; cf. Arnaoutoglou 1998a, p. 65). Legal procedure in public trials in early second-century Paros shows an influence of Classical Athenian law: Lambrinoudakis and Wörrle 1983, 314–16 (Arnaoutoglou 1998a, no. 97).

108. Wilhelm, *KS* 2.1, 175; H. Weber 1908; Accame 1952, 123–27; Robert 1940–1965, vol. 11, 213, on Hellenistic political language and its relation to Attic prose; 524–25 on the Attic form *xumballesthai* in Parian decrees; D. Lewis (a) 1997, 51–59; Gauthier 1985, 127–28, on generalization of "greatest honors" and likely origin in mid-fourth century Athens; Rhodes with Lewis 1997, 550–57; Fröhlich 2004, 116.

109. For instance, in Hellenistic Ionia, the protection of public funds and foundations is ferocious, Athenian-style, but cannot be shown to be directly copied from Athenian law (*Syll.*³ 577, Milētos; 578, Teōs, with careful notes by W. Dittenberger on procedure and parallels). A late fourth-century decree from Thasos mentions judicial procedures (denunciation, arbitration, adversarial oaths, monthly trials) that show quite close resemblance to Athenian practices and indeed can be commented with Athenian parallels, without proof of direct influence: *CITh* 3.9, Salviat 1958.

110. On this theme, below, chapter 17; Ober 2010, Bresson 2016.

111. *IG* 12.6. 17–41 (exile-related decrees), and above, p. 161.

112. Kymē: *SEG* 59.1407, 50.1195. Kōs: *IG* 12.4.1.152 (earlier publication *Tit. Calymnii* XII). Milētos: *I. Delphinion* 139.

113. Decree for Philippidēs: *IG* 2.³ 1.4 857; *IG* 2.² 1191; Tracy 1995, 36–51; Tracy 2003, 9–25 (continuity in mostly democratic institutions compatible with *de facto* Macedonian control); Oetjen 2014, 42–48; Graham 1983.

114. 1291b30-1292a38; 1308a33-1301a12. Simonton 2019 proposes violent *stasis* and a vengeful demagogic aftermath on Tēlos, an alternative path toward convergence.

Chapter 10. The Qualities of the *Polis*

Strange freedom: J. G. Droysen, *Geschichte des Hellenismus* (Hamburg, 1836–1843), 300–1.

1. Matthaei and Zimmermann 2015; Wörrle and Zanker 1995.

2. Housing: Hoepfner and Schwandner 1994. Hērakleia in Lucania: Zuchtriegel 2018, 46–54.

3. On the importance of the Hellenistic period for our understanding of *polis* history, Fröhlich 2004; Hamon 2009; van Nijf and Alston 2011; for a survey of recent debates, and a reading of Polybios in this context, Thornton 2019.

4. Purcell 1990; van Nijf and Alston 2011; Zuiderhoek 2017; Woolf 2020.

5. F. Kolb 2010 for the testcase of central Lykia (which passed from a world of multiple dynastic seats to a big *polis* territory); F. Kolb 2018 for the transition from Achaimenid and dynastic landscape to a *polis* landscape.

6. *Steinepigramme* 01/20/33 (on context, Boulay 2011); on the Neleidai, Polito 2018. On "Archaic" elitism, Duplouy 2006 and above, chapter 6.

7. Grieb 2008 (e.g., on Kōs, Milētos, Rhodes during the high Hellenistic period).

8. *IG* 12.3.66, *SEG* 64.729.

9. A. Chaniotis 1995 (with Ph. Gauthier's meditative remarks, *BE* 96 135); A. Chankowski 2005; Martzavou 2008; R. Parker 2011, 171–223; Chaniotis 2013.

10. On the contexts, the texture, and the meaning of local history, Clarke 2008, Thomas 2019. For a particular instance of local myth, Knoepfler 2010 on Eretria and the myth of Narkissos. Drama: Csapo and Wilson 2020.

11. Kaldellis 2012; on Hellenistic art and its registers, R. Smith 1991, Ma 2006. On issues of canon-formation in antiquity, Netz 2020.

12. Survey of evidence and testcases, in parallel with epigraphical material, in Wörrle and Zanker 1995.

13. Ma 2009.

14. *SEG* 56.418, based on Psychogiou 2006 (unpacking myth and implications, and monumental meanings in the Argive landscape; perhaps a little too specific in positing political allusions; A. Chaniotis, *EBGR* 2007, in *Kernos* 23 (2010), 113.

15. Travelogue: Arenz 2006 (Knoepfler 2013a, 425–27, argues for a dating after 229 BCE). "Kinship diplomacy": Curty 1995; C. Jones 1999a. *Proxenoi* (official guest-hosts of cities), Mack 2015a and http:www.proxenies.csad.ox.ac.uk (accessed September 13, 2023).

16. D. Roussel 1976; N. Jones 1987, 1999.

17. Bousquet and Gauthier 1994, 326–27.

18. Ismard 2010.

19. The material is gathered and studied by P. Hamon in *CITh* 3.

20. Piérart 1983, 1985; Pimouguet 1995; Thonemann 2011.

21. Attica: R. Osborne 1985b; Lohmann 1993; Lohmann and Mattern 2010; Kellogg 2013; Fachard 2017; Knodell, Fachard, and Papangeli 2017; Ackermann 2018. Elsewhere: F. Kolb 2004 (general); and e.g., Lohmann 1999 (Milēsia); Marangou 2002–2005 (Amorgos); F. Kolb 2006, 2008 (Kyaneai in central Lykia); Lolos 2011 (Sikyonia); Fachard 2012 (Eretrias); Lohmann et al. 2014 (Mt Mykalē); Fachard et al. 2020 (Boiotian settlement at Eleutherai).

22. Schilardi 2017, 300.

23. On the importance of the "Kleisthenic" model, Wood 1988, which here I extend to the Hellenistic *polis*.

24. Teōs: *SEG* 35.1132. Geleontes: Rousset 2014, with considerations on the complex articulation of tribe and *genos* within the bicephalic *polis* of Kolophōn. Leros: Manganaro 1963–1964.

25. N. Jones 1987, 188–91 ("vigorous corporate life"), on *IG* 12.2.498, 501, 502, 504, 515 (statue base) and *IG* 12 suppl. pp. 30–32.

26. *IG Locri* 1–37; Migeotte 1992, 197.

27. Generally, Boulay 2014.

28. The case of Milētos, which absorbed neighboring *poleis* such as Myous or Pidasa, raises the question of the integration within the complex phyletic and demotic system; Myous, for one, survived for a while as an undigested *polis*-like mass within the greater Milētos: Herrmann 1965.

29. Briant 1982, 95–135 (wondering whether the *laoi* of Asia Minor ended up being massively enslaved); Ducat 1990. 190–93; Papazoglou 1997; Bertrand 2005a; Zurbach 2021.

30. On the model for Attica, R. Osborne 1985b; Whitehead 1986; Ismard 2010; on its political implications, Wood 1988.

31. Fröhlich and Hamon 2012; Vlassopoulos and Taylor 2015.

32. Rhodes: Pugliese-Carratelli 1939–1940; Thomsen 2020. See also Arnaoutoglou 2003 on "religious" associations; Couvenhes and Milanezi 2007 (centered on Athens); Fröhlich and Hamon 2012. Milētos: Herrmann 1980 (*SEG* 1285, 1139–44).

33. But see further, chapter 15, for the tensions and contradictions embodied and furthered by the associative phenomenon).

34. Cavalrymen: *ISE* 15. Organized bodies: e.g., *I. Priene* B-M 19 (garrison of citizen soldiers); Boulay 2012 (on the example of Hellenistic Teōs). *Neoi*: Kennell 2013; van Bremen 2013b (and also her lectures summarized in *La Lettre du Collège de France*, December 2013).

35. Gauthier 2005, *SEG* 55.1251.

36. *IG* 4.757 (also published with commentary in Maier 1959–1961, no. 32; Migeotte 1992, 21).

37. A. Jones 1940; Gauthier 1984; Rhodes with Lewis 1997; Fröhlich 2004; Ghinatti 2004; Grieb 2008; Hamon 2012, 56–57; Beck 2013.

38. Giangiulio 2004; Greg Anderson 2009.

39. Ma 2018.

40. Ephesos: Walser 2008. Samos: *IG* 12.6.172, 169. Paros: Lambrinoudakis and Wörrle 1983. Generally, Wilhelm 1909, 229–99; Klaffenbach 1960 on the importance both of recordkeeping and of monumental inscriptions of state.

41. On the dynamics of collegiate, non-hierarchized boards of magistrates, Johnstone 2011, 111–26.

42. On the old modes of *charis* in the Hellenistic *poleis*, see Robert 1940–1965, vol. 1, 7–17 and vol. 11–12, 546–47 ("de tous les prytanées s'élève un bruit de vaisselle"); e.g., Bevilacqua 1996 on sacrifices and dedication; *SEG* 22.117 (decree of Ikaria *ca*. 330 BCE); *IG* 11.4.1137–42 for dedications by magistrates, with suitably elitist sentiments; *I. Rhod. Peraia* 355; *BE* 55, 181 reinterpreting and offering parallels for texts published by Kontoleon 1953 as relating to daily sacrifices at the *prytaneion* of Tēnos in the second century BCE (*SEG* 14.553), complete with companions, boys, wine-pourers and piper. Magistracy as a *timē*: Erythrai, with Wilhelm, *KS* 2.1, 359–60 (contrasted with the lot); Gottlieb 1967.

43. Allen 1996 on democratic time; Trümpy 1997; F. Dunn 1998.

44. Specific commission-*archai* are well known in Boiotia: e.g., *I.Oropos* 294; Roesch 1965, 181; Fröhlich 2004, 170, 179, 401, 409 (but also for the practice more generally).

45. The process of extension of written law, by addition, is attested by those documents that lay down and codify earlier practice: Lambrinoudakis and Wörrle 1983; Gauthier et Hatzopoulos 1993 (*I.Beroia* 1, also in *SEG* 43.681, Beroia gymnasiarchical law). Network of offices: e.g. *Syll*.³ 647 (also published as *Staatsverträge* 4.653, *IG* 9.1.32), for magistrates and sacred offices in Steiris, a small *polis* in central Greece in the late second century BCE (D. Rousset, *BE* 21, 6 on date).

46. Wilhelm 1909, 293 on magistrates' cartularies.

47. Robert, *OMS* 1, 535–36 (Chios, matters considered by boards of magistrates and passed on by the monthly presidents thereof).

48. E.g., *Nomima* 1.78, 88, 102; 1.33 (same document published earlier *IG* 9.2.257, *Syll*³. 55), Thetonion in Thessaly.

49. Fines: e.g., *SEG* 48.1037, regulating the powers of magistrates on independent Dēlos (fines to a certain limit, within which each *archē*, including the *boulē*, is *kuria*); *IG* 5.2.3 shows the same practice at Tegea; lists of individuals punished by magistrates with fines can be found at *IG* 12.2.646 (Nasos), *I. Byzantion* S1 (Sēlymbria) and perhaps *IGBulg* 1.314b. Editilary powers: e.g., *IG* 12 suppl. 322 (with Wilhelm 1909, 157–59), a third-century BCE decree from Karthaia, on the powers of magistrates to enforce respect of public spaces, by fines and corporal punishment.

50. Vial 1984 on Dēlos; H. Müller 1995; Hamon 2005; e.g., *I. Olympia* 45 for diplomacy being handled by the *strategoi* and the *boule* at Olympia in 302 BCE; *IG Locri* 1–37 for the Council handling finances in Epizephyrian Lokroi.

51. Halikarnassos: Wilhelm, *KS* 1.1, 298–300, with Rhodes with Lewis 1997, 331; on legal delays, Savalli 1980; for an example, *I. Delphinion* 153 (a crown voted by the Assembly at Milētos, in honor of the Byzantians, is confirmed by a court).

52. *CITh* 3.9.

53. [Aristotle], *Constitution of the Athenians* 47.2–4; Dēlos: V. Chankowski 2019; Lokroi: *IG Locri*. 1–37,

with Costabile 1992 (14–23 on the stone lid, studied by C. Alfaro Giner).

54. SEG 2.579 (also in Chandezon 2003, no. 53), late fourth century BCE.

55. Lambrinoudakis and Wörrle 1983, 351–52 on practice on early second-century Paros (SEG 33.679); F. Gschnitzer, RE suppl. 13, s.v. πρύτανις, 808–9 (the practice is another instance of Athenian influence; its name, "payment for leaders," indicates its origin, in the gifts for the *basileis* sitting in judgment: above, chapter 3.

56. Chandezon 2003, 148 (*prytaneia*).

57. F. Sokolowski 1954.

58. Xanthos: SEG 38.1475. On civic finance and fiscality, Rostovtzeff 1941, 242, and Wiemer 2003, on Syll.³ 1000 (now IG 12.4.293; late second century BCE); Wilhelm, KS 1.3, 265–67; Gauthier 1976, 9; Gauthier 1991; Migeotte 1995; Schuler 2005; Migeotte 2006, and *Studi Ellenistici* 19; Rhodes 2007; Chankowski and Andreau 2007; L. Meier 2012; Migeotte 2014; for a particularly well-documented testcase, Hellenistic Dēlos, V. Chankowski 2019.

59. IG 9.1².188, 213/2 BCE.

60. SEG. 2.579.

61. Gauthier 1991. *Proeisphora*: SEG 59.1407; *I. Priene B-M* 64, lines 33, 51–56, 95.

62. SEG 28.526 (Phayttos in Thessaly, second century BCE) mentions a "direct levy after promise" (*eisphora ex epangelias*) to pay for an honorific statue. On subscriptions and lists of donors, Migeotte 1992; Ellis-Evans 2012; Migeotte 2014, 529–31.

63. L. Meier 2012; Matthaei and Zimmermann 2015.

64. Hamon 2008, 2009, 2021 (on Asia Minor). On Hellenistic judicial workings, Cassayre 2010; Walser 2012; Papazarkadas 2021 (Hellenistic Athens). Fournier 2010, though devoted to the Greek cities under Roman hegemony, then imperial control, is most useful.

65. Herōdas, *Mimiamb* 2.

66. The issues are highlighted by the following three types of institutional provisions: first, the cancellation of decrees as illegal in Dēmētrias: BE 60, 194, Habicht 2008; second, "clearing clauses" to allow decrees to have effect in spite of earlier decrees and laws (e.g., *I. Mag.* 92a, 94, *I.Priene* B-M 112, noted Robert, OMS 5.444–46); third, "entrenchment clauses" that enshrine a decision against later reversal (e.g., *I. Priene* B-M 27; Rhodes with Lewis 1997, 231; in Athens, D. Lewis (a) 1997, 136–49). On decrees having force of law at Magnēsia on Maeander, Wilhelm, KS 2.1, 74–75. On *psēphisma* and *nomos*, Velissaropoulos-Karakastas 2011, vol. 1, 49–63. On worries about voluntary prosecution, BE 02, 536, on ephors in Kyrēnē striking the *poludikoi* with *atimia*, which implies popular courts

and active prosecutors; the same worry lies behind Aristotle's wish for strong penalties against "random" public prosecutions (*Politics*, 6.5 1320a). A tribunal in charge of evaluating laws (*nomothetikon dikastērion*) appears in the democratic *polis* of Kymē, which has already been discussed above: *I. Kyme* 12, SEG 59.1407.

67. For self-correction in earlier periods, see Gomme 1951 on Athenian Assembly; *I. Erythrai* 1 (*ca.* 400 BCE), limiting the renewal of the office of secretary. Iasos: Fabiani 2012, 2015b, with remarks and nuances by P. Fröhlich, BE 13, 379, and by P. Hamon, BE 15, 35. Wilhelm, KS 1.1.298–300, Feyel 2012, 248, on Hellenistic courts confirming decrees.

68. Robert, OMS 3, 1499–1502; Rousset 2014, 75–76 for Kolophōn, discussing Duplouy 2013; Canevaro 2018b. Kōs: Grieb 2008. Magnēsia: *I. Magnesia* 92a (4,678 voters), 94 (3580 voters), in second-century BCE honorific decrees; Halikarnassos: IG 12.4.142 (4,000 voters); Kolophōn: *I. Iasos* 81, SEG 42.1064 (2,050 voters, second century BCE); Priēnē: Kah 2014, 150–54; Delphi: Gauthier 2000.

69. IG 12.3.247–49 (the last inscription registering the number of voters).

70. Secret ballot: Gauthier 1990; BE 09, 302–3 (in Thessaly); Canevaro 2018b, esp. 111–18. For instance, at Kōs: Grieb 2008, 156, and SEG 48.1112; Iasos: SEG 41.929, 57.1046, 65.981; Delphi: Gauthier 2000, 121 (elections of officials).

71. Csapo and Wilson 2019, 515–17 (summarizing hypotheses of M. Amit and E. Robinson).

72. Canevaro 2018b.

73. Rhodes with Lewis 1997, 496–97.

74. On Athenian practice, D. Lewis (a) 1997, 51–59; Rhodes with Lewis 1997 (decline of attested amendments in the Hellenistic period). A wide variety of individual *rogatores* appear in Dēlos, Ōrōpos, Iasos; but these may all be magistrates. Amendments from the floor outside of Athens: Wilhelm, KS 2.1, 75, Robert, OMS 1, 312 n. 3; the Roberts, BE 56, 16 p. 180–81, also suggest that many amendments from the floor were simply integrated into final decisions. Plutarch, *Life of Timoleon* 3.2, if reliable, shows a nomination for office from the floor in mid-fourth century Corinth.

75. Ma 2016c.

76. Already in Athens: discussed by A. Jones, 1957, 120 n.124; [Aristotle], *Constitution of the Athenians* 43.6 on "supplication" to the Assembly, with Rhodes 1981. *ad loc.* with epigraphical examples. Generally, Rhodes with Lewis 1997, index *s.v.* approaches to authorities, Council, or Assembly, on the widespread practice of *prosodos* or *pothodos* (e.g., in the Peloponnese or the islands). See also Wilhelm, KS 2.1, 489–90 ("many people" approaching the authorities at Messēnē, thus generating institutional movement toward a decision);

Robert, *OMS* 2, 969 (on *I. Magnesia* 103); *IG* 12.4.1, 59 with commentary, 42 (Kôs); *CITh* 3, nos. 107 (probably Paros), 110 (Assos), 125 (Smyrna); *I. Iasos* 219 with Fabiani 2019; H. Müller 1995, esp. 49–54; Hamon 2010, 308–10; The right of direct approach to state institutions was also granted as a privilege to foreigners: e.g., Knoepfler 2001c, index s.v. *prosodos* (*ephodos*), *CITh* 3 nos. 15, 16: the point must be to give these special foreigners the same right of access that citizens naturally enjoy. *Prographē*: Hamon 1999, 182.

77. *SEG* 55.1251; Robert, *OMS* 5.347–54, on the *neoi* of Ephesos.

78. *I. Iasos* 219 (ca. 200 BCE, from the letterforms: Fabiani 2019). The officials' *ephodos* probably went to the *boulē*, but individual "additional proposals" might have been put to the Assembly (the verb used is *proeispherein*, "to contribute in addition," cognate to the verb usually used for motions before the Assembly). On procedures at Iasos, Fabiani 2012, 2015b.

79. *I. Erythrai* 114, *SEG* 37.934 are examples of procedurally simple decisions (affecting public space) that the Assembly orders magistrates *not* to decide on or transact administratively, but to refer (*paratheinai*) back to the assembly itself; a similar concept (*ep' anaphorai*) is seen at Teōs (*SEG* 2.580, *Syll.*³ 577). But see further, chapter 18.

80. H. Müller 1976 on Milētos and its college of *epistatai* with military competences; also Grieb 2008, 218–20 on the monarchical temptations of the Classical and early Hellenistic periods, above, pp. 173–74.

81. Rhodes: *prytaneis* serve for six months (Rhodes with Lewis 1997, 273; Grieb 2008, 292). Erythrai: *stratēgoi* serve for four months (Rhodes with Lewis 1997, 370). Kōs: *prostatai* serve for six months, *stratagoi* may also have done (Grieb 2008, 160, 163). At Teōs, the phrourarch in the settlement of Kyrbissos, after its annexation, could serve for four months every five years (*SEG* 26.1306).

82. Ruschenbusch 1984, on a particular island *polis*: "if ever democracy in the sense of the participation of all in office-holding was ever realized anywhere, it was Amorgos."

83. Grieb 2008, 213–14.

84. Allotment: e.g., *OGIS* 229 (third-century Smyrna); *Syll.*³ 633 (*boulē* chosen by lot in Milētos: Grieb 2008, 213–14); Kosmetatou 2013. Tickets for use in allotment machines (probably in relation to jury service in popular courts), are known from a dozen places in the Greek world, from the late fourth century onwards: Kroll 1972; Ph. Gauthier in *BE* 06.331, generally; Thasos (*SEG* 60.946–57); Abydos (*SEG* 55.1306); Olbia (*SEG* 37.671) in Rhodes (Gabrielsen 1997, 27–28); Amphissa (*SEG* 65.2037; provenance insecure since the object comes provenanceless from the antiquities market); on the machine, Dow 1939. Pay and allotment are explicitly attested for the Rhodian jury system (*IG* 12.1.55; Maiuri, *Rodi e Cos* 18 with Fraser 1972). Generally, Bugh 2013.

85. Pottier, Reinach, and Veyries 1887, vol. 1, 206–10 (not completely sure if these are jurors' tickets, but confident that they are related to civic institutions). Allotment tickets are found in graves on Rhodes: *SEG* 30.1035, 47.1257, 59.900.

86. *IG* 2.² 1163 (with Habicht 1982, 64–78 on the priests).

87. The budgetary lines that the Pereians ring-fenced when they joined Meliteia in *sumpoliteia* may have included *misthos* for magistrates; the *misthophoroi* whose salary could not be defaulted on by Milētos, in 211 BCE (leading the city to devise a scheme of public borrowing) were likely officeholders (*I. Delphinion* 147, with Migeotte 1984, republishing the document as no. 97 and translating as "public salaries," even though Vinogradov and Wörrle 1992, 169 n.72, propose mercenaries; I thank Will Mack for discussing this point). Hellenistic *poleis* did not hesitate to offer pensions or subsistence (*trophē*) in certain cases, to prize-winning athletes (Slater 2015) or certain foreigners (Michel, *Recueil* 497 with Wilhelm 1909, 175–77). Payment for jurors is well attested (Rhodes) and may have been met out of court fees (Walser 2012); payment for ambassadors is often attested through the refusal of wealthy citizens to accept such pay (*I. Priene B-M* 67, lines 132–33), but also explicitly (*IG* 12.4.1 56: the *polis* of Kôs gives an ambassador to Sikyōn a sum of money as "crown" for a Sikyonian honorand, travel expenses for six days, and pay, *misthos*). Honorific crowns may have served as a form of compensation, judging by the special mention of magistrates dedicating their crowns (*Tit. Camirenses* 110).

88. On the judicial practice of financial rewards for volunteer prosecution, and its nuances, Rubinstein 2003, 2016.

89. Though Fabiani 2019 sees the whole context as one of crisis; here my emphasis is on the potential of institutional workings.

90. *IG* 9.2.1109 (also published in *Syll.*³ 1157, *LSCG* 83–84).

91. *IG* 12.5.595 with Fröhlich 2004, 243–44.

92. Fröhlich 2004 (accountability), Feyel 2009 (*dokimasia*, the preliminary control of all things public).

93. Teōs: *Syll.*³ 577, line 54. Beroia: (*I. Beroia* 1, earlier in Gauthier and Hatzopoulos 1993 and *SEG* 27.261), lines B88–97, with Fröhlich 2004, 265, 305–19.

94. Rhodes with Lewis 1997, 379.

95. Hedrick 1999; Sickinger 1999; Migeotte 2002; Culasso Gastaldi 2004; Pébarthe 2013. This is notably the case of the reinscription of laws ca. 304/3 BCE in

Athens, after the long period of one-man rule by Demetrios of Phaleron: the writing up of the laws was meant for "whoever wishes to inspect."

96. *I. Lampsakos* 9. See also Wilhelm 1909, 240–42 for figures picked out in red in big Delian accounts; Hedrick 1999; *IG* 2.² 487, *SEG* 33.679; *IG* 12.7.515 (foundation of Kritolaos, Aigiale on Amorgos, late Hellenistic).

97. Gauthier, *BE* 06 175.

98. Fehr 1980. On *polis, topos,* and sharedness, Aristotle, *Pol.* 2.1, 1260 b 39–1261; 3.3, 1276 a 19–22. For a modern, interdisciplinary effort to see the Hellenistic *polis* in its material and social aspects, Matthaei and Zimmermann 2015.

99. Wörrle and Zanker 1995; Matthaei and Zimmermann 2015.

100. I draw the definition from Bell 1993.

101. On the shape, poetics, evolution, and politics of the genre of civic honorific decrees for citizen benefactors Gauthier 1985; Liddel 2009; Forster 2018; Liddel 2021 (analyzing the case of Erythrai).

102. *I. Smyrna* 1–189; the material is abundantly illustrated in Pfuhl and Möbius 1977. See R. Smith 1991, 187–90; Zanker 1993; Robert, *OMS* 7, 641. My analysis here is inspired by D. Bell's essay on communitarianism (1993). On the body language of the reliefs on such gravestones, Masséglia 2015, 53–156.

103. Wilhelm, *KS* 2.1, 416–18 on *dēmosia* in the concrete and abstract sense; see also the essays in *Ktema* 23 (1998); Rousset 2002. Hansen 1998 on public and private, and relation between Athenian democracy and modern liberal democracy.

104. Hennig 1995.

105. E.g., Thucydides 2.37; 7.39.2; see below, p. 469, on the case of M' Salarius Sabinus of Lētē, in the second century CE. See further, chapter 17.

106. Quotation from the Samian decree *IG* 12.6.1 1 (earlier *SEG* 1.366) for the benefactor Boulagoras.

107. Gauthier 1985; Ma 2002.

108. Habicht 2017 (cult as honors); Price 1985 for analytical model, applied in Ma 2002.

109. Gray 2015; earlier Loraux 1997 (2002).

110. On protreptic effect, Robert and Robert 1989, 56 n. 293; Robert, *OMS* 1, 620–3.

111. This sort of explicit declaration appears in late Hellenistic documents: e.g., *I. Priene* B-M 59; *IG* 12.4.1 167 (earlier published in *SEG* 48.1114, decree for a doctor at Kōs); *I. Mylasa* 109.

112. *I. Magnesia* 91; *SEG* 23.447 with *BE* 84, 229; Dēmosthenēs 20.141.

113. Proclamations: Ma 2015a, 34–36; Kokkorou-Alevra 2004, no. 4 (same text republished in *IG* 12.4 364); *IG* 12.4.2 463 (list of honorands at Kōs). Shares from sacrifice: *I. Magnesia* 98.

114. *IG* 12.7.389. On the proclamation of honors, Ceccarelli 2010 (for earlier periods, Wilson 2009).

115. Routine honors: e.g., the short decree from Mesambria *IGBulg* 1.² 308 *ter* (third century BCE, for a *tamias*, treasurer, who performed his duties well and justly). Theater lease by Attic deme of Peiraieus: *Agora* 16, no. 93 (324/3 BCE), with Csapo 2007. Euergetism and financial operations: C. Müller 2011.

116. Gauthier 1985, 31, 34 for a sample of such decrees, from the third and second centuries BCE (for instance at Erythrai, *I. Erythrai* 24, 28, paralleled by the fragments 37.934–35 of similar documents; or Istros, *I. Histria* 12); Forster 2018.

117. Veyne 1976, based on Weberian models; Gauthier 1985; Quass 1993; Wörrle 1995; Habicht 1995; Migeotte 1997; Fröhlich 2005; Domingo Gygax 2006; Brélaz 2009; C. Müller 2011; Ma 2015a; Gygax and Zuiderhoek 2020; Ma 2022.

118. Habicht 1997b on the horsey families of Hellenistic Athens, serving in office. Opportunities: a simple example is the way local elites can enjoy pasturage or wood-collecting rights on the common lands of other *poleis* than their own (Chandezon 2003, 263).

119. Elite families in Athens, Habicht 1982, 178–97; Habicht 1997a, 209, 287–88 (Habicht 2006, 233, 317). In Messēnē: Habicht 1997c; Fröhlich 2008. In Alabanda: Habicht 1999, 19–21 (family attested as officeholding, over 150 years).

120. Elite display: Ma 2015a, 195–239. Elite competition within civic norms: Whitehead 1993.

121. Elite roles: Wilhelm, *KS* 2.1, 408 on the old heroic acceptance of communal tasks (building on an insight by U. von Wilamowitz); Robert, *OMS* 7, 383 n. 6 (*Choix* 503 n. 6) on exposure to military danger (*paraballomai, parabolōs*), with Ma 2003b on possible visual traces of "military culture" among civic elites (but also on military service occasionally commemorated as part of the identity of average citizens in Iōnia: Smyrna, Teōs, Samos). See above, pp. 220–21.

122. Examples are collected in Wilhelm, *KS* 2.1, 268.

123. Hybreas and Euthydēmos: Strabo 14.24; Robert, *OMS* 5, 8.

124. Simonton 2022.

125. Gauthier 1985, 99–100 on Dēmosthenēs, 20.75.

126. For Athens, Hansen 1991, 157, 314 (honors as motivations for good citizens—balanced by punishment in the courts).

127. Jacoby 1945, 185–211; Gauthier 1985, 122–23; Domingo Gygax 2016, 176–77.

128. Gauthier 1985; Domingo Gygax 2016. Aristophanes, *Acharnians* 633, 641.

129. Such honors are richly attested in the epigraphical record: *IG* 2.³ 4, part I.2 (leaving out nos. 128–205): dedications by boards of officials, especially

prytaneis, for being crowned, or even for "winning," after their service, mostly during the fourth century BCE.

130. Faraguna 2011, 2018.

131. Father: e.g., *IGBulg* 1.² 316, an honorific decree starting with explicit mention of the honorand's father and his virtues. Ancestors: an epigram celebrating the Milesian statement of Lichas, after enumerating his glorious services, concludes "no reason to be jealous" (*ou nemesis*), in view of Lichas's glorious ancestry of founders of Iōnia (*Steinepigramme* 01/20/33); similarly, the honorific statue set up by the Kaunians for a fellow citizen completed the normal formula with an epigram celebrating his heroic ancestry, going back to the Bacchiad-led foundation of the city: *Steinepigramme* 01/09/07, earlier published in *I. Kaunos* 83). On fourth-century BCE great-manism, Ferrario 2014.

132. On possible examples of patronage in the *polis*, Garnsey 1988; Gallant 1991; Maehle 2018.

133. Xanthos: *SEG* 38.1476. Milētos: *I. Delphinion* 147 (above, n. 87).

134. *I. Iasos* 244.

135. Ober 2010, Bresson 2016.

136. *IG* 2.² 1174, 367/6 BCE or slightly later; *IG* 2.² 1175; *IG* 2.³ 4 223; Wilhelm, *KS* 2.4, 49–60; 2.1, 197–218, esp. 206–10 on the curse tablet, with photographs (*IG* 3 appendix 24: Wünsch); *PA* 5471, 5474–5; Traill 1994–, 431515, 431520, 431525, 431530; Ma 2012, 139–40; Papakonstantinou 2017, 152–53; Humphreys 2018, vol. 2, 1083–97. The scene of all this drama is known archaeologically: Kouragios 2009–2011. More documents, this time routine, from Halai Aixōnides (recent publications by G. Steinhauer): *SEG* 59.142 (338 BCE), 49.141 (early 3rd century BCE; also 142, 143, fragmentary). On curse tablets, Lamont 2021.

137. *IG* 12.7.221b (earlier published in Michel, *Recueil* 382). Compare *IG* 12.5.129 (unrest on Paros); *I. Priene B-M* 114 (seems to record institutional dysfunction at Erythrai, solved by external judges). Fuks 1984 is inclined to see traces of widespread social discontent. See further, chapter 18.

138. Robert 1963, 474 n.1, with examples (see also *CID* 4.118; *I.Rhamnous* 24). At Amyzōn, "some people" mentioned to the people that public monies had been handed to an excellent (*kalosk'agathos*) and beneficent citizen but never returned, clearly a delicate affair (Robert and Robert 1983, no. 36). A Rhodian association honored one of their members for making someone produce or return 150 drachmas, in spite of "the hatred of some people" (*I. Dor. Inseln* no. 2, datable to the late third or early second century BCE: Baoud 2015, 170, 214), an example of the adoption of civic style in civil society. The trope lived for as long as the *polis*: it is found in Dio Chrysostom's Prousan orations (40.10, 13; 43.10; 48.9) or Libanius (e.g., 56.1).

139. Dēmētrias. Erythrai: *I. Priene B-M* 114 (also *I. Erythrai* 111). Foreign judges: above, p. 215.

140. Vlassopoulos 2007b for the *polis* of Athens as "free spaces"; see chapter 15.

141. E. Harris 2017 on Athenian associations from 340s to late third century BCE; Thomsen 2020 on the civic aspirations of associations in Hellenistic Rhodes.

142. Thomsen 2020; Herrmann 1980; Günther 1995.

143. For a particular case, kinship in democratic Athens, Humphreys 2018; on family, sociability, and *polis*, Gherchanoc 2012.

144. C. Müller 2011; Sosin 2014 on elite rationality in investing and protecting their fortunes.

145. Crowther 1990; 2007b.

146. T. Shear 1978; Gauthier 1985, 77–86. Generally, Paschidis 2008.

147. Bresson 2016, esp. 211–19.

148. Ma 2015a.

149. Walser 2012.

150. *SEG* 62.906 (D. Kah).

151. Mert 2016.

152. Ma 2015a, 144–48.

Part V. *Polis* and Imperium

1. Zimmermann and Schuler 2012 (*SEG* 63.1333).

Chapter 11. The Indian Summer of the *Polis*

Dangerous life, impactful changes: L. Robert, "Théophane de Mytilène à Constantinople," *CRAI* 1969, 42. Republished *OMS* 5, 561–83. Robert goes on with a weighty (but unfulfilled) promise in a footnote: "I have often expressed these ideas and started presenting a synthetic view in my teaching at the Collège de France and the Ecole des Hautes Etudes. I plan to publish . . . a 2-volume history on *The Greek Cities of the Hellenistic Period*."

1. *SEG* 63.1333 (M. Zimmermann, C. Schuler).

2. Polybios 1.4, 3.1; Walbank 2002; Thornton 2020.

3. E.g., Holleaux 1921; Holleaux 1926; Veyne 1975; Derow 1979; W. Harris 1979; A. Sherwin-White 1984; Gruen 1984; Derow 1989; Habicht 1989; R. Kallet-Marx 1995; Bernhardt 1998 (for a sagacious survey of the debates); Nicolet 2001; Derow 2003; Eckstein 2006, 2008; Burton 2011; Dmitriev 2011; Rosenstein 2012a; Eckstein 2013.

4. Hammond 1967, 633–35; Will 1979–82, vol. 2, 283–85; Cabanes 1976, 303–7; Winnifrith 2002, 64–65. On the material forms of civic culture in Hellenistic, especially federal, Ēpeiros before the catastrophe of 167 BCE, Katsikoudis 2005 (with my review at *BMCR* 2008.02.27); Rinaldi 2020.

5. Eckstein 2006, with an image of unrestrained international politics, which is open to challenge on theoretical grounds (Burton 2011) and simplifies Hellenistic international life, where breaches of norms had considerable costs.

6. Eckstein 2013; W. Harris 1979. Maximal suspicion to the point of solipsism: Veyne 1975; Ferrary 1995.

7. Crawford 1977; North 1981; Rosenstein 2011 (on war profits public and private); on the general economic landscape of the Roman Republic, and the impact of war, Kay 2014. Examples: Manlius Vulso, Livy 38.12–27; Polybios 21.33–39; French 1994; a bonanza of plunder and enslavement in Ēpeiros, Livy 45.34–35.

8. Derow 1989; Habicht 1989; Derow 2003.

9. Ma 2002 (derived from work by E. Bickerman). Roman traditions: the notion that Roman foreign policy was determined by a social model of clientage is untenable (Ferrary 1988, 121–24; further thoughts in Jehne and Polo 2015). The Aitolians were dismayed by the consequences of unconditional surrender in 189 BCE (Polybios 20.9): rather than showing some specifically Roman notion of *deditio*, or *fides*, this reflects Aitolian unfamiliarity with this subordinate position (and their effort at achieving the greatest leeway).

10. *RS* 1, no. 12, Knidos, col 3, lines 16–21 (also published as *I. Knidos* 31); Ferrary 2012, 43–60.

11. Defeated: Aitolians, Polybios 21.32. Allies: Lykians, *SEG* 55.1452, lines 9–10.

12. Habicht 1989, 386.

13. Polybios 28.22.

14. Polybios 29.27; Livy 45.12.308; Diodoros 31.2.

15. Polybios 13.1 on Aitolian consumption; Scholten 2000. Polybios, though fiercely anti-Aitolian and fiercely pro-Achaian, identifying the Achaian League with the cause of local liberty, is insensitive to the impact of Achaian expansionism, yet provides insights into it. On Achaian elitism, Champion 2007.

16. I owe much to the doctoral work of T. Ish-Shalom (2023); see also Berlin and Kosmin 2021 on the "middle Macchabees."

17. Mellor 1975; Tuchelt 1979; Salvo 2012.

18. E.g., Polybios 28.13, 28.15; Gruen 1984, 96–131, 481–505. On embassies, Linderski 1995 ("when Rome became the center of the ancient world, it also became the place to which embassies flocked"); Claudon 2015.

19. Polybios 32.3.16. Generally, Deininger 1971 on the protracted attempts at "political resistance" in the face of Roman imperialism; Thornton 2001a.

20. The people of Phoinikē voted to execute politicians who might have been seen as anti-Roman: Polybios 32.6.

21. Polybios 32.7.

22. Polybios 30.20.

23. Ferrary 1988; Dmitriev 2011; Eckstein 2013.

24. *I. Metropolis* 1; Andros: *IG* 12 suppl. 270 with Le Quéré 2015, 30 n. 9.

25. Wörrle 2000; Hamon 2012; Chin 2018.

26. Burton 2011 (based on a constructivist theory of International Relations).

27. Erskine 1994.

28. *I. Lampsakos* 4.

29. Sparta: Kennell 1999; C. Müller 2023 (insisting on the role of Roman intervention); Crete: Petropoulou 1985, 126–29.

30. Deshours 2006; e.g., *SEG* 57.369 is a decree of the *polis* of Pylos for a citizen of Messēnē, even as Pylos is somehow part of a greater Messēnē.

31. Late Hellenistic federalism requires its own study. Chalkis: Knoepfler 1990. Lykia: Knoepfler 2013a. Thessaly: Graninger 2011b; Bouchon and Helly 2013, notably 221–23 on the cults of the "second Thessalian confederation."

32. Thessalian League: Kip 1910, 129–38; Graninger 2011b. Larisa: *SEG* 31.574 and *BE* 83.236; *SEG* 56.638; Tziafalias, Garcia Ramón, and Helly 2006; Helly 2008a, 2008b; Rhodes with Lewis 1997, 179–80. Honors: *SEG* 51.722; 62.635.

33. Ma 2003a, 30–31; Adak and Thonemann 2022, revisiting the whole dossier of Teōs and Abdēra together with an extraordinary new document. Heroism of envoys: *IAegThr* 5, line 22.

34. *I. Delphinion* 148 (*Syll.*[3] 588; also P. Herrmann, *Milet* 6.1.185–89; *Staatsverträge* 4. 654); *I. Priene B-M* 132. I date the peace between Magnēsia and Milētos (and hence a war between these two cities), and the Rhodian arbitration of a conflict between Priēnē and Samos, to the 180s rather than in 196 BCE (Errington 1989; Habicht 2003; Castelli 2017; Bresson, Descat, and Varinlioğlu 2021, 147 n.25; *contra* Wörrle 2004b; Magnetto 2008, followed by Badoud 2012).

35. Crowther 2007a.

36. Robert and Robert 183, nos. 51–54 (Karia: new list of *stephanēphoroi* at Amyzōn "since the Karians were freed"); *Staatsverträge* 4.6688b (from L. Meier 2019,

41–50: alliance between Kibyra and Apollōnia under Salbakē); *TAM* 3.1 2 (also published *Staatsverträge* 4.779) alliance between Termēssos and Adada, probably late Hellenistic).

37. Institutions: Strabo 14.3 with Knoepfler 2013b; on the Lykian League generally, Behrwald 2000; Domingo Gygax 2001. Tyrants: above, p. 216. Orthagoras: *SEG* 18.570; Zimmermann 1993; Rousset 2010.

38. Burton 2011, 205–27 on local agency; Ferrary 1995, 412, on warfare in the 150s and 140s BCE.

39. The late Hellenistic period as a specific moment in the story of the *polis*, rather than as part of an undifferentiated post-Classical decline, emerges clearly in the work of L. Robert (*OMS* 2, 841 n. 3; 5, 561–83) and especially Ph. Gauthier (Gauthier 1985, 53–63). Subsequent work (often by Gauthier's pupils) has nuanced the concept and the periodization: A. Chankowski 1998; Fröhlich and Müller 2005; Grieb 2008; Martzavou 2008; Hamon 2009; Fröhlich and Hamon 2011; C. Müller 2011, 2014.

40. "Indian Summer": Bernhardt 1971; Bernhardt 1984; Λ. Sherwin-White 1984, 249–52; Mikalson 1998, 242–87; Deshours 2007.

41. Rizakis 2008, no. 5 (earlier versions: *RDGE* 43, now superseded; R. Kallet-Marx 1995, whence *SEG* 45.417 *Syll.*³ 684); Ferrary 1988, 186–209. The nature of the proconsul of Macedonia's intervention in southern Greece is unclear: Daux 1937, 355; Accame 1946; Hurlet and Müller 2020, arguing for the existence of a separate province of *Graecia*.

42. Gruen 1984 (for another view, Baronowski 1988); R. Kallet-Marx 1995, ch. 42–96; Epidauros: *IG* 4².63 (with R. Kallet-Marx 1995, 184–97).

43. Livy, *Periocha* 59. Attalid Asia Minor: Thonemann 2013, especially ch. 1.

44. Council: *SEG* 50.1211, Wörrle 2000, 565–70. *Poleis* in the war against Aristonikos: *I. Metropolis* 1; Strabo 14.1.38; Justin 36.4.7; Magie 1950, 147–58; Robert and Robert 1989, 29–35; C. P. Jones 2004 (the chronology of operations is somewhat unclear); Boulay 2014, 481–84.

45. This is the implication of the evidence from *I. Metropolis*; earlier evidence suggested differing statuses within the province of Asia (Bernhardt 1985, 285–94; Ferrary 1991).

46. *I. Metropolis* I, text A. Aristotle, *Politics* 2.8 1268a already comments on the generalization of the practice of state support for war orphans.

47. Ferrary 2017, 317: Apollōnis appears as a free city in Cicero's *In Defence of Flaccus* of 59 BCE (29.70-33.83); on the foundation of Apollōnis, Robert 1962, 255–60.

48. *I. Metropolis* 1; *SEG* 39.1243, col. 1, line 37 (with Robert and Robert 1989, 86, noting the vigor of the expression); Ferrary 1991 (the Kolophonians were exempt from the Roman practice of giving security, *satisdare*, in certain cases), 1999; Lehmann 2000.

49. Roman statesmen later looked back on this period as one of freedom of the *poleis*: Appian, *Mithradatic Wars* 62, *Civil Wars* 5.4.

50. Q. Mucius Scaevola cos. 95: Magie 1950, 159–76; Ferriès and Delrieux 2011; Ferrary 2017, 355–793, 319–20, 325–27. But his father, Q. Mucius Scaevola *augur*, cos. 117, also a governor of Asia, clearly had a legion with him, as shown by the Kolophonian decree for Menippos: Ferrary 2017, 308 n.3, 327; Marek 2016, 259. Both father and son were prosecuted, it seems maliciously, by thwarted Roman tax farmers, for provincial maladministration: see further, pp. 292–93. Thin provincialization: R. Kallet-Marx 1995; attention elsewhere: A. Sherwin-White 1984.

51. Ferrary 2017, 298 n.40.

52. Etienne 1990, 127–34; Le Quéré 2015, 29–130.

53. van Bremen 2010.

54. Pausanias 7.14.7; *SEG* 3.414 with Knoepfler, *BE* 15.254.

55. Kibyratis: Pouilloux, *Choix* 4 (decree from Araxa in Lykia, attesting conflict; on date, Rousset 2010, 127–33, cautious: second half of the second century BCE); Strabo 13.4.17; Rousset 2010 (*SEG* 60.1569); Eilers and Milner 1995.

56. Eurōmos and Mylasa: *SEG* 33.861, Boulay 2014, 170–71. Mētropolis and Kolophōn: *SEG* 39.1244, col. 1, line 50-col 2, line 7, with Robert and Robert 1989, 88–92. Keramos: Robert 1962, 60–62, *I. Keramos* 6. Stratonikeia and Mylasa: Camia 2009, no. 1 (too fragmentary for the subject to be sure); and Rhodes: *SEG* 44.867.

57. Eurōmos: *SEG* 43.709 (exact date unclear, but certainly second century); Ephesos and Sardeis: Laffi 2010.

58. Kōs: *IG* 12.4.293 (earlier *Syll.*³ 1000, cf. Wiemer 2005; navarch, trierarchs, crews of "long ships" and crews of auxiliary cutters); Halikarnassos: *LBW* 3.504. In general (beyond the late Hellenistic period), Boulay 2004, 117–30.

59. Aristotle, *Politics* 7.6 1327a.

60. Horn 1972, 50–63 on funerary reliefs on Samos, at 52 for the representation of arms and armor (abundantly illustrated) with Ma 2003b; *IG* 12.6.464 for citizen soldiers serving at the Heraion under their *skēnarchoi*; Robert, *OMS* 1, 549–68.

61. Milētos: *Inschr. Milet* 1.7 203 (ca. 130 BCE), with Milet 6.1, 199–200 and A. Chankowski 2011, 341–42. Athens: Perrin-Saminadayar 2007, T 26 for a decree on ephebes (earlier *IG* 2.² 1006 + 1031; 123/2 BCE).

62. Camia 2009, on the shape of the phenomenon, and the low-key involvement of Rome in arbitration

(not a tool of Roman power). Milesian arbitration between Messēnē and Sparta, no. 2 (same text in *I. Olympia* 52, *Syll.*³ 683), and the Prienian dispute with Milētos appears in *I. Priene B-M* 376 (first century BCE); earlier R. Kallet-Marx 1995, 161–83. The phenomenon already starts after 168, with significant involvement of Athens: Habicht 2006, 291–307. In the later second and first centuries BCE, examples of arbitration include Ager 1996, nos. 166–67 (involving the Delphic Amphiktiony), 168 (involving Megalēpolis and a neighbor, and probably without any involvement from a reborn Achaian League: the *sunedroi* there are local councilors), 171 (a dispute involving Milētos and Priēnē; see Thonemann 2011, 342–44).

63. Themos and Zavvou 2019, 109–11, no. 2.

64. On the second-century BCE foreign judges, Crowther 1997, 2007a (on foreign judges in and from Thessalian poleis); Fournier 2010, 168 (list), 267–68 (at Sparta).

65. *I. Priene B-M* 101, 48 (Herōdēs at Athens); *I. Priene B-M* 75, lines 20–35, cf. also 65, lines 48–51; 101; 125 (envoy sent to Priēnē by city whose name is now lost). The profusion of embassies mounted by second-century *poleis* is commented on in Robert and Robert 1989, 69.

66. I here argue against the powerful vision offered in Grieb 2008, that the arrival of Rome amounted to the immediate extinction of external freedom and hence the death of democracy in the late Hellenistic city.

67. Generally, Bresson and Descat 2001, including an essay by G. Le Rider on the numismatic patterns; on the latter, Matthaei 2013; and most importantly Meadows 2019.

68. Bombos honored by Larisa: *SEG* 56.638. Thasian history: *CITh* 3 107 (earlier *SEG* 58.952).

69. Wilhelm, *KS* 2.1, 549–53; *KS* 1.3, 275–302; Daux 1937, 371; Mikalson 1998; Martzavou 2008; Lafond 2009; Deshours 2011. Badoud, Fincker, and Moretti 2015–2016 comment on the victories of the athlete Mēnodōros in a whole series of festivals (datable 120-110 BCE).

70. *I. Priene B-M* 65, lines 43–47.

71. *SEG* 39.1243, col. 4, lines 50–2.

72. *LSCG Suppl.* 14; Deshours 2011, 105–13.

73. *Ergastinai* decrees: Mikalson 1998, 256–58; Aleshire and Lambert 2003; Deshours 2011, 131–36.

74. Karila-Cohen 2005a, 2005b, 2009.

75. *I. Magnesia* 100 (*Syll.*³ 695), Deshours 2011, 197–208.

76. *SEG* 45.1508 (new readings reported 64.907); 50.1501; P. Hamon in *BE* 16.452 (summarizing important textual and interpretive work by W. Blümel, R. van Bremen, J.-M. Carbon, and C. Chandezon); Deshours 2011, 261–75.

77. *IG* 9.2.1109 (also in *Syll.*³ 1157, *LSCG* 83–4).

78. Deshours 2006 on *IG* 5.1.1390 (also in *LSCG* 65); Gawlinski 2012 (notably on date).

79. Des Courtils 2001 (challenged in Heinze 2014; not followed here, after discussing the archaeology of the Letoon with L. Cavalier, whom I thank); Le Roy and Hansen 2012.

80. Ferrary and Verger 1999; Kowalleck 2014.

81. Bresson 2006 (reviewing Higbie 2003).

82. *SEG* 65.896 (S. Isager, with remarks by P. Hamon as in *BE* 16.453).

83. Rostovtzeff 1941, 806.

84. Mert 2016 (food market); Hennemeyer 2013 (shrine of Athēna); generally, Raeck, Filges, and Mert 2020.

85. Michels 2009; Clancier 2017.

86. *SEG* 53.1357 with Malay 2018, 101–3; on local identity, Nollé 2010.

87. Chaniotis 1996; Chaniotis 2000 for another possible "dependent" *polis* in Crete; Ma 2000 with some rather lurid images of Hellenistic Crete at war.

88. Rigsby 1996, 289–90 (Teōs); Knäpper 2018, 145.

89. Petropoulou 1985, 104–14, 126; Ghinatti 2004, 107–19. As for the rest of the Hellenistic world, the presence of elite, officeholding families is not enough to disprove the existence of democratic institutions and practices.

90. *IG* 9.2.1109 (also published in *Syll.*³ 1157, *LSCG* 83–84, Deshours 2011, 208–16).

91. Messēnē: Deshours 2006; 2011, 229–31.

92. *I. Magnesia* 100; Fröhlich 2004, 107–8 (for a parallel in *I. Magnesia* 99: prosecution by "whoever wishes" among the citizens).

93. Dēmētrias: *IG* 9.2.1109. Athens: *LSCG* 50 with Martzavou 2013.

94. *SEG* 50.1211; Wörrle 2000, 563, observing that the same situation is described as *eleutheria* in *OGIS* 338.

95. Ferrary 2017, 15–20.

96. Generally, Walser 2012. Rhodes: Maiuri, *Rodi e Cos* 18; Milētos: Camia 2009, no. 3 (earlier *I. Olympia* 52, Ager 1996, no. 159).

97. Papazarkadas 2017; *IG* 2.² 1016 with *SEG* 49.129, *BE* 07, 203; Rizzi 2017 on *IG* 2.² 1013.

98. *IG* 2.³ 4.106–109 with Papazarkadas 2021.

99. Gauthier 2000; Kyriakidis 2014.

100. Larisa: *SEG* 31.574 and *BE* 83.236; *SEG* 56.638; Tziafalias, Garcia Ramón and Helly 2006; Helly 2008a, 2008b; Rhodes with Lewis 1997, 179–80.

101. Tziafalas, Helly, and Bouchon 2016.

102. Royal officers: *SEG* 60.604–5. Proxeny decrees: *SEG* 36.552.

103. Ma 2016b.

104. *IG* 9.2.1109 (*LSCG* 84), line 93.

105. Accountability: Fröhlich 2004; generally, Robert, *OMS* 4, 256–7 on the greater precision of inscribed decisions in the late Hellenistic period; e.g., the institutional culture of Paros, Lambrinoudakis and Wörrle 1983 (368 on the vitality of the late Hellenistic *polis*). *Ennomoi chronoi*: Savalli-Lestrade 1981; Gauthier 2001b, 214–19; Tziafalas, Garcia-Ramon, and Helly 2006 (whence *SEG* 56.636, cf. 638). Complexity: Bertrand 1990 on *I. Lampsakos* 7 (republished *CITh* 3, 109), *I. Assos* 11a (*CITh* 3, 110); constitutional matters are carefully analyzed by P. Hamon in *CITh* 3, 352–61.

106. Habicht 1995 (positing structural continuities in political leadership and elite competition); Fröhlich 2005 on late Hellenistic Priēnē; Hamon 2007 (suggesting leading citizens of late second-century BCE Athens, Rhodes, or Thasos are new arrivals on the political scene).

107. *I. Priene B-M* 51, 92, 93.

108. That is the easiest explanation for the list of payers of taxes related to festivals (*diadikasia*): M. Walbank 2015, *SEG* 65.95.

109. *I. Priene B-M* 144.

110. *SEG* 42.578 (very fragmentary decree from Kalindoia).

111. Livy 34.51.6; Pausanias 7.16.9–10.

112. Sizov 2017.

113. Generally, Touloumakos 1967; R. Kallet-Marx 1995, 65–76; Ferrary 2017, 21–34. *Sunedroi*: Knoepfler 2001c, 415–16; C. Müller 2010, 228, 240 (Boiotia); Deshours 2004 (Messēnē); Piérart 2020, 259–72 on *SEG* 55.409, or rather 63.239 (Argos). As Touloumakos notes, the evidence for oligarchical powers is ambiguous, and the continuities noticeable; see also Ma 2016c on institutional decision-making patterns in various *poleis*, including the Peloponnese of the *sunedroi*.

114. Hamon 2007, based on Robert *OMS* 5, 561–83 (classic paper on Theophanēs of Mytilēnē) and Gauthier 1985 ("late Hellenistic" period); revisited with nuances in Hamon 2012; also Wiemer 2013 (death of democracy ca. 100 BCE).

115. The term of "great decrees" was used by the Roberts (*BE* 68, 445) for the late Hellenistic decrees of Priēnē (some of which run for over 400 lines); Wörrle 1995 on the "stressed-out benefactor" who is the main character of the genre.

116. See the Roberts, *BE* 68, 445; Gauthier 1985, 56–60; Wörrle 1995; Forster 2018, 269–326. E.g., *I. Priene B-M* 63–70, genre-defining (Fröhlich 2005); *OGIS* 339 (Mēnas of Sēstos); *SEG* 44.867 with Savalli 2012 (Poseidōnios of Bargylia); *SEG* 39.1243–44 from Robert and Robert 1989 (Polemaios and Menippos of Kolophōn); *SEG* 33.1035–41 (Archippa of Kymē); *IG* 12.9.236 (Theopompos of Eretria); Salviat 1959 with van Bremen 1996, 25–27 and Dillon 2010, 145–46 (Ēpiē of Thasos); Daux 1965 (Augis of Argos, though the document itself is rather short; inscribed summary of a more fulsome document?). The genre is not attested in Late Hellenistic Athens, where the epigraphical habit abates by the end of the second century BCE.

117. Wörrle 1995 on the fanatical desire (to the point of burnout) to do communitarian good; on the philosophically charged language of the decrees, Gray 2013, 2018, 2022 (extending the interpretive strategies of the "Cambridge School" of political philosophy to study actual civic texts; i.e., decrees and dedications, rather than canonical works of literature by famous thinkers).

118. Polemaios of Kolophōn: *SEG* 39.1243. Aristoboulos of Epidauros: *IG* 4.2¹ 65.

119. For instance, at Priēnē: *I. Priene B-M* 65, lines 94, 106; 75, line 34; 768, 4; 85, line 8; 64, line 28.

120. *SEG* 33.1035–41, with van Bremen 2008 (whom I do not follow on date, but whose reconstruction of the sequence of events is compelling).

121. Fröhlich 2004, 533; 460–61.

122. Fröhlich 2004, 337–8, on *IG* 2.² 956, 958.

123. Tracy 1979.

124. Gauthier 1985, 72–3. On the lack of Roman take-up of royal euergetical roles, Ferrary 2017, 199 (from Ferrary 1997, 201).

125. *I. Priene B-M* 64, 111–17.

126. *SEG* 39.1244, col. 2, lines 46–54.

127. Gauthier 1985, 72–74; Wörrle 1995; Strubbe 2001 (also on the end of this particular political style).

128. *SEG* 39.1243, col. 2, lines 11–33; 39.1244, col. 3, 29–34. The language used for Polemaios is redolent of heroic devotion (*anadechomai, periballomai*).

129. Hamon 2005, 127–29, on Archippa and on *I. Priene B-M* 65, lines 176–82, 192–94, 218–19 (Herōdēs); Hamon 2008, 93–96 (on Moschiōn of Priēnē, *I. Priene B-M* 64, and the sons of magistrates being feasted with their fathers, lines 253–59, with a restoration by Robert and Robert 1989, 96 n.214). On festivities and social imaginary, Rogers 1991a; Chaniotis 1995; Martzavou 2008.

130. Gray 2013.

131. Robert 1937, 37–38; *I. Priene B-M* 64, 253–59; *I. Priene B-M* 65, lines 176–9, 189–92; *I. Priene B-M* 67, 238; *I. I. Priene B-M* 69, 37–39, 54–56, 80–84 (offered by benefactor who happened to be an ex-slave); *I. Priene B-M* 71,12–13; *I. Priene B-M* 84, 3–4. Also (though less spectacularly) at Kolophōn: *SEG* 39.1243, col. 4, lines 31–32; *SEG* 39.1244, col. 2, lines 39–41 (feast for metics and *isoteleis*, resident citizens of different status). Unsurprisingly, Archippa, benefactress of Kymē, also practiced the "humanity" of feasts offered to citizens and noncitizens alike: *SEG* 33.1036–37.

132. *Ergastinai*: above, n. 73; Asklēpios: *SEG* 18.26. Statue: Keesling 2012.

133. Kyriakidis 2014 (Delphi).

134. Fedak 1990, 87; Lohmann 1999, 455; Voigtländer 2004, 282–83.

135. van Bremen 2008 on layout and carving of the whole Archippa dossier, carved posthumously.

136. Sezgin and Aybek 2016.

137. Theopompos: *IG* 12.9.236. A parallel at Pergamon: two statues for the gymnasiarch Pyrrhos son of Athenodoros, two statues of his son: Matthys 2014, Gy 7–9, De 3, with Biard 2017, 444.

138. *I. Priene B-M* 48, 56, 64, 65, 67, 68–70; Raeck 1995 on earlier examples of the phenomenon; Ma 2015a, 133; *SEG* 45.1515 (late second century BCE) is the base of one of four honorific portraits (painted, bronze, marble, and gilt bronze) for Aristodēmos, hereditary priest of Zeus Pigindēnos, honored by the people of Bargasa, in Karia, for his piety, benevolence, justice, and his activity as a benefactor (Debord and Varinlioğlu 2010, 178, no. 13, with 179–80, nos. 14–15, for dedications by the same priest). The multiplication of statues was imitated by communities in post-Attalid inland Asia Minor with aspirations to *polis* culture: *TAM* 5.368b.

139. *SEG* 33.1041, lines 14–15.

140. Aristocratization: Gauthier 1985, 13–14; Hamon 2007.

141. *Pythais*: Karila-Cohen 2007, 2009; ephebes: Perrin-Saminadayar 2007.

142. Thonemann 2021.

143. Alcock 1993a, placing decline in the third century BCE already—too early; Rousset 2004 for qualifications.

144. Habicht 2006, 243–325; Martzavou 2013.

145. F253 Edelstein-Kidd, also *FGrHist / BNJ* 87, F247 (from Athenaios 6.272 e-f).

146. *SEG* 39.1244, col. 2, lines 19–21.

147. Many of the essays in Wörrle and Zanker 1995 are organized around a central idea of late Hellenistic oligarchization.

148. *SEG* 39.1243 1–13.

149. Fröhlich 2005.

150. *I. Priene B-M* 64, with Fröhlich 2005 and Kah 2014, 159–60.

151. Hepding 1907, no. 10 (I am grateful to Helmut Müller for allowing me to see his unpublished text); Wörrle 2007, esp. 512–14; Hamon 2012, 62–64. On democratic affirmation in Pergamon, Ventroux 2017, 108–10 (on Cicero, *In Defence of Flaccus*, 17).

152. *Agora* 16.333, with Habicht 2006, 352, Knoepfler 2014a, 444.

153. Wiemer 2016; Gray 2018b.

154. That Cicero's Greek acquaintances, often philosophically involved or minded, are not teachers and philosophers, but members of the Athenian elite, is explored by Rawson 1985; Menedēmos appears in Cicero, *The Orator*, 1.83. Panaitios, of course, inspired Cicero's *On Duties* (*De officiis*), though the extent to which Panaitios's late Hellenistic concerns can be read in Cicero is unclear (Wiemer 2016).

155. Ferrary 2017, 300–301; earlier Magie 1950, 259–76.

156. Milner and Eilers 1995; L. Meier 2019.

157. Ferrary 2017, 161–94.

158. *SEG* 39.1243; Robert and Robert 1989, notably 39–40; Ferrary 2017, 161–80; on the guarantees, Pont 2015, 65.

159. *RS* 12, Cnidian text, col. 4, lines 5–20, with Ferrary 2017, 128–29, 134.

160. On the law on provincial provinces, Ferrary 2012, 43–60. In the Amphiktionic decree on the Artists (*CID* 4.114), Daux 1937, 371 notes that "la puissance romaine est partout présente dans les délibérations amphictioniques."

161. *Syll.*³ 700.

162. Ferrary 2017, 343–50, on *IG* 12.5.722 (Andros), 12.5.924 (Tēnos).

163. Speaker's *bēma* in Athens: Poseidōnios *FGrHist / BNJ* 87 F 36 ("the speaker's platform built in front of the Stoa of Attalos, for the Roman generals"); Camp 2010, 123–24. L. Gellius: Cicero, *On the Laws*, I. 53, Ferrary 2017, 346–47.

164. Camia 2009, e.g., nos. 3, 4, 5, 6. Chios: *SEG* 22.507 (earlier text in *Syll.*³ 785).

165. Ferrary 2017, 245.

166. Polemaios "met with leading Romans and, seeming worthy of their friendship, he secured its benefit for his fatherland, having established links of *patroneia* with the best men" (*SEG* 39.1243, col. 2, lines 24–31). On individual friends of Rome, Ferrary 2017, 267–70.

167. *OGIS* 438–39; Ferrary 2017, 360 485–86; prefigured by the earlier council of cities convened as part of the Roman settlement (*nomothesia*) of Asia Minor (Wörrle 2000, and above, p. 269).

168. Laffi 2010 with P. Hamon in *BE* 11, 497.

169. Ferrary 2012, 54: the Rhodians are tasked with diffusing the Roman decisions concerning the praetorian provinces; Menippos went on embassies *huper Rhōmaiōn* (*SEG* 39.1244, col. 3, lines 7–8).

170. Walbank 1977 on *IG* 10.2.1s 1668 (milestone); Kaimaris et al. 2010; Ferrary 2017, 125–26.

171. Foucart 1903; S. Mitchell 1999; Ferrary 2017, 331.

172. Mitchell 1999; Campanile 2003a; Fournier 2010, 62–98.

173. Kantor 2014, Eberle 2016.

174. Mitchell 1999; 2008.

175. de Callataÿ 2011; Gatzolis and Psoma 2018.

176. Mitchell 1999; Merola 2001; Mitchell 2008; Corsaro 2010, 120–21; Boulay 2014, 370–78; Ferrary 2017, 298–300. The evidence is the law that regulates the tolls of Asia Minor, as preserved in a much later document dating to the reign of the emperor Nero (Cottier and Corbier 2008); and a speech by Mark Antony given at Ephesos before the Greeks of Asia Minor in winter 42/1 BCE, as preserved or reimagined by a later historian (Appian, *Civil Wars*, 5.4.17): the *poleis* are said to have been left free in 133 BCE, but then exposed to taxes as a share of agricultural production. The latter taxes are the tithes levied by publicans according to the *Lex Sempronia* of 123/2 BCE; the solution I am offering here—aggressive taxation of former royal land held by *poleis*—rests on the insight by Bertrand (2005a) that *poleis* held royal land, and my guess that segments of royal land were taken over by the *poleis*, individually or en masse. A *senatus consultum* of 101 BCE (*RDGE* 12, *SEG* 48.1424) decides on the status of territory owned by Pergamon but claimed by the publicans for taxation—not the whole of Pergamene territory.

177. Artemidōros: Strabo 14.1.26. Kratēs: *I. Priene B-M* 67, with Thonemann 2011, 329–32; see also *I. Ilion* 71.

178. Diodoros 37.5.6–9.

179. The close link between Roman state and entrepreneurial exploitation is minimized in A. Sherwin-White 1984; R. Kallet-Marx 1995.

180. Hatzfeld 1919; Errington 1988; C. Müller and C. Hasenohr 2002; Martzavou 2008, 2010; Eberle and Le Quéré 2017; Eberle 2017; Ferrary 2017, 307–22.

181. Strabo 14.5.2; Coarelli 2005; Coarelli 2014; Mavroiannis 2018.

182. Millar 2002a, 215–30; Lawall 2006; Eberle and Le Quéré 2017.

183. Ferrary and Verger 1999; Ferrary 2017, 379–431 (the statue for M. Antonius in 102 must give a *terminus ante quem* for the monuments of Polemaios and Menippos in their privileged settings).

184. Kirbihler 2007, 2016; Guerber 1995.

185. R. Kallet-Marx 1995, 261–90; Habicht 2006, 327–69.

186. Poseidōnios *FGrHist/BNJ* 87 F 36; Gray 2018b, esp. 140–47.

187. Plutarch, *Life of Sulla*, 26.3.

188. Appian, *Mithradatic Wars*, 54; Plutarch, *Life of Sulla* 19; Pausanias 9.7.4–6.

189. Memnōn of Hērakleia, *FGrH/BNJ* 434.27.

190. Robert and Robert 1954, 97–102, no. 4 (also in *RDGE* 16; Canali de Rossi 1997, no. 350b); *SEG* 45.1825 (Lykia); Campanile 1996.

191. *SEG* 45.1825; 55.1503 (Mithradatic War); 55.1452 (treaty with Rome); Knoepfler 2013b.

192. On Asia Minor, Coudry and Kirbhihler 2010.

193. Wörrle 2009.

194. *SEG* 44.1227 (Mopsouhestia); *I. Stratonikeia* 1101 (Rigsby 1996, no. 210, for the same document); *I. Oropos* 308 (also to be found as Rigsby 1996, no. 6; C. Müller 2019). Generally, Knäpper 2018, 249–69.

195. Sartre 1991, 441–68; Andrade 2013, 94–122; Saliou 2020, 21–42.

196. *oppida impacata redigit in suam potestatem*, Granius Licinianus 35, 82 Criniti.

197. Bertrand 1997. On the period in general, across a Roman-dominated Mediterranean, Crogier-Pétrequin 2014, a thematic issue of the journal *Pallas*, i.e., vol. 96 (2014).

198. Plutarch, *Life of Antony*, 68.4; Millar 2002a, 232; Kirbihler 2013.

199. Robert, *OMS* 5, 561–83; Theopompos: Thériault 2003.

200. Theopompos of Knidos: texts gathered *I. Knidos* 51–60. *MAMA* 11.1 preserves the trace of honors—equestrian statue, temple (*naos*) for a (first-century BCE?) benefactor at Apollōnia in Phrygia (modern Uluborlu).

201. *SEG* 42.755, in contrast with the later inscription published by Robert (above).

202. Laronde 2011.

203. Sparta: Cartledge and Spawforth 2002, 98–106; Magnēsia on Maeander: Strabo 14.1.41; Kōs: Buraselis 2000.

204. Plutarch, *Life of Lucullus* 20; Magie 1950, 251–56; Migeotte 1984, 91–96.

205. Cicero, *Letters to Atticus*, 5.13, 6.1 (50 BCE).

206. Cicero, *Letters to his Friends*, 13.56 addressed to Q. Minucius Thermus (50 BCE); Habicht 1984; Ferriès and Delrieux 2011.

207. Cicero, *Verrines*, 2.1.25–32.

208. Zoumbaki 2013; Eberle and Le Quéré 2017.

209. Kalaitzi 2016, 96–98. Thesssaloniki: Martzavou 2010. Dion: Demaille 2018.

210. Leone 2020.

211. Especially *Letters to Atticus*, 6.1, 6.2.

212. Magie 1950, 416–17; Kirbihler 2011; Ferrary 2017, 217.

213. Plutarch, *Life of Kimon*, 1–2; Hurlet and Müller 2020, 83–84 (arguing that the intervention reflects the absence of any governor in a *provincia Graecia* at that precise moment).

214. Tacitus, *Annals*, 4.56.

215. Thasos: Dunant and Pouilloux 1958, 51–53; Strabo 14.2.24.

216. *SEG* 32.865 (with P. Nigedelis as noted in *SEG* 39.861).

217. *I. Mylasa* 109; Gray 2017.

218. C. Jones 1974; A. Chankowski 1998.

219. *IG* 7.190 with Wilhelm *KS* 2.1, 261–76.
220. *I. Priene* B-M 68–70.
221. *IG* 5.1.11.
222. *SEG* 54.1020.
223. Cicero, *In Defence of Flaccus*, 16; Plutarch, *Life of Brutus*, 30.
224. Strabo 14.2.24; Robert, *OMS* 5, 53; Robert 1969, 306–7 (comparing Hybreas to Dēmosthenēs). The conflict at Magnēsia (on Maeander) between two politicians offers a contemporary parallel: Plutarch, *Precepts of Statecraft* 13–14 (*Mor.* 809B-D).
225. Tēmnos: Cicero, *In Defence of Flaccus*, 44. Courts: Walser 2012.
226. Strabo 12.7.3.
227. On Greek identities in the first century BCE, Schmitz and Wiater 2011, proposing to see a "struggle for identity" by Greeks in the first century BCE.

Chapter 12. The Ends of Liberty

Network of cities: F. Millar, "Empire and City, Augustus to Julian: Obligations, Excuses and Status." *JRS* 73 (1983): 76. Republished in Millar 2004a.

1. Magie 1950 provides a lot of narrative, often relevant, as background to the story of the cities of Asia Minor. See, for examples of dynasty- or emperor-centered studies, Dabrowa 1980 for Asia Minor under the Flavians; Boatwright 2000 on Hadrian and the cities (Hadrian publicized his special care for the Greek cities, *Hellenides poleis*: *I.Thrake Aeg* E 185). It is perfectly true that individual emperors influenced the practical shapes taken by empire at any one moment and is obvious, as in the case of Hadrian, or of Trajan who showered benefits on Milētos (the oracular god Apollōn, at Didyma, had announced his accession to power, probably when he visited the province as a young man in the following of his father, the proconsul of Asia: C. Jones 1975; Ehrhardt and Weiss 2011). On the shape of the Roman empire, see e.g. (among personal favorites), Millar 1967; Millar 1977; Millar 2004a; Potter 2006; Noreña 2011; Mathieu 2014; Ando 2018b; Noreña 2020.

2. Keil 1956, whence *I. Ephesos* 802; Filippini 2019, 165–80.

3. Robert 1940–1965, vol. 5, 29–35; Herrmann 1997; Millar 2004a, 435–64 (originally Millar 1999); C. Jones 2007.

4. On subsidiarity, Jacques 1984; Brélaz 2005; Fournier 2010. Generally, e.g., Millar 1977; Eck 1995–1997; Lendon 1997; Ando 2000; Woolf 2012; Bérenger 2014; W. Harris 2016.

5. Amarelli 2005; Cracco Ruggini 1987. *Municipia* are exceedingly rare in the Greek east: Papazoglu 1986.

6. On the *Constitutio Antoniniana* and Roman citizenship, see for instance Buraselis 2007; Pferdehilt, Scholt, and Barnes 2012; Kantor 2016; Imrie 2018.

7. Parrish 2001; Maupai 2003; Halfmann 2004; Raja 2012. Diōn, *Oration* 47.15, vaunts the advantages of a beautiful, commodious built environment as "worthy of a great city" (admittedly in the context of political struggle over a building project); see below, pp. 350–56.

8. C. Jones 2014 is clearly about a (failed) Augustan-era foundation in Mysia (see p. 323 and n. 121); Hērakleia under Salbakē and Sebastēpolis, in Eastern Karia, respectively late first-century and Augustan-era foundations: Robert and Robert 1954, 153–230, 313–336. The "village of Atys" in Phrygia (*Atyochōrion*) is a *polis*, with institutions and civic culture, by 169 CE: *SEG* 52.1333. Aidēpsos emerged as a separate *polis* only in the late third century CE: Gregory 1979; Goette 2003–2004, on the archaeology of the site. Tymandos and Orkistos: Lenski 2016, 97–11. *Polis* formation in Asia Minor, initiated in the late Hellenistic period, can be seen clearly in the first-century CE list of *poleis* of the province of Asia, grouped by conventus (Habicht 1975; above, p. 275).

9. See the remarks by P. Herrmann, referring to *BE* 83, 426, *ad SEG* 33.1097 (Kimista *vel sim.*, not Kimistēnē, as seems to perpetuate itself in the archeological literature—that form designates a territory); *SEG* 33.1100; Marek 1993, 118–22, 187–210. The site is coming into gradual focus thanks to continuous archaeological work since 2001: Laflı, Christof, and Metcalfe 2012 (historical geography, some inscriptions); Laflı and Şahin 2016 (ceramics).

10. *Annals* 14.27. On cities and earthquakes, C. Jones 2013. On self-governance, Magie 1950, 639–40.

11. Kunnert 2012, 218–20 on "tribes"; on Bithynia, D. Sokolowski 2022. The evidence, however, is patchy.

12. Nörr 1966 on the essential state-like qualities of the Roman *polis* (see further, pp. 325–28); Brunt 1990, 79 n.89 on rivalries and conflicts between cities; Rousset 2004; Fernoux 2009 on city and territory in the Roman period; Heller 2006a, 85–122 on territorial disputes in Roman period.

13. Pausanias 10.4.1.

14. Generally, Brélaz 2008 on the disarmament of the Greek cities; Millar 2004a, 265–97; Veyne 2005, 212; Mecella 2006; Thonemann in *MAMA* 11, p. 27. Thespians: *I. Thespies* 37 with C. Jones 1971a.

15. R. Smith 1998, notably on Ephesian portraits.

16. Gytheion, Chios: Robert, *OMS* 1, 528–34. Athens: *SEG* 47.143, secret ballot with 3616 voters; *IG* 2.² 1035 with Borg 2011 (though Spawforth 2012 would see this as Augustan-inspired antiquarianism).

17. Diōn, *Oration* 44 (Cuvigny 1994, 101 on date).

18. On Diōn, Desideri 1978; C. Jones 1978; Swain 2000. The speeches in Prousa and other Bithynian cities are translated with commentary in Cuvigny 1994. On the high culture of the age, see below, n. 136.

19. Bowman 1971; J. Hanson 2011 on the network of cities in Roman Asia Minor; Lerouxel 2016. On local conflict, Heller 2006a, 2006b.

20. Aphrodisias: Reynolds 1982; de Chaisemartin 2017. Aizanoi: Wörrle 2009.

21. Fernoux 2011, 340–41, generally; Fournier 2010, 493–95 on Kyzikos and other cases; Tacitus, *Annals* 4.36; Suetonius, *Life of Tiberius* 36; Cassius Dio 57.24.6; Plutarch, *Political Precepts* 19 (*Mor*. 815D). Lykia: *SEG* 51.1832; Cassius Dio Cassius 60.17.3; Thornton 2008.

22. Frija 2020.

23. *I. Assos* 26; the later *I. Assos* 28 also shows the same phenomenon of a body of Romans involved in the passing of a decree.

24. *IAegThr* 180. Other examples of Romans involved in decision-making: *SEG* 28.953 (Kyzikos, mid-first century CE); *I. Tralleis* 80; Thonemann 2010, 169 and 2011, 99–100 (the phenomenon endures, anomalously, into the second century at Apameia). Generally, von Andringa 2003; Robu 2019.

25. *MAMA* 11.99; generally, Errington 1988.

26. Thespiai: Robert 1940–1965, vol. 2, 8–9; C. Müller 1996. Mytilēnē: Robert, *OMS* 2, 813–16; Dimopoulou-Piliouni 2015, 650–1. See also, for Asia Minor generally, Kirbihler 2007.

27. A. Jones 1940, 61–64, 132–34; Rizakis 1997, 2001; Salmeri, Raggi, and Baroni 2004; Müller 2014, 197–98; Rizakis 2015; Brélaz 2017, 2018 (monograph on Philippoi); Fernoux 2019 (*coloniae* in northwestern Asia Minor). Generally, for elements of a social history of Roman Greece, Rizakis, Camia and Zoumbaki 2018.

28. *SEG* 57.1432; F. Kolb 2017.

29. Blanco-Perez 2015.

30. Millar 2006a, 223–42; Brélaz 2015.

31. Kirbihler 2007, 20 n.10 (on the disappearance of the Italians as a separate visible social group by 100 CE, with a few exceptions); Vibius Salutaris: Rogers 1991a (a *polis*-friendly interpretation); Kokkinia 2018 for a hard-edged view of Salutaris's benefaction as almost colonialist; further below, p. 351.

32. Sartre 2001b for a survey; see also Millar 2006a, 164–222 on the Roman colonies of the Near East; Brélaz 2015, 2018 (Philippoi's slow Hellenization); generally, Brélaz 2017.

33. Strabo, 12.7.3; 13.4.12; 10.4.9–22. Generally, Clarke 1999; Biraschi and Salmeri 2000.

34. Robert 1940–1965, vol. 2, 37–42; Price 1985; Fujii 2011.

35. *I. Priene B-M* 153 (dedication of temple); Carter 1983, 20–21, 266–67, 283–89.

36. Millar 2004a, 298–312; Price 1985; Campanile 2001; Kantirea 2007; Frija 2012; Wörrle 2014 (on an illuminating testcase, Julio-Claudian Aizanoi); Kolb and Vitale 2016.

37. *SEG* 63.1026; on lower-status Bithynians, W. Ameling on *I. Prusias* 78–79. I owe my understanding of the regions of D. Sokolowski's doctoral research on the Bithynian countryside (2022).

38. *Mnemosyne*: *IThesp* 174 with Marchand 2013; *Karpophoros*: Robert, *OMS* 2, 801–32 (807–9 for assimilation of Julio-Claudian empresses to Demeter, in Asia Minor but also in Syria, based on Riewald 1912; also list in Alexandridis 2004, 290–93). Generally, Camia 2016.

39. Kantiréa 2007, 89–140, on dedications to the People and the *Theoi Sebastoi*.

40. *I. Ephesos* 20 and 1503 with Lytle 2012.

41. R. Smith 2013.

42. Kantiréa 2007 on imperial cult and its responsiveness to the court; Bang 2011; Spawforth 2012 on the importance of court mentality. Impact of monarchy as the outcome of the Roman revolution: Millar 2002a, 292–313.

43. Laffi 1967; Heller 2014, 222–31; Thonemann 2015.

44. Robert, *OMS* 2.835, 5.821–24; Wörrle 1988, 187–88; generally, Frija 2016.

45. Price 1985, 101–32; Chaniotis 2003.

46. Wörrle 1988.

47. Millar 2002a, 314–20.

48. Dupont-Sommer and Robert 1964, 73; Franke 1968, 12; *RPC* 4.3.6180–81.

49. *Oration* 48.11; for a parallel, see the funerary epigram celebrating a Nikaian notable (addressed by his Roman *cognomen*, Sacerdos): "I am he who, when my city was shaken by an earthquake, saved it from Hades thanks to the gifts of Italian Zeus" (*Steinepigramme* 09/05/07, earlier *I. Nikaia* vol. 2, 301a-309a, no. 89; from *AP* 15.7).

50. Robert, *OMS* 2.833 ("divine images" in imperial-era inscriptions from Athens and Adada are statues or busts of the emperors, not cult images).

51. Earthquakes: Magie 1950, 499–500; C. Jones 2013.

52. Generally, Mitchell 1987; Hadrian: Boatwright 2000. Ephesos: *I. Ephesos* 274. Athens: Pausanias, 1.18.6–9; Graindor 1934; Choremi-Spetsieri and Tiginanka 2008.

53. *I. Smyrna* 697, Puech 2002 no. 209; Hallmansecker 2017.

54. Tacitus, *Annals*, 3.60–63 with Price 2005, 123–24; Heller 2006a, 163–237; Lintott 1993, 118. Argos could still honor Ti. Statilius Timokratēs Memmianos for going on embassy "to the Senate and to the kings," meaning the emperors (*IG* 4.590, Hadrianic).

55. *SEG* 56.565.

56. The rather mediocre results of an embassy (or embassies) to the emperor are referred to repeatedly in *Orations* 40, 44, and 45.

57. Robert, *OMS* 6, 211–49, on "glory and hatred" in the relationship of the two cities.

58. Guerber 2009; Fournier 2010 (jurisdiction); Girdvaynte 2020; Kantor 2021.

59. Reynolds 1982; on the structure of the archive, Kokkinia 2015–2016.

60. Reynolds 1982, nos. 14 (Trajan), 21 (Gordian III), 48, 16 (governors' visit); also in *IAph* 8.33, 8.103, 12.34, 8.35.

61. Reynolds 1982, no. 13, also *IAph* 8.32.

62. J. Oliver 1989, no. 34, published earlier in *Syll.*³ 810 (Rhodians), Oliver 1989, no 296, earlier in *IG* 7.2713 (freedom of the Greeks), Suetonius, *Life of Vespasian*, 8.4; J. Oliver 1989, nos. 64–68, also in *IG* 12.3.175–76 (Astypalaia).

63. Alliance: *RDGE* 16, Reynolds 1982, no. 48 (same document in *IAph* 12.34); generally, Guerber 2009, 67–75.

64. *I. Ephesos* 253, 237.

65. Diōn, *Oration* 45.13 (allusive); *MAMA* 11.157.

66. Generally, Guerber 2009; Diōn, *Oration* 35 with Bost Pouderon 2006, vol. 2, 218–23.

67. *SEG* 49.1813; Ritti 2017 on the additional privilege of serving as an assize center.

68. *I. Pergē* 22; Rouechê 1989.

69. *I. Ephesos* 1489, 1489a, 1490 (the Ephesians inscribed the imperial letter at least three times).

70. On festivals, Robert, *OMS* 6.209–19 ("explosion agonistique"); Leschhorn 1998; Nollé 2012b; Slater 2015. Trajan: Pliny, *Letters* 10.118–19.

71. *SEG* 56.1359; Guerber 2009, 215–33.

72. Robert 1987, 22–35; Price 1985, 129; Heller 2006a, 310–13.

73. *SEG* 57.1666.

74. Howgego 2005, 11 on the "magnificent coinage" struck in 139-144 CE; generally Herrmann 2002, Hallmannsecker 2020, 1–4.

75. In addition to the Ionians, Thonemann 2011, 109–17 (Phrygians); Ellis-Evans 2019, 270–76 (*koinon* of cities on Lesbos); *SEG* 41.384 with Knoepfler 2012, 234–35 (Arkadians).

76. For instance, the commission of Boiotarchs sent by *poleis* to represent them at the Boiotian *koinon* (Knoepfler 2012), the *basileus* of the Ionian League (Herrmann 2002), or the various officials of the Macedonian League, whose succession was regulated by a letter of Hadrian (*SEG* 37.593).

77. Deininger 1965; Millar 1977, 385–94; Guerber 2009, 79–213; Edelmann-Singer 2015.

78. Sánchez 2001, 427–36.

79. Vitale 2013, summarizing the very difficult and fragmentary evidence.

80. Generally, Kolb and Vitale 2016, insisting on the importance of the *koina* in determining the shapes of imperial cult. Greece: J. Oliver 1978; Puech 1983; Spawforth and Walker 1985, 1994; Kantiréa 2007 (synthetic). Macedonia: Papazoglou 1998; Herz 2008. Crete: Rouanet-Liesenfelt 1994. Bithynia: Vitale 2012; Edelmann-Singer 2014 (and Madsen 2016, doubtful on any cult under Augustus). Asia Minor: Campanile 1994; Weiss 2002; Campanile 2003b; Kirbihler 2008; Guerber 2009, 125–26; Frija 2012; Ritti 2017, 463–94. Lykia: Reitzenstein 2011. Cyprus: Fujii 2013; *SEG* 63.1436 (decree of Kourion for services performed by gymnasiarch during festival organized by the Cypriot *koinon*).

81. Robert 1940, 270–73, 285 (high priests for the federal cult of the emperors were obligated to give gladiatorial shows, priests for local imperial cult were allowed to). The equivalent of "Asiarch" with the high priest of the emperors at the federal level is established by *I. Sardis* 2.344, with *BE* 20, 388 pp. 576 (J.-Y. Strasser); earlier, see e.g., Kirbihler 2008.

82. Aelius Aristeidēs, *Oration* 50.

83. Burrell 2004; Heller 2006b.

84. *TAM* 5.3.1421; Puech 2004.

85. Bouchon 2016; *I. Beroia* 117.

86. *IG* 7.2711, 2712, 2878; Spawforth 1994, qualified by C. Müller 1997; Knoepfler 2012: the "super-League" is attested between Gaius and Trajan. The super-League is variously called "Pan-hellenes," "Achaians," "Achaians and Pan-hellenes."

87. J. Oliver 1989, no. 124; Laronde 2004.

88. Spawforth and Walker 1985; C. Jones 1996; Spawforth 1999; Gordillo Hervás 2013 on membership.

89. Edelmann-Singer 2015.

90. For a Foucault-informed essay on Roman governmentality and the ambitions of empire, Ando 2010; for surveys of provincial administration, Lintott 1993; Eckhard 2002, 42–59.

91. Plutarch, *Political Precepts* 17 (*Mor.* 813E-F); Kokkinia 2004.

92. Millar 2004a, 313–33 (on military presence but also on the necessity of self-help, as illustrated by Apuleius's novel *The Golden Ass*); Christol and Drew-Bear 1995 for examples of military presence in Asia Minor; Brélaz 2005, 2008.

93. This is the theme of a sustained argument by G. Burton (2000, 2001, 2002, 2004); challenged by Brélaz 2007.

94. Burton 2002, 262, on Pliny, *Letters* 10; Lavan 2018 (on basic authenticity of the collection of administrative letters of the younger Pliny, guaranteed by comparison with documentary material).

95. Fournier 2010; Bérenger 2014, 171–99; Kantor 2015, 2016; Girdvaynte 2020; Kantor 2021; Philostratos, *Lives of the Sophists* 1.15.2 (Polemōn of Smyrna tells his citizens to let the Roman governor monopolize the capital cases).

96. Robert 1940–1965, vol. 1, 143–53 (on an example from Roman Corinth, *Corinth* 8.3.306); Rogers 1991a (Ephesos); Wörrle 1988 (Oinoanda); Kokkinia 2006 (Opramoas).

97. *SEG* 60.1328 for a proconsul of Asia honored by the *polis* of Apollōnia on Rhyndakos as a savior (quite rare); generally, Erkelenz 2003. The example of the governors of Bithynia illustrates conflict and contestation: Pliny, *Letters*, Book 10; 19–115; Diōn, *Oration* 34, 38, 48.

98. Burton 2004, general survey (but his understanding of civic finances as chaotic and in need of firm Roman intervention might be exaggerated; contrast Migeotte 2014, admittedly mostly for an earlier period).

99. Pactumeius Clemens: *ILS* 1067; Liebenam 1897; Camia 2007; *I. Ephesos* 15–16 for the finances of a civic institution, the *gerousia*, supervised by an external official designated by the emperor.

100. Nigdelis and Souris 2005; *SEG* 55.678.

101. Diōn, *Oration* 45.6; 45.10.

102. Diōn, *Oration* 48 (misinterpreted in modern scholarship as referring to the reinstatement of Assembly meetings after their general interdiction, but Diōn refers to meeting "once again," *palin* and in the aorist tense, designating a one-off); a building project was "approved" by the Roman governors (40.6), in fact in a specially summoned meeting (45.15). Aizanoi: Wörrle 2011a (*SEG* 61.1134).

103. Follet and Peppas Delmousou 2019, 767–74.

104. Millar 1977, 139–44. Tithorean perfumes: Pausanias 10.34.19.

105. *Milet* 6.2.666 (imperial slave managing imperially owned purple dyeworks at Milētos); Russell 2013, 42–53.

106. Tacitus, *Annals* 2.47, 12.63; *SEG* 57.1673 (Patara under Vespasian); C. Jones 2013.

107. A. Jones 1938, 138–40; Brunt 1990, 324–432 and 531–40; Scheidel 2015; Le Teuff 2017. Also S. Mitchell 1993, 241–59 (essay on coinage, taxation in kind and the relation between cities and empire); Cottier et al. 2008 (examination of document relevant to reform of tax-farming, under Nero).

108. Nakrason: Herrmann and Polatkan 1969. Poll tax and special foundations: *I. Lampsakos* 10, *I. Assos* 28, *IG* 12.5.946 (Tēnos); Robert and Robert 1954, 175; Le Quéré 2015, 83–85; *SEG* 65.1248 (gift by benefactor to pay for the poll tax of the priests in a rural shrine, at Atyochōrion in Phrygia).

109. Diōn, *Oration* 35.14, 38.26, 40.10; Habicht 1975 (assize network clearly used for collection of some sort of contribution).

110. Amyzōn: *I. Ephesos* 3157; Kolophōn: *SEG* 45.1597; Indeipedion: Malay 2018, with many parallels. Generally, A. Jones 1940, 140–41; and for a parallel in Syria, see the stretch of the road between Damascus and Berytus built by the legate of the province, at the expense of the city of Abila: *ILS* 5864.

111. *I. Tralleis* 601 (in vol. 2).

112. A. Jones 1940, 141–42; S. Mitchell 1976; A. Kolb 2000. (The expression *cursus publicus*, sometimes favored by modern scholars, only appears ca. 300 CE). See notably *I. Sagalassos* 3 (edict of legate of Galatia, under Tiberius, found at Sagalassos), *SEG* 59.1365 and 62.1179 (rescript of Hadrian concerning the movement of soldiers in the province of Asia, two copies: near Priēnē and at Eumeneia in Phrygia), 37.1186 (rescript of Caracalla, found at Takina in Pisidia). The critical expression "state's men" was used by the social anthropologist John Davis to describe local actors who drive interactions into the ambit of the state and increase the latter's reach; I use it here less subtly simply to describe power holders within imperial administration (while noting that such figures had the effect of enmeshing local communities with the state). On Davis, see Dresch and Allen 2018.

113. Pont 2014 (argues against details of S. Mitchell 1976 concerning the interpretation of *SEG* 26.1392; followed here); Ando 2017; Pont 2017, esp. 119–20, 125 on the empire's gaze, both looking down on the reticulation of civic cells and intervening deep into the latter's structure; Pont 2020, 250–71, on the deep impact of instrumentalization by the Roman state through the *munera* system.

114. Pliny, *Letters* 10.19–20; Millar 2004a, 128–31; Brélaz 2005, 71 n. 10 on local prisons in the Roman empire.

115. Blanco-Pérez 2013 (modifying earlier views in Brélaz 2005) on *SEG* 56.1493 (from Akmoneia in Phrygia).

116. Aelius Aristeidēs 50; Jones 2016.

117. Digest 48.3.6.

118. Pliny 10.31–32 (convicts *ad opus publicum*, "for public works" and *in ludum*, "for the games," used as public slaves); Millar 2004a, 120–50.

119. Pont 2020, 80–108 on martyrdom as recurring and total "civic events" in the late second and especially third centuries CE, and their status as response to directives from the Roman state.

120. Birley 1997a, 164; C. Jones 2019b.

121. C. Jones 2014 (my interpretation differs slightly). The presence of Germē and other places as providing councilors shows that they were integrated

in a very large but short-lived Mysian *polis*, founded under Augustus.

122. G. Biard, *BE* 21, 139.

123. *SEG* 51.1832; Thornton 2001b; Wörrle 1988 on uniform, Italian-inspired constitutional measures imposed on Lykian cities.

124. Heller 2009, 2013.

125. Harter-Uibopuu 2008 on *IG* 2.² 1100 (J. Oliver 1989, no. 92).

126. Millar 1963, 1977 (on embassies, 410–47); Millar 2004a, 336–71 (originally 1983); Hauken 1998. Critiques of or nuances on the model of "petition and response": Bleicken 1982; Ando 2006; Connolly 2010; Eich 2012.

127. J. Oliver 1989, nos. 79–81; A. Jones 1971, 84 (on taxes from territory: did they earlier belong to the Roman state?).

128. *IThrake Aeg* E180; Thornton 2007 (contrast Wörrle 2004c who sees oligarchizing capture).

129. Baker and Thériault 2018.

130. On petition and response and its constitutive, performative effect, Brélaz 2007, 130.

131. Price 1985. Nörr 1966, 105–9 (the routinization of imperial cult in the second century reflects the greater integration of the cities in the empire, and the diminution of their autonomy).

132. Veyne 1999, notably 557–66 (on the intellectuals' attempts to "de-Romanize" the Roman emperor).

133. Robert 1969, 286–88; Robert, *OMS* 6. 241–69; Heller 2009, 283–41.

134. Diōn, *Orations* 31, 33, 34, 35; Bost-Pouderon 2006.

135. Cartledge and Spawforth 2002, 154.

136. Bowie 1970; Swain 1996. The cultural history of the Greek cities under the Roman empire is cognate with, but distinct from the "Second Sophistic," which has received much sustained attention (e.g. Bowersock 1969; Schmidt and Fleury 2011) and has been defined expansively. See further below, p. 598, n. 23.

137. Leschhorn 1984; Strubbe 1984–1986; Weiss 1990; Nollé 2012a.

138. Yıldırım 2004; R. Smith 2013. Pergē: Boatwright 1993. Generally, Maupai 2003; Cordovana and Galli 2007; Pont 2010.

139. Price 2004; Robert, e.g., *OMS* 6, 137–68, or Robert 1987, 50–90, with Haymann 2014, for examples

from Kilikia; Harl 1987; Nollé e.g., 2012a; Bennett 2014. More generally, Weiss 2005.

140. Martzavou 2008; Piérart 2010b; Ziegler 1985.

141. Pausanias 10.4.1–4; below, chapter 15.

142. J. Y. Strasser, *BE* 20. 387, on *I. Sardis* 2, index s.v. πόλις.

143. C. Jones 1999a, 112, with other examples (Sidyma, Stratonikeia). Spartan kinship: Cartledge and Spawforth 2002, 114.

144. Veyne 1999.

145. Diōn, *Oration* 38.33; Veyne 1999.

146. On the ideological function of petition for "middling" individuals in the Roman empire, Connolly 2010.

147. Brélaz 2021, 174–76 (while observing the realities of depredation by the military forces deployed by the Roman state).

148. Jacques 1984.

149. Veyne 1961, 97–98.

150. Local communities as sites of identity and agency: Johnston 2017.

151. Lepelley 1993. On the capacities for the western *civitates* to defend their interests through embassies (as shown by two surviving speeches in the late third century CE), Hostein 2012; on the urban settlement ("Autun") as a Roman and imperial city, Woolf 1998, 1–23. The idea is already in Fustel de Coulanges' treatment of Roman Gaul as a mosaic of *civitates* endowed with stately institutions (1994, from the 1891 edition).

152. *IG* 2.² 4193 a-b (and 1997), *Agora* 18, H398 (also *AnnÉpig* 47.69), with *SEG* 59.260; Aymard 1967, 548–57; *SEG* 50.209 (D. Fishwick); Le Roux 2011, 633–48 on Tolosa in general (640 on Q. Trebellius Rufus).

153. Heller 2006a, 2006b (notably on third-century proliferation); Guerber 2009, 325–41.

154. Millar 1964, 8 (on Cassius Dio 54.23.8).

155. Marotta 2005, on the cities' autonomy within the indirect rule of a Roman empire whose intervention is rare.

156. Potter 1990.

157. Robert, *OMS* 6, 211–49.

158. Pausanias 10.34.5. Brélaz 2008.

159. Millar 2004a, 265–97; Pont 2020, 109–80; Harl 1987.

160. Above, pp. 11–12. *SEG* 1.276.

Chapter 13. *Polis*, People, and Power in the Roman Empire

1. de Ste. Croix 1981, 518–37.

2. Liebeschuetz 2000.

3. Maupai 2003 on the politics of urban "beauty"; Ewald 2008, 637, reviewing Cormack 2004; van Nijf 2011, summarizing earlier work, on Termēssos; Ryan 2018 on the "constructed harmony" of unified, oligarchical cityscapes.

4. Syme 1988, 1–20; Halfmann 1979; Birley 1997b; A. Kuhn 2012 on the Quintilii; Adak 2013. Generally, Campanile 2003b; Ferrary 2017, 267–86.

5. Millar 1993a, 116.

6. R. Smith 1998, 73–74; Halfmann 2004, 92–93; Strocka 2009.

7. Graindor 1930; Ameling 1983; Tobin 1997; Galli 2002; Rife 2008. Perrin-Saminadayar 2019 shows how the women surrounding Hērōdēs Atticus are equally grand and exceptional.

8. Boatwright 1993; Gatzke 2020. On the Plancii, S. Jameson 1965; C. Jones 1976.

9. Zōilos: de Chaisemartin 2017, who goes so far as to compare Zōilos, qua "maître d'oeuvre," to Hellenistic kings as city-founders (perhaps excessive); R. Smith 1993.

10. Wörrle 1992; Jes 2007.

11. Steskal 2001; Kalinowski 2002; Kokkinia 2003; generally, Kalinowski 2021. Baths: Steskal and La Torre 2008; Täuber 2015. *Bouleutērion*: Bier 2011, especially 51–52, 57–64.

12. SEG 65.1486; Lepke, Schuler, and Zimmermann 2015, 375.

13. RPC 3.1974–83.

14. On civic honors in this period, Heller and van Nijf 2017; Heller 2020.

15. van Nijf 2011, drawing on an important body of his earlier work (on whose translation, as well as his expression of civic "celebrities," I draw here); TAM 3.1.4.

16. TAM 2.950; Magie 1950, 531–36; Kokkinia 2000; Cormack 2004, 46–47, 274–77; Çevik, Kızgut, Bulut 2010; Ng 2015.

17. TAM 3.500; Hall, Milner, and Coulton 1996.

18. On elite women of the Roman East, van Bremen 1996.

19. Thonemann 2011, 235–41, as an envoi to the world of the cities, before a deep dive in rural Anatolian history (an aspect that this book does not cover).

20. R. Smith 1998.

21. Thür and Aurenhammer 1997; Dillon 1996.

22. Larsen 1938, 465–83 (Greece); Magie 1950, 537–38 (Asia Minor). Landownership in multiple cities is linked to the practice of multiple citizenship: Wörrle 1988, 51; generally, Heller and Pont 2012. Portfolio: Diōn, *Oration* 46; on moneylending, Fernoux 2011, 312–13; food hoarding: Erdkamp 2002. On land concentration in the Greek East, there is a pessimist thesis, based on survey archaeology (Alcock 1993a, 1993b; Bintliff 2012, 313–19) but the picture is in fact unclear: Rousset 2004 (expanded English version, 2008); Rizakis and Lepenioti 2010; Grenet 2011; Rizakis 2014; Lerouxel and Pont 2016; Rizakis, Camia, and Zoumbaki 2018; Girdvainyte 2019. But the whole socioeconomic history of the Eastern part of the Roman empire still remains to be written (there are revisionist, non-miserabilist hints in D. Stewart 2010; Corsten 2016); in the meantime, as part of the recent revolution in the economic history of the Roman empire, Wilson and Bowman 2018.

23. On the "Second Sophistic" and Philostratos (with Civiletti 2002; Bowie and Elsner 2009; Kemezis 2014), see e.g., Boulanger 1923; Bowersock 1969; Bowie 1970, 1982; Graham Anderson 1993; Brunt 1994; Puech 2002; Whitmarsh 2005; Richter and Johnson 2017. Improvisation as Roman: Spawforth 2012, 63–81.

24. On the politics of purism, Swain 1996; Schmitz 1997.

25. Panagopoulos 1977, 226–31; Wörrle 1992, 345–49 (on the particular case of M. Ulpius Appuleius Euryklēs, sent by Aizanoi to the Panhellēnion in Athens in 157 CE); on late Hellenistic culture and politics, Gray 2013, 2018b.

26. R. Smith 2013.

27. Pretzler 2005; Dickenson 2016.

28. Piérart 2010a.

29. Dickenson 2016, 130.

30. Nörr 1966 for the continued sense of *polis* statehood; Leschhorn 1984 on the Hellenistic institution of city-founders; Alcock 1993a (but our understanding of the Hellenistic *polis* has evolved since then); Whitmarsh 2010.

31. Generally, Stephan 2002, 72–113.

32. Robert 1937, 258–89, on the language of *eugeneia* in Roman-era epigraphy; Panagopoulos 1977, 202–5, on gentle birth and natural nobility in Plutarch's civic-ethical writings.

33. Plutarch, *On the Delays of Divine Vengeance* 13 (*Mor.* 558a); Pausanias 9.5.16.

34. Bennett 2014, esp. 29–39, 91–99 on benefactions and distributions; 73–83, 101–2 on "personalized iconography."

35. Robert 1967, 47–51; Bennett 2014, 63–64.

36. R. Smith 1998; Campanile 2003b.

37. Riccardi 2007.

38. Campanile 1994 (*koinon* priests of Asia Minor); Kantirea 2007; Kantirea 2008; Kirbihler 2008; Camia 2011; Frija 2012; Lepke, Schuler, and Zimmermann 2015, 334–40; Camia 2016; Frija 2016.

39. Wörrle 2009a.

40. *Oration* 34.29–30.

41. Gehrke 1993 (using the test case of Boiotian Thisbē); Camia 2009, 36; Hopkins 1980.

42. *IThesp* 37.

43. Aleshire and Lambert 2011.

44. SEG 48.1170. Other examples: *I. Selge* 17; IGR 3.409 (Pogla: councilors, assembly-going citizens and other citizens); IGR 3.800–2.; Rhodes with Lewis 1997, 549.

45. *I. Prusias ad Hypium* 17; Robert 1966b, 69, 87.

46. Ferrary and Rousset 1998 (299–301 on distributions).

47. *IGR* 3.800–2, with Broughton 1938, 785; van Bremen 1994; E. Bauer 2012, 136–37; E. Bauer 2014, 269–74.
48. Wörrle 1988, 253–57.
49. *SEG* 44.1167; these five hundred are likely related to the *ad hoc* group of five hundred, drawn from *bouleutai* and *sitometroumenoi*, which received money in the festival founded by Dēmosthenēs.
50. Ferrary and Rousset 1998; Vatin 1961; *Choix Delphes* 250. The desirability of a study of elite dedications and monuments from Roman Delphi is noted by D. Rousset, *BE* 16, 275.
51. On the Council in the Roman-era *polis*, already I. Lévy 1899; Liebenam 1900, 238–52; A. Jones 1940, 176–77; Magie 1950, 641–43; Wörrle 1988, esp. 123–35; Quass 1993, 382–94; Dmitriev 2005; Hamon 2005; Heller 2009; Fernoux 2011, 347–57; Brélaz 2013, esp. 383–84; Heller 2013; Le Quéré 2015, 216–17.
52. Quass 1993, 383–94.
53. *I. Ephesos* 27A, line 17.
54. *IThesp* 37.
55. Hamon 2005.
56. The title turns up sporadically in different contexts: late second-century CE Tēnos (Etienne 1990, 166–67; Nigdelis 1990, 191–93; Mendone and Zoumbaki 2008, 222); Ephesos (*I. Ephesos* 972, 1044, 1575), Dorylaion in Galatia, Antiocheia under Kragos in Rough Kilikia (Robert 1966b, 87–89 on a discovery by G. Bean and T. B. Mitford), all dating to the third century CE, and in Talmudic sources (I. Lévy 1902) for Askalon. Generally, Robert, *OMS* 7, 675–77; Kleijwegt 1991, 263–72; Dmitriev 2005, 168–72.
57. On such figures, see *TAM* 2.496 (reedited by Balland as *Fouilles de Xanthos* 7.78).
58. Diōn, *Oration* 50; Pliny, *Letters*, 10.79.
59. Dmitriev 2005, 131–32; Giannakopoulos 2008; Bauer 2014.
60. *I. Ephesos* 1487–88; Heller 2013, 210 n. 18.
61. Dmitriev 2005, 154–57.
62. *SEG* 56.1489.
63. Heller 2013.
64. Coudry and Kirbihler 2010 (but the extent of the Roman intervention remains unclear: P. Hamon, *BE* 11, 155; Heller 2013).
65. Pliny, *Letters* 10.78; Fernoux 2004, 129–46; Madsen 2009, 27–59.
66. *SEG* 51.1581 with Thornton 2001b, Heller 2013; *SEG* 51.1832 with Schuler and Zimmermann 2012, 616–18 (list of councilors from Gagai); *SEG* 63.1336 (list of councilors from Patara).
67. Pliny, *Letters* 8.24 (cf. Cicero to his brother, *Letters to Quintus* 1.1).
68. Wörrle 1988, 96–100.
69. A. Jones 1940, 174; on provincialization and Galatia, Mitchell 1993, 61–69.

70. Parthikopolis, founded under Trajan, had an entry fee fixed at 500 drachmas, by Antoninus Pius: *IGBulg* 5.5895.
71. Müller and Staab 2017 (first-century CE?).
72. Rizakis and Camia 2008.
73. Robert 1940–1965, vol. 7, 206–38 on *I.Didyma* 148.
74. On Romanization and elites, Madsen 2002; Rizakis 2007.
75. *SEG* 63.1338.
76. Diōn, *Oration* 34.1.23.
77. Quass 1993, 303–52; Dmitriev 2005, 114–24; more generally, all of the treatment in Veyne 1976, 185–373; Fernoux 2004, 139–40; Dmitriev 2005, esp. 316–19; Zuiderhoek 2008; Ventroux 2017.
78. "All the expenditures": *IG* 5.2.516. Women: van Bremen 1996.
79. Robert 1980, 427, generally; Quass 1993, 328–33 (on gifts and promises in exchange for office), 334–43 (on undertaking "all the offices"); Dmitriev 2005, esp. 223–26, 245–46; Robert, *OMS* 5.234 (on the particular usage of office held "on condition of gifts," e.g., *epi epidosei*).
80. Madsen 2009, 129–30.
81. Diōn, *Oration* 34.23 with C. Jones 1978, 80.
82. A. Jones 1940, 174.
83. Heller 2019a, 61–65.
84. Heller 2013, esp. 206–12.
85. Bartels 2008, 162–76; Haberman 2014, 242–43.
86. Haberman 2014.
87. Hopkins 1983, 121–200 (with G. Burton); Scheidel 1999; Zuiderhoek 2009, 60–66. Vedii: Kalnowski 2021. Sillyon: van Bremen 1996.
88. Lerouxel and Pont 2016.
89. Diōn, *Oration* 46; Fernoux 2004, esp. 280–84; generally, Oppeneer 2018. On the different economical exigencies of large estates and smallholdings, Bresson 2016, 142–70.
90. Generally, van Nijf 1997; Ritti 2016 (Hierapolis, as seen in the record of funerary foundations benefiting associations).
91. Corsten 2016; Wörrle 2004; Pont 2016. Karia: *MAMA* 8.413 (same document *IAph* 12.26), where the debtors of an Aphrodisian seem to be smallholders in the Tabai plateau, at Apollōnia (the Aphrodisian tried to protect his donation against changes by the People).
92. Wörrle 1988, 118–19 and n.247.
93. Dmitriev 2005, 235–6; e.g., *MAMA* 11.60 (Kidyessos).
94. 2.30.
95. Plutarch, *Whether an Old Man Should Engage in Public Affairs* 19 (*Mor.* 794A).
96. Heller 2019b, 2020.
97. Bennett 2014.

98. *SEG* 46.1704 with Wörrle 2004, 300; *I. Perge* 428.

99. Haberman 2014, 244–46. A man of Bithynion (Klaudioupolis), whose tombstone was found some 15 km away from the urban center, is praised by his sons for his activity as a Hesiod-style farmer, alongside his activity as a (local?) judge, his serving (twice) as *archōn*, and his activity as *ekdikos* or public advocate, but with no further mention of benefactions or liturgies (*I. Klaudiopolis* 75, late second century CE?).

100. A. Wilhelm in Heberdey and Wilhelm 1896, 153–54 (but the "eternal best citizen," *aiōnios aristopoliteutēs* at Sparta more likely funded a prize for good citizens rather than inspired citizenry through his everlasting example); Robert 1980, 420 and *OMS* 5, 382–83; Dmitriev 2005, 142–44, 221–22. One example is the Kibyratan benefactor Q. Veranius Philagros (on whom more below), who left an endowment of 400,000 Rhodian drachmas for the gymnasiarchy (*I. Kibyra* 42, 43; Scholz 2015, 87–88).

101. Dēmosthenēs of Oinoanda: Wörrle 1988; S. Mitchell 1990; Rogers 1991b.

102. Dmitriev 2005, notably 152–57. On embassies, the Roman state ensured that compensation was paid to envoys: *Digest* 50.7.3; J. Oliver 1989, nos. 78, 79, 111, 192 (all Antonine-era examples of attention to this matter in imperial letters); *IThrake Aeg* 446 (Traianoupolis in Thrace); *SEG* 56.708b (from Roman Macedonia); *SEG* 59.1424 (in a letter of Hadrian to Pergamon). Conversely, compensation for envoys sent by Byzantion was trimmed by the governor (Pliny, *Letters* 10.43–44).

103. *IG* 10.2.1.5 *1069. Another interesting example of a sanction formula over an honorific monument has recently been published: at Kotenna, on the edge of Pamphylia, three honorific statues were captioned with the full formula on the top molding of the base, *edoxe Kotenneōn tēi boulēi kai tōi dēmōi*, "it seemed good to the Council and the People of the Kotennians" (Adak 2018, republishing more completely a monument found by G. Bean and T. Mitford).

104. Gytheion: *SEG* 11.923. Chios: Robert, *OMS* 1, 518–33. Mytilēnē: Dimopoulou 2017.

105. Diōn, *Oration* 46, esp. 14.

106. La Rocca 2005 gathers the evidence in an important essay on the political culture of the *polis* in the Roman empire; also Chaniotis 2005b (nuanced essay on Aphrodisias); Vujčić 2009.

107. *I Sardis* 1. 8; *Acts of the Apostles* 19; Lewin 1995, 32–33.

108. Mitchell 1993, 201; Lewin 1995, 29–32; La Rocca 2005, 107–8; see also *I. Iasos* 99, 248, with Brélaz 2013, 375–6. Colin 1965 is muddled, confusing acclamations for decrees in pursuit of an oddly biased agenda (showing that the Jewish acclamations during the trial of Jesus had the official force of a decree). Lalla of Tlōs: *SEG* 27.938; on the city, Robert, *OMS* 7, 381–426 (geography); Korkut 2013, 2015 (urban site, territory).

109. Inviting the Council: *Oration* 48.14. *Aprobouleuta psēphismata*: 56.10. Agamemnōn: 49.4.

110. Robert 1994, ch. 7 (with textual notes on the passage, *epizētēsis peri tou artou*).

111. *Oration* 45.16.

112. *I. Ephesos* 27, lines 315–17; *SEG* 38.1462, lines 34–36.

113. *MAMA* 8.413, same document *IAph* 12.26. On entrenchment clauses, Harter-Uibopuu 2013.

114. Fernoux 2005, 2011; Brélaz 2013.

115. Diōn, *Orations* 47 and 48 give a sense of the elite orator dealing with a sovereign assembly.

116. Rhodes with Lewis 1997, 546–48; Lafond 2006, 106 on constitutional continuity in Peloponnesian cities.

117. *IG* 12.9.906, with a vivid summary of the proceedings; Giannakopoulos 2012, 231–36 on the social context.

118. Weiss 1992, modifying earlier views by L. Robert (1967, 55–57).

119. On finances, Migeotte 1996 (for post-classical city more generally). Elections: Lewin 1995, 24–31 and *passim* on the power of the Assembly.

120. Heath 2004, 284–8. For an example of active assembly decision-making: Spawforth in Cartledge and Spawforth 2002, 143–59 and Fournier 2010, 169–76, on Roman Sparta, where a small number of elite families monopolized office, but the Assembly continued to handle business; measures were carried out "as the People wants and the magistrates decide" (*IG* 5.1.18 and 19).

121. Lewin 1995, 43–54, on intra-elite strife in the Roman-era *polis*.

122. Plutarch, *Whether an Old Man Should Engage in Public Life* 18 (*Mor.* 793 D): old men should not compete with the *philarchia* (love of officeholding / thirst for power) of the young.

123. Diōn, *Oration* 7; Bryen 2019. On the political life of Prousa, *Orations* 40; 45.6; 47; Cuvigny 1994; Fuhrmann 2014.

124. Fournier 2010 gathers the meager, ambiguous evidence, and the complex relationship between civic jurisdiction and Roman provincial government; Kantor 2014, 2015.

125. Diōn, *Oration* 31.

126. *Oration* 43.2; I will try to shore up this interpretation elsewhere.

127. *IG* 2.^{2} 1100; Lewin 1995, 34; Harter-Uibopuu 2008, 137–38.

128. Apuleius, *Golden Ass* 3.1–11 (Lucius receives, and declines, an honorific statue for his role in the fes-

tival of Laughter); the People further condemn a witch to stoning (but in an assembly rather than a trial, since the witch took revenge on the introducer of the motion): 1.10. The Christian martyr Pionios is initially heard in the *agora*, before a large crowd (including noncitizens): Robert 1994, ch. 3–7.

129. Lewin 1995, 59–60. Saittai: SEG 40.1063 (four or more tribes, at least two villages, and other civic bodies, including one organization of workers or artisans of some sort).

130. *Orations* 43.11; 46.2; also generally 41, to the Council in Apameia but aware of the People's power. "You, the People": the expression appears in *Orations* 44.10, 45.16.

131. Epameinōndas and "Greek" examples: *Oration* 43. Cheap books: *Oration* 42.

132. SEG 63.1346; Heller 2017. For an even simpler formulation, IGR 3.408, for two men honored by the *polis* of Pogla for filling offices and carrying out *leitourgiai* "according to the decrees."

133. Nörr 1966, 76–79; Fernoux 2011, 40–79; K. Martin 2013.

134. Heller 2006a on conflicts between cities, as a proxy for autonomy (above, pp. 327–28), but also as a means of civic cohesion.

135. Plutarch, *Whether an Old Man Should Engage in Public Life*, 16–17 (*Mor.*792E-F).

136. *I. Tralleis* 31 with Thonemann 2011, 348–49 on date (first century CE).

137. Wörrle 1988, esp. 135–50. Bargylia: SEG 45.1508; 50.1501.

138. Apuleius, *Golden Ass* 1.24–25.

139. *I. Kibyra* 41; Kokkinia 2002 (arguing that Tiberius Neikophoros was not an official but a local speculator on grain prices). For a parallel, note *I. Mylasa* 132 for an individual who served as *zētētēs* (recoverer of public goods?) and *ekdikos*, who did not fear to incur hatred in defending the land of Aphroditē (sacred land under public administration).

140. SEG 61.1024.

141. I borrow this expression from N. McLynn's tribute to the late Mark Whittow, himself the author of a classic study on "Ruling the Late Roman and Early Byzantine City" (1990); but the remark is excised from the published version (*Byzantine and Modern Greek Studies* 45.1 (2021), 2–4) and at time of writing no longer accessible through the website of Corpus Christi College, Oxford.

142. D. Engels 1990. A similar analysis might underlie the picture of the prosperity, urban and rural, of *poleis* in Syria: Antioch, Apameia, Gerasa: Andrade 2013, 150–69; excavations in Kraeling 1938. The link between Stoicism and euergetism is further argued for in Campanile 2016.

143. *Orations* 46; 45.16; 7. 27–45.

144. Migeotte 2014, 177, on the period 100-250 CE as the golden age of the grain fund in Roman Asia Minor.

145. Diōn, *Oration* 46.3; Artemidoros 2.30–31; on subscriptions, including under the Roman empire, Migeotte 1992 (e.g., no. 85 on Diōn's project at Prousa, but also illustrating the continuity of the institution).

146. Corbier 1985; Migeotte 1996; H. Schwartz 2001; Zuiderhoek 2009; Migeotte 2014 (Hellenistic but also Roman-era *polis*).

147. Bouchon 2015.

148. SEG 55.678. The income from the fund given by Q. Veranius Philagros to his city of Kibyra to help with the costs of gymnasiarchy could be used to acquire public lands if the gymnasiarch offered to pay the costs: *I. Kibyra* 43.

149. Halfmann 2004, 85–108.

150. H. Schwarz 2001; Camia 2011.

151. *Oration* 48.9.

152. Pont 2010.

153. Generally, on politics in the Roman-era *polis*, Brélaz 2013; Thornton 2019.

154. On the elitist meanings of Roman-era cityscapes, Ng 2015, 2017; Ryan 2018.

155. Nigdelis and Arvanitaki 2012; Samitz 2013; Wörrle 2004a.

156. SEG 60.644 (Macedonia); TAM 2.838 (list of offices in a consolation decree from Idebēssos in Lykia).

157. SEG 34.1107; Samitz 2013, 44.

158. Millar 2004a, 335–71; *Digest* 50.4.

159. *Digest* 50.12.1; Paparriga-Artemiadi 2020 on the transformation of promises to contractual obligations, liable for penalties on nonpayment and inheritable.

160. Hopkins 1980.

161. Pliny 10.54–55. Andros: a fragmentary decree of the city (*IG* 12.5.724), dating to the "most happy times" of Antoninus Pius, mentions efforts to get the councilors, the *dekaprōtoi* and [the first?] exempted from the poll-tax and (compulsory?) leasing of certain estates: the first was certainly a Roman tax, the latter might have been underwritten by the Roman state, since they are associated as burdens on the elite.

162. *Digest* 50.10.5; cf. 50.8.13 (interest due by private individuals holding public monies after serving in office).

163. *I. Ephesos* 15–16, same document J. Oliver 1989, no. 160, Fant 1981; Pliny *Letters* 10.

164. Orth 1989 on *I Ephesos* 16–17; Dignas 2002, 141–56, 188–96. A fragmentary letter of Hadrian to Nikomēdeia (*TAM* 4.5, same document J. Oliver 1989, no. 93) might concern a similar affair.

165. Zuiderhoek 2011.

166. Diōn, *Oration* 40.1–2; Wörrle 1988, 93–97; Plutarch, *On the Love of Wealth* 5 (*Mor.* 525D): those who want to be the first in their cities and hold office must find sources of money, *porizesthai*.

167. Pont 2019 on misappropriation, profitmaking and corruption (often shielded by local autonomy from the scrutiny of the Roman state, and favored by the weakening of institutional accountability); Pliny 10.110.

168. Plutarch, *Precepts of Statecraft* 13–14 (*Mor.* 808B-809B)

169. Nigdelis and Souris 2005, *SEG* 55.678

170. *SEG* 27.938.

171. Kibyra: *I. Kibyra* 41. Oil at Athens: Harter-Uibopuu 2008.

172. Cassius Dio 69.16.2; Graindor 1934, 79; Follet 1977, 115, 117. A decree of the Areiopagos on public debts incurred by tax farmers may be connected (*Agora* 16, 339).

173. Aelius Aristeidēs, *Oration* 26, 39, 65–67; J. Oliver 1953, 1954; Boatwright 2000, 3–17 (more pessimistic Brunt 1990, 267 n.1: "flagrantly false").

174. Halfmann 2004, 87–89, 110; Fournier 2010, 375–84.

175. Millar 2002, 53 (whence quotation), 161–62 (on Cicero, *Laws* 3.5).

176. Democracy in the Roman Republic: essays gathered in Millar 2002; Hurlet 2012.

177. P. Hamon, *BE* 16, 35, p. 412, on the *prostatai* of Iasos (nuancing the analysis of R. Fabiani), and adducing Fröhlich 2005, 152–55 on the duties of *exetastai*, and other examples of "magistrats à compétence judiciaire défendant l'intérêt public face aux infractions et dont le champ d'intervention a tendance à s'étendre"). Forensic oratory to defend public interests is routinely assumed as part of the occasions for rhetoric in a third-century treatise (alongside private forensic speeches, speeches as ambassadors, and display): Menander Rhetor 1.1 331.

178. Tacitus, *Annals* 2.54.2: the magistrates are local officials rather than Roman governors.

179. Artemidōros and enmity: Chandezon 2014. Polemōn: Swain and Boys-Stones 2007.

180. Diōn, *Oration* 43 (defender of the People, but note 43.5–6, where an orator attacks Diōn to make his name).

181. Graindor 1930; Ameling 1983; Tobin 1997.

182. Stradzins 2022.

183. *IG* 2.² 3606, same document Ameling 1983, vol. 2, no. 190, with vol. 1, 150–51; Tobin 1997, 272–75.

184. Pont 2009 on Aphrodisias; 2016, on Iasos.

185. *SEG* 1.276 (121 CE). On *paraprasis*, see Zuiderhoek 2013.

186. Diōn, *Oration* 48.10; Robert 1940–1965, vol. 7, 80–81.

187. Philostratos, *Lives of the Sophists*, 2.1, 559–63; A. Kuhn 2012; Millar 1977, 3–12, the memorable prologue to the great essay on the Roman emperor; Kennell 1997.

188. C. Jones 1999b; Rife 2008.

189. Philostratos; Ameling 1983, vol. 1, 15–20. On Roman intervention in local feuds, Fournier 2010, 503–91.

190. Thür and Aurenhammer 1997; Halfmann 2004, 85–108; Raja 2012, 55–89. Pliny attended the hearing about Ti. Claudius Aristiōn's case: *Letters* 6.31.

191. Quatember and Scheibelreiter-Gail 2017 for monuments, tombs outside city

192. Philostratos, *Lives of the Sophists* 2.4.

193. The *agora* appears in Diōn, *Oration* 51, as the scene for backbiting and jealousy, in contrast with the utopian rhetoric of civic praise.

Chapter 14. Cooptations, Prolongations, and Endings

Behaving like a Greek city: L. Dirven, "The Imperial Cult in the Cities of the Decapolis, Caesarea Maritima and Palmyra: A Note on the Development of Imperial Cults in the Roman Near East." *ARAM* 23 (2011): 156.

1. Generally A. Jones 1971, 226–94; Millar 1993a; Sartre 2001a; Butcher 2003; Sommer 2018; Saliou 2020, 269–337, 470–85.

2. Sartre 2001a, 640–41. Gerasa: Kennedy 2007.

3. Millar 2006a, 32–50 (classic essay on "a case-study of Hellenisation"); Millar 1993a, 264–95; Bonnet 2015. On post-Seleukid political and cultural landscapes, Ish-Shalom 2023.

4. Millar 2006a, 164–222.

5. *RPC* 1, 4749–50 (under Nero, with portrait of Nero on obverse and reference to the divinized Claudius, *DIVOS CLAUD(ius)*, on reverse).

6. *CIIP* 2, part II.

7. Segal 1997 for a survey of urban form in "Roman Palestine, Syria and Provincial Arabia."

8. Burns 2017.

9. Balty 1988; Butcher 2003, 244–45.

10. de Giorgi 2016, 61–64; de Georgi and Eser 2021, 85–110. The city's mighty colonnaded streets are mentioned in literary sources (Diōn, *Oration* 47.16 and especially the extensive disquisition in Libanios, *Oration in Praise of Antioch*, 196–218, with Downey 1959).

11. Fischer 1995; Boehm, Master, and Le Blanc 2016.

12. *IGLS* 16.1 141, 191 (also in *IGR* 3.1235, 1230); Freyberger et al. 2015; Butler 1919, 346–51; also Freyberger 2000, 2003, 2015, 2017.

13. Andrade 2013, 154–56.

14. *CIL* 3.6687 (same text *ILS* 2683); Millar 1993a, 250–51.

15. Millar 1993a, 253 (for admittedly much later evidence for the territory of Antioch stretching into the Limestone Massif); de Giorgi 2016.

16. *IGLS* 16.1 141–334.

17. Sartre 1981 (republished Sartre 2014, 167–76) on the territory of Kanatha; Millar 1993a, 418–20; Moors 2002, 182–85; Butcher 2003, 158–59, 168; Ando 2017, 132–33. Temples: *IGLS* 16.1 117–39 (Atheila, with doubts about its status), 277–34 (Seeia); generally, Segal 2008, 97–132 (religious life in the Hauran); Mazzilli 2018; Freyberger et al. 2015. Water supply: Freyberger 2004, 2017. *Nymphaeum* of Soada: Sartre-Fauriat 1992; *IGLS* 16.2 331.

18. *IGLS* 13.9801 (*kōmē*), 9810 (*polis* of the Kanathians); 9817 is very similar (Sartre believes the *epimelētai* to be local inhabitants of the villages, entrusted with works by the *polis*). Zeus Greatest: *IGLS* 13.1.9799.

19. Butler 1919, 352–54 and *IGLS* 161. 341–44; *IGLS* 16.1 301 (earlier *SEG* 7.1233); generally, Mazzilli 2018.

20. Millar 1993a, 419, on the *Sēnos Kanōthēnos* and on Thaimos, for whom see also *IGLS* 16.1 145, TI.2 (also *IGF* 131, *IG* 14.2532; found at Genay, 20 kilometers from modern Lyon).

21. De Giorgi 2015, 163–77; generally, on the economy of Roman Syria, Butcher 2003, 135–222.

22. Millar 1993a, 317–19, 399.

23. Millar 1993a; Isaac 1996, 162–67.

24. Sartre 2001a, 815–19; Butcher 2003, 217–20 (notably on the economic aspects of local bronze coinage); Butcher 2004; on Antioch, Neumann 2021, 152–204.

25. Lucian, *On the Syrian Goddess*, 4.

26. Hirt 2015 (mythic connections, but also Roman colonization are celebrated in Tyrian coinage).

27. *IGLS* 4.1298; *RPC* 1.4456–65; 2.2036–38; 3.3812–13.

28. Spijkerman 1979; *RPC* 2.2092.

29. *RPC* 1.4333–78.

30. Petit 1955, 173–76; Millar 2015, 47–70, for the continuation of the story in the fifth century CE.

31. *SEG* 37.1531; Millar 1993a, 6, 378.

32. Andrade 2013, 243–348; Geiger 2014.

33. *IGLS* 4.1346, a milestone set up by "the people of the Klaudieis Apameis Antōninopolis," the *ethnikon* in the plural and the name place in the singular being equated.

34. *RPC* 1.4463, with the coinage labeling Claudius with an honorific accusative; Burnett 2011, 5. The exact circumstances, and the exact relationship between the various geographical concepts, are unclear; it is not quite a matter of Claudius refounding Balaneia as "Claudia Leukas," as often stated. A synoikism may have occurred (the ethnikon is recorded separately by Pliny *Natural History*, 5.82).

35. Sartre 2013, qualified by D. Feissel, *BE* 14, 522; *IGLS* 16.2 39–42. Generally, *IGLS* 16.2 9–84.

36. Pactumeius Clemens: *ILS* 1097. Kanatha: *IGLS* 16.1 184 (also in *SEG* 48.1915, third century CE?).

37. *AE* 1976, 677–78.

38. Small or middling donors at Kanatha: e.g., *IGLS* 16.1 145–51, 153, 154, 155, 199a. Even the city's *ōdeion* benefited from at least two donors (198–99).

39. *I. Gerasa* 1–5, 15.

40. Sartre 1997 for survey of civic institutions in the Roman Levant, and their uniformity; Butler 2003, 223–69.

41. Balaneia: *IGLS* 4.1302, 1303. Kanatha: *IGLS* 16.1 162. On institutions and political culture at Gersasa, Millar 1993a, 408–14.

42. Dionysias (Soada) seems to have had a Council of 140, judging by the numbered seats in the Council house: *IGLS* 16.2 321a.

43. *I. Gerasa* 2–5.

44. *IGLS* 16.1 185 (earlier in *IGR* 3.1224, and even earlier in *I. Syrie* 2330).

45. *IGLS* 16.2 327 shows a notable acting as *pro-ēgoros*, public advocate defending the interests of Dionysias (Soada), and duly honored by the *polis* with statues (including one apparently described as a "golden-mouthed portrait statue"). But see Andrade 2013, 125–47 for an analysis privileging oligarchical city councils.

46. Prosperity of Roman Syria: e.g., Butcher 2003, 135–79; Andrade 2013, 148–70.

47. *IG* $2.^2$ 4210.

48. For another view, Freyberger 2015, insisting on continuities in indigenous culture and society.

49. On the persistence of local styles and traditions in architecture, Ball 2016; but see F. Millar's review of the first edition of this work (Millar 2000), which can yet be nuanced by the visual material gathered in the catalogue of a blockbuster exhibition on the "world between empires," Metropolitan Museum of Art, Spring 2019 (Fowlkes-Childs and Seymour 2019). On the site of Seeia (or Siʿ), Rohmer 2020, 309–39 and on the discontinuities between the material culture of the Iron Age Hauran and the late Hellenistic period, 343–44; the inscriptions are published in *IGLS* 16.1 277–334.

50. Sartre 2017; Millar 1993a, 396.

51. Generally, Starcky and Gawlikoswki 1985; Kaizer 2002; Veyne 2005, 311–451; Sommer 2018; Smedile 2019; Gawlikowski 2021; Yon 2021. Palmyra as *polis*:

Sartre 1996. The urban center was surveyed before and during World War I by Th. Wiegand, the excavator of Priēnē (Wiegand 1932), and excavated from the years of the French Mandate down to the current civil war in Syria (2010–).

52. Matthews 1984; Healey 2009, no. 37; forthcoming in *IGLS* 17.1 (J.-B. Yon); Shifman 2014.

53. On the vast, diverse Palmyrene territory and its villages, Schlumberger 1951; Matthews 1984, 162–72; Teixidor 1984, 77; Seland 2016; Meyer 2017a, 2017b.

54. *IGLS* 17.1 307.

55. Meyer 2017a on the city's concern for "the fields and gardens of the al-Tarfa depression"; *PAT* 0340.

56. Seyrig 1985, 435–36. The *agora* of Palmyra does have a small meeting room, perhaps for officials rather than the Council (Delplace and Dentzer-Feydy 2005, 117–18).

57. A trilingual (Latin, Greek, Aramaic) epitaph might commemorate two freedmen working for the imperial treasury: *IGLS* 17.1 400; also 536 for another trilingual epitaph, possibly for a tax official of the Roman state (as suggested by his Aramaic epitaph).

58. *Logistēs*: *IGLS* 17.1 195; Sartre 1996, 396.

59. Yon 2002, 122–23; Dirven 2011, 153–56.

60. *IGLS* 17.1 351.

61. *IGLS* 17.1 4 (painted on the statue base).

62. Sartre 1996; Kaizer 2002, 38–39; A. Smith 2013.

63. *IGLS* 17.1 224; 53.

64. *IGLS* 17.1 145.

65. *IGLS* 17.1 21.

66. *IGLS* 17.1 150.

67. Ingholt, Seyrig, and Starcky 1955, no. 2, 3, 7, 9.

68. Kaizer 2002, 17, using Savino 1999, 69–75. But the quantitative details might be revised: the 400 hectares of the second-century CE city were not uniformly occupied; for instance, it might be realistic to take a third of that figure, and (with 100–150 inhabitants per hectare) think of ca. 15,000–20,000 inhabitants. As for the territory of Palmyra, I refrain from speculation: it included the valleys around the city, the villages and farmsteads of the uplands, and perhaps settlements served by the Harbaqah dam 69 kilometers southwest of Palmyra, and generally irrigation works to palliate the dry steppe conditions (Schlumberger 1951, 129–34; Meyer 2015; Seland 2016; Meyer 2017a, 28–57; Meyer 2020).

69. Sartre 2001a, 653; Yon 2001; Kaizer 2002, 89–90. On the topography of Palmyra, latest data and interpretations in Schnädelbach 2010.

70. Dijkstra 1995; Andrade 2013, 188–89; Kaizer 2018.

71. Colledge 1976, 88–93; Delplace and Dentzer-Feydy 2005, 339–41; Wielgosz 2010; Dirven 2018; Raja 2018, 292 (tomb-painted images of honorific statues).

72. Dirven 2018.

73. *IGLS* 17.1 18. The term *gbl* (also *IGLS* 17.1 17 dating to 25 CE) is of uncertain etymology (Hoftijzer and Jongeling 1995 *s.v.*).

74. On the problems of the "four tribes," Kaizer 2002, 43–51; A. Smith 2013, 132–43. On tribes in Roman-era *poleis*, Kunnert 2012.

75. *IGLS* 17.1 222, 307; the terminology also appears in fragmentary inscriptions (231, 279).

76. Kalinowski 2002; Kalinowski 2021.

77. On the spaces and rhythms of communal religious life in Roman Palmyra, Kaizer 2002, 2008.

78. Seyrig 1985, 313–32; Ingholt et al. 1955 (no. 8 certainly paid for by the city, but this is a minority in the corpus); Kaizer 2002, 258–59; Raja 2020; Raja 2022 (*non vidi*).

79. E.g., Veyne 2015; Kropp and Raja 2015; Kaizer 2016 (review article).

80. Yon 2001. Temples: Gawlikowski 2021, 113–49. The oft-reproduced reconstruction (by H. Seyrig, R. Amy, and E. Will) of the temple of Bel with two series of Near Eastern-style merlons is in fact not warranted by the material remains: Schmidt-Colinet and Seigne 2022.

81. Cantineau 1935; Millar 1993a, 321–30; D. Taylor 2002.

82. Generally, Colledge 1976; Raja 2018; https://projects.au.dk/palmyraportrait (accessed November 9, 2022).

83. Sommer 2005, arguing against Sartre 1996; nuanced views, notably on institutionalization, in Sommer 2018, 171–209; indigenous culture emphasized, underneath the *polis* institutions, by Graf 2019.

84. Delplace and Dentzer-Feydy 2005, 151–234; *IGLS* 17.1 240–53.

85. On the heavy impact of the army through extraction and consumption, Isaac 1990, 269–310; Pollard 2000, especially 85–110.

86. On Palmyra's long-distance trade, Seland 2016.

87. *IGLS* 17.1 150; Andrade 2012; 2013, 177–203; Magnani and Mior 2017.

88. *IGLS* 17.1 19.

89. Yon 2002; 2017.

90. Colledge 1976 for the diversity of Palmyrene material culture, from architecture to textiles.

91. Heyn 2010; Long 2015; Albertson 2015.

92. *IGLS* 17.1 262 (164 CE, consecration of a man to Bel by his father, at the latter's expense).

93. de Jong 2017.

94. Dirven 2013; Yon 2017; Sommer 2018, 361–93.

95. Schlumberger 1951, on the Roman date of the occupation of the Palmyrene highlands; confirmed but nuanced by Meyer 2017a, 13–16, who notes that some northern villages enjoyed a longer life than Schlumberger allows for.

96. Millar 1993a, 242–47; Lightfoot 2003, 540–47; on the serious playfulness of Lucian's essay, Elsner 2001 is essential.

97. *IGLS* 1.233 (phratry), 234 (public honorific statue set up by Council and People), 235 (epitaph for Roman soldier).

98. *IGLS* 17.1 304.

99. See e.g., Millar 1993a; Butcher 2003; Andrade 2013.

100. *I. Ephesos* 713.

101. Bader and Yon 2018.

102. Lieberman 1946; Sperber 1998; S. Schwartz 2001, 101–75.

103. *CIIP* 4. 3847; Millar 1993a, 376 and *CIIP* 4, p. 890 on the territory. Here I understand the "lords" in *rš mrym* as in the Aramaic translation of "Xanthians" as "lords of Orna" in a fourth-century BCE decree from Lykia (Metzger et al. 1979; above, p. 224): the language of lordship is used to describe the stakeholder citizens of the *polis*.

104. Millar 1993a, 375.

105. Kropp 2013; Rohmer 2020.

106. Millar 1993a, 406–17.

107. The consequence is that the temple architecture, as studied by Freyberger 2015, cannot be used to deduce the social realities of the second-century CE *polis*. On the culture of the "pre-provincial" Hauran, Dentzer 1986, esp. 396–97, 412–13; Rohmer 2020 (who however downdates the temple architecture at Kanatha to the first century CE).

108. Appadana: Feissel and Gascou 1989, 1995; Karrhai: Teixidor, Feissel, and Gascou 1997. See also Edwell 2008 for the density of military occupation on the Mesopotamian frontier; Millar 1993a; de Jong and Palermo 2012 for the long historical and geographical context of the militarization of the frontier.

109. Millar 1993a, 123, 143–45, 153–57, 482, 485.

110. Millar 1993a, 469, on *P. Dura* 4.

111. Generally, Bowman 2000 on urbanization and its connection to institutions; Monson 2012, 262–65 on settlement and status in Roman Egypt; Jördens 2013. On municipalization, Jouguet 1911 (has aged quite badly); Bowman 1986, 37–47, 65–88; Bagnall 1996; Alston 2001; Tacoma 2006; Jördens 2009; Monson 2012, 265–72; Lerouxel 2016.

112. An illustration of Egyptian *polis* life: a decree of Naukratis, passed under Antoninus Pius by "the office-holders and the *dēmos* . . . and the resident Romans and Alexandrians" attests institutional workings (but without a council, replaced by the executive committee of magistrates): *P. Oxy* 3.473 with N. Lewis 1981, 78–80; and Bowman and Rathbone 1992, 121 n.68.

113. Bowman and Rathbone 1992, qualified by the multifactor ecological and economic model proposed by Monson 2012.

114. Hagedorn 2007 on the emergence of *archai* in the *nomos* capitals; Broux 2013 on the privileged orders and their origin (urban population and Greeks in the countryside, centered around village gymnasia), conflated in a single urban elite by Roman administrative reforms; Alston 2001, 193–96 on elite contributions; Bowman 1992 on building.

115. *P. Rylands* 77; A. Jones 1938, 70 was willing to see "a vestigial remnant of popular election," which may be optimistic. Alston 2001, 193–96, notes the considerable expense of running the Egyptian towns, and elite financing.

116. Bagnall 1996, 225–27, 315–16, 319.

117. van Minnen 2002 (but I would argue that the rarity of euergetism is itself typical of *polis* life rather than an exception: see above, pp. 363–65); Alston 2001, 193–96; Drew-Bear 2020, 64–104. Elite contributions: e.g., *P. Oxy* 44.3175, 233 CE (entrance fees to the Council at Oxyrhynchos were paid in the form of a loan taken from the Council's fund and repaid as annuities with interest); 44.3177 (payment of "crown-money").

118. *P. Rylands* 599; *P. Oxy* vol. 40. On the *sitometroumenoi*, Wörrle 1988 (Oinoanda) and above, p. 342.

119. Bowman 1971; Tacoma 2006, 115–62; Drew-Bear 2020 (archives of the Council of Greater Hermoupolis).

120. E.g., Drew-Bear 2020, nos. 19, 20, 21.

121. *P. Oxy* 7.1015

122. *P. Oxy* 1.41; Bowman 1971, 53–67 on the office of *prytanis*; Blume 1989 on the acclamations, the language of "moderation" designating the poor, and legal delays for honors.

123. On the *syndikoi* in Egypt, Bowman 1971, 49, 57, 83.

124. van Minnen 2002; Drew-Bear 2020, 180–95, on no. 43 A (also *SB* 10.10299), arguing that the monuments may have been damaged during unrest.

125. Alston 2001, 268; Parlasca 2007. Generally, de Jong 2017 on Roman-era funerary art as part of a global imperial culture.

126. Literary culture: Bagnall 1996, 99–109. The *Constitution of the Athenians* and *Dēmosthenēs* 21 at Greater Hermoupolis: Otranto 2012 on *P. lit. Lond* 108 (157 n. 3 on provenance); a third-century CE library catalogue from Memphis also mentions the *Constitution* (Pack^2 2089, discussed in Poethke 1974, 1576–57).

127. Cameron 2016.

128. Borg 1998; Riggs 2005.

129. Jacques 1984, 1990 (rich sourcebook in translation); Lepelley 1993; Woolf 1998; Lepelley 2001; Dench 2018.

130. Lenski 2016, 87–113, with improved text of the epigraphical dossier (*MAMA* 7.305); Pont 2020, 408–23.
131. On the military context, Potter 1990, 3–65; on the cities in the crisis, Pont 2020, 109–80.
132. Millar 2004a, 265–97.
133. Harl 1987.
134. Pont 2020, esp. 177–80, 243–45.
135. Barnes 1982; Matthews 2007; S. Mitchell 2015. On the reforms within the continuity of Roman instrumentalization of the *poleis*, Pont 2020, 247–330.
136. Lenski 2016, 103–6.
137. On the problem of local finances, see lately Bransbourg 2008; Lenski 2016, 167–75; Pont 2020, 315–21; Goddard 2020.
138. Pont 2020, 419–20, on the case of Helenopolis in Bithynia.
139. Liebeschuetz 1992, 2000; Wickham 2005, 596–602. For a particular case, Fournier 2018: officeholding ceases to be attested at Thasos in the second half of the third century CE.
140. Lewin 1995, 85–112.
141. Laniado 2002.
142. Theodosius II, *Novel* 23 (Mommsen and Meyer 1905, 2:60–61; translation Pharr 1952, 510–11, slightly modified); Millar 2006b, 9, 92–93; Robert and Robert 1954, 154–55.
143. Petit 1955; Cassella 2010. Willed consensus of the *politeuomenoi*: Oration 56.
144. A. Jones 1940, 251–58; 1964, 2:712–66; generally, Lavan 2008.
145. Brown 2013.
146. R. Smith 2002; contrast the earlier tradition, R. Smith 2006; generally, Smith and Ward-Perkins 2016. On the fate of euergetism, especially in a Christian context, Patlagean 1977, 181–203; Brown 2001; Caner 2021.
147. Robert 1939–1965, vol. 4.
148. Millar 2006b, especially 1–38, notably on the case of Seleukeia on Kalykadnos as seen in the life of St. Thekla (quotation from p. 26–27); also 59–60 (cities of Libya in the time of Synesios), 77–78 (Greek cities on the north coast of the Black Sea, including Chersonesos), 79 (Greek cities in Illyricum and the Adriatic coast), 80 (cities in Greece such as Delphi).
149. Millar 2006b, 98–100 (on the Acts of the Councils as "a sort of gazetteer of a large selection of the cities and provinces which made up Theodosius's Empire"); 133–40 (on competition; see also Millar 2015, 47–70). The cities are listed in the geographical indices of the modern edition of the Acts (E. Schwartz 1928–1938, part 1, 8:25–31; part 2, 6:81–105); compare the earlier list of Fathers at the Council of Nikaia in 325 CE (Honigmann 1939a), and the later list of cities compiled in the sixth century by Hierokles (Honigmann 1939b with Robert 1962, *passim*).
150. Brown 1971, 43–44; though I have earlier mentioned the survival of *polis*-style, stately structures at Flavia Aeduorum (Hostein 2012).
151. C. Jones 2010; the quotation is from *I. Stratonikeia* 1204 (in Jones's translation), from one of several statues awarded to Maximus.
152. Whittow 1990.
153. Saradi 2006; on the general cultural and material context, e.g., Lazaridou 2011.
154. *SEG* 35.1360; Liebeschuetz 2000, 111–12.
155. Petit 1955; Cabouret 2007.
156. Patlagean 1977, 203–31; Liebeschuetz 2000; Laniado 2002; de Oliveira 2020.
157. Waelkens 2006, on the testcase of Sagalassos (clear changes in the fifth century CE, though urban continuity over the next two centuries); Lavan 2009.
158. Patlagean 1977, 228–29; Laniado 2002, 218 (the youth murder a bishop at Kyzikos).
159. Robert 1940–1965, vol. 10, 200; Fowden 1990. Thekla: Dagron 1978.
160. Laniado 2002, 67–68 (landlords), 99, 218 (embassies by bishops; see also Millar 2006b, 143–48). On the Christian takeover of the functions of rhetoric, in dealing with and channeling imperial power, Brown 1992.
161. Brown 2001; Brown 2013; Caner 2020. On Theodoret, Millar 2006b, 28–29, 146–48.
162. See e.g., the survey by Ward 2020; Saliou 2020, 312–19; essay by Elm 2014.
163. I. Jacobs 2013; Dey 2014; I. Jacobs and Elton 2019.
164. Foss 1977, 1979.
165. Foss 1991.
166. Feissel 2010, 251–324; Thonemann 2011, 309–14. On the persistence of a structure of relative statuses of cities in the sixth century CE, Saliou 2020, 282, on Dōrotheos, *Instructions*, 2.34, comparing the increasing awareness of unworthiness of the sinner approaching God to a local notable of Gaza moving to Caesarea, Antioch, and Constantinople.
167. On continuities in the urbanism of the Near East into the Umayyad period, Ward 2020.
168. Haldon 1999, 20–21, 22.
169. *TAM* 5.3. More unusually, the proceedings of the Council of Ephesos in 431 include documents relating to the repression of heresy in Philadelpheia, and a glimpse of households, councillors, rural dwellers, artisans, and immigrants in the Late Roman city: Millar 2004b.
170. Civic autonomy under Byzantine empire: Bratianu 1936. Philadelpheia: *TAM* 5.3 (G. Petzl), for Hellenistic and Roman epigraphy; Schreiner 1969; Ahr-

weiler 1983, vivid but centered on magnates; Ahrweiler 1984. The Catalan mercenary Ramon Muntaner affected to remember Philadelpheia (before which he fought in 1304) as "a noble city, among the great ones in the world," comparable in extent to Rome and Constantinople: Muntaner (ed. Escartí) 1991, vol. 2, ch. 205; translated in Hughes and Hillgarth 2006, 55.

171. For cities in e.g., Asia Minor after the sixth-century watershed, Brandes 1989. On the "Byzantine republic," Kaldellis 2015, insistent on the Roman genealogy of republican practice as part of Byzantine political culture (the word *polis* in the Aristotelian sense does not appear in the index); already Millar 2002b, 46–88.

172. Memnōn of Hērakleia: *FGrHist / BNJ* 434.

Part VI. Making Sense of *Polis*

1. On the potential of the *polis* as form, Castoriadis 2008, with Pébarthe 2012 (and even Allen 2020, distantly); for a critique of the *polis*, especially post-Classical, I draw inspiration from the force of Ando 2018a (but not its details).

Chapter 15. *Polis* as Society

Freedom from the traditional forms of exploitation: E. M. Wood, *Democracy against Capitalism* (Cambridge: 1995), 189–90.

1. For this approach, Bates et al. 1998, offering neo-institutionalist "analytical narratives," which is not quite what I have been doing above. The narrative form is adopted in essays such as Bookchin 1995 (promoting a modern civic autonomy) and Isin 2002 (suspicious and critical of the notion of citizenship), so perhaps there is something to tracing the genealogy and development of political relations in time.

2. On the theoretical issues of narrative history (as an "unpacking" rather than an explanatory form), Veyne 1978.

3. de Ste. Croix 1981; Cartledge 2016, to which the present work is obviously indebted.

4. Weber 1999; Bruhns 2014, 1–85.

5. I hence take a position against van der Spek 1987, 58.

6. Pausanias 10.4.1–4; Petrocheilos and Rousset 2019 (survey of remains, including nekropolis, and epigraphy); Gengler 2020.

7. Generally, pp. 327–28.

8. Aristotle, *Politics* 6.1 1317a.

9. Horden and Purcell 2000; Broodbank 2013; Manning 2018; on resources, Nixon and Price 1990.

10. Fishermen: Aristotle, *Politics* 4.4 1291b, 6.1 1317a (generally, on diversity of *dēmos*); Strabo 14.2.21, *I. Iasos* 34 on the *polis* of Iasos, "living from the sea"; Lytle 2018 on a particular case, fishing by torchlight at Istros on the Black Sea (as the Roman governor of Moesia notes, the city's saltfish industry is its main source of income).

11. Hērakleia: above, pp. 2–8. Ephesos: J. Hanson 2011 (urban center of 224 hectares); the territory may have covered over 400 square kilometers.

12. Gawantka 1985; E. Lévy 1990; Vlassopoulos 2007a.

13. Daverio Rocchi 2011, 25, 28–30; Rousset, Camp, and Minon 2015. The ethnikon "Phanopeus" seems a hybrid, though the political meaning is unclear (Kalliontzis 2020, no. 18, with Rousset, *BE* 21, 233).

14. Millar 1993b; Ma 2000.

15. C. Morgan 1999a for the Early Iron Age and Archaic periods; Nielsen 2007 for the Classical period; Ma 2003a for the Hellenistic. Peloponnese: Adshead 1986; Pariente 1992; Funke and Luraghi 2009; Shipley 2018.

16. Thucydides 4.76.3; *IACP* no. 201; Ma 2016a. Chaniotis 1997 offers nuanced views on the issue of autonomy.

17. Fröhlich 2010; Ma 2018.

18. Ma 2002 drawing on Bikerman 1939a, a critique of Heuss 1937; Capdetrey 2007, 191–224.

19. Hansen in *IACP*, p. 20.

20. van der Vliet 2011.

21. Ober 1989; Canevaro 2017, 2021, for popular/hegemonic culture in Classical Athens; Grieb 2008 for democracy in the third and second centuries BCE; Giangiulio 2015.

22. Grieb 2008 (favoring the internal direction of the definition).

23. Strabo 13.2.3.

24. Hence the interest (indeed, adulation) shown by the Marxist ancient historian G. E. M. de Ste. Croix in Aristotle's social analysis, as compatible with Marx: de Ste. Croix 1981, 69–80.

25. Aristotle, *Politics* 4.13 1297b. On the violence of the rich, Scheid-Tissinier 2004.

26. For a survey of recent debates and of more general theoretical issues, Gray 2022.

27. Wycherley 1957; Thompson and Wycherley 1972; Camp 2010; J. Shear 2011; Paga 2020 (based on a late sixth-century BCE date for the Great Drain, Old

Bouleutērion and the Stoa Basileios). On storage of publicly owned grain at the shrine of Aiakos on the Agora, Stroud 1998, 84–104.

28. Ma 2015a, 103–4; Azoulay 2014a; Baltes 2020; Stewart, Frischen, and Abdelaziz 2022, on the statuary group of the Tyrant-Slayers in the Agora.

29. Millett 1998; Vlassopoulos 2007b; Gottesmann 2014, 26–43. Haircut: Lysias 23.2–3.

30. Gottesman 2014; Hunter 1994.

31. Vlassopoulos 2007b, based on the radical, hopeful essay of Evans and Boyte 1986 on the possibility of agency for the dispossessed (and even compare Gilroy 2002, a radical, race- and class-centered search for free spaces in contemporary Great Britain); Sobak 2015.

32. Akrigg 2015, 155–56. Cf. Crowther 2007b for Iasos.

33. Aristotle, *Politics* 2.1 1261a.

34. Associations in Classical Athens: R. Osborne 1990a; Connor 1996; Arnaoutoglou 1998b; N. Jones 1999; Ismard 2010; Gottesman 2014, 44–76. For the Hellenistic and Roman period, van Nijf 1997; Arnaoutoglou 2003; Martzavou 2008; Fröhlich and Hamon 2012; Gherchanoc 2012 (esp. 208–9); J. Steinhauer 2014; Thomsen 2020. Eckhardt 2016 argues for the impact of the Roman empire on the phenomenon, especially in an urban context. For earlier surveys of the phenomenon, and attempts at historical interpretation, Ziebarth 1896; Poland 1901. Koppenborg, Ascough, and Harland 2011 provide a sourcebook of documentary evidence; and we must await the results of the work of the Copenhagen Associations Project, directed by V. Gabrielsen and C. A. Thomsen; see already the website (and database), https://copenhagenassociations.saxo.ku.dk (accessed July 2023).

35. Leão and Rhodes 2016, fr. 76a; above, p. 87.

36. Herrmann 1980 (whence *SEG* 30.1285 1339–44; cf. 60.1269); W. Günther 1995 (*SEG* 45.1606, also in *Milet* VI 2 795). *Temenitai* also at Mylasa: *SEG* 54.1107, imitating Milētos? (Carbon 2013).

37. Tlos: *SEG* 58.1640 (metalworkers' association beneficiary of a legacy); Thyateira: *TAM* 5.984–87 (with Millar 2004a, 440–41).

38. Funerary foundations: e.g., Ritti 2016 (Roman-era Hierapolis). Rhodes: Thomsen 2020 on e.g., *SEG* 39.737, 185 BCE, or *Lindos* 292.

39. van den Eijnde, Blok, and Strootman 2018 for diachronic collection of essays.

40. Above, p. 87 (with Haggis 2011); p. 283 (with Fröhlich 2005); p. 384.

41. Polybios 20.6.5–7, with Thomsen 2020, 129–30.

42. Taylor and Vlassopoulos 2015; Thomsen 2021.

43. Ma 2015a, Biard 2017 for surveys of the honorific statue habit.

44. C. Müller 2014b on "deconstructing citizenship"; P. Davies 2017b; Azoulay and Ismard 2018.

45. Kamen 2013; Sommerstein 2009 on violence against slaves and citizens alike (admittedly in the topsy-turvy evidence of Attic comedy, often playing with and against boundaries).

46. Xenophon, *Hellenica* 4.5.11.

47. E.g., *SEG* 66.1747 (Roman-imperial Limyra); *Beroia* 59 (citizens and landowners); Baker and Thériault 2018.

48. Boyxen 2018; Vlamos 2022.

49. *IG* 12.3.1270 with Constantakopoulou 2015, 223–31; Thomsen 2020, 137–41. To add to the complexity, it seems that the Rhodian citizen is a member of a Rhodian deme called the *Politai*, and indeed a member of a small community of people from this deme who have settled on Symē.

50. Thomsen 2020, 80–88, on Badoud 2015, no. 22 (picking up on insights by A. Bresson); *I. Pérée Rhodienne*, no. 22 (same text *I. Rhodische Peraia* 501).

51. *TAM* 5.3.1426.

52. Friedrichs 1995; T. Scott 2012.

53. Xenophon, *Hellenica* 4.2.20–21; with Azoulay 2014b.

54. Argos: above, p. 180; Athens: Greco 2020, 27–35; J. Shear 2021. Generally, R. Martin 1951, 164–223 (on survival of old "agonal" function into Roman period).

55. Priēnē: Ma 2015a, 98–99. Smyrna: Bagnall et al. 2016; Robert 1994; Pont 2020, 27–108.

56. Duplouy 2006; Giangiulio 2017; Duplouy 2018b.

57. Connor 1987; Walter 1993; Goldhill and Osborne 1999; Blok 2005, e.g., 19 on recognition as mechanism for admission to society; Duplouy 2006; Duplouy and Brock 2018; Duplouy 2018a-c; Duplouy 2019.

58. Robert and Robert 1989; Kolophonian decrees inscribed at Klaros (*SEG* 39.1243–44; I heard Fergus Millar reflect that one could write a social history of the *polis* out of these documents). Teōs: *SEG* 41.1034. Priēnē: e.g., *I. Priene B-M* 63–70 (and above, pp. 279–84). Generally, Schmitt-Pantel 1990, 1992.

59. Block grants: *SEG* 47.1563, *sumpoliteia* of Latmos and Pidasa (with Wörrle 2003); *SEG* 39.1426, *isopoliteia* of Arsinoē in Kilikia and Nagidos. Analogously, in *IPArk* 18, the Stymphalians gave a share of their sacrifices and rites to the refugee Elateians as a form of participation in public life, and the latter subsequently reciprocate toward their benefactors. Individual grants: for instance, *IG* 12.8.51 (Imbros); *Inschr. Magnesia* 11; Knoepfler 2001c, 38–39. Analogously, in *SEG* 43.709, the *polis* of Eurōmos grants honors to a mercenary, including participation "in the sacred matters of which the other citizens have a share" (the formulation in fact suggests that citizenship was also granted). On grants of citizenship, Mack 2019.

60. E.g., decrees for demarchs at Athens: *IG* 2.² 1178–9; Robert 1940–1965, vol. 1, 1–17. See p. 430 for an example from the *polis* of Karthaia on Keos.

61. Blok 2017, 101; also Blok 2014.

62. Rhodes 1995, esp. 194–95; Blok 2017, 84–85; for a (possibly) parallel usage designating the priority of sacred funds or budget lines in civic finances; Robert, *OMS* 6.595 on *Samothrace* 2.1, no. 5 (P. M. Fraser); *OMS* 7.751.

63. J. Hall 1997b; above, pp. 93, 101–102.

64. Price 2005; Ritter 2002; Matthaei 2013; Caillet et al. 2015.

65. *I. Ilion* 31 with Robert, *OMS* 7, 599–635; Chaniotis 1995; Martzavou 2008 on "festival communities."

66. Connelly 2007; L.-M. Günther 2014a.

67. Zachhuber 2018.

68. *Staatsverträge* 4.653 (also published as *IG* 9.1.32 where it is dated to ca. 135 BCE, *Syll.*³ 647).

69. Blok 2017; Grieb 2008, 139–40; and Dmitriev 2018, 99–100 (Kōs).

70. Sébillotte 2017; R. Osborne 2011, 93–119; Dmitriev 2018, 13–34, 99–100; Blok 2017, esp. 200–206.

71. Here I closely follow Fröhlich 2016.

72. Rumscheid 2014, 174–75, in Matthaei and Zimmermann 2014.

73. Robert 1966a, 89–90.

74. Welles, *RC* 10–13.

75. Ismard 2015.

76. Azoulay 2016.

77. Clastres 1974 (which I read with Gourgouris 2019); also D. Roussel 1976, e.g., 42.

78. Berent 2000, 2004; above, pp. 35–37, 106–12, 183–85, 236–44.

79. Hennig 1995.

80. Ober 1996, 161–87; Canevaro 2017.

81. *IG* 7.1 (on the spelling, Dittenberger argues for the toponym Aigostena, "goat narrows," rather than the Aigosthena, "goat power" known by literary sources and hence generally adopted in secondary literature); generally, Liddel 2009 on Megarian decree culture.

82. Reynolds 1982, no. 2 (also published online as *IAph* 2007, 8.3).

83. Evans, Rueschermeyer, and Skocpol 1985 on "bringing the state back in." S. Johnstone 1999, on the autonomy of legal practice and institutions.

84. On the importance of viewing the political as the intersection of institutions and social practice, Azoulay and Ismard 2007, 306; Ismard 2010; on the autonomy of state functions, Ismard 2015.

85. Grieb 2008, 199–201 on Milētos; I. Savalli-Lestrade in *BE* 19, no. 40, p. 500 (review of Blok 2017), discussing Milet 6.1.1023 (not 1323, by the way), for Milētos but also other cities.

86. [Aristotle], *Constitution of the Athenians*, 55.3.

87. Blok 2017, 201, 207, and generally ch. 5.

88. At Thasos, newly admitted citizens have to argue before the *patra* for acceptance: I believe this simply reproduces procedure for citizen children (material gathered in *CITh* 3, 12, 14, 15, 17, by P. Hamon).

89. *Politics* 5.8 1309a.

90. Fabiani 2017, commenting on new evidence from Iasos; on assembly pay, *RO* 99 (to be dated to the early third rather than the late fourth century: Fabiani 2015b, 259 n.56). "Tribes" in the "Archaic" period: D. Roussel 1976; Hölkeskamp 1993; in the Roman-imperial *polis*: Kunnert 2012.

91. *I. Prusias ad Hypium* 63.

92. *SEG* 45.1508; 50.1501; *BE* 16.452 (P. Hamon).

93. Vernant 1962; Vidal-Naquet 1981.

94. On the role of wine in providing vitamins as well as carbohydrates, Bresson 2016, 122.

95. Chaniotis 2012.

96. Pergamon: Hamon 2012. Consolation decrees: Buresch 1894; Sève 1979; Ehrhardt 1994; Hamon 2016.

97. *Dikaia*; e.g., Xenophon, *Hellenica* 6.3.9; Aristotle, *Politics*, 3.12 1283a.

98. Ma 2015a, 323, based on a metaphor developed by N. Loraux.

99. *SEG* 59.930.

100. Davidson 2012.

101. C. Patterson 1981; Boegehold 1993; Blok 2009; Lape 2010; Blok 2017; above, n. 69 on Kōs.

102. Above, pp. 230–31.

103. Above, pp. 131–32, on the suitors of Agaristē; Gernet 1968, 344–59.

104. On multiple citizenships under the Roman empire, Pont and Heller 2012.

105. van Bremen 1996, showing that female benefactresses do not reflect greater female agency but male family strategies.

106. Aristotle, *Politics*, Book 1; Morris 1987; D'Onofrio 2011.

107. *I. Delphinion* 136 (*isopoliteia* with Olbia); other *isopoliteia* treatises with Milētos are to be found *ibid.* no. 142 (with Phygela, fourth century BCE), 143 (with Seleukeia-Tralleis), 146 (with Mylasa), 150 (with Hērakleia under Latmos, also published as *Staatsverträge* 640); the same terms appear in the treaty of *sumpoliteia* by which Milētos took over Pedasa (149, also published as *Staatsverträge* 638). See P. Herrmann, in *Milet* 6.1. *ad loc.* for dates. Generally, Robert, *OMS* 1, 206 n.1

108. *SEG* 43.703–4; generally see Knoepfler 2001c, esp. pp. 38–39.

109. Ephebic oath: Osborne-Rhodes, *GHI* 88, with Blok 2017, 94–99 arguing for the primacy of the religious. On the "bigness" of the public actor, Ma 2015a; logical primacy of the *polis*: Aristotle, *Politics*, Book 1.

110. I am actually rather dependent on Foucaldian concepts as refracted in P. Veyne (e.g., 2005, 1–116);

also Skornicki 2015 on the difficult problems of Foucault and the state.

111. Fabiani 2017, with P. Hamon in *BE* 18, 408.
112. Aristotle, *Politics*, 3.9 1280b30-9.
113. E. Harris 2017, 114.
114. Thomsen 2020, 129–59.
115. *SGDI* 3090 (also published as *I. Callatis* 43); *ISE* 39.
116. *I.Rhamnous* contains a rich collection of decrees of quasi-civic bodies, dating to the third century BCE; on Symē, Thomsen 2020, 139–41 on *IG* 12.3.1270. As noted above (p. 6), it is possible to wonder whether the decree concerning the goats on the island of Hērakleia (above, pp. 3–11) was passed by such an association, rather than a *polis*: Fröhlich in *BE* 13, 327, on Constantakopoulou 2012.

117. See above, p. 82, on decision-making by kinship groups in early Athens.
118. The importance of the intermediate level for democratic life has been amply recognized, starting with Alexis de Tocqueville's interest in civil society in the United States: e.g., Selznick 1992, Putnam 1994, as studying (or preaching in favor of) pluralistic yet high social-capital polities.
119. P. Jones 2010, 13 (originally published in 1965); critiques in T. Scott 2012, 222.
120. On Roman-era associations, above, p. 348; for an example, Ritti 2016 (Hierapolis in Phrygia).
121. Gray 2013, 2022.
122. Millar 1993a; above, chapter 14.
123. Palmyra: Yon 2019. Qartaba pillar: Gatier 2005; Fowlkes-Childs and Seymour 2019, 138–39.

Chapter 16. *Polis* as Ideals

The state, as problem and as solution: P. Rosanvallon, *L'Etat en France de 1789 à nos jours* (Paris: 1990), 14. **Politics and philosophical convictions:** R. Rorty, *What Can We Hope for? Essays on Politics*, edited by W. P. Malecki and C. Voparil (Princeton: 2022), 35.

1. Robert and Robert 1989, 104.
2. Forster 2018.
3. *IG* 12.9.236.
4. I was complacent enough to congratulate myself on coining this term, but it is the title of a monograph on *Soulcraft and Statecraft in Renaissance Italy*: Hankins 2019.
5. The idea is important to conservative political philosophers, arguing for the inherence of morals in any form of institutions and procedure: Selznick 1992; Heclo 2008 (which entails a cheerful willingness to paint oneself into ethical corners).
6. Hansen 1989a–c, 1991, 1997b; Gauthier 1984, 1985; see especially essays gathered in Ober 1996; issues revisited in Hansen 2010.
7. Ostwald 1986; Hansen 1991; above, pp. 440–41.
8. Dēmosthenēs 21.223–25: law *per se* is just written letters, that cannot come running to save any citizen from harm.
9. Ober 1998.
10. Gray 2013, 2018b.
11. *I. Priene B-M* 25 (second half of the third century BCE).
12. Ober 2012; liberty (not property) as the baseline for membership in the democratic *polis* features heavily in Aristotle's *Politics*, but without clear definition of the meaning of liberty. I would argue for *polis* liberty to be quite similar to the liberty of neoclassical "republicanism" as studied by modern political philosophers (absence of domination): Bock, Skinner, and Viroli 1990 (esp. essays by Q. Skinner on "the prehumanist origins of republican ideas," 121–41, and republican liberty, 293–309); Skinner 1998, esp. 59–99; Pettit 2012—at least similar enough for the essential shared traits to matter more than surface differences in emphasis.

13. Fisher 1992, 498–9, on the democratic *polis*'s project of protecting the poor citizens from violence and injustice; Dēmosthenēs 21 with Ober 1996, 86–106; Aristotle, *Politics*, 6.1–62 1317a-1318a; *SEG* 50.1195, line 38 (attesting the existence of a law against violence (*nomos hubristērios*) at Kymē in the 270s BCE).
14. Thucydides 2.37 (claimed as democratic, Athenian trait); Aristotle, *Politics* 5.9 1310a.
15. Antidemocratic critique: [Xenophon], *Constitution of the Athenians* ("Old Oligarch"); democratic restraint: Lysias, *Oration* 16, provides an example of the high value set on moderation and dislike for big men.
16. Ruzé 2003.
17. On entitlement and its consequences (practical, political), R. Osborne 2009b.
18. Aristotle, *Politics* 5.9 1310a.
19. Fragment 4; above, p. 151; Balot 2001.
20. Lykourgos, *Against Leokratēs*; Diōn, *Oration* 44 (see also 39); generally, Liddel 2007, unpacking civic ideas.
21. As portrayed in Plato's *Kritōn*: Ober 2005, 157–70.
22. *SEG* 39.1243–44 (Klaros); *SEG* 1.276 (Lētē).
23. Hennig 1995.
24. *SEG* 51.1105, line B23; above, 216–17.
25. Bell 1993. Note also a sentiment of M. Horkheimer, from his 1942 essay "Vernunft und Selbsterhaltung": "The presence of the general interest in the par-

ticular one, the representation of their harmony, such was the ideal of the Greek city" (*Die Anwesenheit des allgemeinen im besonderen Interesse, die Vorstellung ihrer Harmonie war der Ideal der griechischen Stadt*, Horkheimer 1997, 320–50, at 324).

26. Aristotle, *Politics* 6.3 1318a.

27. Chirica 2005; Hamon 2012.

28. *IGBulg* 1² 308 bis. As Paraskevi Martzavou remarked to me, the practice might alternatively refer to a funerary ritual, performed individually but across the whole community.

29. Zanker 1993; on the accusative in honorific inscriptions, Ma 2015a, 45–55, developing insights by P. Veyne.

30. On the inscriptions on the bases of honorific statues, Ma 2015a, 15–63. On striving for the finest things in honorific decrees, Robert, *OMS* 1.1080.

31. *Politics* 3.4 1276b.

32. Ober 1998.

33. See for instance, Sherman 1999; Miller 2011; generally, T. Irwin 2020.

34. Lanni 2006, 2016.

35. Ober 2008.

36. Ruzé 2003.

37. T. Irwin 2007, 119–22 (on *ta endoxa*, common opinion, and deliberative method).

38. Ma 2015a, 58–62.

39. *Politics* 3.9, 1310a28.

40. Wörrle 1995; Ober 1989 for "mass and elite" in Classical Athens.

41. Chr. Habicht in *I. Pergamon Asklepieion*, 176–78.

42. Whitehead 1993; Kralli 1999–2000; Forster 2018.

43. Gray 2018a, 205; Wörrle 1995 on the devouring passion for the public good as expected of the good citizen in post-Classical *poleis*; Martzavou 2008 on the "virtuoso" benefactors of the late Hellenistic and early Roman periods, notably in Boiōtia and the Peloponnese.

44. *I. Priene* B-M 64, lines 82–89, with restorations by W. Blümel (for the price being that chosen by the city and not Moschiōn): the text there is missing but Blümel's parallels, the rhetoric of the passage and the usual practice of *paraprasis* are decisive. I also believe that the original inscription omitted, by mistake, an indication of the quantity of grain delivered by Moschiōn.

45. Ma 2002.

46. Broodbank 2013, 696; Konstantidi-Syvridi 2021 (on the case of royal artifacts in early Mycenaean Dendra); Barr-Sharrar 2008 for an example of luxury metalwork in Macedonia (close to Lētē), the famous Derveni crater (above, p. 11).

47. Classic statements of this interpretation of *polis* urbanism in Fehr 1980; Hoepfner and Schwander 1994 (critique in Zuchtriegel 2018); see also Ma 2015b.

48. Matthaei and Zimmermann 2015.

49. Zanker 1993; Neer 2018; R. Osborne 1998b, 157–223, on the authoritarian, even violent potential of the Classical style.

50. Ober 2017.

51. For a historical introduction, Cartledge 2009.

52. Pettit 2012.

53. Robert 1940–1965, vol. 11–12, 213.

54. Ober 2012.

55. On the importance of recognition, Ch. Taylor 1994; Honneth 1996, 2012. I follow here Clements 2012, which draws its orientation from the philosophy of recognition developed by Axel Honneth.

56. Rawls 1999.

57. Arendt 1970.

58. Arendt 1958; on *grandezza*, Q. Skinner in Bock, Skinner, and Viroli 1990, 125–28.

59. Putnam 1994.

60. On civic courage, Balot 2014.

61. *TAM* 2.589; *BE* 50, 183, p. 192; Zimmermann 1993 for context, and above, p. 268.

62. Mert 2016.

63. Robert 1940–1965, vol. 7, 161–70. On traditional agriculture on modern Irakleia, Connell 1980; Gavalas 2010, 67–81, 455 (for plough-oxen); and generally, above, p. 557, n. 12. Modern Irakleia is within the sight of a good harbor, modern Kalantos, and a Hellenistic estate with a tower in southeastern Naxos, connected to the island's road network: Roussos 2017, 256–65; however, Philippson 1959, 144, observes that in modern times, most of the Small Cyclades are not well connected with Naxos, due to the closed nature of the south and western sides of that island (hence the traditional connection with the much more distant Amorgos).

64. Humphreys 2018, 810–11 (on the specific case of decrees and regulation by the demes of Classical Attica); Cocceianus Diōn's speeches, e.g., 43 or 51, reproduce or comment on the utopian self-portrayal of every *polis* as an exemplary *polis*.

65. Agulhon 1979.

66. Vernant 1962, Castoriadis 2008; analytical essay by Pébarthe 2012.

67. On these issues, see pp. 548–52; also volumes such as Arnason and Murphy 2001 or Arnason, Raaflaub, and Wagner 2013, to whose celebratory agenda ancient historians lent themselves gamely.

68. E.g., C. Meier 2001; Vidal-Naquet 2000, 159–80.

69. Fukuyama 1989, then 2006 (originally 1992); I suppose the *polis* citizen, satisfied with recognition and equality, would not be a bad candidate to qualify as Fukuyama's "last man."

70. R. Osborne 1999 on seemingly unitary politics; *tines*: above, p. 252.

71. Loraux 1997, 2002.

72. Thériault 1996.
73. *SEG* 57.1663 (whence *Staatsverträge* 4.726).
74. Balot 2014; Manville 1997.
75. Canevaro 2018b; for comparison, note consensual politics in colonial New England: Zuckerman 1970.
76. Pickard-Cambridge 1988; generally, Csapo and Wilson 2019. On Attic comedy, Dobrov 1997; Bastin-Hammou and Orfanos 2015; Rosen and Foley 2020.
77. On *hubris*, Fisher 1992 (with Canevaro 2018c).
78. Thucydides 6.89.
79. Gray 2015.
80. Veyne 1983.
81. Thomas 2019.
82. Lape 2010 (critical of Athenian nativism); see further below, chapter, 19.
83. *Politics* 5.11, 1313a34-b6.

Chapter 17. *Polis* as Interests

Private property and general interest: T. Piketty, *Une brève histoire de l'égalité* (Paris: 2021), 313.
1. *Orations* 44, 51, 46.
2. Baechler 1985.
3. Horden and Purcell 2000.
4. Scheidel, Morris, and Saller 2007, as opposed to Finley 1973. See also Foxhall 1998; Bresson 2000; Bresson 2016; Harris, Lewis, and Woolmer 2016. Ober 2022 analyzes rationality and calculation as a deep part of ancient Greek culture.
5. This section is inspired by C. Friedrichs's essay on structural features of plurality and governance in the early modern Eurasian city (2010); also Friedrichs 1995.
6. Solon F 13 West (transl. D. Campbell, Loeb).
7. On the related issue of physical infrastructures for market exchange, Chankowski and Karvonis 2012.
8. Perlman 2004 on the economies and economics of Archaic Cretan *poleis*.
9. Hardin 1968; transcended by the institutionalist analyses in Ostrom 1990.
10. Bonnechère 2014; also Eidinow 2007, 344–48, and Dakaris, Vokotopoulou, and Christidis 2013, nos. 2425A, 4016A. Safety (*asphaleia*) is of course a major concern of individual consultants of the oracle (indeed the desire to limit uncertainty is the whole point of the exercise: Eidinow 2007).
11. Nörr 1966, 78.
12. Migeotte 2014; Bresson 2016 on the immense variety of rents levied by the *polis*; already Aristotle, *Politics* 1.11 1259a.
13. A few examples from Priēnē: *I. Priene B-M* 15, 17, 18, 27, 29, 107.
14. On this definition, Levi 1988.
15. North, Wallis and Weingast 2009 on "natural states" based on exploitation.
16. Ostrom 1990; also Tuck 2008 on the philosophical problems of freeriding (and the historiography of the question).
17. Herodotos 1.96–101.
18. I owe my perception of these problems to a brilliant examination paper prepared by Maria Pretzler for the "Aristophanes' Political Comedy" paper in the First Public Examination in the Faculty of Classics at Oxford in 2002.
19. *I. Priene B-M* 19 (330-300 BCE).
20. *Oration* 7; above, 360–61.
21. On constitutional solutions as bargaining, Carugati 2019.
22. R. Osborne 1991.
23. Ma 2015a on the political economy of honors in the *polis*; in the case of Athens, Hansen 1991, 157, 314.
24. The 20 percent default rate on Hellenistic Dēlos is a special case: Bogaert 1968, 143–53, interpreting the evidence as a sign of economic crisis but also noting the reluctance of the *hieropoioi* to foreclose on defaulting loans.
25. Gauthier, *BE* 99, 405, has provocative thoughts on the ability of civic courts to solve problems of intracommunal violence to general satisfaction, but the persistence of economic dissatisfaction; I propose interpreting the latter as a sign of elites being constrained, since they seem to try to appeal to their peers in the form of panels of foreign judges.
26. Harvey 1985 for tolerance of profitmaking in office; Plutarch, in his *Precepts of Statecraft*, takes it for granted that officeholders grant small favors to friends, thus accumulating social capital; above, p. 602, n. 168, for examples of profits to be made out of *polis* institutional workings, open to officeholding elites with access to capital.
27. Parallels abound: e.g., *ancien régime* Provence as studied in Agulhon 1970.
28. Theophrastos, *Characters*, 26; Aristotle, *Politics*, describes the "best" democracy (i.e., most moderate one, that of farmers) as too busy to meet in assembly and "covet the property of others" (*tōn allotriōn ouk epithumousi*), a reference to the redistributive decrees and laws passed by democratic *poleis*: 1318b14, cf. 1320a4, demagogues appeal to the courts to confiscate the property of the rich.
29. [Xenophon], *Constitution of the Athenians*; Thucydides 8.65.3 (in midst of oligarchical coup at Athens); [Aristotle], *Constitution of the Athenians*, 29. On critiques of democracy, above, pp. 197–98; de Ste. Croix 1981, 409–52; Roberts 1997; Ober 1998; Carlier 2005.

30. Cartledge in Cartledge and Spawforth 2002, 38–58; Rostovtzeff 1941, 1368, on lack of forcible redistribution and confiscations. It is true that land redistribution and debt cancellation remained a subject of anxiety (Finley 1983, 108–9; Fuks 1984, more dramatic).

31. Rohde 2019, 231–51.

32. See above, chapter 10 (inspired by Ober 1989); Zuiderhoek 2019.

33. *SEG* 27.938.

34. *Politics* 6.5 1320a is particularly explicit and telling; indeed its terms are quoted in my treatment here.

35. On the practice Zuiderhoek 2013, to whose bibliography add Robert and Robert 1954, 322 n.8; it can be paralleled in the early modern period (Sheppard 1971, 97–98, for the eighteenth-century town of Lourmarin in the Vaucluse, in southern France). The whole transaction is recorded in *SEG* 1.276.

36. Bresson 2007–2008; Ober 2010; Kron 2011; Ober 2015; Bresson 2016.

37. *Political Precepts* 13 (*Mor.* 808 C).

38. Ober 2015; the main testcase for informed quantification (to produce a Gini index of equality, i.e., the divergence from a perfect equal distribution of wealth) is Classical Athens: Kron 2011, Cl. Taylor 2017; Derron 2017 (notably essays by S. von Reden, S. Fachard, N. Purcell, A. Bresson). The "middle class" was much derided as a concept for ancient history by MacMullen 1974, but his assumptions of verticality in ancient city may in turn be challenged.

39. Rostovtzeff 1941 (giving a surprisingly nuanced picture, and constantly aware of the possibility of conflict between "bourgeois" and working class); Morris 2004.

40. For Classical Athens, Millett 1989; but opposing views can be found about patronage in Zelnick-Abramowitz 2000, Alwine 2016, Maehle 2018. See further, chapters 18 and 19.

41. Chwe 2001; Williamson 2013; see already Fukuyama 1995, 21: "[i]n Mark Granovetter's phrase, people are embedded in a variety of social groups—families, neighborhoods, networks, businesses, churches, and nations—against whose interests they have to balance their own," drawing on Granovetter 1985.

42. Humphreys 2018.

43. Herman 2006.

44. Transaction costs: Frier and Kehoe 2007, 117–23. For a "heap" of examples of the practice of trust in the Classical and early Hellenistic world, S. Johnstone 2011; generally, see the liberal essay offered by Fukuyama 1995 (on the modern relationship between social capital in the form of trust outside of the family and industrial structure).

45. Putnam 1994, on the difference between northern and southern Italy, though the historical analyses (plunging deep into time to the Guelf and Ghibelline conflicts) need not convince comparative historians of the city-state; Ober 2008 for Classical Athens (e.g., 156–59); earlier (and not uncontroversially), Banfield 1958; and see S. Johnstone 2011, 4–5 for a critique of Putnam's "social capital" concept as a metaphor, not quite borne out empirically.

46. Above, pp. 208–9; Reger 2004; Chandezon 2013. On the relative position of Aigai and the smaller city of Olympos, Robert 1940–1965, vol. 10, 178–87 (Yeniceköy), as in Chandezon 2003, no. 51, but I have proposed Sakallı Yaylası, 20 kilometers from Aigai (Ma 2013b, 73; *contra*, Boulay 2016, on the territory and history of Aigai more generally.

47. *SEG* 61.1024. On the messiness, inefficiency, and bigness of cities in general, as stimuli for economic growth, J. Jacobs 1969, 1984.

48. Ober 2010, 2015.

49. Mackil 2013, 2014, in an original and compelling new institutionalist framework of analysis.

50. *RO* 96 (earlier published in *SEG* 9.2); Bresson 2011; on absence of Malthusian consequences, Ober 2010.

51. *IG* 9.1.² 750

52. Bresson 2016, 339–80 (low costs); Foxhall 1998 (import and export of staples in collaborative, culturally determined system of exchange).

53. Demography: Hansen 2006, 2008; Bresson 2016, 41–64, 203–6.

54. Acemoglu and Robinson 2012 (a nonspecialized treatment drawing on earlier, more academic work); discussed by J. Blok (2015) while describing the Athenian *diōbelia*, or distribution of 2 obols, as redistributive practice.

55. Costabile 1992; *IG Locri* 1–37.

56. *IG* 12.4 132; Simonton 2019.

57. On such contradictions and conflicts, Gray 2015.

58. C. Jones 1971b; Chandezon 2006-7.

59. This approach is inspired by discourse institutionalism (Schmidt 2010), which gives a place to the actual content of ideas and values, as well as their cost-lowering function.

Chapter 18. Bad *Polis*

Citizenship, particular point of view of the dominant: E. F. Isin, *Being Political. Genealogies of Citizenship* (Minneapolis: 2002), 275.

1. Vidal-Naquet 1975, 837–38, on the eighteenth-century French thinker Volney's critique of Sparta and Athens as based on slavery; Garlan 1985; Steiner 1994, 247 on Rousseau, *Social Contract*, 3.15.

2. Isin 2002 (quotation from p. 51); the programmatic and modernist sections of this work (*Being Political*) are perhaps more useful than the historicizing genealogical surveys of the *polis*, the Roman municipal model, and the mediaeval city. See also Beauregard 2018, for a dissent against optimistic views that cities are inherently democratic and inclusive, rather than generative of inequality and exclusion.

3. The Marxist histories of de Ste. Croix (1981) and Rose (2012), though important projects, do not quite fulfill the premise nor the promise of a radical history of the ancient world.

4. *SEG* 39.606.

5. *I. Keramos* 6. The word *anatasis* also has overtones of bristling opposition, and even actual violent threats (LSJ^9 s.v. 2–3).

6. *SEG* 23.405 with Habicht 2008; *I. Priene B-M* 114.

7. Michel, *Recueil* 382.

8. McDowell 1978, 152–53; Hunter 1994, 120–53; Lanni 2016, 47–74; Aristotle, *Politics*, 6.8 1322b. Petty police operations were ensured, however, by officials: A. Jones 1940, 211–13.

9. Dēmosthenēs 21.11–12; Christ 1998.

10. On Classical Athens, D. Cohen 1995; Riess 2008. 2012; Fisher 2017, 123–25, on violence and the courts, and discussing critically Herman 2006. *Hybris*: Fisher 1992; Canevaro 2018c.

11. D. Cohen 1995, 163–80; Humphreys 2018 is based partly on a rich and hair-raising casebook of family law from late Classical Athens; for Artemidoros's dreamers, Chandezon 2014. On cycles of litigation in Classical Athens, R. Osborne 1985a; D. Cohen 1995.

12. Dēmosthenēs 21; Fisher 1998.

13. Tarsos: Strabo, 14.14; Sardeis: Plutarch, *Precepts of Statecraft* 32 (*Mor.* 825D); *I. Knidos* 34. On violence in public spaces of Hellenistic *polis*, Dickenson 2017.

14. Chandezon 2014.

15. The poetry of Archilochos, at the start of the history of the *polis*, is already full both of solidarities and indications of enmity and conflict as part of a diverse community (F 126, 128, 172 West).

16. Agulhon 1970; Sheppard 1971 (on a particular example, the town of Lourmarin in the Luberon).

17. Plutarch, *Precepts of Statecraft* 14 (*Mor.* 809C-D).

18. Herman 2006, against the view of Athens as vengefully obsessed with honor found in D. Cohen 1995. On violence, see the introductory essay by Vlassopoulos and Xydopoulos in Xydopoulos, Vlassopoulos, and Tounta 2017, 1–27 (engaging with modern historiography of violence, from Norbert Elias to Steven Pinker!). Generally, Bryen 2013, 51–85; earlier, Fisher 1992; Bertrand 2005b.

19. Papakonstantinou 2008, 112–26; Carey, Giannadaki, and Griffith-Williams 2019; Gagarin 2020b, for law and justice in Athens.

20. Plato, *Kriton*; Veyne 2005, 79–116.

21. Constant's essay (in fact a lecture given in February 1819 before a learned society in Paris, the Athénée) "on the liberty of the Ancients compared to that of the moderns" is republished in Constant 2017, 292–311 (text by P. Delbouille, K. Kloocke, G. Paoletti, M. Willems); earlier, Constant 1980 (ed. M. Gauchet), 491–515; Eng. trans. Constant 1988 (B. Fontana). The contrast, as drawn by Constant, inspired a famous essay on "two concepts of liberty" by Isaiah Berlin (1969, based on his inaugural lecture as Gladstone Professor of Government at Oxford, republished and expanded in I. Berlin 2012, as edited by H. Hardy, 166–217).

22. Gossman 2000, 2003, whence I draw the connection between Constant and Burckhardt; S. Bauer 2001, 120 (commenting on a remark in Ehrenberg 1961). The section on the *polis* is to be found in the new publication of the *Griechische Culturgeschichte* (Burckhardt 2002, with the original spelling), vol. 1, 37–254, esp. 39–63; quotation from p. 56. On Burckhardt's cultural history of Greece, see also the selection and translation by S. Stern, edited and presented by O. Murray (Burckhardt 1994; the section on the *polis* is excerpted on pp. 37–62). On the importance of this work in defining (or reifying) the *polis* as an object of study, Gawantka 1985, 12–24, 59–63, 202–3; S. Bauer 2001, esp. 118–38.

23. Still of interest is V. Ehrenberg's reaction to the 1929 edition (originally in the Sudetenland periodical *Hochschulwissen* 7 (1930), 32–36, *non vidi*; revised and translated in Ehrenberg 1946, 53–62). By the time of publication, Burckhardt's work was already quaint, because of its reliance on literary sources without notice of the contributions of the newly professionalized fields of epigraphy or archaeology—to a certain extent, a deliberate choice on his part.

24. On the *Social Contract* (esp. 3.12–15), Steiner 1994, 242–51.

25. Simonde de Sismondi 1818, vol. 16, 353–405; the discussion of ancient and modern liberty is most explicit at 357–59, 369–77. On Sismondi's "Rousseauiste" history of the medieval Italian cities, Waley and Dean 2010, 184–85; on Sismondi as part of a nineteenth-century wave of interest in the medieval commune, Maire Vigueur 1997, 3–6.

26. On forms of patronage in Athens, Alwine 2016; Maehle 2018 (but I would interpret them as dialectical playacting within Athenian democratic practice rather than real, "Mediterranean" patronage).

27. Etzioni-Halevy 1979, 1993.

28. Lukes 2005, revisiting an essay of 1974. On plurality of actors as a brake to the monopoly of power,

Dahl 2005 (revisiting an essay of 1974, indeed one which Lukes responds to).

29. Ober 1989. Seelentag 2015 proposes a model of the Archaic Cretan city in which majoritarian institutions are embedded within social norms and contexts that encourage dependency and defense (inspired by E. Flaig's model of the Roman Republic).

30. *SH* 754 (Theodōros dates before his mention in a late fourth-century BCE treatise *Against Aristotle*).

31. Foxhall 2002; Cl. Taylor 2017.

32. Above, pp. 334–45. Daulis: Grenet 2011, Girdvaynte 2019, on *IG* 9.1.61; I thank S. Fachard for his estimations of the territory of Daulis.

33. Herman 1987; L. Mitchell 1997.

34. R. Osborne 1990c, on Xenophon, *Memorabilia*, 2.9.

35. Thucydides 8. 54.4, 65–66 (cf. Plato, *Theaetetus* 178D); Bearzot 2013, 53–62.

36. Dēmosthenēs 21; Ober 1996, 86–106; Wilson 1998.

37. Plutarch, *Precepts of Statecraft* 13–14 (*Mor.* 808B-809D).

38. Dahl 2005, Flyvbjerg 1998, both analyzed in Lukes 2004.

39. Page, Seawright, and Lacombe 2019.

40. As argued for in Ma 2015a.

41. Elitist tropes: Wörrle 1995. Killos of Paros: *IG* 12.5.129; Bresson 2016, 245–46.

42. Moreno 2007, 208–311.

43. The map is based on the data of the Copernicus program (http://land.copernicus.eu) for 1990: 267 hectares of fields, 535 hectares of grassland, 908 hectares of sclerophyllous cover. The population in 1991 is given in Gavalas 2010, 187–92; on the agriculture of the island, apart from the north-south swathe, Gavalas 2010 also portrays a cultivated valley leading down to the inlet of Livadi, the site of the ancient town.

44. Halstead and Jones 1989; Constantakopoulou 2012. For empirical evidence from modern Irakleia specifically, Connell 1980, e.g., 19–20, on small family gardens, fertilized with goat manure; 64, on domestically produced goatshair tweed.

45. *I. Tralleis* 24.

46. Scheid-Tissinier 2004; Apuleius, *Metamorphoses*, 2.18, 9.35 (*pollensque factionibus et cuncta facile faciens in civitate*), with Millar 2004a, 235.

47. *Oration* 46.7.

48. N. Jones 2004.

Chapter 19. Worst *Polis*

E. Will to Ph. Gauthier: P.-É. Will, "Édouard Will et Pierre Vidal-Naquet." In *Édouard Will historien nancéen du monde grec*, edited by L. Graslin-Thomé and J. Zurbach, 50 (Paris: 2021). The letter discusses Will's critique of Gauthier's institutional history, e.g., Gauthier 1985; the review is republished in É. Will 1998, 811–36.

Polis as state of the slaveholders: F. Engels, *Der Ursprung der Familie, des Privateigentums und des Staats. Im Anschluß an Lewis H. Morgans Forschungen*. Annotated by H. Duncker (Berlin: 1931), 142.

1. Magnēsia: *I. Magnesia* 100. Jews: Ma 2013c on 2 Macc. 6.7–8

2. Ma 2015b.

3. Aristotle, *Politics* 3.1 1275a10.

4. On ancient childhood, Cohen and Rutter 2007; Evans Grubbs and Parkin 2013 on a variety of aspects; Bobou 2015 (Hellenistic representations but also realities); Golden 2015 (Classical Athens); Laes 2011 is ostensibly about the Roman empire, but also draws on the ancient Greek world (and the Greek-speaking East in the Roman world), offering many insights on children as "outsiders within." Infanticide: Bresson 2016, 51–54; Liston, Rotroff, and Snyder 2018, 119–25.

5. Liston, Rotroff, and Snyder 2018.

6. Halperin 1990; Davidson 2007; Lear 2015.

7. Finley 1951, 74–79; on measures of grain, Moreno 2007, 325–26.

8. Women and property: Foxhall 1989; Omitowoju 2002. Shifts in Hellenistic period: Siekerka, Stebnicka, and Wolicki 2021 for an overview of epigraphical material; 99 for examples from Hellenistic central Greece.

9. Harper 2017 (using the evidence of Greek romances written under the Roman empire).

10. *Lysias* 1; Todd 2007, 43–148.

11. Lape 2004; Sommerstein 2014 (notably essays by A. Sommerstein on mistresses and S. James on rape).

12. Xenophon, *Household Management*, 7.4–10.13. But the whole scene is perhaps more ambiguous than first appears: see e.g., Harvey 1984; Murnaghan 1988; Pomeroy 1994, 259–64; Too 2001.

13. Hesiod, *Works and Days*, lines 373–74 with M. West 1978 *ad loc*.

14. T. Morgan 2005; R. Osborne 1994, 1996.

15. D. Cohen 1989; on *gynaikonomoi*, Wehrli 1962; Ogden 2002 (with register of sources; note *CITh* 3.75 for a dedication of statues of Aphroditē by *gynaikonomoi* at Thasos); Piolot 2009.

16. Sommerstein 1998; Veyne 1998 (on ancient sexuality between romance, marriage, and rape); Omitowoju 2002.

17. Glazebrook and Henry 2011; Marshall 2013; Kapparis 2018; Ismard 2019, 81–83.
18. Above, p. 506; Lissarrague 1987; Murray 1990; Debew 2022.
19. *Lysistrata*, e.g., lines 507–20.
20. On slavery in an ancient Greek context, see e.g., Finley 1980; Garlan 1995; duBois 2003; Forsdyke 2012 (on the agency of the enslaved and their imagination); Wrenhaven 2012; D. Lewis (b) 2018; Ismard 2019; Forsdyke 2021. For comparative approaches, Bodel and Scheidel 2017; Lenski and Cameron 2018; and the global comparative survey of slavery and its worlds edited by P. Ismard et al. 2021.
21. Ownership: Finley 1980, D. Lewis (b) 2018. Social death: Vlassopoulos 2011; on the concept, O. Patterson 1982, with Ismard et al. 2021.
22. Finley 1980 on "slave societies" (but I am not following his definition and terminology here); Lenski and Cameron 2018.
23. M. Jameson 1977; Wood 1988. Aristotle, *Politics*, 6.8 1323a (labor of children and wives).
24. Ismard 2019, 80–105.
25. *SEG* 2.579, also Chandezon 2003, no. 53; Adak 2021, 237.
26. Veyne 1998, 32, 35–36, on the slaves' attempting to relieve exhaustion through their apparently casual stances (standing with one leg crossed over the other; "Jack Benny" stance of one arm supporting the chin and in turn propped up at the elbow by the other arm); Masséglia 2015, 53–156 on civic personas, 184–204 on servile bodies (notably on wrist-hold and leg cross).
27. Wood 1988, 61 (though excessively downplaying the economic role fulfilled by enslaved labor for the elite: contrast Bresson 2016, 214–22).
28. Finley 1981, 155. On Chios, Ismard 2021.
29. See e.g., Rihll 1996; E. Harris 2012; D. Lewis (b) 2016, 120–24.
30. Finley 1980, 36; on Reitemeier 1789, Deissler 2000. On the connection between slavery and liberty in ancient Greece, O. Patterson 1991, with Cartledge 1993.
31. *Republic* 578D.
32. *I. Delphinion* 150, lines 87–99 (notes in Herrmann in *Milet* 6.1, p. 186).
33. Zelnick-Abramowitz 2013. Manumission fees in Roman-imperial Thessaly: Bouchon 2009.
34. Plato, *Laws* 777a4-6; *Gorgias* 483b. Generally, Forsdyke 2021, 200–246.
35. Robert and Robert 1983, no. 65.
36. Antiphon, 5.69.
37. On (citizens and) foreigners in the *polis*, Vatin 1984; Lonis 1988; and Baslez 2008 offer excellent overviews.
38. Whitehead 1977; Gauthier 1988; Adak 2003; Niku 2004, 2007 (for post-Classical period).

39. L.-M. Günther 2014b.
40. Herōdas 2 (above, p. 240); Cassayre 2010, 187–89.
41. *SEG* 45.1508; above, p. 429.
42. *SEG* 29.1130bis (P. Herrmann); also in Ager 1996, no. 71.
43. Purcell 1990; Horden and Purcell 2000 (and 2020, esp. 72–83). Collections of papers on various examples and cases of human connectivity in the ancient Greek world: Capdetrey and Zurbach 2012; Olshausen and Sauer 2014; de Ligt and Tacoma 2015; Lo Cascio and Tacoma 2017 (both for the whole Roman empire); Dana and Savalli-Lestrade 2019; Moatti and Chevreau 2021.
44. Baslez 2008 (originally 1984) offers remarkably nuanced views on Hellenistic internationalism coexisting with *polis* institutionalism.
45. The papers are republished in Gauthier 2011, 3–77; for nuances, Mack 2019; Vlassopoulos 2019; Brélaz and Rose 2021, for a (mostly late) Roman perspective.
46. Szanto 1892, 8–66; M. Osborne 1981–1983 (Athens); *CITh* 3.11–17, for Thasos (where new citizens must apply to a civic subdivision, *patra*, for admission). Freed slaves: Akrigg 2015; Sosin 2016.
47. Davies 1978; C. Patterson 1981.
48. R. Thomas 2019.
49. Lape 2010; Diōn, *Orations* 44, 51.
50. Ruschenbusch 1985; Wood 1988 on the Athenian example; Hansen 2004.
51. Ober 2015, 21–44.
52. Ruschenbusch 1985; Hansen 2004. The model is forcefully defended, as one possibility of *polis* life, in Zuchtriegel 2018—but also leveraged into a critique of the *Ackerbürger*-city's exclusionary and exploitative nature. See also Bruhns 2014, 41–54, on the details of Weber's ideal types of "ancient" and "medieval" city.
53. T. Scott 2012.
54. The whole subject of settlement patterns in the ancient world is immense, and sustained by the contribution of survey archaeology (whose findings interact uneasily with the institutional focus of the present book, and indeed challenge it); relevant works (that do not necessarily agree with each other) include R. Osborne 1985b, 1987; Alcock 1993a; Lohmann 1993; Jameson et al. 1994; Brunet 1999; Fachard 2012; Bintliff et al. 2017; Fachard 2017.
55. Price 2011; Witcher 2011.
56. Lohmann et al. 2014; Mack 2015b; Lohmann, Kalaitzogou, and Lüdorf 2017.
57. *I. Priene* B-M 28.
58. Above, p. 121.
59. Price 2011, drawing on F. Kolb's work at Kyaneai (Kolb and Thomsen 2004; F. Kolb 2008); Hailer 2008.
60. Ratté and Commito 2017, summarizing Ratté and de Staebler 2012.

61. Robert and Robert 1983, esp. 271–79 on the breakaway community of the "Amyzonians in Petra," attested only in *I. Priene B-M* 411 and perhaps located at Bağacık, as well the peripheral geography of the *polis*'s territory, drawing on travels by W. R. Paton and J. L. Myres (1896; the Roberts forget to mention the latter); Peschlow-Bindokat 1996a (on the settlement and temple of Zeus Akraios at Bağacık, and the nearby sacred rock at the summit of the mountain, the Tekerlekdağ); 1996b, 46–52.

62. Acheson 1997.

63. Generally, G. Steinhauer 1994, 2017; Lohmann 1993 (Atēnē); Kellogg 2013 (Acharnai); G. Steinhauer 2017 (on the polycentric deme of Halai Aixōnides, which we have seen as the locale of intense local political life: above, pp. 251–52); Ackermann 2018 (Aixōnē); Fachard and Pirsino 2015 on the road network of Attica; Fachard and Bresson 2022. The whole subject is evolving rapidly. Earlier, R. Osborne 1985b had painted a picture of the Attic countryside (and perhaps mainland Greece) as dominated by nucleated settlements for political reasons; see the critique in Brunet 1992.

64. Adak 2021; Adak and Thonemann 2022, docs 2–3, superseding earlier editions (*Nomima* 1.104–5; also in Meiggs-Lewis *GHI* 30; Koerner 1993, nos. 78–79; Osborne-Rhodes *GHI* 102).

65. Robert and Robert 1976, republished *OMS* 7.297–380; generally, Reger 2004.

66. C. Schuchhardt in Bohn with Schuchhardt 1889, 66; Robert 1937, 75–89; Robert 1940–1965, vol. 10, 178–87; Herrmann 1959 (republished in Herrmann 2016, 3–38); Chandezon 2003, no. 51; Ma 2013b, 73 and n.20; Boulay 2016.

67. Boyxen 2018, 42–6; eloquent table, 398, for the territorial expansion of the city.

68. Köcke 2012, 44–45 (using Th. Wiegand's calculations on *I. Didyma* 488).

69. Rhodes: Boyxen 2018 (317: "even if indications of continued appartenance in local forms of social organisation can be discerned, the inhabitants of the incorporated regions were first and foremost citizens of the *polis*").

70. Ando 2017; Zuchtriegel 2018, 154–60, on the possibility that rural dwellers must have been "second-class citizens," *de facto* deprived of access and participation in the social dimension of *polis* life.

71. *Greek Questions* 1 (*Mor.* 201E); see above, p. 150, for parallels at Sikyōn.

72. Wörrle 2011b, 400 n.115; on *paroikoi*, Gauthier 1988; Papazoglou 1997; Schuler 1998; Bertrand 2005b; Kah 2012 (on Priēnē, agnostic on the exact definition of *paroikoi* as opposed to *katoikoi*); Baker and Thériault 2018, 320–22 for the inscription from Xanthos (cautious on meaning of *paroikoi*), to which I feel confident to add *I. Mylasa* 155, for benefactions to citizens, [met]*oikoi, paroikoi* and resident strangers, with Papazoglou 1997, 195; C. Müller 2023.

73. Territory and population of early modern Geneva: Piuz and Mott-Weber 1990 (28–30 on territory and population, D. Zumkeller). Political institutions: O'Mara 1958; Mason 1993; Caesar 2011; Barat 2018, 2022. For the aftermath of upheavals in parallel to (and preceding) the French Revolution, *Révolutions genevoises 1782–1798* (1989); Gür 1992. For our comparative purposes, the interest of the particular case of medieval and early modern Geneva is that its political and social structure was based not on guilds, but an assembly of all citizens (the *Conseil Général*), and furthermore never had a formal aristocracy or patriciate. On the essentially contradictory relations between city and countryside in antiquity, see the bracing, Marxist-inspired notes by East German historian E. Ch. Welskopf (1977).

74. de Ste. Croix 1981, 14, on Galen, *On Good and Bad Humors*, 1.1–7, Kühn 749–52 (on translation of *ospria* and *chedropa*, Ieraci Bio 1987, 115). On the distinction between town and country and Galen, see also *On the Properties of Foodstuffs* 1.7 Kühn 498–500 (which shows Galen walking around Pergamon), 1.14 Kühn 523, 2.38 Kühn 620, 268 Kühn 657, with J. Wilkins in J. Powell 2003, x-xiv.

75. Hansen 1985, 2006 (groundbreaking and field-renewing, but in need of general revision and rethinking). As we have seen, Hansen's model postulates *Ackerbürger* concentrated in the urban center, and a high population density (say 150 people per occupied urban hectare) in thickly inhabited sites. The end results are interestingly plausible, but I might follow historical demographer Colin McEvedy's maverick instinct that ancient cities were underoccupied (2011) and hence that a substantial number of families lived in the countryside. On demographics and Greek history (-writing), Scheidel 2003; Bresson 2016, 41–70.

76. Hansen 1985; G. Oliver 2007; Hansen 2008 (whose one-size-fits-all "shotgun method" I am not following here); Akrigg 2019.

77. The decline in numbers of enfranchised Spartiates (*oliganthrōpia*) is a well-studied problem (Doran 2018), but the demography of the Spartan entity has received much less thought: Figueira 2003.

78. The horrendous agrarian history is illuminated by Gavalas 2010, 67–101.

79. Ross 1843, vol. 2, 35; Philippson 1959, 145 (286 inhabitants in 1928). We could also apply the "shotgun method" of Hansen 2006, but we would need secure data on the size of the urban settlement at Kastro.

80. Kah 2014.

81. Lohmann et al. 2014.

82. Slaves appear often in the epigraphical documentation of Priēnē, in the city (as recipients of largesse

from late second-century BCE benefactors: *I. Priene B-M* 64, 259; 65, 179, 194; 67.239; 69, 39, 56, 77–78, 83; 72, 13; 84,4) and in the countryside (*I. Priene B-M* 11b2, with a possible mention of publicly owned slaves; 30, 6).

83. Kalliontzis 2017; Lucas and Dubach 2023. I thank T. Lucas for discussing the population of Akraiphia, but of course he is not responsible for the speculations here; I have put the figure of twenty conscripts within his demographic models to obtain 700 adult male citizens (between the ages of twenty and sixty), a total of 1,000 male citizens of all ages, and a total free population of 2,040 individuals, to which metics and slaves must be added.

84. Maire Vigueur 2003, esp. 217–19, as noted in Wickham 2015, 14.

85. Vernant 1962; Vernant 1965; Vernant and Vidal-Naquet 1973, Vidal-Naquet 1981 (Eng. translation 1986); Lissarrague 1987, 1990; on the fierce figure of P. Vidal-Naquet, his memoirs (1995–1998), give some incomplete indications but the full intellectual biography of the *Centre Louis Gernet* remains unwritten. For a structuralist account of "self and others," Cartledge 2002b.

86. Hedrick 1994; the invisibility of any subaltern culture in the *polis*, and the high visibility of citizen culture, is emphasized for the case of slaves in Classical Athens by Bäbler 1998 (esp. 200–206), Morris 1998b.

87. Harper 2017. On the complicated topic of ancient Greek attitudes to black-skinned people (and the topic's entanglement with modern racism), Derbew 2022.

88. On the entanglement of Aristotle's political theory with enslavement, Schofield 1999, 101–23; O. Patterson 1991; Monoson 2011; Ismard 2019, esp. 241–47.

89. R. Osborne 1987, e.g., 13–26 (involvement in rural economies, negative image of countryside), 96 (rural profit-seeking); N. Jones 2004; Rosen and Sluiter 2006, notably for essays by J. Bintliff on the interpenetration of rural and urban, H. Cuyller on Aristotle's conceptions of the rural as incapable of political virtues.

90. Caesar 2011, 131, on Todeschini 2007, 225–30 for medieval views of *rusticitas* and poverty as disqualifying.

91. Arendt 1958 with Ismard 2019, esp. 75–79.

92. For an instantiation of this "Arendtian" model, see Roubineau 2021 on the imaginary (but ideologically very coherent) society of Herodas's *Mimiamboi*.

93. On prostitution in the "Archaic" period, M. Henry 2011. Sexual labor might have been a major theme in the poetry of Archilochos, not coincidentally a witness to *polis* formation (e.g., F 42 West); but the negotiation of sexual borders and the frank description of sex also characterize his work (e.g., F 196a West; generally, Swift 2019, 34–36).

94. Rhodes: Bresson, *I. Pérée rhodienne*; Badoud 2011; Held 2015. Mytilēnē: Ellis-Evans 2019. Byzantion

and its Bithynian *peraia*: Phylarchos, *FGrHist* 81 F8, Polybios 4.52.5–10; Robert 1940–1965, vol. 7, 30–44; Papazoglou 1997, 50–2; Avram 2021, 114–16.

95. Julia Gordos: *TAM* 5.687. Tralleis: Malay, Ricl, and Amendola 2018. On *kinaideia*, Sapsford 2022, and note also Robert in Firaltı 1964, 185.

96. Gauthier and Hatzopoulos 1993.

97. Above, pp. 381–87. Women in Palmyra: Yon 2019.

98. Maillot and Zurbach 2021.

99. Bäbler 1998; Roubineau 2012; Futo Kennedy 2014; Lape 2021 (drawing on fragility theory); Vădan 2022 (arguing that foreigners, even resident, were exposed to physical violence).

100. MacDowell 1978, 256.

101. Ogilvie 2003, studying the exclusion of women from guilds and from the advantages of male membership in local communities in early modern Würtenburg,

102. van Bremen 1996. On elite women in the Roman Cyclades, Stavrianopoulou 2006; on elite women and families in Hellenistic Milētos, L.-M. Günther 2014a.

103. *I. Dor. Inseln* 2 with Engelmann 1970; Badoud 2015, 170 on date (late third or early second century BCE? or perhaps rather later, judging by letter forms and in light of a tentative suggestion by Habicht 2003, 555, n.87). The enslaver's name, Merops, might be that of a metic (to be precise, of a man born on Kōs of foreign parents but named, in homage to the island, after Kōs's mythical founder: hence Merops might have been a metic on Kōs and after emigration, a metic on Rhodes—doubly marginal); on the name and its context, Robert, *OMS* 6.694.

104. Boyxen 2018, 318–20; Ismard 2019, 191–22; Thomsen 2020.

105. *IG* 1.³ 1361, Thucydides 2.22.2 on a settlement called "Phrygians" in central Attica. The connection was first made in Wilhelm 1909, 35–37.

106. *FgrHist / BNJ* 572 F4 (from Athenaios, *Sophists at Dinner*, 6, 88–91, 265c-266e). I suppose the "*polis* of slaves" in the hinterland of Kolophōn, mentioned in passing in a decree for a Kolophonian benefactor ca. 100 BCE, was a "maroon" city of runaway slaves: *SEG* 39.1243, line 37. I further suspect the accusations of *androlēpsia*, "man-seizing" that the neighboring *polis* of Mētropolis mounted against Kolophōn had to do with Kolophonian expeditions to recapture people from this settlement and leading to violence and seizures among the rural population of Mētropolis (who may have negotiated and traded with the maroons).

107. S. Schwartz 2010.

108. Millar 1967, 183–84; Brown 1978; Millar 1993a; T. Morgan 2007.

109. Neaira: [Dēmosthenēs] 59; Hamel 2003; C. Müller 2018.

110. Herakleidēs Kritikos fr. 1.4, as arrestingly explained in Knoepfler 2013a, 427 (on date, 425–27).
111. Zuchtriegel 2018. Kyrēnē (*IACG* no. 1029, M. Austin) expanded by expelling the indigenous Libyans (Herodotos 4.139); some remained in the territory of the city: this is implied by the Ptolemaic constitutional law for Kyrēnē (*SEG*. 9.1, republished online as IGCyr 010800), defining citizens as born of two citizen parents, or of a citizen father and of indigenous mothers from a particular, privileged region ("from between the Katabathmos and Authamalax"); generally, Laronde 1987, Marini 2018.
112. van Wees 2003.
113. Macedonia: Ma 2016b, summarizing the work of M. Hatzopoulos. Hellenistic world: G. Cohen 1995, 2006, 2013; on complicity of *poleis* and Hellenistic kings, Strootman 2014. Roman Near East: Millar 1993a, Butcher 2003; for a particular example, Bader and Yon 2018 on the territory of Kapitōlias.
114. Bertrand 2005a.
115. On the Jews, above, n. 1; Andrade 2010. Christians: Pont 2020, 27–108.
116. I simply reproduce the analyses in C. Woodard's suggestive survey of "American nations," specifically his "Tidewater" and "Deep South" (Woodard 2011, 55, 227–29).
117. *Politics* 7.3 1325a.
118. Wood 1988, 38, 121.
119. Towers: argument, and earlier bibliography, in Morris and Papadopoulos 2005; also Chatzidimitriou and Chidiroglou 2014, Seifried and Parkinson 2014 (Euboia), Lambertz 2018 (Naxos). Priēnē: Ma 2013b.
120. Ma 2015b on the exclusionary effect of the beautiful city.
121. See e.g., Shklar 1991; Olson 2004.
122. A. Jones 1940, 259–304; on A. H. M. Jones and the cities in the (Late) Roman empire, Lavan 2008.
123. Purcell 1990, 58.
124. Shklar 1998, notably 1–20 (seminal essay on "the liberalism of fear"), 362–75 on Arendt (370–71 on *The Human Condition*: "Arendt's own political dream remained tied to the *polis*"), 376–85 on Walzer (381, ironical on "Walzer's contempt for the modern state and his quaint addiction to ancient Athens" as well as "his idealization of voluntary associations"); discussions and responses (including by M. Walzer) in Yack 1996.
125. Le Guin 2004, 274–84, originally published in a science-fiction anthology edited by R. Silverberg, *New Dimensions* 3 (New York, 1973), 1–8. I am immensely grateful to my colleague Richard Billows for introducing me (and my family) to Le Guin in general, and this story in particular; and for discussing it with me.
126. Kasimis 2018.
127. Canevaro 2018c; Ismard 2019, 193–202.
128. [Xenophon], *Constitution of the Athenians*, 1.10; Thucydides 3.73. The sense that the democratic *polis* was the least bad state formation in antiquity animates de Ste. Croix 1981.
129. Kron 2012, 212–13.
130. Gray 2013, 2022.
131. Akrigg 2018, 2019.
132. E. Cohen 2000.
133. Diōn, *Oration* 7.
134. Duplouy 2006, 2018a, 2018c, 2019.
135. Cl. Taylor 2011.
136. Filges 2020 on the *Felsheiligtum West* and generally the surprises of the northern fringe (though there also is a civic, albeit marginal, shrine in this area, the well-built and terraced shrine of Demeter).
137. Malay, Ricl and Amendola 2018. The unusual nature of the decree is well brought out in *BE* 19. 446 (P. Hamon).
138. See e.g., Mumford 1979; Zuiderhoek 2017; M. Smith 2019; Woolf 2020.
139. As an example of the appeal of ancient built environments, see the dreamlike reproductions (*Wiederherstellungen*) in Krischen 1938 (I thank Bert Smith for recently reminding me of the Krischen drawings, which I admired in the old Ashmolean Library when working on the Hellenistic *poleis*; the drawings' serene beauty perhaps suggested something about the worthiness and agency of the *poleis*: Ma 2002, 2003). Some are repurposed in this book: figs 10.6, 19.1. On the shift represented by centering cities on local politics and citizenship rather than the economic processes implied by urbanization, Bookchin 1995, deeply inspired by the possibilities offered by the historical model of the *polis*.

Chapter 20. *Polis* of Our Wishes

Middle Ages: U Eco, *Travels in Hyperreality. Essays*. Trans. W. Weaver (San Diego: 1990).
Hundreds of small Greek republics: F. Millar, *The Roman Republic in Political Thought* (Hanover, NH: 2002), 5.

1. For a similar picture of the *polis*, see van Effenterre's essay contrasting this historical model with modern images (republished in van Effenterre 2013, 241–46).
2. Azoulay 2016; for an example of personifications, Elsner 2015 on the decree relief representing Athēna and Hēra embracing (Osborne and Rhodes *GHI* 2); Adak and Thonemann 2022, 201–26. Single person: e.g., *CID* 4.124 (quoted here); Kalliontzis 2020, no. 3.

3. *IACP*=Hansen and Nielsen 2004; above, chapter 1 and *passim*, really.

4. Hansen 2000 (11–19 for checklist); 2002b.

5. Hansen 2000, 141–87; 597–623 (599–600 for a defence against the accusation that the concept of city-state is just the "*polis* in disguise," but it is sidelined into a familiar apology for Hansen's own concept of the *polis*—e.g., debating the concept of autonomy or that of the state).

6. Abélès 1983; Rossi 1987; Muhlberger and Paine 1993; van de Mieroop 1997; Hansen 2000, 611–16; Mahé 2001; Detienne 2003 on the universal desire to *vouloir s'assembler*, the will to assemblies; Graeber and Wengrow 2021.

7. On the "Greek miracle," Lloyd 2022, 32–43, critical of any conception of a Greek miracle (starting with that of E. Renan's *Prière sur l'Acropole*), but still locating Greek philosophy, mathematics, and science among the *polis*'s supposed agonistic culture, political practice of mass persuasion, and contrarian truth-seeking elites. Earlier, I mentioned Arnason, Raaflaub, and Wagner 2013 as an example of celebration of the *polis* as the invention of democracy: p. 611, n. 67.

8. On civic institutions in Mesopotamia, Barjamovic 2004; Kuhrt 2014. Generally, Rossi 1987; Malkin and Hohlfelder 1988; Vlassopoulos 2007c; Sommer 2008, 101–2; Isakhan and Stockwell 2011 (including a well-meaning but not deeply documented attempt by Stockwell to trace archaic Greek democracy to Phoenician models, 42–47); Broodbank 2013; López-Ruiz 2021. India: I depend on Muhlberger and Paine 1993, 35–38 (also Muhlberger 2011); survey in Chakrabarti 2000.

9. On the beginnings of the communal movement in Italy, Wickham 2015; earlier Maire Vigueur 2003 (on the social and political aspect of military service by elites); on civic ideals, Bock, Skinner, and Viroli 1990.

10. Pirenne 1917 (though a piece of Belgian advocacy published during the First World War, this remains a piece of inspired historical analysis). But see, for a non-statist view of late medieval cities, Lantschner 2022.

11. Wickham 2015; Barat 2018.

12. Sheppard 1971; Agulhon 1970.

13. New England: Zuckerman 1970.

14. On discontinuity in the history of democracy, Wood 1995, 204–37; Cartledge 2016; Bringmann 2019; J. Dunn 2019; for a radical history of struggle for equality, Piketty 2021.

15. Yoffee 2005; North, Wallis, and Weingast 2009 (but see van Wees 1999c, 2003, for a vision of "Archaic" Greece determined by violent acquisitiveness); Knodell 2021, 248–62.

16. Kaldellis 2012, 2015 (Byzantine republicanism); P. Jones 1997 (end of communes in Italy); Tarrow 2004 (oligarchies).

17. Millar 1998 (as part of a wider debate about the reality of democracy or popular rule in Republican Rome: Hurlet 2012 on the rejoinder by K.-J. Hölkeskamp).

18. E.g., on different aspects of a "Greek tradition" within different contexts of Western intellectual history, Cambiano 2000 (Middle Ages and early modern periods); Nelson 2004 (early modern Republicanism); Vidal Naquet 1975 (on the French revolution); Urbinati 2002 (Mill); Giangiulio 2015, 13–21 (nineteenth-century unease about democracy, as embodied by the *polis*); long intellectual histories in Bringmann 2019 (with broad scope including continental Europe), J. Dunn 2019 (more canonical and Anglo-American in focus). Millar 2002b, on the modern reception of the Roman Republic, also treats of the importance of Aristotle and his influential model of three constitutions (monarchy, aristocracy, democracy), itself a refinement of a Platonic scheme.

19. See e.g., Champion 2006, illuminating on both ancient and modern aspects of the "Greek tradition" conceived by Nelson 2004.

20. On the modern reception of the Lykian League, and a comparison with the recent epigraphical evidence for it, a wonderful conspectus is given by Knoepfler 2013b.

21. Vidal-Naquet 1975, 826, observing that the note is not humorous or incompetent as was claimed (from the Restoration onwards: Dard 1907, 223–25), but reflects Hérault's knowledge of Plato. The ancient (fourth-century BCE) sense of Crete as endowed with laws of particular antiquity and majesty is an echo of the dynamic lawmaking in "Archaic" Crete from the seventh to the fifth centuries BCE (Gagarin 2008; Gagarin and Perlman 2016; Gagarin 2020a); above, chapters 4 and 5.

22. Gawantka 1985.

23. On this dynamic (as exemplified by eighteenth-century Geneva), and its breakdown as the condition of modern international life, Whatmore 2012; generally, Tilly 1989; Schnettger 2008 on early modern *Kleinstaaten*.

24. Grote: Kierstead 2014. Fustel de Coulanges 1864 (city), 1858 (*Polybe*), with Hartog 1988, 2015.

25. Avlami 2000; Vlassopoulos 2007a. On the reception of the ancient Athenian statesman Periklês, son of Xanthippos, see Azoulay 2014c.

26. Droysen and *polis*: Bravo 1988. Also Bernays 1881 (Phokiōn and his reception); Gawantka 1985; diverse essays in Demoen 2001.

27. On Weber's Orientalism, interesting views in Isin 2002; also Friedrichs 2010, 33–34 (though note that London is excluded from the *polis* model as much as the Oriental city).

28. Islamic city: Abu-Lughod 1987 (engaging with the work of French Orientalist Jean Sauvaget); Faroqhi

1999, 216–17, on the real complexity of Ottoman cities, complete with constituencies and elites capable of agency; Lantschner 2022, on elite-based collective action in "oriental" cities.

29. As examples of thinking about especially Athenian democracy in the aftermath of 1989, e.g., the essays gathered in Euben, Wallace, and Ober 1994. Suspicion before or erasure of the State: e.g., R. Osborne 1998a on ancient colonization as stateless, coalescing in a "Ben-and-Jerry" model (not Osborne's expression, I hasten to add), social rather than organized by state-like institutions; Berent 2000. On Piketty (2013) and the ancient world, see now Koedijk and Morley 2022.

30. Bookchin 1995; Castells 2019.

31. Fukuyama 2011; Aalborg: Flyvbjerg 1998 and above, pp. 492–93. I am not sure M. Hansen has ever talked explicitly and conceptually about a connection between his Danish background and his work on democracy and the *polis*, or his willingness to see the *polis* as an instance of the state.

32. Piketty 2021.

33. Ober 2017 is at least clear on the abstract and theoretical nature of the exercise of finding a usable set of political ideas in the *polis* as a polity (based on equality before liberal rights). What, indeed, would the *polis* be without slavery, exclusion, and patriarchy, if the latter are contingent, connected to the world-historical context, but not to the essence of the *polis* as form? As Max Horkheimer wrote, "[t]he democratic state should, in accordance with its idea, be the Greek *polis* without slaves ([d]er demokratische Staat soll der Idee nach die griechische Polis ohne Sklaven sein) . . . Regard for reason in itself presupposes the factness of the just society, the reality of the *polis* without slaves (*voraus*)," in "Vernunft und Selbsthaltung" (1942, republished in Horkheimer 1997, 320–50, quotations from development at 325–6; the second sentence is written in the capitals which the German philosopher affected for important passages: Horkheimer 1967, 89).

34. G. Parker 2004.

35. I draw inspiration from political philosopher and classicist Danielle Allen's qualified, lucid commitment to the U.S. Constitution in spite of its entanglement with enslavement: Allen 2020; see also the manifesto for political hope and realism in Rorty 2022.

36. Schnapp 2020, 640–45; also above, p. 613, n. 1.

CHRONOLOGY

1420–1200	**BCE Mycenaean palaces**
1200 BCE	End of palaces
1200–1040	**Late Helladic IIIC\Post-Mycenaean period**
1040–900 BCE	Protogeometric period
950 BCE	Lavish monumental burial of couple, Lefkandi
900–700 BCE	**Geometric period**
Ca. 850 BCE	Burial of "Pregnant Rich Lady," Athens
Ca. 800 BCE	Development of Greek alphabetic writing
Ca. 725 BCE	Building of Temple of Apollōn, establishment of West Gate cemetery, Eretria
Ca. 700 BCE?	Early hexameter poems (Homer, Hesiod)
Ca. 700 BCE	Young men of Paros fight against excursions from Naxos; the war-dead buried in two mass graves
675 BCE?	Foundation of Thasos
670–640 BCE	Archilochos's songs
Ca. 660–650 BCE	Building of temple of Artemis, Ephesos
Ca. 650–630 BCE	Law on non-iteration of office of *kosmos*, Drēros
640 BCE?	Kylōn's failed attempt at tyranny, Athens
Ca. 630 BCE	Chigi jug (showing men-at-war clashing in the field, stylized scenes from the realm of myth, and young men's hunt) painted, buried in tomb in Etruria
Ca. 630 BCE	*Korē* of Nikandrē of Naxos set up on Dēlos
621/0 BCE?	Athenian law code, later attributed to Drakōn
Ca. 600 BCE	Alkaios and Sapphō's poetry. Pittakos is *aisymnētēs* in Mytilēnē
594/3 BCE?	Solōn "shakes off the burdens," introduces laws
Ca. 570 BCE	Building of new temple of Apollōn, Corinth; building of Old Temple of Athēna, Akropolis, Athens
Ca. 570 BCE	*Platiwoinarchoi* law is inscribed on a rock, Tiryns

Ca. 550 BCE	Citizens of Chios pass and inscribe complex law on constitutional matters
Ca. 550 BCE	The city of Datala contracts Spensithios as remembrancer in return for payment in kind, citizen status, and privileges
Ca. 525 BCE	Siphnians build treasury at Delphi.
508/7 BCE	Measures proposed by Kleisthenēs, Athens
485–420 BCE	Life of Prōtagoras of Abdēra
490–479 BCE	Persian Wars
478 BCE	Foundation of the league of eastern Greek and western Anatolian communities led by Athens
462–362 BCE	**"Hundred Years' War"**
460 BCE	Athenians massacre Corinthian hoplites at Megara
460–440 BCE	Constitutional reforms in Athens
460–380 BCE	Life of Dēmokritos of Abdēra
448–434 BCE	Spectacular building program on the Athenian Akropolis and across Attica
431–404 BCE	War between Athenian empire and Spartan-led coalition
392 BCE	Massacre at Corinth during the festival of the Eukleia
386 BCE	King's Peace imposed on warring states in Greece by Achaimenid ruler
371 BCE	Defeat of Sparta and allied troops by Thebans at Leuktra
362 BCE	Financial scandal at Halai Aixōnides, intervention by local politician Euthēmōn
359–323 BCE	Reigns of Philippos II and Alexandros III of Macedonia
Ca. 335–322 BCE	Aristotle compiles and writes the *Politics*
334 BCE	Alexandros III declares cities of Asia Minor free and democratic at start of 11-year long expedition across the Achaimenid empire
323–31 BCE	**"Hellenistic" period**
322 BCE	Athens and other cities rise against Macedonia, defeated in Lamian War. Oligarchy in Athens
Ca. 300 BCE	Oligarchs and democrats reconcile on Tēlos
285 BCE	Eretria frees itself from a Macedonian garrison
262 BCE	Athens, Sparta, and other cities unsuccessfully rise against Macedonian king Antigonos Gonatas in Chremonidean War
Ca. 250 BCE	The citizens of the island *polis* of Hērakleia meet to discuss goat-raising, which they ban
229 BCE	Kleomenēs III of Sparta defeated by Macedonian king Antigonos Dōsōn. Athens frees itself from a Macedonian garrison

CHRONOLOGY 625

214–168 BCE	**Roman-Macedonian Wars**
205 BCE	The city of Kytenion in Dōris raises funds to rebuild its walls
196 BCE	Proclamation of freedom of Greeks by T. Quinctius Flamininus
168 BCE	Roman army defeats and slaughters Macedonian forces at Pydna. End of Macedonian kingdom
167 BCE	Rome grants Dēlos to Athens; declares Karian and Lykian cities free
146 BCE	Defeat and dissolution of Achaian League by Rome
Ca. 140 BCE	Arbitration between Messēnē and Sparta
133 BCE	Bequest of Attalid kingdom to Rome. The city of Mētropolis sends troops to fight on Rome's side against an Attalid usurper. Cities of Asia Minor declared free
129 BCE	M' Aquillius builds road in western Asia Minor
128/7 BCE	An Athenian chorus at Delphi sings to the gods, celebrates Roman power
Ca. 120–100 BCE	*Poleis* such as Priēnē, Kolophōn pass long decrees for benefactors
118/7 BCE	Lētē honors M. Annius for services during invasion of Macedonia
Ca. 100 BC	The *polis* of Dēmētrias regulates the oracle of Apollōn Korōpaios; the *polis* of Bargylia honors Artemis Kindyas
94 BCE	Q. Mucius Scaevola the Younger serves as proconsul of Asia Minor
90 BCE	Alliance between Ephesos and Sardeis
88–85 BCE	E First Mithradatic War
69 BCE and later	Diodōros Pasparos, politician of Pergamon, honored for his internal and external activities
49–31 BCE	**Roman civil wars**
27 BCE–14 CE	**Reign of Augustus**
37 CE	Epameinōndas of Akraiphia represents Boiōtian cities in League of Greeks; acts as local benefactor
Ca. 40–ca. 115 CE	Life of Cocceianus Diōn
41–54	**Reign of Claudius**
43 CE	Lykia becomes a Roman province (later united to Pamphylia)
Ca. 45–before 125 CE	Life of Plutarch of Chairōneia
Ca. 90–146 CE	Life of Polemōn of Smyrna, sophist
93 CE	Kolophōn participates in roadbuilding in Ionia
Ca. 101–77 CE	Life of Hērōdēs Atticus
106 CE	Creation of Roman province of Arabia under Trajan
Ca. 109 CE onwards	Pliny the Younger serves as imperial legate in Bithynia

117–38 CE	**Reign of Hadrian**
121/2 CE	The city of Lētē honors the gymnasiarch and benefactor M' Salarius Sabinus
123–152 CE	Benefactions of Opramoas of Rhodiapolis to many Lykian cities
124 CE	Dēmosthenēs of Oinoanda sets up festival in his name in his city
137 CE	Tariff Law of Palmyra
138 CE	Hadrian to writes to confirm the *polis* status of Narykos
138–161 CE	**Reign of Antoninus Pius**
Ca. 150 CE	The city of Tlōs acclaims its benefactress Lalla as "mother of the city"
Ca. 160 CE	Pausanias visits Panopeus and many other *poleis*.
Between 169 and 172 CE	Thespians sends young men to fight with emperor Marcus Aurelius
193–211 CE	**Reign of Septimius Severus**
197 CE	Septimius Severus campaigns in the East against Parthia
Ca. 200 CE	Grant of *polis* status to *nomos*-centers in Egypt
212 CE	Extension of Roman citizenship to free population of empire
Ca. 212–238 CE	Activity of jurist M. Cn. Licinius Rufus of Thyateira
267 CE	P. Herennius Dexippos defends Athens during Herulian invasion of Greece
306–337 CE	**Reign of Constantine I**
324 CE	The people of Orkistos ask for *polis* status
402–450 CE	Reign of Theodosios II
527–565 CE	Reign of Justinian

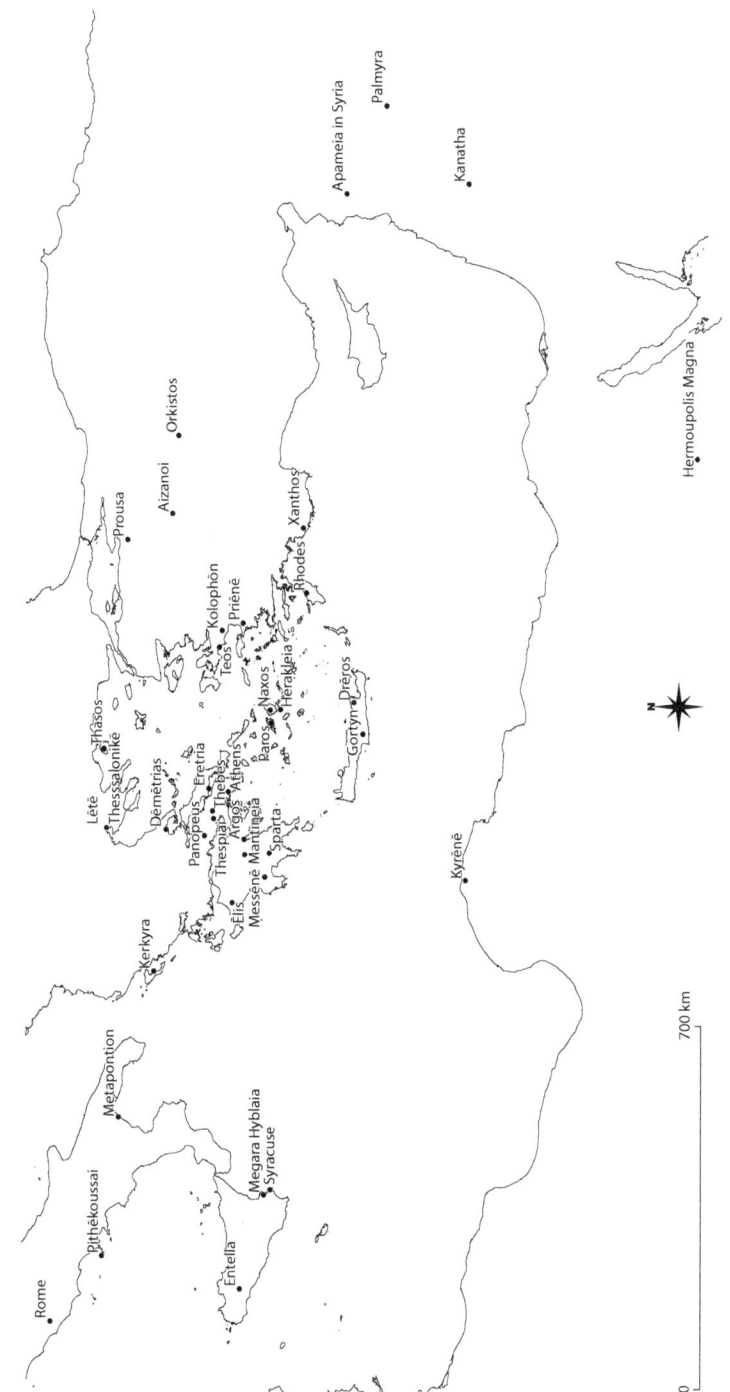

FIGURE 0.1 Orientation map

BIBLIOGRAPHY

All periodicals are abbreviated according to *L'Année Philologique*.

Abélès, M. 1983. *Le lieu du politique*. Paris.
Abu-Lughod, J. L. 1987. "The Islamic City–Historic Myth, Islamic Essence, and Contemporary Relevance." *International Journal of Middle East Studies* 19.2:155–76.
Accame, S. 1946. *Il dominio romano in Grecia dalla guerra acaica ad Augusto*. Rome.
Accame, S. 1952. "Note storiche su epigrafi attiche del V secolo." *RFIC* 80:111–36.
Acemoglu, D., and Robinson, J. A. R. 2012. *Why Nations Fail. The Origins of Power, Prosperity and Poverty*. New York.
Ackermann, D. 2018. *Une microhistoire d'Athènes. Le dème d'Aixônè dans l'Antiquité*. Athens.
Acheson, P. E. 1997. "Does the 'Economic Explanation' Work? Settlement, Agriculture and Erosion in the Territory of Halieis in the Late Classical-Early Hellenistic Period." *JMA* 10.2:165–90.
Adak, M. 2003. *Metöken als Wohltäter Athens. Untersuchungen zum sozialen Austausch zwischen ortsansässigen Fremden und der Bürgergemeinde in klassischer und hellenistischer Zeit (ca. 500-150 v. Chr.)*. Munich.
Adak, M. 2007. "Die rhodische Herrschaft in Lykien und die rechtliche Stellung der Städte Xanthos, Phaselis und Melanippion." *Historia* 56.3:251–79.
Adak, M. 2013. "Claudia Iasonis, eine Asiarchin aus Lykien." *Hermes* 141.4:459–75.
Adak, M. 2018. "Die Melas-Brücke bei Kotenna und die Familie des Stanamoas." *Adalya* 21:211–27.
Adak, M. 2021. "Teos und die hellenistischen Könige von Alexander bis Antiochos III." In *L'Asie Mineure occidentale au IIIe siècle a. C.*, edited by P. Brun, L. Capdetrey, and P. Fröhlich, 231–57. Bordeaux.
Adak. M., and Thonemann, P. J. 2022. *Teos and Abdera. Two Cities in Peace and War*. Oxford.
Adam-Veleni, P., and Tsangari, D., eds. 2015. *Greek Colonisation. New Data, Current Approaches. Proceedings of the Scientific Meeting held in Thessaloniki*. Athens.
Adshead, K. 1986. *Politics of the Archaic Peloponnese. The Transition from Archaic to Classical Politics*. Aldershot.
Agelarakis, A. P. 2017. *Parian Polyandreia. The Late Geometric Funerary Legacy of Cremated Soldiers' Bones on Sociopolitical Affairs and Military Organizational Preparedness in Ancient Greece*. Oxford.
Ager, S. L. 1996. *Interstate Arbitrations in the Greek World, 337-90 B.C.* Berkeley.
Agulhon, M. 1970. *La vie sociale en Provence intérieure au lendemain de la Révolution*. Paris.
Agulhon, M. 1979. *La République au village. Les populations du Var de la Révolution à la IIe République*. Paris.
Ahrweiler, H. 1983. "La région de Philadelphie, au XIVe siècle (1290–1390), dernier bastion de l'hellénisme en Asie Mineure." *CRAI* 127:175–97.
Ahrweiler, H., ed. 1984. *Philadelphie et autres études*. Paris.
Akrigg, B. 2015. "Metics in Athens." In *Communities and Networks in the Ancient Greek World*, edited by C. Taylor and K. Vlassopoulos, 155–73. Oxford.
Akrigg, B. 2019. *Population and Economy in Classical Athens*. Cambridge.
Alba della città, alba delle immagini. Da una suggestione di Bruno d'Agostino. 2008. Athens.
Albertson, F. 2015. "Typology, Attribution, and Identity in Palmyran Funerary Portraiture." In *The World of Palmyra*, edited by A. Kropp and R. Raja, 150–65. Copenhagen.
Alcock, S. E. 1991. "Urban Survey and the Polis of Phlius." *Hesperia* 60:421–63.
Alcock, S. E. 1993a. *Graecia Capta. The Landscapes of Roman Greece*. Cambridge.
Alcock, S. E. 1993b. "Surveying the Peripheries of the Hellenistic World." In *Centre and Periphery in the Hellenistic World*, edited by P. Bilde, 162–75. Aarhus.
Aleshire, S. B., and Lambert, S. D. 2003. "Making the 'Peplos' for Athena: A New Edition of *IG* II² 1060 + *IG* II² 1036." *ZPE* 142:65–86.

Aleshire, S. B., and Lambert, S. D. 2011. "The Attic 'Gene' and the Athenian Religious Reform of 21 B.C." In *Priests and State in the Roman World*, edited by J. H. Richardson and F. Santangelo, 553–75. Stuttgart.
Alexandridis, A. 2004. *Die Frauen des römischen Kaiserhauses. Eine Untersuchung ihrer bildlichen Darstellung von Livia bis Iulia Domna*. Mainz.
Allen, D. S. 1996. "A Schedule of Boundaries: An Exploration, Launched from the Water-Clock of Athenian Time." *G&R* 43.2:157–68.
Allen, D. S. 2010. *Why Plato Wrote*. Malden, MA.
Allen, D. S. 2020. "Why I Love the Constitution." *The Atlantic*. December 2020, 58–63.
Alston, R. 2001. *The City in Roman and Byzantine Egypt*. London.
Alston, R., and van Nijf, O. M., eds. 2008. *Feeding the Ancient Greek City*. Leuven.
Alwine, A. T. 2016. "Freedom and Patronage in the Athenian Democracy." *JHS* 136:1–17.
Amarelli, F., ed. 2005. *Politica e partecipazione nelle città dell'impero romano*. Rome.
Ameling, W. 1983. *Herodes Atticus*. Hildesheim.
Amit, M. 1973. *Great and Small Poleis: A Study in the Relations between the Great Powers and the Small Cities in Ancient Greece*. Brussels.
Ampolo, C. 2001. *Da un'antica città di Sicilia. I decreti di Entella e Nakone: catalogo della mostra*. Pisa.
Anderson, Graham. 1993. *The Second Sophistic. A Cultural Phenomenon in the Roman Empire*. London and New York.
Anderson, Greg. 2003. *The Athenian Experiment. Building an Imagined Political Community in Ancient Attica, 508-490 B.C.* Ann Arbor, MI.
Anderson, Greg. 2005. "Before *Turannoi* Were Tyrants: Rethinking a Chapter of Early Greek History." *ClAnt* 24.2:173–222.
Anderson, Greg. 2009. "The Personality of the Greek State." *JHS* 129:1–22.
Ando, C. 2000. *Imperial Ideology and Provincial Loyalty in the Roman Empire*. Berkeley.
Ando, C. 2006. "The Administration of the Provinces." In *A Companion to the Roman Empire*, edited by D. S. Potter, 177–92. Oxford.
Ando, C. 2010. "Imperial identities." In *Local Knowledge and Microidentities in the Imperial Greek World*, edited by T. Whitmarsh, 17–45. Cambridge.
Ando, C. 2017. "City, Village, Sacrifice: The Political Economy of Religion in the Early Roman Empire." In *Mass and Elite in the Greek and Roman World. From Sparta to Late Antiquity*, edited by R. Evans, 118–36. London.
Ando, C. 2018a. "The Political Economy of the Hellenistic Polis: Comparative and Modern Perspectives." In *The Polis in the Hellenistic World*, edited by H. Börm and N. Luraghi, 9–26. Stuttgart.
Ando, C. 2018b. "Empire as State: The Roman Case." In *State Formations. Histories and Cultures of Statehood*, edited by J. Brooke, G. Anderson, and J. Strauss, 175–89. Cambridge.
Andrade, N. 2010. "Ambiguity, Violence, and Community in the Cities of Judaea and Syria." *Historia* 59.3:342–70.
Andrade, N. J. 2012. "Inscribing the Citizen: Soados and the Civic Context of Palmyra." *Maarav* 19.1–2:65–90.
Andrade, N. J. 2013. *Syrian Identity in the Greco-Roman World*. Cambridge.
Andreau, J. and Chankowski, V. eds. 2007. *Vocabulaire et expression de l'économie dans le monde antique*. Pessac.
Andreioménou, A. K. 1994. "La nécropole d'Akraiphia." In *Nécropoles et sociétés antiques (Grèce, Italie, Languedoc)*, edited by J. D. La Genière, 99–126. Naples.
Andrewes, A. 1956. *The Greek Tyrants*. London.
Andrianou, D. 2006. "Late Classical and Hellenistic Furniture and Furnishings in the Epigraphical Record." *Hesperia* 75.4:561–84.
Antonaccio, C. M. 1995. *An Archaeology of Ancestors. Tomb Cult and Hero Cult in Early Greece*. London.
Aravantinos, V. 2014. "The Inscriptions from the Sanctuary of Herakles at Thebes: An Overview." In *The Epigraphy and History of Boeotia. New Finds, New Prospects*, edited by N. Papazarkadas, 149–210. Leiden.
Aravantinos, V. 2019. "Thebes and Boeotia." In *A Companion to the Archaeology of Early Greece and the Mediterranean*, edited by I. S. Lemos and A. Kotsonas, 763–86. Hoboken, NJ.
Arcenas, S. L. 2018. *Stasis. The Nature, Frequency, and Intensity of Political Violence in Ancient Greece*. Unpublished PhD dissertation. Stanford University.
Arena, E. 2015. "Mycenaean Peripheries during the Palatial Age. The Case of Achaia." *Hesperia* 84.1:1–46.
Arendt, H. 1958. *The Human Condition*. Chicago.
Arendt, H. 1970. *On Violence*. New York.
Arenz, A. 2006. *Herakleides Kritikos "Über die Städte in Hellas": eine Periegese Griechenlands am Vorabend des Chremonideischen Krieges*. Munich.

Arnaoutoglou, I. 1998a. *Ancient Greek Laws. A Sourcebook*. London.
Arnaoutoglou, I. 1998b. "Between *koinon* and *idion*: Legal and Social Dimensions of Religious Associations in Ancient Athens." In *Kosmos. Essays in Order, Conflict, and Community in Classical Athens*, edited by P. Cartledge, P. Millett, and S. von Reden, 68–83. Cambridge.
Arnaoutoglou, I. 2003. Thusias heneka kai sunousias. *Private Religious Associations in Hellenistic Athens*. Athens.
Arnason, J. P., and Murphy, P. W., eds. 2001. *Agon, Logos, Polis. The Greek Achievement and Its Aftermath*. Stuttgart.
Arnason, J.P., Raaflaub, K.A., and Wagner, P., eds. 2013. *The Greek Polis and the Invention of Democracy. A Politicocultural Transformation and its Interpretations*. Malden, MA.
Arrington, N. T. 2010. "Topographic Semantics. The Location of the Athenian Public Cemetery and Its Significance for the Nascent Democracy." *Hesperia* 79.4:499–539.
Arrington, N. T. 2015. *Ashes, Images, and Memories. The Presence of the War Dead in Fifth-Century Athens*. Oxford.
Arrington, N. T. 2022. *Athens at the Margins. Pottery and People in the Early Mediterranean World*. Princeton.
Ashton, N. G. 1991. *Siphnos. Ancient Towers B.C.* Athens.
Ashton, R. H. J. 1999. "The Late Classical/Early Hellenistic Drachms of Knidos." *RN* 154:63–94.
Athanassaki, L., and Bowie, E., eds., 2011. *Archaic and Classical Choral Song. Performance, Politics and Dissemination*. Berlin.
Aupert, P. 1982. "Argos aux VIIIe-VIIe siècles: bourgade ou metropole?" *ASAA* 60:21–31.
Avgerinou, P. 2016. "Water Supply Facilities in Megara during the Archaic and Classical Period." In *Mégarika, Nouvelles recherches sur Mégare, les cités de la Propontide et du Pont-Euxin*, edited by A. Robu and D. Knoepfler, 285–319. Paris.
Avgerinou, P. 2019. "Investigation of the Ancient Underground Aqueduct in Megara (Greece). Preliminary Results." In *Gérer l'eau en Méditerranée au premier milléniare avant J.-C.*, edited by S. Bouffier, O. Belvedere, and S. Vassallo, 39–49. Aix-en-Provence.
Avlami, C., ed. 2000. *L'Antiquité grecque au XIXème siècle: un exemplum contesté*. Paris.
Avram, A. 2021. "Quelle place pour l'esclavage dans les cités pontiques?" In *Statuts personnels et main-d'œuvre en Méditerranée hellénistique*, edited by S. Maillot and J. Zurbach, 93–119. Clermont-Ferrand.
Aymard, A. 1967. *Études d'histoire ancienne*. Paris.
Aytaçlar, N. 2004. "The Early Iron Age at Klazomenai." In *Klazomenai, Teos and Abdera. Metropoleis and Colony*, edited by A. Moustaka and E. Skarlatidou, 17–41. Thessaloniki.
Azoulay, V. 2014a. *Les tyrannicides d'Athènes. Vie et mort de deux statues*. Paris.
Azoulay, V. 2014b. "Repolitiser la cité grecque, trente ans après." *Annales (HSS)* 69.3:689–719.
Azoulay, V. 2014c. *Pericles of Athens*. Translated by J. Lloyd. Princeton.
Azoulay, V. 2016. "Un fantasme monumental: la statue-monde d'Alexandre le Grand." *CCG* 27:229–61.
Azoulay, V. 2017. *The Tyrant-Slayers of Ancient Athens. A Tale of Two Statues*. Translated by J. Lloyd. Oxford.
Azoulay, V. 2019. "Violente amnistie. La réconciliation athénienne de 403 av. J.-C." *Annales (HSS)* 74.2:383–425.
Azoulay, V., and Ismard, P. 2007. "Les lieux du politique dans l'Athènes classique. Entre structures institutionnelles, idéologie civique et pratiques sociales." In *Athènes et le politique. Dans le sillage de Claude Mossé*, edited by P. Schmitt Pantel and F. de Polignac, 271–309. Paris.
Azoulay, V. and Ismard, P. eds. 2011. *Clisthène et Lycurgue d'Athènes: autour du politique dans la cité classique*. Paris.
Azoulay, V., and Ismard, P. 2018. "Honneurs et déshonneurs: autours des statuts juridiques de l'Athènes classique." In *Statuts personnels et espaces sociaux: questions grecques et romaine*, edited by C. Moatti and C. Müller, 213–42. Paris.
Azoulay, V. and Ismard, P. 2020. *Athènes 403: une histoire chorale*. Paris.
Baba, K. 1984. "On Kerameikos Inv. I 388 (SEG XXII, 79): A Note on the Formation of the Athenian Metic-Status." *ABSA* 79:1–5.
Bäbler, B. 1998. *Fleissige Thrakerinnen und wehrhafte Skythen. Nichtgriechen im klassischen Athen und ihre archäologische Hinterlassenschaft*. Stuttgart.
Bader, N., and Yon, J-B. 2018. "Une inscription du théâtre de Bayt Ras/Capitolias." *Syria* 95:155–68.
Badian, E. 1995. "The Ghost of Empire. Reflections on Athenian Foreign Policy in the Fourth Century B.C." In *Die athenische Demokratie im 4. Jahrhundert v. Chr.: Vollendung oder Verfall einer Verfassungsform?*, edited by W. Eder, 79–106. Stuttgart.

Badoud, N. 2015. *Le temps de Rhodes. Une chronologie des inscriptions de la cité fondée sur l'étude de ses institutions.* Munich.
Badoud, N., Fincker, M., and Moretti, J.-C. 2015. "Les monuments érigés à Délos et à Athènes en l'honneur de Ménodôros, pancratiaste et lutteur." *BCH* 139–40.1:345–416.
Baechler, J. 1985. *Démocraties.* Paris.
Bagnall, R. 1976. *The Administration of the Ptolemaic Possessions Outside Egypt.* Leiden.
Bagnall, R. 1996. *Egypt in Late Antiquity.* 2nd ed. Princeton.
Bagnall, R., Casagrande-Kim, R., Ersoy, A., Tanrıver, C., and Yolaçan, B. 2016. *Graffiti from the Basilica in the Agora of Smyrna.* New York.
Baker, P., and Thériault, G. 2019. "Xanthos et la Lycie à la basse époque hellénistique: Nouvelle inscription honorifique xanthienne." *Chiron* 48:301–32.
Ball, W. 2016. *Rome in the East. The Transformation of an Empire.* 2nd ed. Abingdon.
Balot, R. K. 2001. *Greed and Injustice in Classical Athens.* Princeton.
Balot, R. K. 2014. *Courage in the Democratic Polis. Ideology and Critique in Classical Athens.* Oxford.
Baltes, E. P. 2020. "A Monumental Stepped Statue Base in the Athenian Agora." *Hesperia* 89.2:339–77.
Balty, J. C. 1988. "Apamea in Syria in the Second and Third Centuries A.D." *JRS* 78:91–104.
Banfield, E. 1958. *The Moral Basis of a Backward Society.* Glencoe, IL.
Bang, P. F. 2011. "Court And State in the Roman Empire—Domestication and Tradition in Comparative Perspective." In *Royal Courts in Dynastic States and Empires*, edited by J. Duindam, T. Artan, and M. Kunt, 103–28. Leiden.
Barat, R. 2018. *"Les élections que fait le peuple": République de Genève, vers 1680–1707.* Geneva.
Barat, R. 2022. *Voter pour rien. 1691, le jour où les citoyens menacèrent de "faire sauter les vieux."* Paris.
Barjamovic, G. 2004. "Civic Institutions and Self Government in Southern Mesopotamia in the Mid-first Millenium B.C." In *Assyria and Beyond. Studies Presented to Mogens Trolle Larsen*, edited by J. G. Dercksen, 47–98. Leiden.
Barley, N., and Pretzler, M., eds. 2017. *Brill's Companion to Aineias Tacticus.* Leiden.
Barnes, T. D. 1982. *The New Empire of Diocletian and Constantine.* Cambridge, MA.
Baronowski, D. W. 1988. "The Provincial Status of Mainland Greece After 146 B.C. A Criticism of Erich Gruen's views." *Klio* 70:448–60.
Barr-Sharrar, B. 2008. *The Derveni Krater. Masterpiece of Classical Greek Metalwork.* Princeton.
Bartels, J. 2008. *Städtische Eliten im römischen Makedonien. Untersuchungen zur Formierung und Struktur.* Berlin.
Baslez, M. F. 2008. *L'étranger dans la Grèce antique.* 2nd ed. Paris.
Bastin Hammou, M., and Orfanos, C., eds. 2015. *Carnaval et comédie.* Besançon.
Bates, R. H., Greif, A., Levi, M., Rosenthal, J-L., and Weingast, B. R. 1998. *Analytic Narratives.* Princeton.
Bauer, E. 2012. "Old Age as a Principle of Social Organization: Gerousiai in the Poleis of Hellenistic and Roman Southern Asia Minor." In *On Old Age. Approaching Death in Antiquity and the Middle Ages*, edited by C. Krötzl and K. Mustakallio, 127–52. Turnhout.
Bauer, E. 2014. *Gerusien in den Poleis Kleinasiens in hellenistischer Zeit und der römischen Kaiserzeit. Die Beispiele Ephesos, Pamphylien und Pisidien, Aphrodisias und Iasos.* Munich.
Bauer, S. 2001. *Polisbild und Demokratieverständnis in Jacob Burckhardts "Griechischer Kulturgeschichte."* Basel.
Bearzot, C. 1985. *Focione tra storia e trasfigurazione ideale.* Milan.
Bearzot, C. 2004. *Federalismo e autonomia nelle Elleniche di Senofonte.* Milan.
Bearzot, C. 2006. "Argo nel V secolo: ambizioni egemoniche, crisi interne, condizionamenti esterni." In *Argo. Una democrazia diversa*, edited by C. Bearzot and F. Landucci, 105–46. Milan.
Bearzot, C. 2013. *Come si abbatte una democrazia. Tecniche di colpo di Stato nell'Atene antica.* Rome.
Bearzot, C., and Landucci, F., eds. 2006. *Argo. Una democrazia diversa.* Milan.
Beauregard, R. 2018. *Cities in an Urban Age. A Dissent.* Chicago.
Beck, H. 1999. "Ostlokris und die 'Tausend Opuntier': Neue Überlegungen zum Siedlergesetz für Naupaktos." *ZPE* 124:53–62.
Beck, H., ed. 2013. *A Companion to Ancient Greek Government.* Malden, MA.
Beck, H., and Funke, P., eds. 2015. *Federalism in Greek Antiquity.* Cambridge.
Beckman, G., Bryce, T., and Cline, E., eds. 2011. *The Ahhiyawa Texts.* Leiden.
Behrwald, R. 2000. *Der lykische Bund. Untersuchungen zu Geschichte und Verfassung.* Bonn.
Bell, D. 1993. *Communitarianism and its Critics.* Oxford.

Bennett, R. 2014. *Local Elite and Local Coinage. Elite Self-Representation on the Provincial Coinage of Asia, 31 B.C to A.D. 275*. London.

Bérard, C. 1970. *L'hérôon à la porte de l'ouest*. Zürich.

Bérard, C. and Vernant, J.-P. eds. 1984. *La cité des images: Religion et société en Grèce antique*. Paris.

Bérard, R.-M. 2019. "Funerary Practices and the Formation of the Polis at Megara Hyblaea (8th-6th centuries BC)." In *Beyond the Polis. Ritual Practices and the Construction of Social Identity in Early Greece (12th-6th Centuries B.C.)*, edited by I. S. Lemos and A. Tsingarida, 247–58. Brussels.

Bérenger, A. 2014. *Le métier de gouverneur dans l'empire romain de César à Dioclétien*. Paris.

Berent, M. 1998. "Stasis, or the Greek Invention of Politics." *History of Political Thought* 19.3:331–62.

Berent, M. 2000. "Anthropology and the Classics: War, Violence, and the Stateless Polis." *CQ* 50.1:257–89.

Berent, M. 2004. "A Rejoinder to M. H. Hansen." *Polis* 21.1–2, 107–146.

Berg, I. 2019. *The Cycladic and Aegean Islands in Prehistory*. London and New York.

Bergemann, J. 1997. *Demos und Thanatos. Untersuchungen zum Wertsystem der Polis im Spiegel der attischen Grabreliefs des 4. Jahrhunderts v. Chr. und zur Funktion der gleichzeitigen Grabbauten*. Munich.

Berlin, I. 1969. *Four Essays on Liberty*. Oxford.

Berlin, I. 2002. *Liberty*. Edited by H. Hardy. Oxford.

Berlin, A. M., and Kosmin, P. J., eds. 2019. *Spear-Won Land. Sardis from the King's Peace to the Peace of Apamea*. Madison, WI.

Berlin, A. M., and Kosmin, P. J., eds. 2021. *The Middle Maccabees. Archaeology, History, and the Rise of the Hasmonean Kingdom*. Atlanta, GA.

Bernard, A. 1992. *La prose sur pierre dans l'Égypte hellénistique et romaine*. Paris.

Bernays, J. 1881. *Phokion und seine neueren Beurtheiler. Ein Beitrag zur Geschichte der griechischen Philosophie und Politik*. Berlin.

Bernhardt, R. 1971. *Imperium und Eleutheria. Die römische Politik gegenüber den freien Städten des griechischen Ostens*. Hamburg.

Bernhardt, R. 1985. *Polis und römische Herrschaft in der späten Republik (149–31 v. Chr.)*. Berlin.

Bernhardt, R. 1998. *Rom und die Städte des hellenistischen Ostens (3. - 1. Jahrhundert v.Chr.). Literaturbericht 1965–1995*. Berlin.

Berranger, D. 1992. *Recherches sur l'histoire et la prosopographie de Paros à l'époque archaïque*. Clermont-Ferrand.

Bertrand, J.-M. 1989. "Langage et politique: réflexion sur le traité pseudo-xénophontique *De la République des Athéniens*." *Langage et société* 49:25–41.

Bertrand, J-M. 1990. "Formes de discours politiques: décrets des cités grecques et correspondance des rois hellénistiques." In *Du pouvoir dans l'Antiquité. Mots et réalités*, edited by C. Nicolet, 101–16. Paris.

Bertrand, J-M. 1997. "Rome et la Méditerranée Orientale au Ier siècle avant J.-C." In *Rome et la conquête du monde méditerranéen*, vol. 2, edited by C. Nicolet, 789–845. Paris.

Bertrand, J-M. 2000. "La fiction en droit grec. La loi sur l'homicide dans une inscription de Locride." *RD* 78.2:219–31.

Bertrand, J-M. 2005a. "À propos des πάροικοι dans les cités d'Asie Mineure." In *Citoyenneté et participation à la basse époque hellénistique*, edited by P. Fröhlich and C. Müller, 39–49. Geneva.

Bertrand, J-M., ed. 2005b. *La violence dans les mondes grec et romain*. Paris.

Berve, H. 1967. *Die Tyrannis bei den Griechen*. Munich.

Bessios M., Tzifopoulos, G. Z., and Kotsonas A. 2012. *Μεθώνη Πιερίας Ι: Επιγραφές, χαράγματα και εμπορικά σύμβολα στη γεωμετρική και αρχαϊκή κεραμική από το "Υπόγειο."* Thessaloniki.

Bettalli, M. 2012. "Guerra e violenza a Corinto, 392 a. C. (Senofone, *Elleniche*, IV, 5, 1–13)." In *Salvare le poleis, costruire la concordia, progettare la pace*, edited by S. Cataldi, E Bianco, G. Cuniberti, 161–80. Alessandria.

Bevilacqua, G. 1996. "Exitetèria per Afrodite Hegemone da Ramnunte." *Miscellanea greca e romana* 20:55–66.

Beyer, I. 1976. *Die Tempel von Dreros und Prinias A und die Chronologie der kretischen Kunst des 8. und 7. Jhs. v. Chr.* Berlin.

Biard, G. 2017. *La représentation honorifique dans les cités grecques aux époques classique et hellénistique*. Athens.

Bier, L., ed. 2011. *The Bouleuterion at Ephesos*. Vienna.

Bikerman, E. 1938. *Institutions des Séleucides*. Paris.

Bikerman, E. 1939a. "La cité grecque dans les monarchies hellénistiques." *RPh* 13:335–49.

Bikerman, E. 1939b. "Sur une inscription grecque de Sidon." In *Mélanges Syriens offerts à Monsieur René Dussaud Secrétaire Perpétuel de l'Académie des Inscriptions et Belles-Lettres*, 91–9. Paris.
Billows, R. A. 1995. *Kings and Colonists. Aspects of Macedonian Imperialism.* Leiden.
Bintliff, J. L. 1994. "Territorial Behaviour and the Natural History of the Greek Polis." In *Stuttgarter Kolloquium zur Historischen Geographie des Altertums*, edited by E. Olshausen and H. Sonnabend, 207–49. Amsterdam.
Bintliff, J. L. 1997. "Regional Survey, Demography, and the Rise of Complex Societies in the Ancient Aegean: Core-Periphery, Neo-Malthusian, and Other Interpretive Models." *JFA* 24.1:1–38.
Blintiff, J. 2006. "City-Country Relationships in the 'Normal Polis.'" In *City, Countryside, and the Spatial Organization of Value in Classical Antiquity*, edited by R. Rosen and I. Sluiter, 13–32. Leiden.
Bintliff, J. L. 2012. *The Complete Archaeology of Greece: From Hunter-Gatherers to the 20th Century A.D.* Malden, MA.
Bintliff, J., Farinetti, E., Slpapšak, B., and Snodgrass, A. 2017. *Boeotia project. Vol. 2. The city of Thespiai. Survey at a Complex Urban Site.* Cambridge.
Bintliff, J. L., and Howard P. 2007. *Testing the Hinterland. The Work of the Boeotia Survey (1989–1991) in the Southern Approaches of the City of Thespiai.* Cambridge.
Bintliff, J. L., and Snodgrass A. 1988. "Mediterranean Survey and the City." *Antiquity* 62:57–71.
Biraschi, A. M., and Salmeri, G. 2000. *Strabone e l'Asia Minore. Studi di storia e di storiografia.* Perugia.
Birley, A. R. 1997a. *Hadrian. The Restless Emperor.* London.
Birley, A. R. 1997b. "Hadrian and Greek Senators." *ZPE* 116:209–45.
Blackwell, N. G. 2021. "Ahhiyawa, Hatti, and Diplomacy: Implications of Hittite Misperceptions of the Mycenaean World." *Hesperia* 90.2:191–231.
Blanco-Pérez, A. 2013. "C. Claudius Lucianus: An Eirenarch from Akmoneia Selected by the Proconsul M. Sulpicius Crassus: A Note on SEG 56.1493." *ZPE* 186:190–4.
Blanco-Pérez, A. 2015. "Apamea and the Integration of a Roman Colony in Western Asia Minor." In *Processes of Cultural Change and Integration in the Roman World*, edited by S. Roselaar, 136–53. Leiden.
Blandin, B. 2007. *Eretria XVII. Les pratiques funéraires d'époque géométrique à Érétrie.* Lausanne.
Blanshard, A. J. L. 2004. "What Counts as the Demos? Some Notes on the Relationship between the Jury and 'The People' in Classical Athens." *Phoenix* 58.1–2:28–48.
Bleicken, J. 1982. *Zum Regierungsstil des römischen Kaisers: eine Antwort auf Fergus Millar.* Wiesbaden.
Blok, J. H. 2000. "Phye's Procession: Culture, Politics and Peisistratid Rule." In *Peisistratos and the Tyranny. A Reappraisal of the Evidence*, edited by H. Sancisi-Weerdenburg, 17–48. Amsterdam.
Blok, J. H. 2005. "Becoming Citizens. Some Notes on the Semantics of 'Citizen' in Archaic Greece and Classical Athens." *Klio* 87.1:7–40.
Blok, J. H. 2009. "Perikles' Citizenship Law: A New Perspective." *Historia* 58.2:141–70.
Blok, J. 2014. "A 'Covenant' between Gods and Men: *Hiera kai hosia* and the Greek Polis." In *The City in the Classical and Post-Classical World. Changing Contexts of Power and Identity*, edited by C. Rapp and H. Drake, 14–37. Cambridge.
Blok, J. H. 2015. "The *Diôbelia*: On the Political Economy of an Athenian State Fund." *ZPE* 193:87–102.
Blok, J. H. 2017. *Citizenship in Classical Athens.* Cambridge.
Blömer, M., and Raja, R., eds. 2019. *Funerary Portraiture in Greater Roman Syria.* Turnhout.
Blondé, F., Muller, A., and Mulliez, D. 2002. "Évolution urbaine d'une colonie à l'époque archaïque. L'exemple de Thasos." *Pallas* 58:251–65.
Blume, M. 1989. "À propos de P.Oxy I.41. Des acclamations en l'honneur d'un prytane confrontées aux témoignages épigraphiques du reste de l'Empire." In *Egitto e storia dall'Ellenismo all'età araba*, edited by L. Criscuolo and G. Geraci, 271–90. Bologna.
Boardman, J. 1999. *The Greeks Overseas. Their Early Colonies and Trade.* 4th ed. London.
Boatwright, M. T. 1993. "The City Gate of Plancia Magna in Perge." In *Roman Art in Context. An Anthology*, edited by E. D. Ambra, 189–207. Hoboken, NJ.
Boatwright, M. T. 2000. *Hadrian and the Cities of the Roman Empire.* Princeton.
Bobou, O. 2015. *Children in the Hellenistic World. Statues and Representation.* Oxford.
Bock, G., Skinner, Q., and Viroli, M., eds. 1990. *Macchiavelli and Republicanism.* Cambridge.
Bodel, J., and Scheidel, W., eds. 2017. *On Human Bondage. After Slavery and Social Death.* Malden, MA.
Boedeker, D. 1993. "Hero Cult and Politics in Herodotus: The Bones of Orestes." In *Cultural Poetics in Archaic Greece. Cult, Performance, Politics*, edited by C. Dougherty and L. Kurke, 164–77. Cambridge.
Boedeker, D., and Raaflaub, K. A. 1998. *Democracy, Empire, and the Arts in Fifth-century Athens.* Cambridge, MA.

Boegehold, A. L. 1993. "Perikles' Citizenship Law of 451/0 B.C." In *Athenian Identity and Civic Ideology*, edited by A. L. Boegehold and A. C. Scafuro, 57–66. Baltimore.
Boegehold, A. L., and Scafuro, A. C., eds. 1993. *Athenian Identity and Civic Ideology*. Baltimore.
Boehm, R. 2021. "Ritual and Revolution. Artemis Eukleia and the Union of Corinth and Argos Revisited." *Historia* 70.3:315–50.
Boehm, R., Master, D. M., and Le Blanc, R. 2016. "The Basilica, Bouleuterion, and Civic Center of Ashkelon." *AJA* 120.2:271–324.
Boffo, L. 2011. "I decreti 'per difesa / salvezza' della *polis*" una categoria d'archivio." In *Antiqvitas. Scritti di storia antica in onore di Salvatore Alessandrì*, edited by M. Lombardo and C. Marangio, 25–40. Galatina.
Bogaert, R. 1968. *Banques et banquiers dans les cités grecques*. Leiden.
Bohn, R., with Schuchardt, C. 1889. *Altertümer von Aegae*. Berlin.
Bonnechere, P. 2014. "'Gouverner en toute sécurité.' L'oracle de Dodone et l'*Athenaiôn politeia* 43, 4." *ZPE* 189:83–6.
Bonnet, C. 2015. *Les enfants de Cadmos. Le paysage religieux de la Phénicie hellénistique*. Paris.
Bookchin, M. 1995. *From Urbanization to Cities. Toward a New Politics of Citizenship*. London.
Borg, B. 1998. "Der zierlichste Anblick der Welt . . ." *Ägyptische Porträtmumien*. Mainz.
Borg, B. 2011. "Who Cared about Greek Identity? Athens in the First Century BCE." In *The Struggle for Identity. Greeks and their Past in the First Century BCE*, edited by N. Wiater and T. Schmitz, 213–34. Stuttgart.
Boring, T. A. 1979. *Literacy in Ancient Sparta*. Leiden.
Börm, H. 2019. *Mordende Mitbürger. Stasis und Bürgerkrieg in griechischen Poleis des Hellenismus*. Stuttgart.
Borromeo, E. 2004. "Les Cyclades à l'époque ottomane. L'insularité vue par les missionnaires jésuites (1625–1644)." In *Insularités ottomanes*, edited by N. Vatin and G. Veinstein, 123–44. Paris.
Borromeo, E. 2007. *Voyageurs occidentaux dans l'empire ottoman (1600–1644)*. Paris.
Bost Pouderon, C. 2006. *Dion Chrysostome. Trois discours aux villes (Orr. 33–35)*. Salerno.
Botermann, H. 1994. "Wer Baute das Neue Priene? Zur Interpretation der Inschriften von Priene Nr. 1 und 156." *Hermes* 122:162–87.
Bouchon, R. 2009. "La taxe des affranchis et le financement de la vie publique dans les cités thessaliennes: nouvelles lectures de documents du IIe s. apr. J.-C." In *Proceedings of the 2nd Archaeological Meeting of Thessaly and Central Greece*, 395–407.
Bouchon, R. 2015. "Les comptes des épimélètes de la caisse des affranchissements d'Hypata à l'époque impériale: à propos de deux inscriptions récemment publiées ('ΗΟΡΟΣ' 22–25 [2010–2013], p. 327–341)." *ZPE* 193:172–8.
Bouchon, R. 2016. "Les Thessaliens et le culte des empereurs de Rome: tradition, intégration, polycentrisme et jeu d'échelles." In *Kaiserkult in den Provinzen des Römischen Reiches. Organisation, Kommunikation und Repräsentation*, edited by A. Kolb and M. Vitale, 285–307. Berlin.
Bouchon, R., and Helly, B. 2013. "Construire et reconstruire l'État fédéral thessalien (époque classique, époque hellénistique et romaine). Cultes et sanctuaires des Thessaliens." In *Greek Federal States and their Sanctuaries. Identity and integration*, edited by P. Funke and M. Haake, 205–25. Stuttgart.
Boulanger, A. 1923. *Aelius Aristide et la sophistique dans la province d'Asie au IIe siècle de notre ère*. Paris.
Boulay, T. 2011. "La mémoire des faits d'armes dans les cités d'Asie Mineure à l'époque hellénistique: un polyandrion à Milet et Lichas fils d'Hermophantos." In *Pratiques et identités culturelles des armées hellénistiques du monde méditerranéen*, edited by J.-C. Couvenhes, S. Crouzet, and S. Péré-Noguès, 213–25. Bordeaux.
Boulay, T. 2013. "Les 'groupes de référence' au sein du corps civique de Téos." In *Groupes et associations dans les cités grecques (IIIe siècle av. J.-C.–IIe siècle apr. J.-C.)*, edited by P. Fröhlich and P. Hamon, 251–75. Geneva.
Boulay, T. 2014. *Arès dans la cité. Les poleis et la guerre dans l'Asie Mineure hellénistique*. Pisa.
Boulay, T. 2016. "Aigai, Zeus Olympios et le terroir de l'Αἰγαῖς." *RN* 173:95–121.
Bourriot, F. 1976. *Recherches sur la nature du genos. Étude d'histoire sociale athénienne: périodes archaïque et classique*. Lille.
Bourriot, F. 1995. *Kalos kagathos—kalokagathia. D'un terme de propagande de sophistes à une notion sociale et philosophique*. Hildesheim.
Bousquet, J., and Gauthier, P. 1994. "Inscriptions du Létôon de Xanthos." *REG* 107:319–61.
Bowersock, G. W. 1969. *Greek Sophists in the Roman Empire*. Oxford.
Bowie, E. L. 1970. "Greeks and Their Past in the Second Sophistic." *P&P* 46.1:3–41.
Bowie, E. L. 1982. "The Importance of Sophists." In *Later Greek Literature*, edited by J. J. Winkler and G. Williams, 29–60. Cambridge.

Bowie, E. L. 1990. "*Miles ludens*? The Problem of Martial Exhortation in Early Greek Elegy." In *Sympotica. A Symposium on the Symposion*, edited by O. Murray, 221–29. Oxford.

Bowie, E. L. 2014. "Rediscovering Sacadas." In *Patterns of the Past. Epitēdeumata in the Greek Tradition*, edited by A. Moreno and R. Thomas, 39–55. Oxford.

Bowie, E. L., and Elsner, J., eds. 2009. *Philostratus. Greek Culture in the Roman World*. Cambridge.

Bowman, A. K. 1971. *The Town Councils of Roman Egypt*. Toronto.

Bowman, A. K. 1986. *Egypt after the Pharaohs 332 B.C.–A.D. 642. From Alexander to the Arab Conquest*. Berkeley.

Bowman, A. K. 1992. "Public Buildings in Roman Egypt." *JRA* 5:495–503.

Bowman, A. K. 2000. "Urbanisation in Roman Egypt." In *Romanization and the City. Creation, Transformations, and Failures*, edited by E. Fentress and S. E. Alcock, 173–88. Portsmouth.

Bowman, A. K., and Rathbone, D. 1992. "Cities and Administration in Roman Egypt." *JRS* 82:107–27.

Boyxen, B. 2018. *Fremde in der hellenistischen Polis Rhodos. Zwischen Nähe und Distanz*. Berlin.

Braccesi, L. 1998. *I tiranni di Sicilia*. Roma.

Brandes, W. 1989. *Die Städte Kleinasiens im 7. und 8. Jahrhundert*. Berlin.

Bransbourg, G. 2008. "Fiscalité impériale et finances municipales au IVe siècle." *AntTard* 16:255–96.

Braun, T. 1994. "ΧΡΗΣΤΟΥΣ ΠΟΙΕΙΝ." *CQ* 44.1:40–5.

Braund, D. 1994. "The Luxuries of Athenian Democracy." *G&R* 41.1:41–8.

Bravo, B. 1968. *Philologie, histoire, philosophie de l'histoire. Étude sur J. G. Droysen, historien de l'antiquité*. Hildesheim.

Brélaz, C. 2005. *La sécurité publique en Asie mineure sous le principat (Ier - IIIème s. ap. J-C.). Institutions municipales et institutions impériales dans l'Orient romain*. Basel.

Brélaz, C. 2007. "Motifs et circonstances de l'ingérence des autorités romaines dans les cités grecques sous le Principat." In *Amministrare un impero. Roma e le sue province*, edited by A. Baroni, 109–43. Trent.

Brélaz, C. 2008. "L'adieu aux armes: la défense de la cité grecque dans l'empire romain pacifié." In *Sécurité collective et ordre public dans les sociétés anciennes*, edited by C. Brélaz and P. Ducrey, 155–204. Vandœuvres.

Brélaz, C. 2009. "Les bienfaiteurs, "sauveurs" et "fossoyeurs" de la cité hellénistique? Une approche historiographique de l'évergétisme." In *L' huile et l'argent*, edited by O. Curty, S. Piccand and S. Codourey, 37–56. Paris.

Brélaz, C. 2013. "La vie démocratique dans les cités grecques à l'époque impériale." *Topoi (Lyon)* 18.2:367–99.

Brélaz, C. 2015. "La langue des *incolae* sur le territoire de Philippes et les contacts linguistiques dans les colonies romaines d'Orient." In *Interpretatio. Traduire l'altérité culturelle dans les civilisations de l'Antiquité*, edited by F. Colin, O. Huck, and S. Vanseveren, 371–407. Paris.

Brélaz, C., ed. 2017. *L'héritage grec des colonies romaines d'Orient. Interactions culturelles dans les provinces hellénophones de l'empire romain*. Paris.

Brélaz, C. 2018. *Philippes, colonie romaine d'Orient. Recherches d'histoire institutionnelle et sociale*. Athens.

Brélaz, C. 2021. "Deviating Soldiers: Officials on the Move and Local Communities at Risk in Roman Asia Minor and Greece." In *L'expérience de la mobilité de l'Antiquité à nos jours, entre précarité et confiance*, edited by C. Moatti and E. Chevreau, 171–87. Bordeaux.

Brélaz, C., and Rose, E., eds. 2021. *Civic Identity and Civic Participation in Late Antiquity and the Early Middle Ages*. Turnhout.

Bresson, A. 2000. *La cité marchande*. Paris.

Bresson, A. 2006. "Relire la Chronique du temple lindien." *Topoi (Lyon)* 14.2:527–51.

Bresson, A. 2007. *L'économie de la Grèce des cités (fin VIe-Ier siècle a. C.). I. Les structures et la production*. Paris.

Bresson, A. 2008. *L'économie de la Grèce des cités (fin VIe-Ier siècle a. C.). II. Les espaces de l'échange*. Paris.

Bresson, A. 2011. "Grain from Cyrene." In *The Economies of Hellenistic Societies, Third to First Centuries BC*, edited by Z. Archibald, J. K. Davies, V. Gabrielsen, 66–95. Oxford.

Bresson, A. 2016. *The Making of the Ancient Greek Economy. Institutions, Markets, and Growth in the City-States*. Translated by S. Rendall. Princeton.

Bresson, A. 2021. "Closed Economy, Debt and the Spartan Crisis." In *Luxury and Wealth in Sparta and the Peloponnese*, edited by S. Hodkinson and C. Gallou, 77–96. Swansea.

Bresson, A. and Descat, R. 2001. *Les cités d'Asie mineure occidentale au IIe siècle a.C.* Pessac.

Bresson, A., Descat, R., and Varinlioğlu, E. 2021. "Décret des Mogōreis pour le stratège ptolémaïque Moschiôn de Théra." In *L'Asie mineure occidentale au IIIe siècle a.C.*, edited by P. Brun, L. Capdetrey, and P. Fröhlich, 141–71. Bordeaux.

Brett, B. A. 1950. "Athena ΑΛΚΙΔΗΜΟΣ of Pella." *Museum Notes (American Numismatic Society)* 4:55–72.

Briant, P. 1982. *Rois, tributs et paysans. Études sur les formations tributaires du Moyen-Orient ancien.* Besançon.
Briant, P. 1995. "Les institutions de Sardes achéménide. Une note additionnelle." *La Lettre de Pallas* 2:2.
Briant, P. 1996. *Histoire de l'empire perse. De Cyrus à Alexandre.* Paris.
Briant, P. 1998. "Cités et satrapes dans l'empire achéménide: Xanthos et Pixôdaros." *CRAI* 1:305–40.
Briant, P. 2017. *Kings, Countries, Peoples. Selected Studies on the Achaemenid Empire.* Translated by A. Kuhrt. Stuttgart.
Bringmann, K. 2019. *Das Volk regiert sich selbst. Eine Geschichte der Demokratie.* Darmstadt.
Brinkmann, V. 1994. *Die Friese des Siphnierschatzhauses. Beobachtungen zum formalen Aufbau und zum Sinngehalt der Friese des Siphnierschatzhauses.* Munich.
Brinkmann, V. 2003. *Die Polychromie der archaischen und frühklassischen Skulptur.* Munich.
Brisart, T. 2009. "Les pithoi à reliefs de l'atelier d'Aphrati." In *Shapes and Uses of Greek Vases (7th-4th centuries B.C.),* edited by A. Tsingarida, 137–51. Brussels.
Brisart, T. 2011. *Un art citoyen. Recherches sur l'orientalisation des artisanats en Grèce proto-archaïque.* Brussels.
Brock, J. K., and Young, G. M. 1949. "Excavations in Siphnos." *ABSA* 44:1–92.
Brock, R. 1991. "The Emergence of Democratic Ideology." *Historia* 40.2:160–9.
Brock, R. 2009. "Did the Athenian Empire Promote Democracy?" In *Interpreting the Athenian Empire,* edited by J. Ma, N. Papazarkadas, and R. C. T. Parker, 149–66. London.
Brock, R., and Hodkinson, S., eds. 2000. *Alternatives to Athens. Varieties of Political Organization and Community in Ancient Greece.* Oxford.
Broodbank, C. 2013. *The Making of the Middle Sea. A History of the Mediterranean from the Beginning to the Emergence of the Classical World.* London.
Broughton, T. R. S. 1938. "Roman Asia Minor." In *An Economic Survey of Ancient Rome,* vol. 4, edited by T. Frank, 499–918. Baltimore.
Brown, P. 1971. *The World of Late Antiquity AD 150–750.* London.
Broux, Y. 2013. "Creating a New Local Elite: The Establishment of the Metropolitan Orders of Roman Egypt." *APF* 59.1:143–53.
Brunet, M. 1992. "Campagnes de la Grèce antique: le danger du prisme athénien." *Topoi* 2:33–51.
Brown, P. 1978. *The Making of Late Antiquity.* Cambridge, MA.
Brown, P. 1992. *Power and Persuasion in Late Antiquity. Towards a Christian Empire.* Madison, WI.
Brown, P. 2001. *Poverty and Leadership in the Later Roman Empire.* Hanover, NH.
Brown, P. 2013. "From Civic Euergetism to Christian Giving: The Parameters of a Change." In *Religiöser Alltag in der Spätantike,* edited by P. Eich and E. Faber, 23–30. Stuttgart.
Bruhns, H. 1987–89. "La cité antique de Max Weber." In *La cité antique? À partir de l'œuvre de M. I. Finley,* edited by J. Andreau and F. Hartog, 29–42. Florence.
Bruhns, H. 2014. *Max Webers historische Sozialökonomie. L'économie de Max Weber entre histoire et sociologie.* Wiesbaden.
Brulé, P. 2005. "'La cité est la somme des maisons.' Un commentaire religieux." In Ἰδίᾳ καὶ δημοσίᾳ. *Les cadres 'privés' et 'publics' de la religion grecque antique,* edited by V. Dasen and M. Piérart, 27–53. Liège.
Brun, P. 1988. "Mytilène et Athènes au IVème siècle av. J. C." *REA* 90:373–84.
Brun, P. 1989. "L'île de Kéos et ses cités au IVᵉ siècle av. J. C." *ZPE* 76:121–38.
Brun, P., Capdetrey, L., and Fröhlich, P., eds. 2021. *L'Asie mineure occidentale au IIIe siècle a.C.* Bordeaux.
Brunet, M. 1992. "Campagnes de la Grèce antique: le danger du prisme athénien." *Topoi* 2:33–51.
Brunet, M., ed. 1999. *Territoires des cités grecques.* Paris.
Brunet, M. et al. 2019. *Thasos. Heurs et malheurs d'un Eldorado antique.* Paris.
Brunt, P. A. 1990. *Roman Imperial Themes.* Oxford.
Brunt, P. A. 1993. *Studies in Greek History and Thought.* Oxford.
Brunt, P. A. 1994. "The Bubble of the Second Sophistic." *BICS* 39:25–52.
Bryen, A. Z. 2018. *Violence in Roman Egypt. A Study in Legal Interpretation.* Philadelphia.
Bryen, A. Z. 2019. "Politics, Justice, and Reform in Dio's *Euboicus.*" *TAPhA* 149.1:127–48.
Buchner, G., and Ridgway, D. 1993. *Pithekoussai I.* Rome.
Buck, R. J. 1979. *A History of Boeotia.* Edmonton.
Buckler, J. 2003. *Aegean Greece in the Fourth Century BC.* Leiden.
Buckler, J., and Beck, H., 2008. *Central Greece and the Politics of Power in the Fourth Century BC.* Cambridge.
Budelmann, F., ed. 2009. *The Cambridge Companion to Greek Lyric.* Cambridge.

Bugh, G. 2013. "Democracy in the Hellenistic World." In *Belonging and Isolation in the Hellenistic World*, edited by S. L. Ager and R. A. Faber, 111–28. Toronto.

Bultrighini, U., ed. 2005. *Democrazia e antidemocrazia nel mondo greco, Atti del Convegno internazionale di studi*. Alessandria.

Buondelmonti, C. 2018. *Description of the Aegean and Other Islands*. Edited and translated by E. Edon. New York.

Buraselis, K. 2000. *Kos between Hellenism and Rome. Studies on the Political, Institutional and Social History of Kos from ca. the Middle Second Century B.C. until Late Antiquity*. Philadelphia.

Buraselis, K. 2007. *ΘΕΙΑ ΔΩΡΕΑ. Das göttlich-kaiserliche Geschenk: Studien zur Politik der Severer und zur Constitutio Antoniniana*. Vienna.

Burckhardt, J. 1994. *The Greeks and Greek Civilization*. Edited by O. Murray, translated by S. Stern. London.

Burckhardt, J. 2002. *Griechische Culturgeschichte. Die Griechen und ihr Mythus. Die Polis*. Edited by L. Burckhardt, B. von Reibnitz, and J. von Ungern-Sternberg. Munich.

Burckhardt, N. 2012. "Topographische Studie zu den geometrischen Siedlungen der Kykladen—Struktur und Entwicklung der Wohn- und Sakralbauten, Wehranlagen und Grabbezirke." In *Werkraum Antike. Beiträge zur Archäologie und antiken Baugeschichte*, edited by H. Svenshon, M. Boos, and F. Lang, 1–40. Darmstadt.

Buresch, K. 1849. "Die griechischen Trostbeschlüsse." *RhM* 49:424–60.

Burford, A. 1971. "The Purpose of Inscribed Building Accounts." In *Acts of the 5th International Congress of Greek and Latin Epigraphy, Cambridge 1967*. 71–76. Oxford.

Burkert, W. 1965. "Demaratos, Astrabakos und Herakles. Königsmythos und Politik zur Zeit der Perserkriege (Herodot VI, 67–69)." *MH* 22.3:166–77.

Burnett, A. 2011. "The Augustan Revolution Seen from the Mints of the Provinces." *JRS* 101:1–30.

Burns, R. 2017. *Origins of the Colonnaded Streets in the Cities of the Roman East*. Oxford.

Burrell, B. 2004. *Neokoroi. Greek Cities and Roman Emperors*. Leiden.

Burton, G. P. 2000. "The Resolution of Territorial Disputes in the Provinces of the Roman Empire." *Chiron* 30:195–216.

Burton, G. P. 2001. "The Imperial State and its Impact on the Role and Status of Local Magistrates and Councillors in the Provinces of the Empire." In *Administration, Prosopography and Appointment Policies in the Roman Empire*, edited by L. de Blois, 202–14. Amsterdam.

Burton, G. P. 2002. "The Roman Imperial State (A.D. 14–235). Evidence and Reality." *Chiron* 32:249–80.

Burton, G. P. 2004. "The Roman Imperial State, Provincial Governors and the Public Finances of Provincial Cities, 27 B.C.–A.D. 235." *Historia* 53.3:311–42.

Burton, P. J. 2011. *Friendship and Empire: Roman Diplomacy and Imperialism in the Middle Republic (353–146 BC)*. Cambridge.

Butcher, K. 2003. *Roman Syria and the Near East*. Los Angeles.

Butcher, K. 2004. *Coinage in Roman Syria: Northern Syria, 64 BC–AD 253*. London.

Butler, H. C. 1919. *Syria: Publications of the Princeton University Archaeological Expeditions to Syria in 1904–1905 and 1909. Architecture. Section A: Southern Syria*. Leiden.

Cabanes, P. 1976. *L'Épire de la mort de Pyrrhos à la conquête romaine, 272-167 av. J.C.* Paris.

Cabouret, B. 2007. "Les élites urbaines d'Antioche et de Syrie du Nord au IVe siècle." *Topoi (Lyon)* 15:319–41.

Caciagli, S. 2011. *Poeti e società. Comunicazione poetica e formazioni sociali nella Lesbo del VII/VI secolo a. C.* Amsterdam.

Caesar, M. 2011. *Le pouvoir en ville. Gestion urbaine et pratiques politiques à Genève (fin XIIIe-début XVIe siècles)*. Turnhout.

Cahill, N. 2002. *Household and City Organization at Olynthus*. New Haven.

Caillet, J.-P., Destephen, S., Dumézil, B., and Inglebert, H., eds. 2015. *Des dieux civiques aux saints patrons (IVe-VIIe siècle)*. Paris.

Calame, C. 1977. *Les chœurs de jeunes filles en Grèce archaïque*, vols. 1-2. Rome.

Calame, C. 1996. "Sappho's Group: An Initiation into Womanhood." In *Reading Sappho. Contemporary Approaches*, edited by E. Greene, 113–24. Berkeley.

Calame, C. 2001. *Choruses of Young Women in Ancient Greece. Their Morphology, Religious Role, and Social Functions*. Translated by D. Collins and J. Orion. Lanham, MD.

Camassa, G. 1993. "Le istituzioni greche e il nostro tempo storico." *QS* 37:29–41.

Cambiano, G. 2000. *Polis. Un modello per la cultura europea*. Bari.

Cameron, A. 2016. *Wandering Poets and Other Essays on Late Greek Literature and Philosophy*. Oxford.
Camia, F. 2007. "I *curatores rei publicae* nella provincia d'Acaia." *MEFRA* 119.2:409–19.
Camia, F. 2008. "Imperial Priests in Second Century Greece: A Socio-Political Analysis." In *Pathways to Power. Civic Elites in the Eastern Part of the Roman Empire*, edited by D. Rizakis and F. Camia, 23–42. Athens.
Camia, F. 2009. *Roma e le poleis. L'intervento di Roma nelle controversie territoriali tra le comunità greche di Grecia e d'Asia Minore nel secondo secolo a.C.: le testimonianze epigrafiche*. Athens.
Camia, F. 2011. Theoi Sebastoi. *Il culto degli imperatori romani in Grecia (Provincia Achaia) nel secondo secolo D.C.* Athens.
Camia, F. 2016. "Between Tradition and Innovation: Cults for Roman Emperors in the Province of Achaia." In *Kaiserkult in den Provinzen des Römischen Reiches. Organisation, Kommunikation und Repräsentation*, edited by A. Kolb and M. Vitale, 255–84. Berlin.
Camp II, J. McK. 2010. *The Athenian Agora. Site Guide*. Princeton.
Campanile, M. D. 1994. *I sacerdoti del koinon d'Asia (I sec. a. C.-III sec. d. C.). Contributo allo studio della romanizzazione delle élites provinciali nell'Oriente greco*. Pisa.
Campanile, M. D. 1996. "Città d'Asia Minore tra Mitridate e Roma." In *Studi Ellenistici* 8:145–73.
Campanile, M. D. 2001. "Ancora sul culto imperiale in Asia." *MediterrAnt* 4.2:473–88.
Campanile, M. D. 2003a. "L'infanzia della provincia d'Asia: l'origine dei *conventus iuridici* nella provincia." In *Gli stati territoriali nel mondo antico*, edited by C. Bearzot, F. Landucci Gattinoni, and G. Zecchini, 271–88. Milan.
Campanile, M. D. 2003b. "Note sullo studio delle élites locali nelle province orientali in età romana: l'esempio dell'Asia." *RCCM* 45.2:307–16.
Campanile, M. D. 2016. "Stoicismo e propensione evergetica in età romana." *MediterrAnt* 19.1:145–55.
Canali di Rossi, F. 1997. *Le ambascerie dal mondo greco a Roma in età repubblicana*. Rome.
Caner, D. F. 2020. "Bishops and the Politics of Lithomania in Early Byzantium." In *Benefactors and the Polis. The Public Gift in the Greek Cities from the Homeric World to Late Antiquity*, edited by M. Domingo Gygax and A. Zuiderhoek, 267–96. Cambridge.
Canevaro, M. 2017. "The Popular Culture of the Athenian Institutions: 'Authorized' Popular Culture and 'Unauthorized' Elite Culture in Classical Athens." In *Popular Culture in the Ancient World*, edited by L. Grig, 39–65. Cambridge.
Canevaro, M. 2018a. "Demosthenic Influences in Early Rhetorical Education: Hellenistic *Rhetores* and Athenian Imagination." In *The Hellenistic Reception of Classical Athenian Democracy and Political Thought*, edited by M. Canevaro and B. Gray, 73–92. Oxford.
Canevaro, M. 2018b. "Majority Rule vs. Consensus: The Practice of Democratic Deliberation in the Greek Poleis." In *Ancient Greek History and Contemporary Social Science*, edited by M. Canevaro, A. Erskine, B. Gray, and J. Ober, 101–56. Edinburgh.
Canevaro, M. 2018c. "The Public Charge for Hubris Against Slaves: The Honour of the Victim and the Honour of the Hubristēs." *JHS* 138:100–26.
Canevaro, M. 2020. "La délibération démocratique à l'Assemblée athénienne: procédures et stratégies de légitimation." *Annales (HSS)* 74.2:339–81.
Canevaro, M. 2021. "Upside-down Hegemony? Ideology and Power in Ancient Athens." In *Antonio Gramsci and the Ancient World*, edited by E. Zucchetti and A. Cimino, 63–85. London.
Cantineau. J. 1935. *Grammaire du palmyrénien épigraphique*. Cairo.
Capdetrey, L. 2007. *Le pouvoir séleucide. Territoire, administration, finances d'un royaume hellénistique (312-129 avant J.-C.)*. Rennes.
Capdetrey, L., and Zurbach, J., eds. 2012. *Mobilités grecques. Mouvements, réseaux, contacts en Méditerranée, de l'époque archaïque à l'époque hellénistique*. Bordeaux.
Capogrossi Colognesi, L. 1995. "The Limits of the Ancient City and The Evolution of the Medieval City in the Thought of Max Weber." In *Urban Society in Roman Italy*, edited by T. J. Cornell and K. Lomas, 27–37. London.
Capogrossi Colognesi, L. 2000. *Max Weber und die Wirtschaft der Antike*. Göttingen.
Carbon. J.-M. 2013. "Dolphin-Pillars." *EA* 46:27–34.
Carbon, J.-M. and Clackson, J. P. T. 2016. "Arms and the Boy: On the New Festival Calendar from Arkadia." *Kernos* 29:119–58.
Carey, C., Giannadaki, I., and Griffith-Williams, B., eds. 2019. *Use and Abuse of Law in the Athenian Courts*. Leiden.
Carlier, P. 1984. *La royauté en Grèce avant Alexandre*. Strasbourg.

Carlier, P., ed. 1996. *Le IV*ᵉ *s. av. J.-C. Approches historiographiques*. Nancy.
Carlier, P. 2005. "Démocratie et oligarchie dans la *Politique* d'Aristote. Quelques observations." In *Democrazia e antidemocrazia nel mondo greco*, edited by U. Bultrighini, 263–75. Alessandria.
Carlsson, S. 2004. "Koan Democracy in Context." In *The Hellenistic Polis of Kos. State, Economy and Culture*, edited by K. Höghammar, 109–18. Uppsala.
Carstens, A. M. 2009. *Karia and the Hekatomnids. The Creation of a Dynasty*. Oxford.
Carter, J. C. 1983. *The Sculpture of the Sanctuary of Athena Polias at Priene*. London.
Carter, J. C. 1990. "Metapontum-Land, Wealth, and Population." In Butcher, K. 2004. *Coinage in Roman Syria: Northern Syria, 64 BC–AD 253*. London.
Carter, J. C. 2006. *Discovering the Greek Countryside at Metaponto*. Ann Arbor, MI.
Carter, J. C., Morter, J., and Parmly Toxey, A. 1998. *The Chora of Metaponto. The Necropoleis*. Austin.
Carter, D. M. 2011. *Why Athens? A Reappraisal of Tragic Politics*. Oxford.
Cartledge, P. 1978. "Literacy in the Spartan Oligarchy." *JHS* 98:25–37.
Cartledge, P. 1987. *Agesilaos and the Crisis of Sparta*. London.
Cartledge, P. 1993. "Like a Worm I' the Bud? A Heterology of Classical Greek Slavery." *G&R* 40.2:163–80.
Cartledge, P. 2000. "Boiotian Swine F(or)ever? The Boiotian Superstate 395 BC." In *Polis & Politics: Studies in Ancient Greek History Presented to Mogens Herman Hansen on His Sixtieth Birthday*, edited by P. Flensted-Jensen, T. Heine Nielsen and L. Rubinstein, 397–415. Copenhagen.
Cartledge, P. 2002a. *Sparta and Lakonia. A Regional History 1300-362 B.C.* 2nd ed. London and New York.
Cartledge, P. 2002b. *The Greeks. A Portrait of Self and Others*. 2nd ed. Oxford.
Cartledge, P. 2009. *Ancient Greek Political Thought in Practice*. Cambridge.
Cartledge, P. 2012. *Ancient Greek Political Thought in Practice*. Cambridge.
Cartledge, P. 2016. *Democracy. A Life*. Oxford.
Cartledge, P., and Spawforth, A. 2002. *Hellenistic and Roman Sparta. A Tale of Two Cities*. 2nd ed. London.
Carty, A. 2015. *Polycrates, Tyrant of Samos. New Light on Archaic Greece*. Stuttgart.
Carugati, F. 2019. *Creating a Constitution. Law, Democracy, and Growth in Ancient Athens*. Princeton.
Carusi, C. 2003. *Isole e Peree in Asia Minore. Contributi allo studio dei rapporti tra* poleis *insulari e territori continentali dipendenti*. Pisa.
Cassayre, A. 2010. *La justice dans les cités grecques. De la formation des royaumes hellénistiques au legs d'Attale*. Rennes.
Cassella, M. 2010. *Storie di ordinaria corruzione. Libanio, Orazioni LVI, LVII, XLVI*. Messina.
Castelli, T. 2017. "La chronologie des éponymes rhodiens de la fin du IIIᵉ s. et du premier tiers du IIᵉ s. nouvelles hypothèses." *REA* 119.1:3–24.
Castells, M. 2019. *Rupture. The Crisis of Liberal Democracy*. Cambridge.
Castoriadis, C. 2008. *La cité et les lois. Ce qui fait la Grèce 2*. Paris.
Cataldi, S. 2018. Polis ekkletos. *Scritti scelti su Atene antica*. Alessandria.
Cataldi, S., Bianco, E., and Cuniberti, G., eds. 2012. *Salvare le* poleis, *costruire la concordia, progettare la pace*. Alessandria.
Cavanagh, W., Crouwel, J., Catling, R. W. V., and Shipley, G., eds. 2002. *Continuity and Change in a Greek Rural Landscape. The Laconia Survey*. Vol. 1. *Methodology and Interpretation*. London.
Caven, B. 1990. *Dionysius I. Warlord of Sicily*. New Haven.
Cawkwell, G. L. 1996. "The End of Greek Liberty." In *Transitions to Empire. Essays in Greco-Roman History, 360-146 B.C. in Honor of E. Badian*, edited by R. W. Wallace and E. M. Harris, 98–121. Norman, OK.
Cawkwell, G. 2011. *Cyrene to Chaeronea: Selected Essays on Ancient Greek History*. Oxford.
Ceccarelli, P. 1996. "L' Athènes de Périclès: un 'Pays de cocagne'? L'idéologie démocratique et l'αὐτόματος βίος dans la comédie ancienne." *QUCC* 54.3:109–59.
Ceccarelli, P. 2010. "Changing Contexts: Tragedy in the Civic and Cultural Life of Hellenistic City-States." In *Beyond the Fifth Century. Interaction with Greek Tragedy from the Fourth Century BC to the Middle Ages*, edited by I. Gildenhard and M. Revermann, 99–150. Berlin.
Cecchet, L. 2017. "Re-shaping and Re-founding Citizen Bodies: The Case of Athens, Cyrene and Camarina." In *Citizens in the Graeco-Roman World. Aspects of Citizenship from the Archaic period to AD 212*, edited by L. Cecchet and A. Busetto, 50–77. Leiden.
Chakrabarti, D. K. 2000. "Mahajanapada States of Early Historic India." In *A Comparative Study of Thirty City-State Cultures*, edited by M. H. Hansen, 375–91. Copenhagen.

Champion, C. D. 2006. "Review Article—Classical Republicans: Greek and Roman, Ancient and Modern." *Polis* 23.2:387–98.
Champion, C. D. 2007. "Empire by Invitation: Greek Political Strategies and Roman Imperial Interventions in the Second Century B.C.E." *TAPhA* 137.2:255–75.
Chandezon, C. 2003. *L'élevage en Grèce (fin V^e-fin Ier s. a.C.). L'apport des sources épigraphiques.* Bordeaux.
Chandezon, C. 2006-7. "Plutarque et Chéronée. Notes de lecture d'un historien." *Ploutarchos* 4:103–12.
Chandezon, C. 2013. "Les petites cités et leur vie économique. Ou: comment avoir les moyens d'être une *polis*?" *Topoi (Lyon)* 18.1:37–65.
Chandezon, C. 2014. "L'*ekhthra* dans les *Oneirokritika* d'Artémidore de Daldis. Contribution à une réflexion sur l'inimitié et les réseaux dans la société grecque." In *La représentation négative de l'autre dans l'Antiquité. Hostilité, réprobation, dépréciation*, edited by A. Queyrel Bottineau, 23–39. Dijon.
Chaniotis, A. 1995. "Sich selbst feiern? Städtische Feste des Hellenismus im Spannungsfeld von Religion und Politik." In *Stadtbild und Bürgerbild im Hellenismus*, edited by P. Zanker and M. Wörrle, 147–72. Munich.
Chaniotis, A. 1996. *Die Verträge zwischen kretischen Poleis in der hellenistischen Zeit.* Stuttgart.
Chaniotis, A. 1997. Review of M. H. Hansen, *Introduction to an Inventory of 'Poleis'* (Copenhagen, 1996); and M. Hansen and Kurt Raaflaub, eds., *More Studies in the Ancient Greek "Polis"* (Stuttgart, 1996). *BMCR* 1997.07.16.
Chaniotis, A. 2000. "Hellenistic Lasaia (Crete): A Dependent Polis of Gortyn. New Epigraphic Evidence from the Asklepieion near Lasaia." Ευλιμένη 1:55–60.
Chaniotis, A. 2003. "Der Kaiserkult im Osten des Römischen Reiches im Kontext der zeitgenössischen Ritualpraxis." In *Die Praxis der Herrscherverehrung in Rom und seinen Provinzen*, edited by H. Cancik and K. Hitzl, 3–28. Tübingen.
Chaniotis, A. 2005a. *War in the Hellenistic World. A Social and Cultural History.* Malden, MA.
Chaniotis, A. 2005b. "Macht und Volk in den kaiserzeitlichen Inschriften von Aphrodisias." In *Popolo e potere nel mondo antico*, edited by G. Urso, 47–61. Pisa.
Chaniotis, A., ed. 2012. *Unveiling Emotions. Sources and Methods for the Study of Emotions in the Greek World.* Stuttgart.
Chaniotis, A. 2013. "Processions in Hellenistic Cities. Contemporary Discourses and Ritual Dynamics." In *Cults, Creeds and Identities in the Greek City after the Classical Age*, edited by R. Alston, O. M. van Nijf, and C. G. Williamson, 21–47. Leuven.
Chaniotis, A. 2018. *Age of Conquests. The Greek World from Alexander to Hadrian.* Cambridge, MA.
Chankowski, A. S. 1998. "La procédure législative à Pergame au Ier siècle au J.-C.: à propos de la chronologie relative des décrets en l'honneur de Diodoros Pasparos." *BCH* 122.1:159–99.
Chankowski, A. S. 2005. "Processions et cérémonies d'accueil: une image de la cité de la basse époque hellénistique?" In *Citoyenneté et participation à la basse époque hellénistique*, edited by P. Fröhlich and C. Müller, 185–206. Geneva.
Chankowski, A. S. 2011. *L'Éphébie hellénistique: étude d'une institution civique dans les cités grecques des îles de la Mer Égée et de l'Asie Mineure.* Paris.
Chankowksi, V. 2019. *Parasites du dieu. Comptables, financiers et commerçants dans la Délos hellénistique.* Athens.
Chankowski, V., and Karvonis, P., eds. 2012. *Tout vendre, tout acheter. Structures et équipements des marchés antiques.* Bordeaux.
Charalambidou, X. 2018. "Iron Age Mortuary Practices and Material Culture at the Inland Cemetery of Tsikalario on Naxos: Differentiation and Connectivity." *ABSA* 113:143–98.
Chatzidimitriou, A., and Chidiroglou, M. 2014. "Ancient Towers in Central and Southern Euboea." In *Meditations on the Diversity of the Built Environment in the Aegean Basin and Beyond*, edited by D. W. Rupp and J. E. Tomlinson, 311–37. Athens.
Childs, W. A. P. and Demargne, P. 1989. *Le monument des Néréides: le décor sculpté* (Fouilles de Xanthos 8). Paris.
Chin, M. J. H. 2018. "OGIS 332 and Civic Authority at Pergamon in the Reign of Attalos III." *ZPE* 208:121–37.
Chirica, E. 2005. "Funérailles publiques et enterrement au gymnase à l'époque hellénistique." In *Citoyenneté et participation à la basse époque hellénistique*, edited by P. Fröhlich and C. Müller, 207–23. Geneva.
Choremi-Spetsieri, A., and Tinginanka, I., eds. 2008. "Η βιβλιοθήκη του Αδριανού στην Αθήνα. Τα ανασκαφικά δεδομένα." In *Η Αθήνα κατά τη Ρωμαϊκή εποχή. Πρόσφατες ανακαλύψεις, νέες έρευνες / Athens During the Roman Period. Recent Discoveries, New Evidence*, edited by S. Vlizos, 115–32. Athens.
Christ, M. R. 1998. "Legal Self-help on Private Property in Classical Athens." *AJPh* 119.4:521–45.

Christ, M. R. 2006. *The Bad Citizen in Classical Athens*. Cambridge.
Christ, M. R. 2007. "The Evolution of the *Eisphora* in Classical Athens." *CQ* 57.1:53–69.
Christol, M., and Drew-Bear, T. 1995. "Inscriptions militaires d'Aulutrene et d'Apamée de Phrygie." In *La hiérarchie (Rangordnung) de l'armée romaine sous le Haut-Empire*, edited by Y. Le Bohec, 57–92. Paris.
Christophilopoulou, A. 2007. "Domestic space in the Geometric Cyclades. A Study of Spatial Arrangements, Function and Household Activities in Zagora on Andros and Kastro on Siphnos." In *Proceedings of the Danish Institute at Athens*, vol. 5, edited by E. Hallager and J. T. Jensen, 23–34. Athens.
Chwe, M. S.-Y. 2001. *Rational Ritual. Culture, Coordination, and Common Knowledge*. Princeton.
Civiletti, M. 2002. *Filostrato. Vite dei Sofisti. Introduzione, traduzione e note*. Milan.
Clairmont, C. W. 1983. *Patrios nomos. Public Burial in Athens During the Fifth and Fourth Centuries B.C. The Archaeological, Epigraphic-Literary, and Historical Evidence*. Oxford.
Clancier, P. 2017. "The Polis of Babylon: A Historiographical Approach." In *Hellenism and the Local Communities of the Eastern Mediterranean, 400BCE-250CE*, edited by B. Chrubasik and D. King, 53–81. Oxford.
Clarke, K. 1999. *Between Geography and History: Hellenistic Constructions of the Roman World*. Oxford.
Clarke, K. 2008. *Making Time for the Past. Local History and the Polis*. Oxford and New York.
Clastres, P. 1974. *La société contre l'État. Recherches d'anthropologie politique*. Paris.
Claudon, J.-F. 2015. "Les ambassadeurs des cités d'Asie mineure envoyés à Rome." In *La diplomatie romaine sous la République. Réflexions sur une pratique*, edited by B. Grass and G. Strouder, 127–45. Besançon.
Clements, P. 2012. *Rawlsian Political Analysis. Rethinking the Microfoundations of Social Sciences*. Notre Dame, IN.
Cline, E. H. 2021. *1177 B.C.: The Year Civilization Collapsed*. Princeton.
Coarelli, F. 2005. "L'Agora des Italiens': lo statarion di Delo?" *JRA* 18:196–212.
Coarelli, F. 2014. "Delo, la Siria e il commercio degli schiavi." In *Fare storia antica*, 209–13. Rome.
Cobet, J., von Graeve, V., Niemeier, W.-D, Zimmermann, K. 2007. *Frühes Ionien. Eine Bestandsaufname*. Mainz.
Cohen, A. and Rutter, J. B. 2007. *Constructions of Childhood in Ancient Greece and Italy*. Princeton.
Cohen, D. 1989. "Seclusion, Separation, and the Status of Women in Classical Athens." *G&R* 36.1:3–15.
Cohen, D. 1995. *Law, Violence, and Community in Classical Athens*. Cambridge.
Cohen, E. E. 2000. *The Athenian Nation*. Princeton.
Cohen, G. M. 1995. *The Hellenistic Settlements in Europe, the Islands, and Asia Minor*. Berkeley.
Cohen, G. M. 2006. *The Hellenistic Settlements in Syria, the Red Sea Basin, and North Africa*. Berkeley.
Cohen, G. M. 2013. *The Hellenistic Settlements in the East from Armenia and Mesopotamia to Bactria and India*. Berkeley.
Coldstream, J. N. 1976. "Hero-cults in the Age of Homer." *JHS* 96:8–17.
Coldstream, J. N. 1983. "The Meaning of the Regional Styles in the Eighth Century BC." In *The Greek Renaissance of the Eighth Century BC. Tradition and Innovation*, edited by R. Hägg, 17–25. Stockholm.
Coldstream, J. N. 1984. *The Formation of the Greek Polis. Aristotle and Archaeology* Düsseldorf.
Coldstream, J. N. 2003. *Geometric Greece: 900–700 BC*. 2nd edition. London and New York.
Colin, J. 1965. *Les villes libres de l'Orient gréco-romain et l'envoi au supplice par acclamations populaires*. Brussels.
Colledge, M. A. R. 1976. *The Art of Palmyra*. London.
Comparette, T. L. 1906. "The Reorganization of the Municipal Administration under the Antonines." *AJPh* 27.2:166–83.
Congiu, M., Micchiché, C., and Modeo, S., eds. 2011. *Timoleonte e la Sicilia della seconda metà del IV sec. a.C.* Caltanisetta.
Connell, C. 1980. *In the Bee-loud Glade. A Study with Drawings of Greek Village Life on the Southern Cycladic Islands of Amorgos, Donoussa, Schinoussa and Irakleia*. Nauplion.
Connelly, J. B. 2007. *Portrait of a Priestess. Women and Ritual in Ancient Greece*. Princeton.
Connolly, S. 2010. *Lives behind the Laws. The World of the Codex Hermogenianus*. Bloomington, IN.
Connor, W. R. 1987. "Tribes, Festivals and Processions: Civic Ceremonial and Political Manipulation in Archaic Greece." *JHS* 107:40–50.
Connor, W. R. 1993. "The Ionian Era of Athenian Civic Identity." *PAPhS* 137.2:194–206.
Connor, W. R. 1996. "Civil Society, Dionysiac Festival, and the Athenian Democracy." In *Demokratia. A Conversation on Democracies, Ancient and Modern*, edited by J. Ober and C. Hedrick, 217–26. Princeton.
Constant, B. 1980. *De la liberté chez les modernes. Écrits politiques*. Edited by M. Gauchet. Paris.
Constant, B. 1988. *Constant. Political Writings*. Edited and translated by B. Fontana. Cambridge.

Constant, B. 2017. *Œuvres*, vol. 15. *Brochures politiques 1819–1821*. Edited by by K. Kloocke and P. Delbouille. Berlin.
Constantakopoulou, C. 2007. *The Dance of the Islands: Insularity, Networks, the Athenian Empire, and the Aegean World*. Oxford.
Constantakopoulou, C. 2012. "Beyond the Polis: Island Koina and Other Non-Polis Entities in the Aegean." *REA* 114.2:301–21.
Constantakopoulou, C. 2015. "Beyond the Polis: Island *Koina* and Other Non-Polis Entities in the Aegean." In *Communities and Networks in the Ancient Greek World*, edited by Claire Taylor and Kostas Vlassopoulos, 213–36. Oxford.
Constantakopoulou, C. 2007. *The Dance of the Islands. Insularity, Networks, the Athenian Empire, and the Aegean World*. Oxford.
Contamine, P. 1992. *La guerre de Cent Ans*. Paris.
Corbier, M. 1985. "Fiscalité et dépenses locales." In *L'origine des richesses dépensées dans la ville antique*, edited by P. Leveau, 219–32. Aix-en-Provence.
Cordovana, O. M., and Galli, M., eds. 2007. *Arte e memoria culturale nell'età della Seconda Sofistica*. Catania.
Corsaro, M. 2010. "Il nomos di Agirrio e la tassazione diretta del grano nel mondo greco." In *Nuove ricerche sulla legge granaria ateniese del 374/3 a.C.*, edited by A. Magnetto, D. Erdas, and C. Carusi, 99–128. Pisa.
Corsten, T. 1999. *Vom Stamm zum Bund. Gründung und territoriale Organisation griechischer Bundesstaaten*. Munich.
Corsten, T. 2016. "Bauer und Bürger. Einflussmöglichkeiten von Landbesitzern auf das städtische Leben im kaiserzeitlichen Kleinasien." In *Propriétaires et citoyens dans l'Orient romain*, edited by F. Lerouxel and A.-V. Pont, 261–73. Bordeaux.
Costabile, F. 1992. *Polis ed Olympieion a Locri Epizefiri. Costituzione, economia e finanze di una città della Magna Grecia. Editio altera e traduzione delle tabelle locresi*. Soveria Mannelli.
Cottier, M., Crawford, M. H., Crowther, C. V., Ferrary, J.-L., Levick, B. M., Salomies, O., and Wörrle, M., eds. 2008. *The Customs Law of Asia*. Oxford.
Cordano, F. 1992. *Le tessere pubbliche dal Tempio di Atena a Camarina*. Rome.
Cordano, F. 2011. *Camarina. Politica e istituzioni di una città greca*. Tivoli.
Cormack, S. 2004. *The Space of Death in Roman Asia Minor*. Wien.
Coucouzeli, A. 2007. "From megaron to *oikos* at Zagora." In *Building Communities. House, Settlement and Society in the Aegean and Beyond*, edited by R. Westgate, N. Fisher, and J. Whitley, 169–81. London.
Coudin, F. 2009. *Les Laconiens et la Méditerranée à l'époque archaïque*. Naples.
Coudry, M., and Kirbihler, F. 2010. "La *lex Cornelia*, une *lex provinciae* de Sylla pour l'Asie." In *Administrer les provinces de la République romaine*, edited by N. Barrandon and F. Kirbihler, 133–69. Rennes.
Coulson, W. D. E. 1990. *The Greek Dark Ages. A Review of the Evidence and Suggestions for Future Research*. Athens.
Coulton, J. J. 1977. *Ancient Greek Architects at Work. Problems of Structure and Design*. Ithaca.
Couvenhes, J.-C., Crouzet, S., and Péré-Noguès, S., eds. 2011. *Pratiques et identités culturelles des armées hellénistiques du monde méditerranéen*. Bordeaux.
Couvenhes, J.-C., Milanezi, S., eds. 2007. *Individus, groupes et politique à Athènes de Solon à Mithridate*. Tours.
Cracco Ruggini, L. 1987. "La città romana d'età imperiale." In *Modelli di città*, edited by P. Rossi, 127–52. Turin.
Crawford, M. 1977, "Rome and the Greek World: Economic Relationships," *Economic History Review* 30: 42–52.
Crielaard, J. P. 1995. "Homer, History and Archaeology: Some Remarks on the Date of the Homeric World." In *Homeric Questions. Essays in Philology, Ancient History and Archeology*, edited by J.-P. Crielaard, 202–86. Gieben.
Crielaard, J. P. 1998. "Cult and Death in Early 7th-century Euboea: The Aristocracy and the Polis." In *Nécropoles et pouvoir. Idéologies, pratiques et interpretations*, edited by S. Marchegay, M.-T. Le Dinahet, and J.-F. Salles, 43–58. Lyon.
Crielaard, J. P. 2006. "*Basileis* at Sea: Elites and External Contacts in the Euboean Gulf Region from the End of the Bronze Age to the Beginning of the Iron Age." In *Ancient Greece. From the Mycenaean Palaces to the Age of Homer*, edited by S. Deger-Jalkotzy and I. S. Lemos, 271–97. Edinburgh.
Crielaard, J. P. 2007. "Eretria's West Cemetery Revisited: Burial Plots, Social Structure and Settlement Organization During the 8th and 7th Centuries BC." In *Oropos and Euboea in the Early Iron Age*, edited by A. Mazarakis-Ainian, 169–94. Volos.
Crielaard, J. P. 2009a. "The Ionians in the Archaic Period: Shifting Identities in a Changing World." In *Ethnic Constructs in Antiquity. The Role of Power and Tradition*, edited by T. Derks and N. Roymans, 37–84. Amsterdam.

Crielaard, J. P. 2009b. "Cities." In *A Companion to Archaic Greece*, edited by K. A. Raaflaub and H. van Wees, 347–72. Malden, MA.

Crogier-Pétrequin, S., ed. 2014. *Le monde romain de 70 av. J.-C. à 73 apr. J.-C.* Paris.

Croissant, F. 2008. "Batailles géométriques pariennes." In *Alba della città, alba delle immagini*, 31–62. Athens.

Crowther, C. V. 1990. "Iasos in the Second Century BC II: The Chronology of the Theatre Lists." *BICS* 37:143–51.

Crowther, C. V. 1995. "Iasos in the Second Century BC III: Foreign Judges from Priene." *BICS* 40:91–138.

Crowther, C. V. 1996. "I. Priene 8 and the History of Priene in the Early Hellenistic Period." *Chiron* 26:195–250.

Crowther, C. V. 1997. "Inscriptions from the Sparta and Larissa Museums." *ABSA* 92:345–58.

Crowther, C. V. 2007a. "Foreign Judges and Regional Variations in Hellenistic Asia Minor." In *Regionalism in Hellenistic and Roman Asia Minor*, edited by H. Elton and G. Reger, 53–59. Pessac.

Crowther, C. V. 2007b. "The Dionysia at Iasos: Its Artists, Patrons and Audience." In *The Greek Theatre and Festivals. Documentary Studies*, edited by P. J. Wilson, 294–334. Oxford.

Csapo, E. 2007. "The Men Who Built the Theatres: *Theatropolai, Theatronai*, and *Arkhitektones*." *The Greek Theatre and Festivals. Documentary Studies*, edited by P. J. Wilson, 87–121. Oxford.

Csapo, E., and Wilson, P. 2020. *A Social and Economic History of the Theatre to 300 B.C.* Cambridge.

Culasso Gastaldi, E., ed. 2004. *La Prassi della democrazia ad Atene*. Turin.

Curty, O. 1995 *Les parentés légendaires entre cités grecques: Catalogue raisonné des inscriptions contenant le terme συγγένεια et analyse critique*. Geneva.

Cuscunà, C. 2004. "Le *poleis* siceliote tra autonomia ed egemonia nei discorsi di Tucidide." In *Poleis e Politeiai. Esperienze politiche, tradizioni letterarie, progetti costituzionali*, edited by S. Cataldi, 153–65. Alessandria.

Cuvigny, M., ed. 1994. *Dion de Pruse. Discours bithyniens: discours 38–51*. Besançon.

Çevik, N., Kizgut, I., and Bulut, S. 2010. "Rhodiapolis Baths: The First Evaluation Following the Excavations and its Contribution to the Knowledge on Lycian Baths Architecture and Technique." *Adalaya* 13:29–64.

D'Acunto, M. 2013. *Il mondo del vaso Chigi. Pittura, guerra e società a Corinto alla metà del VII secolo a.C.* Berlin.

d'Agostino, B. 2006. "The First Greeks in Italy." In *Greek Colonisation. An Account of Greek Colonies and Other Settlements Overseas*, edited by G. R. Tsetskhladze, 201–37. Leiden.

d'Agostino, B. 2008. "Alba della città, alba delle immagini?" In E. Greco (ed.) *Alba della città, alba delle immagini? Da una suggestione di Bruno d'Agostino* (Tripodes 7): 9–20. Athens.

D'Alessio, G. B. 2004. "Argo e l'Argolide nei canti cultuali di Pindaro." In *La città di Argo. Mito, storia, tradizioni poetiche*, edited by P. Angeli Bernardini, 107–25. Rome.

D'Ercole, M. C., and Zurbach, J. 2019. *Naissance de la Grèce. De Minos à Solon. 3200 à 510 avant notre ère*. Edited by B. Le Guen. Paris.

D'Onofrio, A. M. 2011. "Athenian Burials with Weapons: The Athenian Warrior Graves Revisited." In *The "Dark Ages" Revisited. Acts of an International Symposium in Memory of William D. E. Coulson*, edited by A. Mazarakis-Ainian, 645–73. Volos.

Dąbrowa, E. 1980. *L'Asie mineure sous les Flaviens. Recherches sur la politique provinciale*. Wrocław.

Dagron, G. 1978. *Vie et Miracles de Sainte Thècle*. In coll. with M. Dupré la Tour. Brussels.

Dahl, R. A. 2005. *Who Governs. Democracy and Power in the American City*. 2nd ed. New Haven.

Dakari, S., Vokotopoulou, I., and Christidi, A. F. 2013. Τα χρηστήρια ελάσματα της Δωδώνης των ανασκαφών Δ. Ευαγγελίδη. Athens.

Dana, M., and Savalli-Lestrade, I., eds. 2019. *La cité interconnectée dans le monde gréco-romain (IVᵉ siècle a.C.-IVᵉ siècle p.C.). Transferts et réseaux institutionnels, religieux et culturels aux époques hellénistique et impériale*. Bordeaux.

Danner, P. 1997. "Megara, Megara Hyblaea and Selinus: The Relationship Between the Town Planning of a Mother City, a Colony and a Subcolony in the Archaic Period." In *Urbanization in the Mediterranean in the Ninth to Sixth Centuries BC*, edited by H. D. Andersen et al., 143–66. Copenhagen.

Dard, É. 1907. *Un épicurien sous la terreur. Hérault de Séchelles (1759–1794) d'après des documents inédits*. Paris.

Daux, G. 1937. *Delphes au IIe et au Ier siècle, depuis l'abaissement de l'Étolie jusqu'à la paix romaine, 191-31 av. J.-C.* Paris.

Daux, G., and Hansen, E. 1987. *Fouilles de Delphes. Topographie et architecture. Le trésor de Siphnos*. Paris.

Daverio Rocchi, G. 2008. "Hégémonie et autonomie: Les petites *poleis* dans les *Helléniques* de Xénophon." *AncSoc* 38:1–21.

Daverio Rocchi, G. 2013. "Ethnic Identity, Cults and Territorial Settlement: East and West Locrians." In *Greek Federal States and Their Sanctuaries. Identity and Integration*, edited by P. Funke and M. Haake, 139–61. Stuttgart.

David, E. 1979–1980. "The Influx of Money into Sparta at the End of the Fifth Century BC." *SCI* 5:30–45.

Davidson, J. N. 2007. *The Greeks and Greek Love. A Radical Reappraisal of Homosexuality in Ancient Greece.* London.
Davidson, J. N. 2012. "Bodymaps: Sexing Space and Zoning Gender in Ancient Athens." In *Gender and the City Before Modernity*, edited by L. Foxhall and G. Neher, 107–24. Chichester.
Davies, J. K. 1978. "Athenian Citizenship: The Descent Group and the Alternatives." *CJ* 73.2:105–21.
Davies, J. K. 1997. "The 'Origins of the Greek Polis': Where Should We Be Looking?" In *The Development of the Polis in Archaic Greece*, edited by L.G. Mitchell and P. J. Rhodes, 24–38. London.
Davies, P. A. 2017a. "The Cinadon Conspiracy as Literary Narrative and Historical Source." In *Das antike Sparta*, edited by V. Pothou and A. Powell, 221–43. Stuttgart.
Davies, P. A. 2017b. "Articulating Status in Ancient Greece. Status (In)Consistency as a New Approach." *CCJ* 63:29–52.
Davis, J. L. 2022. *A Greek State in Formation. The Origins of Civilization in Mycenaean Pylos.* With contributions by S. B. Stocker. Oakland, CA.
Dawkins, R. M., ed. 1929. *The Sanctuary of Artemis Orthia at Sparta. Excavated and Described by Members of the British School at Athens, 1906–1910.* London.
De Angelis, F. 1994. "The Foundation of Selinous: Overpopulation or Opportunities?" In *The Archaeology of Greek Colonisation*, edited by F. De Angelis and G. Tsetskhladze, 87–110. Oxford.
De Angelis, F. 2003. *Megara Hyblaia and Selinous. The Development of Two Greek City-states in Archaic Sicily.* Oxford.
De Angelis, F. 2016. *Archaic and Classical Greek Sicily: A Social and Economic History.* Oxford.
Debord, P. 1999. *L'Asie Mineure au IVème siècle: (412–323 a.C.).* Pessac.
Debord, P. 2001. "Les Mysiens: du mythe à l'histoire." In *Origines gentium*, edited by V. Fromentin and S. Gotteland, 135–46. Paris.
Debord, P., and Fröhlich, P. 2018. "Aigai d'Éolide et Colophon-sur-Mer: un nouveau fragment de l'inscription trouvée à Claros." *REA* 120.2:339–65.
Debord, P., and Varinlioğlu, E., eds. 2001. *Les hautes terres de Carie.* Bordeaux.
Debord, P., and Varinlioğlu, E. 2010. *Cités de Carie. Harpasa, Bargasa, Orthosia dans l'Antiquité.* Rennes.
De Callataÿ, F. 1991–92. "Athenian New Style Tetradrachms in Macedonian Hoards." *AJN* 3–4:11–20.
De Callataÿ, F. 2011. "More Than It Would Seem: The Use of Coinage by the Romans in Late Hellenistic Asia Minor (133–63 B.C.)." *AJN* 23:55–86.
De Callataÿ, F. 2012. "Le retour (quantifié) du 'miracle grec.'" In *Stephanèphoros. De l'économie antique à l'Asie Mineure. Hommages à Raymond Descat*, edited by K. Konuk, 63–76. Bordeaux.
de Chaisemartin, N. 2017. "Octavien/Auguste et Aphrodisias: certitudes et perplexités." In *Auguste et l'Asie Mineure*, edited by L. Cavalier, M.-C. Ferriès, and F. Delrieux, 331–43. Bordeaux.
Deene, M. 2013. "Seeking for Honour(s)? The Exploitation of *philotimia* and Citizen Benefactors in Classical Athens." *RBPh* 91:69–88.
Deger-Jalkotzy, S. 1991. "Diskontinuität und Kontinuität Aspekte politischer und sozialer Organisation in mykenischer Zeit." In *La transizione dal Miceneo all'alto arcaismo. Dal palazzo alla città*, edited by D. Musti et al., 53–66. Rome.
Deger-Jalkotzy, S. 1996. "On the Negative Aspects of the Mycenaean Palace System." In *Atti e memorie del Secondo congresso internazionale di Micenologia*, edited by L. De Miro, L. Godard, and A. Sacconi, 715–28. Rome.
Deger-Jalkotzy, S., and Lemos, I. S. 2006. *Ancient Greece. From the Mycenaean Palaces to the Age of Homer.* Edinburgh.
De Giorgi, A. U. 2016. *Ancient Antioch. From the Seleucid Era to the Islamic Conquest.* Cambridge.
De Giorgi, A. U., and Eser, A. A. 2021. *Antioch. A History.* Abingdon.
Deininger, J. 1965. *Die Provinziallandtage der römischen Kaiserzeit von Augustus bis zum Ende des dritten Jahrhunderts n. Chr.* Munich.
Deininger, J. 1971. *Der politische Widerstand gegen Rom in Griechenland 217–86 v. Chr.* Berlin.
Deißler, J. 2000. *Antike Sklaverei und Deutsche Aufklärung im Spiegel von Johann Friedrich Reitemeiers 'Geschichte und Zustand der Sklaverey und Leibeigenschaft in Griechenland' (1789).* Stuttgart.
de Jong, L., and Palermo, R. "Living on the Edge: The Roman Empire in the North Mesopotamian Steppe." In *The Archaeology of Imperial Landscapes. A Comparative Study of Empires in the Ancient Near East and Mediterranean World*, edited by B. S. Düring and T. D. Stek, 240–71. Cambridge.
de Jong, L. 2017. *The Archaeology of Death in Roman Syria. Burial, Commemoration, and Empire.* Cambridge.
Delamarre, J. 1902. "Un nouveau document relatif à la confédération des Cyclades." *RevPhil* 26.3:291–300.

de Libero, L. 1996. *Die archaische Tyrannis*. Stuttgart.
Del Monaco, L. 2013. *Iscrizioni greche d'Italia. Locri*. Rome.
Del Monaco, L. 2018. "Organizzazione civica a Locri Epizefiri." *Mediterraneo Antico*, 21:1–2:71–84.
Delplace, C., and Dentzer-Feydy, J. 2005. *L'agora de Palmyre. Sur la base des travaux de Henri Seyrig, Raymond Duru et Edmond Frézouls*. Pessac.
Demaille, J. 2018. "La population d'origine italienne de la colonie de Dion (Piérie, Macédoine)." In *Les communautés du nord égéen au temps de l'hégémonie romain. Entre ruptures et continuités*, edited by J. Fournier and M. Parissaki, 183–99. Athens.
Demand, N. H. 1990. *Urban Relocation in Archaic and Classical Greece. Flight and Consolidation*. Norman, OK.
Demoen, K. 2001. *The Greek City from Antiquity to the Present. Historical Reality, Ideological Construction, Literary Representation*. Leuven.
Dench, E. 2018. *Empire and Political Cultures in the Roman World*. Cambridge.
Dentzer, J.-M. 1986. "Conclusion: la Syrie du Sud dans la période préprovinciale." In *Hauran I. Recherches archéologiques sur la Syrie du Sud à l'époque hellénistique et romane*, edited by J.-M. Dentzer, 387–420. Paris.
de Oliveira, J. C. M. 2020. "Late Antiquity: The Age of Crowds?" *P&P* 249.1:3–52.
de Polignac, F. 1984. *La Naissance de la cité grecque*. Paris.
de Polignac, F. 1995. *Cults, Territory, and the Origins of the Greek City-State*. Chicago.
de Polignac, F. 2005 "Forms and Processes: Some Thoughts on the Meaning of Urbanization in Early Archaic Greece." In *Mediterranean Urbanization 800–600 B.C.*, edited by R. Osborne and B. Cunliffe, 44–69. Oxford.
de Polignac, F. 2006. "Espaces de communication et dynamiques d'appartenance en Grèce archaïque." *REA* 108.1:9–24.
Derbew, S. 2022. *Untangling Blackness in Greek Antiquity*. Cambridge.
Derow, P. S. 1979. "Polybius, Rome, and the East." *JRS* 69:1–15.
Derow, P. S. 1989. "Rome, the Fall of Macedon and the Sack of Corinth." In *The Cambridge Ancient History*, vol. 8, 2nd ed., edited by A. E. Astin, F. W. Walbank, M. W. Frederiksen, and R. M. Ogilvie, 290–323. Cambridge.
Derow, P. 2003. "The Arrival of Rome: From the Illyrian Wars to the Fall of Macedon." In *A Companion to the Hellenistic World*, edited by A. Erskine, 51–70. Malden, MA.
Derron, P., ed. 2017. *Économie et inégalité. Ressources, échanges et pouvoir dans l'antiquité classique*. Geneva.
Desborough, V. R. d'A. 1964. *The Last Mycenaeans. An Archaeological Survey c. 1200-1000 B.C.* Oxford.
Descat, R. 2000. "Remarques sur les origines du monnayage achéménide." In *Mécanismes et innovations monétaires dans l'Anatolie achéménide. Numismatique et Histoire*, edited by O. Casabonne, 1–8. Paris. Istanbul.
Des Courtils, J. 2001. "Xanthos et le Lètôon au IIè siècle a.C." In *Les cités d'Asie mineure occidentale au IIe siècle a.C.*, edited by A. Bresson and R. Descat, 213–24. Paris.
Deshours, N. 2004. "Les institutions civiques de Messène à l'époque hellénistique tardive." *ZPE* 150:134–46.
Deshours, N. 2006. *Les Mystères d'Andania. Étude d'épigraphie et d'histoire religieuse*. Bordeaux.
Deshours, N. 2011. *L'été indien de la religion civique. Études sur les cultes civiques dans le monde égéen à l'époque hellénistique tardive*. Paris.
Desideri, P. 1978. *Dione di Prusa. Un intellettuale greco nell'Impero romano*. Messina.
de Ste. Croix, G. E. M. 1981. *The Class Struggle in the Ancient Greek World from the Archaic Age to the Arab Conquest*. London.
Detienne, M. 1988. "L'espace de la publicité: ses opérateurs intellectuels dans la cité." In *Les savoirs de l'écriture en Grèce Ancienne*, edited by M. Detienne, 29–81. Lille.
Detienne, M., ed. 2003. *Qui veut prendre la parole?* Paris.
Develin, R. 1989. *Athenian Officials 684–321 B.C.* Cambridge.
Dey, H. W. 2014. *The Afterlife of the Roman City. Architecture and Ceremony in Late Antiquity and the Early Middle Ages*. Cambridge.
Dickenson, C. 2016. "Contested Bones. The Politics of Public Burial in Roman Greece (c. 200 B.C.–200 A.D.)." *AncSoc* 46:95–163.
Dickenson, C. 2017. "Violence, Public Space, and Political Power in the Hellenistic Polis." In *Cultural Perceptions of Violence in the Hellenistic World*, edited by M. Champion and L. O'Sullivan, 21–38. Abingdon.
Dickey, K. 1992. *Corinthian Burial customs, ca. 1100 to 550 B.C.* Unpublished PhD dissertation, Bryn Mawr College.
Dickinson, O. T. P. K. 1994. *The Aegean Bronze Age*. Cambridge.
Dickinson, O. T. P. K. 2006. *The Aegean from Bronze Age to Iron Age. Continuity and Change Between the Twelfth and Eighth Centuries BC*. London.

Dickinson, O. T. P. K. 2014. "How Warlike Were the Mycenaeans, in Reality?" In *Athyrmata. Critical Essays on the Archaeology of the Eastern Mediterranean in Honour of E. Susan Sherratt*, edited by Y. Galanakis, T. Wilkinson, and J. Bennet, 67–72. Oxford.

Dickinson, O. T. P. K. 2019. "What Conclusions Might Be Drawn from the Archaeology of Mycenaean Civilisation about Political Structure in the Aegean." In *From 'LUGAL.GAL' to 'Wanax.' Kingship and Political Organisation in the Late Bronze Age Aegean*, edited by J. M. Kelder and W. J. I. Waal, 31–48. Leiden.

Di Donato, R. 2003. "*Aristeuein*. Lo stato antropologico del guerriero omerico." *IncidAntico* 1:49–66.

Dignas, B. 2002. *Economy of the Sacred in Hellenistic and Roman Asia Minor*. Oxford.

Dijkstra, K. 1995. *Life and Loyalty. A Study in the Socio-Religious Culture of Syria and Mesopotamia in the Graeco-Roman Period Based on Epigraphical Evidence*. Leiden.

Dillery, J. 1995. *Xenophon and the History of His Times*. London.

Dillon, S. *The Female Portrait Statue in the Greek World*. 2010.

Dimitriadou, E. M. 2019. *Early Athens. Settlements and Cemeteries in the Submycenaean, Geometric, and Archaic Periods*. Los Angeles.

Dimitriadou, I. 2020. "Υπομυκηναϊκή Αθήνα (1075/1050-1000 π. Χ.). Από την προϊστορία στην ιστορία." In *Athens and Attica in Prehistory*, edited by N. Papadimitriou, J. C. Wright, S. Fachard, N. Polychronakou-Sgouritsa, and E. Andrikou, 559–74. Oxford.

Dimitsas, M. G. 1896. Ἡ Μακεδονία ἐν λίθοις φθεγγομένοις καὶ μνημείοις σωζομένοις. Ἤτοι πνευματικὴ καὶ ἀρχαιολογικὴ παράστασις τῆς Μακεδονίας ἐν συλλογῇ 1409 ἑλληνικῶν καὶ 189 λατινικῶν ἐπιγραφῶν καὶ ἐν ἀπεικονίσει τῶν σπουδαιοτέρων καλλιτεχνικῶν μνημείων. Athens.

Dimopoulou, A. 2017. "Lesbos sous Auguste: du renouveau des traités à l'apothéose." In *Auguste et l'Asie Mineure*, edited by L. Cavalier, M.-C. Ferriès, and F. Delrieux, 399–412. Bordeaux.

Dimopoulou-Piliouni, A. 2015. Λεσβίων πολιτεῖαι. Πολίτευμα, θεσμοί και δίκαιο των πόλεων της Λέσβου. Αρχαϊκοί, κλασικοί, ελληνιστικοί, ρωμαϊκοί χρόνοι. Athens.

Diogo de Souza, C. 2015. "Considerations about Burials and Funerary Practices in Geometric Argos, Greece (from ca. 900 to 700 B.C.E.)." In *Death as Archaeology of Transition. Thoughts and Materials*, edited by L. Rocha, P. Bueno-Ramirez, and G. Branco, 306–18. Oxford.

Dirven, L. 2011. "The Imperial Cult in the Cities of the Decapolis, Caesarea Maritima and Palmyra: A Note on the Development of Imperial Cults in the Roman Near East." *ARAM* 23:141–56.

Dirven, L. 2013. *Hatra. Politics, Culture and Religion between Parthia and Rome*. Stuttgart.

Dirven, L. 2018. "Palmyrene Sculpture in Context: Between Hybridity and Heterogeneity." In *Palmyra. Mirage in the Desert*, edited by J. Aruz, 120–29. New York.

di Vita, A. 1990. "Town Planning in the Greek Colonies of Sicily from the Time of Their Foundation to the Punic Wars." In *Greek Colonists and Native Population*, edited by J. P. Descoeudres, 344–63. Oxford.

Dmitriev, S. 2005. *City Government in Hellenistic and Roman Asia Minor*. Oxford.

Dmitriev, S. 2011. *The Greek Slogan of Freedom and Early Roman Politics in Greece*. Oxford.

Dmitriev, S. 2018. *The Birth of the Athenian Community. From Solon to Cleisthenes*. Abingdon.

Dobrov, G. W., ed. 1997. *The City as Comedy. Society and Representation in Athenian Drama*. Chapel Hill, NC.

Domingo Gygax, M. 2001. *Untersuchungen zu den lykischen Gemeinden in klassicher und hellenistischer Zeit*. Bonn.

Domingo Gygax, M. 2006. "Les origines de l'évergétisme: échanges et identités sociales dans la cité grecque." *Métis* 4:269–95.

Domingo Gygax, M. 2016. *Benefaction and Rewards in the Ancient Greek City. The Origins of Euergetism*. Cambridge.

Donlan, W. 1997. "The Relations of Power in the Pre-State and Early State Polities." In *The Development of the Polis in Archaic Greece*, edited by L. Mitchell and P.J. Rhodes, 38–48. London.

Donohue, A. A. 2005. *Greek Sculpture and the Problem of Description*. Cambridge.

Doran, T. 2018. *Spartan Oliganthropia*. Leiden.

Doronzio, A. 2018. *Athen im 7. Jahrhundert v. Chr. Räume und Funde der frühen Polis*. Berlin.

Downey, G. 1959. "Libanius' Oration in Praise of Antioch (Oration XI)." *PAPhS* 103.5:652–86.

Dreher, M. 2017. "Die griechische Tyrannis als monarchische Herrschaftsform." In *Monarchische Herrschaft im Altertum*, edited by S. Rebenich, 167–86. Berlin.

Dresch, P., and Allen, R. 2018. "John Horsley Russell Davis." In *Biographical Memoirs of Fellows of the British Academy* 17:121–43.

Drew-Bear, M. 2020. *Les archives du conseil municipal d'Hermoupolis Magna (P. Herm. Boul.)*. Berlin.

Drews, R. 1983. *Basileus. The Evidence for Kingship in Geometric Greece*. New Haven.
Droysen, J. G. 1836–1843. *Geschichte des Hellenismus*. Hamburg.
duBois, P. 2003. *Slaves and Other Objects*. Chicago.
Ducat, J. 1973. "La Confédération béotienne et l'expansion thébaine à l'époque archaïque." *BCH* 97:59–73.
Ducat, J. 1974. "Le mépris des Hilotes." *Annales (HSS)* 29.6:1451–64.
Ducat, J. 1990. *Les Hilotes*. Athens.
Ducat, J. 1994a. "Les conduites et les idéologies intégratrices concernant les esclaves de type hilotique." In *Religion et anthropologie de l'esclavage et des formes de dépendance*, edited by J. Annequin and M. Garrido-Hory, 17–28. Besançon.
Ducat, J. 1994b. *Les Pénestes de Thessalie*. Besançon.
Ducat, J. 1997. "Bruno Helly et les Pénestes." *Topoi (Lyon)* 7.1:183–89.
Ducat, J. 2008. "Le statut des périèques lacédémoniens." *Ktèma* 33:1–86.
Ducat, J. 2010. "The Ghost of the Lakedaimonian State." In *Sparta. The Body Politic*, edited by A. Powell and S. Hodkinson, 183–210. Swansea.
Ducat, J. 2013. "Homoioi." *Ktèma* 38:137–55.
Ducat, J. 2015. "Les hilotes à l'époque archaïque." In *La main-d'œuvre agricole en Méditerranée archaïque. Statuts et dynamiques économiques*, edited by J. Zurbach, 165–95. Bordeaux.
Ducat, J. 2016. "La conspiration de Cinadon (Xénophon, *Helléniques*, III, 3, 4–11)." *Ktèma* 41:343–91.
Ducat, J. 2018. "The *perioikoi*." In *A Companion to Sparta*, edited by A. Powell, 596–614. Hoboken, NJ.
Dunand, F. 1978. "Sens et fonction de la fête dans la Grèce hellénistique: les cérémonies en l'honneur d'Artémis Leucophryéné." *DHA* 4:201–18.
Duchesne, L. 1875. "Une invasion gauloise en Macédoine en l'an 117 avant Jésus-Christ." *RA* 29:6–21.
Dunant, C., and Pouilloux, J. 1958. *Recherches sur l'histoire et les cultes de Thasos. 2. De 196 avant J.-C. jusqu'à la fin de l'Antiquité*. Paris.
Dunn, F. M. 1998. "Tampering with the Calendar." *ZPE* 123:213–31.
Dunn, J. 2019. *Setting the People Free. The Story of Democracy*. 2nd ed. Princeton.
Duplouy, A. 2006. *Le prestige des élites. Recherches sur les modes de reconnaissance sociale en Grèce entre les Xe et Ve siècles avant J.-C.* Paris.
Duplouy, A. 2013. "Les Mille de Colophon 'totalité symbolique' d'une cité d'Ionie (VIe–IIe s. av. J.-C.)." *Historia* 62.2:146–66.
Duplouy, A. 2018a. "Élites, cités et citoyens dans la Grèce archaïque: apports récents et mise au point historiographique." In *Statuts personnels et espaces sociaux. Questions grecques et romaines*, edited by C. Moatti and C. Müller, 19–44. Paris.
Duplouy, A. 2018b. "Pathways to Archaic Citizenship." In *Defining Citizenship in Archaic Greece*, edited by A. Duplouy and R. Brock, 1–49. Oxford.
Duplouy, A. 2018c. "Citizenship as Performance." In *Defining Citizenship in Archaic Greece*, edited by A. Duplouy and R. Brock, 249–74. Oxford.
Duplouy, A. 2019. *Construire la cité. Essai de sociologie historique sur les communautés de l'archaïsme grec*. Paris.
Duplouy, A., and Brock, R., eds. 2018. *Defining Citizenship in Archaic Greece*. Oxford.
Duplouy, A., Mariaud, O., and de Polignac, F. 2010. "Sociétés grecques du VIIème siècle." In *La Méditerranée au VIIème siècle av. J.-C. Essais d'analyses archéologiques*, edited by R. Étienne, 275–309. Paris.
Dupont-Sommer, A., and Robert, L. 1964. *La déesse de Hiérapolis Castabala (Cilicie)*. Paris.
Durkheim, É. 1901. "Francotte, Henri. *Formation des villes, des états, des confédérations et des ligues dans la Grèce ancienne*." *Année sociologique* 6:373–76.
Eberle, L. P. 2016. "Law, Empire, and the Making of Roman Estates in the Provinces during the Late Republic." *Critical Analysis of Law* 3.1:50–69.
Eberle, L. P. 2017. "Making Roman Subjects: Citizenship and Empire Before and After Augustus." *TAPhA* 147.2:321–70.
Eberle, L. P., and Le Quéré, E. 2017. "Landed Traders, Trading Agriculturalists? Land in the Economy of the Italian Diaspora in the Greek East." *JRS* 107:27–59.
Eck, W. 1995. *Der Verwaltung des römischen Reiches in der hohen Kaiserzeit. Ausgewählte und erweiterte Beiträge*. Basel.
Eckhard, S. 2002. *Honoratioren, Griechen, Polisbürger. Kollektive Identitäten innerhalb der Oberschicht des kaiserzeitlichen Kleinasien*. Göttingen.

Eckhardt, B. 2016. "Romanization and Isomorphic Change in Phrygia: The Case of Private Associations." *JRS* 106:147–71.
Eckstein, A. M. 2006. *Mediterranean Anarchy, Interstate War, and the Rise of Rome.* Berkeley.
Eckstein, A. M. 2008. *Rome Enters the Greek East. From Anarchy to Hierarchy in the Hellenistic Mediterranean, 230-170 B.C.* Malden, MA.
Eckstein, A. M. 2013. "Hegemony and Annexation Beyond the Adriatic, 230-146 B.C. " In *A Companion to Roman Imperialism*, edited by B. D. Hoyos, 79–97. Leiden.
Eco, U. 1990. *Travels in Hyperreality. Essays.* Trans. W. Weaver. San Diego.
Edelmann-Singer, B. 2014. "The Provincial Elite in the Provincial Assemblies. Eastern Koina and their Influence on Provincial Identity." *C&M* 65:227–40.
Edelmann-Singer, B. 2015. *Koina und Concilia: Genese, Organisation und sozioökonomische Funktion der Provinziallandtage im römischen Reich.* Stuttgart.
Eder, W., ed. 1995. *Die athenische Demokratie im 4. Jahrhundert v. Chr. Vollendung oder Verfall einer Verfassungsform?* Stuttgart.
Eder, W. 2006. "The World of Telemachus: Western Greece 1200-700 B.C." In *Ancient Greece. From the Mycenaean Palaces to the Age of Homer*, edited by S. Deger-Jalkotzy and I. S. Lemos, 549–79. Edinburgh.
Edwards, A. T. 2004. *Hesiod's Ascra.* Berkeley.
Edwards, M., and Spatharas, D. 2020. *Forensic Narratives in Athenian Courts.* London.
Edwell, P. 2008. *Between Rome and Persia. The Middle Euphrates, Mesopotamia and Palmyra under Roman Control.* London.
Ehrenberg, V. 1933. "Der Damos im archaischen Sparta." *Hermes* 63.3:288–305.
Ehrenberg, V. 1937. "When Did the Polis Rise?" *JHS* 57.2:147–59.
Ehrenberg, V. 1946. *Aspects of the Ancient World. Essays and Reviews.* Oxford.
Ehrenberg, V. 1961. *Von den Grundformen griechischer Staatsordnung.* Heidelberg.
Ehrhardt, N. 1994. "Tod, Trost und Trauer: zur Funktion griechischer Trostbeschlüsse und Ehrendekrete *post mortem*." *Laverna* 5:38–55.
Ehrhardt, N., and Weiss, P. 2011. "Trajans Neubau der Heiligen Strasse von Milet nach Didyma." *Chiron* 41:217–-62.
Eich, P. 2012. "Centre and Periphery: Administrative Communication in Roman Imperial Times." In *Rome, a City and its Empire in Perspective. The Impact of the Roman World through Fergus Millar's Research*, edited by S. Benoist, 85–108. Leiden and Boston.
Eidinow, E. 2007. *Oracles, Curses, and Risk among the Ancient Greeks.* Oxford and New York.
Eilers, C. F., and Milner, N. P. 1995. "Q. Mucius Scaevola and Oenoanda: A New Inscription." *AS* 45:73–89.
Ellinger, P. 1993. *La légende nationale phocidienne: Artémis, les situations extrêmes et les récits de guerre d'anéantissement.* Athens.
Ellis-Evans, A. 2017. "The Coinage and History of Achaiion in the Troad." *REA* 119.1:25–47.
Ellis-Evans, A. 2019. *The Kingdom of Priam. Lesbos and the Troad between Anatolia and the Aegean.* Oxford and New York.
Elm, S. 2014. "Church—Festival—Temple: Reimagining Civic Topography in Late Antiquity." In *The City in the Classical and Post-Classical World. Changing Contexts of Power and Identity*, edited by C. Rapp and H. Drake, 167–82. Cambridge.
Elsner, J. 2001. "Describing Self in the Language of Other: Pseudo (?) Lucian at the Temple of Hierapolis." In *Being Greek Under Rome*, edited by S. Goldhill, 123–53. Cambridge.
Elsner, J. 2015. "Visual Culture and Ancient History: Issues of Empiricism and Ideology in the Samos Stele at Athens." *ClAnt* 34.1:33–73.
Engelmann, H. 1970. "Ehreninschrift eines rhodischen Vereins." *ZPE* 6:279–82.
Engels, D. W. 1990. *Roman Corinth. An Alternative Model for the Classical City.* Chicago.
Engels, F. 1931. *Der Ursprung der Familie, des Privateigentums und des Staats. Im Anschluß an Lewis H. Morgans Forschungen.* Annotated by H. Duncker. Berlin.
Erdkamp, P. 2002. "'A Starving Mob Has No Respect': Urban Markets and Food Riots in the Roman World, 100 B.C.-400 A.D." In *The Transformation of Economic Life under the Roman Empire*, edited by L. De Blois and J. W. Rich, 93–115. Amsterdam.
Eren, K. 2013. "Une relecture archéologique de la géographie historique de l'Ionie à l'époque archaïque." In *L'Anatolie des peuples, des cités et des cultures (IIe millénaire av. J.-C.-Ve siècle ap. J.-C.)*, edited by H. Bru and G. Labarre, 141–49. Besançon.

Erickson, B. L. 2002. "Aphrati and Kato Syme: Pottery, Continuity, and Cult in Late Archaic and Classical Crete." *Hesperia* 71.1:41–90.

Erickson, B. 2005. "Archaeology of Empire: Athens and Crete in the Fifth Century BC." *AJA* 109:619–63.

Erkelenz, D. 2003. *Optimo Praesidi. Untersuchungen zu den Ehrenmonumenten für Amtsträger der römischen Provinzes in Republik und Kaiserzeit*. Bonn.

Errington, R. M. 1988. "Aspects of Roman Acculturation in the East under the Republic." In *Alte Geschichte und Wissenschaftsgeschichte. Festschrift für Karl Christ zum 65. Geburtstag*, edited by P. Kneissl and V. Losemann, 140–57. Darmstadt.

Errington, R. M. 1989. "The Peace Treaty Between Miletus and Magnesia (I. Milet 148)." *Chiron* 19:279–88.

Erskine, A. 1994. "The Romans as Common Benefactors." *Historia* 43.1:70–87.

Ersoy, Y. E. 2007. "Notes on History and Archaeology of Early Clazomenae." In *Frühes Ionien. Eine Bestandsaufnahme*, edited by J. Cobet, V. von Graeve, and W.-D. Niemeier, 149–78. Mainz.

Etienne, R. 1990. *Ténos II. Ténos et les Cyclades. Du milieu du IVe siècle av J.-C. au milieu du IIIe siècle ap. J.-C.* Athens.

Etienne, R. 2004. *Athènes: espaces urbains et histoire des origines à la fin du IIIe siècle ap. J.C.* Paris.

Etienne, R., ed. 2010. *La Méditerranée au VIIe siècle av. J.-C. Essais d'analyses archéologiques*. Paris.

Etzioni-Halevy, E. 1979. *Political Manipulation and Administrative Power. A Comparative Study*. Boston.

Etzioni-Halevy, E. 1993. *The Elite Connection. Problems and Potential of Western Democracy*. Cambridge.

Euben, J., Wallach, J., and Ober, J., eds. 1995. *Athenian Political Thought and the Reconstitution of American Democracy*. Ithaca.

Evans, S. M., and Boyte, C. 1986. *Free Spaces. The Sources of Democratic Change in America*. Chicago.

Evans, P. B., Rueschemeyer, D., and Skocpol, T., eds. 1985. *Bringing the State Back In*. Cambridge.

Evans Grubbs, J. E., and Parkin, T. 2013. *The Oxford Handbook of Childhood and Education in the Classical World*. Oxford.

Ewald, B. C. 2008. "The Tomb as Heterotopia (Foucault's 'hétérotopies'): Heroization, Ritual and Funerary Art in Roman Asia Minor." *JRA* 21:624–34.

Fabiani, R. 2012. "*Dedochtai tei boulei kai toi demoi*: protagonisti e prassi della procedura deliberativa a Iasos." In *'Demokratie' im Hellenismus. Von der Herrschaft des Volkes zur Herrschaft der Honoratioren?*, edited by C. Mann and P. Scholz, 109–65. Mainz.

Fabiani, R. 2014. "Iasos between Maussollos and Athens." In *Euploia. La Lycie et la Carie antiques. Dynamiques des territoires, échanges et identités*, edited by P. Brun et al., 317–30. Bordeaux.

Fabiani, R. 2015a. "Iasos: eine griechische Polis unter hekatomnidischer Herrschaft." In *Zwischen Satrapen und Dynasten. Kleinasien im 4. Jahrhundert v. Chr.*, edited by E. Winter and K. Zimmermann, 49–74. Bonn.

Fabiani, R. 2015b. *I decreti onorari di Iasos. Cronologia e storia*. Munich.

Fabiani, R. 2017. "Suddivisioni civiche: organizzazione, magistrature e culti. Un nuovo decreto di una phylé di Iasos." *Studi Ellenistici* 31:165–204.

Fabiani, R. 2019. "*Kathoti kai proteron*. Un contributo all'interpretazione di *I. Iasos* 219." In *Forme del sacro. Scritti in memoria di Doro Levi*, edited by F. Berti, 111–28. Athens.

Fachard, S. 2012. *La défense du territoire. Étude de la chôra érétrienne et de ses fortifications*. Gollion.

Fachard, S. 2017. "The Resources of the Borderlands: Control, Inequality, and Exchange on the Attic-Boeotian Borders." In *Économie et inégalité. Ressources, échanges et pouvoir dans l'Antiquité classique*, edited by S. Fachard et al., 19–61. Vandœuvres.

Fachard, S., Murray, M. C., Knodell, A.R., and Papangeli, K. 2020. "The Fortress of Eleutherai: New Insights from Survey, Architecture, and Epigraphy." *Hesperia* 89.3:475–549.

Fachard, S., and Bresson, A. 2022. "Athens and the Aegean." In *The Cambridge Companion to the Ancient Greek Economy*, edited by S. von Reden, 106–23. Cambridge.

Fachard, S., and Pirsino, D. 2015. "Roads out of Attica." In *Autopsy in Athens. Recent Archaeological Work on Athens and Attica*, edited by M.M. Miles, 139–53. Oxford.

Fant, J. C. 1981. "The Choleric Roman Official of Philostratus *Vitae Sophistarum* p. 512. L. Verginius Rufus." *Historia* 30.2:240–43.

Faraguna, M. 2003. "I documenti nelle 'Vite dei X oratori' dei *Moralia* plutarchei." In *L'uso dei documenti nella storiografia antica*, edited by A. M. Biraschi et al., 479–503. Naples.

Faraguna, M. 2011. "Lykourgan Athens?" In *Clisthène et Lycurgue d'Athènes. Autour du politique dans la cité classique*, edited by V. Azoulay and P. Ismard, 67–88. Paris.

Faraguna, M. 2012. "*Hektemoroi, Isomoiria, Seisachtheia*: Ricerche recenti sulle riforme economiche di Solone." *Dike* 15:171–93.
Faraguna, M. 2016. "Un filosofo al potere? Demetrio Falereo tra democrazia e tirannide." *MediterrAnt* 19.1–2:35–64.
Faraguna, M. 2018. "Demetrius of Phalerum and Late Fourth-Century Athenian Society. Response to Delfim Leão." In *Symposion 2017*, edited by G. Thür, U. Yiftach, and R. Zelnick-Abramovitz, 457–67. Vienna.
Faroqhi, S. 1999. *Approaching Ottoman History. An Introduction to the Sources*. Cambridge.
Fawcett, P. 2016. "'When I Squeeze You with *Eisphorai*': Taxes and Tax Policy in Classical Athens." *Hesperia* 85.1:153–99.
Fearn, D. 2009. "Oligarchic Hestia: Bacchylides 14B and Pindar, Nemean 11." *JHS* 129:23–38.
Fearn, D., ed. 2011. *Aegina. Contexts for Choral Lyric Poetry. Myth, History, and Identity in the Fifth Century BC*. Oxford.
Fedak, J. 1990. *Monumental Tombs of the Hellenistic Age. A Study of Selected Tombs from the Pre-Classical to the Early Imperial Era*. Toronto.
Fehr, B. 1971. *Orientalische und griechische Gelage*. Bonn.
Fehr, B. 1980. "Kosmos und Chreia: der Sieg der reinen über die praktische Vernunft in der griechischen Stadtarchitektur des 4. Jh." *Hephaistos* 2:155–85.
Feissel, D. 2010. *Documents, droit, diplomatique de l'Empire romain tardif*. Paris.
Feissel, D., and Gascou, J. 1989. "Documents d'archives romains inédits du Moyen Euphrate (IIIe s. ap. J.-C.)." *CRAI* 133.3:535–61.
Feissel, D., and Gascou, J. 1995. "Documents d'archives romains inédits du Moyen Euphrate (IIIe s. après J.-C.). 1: Les pétitions (P. Euphr. 1 à 5)." *JS* 1:65–119.
Fernoux, H.-L. 2004. *Notables et élites des cités de Bithynie aux époques hellénistique et romaine (IIIe siècle av. J.C. – IIIe siècle ap. J.C.): Essai d'histoire sociale*. Lyon.
Fernoux, H.-L. 2005. "Remarques sur la composition sociologique et l'activité politique des assemblées populaires (Ier- IIIe s. p. C.)." In *Survivances et métamorphoses*, edited by H. Duchêne, 19–71. Dijon.
Fernoux, H.-L. 2009. "Frontières civiques et maîtrise du territoire: un enjeu pour la cité grecque sous le Haut-Empire (Ier-IIIe siècle apr. J.-C.)." In *L'Asie mineure dans l'Antiquité. Échanges, populations et territoires*, edited by H. Bru, F. Kirbihler, and S. Lebreton, 135–64. Rennes.
Fernoux, H.-L. 2011. *Le Demos et la cité. Communautés et assemblées populaires en Asie mineure à l'époque impériale*. Rennes.
Fernoux, H.-L. 2019. "Les colonies romaines dans le Nord-ouest de l'Asie mineure (Alexandreia Troas, Lampsaque, Parion et Apamée-Myrléa): les conditions de leur fondation et leur évolution sociologique à l'époque impériale." In *Ancient Cities, 1. Roman Imperial Cities in the East and in Central-Southern Italy*, edited by N. Andrade et al., 107–39. Rome.
Fernoux, H.-L., and Stein, C., eds. 2007. *Aristocratie antique. Modèles et exemplarité sociale*. Dijon.
Ferrario, S. B. 2014. *Historical Agency and the 'Great Man' in Classical Greece*. Cambridge.
Ferrary, J-L. 1988. *Philhellénisme et impérialisme. Aspects idéologiques de la conquête romaine du monde hellénistique, de la seconde guerre de Macédoine à la guerre contre Mithridate*. Paris.
Ferrary, J.-L. 1991. "Le statut des cités libres dans l'empire romain à la lumière des inscriptions de Claros." *CRAI* 1991:557–77.
Ferrary, J.-L. 1995. "*Ius fetiale* et diplomatie." In *Les relations internationales*, edited by E. Frézouls and A. Jacquemin, 411–32. Paris.
Ferrary, J.-L. 1999. "La liberté des cités et ses limites à l'époque républicaine." *Mediterraneo Antico* 2.1:69–84.
Ferrary, J.-L. 2012. *Recherches sur les lois comitiales et sur le droit public romain*. Pavia.
Ferrary, J.-L.2017. *Rome et le monde grec. Choix d'écrits*. Edited by by A. Heller and D. Rousset. Paris.
Ferrary, J.-L., and Rousset, D. 1998. "Un lotissement de terres à Delphes au IIème s. ap. J.-C." *BCH* 122.1:277–342.
Ferrary, J.-L., and Verger, S. 1999. "Contribution à l'histoire du sanctuaire de Claros à la fin du IIe et au Ier siècle av. J.-C.: l'apport des inscriptions en l'honneur des Romains et des fouilles de 1994–1997." *CRAI* 143.3:811–50.
Ferriès, M.-C., and Delrieux, F. 2011. "Quintus Mucius Scaevola, un gouverneur modèle pour les Grecs d'Asie." In *Les gouverneurs et les provinciaux sous la République romaine*, edited by N. Barrandon and F. Kirbihler, 207–30. Rennes.
Feyel, C. 2009. *ΔΟΚΙΜΑΣΙΑ, La place et le rôle de l'examen préliminaire dans les institutions des cités grecques*. Nancy.
Feyel, C., Fournier, J., Graslin-Thomé, L., and Kirbihler, F., eds. 2012. *Communautés locales et pouvoir central dans l'Orient hellénistique et romain*. Nancy.

Feyel, C., and Graslin-Thomé, L. 2017. *Antiochos III et l'Orient.* Paris.
Figueira, J. T. 1981. *Aegina. Society and Politics.* Salem, NH.
Figueira, J. T. 1985. "The Theognidea and Megarian Society." In *Theognis of Megara. Poetry and the Polis,* edited by T. J. Figueira and G. Nagy, 112–58. Baltimore.
Figueira, J. T. 1991. *Athens and Aigina in the Age of Imperial Colonization.* Baltimore.
Figueira, J. T. 1993. *Excursions in Epichoric History. Aiginetan Essays.* Lanham, MD.
Figueira, J. T. 1998. *The Power of Money. Coinage and Politics in the Athenian Empire.* Philadelphia.
Figueira, J. T. 2003. "The Demography of the Spartan Helots." *Helots and Their Masters in Laconia and Messenia. Histories, Ideologies, Structures,* edited by N. Luraghi and S. E. Alcock, 193–239. Cambridge, MA.
Figueira, J. T., and Nagy, G., eds. 1985. *Theognis of Megara. Poetry and the Polis.* Baltimore.
Filges, A. 2020. "Kleinheiligtümer, Wohnviertel, Müllhalden oder Gärten? Forschungen in den nördlichen Hangzonen Prienes." In *Priene von der Spätklassik bis zum Mittelalter. Ergebnisse und Perspektiven der Forschungen seit 1998,* edited by W. Raeck, A. Filges and I. Hakan Mert, 105–16. Bonn.
Filippini, A. 2019. *Efeso, Ulpiano e il Senato. La contesa per il primato nella provincia Asia nel III. sec d. C.* Stuttgart.
Filonik, J., Griffith-Williams, B., and Kucharski, J., eds. 2019. *The Making of Identities in Athenian Oratory.* London.
Finley, M. I. 1951. *Studies in Land and Credit in Ancient Athens 500–200 B.C. The Horos Inscriptions.* New Brunswick, NJ.
Finley, M. I. 1954. *The World of Odysseus.* New York.
Finley, M. I. 1971. *The Ancestral Constitution. An Inaugural Lecture.* London.
Finley, M. I. 1973. *The Ancient Economy.* Berkeley.
Finley, M. I. 1978. "The Fifth-Century Athenian Empire: A Balance Sheet." In *Imperialism in the Ancient World,* edited by P. D. A. Garnsey and C. R. Whittaker, 103–26. Cambridge.
Finley, M. I. 1980. *Ancient Slavery and Modern Ideology,* edited by R. P. Saller and B. D. Shaw. London.
Finley, M. I. 1981. *Economy and Society in Ancient Greece,* edited by R. P. Saller and B. D. Shaw. New York.
Finley, M. I. 1983. *Politics in the Ancient World.* Cambridge.
Finley, M. I. 1985. *Ancient History. Evidence and Models.* London.
Firatlı, N. 1964. *Les stèles funéraires de Byzance gréco-romaine.* Paris.
Fischer, M. 1995. "The Basilica of Ascalon: Marble, Imperial Art, and Architecture in Roman Palestine." In *The Roman and Byzantine Near East. Some Recent Archaeological Research,* edited by J. Humphery, 121–50. Ann Arbor.
Fisher, N. R. E. 1992. *Hybris. A Study in the Values of Honour and Shame in Ancient Greece.* Warminster.
Fisher, N. R. E. 1998. "Violence, Masculinity and the Law in Classical Athens." In *When Men Were Men. Masculinity, Power and Identity in Classical Antiquity,* edited by L. Foxhall and J. Salmon, 68–97. London.
Fisher, N., and van Wees, H., eds. 2015. *'Aristocracy' in Antiquity. Redefining Greek and Roman Elites.* Swansea.
Fischer-Bovet, C. and von Reden, S. eds. 2021. *Comparing the Ptolemaic and Seleucid Empires: Integration, Communication, and Resistance.* Cambridge.
Flannery, K. V. 1988. "The Ground Plans of Archaic States." In *Archaic States,* edited by G. M. Feinman and J. Marcus, 15–58. Santa Fe, NM.
Flyvbjerg, B. 1998. *Rationality and Power. Democracy in Practice.* Translated by S. Sampson. Chicago.
Foley, A. 1988. *The Argolid 800–600 B.C. An Archaeological Survey. Together with an Index of Sites from the Neolithic to the Roman Period.* Göteborg.
Follet, S. 1977. *Athènes au IIe et au IIIe siècle. Études chronologiques et prosopographiques.* Paris.
Follet, S., and Delmousou, P. D. 2019. "Bienfaits de l'empereur Hadrien envers les cités de Sardes et Synnada (*IG* II² 1089, complétée, et *IG* II² 1075, complétée)." *BCH* 143.2:767–83.
Fontana, F. 2010. "Crisi della lega peloponnesiaca e autonomia delle *poleis* in Senofonte: il caso di Fliunte e Corinto." *AncSoc* 40:215–37.
Fontana, F. 2014. *Tra autonomia e dinamiche regionali: storia di Fliunte dall' VIII al IV secolo a.C.* Bari.
Fornara, C. 1971. *Herodotus. An Interpretative Essay.* Oxford and New York.
Forrest, W. G. 2000. "The Pre-polis Polis." In *Alternatives to Athens. Varieties of Political Organization and Community in Ancient Greece,* edited by R. Brock and S. Hodkinson, 280–92. Oxford.
Forsdyke, S. 2005a. *Exile, Ostracism, and Democracy. The Politics of Expulsion in Ancient Greece.* Princeton.
Forsdyke, S. 2005b. "Revelry and Riot in Archaic Megara: Democratic Disorder or Ritual Reversal?" *JHS* 125:73–79.

Forsdyke, S. 2012. *Slaves Tell Tales and Other Episodes in the Politics of Popular Culture in Ancient Greece*. Princeton.
Forsdyke, S. 2021. *Slaves and Slavery in Ancient Greece*. Cambridge.
Forster, F. R. 2018. *Die Polis im Wandel. Ehrendekrete für eigene Bürger im Kontext der hellenistischen Polisgesellschaft*. Göttingen.
Förtsch, R. 2001 *Kunstverwendung und Kunstlegitimation im archaischen und frühklassischen Sparta*. Mainz.
Foss, C. 1977. "Archaeology and the 'Twenty Cities' of Byzantine Asia." *AJA* 81.4:469–86.
Foss, C. 1979. *Ephesus After Antiquity. A Late Antique, Byzantine, and Turkish City*. Cambridge.
Foss, C. 1991. "Cities and Villages of Lycia in the Life of Saint Nicholas of Holy Zion." *The Greek Orthodox Theological Review* 36.3-4:303–39.
Foucart, P. 1903. "La formation de la province romaine d'Asie." *Mémoires de l'Institut national de France* 37.1:297–340.
Fournier, J. 2010. *Entre tutelle romaine et autonomie civique. L'administration judiciaire dans les provinces hellénophones de l'empire romain, 129 av. J.-C–235 ap. J. C*. Athens.
Fournier, J. 2014. "Cyzique à l'époque de l'hégémonie romaine: un modèle d'intégration provinciale?" In *Cyzique, cité majeure et méconnue de la Propontide antique*, edited by M. Sève and P. Schlosser, 309–38. Metz.
Fournier, J. 2018. "Archontes et théores thasiens du Ier au IIIè siècle ap. J.-C." *JS* 1:3–53.
Fowden, G. 1990. "Religious Developments in Late Roman Lycia: Topographical Preliminaries." In Ποικίλα, 343–72. Athens.
Fowler, R., ed. 2004. *The Cambridge Companion to Homer*. Cambridge.
Fowlkes-Child, B., and Seymour, M., eds. 2019. *The World Between Empires. Art and Identity in the Ancient Middle East*. New York.
Foxhall, L. 1989. "Household, Gender and Property in Classical Athens." *CQ* 39.1:22–44.
Foxhall, L. 1997. "A View from the Top: Evaluating the Solonian Property Classes." In *The Development of the Polis in Archaic Greece*, edited by L. Mitchell and P. J. Rhodes, 113–36. London.
Foxhall, L. 1998. "Cargoes of the Heart's Desire: The Character of Trade in the Archaic Mediterranean World." In *Archaic Greece. New Approaches and New Evidence*, edited by N. Fisher and H. Van Wees, 295–309. London.
Foxhall, L. 2002. "Access to Resources in Classical Greece: The Egalitarianism of the Polis in Practice." In *Money, Labour and Land. Approaches to the Economies of Ancient Greece*, edited by P. Cartledge et al., 209–20. London.
Foxhall, L. 2013. "Can We See the 'Hoplite Revolution' on the Ground? Archaeological Landscapes, Material Culture, and Social Status in Early Greece." In *Men of Bronze. Hoplite Warfare in Ancient Greece*, edited by D. Kagan and G. F. Viggiano, 194–221. Princeton.
Franchi, E. 2016. *Die Konflikte zwischen Thessalern und Phokern. Krieg und Identität in der griechischen Erinnerungskultur des 4. Jahrhunderts*. Munich.
Franke, P. R. 1968. *Kleinasien zur Römerzeit. Griechisches Leben im Spiegel der Münzen*. Munich.
Franssen, J. 2011. *Votiv und Repräsentation. Statuarische Weihungen archaischer Zeit aus Samos und Attika*. Heidelberg.
Fraser, P. M. 1972. "Notes on Two Rhodian Institutions." *ABSA* 67:113–24.
Frederiksen, M. 1984. *Campania*. London.
Frederiksen, M. 2011. *Greek City Walls of the Archaic Period, 900–480 B.C*. Oxford.
French. D. 1994. "Isinda and Lagbe." In *Studies in the History and Topography of Lycia and Pisidia. In Memoriam A.S. Hall*, edited by D. French et al., 53–92. Oxford.
Freyberger, K. S. 2000. "The Roman Kanatha: Results of the Campaigns in 1997/1998." *BEO* 52:143–56.
Freyberger, K. S. 2003. "Zur Urbanistik von Kanatha in hochkaiserzeitlicher und spätantiker Zeit." In *Die spatantike Stadt und ihre Christianisierung*, edited by G. Brands and H.-G. Severin, 115–24. Wiesbaden.
Freyberger, K. S., Ertel, C., Tacke, K., and Hatoum, H., eds. 2015. *Kanatha von hellenistischer bis spätantiker Zeit*. Darmstadt.
Freyberger, K. S. 2004. "Die Wasserversorgung von Kanatha (Qanawat) als Spiegel städtischer Kultur der Polisbürger." In *Lokale Identitäten in Randgebieten des Römischen Reiches*, edited by A. Schmidt-Colinet, 59–70. Vienna.
Freyberger, K. S. 2015. *Kanatha von hellenistischer bisspätantiker Zeit*. Darmstadt.
Freyberger, K. S. 2017. "The Sanctuaries at Kanatha and Seeia: Evidence for Religiously Sanctioning the Power to Use Water." In *Contextualizing the Sacred in the Hellenistic and Roman Near East. Religious Identities in Local, Regional, and Imperial Settings*, edited by R. Raja, 143–54. Turnhout.

Friedrichs, C. R. 1995. *The Early Modern City. 1450–1750*. London.
Friedrichs, C. R. 2010. "What Made the Eurasian City Work? Urban Political Cultures in Early Modern Europe and Asia." In *City Limits. Perspectives on the Historical European City*, edited by G. Clark et al., 29–64. Montreal.
Frier, B., and Kehoe, D. 2007. "Law and Economic Institutions." In *The Cambridge Economic History of the Greco-Roman World*, edited by W. Scheidel, I. Morris, and R. Saller, 113–43. Cambridge.
Frija, G. 2012. *Les Prêtres des empereurs. Le culte impérial civique dans la province romaine d'Asie*. Rennes.
Frija, G. 2016. "Les cultes impériaux dans les cités d'Asie Mineure: des spécificités provinciales?" In *Kaiserkult in den Provinzen des Römischen Reiches. Organisation, Kommunikation und Repräsentation*, edited by A. Kolb and M. Vitale, 159–72. Berlin.
Frija, G., ed. 2020. *Être citoyen romain dans le monde grec au IIème siècle de notre ère*. Bordeaux.
Fröhlich, P. 2004. *Les cités grecques et le contrôle des magistrats (IVe-Ier siècle avant J.-C.)*. Geneva.
Fröhlich, P. 2005. "Dépenses publiques et évergétisme des citoyens dans l'exercice des charges à Priène à la basse époque hellénistique." In *Citoyenneté et participation à la basse époque hellénistique*, edited by P. Fröhlich and C. Müller, 225–56. Geneva.
Fröhlich, P. 2008. "Les tombeaux de la ville de Messène et les grandes familles de la cité à l'époque hellénistique." In *Le Péloponnèse d'Épaminondas à Hadrien*, edited by C. Grandjean, 203–27. Bordeaux.
Fröhlich, P. 2010. "L'inventaire du monde des cités grecques: une somme, une méthode et une conception de l'histoire." *RH* 134.3:637–77.
Fröhlich, P. 2013. "Governmental Checks and Balances." In *A Companion to Ancient Greek Government*, edited by H. Beck, 252–66. Malden, MA.
Fröhlich, P. 2016. "La citoyenneté grecque entre Aristote et les modernes." *CCG* 27:91–136.
Fröhlich, P., and Hamon, P., eds. 2012. *Groupes et associations dans les cités grecques (IIIe siècle av. J.-C. - IIe siècle apr. J.-C.)*. Paris.
Fröhlich, P., and Müller, C., eds. 2005. *Citoyenneté et participation à la basse époque hellénistique*. Geneva.
Frullini, S. 2021. "Politics and Landscape in the Argive Plain after the Battle of Sepeia." *JHS* 141:110–35.
Fuhrmann, C. J. 2014. "Dio Chrysostom as a Local Politician: A Critical Reappraisal." In *Aspects of Ancient Institutions and Geography*, edited by L. Brice and D. Slootjes, 161–76. Leiden.
Fujii, T. 2011. "Imperial Cult and Imperial Death in the Roman East: Emperors Represented in Cypriot Inscriptions." In *Mors Omnibus Instat. Aspectos arqueológicos, epigráficos y rituales de la muerte en el Occidente Romano*, edited by J. Andreu, D. Espinosa, and S. Pastor, 159–66. Madrid.
Fujii, T. 2013. *Imperial Cult and Imperial Representation in Roman Cyprus*. Stuttgart.
Fuks, A. 1984. *Social Conflict in Ancient Greece*. Leiden.
Fukuyama, F. 1989. "The End of History?" *The National Interest* 16: 3–18.
Fukuyama, F. 1995. *Trust. The Social Virtues and the Creation of Prosperity*. New York.
Fukuyama, F. 2006. *The End of History and the Last Man*. New York.
Fukuyama. F. 2011. *The Origins of Political Order. From Prehuman Times to the French Revolution*. New York.
Funke, P. 2004. "Sparta und die peloponnesische Staatenwelt zu Beginn des 4. Jahrhunderts und der Dioikismos von Mantineia." *Xenophon and His World*, edited by C. Tuplin, 427–35. Stuttgart.
Funke, P. and Haake, M., eds. 2013. *Greek Federal States and Their Sanctuaries: Identity and Integration*. Stuttgart.
Funke, P., and Luraghi, N., eds. 2009. *The Politics of Ethnicity and the Crisis of the Peloponnesian League*. Washington, DC.
Fustel de Coulanges, N. D. 1858. *Polybe ou la Grèce conquise par les Romains*. Amiens.
Fustel de Coulanges, N. D. 1864. *La Cité antique. Étude sur le culte, le droit, les institutions de la Grèce et de Rome*. Paris.
Fustel de Coulanges, N. D. 1994. *La Gaule romaine*, edited by C. Jullian. Paris.
Futo Kennedy, R. 2014. *Immigrant Women in Athens. Gender, Ethnicity, and Citizenship in the Classical City*. London.
Gabrielsen, V. 1994. *Financing the Athenian Fleet: Public Taxation and Social Relations*. Baltimore, MD.
Gabrielsen, V. 1997. *The Naval Aristocracy of Hellenistic Rhodes*. Aarhus.
Gagarin, M. 2008. *Writing Greek Law*. Cambridge.
Gagarin, M. 2020a. "Cretan Laws and the Early Polis." In *Ιουλιαν Βελισσαροπουλου Επαινεσαι. Studies in Ancient Greek and Roman Law*, edited by A. Dimopoulou, A. Helmis, and D. Karambelas, 97–110. Athens.
Gagarin, M. 2020b. *Democratic Law in Classical Athens*. Austin.
Gagarin, M., and Perlman, P. 2016. *The Laws of Ancient Crete c.650–400 BCE*. Oxford.

Gaignerot-Driessen, F. 2016. *De l'occupation postpalatiale à la cité-état grecque. Le cas du Mirambello (Crète)*. Leuven.

Gaignerot-Driessen, F. 2018. "La formation des cités grecques (XIVème–VIIème s. av. n. è.): approche archéologique à partir de quelques cas crétois." *REG* 131.1:49–73.

Gallant, T. W. 1982. "Agricultural Systems, Land Tenure and the Reforms of Solon." *ABSA* 77:111–24.

Gallant, T. W. 1991. *Risk and Survival in Ancient Greece. Reconstructing the Rural Domestic Economy*. Stanford.

Galli, M. 2002. *Die Lebenswelt eines Sophisten. Untersuchungen zu den Bauten und Stiftungen des Herodes Atticus*. Mainz.

Garlan, Y. 1995. *Les esclaves en Grèce ancienne*. 2nd ed. Paris.

Garnsey, P. A. D. 1988. *Famine and Food Supply in the Graeco-Roman World: Responses to Risk and Crisis*. Cambridge.

Gartland, S. D., ed. 2016a. *Boiotia in the Fourth Century BC*. Philadelphia.

Gartland, S. D. 2016b. "A New Boiotia? Exiles, Landscapes, and Kings." In *Boiotia in the Fourth Century B.C.*, edited by S. D. Gartland, 147–64. Philadelphia.

Gassner, V., Muss, U., and Grammer, B. 2017. "The Urban Organization of Kolophon and its Necropoleis. The Results of the 2011–2014 Surveys." *Hesperia* 86.1:43–81.

Gatier, P.-L. 2005. "La 'colonne de Qartaba' et la romanisation de la montagne libanaise." In *Aux pays d'Allat. Mélanges offerts à Michał Gawlikowski*, edited by P. Bieliński and F. M. Stępniowski, 77–97. Warsaw.

Gatzke, A. F. 2020. "The Gate Complex of Plancia Magna in Perge: A Case Study in Reading Bilingual Space." *CQ* 70.1:385–96.

Gatzolis, C. and Psoma, S. 2018. "Coinages Issues to Serve Roman Interests and the Case of Histiaia." In *Les communautés du nord égéen au temps de l'hégémonie romaine. Entre ruptures et continuités*, edited by J. Fournier and M.-G. G. Parissaki, 63–77. Athens.

Gauthier, P. 1966. "Les clérouques de Lesbos et la colonisation athénienne au Vème siècle." *REG* 79.373:64–88.

Gauthier, P. 1976. *Un commentaire historique des Πόροι de Xénophon*. Geneva.

Gauthier, P. 1982. "Notes sur trois décrets honorant des citoyens bienfaiteurs." *RPh* 56.2:215–31.

Gauthier, P. 1984. "Les cités hellénistiques: épigraphie et histoire des institutions et des régimes politiques, I." In Πρακτικά τοῦ Η' διεθνοῦς συνεδρίου Ἑλληνικῆς καὶ Λατινικῆς ἐπιγραφικῆς, 82–107. Athens.

Gauthier, P. 1985. *Les cités grecques et leurs bienfaiteurs (IVᵉ-Iᵉʳ siècle avant J.-C.). Contribution à l'histoire des institutions*. Paris.

Gauthier, P. 1987–89. "Grandes et petites cités: hégémonie et autarcie." *Opus* 6–7:187–202.

Gauthier, P. 1988. "Métèques, périèques et paroikoi." In *L'étranger dans le monde grec*, edited by R. Lonis, 23–46. Nancy.

Gauthier, P. 1989. *Nouvelles inscriptions de Sardes II*. Geneva.

Gauthier, P. 1990. "Quorum et participation civique dans les démocraties grecques." In *Du pouvoir dans l'Antiquité. Mots et réalités*, edited by C. Nicolet, 73–99. Paris.

Gauthier, P. 1991. "Ἀτέλεια τοῦ σώματος." *Chiron* 21:49–68.

Gauthier, P. 1993. "Décrets d'Érétrie en l'honneur de juges étrangers." *REG* 106.506:589–98.

Gauthier, P. 1994. "Les rois hellénistiques et les juges étrangers: à propos de décrets de Kimôlos et de Laodicée du Lykos." *JS* 2:165–95.

Gauthier, P. 2000. "Les institutions politiques de Delphes au IIe siècle a. C." In *Delphes cent ans après la grande fouille. Essai de bilan*, edited by A. Jacquemin 109–39. Athens.

Gauthier, P. 2001a. "Les Pidaséens entrent en sympolitie avec les Milésiens: la procédure et les modalités institutionnelles." In *Les cités d'Asie mineure occidentale au IIᵉ siècle a.C.*, edited by A. Bresson and R. Descat, 117–27. Paris.

Gauthier, P. 2001b. "Les assemblées électorales et le calendrier de Samos à l'époque hellénistique." *Chiron* 31:211–27.

Gauthier, P. 2003. "Le décret de Colophon l'Ancienne en l'honneur du Thessalien Asandros et la sympolitie entre les deux Colophon." *JS* 1:61–100.

Gauthier, P. 2005. "Un gymnasiarque honoré à Colophon." *Chiron* 35:101–12.

Gauthier, P. 2011. *Études d'histoire et d'institutions grecques. Choix d'écrits*. Geneva.

Gauthier, P., and Hatzopoulos, M. V., eds. 1993. *La Loi gymnasiarchique de Béroia*. Athens.

Gavalas, P. 2010. Η Ηρακλειά του χθες και του σήμερα. Irakleia.

Gawantka, W. 1985. *Die sogenannte Polis. Zur Entstehung, Geschichte und Kritik der modernen althistorischen Grundbegriffe, der griechische Staat, die griechische Staatsidee, die Polis*. Wiesbaden.

Gawlikowski, M. 2021. *Tadmor - Palmyra. A Caravan City Between East and West*. Cracow.

Gawlinski, L. 2012. *The Sacred Law of Andania. A New Text with Commentary*. Berlin.

Gehrke, H.-J. 1985. *Stasis. Untersuchungen zu den inneren Kriegen in den griechischen Staaten des 5. und 4. Jh. v. Chr.* Munich.

Gehrke, H.-J. 1986. *Jenseits von Athen und Sparta. Das dritte Griechenland und seine Staatenwelt.* Munich.

Gehrke, H.-J. 1993. "Thisbe in Boiotien: eine Fallstudie zum Thema 'Griechische Polis und Römisches Imperium.'" *Klio* 75:145–54.

Gehrke, H.-J. 1997. "Gewalt und Gesetz: Die soziale und politische Ordnung Kretas in der Archaischen und Klassischen Zeit." *Klio* 79:23–68.

Geiger, J. 2014. *Hellenism in the East: Studies on Greek Intellectuals in Palestine.* Stuttgart.

Genevrois, G. 2017. *Le vocabulaire institutionnel crétois d'après les inscriptions (VIIe-IIe s. av. J. C.).* Geneva.

Gengler, O. 2020. "Pausanias et la ville grecque: autour de la description de Panopée." In *Dire la ville en grec aux époques antique et byzantine,* edited by L. Lopez-Rabatel, V. Mathé, and J.-C. Moretti, 305–24. Lyon.

Gernet, L. 1968. *Anthropologie de la Grèce antique.* Paris.

Gherchanoc, F. 2012. *L'oikos en fête. Célébrations familiales et sociabilité en Grèce ancienne.* Paris.

Ghinatti, F. 2004. *I decreti dalla Grecia a Creta.* Alessandria.

Giangiulio, M. 2001. "Constructing the Past: Colonial Traditions and the Writing of History: The Case of Cyrene." In *The Historian's Craft in the Age of Herodotus,* edited by N. Luraghi, 116–37. Oxford.

Giangiulio, M. 2004. "Stato e statualità nella *polis*: riflessioni storiografiche e metodologiche. Ovvero del buon uso di Max Weber e del paradigma dello stato moderno." In *Poleis e Politeiai. Esperienze politiche, tradizioni letterarie, progetti costituzionali,* edited by S. Cataldi, 31–53. Alessandria.

Giangiulio, M. 2015. *Democrazie greche. Atene, Sicilia, Magna Grecia.* Rome.

Giangiulio, M. 2017. "Looking for Citizenship in Archaic Greece: Methodological and Historical Problems." In *Citizens in the Graeco-Roman World. Aspects of Citizenship from the Archaic Period to AD 212,* edited by L. Cecchet and A. Busetto, 33–49. Leiden.

Giangiulio, M. 2018. "Oligarchies of 'Fixed Number' or Citizen Bodies in the Making?" In *Defining Citizenship in Archaic Greece,* edited by A. Duplouy and R. W. Brock, 275–92. Oxford.

Giannakopoulos, N. 2008. Ο θεσμός της Γερουσίας των ελληνικών πόλεων κατά τους ρωμαϊκούς χρόνους: οργάνωση και λειτουργίες. Thessaloniki.

Giannakopoulos, N. 2012. Θεσμοί και λειτουργία των πόλεων της Εύβοιας: κατά τους ελληνιστικούς και τους αυτοκρατοριούς χρόνους / *Institutions and Function of the Euboean Cities in the Hellenistic and the Imperial Period.* Thessaloniki.

Gillone, D. 2004. "I Lacedemoni e l'autonomia degli alleati peloponnesiaci." In *Il Peloponneso di Senofonte,* edited by G. Daverio Rocchi and M. Cavalli, 115–41. Milan.

Gilroy, P. 2002. *"There Ain't No Black in the Union Jack." The Cultural Politics of Race and Nation.* London.

Gilula, D. 2000. "Hermippus and his Catalogue of Goods (fr. 63)." *The Rivals of Aristophanes. Studies in Athenian Old Comedy,* edited by D. Harvey et al., 75–90. Swansea.

Girdvaynte, L. 2019. "Memmius Antiochos and Daulis (IG IX.1 61): Between Roman Procedure and Local Law?" *ZPE* 209:159–74.

Girdvaynte, L. 2020. "Law and Citizenship in Roman Achaia: Continuity and Change." In *Law in the Roman Provinces,* edited by K. Czajkowski, B. Eckhardt, and M. Strothmann, 210–42. Oxford.

Glaser, H. 1983. *Antike Brunnenbauten (KPHNAI) in Griechenland.* Vienna.

Glazebrook, A., and Henry, M. H., eds. 2011. *Greek Prostitutes in the Ancient Mediterranean, 800 BCE–200 CE.* Madison, WI.

Goddard, C. J. 2021. "Euergetism, Christianity and Municipal Culture in Late Antiquity, from Aquileia to Gerasa (Fourth to Sixth Centuries CE)." In *Benefactors and the Polis. The Public Gift in the Greek Cities from the Homeric World to Late Antiquity,* edited by M. D. Gygax and A. Zuiderhoek, 297–329. Cambridge.

Goette, H. R. 2003–2004. "Ο γλυπτός διάκοσμος των >Θερμών του Σύλλα< στην Αιδιψό." *Αρχέιον Ευβοϊκών Μελετών* 35:45–52.

Golden, M. 2015. *Children and Childhood in Classical Athens.* 2nd ed. Baltimore.

Goldhill, S., and Osborne, R., eds. 1999. *Performance Culture and Athenian Democracy.* Cambridge.

Gomme, A. W. 1933. *The Population of Athens in the Fifth and Fourth Centuries B.C.* Oxford.

Gomme, A. W. 1951. "The Working of the Athenian Democracy." *History* 36.126–127:12–28.

Gordillo Hervás, R. 2013. "Il Panhellenion e i suoi membri: un riesame della documentazione epigrafica relativa alla composizione della lega." *MediterrAnt* 16.1:101–21.

Gossman, L. 2000. *Basel in the Age of Burckhardt. A Study in Unseasonable Ideas.* Chicago.

Gossman, L. 2003. "Per me si va nella città dolente: Burckhardt and the *Polis*." In *Out of Arcadia. Classics and Politics in Germany in the Age of Burckhardt, Nietzsche and Wilamowitz*, edited by I. Gildenhard and M. Ruehl, 47–59. London.
Gottesman, A. 2014. *Politics and the Street in Democratic Athens*. Cambridge.
Gottlieb, G. 1967. *Timuchen. Ein Beitrag zum griechischen Staatsrechts*. Heidelberg.
Gounaris, A. 1999. "Έρευνες οικιστικής των Πρωτογεωμετρικών—Γεωμετρικών Κυκλάδων και τα ζητούμενα της Κυκλαδικής πρωτοϊστορίας." In *Φώς Κυκλαδικόν. Τιμητικός τόμος στη μνήμη του Νίκου Ζαφειροπούλου*, edited by N. Zapheiropoulos, 96–113. Stampolidēs.
Gounaris, A. 2005. "Cult Places in the Cyclades during the Protogeometric and Geometric Periods: Their Contribution in Interpreting the Rise of the Cycladic *Poleis*." In *Architecture and Archaeology in the Cyclades. Papers in Honour of J. J. Coulton*, edited by M. Yeroulanou and M. Stamatopoulou, 13–68. Oxford.
Gourgouris, S. 2019. *The Perils of the One*. New York.
Graeber, D., and Wengrow, D. 2021. *The Dawn of Everything. A New History of Humanity*. New York.
Graf, D. 1985. "Greek Tyrants and Achaemenid Politics." In *The Craft of the Ancient Historian. Essays in Honor of C. G. Starr*, edited by J. Eadie and J. Ober, 79–123. Lanham, MD.
Graf, D. 2019. "Palmyra: The Indigenous Factor." In *Roman Imperial Cities in the East and in Central-Southern Italy*, edited by N. Andrade et al., 295–324. Rome.
Graham, A. J. 1983. *Colony and Mother City in Ancient Greece*. 2nd ed. Chicago.
Graindor, P. 1930. *Un milliardaire antique. Hérode Atticus et sa famille*. Cairo.
Graindor, P. 1934. *Athènes sous Hadrien*. Cairo.
Grandjean, Y. 1988. *Recherches sur l'habitat thasien à l'époque grecque*. Athens.
Grandjean, Y., and Salviat. F. 2000. *Guide de Thasos*. 2nd ed. Athens.
Graninger, D. 2011a. "'In As Much Land as the Pheraioi Rule': A Note on SEG 23, 418." *Tyche* 11.2:88–90.
Graninger, D. 2011b. *Cult and Koinon in Hellenistic Thessaly*. Leiden.
Granovetter, M. 1985. "Economic Action and Social Structure: The Problem of Embeddedness." *American Journal of Sociology* 91.3:481–510.
Gray, B. 2013. "The Polis Becomes Humane? φιλανθρωπία as a Cardinal Civic Virtue in Later Hellenistic Honorific Epigraphy and Historiography." *Parole in movimento. Linguaggio politico e lessico storiografico nel mondo ellenistico*, edited by M. Mari and J. Thornton, 137–62. Pisa.
Gray, B. 2015. Stasis *and Stability. Exile, the Polis and Political Thought, c. 404–146 B.C.* Oxford.
Gray, B. 2018a. "A Civic Alternative to Stoicism: The Ethics of Hellenistic Honorary Decrees." *ClAnt* 37.2:187–235.
Gray, B. 2018b. "A Later Hellenistic Debate about the Value of Classical Athenian Civic Ideals? The Evidence of Epigraphy, Historiography and Philosophy." In *The Hellenistic Reception of Classical Athenian Democracy and Political Thought*, edited by M. Canevaro and B. Gray, 139–76. Oxford.
Gray, B. 2022. "L'invention du social? Délimiter la politique dans la cité grecque (de la fin de la période classique au début de l'époque impériale." *Annales (HSS)* 77.4:633–71.
Greco, E. 2020. *En Grèce et en Grande Grèce. Archéologie, espace et sociétés*. Naples.
Green, D. 2014. *The Hundred Years War. A People's History*. New Haven.
Green, J. R. 1990. "Zagora–Population Increase and Society in the Late Eighth Century." In ΕΥΜΟΥΣΙΑ. *Ceramic and Iconographic Studies in Honour of Alexander Cambitoglou*, edited by J.-P. Descoeudres, 41–47. Sydney.
Greenhalgh, P. A. L. 1973. *Early Greek Warfare*. Cambridge.
Gregory, T. E. 1979. "Roman Inscriptions from Aidepsos." *GRBS* 20:255–77.
Grenet, C. 2011. "Un litige foncier à Daulis au IIe ap. J.-C. (*IG* IX, 1, 61)." In *Philologos Dionysios. Mélanges offerts au professeur Denis Knoepfler*, edited by N. Badoud, 103–48. Geneva.
Grieb, V. 2008. *Hellenistische Demokratie. Politische Organisation und Struktur in freien griechischen Poleis nach Alexander dem Grossen*. Stuttgart.
Griesbach, J. 2016. "Wechselnde Standorte: Griechische Porträtstatuen und die Neu-Konfiguration von Erinnerungsräumen." In *Eikones. Portraits en contexte. Recherches nouvelles sur les portraits grecs du Ve au Ier s. av. J.-C.*, edited by F. Queyrell et al., 149–85. Venosa.
Grote, O. 2016. "Die Genese der griechischen Polis als Ausdifferenzierung von Systemen." *Gymnasium* 123.5:467–89.
Gruben, G. 2001. *Griechische Tempel und Heiligtümer*. 5th ed. Munich.
Gruen, E. S. 1984. *The Hellenistic World and the Coming of Rome, I-II*. Berkeley.

Gschnitzer, F. 2001–3. *Kleine Schriften zum griechischen und römischen Altertum*. Stuttgart.
Guerber, É. 1995. "Cité libre ou stipendiaire? À propos du statut juridique d'Éphèse à l'époque du Haut-Empire Romain." *REG* 108.2:388–409.
Guerber, É. 2009. *Les cités grecques dans l'Empire romain. Les privilèges et les titres des cités de l'Orient hellénophone d'Octave Auguste à Dioclétien*. Rennes.
Guía Valdés, M. A. 2019. "The Social and Cultural Background of Hoplite Development in Archaic Athens: Peasants, Debts, Zeugitai and Hoplethes." *Historia* 68.4:388–412.
Günther, L.-M. 2014a. *Bürgerinnen und ihre Familien im hellenistischen Milet. Untersuchungen zur Rolle von Frauen und Mädchen in der Polis-Öffentlichkeit*. Wiesbaden.
Günther, L.-M. 2014b. "Überlegungen zur sozialen Mobilität von Metöken in hellenistischen Poleis." In *Mobilität in den Kulturen der antiken Mittelmeerwelt*, edited by V. Sauer and E. Olshausen, 267–74. Stuttgart.
Günther, W. 1970. "Zwei neue Temenitenverzeichnisse aus Milet." *Chiron* 25:43–54.
Günther, W. 1995. "Zwei neue Temenitenverzeichnisse aus Milet." *Chiron* 25:43–53.
Gür, A. 1992. "L'émeute genevoise de janvier 1789 avait-elle un caractère insurrectionnel?" In *Regards sur la Révolution genevoise, 1792–1798*, 37–67. Geneva.
Gygax, M. D., and Zuiderhoek, A., eds. 2020. *Benefactors and the Polis. The Public Gift in the Greek Cities from the Homeric World to Late Antiquity*. Cambridge.
Haberman, W. 2014. "Bemerkungen zur Größe von Stadträten im kaiserzeitlichen griechischen Osten." *MBAHWS* 32:227–47.
Habicht, C. 1975. "New Evidence on the Province of Asia." *JRS* 55:64–91.
Habicht, C. 1982. *Studien zur Geschichte Athens in hellenistischer Zeit*. Göttingen.
Habicht, C. 1984. "Zur Personenkunde des griechisch-römischen Altertums." *BASP* 21.1–4:69–75.
Habicht. C. 1989. "The Seleucids and their Rivals." In *Cambridge Ancient History*, 2nd ed., edited by A. E. Astin et al., 324–87. Cambridge.
Habicht, C. 1995. "Ist ein 'Honoratiorenregime' das Kennzeichen der Stadt im späteren Hellenismus?" In *Stadtbild und Bürgerbild im Hellenismus*, edited by M. Wörrle and P. Zanker, 87–92. Munich.
Habicht, C. 1997a. *Athens from Alexander to Antony*. Cambridge, MA.
Habicht, C. 1997b. "Ein neues Zeugnis der athenischen Kavallerie?" *ZPE* 15:121–4.
Habicht, C. 1997c. "Zwei Familien aus Messene." *ZPE* 115:125–27.
Habicht, C. 1999. "Zu griechischen Inschriften aus Kleinasien." *EA* 31:19–29.
Habicht, C. 2003. "Rhodian Amphora Stamps and Rhodian Eponyms." *REA* 105.2:541–78.
Habicht. C. 2006. *Athènes hellénistique: histoire de la cité d'Alexandre le Grand à Marc Antoine*. Translated by M. and D. Knoepfler. 2nd edition. Paris.
Habicht, C. 2007. "Neues zur hellenistischen Geschichte von Kos." *Chiron* 37: 123–152.
Habicht, C. 2008. "Judicial Control of the Legislature in Greek States." *Studi Ellenistici* 20:17–23.
Habicht, C. 2017. *Divine Honors for Mortal Men in Greek Cities. The Early Cases*. Translated by J. N. Dillon. Ann Arbor, MI.
Hägg, R. 1982. "Zur Stadtwerdung des dorischen Argos." In *Palast und Hütte. Beiträge zum Bauen und Wohnen im Altertum*, edited by D. Papenfuss and V. Strocka, 297–307. Mainz.
Hägg, R. 1983a. *The Greek Renaissance of the Eighth Century B.C. Tradition and Innovation*. Stockholm.
Hägg, R. 1983b. "Burial Customs and Social Differentiation in 8th-century Argos." In *The Greek Renaissance of the Eighth Century B.C. Tradition and Innovation*, edited by R. Hägg, 27–31. Stockholm.
Haggis, C. D., et al. 2011. "Excavations in the Archaic Civic Buildings at Azoria in 2005–2006." *Hesperia* 80.1:1–70.
Hailer, U. 2008. *Einzelgehöfte im Bergland von Yavu (Zentrallykien)*. Bonn.
Haldon, J. 1999. "The Idea of the Town in the Byzantine Empire." In *The Idea and Ideal of the Town Between Late Antiquity and the Early Middle Ages*, edited by G. P. Brogiolo and B. Ward-Perkins, 1–23. Leiden.
Halfmann, H. 1979. *Die Senatoren aus dem östlichen Teil des Imperium Romanum bis zum Ende des 2. Jahrhunderts n. Chr.* Göttingen.
Halfmann, H. 2004. *Éphèse et Pergame. Urbanisme et commanditaires en Asie mineure romaine*. Pessac.
Hall, A. S., Milner N. P., and Coulton, J. J. 1996. "The Mausoleum of Licinnia Flavilla and Flavianus Diogenes of Oinoanda: Epigraphy and Architecture." *AN* 46:111–44.
Hall, J. M. 1995. "The Political and Cultic Geography of the Argive Plain, 900–400 B.C." *American Journal of Archaeology* 99.4:577–613.
Hall, J. M. 1997a. *Ethnic Identity in Greek Antiquity*. Cambridge.

Hall, J. M. 1997b. "Alternative Responses within *Polis* Formation: Argos, Mykenai and Tiryns." In *Urbanization in the Mediterranean in the 9th to 6th Centuries BC.*, edited by H. D. Andersen et al., 89–109. Copenhagen.
Hall, J. M. 2002. *Hellenicity. Between Ethnicity and Culture*. Chicago.
Hall, J. M. 2007. "Politics and Greek Myth." In *The Cambridge Companion to Greek Mythology*, edited by R. Woodard, 331–54. Cambridge.
Hall, J. M. 2013. "The Rise of State Action in the Archaic Age." In *A Companion to Ancient Greek Government*, edited by H. Beck, 7–21. Malden, MA.
Hallmannsecker, M. 2017. "Heracles Hoplophylax, Iudaioi, and a Palm Grove: A Fresh Look at I. Smyrna 697." *EA* 50:109–27.
Hallmannsecker, M. 2020. "The Ionian Koinon and the Koinon of the 13 Cities at Sardis." *Chiron* 50:1–27.
Halperin, M. D. 1990. *One Hundred Years of Homosexuality and Other Essays on Greek Love*. London.
Halstead, P. 1996. "The Development of Agriculture and Pastoralism in Greece: When, How, Who and What?" In *The Origins and Spread of Agriculture and Pastoralism in Eurasia*, edited by D. Harris, 296–309. Washington.
Halstead, P. 2014. *Two Oxen Ahead. Pre-Mechanized Farming in the Mediterranean*. Hoboken, NJ.
Halstead, P., and Jones, G. 1989. "Agrarian Ecology in the Greek Islands: Time Stress, Scale and Risk." *JHS* 109:41–55.
Hamel, D. 2003. *Trying Neaira. The True Story of a Courtesan's Scandalous Life in Ancient Greece*. New Haven.
Hamilton, C. D. 1979. *Sparta's Bitter Victories. Politics and Diplomacy in the Corinthian War*. Ithaca, NY.
Hammer, D. 2002. *The Iliad as Politics. The Performance of Political Thought*. Norman, OK.
Hammer, D. 2004. "Ideology, the Symposium, and Archaic Politics." *AJP* 125.4:479–512.
Hammond, N G. L. 1967. *Epirus. The Geography, the Ancient Remains, the History and Topography of Epirus and Adjacent Areas*. Oxford.
Hamon, P. 1999. "Juges thasiens à Smyrne: I. Smyrna 582 complété." *BCH* 123.1:175–94.
Hamon, P. 2005. "Le Conseil et la participation des citoyens: les mutations de la basse époque hellénistique." In *Citoyenneté et participation à la basse époque hellénistique*, edited by P. Fröhlich and C. Müller, 121–44. Geneva.
Hamon, P. 2007. "Élites dirigeantes et processus d'aristocratisation à l'époque hellénistique." In *Aristocratie antique. Modèles et exemplarité sociale*, edited by H.-L. Fernoux and C. Stein, 77–98. Dijon.
Hamon, P. 2008. "Kymè d'Éolide, cité libre et démocratique, et le pouvoir des stratèges." *Chiron* 38:63–106.
Hamon, P. 2009. "Démocraties grecques après Alexandre: à propos de trois ouvrages récents." *Topoi (Lyon)* 16.2:347–82.
Hamon, P. 2010. "Études d'épigraphie thasienne, III: Un troisième fragment de la Stèle des Braves et le rôle des polémarques à Thasos." *BCH* 134.1:301–15.
Hamon, P. 2012. "Gleichheit, Ungleichheit und Euergetismus: die *isotes* in den kleinasiatischen Poleis der hellenistischen Zeit." In *Demokratie im Hellenismus. Von der Herrschaft des Volkes zur Herrschaft der Honoratioren?*, edited by C. Mann and P. Schol, 56–73. Manz.
Hamon, P. 2016. "La Moire à Apollonia de Phrygie: deux décrets de consolation de l'époque d'Hadrien." *Chiron* 46:265–84.
Hamon, P. 2021. "Conclusion: profits et pertes de la haute époque hellénistique—un essai d'inventaire en Asie Mineure." In *L'Asie Mineure occidentale au IIIe siècle a. C.*, edited by P. Brun, L. Capdetrey, and P. Fröhlich, 397–413. Bordeaux.
Hagedorn, D. 2007. "The Emergence of Municipal Offices in the Nome-capitals of Egypt." In *Oxyrhynchus. A City and Its Texts*, edited by A. K. Bowman et al., 194–204. London.
Hankins, J. 2019. *Virtue politics. Soulcraft and Statecraft in Renaissance Italy*. Cambridge, MA.
Hansen, M. H. 1980. "Seven Hundred *archai* in Classical Athens." *GRBS* 21.2:151–73.
Hansen, M. H. 1985. *Demography and Democracy. The number of Athenian Citizens in the Fourth Century B.C.* Herning.
Hansen, M. H. 1989a. "Demos, ekklesia, and dikasterion. A Reply to Martin Ostwald and Josiah Ober." *C&M* 40:101–6.
Hansen, M. H. 1989b. "On the Importance of Institutions in an Analysis of Athenian Democracy." *C&M* 40:107–13.
Hansen, M. H. 1989c. "Athenian Democracy. Institutions and Ideology." *CPh* 84.2:137–48.
Hansen, M. H. 1991. *The Athenian Democracy in the Age of Demosthenes. Structure, Principles and Ideology*, trans. J. A. Crook. Oxford.

Hansen, M. H. 1995. "The 'Autonomous City-State': Ancient Fact or Modern Fiction?" In *Studies in the Ancient Greek Polis*, edited by M. H. Hansen and A. K. Raaflaub, 21–43. Stuttgart.

Hansen, M. H 1997a. "The *Polis* as an Urban Centre: The Literary and Epigraphical Evidence." In *The Polis as an Urban Centre and as a Political Community*, edited by M. Hansen, 9–86. Copenhagen.

Hansen, M. H. 1997b. "One Hundred and Sixty Theses about Athenian Democracy." *C&M* 48:204–65.

Hansen, M. H., ed. 1998. *Polis and City-state. An Ancient Concept and its Modern Equivalent*. Copenhagen.

Hansen, M. H., ed. 2000. *A Comparative Study of Thirty City-State Cultures. An Investigation Conducted by the Copenhagen Polis Centre*. Copenhagen.

Hansen, M. H. 2002a. "Was the *Polis* a State or a Stateless Society?" In *Even More Studies in the Ancient Greek Polis*, edited by T. H. Nielsen, 17–47. Stuttgart.

Hansen, M. H., ed. 2002b. *A Comparative Study of Six City-State Cultures. An Investigation Conducted by the Copenhagen Polis Centre*. Copenhagen.

Hansen, M. H. 2004. "The Concept of the Consumption City Applied to the Greek *Polis*." In *Once Again. Studies in the Ancient Greek Polis*, edited by T. Heine Nielsen, 9–47. Stuttgart.

Hansen, M. H. 2006. *The Shotgun Method. The Demography of the Ancient Greek City-State Culture*. Columbia, MO.

Hansen, M. H. 2008. "An Update on the Shotgun Method." *GRBS* 48.3:259–86.

Hansen, M. H. 2010. "The Concepts of *Demos*, *Ekklesia*, and *Dikasterion* in Classical Athens." *GRBS* 50.4:499–536.

Hansen, M. H. 2013. Review of E. Robinson, "Democracy beyond Athens: Popular Government in the Greek Classical Age." *BMCR* 2013.01.17.

Hanson, V. D. 1999. *The Wars of the Ancient Greeks and Their Invention of Western Military Culture*. London.

Hanson. J. W. 2011. "The Urban System of Roman Asia Minor and Wider Urban Connectivity." In *Settlement, Urbanization, and Population*, edited by A. Bowman and A. Wilson, 229–75. Oxford.

Hardin, G. 1968. "The Tragedy of the Commons." *Science* 162.3859:1243–48.

Harl, K. W. 1987. *Civic Coins and Civic Politics in the Roman East, A.D. 180–275*. Berkeley.

Harper, K. 2017. "Freedom, Slavery and Female Sexual Honor in Antiquity." *On Human Bondage. After Slavery and Social Death*, edited by J. Bodel and W. Scheidel, 109–21. Malden, MA.

Harris, E. M. 2012 "Homer, Hesiod, and the 'Origins' of Greek Slavery." *REA* 114.2:345–66

Harris, E. M. 2017. "Applying the Law about the Award of Crowns to Magistrates (Aeschin. 3.9–31; Dem. 18.113–117): Epigraphic Evidence for the Legal Arguments at the Trial of Ctesiphon." *ZPE* 202:105–17.

Harris, E. M., Lewis D. M., and Woolmer, M., eds. 2016. *The Ancient Greek Economy. Markets, Households and City-States*. Cambridge.

Harris, E., and Lewis, D. 2022. "What Are Early Greek Laws About? Substance and Procedure in Archaic Statutes, c. 650–450 BC." In *From Homer to Solon. Continuity and Change in Archaic Greece*, edited by J. C. Bernhardt and M. Canevaro, 227–62. Leiden.

Harris, W. V. 1979. *War and Imperialism in Republican Rome 327-70 B.C*. Oxford.

Harris, W. V. 2016. *Roman Power. A Thousand Years of Empire*. Cambridge.

Harrison, T., and Irwin, E., eds. 2018. *Interpreting Herodotus*. Oxford.

Harter-Uibopuu, K. 2008. "Hadrian and the Athenian Oil Law." In *Feeding the City*, edited by R. Alston and O. van Nijf, 127–41. Leuven.

Harter-Uibopuu, K. 2013. "Bestandsklauseln und Abänderungsverbote: der Schutz zweckgebundener Gelder in der späthellenistischen und kaiserzeitlichen Polis." *Tyche* 28:51–96.

Hartog, F. 1988. *Le XIXème siècle et l'histoire. Le cas Fustel de Coulanges*. Paris.

Hartog, F. 2015. *Partir pour la Grèce*. Paris.

Harvey, F. D. 1965. "Two Types of Equality." *C&M* 26:101–46.

Harvey, F. D. 1966. "Corrigenda to *C&M* XXVI 1965 101–46." *C&M* 27:99–100.

Harvey, F. D. 1984. "The Wicked Wife of Ischomachos." *EMC* 28:68–70.

Harvey, F. D. 1985 "*Dona ferentes*: Some Aspects of Bribery in Greek Politics." In *Crux. Essays in Greek History Presented to G. E. M. de Ste. Croix on His 75th Birthday*, edited by P. A. Cartledge and F. D. Harvey, 76–117. Exeter & London.

Hatzfeld, J. 1919. *Les trafiquants italiens dans l'Orient hellénique*. Paris.

Hatzopoulos, M. B. 1994. *Cultes et rites de passage en Macédoine*. Athens.

Hatzopoulos, M. B. 1996. *Macedonian Institutions under the Kings. A Historical and Epigraphic Study*. Athens.

Haubold, J. 2000. *Homer's People. Epic Poetry and Social Formation*. Cambridge.

Hauken, T. 1998. *Petition and Response. An Epigraphic Study of Petitions to Roman Emperors, 181–249*. Bergen.

Haussoullier, B. 1910. "Jules Delamarre." *JS* 8:40–1.
Hawke, J. 2011. *Writing Authority. Elite Competition and Written Law in Early Greece.* DeKalb, IL.
Haymann, F. 2014. *Untersuchungen zur Geschichte und Identitätskonstruktion von Aigeai im römischen Kilikien (20 v.–260 n. Chr.).* Bonn.
Healey, J. F. 2009. *Aramaic Inscriptions and Documents of the Roman Period.* Oxford.
Heath, M. 2004. *Menander. A Rhetor in Context.* Oxford
Heberdey, R., and Wilhelm, A. 1896. *Reisen in Kilikien, ausgeführt 1891 und 1892.* Vienna.
Heclo, H. 2008. *On Thinking Institutionally.* Boulder, CO.
Hedrick, C. 1994. "The Zero Degree of Society: Aristotle and the Athenian Citizen." In *Athenian Political Thought and the Reconstruction of American Democracy*, edited by J. P. Euben, J. R. Wallace, and J. Ober, 289–318. Ithaca, NY.
Hedrick, C. W. 1999. "Democracy and the Athenian Epigraphical Habit." *Hesperia* 68.3:387–439.
Heinze, L. 2014. "Modernisierte Hüllen? Das Letoon Bei Xanthos Und Die Verwendung Von Tempeln Als Medium Der Erinnerungskultur in Hellenistischen Heiligtümern." In *Stadtkultur im Hellenismus*, edited by M. Zimmermann, 76–96. Mainz.
Heisserer, A. J. 1980. *Alexander the Great and the Greeks. The Epigraphic Evidence.* Norman, OK.
Held, W., and C. Wilkening-Aumann. 2015. "Vom karischen Bund zur griechischen Polis. Archäologischer Survey in Bybassos und Kastabos auf der karischen Chersones." In *Urbane Strukturen und bürgerliche Identität im Hellenismus*, edited by A. Matthaei and M. Zimmermann, 74–98. Heidelberg.
Heller, A. 2006a. *Les Bêtises des Grecs. Conflits et Rivalités entre Cités d'Asie et de Bithynie à l'époque Romaine (129 A.C.–235 P.C.).* Bordeaux.
Heller, A. 2006b. "Titulatures de cités et contrôle du pouvoir central: le cas de la troisième néocorie d'Éphèse." In *La 'crise' de l'Empire romain de Marc Aurèle à Constantin. Mutations, continuités, ruptures*, edited by M.-H. Quet et al., 279–306. Paris.
Heller, A. 2009. "La cité grecque d'époque impériale: vers une société d'ordres?" *Annales (HSS)* 64.2:341–73.
Heller, A. 2013. "Les institutions civiques grecques sous l'Empire: romanisation ou aristocratisation?" In *Les Grecs héritiers des Romains*, edited by P. Derron, 203–42. Vandœuvres.
Heller, A. 2014. "Domination subie, domination choisie: les cités d'Asie Mineure face au pouvoir romain, de la république à l'empire." *Pallas* 96:217–32.
Heller, A. 2017. "Priesthoods and Civic Ideology: Honorific Titles for *Hiereis* and *Archiereis* in Roman Asia Minor." In *Empire and Religion. Religious Change in Greek Cities under Roman Rule*, edited by E. M Gijavlo, J. M. C. Copete and F. L. Gómez, 1–20. Leiden.
Heller. A. 2019a. "Greek Citizenship in the Roman Empire: Political Participation, Social Status and Identities/" In *In The Crucible of Empire. The Impact of Roman Citizenship upon Greeks, Jews and Christians*, edited by K. Berthelot and J. Price, 55–72. Leuven.
Heller. A. 2019b. "Leading Families in the Cities of Roman Asia Minor: A Quantitative Approach." In *Roman Imperial Cities in the East and in Central-Southern Italy*, edited by N. Andrade, C. Marcaccini, G. Marconi, and D. Viola, 93–103. Rome.
Heller, A. 2020. *L'âge d'or des bienfaiteurs. Titres honorifiques et sociétés civiques dans l'Asie Mineure d'époque romaine Ier s. av. J.-C.—IIIe apr. J.-C.* Geneva.
Heller, A., and Pont, A.-V. 2012. eds. *Patrie d'origine et patries électives: les citoyennetés multiples dans le monde grec d'époque romaine.* Pessac.
Heller, A., and van Nijf, O. ed. 2017. *The Politics of Honour in the Greek Cities of the Roman Empire.* Leiden.
Helly, B. 1995. *L'État thessalien. Aleuas le Roux, les tétrades et les tagoi.* Lyon.
Helly, B. 2008a. "Encore le blé thessalien: trois décrets de Larisa (*IG* IX 2, 506), accordant aux Athéniens licence d'exportation et réduction des droits de douane sur leurs achats de blé." *Studi ellenistici* 20:25–108.
Helly, B. 2008b. "Un décret pour des juges de Messène: le décret *IG* V 1, 1428 + *addenda* p. 311 (L. Robert, *OMS* I, p. 51–56)." *RPh* 81.1:129–43.
Helly, B. 2009. "La Thessalie au 3ᵉ siècle av. J.-C." In *Αρχαιολογικό έργο Θεσσαλίας και Στερεάς Ελλάδας. 2, Πρακτικά επιστημονικής συνάντησης*, edited by A. Mazarakis-Ainian, 339–68. Volos.
Helly, B., and Tziafalias, A. 2013. "Décrets inédits de Larisa organisant la vente de terres publiques attribuées aux cavaliers." *Topoi (Lyon)* 18.1:135–249.
Hennemeyer, A. 2013. *Das Athenaheiligtum von Priene. Die Nebenbauten. Altar, Halle und Propylon und die bauliche Entwicklung des Heiligtums.* Munich.

Hennig, D. 1995. "Staatliche Ansprüche an privaten Immobilienbesitz in der klassischen und hellenistischen Polis." *Chiron* 25:235–82.

Henry, M. M. 2011. "The Traffic in Women: From Homer to Hipponax, from War to Commerce." In *Greek Prostitutes in the Ancient Mediterranean, 800 BCE–200 CE*, edited by A. M. J. Glazebrook and M. M. Henry, 14–33. Madison, WI.

Henry, O., ed. 2013. *4th Century Karia. Defining a Karian Identity under the Hekatomnids*. Istanbul.

Hepding, H. 1907. "Die Arbeiten zu Pergamon 1904–1905. 2. Die Inschriften." *MDAI(A)* 32:241–377.

Herda, A. 2006. "Panionion-Melia, Mykalessos-Mykale, Perseus und Medusa. Überlegungen zur Besiedlungsgeschichte der Mykale in der frühen Eisenzeit." *MDAI(I)* 56:43–102.

Herda, A. 2009. "Karkisa-Karien und die sogennante Ionische Migration." In *Die Karer und die Anderen*, edited by F. Rumscheid, 27–108. Bonn.

Herman, G. 1987. *Ritualised Friendship and the Greek City*. Cambridge.

Herman, G. 2006. *Morality and Behaviour in Democratic Athens. A Social History*. Cambridge.

Herrmann, P. 1959. *Neue Inschriften zur historischen Landeskunde von Lydien und angrenzenden Gebieten*. Vienna.

Herrmann, P. 1965. "Neue Urkunden zur Geschichte von Milet im 2. Jahrhundert v. Chr." *MDAI(I)* 15:71–117.

Herrmann, P. 1980. "Urkunden milesischer Temenitai." *MDAI(I)* 30:223–39.

Herrmann, P. 1981. "Teos und Abdera im 5. Jahrhundert v. Chr. Ein neues Fragment der *Teiorum Dirae*." *Chiron* 11:1–30.

Herrmann, P. 1993. "Epigraphische Notizen: 10. πολιτεία—πολιτεύεσθαι. 11. Ein scriniarius. 12. ἴδρις: zu Grabepigrammen aus Selge und Hadrianoi." *EA* 21:71–76.

Herrmann, P. 1997. "Die Karriere eines prominenten Juristen aus Thyateira." *Tyche* 12:111–24.

Herrmann, P. 2001. "Milet au IIe siècle a.C." In *Les cités d'Asie mineure occidentale au IIe siècle a.C.*, edited by A. Bresson and R. Descat, 109–16. Paris.

Herrmann, P. 2002. "Das κοινὸν τῶν Ἰώνων unter römischer Herrschaft." In *Widerstand-Anpassung-Integration. Die griechische Staatenwelt und Rom. Festschrift für Jürgen Deininger zum 65. Geburtstag*, edited by N. Ehrhardt and L.-M. Günther, 207–22. Stuttgart.

Herrmann, P. 2016. *Kleinasien im Spiegel epigraphischer Zeugnisse: ausgewählte kleine Schriften*, edited by W. Blümel. Berlin.

Herrmann, P., and Polatkan, K. Z. 1969. *Das Testament des Epikrates und andere neue Inschriften aus dem Museum von Manisa*. Vienna.

Herz, P. 2008. "Überlegungen zur Geschichte des makedonischen Koinon im dritten Jahrhundert." In *Festrituale in der römischen Kaiserzeit*, edited by J. Rüpke, 115–32. Tübingen.

Heuss, A. 1937. *Stadt und Herrscher des Hellenismus in ihren staats- und völkerrechtlichen Beziehungen*. Leipzig.

Heyn, M. 2010. "Gesture and Identity in the Funerary Art of Palmyra." *AJA* 114.4:631–61.

Higbie, C. 2003. *The Lindian Chronicle and the Greek Creation of Their Past*. Oxford.

Hignett, C. 1952. *A History of the Athenian Constitution to the End of the Fifth Century B.C.* Oxford.

Hirt, A. 2015. "Beyond Greece and Rome: Foundation Myths on Coinage in the Third Century AD." In *Foundation Myths in Ancient Societies. Dialogues and Discourses*, edited by N. Mac Sweeney, 190–226. Philadelphia.

Hodkinson, S. 2000. *Property and Wealth in Classical Sparta*. London.

Hodkinson, S. 2009. "Was Sparta an Exceptional Polis?" In *Sparta: Comparative Approaches*, edited by T. Barnes and S. Hodkinson, 417–72. Swansea.

Hodkinson, S., and Hodkinson, H. 1981. "Mantineia and the Mantinike: Settlement and Society in a Greek Polis." *BSA* 76:239–96.

Hodkinson, S., Morris I. M., and Christesen, P., eds. 2012. *Sparta in Modern Thought. Politics, History and Culture*. Swansea.

Hodkinson, S., and Powell, A., eds. 2002. *Sparta. Beyond the Mirage*. London.

Hoepfner, W., and Schwandner, E.-L. 1994. *Haus und Stadt im klassischen Griechenland*. Munich.

Hoffmann, H. 1972. *Early Cretan Armorers*. Mainz.

Hoftijzer, J., and Jongeling, K. 1995. *Dictionary of the North-West Semitic Inscriptions*. Leiden.

Hölbl, G. 2004. *Geschichte des Ptolemäerreiches. Politik, Ideologie und religiöse Kultur von Alexander dem Grossen bis zur römischen Eroberung*. Stuttgart.

Hölkeskamp, K.-J. 1992. "Written Law in Archaic Greece." *PCPhS* 38:87–117.

Hölkeskamp, K.-J. 1993. "Demonax und die Neuordnung der Bürgerschaft von Kyrene." *Hermes* 121.4:404–21.

Hölkeskamp, K.-J. 1997. "*Agorai* bei Homer." In *Volk und Verfassung im vorhellenistischen Griechenland*, edited by W. Eder and K.-J. Hölkeskamp, 1–19. Stuttgart.

Holleaux, M. 1921. *Rome, la Grèce et les monarchies hellénistiques au IIIe siècle avant J. C. (273–205)*. Paris.
Holleaux, M. 1926. "La politique romaine en Grèce et dans l'Orient hellénistique au IIIe siècle." *RPh* 50:46–66.
Hölscher, T. 1998. *Öffentliche Räume in frühen griechischen Städten*. Heidelberg.
Holtzmann, B. 2003. *L'Acropole d'Athènes. Monuments, cultes et histoire du sanctuaire d'Athéna Polias*. Paris.
Honigmann, E. 1939a. "La liste originale des Pères de Nicée: à propos de l'Évêché de 'Sodoma' en Arabie." *Byzantion* 14.1:17–76.
Honigmann E. 1939b. *Le synekdèmos d'Hiéroklès et l'opuscule géographique de Georges de Chypre*. Brussels.
Honneth, A. 1996. *The Struggle for Recognition. The Moral Grammar of Social Conflicts*. Cambridge, MA.
Honneth, A. 2012. *The I in We. Studies in the Theory of Recognition*. Cambridge, MA.
Hopkins, K. 1980. "Taxes and Trade in the Roman Empire (200 B.C.–A.D. 400)." *JRS* 70:101–25.
Hopkins, K. 1983. *Death and Renewal. Sociological Studies in Roman History II*. Cambridge.
Horden, P., and Purcell, N. 2000. *The Corrupting Sea. A Study of Mediterranean History*. Oxford.
Horden, P., and Purcell, N. 2020. *The Boundless Sea. Writing Mediterranean History*. London.
Horkheimer. M. 1967. *Autoritärer Staat. Die Juden und Europa. Vernunft und Selbsterhaltung. Aufsätze 1939–1941*. Amsterdam.
Horkheimer, M. 1997. *Gesammelte Schriften Band 5. 'Dialektik der Aufklärung' und Schriften 1940–1950*. 2nd ed. Frankfurt.
Horn, R. 1972. *Hellenistische Bildwerke auf Samos*. Bonn.
Hornblower, S., ed. 1994. *Greek Historiography*. Oxford.
Hornblower, S. 2004. *Thucydides and Pindar. Historical Narrative and the World of Epinikian Poetry*. Oxford.
Hornblower, S., and Morgan, C., eds. 2007. *Pindar's Poetry, Patrons, and Festivals: From Archaic Greece to the Roman Empire*. Oxford.
Hornblower, S. 2011. *The Greek World*. 4th ed. London.
Hostein, A. 2012. *La cité et l'empereur. Les Éduens dans l'Empire romain d'après les Panégyriques latins*. Paris.
Houby-Nielsen, S. 1992. "Interaction between Chieftains and Citizens? 7th Century BC Burial Customs in Athens." *ActaHyp* 4:343–74.
Houby-Nielsen, S. H. 1995. "'Burial Language' in Archaic and Classical Kerameikos." *Proceedings of the Danish Institute in Athens* 1:129–91.
Howgego, C. 2005. "Coinage and Identity in the Roman Provinces." In *Coinage and Identity in the Roman Provinces*, edited by C. Howgego, V. Heuchert, and A. Burnett, 1–17. Oxford.
Hughes, R., and Hillgarth, J. 2006. *The Catalan Expedition to the East. From the Chronicle of Ramon Muntaner*. Translated by R. Hughes. Barcelona.
Humphreys, S. C. 1978. *Anthropology and the Greeks*. London.
Humphreys, S. C. 2018. *Kinship in Ancient Athens. An Anthropological Analysis*. Oxford.
Hunt, P. 2010. *War, Peace and Alliance in Demosthenes' Athens*. Cambridge.
Hunt, P. 2017. "Slaves or Serfs? Patterson on the Thetes and Helots of Ancient Greece." In *On Human Bondage. After Slavery and Social Death*, edited by J. Bodel and W. Scheidel, 55–80. Malden, MA.
Hunter, V. J. 1994. *Policing Athens. Social Control in the Attic Lawsuits, 420–320 B.C*. Princeton.
Hurlet, F. 2012. "Démocratie à Rome? Quelle démocratie? En relisant Millar (et Hölkeskamp)." In *Rome. A City and its Empire in Perspective: The Impact of the Roman World through Fergus Millar's Research*, edited by S. Benoist, 19–43. Leiden.
Hurlet, F., and Müller, C. 2020. "L'Achaïe à l'époque républicaine (146–27 av. J.-C.): une province introuvable?" *Chiron* 50:49–100.
Hurwit, J. M. 1999. *The Athenian Acropolis. History, Mythology, and Archaeology from the Neolithic Era to the Present*. Cambridge.
Hurwit, J. M. 2002. "Reading the Chigi Vase." *Hesperia* 71.1:1–22.
Hurwit, J. M. 2004. *The Acropolis in the Age of Pericles*. Cambridge.
Ieraci Bio, A. M. 1987. *Galeno. De bonis malisque sucis*. Naples.
Igelbrink, C. 2015. *Die Kleruchien und Apoikien Athens im 6. und 5. Jahrhundert v. Chr. Rechtsformen und politische Funktionen der athenischen Gründungen*. Berlin.
Imhoof Blumer, F. 1890. *Griechische Münzen*. Munich.
Imrie, A. 2018. *The Antonine Constitution. An Edict for the Caracallan Empire*. Leiden.
Ingholt, H., Seyrig, H., and Starcky, J. 1955 *Recueil des tessères de Palmyre*. Paris.

Irwin, E. 2005. *Solon and Early Greek Poetry. The Politics of Exhortation*. Cambridge.
Irwin, T. 2007. *Development of Ethics. Volume 1. From Socrates to the Reformation*. Oxford.
Irwin, T. 2020. *Ethics Through History. An Introduction*. Oxford.
Isaac, B. 1990. *The Limits of Empire. The Roman Army in the East*. Oxford.
Isaac, B. H. 1996. "Eusebius and the Geography of Roman Provinces." In *The Roman Army in the East*, edited by D. L. Kennedy, 153–68. Ann Arbor, MI.
Isakhan, B., and Stockwell, S., eds. 2011. *The Secret History of Democracy*. London.
Ish-Shalom, T. 2023. *State Formation and Ethnic Identity in the Late-Seleucid Levant (200–63 BCE)*. Unpublished PhD dissertation. Columbia University.
Isin, E. F. 2002. *Being Political. Genealogies of Citizenship*. Minneapolis.
Ismard, P. 2007. "Les associations en Attique de Solon à Clisthène." In *Individus, groupes et politique à Athènes de Solon à Mithridate*, edited by J. Couvenhes and S. Milanezi, 17–33. Tours.
Ismard, P. 2010. *La cité des réseaux. Athènes et ses associations. VIe–Ier siècle av. J.-C.* Paris.
Ismard P. 2013 *L'événement Socrate*. Paris.
Ismard, P. 2015. *La démocratie contre les experts. Les esclaves publics en Grèce ancienne*. Paris.
Ismard, P. 2019. *La cité et ses esclaves. Institutions, fictions, expériences*. Paris.
Ismard, P. 2021. "L'invention de l'esclavage-marchandise? L'île de Chios, VIe–Ier siècles avant notre ère." In *Les mondes de l'esclavage. Une histoire comparée*, edited by P. Ismard, B. Rossi, and C. Vidal, 43–53. Paris.
Ismard, P., Rossi, B., and Vidal. C., eds. 2021. *Les Mondes de l'esclavage. Une histoire comparée*. Paris.
Jackson, A. 2000. "Argos' Victory over Corinth. ΑΡΓΕΙΟΙ ΑΝΕΘΕΝ ΤΟΙ ΔΙFΙ ΤΟΝ ϘΟΡΙΝΘΟΘΕΝ." *ZPE* 132:295–311.
Jacobs, I. 2013. *Aesthetic Maintenance of Civic Space. The 'Classical' City from the 4th to the 7th c. AD*. Leuven.
Jacobs, I., and Elton, H., eds. 2019. *Asia Minor in the Long Sixth Century. Current Research and Future Directions*. Oxford.
Jacobs, J. 1969. *The Economy of Cities*. New York.
Jacobs, J. 1984. *Cities and the Wealth of Nations. Principles of Economic Life*. New York.
Jacoby, F. 1945. "Some Athenian Epigrams from the Persian Wars." *Hesperia* 14.3:157–211.
Jacques, F. 1984. *Le privilège de liberté. Politique impériale et autonomie municipale dans les cités de l'Occident romain (161–244)*. Rome.
Jacques, F. 1990. *Les cités de l'occident romain. Du Ier siècle avant J.-C. au VIe siècle après J.-C. Documents traduits et commentés*. Paris.
James, J. 2024. "Indicting the Athenians in the Melian Dialogue." *JHS* 144:164–181.
Jameson, M. H. 1977. "Agriculture and Slavery in Classical Athens." *CJ* 73.2:122–45.
Jameson, M. H. et al., eds. 1994. *A Greek Countryside. The Southern Argolid from Prehistory to the Present Day*. Stanford, CA.
Jameson, S. 1965. "Cornutus Tertullus and the Plancii of Perge." *JRS* 55.1–2:54–58.
Jeffery, L. H. 1976. *Archaic Greece. The City-States c. 700–500 B.C.* New York.
Jeffery, L. H. 1990. *The Local Scripts of Archaic Greece. A Study of the Origin of the Greek Alphabet and its Development from the Eighth to the Fifth Centuries B.C.* 2nd ed. Edited by A. W. Johnston. Oxford.
Jehne, M. 1991. "Die Friedensverhandlungen von Sparta 392/1 v. Chr. und das Problem der kleinasiatischen Griechen." *Chiron* 21:265–76.
Jehne, M., and Polo, F. P., eds. 2015. *Foreign clientelae in the Roman Empire. A Reconsideration*. Stuttgart.
Jes, K. 2007. "Eine Stadt von edler Abkunft und hohem Alter: kulturelles Gedächtnis in Aizanoi im 2. Jh. n. Chr." In *Arte e memoria culturale nell'età della Seconda Sofistica*, edited by O. Cordovana and M. Galli, 153–68. Catania.
Johnston, A. 2017. *The Sons of Remus. Identity in Roman Gaul and Spain*. Cambridge, MA.
Johnstone, S. 1999. *Disputes and Democracy. The Consequences of Litigation in Ancient Athens*. Austin, TX.
Johnstone, S. 2011. *A History of Trust in Ancient Greece*. Chicago.
Jones, A. H. M. 1938. "The Election of the Metropolitan Magistrates in Egypt." *JEA* 24.1:65–72.
Jones, A. H. M. 1940. *The Greek City from Alexander to Justinian*. Oxford.
Jones, A. H. M. 1957. *Athenian Democracy*. Oxford.
Jones, A. H. M. 1964. *The Later Roman Empire 284–602*. Oxford.
Jones, A. H. M., et al., eds. 1971. *The Cities of the Eastern Roman Provinces*. Oxford.
Jones, C. P. 1971a. "The Levy at Thespiae under Marcus Aurelius." *GRBS* 12.1:45–48.
Jones, C. P. 1971b. *Plutarch and Rome*. Oxford.
Jones, C. P. 1974. "Diodoros Pasparos and the Nikephoria of Pergamon." *Chiron* 4:183–205.

Jones, C. P. 1975. "An Oracle Given to Trajan." *Chiron* 5:403–6.
Jones, C. P. 1976. "The Plancii of Perge and Diana Planciana." *HSPh* 80:231–37.
Jones, C. P. 1978. *The Roman World of Dio Chrysostom*. Cambridge, MA.
Jones, C. P. 1996. "The Panhellenion." *Chiron* 26:29–56.
Jones, C.P. 1999a. *Kinship Diplomacy in the Ancient World*. Cambridge, MA.
Jones, C. P. 1999b. "Interrupted Funerals," *PAPhS* 143.4:588–600.
Jones, C. P. 2004. "Events Surrounding the Bequest of Pergamon to Rome and the Revolt of Aristonicos: New Inscriptions from Metropolis." *JRA* 17:469–85.
Jones, C. P. 2007. "Juristes romains dans l'Orient grec." *CRAI* 151.3:1331–59.
Jones, C. P. 2010. "New Late Antique Epigrams from Stratonicea of Caria." *EA* 42:145–51.
Jones, C. P. 2013. "Earthquakes and Emperors." In *Infrastruktur und Herrschaftsorganisation im Imperium Romanum*, edited by A. Kolb, 52–65. Zürich.
Jones, C. P. 2014. "Louis Robert in Central Mysia." *Chiron* 44:23–54.
Jones, C. P. 2019a. "Aelius Aristeides in Mysia." In *Panegyrikoi Logoi. Festschrift für Johannes Nollé zum 65. Geburtstag*, edited by M. Nollé et al., 301–6. Bonn.
Jones, C. P. 2019b. "The Siege of Colophon and the Immunity of Claros." *ZPE* 210:137–46.
Jones, N. F. 1987. *Public Organization in Ancient Greece. A Documentary Study*. Philadelphia.
Jones, N. F. 1999. *The Associations of Classical Athens. The Response to Democracy*. Oxford.
Jones, N. F. 2004. *Rural Athens under the Democracy*. Philadelphia.
Jones, P. 1997. *The Italian City-State. From Commune to Signoria*. Oxford.
Jones, P. 2010. "Communes and Despots: The City State in Late-Medieval Italy." In *Communes and Despots in Medieval and Renaissance Italy*, edited by B. Paton and J. E. Law, 3–24. London.
Jördens, A. 2009. *Statthalterliche Verwaltung in der römischen Kaiserzeit. Studien zum praefectus Aegypti*. Stuttgart.
Jördens, A. 2013. "Roms Herrschaft über Ägypten." *JJP* 43:51–71.
Jouguet, P. 1911. *La vie municipale dans l'Egypte romaine*. Paris.
Kah, D. 2012. "'Paroikoi' und Neubürger in Priene." In *Migration und Bürgerrecht in der hellenistischen Welt*, edited by L.-M. Günther, 51–71. Wiesbaden.
Kah, D. 2014. "Demokratie in der Kleinstadt. Überlegungen Zu Demographie und Partizipation am Beispiel des Hellenistischen Priene." In *Stadtkultur im Hellenismus*, edited by A. Matthei and M. Zimmermann, 148–72. Mainz.
Kaimaris, D., Georgoula, O., Karadedos, G., and Patias, P. 2010. "Εναέρια και δορυφορική αρχαιολογία: εντοπισμός της Εγνατίας οδού και άλλων αρχαιολογικών θέσεων κατά μήκος της διαδρομής της, από την Αμφίπολη έως τους Φιλίππους." In *Το αρχαιολογικό έργο στη Μακεδονία και στη Θράκη. 21, 2007*, edited by P. Adam-Veleni and K. Tzanavari, 371–82. Thessaloniki.
Kaizer, T. 2002. *The Religious Life of Palmyra. A Study of the Social Patterns of Worship in the Roman Period*. Stuttgart.
Kaizer, T. 2008. *The Variety of Local Religious Life in the Near East. In the Hellenistic and Roman Periods*. Leiden.
Kaizer, T. 2016. "The Future of Palmyrene Studies." *JRA* 29:924–31.
Kaizer, T. 2018. "'Ich Bin Ein Palmyrerener' or 'Je Suis Tadmor': On How to Be a Proper Citizen of the Queen of the Desert." In *Palmyra: Mirage in the Desert*, edited by Joan Aruz, 76–89. New York.
Kalaitzi, M. 2016. *Figured Tombstones from Macedonia. Fifth to First Centuries BC*. Oxford.
Kaldellis, A. 2012. "The Byzantine Role in the Making of the Corpus of Classical Greek Historiography: A Preliminary Investigation." *JHS* 132:71–85.
Kaldellis, A. 2015. *The Byzantine Republic. People and Power in New Rome*. Cambridge.
Kalinowski, A. 2002. "The Vedii Antonini: Aspects of Patronage and Benefaction in Second-Century Ephesos." *Phoenix* 56:109–49.
Kalinowski, A. 2021. *Memory, Family and Community in Roman Ephesos*. Cambridge.
Kallet, L. 2013. "The Origins of the Athenian Economic Arche." *JHS* 133:43–60
Kallet L. and Kroll, J. 2020. *The Athenian Empire. Using Coins as Sources*. Cambridge.
Kallet-Marx, L. 1989. "Did Tribute Fund the Parthenon?" *Classical Antiquity* 8:252–66.
Kallet-Marx, R. M. 1985. "Athens, Thebes and the Foundation of the Second Athenian League." *ClAnt* 4:127–51.
Kallet-Marx, R. M. 1995. *Hegemony to Empire. the Development of the Roman Imperium in the East from 148 to 62 B.C.* Berkeley.
Kalliontzis, Y. 2017. "Akraiphia et la guerre entre Démétrios Poliorcète et les Béotiens." *BCH* 141.2:669–96.

Kalliontzis, Y. 2020. *Contribution à l'épigraphie et à l'histoire de la Béotie hellénistique. De la destruction de Thèbes à la bataille de Pydna*. Athens.

Kamen, D. 2013. *Status in Classical Athens*. Princeton.

Kaninia, E., and Schierup, S. 2017. "Vroulia Revisited: From K.F. Kinch's Excavations in the Early 20th Century to the Present Archaeological Site." *Proceedings of the Danish Institute at Athens* 8:89–129.

Kantirea, M. 2007. *Les dieux et les dieux augustes. Le culte impérial en Grèce sous les Julio-claudiens et les Flaviens*. Athens.

Kantirea, M. 2008. "Une famille sacerdotale du culte impérial de Sicyone (Syll³ 846 et *IG* IV 399)." In *Pathways to Power. Civic Elites in the Eastern Part of the Roman Empire*, edited by A. D. Rizakis and F. Camia, 15–22. Athens.

Kantirea, M., and Camia, F. 2010. "The Imperial Cult in the Peloponnese." In *Roman Peloponnese III. Society, Economy and Culture under the Roman Empire, Meletemata* 63, edited by A. D. Rizakis and C. Lepenioti, 375–406. Athens.

Kantor, G. 2014. "Roman Legal Administration in the Province of Asia: Hellenistic Heritage vs. Innovation." In *L'imperium Romanum en perspective. Les savoirs d'empire dans la République romaine et leur héritage dans l'-Europe médiévale et moderne*, edited by J. Dubouloz, S. Pittia, and G. Sabatini, 243–68. Besançon.

Kantor, G. 2015. "Greek Law under the Romans." In *The Oxford Handbook of Ancient Greek Law*, edited by E. M. Harris and M. Canevaro. Oxford.

Kantor, G. 2016. "Local Law in Asia Minor after the Constitutio Antoniniana." In *Citizenship and Empire in Europe 200–1900. The Antonine Constitution after 1800 Years*, edited by C. Ando, 45–62. Stuttgart.

Kantor, G. 2021. "Citizenships and Jurisdictions: The Greek City Perspective." In *Roman and Local Citizenship in the Long Second Century CE*, edited by M. Lavan and C. Ando, 231–54. Oxford.

Kantzios, I. 2018. "Alcaeus Fragment 130b V and the Literature of Exile." *Arethusa* 51.3:191–207.

Kapparis, K. 2018. *Prostitution in the Ancient Greek World*. Berlin.

Karila-Cohen, K. 2005a. "Apollon, Athènes et la Pythaïde: mise en scène 'mythique' de la cité au IIe siècle av. J.-C." *Kernos* 18:219–39.

Karila-Cohen, K. 2005b. "Les pythaïstes athéniens et leurs familles: l'apport de la prosopographie à la connaissance de la religion à Athènes au IIᵉ siècle avant notre ère." In *Prosopographie et histoire religieuse*, edited by M.-F. Baslez and F. Prévot. 69–83. Paris.

Karila-Cohen, K. 2009. "Les filles d'Athènes à Delphes: femmes, religion et société à travers l'exemple des canéphores de la Pythaïde." In *Chemin faisant. Mythes, cultes et société en Grèce ancienne. Mélanges en l'honneur de Pierre Brulé*, edited by L. Bodiou, 133–42. Rennes.

Kasimis, D. 2018. *The Perpetual Immigrant and the Limits of Athenian Democracy*. Cambridge.

Katsikoudis, I. 2005. Δωδώνη. Οι τιμητικοί ανδριάντες. Ioannina.

Katsonopoulou, D., Petropoulos, I., and Katsarou, S., eds. 2008. *Paros II* : Ο Αρχίλοχος και η εποχή του. Athens.

Kay, P. 2014. *Rome's Economic Revolution*, Oxford.

Kaye, N. 2022. *The Attalids of Pergamon and Anatolia. Money, Culture, and State Power*. Cambridge.

Kayser, F. 2017. "Ptolémaïs de Haute-Égypte: une cité grecque dans son environnement égyptien." In *Communautés nouvelles en Égypte hellénistique et romaine*, edited by F. Kayser and L. Medini, 15–67. Chambéry.

Keesling, C. 2003. *The Votive Statues of the Athenian Acropolis*. New York.

Keesling, C. 2012. "Syeris, Diakonos of the Priestess Lysimache on the Athenian Acropolis (IG II2 3464)." *Hesperia* 81:467–505.

Keil, J. 1956. *Ein ephesischer Anwalt des 3. Jahrhunderts durchreist das Imperium Romanum*. Munich.

Kelly, T. 1976. *A History of Argos to 500 B.C*. Minneapolis.

Kellogg, D. L. 2013. *Marathon Fighters and Men of Maple. Ancient Acharnai*. Oxford.

Kemezis, A. M. 2014. *Greek Narratives of the Roman Empire under the Severans. Cassius Dio, Philostratus and Herodian*. Cambridge.

Kennedy, D. L. 2001 "Nabataean Archaeology from the Air." *Adumatu* 4:21–40.

Kennedy, D. L. 2007. *Gerasa and the Decapolis. A "Virtual Island" in Northwest Jordan*. London.

Kennell, N. M. 1997. "Herodes Atticus and the Rhetoric of Tyranny." *CPh* 92.4:346–62.

Kennell, N. M. 1999. "From 'Perioikoi' to 'Poleis': The Laconian Cities in the Late Hellenistic Period." In *Sparta. New Perspectives*, edited by S. Hodkinson and A. Powell, 189–210. London.

Kennell, N. 2013. "Who Were the Neoi?" In *Epigraphical Approaches to the Post-Classical Polis. 4th century B.C. to 2nd century A.D.*, edited by P. Martzavou and N. Papazarkadas, 217–32. Oxford.

Kerschner, M. 2020. "The Archaic Temples in the Artemision and the Archaeology of the 'Central Basis.'" In *White Gold. Studies in Early Electrum Coinage*, edited by. P. van Alfen and U. Wartenberg, 191–262. New York.
Kerschner, M., and Prochaska, W. 2011. "Die Tempel und Altäre der Artemis in Ephesos und ihre Baumaterialien." *JÖAI* 80:73–153.
Kienast, H. J. 1978. *Die Stadtmauer von Samos*. Bonn.
Kienast, H. J. 1995. *Die Wasserleitung von Eupalinos auf Samos*. Bonn.
Kienast, D. 2005. "Die Funktion der attischen Demen von Solon bis Kleisthenes." *Chiron* 35:69–100.
Kierstead, J. 2014. "Grote's Athens: The Character of Democracy." In *Brill's Companion to George Grote and the Classical Tradition*, edited by K. Demetriou, 161–210. Leiden.
Kierstead, J. 2017. "Associations and Institutions in Athenian Citizenship Procedures." *CQ* 67.2:444–59.
Kilian-Dirlmeier, I. 1998. "Elitäres Verhalten vom Ende der Bronzezeit bis zum Beginn der Eisenzeit." In *The History of the Hellenic Language and Writing from the Second to the First Millenium BC. Break or Continuity?*, edited N. Dimoudis and A. Kyriatsoulis, 305–30. Altenburg.
Kinch, K. F. 1914. *Vroulia*. Berlin.
Kip, G. 1910. *Thessalische Studien. Beiträge zur politischen Geographie, Geschichte und Verfassung der thessalischen Landschaften*. Halle.
Kirbihler, F. 2007. "Die Italiker in Kleinasien, mit besonderer Berücksichtigung von Ephesos (133 v. Chr-1 Jhdt. n. Chr.)." In *Neue Zeiten-Neue Sitten. Zur Rezeption und Integration römischen und italienischen Kulturguts in Kleinasien*, edited by M. Meyer, 19–35. Vienna.
Kirbihler, F. 2008. "Les grands-prêtres d'Éphèse: aspects institutionnels et sociaux de l'asiarchie." In *Pathways to Power. Civic Elites in the Eastern Part of the Roman Empire*, edited by A. Rizakis and F. Camia, 107–49. Athens.
Kirbihler, F. 2011. "Servilius Isauricus proconsul d'Asie: un gouverneur populaire." In *Les gouverneurs et les provinciaux sous la République romaine*, edited by N. Barrandon and F. Kirbihler, 249–72. Rennes.
Kirbihler, F. 2013. "Brutus et Cassius et les impositions, spoliations et confiscations en Asie Mineure durant les guerres civiles (44–42 a. C.)." In *Spolier et confisquer dans les mondes grec et romain*, edited by M.-C. Ferriès and F. Delrieux, 345–66. Chambéry.
Kirbihler, F. 2016. *Des Grecs et des Italiens à Éphèse. Histoire d'une intégration croisée (133 a.C.–48 p.C.)*. Bordeaux.
Kirsten, E. 1956. *Die griechische Polis als historisch-geographisches Problem des Mittelmeerraumes*. Bonn.
Klaffenbach, G. 1960. *Bemerkungen zum griechischen Urkundenwesen*. Berlin.
Kleijwegt, M. 1991. *Ancient Youth. The Ambiguity of Youth and the Absence of Adolescence in Greco-Roman Society*. Amsterdam.
Kleiner, D. E. E. 1983. *The Monument of Philopappos in Athens*. Rome.
Kloppenborg, J. S., Ascough, R. S., and Harlan, P. H., eds. 2011. *Greco-Roman Associations. Texts, Translations, and Commentary*. Berlin.
Knäpper, K. 2018. *Hieros Kai Asylos. Territoriale Asylie im Hellenismus in ihrem historischen Kontext*. Stuttgart.
Knodell, A. R. 2021. *Societies in Transition in Early Greece. An Archaeological History*. Oakland.
Knodell, A. R., Fachard, S., and Papangeli, K. 2017. "The Mazi Archaeological Project 2016: Survey and Settlement Investigations in Northwest Attica (Greece)." *AK* 60:146–63.
Knoepfler, D. 1990. "Contributions à l'épigraphie de Chalcis." *BCH* 114:473–98.
Knoepfler, D. 1997. "Le territoire d'Érétrie et l'organisation politique de la cité (*démoi, chôroi, phylai*)." In *The Polis as an Urban Centre and as a Political Community*, edited by M. H. Hansen, 352–449. Copenhagen.
Knoepfler, D. 2001a. "Loi d'Érétrie contre la tyrannie et l'oligarchie, 1." *BCH* 125.1:195–238.
Knoepfler, D. 2001b. "La réintégration de Thèbes dans le 'Koinon' béotien après son relèvement par Cassandre, ou les surprises de la chronologie épigraphique." In *Recherches récentes sur le monde hellénistique*, edited by R. Frei-Stolba and K. Gex, 11–26. Bern.
Knoepfler, D. 2001c. *Décrets érétriens de proxénie et de citoyenneté*. Lausanne.
Knoepfler, D. 2002. "Loi d'Érétrie contre la tyrannie et l'oligarchie, 2." *BCH* 126.1:149–204.
Knoepfler, D. 2004. "'Pauvres et malheureux Érétriens': Démosthène et la nouvelle loi d'Érétrie contre la tyrannie." In *Poleis e Politeiai. Esperienze politiche, tradizioni letterarie, progetti costituzionali*, edited by S. Cataldi, 403–19. Alessandria.
Knoepfler, D. 2010. *La Patrie de Narcisse*. Paris.

Knoepfler, D. 2012. "L'exercice de la magistrature fédérale béotienne par des 'étrangers' à l'époque impériale: conséquence de l'extension du Koinon en dehors des frontières de la Béotie ou simple effet d'une multi-citoyenneté individuelle?" In *Patrie d'origine et patries électives. Les citoyennetés multiples dans le monde grec d'époque romaine*, edited by A. Heller and A.-V. Pont, 223–47. Paris.

Knoepfler, D. 2013a. "Épigraphie et histoire des cités grecques." *ACF* 11:425–48.

Knoepfler, D. 2013b. "Un modèle d'une belle république fédérative? Montesquieu et le système politique politique des Lyciens, de la genèse de l'*Esprit des Lois* aux découvertes épigraphiques les plus récentes en Asie Mineure méridionale." *JS* 1:111–54.

Knoepfler, D. 2014a. "Épigraphie et histoire des cités grecques." *ACF* 113:427–47.

Knoepfler, D. 2014b. "ΕΧΘΟΝΔΕ ΤΑΣ ΒΟΙΩΤΙΑΣ: The Expansion of the Boeotian *Koinon* towards Central Euboia in the Early Third Century BC." In *The Epigraphy and History of Boiotia. New Finds, New Prospects*, edited by N. Papazarkadas, 68–94. Leiden.

Köcke, L. S. 2012. "Milet stirbt aus?!—demographische Überlegungen zu Neubürgern in einer hellenistischen Grossstadt." In *Migration und Bürgerrecht in der hellenistischen Welt*, edited by L.-M. Günther, 41–49. Wiesbaden.

Kockel, V. 2012. "Rekonstruktion oder Entwurf? Zweimal Priene aus der Vogelschau." In *Werkraum Antike— Beiträge zur Archäologie und antiken Baugeschichte*, edited by F. Lang, M. Boss, and H. Svenshon, 211–28. Darmstadt.

Koedijk, M., and Morley, N., eds. 2022. *Capital in Classical Antiquity*. London.

Koerner, R. 1993. *Inschriftliche Gesetzestexte der frühen griechischen Polis*. Edited by K. Hallof. Cologne.

Kõiv, M. 2003. *Ancient Tradition and Early Greek History. The Origins of States in Early-Archaic Sparta, Argos and Corinth*. Tallinn.

Kõiv, M. 2016. "Basileus, Tyrannos and Polis: The Dynamics of Monarchy in Early Greece." *Klio* 98.1:1–89.

Kõiv, M. 2019. "Reading Ancient Tradition: The Rulers of Ancient Corinth." *Chiron* 49:93–129.

Kokkinia, C. 2000. *Die Opramoas-Inschrift von Rhodiapolis. Euergetismus und soziale Elite in Lykien*. Bonn.

Kokkinia, C. 2002. "Grain for Cibyra: Vernius Philagros and the 'Great Conspiracy.'" In *Feeding the Ancient Greek City*, edited by R. Alston and O. van Nijf, 143–58. Leuven.

Kokkinia, C. 2003. "Letters of Roman Authorities on Local Dignitaries: The Case of Vedius Antoninus." *ZPE* 142:197–213.

Kokkinia, C. 2004. "Ruling, Inducing, Arguing: How to Govern (and Survive) a Greek Province." In *Roman Rule and Civic Life. Local and Regional Perspectives*, edited by L. de Ligt, E.A. Hemelrijk, and H.W. Singor, 39–58. Amsterdam.

Kokkinia, C. 2006. "The Governor's Boot and the City's Politicians: Greek Communities and Rome's Representatives under the Empire." In *Herrschaftsstrukturen und Herrschaftspraxis. Konzepte, Prinzipien und Strategien der Administration in römischen Kaiserreichs*, edited by A. Kolb, 181–89. Berlin.

Kokkinia, C. 2015–2016. "The Design of the 'Archive Wall' at Aphrodisias." *Tekmeria* 13:9–55.

Kokkinia, C. 2018. "A Roman Financier's Version of Euergetism: C. Vibius Salutaris and Ephesos." *Tekmeria* 14:215–52.

Kokkorou-Aleura, G. 2004. *Οι επιγραφές*. Athens.

Kokkorou-Alevras, G. 2018. "The Painted Decoration on the Dress of the Nikandre Statue." In *Les arts de la couleur en Grèce ancienne... et ailleurs. Approches interdisciplinaires*, edited by P. Jockey, 115–30. Paris.

Kolb, A. 2000. *Transport und Nachrichtentransfer im Römischen Reich*. Berlin.

Kolb, A., and Vitale, M., eds. 2016. *Kaiserkult in den Provinzen des römischen Reiches*. Berlin.

Kolb, F., ed. 2004. *Chora und Polis*. Munich.

Kolb, F., ed. 2006. *Die Chora von Kyaneai. Untersuchungen zur politischen Geographie, Siedlungs- und Agrarstruktur des Yavu-Berglandes in Zentrallykien*. Bonn.

Kolb, F., ed. 2008. *Burg - Polis - Bischofssitz. Geschichte der Siedlungskammer von Kyaneai in der Südwesttürkei*. Mainz.

Kolb, F. 2010. "Die Einführung der Polis in Zentrallykien: Modernisierung und Traditionalismus der politischen und gesellschaftlichen Strukturen." In *Società indigene e cultura greco-romana*, edited by E. Migliario, L. Troiani, and G. Zecchini, 77–93. Rome.

Kolb, F. 2017. "La Lycie sous Auguste: une région entre *libertas* et *provincia*." In *Auguste et l'Asie Mineure*, edited by L. Cavalier, F. Delrieux, and M.-C. Ferriès, 91–99. Bordeaux.

Kolb, F. 2018. *Lykien. Geschichte einer antiken Landschaft*. Darmstadt.

Kolb, F., and Thomsen, A. 2004. "Forschungen zu Zentralorten und Chora auf dem Gebiet von Kyaneai (Zentrallykien): Methoden, Ergebnisse, Probleme." In *Chora und Polis*, edited by F. Kolb, 1–42. Munich.

Kolodny, E. Y. 1974. *La population des îles de la Grèce. Essai de géographie insulaire en Méditerranée Orientale*. Aix-en-Provence.
Konstantinidi-Syvridi, E. 2021. "Artisans in the Service of the Royalty at Dendra and their Role in the Formation of Fashion Trends." In *(Social) Place and Space in Early Mycenaean Greece. International Discussions in Mycenaean Archaeology*, edited by B. Eder and M. Zavadil, 510–15. Vienna.
Kontoleon, N. M. 1953. "Ἐπιγραφαὶ ἐκ Τήνου." In *Geras Antoniou Keramopoullou. Epistemonikai Pragmateiai*, edited by D. A. Keramopoullos, 224–40. Athens
Kontoleon, N. M. 1964. "Archilochos und Paros." In *Archiloque. Sept exposés et discussion*, edited by J. Pouilloux et al., 37–73. Vandœuvres.
Korkut, T. 2013. "Die Ausgrabungen in Tlos." In *Euploia. La Lycie et la Carie antiques. Dynamiques des territoires, échanges et identités*, edited by P. Brun, L. Cavalier, K. Konuk, and F. Prost, 333–44. Bordeaux.
Korkut, T. 2015. *Tlos. Akdağlar'ın yamacında bir Likya kenti*. Istanbul.
Kosmetatou, E. 2013. "Tyche's Force: Lottery and Chance in Greek Government." In *A Companion to Ancient Greek Government*, edited by H. Beck, 235–51. Malden, MA.
Kosmin, P. J. 2014. *Land of the Elephant Kings. Space, Territory, and Ideology in the Seleucid Empire*. Cambridge, MA.
Kosmin, P. J. 2015. "A Phenomenology of Democracy: Ostracism as Political Ritual." *ClAnt* 34.1:121–61.
Kotsonas, A. 2002. "The Rise of the Polis in Central Crete." *Εὐλιμένη* 3:37–74.
Kotsonas, A. 2016. "Politics of Periodization and the Archaeology of Early Greece." *AJA* 120.2:239–270.
Kouragios, Y. 2009–2011. "Ο αρχαίος δήμος των Αιξωνιδών Αλών Αττικής." *Εὐλιμένη* 10–12:33–62.
Kourou, N. 2011. "From the Dark Ages to the Rise of the Polis in the Cyclades: The Case of Tenos." In *Dark Ages Revisited*, edited by A. Mazarakis-Ainian, 399–414. Volos.
Kourou, N. 2013. "Η αρχαία πολη στο Ξώμπουργο." In *Η αρχαία Τήνος*, edited by R. Etienne, N. Kourou, and E. Simantoni-Bournia, 75–97. Athens.
Kowalleck, I. 2014. "Alte Votive in neuen Kontesten. Zur Weiter- und Widerverwendung archaischer Votivstatuen in Ionien." In *Weiter- und Wiederverwendungen von Weihestatuen in griechischen Heiligtümern*, edited by C. Leypold, M. Mohr, and C. Russenberger, 87–104. Rahden.
Kraeling, C. H. 1938. *Gerasa, City of the Decapolis*. New Haven.
Kralli, I. 1999–2000. "Athens and her Leading Citizens in the Early Hellenistic Period (338–261 B.C.): the Evidence of the Decrees Awarding the Highest Honours." *Ἀρχαιογνωσία* 10:133–62.
Kralli, I. 2017. *The Hellenistic Peloponnese. Interstate Relations. A Narrative and Analytic History, from the Fourth Century to 146 B.C.* Swansea.
Kramer-Hajos, M. 2008. *Beyond the Palace. Mycenaean East Lokris*. Oxford.
Krischen, F. 1938. *Die griechische Stadt. Wiederherstellungen*. Berlin.
Kritzas, C. 2006. "Nouvelles inscriptions d'Argos: les archives des comptes du trésor sacré (IVe s. av. J.-C.)." *CRAI* 2006:397–434.
Kritzas, C. and Prignitz, S. 2020. "The 'Stele of Punishments': A New Inscription from Epidauros." *AE* 159:1–61.
Kroll, J. H. 1972. *Athenian Bronze Allotment Plates*. Cambridge, MA.
Kroll, J. H. 2015. "A Bronze Allotment Plate from Central Greece." In *Ἄξων. Studies in Honor of Ronald S. Stroud*, edited by A. P. Matthaiou and N. Papazarkadas, 595–98. Athens.
Kroll, J. H. 2020. "The Inscribed Account on Lead from the Ephesian Artemisium." In *White Gold. Studies in Early Electrum Coinage*, edited by P. van Alfen and U. Wartenberg, 49–63. New York.
Kron, G. 2011. "The Distribution of Wealth in Athens in Comparative Perspective." *ZPE* 179:129–38.
Kron, G. 2012. "Nutrition, Hygiene and Mortality: Setting Parameters for Roman Health and Life Expectancy Consistent with our Comparative Evidence." In *Impatto della peste Antonina*, edited by E. Lo Cascio, 193–252. Bari.
Kropp, A. 2013. *Images and Monuments of Near Eastern Dynasts, 100 BC–AD 100*. Oxford.
Kropp, A. and Raja, R., eds. 2015. *The World of Palmyra*. Copenhagen.
Kübler, K. 1973. "Eine archaische Grabanlage vor dem Heiligen Tor und ihre Deutung." *AA* 88:173–93.
Kuhn, A. B. 2012. "Herodes Atticus and the Quintilii of Alexandria Troas: Elite Competition and Status Relations in the Graeco-Roman East." *Chiron* 42:421–58.
Kuhrt, A. 2014. "Even a Dog in Babylon is Free." in *The Legacy of Arnaldo Momigliano*, edited by T. Cornell and O. Murray, 77–87. London.
Kunnert, U. 2012. *Bürger unter sich. Phylen in den Städten des kaiserzeitlichen Ostens*. Basel.
Kurke, L. 1991. *The Traffic in Praise. Pindar and the Poetics of Social Economy*. Ithaca, NY.
Kurke, L. 1999. *Coins, Bodies, Games, and Gold. The Politics of Meaning in Archaic Greece*. Princeton.

Kurke, L. and Neer, R. 2019. *Pindar, Song, and Space: Toward a Lyric Archaeology*. Baltimore.
Kyriakidis, N. 2014. "Les Delphiens au miroir de leurs offrandes monumentales: élite sociale et notabilité politique dans une petite cité de Grèce centrale (IVᵉ s.—Iᵉʳ s. av. J.C.)." *BCH* 138.1:103–29.
Kyrieleis, H. 2006. *Anfänge und Frühzeit des Heiligtums von Olympia. die Ausgrabungen am Pelopion 1987–1996*. Berlin.
Laes, C. 2011. *Children in the Roman Empire. Outsiders Within*. Cambridge.
Laffi, U. 1967. "Le iscrizioni relative all'introduzione nel 9 a.C. del nuovo calendario della Provincia d'Asia." *SCO* 16:5–98.
Laffi, U. 2010. *Il trattato fra Sardi ed Efeso degli anni 90 a.C.* Pisa.
Laflı, E., Christof, E., and Metcalfe, M. 2012. *Hadrianopolis I. Inschriften Aus Paphlagonia*. Oxford.
Laflı, E., and Şahin, G. K. 2016. *Hadrianopolis III. Ceramic Finds from Southwestern Paphlagonia*. Oxford.
Lafond, Y. 2006. *La mémoire des cités dans le Péloponnèse d'époque romaine. IIᵉ siècle avant J.-C.—IIIᵉ siècle après J.-C.* Rennes.
Lafond, Y. 2009. "Normes religieuses et identité civique dans les cités de Grèce égéenne (IIᵉ s. av. J.-C.—IIIᵉ s. ap. J.-C.)." In *La norme en matière religieuse en Grèce ancienne*, edited by P. Brulé, 321–34. Rennes.
Lagogianni-Georgakarakou, M. 2007. *Πολιτεύεσθαι τους Κείους κατά πόλεις. η διασπάση ως μέσον πολιτικού ελέγχου*. Athens.
Lambert, S. D. 2018. *Inscribed Athenian Laws and Decrees in the Age of Demosthenes. Historical Essays*. Leiden.
Lambertz, M. 2018. "Hellenistische Türme und Turmgehöfte auf Naxos." *MDAI(A)* 133:185–238.
Lambrinoudakis, V. 1982. "Antike Niederlassungen auf dem Berge Aipos von Chios." In *Palast und Hütte, Beiträge zum Bauen und Wohnen in Altertum*, edited by D. Papenfuss and V. M. Strocka, 375–94. Mainz.
Lambrinoudakis, V. K. 1988. "Veneration of Ancestors in Geometric Naxos." In *Early Greek Cult Practice*, edited by R. Hägg, N. Marinatos, and G. Nordquist, 235–46. Stockholm.
Lambrinoudakis, V. K. 1991. "The Sanctuary of Iria on Naxos and the Birth of Monumental Greek Architecture." In *New Perspectives in Early Greek Art*, edited by D. Buitron-Oliver, 173–88. Hanover, NJ.
Lambrinoudakis, V. K. 2001. "The Emergence of the City-State of Naxos in the Aegean." In *The Two Naxos Cities. A Fine Link Between the Aegean Sea and Sicily*, edited by M. C. Lentini, 13–22. Naxos.
Lambrinoudakis, V. K. 2004. "The Emergence of the City-State of Naxos in the Aegean." In *Le due città di Naxos*, edited by M. C. Lentini, 61–74. Milan.
Lambrinoudakis, V. K., and Wörrle, M. 1983. "Ein hellenistisches Reformgesetz über das Urkundenwesen von Paros." *Chiron* 13:283–368.
Lamont, J. 2021. "Cold and Worthless: The Role of Lead in Curse Tablets." *TAPA* 15.1: 35–68
Lane Fox, R. 2000. "Theognis: An Alternative to Democracy." In *Organization and Community in Ancient Greece*, edited by R. Brock and S. Hodkinson, 35–51. Oxford.
Lane Fox, R. 2008. *Travelling Heroes. Greeks and their Myths in the Epic Age of Homer*. New York.
Lang, F. 1996. *Archäische Siedlungen in Griechenland. Struktur und Entwicklung*. Berlin.
Lang, F. 2007. "House-Community-Settlement: The New Concept of Living in Archaic Greece." In *Building Communities. House, Settlement and Society in the Aegean and Beyond*, edited by R. Westgate, N. Fisher, and J. Whitley, 183–93. Athens.
Langdon, S. 1998. Review of Mazarakis-Ainian 1997. *AJA* 102.4:835–36.
Laniado, A. 2002. *Recherches sur les notables municipaux dans l'Empire protobyzantin*. Paris.
Lanni, A. 2006. *Law and Justice in the Courts of Classical Athens*. Cambridge.
Lanni, A. 2016. *Law and Order in Ancient Athens*. Cambridge.
Lantschner, P. 2022. "City States in the Later Medieval Mediterranean World." *P&P* 254.1:3–49.
Lanzilotta, E. 2000. "Elementi di diritto costituzionale nelle iscrizioni greche del IV secolo a.C." *RFIC* 138:144–54.
Lapatin, K. 2007. "Art and Architecture." In *The Cambridge Companion to the Age of Pericles*, edited by L. Samons II, 125–52. Cambridge.
Lape, S. 2004. *Reproducing Athens: Menander's Comedy, Democratic Culture, and the Hellenistic City*. Princeton.
Lape, S. 2010. *Race and Citizen Identity in the Classical Athenian Democracy*. Cambridge.
Lape, S. 2021. "The Precarity of Female Immigrants in Graeco-Roman Comedy and Athenian Culture." In *L'expérience de la mobilité de l'Antiquité à nos jours, entre précarité et confiance*, edited by C. Moatti and E. Chevreau, 31–48. Bordeaux.
Lardinois, A. 1996. "Who Sang Sappho's Songs?" In *Reading Sappho. Contemporary Approaches*, edited by E. Greene, 150–72. Berkeley.

La Rocca, A. 2005. "Diritto di iniziativa e potere popolare nelle assemblee cittadine greche." In *Politica e partecipazione nelle città dell'impero romano*, edited by F. Amarelli and A. Schiavone, 93–118. Rome.
Laronde, A. 1987. *Cyrène et la Libye hellénistique. Libykai historiai de l'époque républicaine au principat d'Auguste*. Paris.
Laronde, A. 2004. "Les rivalités entre les cités de la Cyrénaïque à l'époque impériale." In *L'hellénisme d'époque romaine. Nouveaux documents, nouvelles approches. (Ier s. a C.—IIIe s. p. C.)*, edited by S. Follet, 187–93. Paris.
Laronde, A. 2011. "Cyrène au début du Ier siècle." *MI* 3:59–63.
Larsen, J. A. O. 1938. "Roman Greece." In *An Economic Survey of Ancient Rome*, vol. 4, edited by T. Frank, 259–498. Baltimore.
Latacz, J. 1977. *Kampfparänese, Kampfdarstellung und Kampfwirklichkeit in der Ilias, bei Kallinos und Tyrtaios*. Munich.
Latte, K. 1968. *Kleine Schriften zu Religion, Recht, Literatur und Sprache der Griechen und Römer*, edited by O. Gigon, W. Buchwald and W. Kunkel. Munich.
Lavan, L. A. 2008. "A. H. M. Jones and 'The Cities' 1964–2004." In *A. H. M. Jones and the Later Roman Empire*, edited by D. Gwynn, 167–91. Leiden.
Lavan, L. A. 2009. "What Killed the Ancient City? Chronology, Causation and Traces of Continuity." *JRA* 22:803–12.
Lavan, M. 2018. "Pliny *Epistles* 10 and Imperial Correspondence. The Empire of Letters." In *Roman Literature under Nerva, Trajan and Hadrian. Literary Interactions, AD 96–138*, edited by A. König and C. Whitton, 280–301. Cambridge.
Lawall, M. 2006. "Consuming the West in the East: Amphoras of the Western Mediterranean in the Aegean before 86 B.C." In *Old Pottery in a New Century*, edited by D. Malfitana, J. Poblome, and J. Lund, 265–86. Catania.
Lazaridou, A. 2011. *Transition to Christianity Art of Late Antiquity, 3rd–7th century AD*. New York.
Leão, D. F. 2018. "Plutarch on Demetrius of Phalerum: The Intellectual, the Legislator and the Expatriate." *Symposion*, edited by G. Thür, U. Yiftach, and R. Zelnick-Abramovitz, 441–57. Vienna.
Leão, D. F., and Rhodes, P. J. 2016. *The Laws of Solon. A New Edition with Introduction, Translation and Commentary*. London.
Lear, A. 2015. "Was Pederasty Problematized? A Diachronic View." In *Sex in Antiquity. Exploring Gender and Sexuality in the Ancient World*, edited by M. Masterson, N. S. Rabinowitz, and J. Robson, 115–36. London.
Lefèvre, F. 1998. *L' Amphictionie pyléo-delphique: histoire et institutions*. Athens.
Lefèvre-Novaro, D. 2007. "Les débuts de la polis (l'exemple de Phaistos-Crète)." *Ktèma* 32:467–96.
Legon, R. 1981. *Megara. The Political History of a Greek City-State to 336 B.C.* Ithaca, NY.
Le Guen, B., ed. 1997. *De la scène aux gradins. Théâtre et représentations dramatiques après Alexandre le Grand*. Toulouse.
Le Guin, U. K. 2004. *The Wind's Twelve Quarters*. New York.
Lehmann, G. A. 2000. "Polis-Autonomie und römische Herrschaft an der Westküste Kleinasiens. Kolophon/Klaros nach der Aufrichtung der Provincia Asia." In *Politics, Administration and Society in the Hellenistic and Roman World*, edited by L. Mooren, 215–38. Leuven.
Lemos, I. S. 2002. *The Protogeometric Aegean. The Archaeology of the Late Eleventh and Tenth Centuries BC*. Oxford.
Lemos, I. S. 2007. "'... ἐπεὶ πόρει μύρια ἕδνα...' (Iliad 22,472): Homeric Reflections in Early Iron Age Elite Burials." In *The Formation of Elites and Elitist Lifestyles from Mycenaean Palatial Time to the Homeric Period*, edited by E. Alram-Stern and G. Nightingale, 274–83. Vienna.
Lemos, I. 2014. "Communities in Transformation: An Archaeological Survey from the 12th to the 9th Century BC." *Pharos* 20.1:163–94.
Lemos, I. and Deger-Jalkotzy, S. 2006. *Ancient Greece from the Mycenaean Palaces to the Age of Homer*. Edinburgh.
Lemos, I., and Kotsonas, A. eds. 2019. *A Companion to the Archaeology of Early Greece and the Mediterranean*. Hoboken, NJ.
Lemos, I., Livieratou, A., and Thomatos, M. 2009. "Post-Palatial Urbanization: Some Lost Opportunities." In *Inside the City in the Greek World. Studies of Urbanism from the Bronze Age to the Hellenistic Period*, edited by S. Owen and L. Preston, 62–84. Oxford.
Lendon, J. E. 1997. *Empire of Honour. The Art of Government in the Roman World*. Oxford.
Lendon, J. E. 2005. *Soldiers and Ghosts. A History of Battle in Classical Antiquity*. New Haven.

Lenski, N. 2016. *Constantine and the Cities. Imperial Authority and Civic Politics.* Philadelphia.
Lenski, N., and Cameron, C. M., eds. 2018. *What Is a Slave Society? The Practice of Slavery in Global Perspective.* Cambridge.
Lentini, M. C., and Whitbread, I. K. 2012. "Recent Investigation of the Early Settlement Levels at Sicilian Naxos." *MedArch* 25:309–15.
Leone, S. 2020. *Polis, Platz und Porträt. Die Bildnisstatuen auf der Agora von Athen im Späthellenismus und in der kaiserzeit (86 v. Chr.—267 n. Chr.).* Berlin.
Lepelley, C. 1993. "Universalité et permanence du modèle de la cité dans le monde romain." In *Ciudad y comunidad cívica en Hispania. Siglos II y III d. C.*, 13–23. Madrid.
Lepelley, C. 2001. *Aspects de l'Afrique romaine. Les cités, la vie rurale, le Christianisme.* Bari.
Lepke, A., Schuler, C., and Zimmermann, K. 2015. "Neue Inschriften aus Patara III: Elitenrepräsentation und Politik in Hellenismus und Kaiserzeit." *Chiron* 45:291–384.
Leppin, H. 2013. "Unlike(ly) Twins? Democracy and Oligarchy in Context." In *A Companion to Ancient Greek Government*, edited by H. Beck, 146–58. Malden, MA.
Le Quéré, E. 2015. *Les Cyclades sous l'Empire romain. Histoire d'une renaissance.* Rennes.
Lerat, L. 1952. *Les Locriens de l'ouest.* Paris.
Le Rider, G. 2001. *La naissance de la monnaie. Pratiques monétaires de l'Orient ancien.* Paris.
Le Roux, P. 2011. *La toge et les armes. Rome entre Méditerranée et Océan.* Rennes.
Lerouxel, F. 2016. "Y a-t-il des riches en Égypte romaine au Ier s.?" In *Propriétaires et citoyens dans l'Orient romain*, edited by F. Lerouxel and A.-V. Pont, 213–31. Bordeaux.
Lerouxel, F., and Pont, A.-V., eds. 2016. *Propriétaires et citoyens dans l'Orient romain.* Bordeaux.
Le Roy, C., and Hansen, E. 2012. *Le Temple de Léto au Létoon de Xanthos: étude architecturale.* Fouilles de Xanthos 11. Aarhus.
Leschhorn, W. 1984. *Gründer der Stadt. Studien zu einem politisch-religiösen Phänomen der griechischen Geschichte.* Stuttgart.
Leschhorn, W. 1998. "Die Verbreitung von Agonen in den östlichen Provinzen des Römischen Reiches." *Stadion* 24.1:31–57.
Le Teuff, B. 2017. "La fiscalité de la province d'Asie au tournant de l'ère augustéenne. Un bilan." In *Auguste et l'Asie Mineure*, edited by L. Cavalier, M.-C. Ferriès, and F. Delrieux, 61–73. Bordeaux.
Lévêque, P., and Vidal-Naquet, P. 1964. *Clisthène l'Athénien.* Paris.
Levi, M. 1988. *Of Rule and Revenue.* Berkeley.
Levick, B. 1967. *Roman Colonies in Southern Asia Minor.* Oxford.
Lévy, E. 1978. "Notes sur la chronologie athénienne au VIe siècle." *Historia* 27.4:513–21.
Lévy, E. 1983. "Αὐτονομία et ἐλευθερία au Ve siècle." *RPh* 57.2:249–70.
Lévy, E. 1990. "La cité grecque. Invention moderne ou réalité antique?" In *Du pouvoir dans l'Antiquité. Mots et réalités*, edited by C. Nicolet, 53–67. Geneva.
Lévy, I. 1899. "Études sur la vie municipale de l'Asie Mineure sous les Antonins." *REG* 12.47:255–89.
Lévy, I. 1902. "Les Πατρόβουλοι dans l'épigraphie grecque et la littérature talmudique." *RPh* 26.3:272–78.
Lewin, A. 1995. *Assemblee popolari e lotta politica nelle città dell'impero romano.* Florence.
Lewis, D. M. (a) 1984. "Democratic Institutions and Their Diffusion, I." In *Πρακτικὰ τοῦ η' διεθνοῦς συνεδρίου ἑλληνικῆς καὶ λατινικῆς ἐπιγραφικῆς*, 55–61. Athens.
Lewis, D. M. (a) 1997. *Selected Papers in Greek and Near Eastern History*, edited by P. Rhodes. Oxford.
Lewis D. M. (b) 2018. *Greek Slave Systems in their Eastern Mediterranean context, c.800–146 B.C.* Oxford.
Lewis, N. 1981. "*Notationes legentis.*" *BASP* 18:73–81.
Lewis, S. 2004. "Καὶ σαφῶς τύραννος ἦν: Xenophon's Account of Euphron of Sicyon." *JHS* 124:65–74.
Liddel, P. 2007. *Civic Obligation and Individual Liberty in Ancient Athens.* Oxford.
Liddel, P. 2009. "The Decree Cultures of the Ancient Megarid." *CQ* 59.2:411–36.
Liddel, P. 2020. *Decrees of Fourth-Century Athens (403/2–322/1 B.C.). Political and Cultural Perspectives.* Cambridge.
Liddel, P. 2021. "The Discourses of Identity in Hellenistic Erythrai: Institutions, Rhetoric, Honour and Reciprocity." *Polis* 38.1:74–107.
Liebenam, W. 1897. "*Curator rei publicae.*" *Philologus* 56:290–325.
Liebenam, W. 1900. *Städteverwaltung im römischen Kaiserreiche.* Leipzig.
Lieberman, S. 1946. "Palestine in the Third and Fourth Centuries." *Jewish Quarterly Review* 36:329–41.

Liebeschuetz, W. 1992. "The End of the Ancient City." In *The City in Late Antiquity*, edited by J. W. Rich, 1–49. London.
Liebeschuetz, W. 2000. *The Decline and Fall of the Roman City*. Oxford.
Lightfoot, J. L. 2003. *Lucian. On the Syrian Goddess. Edited with Introduction, Translation, and Commentary*. Oxford.
Linderski, J. 1995. "Ambassadors Go to Rome." In *Les Relations internationales*, edited by E. Frézouls and A. Jacquemin, 453–78. Paris.
Lintott, A. 1982. *Violence, Civil Strife and Revolution in the Classical City, 750–330 B.C.* Baltimore.
Lintott, A. 1993. *Imperium Romanum. Politics and Administration*. London.
Lissarrague, F. 1987. *Un flot d'images. Une esthétique du banquet grec*. Paris.
Lissarrague, F. 1990. *L'autre guerrier. Archers, peltastes, cavaliers dans l'imagerie attique*. Rome.
Liston, M. A., Rotroff, I., and Snyder, L. M. 2018. *The Agora Bone Well*. Princeton.
Lloyd, G. E. R. 2022. *Expanding Horizons in the History of Science. The Comparative Approach*. Cambridge.
Lo Cascio, E., and Tacoma, L. E., eds. 2017. *The Impact of Mobility and Migration in the Roman Empire*. Rome.
Lohmann, H. 1993. *Atēnē. Forschungen zu Siedlungs- und Wirtschaftsstruktur des klassischen Attika*. Athens.
Lohmann, H. 1996. Review of Ashton 1991. *Gnomon* 68.3:241–45.
Lohmann, H. 1999. "Survey in der Chora von Milet: Vorbericht über die Kampagnen der Jahre 1996 und 1997." *AA* 3:439–73.
Lohmann, H., and Mattern, T., eds. 2010. *Attika. Archäologie einer 'zentralen' Kulturlandschaft*. Wiesbaden.
Lohmann, H., Kalaitzoglou, G., and Lüdorf, G., eds. 2014. *Forschungen in der Mykale. I, 2 Survey in der Mykale. Ergänzende Studien*. Bonn.
Lohmann, H., Kalaitzoglou, G., and Lüdorf, G., eds. 2017. *Forschungen in der Mykale. Landeskunde eines westkleinasiatischen Gebirgszuges vom Chalkolithikum bis in spätosmanische Zeit*. Bonn.
Lolos, Y. A. 2005. "The Sanctuary of Titane and the City of Sikyon." *ABSA* 100:275–98.
Lolos, Y. A. 2011. *Land of Sikyon. Archaeology and History of a Greek City-State*. Princeton.
Lomas, K. 2006. "Tyrants and the *Polis*: Migration, Identity and Urban Development in Sicily." In *Ancient Tyranny*, edited by S. Lewis, 95–118. Edinburgh.
Lombardo, M. 2005. "Le prime 'democrazie' in Magna Grecia." In *Democrazia e antidemocrazia nel mondo greco*, edited by U. Bultrighini, 109–18. Alessandria.
Long, T. 2016. "Facing the Evidence: How to Approach the Portraits." In *The World of Palmyra*, edited by A. Kropp and R. Raja, 135–49. Copenhagen.
Longo, F. 2009. "L'ἀγορή di Omero. Rappresentazione poetica e documentazione archeologica." In *Lo Scudo di Achille dell'Iliade. Esperienze ermeneutiche a confronto*, edited by M. D'Acunto and R. Palmisciano, 199–224. Pisa.
Lonis, R., ed. 1988. *L'étranger dans le monde grec*. Nancy.
Lonis, R. 1994. *La cité dans le monde grec. Structures, fonctionnement, contradictions*. Paris.
López-Ruiz, C. 2021. *Phoenicians and the Making of the Mediterranean*. Cambridge, MA.
Loraux, N. 1981. *L'invention d'Athènes. Histoire de l'oraison funèbre dans la 'cité classique.'* 2nd edition. Paris.
Loraux, N. 1986. "Thucydide a écrit la Guerre du Péloponnèse." *Mètis* 1.1:139–61.
Loraux N. 1993. *L'invention d'Athènes. Histoire de l'oraison funèbre dans la 'cité classique.'* Paris.
Loraux, N. 1996. *Né de la terre. Mythe et politique à Athènes*. Paris.
Loraux, N. 1997. *La cité divisée. L'oubli dans la mémoire d'Athènes*. Paris.
Loraux, N. 2002. *The Divided City. On Memory and Forgetting in Ancient Athens*. Translated by C. Pache and J. Fort. Princeton.
Low, P. 2007. *Interstate Relations in Classical Greece. Morality and Power*. Cambridge.
Low, P., ed. 2008. *The Athenian Empire*. Edinburgh.
Low, P. 2010. "Commemoration of the War Dead in Classical Athens. Remembering Defeat and Victory." In *War, Democracy and Culture in Classical Athens*, edited by D. Pritchard, 341–58. Cambridge.
Luke, J. 2003. *Ports of Trade, Al Mina and Geometric Greek Pottery in the Levant*. Oxford.
Lukes, S. 2005. *Power. A Radical View*. 2nd ed. Basingstoke.
Lucas, T., and Dubach, G. 2023. "Counting Boiotians: Conscription Lists, Military Forces, and Demography in Hellenistic Boiotia." *Hesperia* 92.3:481–513.
Lulli, L. 2011. *Narrare in distici: l'elegia greca arcaica e classica di argomento storico-mitico*. Rome.
Luraghi, N. 1994. *Tirannidi arcaiche in Sicilia e Magna Grecia. Da Panezio di Leontini alla caduta dei Dinomenidi*. Florence.
Luraghi, N. 1998. "Il Gran Re e i tiranni." *Klio* 80:22–46.

Luraghi, N. 2002. "Becoming Messenian." *JHS* 122:45–69.
Luraghi, N. 2005. "Pausania e i Messenii: interpretazioni minime." *RFIC* 133.2:177–201.
Luraghi, N. 2008. *The Ancient Messenians. Constructions of Ethnicity and Memory*. Cambridge.
Luraghi, N., and Alcock, S. eds. 2003. *Helots and Their Masters in Laconia and Messenia: Histories, Ideologies, Structures*. Washington, D.C.
Luther, A., Meier, M., and Thommen, L., eds. 2006. *Das frühe Sparta*. Stuttgart.
Lynch, K. 2011. *The Symposium in Context. Pottery from a Late Archaic House near the Athenian Agora*. Princeton.
Lytle, E. 2012. "A Customs House of Our Own: Infrastructure, Duties and a Joint Association of Fishermen and Fishmongers (IK, 11.1a-Ephesos, 20)." In *Tout vendre, tout acheter. Structures et équipements des marchés antiques*, edited by V. Chankowski and P. Karvonis, 213–24. Bordeaux.
Lytle, E. 2013. "Farmers into Sailors: Ship Maintenance, Greek Agriculture, and the Athenian Monopoly on Kean Ruddle. (*IG* II^2 1128)." *GRBS* 53:520–50.
Lytle, E. 2018. "Fishing with Fire: Technology, Economy and Two Greek Inscriptions." *Historia* 67.1:61–102.
Lyttkens, C. H. 2006. "Reflections on the Origins of the Polis: An Economic Perspective on Institutional Change in Ancient Greece." *Constitutional Political Economy* 17:31–48.
Ma, J. 2000. "Fighting Poleis of the Hellenistic World." In *War and Violence in Ancient Greece*, edited by H. van Wees, 337–76. Swansea.
Ma, J. 2002. *Antiochos III and the Cities of Western Asia Minor*. 2nd. ed. Oxford.
Ma, J. 2003a. "Peer Polity Interaction in the Hellenistic Age." *P&P* 180:9–39.
Ma, J. 2003b. "Une culture militaire en Asie Mineure?" In *Les Cités grecques et la guerre en Asie mineure à l'époque hellénistique*, edited by J.-C. Couvenhes and H. Fernoux, 199–220. Paris.
Ma, J. 2006. "The Two Cultures: Connoisseurship and Civic Honours." *Art History* 29.2:325–38.
Ma, J. 2009. "City as Memory." In *The Oxford Handbook of Hellenic Studies*, edited by G. Boys-Stones, B. Graziosi, and P. Vasunia, 248–59. Oxford.
Ma, J. 2012. "Epigraphy and Authority." In *Epigraphy and the Historical Sciences*, edited by J. Davies and J. Wilkes, 133–58. London.
Ma, J. 2013a. "Hellenistic Empires." In *The Oxford Handbook of the State in the Ancient Near East and Mediterranean*, edited by P. F. Bang and W. Scheidel, 324–57. Oxford.
Ma, J. 2013b. "Grandes et petites cités au miroir de l'épigraphie classique et hellénistique." *Topoi (Lyon)* 18:67–86.
Ma, J. 2013c. "Re-examining Hanukkah." Marginalia Review of Books. July 9, 2013. https://themarginaliareview.com/re-examining-hanukkah/
Ma, J. 2015a. *Statues and Cities. Honorific Portraits and Civic Identity in the Hellenistic World*. 2nd ed. Oxford.
Ma, J. 2015b. "Space and/as Conflict in the Hellenistic Period." In *Continuity and Destruction in the Greek East. The Transformation of Monumental Space from the Hellenistic Period to Late Antiquity*, edited by S. Chandrasekaran and A. Kouremenos, 3–10. Oxford.
Ma, J. 2016a. "The Autonomy of the Boiotian Poleis." In *Boiotia in the Fourth Century B.C.*, edited by S. D. Gartland, 32–41. Philadelphia.
Ma, J. 2016b. "The *Polis* in a Cold Climate: Propositions, Consequences, Questions." In Βορειοελλαδικά. *Tales from the Lands of the ethne*, edited by M. Kalaitzi et al., 309–28. Athens.
Ma, J. 2016c. "*Gnômê tou dêmou*: quand le peuple propose et dispose." *CCG* 27:171–88.
Ma, J. 2016d. "Élites, élitisme et communauté dans la polis archaïque." *Annales (HSS)* 71.3:633–58.
Ma, J. 2018. "Whatever Happened to Athens? Thoughts on the Great Convergence and Beyond." In *The Hellenistic Reception of Classical Athenian Democracy and Political Thought*, edited by B. Gray and M. Canevaro, 277–97. Oxford.
Ma, J. 2022. Review of Gygax and Zuiderhoek 2020. *BMCR* 2022.10.36.
Ma, J., Papazarkadas, N., and Parker, R., eds. 2009. *Interpreting the Athenian Empire*. London.
Maass, M. 1978. *Die geometrischen Dreifüsse von Olympia*. Berlin.
MacDowell, D. M. 2009. *Demosthenes the Orator*. New York.
MacDowell, D. M. 1978. *The Law in Classical Athens*. Ithaca.
Mack, W. 2013. "Communal Interests and Polis Identity under Negotiation: Documents Depicting Sympolities between Cities Great and Small." *Topoi (Lyon)* 18.1:87–116.
Mack, W. 2015a. *Proxeny and Polis. Institutional Networks in the Ancient Greek World*. Oxford.
Mack, W. 2015b. "Shepherds Beating the Bounds? Territorial Identity at a Dependent Community (*IPriene* 361-63)." *JHS* 135:51–77.

Mack, W. 2019. "Beyond Potential Citizenship: A Network Approach to Understanding Grants of Politeia." In *La cité interconnectée dans le monde gréco-romain (IVe siècle a.C.–IVe siècle p.C.). Transferts et réseaux institutionnels, religieux et culturels aux époques hellénistique et impériale*, edited by M. Dana and I. Savalli-Lestrade, 61–82. Bordeaux.
Mackil, E. 2004. "Wandering Cities: Alternatives to Catastrophe in the Greek Polis." *AJA* 108.4:493–516.
Mackil, E. 2013. *Creating a Common Polity. Religion, Economy, and Politics in the Making of the Greek Koinon*. Berkeley.
Mackil, E. 2014. "Creating a Common Polity in Boeotia." In *The Epigraphy and History of Boeotia. New Finds, New Prospects*, edited by N. Papazarkadas, 45–67. Leiden.
Mackil, E. 2018. "Property Security and its Limits in Classical Greece." In *Ancient Greek History and Contemporary Social Science*, edited by M. Canevaro, A. Erskine, B. Gray, and J. Ober, 315–43. Edinburgh.
MacMullen, R. 1974. *Roman Social Relations, 50 B.C. to A.D. 284*. New Haven.
Mac Sweeney, N. 2013. *Foundation Myths and Politics in Ancient Ionia*. Cambridge.
Mac Sweeney, N. 2016. "Anatolian-Aegean Interactions in the Early Iron Age: Migration, Mobility, and the Movement of People." In *Of Odysseys and Oddities. Scales and Modes of Interaction Between Prehistoric Aegean Societies and Their Neighbours*, edited by B. Malloy, .411–34. Oxford.
Mac Sweeney, N. 2017. "Separating Fact from Fiction in the Ionian Migration." *Hesperia* 86.3:379–421.
Madsen, J. M. 2002. "The Romanization of the Greek Elite in Achaia, Asia and Bithynia: Greek Resistance or Regional Discrepancies?" *OTerr* 8:87–113.
Madsen, J. M. 2009. *Eager to be Roman. Greek Response to Roman Rule in Pontus and Bithynia*. London.
Madsen, J. M. 2016. "Who Introduced the Imperial Cult in Asia and Bithynia? The Koinon's Role in the Early Worship of Augustus." In *Kaiserkult in den Provinzen des Römischen Reiches. Organisation, Kommunikation und Repräsentation*, edited by A. Kolb and M. Vitale, 21–36. Berlin.
Maehle, I. B. 2018. "The Economy of Gratitude in Democratic Athens." *Hesperia* 87.1:55–90.
Magie, D. 1950. *Roman Rule in Asia Minor*. Princeton.
Magnani, S., and Mior, P. 2017. "Palmyrene Elites: Aspects of Self-Representation and Integration in Hadrian's Age." In *Official Power and Local Elites in the Roman Provinces*, edited by R. Varga and V. Rusu-Bolindet, 96–114. London.
Magnetto, A. 2008. *L'arbitrato di Rodi fra Samo e Priene. Testi e Commenti*. Pisa.
Magnetto, A. 2015. "L'arbitrato dei Romani del rapporto con la diplomazia dei Greci: alcuni spunti di riflessione." In *La diplomatie romaine sous la république. Réflexions sur une pratique*, edited by B. Grass and G. Stouder, 65–86. Besançon.
Magnetto, A. 2016. "Interstate Arbitration and Foreign Judges." In *The Oxford Handbook of Ancient Greek Law*, edited by E. M. Harris and M. Canevaro. Oxford.
Mahé, A. 2001. *Histoire de la Grande Kabylie, XIXe–XXe siècle. Anthropologie historique du lien social dans les communautés villageoises*. Saint-Denis.
Maier, F. G. 1959–61 *Griechische Mauerbauinschriften*, 2 vols. Heidelberg.
Maillot, S., and Zurbach, J., eds. 2021. *Statuts personnels et main-d'œuvre en Méditerranée hellénistique*. Clermont-Ferrand.
Maire Vigueur, J.-C. 1997. "Il problema storiografico: Firenze come modello (e mito) di regime popolare." In *Magnati e popolari dell'Italia comunale*, 1–16. Pistoia.
Maire Vigueur, J.-C. 2003. *Cavaliers et citoyens. Guerre, conflits et société dans l'Italie communale, XIIe–XIIIe siècles*. Paris.
Malay, H. 2018. "A Provisional Publication: Some Copies of Inscriptions from P. Hermann's Papers. Record of Road Work by the Indipeidatai (Revision on SEG 45,1661)." *EA* 51:98–104.
Malay, H., Ricl, M., and Amendola, D. 2018. "The City of Tralleis Combats Immorality: Measures Taken against οἱ ἐν κιναιδείᾳ βιοῦντες in a New Civic Decree." *EA* 51:91–97.
Malkin, I. 1987. *Religion and Colonization in Ancient Greece*. Leiden.
Malkin, I. 1998. *The Returns of Odysseus. Colonization and Ethnicity*. Berkeley.
Malkin, I. 2002. "Exploring the Concept of 'Foundation': A Visit to Megara Hyblaia." In *Oikistes. Studies in Constitutions, Colonies and Military Power in the Ancient World Offered in Honor of A. J. Graham*, edited by V. B. Gorman and E. W. Robinson, 195–225. Leiden.
Malkin, I. 2003. "'Tradition' in Herodotus: The Foundation of Cyrene." In *Herodotus and His World*, edited by P. Derow and R. Parker, 153–70. Oxford.
Malkin, I., and Hohlfelder, R. L. 1988. *Mediterranean Cities. Historical Perspectives*. London.
Manganaro Perrone, G. 1963–1964. "Le iscrizioni delle isole milesie." *ASAA* 25-6:293–349.
Manganaro Perrone, G. 1974. "SGDI, IV, 4 n. 49 (DGE, 707) e il bimetallismo monetale di Creso." *Epigraphica* 36:55–77.

Mann, C., and Scholz, P. S., eds. 2011. *"Demokratie" im Hellenismus. Von der Herrschaft des Volkes zur Herrschaft der Honoratioren? Die hellenistische Polis als Lebensform, 2.* Berlin.
Manning, J. G. 2018. *The Open Sea: The Economic Life of the Ancient Mediterranean World from the Iron Age to the Rise of Rome.* Princeton.
Manville, B. 1990. *The Origins of Citizenship in Ancient Athens.* Princeton.
Manville, P. B. 1997. "Pericles and the 'Both/And' Vision for Democratic Athens." In *Polis and Polemos,* edited by C. D. Hamilton and P. Krentz, 73–84. Claremont, CA.
Marangou, L .I. 2002–2005. *Amorgos.* Athens.
Marcaccini, C. 2001 *Costruire un'identità, scrivere la storia. Archiloco, Paro e la colonizzazione di Taso.* Florence.
Marchand, F. 2013. "The Statilii Tauri and the Cult of the Theos Tauros at Thespiai." *JAH* 1.2:145–69.
Marchetti, P. 1994. "Recherches sur les mythes et la topographie d'Argos." *BCH* 118.1:131–60.
Marchiandi, D. 2011. *I periboli funerari nell'Attica classica. Lo specchio di una "borghesia."* Athens.
Marek, C. 1993. *Stadt, Ära und Territorium in Pontus-Bithynia und Nord-Galatia.* Tübingen.
Marek, C. 2016. *In the Land of a Thousand Gods. A History of Asia Minor in the Ancient World.* Translated by S. Rendall. Princeton.
Marginesu, G. 2005. *Gortina di Creta. Prospettive epigrafiche per lo studio della forma urbana.* Athens.
Marini, S. 2018. *Grecs et Libyens en Cyrénaïque dans l'Antiquité. Aspects et vicissitudes d'un rapport millénaire.* Paris.
Marotta, V. "Conflitti politici cittadini e governo provinciale." In *Politica e partecipazione nelle città dell'Impero romano,* edited by F. Amarelli, 119–202. Rome.
Marshall, C. W. 2013. "Sex Slaves in New Comedy." In *Slaves and Slavery in Ancient Greek Comic Drama,* edited by B. Akrigg and R. Tordoff, 173–96. Cambridge.
Martin, K. 2013 *Demos-Boule-Gerousia. Personifikationen städtischer Institutionen auf kaiserzeitlichen Münzen aus Kleinasien.* Bonn.
Martin, R. 1951. *Recherches sur l'agora grecque. Études d'histoire et d'architecture urbaines.* Paris.
Martzavou, P. 2008. *Recherches sur les communautés festives dans la "vieille Grèce" entre le IIème siècle a.C. et le IIIème siècle p.C.* Unpublished Ph.D. dissertation. Paris, École Pratique des Hautes Etudes, IVème section.
Martzavou, P. 2010. "Les cultes isiaques et les Italiens entre Délos, Thessalonique et l'Eubée." *Pallas* 84:181–205.
Martzavou, P. 2013. "Isis et Athènes: épigraphie, espace et pouvoir à la basse époque hellénistique." In *Power, Politics and the Cults of Isis,* edited by L. Bricault and J.-M. Versluys, 163–91. Leiden.
Marzari, F. 2006. "I *mythietai* di Anacreonte." *SIFC* 4.2:201–9.
Mason, P. A. 1993. "The Genevan Republican Background to Rousseau's *Social Contract.*" *HPTh* 14.4:547–72.
Masséglia, J. 2015. *Body Language in Hellenistic Art and Society.* Oxford.
Masson, O. 1992. "Les lamelles de plomb de Styra, *IG* XII 9,56: essai de bilan." *BCH* 116.1:61–72.
Mathieu, N. ed. 2014. *Le monde romain de 70 av. J.-C. à 73 apr. J.-C. Voir, dire, lire l'empire.* Rennes.
Matthaei, A. 2013. *Münzbild und Polisbild. Untersuchngen zur Selbstdarstellung kleinasiatischer Poleis im Hellenismus.* Munich.
Matthaei, A., and Zimmermann, M., eds. 2014. *Stadtkultur im Hellenismus. Die hellenistische Polis als Lebensform.* Göttingen.
Matthaei, A., and Zimmermann, M., eds. 2015. *Urbane Strukturen und bürgerliche Identität im Hellenismus.* Heidelberg.
Matthaiou, A. P. 2014. "Four Inscribed Bronze Tablets from Thebes: Preliminary Notes." In *The Epigraphy and History of Boeotia. New Finds, New Prospects,* edited by N. Papazarkadas, 211–22. Leiden.
Matthews, J. F. 1984. "The Tax Law of Palmyra: Evidence for Economic History in a City of the Roman East." *JRS* 74:157–80.
Matthews, J. F. 2007. *The Roman Empire of Ammianus.* Ann Arbor, MI.
Matthys, M. 2014. *Architekturstiftungen und Ehrenstatuen. Untersuchungen zur visuellen Repräsentation der Oberschicht im späthellenistischen und kaiserzeitlichen Pergamon.* Darmstadt.
Maupai, I. 2003. *Die Macht der Schönheit. Untersuchungen zu einem Aspekt des Selbstverständnisses und der Selbstdarstellung griechischer Städte in der Römischen Kaiserzeit.* Bonn.
Mavridis F., Tankosić, Ž., and Kotsonas, A. 2018. "The Irakleia Caves Exploration Project and the Importance of Cave Research for the Archaeology of the Cyclades. A Brief Note." In *Cycladic Archaeology and Research. New Approaches and Discoveries,* edited by E. Angliker and J. Tully, 249–60. Oxford.

Mavroiannis, T. 2018. "Le commerce des esclaves syriens (143–88 av. J.-C.)." *Syria* 95:245–74.
Mazarakis-Ainian, A. 1987. "Geometric Eretria." *AK* 30.1:3–24.
Mazarakis-Ainian, A. 1997. *From Rulers' Dwellings to Temples. Architecture, Religion and Society in Early Iron Age Greece (1100–700 B.C.)*. Jonsered.
Mazarakis-Ainian, A. 2002. "Les fouilles d'Oropos et la fonction des périboles dans les agglomérations du début de l'Âge du Fer." In *Habitat et urbanisme dans le monde grec de la fin des palais mycéniens à la prise de Milet 494 av. J.-C.*, edited by J. M. Luce, 183–227. Toulouse.
Mazarakis-Ainian, A. 2007. "Architecture and Social Structure in EIA Greece." In *Building Communities. House, Settlement and Society in the Aegean and Beyond*, edited by R. Westgate, N. Fisher, and J. Whitley, 157–68. London.
Mazarakis-Ainian, A. 2007–2008. "Buried Among the Living in Early Iron Age Greece: Some Thoughts." In *Sepolti tra i vivi. Buried Among the Living. Evidenza ed interpretazione di contesti funerari in abitato*, edited by G. Bartoloni and M. G. Benedettini, 365–98. Rome.
Mazarakis-Ainian, A. 2012. "Des quartiers spécialisés d'artisans à l'époque géométrique." In *'Quartiers' artisanaux en Grèce ancienne. Une perspective méditerranéenne*, edited by A. Esposito and G. M. Sanidas, 135–54. Villeneuve d'Ascq.
Mazarakis-Ainian, A., ed. 2017. *Les sanctuaires archaïques des Cyclades*. Rennes.
Mazarakis Ainian, A., and Livieratou, A. 2010. "The Academy of Plato in the Early Iron Age." *Attika. Archäologie einer 'zentralen' Kulturlandschaft*, edited by H. Lohmann and T. Mattern, 87–100. Wiesbaden.
Mazarakis-Ainian, A., and Mouliou, M. 2008. *Archaeological Quests. Excavations at Homeric Graia*. Volos.
Mazzilli, F. 2018. *Rural Cult Centres in the Hauran. Part of the Broader Network of the Near East (100 BC–AD 300)*. Oxford.
McDonald, B. R. 1983. "The Megarian Decree." *Historia* 32.4:385–410.
McEvedy, C. 2011. *Cities of the Classical World. An Atlas and Gazetteer of 120 Centres of Ancient Civilization*, edited by D. S. Oles. London.
McGlew, J. F. 1993. *Tyranny and Political Culture in Ancient Greece*. Ithaca.
McInerney, J. 1999. *The Folds of Parnassos: Land and Ethnicity in Ancient Phokis*. Austin, TX.
McNicoll, A.W. 1997. *Hellenistic Fortifications from the Aegean to the Euphrates*. Oxford.
Meadows, A. R. 2019. "The Great Transformation: Civic Coin Design in the Second Century BC." In *ΤΥΠΟΙ. Greek and Roman Coins Seen Through Their Images. Noble Issuers, Humble Users?*, edited by P. P. Iossif et al., 287–318. Liège.
Mecella, L. 2006. "Publio Herennio Dexippo: osservazioni in margine ad una nuova edizione dei frammenti." *MedAnt* 9.1:9–31.
Mee, C., and Forbes, H., eds. 1997 *A Rough and Rocky Place. The Landscape and Settlement History of the Methana Peninsula, Greece*. Liverpool.
Meier, C. 2001. "The Greeks: The Political Revolution in World History." In *Agon, Logos, Polis. The Greek Achievement and Its Aftermath*, edited by J. P. Arnason and P. Murphy, 56–71. Stuttgart.
Meier, C. 2011. *Griechen und Europa. Die grosse Herausforderung der Freiheit im fünften Jahrhundert v. Chr.* Saarbrücken.
Meier, L. 2012. *Die Finanzierung öffentlicher Bauten in der hellenistischen Polis*. Mainz.
Meier, L. 2019. *Kibyra in hellenistischer Zeit. Neue Staatsverträge und Ehreninschriften*. Vienna.
Meier, M. 1998. *Aristokraten und Damoden. Untersuchungen zur inneren Entwicklung Spartas im 7. Jahrhundert v. Chr. und zur politischen Funktion der Dichtung des Tyrtaios*. Stuttgart.
Meiggs, R. 1972. *The Athenian Empire*. Oxford.
Meister, J. B. 2020. *"Adel" und gesellschaftliche Differenzierung im archaischen und frühklassischen Griechenland*. Stuttgart.
Mellor, R. 1975. ΘΕΑ ΡΩΜΗ. *The Worship of the Goddess Roma in the Greek World*. Göttingen.
Mendone, L. G., and Zoumbaki, S. 2008. *Roman Names in the Cyclades, Part 1*. Athens.
Meritt, B. D., Wade-Gery, H. T., and McGregor, M. F. 1930–53. *Athenian Tribute Lists*. Princeton.
Merola, G. D. 2001. *Autonomia locale, governo imperiale. Fiscalità e amministrazione nelle province asiane*. Bari.
Mersch, A. 1997. "Urbanization of the Attic Countryside from the Late 8th Century to the 6th Century BC." In *Urbanization in the Mediterranean in the 9th to 6th centuries BC*, edited by H. D. Andersen, 45–62. Copenhagen.
Mert, İ. H. 2016. "Priene'deki Gida Pazari: der sog. Lebensmittelmarkt von Priene." *Olba* 24:365–418.

Metcalf, W. E., ed. 2012. *Oxford Handbook of Greek and Roman Coinage.* Oxford.
Metzger, H., Laroche, E., Dupont-Sommer, A., Mayrhofer, M., and Demargne, P. 1979. *Fouilles de Xanthos, VI. La stèle trilingue du Létoon.* Paris.
Meyer, J. C. 2015. "Palmyrena: Settlements, Forts and Nomadic Networks." In *The World of Palmyra,* edited by A. Kropp and R. Raja, 88–104. Copenhagen.
Meyer, J. C. 2017a. *Palmyrena. Palmyra and the Surrounding Territory from the Roman to the Early Islamic Period.* Oxford.
Meyer, J. C. 2017b. "The Bride of the Dry Steppe: Palmyra and the Surrounding Territory." In *Palmyra. Mirage in the Desert,* edited by J. Aruz, 28–39. New York.
Meyer, J. C. 2020. "Palmyra: Marginal Agriculture in a Marginal Landscape?" In *Inter duo Imperia. Palmyra between East and West,* edited by M. Sommer, 47–64. Stuttgart.
Michels, C. M. 2009. *Kulturtransfer und monarchischer "Philhellenismus." Bithynien, Pontos und Kappadokien in hellenistischer Zeit.* Göttingen.
Michetti, L. M., and van Kampen, I. eds. 2014. *Il Tumulo di Monte Aguzzo a veio e la collezione Chigi, Ricostruzione del contesto dell'olpe Chigi e note sulla formazione della collezione archeologica della famiglia Chigi a formello.* Rome.
Middleton, G. 2020. *Collapse and Transformation. The Late Bronze Age to Early Iron Age in the Aegean.* Oxford.
Migeotte, L. 1984. *L'emprunt public dans les cités grecques: recueil des documents et analyse critique.* Quebec and Paris.
Migeotte, L. 1992. "Sur les rapports financiers entre le sanctuaire et la cité de Locres." In *Comptes et inventaires dans la cité grecque,* edited by D. Knoepfler, 191–203. Neuchâtel.
Migeotte, L. 1995. "Les finances publiques des cités grecques: bilan et perspectives de recherche." *Topoi (Lyon)* 5.1:7–32.
Migeotte, L. 1996. "Les finances des cités grecques au-dela du primitivisme et du modernisme." In *Energeia. Studies on Ancient History and Epigraphy Presented to H. W. Pleket,* edited by J. H. M. Strubbe, 79–96. Leiden.
Migeotte, L. 1997. "L'évergétisme des citoyens aux périodes classique et hellénistique." In *Actes du Xe congrès international d'épigraphie grecque et latine,* edited by M. Christol and O. Masson, 183–97. Paris.
Migeotte, L. 2002. "Information et vie politique dans la cité grecque." In *L'information et la mer dans le monde antique,* edited by J. Andreau and C. Virlouvet, 21–32. Rome.
Migeotte, L. 2006. "La haute administration des finances publiques et sacrées dans les cités hellénistiques." *Chiron* 36:379–94
Migeotte, L. 2014. *Les finances des cités grecques. Aux périodes classique et hellénistique.* Paris.
Mikalson, J. 1998. *Religion in Hellenistic Athens.* Berkeley.
Milan, S. 2018. "Polis and Dependency in Epirus: The Case of Cassope and the Poleis of Cassopaea." In *Politics, Territory and Identity in Ancient Epirus,* edited by A. J. Dominguez, 101–34. Milan.
Miles, M. 2011. "The *lapis primus* and the Older Parthenon." *Hesperia* 80.4:657–75.
Mili, M. 2014. *Religion and Society in Ancient Thessaly.* Oxford.
Millar, F. 1964. *A Study of Cassius Dio.* Oxford.
Millar, F. 1965. "Epictetus and the Imperial Court." *JRS* 55.1–2:141–48.
Millar, F. 1967. *The Roman Empire and Its Neighbours.* London.
Millar, F. 1977. *The Emperor in the Roman World (31 BC–AD 337).* London.
Millar, F. 1981. "The World of the Golden Ass." *JRS* 71:63–75.
Millar, F. 1993a. *The Roman Near East. 31 BC–AD 337.* Cambridge, MA.
Millar, F. 1993b. "City-States." *CR* 43.1:123–4.
Millar, F. 1998. *The Crowd in Rome in the Late Republic.* Ann Arbor, MI.
Millar, F. 2000. Review of W. Ball, *Rome in the East. The Transformation of an Empire. Topoi (Lyon)* 10.2:485–92.
Millar, F. 2002a. *The Roman Republic and the Augustan Revolution.* Edited by by H. Cotton and G. Rogers. Chapel Hill, NC.
Millar, F. 2002b. *The Roman Republic in Political Thought.* Hanover, NH.
Millar, F. 2004a. *Government, Society, and Culture in the Roman Empire.* Edited by H. Cotton and G. Rogers. Chapel Hill, NC.
Millar, F. 2004b. "Repentant Heretics in Fifth-Century Lydia: Identity and Literacy." *SCI* 23:111–30.
Millar, F. 2006a. *The Greek World, the Jews, and the East.* Edited by H. Cotton and G. Rogers. Chapel Hill, NC.
Millar, F. 2006b. *A Greek Roman Empire. Power and Belief under Theodosius II (408–450).* Berkeley.
Millar, F. 2015. *Empire, Church and Society in the Late Roman Near East. Greeks, Jews and Saracens.* Leuven.

Miller, J. 2011. *Aristotle's Nicomachean Ethics. A Critical Guide.* Cambridge.
Millett, P. 1989. "Patronage and its Avoidance in Classical Athens." In *Patronage in Ancient Society,* edited by A. Wallace-Hadrill, 15–47. London.
Millett, P. 1998. "Encounters in the Agora." In *Kosmos. Essays in Order, Conflict and Community in Classical Athens,* edited by P. Cartledge, P. Millett, and S. von Reden, 203–28. Cambridge.
Millett, P. 2000. "Mogens Hansen and the Labelling of Athenian Democracy." In *Polis and Politics. Studies in Ancient Greek History,* edited by P. Flensted-Jensen, T. H. Nielsen, and L. Rubinstein, 355–62. Copenhagen.
Minon, S. 2007. *Les inscriptions éléennes dialectales (VIe–IIe siècle avant J.-C.).* Geneva.
Mitchell, L. 1997. *Greeks Bearing Gifts. The Public Use of Private Relationships in the Greek World, 435–323 B.C.* Cambridge.
Mitchell, L. 2013. *The Heroic Rulers of Archaic and Classical Greece.* London.
Mitchell, S. 1976. "Requisitioned Transport in the Roman Empire: a New Inscription from Pisidia." *JRS* 66:106–31.
Mitchell, S. 1987. "Imperial Building in the Eastern Roman Provinces." *HSPh* 91:333–65.
Mitchell, S. 1990. "Festivals, Games, and Civic Life in Roman Asia Minor." *JRS* 80:183–93.
Mitchell, S. 1993. *Anatolia: Land, Men, and Gods in Asia Minor.* Oxford.
Mitchell, S. 1999. "The Administration of Roman Asia from 133 BC to AD 250." In *Lokale Autonomie und römische Ordnungsmacht in den kaiserzeitlichen Provinzen vom 1. bis 3. Jahrhundert,* edited by W. Eck and E. Müller-Luckner, 17–46. Munich.
Mitchell, S. 2008. "Geography, Politics, and Imperialism in the Asian Customs Law." In *The Customs Law of Asia,* edited by M. Cottier et al., 165–201. Oxford.
Mitchell, S. 2015. *A History of the Later Roman Empire, AD 284–641.* 2nd ed. Malden, MA.
Moatti, C., and Chevreau, E., eds. 2021. *L'expérience de la mobilité de l'Antiquité à nos jours, entre précarité et confiance.* Pessac.
Moggi, M. 1976. *I sinecismi interstatali greci.* Pisa.
Momigliano, A. 1934. *Filippo il Macedone.* Florence.
Mommsen, T., and Meyer, P. 1905. *Theodosiani libri XVI cum Constitutionibus Sirmondianis. Et Leges novellae ad Theodosianum pertinentes.* 2 vols. Berlin.
Monoson, S. 2011. "Navigating Race, Class, Polis, and Empire: The Place of Empirical Analysis in Aristotle's Account of Natural Slavery." In *Reading Ancient Slavery,* edited by R. Alston, E. Hall, and L. Proffitt, 133–51. London.
Monson, A. 2012. *From the Ptolemies to the Romans. Political and Economic Change in Egypt.* Cambridge.
Moors, S. 2002. "The Decapolis: City Territories, Villages and Bouleutai." In *After the Past. Essays in Ancient History in Honour of H. W. Pleket,* edited by W. Jongman and M. Kleiijwegt, 157–207. Leiden.
Moreno, A. 2007. *Feeding the Democracy. The Athenian Grain Supply in the Fifth and Fourth Centuries B.C.* Oxford.
Moreno, A. 2009. "'The Attic Neighbor': The Cleruchy in the Athenian Empire." In *Interpreting the Athenian Empire,* edited by J. Ma, N. Papazarkadas, and R. C. Parker, 211–21. London.
Morgan, C. 1990. *Athletes and Oracles. The Transformation of Delphi in the Eighth Century BC.* Cambridge.
Morgan, C. 1999a. *Isthmia. Vol. VIII The Late Bronze Age Settlement and Early Iron Age Sanctuary.* Princeton.
Morgan, C. 1999b. "Some Thoughts on the Production and Consumption of Early Iron Age Pottery in the Aegean." In *The Complex Past of Pottery. Production, Circulation and Consumption of Mycenean and Greek Pottery,* edited by J. P. Crielaard, V. Stissi, and G. J. van Wijngaarden, 213–59. Leiden.
Morgan, C. 2003. *Early Greek States Beyond the Polis.* London.
Morgan, C. 2006. "*Ethne* in the Peloponnese and Central Greece." In *Ancient Greece from the Mycenean Palaces to the Age of Homer,* edited by S. Deger-Jalkotzy and I. S. Lemos, 233–54. Edinburgh.
Morgan, C. 2009. "The Early Iron Age." In *A Companion to Archaic Greece,* edited by K. A. Raaflaub and H. van Wees, 41–63. Malden, MA.
Morgan, C. 2011. "The Elite of Aetos: Religion and Power in Early Iron Age Ithaka." In *The "Dark Ages" Revisited. Acts of an International Symposium in Memory of William D.E. Coulson,* edited by A. Mazarakis-Ainian, 113–25. Volos.
Morgan, C., and Whitelaw, T. 1991. "Pots and Politics: Ceramic Evidence for the Rise of the Argive State." *AJA* 95:79–108.
Morgan, T. 2005. "The Wisdom of Semonides fr. 7." *CCJ* 51:72–85.

Morgan, T. 2007. *Popular Morality in the Early Roman Empire*. Cambridge.
Morris, I. 1986. "The Use and Abuse of Homer." *ClAnt* 5.1:81–138.
Morris, I. 1987. *Burial and Ancient Society. The Rise of the Greek City-State*. Cambridge.
Morris, I. 1992. *Death-Ritual and Social Structure in Classical Antiquity*. Cambridge.
Morris, I. 1993. "Everyman's Grave." In *Athenian Identity and Civic Ideology*, edited by A. L. Boegehold and A. C. Scafuro, 67–101. Baltimore.
Morris, I. 1996. "The Strong Principle of Equality and the Archaic Origins of Greek Democracy." In *Demokratia. A Conversation on Democracies, Ancient and Modern*, edited by J. Ober and C. Hedrick, 19–48. Princeton.
Morris, I. 1998a. "Archaeology and Archaic Greek History." In *Archaic Greece. New Approaches and New Evidence*, edited by N. Fisher and H. van Wees, 1–92. Swansea.
Morris, I. 1998b. "Remaining Invisible: The Archaeology of the Excluded in Classical Athens." In *Women and Slaves in Greco-Roman Culture. Differential Equations*, edited by S. R. Joshel and S. Murnaghan, 193–220. London.
Morris, I. 2000. *Archaeology as Cultural History: Words and Things in Iron Age Greece*. Malden, MA.
Morris, I. 2004. "Economic Growth in Ancient Greece." *Journal of Institutional and Theoretical Economics* 160:709–42.
Morris, I. 2006. "The Collapse and Regeneration of Complex Society in Greece, 1500–500 B.C." In *After Collapse. The Regeneration of Complex Societies*, edited by G. M. Schwartz and J. J. Nichols, 72–84, Tucson.
Morris, I. 2009a. "The Eighth-Century Revolution." In *A Companion to Archaic Greece*, edited by K. A. Raaflaub and H. van Wees, 64–80. Malden, MA.
Morris, I. 2009b. "The Greater Athenian State." In *The Dynamics of Ancient Empires. State Power from Assyria to Byzantium*, edited by I. Morris and W. Scheidel, 99–177. Oxford.
Morris, S. P., and Papadopoulos, J. 2005. "Greek Towers and Slaves: an Archaeology of Exploitation." *AJA* 109.2:155–225.
Mossé, C. 1978. "Le thème de la patrios politeia dans la pensée grecque du IVe siècle." *Eirene* 16:81–89.
Moustaka, A., Skarlatidou, E. C., Tzannes, M.-C., and Ersoy, Y., eds. 2004. *Klazomenai, Teos and Abdera. Metropoleis and Colony*. Thessaloniki.
Muhlberger, S. 2011. "Republics and Quasi-Democratic Institutions in Ancient India." In *The Secret History of Democracy*, edited by B. Isakhan and S. Stockwell, 49–59. Basingstoke.
Muhlberger, S., and Paine, P. 1993. "Democracy's Place in World History." *Journal of World History* 4.1:23–45.
Müllenhoff, M. 2005. *Geoarchäologische, sedimentologische und morphodynamische Untersuchungen im Mündungsgebiet des Büyük Menderes (Mäander), Westtürkei*. Marburg.
Müller, C. 1996. "Les *nomina romana* à Thespies du IIe s. a. C. à l'édit de Caracalla." In *Roman Onomastics in the Greek East. Social and Political Aspects*, edited by A. D. Rizakis, 157–66. Paris.
Müller, C. 1997. "Les débuts du culte impérial en Béotie." *REG* 110.1:xix–xxi.
Müller, C. 2010. "Les élites béotiennes et la richesse du IVe au IIe s. a. C. Quelques pistes de réflexion." In *La Cité et ses élites. Pratiques et représentation des formes de domination et de contrôle social dans les cités grecques*, edited by L. Capdetrey and Y. Lafond, 225–44. Bordeaux.
Müller, C. 2011. "Évergétisme et pratiques financières dans les cités de la Grèce hellénistique." *REA* 113.2:345–63.
Müller, C. 2014a. "Les Romains et la Grèce égéenne du Ier s. av. J.-C. au Ier s. apr. J.-C.: un monde en transition?" *Pallas* 96:193–216.
Müller, C. 2014b. "(De)constructing Politeia: Reflections on Citizenship and the Bestowal of Privileges upon Foreigners in Hellenistic Democracies." *Annales (HSS)* 69.3:533–54.
Müller, C. 2018. "Itinéraires d'une prostituée. Néaira et les espaces de la cité au IVe siècle av. J-C." In *Statuts personnels et espaces sociaux. Questions grecques et romaines*, edited by C. Moatti and C. Müller, 243–69. Paris.
Müller, C. 2019. "Les méandres de la taxation romaine en Grèce à la fin de l'époque hellénistique. Une vue d'Oropos (à propos de RDGE 23)." In *Philorhômaios kai Philhellèn. Hommages à Jean-Louis Ferrary*, edited by A. Heller, C. Müller, and A. Suspène, 391–417. Geneva.
Müller, C. 2023. "How (Not) to Be a Citizen. Subordination and Participation of the *perioikoi* in Hellenistic Sparta (and Elsewhere)." In *Politeia and Koinonia. Studies in Ancient Greek History in Honour of Josine Blok*, edited by V. Pirenne-Delforge and M. Wecowski, 65–88. Leiden.
Müller, C., and Hasenohr, C., eds. 2002. *Les Italiens dans le monde grec. IIème siècle av. J.-C.—Ier siècle ap. J.-C. Circulation, activités, intégration*. Athens.
Müller, H. 1976. *Milesische Volksbeschlüsse. Eine Untersuchung zur Verfassungsgeschichte der Stadt Milet in hellenistischer Zeit*. Göttingen.

Müller, H. 1995. "Bemerkungen zu Funktion und Bedeutung des Rats in den hellenistischen Städten." In *Stadtbild und Bürgerbild im Hellenismus*, edited by M. Wörrle and P. Zanker, 41–54. Munich.
Müller, H., and Staab, G. 2017. "Dion. Ein pergamenischer Politiker im Himmel." *Chiron* 47:339–65.
Mumford, L. 1970. *The Culture of Cities*. 2nd ed. New York.
Munn, M. 2000. *The School of History. Athens in the Age of Socrates*. Berkeley.
Muntaner, R. 1999 *Crònica*. Edited by V. J. Escartí. Valencia.
Murnaghan S. 1988. "How a Woman Can Be More Like a Man: The Dialogue between Ischomachus and His Wife in Xenophon's *Oeconomicus*." *Helios* 15.1:9–22.
Murray, O., ed. 1990. *Sympotica: A Symposium on the Symposion*. Oxford.
Murray, O. 1993. *Early Greece*. Cambridge, MA.
Murray, O. 1997. "Rationality and the Greek City: The Evidence from Kamarina." In *The Polis as an Urban Centre and as a Political Community*, edited by M. H. Hansen, 493–504. Copenhagen.
Murray, O., and Price, S. R. F., eds. 1990. *The Greek City from Homer to Alexander*. Oxford.
Murray, S. C. 2017. *The Collapse of the Mycenaean Economy. Imports, Trade, and Institutions, 1300–700 BCE*. Cambridge.
Murray, S. C. 2018 "Lights and Darks: Data, Labeling, and Language in the History of Scholarship on Early Greece." *Hesperia* 87.1:17–54.
Musti, D. 2000. "Il tema dell'autonomia nelle *Elleniche* di Senofonte." *RFIC* 128.2:170–81.
Nafissi, M. 1991. *La nascita del kosmos: studi sulla storia e la società di Sparta*. Naples.
Nafissi, M. 2001. *La Nascita del Kosmos. Studi sulla storia e la società di Sparta*. Perugia.
Nafissi, M. 2009. "Sparta." In *The Blackwell Companion to Archaic Greece*, edited by K. A. Raaflaub and H. van Wees, 117–37. Malden, MA.
Nafissi, M. 2010. "The Great *rhetra* (Plut. Lyc. 6): A Retrospective and Intentional Construct?" In *Intentional History. Spinning Time in Ancient Greece*, edited by L. Foxhall, H.-J. Gehrke, and N. Luraghi, 89–119. Stuttgart.
Nails, D. 2009. "The Trial and Death of Socrates." In *A Companion to Greek and Roman Political Thought*, edited by R. K. Balot, 321–38. Malden, MA.
Nakassis, D. 2013. *Individuals and Society in Mycenaean Pylos*. Leiden.
Nakassis, D. 2020. "The Economy." In *A Companion to the Archaeology of Early Greece and the Mediterranean*, vol. 1, edited by I. Lemos and A. Kotsonas, 271–91. Hoboken, NJ.
Neer, R. T. 2001. "Framing the Gift: The Politics of the Siphnian Treasury at Delphi." *ClAnt* 20.2:273–344.
Neer, R. T. 2018. *Greek Art and Archaeology c. 2500–c. 150 BCE*. 2nd ed. New York.
Nelson, E. 2004. *The Greek Tradition in Republican Thought*. Cambridge.
Netz, R. 2020. *Scale, Space and Canon in Ancient Literary Culture*. Cambridge.
Nevett, L. 2012. "Towards a Female Topography of the Ancient Greek City: Case Studies from Late Archaic and Early Classical Athens (c.520–400 BCE)." In *Gender and the City before Modernity*, edited by L. Foxhall and G. Neher, 86–106. Malden, MA.
Nevett, L., et al. 2020. "Constructing the 'Urban Profile' of an Ancient Greek City: Evidence from the Olynthos Project." *ABSA* 115:329–78.
Neumann, K. M. 2021. *Antioch in Syria. A History from Coins (300 BCE–450 CE)*. Cambridge.
Ng, D. Y. 2015. "Commemoration and Élite Benefaction of Buildings and Spectacles in the Roman World." *JRS* 105:101–23.
Ng, D.Y. 2017. "The Salutaris Foundation: Monumentality through Periodic Rehearsal." In *Roman Artists, Patrons and Public Consumption. Familiar Works Reconsidered*, edited by B. Longfellow and E. Perry, 63–87. Ann Arbor.
Nicolet, C. 2001. *Rome et la conquête du monde méditerranéen (264–27 avant J.-C.)*. 6th ed. Paris.
Nielsen, T. H. 2000. "Epiknemidian, Hypoknemidian, and Opountian Lokrians: Reflections on the Political Organisation of East Lokris in the Classical Period." In *Further Studies in the Ancient Greek Polis*, edited by P. Flensted-Jensen, 91–120. Stuttgart.
Nielsen, T. H. 2002. *Arkadia and its Poleis in the Archaic and Classical Period*. Göttingen.
Nielsen, T. H. 2007. *Olympia and the Classical Hellenic City-State Culture*. Copenhagen.
Nielsen, T. H. 2014. "Foreign Entrants at Minor Athletic Festivals in Late-Archaic and Classical Greece." *Nikephoros* 27:91–158.
Nielsen, T. H. 2015. "The Arkadian Confederacy." In *Federalism in Greek Antiquity*, edited by H. Beck and P. Funke, 250–68. Cambridge.

Niemeier, W.-D. 2002. *Der Kuros vom heiligen Tor. Überraschende Neufunde archaischer Skulptur im Kerameikos in Athen.* Mainz.

Nieto Izquierdo, E. 2019. *Recueil d'inscriptions grecques dialectales. L'Argolide.* Nancy.

Nigdelis, P. 1990. *Πολίτευμα και κοινωνία των πόλεων των Κυκλάδων κατά την ελληνιστική και αυτοκρατορική εποχή.* Thessaloniki.

Nigdelis, P. M., and Arvanitaki, A. 2012. "Direct Taxation in Roman Macedonia: A New Votive Inscription of a δεκάπρωτος in an Unknown City of Western Pieria." *Chiron* 42:271–86.

Nigdelis, P. M., and Souris, G. A. 2005. *Ανθύπατος λεγει. Ένα διαταγμα των αυτοκρατορικών χρόνων για το γυμνάσιο της Βέροιας.* Thessaloniki.

Niku, M. 2004. "When and Why Did the Athenian μετοίκια System Disappear? The Evidence of Inscriptions." *Arctos* 38:75–93.

Niku, M. 2007. *The Official Status of the Foreign Residents in Athens, 322–120 B.C.* Helsinki.

Nixon, L., and Price, S. R. F. 1990. "The Size and Resources of Greek Cities." In *The Greek City from Homer to Alexander*, edited by O. Murray and S. R. F. Price, 137–70. Oxford.

Nollé, J. 2010. "Beiträge zur kleinasiatischen Münzkunde und Geschichte." *Gephyra* 7:71–124.

Nollé, J. 2012a. "Zum Kult der Anaïtis Artemis von Hypaipa und zu einigen Patriatraditionen der torrhebischen Kaÿstertal-Stadt." *JNG* 62:127–95.

Nollé, J. 2012b. "Stadtprägungen des Ostens und die 'explosion agonistique': Überlegungen zu Umfang, Aussagen und Hintergründen der Propagierung von Agonen auf den Prägungen der Städte des griechischen Ostens." In *L'organisation des spectacles dans le monde romain*, edited by J. Nollé et al., 1–39. Geneva.

Noreña, C. F. 2011. *Imperial Ideals in the Roman West. Representation, Circulation, Power.* Cambridge.

Noreña, C. F. 2020. "Emperors, Benefactions and Honorific Practice in the Roman Imperial Greek Polis." In *Benefactors and the Polis. The Public Gift in the Greek Cities from the Homeric World to Late Antiquity*, edited by M. D. Gygax and A. Zuiderhoek, 201–21. Cambridge.

Nörr, D. 1966. *Imperium und Polis in der hohen Prinzipatszeit.* Munich.

North, J. A. 1981. "The Development of Roman Imperialism." *JRS* 71:1–9.

North, D. C., Wallis, J. J., and Weingast, B. R. 2009. *Violence and Social Orders. A Conceptual Framework for Interpreting Recorded Human History.* Cambridge.

Oakley, J. H. 2004. *Picturing Death in Classical Athens: The Evidence of the White Lekythoi.* Cambridge.

Ober, J. 1989. *Mass and Elite in Democratic Athens: Rhetoric, Ideology, and the Power of the People.* Princeton.

Ober, J. 1996. *The Athenian Revolution. Essays on Ancient Greek Democracy and Political Theory.* Princeton.

Ober, J. 1998. *Political Dissent in Democratic Athens. Intellectual Critics of Popular Rule.* Princeton.

Ober, J. 2001. "The Debate over Civic Education in Classical Athens." In *Education in Greek and Roman Antiquity*, edited by Y. L. Too, 175–207. Leiden.

Ober, J. 2005. *Athenian Legacies. Essays on the Politics of Going on Together.* Princeton.

Ober, J. 2008. *Democracy and Knowledge. Innovation and Learning in Classical Athens.* Princeton.

Ober, J. 2010. "Wealthy Hellas." *TAPA* 140.2:241–86.

Ober, J. 2012. "Democracy's Dignity." *The American Political Science Review* 106.4:827–46.

Ober, J. 2015. *The Rise and Fall of Classical Greece.* Princeton.

Ober, J. 2017. *Demopolis. Democracy Before Liberalism in Theory and Practice.* Cambridge.

Ober, J. 2022. *The Greeks and the Rational. The Discovery of Practical Reason.* Princeton.

Ober, J., Wallace, R., and Raaflaub, K. 2007. *Origins of Democracy in Ancient Greece.* Berkeley.

Oetjen, R. 2014. *Athen im dritten Jahrhundert v. Chr. Politik und Gesellschaft in den Garnisonsdemen auf der Grundlage der inschriftlichen Überlieferung.* Düsseldorf.

Ogden, D. 1994. "Crooked Speech: The Genesis of the Spartan Rhetra." *JHS* 114:85–102.

Ogden, D. 1997. *The Crooked Kings of Ancient Greece.* London.

Ogden, D. 2002. "Controlling Women's Dress: Gynaikonomoi." In *Women's Dress in the Ancient Greek World*, edited by L. Llewellyn-Jones and S. Blundell, 202–25. Swansea.

Ogilvie, S. 2003. *A Bitter Living. Women, Markets, and Social Capital in Early Modern Germany.* Oxford.

Oliva, P. 1971. *Sparta and Her Social Problems.* Hakkert.

Oliver, G. J. 2007. *War, Food, and Politics in Early Hellenistic Athens.* Oxford.

Oliver, J. H. 1953. *The Ruling Power. A Study of the Roman Empire in the Second Century after Christ through the Roman Oration of Aelius Aristides.* Philadelphia.

Oliver, J. H. 1954. "The Roman Governor's Permission for a Decree of the Polis." *Hesperia* 23.2:163–67.

Oliver, J. H. 1978. "Panachaeans and Panhellenes." *Hesperia* 47.2:185–91.

Oliver, J. H. 1989. *Greek Constitutions of Early Roman Emperors from Inscriptions and Papyri*. Philadelphia.
Ollier, F. 1933–1943. *Le mirage spartiate. Étude sur l'idéalisation de Sparte dans l'antiquité grecque du début de l'école cynique jusqu'à la fin de la cité*. Paris.
Olshausen, E., and Sauer, V. 2014. *Mobilität in den Kulturen der antiken Mittelmeerwelt*. Stuttgart.
Olson, J. 2004. *The Abolition of White Democracy*. Minneapolis.
O'Mara, P. F. 1958. "Jean-Jacques and Geneva: The Petty Bourgeois Milieu of Rousseau's Thought." *The Historian* 20.2:127–52.
Omitowoju, R. 2002. *Rape and the Politics of Consent in Classical Athens*. Cambridge.
Oppeneer, T. 2018. "Assembly Politics and the Rhetoric of Honour in Chariton, Dio of Prusa and John Chrysostom." *Historia* 67.2:223–43.
Orth, W. 1989. "Demos-freundliche Tendenzen in der Zeit des Kaisers Claudius." In *Migratio et commutatio: Studien zur alten Geschichte und deren Nachleben*, edited by H.-J. Drexhage and J. Sünskes Thompson. 50–59. Sankt Katharinen.
Osborne, M. J. 1981–1983. *Naturalization in Athens*. Brussels.
Osborne, R. 1985a. "Law in Action in Classical Athens." *JHS* 105:40–58.
Osborne, R. 1985b. *Demos. The Discovery of Classical Attika*. Cambridge.
Osborne, R. 1987. *Classical Landscape with Figures. The Ancient Greek City and its Countryside*. London.
Osborne, R. 1989. "A Crisis in Archaeological History? The Seventh Century BC in Attica." *ABSA* 84:297–322.
Osborne, R. 1990a. "The Demos and its Divisions in Classical Athens." In *The Greek City from Homer to Alexander*, edited by O. Murray and S. R. F. Price, 265–93. Oxford.
Osborne, R. 1990b. "What Was a Demagogue?" *Omnibus* 19:11–13.
Osborne, R. 1990c. "Vexatious Litigation in Classical Athens: Sykophancy and the Sykophant." In *Nomos. Essays in Athenian Law, Politics and Society*, edited by P. Cartledge, P. Millett, and S. R. Todd, 83–102. Cambridge.
Osborne, R. 1991. "Pride and Prejudice, Sense and Subsistence: Exchange and Society in the Greek City." In *City and Country in the Ancient World*, edited by J. W. Rich and A. Wallace-Hadrill, 119–45. London.
Osborne, R. 1994. "Looking On—Greek Style: Does the Sculpted Girl Speak to Women Too?" In *Classical Greece. Ancient Histories and Modern Archaeologies*, edited by I. M. Morris, 81–96. Cambridge.
Osborne, R. 1996. "Desiring Women on Athenian Pottery." In *Sexuality in Ancient Art. Near East, Egypt, Greece and Italy*, edited by N. B. Kampen, 65–80. Cambridge.
Osborne, R. 1996–1997. "The Spartan Exception." In *Debating Dark Ages. Papers on Mediterranean Archaeology*, edited by M. Kleibrink, 19–24. Groningen.
Osborne, R. 1997. "Law and Laws: How Do We Join Up the Dots?" In *The Development of the Polis in Archaic Greece*, edited by L. G. Mitchell and P. J. Rhodes, 74–82. London.
Osborne, R. 1998a. "Early Greek Colonisation? The Nature of Greek Settlement in the West." In *Archaic Greece. New Approaches and New Evidence*, edited by N. Fisher and H. Van Wees, 251–69. London.
Osborne, R. 1998b. *Archaic and Classical Greek art*. Oxford.
Osborne, R. 1999. "Inscribing Performance." In *Performance Culture and Athenian Democracy*, edited by S. Goldhill and R. Osborne, 341–58. Cambridge.
Osborne, R. 2000. "Religion, Imperial Politics, and the Offering of Freedom to Slaves." In *Law and Social Status in Classical Athens*, edited by V. Hunter and J. Edmondson, 74–92. Oxford.
Osborne, R. 2004. "Homer's Society." In *The Cambridge Companion to Homer*, edited by R. Fowler, 206–19. Cambridge.
Osborne, R. ed. 2007. *Debating the Athenian Cultural Revolution: Art, Literature, Philosophy, and Politics, 430–380 BC*. Cambridge.
Osborne, R. 2009a. *Greece in the Making 1200–479 B.C.* 2nd ed. London.
Osborne, R. 2009b. "Economic Growth and the Politics of Entitlement." *CCJ* 55:97–125.
Osborne, R. 2010. *Athens and Athenian Democracy*. Cambridge.
Osborne, R. 2011. *The History Written on the Classical Greek Body*. Cambridge.
Osborne, R. 2018. *The Transformation of Athens. Painted Pottery and the Creation of Classical Greece*. Princeton.
Osborne, R., and Cunliffe, B. 2005. *Mediterranean Urbanization 800–600 BC*. Oxford.
Ostrom, E. 1990. *Governing the Commons. The Evolution of Institutions for Collective Action*. Cambridge.
Ostwald, M. 1982. *Autonomia. Its Genesis and Early History*. Chico, CA.

Ostwald, M. 1986. *From Popular Sovereignty to the Sovereignty of Law. Law, Society, and Politics in Fifth-century Athens.* Berkeley.
Ostwald, M. 2000. "Oligarchy and Oligarchs in Ancient Greece." In *Polis & Politics. Studies in Ancient Greek History*, edited by P. Flensted-Jensen, T. H. Nielsen, and L. Rubinstein, 385–96. Copenhagen.
O'Sullivan, L. 2009. *The Regime of Demetrius of Phalerum in Athens. A Philosopher in Politics.* Leiden.
Otranto, R. 2012. "Demostene e Callimaco nel P.Lit.Lond. 108." *Aegyptus* 92:157–72.
Owen, S. 2009. "The 'Thracian' Landscape of Archaic Thasos." In *Inside the City in the Greek World: Studies of Urbanism from the Bronze Age to the Hellenistic Period*, edited by L. Preston, S. Owen, 85–98. Oxford.
Özyiğit, Ö. 1994. "The City Walls of Phokaia." *REA* 96.2:77–109.
Paga, J. 2020. *Building Democracy in Late Archaic Athens.* New York.
Page, B. I., Seawright, J., and Lacombe, M. J. 2019. *Billionaires and Stealth Politics.* Chicago.
Palaima, T. 2003. "'Archives' and 'Scribes' and Information Hierarchy in Mycenaean Greek Linear B Records." In *Ancient Archives and Archival Traditions. Concepts of Record-Keeping in the Ancient World*, edited by M. Brosius, 153–94. Oxford.
Panagopoulos, C. 1977. "Vocabulaire et mentalité dans les *Moralia* de Plutarque." *DHA* 3:197–235.
Pandermalis, D. 2012. *Archaic Colors.* Translated by L. Psarrou. Athens.
Papadimitriou, A. 2006. "The Early Iron Age in the Argolid: Some New Aspects." In *Ancient Greece. From the Mycenaean Palaces to the Age of Homer*, edited by S. Deger-Jalkotzy and I. S. Lemos, 532–48. Edinburgh.
Papadimitriou, N., and Cosmopoulos, M. B. 2020. "The Political Geography of Attica in the Middle and the Late Bronze Age." In *Athens and Attica in Prehistory*, edited by N. Papadimitriou et al., 373–86. Oxford.
Papadopoulos, J. K. 1996. "Dark Age Greece." In *The Oxford Companion to Archaeology*, edited by B. M. Fagan, 253–55. Oxford.
Papadopoulos, J. K. 1997. "Phantom Euboians." *JMA* 10.2:191–219.
Papadopoulos, J. K. 2001. Review of Ἀνασκαφὲς Νάξου. Τὸ Νότιο Νεκροταφεῖο τῆς Νάξου κατὰ τη Γεωμετρικῆ Περίοδο. Ἔρευνες τῶν Ἕλων 1931–1939 (Nota Kourou). *AJA* 105.2:349–50.
Papadopoulos, J. K. 2002. "Παίζω η χέζω? A Contextual Approach to *pessoi* (Gaming Pieces, Counters or Convenient Wipes?)," *Hesperia* 71.4:423–27.
Papadopoulos, J. K. 2003. *Ceramicus Redivivus. The Early Iron Age Potters' Field in the Area of the Classical Athenian Agora.* With a contribution by K. Schilling. Princeton.
Papadopoulos, J. K. 2005. *The Early Iron Age Cemetery at Torone. Excavations Conducted by the Australian Archaeological Institute at Athens in Collaboration with the Athens Archaeological Society.* Los Angeles.
Papadopoulos, J. K. 2016. "*Komai*, Colonies and Cities in Epirus and Southern Albania: The Failure of the Polis and the Rise of Urbanism on the Fringes of the Greek World." In *Of Odysseys and Oddities. Scales and Modes of Interaction between Prehistoric Aegean Societies and their Neighbours*, edited by B. Molloy, 435–60. Oxford.
Papadopoulos, J. K., and Lord Smithson, E. 2002. "The Cultural Biography of a Cycladic Geometric Amphora: Islanders in Athens and the Prehistory of Metics." *Hesperia* 71.2:149–99.
Papadopoulos, J. K., and Lord Smithson, E. 2017. *The Early Iron Age. The Cemeteries. Athenian Agora* 36. Princeton.
Papadopoulos, J. K., and Schilling, M. R. 2003. *Ceramicus Redivivus. The Early Iron Age Potters' Field in the Area of the Classical Athenian Agora.* Princeton.
Papadopoulou, Z. 2016. "Ὅρος ἀπὸ τὴν Νάξο." *Grammateion* 5:29–32.
Papakonstantinou, Z. 2008. *Lawmaking and Adjudication in Archaic Greece.* London.
Papakonstantinou, Z. 2010. "Agariste's Suitors: Sport, Feasting and Elite Politics in Sixth-Century BC Greece." *Nikephoros* 23:71–93.
Papakonstantinou, Z. 2017. "Binding Curses, Agency and the Athenian Democracy." In *Violence and Community Law, Space and Identity in the Ancient Eastern Mediterranean World*, edited by I. K. Xydopoulos, K. Vlassopoulos, and E. Tounta, 142–58. London.
Papakosta, L. 1991. "Παρατηρήσεις σχετικά με την τοπογραφία του αρχαίου Αιγίου." In *Achaia und Elis in der Antike*, edited by A. D. Rizakis, 235–40, Athens.
Papalexandrou, A. 2005. *The Visual Poetics of Power. Warriors, Youths, and Tripods in Early Greece.* Lanham, MD.
Papalexandrou, A. 2008. "Boiotian Tripods: The Tenacity of a Panhellenic Symbol in a Regional Context." *Hesperia* 77.2:251–82.

Paparriga-Artemiadi, L. 2020. "'Ἐπαγγελία' (*pollicitatio apud rem publicam*): l'évolution de la nature juridique de l'évergésie et ses effets sur le fonctionnement des cités (IIIe s. avant–VIe s. après notre ère." In *Ἰουλίαν Βελισσαροπούλου Ἐπαινέσαι. Studies in Ancient Greek and Roman Law*, edited by A. Dimopoulou, A. Helmis, and D. Karambelas, 165–90. Athens.

Papazarkadas, N. 2009. "Epigraphy and the Athenian Empire: Re-shuffling the Chronological Cards." In *Interpreting the Athenian Empire*, edited by J. Ma, N. Papazarkadas, and R. Parker, 67–88. London.

Papazarkadas, N. 2017. "Judicial and Financial Administration in Late Hellenistic Athens: A New Decree of the Athenian Council." *Hesperia* 86.1:325–57.

Papazarkadas, N. 2021. "Courts, Magistrates and Allotment Procedures: A New Inscribed Kleroterion from Hellenistic Athens." In *Vorträge zur griechischen und hellenistischen Rechtsgeschichte*, edited by K. Harter-Uibopuu and W. Riess, 105–24. Vienna.

Papazoglu, F. 1986. "Oppidum Stobi civium Romanorum et municipium Stobensium." *Chiron* 16:213–37.

Papazoglou, F. 1988. *Les villes de Macédoine à l'époque romaine*. Athens.

Papazoglou, F. 1997. *Laoi et paroikoi. Recherches sur la structure de la société hellénistique*. Belgrade.

Papazoglou, F. 1998. "Le koinon macédonien et la province de Macédoine." *Thracia* 12:133–39.

Pappi, E. 2006. "Argive Geometric Figured Style: The Rule and the Exception." In *Pictorial Pursuits. Figurative Painting on Mycenaean and Geometric Pottery*, edited by E. Rystedt and B. Wells, 229–37. Stockholm.

Pappi, E., and Triantaphyllou, S. 2011. "Mortuary Practices and the Human Remains: A Preliminary Study of the Geometric Graves in Argos, Argolid." In *The "Dark Ages" Revisited*, edited by A. Mazarakis Ainian, 673–88. Volos.

Pariente, A. 1992. "Le monument argien des Sept contre Thèbes." In *Polydipsion Argos. Argos de la fin des palais mycéniens à la constitution de l'état classique*, edited by M. Piérart, 195–229. Athens.

Parker, G. 2004. *Sovereign City. The City-State Ancient and Modern*. London.

Parker, R. 1983. *Miasma. Pollution and Purification in Early Greek Religion*. Oxford.

Parker, R. 2010. "The Convention of the Basaidai and the Four Families." *ZPE* 173:87–88.

Parker, R. 2011. *On Greek Religion*. Ithaca.

Parlasca, K. 2007. "Grave Reliefs and Architectural Sculpture." In *Oxyrhynchus. A City and its Texts*, edited by A. K. Bowman et al., 91–103. London.

Parrish, D. 2001. *Urbanism in Western Asia Minor. New Studies on Aphrodisias, Ephesos, Hierapolis, Pergamon, Perge and Xanthos*. Portsmouth.

Paschidis, P. 2008. *Between City and King. Prosopographical Studies on the Intermediaries between the Cities of the Greek Mainland and the Aegean and the Royal Courts in the Hellenistic Period, 322–190 B.C.* Paris.

Pascual, J., and Papakonstantinou, M.-F., eds. 2013. *Topography and History of Ancient Epicnemidian Locris*. Leiden.

Patlagean, E. 1977. *Pauvreté économique et pauvreté sociale à Byzance. 4e–7e siècles*. Paris.

Paton, B., and Law, J. E., eds. 2016. *Communes and Despots in Medieval and Renaissance Italy*. Routledge.

Paton, W. R., and Myres, J. L. 1896. "Karian Sites and Inscriptions." *JHS* 16:188–271.

Patterson, C. 1981. *Pericles' Citizenship Law of 451–50 B.C.* New York.

Patterson, O. 1982. *Slavery and Social Death. A Comparative Study*. Cambridge, MA.

Patterson, O. 1991. *Freedom in the Making of Western Culture*. New York.

Pawlak, M. 2010. "From Messene to Rome: Ti. Claudius Saithidas and His Family." In *Hortus Historiae. Studies Dedicated to Prof. Jozef Wolski*, edited by M. Dzielska et al., 411–24. Kraków.

Pébarthe, C. 2005. "La perception des droits de passage à Chalcis (*IG* I^3 40, 446 a.C.)." *Historia* 54.1:84–92.

Pébarthe, C. 2006. *Cité, démocratie et écriture. Histoire de l'alphabétisation d'Athènes à l'époque classique*. Paris.

Pébarthe, C. 2009. "Émigrer d'Athènes: Clérouques et colons aux temps de la domination athénienne sur l'Égée au Ve siècle a.C." In *Le monde de l'itinérance en Méditerranée de l'Antiquité à l'époque moderne. Procédures de contrôle et d'identification*, edited by W. Kaiser, C. Moatti, and C. Pébarthe, 367–90. Paris.

Pébarthe, C. 2012. "Faire l'histoire de la démocratie athénienne avec Cornelius Castoriadis." *REA* 114.1:139–57.

Pébarthe, C. 2013. "Les archives de la cité de raison: Démocratie athénienne et pratiques documentaires à l'époque classique." In *Archives and Archival Documents in Ancient Societies*, edited by M. Faraguna, 107–25. Trieste.

Pellagatti, P. 1983. "Bilancio degli scavi di Naxos per l'VIII e il II sec. a. C." *ASAA* 59:291–311.

Pellegrin, P. 2017. *L'excellence menacée. Sur la philosophie politique d'Aristote*. Paris.

Pellegrino, M. 2000. *Utopie e immagini gastronomiche nei frammenti dell'Archaia*. Bologna.

Perlman, P. 1995. "ΘΕΩΡΟΔΟΚΟΥΝΤΕΣ ΕΝ ΤΑΙΣ ΠΟΛΕΣΙΝ: Panhellenic Epangelia and Political Status." In *Sources for the Ancient Greek City-State*, 2nd ed., edited by M. H. Hansen, 113–64. Copenhagen.

Perlman, P. 2000a. *City and Sanctuary in Ancient Greece. The Theorodokia in the Peloponnesus.* Göttingen.
Perlman, P. 2000b. "Gortyn: The First Seven Hundred Years Part I." In *Polis and Politics. Studies in Ancient Greek History,* edited by P. Flensted-Jensen, T. H. Nielsen, and L. Rubinstein, 59–89. Copenhagen.
Perlman, P. 2002. "Gortyn: The First Seven Hundred Years. Part II. The Laws from the Temple of Apollo Pythios." In *Even More Studies in the Ancient Greek Polis,* edited by T. H. Nielsen, 187–227. Stuttgart.
Perlman, P. 2004. "Tinker, Tailor, Soldier, Sailor: The Economies of Archaic Eleutherna, Crete." *ClAnt* 23.1:95–136.
Perlman, P. 2010. "Of Battle, Booty, and Citizen Women: A 'New' Inscription from Axos, Crete (*IC* II v 5 + *IC* II v 6)." *Hesperia* 79.1:79–112.
Perlman, P. 2014. "Reading and Writing Archaic Cretan Society." In *Cultural Practices and Material Culture in Archaic and Classical Crete,* edited by G. Seelentag and O. Pilz, 177–206. Berlin.
Perrin-Saminadayar, E. 2007. *Éducation, culture et société à Athènes. Les acteurs de la vie culturelle Athénienne (229–88): un tout petit monde.* Paris.
Perrin-Saminadayar, E. 2019. "Les femmes de l'entourage d'Hérode Atticus." In *Femmes grecques de l'Orient romain,* edited by S. Lalanne, 155–68. Besançon.
Peschlow-Bindokat, A. 1996a. "Der Kult des anatolischen Regen- und Wettergottes auf dem Gipfel des Latmos und das Heiligtum des Zeus Akraios im Tal von Dikilitaş." *MDAI(I)* 46:217–25.
Peschlow-Bindokat, A. 1996b. *Der Latmos. Eine unbekannte Gebirgslandschaft an der türkischen Westküste.* Mainz.
Petit, P. 1955. *Libanius et la vie municipale à Antioche au IVe siècle après J.-C.* Paris.
Petrocheilos, N., and Rousset, D. 2019. "Contribution à l'histoire et l'épigraphie de Panopeus en Phocide." *BCH* 143.2:795–815.
Petropoulou, A. 1985. *Beiträge zur Wirtschafts- und Gesellschaftsgeschichte Kretas in hellenistischer Zeit.* Frankfurt.
Pettit, P. 2012. *On the People's Terms. A Republican Theory and Model of Democracy.* Cambridge.
Pferdehirt, B., Scholz, M., and Barnes, T. D. eds. 2012. *Bürgerrecht und Krise: die "Constitutio Antoniniana" 212 n. Chr. und ihre innenpolitischen Folgen.* Mainz.
Pfuhl, E., and Möbius, H. 1977. *Die ostgriechischen Grabreliefs.* Mainz.
Pharaklas, N. 1998. Θηβαϊκά. Athens.
Pharr, C. 1952. *The Theodosian Code and Novels and the Sirmondian Constitutions.* Princeton.
Philaniotou, O. 2006. "Herakleia." In *Archaeology. Aegean Islands,* edited by A. G. Vlachopoulos, 289. Athens.
Philippa-Touchais, A. 2011. "'Cycles of Collapse in Greek Prehistory': Reassessing Social Change at the Beginning of the Middle Helladic and the Early Iron Age." In *The "Dark Ages" Revisited,* edited by A. Mazarakis Ainian, 31–44. Volos.
Philippson, A. 1912. *Reisen und Forschungen im westlichen Kleinasien,* part 2. *Ionien und das westliche Lydien.* Gotha.
Philippson, A. 1959. *Die griechischen Landschaften; eine Landeskunde.* Vol. 4. *Das Ägäische Meer und seine Inseln.* Edited by E. Kirsten. Frankfurt am Main.
Phillips, D. D. 2013. *The Law of Ancient Athens.* Ann Arbor, MI.
Piccirilli, L. 1974. "Fliunte e il presunto colpo di stato democratico." *ASNP* 4.1:57–70.
Pickard-Cambridge, A. W. 1988. *The Dramatic Festivals of Athens.* 2nd ed. London.
Piepenbrink, K. 2014. "Zwischen archäischem Verhaltenscodex und Polisbezug: Die Argumentation mit 'Zorn' in attischen Gerichtsprozessen." *Hermes* 142.2:162–80.
Piérart, M. 1983. "I: Tribus et dèmes." *Museum Helveticum* 40:1–18.
Piérart, M. 1985. "Modèles de répartition des citoyens dans les cités ioniennes." *REA* 87:169–90.
Piérart, M. 1997. "L'attitude d'Argos à l'égard des autres cités d'Argolide (600–300 a.C.)." In *The Polis as an Urban Centre and as a Political Community,* edited by M. H. Hansen, 321–51. Copenhagen.
Piérart, M. 2010a. "Argos romaine: la cité des Perséides." In *Roman Peloponnese III. Society, Economy and Culture under the Roman Empire,* edited by A. D. Rizakis and C. Lepenioti, 19–42. Athens.
Piérart, M. 2010b. "Feasts and Games of *Paides* in the Peloponnese of the Imperial Period." In *Roman Peloponnese III. Society, Economy and Culture under the Roman Empire,* edited by A. D. Rizakis and C. Lepenioti, 309–27. Athens.
Piérart, M. 2020. *Klyton Argos. Histoire, société et institutions d'Argos. Choix d'articles de Marcel Piérart.* Ed. O. Curty. Bordeaux.
Piérart, M. and Touchais, G. 1996. *Argos. Une ville grecque de 6000 ans.* Paris.
Piketty. T. 2013. *Le capital au XXIe siècle.* Paris.
Piketty, T. 2021. *Une brève histoire de l'égalité.* Paris.

Pikoulas, Y. A. 2000. "The Road Network of Arkadia." In *Defining Ancient Arkadia*, edited by T. Heine Nielsen and J. Roy, 248–319. Copenhagen.
Pimouguet, I. 1995. "Défense et territoire: l'exemple milésien." *DHA* 21.1:89–109.
Piolot, L. 2009. "À l'ombre des maris." In *Chemin faisant. Mythes, cultes et société en Grèce ancienne*, edited by L. Bodiou et al., 87–113. Rennes.
Pirenne, H. 1917. *Les anciennes démocraties des Pays-Bas*. Paris.
Pires Aurelio, D., and Santos Campos, A., eds. 2022. *Machiavelli's Discourses on Livy. New Readings*. Leiden.
Piuz, A.-M., and Mottu-Weber, L., eds. 1990. *L'économie genevoise, de la Réforme à la fin de l'Ancien Régime. XVIe–XVIIe siècles*. Geneva.
Poethke, G. 1974. "Griechische Literatur des ausgehenden 5. und 4. Jh. in Ägypten." In *Hellenische Poleis. Krise-Wandlung-Wirkung*, edited by E. C. Weiskopf, vol. 4, 1570–88. Berlin.
Poland, F. 1909. *Geschichte des griechischen Vereinswesens*, Leipzig.
Polito, M. 2018. "Nélée héros fondateur et l'identité communautaire: Milet et les Ioniens." In *Héros fondateurs et identités communautaires dans l'Antiquité entre mythe, rite et politique*, edited by M. Castiglioni, R. Carboni, M. Giuman, and H. Bernier-Farella, 153–68. Perugia.
Pollard, N. 2000. *Soldiers, Cities and Civilians in Roman Syria*. Michigan.
Pomeroy, S. 1994. *Xenophon, Oeconomicus. A Social and Historical Commentary*. Oxford.
Pontier, P. 2007. "Xénophon, Sparte et Phlionte." *Ktèma* 32:363–77.
Pont, A.-V. 2008. "Évergètes bâtisseurs à Aphrodisias au Haut-Empire." In *Pathways to Power. Civic Elites in the Eastern Part of the Roman Empire*, edited by A. D. Rizakis and F. Camia, 181–208. Athens.
Pont, A.-V. 2010. *Orner la cité. Enjeux culturels et politiques du paysage urbain dans l'Asie gréco-romaine*. Paris.
Pont, A.-V. 2014. "*In singulis ciuitatibus et uicis*: Liturgies des routes et autonomie civique d'après le dossier de Sagalassos." In *Se déplacer dans l'Empire romain. Approches épigraphiques*, edited by S. Demougin and M. Navarro Caballero, 69–83. Bordeaux.
Pont, A.-V. 2015. "'Ne pas promettre de caution le jour de sabbat' (ΕΓΓΥΑΣ ΜΗ ΟΜΟΛΟΓΕΙΝ): Flavius Josèphe, *Antiquités juives*, XVI 163 et 168 à la lumière des sources épigraphiques." *ZPE* 194:63–67.
Pont, A.-V. 2016. "Élites civiques et propriété foncière: les effets de l'intégration à l'Empire romain sur une cité grecque moyenne, à partir de l'exemple d'Iasos." In *Propriétaires et citoyens dans l'Orient romain*, edited by F. Lerouxel and A.-V. Pont, 233–60. Bordeaux.
Pont, A.-V. 2017. "Cités grecques et administration romaine en Asie mineure à l'époque augustéenne: l'interaction des normes civiques grecques et des dispositions romaines à travers la question des 'droits' des juifs." In *Auguste et l'Asie Mineure*, edited by L. Cavalier, M.-C. Ferriès, and F. Delrieux, 117–26. Bordeaux.
Pont, A.-V. 2019. "Les malversations financières dans les cités d'Asie Mineure d'Auguste à Dioclétien: enjeux judiciaires, sociaux et politiques." In *Philorhômaios kai Philhellèn. Hommage à Jean-Louis Ferrary*, edited by C. Müller and A. Suspène, 289–306. Geneva.
Pont, A.-V. 2020. *La fin de la cité grecque. Métamorphoses et disparition d'un modèle politique et institutionnel local en Asie Mineure, de Trajan Dèce à Constantin*. Geneva.
Pont, A.-V., and Heller, A. 2012. *Patrie d'origine et patries électives. Les citoyennetés multiples dans le monde grec d'époque romaine*. Bordeaux.
Popham, M. R., and Lemos, I. S. 1995. "An Euboean Warrior Trader." *OJA* 14.2:151–57.
Potter, D. S. 1990. *Prophecy and History in the Crisis of the Roman Empire. A Historical Commentary on the Thirteenth Sibylline Oracle*. Oxford.
Potter, D. S., ed. 2006. *A Companion to the Roman Empire*. Malden, MA.
Pottier, E., Reinach, S., and Veyries, A. 1887. *La nécropole de Myrina*. Paris.
Pouilloux, J. 1964. "Archiloque et Thasos histoire et poésie." In *Archiloque. Sept exposés et discussion*, edited by J. Pouilloux, 1–27. Geneva.
Powell, A. 2001. *Athens and Sparta. Constructing Greek Political Social History from 478 B.C.* 2nd ed. London.
Powell, A., and Meidani, K., eds. 2016. *"The Eyesore of Aigina." Anti-Athenian Attitudes in Greek, Hellenistic and Roman History*. Swansea.
Powell, J. 2003, *Galen. On the Properties of Foodstuffs*. Cambridge.
Prandi, L. 1988. *Platea. Momenti e problemi della storia di una polis*. Padua.
Prestwich, M. 2018. *A Short History of the Hundred Years War*. London.
Pretzler, M. 2005. "Pausanias at Mantinea: Invention and Manipulation of Local History." *CCJ* 51:21–34.
Price, S. R. F. 1985. *Rituals and Power. The Roman Imperial Cult in Asia Minor*. Cambridge.

Price, S. R. F. 2005. "Local Mythologies in the Greek East." In *Coinage and Identity in the Roman Provinces*, edited by C. Howgego, V. Heuchert, and A. Burnett, 115–24. Oxford.

Price, S. R. F. 2011. "Estimating Ancient Greek Populations: The Evidence of Field Survey." In *Settlement, Urbanization, and Population*, edited by A. K. Bowman and A. Wilson, 17–35. Oxford.

Prost, F. 2010a. "Législateurs, tyrans, lois somptuaires ou comment définir un groupe social en Grèce ancienne." In *La cité et ses élites. pratiques et représentation des formes de domination et de contrôle social dans les cités grecques*, edited by L. Capdetrey and Y. Lafond, 187–210. Pessac.

Prost, F. 2010b. "Quelle place pour les dieux dans la cité grecque?" In *La Méditerranée au VIIe siècle. Essais d'analyses archéologiques*, edited R. Etienne, 223–33. Paris.

Psalti, A. 2006. "Νεα Τοπογραφικά Δεδομένα για την Πλατεία Αγοράς της Ερέτριας Ἡ Ανασκαφή του Οικοπέδου Αν. Αλεξάνδρη." *Αρχαιολογικό Έργο Θεσσαλίας καί Στερεάς Ελλάδας* 2:1019–38.

Psychogiou, O. 2006. "Επιτύμβια Επιγραφή του Φορωνέος από την Οδό Γούναρη στο Άργος." In *Α' Ἀρχαιολογικὴ Σύνοδος Νοτίας καὶ Δυτικῆς Ἑλλάδος*, edited by M. Kazakou, 299–316. Athens.

Puech, B. 1983. "Grands-prêtres et helladarques d'Achaïe." *REA* 85.2:15–43.

Puech, B. 2002. *Orateurs et sophistes grecs dans les inscriptions d'époque impériale.* Paris.

Puech, B. 2004. "Des cités-mères aux métropoles." In *L'hellénisme d'époque romaine. Nouveaux documents, nouvelles approches (Ier s. a C.–IIIème s. p. C.)*, edited by S. Follet, 357–404. Paris.

Pugliese-Carratelli, G. 1939–1940. "Per la storia delle associazioni in Rodi antica." *ASAA* 1–2:147–200.

Purcell, N. 1990. "Mobility and the Polis." In *The Greek City from Homer to Alexander*, edited by O. Murray and S. R. F. Price, 29–58. Oxford.

Purcell, N. 1994. "South Italy in the Fourth Century BC." In *The Cambridge Ancient History.* Vol. 6, 2nd ed., edited by D. M. Lewis, J. Boardman, S. Hornblower, and M. Ostwald, 381–403. Cambridge.

Purcell, N. 2005. "Statics and Dynamics: Ancient Mediterranean Urbanism." In *Mediterranean Urbanization 800–600 B.C.*, edited by R. Osborne and B. W. Cunliffe, 249–72. Oxford.

Putnam, R. D. 1994. *Making Democracy Work. Civic Traditions in Modern Italy.* Princeton.

Quass, F. 1993. *Die Honoratiorenschicht in den Städten des griechischen Ostens: Untersuchungen zur politischen und sozialen Entwicklung in hellenistischer und römischer Zeit.* Stuttgart.

Quatember, U., and Scheibelreiter-Gail, V. 2017. "T. Flavius Damianus und der Grabbau seiner Familie." *JÖAI* 86:221–354.

Raaflaub, K. A. 1998. "A Historian's Headache: How to Read 'Homeric Society'?" In *Archaic Greece. New Approaches and New Evidence*, edited by N. R. E. Fisher and H. van Wees, 169–93. London and Swansea.

Raaflaub, K. A. 2009. "Learning from the Enemy? Athenian Imperial Policies and Persian 'Instruments of Empire.'" In *Interpreting the Athenian Empire. New Essays*, edited by J. Ma, N. Papazarkadas, and R. Parker, 89–124. London.

Raeck, W. "Der mehrfache Apollodoros: Zur Präsenz des Bürgers im hellenistischen Stadtbild am Beispiel von Priene." In *Stadtbild und Bürgerbild im Hellenismus*, edited by M. Wörrle and P. Zanker, 231–38. Munich.

Raeck, W., Filges, A., and Mert I. H., eds. 2020. *Priene von der Spätklassik bis zum Mittelalter. Ergebnisse und Perspektiven der Forschungen seit 1998.* Bonn.

Raeder, J. 1984. *Priene, Funde aus einer griechischen Stadt im Berliner Antikenmuseum.* Berlin.

Raggi, A. 2006. *Seleuco di Rhosos. Cittadinanza e privilegi nell'Oriente greco in età tardo-repubblicana.* Pisa.

Raja, R. 2012. *Urban Development and Regional Identity in the Eastern Roman Provinces, 50 BC–AD 250. Aphrodisias, Ephesos, Athens, Gerasa.* Copenhagen.

Raja, R. 2018. "Stacking Aesthetics in the Syrian Desert: Displaying Palmyrene Sculpture in the Public and Funerary Sphere." In *Visual Histories of the Classical World. Essays in Honour of R. R. R. Smith*, edited by C. M. Draycott et al., 281–98. Turnhout.

Raja, R. 2020. "Come and Dine with Us: Invitations to Ritual Dining as Part of Social Strategies in Sacred Spaces in Palmyra." In *Lived Religion in the Ancient Mediterranean World. Approaching Religious Transformations from Archaeology, History and Classics*, edited by V. Gasparini et al., 385–404. Berlin.

Raja, R., ed. 2022. *The Small Stuff of the Palmyrenes. Coins and Tesserae from Palmyra.* Turnhout.

Ramgopal, S. 2017. "One and Many: Associations of Roman Citizens in Greece." In *Social Dynamics under Roman Rule. Mobility and Status Change in the Provinces of Achaia and Macedonia*, edited by A. D. Rizakis, F. Camia, and S. Zoumbaki, 407–25. Athens.

Ratté, C. J., and Commito, A. 2017. *The Countryside of Aphrodisias.* Ann Arbor, MI.

Ratté, C. J., and de Staebler, P. D., eds. 2012. *The Aphrodisias Regional Survey.* Darmstadt.

Raubitschek, A. E. 1949. *Dedications from the Athenian Akropolis. A Catalogue of the Inscriptions of the Sixth and Fifth Centuries BC.* Cambridge, MA.
Rawlings, L. 2000. "Alternative Agonies: Hoplite Martial and Combat Experiences Beyond the Phalanx." In *War and Violence in Ancient Greece,* edited by H. van Wees, 233–60. London.
Rawls, J. 1999. *A Theory of Justice.* Cambridge. MA.
Rawson, E. 1985. "Cicero and the Areopagus." *Athenaeum* 63:44–67.
Rawson, E. 1991. *The Spartan Tradition in European Thought.* 2nd ed. Oxford.
Raynor, B. 2016. "*Theorodokoi, Asylia,* and the Cities of Macedonia." *GRBS* 56.2:225–62.
Reddé, M., Dubois, L., Briquel, D., Lavagne, H., and Queyrel, F., eds. 2003. *La naissance de la ville dans l'antiquité.* Paris.
Reger, G. L. 2004. "*Sympoliteiai* in Hellenistic Asia Minor." In *Greco-Roman East. Politics, Culture, Society,* edited by S. Colvin, 145–80. Cambridge.
Reitemeier, F. 1789. *Geschichte und Zustand der Sklaverey und Leibeigenschaft in Griechenland.* Berlin.
Reitzenstein, D. 2011. *Die lykischen Bundespriester. Repräsentation der kaiserzeitlichen Elite Lykiens.* Berlin.
Révolutions genevoises: 1782–1798. 1989. Geneva.
Reynolds, J. M. 1982. *Aphrodisias and Rome. Documents from the Excavation of the Theatre at Aphrodisias Conducted by Professor Kenan T. Erim, Together with Some Related Texts.* London.
Rhodes, P. J. 1995. "*Ekklesia Kyria* and the Schedule of Assemblies in Athens." *Chiron* 25:187–98.
Rhodes, P. J. 2004. "Keeping to the Point." In *The Law and the Courts in Ancient Greece,* edited by E. M. Harris and L. Rubinstein, 137–58. London.
Rhodes, P. J. 2005. "Democracy and Its Opponents in Fourth-Century Athens." In *Democrazia e antidemocrazia nel mondo greco,* edited by U. Bultrighini, 275–89. Alessandria.
Rhodes, P. J. 2006. "The Reforms and Laws of Solon: An Optimistic View." In *Solon of Athens. New Historical and Philological Approaches,* edited by J. Blok and A. Lardinois, 248–60. Leiden.
Rhodes, P. J. 2007. "διοίκησις." *Chiron* 37:359–62.
Rhodes, P. J. 2008. "After the Three-Bar 'Sigma' Controversy: The History of Athenian Imperialism Reassessed." *CQ* 58.2:500–6.
Rhodes, P. J. 2009. *Athens in the Fourth Century B.C.* Athens.
Rhodes, P. J., with Lewis, D. M. 1997. *The Decrees of the Greek States.* Oxford.
Rhodes, R. F. 2003. "The Earliest Greek Architecture in Corinth, and the 7th-Century Temple on Temple Hill." *Corinth* 20:85–94.
Riccardi. L.-A. 2007. "The Bust-Crown, the Panhellenion, and Eleusis." *Hesperia,* 76.2:365–90.
Richer, N. 1998. *Les éphores. Études sur l'histoire et sur l'image de Sparte (VIIIᵉ-IIIᵉ siècle avant Jésus-Christ).* Paris.
Richter, D. S., and Johnson, W. A., eds. 2017. *The Oxford Handbook of the Second Sophistic.* New York.
Richter, G. M. A. 1968. *Korai. Archaic Greek Maidens: A Study of the Development of the Kore Type in Greek Sculpture.* London.
Riess, W. 2008. "Private Violence and State Control: The Prosecution of Homicide and its Symbolic Meanings in Fourth-Century BC Athens." In *Sécurité collective et ordre public dans les sociétés anciennes,* edited by H. van Wees, P. Ducrey, and C. Brélaz. 49–94. Geneva.
Riess, W. 2012. *Performing Interpersonal Violence. Court, Curse, and Comedy in Fourth-Century BCE Athens.* New York.
Riewald, P. 1912. *De imperatorum Romanorum cum certis dis et comparatione et aequatione.* Halle.
Rife, J. L. 2008. "The Burial of Herodes Atticus: Elite Identity, Urban Society, and Public Memory in Roman Greece." *JHS* 128:92–127.
Riggs, C. 2005. *The Beautiful Burial in Roman Egypt. Art, Identity, and Funerary Religion.* Oxford.
Rigsby, K. 1991. "Nouvelles Inscriptions de Sardes, P. Gauthier." *GGA* 243:45–52.
Rigsby, K. J. 1996. *Asylia. Territorial Inviolability in the Hellenistic World.* Berkeley.
Rihll, T. E. 1991. "Hektemoroi: Partners in Crime?" *JHS* 111:101–27.
Rihll, T. E. 1993. "War, Slavery, and Settlement in Early Greece." In *War and Society in the Greek World,* edited by J. Rich and G. Shipley, 77–107. London.
Rihll, T. E. 1996. "The Origin and Establishment of Ancient Greek Slavery." In *Serfdom and Slavery. Studies in Legal Bondage,* edited by M. L. Bush, 89–111. London.
Rinaldi, E. 2020. *Agorai ed edilizia pubblica civile nell'Epiro di età ellenistica.* Bologna.
Ritter, S. 2002. *Bildkontakte. Götter und Heroen in der Bildsprache griechischer Münzen des 4. Jahrhunderts v. Chr.* Berlin.

Ritti, T. 2016. *Per la storia sociale ed economica di Hierapolis di Frigia. Le fondazioni sociale e funerarie.* Rome.

Ritti, T. 2017. *Hierapolis di Frigia IX. Storia e istituzioni di Hierapolis.* Istanbul.

Rix, E. M. 2016. *Tombs and Territories. The Epigraphic Culture of Lycia, c. 450–197 B.C.* Unpublished Ph.D. dissertation. Oxford University.

Rizakis, A. D. 1997. "Roman Colonies in the Province of Achaia: Territories, Land and Populations." In *The Early Roman Empire in the East,* edited by S. Alcock, 15–36. Oxford.

Rizakis, A. D. 2001. "La constitution des élites municipales dans les colonies romaines de la province d'Achaïe." In *The Greek East in the Roman Context,* edited by O. Salomies, 107–30. Helsinki.

Rizakis, A. D. 2007. "Les Ti. Claudii et la promotion des élites péloponnésiennes." In *Rome, l'Italie et la Grèce. Hellénisme et philhellénisme au premier siècle ap. J.-C.,* edited by Y. Perrin, 183–95. Brussels.

Rizakis, A. D. 2008. *Les cités achéennes. Épigraphie et histoire.* Athens.

Rizakis, A. D. 2014. "Town and Country in Early Imperial Greece." *Pharos* 20.1:241–67.

Rizakis, A. D. 2015. "Expropriations et confiscations des terres dans le cadre de la colonisation romaine en Achaïe et en Macédoine." *MEFRA* 127.2:469–85.

Rizakis, A. D. 2016. "Statut foncier, habitat rural et pratiques agricoles en Grèce sous l'Empire. In *Propriétaires et citoyens dans l'Orient romain,* edited by F. Lerouxel and A.-V. Pont, 51–67. Bordeaux.

Rizakis, A. D., and Camia, F. 2008. *Pathways to Power: Civic Elites in the Eastern Part of the Roman Empire.* Athens.

Rizakis, A. D., and Lepenioti, C., eds. 2010. *Roman Peloponnese III. Society, Economy and Culture under the Roman Empire.* Athens.

Rizakis, A. D., Camia F., and Zoumbaki, S., eds. 2018. *Social Dynamics under Roman Rule. Mobility and Status Change in the Provinces of Achaia and Macedonia.* Athens.

Rizzi, M. 2017. *Marktbezogene Gesetzgebung im späthellenistischen Athen—der Volksbeschluss über Maße und Gewichte. Eine epigraphische Untersuchung.* Munich.

Robert, L. 1937. *Études Anatoliennes. Recherches sur les inscriptions grecques de l'Asie Mineure.* Paris.

Robert, L. 1940. *Gladiateurs dans l'Orient grec.* Paris.

Robert, L. 1940–1965. *Hellenica. Recueil d'épigraphie de numismatique et d'antiquités grecques.* Paris.

Robert, L. 1948. "Un juriste romain dans une inscription de Beroia." *Hellenica* 5:29–34.

Robert, L. 1960. *Hellenica. Recueil d'épigraphie de numismatique et d'antiquités africaines.* Vols. 11–12. Paris.

Robert, L. 1962. *Villes d'Asie Mineure. études de géographie antique.* 2nd ed. Paris.

Robert, L. 1963. *Noms indigènes dans l'Asie Mineure gréco-romaine.* Vol. 1. Paris.

Robert, L. 1966a. *Monnaies antiques en Troade.* Geneva.

Robert, L. 1966b. *Documents de l'Asie Mineure méridionale.* Geneva.

Robert, L. 1967 *Monnaies grecques. Types, légendes, magistrats monétaires et géographie.* Geneva.

Robert, L. 1969. "Inscriptions." In *Laodicée du Lycos, Le Nymphée. Campagnes 1961–1963,* edited by J. des Gagniers et al., 247–390. Quebec.

Robert, L. 1980. *A travers l'Asie Mineure. poètes et prosateurs, monnaies grecques, voyageurs et géographie.* Athens.

Robert, L. 1987. *Documents d'Asie Mineure.* Athens.

Robert, L. 1994. *Le martyre de Pionios, prêtre de Smyrne.* Edited by G. W. Bowersock and C. P. Jones. Washington, DC.

Robert, L., and Robert, J., 1954. *La Carie,* vol. 2. *Le Plateau de Tabai.* Paris.

Robert, L., and Robert, J. 1976. "Une inscription grecque de Téos en Ionie; l'union de Téos et de Kyrbissos." *JS* 3–4:153–235.

Robert, L., and Robert, J. 1983. *Fouilles d'Amyzon en Carie. Tome I. Exploration, histoire, monnaies et inscriptions.* Paris.

Robert, L., and Robert, J. 1989. *Claros,* vol. 1. *Décrets hellénistiques.* Paris.

Roberts, J. T. 1997. *Athens on Trial. The Antidemocratic Tradition in Western Thought.* Princeton.

Roberts, J. T. 2017. *The Plague of War. Athens, Sparta, and the Struggle for Ancient Greece.* New York.

Robinson, B. A. 2011. *Histories of Peirene. A Corinthian Fountain in Three Millennia.* Princeton.

Robinson, E. W. 1997. *The First Democracies. Early Popular Government Outside Athens.* Stuttgart.

Robinson, E. W. 2011. *Democracy Beyond Athens. Popular Government in the Greek Classical Age.* Cambridge.

Robu, A. 2019. "La participation des Rhômaioi à la vie civique et religieuse des cités grecques (IIe-Ier siècles a.C.): continuités et adaptations institutionnelles." In *La cité interconnectée dans le monde gréco-romain, IVe siècle a.C.–IVe siècle p.C. Transferts et réseaux institutionnels, religieux et culturels aux époques hellénistique et impériale,* edited by M. Dana and I. Savalli-Lastrade, 327–38. Bordeaux.

Roebuck, C. A. 1972. "Some Aspects of Urbanization in Corinth." *Hesperia* 41.1:96–127.
Roesch, P. 1965. *Thespies et la confédération béotienne*. Paris.
Rogers, G. M. 1991a. *Sacred Identity of Ephesos. Foundation Myths of a Roman City*. London.
Rogers, G. M. 1991b. "Demosthenes of Oenoanda and Models of Euergetism." *JRS* 81:91–100.
Rohde, D. 2017. "'Weder haben wir in der gemeinsamen Kasse Geld, noch zahlen wir mit Lichtigkeit aus underen eigenen Mitteln': Die öffentlichen Finanzen Spartas in klassischer Zeit." In *Das antike Sparta*, edited by V. Pothou and A. Powell, 245–70. Stuttgart.
Rohde, D. 2019. *Von der Deliberations-demokratie zur Zustimmungs-demokratie. Die öffentlichen Finanzen Athens und die Ausbildung einer Kompetenzelite im 4. Jahrhundert v. Chr.* Berlin.
Rohmer, J. 2020. *Hauran VI. D'Aram à Rome. La Syrie du Sud de l'âge du fer à l'annexion romaine (XIIe siècle av. J.-C.–Ier siècle apr. J.-C.)*. Beirut.
Rombos, T. 1988. *The Iconography of Attic Late Geometric II Pottery*. Partille.
Romiopoulou, K. 1999. "Οι αποικίες της Άνδρου στο βόρειο Αιγαίο." In *Phos Kykladikon*, edited by M. P. Stampolidis, 126–31. Athens.
Rood, T. 1998. *Thucydides: Narrative and Explanation*. Oxford.
Rood, T. 2004. "Xenophon and Diodorus: Continuing Thucydides." In *Xenophon and His World*, edited by C. J. Tuplin, 341–95. Stuttgart.
Rood, T. 2007. "The Development of the War Monograph." In *A Companion to Greek and Roman Historiography*, edited by J. Marincola, 131–41. Malden, MA.
Rorty, R. 2022. *What Can We Hope for? Essays on Politics*. Edited by W. P. Malecki and C. Voparil. Princeton.
Rosanvallon, P. 1990. *L'Etat en France de 1789 à nos jours*. Paris.
Rose, P. W. 2012. *Class in Archaic Greece*. Cambridge.
Rosen, K. 1987. "Ehrendekrete, Biographie und Geschichtsschreibung. Zum Wandel der griechischen Polis im frühen Hellenismus." *Chiron* 17:277–92
Rosen, R. M., and Foley, H. P., eds. 2020. *Aristophanes and Politics. New Studies*. Leiden.
Rosen, R. M., and Sluiter, I. 2006. *City, Countryside, and the Spatial Organization of Value in Classical Antiquity*. Leiden.
Rosenbloom, D. S. 2004a. "*Poneroi* vs. *Chrestoi*: The Ostracism of Hyperbolos and the Struggle for Hegemony in Athens after the Death of Perikles, Part I." *TAPhA* 134.1:55–100.
Rosenbloom, D. S. 2004b. "*Poneroi* vs. *Chrestoi*: The Ostracism of Hyperbolos and the Struggle for Hegemony in Athens after the Death of Perikles, Part II." *TAPhA* 134.2:323–58.
Rosenstein, N. S. 2011. "War, Wealth and Consuls." In *Consuls and Res Publica. Holding High Office in the Roman Republic*, edited by H. Beck et al., 133–58. Cambridge.
Rosenstein, N. S. 2012a. *Rome and the Mediterranean 290–146 B.C. The Imperial Republic*. Edinburgh.
Rosenstein, N. S. 2012b. "Integration and Armies in the Middle Republic." In *Processes of Integration and Identity Formation in the Roman Republic*, edited by S. T. Roselaar, 85–103. Leiden.
Roscalla, F. 2004. "'Kalokagathia' e 'kaloi kagathoi' in Senofonte." In *Xenophon and his World*, edited by C. J. Tuplin, 115–24. Stuttgart.
Rosivach, V. J. 1987. "Autochthony and the Athenians." *CQ* 37.2:294–306.
Ross, L. 1843. *Reisen auf den griechischen Inseln des ägäischen Meeres*. Stuttgart and Tübingen.
Rossi, P., ed. 1987. *Modelli di città. Strutture e funzioni politiche*. Turin.
Rostovtzeff, M. 1941. *The Social and Economic History of the Hellenistic World*. Oxford.
Rouanet-Liesenfelt, A.-M. 1994. "Remarques sur l'assemblée provinciale crétoise et son grand-prêtre à l'époque du Haut-Empire." *Ktèma* 19:7–25.
Roubineau, J.-M. 2007. "Les hektémores." In *Vocabulaire et expression de l'économie dans le monde antique*, edited by J. Andreau and V. Chankowski, 177–209. Pessac.
Roubineau, J.-M. 2012. "La condition d'étranger de passage dans les cités grecques: statue de droit ou position hors-la-cité." In *Mobilités grecques. Mouvements, réseaux, contacts en Méditerranée de l'époque archaïque à l'époque hellénistique*, edited by L. Capdetrey and J. Zurbach, 157–72. Paris.
Roubineau, J.-M. 2015. *Les cités grecques. VIe-IIe siècle avant J.-C. Essai d'histoire sociale*. Paris.
Roubineau, J.-M. 2021. "Statut, travail et identité sociale dans les Mimes d'Hérondas." In *Statuts personnels et main-d'œuvre en Méditerranée hellénistique*, edited by. S. Maillot and J. Zurbach, 33–46. Clermont-Ferrand.
Roueché, C. 1989. "Floreat Perge!" In *Images of Authority*, edited by C. Roueché and M. M. Mackenzie, 206–28. Cambridge.
Roussel, D. 1976. *Tribu et cité. Études sur les groupes sociaux dans les cités grecques aux époques archaïque et classique*. Paris.

Roussel, P. 1911. "La Confédération des Nésiotes." *BCH* 35:441–55.
Rousset, D. 2002. "Terres sacrées, terres publiques et terres privées à Delphes." *CRAI* 146.1:215–41.
Rousset, D. 2004. "La cité et son territoire dans la province d'Achaïe et la notion de 'Grèce romaine.'" *Annales (HSS)* 59.2:363–83.
Rousset, D. 2004–5. "Épigraphie grecque et géographie historique du monde hellénique." *AEHE IV* 20:114–18.
Rousset, D. 2008. "The City and Its Territory in the Province of Achaea and 'Roman Greece.'" *HSCPh* 104:303–37.
Rousset, D. 2010. *De Lycie en Cabalide. La convention entre les Lyciens et Termessos près d'Oinoanda*. Geneva.
Rousset, D. 2014. "La stèle des Géléontes au sanctuaire de Claros." *CRAI* 158.1:9–20.
Rousset, D. 2020. "Les Locriens de l'Est et les Phocidiens de la guerre du Péloponnèse au début de l'époque hellénistique." *REA* 122.2:389–443.
Rousset, D., Camp, J., and Minon, S. 2015. "The Phokian City of Panopeus/Phanoteus, Three New Rupestral Inscriptions, and the Cippus of the Labyadai of Delphi." *AJA* 119.4:441–63.
Roussos, K. 2017. *Reconstructing the Settled Landscape of the Cyclades. The Islands of Paros and Naxos during the Late Antique and Early Byzantine Centuries*. Leiden.
Roy, J. 2000. "The Frontier between Arkadia and Elis in Classical Antiquity." In *Polis and Politics. Studies in Ancient Greek History*, edited by P. Flensted-Jensen, T. H. Nielsen and L. Rubinstein, 133–56. Copenhagen.
Roy, J. 2006. "Elean Voting-Tokens and Courts at Psophis in the Later Third Century." *ZPE* 156:129–40.
Roy, J. 2009a. "Elis." In *The Politics of Ethnicity and the Crisis of the Peloponnesian League*, edited by P. Funke and N. Luraghi, 30–48. Cambridge, MA.
Roy, J. 2009b. "The Spartan-Elean War of c. 400." *Athenaeum* 97.1:69–86.
Rubinstein, L. 2003. "Volunteer Prosecutors in the Greek World." *Dike* 6:87–113.
Rubinstein, L. 2016. "Reward and Deterrence in Classical and Hellenistic Enactments." In *Symposion 2015. Conferências sobre a História do Direito grego e helenístico*, edited by G. Thür and D. Leão, 419–49. Vienna.
Ruggeri, C. 2004. *Gli stati intorno a Olimpia. Storia e costituzione dell'Elide e degli stati formati dai perieci elei (400–362 a. C.)*. Stuttgart.
Rumscheid, F. 1998. *Priene. A Guide to the 'Pompeii of Asia Minor.'* Istanbul.
Rumscheid, F. 2006. *Die figürlichen Terrakotten von Priene: Fundkontexte, Ikonographie und Funktion in Wohnhäusern und Heiligtümern im Licht antiker Parallelbefunde*. Wiesbaden.
Rumscheid, F. 2014. "Ursprünglicher Bebauungsplan, Erstbebauung und Veränderungen im hellenistischen Stadtbild Prienes als Ergebnis öffentlicher und privater Ambitionen." In *Stadtkultur im Hellenismus*, edited by A. Matthaei and M. Zimmermann, 173–90. Heidelberg.
Runciman, W. G. 1982. "Origins of States: The Case of Archaic Greece." *Comparative Studies in Society and History* 24.3:351–77.
Ruppenstein, F. 2020. "The End of the Bronze Age in Attica and the Origin of the *Polis* of Athens." In *Athens and Attica in Prehistory*, edited by N. Papadimitriou et al., 569–74. Oxford.
Ruschenbusch, E. 1984. "Modell Amorgos." In *Aux origines de l'hellénisme. La Crète et la Grèce. Hommage à Henri van Effenterre*, 265–71. Paris.
Ruschenbusch, E. 1985. "Die Zahl der griechischen Staaten und Arealgrösse und Bürgerzahl der 'Normalpolis.'" *ZPE* 59:253–63.
Russell, B. 2013. *The Economics of the Roman Stone Trade*. Oxford.
Rutishauser, B. 2012. *Athens and the Cyclades. Economic Strategies 540–314 B.C.* Oxford.
Ruzé, F. 1985. "Le style ionien dans la vie politique archaïque." *REA* 87.1–2:157–67.
Ruzé, F. 1997. *Délibération et pouvoir dans la cité grecque. De Nestor à Socrate*. Paris.
Ruzé, F. 2003. *Eunomia. À la recherche de l'équité*. Boulogne-sur-Mer.
Ryan, G. 2018. "Building Order: Unified Cityscapes and Elite Collaboration in Roman Asia Minor." *ClAnt* 37.1:151–85.
Ryder, T. T. B. 1965. *Koine Eirene. General Peace and Local Independence in Ancient Greece*. New York.
Saliou, C. 2020. *Le Proche-Orient. De Pompée à Muhammad. Ier s. av J.-C.–VIIe s. apr. J.-C.* Paris.
Salmeri, G., Raggi, A., and Baroni, A., eds. 2004. *Colonie romane nel mondo greco*. Rome.
Salmon, J. B. 1984. *Wealthy Corinth. A History of the City to 338 B.C.* Oxford.
Salomon, N. 1997. *Le cleruchie di Atene. Caratteri e funzione*. Pisa.
Salviat, F. 1958. "Une nouvelle loi thasienne: institutions judiciaires et fêtes religieuses à la fin du VIe siècle av. J.C." *BCH* 82:193–267.

Salviat, F. 1959. "Décrets pour Épié, fille de Dionysios: déesses et sanctuaires thasiens." *BCH* 83:362–97.
Salvo, I. 2012. "Romulus and Remus at Chios Revisited: A Re-examination of SEG XXX 1073." In *Epigraphical Approaches to the Post-Classical Polis: Fourth Century BC to Second Century AD*, edited by P. Martzavou and N. Papazarkadas, 125–138. Oxford.
Samitz, C. 2013. "Die Einführung der Dekaproten und Eikosaproten in den Städten Kleinasiens und Griechenlands." *Chiron* 42:1–61.
Sánchez, P. 2001. *L'Amphictionie des Pyles et de Delphes. Recherches sur son rôle historique, des origines au IIe siècle de notre ère*. Stuttgart.
Santagati, E. 2018. *Timoleonte. Hieros anēr tra storia e propaganda*. Lanciano.
Santamaría, M. A., ed. 2019. *The Derveni Papyrus. Unearthing Ancient Mysteries*. Leiden.
Sapsford, T. 2022. *Performing the Kinaidos. Unmanly Men in Ancient Mediterranean Cultures*. Oxford.
Saradi, H. G. 2006. *The Byzantine City in the Sixth Century. Literary Images and Historical Reality*. Athens.
Sartre, M. 1981. "Le territoire de Canatha." *Syria* 58:343–57.
Sartre, M. 1991. *L'Orient romain: provinces et sociétés provinciales en Méditerranée orientale d'Auguste aux Sévères (31 avant J.-C-235 après J.-C.)*. Paris.
Sartre, M. 1996. "Palmyre, cité grecque." *AArchSyr* 42:385–405.
Sartre, M. 1997. "Vie municipale et intégration des notables dans la Syrie et l'Arabie romaine." *Antiquitas* 22:153–74.
Sartre, M. 2001a. *D'Alexandre à Zénobie. Histoire du Levant antique, IVe siècle av. J.-C.-IIIe siècle ap. J.-C.* Paris.
Sartre, M. 2001b. "Les colonies romaines dans le monde grec. Essai de synthèse." *Electrum* 5:111–52.
Sartre, M. 2013. "Dionysias d'Arabie." In *Le voyage des légendes: Hommages à Pierre Chuvin*, edited by D. Lauritzen and M. Tardieu, 123–38. Paris.
Sartre, M. 2014. *L'historien et ses territoires. Choix d'articles*. Edited by by P. Brun. Bordeaux.
Sartre, M. 2017. "Panthéons civiques du Hauran." In *Contextualizing the Sacred in the Hellenistic and Roman Near East. Religious Identities in Local, Regional and Imperial Settings*, edited by R. Raja, 169–80. Turnhout.
Sartre-Fauriat, A. 1992. "Le nymphée et les adductions d'eau à Soada-Dionysias de Syrie au IIe siècle ap. J.-C." *Ktèma: civilisations de l'Orient, de la Grèce et de Rome antiques* 17:133–51.
Savalli-Lestrade, I. 1981. "La clausola 'ἐν τοῖς ἐννόμοις χρόνοις' nei decreti greci di cittadinanza d'età ellenistica." *ASNP* 3.11.3:615–40.
Savalli-Lestrade, I. 1998. *Les philoi royaux dans l'Asie hellénistique*. Geneva.
Savalli-Lestrade, I. 2012. "Élites civiques et compétences étrangères dans les affaires judiciaires et diplomatiques des cités grecques aux époques hellénistique et impériale." *CCG* 23:131–39.
Savino, E. 1999. *Città di frontiera nell'Impero romano. Forme della romanizzazione da Augusto ai Severi*. Bari.
Schaps, D. M. 2004. *The Invention of Coinage and the Monetization of Ancient Greece*. Ann Arbor, MI.
Schaub, J. F. 2005. "La notion d'État Moderne est-elle utile? Remarques sur les blocages de la démarche comparatiste en histoire." *Cahiers du monde russe* 46.1–2:51–64.
Schede, M. 1964. *Die Ruinen von Priene. Kurze Beschreibung*. 2nd ed. Berlin
Scheid-Tissinier, E. 2004. "Classe dirigeante, classe dangereuse? Une représentation des élites dans l'Athènes du IVe siècle." *Histoire urbaine* 10:27–41.
Scheidel, W. 1999. "Emperors, Aristocrats, and the Grim Reaper: Towards a Demographic Profile of the Roman Élite." *CQ* 49.1:254–81.
Scheidel, W. 2003. "The Greek Demographic Expansion: Models and Comparisons." *JHS* 123:120–40.
Scheidel, W. 2015. "The Early Roman Monarchy." In *Fiscal Regimes and the Political Economy of Premodern States*, edited by A. Monson and W. Scheidel, 229–57. Cambridge.
Scheidel, W. 2019. *Escape from Rome. The Failure of Empire and the Road to Prosperity*. Princeton.
Scheidel, W., Morris, I., and Saller, R., eds. 2007. *The Cambridge Economic History of the Greco-Roman World*. Cambridge.
Schede, M. 1964. *Die Ruinen von Priene. Kurze Beschreibung*. 2nd ed. Edited by W. Kleiss and G. Kleiner. Berlin.
Schilardi, D. 1983. "The Decline of the Geometric Settlement of Koukounaries at Paros." In *The Greek Renaissance of the Eighth Century BC. Tradition and Innovation*, edited by R. Hägg, 173–83. Stockholm.
Schilardi, D. 2002. "The Emergence of Paros the Capital." *Pallas* 58:229–49.
Schilardi, D. 2017. "Koukounaries and the Cult of Athena." In *Les sanctuaires archaïques des Cyclades*, edited by A. Mazarakis-Ainian, 287–305. Rennes.
Schlumberger, D. 1951. *La Palmyrène du nord-ouest. Villages et lieux de culte de l'époque impériale. Recherches archéologiques sur la mise en valeur d'une région du désert par les Palmyréniens*. Paris.

Schmidt, T., and Fleury, P., eds. 2011. *Perceptions of the Second Sophistic and Its Times*. Toronto.

Schmidt, V. A. 2010. "Taking Ideas and Discourse Seriously: Explaining Change through Discursive Institutionalism as the Fourth 'New Institutionalism.'" *European Political Science Review* 2:1:1–25.

Schmidt-Colinet, A., and Seigne, J. 2022. "Die Bekrönung der Tempel im hellenistisch-römischen Syrien: neue Überlegungen zu den Zinnen im Belheiligtum von Palmyra." *RA* 2022.1:57–77.

Schmitt-Pantel, P. 1990. "Collective Activities and the Political in the Greek City." In *The Greek City from Homer to Alexander*, edited by O. Murray and S. R. F. Price, 199–213. Oxford.

Schmitt Pantel, P. 1992. *La cité au banquet. Histoire des repas publics dans les cités grecques*. Paris.

Schmitt-Pantel, P. 1997. "Public Feasts in the Hellenistic Greek City: Forms and Meanings." In *Conventional Values of the Hellenistic Greeks*, edited by P. Bilde, 29–47. Aarhus.

Schmitz T. 1997. *Bildung und Macht. Zur sozialen und politischen Funktion der zweiten Sophistik in der griechischen Welt der Kaiserzeit*. Munich.

Schmitz, T., and Wiater, N. eds. 2011. *The Struggle for Identity. Greeks and Their Past in the First Century BCE*. Stuttgart.

Schnädelbach, K. 2010. *Topographia Palmyrena 1. Topography*. Damascus.

Schnapp, A. 1997. *Le chasseur et la cité. Chasse et érotique en Grèce ancienne*. Paris.

Schnapp, A. 2020. *Une histoire universelle des ruines: des origines aux Lumières*. Paris.

Schneider, P. 1987. "Zur Topographie der Heiligen Straße von Milet nach Didyma." *AA* 1:101–29.

Schnettger, M. 2008. "Kleinstaaten in der Frühen Neuzeit: Konturen eines Forschungsfeldes (Small States in Early Modern Times: Contours of a Field of Research)." *HZ* 286.3:605–40.

Schofield, M. *Saving the City: Philosopher-kings and Other Classical Paradigms*. London.

Scholl, A. 2006. "Ἀναθήματα τῶν ἀρχαίων: Die Akropolisvotive aus dem 8. bis frühen 6. Jdt v Chr. und die Staatswerdung Athens." *JDAI* 121:1–173.

Scholten, J. B. 2000. *The Politics of Plunder. Aitolians and their Koinon in the Early Hellenistic Era, 279–217 B.C.* Berkeley.

Scholz, P. 2000. "Der Prozess gegen Sokrates: ein 'Sündenfall' der athenischen Demokratie?" In *Grosse Prozesse im antiken Athen*, edited by L. A. Burckhardt, A. Leonhard, and J. von Ungern-Sternberg, 157–73. Munich.

Scholz. P. 2015. "Städtische Honoratiorenherrschaft und Gymnasiarchie in der Kaiserzeit." In *Das kaiserzeitliche Gymnasion*, edited by P. Scholz and D. Wiegandt, 79–98. Berlin.

Schreiner, P. 1969. "Zur Geschichte Philadelpheias im 14 Jhdt (1293–1390)." *OCP* 35:375–429.

Schröder, J. 2020. *Die Polis als Sieger. Kriegsdenkmäler im archaisch-klassischen Griechenland*. Berlin.

Schuler, C. 1998. *Ländliche Siedlungen und Gemeinden im hellenistischen und römischen Kleinasien*. Munich.

Schuler, C. 2005. "Die διοίκησις τῆς πόλεως im öffentlichen Finanzwesen der hellenistischen Poleis." *Chiron* 35:85–403.

Schuler, C., and Zimmermann, K. 2012. "Neue Inschriften aus Patara. 1, Zur Elite der Stadt in Hellenismus und früher Kaiserzeit." *Chiron* 42:567–626.

Sciacchitano, R. 2018. "Il *kosmos* cretese in età arcaica e classica: alcune considerazioni." *ZPE* 206:68–76.

Scott, J. C. 2017. *Against the Grain. A Deep History of the Earliest States*. New Haven.

Scott. T. 2012. *The City-State in Europe, 1000–1600. Hinterland, Territory, Region*. Oxford.

Schwartz, A. 2009. *Reinstating the Hoplite. Arms, Armour and Phalanx Fighting in Archaic and Classical Greece*. Stuttgart.

Schwartz, S. 2001. *Imperialism and Jewish Society, 200 B.C.E. to 640 C.E.* Princeton.

Schwartz, S. 2010. *Were the Jews a Mediterranean Society? Reciprocity and Solidarity in Ancient Judaism*. Princeton.

Schwarz. E. 1928–1938. *Acta Conciliorum Œcumenicorum*. Berlin.

Schwarz, H. 2001. *Soll oder Haben? Die Finanzwirtschaft kleinasiatischer Stadte in der römischen Kaiserzeit am Beispiel von Bithynien, Lykien und Ephesos (29 v. Chr.–284 n. Chr.)*. Bonn

Scully, H. 1990. *Homer and the Sacred City*. Ithaca, NY.

Seager, R., and Tuplin, C. J. 1980. "The Freedom of the Greeks of Asia: On the Origins of a Concept and the Creation of a Slogan." *JHS* 100:141–54.

Sébillotte, V. 2017. "'Gender studies' et domination masculine: les citoyennes de l'Athènes classique, un défi pour l'historien des institutions." *CCG* 28:7–30.

Seelentag, G. 2009. "Regeln für den Kosmos: Prominenzrollen und Institutionen im archaischen Kreta." *Chiron* 39:65–99.

Seelentag, G. 2015. *Das archaische Kreta. Institutionalisierung im frühen Griechenland*. Berlin.

Segal, A. 1997. *From Function to Monument. Urban Landscapes of Roman Palestine, Syria and Provincial Arabia*. Oxford.
Segal, A. 2008. *The Variety of Local Religious Life in the Near East in the Hellenistic and Roman Periods*. Leiden.
Seifried, R. M., and Parkinson, W. A. 2014. "The Ancient Towers of the Paximadi Peninsula, Southern Euboia." *Hesperia* 83.2:277–313.
Seland, E. H. 2016. *Ships of the Desert and Ships of the Sea. Palmyra in the World Trade of the First Three Centuries CE*. Wiesbaden.
Selznick, Ph. 1992. *The Moral Commonwealth. Social Theory and the Promise of Community*. Berkeley.
Senff, R. 2006. "Die Ergebnisse der neuen Grabungen im archaischen Milet: Stratigraphie und Chronologie." In *Frühes Ionien. Eine Bestandsaufnahme*, edited by J. Cobet et al., 319–26. Mainz.
Sève, M. 1979. "Un décret de consolation à Cyzique." *BCH* 103.1:327–59.
Seyrig, H. 1985. *Scripta Varia. Mélanges d'archéologie et d'histoire*. Paris.
Sezgin, Y., and Aybek, S. 2016. "A Group of Portrait Statues from the Bouleuterion of Aigai: A Preliminary Report." In *Eikones: Portrais en contexte: Recherches sur les portraits grecs*, edited by R. von den Hoff, F. Queyrel, and E. Perrin-Saminadayar, 17–43. Venosa.
Shanks, M. 1999. *Art and the Greek City State. An Interpretive Archaeology*. Cambridge.
Shapiro, A. 1991. "The Iconography of Mourning in Athenian Art." *AJA* 95.4:629–56.
Shear, I. M. 2000. *Tales of Heroes. The Origins of the Homeric Texts*. New York.
Shear, I. M. 2004. *Kingship in the Mycenaean World and its Reflections in the Oral Tradition*. Philadelphia.
Shear, J. 2011. *Polis and Revolution. Responding to Oligarchy in Classical Athens*. Cambridge.
Shear, J. 2021. *Serving Athena: The Festival of the Panathenaia and the Construction of Athenian Identities*. Cambridge.
Shear, T. L. Jr. 1978. *Kallias of Sphettos and the Revolt of Athens in 286 B.C.* Princeton.
Shear, T. L. Jr. 2016. *Trophies of Victory. Public Building in Periklean Athens*. Princeton.
Sheedy, K. A. 2006–2007. "The Marble Walls of Siphnos." *MedArch* 19–20:67–74.
Sheedy, K. A. 2012. "Aegina, the Cyclades, and Crete." In *The Oxford Handbook of Greek and Roman Coinage*, edited by W. E. Metcalf, 105–27. Oxford.
Shelmerdine, C. W. 2006. "Mycenaean Palatial Administration." In *Ancient Greece: From the Mycenaean Palaces to the Age of Homer*, edited by S. Deger-Jalkotzy and I. S. Lemos, 73–86. Edinburgh.
Shelmerdine, C. W. 2008. *The Cambridge Companion to the Aegean Bronze Age*. Cambridge.
Shelmerdine, C. and Bennet, J. 2008. "Mycenean States: Economy and Administration." In *The Cambridge Companion to the Aegean Bronze Age*, edited by C. W. Shelmerdine, 289–30. Cambridge.
Sheppard, T. F. 1971. *Lourmarin in the Eighteenth Century. A Study of a French Village*. Baltimore.
Sherman, N., ed. 1999. *Aristotle's Ethics. Critical Essays*. Lanham, MD.
Sherratt, S. 2001. "Potemkin Palaces and Route-Based Economies." In *Economy and Politics in the Mycenaean Palace States*, edited by S. Voutsaki and J. Killen, 214–38. Cambridge.
Sherwin-White, A. N. 1984. *Roman Foreign Policy in the East, 168 B.C. to A.D. 1*. Norman, OK.
Sherwin-White S. 1978. *Ancient Cos. An Historical Study from the Dorian Settlement to the Imperial period*. Göttingen.
Shifman, I. S. 2014. *The Palmyrene Tax Tariff*. Translated by S. Khobnya. Oxford.
Shipley, G. J. 1987. *A History of Samos, 800–188 B.C.* Oxford.
Shipley, G. J. 2018. *The Early Hellenistic Peloponnese. Politics, Economies, and Networks 338–197 B.C.* Cambridge.
Shklar, J. N. 1991. *American Citizenship. The Quest for Inclusion*. Cambridge, MA.
Shklar, J. N. 1998. *Political Thought and Political Thinkers*. Edited by S. Hoffmann. Chicago.
Sickinger, J. P. 1999. *Public Records and Archives in Classical Athens*. Chapel Hill, NC.
Sickinger, J. P. 2017. "New Ostraka from the Athenian Agora." *Hesperia* 86.3:443–508.
Siekierka, P., Stebnicka, K., and Wolicki, A. 2021. *Women and the Polis. Public Honorific Inscriptions for Women in the Greek Cities from the Late Classical to the Roman Period*. Berlin.
Siewert, P. 2002. *Ostrakismos-Testimonien. Die Zeugnisse antiker Autoren, der Inschriften und Ostraka über das athenische Scherbengericht*. Stuttgart.
Siewert, P. 2006. "Kultische und politische Organisationsformen im frühen Olympia und in seiner Umgebung." In *Kult–Poltik–Ethnos. Überregionale Heiligtümer im Spannungsfeld von Kult und Politik*, edited by K. Freitag, P. Funke, and M. Haake, 43–55. Stuttgart.
Simantoni-Bournia, E. 2004. *La céramique grecque à reliefs. Ateliers insulaires du VIIIe au VIe siècle avant J.-C.* Geneva.

Simantoni-Bournia, 2013. "Η Τήνος καὶ η γέννηση της Ελληνικής εικονογραφίας. Η ανάγλυφη κεραμεική." In *Η αρχαία Τήνος*, edited by R. Etienne, N. Kourou, and E. Simantoni-Bournia, 98–122. Athens.
Simon, P., and Verdan, S. 2014. "'Hippotrophia': chevaux et élites eubéennes à la période géométrique." *AK* 57:3–24.
Simonton, M. 2017. *Classical Oligarchy. A Political History*. Princeton.
Simonton, M. 2019. "The Telos Reconciliation Dossier (*IG* XII.4.132): Democracy, Demagogues and Stasis in an Early Hellenistic Polis." *JHS* 139:187–209.
Simonton, M. 2022. "Demagogues and Demagoguery in Hellenistic Greece." *Polis* 39.1:35–76.
Simonde de Sismondi, J. C. L. 1818. *Histoire des républiques italiennes du Moyen Âge*. 2nd ed. Paris.
Sinclair, R. K. 1988. *Democracy and Participation in Athens*. Cambridge.
Sizov, S. 2017. "On the Composition of the Achaian *Synodos* in Polybios' Time." *AAntHung* 57.4:381–414.
Sjöberg, B. 2004. *Asine and the Argolid in the Late Helladic III Period. A Socio-Economic Study*. Oxford.
Skinner, Q. 1998. *Liberty before Liberalism*. Cambridge.
Skornicki, A. 2015. *La grande soif de l'État. Michel Foucault avec les sciences sociales*. Paris.
Slater, W. J. 2015. "Victory and Bureaucracy: The Process of Agonistic Rewards." *Phoenix* 69:147–59.
Slawisch, A. 2009. "Epigraphy versus Archaeology: Conflicting Evidence for Cult Continuity in Ionia during the Fifth Century BC." In *Sacred Landscapes in Anatolia and Neighbouring Regions*, edited by C. Gates, J. Morin, and, T. Zimmermann, 29–34. Oxford.
Slawisch, A., and Wilkinson, T. C. 2018. "Processions, Propaganda, and Pixels: Reconstructing the Sacred Way between Miletos and Didyma." *AJA* 122.1:101–43.
Slot, B. 1982. *Archipelagus Turbatus. Les Cyclades entre colonisation latine et occupation ottomane c. 1500–1718*. Istanbul.
Small, D. B. 2010. "The Archaic *polis* of Azoria: A Window into Cretan 'Polital' Social Structure." *JMA* 23.2:197–217.
Smarczyk, B. 1990. *Untersuchungen zur Religionspolitik und politischen Propaganda Athens im Delisch-Attischen Seebund*. Munich.
Smarczyk, B. 2003. *Timoleon und die Neugründung von Syrakus*. Göttingen.
Smedile, V. 2019. *Palmira. Dinamiche politico-economiche e fenomeni culturali nei primi tre secoli dell'Impero*. Canterano.
Smith, A. 2013. *Roman Palmyra. Identity, Community, and State Formation*. Oxford.
Smith, M. L. 2019. *Cities. The First 6,000 Years*. New York.
Smith, R. R. R. 1991. *Hellenistic Sculpture. A Handbook*. London.
Smith, R. R. R. 1993. *The Monument of C. Julius Zoilos*. Mainz.
Smith, R. R. R. 1998. "Cultural Choice and Political Identity in Honorific Portrait Statues in the Greek East in the Second Century A.D." *JRS* 88:56–93.
Smith R. R. R. 2002. "The Statue Monument of Oecumenius: A New Portrait of a Late Antique Governor from Aphrodisias." *JRS* 92:134–56.
Smith, R. R. R. 2006. *Roman Portrait Statuary from Aphrodisias*. Mainz.
Smith, R. R. R. 2007. "Pindar, Athletes and the Early Statue Habit." In *Pindar's Poetry, Patrons, and Festivals. From Archaic Greece to the Roman Empire*, edited by S. Hornblower and C. Morgan, 83–139. Oxford.
Smith, R. R. R. 2013. *The Marble Reliefs from the Julio-Claudian Sebasteion*. Darmstadt.
Smith, R. R. R., and Ward-Perkins, B. 2016. *The Last Statues of Antiquity*. Oxford.
Snodgrass, A. M. 1977. *Archaeology and the Rise of the Greek State*. Cambridge.
Snodgrass, A. M. 1981. *Archaic Greece. The Age of Experiment*. London.
Snodgrass, A. M. 1986. "Interaction by Design: The Greek City State." In *Peer Polity Interaction and Socio-Political Change*, edited by C. Renfrew and J. F. Cherry, 47–58. Cambridge.
Snodgrass, A. M. 1993. "The Rise of the Polis: The Archaeological Evidence." In *The Ancient Greek City-State*, edited by M. H. Hansen, 30–40. Copenhagen.
Snodgrass, A. M. 2000. *The Dark Age of Greece. An Archaeological Survey of the Eleventh to the Eighth Centuries BC*. Edinburgh.
Snodgrass, A. M. 2006. *Archaeology and the Emergence of Ancient Greece. Collected Papers on Early Greece and Related Topics (1965–2002)*. Edinburgh.
Snodgrass, A. M. 2008. "Descriptive and Narrative Art at the Dawn of the Polis." In *Alba della città, alba delle immagini. Da una suggestione di Bruno d'Agostino*, 21–30. Athens.

Sobak, R. 2015. "Sokrates among the Shoemakers." *Hesperia* 84.4:669–712.
Sokolowski, F. 1954. "Fees and Taxes in the Greek Cults." *HThR* 47.3:153–64.
Sokolowski, D. 2022. *Inventing Roman Bithynia. Rural Cultures and Identities in the 1st-3rd Centuries CE.* Unpublished Ph.D. dissertation. New York, Columbia University.
Sommer, M. 2005. "Palmyra and Hatra. 'Civic' and 'Tribal' Institutions at the Near Eastern Steppe Frontier." In *Cultural Borrowings and Ethnic Appropriations in Antiquity*, edited by E. S. Gruen, 285–96. Stuttgart.
Sommer, M. 2018. *Roms orientalische Steppengrenze. Palmyra-Edessa-Dura-Europos-Hatra. Eine Kulturgeschichte von Pompeius bis Diocletian.* 2nd ed. Stuttgart.
Sommerstein, A. H. 1998. "Rape and Young Manhood in Athenian Comedy." In *Thinking Men. Masculinity and its Self-Representation in the Classical Tradition*, edited by L. Foxhall and J. Salmon, 100–14. London.
Sommerstein, A. H. 2005. "An Alternative Democracy and an Alternative to Democracy in Aristophanic Comedy." In *Democrazia e antidemocrazia nel mondo greco*, edited by U. Bultrighini, 195–207. Alessandria.
Sommerstein, A. H. 2009. "Slave and Citizen in Aristophanic Comedy." In *Talking about Laughter and Other Studies in Greek Comedy*, edited by A. H. Sommerstein, 136–54. Oxford.
Sommerstein, A. H., ed. 2014. *Menander in Contexts.* London.
Sosin, J. D. 2014. "Endowments and Taxation in the Hellenistic Period." *AncSoc* 44:43–89.
Sosin, J. D. 2016. "A Metic was a Metic." *Historia* 65.1:2–13.
Spawforth, A. J. S. 1994. "Corinth, Argos, and the Imperial Cult: Pseudo-Julian, Letters 198." *Hesperia* 63.2:211–32.
Spawforth, A. J. S. 1999. "The Panhellenion Again." *Chiron* 29:339–52.
Spawforth, A. J. S. 2006. *The Complete Greek Temples.* London.
Spawforth, A. J. S. 2012. *Greece and the Augustan Cultural Revolution.* Cambridge.
Spawforth, A. J. S., and Walker, S. 1985. "The World of the Panhellenion I: Athens and Eleusis." *JRS* 75:78–104.
Sperber, D. 1998. *The City in Roman Palestine.* New York and Oxford.
Spijkerman, A. 1979. *The Coins of the Decapolis and Provincia Arabia.* Edited by M. Piccirillo. Jerusalem.
Sprawski, S. 1999. *Jason of Pherae. A Study on History of Thessaly in Years 431-370 B.C.* Kraków.
Sprawski, S. 2004. "Were Lycophron and Jason Tyrants of Pherae? Xenophon on the History of Thessaly." In *Xenophon and His World*, edited by C. J. Tuplin, 437–52. Stuttgart.
Sprawski, S. 2012. "Remarks on Aristotle's *Thettalon* Politeia." In *The Greek World in the 4th and 3rd Centuries BC*, edited by E. Dąbrowa, 137–48. Kraków.
Stahl, M. 1987. *Aristokraten und Tyrannen im archaischen Athen. Untersuchungen zur Überlieferung, zur Sozialstruktur und zur Entstehung des Staates.* Stuttgart.
Stampolidis, N. C. 2004. "The Necropolises." In *Eleutherna. Polis-Acropolis-Necropolis*, edited by N. C. Stampolidis, 116–43. Athens.
Stampolidis, N. C. 2008. *Ancient Eleutherna. West Sector.* Translated by T. Cullen and A. Oikonomou. Athens.
Stampolidis, N. Chr., 2019. "Eleutherna." In *Crete. Emerging Cities. Aptera Eleutherna Knossos*, edited by N. C. Stampolidis et al., 98–162. Athens.
Stanton, G. R. 1984. "The tribal reform of Kleisthenes the Alkmeonid." *Chiron* 14:1–41.
Starcky, J., and Gawlikoswky, M. 1985. *Palmyre.* 2nd ed. Paris.
Starr, C. 1957. "The Early Greek City-State." *PP* 12:97–108.
Starr, C. 1961. *The Origins of Greek Civilization, 1100–650 B.C.* New York.
Stavrianopoulou, E. 2006. *'Gruppenbild mit Dame.' Untersuchungen zur rechtlichen und sozialen Stellung der Frau auf den Kykladen im Hellenismus und in der römischen Kaiserzeit.* Stuttgart.
Stefanaki, V. 2008. "The Coinage of Telos in the Late Classical and Early Hellenistic Periods." *NC* 168:21–32.
Stein-Hölkeskamp, E. 1989. *Adelskultur und Polisgesellschaft. Studien zum griechischen Adel in archaischer und klassischer Zeit.* Stuttgart.
Steiner, D. T. 1994. *The Tyrant's Writ. Myths and Images of Writing in Ancient Greece.* Princeton.
Steinhauer, G. 1994. "Παρατηρήσεις στην οικιστική μορφή των αττικών δήμων." In *The Archaeology of Athens and Attica Under the Democracy*, edited by W. D. E. Coulson and O. Palagia, 175–89. Oxford.
Steinhauer, G. 1998. "Demendekrete und ein neuer Archon des 3. Jahrhunderts v. Chr. Aus dem Aphrodision von Halai Aixonides." *MDA(A)* 113:235–48.
Steinhauer, G. 2017. "Attic Demoi." In *Athens and Attica. History and Archaeology*, ed A. Vlachopoulos, 107–27. Athens.
Steinhauer, J. 2014. *Religious Associations in the Post-Classical Polis.* Stuttgart.

Stephan, E. 2002. *Honoratioren, Griechen, Polisbürger. Kollektive Identitäten innerhalb der Oberschicht des kaiserzeitlichen Kleinasien.* Göttingen.

Stephani, E., Tsangaraki, E., and Arvanitaki, A., eds. 2019. *Από τον Νότο στον Βορρά. Αποικίες των Κυκλάδων στο Βόρειο Αιγαίο.* Thessaloniki.

Steskal, M. 2001. "Zu den Stiftungen des M. Claudius P. Vedius Antoninus Phaedrus Sabinianus und ihrem Echo in Ephesos." *Tyche* 16:177–88.

Steskal, M., and La Torre, M. 2008. *Das Vediusgymnasium in Ephesos. Archäologie und Baubefund.* Vienna.

Stewart, A. 1990. *Greek Sculpture: An Exploration.* New Haven.

Stewart, A., Frischer, B., and Abdelaziz, M. 2022. "Fear and Loathing in the Hellenistic Agora: Antenor's Tyrannicides Return." *Hesperia* 91.2:311–50.

Stewart, D. R. 2010. "The Rural Roman Peloponnese: Continuity and Change." In *Roman Peloponnese 3. Studies on Political, Economic and Socio-Cultural History*, edited by A. D. Rizakis and C. E. Lepeniotti, 217–33. Athens.

Stewart, A., Frischer, B., and Abdelaziz, M. 2022. "Fear and Loathing in the Hellenistic Agora: Antenor's Tyrannicides Return." *Hesperia* 91.2:311–50.

Stocker, S. R., and Davis, J. L. 2017. "The Combat Agate from the Grave of the Griffin Warrior at Pylos." *Hesperia* 86.4:583–605.

Stone. I. F. 1988. *The Trial of Socrates.* Boston.

Strauss, B. 2013. "The Classical Greek Polis and Its Government." In *The Blackwell Companion to Classical Greek Government*, edited by H. Beck, 22–37. Oxford.

Stradzins, E. 2022. "Herodes Atticus and the Sanctuaries of Achaea: Re-interpreting the Roman Present via the Greek Past." In *The Province of Achaea in the Second Century CE.*, edited by A. Kouremenos, 166–90. Abingdon.

Strauss Clay, J., Malkin, I., and Tzifopoulos, Y. Z., eds. 2017. *Panhellenes at Methone. Graphê in Late Geometric and Protoarchaic Methone.* Berlin.

Strocka, M. 2009. "Die Celsusbibliothek als Ehrengrab am Embolos." In *Neue Forschungen zur Kuretenstraße von Ephesos*, edited by S. Ladstätter, 247–59. Vienna.

Strootman, R. 2014. "Hellenistic Imperialism and the Ideal of World Unity." In *The City in the Classical and Post-Classical World. Changing Contexts of Power and Identity*, edited by C. Rapp and H. A. Drake, 38–61. Cambridge.

Stroud, R. 1969. *Drakon's Law on Homicide.* Berkeley.

Stroud, R. S. 2008. *The Athenian Grain-Tax Law of 374/3 B.C.* Princeton.

Strong, R. 1984. *Art and Power. Renaissance Festivals, 1450–1650.* Berkeley.

Strubbe, J. H. M. 1984–1986. "Gründer kleinasiatischer Städte: Fiktion und Realität." *Ancient Society* 15–17:253–304.

Strubbe, J. H. M. 2001. "Bürger, Nichtbürger und Polis-Ideologie." In *The Greek City from Antiquity to the Present. Historical Reality, Ideological Construction, Literary Representation*, edited by K. Demoen, 27–39. Leuven.

Stylianou, P. J. 1998. *A Historical Commentary on Diodorus Siculus Book 15.* Oxford.

Sumption, J. 1990–2023. *The Hundred Years War*, 5 vols. London.

Swain, S. C. R. 1996. *Hellenism and Empire. Language, Classicism, and Power in the Greek World AD 50–250.* Oxford.

Swain, S. C. R., ed. 2000. *Dio Chrysostom. Politics, Letters, and Philosophy.* Oxford.

Swain, S. C. R., and Boys-Stones, G. R., eds. 2007. *Seeing the Face, Seeing the Soul. Polemon's Physiognomy from Classical Antiquity to Medieval Islam.* Oxford.

Swift, L. 2019. *Archilochos. The Poems. Introduction, Text, Translation, and Commentary.* Oxford.

Swoboda, H. 1890. *Griechischen Volksbeschlusse. Epigraphische Untersuchungen.* Leipzig.

Szanto, E. 1892. *Das griechische Bürgerrecht.* Freiburg im Breisgau.

Syme, R. 1988. *Roman Papers*, vol. 8. Edited by A. R. Birley. Oxford.

Tacoma, L. E. 2006. *Fragile Hierarchies. The Urban Elites of Third Century Roman Egypt.* Leiden.

Taita, J. 2007. *Olimpia e il suo vicinato in epoca arcaica.* Milan.

Talamo, C. 2003. "Aspetti dell'organizzazione del territorio a Mileto." In *Gli stati territoriali nel mondo antico*, edited by C. Bearzot, F. Landucci and G. Zecchini, 159–78. Milan.

Talbert, R. J. A. 1974. *Timoleon and the Revival of Greek Sicily, 344–317 B.C.* Cambridge.

Tandy, D. W. 1997. *Warriors into Traders. The Power of the Market in Early Greece.* Berkeley.

Tarrow, S. 2004. "From Comparative Historical Analysis to Local Theory." *Theory and Society* 33:443–471.

Täuber, H. 2015. "Ein Kaiserbrief des Antoninus Pius zu einem bisher unbekannten Erdbeben in Ephesos." *JÖAI* 84:301–10.

Taylor, Ch. 1994. "The Politics of Recognition." In *Multiculturalism. Examining the Politics of Recognition*, edited by A. Gutman, 25–73. Princeton.

Taylor, Cl. 2011. "Migration and the Demes of Attica." In *Demography and the Graeco-Roman World. New Insights and Approaches*, edited by C. Holleran and A. Pudsey, 117–34. Cambridge.

Taylor, Cl. 2017. *Poverty, Wealth, and Well-Being. Experiencing* penia *in Democratic Athens*. Oxford.

Taylor, D. G. K. 2002. "Bilingualism and Diglossia in Late Antique Syria and Mesopotamia." In *Bilingualism in Ancient Society. Language Contact and the Written Text*, edited by J. N. Adams, M. Janse, and S. Swain, 298–331. Oxford.

Taylor, Cl., and Vlassopoulos, K., eds. 2015. *Communities and Networks in the Ancient Greek World*. Oxford.

Teegarden, D. 2014. *Death to Tyrants! Ancient Greek Democracy and the Struggle Against Tyranny*. Princeton.

Teixidor, J. 1984. *Un port romain du désert. Palmyre et son commerce d'Auguste à Caracalla*. Paris.

Teixidor, J., Feissel, D., and Gascou, J. 1997. "Documents d'archives romains inédits du Moyen Euphrate (IIIe siècle après J-C)." *JS* 1:3–57.

Televantou, C. A. 1999. "Ἄνδρος. Τὸ ἱερὸ τῆς Ὑψιλῆς." In *Φῶς Κυκλαδικόν. Τιμητικὸς τόμος στη μνήμη του Νίκου Ζαφειρόπουλου*, edited by N. C. Stampolidis, 132–37. Athens.

Televantou, C. A. 2000 (2009). "Ἀρχαιολογικὸς χῶρος Ὑψιλῆς." *AD* 55:965–66.

Themelis, P. G. 2010. "The Economy and Society of Messenia under Roman Rule." In *Roman Peloponnese 3. Society, Economy and Culture under the Roman Empire. Continuity and Innovation*, edited by A. D. Rizakis and C. E. Lepeniotis, 89–110. Paris.

Themelis, P. G., and Touratsoglou, I. P. 1997. *Οἱ τάφοι τοῦ Δερβενίου*. Athens.

Themos, N., and Zavvou, E. 2019. "New Hellenistic Inscriptions from Phigaleia (Arcadia)." In *From Document to History. Epigraphic Insights into the Greco-Roman World*, edited by C. F. Noreña and N. Papazarkadas, 103–19. Leiden.

Thériault, G. 1996. *Le culte d'Homonoia dans les cités grecques*. Quebec.

Thériault, G. 2003. "Évergétisme grec et administration romaine: la famille cnidienne de Gaios Ioulios Théopompos." *Phoenix* 57.3–4:232–56.

Thomas, C. G. 2005. *Finding People in Early Greece*. Columbia, MO.

Thomas, R. 2007. "Fame, Memorial, and Choral Poetry. The Origins of Epinikian Poetry: An Historical Study." In *Pindar's Poetry, Patrons, and Festivals. From Archaic Greece to the Roman Empire*, edited by S. Hornblower and C. A. Morgan, 141–66. Oxford.

Thomas, R. 2019. *Polis Histories. Collective Memories and the Greek World*. Cambridge.

Thompson, H. A., and Wycherley, R. E. 1972. *The Agora of Athens. The History, Shape, and Uses of an Ancient City Center. Athenian Agora 14*. Princeton.

Thomsen, C. 2020. *The Politics of Association in Hellenistic Rhodes*. Edinburgh.

Thonemann, P. J. 2010. "The Women of Akmoneia." *JRS* 100:163–78.

Thonemann, P. J. 2011. *The Maeander Valley. A Historical Geography from Antiquity to Byzantium*. Cambridge.

Thonemann, P. J., ed. 2013. *Attalid Asia Minor. Money, International Relations, and the State*. Oxford.

Thonemann, P. J. 2015. "The Calendar of the Roman Province of Asia." *ZPE* 196:123–41.

Thonemann, P. J. 2021. "Estates and the Land in Hellenistic Asia Minor: An Estate Near Antioch on the Maeander." *Chiron* 51:1–36.

Thornton, J. 2001a. *Lo storico, il grammatico, il bandito. Momenti della resistenza greca all'*Imperium Romanum. Catania.

Thornton, J. 2001b. "Gli aristoi, l'akriton plethos e la provincializzazione della Licia nel monumento di Patara." *MediterrAnt* 4:427–46.

Thornton, J. 2007. "*Nomoi, eleutheria* e democrazia a Maronea nell'età di Claudio." In *Incontri tra culture nell'oriente ellenistico e romano*, edited by T. Gnoli and F. Muccioli, 139–66. Milan.

Thornton, J. 2008. "*Lesteiai* nella dedica a Claudio del monumento di Patara: una sommessa proposta d'interpretazione." *MediterrAnt* 11:175–98.

Thornton, J. 2019. "Istituzioni democratiche e tensioni sociali: dalla *polis* ellenistica alla città imperiale." In *Roman Imperial Cities in the East and in Central-Southern Italy*, edited by N. Andrade et al., 55–90. Rome.

Thornton, J. 2020. *Polibio. Il politico e lo storico*. Rome.

Thür, H., and Aurenhammer, M. 1997. '... *und verschönerte die Stadt* ...' καὶ κοσμήσαντα τὴν πόλιν. *Ein Ephesischer Priester des Kaiserkultes in seinem Umfeld*. Vienna.

Tiersch, C. ed. 2016. *Die Athenische Demokratie im 4. Jahrhundert: zwischen Modernisierung und Tradition*. Stuttgart.

Tilly, C. 1989. "Cities and States in Europe 1000–1800." *Theory and Society* 18.5:563–84.

Tiré, C., and van Effenterre, H. 1966. *Guide des fouilles françaises en Crète*. Athens.

Tiverios, M. 2008. "Greek Colonisation in the Northern Aegean." In *Greek Colonisation. An Account of Greek Colonies and Other Settlements Overseas*, edited by G. R. Tsetskhladze, 1–154. Leiden.

Tobin, J. 1997. *Herodes Attikos and the City of Athens. Patronage and Conflict Under the Antonines*. Amsterdam.

Todd, S. C. 2007. *A Commentary on Lysias, Speeches 1–11*. Oxford.

Todeschini, G. 2007. *Visibilmente crudeli: Malviventi, persone sospette e gente qualunque dal medioevo all'eta moderna*. Bologna.

Too, Y.-L. 2001. "The Economies of Pedagogy: Xenophon's Wifely Didactics." *CCJ* 47:65–80.

Touchais, G., and Divari-Valakou, N. 1998. "Argos du Néolithique à l'époque géométrique: synthèse des données archéologiques." In *Argos et l'Argolide. Topographie et urbanisme*, edited by A. Pariente and G. Touchais, 8–21. Athens.

Touloumakos, J. 1967. *Der Einfluss Roms auf die Staatsform der griechischen Stadtstaaten des Festlandes und der Inseln der ersten und zweiten Jhdt. V. Chr*. Göttingen.

Tracy, S. V. 1979. "Athens in 100 B.C." *HSPh* 83:213–35.

Tracy, S. V. 1982. I.G. II^2 2336. *Contributors of First Fruits for the Pythais*. Meisenheim.

Tracy, S. V. 1995. *Athenian Democracy in Transition. Attic Letter-Cutters of 340 to 290 B.C*. Berkeley.

Tracy, S. V. 2003. *Athens and Macedon. Attic Letter-Cutters of 300 to 229 B.C*. Berkeley.

Tracy, S. V. 2014. "Downdating Some Athenian Decrees with Three-Bar Sigma: A Palaeographic Approach." *ZPE* 190:105–15.

Tracy, S. V. 2016. *Athenian Lettering of the Fifth Century B.C. The Rise of the Professional Letter Cutter*. Berlin.

Traill, J. 1994. *Persons of Ancient Athens*. Toronto.

Tréziny, H. 2006. "L'urbanisme archaïque des villes ioniennes: un point de vue occidental." *REA* 108.1:225–47.

Tréziny, H. 2018. *Mégara Hyblaea 7. La ville classique, hellénistique et romaine*. Rome.

Tritle, L. 2014. *Phocion the Good*. London.

Trümpy, C. 1997. *Untersuchungen zu den altgriechischen Monatsnamen und Monatsfolgen*. Heidelberg.

Tsakos, K. 2007. "Die Stadt Samos in der geometrischen und archaischen Epoche." In *Frühes Ionien. Eine Bestandsaufnahme*, edited by J. Cobet, 189–99. Mainz.

Tsetskhladze, G., ed. 2006–2008. *Greek Colonization. An Account of Geek Colonies and Other Settlements Overseas*. Leiden.

Tuchelt, K. 1979. *Frühe Denkmäler Roms in Kleinasien: Beiträge zur archäologischen Überlieferung aus der Zeit der Republik und des Augustus*. Tübingen.

Tuchelt, K., Schneider, P., and Schattner, T. G. 1996. *Ein Kultbezirk an der Heiligen Straße von Milet nach Didyma*. Berlin.

Tuck, R. 2008. *Free Riding*. Cambridge.

Tuplin, C. J. 1986. "The Fate of Thespiae during the Theban Hegemony." *Athenaeum* 64:321–41.

Tuplin, C. J. 1993. *The Failings of Empire. A Reading of Xenophon* Hellenica 2.3.11–7.5.27. Stuttgart.

Tuplin, C. J. 2007. "Continuous Histories (*Hellenica*)." In *A Companion to Greek and Roman Historiography*, edited by J. Marincola, 143–53. Malden, MA.

Tzanavari, K. 2019. "Αρχαία Λητή. Η πόλη και τα νεκροταφεία της." In *Η αρχαία Λητή και η περιοχή της*, edited by †E. Stephani, P. Photiadis, N. Trivizadakis, and N. Minaoglou, 19–38. Thessaloniki.

Tziafalias, A., Garcia-Ramon, J. L., and Helly, B. 2006. "Décrets inédits de Larissa (2)." *BCH* 130.1:435–83.

Tziafalias, A., Helly, B., and Bouchon, R. 2016. "Lois de Larisa: règlement relatif à des célébrations religieuses à Zeus et à Ennodia." *Studi ellenistici* 30:69–102

Ulf, C. 2007. "Elite oder Eliten in den Dark Ages und der Archaik: Realitäten und Modelle." in *Keimelion: The Formation of Elites and Elitist Lifestyles from Mycenaean Palatial Time to the Homeric Period*, edited by E. Alram-Stern and G. Nightingale, 316–24. Vienna.

Urbinati, N. 2002. *Mill on Democracy. From the Athenian Polis to Representative Government*. Chicago.

Vădan, P. 2022. "Migration, Mobility, and the Hierarchy of Violence in the Classical and Early Hellenistic Polis." *TAPhA* 152.2:381–425.

van Alfen, P., and Wartenberg, U. 2020. *White Gold: Studies in Early Electrum Coinage*. New York.

Van Andringa, W. 2003. "Cités et communautés d'expatriés installées dans l'Empire romain: le cas des 'cives Romani consistentes.'" In *Les communautés religieuses dans le monde gréco-romain. Essais de définition*, edited by N. Belayche and S. C. Mimouni, 49–60. Turnhout.

Van den Eijnde, F., Blok, J. J., and Strootman, R. 2018. *Feasting and Polis Institutions*. Leiden.

van Bremen, R. 1996. *The Limits of Participation: Women and Civic Life in the Greek East in the Hellenistic and Roman Periods*. Amsterdam.

van Bremen, R. 2008. "The Date and Context of the Kymaian Decrees for Archippe (SEG 33, 1035–1041)," *REA* 110.2:357–382.

van Bremen, R. 2010. "The Inscribed Documents on the Temple of Hekate at Lagina and the Date and Meaning of the Temple Frieze." In *Hellenistic Karia: Proceedings of the First International Conference on Hellenistic Karia, Oxford, 29 June–2 July 2006*, edited by R. van Bremen and M. Carbon, 483–504. Pessac.

van Bremen, R. 2013a. "A Property Transaction between Kindye and Mylasa: I.Mylasa 11 Reconsidered." *Epigraphica Anatolica* 46:1–26.

van Bremen, R. 2013b. "Neoi in Hellenistic Cities: Age Class, Institution, Association?" In *Groupes et Associations dans le monde grec: structures d'appartenance et dynamique sociales dans les poleis de l'époque hellénistique et impériale (IIIe s. a.C-IIe s. p. C)*, edited by P. Fröhlich and P. Hamon, 31–59. Geneva.

van Bremen, R., and Carbon, M. 2010. *Hellenistic Karia: Proceedings of the First International Conference on Hellenistic Karia*. Pessac.

Van der Spek, R. 1987. "The Babylonian City." In *Hellenism in the East. The Interaction of Greek and Non-Greek Civilizations from Syria to Central Asia after Alexander*, edited by A. Kuhrt and S. Sherwin-White, 57–74. London.

Van der Vliet, E. C. L. 2011. "The Early Greek Polis: Regime Building, and the Emergence of the State." In *State Formation in Italy and Greece. Questioning the Neoevolutionist Paradigm*, edited by D. C. Haggis and N. Terrenato, 119–34. Oxford.

Van Dommelen, P. 2017. "Classical Connections and Mediterranean Practices: Exploring Connectivity and Local Interactions." In *The Routledge Handbook of Archaeology and Globalization*, edited by T. Hodos, 618–33. London.

Van Effenterre, H. 1979. "Réflexions sur la fiscalité dans la Grèce des cités archaïques." In *Points de vue sur la fiscalité antique*, edited by H. van Effenterre, 19–30. Paris.

Van Effenterre, H. 1986. *Les Egéens aux origines de la Grèce. Chypre, Cyclades, Crète et Mycènes*. Paris.

Van Effenterre, H. 2009. *La nécropole de Dréros*. Edited by M. Perna. Athens.

Van Effenterre, H. 2013. *Minos et les Grecs. La cité revisitée*. Edited by F. Ruzé. Paris.

Van Minnen, P. 2002. "Hermopolis in the Crisis of the Roman Empire." In *After the Past. Essays in Ancient History in Honour of H.W. Pleket*, edited by W. Jongman and M. Kleiwegt, 185–204. Leiden.

Van Nijf, O. M. 1997. *The Civic World of Professional Associations in the Roman East*. Amsterdam.

Van Nijf, O. M. 2011. "Public Space and the Political Culture of Roman Termessos." In *Political Culture in the Greek City After the Classical Age*, edited by O. M. van Nijf, R. Alston, and C. G. Williamson, 215–42. Leuven.

van Nijf, O., and Alston, R. eds. 2011. *Political Culture in the Greek City after the Classical Age*. London.

Van Wees, H. 1994a. "The Homeric Way of War: The *Iliad* and the Hoplite Phalanx (I)." *G&R* 41.1:1–18.

Van Wees, H. 1994b. "The Homeric Way of War: The *Iliad* and the Hoplite Phalanx (II)." *G&R* 41.2:131–55.

Van Wees, H. 1995. "Princes at Dinner: Social Event and Social Structure in Homer." In *Homeric Questions*, edited by J.-P. Crielaard, 147–82. Amsterdam.

Van Wees, H. 1996. "Heroes, Knights and Nutters: Warrior Mentality in Homer." In *Battle in Antiquity*, edited by A. B. Lloyd, 1–86. London.

Van Wees, H. 1997. "Homeric Warfare." In *A New Companion to Homer*, edited by I. Morris and B. Powell, 668–93. Leiden.

Van Wees, H. 1998. "Greeks Bearing Arms: The State, the Leisure Class, and the Display of Weapons in Archaic Greece." In *Archaic Greece. New Approaches and New Evidence*, edited by N. Fisher and H. van Wees, 333–78. London.

Van Wees, H. 1999a. "Homer and Early Greece." In *Homer. Critical Assessments*, vol. 2. *The Homeric World*, edited by I. J. de Jong, 1–32. London.

Van Wees H. 1999b. "Tyrtaeus' Eunomia: Nothing to Do with the Great Rhetra." In *Sparta, New Perspectives*, edited by S. Hodkinson and A. Powell, 1–41. London.

Van Wees 1999c. "The Mafia of Early Greece. Violent Exploitation in the Seventh and Sixth centuries BC." In *Organized Crime in Antiquity*, edited by Keith Hopwood, 1–51. London.

Van Wees, H. 2000. "Megara's Mafiosi: Timocracy and Violence in Theognis." In *Alternatives to Athens. Varieties of Political Organization and Community in Ancient Greece*, edited by R. Brock and S. Hodkinson, 52–67. Oxford.

Van Wees, H. 2003. "Conquerors and Serfs: Wars of Conquest and Forced Labour in Archaic Greece." In *Helots and their Masters in Laconia and Messenia. Histories, Ideologies, Structures*, edited by N. Luraghi and S. Alcock, 33–80. Cambridge, MA.

Van Wees, H. 2004. *Greek Warfare, Myth and Realities*. London.

Van Wees, H. 2006a. "From Kings to Demigods: Epic Heroes and Social Change, c. 750–600 B.C." In *Ancient Greece. From the Mycenaean Palaces to the Age of Homer*, edited by S. Deger-Jalkotzy and I. Lemos, 363–79. Edinburgh.

Van Wees, H. 2006b. "'The Oath of the Sworn Bands': The Acharnae Stela, the Oath of Plataea and Archaic Spartan Warfare." In *Das Frühe Sparta*, edited by A. Luther, M. Meier, and L. Thommen, 125–64. Stuttgart.

Van Wees, H. 2009a. *A Companion to Archaic Greece*. Chichester.

Van Wees, H. 2009b. "The Economy." In *A Companion to Archaic Greece*, edited by H. van Wees, 444–67. Chichester.

Van Wees, H. 2013. *Ships and Silver. Taxes and Tribute. A Fiscal History of Archaic Athens*. London.

Vatin, C. 1961. "Démiurges et épidamiurges à Delphes." *BCH* 85:236–55.

Vatin, C. 1984. *Citoyens et non-citoyens dans le monde grec*. Paris.

Vecchio, L. 2019. "La 'grande iscrizione' e la città agli inizi dell'età ellenistica: aspetti e problemi." In *Colofone, città della Ionia. Nuove ricerche e studi*, edited by L. Vecchio, 149–79. Salerno.

Velisarropoulos-Karakostas, J. 2011. *Droit grec d'Alexandre à Auguste (323 av. J.-C-–14 ap. J.-C.): personnes, biens, justice*. Athens.

Veneciano, G. 2014. "The Structure of the Legal Norm in Archaic Greece: A Case Study (*IvO* 7)." *ZPE* 192:143–55.

Ventroux, O. 2017. *Pergame. Les élites d'une ancienne capitale royale à l'époque romaine 133 av. J.-C.–IIIe s. apr. J.-C.* Rennes.

Verdan, S. 2013. *Le Sanctuaire d'Apollon Daphnéphoros à l'époque géométrique*. Lausanne.

Vernant, J.-P. 1962. *Les origines de la pensée grecque*. Paris.

Vernant, J.-P. 1965. *Mythe et pensée chez les Grecs. Études de psychologie historique*. Paris.

Vernant, J.-P., and Vidal-Naquet, P. 1973. *Mythe et tragédie en Grèce ancienne*. Paris.

Vernant, J.-P., and Vidal-Naquet, P. 1988. *Myth and Tragedy in Ancient Greece*. Translated by Janet Lloyd. New York.

Veyne. P. 1961. "Le Marsyas 'colonial' et l'indépendance des cités." *RPh* 35:87–98.

Veyne, P. 1975. "Y a-t-il eu un impérialisme romain?" *MEFRA* 87:793–855.

Veyne, P. 1976. *Le pain et le cirque. Sociologie historique d'un pluralisme politique*. Paris.

Veyne, P. 1978. *Comment on écrit l'histoire. Essai d'épistémologie. Suivi de Foucault révolutionne l'histoire*. Paris.

Veyne, P. 1983. *Les Grecs ont-ils cru à leurs mythes? Essai sur l'imagination constituante*. Paris.

Veyne, P. 1998. "La fresque dite des Mystères à Pompéi." In *Les mystères du gynécée*, edited by P. Veyne, F. Lissarrague, and F. Frontisi-Ducroux, 13–153, Paris.

Veyne, P. 1999. "L'identité grecque devant Rome et l'empereur." *REG* 112.2:511–67.

Veyne, P. 2005. *L'empire gréco-romain*, Paris.

Veyne, P. 2015. *Palmyre. L'irremplaçable trésor*. Paris.

Vidal-Naquet, P. 1975. "Le mirage grec et la Révolution française." *Esprit* 452.12:825–39.

Vidal-Naquet, P. 1981. *Le chasseur noir. Formes de pensée et formes de société dans le monde grec*. Paris.

Vidal-Naquet, P. 1986. *The Black Hunter. Forms of Thought and Forms of Society in the Greek World*. Translated by A. Szegedy-Maszak. Baltimore.

Vidal-Naquet, P. 1995–1998. *Mémoires*. 2 vols. Paris.

Vidal-Naquet, P. 2000. *Les Grecs, les historiens, la démocratie. Le grand écart*. Paris.

Viglaki-Sofianou, M. 2004. "Γεωμετρική νεκρόπολη Αρχαίας Σάμου." In *Το Αιγαίο στην Πρώιμη Εποχή του Σιδήρου*, edited by N. C. Stampolidis and A. Giannikouri, 189–96. Athens.

Viglaki-Sofianou, M. 2013. "Ανάδειξη της Γεωμετρικής νεκρόπολης των τύμβων της αρχαίας πόλης της Σάμου." In Νησιωτικές Ταυτότητες: η συμβολή της Γενικής Γραμματείας Αιγαίου και Νησιωτικής Πολιτικής στην έρευνα και ανάδειξη του πολιτισμού του αρχιπελάγους, edited by M. Alvanou, 21–23. Mytilene.

Vink, M C. 1997. "Urbanization in Late and Sub-Geometric Greece: Abstract Considerations and Concrete Case Studies of Eretria and Zagora c. 700 B.C." *ActHyp* 7:111–41.

Vinogradov, J. G., and Wörrle, M. 1992. "Die Söldner von Phanagoreia." *Chiron* 22:159–70.
Vinogradov, J. G., and Zolotarev, M. I. 1999. "L'ostracismo e la storia della fondazione di Chersonesos Taurica: analisi comparata con gli ostraka dal Kerameikos di Atene." *MEP* 2:110–31.
Vitale, M. 2012. "Hellenische Poleis, Hellenarchen und 'koina' der Hellenen fern der 'Heimat': die Hellenen-Titulatur vom Schwarzen Meer bis zur syrischen Wüstensteppe." *Tyche* 27:153–92.
Vitale, M. 2013. *Koinon Syrias. Priester, Gymnasiarchen und Metropoleis der Eparchien im kaiserzeitlichen Syrien.* Berlin.
Viviers, D. 1994. "La cité de Dattalla et l'expansion de Lyktos en Crète centrale." *BCH* 118.1:229–59.
Vlachopoulos, A. G., and Charalambidou, X. 2019. "Naxos and the Cyclades." In *A Companion to the Archaeology of Early Greece and the Mediterranean*, edited by A. Kotsonas and I. Lemos, 1007–28. Hoboken, NJ.
Vlamos, A. 2022. "Redéfinir l'État rhodien: la question des tribus et des anciennes poleis dans l'organisation publique de Rhodes de l'époque hellénistique." *REA* 124.1:125–42.
Vlassopoulos, K. 2007a. *Unthinking the Greek Polis. Ancient Greek History beyond Eurocentrism.* Cambridge.
Vlassopoulos, K. 2007b. "Free Spaces: Identity, Experience and Democracy in Classical Athens." *CQ* 57.1:33–52.
Vlassopoulos, K. 2007c. "Between East and West: The Greek *Poleis* as Part of a World-System." *Ancient West and East* 6:91–111.
Vlassopoulos, K. 2011. "Greek Slavery: From Domination to Property and Back Again." *JHS* 131:115–30.
Vlassopoulos, K. 2013. *Greeks and Barbarians.* Cambridge.
Vlassopoulos, K. 2019. "Historicising the Closed City." In *La cité interconnectée dans le monde gréco-romain (IVᵉ siècle a. C.–IVᵉ siècle p. C.). Transferts et réseaux institutionnels, religieux et culturels aux époques hellénistique et impériale*, edited by M. Dana and I. Savalli-Lestrade, 43–57. Bordeaux.
Vlassopoulos, K., and Taylor, C., eds. 2015. *Communities and Networks in the Ancient Greek World.* Oxford.
Voigtländer, W. 2004. *Teichiussa. Näherung und Wirklichkeit.* Westphalia.
Von Kienlin, A. 2004. *Die Agora von Priene.* Unpublished PhD dissertation, Technical University, Munich.
Vujčić, N. 2009. "Greek Popular Assemblies in the Imperial Period and the Discourses of Dio of Prusa." *EA* 42:157–69.
Wace, A., and Stubbings, F., eds. 1963. *A Companion to Homer.* London.
Waelkens, M. 2006. "The Late Antique to Early Byzantine City in Southwest Anatolia: Sagalassos and Its Territory: A Case Study." In *Die Stadt in der Spätantike—Niedergang oder Wandel?*, edited by J.-U. Krause and C. Witschel, 199–255.
Walbank, F. W. 1977. "The Original Extent of the Via Egnatia." *LCM* 2:73–74.
Walbank, F. W. 2002. *Polybius, Rome, and the Hellenistic World. Essays and Reflections.* Cambridge.
Walbank, M. 2015. "Athens in 143/2 B.C.: Three Decrees and a Diadikasia." *ZPE* 193:118–32.
Waley, D., and Dean, T. 2010. *The Italian City Republics.* 4th ed. London.
Wallace, R. W. 2013. "Councils in Greek Oligarchies and Democracies." In *A Companion to Ancient Greek Government*, edited by H. Beck, 191–204. Malden, MA.
Wallace, Sara. 2010. *Ancient Crete. From Successful Collapse to Democracy's Alternatives.* Cambridge.
Wallace, Sara. 2020. "Economies in Crisis: Subsistence and Landscape Technology in the Aegean and East Mediterranean after c. 1200 B.C." In *Collapse and Transformation. The Late Bronze Age to Early Iron Age in the Aegean*, edited by G. D. Middledon, 247–58. Oxford.
Wallace, Shane. 2016. "The Rescript of Philip III Arrhidaios and the Two Tyrannies at Eresos." *Tyche* 31:239–58.
Wallace, Shane. 2018. "Alexander the Great and Democracy in the Hellenistic World." In *The Hellenistic Reception of Classical Athenian Democracy and Political Thought*, edited by M. Canevaro and B. D. Gray, 45–72. Oxford.
Wallinga, H. T. 2000. "The Athenian 'naukraroi.'" In *Peisistratos and the Tyranny. A Reappraisal of the Evidence*, edited by H. Sancisi-Weerdenburg, 131–46. Amsterdam.
Walser, A. V. 2008. *Bauern und Zinsnehmer. Politik, Recht und Wirtschaft im frühhellenistischen Ephesos.* Munich.
Walser, A. V. 2012. "ΔΙΚΑΣΤΗΡΙΑ—Rechtsprechung und Demokratie in den hellenistischen Poleis." In *"Demokratie" im Hellenismus. Von der Herrschaft des Volkes zur Herrschaft der Honoratioren?*, edited by C. Mann and P. Scholz, 74–108. Mainz.
Walter, U. 1993. *An der Polis teilhaben. Bürgerstaat und Zugehörigkeit im archaischen Griechenland.* Stuttgart.
Ward, W. D. 2020. *Near Eastern Cities from Alexander to the Successors of Muhammad.* Abingdon.
Watson, J. 2011. "Rethinking the Sanctuary of Aphaia." In *Aegina. Contexts for Choral Lyric Poetry. Myth, History, and Identity in the Fifth Century BC*, edited by D. Fearn, 79–113, Oxford.
Weber, H. 1908. *Attisches Prozessrecht in den attischen Seebundstaaten.* Paderborn.

Weber, M. 1999. *Gesamtausgabe*. Vol. I/22,5. *Wirtschaft und Gesellschaft. Die Stadt*. Edited by W. Nippel. Tübingen.
Węcowski, M. 2011. "On the Historicity of the 'Homeric World': Some Methodological Considerations." In *Dark Ages Revisited*, edited by A. Mazarakis Ainian, 73–81. Volos.
Węcowski, M. 2014. *The Rise of the Greek Aristocratic Banquet*. Oxford.
Węcowski, M. 2022. *Athenian Ostracism and Its Original Purpose. A Prisoner's Dilemma*. Oxford.
Wehrli, C. 1962. "Les gynéconomes." *MH* 19.1:33–8.
Weiberg, E., and Finné, M. 2018. "Resilience and Persistence of Ancient Societies in the Face of Climate Change: A Case Study from Late Bronze Age Peloponnese." *World Archaeology* 50.4:584–602.
Weiss, P. 1990. "Mythen, Dichter und Münzen von Lykaonien." *Chiron* 20:221–37.
Weiss, P. 1992. "Zu Münzprägungen mit den Formeln ΑΙΤΗΣΑΜΕΝΟΥ und ΕΙΣΑΓΓΕΙΛΑΝΤΟΣ." In *Studien zum antiken Kleinasien 2*, 167–80. Bonn.
Weiss, P. 2002. "Asiarchen sind *Archiereis Asias*. Eine Antwort auf S. J. Friesen." In *Widerstand—Anpassung—Integration. Die griechische Staatenwelt und Rom. Festschrift für Jürgen Deininger zum 65. Geburtstag*, edited by L. Ehrhardt and L.-M. Günther, 241–54. Stuttgart.
Weiss, P. 2005. "The Cities and Their Money." In *Coinage and Identity in the Roman Provinces*, edited by C. Howgego, V. Heuchert, and A. Burnett, 57–68. Oxford.
Welskopf, E. C. 1977. "*Polis* und *Chora*: konnte die Diskontiuität der Stadt vom Lande her überbrückt werden?" In *Thèmes de recherche sur les villes antiques d'occident*, edited by P.-M. Duval and E. Frézouls, 153–55, Paris.
Welwei, K.-W. 1981. "Adel und Demos in der frühen Polis." *Gymnasium* 88:1–23.
Welwei, K.-W. 1992. *Athen vom neolithischen Siedlungsplatz zur archaischen Polis*. Darmstadt.
Welwei, K.-W. 1998. *Die griechische Polis. Verfassung und Gesellschaft in archaischer und klassischer Zeit*. 2nd ed. Stuttgart.
Welwei, K.-W. 2004. "Orestes at Sparta: The Political Significance of the Grave of the Hero." In *Spartan Society*, edited by T. J. Figueira, 219–30. Swansea.
Werlings, M.-J. 2010. *Le démos avant la démocratie. Mots, concepts, réalités historiques*. Paris.
West, M. L. 1978. *Hesiod. Works & Days*. Oxford.
West, M. L. 1997. *The East Face of Helicon. West Asiatic Elements in Greek Poetry and Myth*. Oxford.
West, M. L. 2011. *The Making of the Iliad. Disquisition and Analytical Commentary*. Oxford.
West, W. C. 2015. "Informal and Practical Uses of Writing on Potsherds from Azoria, Crete." *ZPE* 193:151–63.
Westgate, R. 2015. "Space and Social Complexity in Greece from the Early Iron Age to the Classical Period." *Hesperia* 84.1:47–95.
Westlake, H. D. 1935. *Thessaly in the Fourth Century BC*. London.
Westlake, H. D. 1952. *Timoleon and his Relations with Tyrants*. Manchester.
Whatmore, R. 2012. *Against War and Empire. Geneva, Britain, and France in the Eighteenth Century*. New Haven.
Whibley, L. 1896. *Greek Oligarchies. Their Character and Organisation*. London.
Whitehead, D. 1977. *The Ideology of the Athenian Metic*. Cambridge.
Whitehead, D. 1986. *The Demes of Attica 508/7–ca. 250 B.C. A Political and Social Study*. Princeton.
Whitehead, D. 1993. "Cardinal Virtues: The Language of Public Approbation in Democratic Athens." *C&C* 44:37–75.
Whitehead, D. 2002. *How to Survive Under Siege. Aineias the Tactician. A Historical Commentary*. 2nd ed. Bristol.
Whitley, J. 1991. *Style and Society in Dark Age Greece. The Changing Face of a Pre-literate Society 1100–700 B.C.* Cambridge.
Whitley, J. 1994. "The Monuments That Stood Before Marathon: Tomb Cult and Hero Cult in Archaic Attica." *AJA* 98.2:213–30.
Whitley, J. 1995. "Tomb Cult and Hero Cult: The Uses of the Past in Archaic Greece." In *Time, Tradition, and Society in Greek Archaeology. Bridging the "Great Divide,"* edited by N. Spencer, 43–63. London.
Whitley, J. 1997. "Cretan Laws and Cretan Literacy." *AJA* 101.4:635–61.
Whitley, J. 2001. *The Archaeology of Ancient Greece*. Cambridge.
Whitley, J. 2004. "Cycles of Collapse in Greek Prehistory: The House of Tiles at Lerna and the 'Heroon' at Lefkandi." In *Explaining Social Change. Studies in Honour of Colin Renfrew*, edited by J. Cherry, C. Scarre, and S. Shennan, 193–201. Cambridge.
Whitmarsh, T. 2005. *The Second Sophistic*. Oxford.

Whitmarsh, T., ed. 2010. *Local Knowledge and Microidentities in the Imperial Greek World*. Cambridge.
Whittaker, R. 1995. "Do Theories of the Ancient City Matter?" In *Urban Society in Roman Italy*, edited by T. J. Cornell and K. Lomas, 9–26. London and New York.
Whittow, M. 1990. "Ruling the Late Roman and Early Byzantine City: A Continuous History." *PP* 129:3–29.
Wickham, C. 2005. *Framing the Early Middle Ages. Europe and the Mediterranean 400–800*. Oxford.
Wickham, C. 2015. *Sleepwalking into a New World. The Emergence of Italian City Communes in the Twelfth Century*. Princeton.
Wiegand, T. 1910. *Priene. Ein Begleitwort zur Rekonstruktion von A. Zippelius*. Leipzig.
Wiegand, T. 1932. *Palmyra. Ergebnisse der Expeditionen von 1902 und 1917*. Berlin.
Wiegand, T., and Schrader, H. 1904. *Priene. Ergebnisse der Ausgrabungen und Untersuchungen in den Jahren 1895–1898*. Berlin.
Wielgosz, D. 2010. "La sculpture en marbre à Palmyre." In *Studia Palmyreńskie IX*, edited by M. Gawlikowski, 75–106. Warsaw.
Wiemer, H.-U. 2003. "Die koische Opfergebotsliste Syll. 1000: 'diagrapha' oder 'nomos'?" *ZPE* 145:117–22.
Wiemer, H.-U. 2013. "Hellenistic Cities: The End of Greek Democracy?" In *A Companion to Ancient Greek Government*, edited by H. Beck, 54–69. Malden, MA.
Wiemer, H.-U. 2016. "Römische Aristokraten oder griechische Honoratioren? Kontext und Adressaten der Verhaltenslehre des Stoikers Panaitios." *Chiron* 46:1–45.
Wilhelm, A. 1909. *Beiträge zur griechischen Inschriftenkunde mit einem Anhange über die öffentliche Aufzeichung von Urkunden*. Vienna.
Will, E. 1955–1957. "Miltiade et Dorieus." *La Nouvelle Clio* 7–9:127–32.
Will, E. 1956. *Doriens et Ioniens: essai sur la valeur du critère ethnique appliqué à l'étude de l'histoire et de la civilisation grecques*. Paris.
Will, E. 1979–82. *Histoire politique du monde hellénistique (323–30 av. J.C.)*. 2nd ed. 2 vols. Nancy.
Will, E. 1998. *Historica Graeco-Hellenistica. Choix d'écrits 1953–1993*. Paris.
Will, P.-É. 2021. "Édouard Will et Pierre Vidal-Naquet." In *Édouard Will historien nancéen du monde grec*, edited by L. Graslin-Thomé and J. Zurbach, 33–53. Paris.
Williams, C. K. 1984. "The Early Urbanization of Corinth." *ASAA* 60:9–19.
Williamson, C. G. 2013. "As God Is My Witness: Civic Oaths in Ritual Space as a Means Towards Rational Cooperation in the Hellenistic Polis." In *Cults, Creeds and Identities in the Greek City after the Classical Age*, edited by R. Alston, O. M. van Nijf, and C. G. Williamson, 119–74. Leuven.
Wilson, P. 1998. "People Power." *CR* 48.2:374–76.
Wilson, P. 2000. *The Athenian Institution of the Khoregia. The Chorus, the City and the Stage*. Oxford.
Wilson, P., ed. 2007. *The Greek Theatre and Festivals. Documentary Studies*. Oxford.
Wilson, P. 2009. "Tragic Honours and Democracy: Neglected Evidence for the Politics of the Athenian Dionysia." *CQ* 59.1:8–29.
Wilson, A., and Bowman, A. K. 2018. *Trade, Commerce, and the State in the Roman World*. Oxford.
Winkler, J. J., and Zeitlin, F., eds. 1990. *Nothing to Do with Dionysos? Athenian Drama in its Social Context*. Princeton.
Winnifrith. T. J. 2002. *Badlands - Borderlands. A History of Southern Albania - Northern Epirus*. London.
Witcher, R. 2011 "Missing Persons? Models of Mediterranean Regional Survey and Ancient Populations." In *Settlement, Urbanization, and Population*, edited by A. K. Bowman and A. I. Wilson, 36–75. Oxford.
Wood, E. M. 1988. *Peasant-Citizen and Slave. The Foundations of Athenian Democracy*. London.
Wood, E. M. 1995. *Democracy against Capitalism*. Cambridge.
Woodard, C. 2011. *American Nations. A History of the Eleven Rival Regional Cultures of North America*. New York.
Woolf, G. 1998. *Becoming Roman. The Origins of Provincial Civilization in Gaul*. Cambridge.
Woolf, G. 2012. *Rome. An Empire's Story*. Oxford.
Woolf, G. 2020. *The Life and Death of Ancient Cities. A Natural History*. Oxford.
Wörrle, M. 1988. *Stadt und Fest im kaiserzeitlichen Kleinasien. Studien zu einer agonistischen Stiftung aus Oinoanda*. Munich.
Wörrle, M. 1992. "Neue Inschriftenfunde aus Aizanoi 1." *Chiron* 22:337–76.
Wörrle, M. 1995. "Vom tugendsamen Jüngling zum gestressten Euergeten. Überlegungen zum Bürgerbild Hellenistischer Ehrendekrete." In *Stadtbild und Bürgerbild im Hellenismus*, edited by M. Wörrle and P. Zanker, 241–50. Munich.
Wörrle, M. 2000. "Pergamon um 133 v. Chr." *Chiron* 30:543–76.

Wörrle, M. 2003. "Pidasa du Grion et Héraclée du Latmos: deux cités sans avenir." *CRAI* 147.4:1361–79.
Wörrle, M. 2004a. "Ermandyberis von Limyra, ein prominenter Bürger aus der Chora." In *Chora und Polis*, edited by F. Kolb, 291–302. Munich.
Wörrle, M. 2004b. "Der Friede zwischen Milet und Magnesia: methodische Probleme einer Communis opinio." *Chiron* 34:45–57.
Wörrle, M. 2004c. "Maroneia im Umbruch: Von der hellenistischen zur kaiserzeitlichen Polis." *Chiron* 34:149–67.
Wörrle, M. 2007. "Zu Rang und Bedeutung von Gymnasion und Gymnasiarchie im hellenistischen Pergamon." *Chiron* 37:501–16.
Wörrle, M. 2009. "Neue Inschriftenfunde aus Aizanoi 5: Aizanoi und Rom 1." *Chiron* 39:409–44.
Wörrle, M. 2011a. "Neue Inschriftenfunde aus Aizanoi 6: Aizanoi und Rom 2." *Chiron* 41:357–76.
Wörrle, M. 2011b. "Epigraphische Forschungen zur Geschichte Lykiens 10: Limyra in seleukidischer Hand." *Chiron* 41:377–415.
Wörrle, M. 2014. "Neue Inschriftenfunde aus Aizanoi 7. Aizanoi und Rom 3: Der julisch-claudische Kaiserkult in Aizanoi." *Chiron* 44:439–511.
Wörrle, M., and Zanker, P. eds. 1995. *Stadtbild und Bürgerbild im Hellenismus*. Munich.
Wrenhaven, K. L. 2012. *Reconstructing the Slave. The Image of the Slave in Ancient Greece*. London.
Wriedt Sørensen, L. 2002. "The Archaic Settlement at Vroulia on Rhodes and Ian Morris." *ActaHyp* 9:243–53.
Wycherley, R. E. 1957. *Literary and Epigraphical Testimonia, Athenian Agora 3*. Princeton.
Xydopoulos, I., Vlassopoulos, K., and Tounta, E., eds. 2017. *Violence and Community. Law, Space and Identity in the Ancient Eastern Mediterranean World*. London.
Yack, B., ed. 1996. *Liberalism without illusions. Essays on Liberal Theory and the Political Vision of Judith N. Shklar*. Chicago.
Yasur-Landau, A. 2010. *The Philistines and Aegean Migration at the End of the Late Bronze Age*. Cambridge.
Yıldırım, B. 2004. "Identities and empire: Local mythology and the self-representation of Aphrodisias." *Paideia. The World of the Second Sophistic*, edited by B. E. Borg, 23–52. Berlin.
Yoffee, N. 2005. *Myths of the Archaic State. Evolution of the Earliest Cities, States and Civilizations*. Cambridge.
Yoffee, N., ed. 2015. *Early Cities in Comparative Perspective, 4000 BCE–1200 CE*. Cambridge.
Yon, J.-B. 2001. "Evergetism and Urbanism in Palmyra." In *Recent Research in Late-Antique Urbanism*, edited by L. Lavan, 173–81. Portsmouth, RI.
Yon, J.-B. 2002. *Les notables de Palmyre*. Beirut.
Yon, J.-B. 2017. "Le reflet des honneurs." In *The Politics of Honour in the Greek Cities of the Roman Empire*, edited by A. Heller and O. van Nijf, 496–526. Leiden.
Yon, J.-B. 2019. "Femmes de Palmyre." In *Femmes grecques de l'Orient romain*, edited by S. Lalanne, 183–203. Besançon.
Yon, J.-B. 2021. "Palmyra." In *A Companion to the Hellenistic and Roman Near East*, edited by T. Kaizer, 284–94. Hoboken, NJ.
Youni, M. 2007. "An Inscription from Teos Concerning Abdera." In *Thrace in the Graeco-Roman World*, edited by A. Iakovidou, 724–36. Athens.
Zaccarini, M. 2013. "Dalla 'triere leggera' alla 'triere pesante': l'evoluzione della marina ateniese tra Temistocle e Cimone." *Rivista di Storia Militare* 2:7–27.
Zaccarini, M. 2017. *The Lame Hegemony. Cimon of Athens and the Failure of Panhellenism, ca. 478–450 B.C.* Bologna.
Zachhuber, J. 2018. "The Lost Priestesses of Rhodes? Female Religious Offices and Social Standing in Hellenistic Rhodes." *Kernos* 31:82–110.
Zachos, G. A. 2016. *Tabula Imperii Romani. J34- Athens: Achaia Phthiotis- Malis-Aenis-Oitaia-Doris-Eurytania-East and West Locris-Phokis-Aitolia-Akarnania*. Athens.
Zahnrt, M. 1971. *Olynth und die Chalkidier. Untersuchungen zur Staatenbildung auf der Chalkidischen Halbinsel im 5. und 4. Jahrhundert v. Chr.* Munich.
Zanker, P. 1993. "The Hellenistic Grave Stelai from Smyrna: Identity and Self-Image in the Polis." In *Images and Ideologies. Self-Definition in the Hellenistic World*, edited by A. Bulloch et al., 212–30. Berkeley.
Zannis, A. G. 2014. *Le pays entre le Strymon et le Nestos. Géographie et histoire (VIIe–IVe siècle avant J.-C.)*. Athens.

Zaphiropoulou, P. 1994. "Une nécropole à Paros." In *Nécropoles et sociétés antiques*, edited by J. de la Genière, 127–52. Naples.
Zaphiropoulou, P. 1999. "I due *polyandria* dell'antica necropoli di Paros." *AION* 6:13–24.
Zelnick-Abramovitz, R. 2000. "Did Patronage Exist in Classical Athens?" *AC* 69:65–80.
Zelnick-Abramovitz, R. 2013. *Taxing Freedom in Thessalian Manumission inscriptions*. Leiden.
Ziebarth, E. 1896. *Das griechische Vereinswesen*. Leipzig.
Ziegler, R. 1985. *Städtisches Prestige und kaiserliche Politik. Studien zum Festwesen im Ostkilikien im 2. und 3. Jhdt n. Chr.* Düsseldorf.
Zimmermann, M. 1993. "Bemerkungen zur rhodischen Vorherrschaft in Lykien (189/88–167 v. Chr.)." *Klio* 75:110–30.
Zoumbaki, S. 2013. "In Search of the Horn of Plenty: Roman Entrepreneurs in the Agricultural Economy of the Province of Achaia." In *Villae Rusticae. Family and Market-Oriented Farms in Greece under Roman Rule*, edited by A. D. Rizakis and I. P. Touratsoglou, 52–73. Athens.
Zuckerman, M. 1970. *Peaceable Kingdoms. New England Towns in the Eighteenth Century*. New York.
Zuiderhoek, A. J. 2008. "On the Political Sociology of the Imperial Greek City." *GRBS* 48.4:417–45.
Zuiderhoek, A. J. 2009. *The Politics of Munificence in the Roman Empire. Citizens, Elites and Benefactors in Asia Minor.* Cambridge.
Zuiderhoek, A. J. 2011. "Oligarchs and Benefactors: Elite Demography and Euergetism in the Greek East of the Roman Empire." In *Political Culture in the Greek East After the Classical Age*, edited by O. van Nijf and R. Alston, 185–95. Leuven.
Zuiderhoek, A. J. 2013. "No Free Lunches: *paraprasis* in the Greek Cities of the Roman East." *HSPh* 107:297–321.
Zuiderhoek, A. J. 2017. *The Ancient City*. Cambridge.
Zuiderhoek, A. J. 2019. "Benefactors, Markets and Trust in the Roman East. Civic Munificence as Extramercantile Exchange." In *The Extramercantile Economies of Greek and Roman Cities. New Perspectives on the Economic History of Classical Antiquity*, edited by D. Hollander, T. R. Blanton IV, and J. T. Fitzgerald, 51–62. Abingdon.
Zurbach, J. 2006. "L'Ionie à l'époque mycénienne: essai de bilan historique." *REA* 108.1:271–96.
Zurbach, J. 2013. "La formation des cités grecques: statuts, classes et systèmes fonciers." *Annales (HSS)* 68.4:957–98.
Zurbach, J. 2017. *Les hommes, la terre et la dette en Grèce c. 1400–c. 500 a.C.*, vols 1–2. Bordeaux.
Zurbach, J. 2021. "La main-d'œuvre agricole dans les cités d'Asie, fin IVe–fin Ier siècle." In *Statuts personnels et main-d'œuvre en Méditerranée hellénistique*, edited by J. Zurbach and S. Maillot, 225–60. Clermont-Ferrand.
Zuchtriegel, J. 2018. *Colonization and Subalternity in Classical Greece. Experience of the Non-Elite Population.* Cambridge.

ILLUSTRATIONS CREDITS

0.1. Map by Giovanni Lovisetto
1.1. Photograph Zarko Tankosic, 2016.
1.2. Map by Giovanni Lovisetto.
1.3. From Delamarre, 1902.
1.4. Published by permission of the German Archaelogical Institute. Zippelius, Negative no. D-DAI-IST-70-21.
1.5. Map by Giovanni Lovisetto (based on Müllenhoff 2005, fig. 50).
1.6. From Ober 2015, Princeton University Press.
2.1. Map by Giovanni Lovisetto.
2.2. Published by permission of the Trustees of the American School of Classical Studies at Athens.
2.3. Dimitriadou, Eirini M., 2019. "Figure 3.47: Athens. The sites of the Protogeometric cemeteries" from *Early Athens: Settlements and Cemeteries in the Submycenaean, Geometric, and Archaic Periods*. Version 1. Cotsen Institute of Archaeology Press. https://doi.org/10.25346/S6/32LBDJ. Map modified by Giovanni Lovisetto.
2.4. Published by permission of the British School at Athens.
2.5. Published by permission of the École Française d'Athènes, 19312, Argos, époque géométrique. EFA/ V. Philippa - Y. Rizakis, and of the Ephorate of Antiquities of the Argolid. © Hellenic Ministry of Culture and Sports, Ephorate of Antiquities of Argolis.
2.6. Published by permission of the Trustees of the American School of Classical Studies at Athens.
2.7. Published by permission of the École Française d'Athènes, 26336, Argos, armure de bronze. EFA/ Émile Sérafis, and of the Ephorate of Antiquities of the Argolid. © Hellenic Ministry of Culture and Sports, Ephorate of Antiquities of Argolis.
3.1. Photograph John Ma, 2017.
3.2. Photographs Renaud Hirsch, 2018. © Ministry of Culture, Hellenic Republic / Ephoreia of Antiquities, Cyclades
4.1. Published by permission of the Centre for the Study of Ancient Documents, Oxford.
4.2. After H. Pfuhl, Malerei und Zeichnung der Griechen (Munich, 1923).
4.3. Published by permission of the Danish Institute in Athens, and of Eriphylē Kaninia and Stine Schierup.

4.4. Published by permission of the Ecole Française d'Athènes, 22551, Thasos, Mnéma de Glaucos (photographer: unknown). © Hellenic Republic, Ministry of Culture and Sports, General Directorate of Antiquities and Cultural Heritage, Ephorate of Antiquities of Kavala.

5.1. Published by permission of the Trustees of the American School of Classical Studies at Athens.

5.2. Acr. 3, © Acropolis Museum, photo: Socratis Mavrommatis, 2011.

5.3. Published by permission of the Centre for the Study of Ancient Documents, Oxford.

5.4. Published by permission of the École Française d'Athènes, 46497, Argos, borne de l'enclos, Hérôon des sept contre Thèbes. EFA/ A. Pariente. Photograph by John Ma, 2023.

5.5. Metropolitan Museum of Art, New York, Fletcher Fund, 1938, 38.11.7.

5.6. Photograph by Kondephy, 2015, under Creative Commons Attribution-Share Alike 4.0 International license. https://creativecommons.org/licenses/by-sa/4.0/deed.en

5.7. Published by permission of the École Française d'Athènes, 18083, Delphes, Trésor de Siphnos, perspective restituée, EFA/Hansen, Erik, 1954.

5.8. Published by permission of the École Française d'Athènes, 18094, Delphes, Trésor de Siphnos, façade Nord, EFA/ Hansen, Erik, 1954.

6.1. Metropolitan Museum of Art, New York, Fletcher Fund, 1932, 32.11.1

6.2. Reproduced by permission of Elisabeth Walter-Karydi.

6.3. By permission of Georgia Kokkorou-Alevra and the École Française d'Athènes (drawing Aspasia Drigkopoulou)

6.4. Reproduced by permission of Sanne Houby-Nielsen.

6.5. Published by permission of the National Archaeological Museum, Athens (photographer: Eleftherios Galanopoulos). © Hellenic Ministry of Culture and Sports/ Organization of Cultural Resources Development (H.O.C.RE.D.).

6.6. Published by permission of the German Archaeological Institute, Athens.

6.7. Metropolitan Museum of Art, New York, Gift of A. J. B. Wace, 1923 and 19244, 24.195.15, 24.195.97, 24.195.80, 24.195.101, 24.195.67, 24.195.46.

7.1. Reproduced with permission of Edinburgh University Press through PLSclear.

7.2. Map by Giovanni Lovisetto.

7.3. Map by Giovanni Lovisetto.

8.1. Published by permission of © Nicholas Cahill.

8.2. Published by permission of the Ephorate of Antiquities of Athens-Ancient Agora Excavations/ American School of Classical Studies Archive © Hellenic Ministry of Culture and Sports/ Organization of Cultural Resources Development (H.O.C.RE.D.)

8.3. Metropolitan Museum of Art, New York, Fletcher Fund, 1959, 59.11.27.

9.1. By permission of the German Archaeological Institute at Athens, Negative no. D-DAI-ATH-Grabrelief-0550 (photographer: unknown)

9.2. Map by Giovanni Lovisetto.

9.3. Photograph John Ma, 2017.

9.4. Published by permission of C. Ampolo and Scuola Normale Superiore di Pisa.

9.5. Bibliothèque Nationale de France.

10.1. Published by permission of Denis Rousset.

10.2. Published by permission of Feliciantonio Costabile.

10.3. From Pottier, Reinach and Veyries 1887.

10.4. J. Paul Getty Museum 71.AA.288.

10.5. From Richard Wünsch, IG 3 appendix (1897).

10.6. From Krischen 1938. Composition by Giovanni Lovisetto.

11.1. The rights on the depicted monument, which falls under the jurisdiction of the Ephorate of Antiquities of Fokida, belong to the Ministry of Culture and Sports (Law 4858/2021). © Hellenic Ministry of Culture and © Sports/Hellenic Organization of Cultural Resources Development.

11.2. Plan by Giovanni Lovisetto.

11.3. By permission of Alexander von Kienlin. Composition by Giovanni Lovisetto.

11.4. Photograph by Jean-Charles Moretti.

12.1. By permission of New York University Excavations at Aphrodisias (Guido Petruccioli).

12.2. By permission of New York University Excavations at Aphrodisias (Guido Petruccioli).

12.3. By permission of the Münzkabinett, Staatliche Museen zu Berlin - Stiftung Preußischer Kulturbesitz, 18304385, photograph: Münzkabinett, Staatliche Museen zu Berlin, Bernhard Weisser.

12.4. Published by permission of Christina Kokkinia.

12.5. Bibliothèque Nationale de France.

12.6. Map by Giovanni Lovisetto.

13.1. Photograph by Lensmatter, under Creative Commons 2.0 license. https://creativecommons.org/licenses/by/2.0/

13.2. Photograph Carole Raddato, under Creative Commons Attribution-ShareAlike 2.0 Generic license. https://creativecommons.org/licenses/by-sa/2.0/deed.en

13.3. Bibliothèque Nationale de France.

13.4. Published by permission of the Ephorate of Antiquities of Athens-Ancient Agora Excavations and the American School of Classical Studies Archive. © Hellenic Ministry of Culture and Sports/ Organization of Cultural Resources Development (H.O.C.RE.D.)

13.5. Published by permission of the Ephorate of Antiquities of the City of Thessaloniki. Photograph by John Ma, 2019.

14.1. Photograph by Bernard Gagnon, 2010, under Creative Commons 3.0 license. https://creativecommons.org/licenses/by-sa/3.0/deed.en

14.2. Published by permission of Ryan Boehm.

14.3. Published by permission of the American Society of Overseas Research.

14.4. Map by Giovanni Lovisetto.

14.5. Published by permission of Eivind Heldaas Seland. Basemap © ESRI 2014.

14.6. Published by permission of Klaus Schnädelbach.

14.7. Published by permission of Christine Delplace, Thibaut Fournet, and Ausonius Éditions.

14.8. Metropolitan Museum of Art, New York, Purchase, 1902, 02.29.4.

14.9. Metropolitan Museum of Art, New York, Rogers Fund, 1911, 11.139.

14.10. Published by permission of Aphrodisias Excavations (Guido Petruccioli).

15.1. Photograph by Sylvian Fachard, 2008.

15.2. Map by Giovanni Lovisetto.

15.3. Published by permission of the Ministry of Culture, Directorate General of Antiquities, Lebanon.

17.1. Map by Giovanni Lovisetto.

17.2. Map by Giovanni Lovisetto.

18.1. Metropolitan Museum of Art, New York, Gift of Renée E. and Robert A. Belfer, 2001, 2001.443.

18.2. Map by Giovanni Lovisetto.

19.1. From Krischen 1938 (drawing by H. Horn).

20.1. From Volney, *Les ruines*, 1826 edition, frontispiece.

20.2. Photograph by Zarko Tankosic, 2016.

INDEX

accountability: in Classical Athens, 182; in early *polis*, 111; after great convergence, 243–44, 249
Achaimenid empire, 70–71, 165; defeat of, 162
Ackerbürger, 513–14, 516
adult male citizen, 517–19; ideological centrality of, 430, 504, 520–22, 529
agora, 9, 39, 49, 54, 80, 82, 87, 97, 98, 99, 100, 103, 115, 121, 179–80, 202, 254–55, 336, 337, 423; of Argos, 39, 115, 339; of Athens, 32, 291, 294, 298, 417, 504; and conflict, 602n193; diversity in, 419; of Palmyra, 380, 382, 385; and performance, 422; of Priēnē, 256–57, 275, 279, 287, 451, 482; title of pamphlet, 367
Aischinēs, 184–85
aisymnētēs, 137
aitēsis, 576n40
Aitolians, 265, 587n9
alibi for rule, 528–31, 536
Alkaios, 80, 118, 136, 141–42
allotment, use of to fill office, 154, 180, 182, 242, 477, 425, 584n84
anatasis, 482–83
antiquarianism, 231–32, 272, 274–75; and community, 354; links with elite, 339; Roman, 325–28. *See also* myth; mythical kinship
arbitration: modified by Roman interference, 291; between *poleis*, 10, 213, 222, 267, 271, 276
archaeology, and social history of the Early Iron Age, 22–24, 49–50
"Archaic" period, 72–73; art of, 89–90, 565n53; statue habit, during, 128–31
archē: Athenian, 162–67; as empire, 165–66; exceptionalism, 172; influence or lack of, on other *poleis*, 166–67, 227
Archilochos, 88, 97–98, 141–42
Areiopagos, 81, 183
Arendt, H., 450–51, 522
Argos, as Classical democracy, 190–91; in the Early Iron Age, 38–39, 44–45; early law in, 106
Aristophanes, 455–56, 464, 529–30
aristopoliteutēs, 600n100
Aristotle: approach to *polis*, xvii, 18–19, 407–8; on Athenian constitution, 183–84; *Nikomachean Ethics*, 445; *Politics*, 217–18, 228, 255, 416–17, 433, 443–47,

460, 468, 478, 480, 521–22, 529; pragmatism, 445; witness to great convergence, 217–18
Arkadia, peer-polity interaction in, 120
Assembly, 6, 186, 220–22, 240–41, 361, 441, 465, 482, 535; acclamations in, 381; business in, 351–52, 423, 427; disappearance of, 396; in early *polis*, 78, 80, 81, 84, 106, 114, 125, 138; Homeric, 59–61, 79; meetings of, 59–60, 80, 240–42; religious business in, 423; in Roman-era *polis*, 349–52, 362, 365, 600n120; social composition of, 99, 346, 352–53, 381, 516, 519, 536; in Sparta, 194
assignment of cities to others, 303, 313, 395
associations, 235–36, 253–54, 417–18, 433–34, 608n34; in early *polis*, 84–87, 112–13, 143–44; as invented institution, 85–87; kinship groups, 86; *polis* as association of associations, 417–19; as synekdoche, 144. *See also* civic subdivisions; dining groups
Athens: "Archaic" institutions of, 81–83, 86–87; in the "Archaic" period, 140; and *archē*, 162–67, 573n9, 172, 175, 190–91; artistic production, 187; citizenship at, 115, 517–18, 527; civic identity of, 187–88; in the classical period, 156, 419, 440–41, 446–47, 524; complexity in, 188–89; constitutional development in Classical period, 125–26, 182–83; contradictions in, 187–89; as democracy, 182–93, 447, 455–56, 471, 485–86, 489–91, 535; in the Early Iron Age, 32–35, 37, 39–40, 44–45; foreigners in, 510–12; in fourth-century BCE, 169, 183, 187, 471; institutions in early Athens, 81–82, 108–9, 147, 149–50; late Hellenistic, 272, 283–85, 288, 294–95; law in, 95, 113–14, 182–86; limited influence on other *poleis*, 191, 580n107, 581n109; oligarchical coups in, 183; slavery in, 507, 510; stateness of, 183–85; women in, 504
Attica, 81, 95, 515; "Archaic" social structure in, 134, 147–50; funerary practice in, 130. *See also* Athens
autonomy, 16, 169, 176–78, 306, 325–26, 414–16; connection with citizen dignity, 443; connection with democracy, 222, 333, 415, 443; end of, 328–29; expressed by stateness, 236, 325–26, 361, 415; in "Indian Summer," 269, 289–90, 298; as part of great convergence, 210–13; in Roman empire, 306, 311, 325–31; in second century BCE, 267–68; as status in empire, 206, 293–94, 311, 415; survival, 329–32. *See also polis*, agency in the face of big powers

bargaining, social, in *polis*, 250–51, 361–67, 376, 466–69
big and small *poleis*, 71–72, 170–74; and local resistance, 174, 176
bishops, 399, 400
body, 53, 134–35
Boiotian League, 119–20, 168, 174, 197, 209–10, 212, 317
budget. *See* civic finances
burials in Early Iron Age, 30, 34, 36–38, 38–39, 44–49
burnout, 590n117

Castoriadis, C., 452–53, 465, 476
Catalans, 607n170
children, 90, 232, 424, 427, 503–4; elite, 345, 431
Chios: ally of Rome, 291; as classical oligarchy, 197; law of, 107–8, 114; and slavery, 508, 526
Cicero, 298
citizenship: as descent from two citizen parents, 187, 230–31, 431, 504, 510–11, 619n111; in early polis, 113–15, 144–49; end of, 400; and exclusion, 113–15; in multiple cities, 431, 510, 598n22; as performance, 131, 421–23, 429, 536; porosity of access to, 535–6; restrictions to, in Roman-era *polis*, 342; Roman, 259, 302
civic finances, 139, 190–91, 238–39, 251, 356–57, 596n98. *See also* budget; public goods; taxation: civic
civic ideology, 185–86, 244–47, 289, 441–48; as institution, 479
civic society, 428–33; and civic capital, 433; entrenching civic ideology, 428. *See also* civic subdivisions
civic subdivisions, 180, 232–34, 384, 458, 470–71; link with equality, 233. *See also* associations
civil society, 433–35, 525–26
civil war, 179–80, 199–201; end of, 214–15; overcoming, 220
Classical period, 159–60, 205; democracies in, 189–91, 200–201; oligarchies in, 193, 197–200; rich evidence for, 156; short Athenian century as, 162–65; wars in, 160
closed polities, 144–45, 153; end of, 218; evolving into Classical oligarchy, 193–94
clustervilles, 32–35
Cocceianus Diōn (Dio Chrysostom), 304, 350, 353, 355–56, 359, 362–63, 441–42, 459, 497, 536
coinage, 112, 122; Athenian New Style, 292, 294; as benefaction, 337; bronze, 328, 339, 347, 352, 395; cistophoric, 292; *DAMOKRATIA* bronze coinage, 219; and local identity, 315, 327, 374, 388; regional, 119, 315; and Roman power, 306; wreath-bearing, 272
collaboration, between *poleis*, 70–71, 161, 167, 174–76, 216, 227–28, 271, 474. *See also* peer-polity interaction
collaboration: as exclusion, 525; within *polis*, 139, 148, 365, 476; and rational rituals, 471–72

"colonization," Greek, 97–99
communitarian politics, 444–48, 449; as utilitarianism, 486
community, control over elites, 48–49, 58–61, 65–67, 139–42, 248–50, 612n25; institutional, 466–67; in Late Roman city, 399; in Roman-era *polis*, 353
community, logical primacy of, 443, 450; and virtue politics, 467. *See also* public good
competition: in "Archaic" open polities, 147–48; in democracy, 185–86; in early *polis*, 132–34, 136, 149–50; escalation of, 136–37; after great convergence, 342; in *polis*, 214; in Roman-era *polis*, 352, 362. *See also* conflict; elites; tragedy of the elites
concord, 455; exacerbating conflict, 247, 456, 482–83
conflict, 251–53, 362, 366, 481–88
constitutional experiments, 240
constitutionalism, 259, 334, 350, 583n66, 590n105. *See also* great intensification
consumer city, 233, 513
Copenhagen Polis Centre, 17–18, 208, 543–44
Corinth: civil war in, 179; in Early Iron Age, 39–42
Corinthian vases: and "Archaic" Greek society, 90
costs: of institutions, 463, 471–73, 476–77; moral and social, 486–88, 520–22, 524–25, 532–33
couch, dining, 74, 425, 520
Council, 80, 199, 237, 240–43, 241, 249; in Athens, 182–83; censitary requirement, scanty evidence for, 345; citizens' access to, 241; in early Chios, 108; in early *polis*, 80, 81, 84, 108, 125; entry-fees, 343; large membership of, 345; in leagues, 197, 269; not equivalent to curial class, 345; in oligarchies, 137, 183, 197; privileged during "Indian Summer," 283; in Roman Egypt, 391–92; in Roman-era *polis*, 305, 324, 342–45, 381; *sunedrion*, 278
cows, as gifts, 482
Crete: dining groups from, 87, 113; palatial polities in, 28

"Dark Ages," 23, 30, 64–65
decision-making, democratic, 240–42
decrees, 220, 221, 224, 241, 277, 278; honorific, 247–49; long decrees during "Indian Summer," 256, 279–88; read in public, 244; in Roman-era *polis*, 304, 349
dekaprōtos, 347, 358
demagogy, 200; in Classical Athens, 183–93; after great convergence, 249; in Roman-era *polis*, 349–51, 356, 464
democracy: Athenian, 185–86; diffusion, 220–23; in early *polis*, 121–27; economic aspects of, 192–93; generalization of, 213–22; after great convergence, 240–44, 415–16; during the "Hundred Years," 189–93; in "Indian Summer," 276–79, 285–87, 299; as institutions, 182–85, 220; not dead after Classical period, 409–10; pragmatism of, 442; in Roman Egypt, 392–93; in Roman-era *polis*, 348–53; on

spectrum with oligarchy, 200–201, 527–28; sustained by kings, 218–19
democratic elite theory, 489
demography, 38, 91, 604n68, 617n75, 618n83; and power, 517–20
Dēmosthenēs, 184–85, 491
dependent polis. See subordination
dignity, 442, 449
dilemma of access, 144–49, 522
dining groups, 87–89, 110, 113. See also sumposion
dioikēsis. See budget; civic finances
distinction, in Early Iron Age, 44–47
distributions, 120–22, 342; refused by Hērōdēs Atticus, 364
diversity, social, 413; in "Archaic" period, 97–98; in Early Iron Age, 44–49, 58, 65–67; in types of poleis, 12, 71–72, 412–13
dokimasia. See scrutiny
Drakōn: homicide law, 82–83; law code, 83
Drēros, law of, 75–79, 85, 95–96, 453, 461, 464
Dusty-feet, 516, 572n95

Early Iron Age: chronological schemes in, 23; clustervilles in, 32–38, 66; and core geography of polis development, 23; fluidity, social during, 44–49, 58, 65–67; and Homeric epic, 62; mobility during, 35–36; settlement patterns during, 32–35, 49–50; and social structure, 36–38, 44–49, 51–58
early state theory, 558n36
economic boom, late Classical, 178, 469–70
economics: New Institutional, 460, 550; in polis, 180, 346, 381, 459–60, 466, 469–74
egalitarianism, 6, 8, 218, 244, 449; in early polis, 88, 124–27, 150; during "Indian Summer," 288; and slavery, 506–7; in Sparta, 145, 194
eirenarch, 323–24
eisphora. See wealth-tax
ekdikos, 361, 397, 465
Eleutherna, 46–47; early law in, 105
Ēlis, citizenship at, 115; early law in, 69, 106–7
elites: acquisitiveness, 35–36, 132–36; benefactions by, 247–50, 336–37, 355, 375–76, 380–81, 443; controlling agenda, 489–95; diversity of, 55–56, 346–48, 381; in Early Iron Age, 36–38, 44–49, 51–57; in early polis, 128–39; economic strategies of, in Roman empire, 359–60, 598n22; as explanation for everything, 139–40, 338; after great convergence, 247–50, 255–57; in "Indian Summer," 279–83, 298–99; in Roman-era polis, 334–41; and slavery, 507–8; spreading Roman-style institutions, 344–45; violence of, 133–34, 496–98; and wealth, 248, 284–85, 338, 362. See also competition; factions; oligarchical culture; oligarchy
elitism, within democracy, 147–48, 248, 283–87, 586n131

end of history: as function of empire, 291, 300, 306; as function of polis, 251, 454
ephebes, 271, 284, 288, 366; oath of, 432–33
epigraphy, as source for polis history, xvi, 5, 229, 303, 573n9, 611n30, and passim. See also inscriptions
Eretria, law of, 216–17. See also Euboia
ethnikon, 6, 374–75, 425, 607n13; internal use, 342
Euboia: citizenship on, 115; in Early Iron Age, 34–36
euergetism, 248–50, 468; end of, 396; as flight from polis, 363–66; Late Roman survivals of, 397, 399; as mise en abyme, 367; misleading term, 248. See also elites: benefactions by

Fabergé effect, not present in polis, 448
factions, 136–38, 199–201, 204–5
festivals, 118–19, 231, 272; festival communities, 609n65; modified by ruler cult, 307; in Roman empire, 314–15
fish, 295, 297, 307, 354
fishermen, 413; as name of faction, 136
foreigners, resident, 114–15, 417, 429, 510–11, 520
foreign judges, 215, 253, 267, 271; under Rome, 327
forensic oratory, 184–85, 250, 352, 441, 443, 444, 485, 497, 527; in Roman empire, 352, 367, 442, 602n177
fortifications, 8, 12, 210, 231, 236, 239; in early polis, 93, 94, 103; of Panopeus, 411–12
freebooting, 35–36, 56, 60, 133–34
freedom, collective. See autonomy
freedom, individual, 443, 446, 449, 497, 610n12; as alibi for rule, 528–31
freeriding, 434–65
free spaces, 435–36, 535–37; and violence, 499–500
"friends": of kings, 255, 265; of Roman emperor, 311; of Romans, 296–97

Gaul, 330–31, 597n151
gender, 423–24; as proxy for institutional power, 430–31
Geneva, xv–xvi, 487; absence of guilds and patriciates, 545, 617n73; territory and population, 517
Geometric period. See Early Iron Age
global history of city-states, 543–46; discontinuities, 546
goats, 3, 451, 461–62, 483, 495
Goldilocks, 475–76, 479; no to, 480
Gortyn, law of, 80, 104–5
great convergence, 203–57, 466; normalization, 277; persistence, 367
great intensification, 276–79, 303–4, 349
"Greek miracle," 408, 545, 546, 550
groups. See associations

hegemony, 167–68, 172–73; end of, 205–10, 231–32. See also archē
hegoumenoi ("rulers"), used for Romans, 318–19

Hellenistic period, 230, 254–55; definition of, 156–57, 230; democratic culture of, 220–22; end of high Hellenistic system, 265; Hellenistic empires, 206–8, 223–25; institutions, 240–44, 247–49; late second century BCE benefactors, 279, 281, 283–85; Leagues, 211–12, 265–68; peer-polity interaction in, 212–13, 215, 225–27, 267, 272, 291; *poleis* during the late Hellenistic period, 269–76, 285–87; ruler cult during, 307–9; stateness in, 236–37. *See also* Roman Republic
helots, 92, 134, 194, 576n75; end of, 233–35, 267
Hērakleia, 3–8, 481, 518; citizens of, 4, 6, 427, 451, 501–2, 513; inscribed decree, 3–5, 557n1, 455, 461–62, 465, 483–84, 495; institutions of, 4–8, 229, 238; women in, 504
Hermippos, 164–65
Hērōdēs Atticus, 335, 364–66
Herodotos, 70, 72, 121
Hesiod, 51, 56, 58, 60–63, 170
Hesiodic poems. *See* Hesiod
historiography, of *polis*, 17–18, 549–52
Hittite empire, and Mycenaean polities, 27–28
Homer: as headache for the historian, 22, 61–62; *Iliad*, 51–53, 57, 60–61; *Odyssey*, 51, 53, 58; poems, 22; portrayal of communities, 59–61, 83, 86; portrayal of lords, 51–59, 78–79
homonoia. *See* concord
honors, 186–87, 244–47, 249–50, 259, 277, 416, 439–40, 442, 444; by associations, 434; as communitarian form, 445; cultic, for Roman emperor, 307; as exchange, 468–69; intensified during "Indian Summer," 279–84, 296, 299; and resentment, 482; in Roman-era *polis*, 317, 337, 339, 342–43, 352–53, 366, 375, 386, 392; for Romans, 266–68
Hundred Years' War (Greece), 157, 160–61, 174, 200, 415

Iasōn of Pherai, 173–74
immigration and immigrants, 113–14, 254–55
inequality, 230, 399, 490; in Sparta, 194–95; source of social power, 490–95; tamed by political equality, 449
infernal equation, 203–5
inheritance, 255, 424, 344; partible, 513, 571n78
inscriptions: in Aramaic, 377, 384, 386; and associations, 434; in early Greece, 70; and elite, 338, 341; in Greek, 374; in Latin, 369; as normed genre, 430, 445; and popular sovereignty, 244; and transparency, 244. *See also* epigraphy; honors; law; literacy; scrutiny
institutions, 13–16, 436–38, 452–53; civic rituals as metaphor for, 429–30; and power, 427–28
institutions *vs* ideology in study of *polis*, 440–41
isopoliteia, 609n107
Italian settlers, 293, 297, 305

jury-courts, 184–85, 190, 242, 277, 299
Justinian, 401

Kanatha, as a Roman imperial *polis*, 370–77
Kinadōn, 196
kings, 205, 215, 223, 226; and civic honors, 215, 245–46. *See also polis*, agency in the face of big powers
Kleisthenēs, 113, 131
koinon: association, 6, 415, 434; common treasury of, 6, 238, 251, 426; as commonwealth / community / society, 6, 13, 250, 253, 277, 425, 451, 463, 501, 502; as federal organization, 277, 301, 302, 315–17, 291; poetics of, 6, 16–17, 427–28, 446, 481, 483, 501–2

landlordism, in contrast with *polis*, 5, 470
Late Antique City, 399–402
Late Bronze Age: collapse of, 29–31; polities of, 25–27
Late Hellenistic period, 588n39
law: "Archaic," 69, 77–80, 104–9, 139–41; in Classical Athens, 184–85; distinguished from decree, 78, 106, 240, 583n66; "open texture," 185, 486, 575n27
leagues: "Archaic," 118–20; classical, 174–75; in great convergence, 209–12; under Roman empire, 315–17; in second century BCE, 267–68. *See also* super-League
leitourgia, 186, 191, 239, 361, 466; during "Indian Summer," 279, 286; in Late Roman *polis*, 396–97, 399; in Roman-era *polis*, 358–59, 361–62, 376
Lētē: benefactor of, 290, 333, 365, 469; as *polis*, 11
Lex Pompeia, 344, 345
literacy: in early *polis*, 139–41, 571n62; in Sparta, 577n79
loans, to cities, 239
Lokris, early law in, 110, 153–55; regionalization and differentiation, 153–55

Macedonia: defeat of, 265; Macedonian conquests, 205–6; Macedonian national kingdom, 446; single rule in, 138
magistrates, 236–37, 242, 582n45; in early *polis*, 76–77, 81–82, 104–8; as function of stateness, 237, 354–55; in Roman-era *polis*, 346–48, 354, 380
Mantineia: democracy and oligarchy in, 203; integration of *polis*, 177–78
maroons, 526, 609n108
mass and elite, 182–89, 338, 431, 432, 468, 477, 509; and conflictual dynamics, 485; in later contests, 545; in modern times, 550; replaced by "elite and community," 445–46. *See also* Athens; democracy; rich and poor
meals, communal, 81–88, 110–11
Megara: violence at, 160; water-supply at, 103, 566n16
metoikoi. *See* foreigners, resident
misthos. *See* pay

mobility: in "Archaic" age, 97–98, 114; and citizenship, 511; in Early Iron Age, 35–36; in Hellenistic age, 254–55
moralizing discourse, in *polis*, 245, 248–49
Mycenaean polities, 27–30
myth, and community, 115–16, 231, 328, 374
mythical kinship, 213, 230, 331
Mytilēnē: cities subordinate to, 171; magistrates dining in, 87; as *polis*, 80; resist Spartan hegemony, 176; strife at, 136–38

narrative form, 607n1 (chap. 15)
nativism, 511–12; ideological consequences, 521
naukraroi, 81–82
Naxos, in Early Iron Age, 37–38, 41–42, 67–68
new city foundations, 180, 215, 223; in Roman empire, 302–3, 323–25, 392–93

oligarchical culture, after great convergence, 250
oligarchism, zombie, 488–89
oligarchy, 193–99; contradictions, 198–99; end of, 215, 217–18; ideology of, 197–98; as innovation, 198–99; institutions in, 197; and rationality, 198; on spectrum with democracy, 200–201, 527–28; threat of, 488–95
open polities, 145–49, 154
ostrakismos, 125–26, 186, 191

palatial polities, 25–29; in historiography of polis, 28
Palmyra, 377–87; Customs Law, 377–82; institutions of, 12; material culture of, 384–87; normalcy, 387–88; political economy, 524; public bilingualism, 385–87; as a Roman imperial *polis*, 379–84, 387–88; size, 381, 604n68; villages of, 604n95
Pan-Hellenion, 318
Panopeus, 12, 303, 410–14
Paros, in Early Iron Age, 67–68
Parthenon, Athens, 573n14
participation, 114, 121, 186, 192, 242, 421–23; as mystification, 432; at Palmyra, 386; wide, in office holding, 347–48
patrobouloi, 243
patronage, lack of, 248, 470; possibly hidden, 495–98, 527
pay, 182, 242, 348, 584n87
peer-polity interaction, 10–11, 120, 212–13, 267, 271–72, 287; and diffusion of *polis*, 225–26; Late Roman survival of, 399; in Roman empire, 291, 315, 318, 328, 331–32. *See also* collaboration, between *poleis*
People, 6, 11, 12, 185, 241, 286; in early *polis*, 84–85, 106, 108, 125; as non-elite, 125, 126, 141, 183, 376; in Roman-era *polis*, 348–53, 357, 381; as whole community, 194, 354, 427, 446–47, 465
Periklēs, 166

perioikism, 95–96, 118, 144; disappearance of, 266
personification, of *polis*, 354, 426, 541–42
petition and response, 325
philosophy, 186, 192, 217; during "Indian Summer," 288–89
Phokiōn, 199, 577n107
phulakē, 4, 6, 7
platiwoinarchoi, 81
Plato, 186, 192, 445–46, 509
playacting, 144–45, 194, 254
Plutarch, 84
policing: in cities during crisis, 201; by *poleis* in Roman empire, 323–24; in *polis*, 462, 498; in Sparta, 196
Polis: in the absolute, 8, 79; agency in the face of big powers, 206–7, 223–24, 231–32, 289–90, 306, 326, 329–32; "biography" of, 17; complexity of, 142–49, 189, 419–21, 457, 460–61; contradictions in, 251–53, 455–57, 476–77; defense of, 533–36; definition of, 6, 13, 424; as descent group, 230–31, 511–12; diffusion of model of, 224–26, 275; end of, 399–400; as exclusion, 481, 502; as fiction, 501–2; fostered by kings, 275; without Greek miracle, 408; as ideological elision, 426–27; influence on Roman empire, 329–32; and injustice, 532–33; instrumentalized by Roman empire, 319–25, 388–91, 393; investment in concept of, as origin of "West," 72–73, 550; as justice, 443, 447; limits of ethics, 525–27, 533; materiality, 8, 12, 101–5, 448; military means of, 71, 89, 206–7, 303, 322, 332–33; non-liberal nature of, 486–87; not stateless society, 107, 426; as plurality, 253–54; as political form, 407; political institutions of, 11, 75–85; as regulatory entity, 112, 461–62, 466; as religious organization, 421–24; in Roman Egypt, 390–93; size of, 13; as society of, 253, 416–21; as state, 13–16, 183–85, 236–39, 377–79; territory of, 9, 95–96, 180, 303, 304, 354, 371–73, 378, 512–16 (*see also* structuration of territory); unity of phenomenon, 12–17, 99, 229–30, 377–76, 410–11; and utopianism, 41–52; as violence, 482–88. *See also* autonomy; democracy; dilemma of access; *koinon*; reception of *polis*; stateness
polis dēmokratoumenē, 222, 415, 443
political speech, 183, 241, 299, 441, 485–86; in Roman-era *polis*, 304, 352, 441–42. *See also* demagogy
political union, 179, 208–9, 211, 472–73, 514–15
politics, invention of, 452; as labor or work, 450–51, 458
Polybios, 263–64
popular sovereignty: in Classical Athens, 183–86, 189; in early *polis*, 125; as epistemology, 445–46; after great convergence, 240–42; during "Indian Summer," 277–78, 285–86; in Roman-era *polis*, 360–62
populism: archaic, 126, 150; in Athens, 183, 189. *See also* demagogy

power, Arendt-style, 450–51
Priēnē: citizens of, 425, 518–19; as a Hellenistic *polis*, 255–57, 279–81, 286–87, 447, 451; peer-polity interaction and, 10–11; urban settlement in, 8–9, 502, 514, 537
procedure, 83, 105, 240; and popular sovereignty, 445; in Roman-era *polis*, 304, 349, 351; second-century BCE intensification, 278
prohairesis, 216–17, 246
prosecution, voluntary, 186, 243–44, 276
Protogeometric pause, 30–32, 38
public actor, 353–57, 376, 382, 432–33
public and private, 245, 386–87, 466–67
public good, 59–60, 185–86, 216–17, 220–22, 247, 443–44, 462, 476
public goods, 190, 193, 201, 237–39, 255, 357, 404, 425–29, 465–72, 529, 531, 536; and autonomy, 415; in early *polis*, 106, 109–13, 121–24, 476–77; entanglement of, with slavery, 507–8; and free-riding, 463–65; in Homeric world, 62; moral valence of, 443–47; in Roman-era *polis*, 326, 355–63, 379, 397, 465; unequal access to, 515–16. *See also* elite: benefactions by; *leitourgia*; taxation: civic
public money, 81–82, 237–39
public writing, 69–70, 75–80, 81, 82, 107–8, 139, 141, 244. *See also* epigraphy; inscriptions

rationality, 104–9, 192, 245–47, 278, 456, 464; and rituals, 470–71
Rawls, J. R., 449
reception of *polis*, 546–49
redistribution, 87, 193, 200, 218, 228, 286, 387, 416, 470, 612n28; unclear scale of, 490
religion, 78, 231, 384; activity during "Indian Summer," 272–75; as mystification, 432–33; as participation, 423–24; as proxy for institutional power, 430, 471. *See also* festivals; shrines, extra-urban; temple-building
rhetra, 69, 106, 125, 564n23
Rhodes, as *polis*, 420
rich and poor, 126, 144, 248, 252, 356, 362, 416, 438
road-building, and "Archaic" connectivity, 120; as corvée, 321–22; and Roman power, 292
Robert, Louis, and history of *polis*, 586, and *passim*
Roman citizens, living in *poleis*, 305
Roman Empire, 310–18, 319, 320–21, 375; Assembly in the *poleis* of, 350–53; Council in the *poleis* of, 342–45; elite benefaction, 337–39; fostering *poleis* in Egypt, 390–93; fostering *polis* life, 357–61, 388–90; and foundation of Roman colonies, 305–6, 368–77, 388–90, 393, 436, 475; Greek *poleis* within, 301–6, 327, 475, 490; imperial cult, 308–11, 316–17, 340–41, 375; as imperial state, 319–24, 331; as Late Roman state, 396–97, 399, 401; leagues under, 315–18; and *leitourgiai*-system, 358–60; as New Empire, 395–96; officeholding under, 345–48
Roman Near East, 296; historical genesis of, 368–69; indigenous cultures in, 377, 384–87, 388, 603n49, 605n107; urbanism in, 370–71
Roman Republic: disorderly, in first century BCE, 296–97; imperialism, 263–66; initial looseness of control, 267–69; power of over Hellenistic *poleis*, 259–61, 263–68, 289–300; violence by, 264
Rome: armies of, in provinces, 588n50, 595n92; control of local finances by, 320; governor, 289, 290, 293, 298, 313, 319–20; intervention in *poleis* by, 269, 278, 324, 344, 357–59, 375; and power, 259–61, 263–68, 289–300, 304, 318–19; provincial administration of, 289–93, 318–24, 357–59, 379–80; republican heritage of, 360–61, 402; underwriting *polis*, 357. *See also* statuses: in Roman empire
ruler-cult: and agency, 247, 326–27; and elites, 340–41; under Roman empire, 306–10, 316–18
rural settlement, 232, 514–15; in Asia Minor, 514; in sixth century BCE, 104, 124–25

Sakadas, 568n71
scrutiny, 182, 232, 240–49, 343. *See also* accountability
"Second Sophistic," 304, 338–39, 597n136
self-interest, 254
Sēmonidēs, 505
serfdom, 26, 92, 134, 144, 150, 194. *See also* helots
settlement patterns, 32–35, 38–42, 49–50, 124–25, 616n54, 617n75
sexuality, 504, 506, 521–24, 537
Shklar, J., 533
shrines, extra-urban, 40–42, 561n87
Sicily: democracies in, 191, 216; dropped out of main *polis* story, 368; Greek settlements in, 98; hegemony in, 171–73, 201; tyranny in, 138, 226
signorial turn, 226, 546. *See also* single rule
Sikyōn, rural development in, 104, 124
single rule, 137–39, 143, 173–74, 201–2, 218, 297–99; end of, 215–16, 226
Siphnos, as "Archaic" city-state, 121–24
slavery, 35, 55–56, 66, 114, 122, 133, 145, 164, 194, 567n65; constituent part of *polis*, 506–10, 522–23
social capital, 435, 468, 471, 610n118; and elite competition, 362; and elite power, 140
social structure: in Early Iron Age, 44–46; after great convergence, 348, 470
Solōn: legislation of, 83, 86–87, 108–9, 113–14, 147, 151; political poetry, 441, 443, 460–61
song, and society, 88. *See also sumposion*
Sophists, and democracy, 192
Sparta: "Archaic" retro-charter at, 84; citizenship at, 115, 518; in the classical period, 194, 419; dining groups at, 87, 113; early institutions of, 83–85;

hegemony of, 167–68; institutional power in, 84–85; law in, 107; literacy in, 184; as plutocracy, 194–95; power in the Peloponnese, 118; Spartiate political style, 145; sub-divisions of, 84; tyranny in, 139; and warfare, 71, 92. *See also* playacting

speech-act theory, 78, 264, 318–19, 324–25, 328, 422, 462, 487, 536

stasis. *See* civil war

stateness: of Classical Athens, 183–84; in early *polis*, 79–80, 107; in the form of society-state, 425–27; of *polis*, 236–40, 416; under Rome, 325–28, 360–61. *See also* magistrates; public money; taxation: civic

statues, honorific: and communitarianism, 445; and elites, 187, 217, 227, 245, 249–50, 255, 259, 591n138; as ethical genre, 439–40; in "Indian Summer," 284–87; as mystification, 493; "private honorific," 189, 254, 255, 381, 419; in Roman-era *polis*, 337, 338–41, 365, 380, 383, 592n200; for Roman governors, 266, 294; as sign of public decision, 349–50, 446

status: granted by community, 187, 286; in *polis*, 129–31, 132

statuses of cities, 172; in late antiquity, 401, 606n166; in Roman empire, 293, 295–96, 311–15, 327, 342

statuses within *polis*, 147, 149, 153, 194, 195, 419–20, 435

Strabo, 306

stratification, 341–45, 421, 516–17; unclear evidence for, 345–46

structuration of territory, 10, 21, 473; in Early Iron Age, 42, 62–64; in early *polis*, 92, 95, 99–100; and inequality, 498, 512–17, 521–22, 569n117; interference with, by Roman empire, 322–23; regional, 42–44, 96, 115–21; in Roman-era *polis*, 303, 342; in Roman Near East, 371–74; at Xanthos, 224. *See also* rural settlement; shrines, extra-urban; subordination

subordination, 64, 92, 95–96, 118, 144, 154, 170–72, 208, 276, 395, 415; end of, 208–10; persistence, 578n19. *See also* perioikism

sumpoliteia. *See* political union

sumposion, 87–89, 130, 136; as site of othering, 506

sunoikismos. *See* political union

super-League, of Greek cities, 317–18

supra-*polis* rulers, 204–6, 215, 224–25, 227–28, 275. See also *polis*, agency in the face of big powers; ruler-cult

taxation: in Athens, 186; civic, 237–38, 462, 468; in early *polis*, 80–81, 109–10; in Roman-era *polis*, 356, 378–79; in Sparta, 195. *See also* public money

taxation, imperial, 162, 167, 177, 206, 320–21, 358, 592n176

temple-building: in early *polis*, 93, 101–3; in Early Iron Age, 39–40; during "Indian Summer," 274

Thebes, supremacy of, 168–70, 173. *See also* Boiotian League

Thespiai, 62–63, 170

three-dimensional power, 489–95

Thucydides, 162, 172, 175

tines (unnamed evil-doers), 253, 455

titles, of cities in Roman empire, 315

Tlōs: and benefactress Lalla, 350, 468; decree of, 450

tragedy of the commons, 462

tragedy of the elites, 249, 359–65, 466–67, 498–99; and violence, 484–86

tribes (not primitive), 43, 113. *See also* civic subdivisions; groups

tribute. *See* taxation, imperial

trust, 471–72

tyrant-slaying, 216–17

Tyrtaios, 83–84, 90, 92; slightly repetitive, 90

urbanism, 32–35, 38–40, 61, 93–94, 97–99, 101–5, 180; and conflict, 351, 363, 382; and egalitarianism, 229, 474–75; and exclusion, 502, 531; grid plan in, 8–9, 180, 229, 245, 425, 474; Late Antique, 401; and politics, 538; in Roman-era *polis*, 334–36, 360; in Roman Near East, 370–71, 381–82. *See also agora*; temple-building

utilitarianism, 486

Vernant, J.-P., 452–53, 465, 476

virtue politics, 440–47; efficacy, 454; and exclusion, 529

Volney, 613n1

voters, numbers of, 240–41, 519, 594n16

Vroulia, settlement at, 93–94

vulnerability, 524–25

war: in "Archaic" Greece, 89–92, 117–18, 134, 275–76; in Classical Greece, 159–60; in Classical Sparta, 195–96; and civic subdivisions, 86, 91, 233, 236; in Early Iron Age, 64, 67–68; after great convergence, 213, 585n121; Homeric, 51–52; in "Indian Summer," 269–71, 588n60; and Late Roman *polis*, 393; and stateness, 91. See also *Polis*: military means

warships, 70–72, 111, 270–71

waterworks, 104

wealth-tax, 6, 186, 230, 251, 279

weekend, working during, 554–55

women: beauty contest of, 118; as citizens, 423–24, 431; complementary to male citizens, 305; of elite, 128, 148, 338, 431; excluded, 88, 187, 504–6; as magistrates, 345; at Palmyra, 524; and religion, 272

Xenophon, 175–76, 421, 491, 505

GPSR Authorized Representative: Easy Access System Europe - Mustamäe tee
50, 10621 Tallinn, Estonia, gpsr.requests@easproject.com

www.ingramcontent.com/pod-product-compliance
Lightning Source LLC
Jackson TN
JSHW020706080326
98924JS00002B/484